Principles of Behavioral Economics

Principles of Behavioral Economics, written by an acknowledged leader in the field, provides a comprehensive introduction to one of the most exciting areas of modern economics. It demonstrates how models of economic theory can be enriched by using interdisciplinary insights from psychology, sociology, evolutionary biology, and neuroscience to build the basis for a more empirically supported set of economic principles. Unique in its level of completeness, rigor, and lucidity, the book highlights the important link between theoretical and empirical economics by demonstrating the usefulness of a range of data sources such as observational data, lab data, survey data, and neuroeconomic data. This field-defining textbook argues that behavioral economics is not just a supplement to mainstream economics. Taking behavioral economics seriously requires a total rethink, and eventual transformation, of potentially every area of economics.

- Written in an engaging style suitable for a broad range of students, with calculus only used as and when necessary
- Covers both basic theory and promising topics on the current research frontiers, highlighting the link between theoretical and empirical economics
- Extensive set of end-of-chapter exercises with a full solutions manual for lecturers available online
- An online only chapter on neuroeconomics.

Sanjit Dhami is Professor of Economics at the University of Leicester. He is the author of the seven-volume book, *The Foundations of Behavioral Economic Analysis* (2020), the leading graduate book in the area. He is also the coauthor, with Cass Sunstein, of *Bounded Rationality: Heuristics, Judgement, and Public Policy* (2022). His research has addressed fundamental questions in behavioral economics and has spanned some of its major areas, such as decision making under risk and uncertainty, other-regarding preferences, time discounting, game theory, and bounded rationality.

"Again, Sanjit Dhami has written an utterly fascinating book – this time aimed at teaching behavioral economics to undergraduates. It is the perfect book for that. But it is also the perfect book for anyone who wants to know how behavioral economics fits into standard economics, and then, further, how it fits into the social sciences as a whole. Every economist, and every social scientist, will learn a lot and find great pleasure in *Principles of Behavioral Economics*."

George Akerlof, Nobel Laureate in Economics 2001; University Professor, Georgetown University

"A masterful blend of theory and empirical evidence, this is an essential resource for students and researchers, and a must-read for anyone interested in the future of economic thought."

Ernst Fehr, Professor of Economics, University of Zurich

"Sanjit Dhami, author of the definitive graduate textbook on behavioral economics, has brought his wisdom, eloquence, and clarity of writing to the creation of an equally impressive volume aimed at undergraduates. In-depth and comprehensive, this book is perfect for year-long course sequences or for intelligent laypeople who want to gain a deep familiarity with the field."

George Loewenstein, Herbert A. Simon University Professor of Economics and Psychology, Carnegie Mellon University

"Because of its rapid growth and many connections to other disciplines, behavioral economics has sometimes appeared to be a rich but somewhat disparate collection of theories and models, empirical findings, and puzzles. With this landmark textbook, we finally have a comprehensive, unified, and remarkably pedagogical treatment of the entire field, seamlessly integrated with micro and game theory, experiments, and real-world applications. It will undoubtedly become the reference textbook for undergraduate courses on the subject, and the natural entry point into the field for many other readers."

Roland Bénabou, Theodore A. Wells '29 Professor of Economics and Public Affairs, Princeton University

"In *Principles of Behavioral Economics: Microeconomics and Human Behavior*, Sanjit Dhami offers a companion volume, accessible to undergraduates, to his landmark graduate-level survey of behavioral economics, *Foundations of Behavioral Economic Analysis*. Like its predecessor, the companion volume is distinguished by its detailed yet readable coverage of theory and evidence and its balanced discussion of the philosophical and methodological differences and similarities between behavioral and neoclassical approaches to microeconomics. Interested undergraduates will gain from reading this masterful book."

Vincent P. Crawford, Professor, University of California, San Diego and University of Oxford

"This is an outstanding undergraduate textbook in behavioral economics. It not only highlights key results in the field but also conveys the excitement of our ongoing quest to make economics truer. I highly recommend it to all."

Xavier Gabaix, Pershing Square Professor of Economics and Finance, Harvard University

Principles of Behavioral Economics

Microeconomics and Human Behavior

Sanjit Dhami
University of Leicester

CAMBRIDGE
UNIVERSITY PRESS

CAMBRIDGE
UNIVERSITY PRESS

Shaftesbury Road, Cambridge CB2 8EA, United Kingdom

One Liberty Plaza, 20th Floor, New York, NY 10006, USA

477 Williamstown Road, Port Melbourne, VIC 3207, Australia

314-321, 3rd Floor, Plot 3, Splendor Forum, Jasola District Centre, New Delhi - 110025, India

103 Penang Road, #05–06/07, Visioncrest Commercial, Singapore 238467

Cambridge University Press is part of Cambridge University Press & Assessment, a department of the University of Cambridge.

We share the University's mission to contribute to society through the pursuit of education, learning and research at the highest international levels of excellence.

www.cambridge.org
Information on this title: www.cambridge.org/highereducation/isbn/9781009422338

DOI: 10.1017/9781009422314

First published 2025

Printed in the United Kingdom by CPI Group Ltd, Croydon CR0 4YY

A catalogue record for this publication is available from the British Library

A Cataloging-in-Publication data record for this book is available from the Library of Congress

ISBN 978-1-009-42233-8 Hardback
ISBN 978-1-009-42229-1 Paperback

Additional resources for this publication at www.cambridge.org/dhami

Dedicated

To my parents

Contents

13 Neuroeconomics

This chapter is online only and can be found at http://cambridge.org/dhami

Figures

Tables

Preface

Authors who write graduate books do not often publish an undergraduate book on the same subject. Perhaps writing the graduate book imparts a sobering recognition of the potential challenges of writing an undergraduate book. In 2016, I completed an advanced treatment of behavioral economics that took me nearly 12 years to write.[1] While immensely rewarding, this involved major sacrifices in my professional and personal life. I did not imagine then that I would write an undergraduate book on behavioral economics. Several factors contributed to my decision to write such a book.

First, despite several books on the subject at this level, I felt that a comprehensive and definitive treatment that could potentially define behavioral economics at the undergraduate level was missing. Behavioral economics is relatively young, and it is the next generation of economists who are pursuing their undergraduate degrees now that are likely to make the most exciting and important advances in the future. In my view, in order to fire their imagination and interest, they needed a book that would not just collect, in one place, the most important principles of the subject, but also bring the cutting edge of research in the field within their grasp.

Second, the widespread and pernicious practice of teaching empirics-free, theory-only, courses in microeconomics and game theory in universities is hugely damaging. It flies in the face of everything that we know about the scientific method in the natural sciences. For this reason, this book is also intended to serve as a companion text for traditional courses in economic theory in order to provide students with the relevant empirical evidence for traditional and behavioral theories. In a welcome and growing trend, a few enlightened instructors in microeconomics and game theory courses have already introduced some of the insights from behavioral economics, often gratifyingly from my advanced book, into their courses.

Third, in economics, there is still a great deal of confusion caused by homespun methodological positions taken by some of the leaders in economic theory. Yet, these positions bear no relation to the scientific method and are inimical to progress. Several undergraduate offerings in behavioral economics try to tread a delicate diplomatic path in the middle, which muddies the waters further and sometimes serves to confuse and misguide students on the purpose of economic theory. I wished to write a book that would outline the scientific approach quite clearly in the introduction and follow it up in the rest of the book. In the natural sciences, teaching and research is already steeped in these methods.

[1] Dhami (2016). *The Foundations of Behavioral Economic Analysis.* Oxford University Press: Oxford. This was subsequently edited, updated, and split into seven volumes published by Oxford University Press in 2019–2020.

Fourth, I wished to convey the excitement and fun offered by a course in behavioral economics. This is only possible by tightly weaving theory and empirics together, tracing out the feedback process between the two, and solving concrete and tangible problems that students can relate to. In this, I simply follow the best practice in the natural sciences, although to some in economics this may appear to be novel.

I started by pointing out that authors of graduate books do not typically write undergraduate books. However, economists know of at least two well-known and celebrated exceptions. The first is Hal R. Varian's books on microeconomics and the second is Walter Rudin's books on mathematical and functional analysis. I was greatly encouraged by both while thinking through the plan for writing this book. In particular, Walter Rudin's undergraduate book *Principles of Mathematical Analysis* that many PhD students in economics are required to master, provided the motivation for the title of this book.

I had initially planned on writing a short introduction to behavioral economics not just for economists but also for other social and behavioral scientists. As a matter of fact, I started writing such a book for the Cambridge University Press' Elements Series. However, it soon became clear that this format was too restrictive for the sort of book I had in mind. In the event, this book offers the reader a comprehensive, lucid, state of the art treatment of the subject matter. I have not shied away from including advanced and challenging material in the book, but the main technical requirement to read the book is modestly set at basic high school maths. Calculus is sparingly used, and only when absolutely essential. As such, the book can be taught at any stage of the undergraduate degree, although it might perhaps be more suitable for second and third year students.

I am greatly indebted to Ernst Fehr for drawing up a template for a significant and important chapter on neuroeconomics that is only available online to keep the length of the printed version more manageable. I learned a great deal from Ernst's comments and suggestions, not just on this chapter, but also on other parts of the book, particularly Part II. Vincent Crawford kindly shared some of his exercises for Part IV.

Teimuraz Gogsadze spent considerable time to carefully read the entire book at all stages, offering invaluable comments and corrected several typos and errors. Mehar Chauhan offered useful suggestions on several parts of the book. She also used her background in psychology and neuroscience to painstakingly draw many illustrations, in color, for the chapter on neuroscience. Narges Hajimoladarvish, Junaid Arshad, Emma Manifold, Ayush Agarwal, and Caspar Kaisar read selected parts of the book and offered very useful advice and suggestions. Jacob Seifert and Paul Schaefer assisted with proofreading parts of the final draft. I am extremely grateful to all these individuals who understood the public goods nature of this project and generously offered their time and advice.

A separate solutions manual, written jointly with Teimuraz Gogsadze, is available to instructors. It contains the solutions to all exercises at the end of each part of the book. It also contains unsolved problems for further thought that are not present in the book.

Over the years I have been supported and encouraged in my work by many individuals and they have significantly contributed to my understanding of the subject in their diverse roles as friends, mentors, coauthors, and academic referees. Without implicating any of them for the shortcomings of this book, I would like to thank Ali al-Nowaihi, Vincent Crawford, Martin

Dufwenberg, Ernst Fehr, Herbert Gintis, Klaus Schmidt, Dennis Snower, Cass Sunstein, and Peter Wakker.

A project of this size always requires enormous support from the family. I would like to thank my entire family for their support and encouragement. My son, Sahaj, helped me to choose the book cover. I dedicate this book to my parents, Manohar and Baljeet, my two role models in life, who have always been a source of unconditional love, support, strength, and encouragement.

Introduction

Taught undergraduate and graduate programs in economics largely conform to the dominant paradigm, *neoclassical economics*, that models "real" humans through the lens of a "fictitious" being, *homo-economicus*. Throughout this book, we use the term "neoclassical economics" to refer only to its "actual practice" in mainstream economics rather than the original intent and motivation of its founding fathers.

Homo-economicus is an entirely *self-regarding*, *amoral*, *emotionless*, *utility maximizing* being that possesses *unbounded rationality*. Thus, homo-economicus will happily break a promise, lie, cheat, and violate social norms, if that leads to greater net expected monetary gains. Lacking emotions, this being also experiences no guilt or shame from such actions. Homo-economicus does not consider the morality of its own actions, or the actions of others, or the fairness of procedures, provided that its actions maximize material gains. In making decisions, homo-economicus believes that any other individual is also, well, another homo-economicus.

Unbounded rationality is slightly harder to define without invoking formal technical jargon to first define rationality, which we do later in this book. Unlike the usage of the term "rationality" in common discourse and in some of the other social and behavioral sciences, in economics rationality has a clear definition with falsifiable implications. Unbounded rationality requires *unlimited attention*; *unlimited and perfect memory*; *unlimited computational ability* that matches the fastest computers; *unlimited knowledge and use of existing mathematics and statistics*; and *unlimited ability to see through alternative methods of framing identical information*. But this does not exhaust the sense in which we may use the prefix "unlimited" to the mental gifts that homo-economicus possesses, as we shall see in various parts of the book.[1] These features of homo-economicus are typically considered relatively uncontroversial in courses in economic theory, and indeed in much research in economics.

All science proceeds on the basis of observations and intuition to formulate testable hypotheses. These hypotheses are then stringently tested with the aim of falsifying, not confirming, them. It was entirely reasonable for neoclassical economics to proceed in the manner laid out above, from the early part of the twentieth century onwards. Homo-economicus was a useful first hypothesis or model of actual humans. However, when tested stringently, many of its central assumptions and predictions failed the empirical test, often quite dramatically.

Neoclassical economics relies on *marginalist principles*. Roughly, the optimal action taken by homo-economicus in any given situation ensures that the marginal benefit of the action equals its

[1] Alfred Marshall's *Principles of Economics*, published in 1890, and Paul Samuelson's *Foundations of Economic Analysis*, published in 1947, are important early texts on neoclassical economics. These texts laid the foundations of what was to come later. While Marshall relied on a verbal/diagrammatic method, Samuelson used the language, methods, and techniques, from mathematics and statistics, that have since become characteristic of the subject.

marginal cost. This, of course, requires homo-economicus to be aware of the marginal benefits and marginal costs of all actions. The Hall and Hitch Committee Report was published in 1939 by a group of Oxford economists, and was based on interviews with UK businessmen. It showed that firms do not use marginalist principles (in this case, marginal revenue equals marginal cost) in deciding on their prices or quantities.

The evidence accumulated from the work of several Nobel Prize winners in the Economic Sciences has rejected the homo-economicus model and some of the central theories in neoclassical economics. We outline some of this work below and discuss it in the book in much detail, although a great deal of it finds, at best, an honorable mention in a footnote in many courses in economic theory.

Allais (1953) showed that under risk and uncertainty, humans do not follow *expected utility theory,* the main decision theory under risk in neoclassical economics. In his Nobel Prize acceptance speech in 1978, Simon (1978), who also invented Artificial Intelligence in his other avatar, pointed out that there is no evidence that firms produce at the point where marginal revenue equals marginal cost. This is almost as significant as a Nobel Prize winning physicist arguing in their acceptance speech that atoms are a figment of our imagination. Simon also made important contributions to the literature on bounded rationality; for a summary, see Simon (2000).

In the early 1970s, Tversky and Kahneman (1971, 1973, 1974), showed that many important predictions of the homo-economicus model were decisively rejected; for a lucid introduction, see Kahneman (2011). Kahneman and Tversky (1979) then showed, in the second most cited paper in economics, that expected utility theory is rejected, and proposed the best known alternative in behavioral economics under risk and uncertainty, *prospect theory*. Reinhard Selten, who made important contributions to classical game theory, also expressed an interest in experiments in the 1960s, and in modeling bounded rationality. He remained, throughout the rest of his life, a strong and vocal critic of the homo-economicus model (Selten, 1998, 2001).

In the 1980s and beyond, Richard Thaler showed that some of the key assumptions of the neoclassical model are violated. People do not calculate opportunity costs very well, and cannot write budget constraints in the usual way (total expenditure equals total income) due to *mental accounting*. For an engaging account of Thaler's diverse contributions to behavioral economics and behavioral finance, see Thaler (2015). In the early 1980s, Akerlof (1982) showed that fairness played a key role in the determination of market wages and tried to integrate theories from sociology into economics. Shiller (1981) showed that the efficient markets hypothesis, a cornerstone of finance, is rejected by the empirical evidence, so stock markets are not as efficient as they were thought to be.

It would be remiss not to mention the work of Smith (1962) who showed that double auction experiments lead to outcomes consistent with a competitive general equilibrium. However, Smith "assigned" values of objects to subjects; that is, an experimenter determines how much an object, say, a mug, is worth to a subject rather than the subjects determining the value of the object. By contrast, when subjects are free to assign values to objects, which appears to be the more natural method, systematic departures from the competitive equilibrium outcome are found, as in the classic *endowment effect* experiments (Kahneman et al., 1991; Thaler, 2015).

In addition, many influential pioneers within economics, several who are likely to join the elusive Nobel club, have conducted pathbreaking work in highlighting the serious shortcomings of the basic neoclassical framework. You will have ample opportunity to be introduced to their pathbreaking work over the course of this book.

In science, there is only one tenable response to the problem of lack of conformity of the data with the predictions of a theory, once all confounds have been accounted for. The theory must either be reformed, enriched, or altered, to account for the evidence. If it is non-salvageable, then it should be jettisoned. The empirical refutation of some of the key features of neoclassical economics set the stage for the development of *behavioral economics*, arguably the most significant development in economics, perhaps of all time.

The rest of this introduction attempts to put the reader in the right frame of mind to read this book. This does not necessarily take the form of explaining behavioral theories and the associated evidence; the book does enough of that. Rather, it takes the form of thinking through a few central questions. How should economists practice their craft? What is good science? What is the role of, and the relation between, theory and evidence? What are some of the potential misconceptions about behavioral economics?

In addition, we spend a bit of time outlining the philosophy behind the book and how one might design a good, well-rounded, course in behavioral economics. Lest some of the material in this chapter looks like sweeping assertions, note that references and details are kept to a minimum whenever the corresponding material is discussed and referenced later in the book.

0.1 The Broad Road Map of Behavioral Economics

In first year courses, economics is typically defined as *the science of allocation of scarce resources among competing uses*. I often cringe when I hear this – indeed I was taught the same definition in my first year in university. This is an unnecessarily narrow and mechanistic vision of economics; and a misunderstanding of the scope of the social and behavioral sciences, of which economics is an important part.

For the purposes of this book, the reader may use the following definition of behavioral economics.

Definition 0.1 *Behavioral economics is an interdisciplinary approach to the social and behavioral sciences that draws insights from economics, psychology, sociology, anthropology, evolutionary biology, sociobiology, and neuroscience. It aims to address the following two central questions.*

(1) How do humans exercise their judgment and make decisions?
(2) How and why do humans cooperate, compete, and coordinate, in small and large groups?

Behavioral economics draws on a rich body of interdisciplinary theory and evidence on human behavior. By contrast, neoclassical economics has been conspicuous in its neglect of the other social and behavioral sciences. Economists are sometimes surprised at how much work has been done in the other social and behavioral sciences on each of the central questions posed above. For instance, judgment and decision making, which is highlighted in the first question, is already an important and thriving part of psychology and management. The second central question, in particular, broadens the scope of behavioral economics beyond the allocation of scarce resources to make it consistent with the general scope of the social and behavioral sciences.

The broad approach, and methods, of behavioral economics may be described as follows.

Behavioral economic theories aim to derive clear, testable, falsifiable, predictions in a rigorous manner, employing as much mathematics and statistics as is required. Behavioral economics is committed to jettisoning theories that are rejected by the data, once all reasonable confounds have been accounted for. It uses data from the lab, field, surveys; observational data; and data using neuroscientific methods. It does not necessarily assign any hierarchical preference among the source of the data in forming inferences about human behavior, and in testing competing theories.

The first part of the approach outlined above shows that the methods of behavioral economics, that is, the mathematical and statistical models used to derive clear, testable, and falsifiable predictions, are rooted in neoclassical economics. However, the second part, a commitment to getting rid of rejected theories, is much stronger relative to the current practice within neoclassical economics (more on this below). The final part of the approach shows that behavioral economics relies on richer and novel sources of data relative to neoclassical economics, which typically uses only observational data, and sometimes views the other data sources with suspicion.

Behavioral economics is still relatively young. Some of the ideas can be traced back to a long lineage, extending back to Adam Smith's *The Theory of Moral Sentiments*, published in 1759, and developments in the related social and behavioral sciences; readers interested in a historical account can consult Camerer and Loewenstein (2004) and Ashraf et al. (2005). The work by Maurice Allais and Herbert Simon in the 1950s, followed by important work on behavioral theories of the firm in the 1960s by Cyert and March (1963), was largely ignored in mainstream economics, despite its importance and originality. However, the key developments that led to an explosion in the modern literature on behavioral economics occurred throughout the 1970s, in great part due to Daniel Kahneman and Amos Tversky, and gathered pace thereafter.

Behavioral economics does not always provide a fully satisfactory account of all the empirical evidence that we have at our disposal, nor has it been applied to every problem that neoclassical economics has been applied to. However, it has already been applied to a very wide range of problems, and when pitted against the neoclassical predictions, its record in explaining the data is significantly better. Its ability to explain the empirical evidence on human behavior is unprecedented in economics, and ignorance of its subject matter ought no longer be a viable option for any serious economist.

This book is an introductory account of the principles of behavioral economics, and a record of its predictions, when pitted against the data. It also demonstrates the fruitfulness of a constant feedback between the evidence and theory, which is one of the hallmarks of the natural sciences.

Sometimes a distinction is drawn between *behavioral economics* and *experimental economics*. Given the close feedback between theory and evidence in behavioral economics, such distinctions are artificial for most practical purposes. Experiments, unless they are underpinned by the relevant theory, may lack discipline and direction, although it is also true that in some cases there is no established theory yet to account for important experimental evidence. Conversely, behavioral theory, unless it is supported by the data, is not tenable.

0.2 What Constitutes Good Science?

The key to doing good economics, whether in research or teaching, relies on understanding what constitutes good science. I would encourage students and instructors to spend some time thinking about these issues that lie at the heart of their subject.

0.2.1 The Scientific Method

The scientific method is essentially a series of prescriptions in order to do good science. A researcher typically begins with some observations about the real world, or conjectures about a phenomenon. The researcher then generates predictions based on known theory, or new theory that the researcher may formulate. In order to test the predictions, the researcher then forms clear hypotheses to either explain the observations, or verify the conjectures. The hypotheses, based on the relevant theory, specify the circumstances under which the predictions of the theory will fail or succeed. This ensures that the relevant theory is falsifiable, a minimum requirement for any theory. Finally, the researcher will design experiments to collect data, or use existing data, to test the theory using appropriate statistical methods.

The tests are designed to *falsify rather than confirm* the theory; this is the sense in which they are "stringent tests of the theory." Any particular dataset may confirm the theory for now, but the theory might well be rejected by future data. Scientific progress is achieved as newer, and better, theories are formulated that explain everything that the older theories could explain, but also explain some new phenomena that the old theories could not explain. We may never discover the objectively true underlying theory, but so long as we successfully construct a succession of theories that do better at explaining the data, we make progress. Relative to the "true" underlying theory, the succession of intermediate theories may well be "wrong" but this is not a valid argument to avoid continually formulating better, or less wrong, theories. We come back to this point below because it has been misused in economics to protect existing theories from testing and refutation on the grounds that "all theories are wrong anyways."

The description of the scientific method above is roughly consistent with the justly celebrated work of Popper (1934, 1963). Subsequent work by Kuhn (1962) argued that scientific progress arises by periodic paradigm shifts (abrupt changes in theories) and science does not accumulate in a linear fashion. Kuhn describes a nonlinear process of scientific progress in which "paradigm changes" eventually occur as anomalies begin to accumulate against existing theories, leading to a tipping point where the existing theories become untenable.

Meanwhile several important developments took place in the Popperian position, which make it, in the view of this book, the only tenable framework to follow as good practice in economics. The Duhem–Quine thesis points out that a test of any theory is a joint test of the theory and the auxiliary assumptions. For instance, the data might reject a theory, not because it is incorrect, but because the experimental instructions were flawed, or the subject pool was inappropriate, or proper incentives were not offered. Hence, a single test of a theory may not reject it. One must, therefore, control for all reasonable auxiliary and confounding factors before one concludes that a theory is rejected.

In an important development in the Popperian tradition, Lakatos (1970) proposed *the methodology of scientific research programs*. He distinguished between the non-expendable hard core of a research program and an expendable auxiliary part. As anomalies to the research program begin to surface, the hard core is protected while the auxiliary assumptions are modified to address the anomalies. If such a process leads also to the generation of novel predictions, then it is referred to as *theoretically progressive*. If the novel predictions are not refuted by new data, then the research program is termed as *empirically progressive*. If, however, anomalies to the research program continue to accumulate and the program loses its theoretical and empirical progressivity, then the research program is doomed and likely to be replaced by a new research program.

0.2.2 The Scientific Method in the Natural Sciences

The scientific method, described above, is the critical blueprint on which the natural sciences are based and this should, in principle, apply equally well to economics. However, there is an unfortunate, and uncalled for, divergence of views between the natural sciences and economics on the purpose of the relevant theory. In the natural sciences, the purpose of the relevant theory is to explain the natural world, and researchers try hard to falsify existing theory by designing stringent tests to fail the theory. For, if a theory were to fail, then it provides scientists with an exciting opportunity to understand the real world better and drive further progress in their field. This takes the form of a relatively quick process of accepting refutations of the existing theory and then a stiff competition among competing research groups throughout the world to formulate new theories. For instance, there was a great deal of excitement in the scientific community when the large Hadron Collider was to begin running experiments, in the hope that the shortcoming in existing theories would be revealed, leading to important new advances.

In particular, there is no religious adherence to existing theories in the natural sciences. Let us see what this means. In one of the most celebrated results in physics, Einstein formulated the theory of relativity in 1915. He proposed three tests of the theory. The first, related to observations of the orbit of the planet Mercury, which Newtonian physics failed to explain and relativity could explain, was a known problem. The second, bending of light as it passes through the gravitational field of a stellar body, was a new prediction that needed to be tested, and it was clear how to test it. The third, gravitational redshift (electromagnetic waves traveling out of a gravitational field lose energy leading to an increase in their wavelength) was also a new prediction, but it was completely unclear how to test it.

In a letter to the *London Times* on 28 November 1919, Einstein wrote: “The chief attraction of the theory lies in its logical completeness. If a single one of the conclusions drawn from it proves wrong, it must be given up.” In the event, the second prediction was confirmed by new experiments in 1919, but “proper” confirmation of the third prediction took many more years with significant breakthroughs in 1954 and continuing on to recent years. In every single test, not a single deviation from the predictions of the theory of relativity was found.

In economic theory, there is no comparable example to Einstein’s clear road map to reject his own theory. Yet Einstein’s approach is not uncommon in the natural sciences, and it is a major reason for the success of the natural sciences. In particular, natural sciences have inbuilt mechanisms that do not allow theories to be shielded from refutation, or to hide behind defensive positions.

It can take many years, decades, and sometimes centuries, to develop fully satisfactory theories in the face of constant empirical challenges. For instance, the germ theory of disease was initially proposed in 1549, and then through a series of discoveries, placed on a much firmer footing around the 1890s, particularly following the seminal work of Louis Pasteur and Robert Koch. The molecular basis of life, DNA, was first discovered by a Swiss chemist, Johann Friedrich Miescher, in the 1860s. Yet, he resisted in publishing his findings until 1874 as it was generally believed that the nucleus was too small to contain the building blocks of life. Finally, the structure of DNA was discovered about 80 years later in the 1950s by Francis Crick and James Watson, although several other teams, particularly the one led by Rosalind Franklin, appeared to be arriving at the same result. In other words, scientific discoveries are the results of long periods of persistence and grind.

One last example. The Higgs Boson particle was discovered in 2012, and hailed as the "God Particle" by the popular media. However, the theory behind it was originally published in 1964 by Peter Higgs, among others. However, it took decades to build the necessary equipment, in this case the large Hadron Collider, in order to test it. Peter Higgs received the Nobel Prize in physics in 2013, but he did not receive the prize until his theory had been stringently tested and confirmed. This is reflective of the standards for receiving a Nobel Prize in the natural sciences.

It would, however, appear from the track record of past winners of the Nobel Prize in the Economic Sciences that somewhat different standards of conformity of theory with the empirical evidence apply. A retrospective analysis of past winners in economics to examine what fraction of the winners have not had their theories rejected by the empirical evidence might not make for exhilarating reading. Curiously, in 2013, the Nobel Prize in the Economic Sciences was awarded jointly to Eugene Fama and Robert Shiller. Shiller received it for showing that financial markets are inefficient and Fama for showing that financial markets are not efficient; although both also made other notable contributions that were likely taken into account for the prize.[2] A situation such as this is unlikely to arise for the Nobel Prize in the natural sciences.

0.2.3 The Scientific Method in Economics

Many of you are likely to be pursuing an economics degree. Have you ever wondered why your typical microeconomics courses, or your game theory courses, hardly contain a shred of empirical evidence that offers "stringent" tests of the theory?

At best, unless you were taught by an exceptionally enlightened instructor, it might have been mentioned that people act "as if" they behave in conformity with the taught models. The "as if" condition does not require the factual accuracy of all the assumptions made in the model; such as checking if the relevant bordered Hessian in your optimization problem when you buy your next meal at the university cafeteria is negative semi-definite. The "as if" condition holds if, despite making assumptions that might not be literally true, the predictions of these models are indistinguishable from actually observed behavior. For instance, the moon, sun, and earth are

[2] To be sure, both winners also made sterling contributions in other areas too, deserving of the prize.

satisfactorily modeled for many purposes as just three point masses (the so called "three body problem"), even if this is not literally true.

The "as if" assumption is central to neoclassical economics, and it was forcefully advocated by Friedman (1953) whose views on methodology are widely subscribed to in economics. Friedman (1953, p. 14) argued:

> Truly important and significant hypotheses will be found to have "assumptions that are wildly inaccurate descriptive representations of reality, and, in general, the more significant the theory, the more unrealistic the assumptions .... To be important, therefore, a hypothesis must be descriptively false in its assumptions."

These insights form the basis on which most neoclassical economic theory has been constructed and it is the basis on which many economic theorists practice their craft. In principle, the "as if" assumption is not problematic, provided, and this is the critical caveat, the predictions are stringently tested against the data.

One of the enduring contributions of Kahneman and Tversky in their work in the 1970s was to show that the predictions of neoclassical economic models do not hold even in an "as if" sense (Tversky and Kahneman, 1971, 1973, 1974; Kahneman and Tversky, 1979). A mountain of evidence has supported and added massively to the work of Kahneman and Tversky in subsequent years. This book gives an account of this evidence. However, this work is conspicuous by its absence in the typical course in economic theory.

Consider again the failure of most of your microeconomics and game theory courses to mention the relevant empirical evidence. How are corresponding "theory" courses in the natural sciences taught? Should you expect a course in, say, theoretical physics to stay relatively silent on the relevant empirical evidence? Here is a quote from one of the leading social and behavioral scientists of our times who is also well versed in physics. Gintis (2009, p. xvi) mentions:

> Economic theory has been particularly compromised by its neglect of the facts concerning human behavior ... I happened to be reading a popular introductory graduate text on quantum mechanics, as well as a leading graduate text in microeconomics. The physics text began with the anomaly of blackbody radiation, ... The text continued, page after page, with new anomalies ... and new, partially successful models explaining the anomalies. In about 1925, this culminated with Heisenberg's wave mechanics and Schrödinger's equation, which fully unified the field. By contrast, the microeconomics text, despite its beauty, did not contain a single fact in the whole thousand-page volume. Rather the authors built economic theory in axiomatic fashion, making assumptions on the basis of their intuitive plausibility, their incorporation of the "stylized facts" of everyday life, or their appeal to the principles of rational thought .... We will see that empirical evidence challenges some of the core assumptions in classical game theory and neoclassical economics.

What accounts for this unusual state of affairs? The chief contributory factor has been the inability of neoclassical economics to internalize and practice the scientific method. In its place, the economics profession has adopted a range of homespun methodological positions. In some cases, these homespun positions reflect a misunderstanding of the purpose of economic theory; in other cases they are overly pessimistic of the possibilities for economic models. In yet other cases, they appear to serve a vested purpose in protecting existing economic models from refutation. Whatever the underlying reason, this has in many cases been pernicious for progress in developing neoclassical economic theories that are in sound conformity with the evidence.

Here is a set of quotes, taken from published papers by some of the leaders in economic theory, that amply demonstrate the range of views, yet they share a common intellectual position that goes back to Friedman's "as if" position. It is worth stating these views in some detail because they are so widely subscribed to in economics, yet they have little basis in the scientific method.

> Hence the choice of a model will depend on the purpose for which the model is used, the modeler's intuition, and the modeler's subjective judgment of plausibility .... One economist may reject another's intuition, and, ultimately, the marketplace of ideas will make some judgments. Dekel and Lipman (2010, p. 264).

> In particular, we agree that: economic models are often viewed differently than models in the other sciences; economic theory seems to value generality and simplicity at the cost of accuracy; models are expected to convey a message much more than to describe a well-defined reality; these models are often akin to observations, or to *gedankenexperiments*; and the economic theorist is typically not required to clearly specify where his model might be applicable and how. Gilboa et al. (2014, p. F. 516).

> As in the case of fables, models in economic theory are derived from observations of the real world, but are not meant to be testable. As in the case of fables, models have limited scope. As in the case of a good fable, a good model can have an enormous influence on the real world, not by providing advice or by predicting the future, but rather by influencing culture. Yes, I do think we are simply the tellers of fables, but is that not wonderful? Rubinstein (2006, p. 882)

> Theories are never correct, and in the case of the social sciences they tend to be almost always wrong. The question, therefore, is not whether they are right or wrong, but whether they are wrong in a way that invalidates the conclusions drawn from them. Gilboa (2009, p. 104, in his Section 8.1 titled "Theories Are Always Wrong")

In these views, the arbiter between competing theoretical models is not the empirical evidence, but the "marketplace of ideas." Economic models are also justified as having a "special status" distinct from models in the natural sciences in several respects. They are expected to convey a message, not describe a well-defined reality, or even be testable; theorists are not even required to specify where their models might be applicable; and economic models are akin to fables that are designed to influence culture. I suspect that most neoclassical economists will agree with these views to varying degrees.

All this makes it very difficult, if not impossible, to distinguish between competing theories designed to explain the same reality. This is a recipe for the proliferation of "styles" and "fashions" in economic models; ad-hoc untestable explanations of supposed stylized facts; and loose hand-waving to cherry pick supposed stylized facts that are consistent with a given theory. None of these views wishes to expose economic theories to stringent tests designed to reject theories, as compared to tests that confirm them. Indeed, since all theories in the social sciences are presumed to be wrong anyways, and only required to be internally logically consistent, the claim is that there is no point at all in stringently testing them with the data. This book does not subscribe to any of these views.

One argument for demanding a special status for economic theories has been to plead that they are difficult, if not impossible, to test. Furthermore, it is argued, testing of theories is easier in the natural sciences where the subjects are atoms and natural phenomena, rather than idiosyncratic humans and human behavior. Nothing could be farther from the truth. These arguments reveal ignorance about empirical testing in the natural sciences and the development of empirical regularities in behavioral economics.

Testing can be incredibly difficult and challenging in the natural sciences, as evidenced by our brief discussion in Section 0.2.2. But scientists exploring, say, the chemical composition at the core of a distant star, or the origins of life, or the origin of the Universe, or what causes particular diseases, did not plead for a special status for their subjects. They got on with the very difficult and dogged job of finding the answers, sometimes taking centuries in the process to arrive at a satisfactory answer.

It is true that human behavior is very different from the behavior of atoms. It is, for instance, more heterogeneous. But that does not prevent us from constructing economic theories that allow for this heterogeneity. Physicists did not throw up their hands in despair when asked to model particles in Brownian motion. They got on with developing the appropriate theoretical tools that would allow them to predict the probability that a particle was at a particular location at a given time. This can be tested, and when tested, the theory was confirmed. Nothing prevents economists from engaging in such an exercise.

Economics can, and should, do better in two ways. First, by accepting that the purpose of economic models is to explain a well-defined reality. Second, by showing willingness to subject their theories to stringent empirical testing, with a variety of methods and sources of data, and by jettisoning empirically rejected theories. This allows one to make a choice between competing theories, and point to the way forward, based on the only tenable arbiter – the relevant empirical evidence.

But this is largely what the emerging field of behavioral economics is already engaged in, and this task is facilitated by the close feedback between theory and experiments. Students taking a *well-designed course in behavioral economics* (more on this below) are often palpably excited by the ability to understand human behavior in such a comprehensive manner.

0.3 Data and Methods in Behavioral Economics

The ability to perform controlled experiments is the hallmark of all good science. Experiments not only inform us which of the competing theories explains the data, they might themselves provide the basis for future theoretical developments. Economics has been a relative latecomer to controlled lab and field experiments. It has typically relied on using observational data to draw inferences about actual behavior, or to test theories. Such data is often collected for entirely different purposes (e.g., government statistics collected for annual reports), hence, it is a challenging task to control for all possible reasonable confounds and to ensure exogenous variation in just the right variables. Despite the use of sophisticated econometric techniques, in actual practice it is doubtful how well all possible reasonable confounds can be controlled for.

Data collected from lab and field experiments provides the gold standard in science that gives rise to true exogenous variation in one variable while keeping everything else fixed. *Randomized control trials* (RCTs) in medicine are an example of such field data. This process was played out in public during the recent developments of new vaccines for Coronavirus as clinical trials for several candidate vaccines began in 2020. A control group was given a placebo and a treatment group was given the actual vaccine to be tested. Subjects in the experiment were randomly allocated to the control and the treatment groups without the subjects and the experimenter knowing which group any subject belonged to (double blind trials). If the sample size is high enough in such trials, then a contrast between the control and the treatment group provides evidence for the efficacy of the vaccine and any potential side effects; hence, the term "controlled experiments". This is the basic method followed in RCTs and it must be mentioned, lest there is any confusion, in lab experiments too.

Controlled lab experiments and field experiments have played a major role in the development and success of behavioral economics. The results from these experiments have challenged the predictions of neoclassical economics, hence, for an extended period of time, there was hostility to these new methods, often on weak grounds. However, all this has changed, and is changing, for the better. This change has been accomplished by the ability of behavioral economists to systematically address the objections to the use of these newer data sources. All top journals in economics now routinely publish research based on these methods. Instructors teaching any course in economics can now draw on the evidence from behavioral economics with considerable confidence.

We also wish, in this section, to offer a defense of lab experiments as this method has been sometimes much misunderstood and maligned, not only in neoclassical economists, but also by some applied economists who solely push the virtues of RCTs at the expense of lab experiments. However, our purpose is not to argue that any particular method is always superior to the other methods, but rather to make a case for a non-hierarchical respect for these alternative sources of data.

Let us briefly consider a few objections that were raised against lab experimental methods; a more detailed discussion with references follows later in the book, particularly in Part II.[3]

1. *The student subject pool*: The university/college student subject pool that was predominantly used in some of the early lab experiments was a target for the critics. However, in most areas, experiments have now been performed with diverse subject pools, sustaining the core insights derived from experiments with student subjects. Students are a well-educated subject pool that is likely to understand the experimental instructions well. After all, economic theory does not exempt students from its predictions. If anything, experiments with student subject pools on prosociality have shown better conformity with neoclassical theory as compared to non-student subject pools. However, both subject pools reject several critical assumptions and findings of neoclassical economics.
2. *Lack of incentives*: The critics have argued that incentives in experiments were too small to take refutations of the predictions of neoclassical economics seriously. Yet, economic theory does not specify how high the incentives ought to be for them to hold. It is worth pointing out that it was only through experiments that *stake size effects*, that is, the dependence of human behavior on the size of the incentives, was discovered. The general lesson is that increasing

[3] For a discussion of the objections to various aspects of the findings from experimental economics, see Levitt and List (2007). For a defense of the experimental method against these objections see Falk and Heckman (2009), Camerer (2015). Several important papers are contained in the edited book by Fréchette and Schotter (2015). For a wide-ranging discussion of the experimental method, see Roth (1995) and Bardsley et al. (2010).

the size of incentives in experiments may reduce the variance of responses in some types of experiments, but this does not change the qualitative results, say, the signs of the comparative static effects. There are no known major reversals of qualitative results in the presence of incentives, although incentives may have quantitative effects.

3. *External validity*: Are the findings from lab experiments portable/applicable to the real world? The initial suspicion was that they might not be. This is known as the problem of *external validity* of lab findings. However, there is no a priori reason why the findings of well-designed lab experiments should not be relevant to the real world, particularly when lab experiments are conducted with diverse subject pools. There is now persuasive evidence on the external validity of lab experiments from many different domains. For instance, subjects who are more prosocial in the lab are also more prosocial in real life; for the evidence, see Part II.

While RCTs, which are field experiments, are often cited as the gold standard in testing, this book does not place them hierarchically above lab experiments in order of importance. Both methods are important in their own ways and both have limitations. The key feature of both sorts of experiments is that they are able to induce exogenous variation in one variable of interest, while keeping all other variables fixed.

In RCTs, one group of subjects is randomly allocated by the experimenter to a treatment group (there can also be multiple treatment groups). The behavior of this group can then be compared to the rest (the control group). A lab experiment also works on the same principle by randomly assigning subjects in the lab to different treatment groups whose behavior relative to a control group can be studied. Since RCTs are often run with larger budgets, they typically have the advantage of employing larger sample sizes and, hence, imparting greater statistical power to tests of competing hypotheses. Such "scaling up" of sample size is important to learn more about the quantitative effects of a phenomenon (Muralidharan and Niehaus, 2017). However, in principle, nothing prevents us from using large sample sizes in lab experiments, provided that we have appropriate resources to do so.

For a wide-ranging discussion of the misperceptions about RCTs that have led many to place RCTs above all other forms of data, the interested reader may wish to consult Deaton and Cartwright (2018).[4] In particular, they challenge the greater presumed external validity of RCTs and claims about the average treatment effects (ATEs), which is the average difference in the effect found between the treatment and the control groups. They write (p. 10): "More fundamentally, we strongly contest the often-expressed idea that the ATE calculated from an RCT is automatically reliable, that randomization automatically controls for unobservables, or worst of all, that the calculated ATE is true. If, by chance, it is close to the truth, the truth we are referring to is the truth in the trial sample only."

It is typically possible to engage in more complex manipulation of the experimental conditions by the experimenter in lab experiments relative to RCTs, increasing the scope of the phenomena that can be studied. RCTs may not allow the complex treatment manipulation that is required in order to test many different economic theories. These points may be difficult to understand in the abstract. Hence, we give a concrete example below that illustrates several features of how data is collected and how treatments are designed in behavioral economics.

[4] Angus Deaton is the 2015 Nobel Prize winner in economics.

Consider, for instance, a researcher who is interested in a problem where social norms play a key role. Social norms underpin a great deal of human behavior and they require several important ingredients that need to be manipulated in order to test theories based on them (Bicchieri, 2006; Elster, 2011; Fehr and Schurtenberger, 2018). Conformity with social norms requires the presence of *empirical expectations* (one's expectations of the actions of others, based on observations of the "actual behavior" of others) and *normative expectations* (one's expectations of how the relevant social group expects others "ought to behave"). Successful social norms require that these two forms of expectations should not be in conflict with each other. Furthermore, the emotion of shame from breaking a social norm, and punishments from the social group for norm violation act, respectively, as internal and external deterrents to violate norms. It may be difficult to sustain social norms in the absence of these deterrents.

But this does not fully capture the inherent complexity present in many important economic situations and theories. Not only are individuals often subject to social norms, but they might also interact within several kinds of economic partnerships and team environments. In these settings, individuals might additionally suffer from the emotion of guilt from letting down a partner's expectation. Such situations are pervasive in human cooperation across many domains.

With so many moving components (empirical expectations, normative expectations, punishments, guilt, shame) is it realistic to expect an RCT to provide us with a stringent test of the relevant economic theory? Would lab experiments, or the traditionally used field/observational data, be more appropriate?

The answer depends on the research questions that one is interested in. Rather than talk in the abstract, consider a concrete example below from microfinance contracts where all these moving parts play an important role. This example also allows us to introduce the 2×2 experimental design, a widely used method in experimental economics; and also introduces readers to some other useful considerations in experimental design.

Microfinance borrowers are small borrowers who lack collateral to borrow money for potentially profitable, but risky projects. The formal banking sector is unwilling to lend them any money in the absence of collateral, yet the borrower and the lender might be better off if such lending were available; we may term this as the *microfinance problem*. The Grameen Bank, and its founder Muhammad Younus, who did his PhD in economics, won the 2006 Nobel Peace Prize, for solving the microfinance problem through cleverly devised contracts. These contracts often have the following two interesting dimensions.

1. *The type of liability:* In a *joint liability* (JL) contract, a microfinance bank lends money to a group of borrowers. Each borrower in the group engages in an independent and risky project that requires the input of costly effort that is not observed by the bank. However, if any borrower in the group defaults on their loan, all the other borrowers in the group are refused a future loan by the bank, even if they have repaid their own loans. This is the sense in which joint liability applies. This provides a powerful incentive for borrowers to exert "peer pressure" on others in the group to work hard to repay the loan. By contrast, in an individual liability loan (IL), each borrower borrows money individually and if they repay their own loan, they qualify for a future loan. We may take the type of the liability, JL or IL, to be the first dimension of the microfinance contracts.

Table 0.1 A 2 × 2 experimental design for microfinance contracts in a simple two period model.

Repayment / Liability	Private (I) Unobservable to a third party	Public (P) Observable to a third party
Individual Liability (IL) Borrower gets 2nd period loan only if the 1st period loan is repaid.	***ILI*** Emotions absent No Private Signal No Public Signal	***ILP*** Shame No Private Signal Public Signal s
Joint Liability (JL) Borrower gets 2nd period loan only if all group members repay their 1st period loans.	***JLI*** Guilt Private Signal θ_i No Public Signal	***JLP*** Guilt & Shame Private Signal θ_i Public Signal s

Source: Dhami et al. (2022).

2. *Mode of repayment:* The loan officer visits groups of borrowers, say in a village, at discrete intervals of time, perhaps weekly or once every month. The borrowers in a village are gathered together to meet the loan officer and their loan repayment decision is "publicly observed" by others. This is the sense in which there is *public repayment* (P) of loans.
   By contrast, under private/individual repayment (I), the loans are repaid privately to the bank and the repayment/default decision is not publicly observed by others.

Since loan defaults have future consequences in microfinance contracts, the simplest setting to think about this problem is of two time periods. Putting the two dimensions together in a 2 × 2 design, we get the four different types of microfinance contracts shown in Table 0.1: *ILI* (individual liability, private repayment), *ILP* (individual liability, public repayment), *JLI* (joint liability, private repayment), *JLP* (joint liability, public repayment). We explain the contents of Table 0.1 in more detail below.

The two main foundational questions in microfinance contracts are the following:

1. What determines the type of microfinance contract (ILI, ILP, JLI, or JLP) offered by lenders?
2. What are the determinants of effort and repayments by loan borrowers?

How might we answer these questions through three different methods by which data can be generated, RCTs, lab experiments, and classical testing within economics that uses observational field data?

Researchers interested in these questions have typically suggested the roles of *peer pressure* and *social capital* in inducing borrowers in a JL contract to repay their loans. Social norms of repayment have also been highlighted in the literature. However, despite impressive progress in the literature, answering the two fundamental questions has proved elusive, moving the 2019 Nobel Prize winner in the Economic Sciences to remark:

> We still seem to be missing the right experiment here, and I am not entirely sure what that would be... it is entirely possible that the theory is missing something essential. On the theoretical side, the idea that behavioral issues are key to understanding borrower and lender behavior is in the air... Banerjee (2013, pp. 494, 495, 514).

It is clear that satisfactory answers to the two questions above require a formalization of peer pressure and social capital within a theory of social norms of some sort. A researcher wishing to use RCTs will, therefore, have to look for data that provides them with exogenous variation in each of the relevant elements keeping everything else fixed. The relevant elements here include the types of contracts, keeping all other contractual terms fixed; empirical expectations; normative expectations; punishments for norm violations; peer pressure; and social capital.

But it is still unclear how observed exogenous variation in one of the elements listed above can provide a complete answer to the questions we have posed. For starters, there is no presumption that the "other elements" can be held fixed over the long time period that the RCTs typically take to complete. Furthermore, the claim is often made that RCTs are theory-free. This creates difficulties in first constructing a theoretical model, and then carefully designing purpose-built experiments to test the predictions of the theory. Hence, this circumscribes the scope of the research questions that can be posed.

A researcher wishing to use observational data in economics will look for the best available proxies of the various elements that are listed above (contractual structure, empirical expectations, normative expectations, punishments, peer pressure, social capital). The researcher will then attempt to relate them statistically to contractual choices by lenders, and effort choices by borrowers. This is fine in principle, but it is never as straightforward in practice. Good proxies may be hard, or impossible, to obtain. The various elements may themselves be correlated, which precludes using them together. Good instruments for the relevant variables might not be available. Researchers interested in observational field studies may also look for natural exogenous variation in any of the relevant elements. However, this data is not custom-generated and finding such exogenous variation in just one element, keeping the rest fixed, is often down to pure luck. This may also hamper the process of first writing the relevant theory, deriving the relevant predictions, and then inducing custom-made exogenous variation in the data to stringently test the theory.

For other, simpler, research questions, RCTs and observational studies have been enormously insightful and useful. To be sure, there has been a large empirical literature using RCTs and observational studies to answer the two foundational questions in microfinance. But there has been limited success. As noted in Banerjee's quote above, that is partly due to the shortcomings of the methods noted earlier. Other contributory factors include a lack of formal definitions for peer pressure/social capital, and the inability to hold the contractual terms fixed when comparing different contracts. For instance, it is not very illuminating to compare JL contracts with IL contracts if their associated contractual terms (interest rates, duration, type of borrowers) are different. For a sample of papers that reference these issues, see Banerjee (2013), Giné and Karlan (2014), Dhami et al. (2022).

Dhami et al. (2022) propose using lab experiments to answer the two foundational questions listed above. To induce greater realism in their experiments, they use experienced microfinance borrowers as their subjects. Lab experiments conducted in the field with real subjects are known as *lab in the field experiments*, and sometimes as *artefactual field experiments*. The authors begin with a formal theoretical, beliefs-based, model that relies on *psychological game theory* (see Section 8.6 of the book) and define peer pressure and social capital in a precise manner. This allows them to derive testable theoretical predictions. They then use the 2×2 experimental design shown in Table 0.1 that allows for stringent empirical tests of their predictions. We consider their results in more detail in Part IV, but for now we offer some insights from their work which show why an RCT may not be well suited to the task.

Peer pressure arises in JL contracts (JLI, JLP) but not in IL contracts (ILI, ILP). Borrower i in a JL contract may feel "guilty" from letting down the effort expectations of other group members to whom the loan has jointly been given. For, if one member defaults, the others lose future borrowing privileges. In the experiments, this requires that borrower i receive a signal θ_i of the effort expectations of their partners in the group. All this is underpinned by a theoretical model of guilt-aversion, which we describe in more detail in Section 8.6. Valuable social capital can be lost by defaulting in front of one's social group, which is the case in public repayment contracts (ILP, JLP) but not in private repayment contracts (ILI, JLI). Borrowers under public repayment contracts receive some signal, s, of the underlying normative expectations of the relevant social group. Thus, a default in front of one's social group invokes shame from falling below the normative expectations set by the social group. Table 0.1 shows the emotions invoked in each contract and the signals (θ_i, s) available in each type of contract.

1. Holding fixed the method of repayment (public or individual basis), but varying the liability structure (IL to JL), allows us to isolate the effects of peer pressure alone. This arises from the guilt experienced by borrower i from putting in an effort below the expectation of the partner, as captured by the signal θ_i of the partner's expectations. This requires us to compare the outcomes in the following pairs of contracts: ILI versus JLI and ILP versus JLP.
2. Holding fixed the liability structure (IL or JL) but varying the method of repayment, we can study the effect of social capital alone that arise from defaults, and social punishment from peers that invokes the emotion of shame. The emotion of shame arises from putting in effort below the expectations of the social group, as captured by the signal s of the effort expectations of the social group. For this we need to compare the outcomes in the following pairs of contracts: ILI versus ILP and JLI versus JLP.
3. Finally, a comparison of the contract JLI with ILP gives us a comparison of the joint effects of peer pressure and social capital; the authors use this to compare the relative importance of guilt and shame in influencing the effort level of workers.

Furthermore, we can compare the effort levels under the various contracts to examine the determinants of effort. In other words, in order to answer the fundamental questions in microfinance, it becomes imperative to use

(i) the 2×2 treatment design shown in Table 0.1, and
(ii) either lab, or artefactual field experiments.

It is important to note that the precise formulation of such a design is facilitated by first specifying the predictions of the relevant theoretical model. It allows us to answer both fundamental questions in microfinance posed above. The authors find that peer pressure (underpinned by guilt aversion) and social capital (underpinned by shame aversion) are enormously important determinants of not just contractual choices offered by the lenders but also the effort choices by borrowers. Social norms play a key role in the effort choices of borrowers. When both emotions, guilt and shame, are in play, it is the shame experienced from violating norms within a social group, rather than guilt experienced from letting down a partner's expectation, that is more important. We describe the results in more detail in Part IV. However, for the moment, this exercise allows us to think about the usefulness of alternative sources of data and why, in particular, lab-in-the-field experiments are often a very useful source of data.

Note some of the following take-away lessons from this exercise. We are not arguing in this book that RCTs are inferior to lab experiments or to any other method. However, we do argue that there should be no presumption that lab experiments are hierarchically inferior to RCTs, or to observational field experiments in economics, for the following reasons.

1. In many cases, particularly for theories that have complex moving parts, careful lab experimental design might be the best available option. Extra realism can be imparted by using real life subjects as in artefactual field studies.
2. Enormous budgets are typically required to run RCTs, while lab experiments are cheaper to run, allowing for quicker replication, and faster progress.
3. The time duration for running RCTs may make it difficult to hold fixed everything else. For instance, in an RCT lasting over two years for the microfinance experimental design reported above, when exactly should the signals θ_i and s be given to the subjects? Will the effects of these signals wear off? Will these signals given to the treatment group also influence the behavior of the control group as the two groups meet and share information in the real world? The anonymity and experimental control in lab experiments on the other hand allows for clean and unambiguous results.
4. While we know a great deal about replication of results in experimental economics, much less is known about the replication of results from RCTs, given the time, effort, and resource intensity required to conduct RCTs. In behavioral economics, the outcomes are often found to be context, frame, and culture dependent, hence exact replication may not always be possible. However, replication is an important part of establishing confidence in the results from a particular method and there is growing interest in replications of existing experimental studies (Camerer et al., 2016; Camerer et al., 2018). One suggestion for enhancing replication success rates is to increase the significance level required for new results (Benjamin et al., 2018). However, some of the most important experiments in behavioral economics that establish systematic departures from the neoclassical model have been successfully replicated. A small sample of these experiments includes experiments to establish reference dependence, loss aversion, non-linear probability weighting, prosocial preferences, conditional reciprocity, present-biased preferences, limited attention, limited and subjective recall of memory, the use of judgment heuristics, and the inability to conform to some of the central predictions in models of classical game theory.
5. The portability of the results from RCTs to other contexts and economic situations is not always clear, while experiments, because they are less resource intensive, can be more readily run to check for portability. The finding of *prosocial punishment* in public goods games in richer countries in the West and *anti-social punishment* in some poorer, more traditional, societies, is an example (see Part II of the book for the details).
6. Finding precise exogenous variation in several kinds of variables is extremely difficult in RCTs. This is also the case in observational field data. As an illustrative example, consider the manipulation of higher order beliefs that underpin, say, guilt aversion and shame aversion in

the microfinance experiments reported above. By contrast, such belief manipulation is readily achieved in lab experiments. For instance, with two players A and B, the first order beliefs of A about B are what A expects B to do. The second order beliefs of player B are beliefs about the first order beliefs of player A. The definitions of guilt aversion and shame aversion require precise manipulation of second order beliefs as we shall show in Part IV. It is highly unlikely that the required manipulation of beliefs can be cleanly achieved in an RCT or an observational field study.

0.4 Some Misconceptions about Behavioral Economics

Given that behavioral economics is still young, there are several misconceptions and questions about the subject that need to be clarified. In what follows, the misconception/question is stated in italics, followed by an assessment.

1. *Behavioral economics is a "soft" option*: Behavioral economics is as theoretically rigorous as neoclassical economics. It is essentially microeconomic theory that is interdisciplinary, and strongly grounded in the empirical evidence. Some of the main theories, for example, prospect theory, hyperbolic discounting, and some theories of other-regarding preferences, are axiomatically founded, as in neoclassical economics. But more importantly, they explain the evidence much better.
2. *Is behavioral economics a science or more generally, is economics a science?* The approach taken in this book is in the affirmative in the following sense. The best work in behavioral economics is done by rigorously formulating the relevant interdisciplinary theory, clearly specifying the circumstances under which it fails, and then stringently testing it using rigorous statistical methods. In the event that a theory is rejected after controlling for all reasonable confounds, the researcher respects the empirical rejection. But this is essentially the template from the natural sciences. We do not subscribe to the erroneous view, examined in detail above, that testing of theories is somehow more complicated in economics relative to the natural sciences, or that a special status is needed for economic theories that protect them from being refuted. Doing so would be defeatist, a blatant cop out, retrogressive, and inimical to further progress.
3. *There is no finding in behavioral economics that cannot be accommodated within neoclassical economics*: This view is in error in many different ways. Consider the von-Neumann–Morgenstern axioms that give rise to an expected utility representation of preferences in neoclassical economics (see Chapter 1). The most satisfactory alternative in behavioral economics under risk and uncertainty is prospect theory (see Chapter 2). While elements of prospect theory, in particular reference dependence and loss aversion, can be accommodated within the von-Neumann–Morgenstern axioms, a key element, non-linear probability weighting, cannot be. Furthermore, neoclassical economics has made little, if any, use of reference dependence and loss aversion even if these features can be accommodated within its ambit. In particular, neoclassical economics offers no interesting predictions by using these elements because it has no theory about how human behavior differs in the domains of gains and losses relative to a reference point.

Bounded rationality in the form of non-optimizing behavior, say in the use of heuristics that are sometimes prone to error, is not consistent with utility maximizing behavior in neoclassical economics. Non-optimizing behavior could also arise due to limited attention, overconfidence, and cognitive limitations (Parts V and VI) or due to true uncertainty (where the future consequences of one's actions are totally unimaginable).

It is sometimes useful to formulate models that are behavioral for some parameter values, and neoclassical for other parameter values. Indeed, this is a feature of many behavioral models. However, in general, behavioral economics need not be a special case of neoclassical economics (e.g., prospect theory is not a special case of expected utility). Nor is neoclassical economics necessarily a special case of behavioral economics (optimizing behavior need not be a special case of using simple rules of thumb). Hence, statements such as "if you generalize neoclassical economics enough you get behavioral economics" are not only imprecisely formulated and unhelpful in gaining any further understanding of the subject, they are also erroneous.

4. *Given enough experience, the behavior of subjects conforms to the predictions of neoclassical economics*: This assertion is not empirically supported. The behavior of experienced subjects still departs in important ways from the predictions of neoclassical economics. A wealth of data, particularly the field data reviewed in this book, shows that experienced subjects exhibit a range of behavioral features. These features include reference dependence, loss aversion, non-linear probability weighting, conditional reciprocity, guilt, shame, moral values, present-focused preferences, limited attention, imperfect memory and recall, heuristics, social and moral norms-based behavior rather than optimizing behavior, and limited steps of reasoning in strategic situations. Each of these features creates important departures from the predictions of the neoclassical model.
5. *Behavioral economics is a subfield of economics*: Behavioral economics does share a common toolkit with neoclassical economics, for example, formal mathematical models to generate predictions and stringent empirical testing. However, behavioral economics is interdisciplinary, applies to all areas of economics, and offers novel testable predictions that are sometimes absent in neoclassical economics. As such, teaching behavioral economics as another optional course in an undergraduate degree gives a misleading signal of its importance and scope (more on this below).
6. *Behavioral economics mainly comprises a few carefully chosen nudges and disorganized sets of heuristics*: Nudges play a critically important role in public policy and have been enormously successful in producing policy affects that compare favorably with other economic incentives. However, a quick look at this book will show that the topic of nudges, which is a subset of behavioral welfare economics (see Chapter 12), is overall a smaller part of behavioral economics, relative to its portrayal in common discourse. Furthermore, understanding the need for nudges requires one to master the material from several parts of the book, such as present-focused preferences, cognitive limitations, limited attention, mental models, and models of habit formation.

Heuristics are rules of thumb that people use to solve problems (see Part V of the book). As such, they offer an alternative to mathematical optimization (that economics undergraduates are well trained in) to solve economic problems. A common criticism is that there are too many heuristics and they comprise an unorganized and arbitrary set of rules of behavior. This criticism is misplaced. The work of Kahneman and Tversky that we examine in Part V, does highlight the context and the frame in which these heuristics are useful. It is also possible to give formal definitions of several heuristics and derive testable implications that have been successfully tested against the data. Some heuristics are defined as belonging to a larger family of heuristics. For instance, the gambler's fallacy and the hot hand fallacy, although leading to a different set of behaviors, are just different forms of the representativeness heuristic. Thus, the heuristics are nicely organized into suitable subgroups, and their context is quite clear. However, we do certainly need more progress in this area.

0.5 About This Book

This book is designed for several different purposes. The entire book is too long to be taught in a single semester in its entirety, but it offers a rich menu of potential options for instructors wishing to use it for a single semester course. The book would ideally be taught in a two to three semester course in behavioral economics.

The book can also be taught, as an essential part of a microeconomics or game theory course, at the second or third year undergraduate levels. The pernicious and, sadly, widespread practice in economics of teaching empirics-free courses in microeconomics and game theory needs to be strongly discouraged. Students need to cast their vote through the end of year course evaluations in demanding more empirically founded courses in economic theory. In doing so, they would not just be following the lead from the natural sciences, but ensuring that they achieve a better understanding of the real world, where they are likely eventually to end up working.

Other courses in applied microeconomics such as industrial organization, labor economics, public economics, contract theory, regulation, law and economics, are also likely to find parts of the book useful. While there exist advanced books in behavioral economics for those who are interested in pursuing a graduate course[5] or those conducting research, this book can also be a useful entry point for the advanced reader who has had no prior grounding in behavioral economics.

The book is divided into seven parts. These parts are, in order, *Behavioral Decision Theory*, *Other-Regarding Preferences*, *Behavioral Time Discounting*, *Behavioral Game Theory*, *Bounded Rationality*, and *Further Topics in Behavioral Economics*. Within the last part of the book titled *Further Topics in Behavioral Economics*, we have a chapter on a smorgasboard of topics such as limited attention, salience, happiness economics, complexity economics, learning models, and behavioral industrial organization. This is followed by two further chapters on, respectively, behavioral welfare economics, and an ambitious chapter on neuroeconomics, which is available only on Cambridge's Higher Education website and it is freely accessible at

[5] For a graduate-level treatment of behavioral economics, see Dhami (2016) which was subsequently updated and split into seven volumes published by Oxford University Press. There are also several handbooks and collections of articles that are likely to be useful for such a reader.

www.cambridge.org/dhami. The table of contents gives a detailed account of all that is inside the book covers. Section 0.6 discusses the book contents further.

This book is a comprehensive, state of the art, introduction to the most important principles of behavioral economics. It does not shy away from difficult and challenging questions and topics. Indeed it makes particular virtue out of discussing them in a straightforward, clear, and lucid manner. Only as much mathematics as is absolutely necessary is used. In particular, calculus is sparingly used and no more than high school algebra is required in most places. As such, the book can be taught at any stage in an undergraduate degree. There are problems and references at the end of each part of the book. The only exception is Part VI, where the three chapters do not have a common theme, so there are separate references for each chapter and problems at the end of each chapter except the neuroeconomics chapter that does not have any associated problems.

The book is written in a modular way, so that readers can dip into almost any chapter at will without worrying about reading the book in a linear fashion. The existing structure follows, roughly, the typical sequence that is used in microeconomics courses. The one notable exception is that microeconomics courses begin with a chapter on consumption choices under certainty, while this book begins with choice under risk and uncertainty. The reason for this is that choice under certainty in behavioral economics is meshed with several other topics. For instance, the prospect theory utility function under risk and uncertainty also applies under certainty. Choice under certainty in behavioral economics also has elements of limited attention, salience, anticipal utility, experienced versus transaction utility, self-regarding versus other-regarding preferences, and so on. For all these reasons, there is not a compelling case to begin with a chapter on certainty in a book on behavioral economics. The structure of the book also mirrors the one in my more advanced book (Dhami, 2016) and the seven subsequent book volumes. This should enable readers to transit seamlessly from undergraduate courses in behavioral economics to more advanced graduate courses in behavioral economics.

0.6 Designing Courses in Behavioral Economics

This brief section is addressed to two types of audience. First, instructors who teach courses in behavioral economics, or experimental economics, or some combination of the two. Second, students who wish to gain greater familiarity with the contents of this book and wish to read parts of it on their own.

It can be difficult to fit an entire course in behavioral/experimental economics within a single semester. Undergraduate programs in several universities have successfully made a strong case to have a two-semester course on the subject. Instructors in many microeconomics courses increasingly incorporate evidence from behavioral economics, which is a positive development that should be built on by those who might have failed to notice that they are behind the curve.

I am moved to share my dismay at the proliferation of fairly idiosyncratic course outlines in behavioral/experimental economics that revolve around a few topics of personal interest to instructors. This would normally be fine for a topics course in behavioral economics. However, a behavioral/experimental economics course, particularly when it is the only such course offering in the undergraduate degree, needs a solid core of standardized material that does justice to the subject. Behavioral economics is still young and well-designed undergraduate courses will play a key role in motivating the next generation of students to work in this exciting area and make important contributions to it. Conversely nothing puts off students more than an idiosyncratic and poorly designed course.

I invite instructors in behavioral/experimental courses to imagine a course in microeconomics, the closest analogue within the standard curriculum. Suppose that an instructor, primarily interested in empirical estimation of production functions, teaches an entire microeconomics course based on just a few applied, but famous, papers on empirical estimation of the production function. There would be an absolute outcry if this happened, and it never does happen. Yet, some current offerings in behavioral and experimental economics are, sadly, not far off from this hypothetical case. Many undergraduate students will only see a single course offered on the subject, typically in experimental economics, that is theory-free, and based on a few, well-published, empirical papers of personal interest to the instructor. The exams are often uninspiring and based on memorizing the details in these papers. This is an undesirable state of affairs that needs to change. It is also an important concern that led to this book being written. I have responded by offering a template for a systematic and standardized approach to the most important principles of behavioral economics.

Many different types of well-designed single-semester courses in behavioral economics are feasible. Each of these courses might wish to consider several core elements taken from the first four parts of the book. The remaining topics could be picked from Parts V and VI of the book, depending on the instructor's interests.

Among the possible topics, based on my own one-semester third-year undergraduate course at Leicester, delivered with a combination of lectures and workshops over 30 hours of contact time, are the following. Each of these topics is treated in detail in this book. Instructors in the United Kingdom, of which the semester at Leicester is representative, are likely to find it difficult to cover all of these topics in detail in a semester-length course. Hence, for some of these topics, depending on their interest, instructors may wish to provide just a broad outline and comment on the empirical findings. As part of a good education in a university, some of the students can then chase up these topics in more detail from the book, depending on their own interests. The North American semester tends to be longer, although of variable length, which should permit many of these topics to be covered in more detail.

1. Topic-1 (Behavioral Decision Theory): It is best to begin with expected utility theory and its refutations. The main focus should be on a formal exposition of prospect theory that includes non-linear probability weighting. This can be followed by selected applications such as the endowment effect, tax evasion puzzles, implications for optimal contracts, and prospect theory preferences in primates. The instructor should also probably articulate where prospect theory explains well the evidence from risk, uncertainty, and ambiguity, and where it does not. Students should also be invited to consider if this machinery can help us to understand true uncertainty or *Knightian uncertainty* (unknown unknowns).
2. Topic-2 (Other-Regarding Preferences): It is best to begin with a description of the experimental games (ultimatum game, gift exchange game, trust game, public goods game) and the

associated evidence on human prosociality and conditional reciprocity. This can be followed by a discussion of the theoretical models that try to explain the relevant evidence. These models could include the Fehr–Schmidt model, the Bolton–Ockenfels model, the Charness–Rabin model, and models of intentions driven reciprocity. It is important to emphasize to the students what sort of dynamics we should expect when there is a mixture of self-regarding and other-regarding preferences. The instructor could also discuss applications to the theory of incentives and how behavioral factors have painted a very nuanced picture of the economic effects of incentives.

3. Topic-3 (Behavioral Time Discounting): The instructor may find it useful to begin with the exponential discounting utility model and the empirical evidence which refutes it (common difference effect, gain-loss asymmetry, magnitude effect, subadditive discounting, dependence of utility on the shapes of consumption profiles). Of these refutations, it is probably best to focus on the common difference effect in some detail and show that hyperbolic discounting provides a resolution to the observed refutation. Time/interest permitting, some of the resolutions to the other refutations can be taken up. Among applications, students typically express interest in the implications for lifecycle models of consumption/savings and the applications of the perception-perfect equilibrium concept to, say, procrastination and its flip side, preproperation.
4. Topic-4 (Behavioral Game Theory): It is best to begin with the static prisoners' dilemma game and the evidence as motivation for the topic, followed by the evidence on Nash equilibrium and subgame perfect equilibrium. One can then show how relaxing the assumptions of the classical equilibrium concepts in game theory leads to the level-k model, the quantal response equilibrium model, cursed equilibrium, and evidential reasoning. There are plenty of applications of these models in the book. It is also worth pointing out to students the critical distinction between private rationality and social rationality, and how a correlated equilibrium might play the role of social norms. Some courses might wish to have a major behavioral game theory component, and indeed this could be a stand-alone course in its own right. For such courses, there is a rich menu of options available in a separate "topics in behavioral game theory" chapter in the book that includes psychological game theory (an absolute must), auction theory, bargaining theory, elements of evolutionary game theory, and the usefulness of the mouselab software.
5. Topic-5 (Miscellaneous): Most instructors will find that by now they have run out of time in a single-semester course, hence, the usefulness of having a two-semester course, which many universities have already moved towards. This will allow many exciting topics to be chosen from Parts V and VI of the book. There are too many topics to list here and I suggest that instructors exercise their own preferences. However, I will take the liberty to point out a few.

   It is important to emphasize the role of *judgment heuristics*, *aspiration adaptation*, and *mental accounting* (Part V). These methods provide non-optimization alternatives to the standard optimization methods in economics. There should be no presumption that optimization methods are somehow superior, although this is the implicit position taken by many economists. This position is largely based on the technical convenience arising from the use of optimization methods, rather than any clinching empirical evidence. Ultimately, the empirical evidence must decide which way we go. For a thorough discussion of these issues, including instances where optimization and non-optimization methods produce similar results, see Dhami and Sunstein (2022).

The first of three chapters in Part VI contains a host of topics that many instructors will find too tempting to ignore, such as behavioral industrial organization, limited attention, salience, and happiness economics. However, I would like to draw particular attention to complexity economics, which receives generous space in the book. It provides an alternative to the existing macroeconomic frameworks by thinking in terms of complex adaptive dynamic systems, using low-level rationality, that produce emergent phenomena and chaos. Together with the material on judgment heuristics and non-optimizing choices in Part V, it provides us with a set of possibilities to think about how humans might make choices under true uncertainty.

Undergraduate students must at some point in their degrees be made aware of the limitations of neoclassical welfare economics that relies purely on the homo-economicus model, compromising on its practical usefulness. The second of the three chapters in Part VI on behavioral welfare economics explores these issues. It is also an introduction to the hugely important behavioral public policy instrument, nudges, that falls under the theory of libertarian paternalism. Students should be encouraged to think through some of the foundational issues behind libertarian paternalism and also the practical successes of nudges in producing changes in human behavior that would take unrealistically high economic incentives to achieve.

The final chapter in Part VI is an introduction to the cutting edge of issues in modern neuroeconomics for those who wish to learn about this important, and sometimes elusive, area. In particular, we discuss the areas of the brain that are particularly relevant for the neuroeconomics literature; alternative measurement and manipulation techniques; brain areas that encode subjective value and prediction errors; the drift diffusion model that underlies perceptual decision making, with applications to limited attention and response times; and how we might establish causality in neuroeconomics.

References

Akerlof, George A. (1982). Labor Contracts as Partial Gift Exchange. *The Quarterly Journal of Economics* 97(4): 543–569.

Allais, M. (1953). La psychologie de lhomme rationnel devant le risque: critique des postulats et axiomes de lécole Américaine. *Econometrica* 21: 503–546.

Ashraf, N., Camerer, C. F., and Loewenstein, G. (2005). Adam Smith, Behavioral Economist. *Journal of Economic Perspectives* 19(3): 131–145.

Banerjee, A. V. (2013). Microcredit Under the Microscope: What Have We Learned in the Past Two Decades, and What Do We Need to Know? *Annual Review of Economics* 5(1): 487–519.

Bardsley, N., Cubitt, R., Loomes, G., Peter Moffatt, P., Starmer, C., and Sugden, R. (2010). *Experimental Economics: Rethinking the Rules.* Princeton University Press: Princeton.

Benjamin, D. J., Berger, J. O., Johannesson, M., Nosek, B. A., Wagenmakers, E. J., Berk, R., and Morgan, S. L. (2018). Redefine Statistical Significance. *Nature Human Behaviour* 2(1): 6–10.

Bicchieri, C. (2006). *The Grammar of Society: The Nature and Dynamics of Social Norms.* Cambridge University Press: New York.

Camerer, C. F. (2015). The Promise and Success of Lab-Field Generalizability in Experimental Economics: A Critical Reply to Levitt and List. in G. R. Fréchette and A. Schotter (eds.), *Handbook of Experimental Economic Methodology*. Oxford University Press: Oxford. pp. 249–295.

Camerer, C. F., Dreber, A., Forsell, E., Ho, T.-H., Huber, J., Johannesson, M., Kirchler, M., Almenberg, J., Altmejd, A., Chan, T., Heikensten, E., Holzmeister, F., Imai, T., Isaksson, S., Nave, G., Pfeiffer, T., Razen, M., Wu, H. (2016). Evaluating Replicability of Laboratory Experiments in Economics. *Science* 351: 1433–1436.

Camerer, C. F., Dreber, A., Holzmeister, F., Ho, T.-H., Huber, J., Johannesson, M., Kirchler, M., Nave, G., Nosek, B. A., Pfeiffer, T., Altmejd, A., Buttrick, N., Chan, T., Chen, Y., Forsell, E., Gampa, A., Heikensten, E., Hummer, L., Imai, T., Isaksson, S., Manfredi, D., Rose, J., Wagenmakers, E.-J., Wu, H. (2018). Evaluating Replicability of Social Science Experiments Published in Nature and Science between 2010 and 2015. *Nature Human Behavior* 2: 637–644.

Camerer, C. and Loewenstein, G. (2004). Behavioral Economics: Past, Present, Future. In C. Camerer, G. Loewenstein, and M. Rabin (eds.), *Advances in Behavioral Economics*. New York: Russell Sage Foundation, pp. 3–51.

Cyert, R. and March, J. G. (1963). *A Behavioral Theory of the Firm*. Prentice-Hall: Englewood Cliffs, NJ.

Deaton, A. and Cartwright, N. (2018). Understanding and Misunderstanding Randomized Controlled Trials. *Social Science & Medicine* 210: 2–21.

Dekel, E. and Lipman, B. L. (2010). How (Not) to Do Decision Theory. *Annual Review of Economics* 2: 25782.

Dhami, S. (2016). *The Foundations of Behavioral Economic Analysis.* Oxford University Press: Oxford.

Dhami, S., Arshad, J., and al-Nowaihi, A. (2022). Psychological and Social Motivations in Microfinance Contracts: Theory and Evidence. *Journal of Development Economics* 158. https://www.sciencedirect.com/science/article/pii/S0304387822000712

Dhami, S. and Sunstein, C. (2022). *Bounded Rationality: Heuristics, Judgment, and Public Policy.* MIT Press: Massachusetts.

Elster, J. (2011). Norms. In P. Bearman and P. Hedström (eds.), *The Oxford Handbook of Analytical Sociology*. Oxford University Press: Oxford, pp. 195–217.

Falk, A. and Heckman, J. J. (2009). Lab Experiments Are a Major Source of Knowledge in the Social Sciences. *Science* 326: 535–538.

Fehr, E. and Schurtenberger, I. (2018). Normative Foundations of Human Cooperation. *Nature Human Behaviour* 2(7): 458–468.

Fréchette, G. R. and Schotter, A. (2015). *Handbook of Experimental Economic Methodology*. Oxford University Press: Oxford.

Friedman, M. (1953). *The Methodology of Positive Economics.* University of Chicago Press: Chicago.

Gilboa, I. (2009). *Theory of Decision under Uncertainty.* Cambridge University Press: Cambridge.

Gilboa, I., Postlewaite, A., Samuelson, L., and Schmeidler, D. (2014). *Economic Models as Analogies*. Economic Journal 124: F513–F533.

Giné, X. and Karlan, D. S. (2014). Group versus Individual Liability: Short and Long Term Evidence from Philippine Microcredit Lending Groups. *Journal of Development Economics* 107: 65–83.

Gintis, H. (2009). *The Bounds of Reason: Game Theory and the Unification of the Behavioral Sciences*. Princeton University Press: Princeton.

Kahneman, D. (2011). *Thinking Fast and Slow.* Farrar, Strauss, Giroux: New York.

Kahneman, D., Knetsch, J. L., and Thaler, R. H. (1991). Anomalies: The Endowment Effect, Loss Aversion, and Status Quo Bias. *Journal of Economic Perspectives* 5(1): 193–206.

Kahneman, D. and Tversky, A. (1979). Prospect Theory: An Analysis of Decision under Risk. *Econometrica* 47(2): 263–291.

Kuhn, T. S. (1962). *The Structure of Scientic Revolutions.* University of Chicago Press: Chicago.

Lakatos, I. (1970). Falsification and the Methodology of Scientific Research Programmes. In I. Lakatos and A. Musgrave (eds.), *Criticism and the Growth of Knowledge*. Cambridge University Press: Cambridge.

Levitt, S. D. and List, J. A. (2007). What Do Laboratory Experiments Measuring Social Preferences Reveal About the Real World? *Journal of Economic Perspectives* 21(2): 153–174.

Muralidharan, K. and Niehaus, P. (2017). Experimentation at Scale. *Journal of Economic Perspectives* 31(4): 103–124.

Popper, K. (1934). *Logik der Forschung* (Hutchinson & Company published the translation by Karl Popper titled The Logic of Scientific Discovery in 1959).

Popper, K. (1963). *Conjectures and Refutations: The Growth of Scientific Knowledge.* Routledge and Kegan Paul: London.

Roth, A. E. (1995). Introduction to Experimental Economics. In J. H. Kagel, and A. E. Roth, (eds.), *The Handbook of Experimental Economics*. Princeton University Press: Princeton, pp. 3–109.

Rubinstein, A. (2006). Dilemmas of an Economic Theorist. *Econometrica* 74(4): 865–883.

Selten, R. (1998). Features of Experimentally Observed Bounded Rationality. *European Economic Review* 42(3–5): 413–436.

Selten R. (2001). What Is Bounded Rationality? In G. Gigerenzer and R. Selten (eds.), *Bounded Rationality: The Adaptive Toolbox. Dahlem Workshop Report.* MIT Press: Cambridge, MA, pp. 1–12.

Shiller, R. (1981). Do Stock Prices Move Too Much to Be Justified by Subsequent Changes in Dividends? *American Economic Review* 71: 421–436.

Simon, H. A. (1978). Rational Decision-Making in Business Organizations. Nobel Memorial Lecture, December 8, 1978.

Simon, H. A. (2000). Bounded Rationality in Social Science: Today and Tomorrow. *Mind and Society* 1(1): 25–39.

Smith, V. L. (1962). An Experimental Study of Competitive Market Behavior. *Journal of Political Economy* 70(2): 111–137.

Thaler, R. H. (2015). *Misbehaving: The Making of Behavioral Economics*. W. W. Norton and Company: New York.

Tversky, A. and Kahneman, D. (1971). Belief in the Law of Small Numbers. *Psychological Bulletin* 76: 105–110.

Tversky, A. and Kahneman, D. (1973). Availability: A Heuristic for Judging Frequency and Probability. *Cognitive Psychology* 5(2): 207–232.

Tversky, A. and Kahneman, D. (1974). Judgment under Uncertainty: Heuristics and Biases. *Science* 185: 1124–1130.

Part I

Behavioral Decision Theory

Introduction to Part I

We often take actions that have consequences that cannot be entirely predicted with certainty, for example, a student choosing a university for higher studies; an investor investing in the stock market; a couple deciding to have one more child; an employee choosing a pension plan; a firm planning to enter a new market; or a government mulling over alternative policy actions on climate change. Animals too need to take actions whose consequences they cannot predict with certainty. For instance, the hunting success rate of the big cats, lions, and tigers, is probably less than 30%.

Yet, humans and animals need to make decisions, and do make decisions, even when their actions have *unpredictable consequences*. Part I of the book is a study of the choice of such actions, but mostly for humans, although we shall also explore an important relation between the risk preferences of humans and closely related primate relatives.

A refinement of the term "unpredictable consequences" can lead to a more nuanced understanding of human decision making. In particular, we find it convenient to distinguish between *risk*, *subjective uncertainty*, *ambiguity*, and *true uncertainty*. Risk refers to situations where all possible outcomes arising from a decision, and the associated probabilities of the outcomes, are objectively known. Subjective uncertainty arises when these probabilities are not objectively known, but subjective probability estimates are available. Ambiguity arises when no subjective or objective probabilities can explain actual choices. True uncertainty (sometimes known as Knightian uncertainty), pervasive in the real world, arises when all possible outcomes from one's actions cannot even be imagined; this is sometimes known as the case of "unknown unknowns."

Despite the overwhelming importance of true uncertainty, economics has surprisingly little to offer by way of predictions in this case. Courses in economics may, at best, mention the term "true uncertainty" tangentially, and in passing. This is a theme that we return to several times in this book. Most of Part I of the book is about decision making under risk and subjective uncertainty.

We organize our discussion into two chapters. In Chapter 1 we explore the traditional approach to decision making under risk and uncertainty in neoclassical economics. This approach assumes that decision makers follow *expected utility theory* (EUT). Moreover, EUT underpins most economic models, and it is the main theory under risk that is taught in microeconomic theory courses, to the almost complete exclusion of other theories. Empirical evidence decisively rejects EUT.

Two features of EUT are rejected by the evidence. First, decision makers do not derive utility from the final levels of income or wealth but from "changes" in these levels from some reference level. This is not inconsistent with the axiomatic foundations of EUT, but EUT has little to offer by way of new predictions even if we relaxed this assumption. Second, decision makers weight probabilities nonlinearly, in contrast to the linear weighting of probabilities under EUT. These two features of EUT led to a large number of rejections of its predictions that have been well documented since the 1950s.

In Chapter 2, we focus on providing alternatives to EUT that address its two main drawbacks mentioned above. We first draw on the empirical evidence to demonstrate how humans weight probabilities nonlinearly, using a *probability weighting function*, which is an essential ingredient in most alternatives to EUT. We follow this up by outlining *rank dependent utility theory* (RDUT), which introduces nonlinear probability weighting. Moreover, RDUT can explain some of the well-known paradoxes of EUT, such as the Allais paradox, which we consider in Chapter 1.

We then discuss *prospect theory* that arose from a detailed consideration of the evidence from human decision making under risk and subjective uncertainty. Associated with the names of Daniel Kahneman and Amos Tversky, who first published it in 1979, and then revised it in 1992, it is one of the most stellar achievements in the social and behavioral sciences. Prospect theory is currently the most satisfactory decision theory as it can explain human choices under risk, subjective uncertainty, and ambiguity. It is also the most tested decision theory, so there is also evidence against it in some domains, which calls for an improvement of the underlying theory. We point out some of this evidence. We consider a large number of applications of prospect theory to a range of domains to illustrate the general usefulness of the theory.

1 The Traditional Approach to Decision Making under Risk and Subjective Uncertainty

1.1 Introduction

In this chapter we explore decision making under risk and subjective uncertainty when decision makers follow *expected utility theory* (EUT). This is the traditional approach taken in neoclassical economics and it has a preeminent position in research and teaching in economics. It is also rejected by the evidence.

Undergraduate students in economics will be familiar with EUT, as it is the main, perhaps the only, model of decision making taught in such courses. However, there will be variation in the courses offered and some courses might have highlighted the connection between the preference foundations of the theory and the convenient functional form that makes this theory so accessible to use. The purpose of this chapter is to partly enable students with diverse backgrounds to achieve a common understanding of EUT that includes the preference foundations.

The preference foundations of EUT are important to explore. Some of the presumed rejections of EUT that have been highlighted in the empirical literature are consistent with its preference foundations. For instance, the concept of *reference dependence* that partitions the domain of outcomes into gains and losses (relative to a reference point), and plays a key role in prospect theory in Chapter 2, is also consistent with EUT. However, this is not a justification for the continued use of EUT, because it lacks any insights on how human behavior might be different in the domains of gains and losses. By contrast, prospect theory is based on critical insights and evidence on precisely this difference in human behavior in the two domains.

Other rejections of EUT, such as nonlinear weighting of probabilities, are inconsistent with the preference foundations of EUT. We now have good, robust, evidence on nonlinear probability weighting and it contradicts the axioms that give rise to EUT. The Allais paradox that we examine in this chapter is an example of empirical evidence that directly contradicts linear probability weighting under EUT. It used to be fashionable to mention the Allais paradox in microeconomics books (perhaps because Maurice Allais was an economic theorist who won the Nobel Prize in 1988) as a curious anomaly, but no more. However, it was shown later that this paradox is actually based on good underlying empirical support for nonlinear probability weighting. Allais, who lived to a ripe old age of 99 and died in 2010, might have been somewhat pleased with the developments in behavioral decision theory that he himself spurred in the early 1950s.

Another feature of EUT that we highlight in this chapter is that attitudes to risk are captured entirely by the shape of the utility function. This could be puzzling to some who might believe that attitudes to risk have something to do with probabilities. However, this counterintuitive result, which is not a feature of any of the alternatives to EUT considered in Chapter 2, simply follows from the logic of EUT.

1.2 A Taxonomy of Situations

Suppose that a *decision maker* takes an action "A" that leads to n possible outcomes denoted by $x_1 < x_2 < \ldots < x_n$. The outcomes can be monetary, say, different income levels arising from stock market investment; or nonmonetary, say, different degrees of job satisfaction from a job. When taking the action A, the decision maker does not know which outcome will materialize in the future, and in this sense the consequences are unpredictable. Denote the probabilities associated with the n outcomes by, respectively, $p_1, p_2, \ldots, p_n$, which are nonnegative and sum up to 1. The simplest case arises when $n = 2$, so there are two outcomes $x_1 < x_2$, such that x_1 occurs with probability $p_1 \geq 0$ and x_2 occurs with probability $p_2 \geq 0$, and $p_1 + p_2 = 1$. This is shown in Figure 1.1 using a simple *decision tree*.

For the case of n outcomes, we can conveniently summarize the unpredictable consequences from an action, and the associated probabilities, by using the shorthand notation of a *lottery*, L (not to be confused with lotteries in ordinary parlance):

$$L = (x_1, p_1; x_2, p_2; \ldots; x_n, p_n). \tag{1.1}$$

In (1.1) each of the n outcome-probability pairs is separated by a semicolon. For instance, suppose that the relevant action, A, is a stock market investment, and there are only two possible outcomes ($n = 2$). Then, the two-outcome lottery $L = (-10, 0.3; 15, 0.7)$ informs us that the investment yields an outcome -10 with a 30% probability and an outcome 15 with a 70% probability. When $n = 1$, so that an outcome x is received with probability 1, a situation of complete certainty, the corresponding lottery is written as

$$L = (x, 1). \tag{1.2}$$

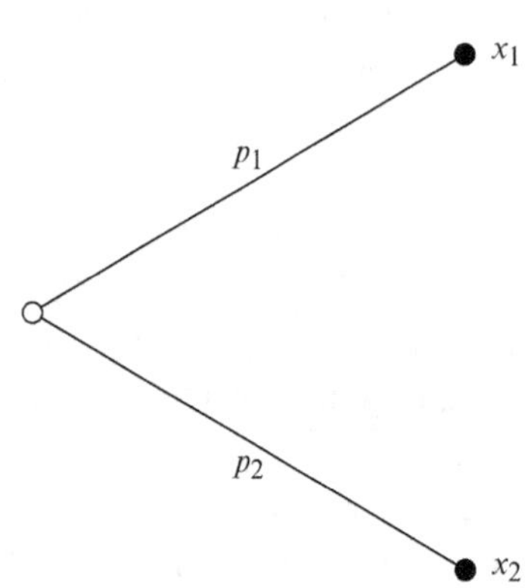

Figure 1.1 A simple decision tree when there are two outcomes, $n = 2$

More generally, one can imagine a decision maker choosing among m different actions $A_1, \ldots, A_m$. For instance, each action could be an investment in a different asset. Each action has potentially unpredictable consequences; perhaps each investment leads to a set of possible returns with associated probabilities. Thus, we may think of the m actions $A_1, \ldots, A_m$ giving rise to, respectively, m lotteries $L_1, \ldots, L_m$. This is also known as a *game against nature* because the individual chooses an action and then nature probabilistically chooses an outcome from the lottery corresponding to that action.

The basic problem in the economics of risk and uncertainty is to choose the optimal action among the m available actions when they lead to probabilistic outcomes. But since each action results in a unique lottery, we can dispense with actions altogether and simply ask which of the m different lotteries $L_1, \ldots, L_m$ the decision maker prefers the most. If lottery L_i is preferred the most, then the action that led to it, A_i, is also the preferred action. The rest of this chapter addresses this question.

It is important to sharpen the use of the term "unpredictable consequences" above, into four different categories: risk, subjective uncertainty, ambiguity, and true uncertainty. We now explain these categories.

1.2.1 Risk

Suppose that a decision maker knows all the outcomes, $x_1 < \ldots < x_n$, in a lottery. If the associated probabilities, $p_1, \ldots, p_n$, are "objectively known," then we have a situation of *risk*. Suppose you agree to the following bet with a friend. A fair six-sided die with six possible outcomes, $1, \ldots, 6$, will be thrown. If an even number comes up, your friend will give you \$1, and if an odd number comes up, then you will give your friend \$1. Before the die is tossed, it is reasonable for both decision makers to assign an objective probability of 50% to winning the bet and an objective probability of 50% to losing the bet. In effect, each friend faces the two-outcome lottery $L = (-1, 0.5; 1, 0.5)$. This is a situation of risk.

1.2.2 Subjective Uncertainty

Suppose that decision makers know all the outcomes, $x_1 < \ldots < x_n$, arising from their actions. In some cases no objective probabilities can be assigned to events. Suppose, for instance, that a friend offers you the following bet. If a Democratic candidate wins the US presidential elections in 2034, the friend will pay you \$100, and if a Republican candidate wins the election you will pay him \$100. Should you accept the bet?

This is a non-trivial problem because no objective probabilities exist for such events. Evaluating this bet will require you to "subjectively" estimate the winning probability of the candidates from the two political parties, looking ahead more than 10 years. Yet, some decision makers might be willing to take on such a bet. This suggests that they might be able to form valid "subjective estimates" based, say, on past data and their subjective assessments. The estimates must be valid in the sense that the subjective probabilities of the two events (either a Democrat or a Republican candidate wins) are nonnegative and sum up to 1. This is known as a situation of *subjective uncertainty* and it is often represented by a special construct known as a *Savage act*.

Denote the event "Democratic party candidate wins" by D and the event "Republican candidate wins" by R. Then, we can write a Savage act, f, for "you" as

$$f = (D, 100; R, -100), \tag{1.3}$$

that is, you win \$100 if the event D takes place and you lose \$100 if the event R takes place. By contrast, the Savage act for your friend, g, can be written as $g = (D, -100; R, 100)$.

Suppose, however, that you are able to assign valid subjective probability estimates of $q_1 \geq 0$ and $q_2 \geq 0$, respectively, to the two events, D and R, such that $q_1 + q_2 = 1$. In this case, we say that the assumption of *probabilistic sophistication* is met. We can now write the Savage act f in its equivalent lottery representation as

$$L = (100, q_1; -100, q_2). \tag{1.4}$$

It follows that under the assumption of probabilistic sophistication, we can treat subjective uncertainty in a manner similar to risk. This essentially allows us to focus on risk in this part of the book, while subjective uncertainty can be analyzed with the same tools.

1.2.3 Ambiguity

Suppose that a decision maker knows that an action leads to a set of n possible outcomes, $x_1 < \ldots < x_n$. A situation of *ambiguity* arises if, using EUT, it is "impossible" to assign either objective or subjective probabilities to the outcomes. We shall discuss this in more detail in Section 2.6. The most famous example is the *Ellsberg paradox*, named after Daniel Ellsberg who released the Pentagon Papers in 1971, which led to a national political controversy in the US. Imagine that we have two urns. A "known urn" (K) contains 50 red and 50 black balls. An "unknown urn" (U) contains a mixture of 100 balls that are either red or black but the exact mixture is unknown.

Most people correctly assign an objective probability of 0.5 to randomly drawing a red ball from the known urn. Appearing to use the *principle of insufficient reason*,[1] they also assign an identical probability 0.5 of randomly drawing a red ball from the unknown urn. Now suppose that the decision maker is offered the following bet. A ball is randomly chosen from one of the the urns. The decision maker receives a prize of \$$z$ if it is a red ball ("event R") and a prize of \$0 if it is a black ball ("event B"). Which urn should the decision maker choose to bet on? In effect, from any of the urns, K and U, the decision maker faces the following Savage act

$$f = (B, 0; R, z). \tag{1.5}$$

Given that the probability assigned by the decision maker to drawing a red ball from each of the two urns is 0.5, and using the principle of probabilistic sophistication (see Section 1.2.2), we can write the Savage act, from any of the two urns, in (1.5) as the lottery

$$L = (0, 0.5; z, 0.5). \tag{1.6}$$

[1] The principle of insufficient reason suggests that a decision maker should assign the same a priori probability to two competing hypotheses if there is no compelling reason for choosing one over the other.

Since the decision maker faces an identical lottery from both urns, one may reasonably expect the decision maker to be indifferent between picking which urn to bet on. By contrast, the empirical evidence shows that most people pick the known urn over the unknown urn. In effect, no objective or subjective probabilities can be assigned that justify the given choice (ambiguity).

1.2.4 True Uncertainty

Risk, subjective uncertainty, and ambiguity do not exhaust the set of all possible situations of interest. Suppose that all the outcomes arising from an action cannot even be imagined then we have a situation of *true uncertainty*, or *Knightian uncertainty*.[2] Imagine, at the time of proposing marriage to your partner, being asked to imagine and write down all the possible marital outcomes that could arise in the future. Firms often face true uncertainty in trying to guess future developments in technology. For instance, in 1943, Thomas Watson, President of IBM, guessed that there is a world market for about five computers. The future can often be truly unimaginable.

True uncertainty is pervasive in the real world. Arguably, of the four categories in this section, it is probably the most important and perhaps the most prevalent. But, curiously, it is the least studied of the four. It is probably fair to say that economics has no direct predictions to offer under true uncertainty. Yet humans routinely make decisions under true uncertainty. People do propose marriage to others, and firms do make decisions on investment and capital restructuring that require imagining unknown unknowns over a long time horizon. Behavioral economics contains work on social norms, mental models, and heuristics that might ultimately prove important to address this problem. You will see some of this work later in the book.

1.3 The Neoclassical Approach to Risk

A simple criterion to choose between lotteries is to pick the lottery whose *expected value* (or average value) is highest. The expected value of the n outcome lottery in (1.1) is given by

$$E(L) = \sum_{i=1}^{n} p_i x_i = p_1 x_1 + \ldots + p_n x_n. \tag{1.7}$$

The expected value corresponds to "average value" in common usage where each possible outcome is multiplied by the probability of its occurrence, and then we add across all outcomes. However, this criterion ignores the relative riskiness of the lotteries. For instance, the lotteries $L_1 = (-10, 0.5; 10, 0.5)$ and $L_2 = (-15, 0.25; -5, 0.25; 10, 0.5)$ have an identical expected value

[2] Donald Rumsfeld, the former US secretary of defence, famously referred to true uncertainty as "unknown unknowns." The following quote is attributed to him in 2012, in response to a question on whether Iraq possessed weapons of mass destruction: "Reports that say that something hasn't happened are always interesting to me, because as we know, there are known knowns; there are things we know we know. We also know there are known unknowns; that is to say we know there are some things we do not know. But there are also unknown unknowns – the ones we don't know we don't know. And if one looks throughout the history of our country and other free countries, it is the latter category that tends to be the difficult ones."

of 0 and so an expected value maximizer should be indifferent between them. Yet, lottery L_2 appears to be "riskier" as the outcomes are more "spread out" and many people may, for that reason, prefer L_1 to L_2.

1.3.1 Expected Utility Theory

Expected utility theory (EUT), the dominant approach in neoclassical economics, takes account of the expected value of a lottery as well as its "riskiness." Suppose that outcomes are drawn from a set X of real-valued outcomes. A utility function takes any outcome x from the set X and assigns a real number to it, $u(x)$. We write this as $u : X \to \mathbb{R}$, where $\mathbb{R}$ is the set of real numbers. Suppose that a utility function exists. A decision maker who follows EUT, evaluates the n outcome lottery in (1.1) by multiplying the utility from each outcome by the corresponding probability and then summing across all possible outcomes.

$$EU(L) = \sum_{i=1}^{n} p_i u(x_i). \tag{1.8}$$

EUT is simply a hypothesis about how decision makers evaluate lotteries. A determination of its usefulness as a theory must rely on stringent empirical tests of its predictions. The formula in (1.8) is sometimes also known as the "von Neumann Morgenstern expected utility function" after the name of the two authors who proposed the first axiomatic derivation.

The derivation of the functional form in (1.8) is based on underlying binary preferences over the set of all possible lotteries and then assigning restrictions, or axioms, on these preferences. Under a set of plausible restrictions on these preferences, we get the expected utility form in (1.8); conversely, the functional form in (1.8) implies that the decision maker must follow these axioms. The underlying axioms define what it means for a decision maker to be classified as "rational" under risk, and hence, they are also known as the *axioms of rationality under risk*. Given the equivalence between the axioms and the expected utility form in (1.8), we can say that decision makers who are rational under risk subscribe to EUT. This is all that rationality means in this context, and we describe the essentials in Section 1.4 below. Readers with an appetite for a more rigorous approach can consult Wakker (2010) and Dhami (2019a).

Two features of EUT stand out in (1.8).

1. The objective function is *linear in probabilities*.[3]
2. The individual derives utility, $u(x)$, from the *final level of an outcome* only.

By contrast, most people *weight probabilities nonlinearly* and derive utility from *changes in outcomes relative to a reference point*. This has spurred developments in *behavioral decision theory* that are explored later in the chapter, but for the moment let us consider these features a bit more.

[3] Visual inspection of (1.8) directly reveals that the RHS is *linear* in probabilities; for instance, terms such as p_i^2 or $\sqrt{p_i}$, if they had been present, would have made the RHS nonlinear in probabilities. Here is a slightly more formal definition of linearity. Suppose that there are two lotteries, L_1 and L_2. The decision maker receives a *compound lottery* of the form $(L_1, p; L_2, 1-p)$, $p > 0$. Compound lotteries are defined later in this chapter, but here it simply means that with probability p the decision maker gets to play the lottery L_1, and with probability $1-p$ the decision maker gets to play the lottery L_2. Then, linearity implies that $EU(L_1, p; L_2, 1-p) = pEU(L_1) + (1-p)EU(L_2)$.

In the 1978 film, *The Deer Hunter*, in an intriguing scene involving Robert De Niro, a group of American soldiers, dehumanized by the Vietnam war, play a game of *Russian roulette* (readers can view the clip on YouTube). The game is a bet with risky consequences. For a given reward or prize, one randomly spins a revolver cylinder that has less than six bullets, points the revolver to one's head, and fires. If you are compelled to play Russian roulette, how much money would you pay to remove one bullet from the revolver in the following two cases?

1. The number of bullets in the revolver is one.
2. The number of bullets in the revolver is five.

The removal of a single bullet in any of these two cases reduces the probability of dying by an identical magnitude, $\frac{1}{6}$. Under EUT, the linearity in probabilities implies that you should be willing to pay the same amount of money in both cases (one of the exercises asks you to prove this formally). However, most people are willing to pay relatively more in case 1, that is, to remove one bullet and achieve certainty of staying alive, rather than reduce the probability of dying from $\frac{5}{6}$ to $\frac{4}{6}$ in case 2. This violates EUT.

To motivate the violation of the second feature of EUT, suppose that push-up loving twins Tim and John normally do 50 push-ups. Today John sets an ambitious "target" of 54 push-ups, while Tim sets a more conservative "target" of 50 push-ups. Both brothers manage 52 push-ups. Who is the happier of the two? Surely Tim because he has exceeded his target by two, while John falls short by two. However, if the brothers derived utility *only* from the final level of the outcome, 52 push-ups, then they must experience an identical utility, $u(52)$, and must be equally happy; for more examples of this sort, see Heath et al. (1999). Empirical evidence from several domains strongly suggests that decision makers have a target or *reference point*, say, an income target or some *goal*, and they derive utility from the size of the outcome relative to the target. This plays a central role in prospect theory in Section 2.4.

Before we continue our analysis of EUT under risk, we briefly outline the approach under subjective uncertainty. Suppose that (i) a sample space, S, of possible outcomes arises from the actions of a decision maker, and (ii) these outcomes can be partitioned into "mutually exclusive events" $S_1, S_2, \ldots, S_n$, so that the union of these subsets is S. Let the decision maker face the following Savage act (see Section 1.2.2),

$$f = (S_1, x_1; S_2, x_2; \ldots; S_n, x_n), \tag{1.9}$$

which specifies an outcome x_i to be received by the decision maker if the event S_i, $i = 1, \ldots, n$ occurs. Suppose that the decision maker assigns the subjective probability $q_i \geq 0$ to the event S_i and $\sum_{i=1}^{n} q_i = 1$. If the assumption of probabilistic sophistication (see Section 1.2.2) holds, then we can write the Savage act in (1.9) as the following lottery in the standard form where subjective probabilities replace objective probabilities

$$L = (x_1, q_1; x_2, q_2; \ldots; x_n, q_n). \tag{1.10}$$

In a remarkable result, Savage (1954), building on earlier insights by de Finetti (1937), proposed an axiomatically founded approach to decision making under subjective uncertainty called *subjective expected utility* (SEU). Under SEU, the Savage act (1.9) is evaluated as

$$SEU(L) = \sum_{i=1}^{n} q_i u(x_i). \tag{1.11}$$

Notice the similarity in (1.8) and (1.11). Yet these utility representations are derived under different axiom systems. In the axiomatic derivation of SEU, there are no subjective probabilities, nor is probabilistic sophistication required. The decision maker is only required to have preferences over pairs of all possible Savage acts and these preferences must satisfy certain conditions, or axioms. Yet, the final representation in (1.11) turns out to be quite similar to (1.8), and the unique set of numbers $q_1, \ldots, q_n$ can be interpreted as the subjective probabilities of the decision maker corresponding to the events $S_1, \ldots, S_n$.[4] The bottom line is that we can analyze subjective uncertainty using tools similar to the ones that we have developed under risk. For this reason, we do not discuss subjective uncertainty further in this chapter.

1.3.2 Attitudes to Risk under EUT

The lottery $L = (16, 0.4; 36, 0.6)$ has expected value $E(L) = 0.4 \times 16 + 0.6 \times 36 = 28$. Suppose that the utility function of a decision maker is *strictly concave*, say, $u(x) = \sqrt{x}$. The expected utility of this lottery is

$$EU(L) = 0.4 \times \sqrt{16} + 0.6 \times \sqrt{36} = 5.2. \tag{1.12}$$

Let us now preform a thought experiment. Consider the sure amount, C_L, received with probability 1, that is, the lottery $(C_L, 1)$. Can we find an amount C_L such that the decision maker is indifferent between the lottery L and the lottery $(C_L, 1)$? If yes, then C_L is known as the *certainty equivalent* of the lottery L. We have $u(C_L) = \sqrt{C_L}$, hence, using (1.8), $EU(C_L, 1) = 1 \times \sqrt{C_L}$.

The fact that the decision maker is indifferent between the lottery L and the lottery $(C_L, 1)$, implies that a decision maker who uses EUT satisfies,

$$EU(C_L, 1) = EU(L). \tag{1.13}$$

From the calculations above, this implies that $\sqrt{C_L} = 5.2$, or $C_L = 27.04$. Thus, we find that the inequality $C_L < E(L)$ holds because $27.04 < 28$. When this inequality holds, the decision maker is said to be risk averse because the decision maker is willing to accept an amount C_L, that is even lower than the expected value of the lottery in order to avoid playing the lottery.

The calculation of C_L depends on the utility function, u, for outcomes and the particular decision theory that we use, which in this case is EUT. We can state the certainty equivalent of a lottery for any decision theory. Consider a decision theory DT (EUT is one possible example) that takes any lottery L in the set of possible lotteries $\mathcal{L}$ and assigns it some value which is a real number, that is, $DT : \mathcal{L} \longrightarrow \mathbb{R}$. EUT is a special case of DT which evaluates the lottery L by assigning it a real number according to (1.8).

Definition 1.1 *(Certainty equivalent) Consider the lottery L in (1.1) and a decision theory* $DT : \mathcal{L} \longrightarrow \mathbb{R}$. *The certainty equivalent of the lottery L is an outcome* C_L *offered to the decision maker*

[4] For more details, the advanced reader can consult Wakker (2010).

with probability 1, $(C_L, 1)$, such that the decision maker is indifferent between the lotteries $(C_L, 1)$ and L. In other words,

$$DT(C_L, 1) = DT(L). \tag{1.14}$$

The special case of (1.14) for EUT is stated in (1.13). We show next why for a given lottery, L, the comparison between C_L and $E(L)$ is important.

Definition 1.2 *(Risk attitudes) A decision maker who faces the lottery L in (1.1) is said to be*

1. *risk averse if $C_L < E(L)$;*
2. *risk loving if $C_L > E(L)$; and*
3. *risk neutral if $C_L = E(L)$.*

The worth of a lottery L to a *risk averse decision maker* is even lower than the expected value of the lottery, $E(L)$. In other words, such a decision maker will gladly forego the lottery in return for a sure amount that is even lower than the expected value of the lottery. In the converse case, $C_L > E(L)$, a *risk loving decision maker* will ask for a sure amount greater than the expected value of the lottery in order to forego the chance of facing the lottery. A risk neutral decision maker will be indifferent between the expected value of the lottery and the lottery.

Under EUT, attitudes to risk are captured entirely by the shape of the utility function, u, for outcomes, as shown in the next proposition.

Proposition 1.1 *Suppose that a decision maker follows EUT and faces the lottery L in (1.1). The utility function for outcomes is as defined above, $u : X \to \mathbb{R}$. Then,*

1. *$C_L < E(L)$, or risk averse behavior, is equivalent to a strictly concave u;*
2. *$C_L > E(L)$, or risk loving behavior, is equivalent to a strictly convex u; and*
3. *$C_L = E(L)$, or risk neutral behavior, is equivalent to a linear u.*

Commonly used examples of (i) concave utility are $u(x) = \sqrt{x}$ and $u(x) = lnx$, (ii) convex utility are $u(x) = x^2$ and $u(x) = e^x$, and (iii) linear utility are $u(x) = x$ and $u(x) = 2 + 6x$. A simple application of Jensen's inequality proves the result in Proposition 1.1; you are asked to prove it in one of the exercises. A diagrammatic treatment for the two-outcomes case can be found in any basic undergraduate microeconomics book, so we omit it.

To most non-economists, attitudes to risk appear to have something to do with the probabilities, or the chance, with which the outcomes in a lottery are received, and not the shapes of utility functions. Indeed, the non-economists' suspicion is well supported by the theory and the evidence, as we shall demonstrate in later sections.

Suppose that we have two different lotteries, L_P and L_Q, which have identical outcomes, $x_1 < \ldots < x_n$, but they differ in the probabilities with which the outcomes are received.

$$L_P = (x_1, p_1; \ldots; x_n, p_n) \,; \; L_Q = (x_1, q_1; \ldots; x_n, q_n). \tag{1.15}$$

In the lottery L_P, the respective probabilities of the n outcomes are $p_1, \ldots, p_n$, while in the lottery L_Q these probabilities are $q_1, \ldots, q_n$. As usual, both sets of probabilities are non-negative and sum up to 1. Denote the cumulative probability distributions for these lotteries by P and Q, respectively. Thus, the cumulative probability of getting an outcome equal to or lower than x_i,

Table 1.1 The cumulative distribution functions *P*, *Q* corresponding to the respective lotteries L_P and L_Q

	30	60	100
Q	0.3	0.6	1.0
P	0.1	0.4	1.0

$i = 1, \ldots, n$, (i) in lottery L_P is $P(x_i)$, and (ii) in lottery L_Q is $Q(x_i)$. We first state the concept of *first order stochastic dominance* and then explain it.

Definition 1.3 *(First order stochastic dominance) Consider the two lotteries L_P, L_Q in (1.15), with the associated cumulative distribution functions P and Q, respectively. Then, the lottery L_P first order stochastically dominates L_Q if $P(x_i) \leq Q(x_i)$ for all $i = 1, \ldots, n$. First order stochastic dominance is strict if for at least one value of $i = 1, \ldots, n$ we have $P(x_i) < Q(x_i)$.*

Consider the case $n = 3$ and $L_P = (30, 0.1; 60, 0.3; 100, 0.6)$, $L_Q = (30, 0.3; 60, 0.3; 100, 0.4)$. Table 1.1 shows the respective cumulative distribution functions, P and Q. We have $P(30) < Q(30)$, $P(60) < Q(60)$, and $P(90) = Q(90)$, so the lottery L_P strictly first order stochastically dominates the lottery L_Q. Thus, under the lottery L_P, there is a relatively smaller probability of getting lower outcomes and a relatively higher probability of getting higher outcomes. Why should we be interested in the concept of stochastic dominance, other than to find an alternative way of determining which of two lotteries is the riskier one? There are two reasons.

1. We may, a priori, require decision makers to be rational in the sense that they cannot choose stochastically dominated options, perhaps on the grounds that it is akin to leaving money on the table. On this criterion, we may then reject any decision theory that allows for the choice of stochastically dominated options. This is pretty much the default position in economics. Indeed, this argument was used to reject the decision weighted model of utility (see the discussion in Section 2.2 below).
2. We could take another position that is in better conformity with the best practice in the natural sciences. We initially hypothesize that "decision makers do not choose stochastically dominated options" and then test the hypothesis against the data, but we do not use it as a precondition for the acceptance of any decision theory. Indeed, the experiments of Kahneman and Tversky (1979) suggest that when stochastic dominance is easy to spot, then decision makers do not choose stochastically dominated options. However, when such dominance is hard to spot, as, for instance, when there are several outcomes in a lottery, then decision makers may indeed violate stochastic dominance. This is a more satisfactory position because if stochastic dominance is violated, then further experiments may reveal the reasons why, and lead to further revisions and improvements in the theory.

1.3.3 The Allais Paradox

The classic demonstration of non-linear probability weighting, the *Allais paradox*, was given by the Nobel Prize winning economist Maurice Allais (1953). We use an example from Kahneman and Tversky (1979) below to illustrate the paradox.

Consider a choice between the following lotteries, where the outcomes are monetary amounts.

$$L_1 = (3000, 1) \text{ versus } L_2 = (0, 0.2; 4000, 0.8). \tag{1.16}$$

Most people prefer the lottery L_1 to the lottery L_2 because having 3000 for sure appears more attractive than risking a 20% chance of receiving nothing even if there is an 80% chance of gaining an extra 1000.

Now consider a second choice between another pair of lotteries.

$$L_3 = (0, 0.8; 4000, 0.2) \text{ versus } L_4 = (0, 0.75; 3000, 0.25) \tag{1.17}$$

Most people prefer the lottery L_3 to the lottery L_4. The likely reason is that most people perceive the probabilities 20% and 25% as similar, so they pick the lottery L_3 which offers the higher amount 4000.

All this is reasonable. But it contradicts EUT. To see this, suppose that the utility from an outcome of 0 is also zero, so $u(0) = 0$. The observed preference for L_1 over L_2 under EUT implies

$$u(3000) > 0.8u(4000). \tag{1.18}$$

The observed preference for L_3 over L_4 under EUT implies

$$0.2u(4000) > 0.25u(3000). \tag{1.19}$$

Multiply the inequality in (1.19) by 4 on both sides to get

$$u(3000) < 0.8u(4000). \tag{1.20}$$

The inequalities in (1.18) and (1.20) directly contradict each other. Hence, EUT cannot simultaneously explain both sets of choices. The majority choices hint that in the choice between L_1 and L_2, the decision maker is particularly sensitive to the change in probabilities close to the endpoints of the probability interval (between 80% to 100%). However, in the choice between L_3 and L_4, the decision maker is not as sensitive to changes in probabilities in the middle ranges (between 20% to 25%). This differing sensitivity to probabilities, depending on where on the probability interval $[0, 1]$ they occur, gives rise to nonlinear probability weighting; we explore this in more detail in Section 2.2.

There is nothing specific about the numbers that are used in the lotteries in (1.16) and (1.17). The Allais paradox applies to any such pairs of lotteries where each lottery has only 1 non-zero outcome and the ratio of probabilities in the two pairs of lotteries corresponding to the non-zero outcomes is identical; in this case $\frac{0.8}{1} = \frac{0.2}{0.25}$. For this reason, such violations are known as the *common-ratio form* of the Allais paradox.

Two of the finest theorists of the time, both well versed in EUT, including the Nobel Prize winner Paul Samuelson, and Leonard Savage who developed SEU, were used as test subjects by Maurice Allais in a 1952 Paris conference. Both picked L_1 in the first choice and L_3 in the second, violating EUT (Allais used a different set of numbers from the lotteries in (1.16) and (1.17)). There is now a massive body of refutations of EUT and it would be pointless to continue testing

EUT any further because the nature of violations of EUT is well established.[5] Furthermore, there are much better behavioral alternatives, such as prospect theory that we discuss below.

In an interesting result that should have been obvious much earlier, Rabin (2000) demonstrated the following puzzle. Suppose that a decision maker has wealth $w > 0$ and faces two possible lotteries. Lottery $L_1 = (w, 1)$ is essentially the status-quo where the decision maker retains their wealth w with certainty. Lottery $L_2 = (w - 10, 0.5; w + 11, 0.5)$ offers a 50–50 chance of losing 10 and gaining 11, for a small net gain 0.5, so that the expected value of L_2 is slightly above w. Suppose that the decision maker prefers L_1 over L_2 for any level of wealth. This implies that the decision maker is risk averse over small stake gambles. The reason we can conclude this is that $EL_2 = w + 0.5$, and the certainty equivalent of L_2 is no higher than w (otherwise L_1 would not have been preferred to L_2). Since certainty equivalent is lower than the expected value, the decision maker must be risk averse.

Rabin (2000) then showed that the preference for L_1 over L_2 implies that an EUT decision maker will be risk averse to an absurd degree over large stakes in the following sense. Define a third lottery, $L_3 = (w - 100, 0.5; w + A, 0.5)$, which gives a 50–50 chance of losing 100 or gaining an amount A, which can be as large as we want it to be. Then, the preference for L_1 over L_2 implies that the EUT decision maker will prefer the lottery L_2 over the lottery L_3, which offers a 50% chance of winning a potentially infinite amount. This absurdly high risk aversion over large stakes is known as *Rabin's paradox*.

What is going on here? The basic problem is that the rejection of a small stakes gamble (L_2 over L_1) implies that the utility function of a decision maker who follows EUT must be too concave in order to capture risk aversion over small stakes. If we extend such a utility function in either direction, it ends up being excessively curved in a concave manner, leading to fantastic risk aversion over large stakes. It is "absurdly highly curved" because the marginal utility of wealth (slope of the utility function) drops off too quickly over small intervals. Hence, over larger intervals, the drop in marginal utility is too steep to be accounted for by the evidence. In the other decision theories that we consider in this chapter, where probabilities are weighted nonlinearly, risk attitudes are not determined entirely by the shape of the utility function in a sense that we will make precise later. It can also be shown that Rabin's paradox does not apply to prospect theory; for a numerical example see Dhami (2019a).

1.4 Preference Foundations

Neoclassical economics treats individual preferences as the primitives on which human behavior is based. It is customary to describe the preference foundations first, followed by the appropriate theory, such as expected utility theory. However, students can sometimes be put off by axiomatic foundations. For this reason, our exposition is in the reverse order and we present the preference foundations last. Instructors who wish to reverse the order can simply cover this section first, before introducing the expected utility function.

[5] For a survey of the empirical evidence, see Kahneman and Tversky (2000), Starmer (2000), Wakker (2010), and Dhami (2019a, Vol. 1).

Suppose that a decision maker must make a choice from some set of alternatives in a set

$$X = \{x_1, x_2, \ldots, x_n\}. \tag{1.21}$$

We assume that for any two alternatives $x, y \in X$, the decision maker can engage in a binary comparison by virtue of possessing a binary preference relation $\succeq$, which means "at least as good as." For instance, if $x \succeq y$, then in terms of the decision maker's preferences, the alternative x is at least as good as the alternative y. We can also state the "strict" binary preference relation, $\succ$, so that $x \succ y$ implies that x is strictly preferred to y. In this case, it is never the case that $y \succeq x$. Another useful binary preference relation is the indifference relation, $\sim$, so that $x \sim y$ implies that both $x \succeq y$ and $y \succeq x$ are simultaneously true. The negation of the binary relation $\succeq$ is denoted by $\not\succeq$. Thus, $x \not\succeq y$ means that it is "not the case that x is at least as good as y."

The properties of these underlying preferences, or the restrictions on these preferences, are referred to as *axioms*. Can we impose "sensible and plausible" axioms? Consider the following axioms on preferences, which we state first followed by a discussion.

Axiom 1.1 *Reflexivity: For any $x \in X$, we have $x \succeq x$.*

Axiom 1.2 *Completeness: For any two alternatives $x, y \in X$, we have the following possibilities.*
(1) (Strict Preference) $x \succeq y$ but $y \not\succeq x$. This implies that $x \succ y$.
(2) (Strict Preference) $y \succeq x$ but $x \not\succeq y$. This implies that $y \succ x$.
(3) (Indifference) $x \succeq y$ and $y \succeq x$. This implies that $x \sim y$.

Axiom 1.3 *Transitivity: Consider any three alternatives $x, y, z \in X$. If $x \succeq y$ and $y \succeq z$, then $x \succeq z$.*

The reflexivity axiom simply says that any alternative is at least as good as itself. Completeness requires the decision maker to be able to make binary comparisons between all pairs of alternative choices that there are in the universe of choices. We list all three possibilities – one alternative is strictly preferred to the other, or the decision maker is indifferent between the two alternatives. Completeness would be violated if, for instance, the decision maker said: "I cannot make up my mind between $x, y \in X$" or that "I am in two minds over which of $x, y \in X$ I should choose." Sometimes the property of reflexivity is subsumed under completeness by setting $x = y$. Transitivity implies that if one alternative is at least as good as the second, and the second is at least as good as the third, then the first alternative is at least as good as the third. The decision maker is then assumed to pick an alternative $x^* \in X$ such that $x^* \succeq y$ for all $y \in X$; x^* is sometimes known as the best alternative in X. This does not rule out the possibility that multiple alternatives satisfy the criterion for being the best element in the set X.

Ex-ante, the axioms might well appear to be sensible and plausible. However, until they are tested stringently, the axioms are simply hypotheses about human behavior. The real test of these axioms is in their empirical testing. If the axioms turn out to be empirically rejected, then the theory gives an incorrect description of underlying human behavior. Humans have no obligations to conform to the axioms written down by economic theorists, and economic theorists should be willing to accept empirical refutations of these axioms once they are stringently tested. We consider the empirical evidence for these axioms in several parts of the book.

Preferences that satisfy the three axioms, reflexivity, completeness, and transitivity are said to be *consistent preferences*. These are also known as the *axioms of rationality*, in the sense that this is the minimum requirement that economists impose on human behavior to be classed as rational.

Economists like to analyze human behavior in terms of utility functions, and it is often more convenient to do so.

Definition 1.4 *A utility function, $u : X \rightarrow \mathbb{R}$ represents the preference relation, $\succeq$, if whenever $x, y \in X$ and $x \succeq y$, we have $u(x) \geq u(y)$. Conversely, if $u(x) \geq u(y)$, then $x \succeq y$ must be true. This is sometimes written as $x \succeq y \Leftrightarrow u(x) \geq u(y)$.*

In Definition 1.4, a utility function is not designed to capture the intensity of preferences. If $x \succeq y$, then all we can say, if a utility function exists, is that the utility from the alternative x is relatively higher than from the alternative y. But we cannot say, by how much higher. In this sense, the measurement of utility is ordinal, not cardinal. From Definition 1.4, the status of a utility function and the underlying preferences are identical in the following sense. One may either test the underlying axioms to falsify the theory, or test the associated utility function that represents these preferences. Any of these two methods of testing is equally valid. Since utility functions are unobserved, it is sometimes easier to test the individual axioms.

Additional assumptions on preferences are typically introduced in microeconomics in order to make the analysis more tractable. For instance, a technical assumption on preferences, the *continuity axiom*, allows us to draw continuous utility functions. Furthermore, the assumption of *monotonicity* on preferences allows us to infer that the utility function is increasing in outcomes.

We now outline the preference axioms that lead to an expected utility representation of preferences. Consider a situation of risk. Let $\mathcal{L}$ be the set of all lotteries of the form given in (1.1). The set of outcomes continues to be given in (1.21) with

$$x_1 < x_2 < \ldots < x_n.$$

Suppose that the decision maker has preferences, denoted by $\succeq$, over any two alternative lotteries in $\mathcal{L}$.[6] Thus, the notation $L_1 \succeq L_2$ means that the lottery L_1 is "at least as good as" the lottery L_2. The preference relation $\succeq$ is sometimes known as a weak preference relation. The "strict" preference relation, $\succ$, can also be defined. Thus $L_1 \succ L_2$ means that the decision maker strictly prefers the lottery L_1 to the lottery L_2. Similarly the indifference relation, $\sim$, is interpreted as follows. If $L_1 \sim L_2$, then the decision maker is indifferent between the two lotteries.

As in the case of certainty, we seek out sensible and plausible restrictions on preferences over the set of lotteries that will allow us to represent preferences by some utility function. Consider the set $\mathcal{L}$ of all lotteries of the form (1.1) under risk. The decision maker has a binary preference relation, $\succeq$, over the set $\mathcal{L}$ which satisfies the following axioms, Axioms 1.4 to 1.8, also known as the *axioms of rationality under risk*. We first state the axioms, followed by a discussion.

[6] It is important to stress that $\succeq$ is not the same binary preference relation which we introduced for the case of certainty in Definition 1.4. The preference relation under certainty was defined over the set of outcomes X, rather than over the set of lotteries $\mathcal{L}$. It would be more satisfactory to denote the new preference relation over $\mathcal{L}$ by a separate symbol, such as $\succeq_L$ or $\succeq_{EU}$. But in order to reduce notational clutter we continue to use $\succeq$.

Axiom 1.4 *Completeness: For all lotteries $L_1, L_2 \in \mathcal{L}$, we have the following three possibilities.*
(ai) $L_1 \succeq L_2$ but $L_2 \not\succeq L_1$. In this case $L_1 \succ L_2$.
(aii) $L_2 \succeq L_1$ but $L_1 \not\succeq L_2$. In this case $L_2 \succ L_1$.
(aiii) $L_1 \succeq L_2$ and $L_2 \succeq L_1$. In this case $L_1 \sim L_2$.

Axiom 1.5 *Transitivity: For all lotteries $L_1, L_2, L_3 \in \mathcal{L}$, $L_1 \succeq L_2$ and $L_2 \succeq L_3 \Rightarrow L_1 \succeq L_3$.*

Axiom 1.6 *(Best and worst) There exists a best lottery $(x_n, 1)$ and a worst lottery $(x_1, 1)$ such that $(x_n, 1) \succ (x_1, 1)$.*

Axiom 1.7 *(Continuity) For each lottery, $L \in \mathcal{L}$, there exists some probability $p \in [0, 1]$ such that $L \sim (x_1, 1 - p; x_n, p)$.*

Axiom 1.8 *(Independence) For all lotteries $L_1, L_2, L \in \mathcal{L}$, and all probabilities $p \in [0, 1]$,*

$$L_1 \succeq L_2 \Leftrightarrow (L_1, p; L, 1 - p) \succeq (L_2, p; L, 1 - p).$$

The completeness axiom, Axiom 1.4, and the transitivity axiom, Axiom 1.5, are analogous to similar axioms defined for the case of certainty except that they are defined over the set of lotteries, $\mathcal{L}$. Axiom 1.6 requires the decision maker to strictly prefer the highest outcome with certainty to receiving the lowest outcome with certainty. The continuity axiom, Axiom 1.7, requires that some combination of the worst and best lotteries makes the decision maker indifferent to any other lottery. The most critical axiom is the *independence axiom*, Axiom 1.8. It requires that the preference relation is unchanged when each lottery is mixed with the same third lottery, L. The lottery $(L_1, p; L, 1 - p)$ in Axiom 1.8 is known as a lottery of lotteries, or a *compound lottery*. It specifies that the decision maker receives a "mixture" of two lotteries, L_1 and L, such that L_1 is received with probability p and L with probability $1 - p$. In evaluating mixtures of lotteries, the decision maker uses the *reduction of compound lotteries axiom*. This axiom requires us to use the product law of probabilities in the presence of compound outcomes whenever probabilities are independent, as shown in the next example. The reduction of compound lotteries axiom is implicitly a part of the axioms of rationality under risk, although it is often not stated formally as such.

Example 1.1 *Consider two lotteries $L_1 = (x_1, p; x_2, 1 - p)$ $p \in [0, 1]$ and $L_2 = (z_1, q; z_2, 1 - q)$, $q \in [0, 1]$. The compound lottery $L_3 = (L_1, s; 0, 1 - s)$, $s \in [0, 1]$ specifies that the decision make receives the lottery L_1 with probability s and the outcome 0 with probability $1 - s$. Thus, we can write L_3 as*

$$L_3 = ((x_1, p; x_2, 1 - p), s; 0, 1 - s).$$

The reduction of compound lotteries axiom now enables us to evalute the lottery L_3 as

$$L_3 = (x_1, ps; x_2, (1 - p)\, s; 0, 1 - s).$$

The reader can check that the probability of each outcome is non-negative and the probabilities sum up to 1. For more complicated compound lotteries such as $L_4 = (L_1, s; L_2, 1 - s)$, where L_1 and L_2 are defined above, the axiom is only slightly more tedious to implement but the principle stays the same, as shown below.

$$L_4 = ((x_1, p; x_2, 1 - p), s; (z_1, q; z_2, 1 - q), 1 - s)$$

or,

$$L_4 = (x_1, ps; x_2, (1-p)\, s; z_1, q\,(1-s)\,; z_2, (1-q)\,(1-s)).$$

We now ask if there exists a utility function which represents preferences that satisfy the axioms of rationality under risk.

Definition 1.5 *Suppose that $\succeq$ is a binary relation on the set of lotteries, $\mathcal{L}$. A utility function $U : \mathcal{L} \to \mathbb{R}$ represents these preferences if, for any $L_1, L_2 \in \mathcal{L}$, whenever $L_1 \succeq L_2$ we have $U(L_1) \geq U(L_2)$.*

In a seminal result, the mathematician von Neumann and the mathematical economist Oskar Morgenstern showed that the expected utility function represents preferences that satisfy the axioms of rationality under risk.

Proposition 1.2 *(von Neumann–Morgenstern expected utility function): Let $\succeq$ be a binary relation on the set of lotteries, $\mathcal{L}$, that satisfies the axioms of rationality under risk, Axioms 1.4 to 1.8. Then, for any $L_1, L_2 \in \mathcal{L}$, whenever $L_1 \succeq L_2$, we have $EU(L_1) \geq EU(L_2)$, where the EU function is defined in (1.8). Conversely, if $EU(L_1) \geq EU(L_2)$, then the preferences $\succeq$ satisfy the axioms of rationality under risk.*[7]

One advantage of developing the appropriate axioms and results such as the one in Proposition 1.2 is that one can either test the rationality axioms, or equivalently, the expected utility representation of preferences. They have identical status. However, testing the axioms is often easier because we cannot directly observe the utility functions of individuals. The axioms of rationality under risk are merely hypotheses about actual human behavior. In particular, humans could not be classified as irrational, or mad, if they violated the axioms of rationality under risk. All that we can conclude from such an exercise would be that the axioms of rationality are not good enough hypotheses about human behavior under risk. The word "rationality" in this case does not have any normative or injunctive connotations.

An interesting application of the axioms of rationality is to the Allais paradox. In Section 1.3.3, we directly showed that the Allais paradox violates expected utility theory. Proposition 1.2 implies that one or more of the axioms of rationality must have been violated. The independence axiom fails in this case, as we show below.

In Section 1.3.3, most decision makers choose lottery L_1 over lottery L_2, where L_1, L_2 are given by:

$$L_1 = (3000, 1) \text{ and } L_2 = (0, 0.2; 4000, 0.8). \tag{1.22}$$

Let us now pick a third lottery $L = (0, 1)$ which gives an outcome of zero with probability 1. Then, the independence axiom, Axiom 1.8, implies that, for $p = \frac{1}{4}$,

$$L_1 \succeq L_2 \Leftrightarrow \left(L_1, \frac{1}{4}; L, \frac{3}{4}\right) \succeq \left(L_2, \frac{1}{4}; L, \frac{3}{4}\right).$$

[7] The proof of this proposition can be found in any advanced undergraduate or postgraduate book in microeconomics and there is little merit in repeating that proof here.

Substituting the lotteries L_1 and L_2, this implies that

$$L_1 \succeq L_2 \Leftrightarrow \left((3000,1), \frac{1}{4}; (0,1), \frac{3}{4}\right) \succeq \left((0,0.2;4000,0.8), \frac{1}{4}; (0,1), \frac{3}{4}\right). \tag{1.23}$$

The reduction of compound lotteries axiom allows us to simplify (1.23) as

$$L_1 \succeq L_2 \Leftrightarrow (0,0.75;3000,0.25) \succeq (0,0.8;4000,0.2). \tag{1.24}$$

Noting, from Section 1.3.3, that

$$L_3 = (0,0.8;4000,0.2) \text{ and } L_4 = (0,0.75;3000,0.25), \tag{1.25}$$

we can rewrite (1.24) as

$$L_1 \succeq L_2 \Leftrightarrow L_4 \succeq L_3.$$

Thus, the independence axiom predicts that if a decision maker chooses lottery L_1 over lottery L_2, they must necessarily choose the lottery L_4 over lottery L_3. However, the evidence shows that most people choose the lottery L_3 over the lottery L_4, which gives rise to the Allais paradox. Hence, the independence axiom is violated.

The alert reader would have noted that we invoked two axioms in our proof above. The independence axiom, and the reduction of compound lotteries axiom. Hence, we cannot be sure which, or both, of the axioms lead to the Allais paradox in expected utility theory. The evidence shows that the reduction of compound lotteries axiom too is violated (Fan et al., 2019). Hence, it is possible both axioms are violated.

2 Modern Approaches to Decision Making under Risk and Subjective Uncertainty

2.1 Introduction

In this chapter we study the behavioral alternatives to EUT under risk and uncertainty.

We begin, in Section 2.2, with an introduction to *nonlinear probability weighting*. A *probability weighting function* is one's subjective evaluation of underlying objective probabilities. The evidence indicates that there is heterogeneity among people in how they weight probabilities, but the median shape is an inverse S-shape. This implies that people overweight small probabilities but underweight large probabilities. Furthermore, people display two kinds of behavior for very small, but economically meaningful probabilities. Some people take account of these probabilities, overweighting them, while others just ignore them and, for instance, refuse to buy any insurance even when offered on actuarially overfair terms.

In Section 2.3, we outline *rank dependent utility theory* (RDUT), which amends EUT to include nonlinear probability weighting. As such, it is able to explain several paradoxes of EUT, including the Allais paradox. Attitudes to risk under RDUT depend jointly on the shapes of the utility function and the probability weighting function. Thus, for instance, it is possible that a decision maker with a convex utility function might be risk averse and a decision maker with a concave utility function might be risk loving. We also show that RDUT captures in a simple way, the notions of *optimism* and *pessimism*.

Section 2.4 takes up the study of *prospect theory*. The starting point of the theory is a *reference point*, or a goal, or a target, relative to which decision makers evaluate outcomes. Outcomes better than the reference point are classified as *gains* and outcomes worse than the reference point as *losses*. Importantly, prospect theory describes why it is important to split the domain of outcomes into gains and losses. Namely, that human decision making is very different in the two domains. There are two important differences. First, *loss aversion* ensures that losses bite more than equivalent gains with the typical median estimate being about "two" times more. Second, attitudes to risk are different in the two domains. We describe the *fourfold pattern of risk attitudes* under prospect theory, which is consistent with the evidence. Notably other decision theories struggle to explain it.

Prospect theory explains everything that RDUT can explain. RDUT, in turn, can explain everything that EUT can explain. However, RDUT and EUT fail under ambiguity but prospect theory also explains the evidence from ambiguity in Ellsberg-type experiments, based on the notion of *source-dependent uncertainty*. Prospect theory does have more parameters than RDUT and EUT. However, there is independent and reasonably strong experimental and neuroeconomic support for the extra parameters responsible for reference points and loss aversion.

Finally, in Section 2.5 we outline several applications of prospect theory, which demonstrate the usefulness and scope of the theory that encompasses virtually the entirety of economics. These include applications to the endowment effect; labor supply of taxi drivers; tax evasion behavior; the link between loss aversion and evolution; and applications in finance and in organizations. Currently prospect theory is the most satisfactory decision theory.

2.2 Nonlinear Probability Weighting

We considered two examples of nonlinear probability weighting in Chapter 1: The Russian roulette example, and the Allais paradox. There is overwhelming evidence of nonlinear probability weighting from almost all domains in economics.[1] We now consider attempts at formalizing this evidence.

Suppose that there is some *objective probability* $0 \leq p \leq 1$ corresponding to an outcome, x. Denote the *subjective probability weight* accorded by a decision maker to this outcome by $w(p)$, where $0 \leq w(p) \leq 1$. It is reasonable to expect that decision makers assign (i) zero subjective weight to impossible outcomes, so $w(0) = 0$, (ii) maximum possible subjective weight to outcomes received with probability 1, so $w(1) = 1$, and (iii) the subjective probability weight $w(p)$ must increase as the probability, p, increases. This motivates the following definition of a *probability weighting function* (PWF) that plays a key role in behavioral alternatives to EUT.

Definition 2.1 *(Probability weighting function) A probability weighting function is a strictly increasing function* $w : [0,1] \to [0,1]$ *such that* $w(0) = 0$ *and* $w(1) = 1$.

In words, $w : [0,1] \to [0,1]$ means that the function w takes any probability $p \in [0,1]$ and determines a corresponding subjective weight $w(p) \in [0,1]$. Well-known methods exist that enable us to elicit the PWF for individuals. We shall omit this discussion, but for the details see Wakker (2010) and Dhami (2019a). Empirical evidence shows that there is a great deal of heterogeneity in the elicited PWFs of decision makers, and that for the same decision maker, the elicited PWF depends on the context in which they are elicited. Such context dependence of the PWF plays a major role in explaining the Ellsberg paradox under ambiguity; see Section 2.6 below.

In principle, there is an infinite number of functions that satisfy the restrictions in Definition 2.1. Figure 2.1 plots two PWFs (the continuous curve and the dotted curve); probability $0 \leq p \leq 1$ is measured on the horizontal axis, and the subjective weight $0 \leq w(p) \leq 1$ on the vertical axis. We have also drawn a diagonal line which is equidistant from both axes, so that along this line, we always have linear probability weighting $w(p) = p$, as in EUT. Departures from the diagonal line indicate the extent of nonlinear probability weighting.

[1] For a richer survey of the evidence, the interested reader can consult Kahneman and Tversky (2000), and Dhami (2019a).

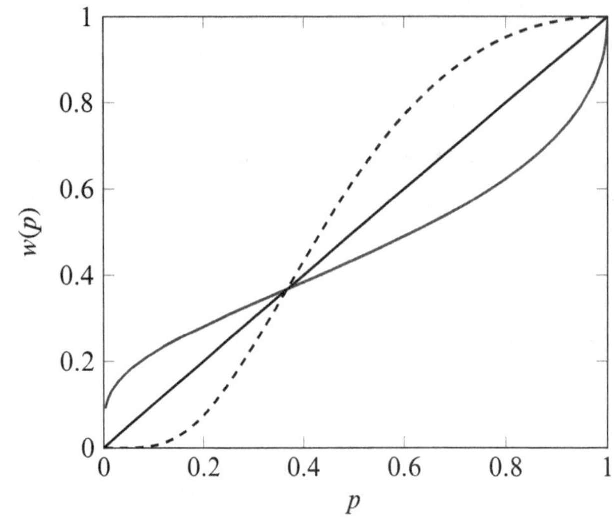

Figure 2.1 Plots of two Prelec probability weighting functions

For future reference, we formally define a *fixed point* and a *point of inflection*, and we shall illustrate both points below in our discussion. Intuitively, a fixed point maps a probability into an identical subjective weight; while a point of inflection is such that the second derivative of the PWF is zero at that point.

Definition 2.2 *Consider a probability weighting function* $w : [0, 1] \to [0, 1]$.
(a) (Fixed point) A fixed point of the PWF, p^*, *satisfies* $w(p^*) = p^*$, *where* $p^* \in [0, 1]$.
(b) (Point of inflection) The point of inflection of the PWF, $\widetilde{p}$, *if it exists, is defined as* $w''(\widetilde{p}) = 0$, *where* $\widetilde{p} \in [0, 1]$.

The bulk of the empirical evidence suggests that many decision makers have the continuous *inverse S-shaped PWF shown in* Figure 2.1. There is a point at which this PWF cuts the diagonal line. From Definition 2.2, this is an "interior" *fixed point* which satisfies $w(p^*) = p^*$. Two other "extreme" fixed points, $p^* = 0$ and $p^* = 1$, are already built into the definition of a PWF in Definition 2.1 because $w(0) = 0$ and $w(1) = 1$. In our discussion below, we shall be mainly interested in the interior fixed point. Since the PFW is strictly increasing, the interior fixed point, if it exists, is unique.

Consider the *inverse S-shaped PWF* in Figure 2.1 and the interior fixed point, p^*. To the left of p^*, the PWF lies strictly above the diagonal ($w(p) > p$, except at $p = 0$), *so small probabilities are overweighted.* To the right of p^*, the PWF lies strictly below the diagonal ($w(p) < p$, except at $p = 1$), *so large probabilities are underweighted.* By contrast, the second PWF in Figure 2.1, shown as the dashed *S-shaped* PWF, illustrates the opposite pattern – *underweighting of small probabilities and overweighting of large probabilities.*

In Figure 2.1 we have plotted the *Prelec probability weighting function* (Prelec, 1998). This function has proved popular in applied work; it is tractable; and it has axiomatic foundations. We give a formal definition of it below that will enable the reader to plot it for various parameter values.

Definition 2.3 *(Prelec function) The Prelec (1998) function,* $w : [0,1] \to [0,1]$*, is given by* [2]

$$w(p) = e^{-\beta(-\ln p)^{\alpha}}, \; p \in [0,1], \; \alpha > 0, \; \beta > 0. \tag{2.1}$$

In Definition 2.3, α, β are the two parameters. To check that the Prelec function is indeed a PWF, we need to check the conditions required in Definition 2.1. We give these calculations here in order to make readers familiar with handling such functions.

1. $w(0) = e^{-\beta(-\ln 0)^{\alpha}}$. Using $ln 0 = -\infty$, we have $w(0) = \frac{1}{e^{\infty}} = 0$.
2. $w(1) = e^{-\beta(-\ln 1)^{\alpha}}$. Using $ln 1 = 0$, we have $w(1) = e^{0} = 1$.
3. To check that w is an increasing function when $p \in (0,1)$, we take logs on both sides of (2.1) to get

   $$lnw(p) = -\beta(-\ln p)^{\alpha}. \tag{2.2}$$

   Since $ln(x)$ is a strictly increasing function when it is defined, checking that $lnw(p)$ is a strictly increasing function for $p \in (0,1)$ implies that $w(p)$ is a strictly increasing function for $p \in (0,1)$. Differentiating (2.2) with respect to p, we get $\frac{lnw(p)}{dp} = \frac{\alpha\beta}{p}(-\ln p)^{\alpha-1} > 0$ for all $p > 0$.

Thus, the Prelec function satisfies the conditions required for it to be a PWF.

The parameters α, β give important insights about the underlying behavior of decision makers. The parameter α determines the concavity or convexity of the function.

1. If $\alpha < 1$ we get an inverse S-shaped PWF. In Figure 2.1, the inverse S-shaped PWF is drawn for the case $\alpha = 0.5 < 1$. This PWF is first concave ($w'' < 0$), and then it becomes convex ($w'' > 0$). In between this change in the second derivative, for some probability $\widetilde{p}$ we have the *point of inflection*, which we know from Definition 2.2, is defined as $w''(\widetilde{p}) = 0$.
2. If $\alpha > 1$ we get the dashed S-shaped PWF in Figure 2.1, which has been drawn for the case of $\alpha = 2 > 1$. This function is first convex, then concave, and the two segments are separated by a point of inflection, $\widetilde{p}$, where $w''(\widetilde{p}) = 0$.

The second parameter β controls the elevation, or height, of the PWF; or, in other words, the height of the point of inflection. In Figure 2.1, we have used the value $\beta = 1$. In this special case only, the point of inflection lies on the diagonal 45° line and coincides with the fixed point, so $\widetilde{p} = p^*$.

Figure 2.2 shows three Prelec functions for three different values of β, but $\alpha = 0.5$ in each case.

1. The case $\beta = 1$ is shown by the continuous Prelec curve in the middle, and we have discussed this special case above.
2. When $\beta < 1$, the elevation increases and the point of inflection lies above the diagonal, so $\widetilde{p} < p^*$. See the case $\beta = 0.25 < 1$ shown as the dashed uppermost curve in Figure 2.2.
3. When $\beta > 1$, the point of inflection lies below the diagonal and the elevation of the function decreases. See the case $\beta = 2 > 1$ shown as the dotted lowermost curve in Figure 2.2. In this case we have $\widetilde{p} > p^*$.

[2] The notation $w : [0,1] \to [0,1]$ means that the PWF takes an element from the probability interval $p \in [0,1]$ and maps it into a corresponding subjective probability weight $w(p) \in [0,1]$.

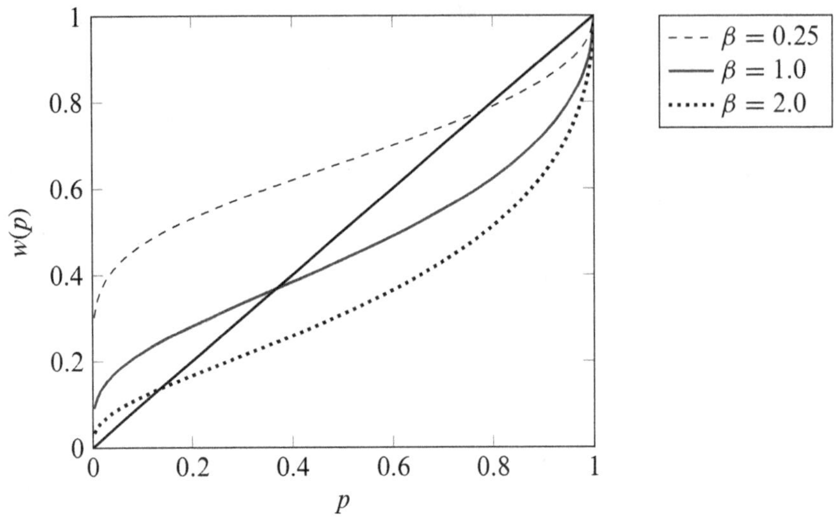

Figure 2.2 The effect of changing β on the Prelec probability weighting function

EUT, which presupposes linear weighting, $w(p) = p$, corresponds to the diagonal line in Figure 2.1. It is a special case of the Prelec function when $\alpha = \beta = 1$. Substituting $\alpha = \beta = 1$ in (2.1), we get

$$w(p) = e^{-1(-\ln p)^1} = e^{lnp} = p, \tag{2.3}$$

where the last equality uses the fact that the *ln* and exponential functions are inverses of each other. Clearly, there is no psychological or evolutionary reason why humans should possess the specific preference parameters $\alpha = \beta = 1$ among all the infinite number of possible values of α, β.

While the "typical" PWF is inverse S-shaped, data suggests significant heterogeneity across decision makers. Some decision makers have strictly convex PWFs throughout (e.g., $w(p) = p^2$) while others have strictly concave PWFs throughout (e.g., $w(p) = \sqrt{p}$).

Note that, by itself, a PWF cannot make any predictions. It needs to be embedded within a decision theory in order for it to have predictive content. One may, as a first pass, propose to make EUT more empirically relevant by replacing objective probabilities $p_1, \ldots, p_n$ by the subjective probability weights $w(p_1), \ldots, w(p_n)$. This gives rise to the *decision weighted utility* (compare with (1.8))

$$DWU(L) = \sum_{i=1}^{n} w(p_i)u(x_i). \tag{2.4}$$

When $w(p) = p$, (2.4) reduces to the case of EUT in (1.8). However, it was soon discovered that decision makers who follow DWU could choose *first order stochastically dominated options*, which was unacceptable to decision theorists.[3] Hence, this idea was not pursued further.

[3] Readers interested in a proof can consult Dhami (2019a, Vol. I).

2.3 Rank Dependent Utility

In order to avoid the choice of stochastically dominated options, yet take account of the empirical evidence on nonlinear probability weighting, Quiggin (1982) proposed *rank dependent utility theory* (RDUT). Suppose that the decision maker faces the n outcome lottery in (1.1) and all probabilities are strictly positive, $p_i > 0, i = 1, \dots, n$. Otherwise, if any $p_i = 0$, then we would write (1.1) as an $n-1$ outcome lottery.

The evaluation of the lottery L under rank dependent utility

$$RDU(L) = \sum_{i=1}^{n} \pi_i u(x_i). \tag{2.5}$$

Comparing with the EUT formula in (1.8), RDUT uses the same utility function, u, but it replaces the objective probabilities $p_1, \dots, p_n$ by non-negative numbers known as *decision weights* $\pi_1, \dots, \pi_n$ (explained below). RDUT is a generalization of EUT. Hence, it can explain everything that EUT can and, in addition, it can explain the violations arising from nonlinear probability weighting, such as the Russian roulette game and the Allais paradox. Hence, it is an improvement.

The construction of decision weights under RDUT is no more complicated than computing the cumulative distribution function of lotteries. We shall show that decision weights essentially account for *optimism* and *pessimism* of decision makers, relative to a decision maker who follows EUT.

Definition 2.4 *(Decision weights under RDUT) Suppose that a decision maker faces the lottery* $L = (x_1, p_1; \dots; x_n, p_n)$, $x_1 < \dots < x_n$, *and has the probability weighting function* $w(p)$. *Then, the decision weights* $\pi_1, \dots, \pi_n$ *corresponding to the outcomes* $x_1 < \dots < x_n$ *are given respectively by*

$\pi_n = w(p_n)$

$\pi_{n-1} = w(p_{n-1} + p_n) - w(p_n)$

$\pi_{n-2} = w(p_{n-2} + p_{n-1} + p_n) - w(p_{n-1} + p_n)$

.

.

.

$\pi_2 = w(p_2 + p_3 + \dots + p_n) - w(p_3 + p_4 + \dots + p_n)$

$\pi_1 = w(p_1 + p_2 + \dots + p_n) - w(p_2 + p_3 + \dots + p_n) = 1 - w(p_2 + p_3 + \dots + p_n).$

Notice the following features of the construction of decision weights in Definition 2.4. First, we employ the calculations needed to compute a cumulative distribution function (as, say, in Table 1.1). Second, instead of starting from the smallest outcome and then moving upwards, one outcome at a time, as in Table 1.1, we proceed in the opposite direction. We begin with the highest outcome x_n, and then go downwards one outcome at a time, until we end up with the smallest outcome x_1. Third, instead of cumulating the probabilities directly, we use cumulative transformations of the PWF, w. Finally, in the calculation of π_1, we use $w(1) = 1$.

Decision weights have two properties. First, note from Definition 2.4 that each decision weight is non-negative because w is a strictly increasing function. For instance, $\pi_{n-1} = w(p_{n-1} + p_n) - w(p_n) > 0$ because $p_{n-1} + p_n > p_n$, so $w(p_{n-1} + p_n) > w(p_n)$. Second, if we sum up all the decision weights they add up to 1; to prove it, start from π_n and keep going down, cancelling the second term in any row with the first term in the previous row.

Example 2.1 *Consider the case $n = 3$ and the lottery $L = (4, 0.2; 9, 0.3; 16, 0.5)$. Suppose that the utility function is $u(x) = \sqrt{x}$ and the probability weighting function is a Prelec function with $\beta = 1$ and $\alpha = 0.5$, i.e., $w(p) = e^{-(-\ln p)^{0.5}}$. The RDU of this lottery is*

$$RDU(L) = \pi_1\sqrt{4} + \pi_2\sqrt{9} + \pi_3\sqrt{16}.$$

The decision weights can be calculated using Definition 2.4 for the case $n = 3$. We will need to use the rows corresponding to π_n, π_{n-1}, and π_{n-2} in Definition 2.4.
$\pi_3 = w(0.5) = e^{-(-\ln 0.5)^{0.5}} = 0.4349$
$\pi_2 = w(0.3 + 0.5) - w(0.5) = e^{-(-\ln 0.8)^{0.5}} - e^{-(-\ln 0.5)^{0.5}} = 0.1886$
$\pi_1 = w(0.2 + 0.3 + 0.5) - w(0.3 + 0.5) = 1 - e^{-(-\ln 0.8)^{0.5}} = 0.3765$
Thus,

$$RDU(L) = 0.3765 \times 2 + 0.1886 \times 3 + 0.4349 \times 4 = 2.9416.$$

2.3.1 Optimism and Pessimism

Let us compare EUT and RDU for a two-outcome ($n = 2$) lottery $L = (x_1, p_1; x_2, p_2)$, where $x_1 < x_2$. The relevant calculations are

$$\begin{cases} EU(L) = p_1u(x_1) + p_2u(x_2) \\ RDU(L) = \pi_1u(x_1) + \pi_2u(x_2) \end{cases}. \tag{2.6}$$

The utilities from the two outcomes, $u(x_1), u(x_2)$, are identical in both expressions. So if $\pi_2 > p_2$ and $\pi_1 < p_1$, then the decision maker who follows RDUT places a relatively higher weight on the higher outcome and a relatively lower weight on the lower outcome. Such a decision maker is said to be *optimistic*. In the converse case ($\pi_2 < p_2$ and $\pi_1 > p_1$) the decision maker is said to be *pessimistic*. Both cases can arise under RDUT.

For $n = 2$, Definition 2.4 implies the following decision weights (use the rows corresponding to π_n and π_{n-1}).

$$\pi_2 = w(p_2) \text{ and } \pi_1 = 1 - w(p_2). \tag{2.7}$$

For pedagogic ease, suppose that the PWF is a convex function throughout, $w(p) = p^2$. From basic arithmetic, for any number $0 < p < 1$, we have $p^2 < p$. Thus, $\pi_2 = w(p_2) = p_2^2 < p_2$ and it can be shown that $\pi_1 > p_1$.[4] It follows that the decision maker who follows RDUT is pessimistic relative to a EU decision maker. If, however, the PWF is concave throughout, for example, $w(p) = \sqrt{p}$, then for all $0 < p < 1$ we have $w(p) = \sqrt{p} > p$. Here, we have the opposite case, $\pi_2 > p_2$ and $\pi_1 < p_1$, and the decision maker who follows RDUT acts in a relatively *optimistic* manner. If the decision maker has an inverse S-shaped PWF, then optimism and pessimism depend on the magnitude of p_2.

[4] Here is the relevant calculation. We have $\pi_1 = 1 - w(p_2) = 1 - p_2^2$. Using the identity $p_1 + p_2 = 1$, we can rewrite $\pi_1 = p_1 + p_2 - p_2^2 = p_1 + p_2(1 - p_2) > p_1$.

Thus, the calculations on decision weights under RDUT capture the underlying degrees of optimism and pessimism relative to EUT. This formalization also gives us a handle on what these underlying emotional states might mean in decision theory, although this is not the only sense in which optimism and the related term, overconfidence, has been used in the behavioral economics literature. More on this later in the book.

2.3.2 Attitudes to Risk under RDUT

Recall that attitudes to risk under EUT depend only on the shape of the utility function (Proposition 1.1). By contrast, RDUT allows attitudes to risk to be determined *jointly by the shapes of the PWF, and the utility function.* Suppose for the two-outcome lottery, evaluated in (2.6), the utility function is linear, e.g., $u(x) = x$, hence,

$$RDU(L) = \pi_1 x_1 + \pi_2 x_2. \tag{2.8}$$

Recall, under EUT, a linear utility function implies risk neutrality (Proposition 1.1). However, suppose that p_2 is small and the PWF is inverse S-shaped (see the continuous PWF in Figure 2.1). Since low probabilities are overweighted, hence, using (2.7),

$$\pi_2 = w(p_2) > p_2$$

In other words, a decision maker who follows RDUT may assign an inordinately high subjective weight to high outcomes, appearing to an outside observer as risk loving (despite a linear utility function). If, on the other hand, p_2 is high, then since high probabilities are underweighted, and a low a subjective weight may be assigned to the high outcome, x_2, that is,

$$\pi_2 = w(p_2) < p_2$$

In this case, the decision maker may appear to an outside observer as risk averse (despite the linear utility). We illustrate these ideas through examples.

Example 2.2 *Let* $L = (20, 0.85; 200, 0.15)$, $w(p) = p^2$, *and* $u(x) = x$, *so that someone trained in EUT might imagine the decision maker to be risk neutral because the utility function is linear. The expected value of the lottery is*

$$E(L) = 20 \times 0.85 + 200 \times 0.15 = 47.$$

Using (2.6), (2.7), the RDU of the lottery is

$$RDU(L) = (1 - w(0.15))20 + w(0.15)200.$$

We have $w(0.15) = (0.15)^2 = 0.0225$. *Thus,* $RDU(L) = (1-0.0225)\times 20 + 0.0225 \times 200 = 24.05$. *To calculate attitudes to risk (see Definition 1.2), we need to calculate the certainty equivalent,* C_L, *of the lottery. We have* $RDU(C_L, 1) = w(1) \times C_L = C_L$ *(using* $w(1) = 1$*). From the definition of the certainty equivalent, we have* $RDU(C_L, 1) = RDU(L)$, *hence,* $C_L = 24.05 < E(L) = 47$. *Thus, the decision maker is risk averse (Definition 1.2) despite having a linear utility function.*

In Example 2.2, all probabilities are underweighted because $p^2 < p$. Let us now consider the other case where all probabilities are overweighted, as in the case of $w(p) = \sqrt{p}$.

Example 2.3 *Suppose that everything is as in Example 2.2, but* $w(p) = \sqrt{p}$. *We now have* $w(0.15) = \sqrt{0.15} = 0.3873$. *Hence,* $RDU(L) = (1 - 0.3873) \times 20 + 0.3873 \times 200 = 89.71$. *Proceeding as in Example 2.2, the certainty equivalent is given by* $C_L = 89.71 > E(L) = 47$. *Thus, the decision maker is risk loving (Definition 1.2) despite having a linear utility function.*

The calculations in Examples 2.2 and 2.3 show that the calculation of risk aversion is not as straightforward as is made out under EUT. A tremendous amount of intellectual effort has been sunk into estimating the risk aversion parameter under EUT by assuming specific functional forms such as constant relative risk aversion utility. However, by not taking into account non-linear probability weighting, the resulting estimates cannot be trusted. Furthermore, under prospect theory, which we examine next, there might be no risk aversion left once we account for loss aversion.

2.3.3 An Example Where EUT and RDUT Fail

Both EUT and RDUT fail the empirical test in situations where the reference point plays an important role. Consider the following example.

Example 2.4 *(A refutation of both EUT and RDUT): Consider Problems 11 and 12 from Kahneman and Tversky (1979). Units are in Israeli pounds. A decision maker (referred to as "you") has initial wealth y and is given two different additional amounts in two different problems. In each problem the decision maker is then asked to make a choice between two lotteries.*
Problem 11: Suppose that you have been given an additional amount 1000 *over and above your wealth y. You are now asked to choose between the two lotteries*

$$L_1 = (y + 1000, 0.5; y + 2000, 0.5) \text{ and } L_2 = (y + 1000, 0; y + 1500, 1).$$

In effect, over and above the initial wealth $y + 1000$, *in lottery* L_1 *the decision maker is given* 1000 *with probability* 0.5 *and in lottery* L_2, *an extra* 500 *with probability 1. The vast majority of subjects, 84%, chose* L_2 *and the rest, 16%, chose* L_1. *Suppose that decision makers follow RDUT. Then, the observed behavior of the majority of the subjects suggests that* $RDU(L_2) > RDU(L_1)$. *Using (2.5) and Definition 2.4, we get that for the majority choices*

$$RDU(L_2) > RDU(L_1) \iff u(y + 1500) > (1 - w(0.5))\, u(y + 1000) + w(0.5)u(y + 2000). \quad (2.9)$$

Problem 12: Suppose that you have been given an additional amount 2000 *over and above your wealth y. You are now asked to choose between*

$$L_3 = (y + 1000, 0.5; y + 2000, 0.5) \text{ and } L_4 = (y + 1500, 1; y + 2000, 0).$$

In effect, over and above the initial wealth $y + 2000$, *in lottery* L_3 *the decision maker faces a loss of* 1000 *with probability* 0.5 *while in lottery* L_4, *a loss of* 500 *with probability 1. In this case, the majorty of subjects, 69%, chose* L_3 *while 31% chose* L_4. *Using (2.5) and Definition 2.4, we get that for the majority choices*

$$RDU(L_4) < RDU(L_3) \iff u(y+1500) < (1 - w(0.5))\, u(y+1000)+w(0.5)u(y+2000). \quad (2.10)$$

The two conditions (2.9), (2.10) contradict each other. In other words, the data for the two sets of choices in Problems 11 and 12 is not consistent with a decision maker who follows RDUT. In Problem 11, the decision maker has an endowment of $y + 1000$ *and in Problem 12, an endowment of* $y + 2000$*. The status quo, or the current endowment, turns out to be a powerful determinant of reference points. However, RDUT is not able to take account of changes in the reference point in the two cases. By contrast, prospect theory, which is based on an evaluation of lotteries that takes account of reference points, predicts the pattern of choices that we observe in Problems 11 and 12 (one of the exercises takes up this question).*

2.4 Prospect Theory

Based on experiments conducted in the 1960s and 1970s, Kahneman and Tversky (1979) proposed *original prospect theory* (OPT). This was similar to decision weighted utility in (2.4), albeit with a different utility function that took reference dependence into account (see below). Since decision weighted utility allowed stochastically dominated options to be chosen, OPT faced criticism within economics. Tversky and Kahneman (1992) used insights from RDUT, which precluded the choice of stochastically dominated options, to give a revised account, *prospect theory* (PT), sometimes also known as *cumulative prospect theory*. Our exposition below uses PT.

The idea that all forms of life, plants and animals, evaluate changes relative to some reference point, or are more sensitive to *changes* than *levels*, is well established in psychology and biology. In a famous experiment in psychology, an individual first dips the left hand in hot water and the right hand in cold water, allowing the hands to get used to the temperature, then takes both hands out simultaneously and dips them into lukewarm water. The left hand reports the temperature of the lukewarm water as 'cold' while the right hand reports the temperature as 'hot' indicating reference dependence, or sensitivity to "changes in levels." The status quo is a powerful reference point in many human decisions. Reference points might also be determined by fairness considerations, or by social norms, or by expectations of future outcomes.

2.4.1 Lotteries in Incremental Form

Suppose that decision makers care for outcomes, $x_1 < \ldots < x_n$ relative to a reference point, r. Then, decision makers in PT are interested in *lotteries in incremental form* that subtract r from each outcome. Such a lottery is given by

$$L = (x_1 - r, p_1; x_2 - r, p_2; \ldots; x_n - r, p_n). \tag{2.11}$$

The reference point splits outcomes into the domain of gains ($x - r \geq 0$) and the domain of losses ($x - r < 0$). Let us define

$$y = x - r \tag{2.12}$$

as the generic outcome relative to the reference point. More generally, suppose that we have l outcomes in the domain of losses, g outcomes in the domain of gains, and 1 outcome that equals the reference point, for total of $l + 1 + g = n$ outcomes. These outcomes are ordered as follows

$$y_{-l} < y_{-l+1} < y_{-l+2} < \ldots < y_{-1} < y_0 = 0 < y_1 < y_2 < \ldots < y_g,$$

where $y_i = x_i - r$ is the *ith outcome relative to the reference point* that, for brevity, we henceforth refer to as *outcome* only. Thus, the lottery in incremental form in (2.11) can be written as

$$L = (y_{-l}, p_{-l}; y_{-l+1}, p_{-l+1}; \ldots; y_{-1}, p_{-1}; y_0, p_0; y_1, p_1; y_2, p_2; \ldots; y_g, p_g). \tag{2.13}$$

We denote the set of all possible outcomes relative to the reference point by $Y \subset \mathbb{R}$. Denote the set of all lotteries in incremental form by $\mathbf{L}_I$.

2.4.2 Utility Function under Prospect Theory

The reference point splits the domain of outcomes into gains and losses. This is not merely semantics. The behavior of decision makers is fundamentally different in the domains of gains and losses in several respects. First, individuals exhibit *loss aversion*, that is, losses bite more than equivalent gains; the median estimates suggest a figure of approximately two times more. Thus, a gain of \$100 may feel like a gain of \$100, but a loss of \$100 feels like a loss of about \$200. Second, if probabilities are not too small, and this is an important caveat as we shall see later, decision makers are risk averse in gains and risk loving in losses, as illustrated in the following experiment in Tversky and Kahneman (1981), where subjects were given the following instructions.

Imagine that the US is preparing for the outbreak of an unusual Asian disease, which is expected to kill 600 people. Two alternative programs to combat the disease have been proposed and subjects must choose one of them. Assume that the exact scientific estimates of the consequences of the programs are as follows.

"Lives saved" framing: If program A is adopted, 200 people will be saved. If program B is adopted, there is a one-third probability that 600 people will be saved and a two-thirds probability that no people will be saved. [72% chose the safe program A, 28% chose the risky program B]

"Lives lost" framing: If program C is adopted, 400 people will die. If program D is adopted, there is a one-third probability that nobody will die and a two-thirds probability that 600 people will die. [78% chose D, the risky program, and 22% chose the safe program C]

If the reference point is the status quo then "lives saved" puts one in the domain of gains and "lives lost" in the domain of losses. The pair of options A and C have identical information content, so do B and D, but they are described differently – one in terms of lives saved and the other in terms of lives lost. Under the neoclassical assumption of *description invariance*, alternative, but informationally equivalent, ways of presenting the same information should not affect behavior. Yet, subjects pick the safe option in gains and the risky option in losses. Thus, reference points are important, description invariance does not hold, and risk attitudes are domain-specific. These specific findings have been replicated successfully with medical practitioners, and the general findings have been replicated repeatedly.

The utility function under PT, denoted by v, to differentiate it from the utility function u in EUT and RDUT, is shown in Figure 2.3. Along the horizontal axis, we measure, y, the outcomes net of the reference point. Along the vertical axis, we measure the utility, $v(y)$, arising from y. The origin corresponds to the point where $y = 0$. The utility function is concave in gains, which

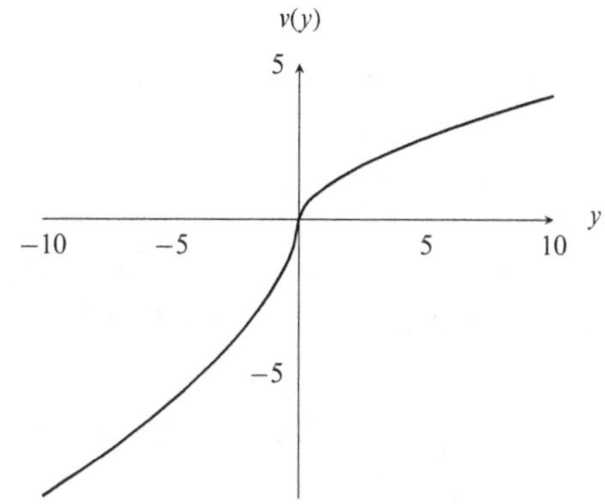

Figure 2.3 The utility function under prospect theory for empirically relevant values of the parameters

inclines the decision maker towards risk aversion, and is convex in losses which inclines the decision maker towards risk loving behavior. This is exactly what occurs in the lives saved/lives lost example above. However, attitudes to risk are more complex under PT once we take account of low probability events; see Section 2.4.4. There is also a kink at the origin in Figure 2.3, where loss aversion just begins to bite in the domain of losses and marginal utility falls dramatically.

We can summarize this information in the following more formal definition.

Definition 2.5 *(Utility function under PT). Let $Y \subset \mathbb{R}$ be the set of all outcomes (relative to the reference point). A utility function, $v : Y \to \mathbb{R}$ is a continuous and strictly increasing function with the following properties:*
a. $v(0) = 0$ (reference dependence).
b. v is concave in gains and convex in losses (Diminishing marginal utility).
c. $-v(-y) > v(y)$ for $y > 0$ (loss aversion).

Definition 2.5b, concavity and convexity of the utility function, respectively, implies diminishing sensitivity to gains and losses. The outcome $y > 0$ when experienced as a gain results in the utility $v(y)$, and when experienced as a loss, $-y$, results in the disutility $v(-y) < 0$. Loss aversion (Definition 2.5c) implies that the absolute value of this disutility, $-v(-y)$, is relatively higher.

An example of a utility function that satisfies Definition 2.5 is the following power form of the utility function that is empirically supported.

$$v(y) = \begin{cases} y^{\gamma} & \text{if } \ y \geq 0 \\ -\lambda(-y)^{\gamma} & \text{if } \ y < 0 \end{cases} ; \lambda > 1,\ 0 < \gamma < 1. \tag{2.14}$$

In (2.14), the parameter $0 < \gamma < 1$ controls the curvature of the utility function, and the loss aversion parameter $\lambda > 1$ captures the size of loss aversion. Tversky and Kahneman (1992) find that the median values of these parameters are $\gamma = 0.88$ and $\lambda = 2.25$. In Figure 2.3, we have plotted the function in (2.14) for the parameter values $\lambda = 2.25$ and $\gamma = 0.60$. The value $\gamma = 0.88$ is close to $\gamma = 1.0$ (linear utility function) and it is visually difficult to distinguish a utility function with $\gamma = 0.88$ from a straight line. Since straight line utility functions are associated with risk neutrality under EUT (Proposition 1.1), much of what we observe as cautionary behavior under risk probably arises from loss aversion and nonlinear probability weighting, rather than from risk aversion. This is an important insight of PT. The special case $\gamma = 1$ gives rise to a *piecewise linear utility function*, and it is popular in applied work.

2.4.3 The Prospect Theory Value Function

Analogous to the objective functions under EUT and RDUT given in (1.8), (2.5), the objective function under PT, sometimes known as a *value function*, $V : \mathbf{L}_I \longrightarrow \mathbb{R}$, is given by

$$PT(L) \equiv V(L) = \sum_{i=-l}^{g} \pi_i v(y_i), L \in \mathbf{L}_I. \tag{2.15}$$

In (2.15), the lottery L in incremental form is given in (2.13), the utility function v is given in Definition 2.5, the set of all lotteries in incremental form is given by $\mathbf{L}_I$, and the index on the summation sign runs from the smallest outcome to the largest outcome. The main difference between the objective functions under RDUT and PT, (2.5) and (2.15), is that the utility functions, u and v, are different. The decision weights in (2.15) are computed separately in each domain. To see this, let us rewrite (2.15).

$$PT(L) = \pi_{-l} v\left(y_{-l}\right) + \pi_{-l+1} v\left(y_{-l+1}\right) + \ldots + \pi_{-1} v\left(y_{-1}\right) + \pi_0 v\left(0\right) + \pi_1 v\left(y_1\right) + \ldots + \pi_g v\left(y_g\right). \tag{2.16}$$

For the domain of gains, the decision weights $\pi_1, \pi_2, \ldots, \pi_g$ are calculated exactly as under RDUT in Definition 2.4. The calculation of the decision weights in the domain of losses, $\pi_{-l}, \pi_{-l+1}, \ldots, \pi_{-1}$, is analogous, except that we begin with the decision weight, π_l corresponding to the lowest outcome and then keep going up one outcome at a time towards the reference point. The relevant calculations are summarized in the next definition.

Definition 2.6 *(Decision weights under PT) Suppose that the decision maker faces the lottery L in (2.13),*

$$L = \left(y_{-l}, p_{-l}; y_{-l+1}, p_{-l+1}; \ldots; y_{-1}, p_{-1}; y_0, p_0; y_1, p_1; y_2, p_2; \ldots; y_g, p_g\right), \tag{2.17}$$

and has the probability weighting function w(p). Then, the decision weights are given as follows.

(i) Decision weights in the domain of gains

$$\pi_g = w(p_g)$$
$$\pi_{g-1} = w(p_{g-1} + p_g) - w(p_g)$$
$$\pi_{g-2} = w(p_{g-2} + p_{g-1} + p_g) - w(p_{g-1} + p_g)$$
$$\vdots$$
$$\pi_1 = w(p_1 + p_2 + \ldots + p_g) - w(p_2 + p_3 + \ldots + p_g)$$

(ii) Decision weights in the domain of losses

$$\pi_{-l} = w(p_{-l})$$
$$\pi_{-l+1} = w(p_{-l+1} + p_{-l}) - w(p_{-l})$$
$$\pi_{-l+2} = w(p_{-l+2} + p_{-l+1} + p_{-l}) - w(p_{-l+1} + p_{-l})$$

.

.

.

$$\pi_{-1} = w(p_{-1} + p_{-2} + \ldots + p_{-l+1} + p_{-l}) - w(p_{-2} + \ldots + p_{-l+1} + p_{-l}).$$

As under RDUT, all decision weights are positive. However, unlike the decision weights under RDUT which add up to 1, the decision weights under PT do not add up to 1 unless (i) all outcomes are in gains, or (ii) all outcomes are in losses. The reader can directly check this using Definition 2.6. In Definition 2.6, we have not assigned any decision weight, π_0, to the reference outcome. The reason is that since $v(0) = 0$ (Definition 2.5a), the term $\pi_0 v(0)$ in (2.16) equals zero, so we may assign any finite number to π_0. One proposal is to adjust the value of π_0 so that when the decision weights are added, inclusive of π_0, they add up to 1.

It is conceivable that the decision maker uses different PWFs in gains and in losses. If, for instance, decision makers use a Prelec PWF, then the two parameters α, β might be different in the two domains. There is some evidence that α, which controls curvature, is similar across the two domains, but β, which controls elevation, may be different in the two domains.

The numerical examples below should enable readers to gain familiarity with computing the prospect theory evaluation of lotteries.

Example 2.5 *Consider the lottery* $(4, 0.2; 9, 0.3; 16, 0.5)$ *in Example 2.1. Suppose that the reference point of the decision maker is* $r = 9$*; the probability weighting function is a Prelec function with* $\beta = 1$ *and* $\alpha = 0.5$*, that is,* $w(p) = e^{-(-lnp)^{0.5}}$*; and the utility function is given in (2.14) with* $\gamma = 0.88$ *and* $\lambda = 2.25$*, so*

$$v(y) = \begin{cases} y^{0.88} & \text{if } y \geq 0 \\ -2.25(-y)^{0.88} & \text{if } y < 0 \end{cases}. \tag{2.18}$$

The first step is to subtract the reference point $r = 9$ *from each outcome in the given lottery to express the lottery in incremental form*

$$L = (-5, 0.2; 0, 0.3; 7, 0.5).$$

There is one outcome each in gains and losses, so this is the special case where $l = 1$ *and* $g = 1$*. The prospect theory evaluation of this lottery is given by*

$$PT(L) = \pi_{-1} v(-5) + \pi_0 v(0) + \pi_1 v(7). \tag{2.19}$$

Using Definition 2.6, the decision weights are given by (we will need the rows corresponding to π_g *and* π_{-l} *in Definition 2.6 because* $g = 1$ *and* $l = 1$*)*

$$\pi_1 = w(0.5),$$
$$\pi_{-1} = w(0.2).$$

Using the utility function in (2.18), we get:

$$v(7) = 7^{0.88} = 5.5423; \; v(0) = 0; \; v(-5) = -2.25\,(5)^{0.88} = -9.2742.$$

We can also use the probability weighting function $w(p) = e^{-(-lnp)^{0.5}}$ *to calculate:*

$$\pi_1 = w(0.5) = e^{-(-ln0.5)^{0.5}} = 0.4349; \pi_{-1} = w(0.2) = e^{-(-ln0.2)^{0.5}} = 0.2812.$$

Substituting this information in (2.19), we get

$$PT(L) = 0.2812\,(-9.2742) + 0.4349\,(5.5423) = -0.1976.$$

The overall prospect theory evaluation of the lottery is negative because the loss of 5, relative to the reference point, is aversive and $v(-5) = -9.2742$, which swamps the gains from the positive outcome.

Example 2.6 *Consider the following lottery in incremental form (the reference point has already been subtracted from the outcomes) that has two outcomes each in gains and losses ($l = 2$, $g = 2$):*

$$L = (-10, 0.3; \ -5, 0.2; 5, 0.4; 10, 0.1).$$

The probability weighting function of the decision maker is $w(p) = p^2$, and the utility function is piecewise linear ($\gamma = 1$) with the parameter of loss aversion $\lambda = 2.25$, that is

$$v\,(y) = \begin{cases} y & \text{if} \quad y \geq 0 \\ -2.25\,(-y) & \text{if} \quad y < 0 \end{cases}. \tag{2.20}$$

The prospect theory evaluation of this lottery is

$$PT(L) = \pi_{-2}v(-10) + \pi_{-1}v(-5) + \pi_1 v(5) + \pi_2 v(10). \tag{2.21}$$

Using the rows corresponding to π_g, π_{g-1}, π_{-l}, and π_{-l+1} in Definition 2.6, the decision weights can be calculated as follows.

$$\begin{aligned} \pi_2 &= w(0.1) = (0.1)^2 = 0.01 \\ \pi_1 &= w(0.4 + 0.1) - w(0.1) = (0.5)^2 - (0.1)^2 = 0.24 \\ \pi_{-2} &= w(0.3) = (0.3)^2 = 0.09 \\ \pi_{-1} &= w(0.2 + 0.3) - w(0.3) = (0.5)^2 - (0.3)^2 = 0.16. \end{aligned}$$

Using the piecewise linear utility function, we have:

$$v(10) = 10; v(5) = 5; v(-5) = -2.25\,(5) = -11.25; v(-10) = -2.25\,(10) = -22.5.$$

Substituting these calculations in (2.21) we get

$$PT(L) = 0.09(-22.5) + 0.16(-11.25) + 0.24(5) + 0.01(10) = -2.525.$$

Loss aversion is a central feature of PT, as well as in the modifications of PT, such as the Köszegi and Rabin model that we outline below. An emerging literature has highlighted the possibility that a fraction of experimental subjects might be loss seeking, rather than loss averse; for a metastudy see Brown et al. (2024). In terms of (2.14) loss seeking corresponds to the case $\lambda < 1$. For instance, Campos-Mercade et al. (2024) show that three quarters of their subjects are loss averse, while a quarter of the subjects are loss seeking. However, their estimation is undertaken within a Köszegi–Rabin model with linear underlying probabilities. Insofar as we have robust empirical evidence in favor of nonlinear probability weighting, it is not clear what effects the assumption of linear probability weighting might have had on the estimated values of loss aversion.

It is important to note that the estimation of the parameters of prospect theory requires a joint estimation of the parameters of the probability weighting function and the utility function. An important determinant of loss aversion could be stake sizes. When the stakes are really high, would some of the loss-seeking subjects act as loss averse instead? The answers to questions such as these are not well understood yet.

Köszegi and Rabin (2006, 2007) propose a slightly different form of preferences that take account of utility arising from two different sources.

(i) The utility, u, from the *absolute level of an outcome*, x, and
(ii) gain–loss utility, g, that arises from *changes in outcomes relative to a reference point*, $y = x - r$, where r is the reference point.

In particular, gain–loss utility takes the same form as (2.14) but with $\gamma = 1$. Thus, the Köszegi–Rabin utility function, v^* (to distinguish it from the PT utility function in (2.14), v), is written

$$v^*(x, r) = u(x) + \mu g(x - r); \mu > 0, \tag{2.22}$$

where $\mu > 0$ is the relative weight assigned to the gain–loss utility function, g, which is given by

$$g\left(x - r\right) = \begin{cases} x - r & \text{if} \quad x \geq r \\ -\lambda\left(r - x\right) & \text{if} \quad x < r \end{cases} ; \lambda > 1. \tag{2.23}$$

In their formulation of the value function under prospect theory, the analogue of (2.15), Köszegi and Rabin use linear probability weighting, as under EUT, that is, $\pi_i = p_i$.

The Köszegi–Rabin model is popular in economics and has been widely applied to issues in macroeconomics, industrial organization, and contract theory. Its main attraction for economists, particularly for neoclassical economists, is the promise that it gives rise to an *endogenous reference point*, r, that is determined inside the model. The reference point is determined using the same method as rational expectations in macroeconomics, or the notion of sequential rationality in game theory (see Chapters 5, 6). Informally described, decision makers have initial expectations about the probabilistic outcomes of their actions, so they form reference points based on these expectations, and, on average, these expectations turn out to be correct.

A common perception in economics appears to be that the Köszegi–Rabin model is a superior theory as compared to the standard PT, because we get something (endogenous reference point) for nothing. This perception is mistaken.

1. It is not the case that we get something for nothing; this almost never happens in economic theory. The use of this framework requires the heroic assumption that decision makers follow rational expectations in forming reference points. The authors suggest relaxing this assumption, but no concrete empirically relevant suggestions have been proposed so far.
2. The usefulness of the assumption of rational expectations cannot be decided on theoretical criteria. In science, the usefulness of a theory arises from its ability to explain the empirical evidence. Direct tests of the rational expectations assumption in forming reference points are incredibly difficult. Empirical evidence does, however, indicate that expectations may play an important role in forming reference points (Abeler et al., 2011; Ericson and Fuster, 2011). However, the experimental results in Cerulli-Harms et al. (2019) reject the predictions of the

Köszegi–Rabin model. They show that the endowment effect (see Section 2.5.1) exists even for those probabilities that the Köszegi–Rabin model predicts that they should not, and the results are very sensitive to relatively minor features of the experimental instructions.

3. The informational and cognitive requirements to form rational expectations are incredibly cognitively and informationally challenging. In contrast to the "equilibrium in beliefs" approach implicit in rational expectations, we consider evidence in Part IV of models based on *disequilibrium beliefs* that are supported by the empirical evidence, and run counter to rational expectations.
4. There is much evidence on nonlinear probability weighting that cannot be taken account of in the Köszegi–Rabin model because it assumes linear probability weighting.

Nevertheless, the formulation in (2.22) and (2.23) is an important contribution to the literature. We consider an application of these preferences to renegotiation of contracts in Section 2.5.9 below, but without the other features of the Köszegi–Rabin model.

There have been other attempts to model behavior under risk that are based on *regret-aversion* and *disappointment-aversion*, as well as using the *salience of outcomes* to construct the decision weights. However, reference dependence and loss aversion already reflect, in a reduced form manner, the emotions of regret and disappointment from receiving an outcome lower than the reference point. We consider salience theory and limited attention in Part VI of the book and the specific features of these models continue to be tested. Overall, looking at the broad sweep of the available evidence, PT currently provides the most satisfactory description of human behavior under risk, uncertainty, and ambiguity.

2.4.4 Attitudes to Risk under Prospect Theory

As under RDUT, attitudes to risk under PT are determined jointly by the shapes of the PWF and the utility function. However, attitudes to risk are even more interesting under PT because of the existence of separate domains of gains and losses, and the different shapes of the utility functions in each domain. For instance, in the domain of gains, the concavity of utility creates a predisposition towards risk aversion, and the convexity of utility in losses a predisposition towards risk seeking. Yet, since low probabilities are overweighted in the PWF, these predispositions can be overridden. For instance, overweighting of the small probability of a gain may actually make the decision maker more willing to take risks, countering the tendency of the concave utility function to impart caution. The opposite occurs in the domain of losses.

Tversky and Kahneman (1992) provide evidence on the *fourfold pattern of attitudes to risk* under PT. Consider two-outcome lotteries in incremental form given by

$$L = (0, 1 - p; y, p),$$

where $y = x - r$, is a gain, $y > 0$, or a loss, $y < 0$. With probability $1 - p$, we have $x - r = 0$. In Table 2.1, we consider either a low probability ($p = 0.05$) or a high probability ($p = 0.95$), and either gains ($y = 100 > 0$) or losses ($y = -100 < 0$). This gives rise to 4 lotteries, shown in each cell of Table 2.1 along with the associated certainty equivalents and expected values.

Table 2.1 Fourfold classification of risk under prospect theory

Probability	Domain of Gains	Domain of Losses
Low	$L = (100, 0.05; 0, 0.95)$ $C_L = 14, E(L) = 5$	$L = (-100, 0.05; 0, 0.95)$ $C_L = -8, E(L) = -5$
High	$L = (100, 0.95; 0, 0.05)$ $C_L = 78, E(L) = 95$	$L = (-100, 0.95; 0, 0.05)$ $C_L = -84, E(L) = -95$

Recall, from Definition 1.2, that a decision maker is either risk averse ($C_L < E(L)$), or risk loving ($C_L > E(L)$), or risk neutral ($C_L = E(L)$). In Table 2.1, for low probabilities ($p = 0.05$), there is risk seeking in gains, but for high probabilities ($p = 0.95$), there is risk aversion in gains. The opposite situation is found in losses – risk aversion for low probabilities, but risk seeking for high probabilities. This fourfold pattern is hard to explain under theories other than PT.

The fourfold pattern of risk attitudes is not dependent on the particular numbers that we have chosen in the lotteries in Table 2.1. One of the exercises asks you to derive a more general result. The next example goes through the steps required to determine attitudes to risk under PT, for a slightly more complicated lottery. The same template can be used to determine attitudes to risk in any problem in PT.

Example 2.7 *Consider Example 2.5 where we used the lottery* $L = (4, 0.2; 9, 0.3; 16, 0.5)$ *and calculated* $PT(L) = -0.1976$ *using the reference point* $r = 9$*. The expected value of the lottery is* $E(L) = 11.5$*. The certainty equivalent is a lottery of the form* $(C_L, 1)$*. We first need to convert it into incremental form, using the reference point* $r = 9$*, which gives* $(C_L - 9, 1)$*.*
Since $PT(L) < 0$*, let us conjecture that the certainty equivalent relative to the reference point is a negative number,* $C_L - 9 < 0$*. Thus,* $PT(C_L - 9, 1) = -2.25\,(-(C_L - 9))^{0.88}$*. Since the certainty equivalent makes a decision maker indifferent to the lottery, and* $PT(L) = -0.1976$*, we can solve* C_L *from the condition* $PT(C_L - 9, 1) = PT(L)$*, or* $-2.25\,(-(C_L - 9))^{0.88} = -0.1976$*, to get* $C_L = 8.937 < E(L) = 11.5$*. Thus, the decision maker is risk averse.*

2.5 Applications of Prospect Theory

The scope of applications of PT is vast, and encompasses most of economics. We consider selected applications of PT in this section.

2.5.1 The Endowment Effect

Among animals, the owners of territories are typically able to defeat the intruders. Animals may even develop conventions such as "First one there wins, later arrivals retreat" (Smith and Parker, 1976) which are stable in an evolutionary sense (see Part IV for the concept of evolutionary stability). Thus, owners of territories act as if they have more to lose than intruders gain from occupying the same territory. It is "as if" owners of territories place relatively greater value on their territories simply because that is their status-quo position, so they defend it vigorously and are often able to repel intruders. Among humans, several experiments find that owners of objects whose status-quo position is physical ownership of the object, value objects more than potential bidders for the object; this is known as the *endowment effect*.

Kahneman et al. (1990) gave half of their student subjects a university mug to own (with known value to students) and the other half were assigned a monetary endowment which they could use to bid for the mug. The median minimum selling price (or *minimum willingness to accept*, *WTA*) by the owners was "more than twice" the median maximum buying price (or the *maximum willingness to pay*, *WTP*) stated by potential buyers. Loss aversion provides the leading explanation of this phenomenon.

Suppose that the seller and the buyer have a piecewise linear utility function (set $\gamma = 1$ in (2.14)). The seller is endowed with the mug, hence, the reference point of the seller is one mug ($r = 1$), while that of the buyer is zero mug ($r = 0$). Foregoing the mug in return for a price P, imposes a utility loss on the seller equal to loss aversion, λ, times 1 mug, which equals λ. Thus, the WTA of the seller equals his utility loss, that is, $WTA = \lambda$. The gain to the buyer from buying 1 mug relative to the reference point of 0 mug is simply equal to 1, so the WTP of the buyer equals $WTP = 1$. Thus, we have

$$\frac{WTA}{WTP} = \lambda \approx 2.$$

The ratio of WTA to WTP which can be easily elicited from subjects in experimental studies, thus, indicates loss aversion. It is found to be approximately equal to 2. One potential concern with estimating loss aversion in this manner is that sellers might be artificially inflating their WTA in order to increase profits. In order to address this concern, the authors run a separate treatment in which the exchange price between the buyer and the seller is chosen randomly. Thus, the actual WTA stated by the sellers has no influence on the price used in the transaction, and they do not benefit from overstating it. Yet, the observed size of the endowment effect was found to be similar.

Is the physical ownership of the mug, the key transmission mechanism that explains the endowment effect? In order to answer this question, the authors introduce a separate group of subjects, the *choosers*, in addition to the buyers and the sellers. For any price P that is being negotiated between the seller and the buyer, the choosers were given the option of either accepting the price P or receiving the mug. Thus, their choice was very much like the choice facing a seller, except that while sellers had physical possession of the mug, choosers did not. Hence, any difference in the behavior between sellers and choosers is expected to arise on account of the difference in the physical possession of the object for sale. It was found that choosers behaved just like buyers in terms of the value that they placed on the mug, and not like sellers. Hence, the endowment effect does arise from physical possession of the object.

The results of the endowment effect studies have been successfully replicated with many diverse items of exchange such as pizza toppings, hunting permits, wine, and college basketball tickets. The endowment effect is found to be influenced by a range of factors which include the duration of ownership of an object; the framing of questions that highlights alternative uses of the mug to the seller and alternative uses of the money to the buyer; the emotional states of sellers and buyers; age and education of the subjects; the nature of the good being exchanged, for example, whether it is a health or a nonhealth good. One also finds substantial heterogeneity among subjects in measured loss aversion.

Hartzmark et al. (2021) present evidence to show that ownership of an object alters the processing of positive and negative information about the object. Owners overshoot in their processing of positive and negative information. A positive signal about the quality of the good leads owners to overestimate the future price of the object, and a negative signal leads them to underestimate it. By contrast, non-owners update their expectation of the price in a manner consistent with standard Bayesian updating. The main implication is that positive news increases the endowment effect and negative news decreases it. If the signal is negative enough, then the endowment effect disappears.

In an interesting application, Fryer et al. (2012) assign school teachers randomly to two treatments in Chicago. In the first treatment, teachers are given upfront monetary payments, and they are assigned "achievement targets" for their students. However, if at the end of the year, students fail to achieve the assigned targets, then teachers need to return back their monetary payments. In the second treatment, teachers are promised the same monetary payments for the same "achievement targets" but the payments are made only if the targets are achieved. At the end of the year, teachers in both treatments earn identical amounts of money. If we ignore discounting, then under expected utility theory, teachers in both treatments are predicted to work equally hard to achieve the targets.

Under prospect theory, things are a bit different. In the first treatment, the monetary payments might become a part of the reference point of the teachers, and teachers might feel entitled to these payments, much like the owners of mugs in the endowment effect. Hence, the possibility of losing these upfront payments at the end of the year, should the targets not be met, is likely to invoke loss aversion. This is not the case in the second treatment where the payments are made at the end of the year. Hence, teachers in the first treatment have an extra incentive to work harder to achieve the targets in order to avoid loss aversion. This is exactly what the data shows. Performance-based teacher pay is more effective in inducing student achievement in the first treatment.

But what if we gave teachers a choice between the contracts in the two treatments. Would teachers in the first treatment not wish to be in the second treatment, in order to avoid loss aversion from potentially losing their upfront payments. In other words, would not many teachers avoid contracts that put them in the loss domain relative to the gain domain. While this question has not been specifically tested for school teachers, Imas et al. (2016) show that people in fact prefer contracts of the form in the first treatment above, where loss aversion bites, rather than the second treatment. Their preferred explanation is that such contracts provide a commitment technology to people, inducing them to work harder. This also indicates that people have an awareness of loss aversion.

2.5.2 Why Is It So Hard to Find a Taxi on a Rainy Day in New York?

One expects taxis to be a little bit harder to find on a rainy day in New York because more people are using taxis at any given time. However, it is puzzling why many taxi drivers quit work earlier on a rainy day. After all, there are lower waiting times between successive taxi trips, so the effective wage per hour of taxi drivers is higher. Why do they then reduce their labour supply? Neoclassical economics allows for a backward bending labour supply curve but it is based on opposing income and substitution effects of a change in real wage that are hard to verify with field data. By contrast, the behavioral explanation given by Camerer et al. (1997) is straightforward. Around the mid-1990's, taxi drivers had a daily income target (or reference point), say, of about \$100. They continue to work until they hit the target, otherwise they would end up in the domain of losses, where loss aversion bites. Once they hit the target, which is quicker on a rainy day, they may quit for the day. Hence, we observe earlier quits.

The intuition is straightforward, but empirical testing poses problems. First, we need to identify subjects pools that have a real choice in working hours, for example, bicycle messengers or sports stadium vendors who choose how long to work on a particular day. Second, the reference point might itself vary on different days, and there could be several confounding factors such as driver fixed effects, luck, and prior earnings. Despite several mixed empirical results, subsequent research shows that the weight of the evidence is supportive of the effect (Fehr and Goette, 2007; Crawford and Meng, 2011). There is also some evidence that more experienced drivers may be less prone to quitting early, countering the effects arising from loss aversion.

2.5.3 Why Do People Pay Taxes?

In Western democracies, amateur tax evaders face a probability of detection, p, that lies between 1%–5%. If caught, a tax evader pays back the evaded tax plus a fine, θ, which, for Western democracies, ranges between one half to two times the evaded tax payments. For illustrative purposes, suppose that we took the intermediate values, $p = 3\%$ and $\theta = 1$. Consider a taxpayer wishing to evade \$1 in taxes. If caught, with probability p, he must pay back the \$1 in evaded tax, plus the fine, θ; so he is left with an income of $-\theta$. If not caught, with probability $1 - p$, the taxpayer can keep the \$1 in evaded tax. It follows that the expected return on \$1 of evaded tax is

$$(1 - p) - p\theta. \tag{2.24}$$

Substituting $p = 0.03$ and $\theta = 1$ in (2.24), the expected return on a dollar of evaded tax is 94%. It is hard to find an asset which offers a comparable return. This begs the question: Why do people pay taxes? The evidence shows that among those who have a chance to evade taxes (e.g., their taxes are not witheld at source), about 30% do evade taxes. However, EUT predicts that all taxpayers should evade taxes at such high returns. Even taking account of plausible stigma costs from being caught evading taxes, one explain the puzzle.

Dhami and al-Nowaihi (2007) took the legal after-tax income as the reference point to explain this puzzle. They also used all components of PT and accounted also for plausible stigma costs.[5] They show that overweighting of the small probability of being caught (see the inverse S-shaped PWF in Figure 2.1) and loss aversion from paying the fine if caught, jointly offer sufficient deterrence so that about 70% of taxpayers will not wish to evade.

[5] Readers interested in following up the comprehensive literature on the subject and the insights that preceeded and succeeded this paper can consult Alm (2019).

In order to understand these insights better, consider an illustrative example that makes the following assumptions. (i) The decision maker, a potential tax evader, follows prospect theory and has the Prelec probability weighting function $w(p) = e^{-0.8(-lnp)^{0.3}}$, so $\alpha = 0.3$ and $\beta = 0.8$. (ii) If caught evading taxes, the decision maker is in the domain of losses, and if not caught, in the domain of gains. Indeed, this is automatically ensured for any level of declared income if the reference point is the legal after-tax income; for the proof, see Dhami and al-Nowaihi (2007). (iii) The utility function is piecewise linear as in (2.20) and $\lambda = 2.25$.

Under these assumptions, the analogue of (2.24) is

$$w(1-p) - \lambda w(p)\theta. \tag{2.25}$$

Substituting $p = 0.3$, $\lambda = 2.25$, and the Prelec function with $\alpha = 0.3$, $\beta = 0.8$ in (2.25), we get

$$e^{-0.8(-ln0.97)^{0.3}} - 2.25e^{-0.8(-ln0.03)^{0.3}} = 0.05387.$$

Thus, the perceived return on tax evasion is only 5.38%. Furthermore, if there are stigma costs of being caught evading taxes, the return on tax evasion is reduced even further. Since there is likely to be a distribution of stigma costs among taxpayers, some will find it optimal to evade, while others will not. Under plausible conditions, we get a reasonable match between the theory and the tax evasion data.

The bulk of the empirical evidence shows that an increase in the tax rate induces taxpayers to evade more. The prediction under EUT, under the plausible assumption of *decreasing absolute risk aversion* (DARA), is the opposite, namely, that as the government raises taxes, people evade less taxes. One of the exercises asks you to supply the relevant intuition. In any case, the EUT prediction is not only counterintuitive but also empirically rejected; this is known as the *Yitzhaki puzzle*. The puzzle can be explained under prospect theory, using the following rough intuition, although a formal analysis requires a more nuanced explanation under the conditions of the model. An increase in the tax rate pushes tax evaders in the domain of losses where they are risk seeking (see the convex utility function in losses in Figure 2.3), hence, they are more likely to choose the risky activity of tax evasion rather than the safe activity of paying taxes. Thus, an increase in taxes increases tax evasion.

2.5.4 Evolution and Loss Aversion

Capuchin monkeys, found in South America, separated from the evolutionary line that led to present day humans, about 35 million years ago. They are a particularly sociable monkey and can be trained to exchange tokens for food. In particular, they are given an endowment of tokens, and they learn to exchange evolutionary salient items with experimenters, such as apple slices or peanut butter for the tokens; see the illustration in Figure 2.4. Empirical evidence gathered from such transactions between experimenters and capuchins has revealed that their utility function is similar to the PT utility function in Figure 2.3.

In the experiments by Chen et al. (2006), two experimenters stood at two ends of a cage with a trained capuchin monkey inside the cage who was given an endowment of tokens. Experimenter 1 initially held out one slice of apple in exchange for a token. However, on receiving a token, the experimenter offered the following lottery in apple slices to the monkey: $L = (1, 0.5; 2, 0.5)$,

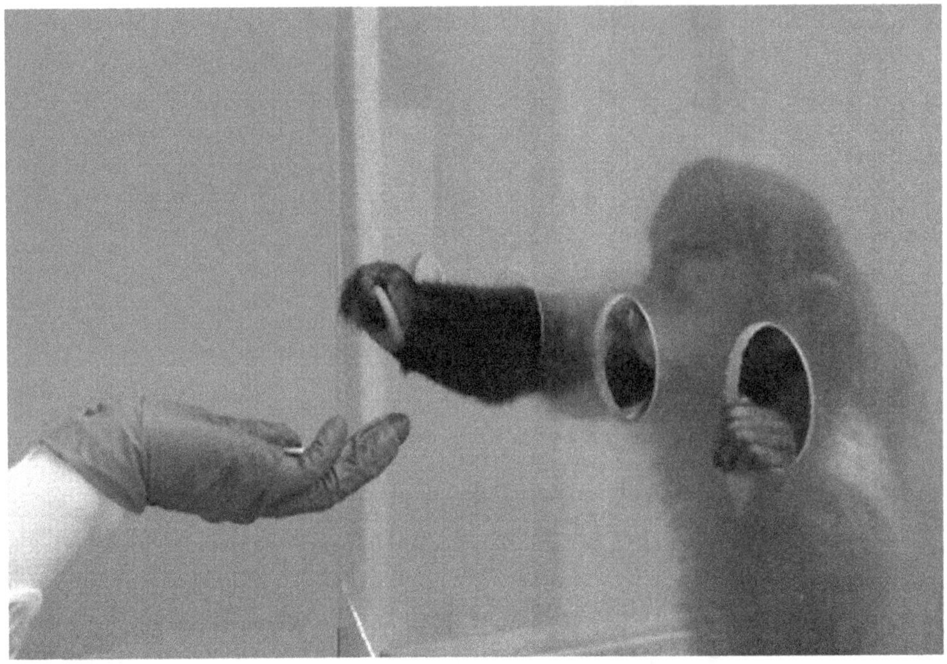

Figure 2.4 Trading evolutionary salient items for tokens with capuchin monkeys to determine their attitudes to risk. Source: Lakshminarayanan et al. (2008)

which is a 50–50 chance of giving one slice or two slices. By contrast, Experimenter 2 initially held out two slices of apple but on receiving a token from the capuchin, also offered the same lottery L as Experimenter 1. Since both experimenters offer identical lotteries, under EUT and RDUT, a capuchin monkey should be indifferent between trading with the two experimenters. However, 71% of the monkeys traded with Experimenter 1.

This behavior is consistent with PT. The capuchin appears to take the initial offering by the experimenters as the reference point for trade. Trading with Experimenter 1, the exchange always places the capuchin in the domain of gains (outcome at least as high as the reference point). However, trading with Experimenter 2, places the capuchin in the domain of losses (outcome strictly lower than the reference point) 50% of the time, with no extra gains for the remaining 50% of the time relative to Experimenter 1. The capuchin wishes to avoid these losses with Experimenter 2, hence, trades less with this experimenter. Thus, reference points appear to be an important determinant of behavior for capuchin monkeys.

In another experiment, Experimenter 1 initially held out two apple slices to trade and on receiving a token from the capuchin always offered one apple slice in return. Experimenter 2 initially held out one apple slice, and on receiving a token from the capuchin, always offered one apple slice in return. Under EUT and RDUT, because the final outcome is identical for each experimenter (receipt of one apple slice for one token), a capuchin monkey should be indifferent between the two experimenters. However, 80% of the trades took place with Experimenter 2. This is consistent with loss aversion. Trading with Experimenter 1, capuchins always receive one

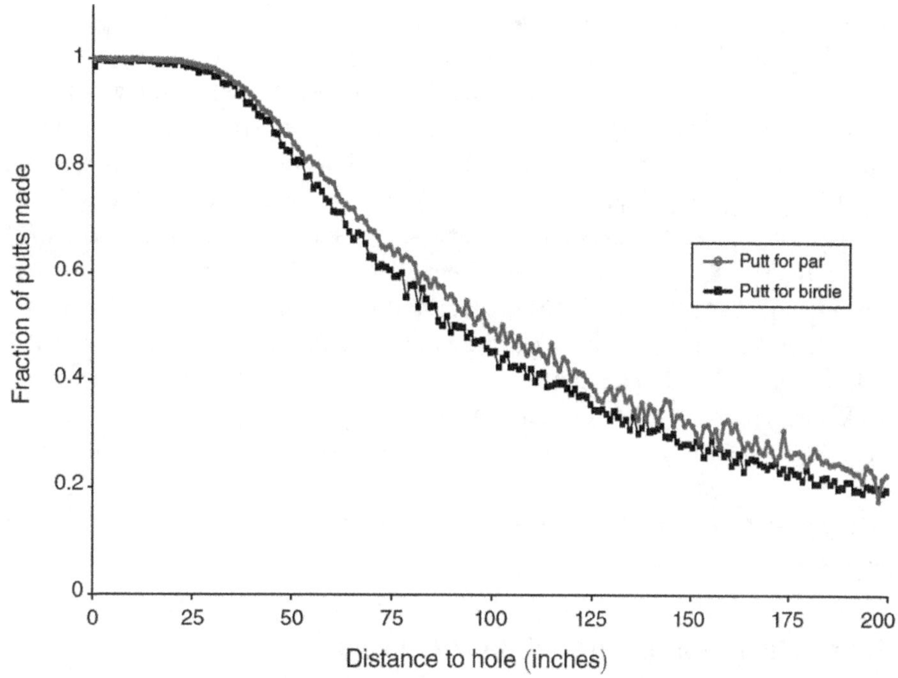

Figure 2.5 Fraction of par and birdie putts that were successful, depending on the distance to the hole. Based on data from 2,525,161 putts. Source: Pope and Schweitzer (2011)

apple slice less relative to the reference point of one apple slice, hence, they are less willing to trade with him. Subsequent results have also found an endowment effect in capuchin monkeys, which arises from loss aversion, and, remarkably, risk aversion in gains and risk seeking in losses just as for human subjects (Lakshminarayanan et al., 2011).

The close connection between human and capuchin behavior under risk is a tremendously important finding. It shows that human risk preferences, in particular, loss aversion, predate the evolutionary separation of capuchin monkeys 35 million years ago from the evolutionary chain that lead to homo sapiens. Thus, such risk preferences are inherited from a common ancestor. Applied to humans, this means that risk preferences, particularly in the form of loss aversion, are hardwired in humans.

2.5.5 Is Tiger Woods Loss Averse?

Each hole on a golf course has an associated *par score*. Starting with a tee, this is the typical number of shots taken by a skilled golfer to sink the putt into the hole. The par score depends on the level of difficulty of the golf course. A golfer is said to make a *birdie* (respectively, a *bogie*), if she sinks the putt into the hole using one stroke less (respectively, more) than the par score.

Pope and Schweitzer (2011) argued that the par score for a golf course acts as a reference point. When putting for par, golfers are mindful that if they miss the shot they will be shooting for a bogie that pushes them into the domain of losses where loss aversion bites. Hence, they need to be extra careful for that shot. By contrast, when golfers are putting for a birdie, they have the cushion of an extra shot left for par, hence, they might be less careful. The authors control for the level of difficulty of the shot, and use 2.5 million data points from actual shots taken from the PGA circuit using laser measurements. They find that golfers are indeed more successful on par shots as compared to birdie shots by two to three percentage points, despite the two shots being of similar level of difficulty; see Figure 2.5. Although this might seem like a small difference, if professional golfers were to shed the trait of loss aversion they would each make an extra \$1.2 million. So, yes, Tiger Woods and other professional golfers are loss averse and experienced players in high stakes situations are also likely to be loss averse.

There have been concerns in the literature that the behavioral features of PT that distinguish it from EUT might be eliminated if one uses field data, highly experienced subject pools, or high stakes experiments. These concerns have been laid to rest by the weight of the evidence. To be sure, individuals might learn to partially override some behavioral features such as loss aversion if it reduces their payoffs. But the effects are quantitatively modest and, in actual practice, the observed economic outcomes arise jointly from the behavior of experienced and inexperienced subjects.

2.5.6 Human Behavior for Low Probability Events

Recall the inverse S-shaped PWF in Figure 2.1. Notice how steep it is close to the origin. Small probabilities are massively overweighted.[6] Thus, humans ought to be hypersensitive to small probability events. We ought to, for instance, be desperate to take up insurance against low probability natural catastrophes such as earthquakes and floods. Yet, the evidence shows that people exhibit great reluctance to buy such insurance even when it is offered on extremely favourable terms and subsidized by the government; the classic study is by Kunreuther et al. (1978).

Many humans also appear to be insensitive to the *small probability of a large loss*. The evidence comes from many sources, such as running red traffic lights; the inability of capital punishment to completely deter crime; not wearing seat belts; dismal take up of free breast cancer examinations in the early days before the well-publicized mastectomies of the US first ladies Betty Ford and Happy Rockefeller; and the decision by some to not take up the MMR and Covid-19 vaccines.

In each of these cases, PT coupled with an inverse S-shaped PWF is not able to explain the stylized facts. al-Nowaihi and Dhami (2010) in their proposal for *composite prospect theory* show that such behavior can be explained by a fraction of the population having the S-shaped PWF (dashed curve in Figure 2.1) for low probabilities, but otherwise having an inverse S-shaped PWF for nonextreme probabilities. The resulting probability weighting function is found by smooth pasting three Prelec functions, and it is axiomatically founded. They are able to explain all the puzzles listed above in this subsection. However, while plausible, this proposal needs to be stringently empirically tested, before we can be sure.

[6] al-Nowaihi and Dhami (2010) formalize the precise sense in which this is true, namely, that the ratio of probability weight to the probability becomes infinitely large as probabilities approach zero, that is, $lim_{p\to 0}\frac{w(p)}{p}=\infty$.

Kahneman and Tversky (1979) were well aware of human behavior towards low probabilities and explicitly incorporated it into original prospect theory (OPT), although these insights were not pursued much in the subsequent work. In our notation, they write (pp. 282–283):

> The sharp drops or apparent discontinuities of $w(p)$ at the end-points are consistent with the notion that there is a limit to how small decision weight can be attached to an event, if it is given any weight at all. A similar quantum of doubt could impose an upper limit on any decision weight that is less than unity ... the simplification of prospects can lead the decision maker to discard events of extremely low probability and to treat events of extremely high probability as if they were certain. Because people are limited in their ability to comprehend and evaluate extreme probabilities, highly unlikely events are either ignored or overweighted, and the difference between high probability and certainty is either neglected or exaggerated. Consequently $w(p)$ is not well-behaved near the end-points.

We briefly note the difference between OPT and PT. In OPT, when decision makers face a lottery, they engage in two different phases. In the *editing phase*, they scan the lottery to simplify the given information so that it is cognitively easier to evaluate. For instance, if first order stochastic dominance is immediately obvious, they might discard dominated lotteries; this does not take place if dominance is not obvious. If an outcome in a lottery appears multiple times with different probabilities, the resulting probabilities are added. If two identical or "similar" outcomes in two different lotteries occur with identical or "similar" probabilities, then the outcomes are cancelled in both lotteries. Once the lotteries are edited in this manner, in the *evaluation phase* the edited lotteries are evaluated using the decision weighted utility (DWU) model in (2.4) but using the prospect theory utility function in Definition 2.5. As noted earlier, the DWU model may lead to the choice of stochastically dominated options, hence OPT was initially criticized, but this problem was addressed in the proposal for PT (Tversky and Kahneman, 1992) using the machinery on decision weights borrowed from RDUT.

2.5.7 Prospect Theory and Finance

Prospect theory (PT) has revolutionized the study of finance, giving rise to the field of *behavioral finance*. We present a flavour of some of the results that arise from applying PT to finance. For a survey of behavioral finance and the references, see Barberis and Thaler (2003) and Dhami (2020, Vol. V). We return to these themes in several places in the book when we discuss issues of bounded rationality.

From 1926–1997, the return on treasury bills, a completely safe asset that offers a fixed interest rate, has been less than 1%, while the annual average real return on risky stocks has been 7%. This difference of 6% cannot be explained by the difference in riskiness of the two assets or by the degree of risk aversion of investors. This is known as the *equity-premium puzzle*; one of the exercises at the end of the chapter asks you to work through a numerical example. Benartzi and Thaler (1995) provide an explanation based on loss aversion. Stocks fluctuate a great deal in value, often falling in value below the reference point where loss aversion bites, magnifying the downward stock movements by about two times, on average. Hence, investors require higher returns on stocks to compensate them for the extra downside risk created by loss aversion. Investors might also feel anxious on observing fluctuating stock returns. It has been shown that the extra return on stocks may also be on account of an *anxiety premium* from holding them.

Typically investors have subjective belief distributions about unknown stock market returns. From the inverse S-shaped PWF in Figure 2.1, we know that they overweight small probabilities. Hence, they may give undue attention to events that are fairly unlikely, such as the small probability of a crash, or the small probability of a high return. Taking account of these factors provides a better explanation for stock prices. Furthermore, skewness in asset returns may actually be reflected in the price of assets on account of nonlinear probability weights (Barberis, 2013).

Our final application is the *disposition effect*. Suppose that an investor purchases an asset, say, a house for $\$X$. The purchase price often becomes the reference point for the perceived worth of the house, perhaps adjusting for inflation. Investors may then be reluctant to sell the asset for less than $\$X$, even if it makes good economic sense to sell.

Consider the following example, adapted from the behavior of a university faculty member in Finance that I once knew, and who for anonymity I will refer to as John. John initially lived in city A where he owned a house that he purchased for $\$X$ at a time of a property boom. He was then offered an attractive job in city B, and he relocated to city B because the commuting distance between the two cities made travel infeasible. However, in the meantime, the price of houses had dropped throughout the country. John's house in city A was evaluated at a price $\$Y < \$X$ and he felt that if he were to sell the house, he would be in the domain of losses, where loss aversion bites, and inflate the loss $X - Y$ by approximately two times. He planned on waiting it out and rented a house in city B while making regular and costly trips back to city A to try to sell the house. He also suffered emotional stress during the period. It did not make good economic sense to continue this arrangement because the prices of houses had fallen throughout the country, including in city B. So if John had sold the house in city A at a price of $\$Y$, he could have purchased a cheaper house in city B, saving money on rents, costly travel, and avoiding emotional stress. Indeed, this is what John was likely to teach in his lectures on financial economics, although he sometimes found it difficult to follow his own advice.

In finance, the disposition effects may induce investors to hold on to loss making stock for too long because they find that the current price is too low relative to the purchase price. Thus, there is a tendency to hold on to losing stock for too long, while selling off winning stock too early. We review this evidence later in the book.

2.5.8 Incentives in Organizations

In neoclassical economics and under moral hazard (when the workers' effort is hard to observe or verify to a third party), incentives are predicted to be *high-powered*, that is, wages depend too closely on actual outcomes. Yet, observed incentives are not as high-powered as predicted, and most employees are paid a sizeable fixed wage component. Loss aversion provides a potential explanation. Under high-powered incentives, when the outcome is bad, workers will be paid a low wage, possibly below their reference point, and workers are driven into the domain of losses where loss aversion applies. The result is that low wages are perceived to be even lower by workers, reducing worker morale and job satisfaction. Furthermore, in order to compensate workers and ensure that their participation constraint is satisfied, firms will have to offer them even higher wages when the outcomes are good, which reduces the expected profits of firms. Thus, firms might instead prefer to offer a relatively flat wage schedule.

Let us consider a simple example. Suppose that a firm employs a single worker, whose effort is unobserved by the firm, or it is unverifiable to a third party. Thus, the effort level cannot be written down in a wage contract. The worker can exert only two levels of effort: $e = 0$ (shirking) or $e = 1$ (working hard). Effort is costly to the worker and the cost of effort $c(e)$ is given by $c(0) = 0$ (shirking is costless), and $c(1) = c > 0$ (working is costly). The outside option of the worker, should the worker quit this job and work elsewhere, gives the worker a level of utility $\overline{v} > 0$.

The production function of the firm is $f(e)$. If the worker shirks, then no output is produced, that is, $f(0) = 0$. If the worker works hard, $e = 1$, then there are the following two equally likely outcomes that occur with probability 0.5 each. In the *good state* of the world a positive output $f(1) = z > 0$ is produced, and in the *bad state*, a zero output, $f(1) = 0$, is produced. The firm is risk neutral so it cares only about maximizing expected profit.

The only observable and verifiable signal of the worker's effort is the output produced. Hence, the firm can only condition wage payments on the observed output. Suppose that the firm offers the contract (w_H, w_L), which states that if the output is high, $z > 0$, the worker will receive the wage w_H, and when the output is low, 0, the worker will receive the wage w_L.

We assume that the worker follows prospect theory, but weights probabilities linearly, so $w(p) = p$. The reference wage from wage income is r and the utility function of the worker from wages is piecewise linear, which is given by substituting $\gamma = 1$ in (2.14):

$$v(y) = \begin{cases} y & \text{if } y \geq 0 \\ -\lambda(-y) & \text{if } y < 0 \end{cases}.$$

Consider the benchmark results under EUT. Since the utility function of the worker is linear, under EUT, which lacks a reference point, the worker is risk neutral. Thus, the prediction under neoclassical incentive theory is that the optimal contract should make the worker a residual claimant, that is, the firm should sell the project to the worker in return for a fixed rent, R. The worker then fully bears all the risk from the project, which is not a problem for risk-neutral workers. This arrangement ensures that once the rent is paid, the worker receives the full marginal product from their effort levels, which eliminates the moral hazard problem. Let us now return back to the problem where the worker uses prospect theory.

We assume that the firm wishes to induce only the high effort level, $e = 1$.

In the bad state of the world where the output is 0, the worker is paid a wage w_L. The utility of a worker who shirks, $e = 0$, is denoted by $v(w_L, 0)$ and the utility of a worker who works hard, $e = 1$, is denoted by $v(w_L, 1)$. The reference point r is assumed to apply to wage income alone, and not the effort costs. In a more complete model, the worker might also have a separate reference point for effort costs; we abstract from these considerations. The utility function of the worker, in the bad state of the world, for the two levels of effort $e = 0$ and $e = 1$, is defined as follows.

$$v(w_L, 0) = \begin{cases} w_L - r & \text{if } w_L \geq r \\ -\lambda(-(w_L - r)) & \text{if } w_L < r \end{cases}. \tag{2.26}$$

$$v(w_L, 1) = \begin{cases} w_L - r - c & \text{if } w_L \geq r \\ -\lambda(-(w_L - r)) - c & \text{if } w_L < r \end{cases}. \tag{2.27}$$

The only difference between (2.26) and (2.27) is that the worker incurs an effort cost $c > 0$ from working hard. By assumption, the reference point applies to wages but not effort.

In the good state of the world, the output turns out to be high, z, and the worker is paid the wage w_H. This possibility only arises when the worker works hard, $e = 1$. The prospect theory utility of the worker in this case is

$$v(w_H, 1) = \begin{cases} w_H - r - c & \text{if} \quad w_H \geq r \\ -\lambda\left(-\left(w_H - r\right)\right) - c & \text{if} \quad w_H < r \end{cases}. \tag{2.28}$$

If $w_L < r$ and $w_H < r$ then the worker will not work for the firm because the outside option of the worker, net of the reference point, is positive, $\overline{v} > 0$. If, on the other hand, $w_L > r$ and $w_H < r$, then the worker will always prefer to shirk, $e = 0$, rather than put in the costly high effort, $e = 1$. Hence, we can rule this case out. We rule out the case $w_L > r$ and $w_H > r$. This might occur, for instance, if the cost of effort, c, of the worker is too high, and the participation constraint is very costly for the firm to implement. In this case, the worker is never in the domain of losses and, hence, loss aversion never bites and we are back in the world of neoclassical incentive theory. Thus, the only case that we consider below is $w_L < r$ and $w_H > r$.

It is possible that the firm does not have sufficient means to pay the worker in the bad state of the world, where output is zero. For this reason, the maximum wage that the firm can pay the worker in the bad state is assumed to satisfy

$$\overline{w}_L < r.$$

Assume to begin with that, in the bad state, the firm pays the worker some wage

$$w_L \leq \overline{w}_L.$$

Using the arguments above, $w_H > r$, otherwise the worker will just choose the outside option. It follows from (2.26) that the utility of the worker from shirking is

$$v(w_L, 0) = -\lambda\left(r - w_L\right) < 0. \tag{2.29}$$

Since the worker's outside option is $\overline{v} > 0$, and $v(w_L, 0) < 0$, the worker never shirks while working for the firm. Hence, the only possible options are to (i) either work hard for the firm, or (ii) not work for the firm at all. Thus, we have checked the *incentive compatibility condition* which requires that the worker prefers to work rather than shirk. We now need to check the *participation constraint* of the worker. Using (2.27) and (2.28), from working hard, $e = 1$, the worker gets the following prospect theory utility, V_w (recall we have assumed linear probability weighting),

$$V_w = 0.5\left[-\lambda\left(r - w_L\right) - c\right] + 0.5\left(w_H - r - c\right). \tag{2.30}$$

The worker's participation constraint, $V_w \geq \overline{v}$, must hold for the worker to work for the firm rather than exercise the outside option. Using (2.30), this implies that

$$0.5\left[-\lambda\left(r - w_L\right) - c\right] + 0.5\left(w_H - r - c\right) \geq \overline{v}. \tag{2.31}$$

Since paying a higher wage reduces the expected profits of the firm, a profit maximizing firm will ensure that the inequality in (2.31) is an equality. Hence, can solve out for w_H to get

$$w_H = 2\overline{v} + c - \lambda w_L + r(1 + \lambda). \tag{2.32}$$

We can now derive the effects on the optimal wage in the good state w_H that are caused by changes in $\overline{v}, c, \lambda, r, w_L$. By direct observation, or by differentiating both sides of (2.32) with respect to these parameters, it is straightforward to show the following. The wage w_H is *increasing* in (i) the outside option, $\overline{v}$; (ii) the cost, c, of putting in a high effort level; (iii) the reference point, r, of the worker; and (iv) the magnitude of the loss aversion parameter, λ. However, w_H is *decreasing* in the wage paid in the bad state, w_L.

The intuition for the main results is as follows. Loss aversion increases the disutility felt by the worker in the bad state from receiving a wage below the reference point, and an increase in the reference point increases the size of the loss felt in the bad state, which is multiplied by the loss aversion parameter. Both factors reduce the expected utility of the worker from working hard, V_w, and hence, require a higher wage in the good state to ensure that the participation constraint $V_w \geq \overline{v}$ is satisfied. The wage paid in the bad state, w_L, directly increases the worker's expected utility, V_w, hence, mitigating the need to increase w_H to ensure that the participation constraint $V_w \geq \overline{v}$ is met.

The result that the wage in the good state, w_H, is increasing in the size of loss aversion is not the only novel implication of the model. Consider the problem of the firm. It wishes to minimize the expected wage payment, Ew, to the worker,

$$Ew = 0.5w_H + 0.5w_L, \tag{2.33}$$

subject to the constraint that it wishes to induce a high effort level, $e = 1$. Substituting w_H from (2.32) into (2.33), we get

$$Ew = \frac{1}{2}\left[2\overline{v} + c - (\lambda - 1)\, w_L + r(1 + \lambda)\right]. \tag{2.34}$$

Since $\lambda > 1$, the RHS of (2.34) is decreasing in w_L. The reason is that an increase in w_L by an amount $\Delta > 0$, increases Ew by 0.5Δ units (see (2.33)). However, from (2.32), this reduces the wage in the good state, w_H, by $\lambda\Delta$. From (2.33), the effect of this on the expected wage paid by the firm is $-0.5\lambda\Delta$. Thus, the net effect on the expected wage is $-0.5\lambda\Delta + 0.5\Delta = -0.5\Delta\,(\lambda - 1) < 0$. In other words, the firm will find it optimal to increase the wage in the bad state, w_L, as much as possible because it reduces the aggregate expected wage bill. Since $w_L \leq \overline{w}_L$, the firm will find it profit maximizing to set $w_L = \overline{w}_L$.

In other words, loss aversion pushes up the wage in the bad state of the world and pushes down the wage in the good state of the world. But this is exactly what firms do when they wish to insure workers. However, neoclassical theory predicts that with risk-neutral firms and risk-neutral workers, there should be no role for insurance, and no conflict between insurance and incentives. Yet, we find the opposite, on account of loss aversion. Thus, loss aversion is likely to lead to a tendency towards fixed wage payments, although showing this more formally will require a more complete analysis of the problem. Readers interested in pursuing these issues further can consult Dhami (2019a, Section 3.10).

2.5.9 Reference Points, Renegotiation, and the Formation of Firms

Incomplete contracts arise when parties to a contract cannot objectively specify all possible eventualities that might arise and, hence, cannot write these contingencies into the contract. Loss aversion plays an important role in the formation of firms under incomplete contracts.

In the presence of incomplete contracts, trading partners might need to renegotiate their contracts, ex-post, in the event that an unforeseen eventuality arises. However, the initial contract creates a reference point and renegotiation is likely to lead one of the two parties (if not both) to fall below their reference point, where loss aversion bites. The result is that parties might not agree to renegotiation even when it is efficient (Herweg and Schmidt, 2013). One potential solution is for the trading parties to get together to form a limited liability firm instead. The evidence is supportive of this mechanism; see Fehr et al. (2011).

Let us use a simple model to illustrate these points. Consider two time periods, $t = 0$ and $t = 1$. At time $t = 0$, buyers and sellers look for trading partners under perfectly competitive conditions. Once a buyer–seller pair meet each other and decide to sign a long-term contract, they effectively turn a competitive situation into a bilateral monopoly. The two parties then, at time $t = 0$, write a long-term incomplete contract in which the seller agrees to provide 1 unit of a good at a price P_0, at time $t = 1$.

The contract is incomplete in the sense that at time $t = 0$, both parties cannot imagine the quality, q, of the good that will be needed at time $t = 1$. Hence, a time $t = 0$ contract specifies that the seller will sell one unit of the generic quality, q_0, of the good to the buyer, at a price $P_0 > 0$ at time $t = 1$. The value of the one unit of the generic quality good to the buyer is $\theta_0 > 0$ and the seller's cost of supplying the generic quality is $c_0 > 0$.

At the beginning of time $t = 1$, suppose that the buyer discovers that the most appropriate quality is not the generic quality, q_0, but rather the quality q_1, which has value θ_1 to the buyer. It costs the seller $c_1 > c_0$ to supply the new quality q_1 and $c_1 < \theta_1$; perhaps the seller has to incur new research costs to implement the new designs. The two parties can, at time $t = 1$, renegotiate the time $t = 0$ contract so that the seller can supply the buyer the quality q_1 by incurring a cost $c_1 < \theta_1$. The renegotiation specifies the new price P_1 at which the one unit should be exchanged between the seller and the buyer. The economic surplus from the renegotiated exchange is $\theta_1 - c_1 > 0$ so it is economically efficient to renegotiate.

One of the insights of the new *contracts as reference points* literature is that the original contracts set the entitlements or reference points of the trading parties. Thus, we assume that the originally agreed upon price, P_0, becomes the reference point of the buyer and the seller. We also assume in the discussion below that the renegotiated price increases because the new quality is more expensive to produce ($c_1 > c_0$). Thus, we have

$$P_0 < P_1. \tag{2.35}$$

Let us use the Köszegi–Rabin preferences, v^*, in Section 2.4.3, whereby decision makers derive utility from the absolute level of an outcome and a gain–loss term. We restrict $\mu = 1$ for simplicity, so that absolute utility and gain–loss utility are equally weighted. Thus, the buyer renegotiates if

$$v_B^*(P_1, P_0) \geq v_B^*(P_0, P_0), \tag{2.36}$$

where $v_B^*(P_1, P_0)$ is the utility of the buyer if renegotiation takes place and the new price is P_1; and $v_B^*(P_0, P_0)$ is the utility of the buyer if renegotiation does not take place. The reference outcome is the time $t = 0$ negotiated price, P_0. Assume that gain-loss utility is only with respect to the change in price. Using (2.22) and (2.23), rewrite 2.36 as

$$(\theta_1 - P_1) + g_B(P_0 - P_1) \geq (\theta_0 - P_0) + g_B(P_0 - P_0). \tag{2.37}$$

Each of these utilities is made up of two terms. The first term on each side gives the absolute utility from an outcome to the buyer, respectively, $\theta_1 - P_1$ and $\theta_0 - P_0$. The second term on each side gives the gain–loss utility of the buyer, respectively, $g_B(P_0 - P_1)$ and $g_B(P_0 - P_0) = 0$; the second of these terms is zero because if there is no renegotiation, there is neither a gain nor a loss to the buyer.

Thus, we can rewrite (2.37) as

$$(\theta_1 - \theta_0) \geq -g_B(P_0 - P_1) - (P_0 - P_1). \tag{2.38}$$

The gain–loss utility of the buyer is given by

$$g_B = \begin{cases} P_0 - P_1 & \text{if} \quad P_0 \geq P_1 \\ -\lambda_B\,[P_1 - P_0] & \text{if} \quad P_0 < P_1 \end{cases}, \tag{2.39}$$

where we have allowed for the possibility of buyer-specific parameter of loss aversion, λ_B. From (2.35), $P_1 > P_0$, hence, from the second row of (2.39) the buyer is in the domain of losses. Substituting (2.39) in (2.38), and simplifying, the buyer renegotiates if

$$(\theta_1 - \theta_0) \geq (1 + \lambda_B)\,(P_1 - P_0)\,. \tag{2.40}$$

Similarly, the seller renegotiates if the seller's utility from renegotiation, $v_S^*(P_1, P_0)$, is greater than the seller's utility from not renegotiating, $v_S^*(P_0, P_0)$. Assume that gain-loss utility is only with respect to the change in price. Using (2.22) and (2.23), the condition $v_S^*(P_1, P_0) \geq v_S^*(P_0, P_0)$ implies

$$(P_1 - c_1) + g_S(P_1 - P_0) \geq (P_0 - c_0) + g_S(P_0 - P_0), \tag{2.41}$$

where the gain–loss utility of the seller is

$$g_S = \begin{cases} P_1 - P_0 & \text{if} \quad P_1 \geq P_0 \\ -\lambda_S\,[P_0 - P_1] & \text{if} \quad P_1 < P_0 \end{cases}. \tag{2.42}$$

and λ_S is the loss aversion parameter of the seller. Since $P_1 > P_0$ and $v_S^*(0) = 0$, we can use the first row of (2.42) in (2.41) and simplify to get

$$P_1 - P_0 \geq \frac{1}{2}\,(c_1 - c_0). \tag{2.43}$$

From (2.40) and (2.43), renegotiation takes place for all price levels, P_1, if

$$\frac{1}{2}\,(c_1 - c_0) + P_0 \leq P_1 \leq \frac{\theta_1 - \theta_0}{1 + \lambda_B} + P_0. \tag{2.44}$$

From (2.44), the presence of loss aversion, λ_B, reduces the upper bound on P_1 in a successful renegotiation, hence, reducing the set of potential agreements that are possible ex-post at time $t = 1$. For instance, if $P_0 = 15$, $c_1 - c_0 = 8$, and $\theta_1 - \theta_0 = 10$, then in the absence of loss aversion ($\lambda_B = 0$) the contract is successfully renegotiated if $19 \leq P_1 \leq 25$. Suppose that the loss aversion of the buyer is $\lambda_B = 2.25$, then the contract is successfully renegotiated if $19 \leq P_1 \leq 19.44$, which is a more restrictive interval and less likely to be satisfied. Recall that 2.25 was the median value of loss aversion in Tversky and Kahneman (1992) with significant heterogeneity across subjects. If the loss aversion parameter of the buyer is slightly higher, say, $\lambda_B = 2.55$, then for successful renegotiation, the required condition, $19 \leq P_1 \leq 18.92$, can never be satisfied.

Thus, the presence of loss aversion may preclude the possibility of ex-post efficiency enhancing trades in such bilateral trading relations with independent traders. One possible market solution to this problem may be to merge the two parties as two divisions within one firm where such internal renegotiation problems can be resolved by the manager of the firm.

2.6 A Note on the Ellsberg Paradox

Recall our discussion of the Ellsberg paradox in Section 1.2.3. Let us first make precise the sense in which no subjective probabilities can be used to explain the Ellsberg paradox under EUT. Recall from Section 1.2.3 that from the known urn, K, which contains a known mixture of red and black balls, the decision maker faces the following lottery

$$L = (0, 0.5; z, 0.5),$$

that is, it gives a prize of z if a randomly drawn ball is red. Thus the expected utility from playing this lottery from the known urn is

$$EU(L \mid K) = 0.5u(z).$$

By contrast, the unknown urn, U, contains an unknown mixture of red and black balls. Suppose that the decision maker assigns the subjective probabilities p_R and p_B to randomly drawing a red and a black ball from urn, U, such that $p_R + p_B = 1$. Then, in effect, for U, the decision maker faces the lottery

$$L = (0, p_B; z, p_R),$$

which gives the expected utility from betting on urn U,

$$EU(L \mid U) = p_R u(z).$$

Thus, the preference for betting on K rather than U indicates that

$$0.5u(z) > p_R u(z) \Rightarrow p_R < 0.5.$$

But this contradicts the assignment of the probability $p_R = 0.5$ to drawing a red ball from U, which is the probability assigned by decision makers to this event, using the principle of insufficient reason, when they view urn U in isolation.

Abdellaoui et al. (2011) test the idea that each urn is a different "source" of subjective uncertainty. They are different sources in the sense that an individual's preferences are found to vary between the two urns in terms of the measured parameters of the Prelec probability weighting function. They estimate the two parameters of the Prelec function for the known urn to be $\alpha = 0.88, \beta = 0.93$ and for the unknown urn to be $\alpha = 0.64, \beta = 1.03$. In other words, the inverse S-shaped Prelec function for the known urn (relative to the unknown urn) has a more pronounced departure from the diagonal line in Figure 2.1, and it is slightly less elevated. Thus, the manner in which small probabilities are overweighted and large ones underweighted is quite different for both the urns. This can potentially account for the preference for the known urn over the unknown urn. We may refer to this as *ambiguity aversion*.

But things get more interesting when we reduce the probability of drawing a red ball from 0.5 to smaller numbers. This is achieved by introducing balls of several colors in the urn. For instance, if there are balls of five colors in each urn, including the color red, then the probability of drawing a red ball is 0.2. For balls of 10 different colours, this probability drops to 0.1. While *ambiguity-aversion* (preference for the known urn over the unknown urn) arises for high probabilities, we observe *ambiguity-seeking* (relative preference for the unknown urn) for low probabilities of drawing a red ball. Currently, none of the available decision theories in an already large literature are able to explain the simultaneous occurrence of *ambiguity aversion for high probabilities and ambiguity seeking for low probabilities*; see Wakker (2010) and Dhami (2019a) for a survey of this literature. Indeed, this evidence rejects most of the existing models of ambiguity aversion. al-Nowaihi and Dhami (2017) propose a model using quantum physics to explain this phenomena. While this will take us well beyond the scope of the current book, and requires familiarity with quantum physics, it illustrates the wide scope of behavioral economics, and the promise of interdisciplinary research.

References

Abdellaoui, M. A., Baillon, A., Placido, L., and Wakker, P. P. (2011). The Rich Domain of Uncertainty: Source Functions and Their Experimental Implementation. *American Economic Review* 101(2): 695–723.

Abeler, J., Falk, A., Goette, L., and Huffman, D. (2011). Reference Points and Effort Provision. *American Economic Review* 101(2): 470–492.

Alm, J. (2019). What Motivates Tax Compliance. *Journal of Economic Surveys* 33(2): 353–388.

al-Nowaihi, A. and Dhami, S. (2010). Composite Prospect Theory: A Proposal to Combine Prospect Theory and Cumulative Prospect Theory. University of Leicester. Discussion Paper 10/11.

al-Nowaihi, A. and Dhami, S. (2017). The Ellsberg Paradox: A Challenge to Quantum Decision Theory? *Journal of Mathematical Psychology* 78: 40–50.

Allais, M. (1953). Le comportement de l'homme rationnel devant le risque, critique des postulats et axiomes de l'ecole Americaine. *Econometrica* 21: 503–546.

Barberis, N. (2013). The Psychology of Tail Events: Progress and Challenges. *American Economic Review* 103(3): 611–616.

Barberis, N. and Huang, M. (2001). Mental Accounting, Loss Aversion, and Individual Stock Returns. *Journal of Finance* 56: 1247–1292.

Barberis, N. and Thaler, R. H. (2003). A Survey of Behavioral Finance. In G. M. Constantinides, M. Harris, and R. M. Stulz (eds.), *Handbook of the Economics of Finance*, Volume 1. 1st edition. Amsterdam: Elsevier, ch. 18, pp. 1053–1128.

Benartzi, S. and Thaler, R. H. (1995). Myopic Loss–Aversion and the Equity Premium Puzzle. *Quarterly Journal of Economics* 110(1): 73–92.

Brown, A. L., Imai, T., Vieider, F., and Camerer, C. (2024). Meta-analysis of Empirical Estimates of Loss-Aversion. *Journal of Economic Literature* 62(2): 485–516.

Camerer, C. F., Babcock, L., Loewenstein, G., and Thaler, R. H. (1997). Labor Supply of New York City Cabdrivers: One Day at a Time. *Quarterly Journal of Economics* 112(2): 407–441.

Campos-Mercade, P., Goette, L., Graeber, T., Kellogg, A., and Sprenger, C. (2024). "De Gustibus" and Disputes about Reference Dependence. Harvard Business School Working Paper 24–046.

Cerulli-Harms, A., Goette, L., and Sprenger, C. (2019). Randomizing Endowments. *American Economic Journal: Microeconomics* 11(1): 185–207.

Chen, M. K., Lakshminarayanan, V., and Santos, L. (2006). How Basic Are Behavioral Biases? Evidence from Capuchin Monkey Trading Behavior. *Journal of Political Economy* 114(3): 517–532.

Crawford, V. P. and Meng, J. (2011). New York City Cab Drivers' Labor Supply Revisited: Reference-Dependent Preferences with Rational Expectations Targets for Hours and Income. *American Economic Review* 101(5): 191–232.

de Finetti, B. (1937). La prevision: ses lois logiques, ses sources subjectives. *Annales de l'Institute Henri Poincare* 7(1): 1–68.

Dhami, S. (2019a). *Foundations of Behavioral Economic Analysis: Volume I: Behavioral Decision Theory*. Oxford University Press: Oxford.

Dhami, S. (2020). *Foundations of Behavioral Economic Analysis: Volume V: Bounded Rationality*. Oxford University Press: Oxford.

Dhami, S. and al-Nowaihi, A. (2007). Why Do People Pay Taxes: Expected Utility versus Prospect Theory. *Journal of Economic Behaviour and Organization* 64: 171–192.

Dhami, S. and al-Nowaihi, A. (2021). Behavioral Economics and Rationality. In M. Knauff and W. Spohn (eds.), *Handbook of Rationality*. MIT Press: Cambridge, MA.

Ericson, K. M. M. and Fuster, A. (2011). Expectations as Endowments: Evidence on Reference-Dependent Preferences from Exchange and Valuation Experiments. *Quarterly Journal of Economics* 126(4): 1879–1907.

Fan, Y., Budescu, D. V., and Diecidue, E. (2019). Decisions with Compound Lotteries. *Decision* 6(2): 109–133.

Fehr, E. and Goette, L. (2007). Do Workers Work More if Wages Are Higher? Evidence from a Randomized Field Experiment. *American Economic Review* 97(1): 298–317.

Fehr, E., Hart, O., and Zehnder, C. (2011). Contracts as Reference Points: Experimental Evidence. *American Economic Review* 101(2): 493–525.

Fryer, Roland G., Levitt, Steven D., List, John A. and Sadoff, Sally. Enhancing the Efficacy of Teacher Incentives through Loss Aversion: A Field Experiment (July 2012). NBER Working Paper No. w18237, available at SSRN: https://ssrn.com/abstract=2114863.

Hartzmark, S. M., Hirshman, S. D., Imas, A. (2021). Ownership, Learning, and Beliefs. *The Quarterly Journal of Economics* 136(3): 1665–1717.

Heath, C., Larrick, R. P., and Wu, G. (1999). Goals as Reference Points. *Cognitive Psychology* 38(1): 79–109.

Herweg, F. and Schmidt, K. M. (2013). Loss Aversion and Inefficient Renegotiation. *Review of Economic Studies* 82: 297–332.

Imas, A., Sadoff, S., and Samek, A. (2016). Do People Anticipate Loss Aversion? *Management Science* 63(5): 1271–1284.

Kahneman, D., Knetsch, J. L., and Thaler, R. H. (1990). Experimental Tests of the Endowment Effect and the Coase Theorem. *Journal of Political Economy* 98(6): 1325–1348.

Kahneman, D. and Tversky, A. (1979). Prospect Theory: An Analysis of Decision under Risk. *Econometrica* 47(2): 263–291.

Kahneman, D. and Tversky, A. (2000). *Choices, Values, and Frames*. Cambridge University Press: Cambridge.

Köszegi, B. and Rabin, M. (2006). A Model of Reference-Dependent Preferences. *Quarterly Journal of Economics* 121(4): 1133–1165.

Köszegi, B. and Rabin, M. (2007). Reference-Dependent Risk Attitudes. *American Economic Review* 97(4): 1047–1073.

Kunreuther, H., Ginsberg, R., Miller, L., et al. (1978). *Disaster Insurance Protection: Public Policy Lessons*. New York: Wiley.

Lakshminarayanan, V., Chen, M. K., and Santos, L. R. (2008). Endowment Effect in Capuchin Monkeys. *Philosophical Transactions of the Royal Society* B 363: 3837–3844.

Lakshminarayanan, V., Chen, M. K., and Santos, L. R. (2011). The Evolution of Decision-Making under Risk: Framing Effects in Monkey Risk Preferences. *Journal of Experimental Social Psychology* 47(3): 689–693.

Pope, D. and Schweitzer, M. (2011). Is Tiger Woods Loss Averse? Persistent Bias in the Face of Experience, Competition, and High Stakes. *American Economic Review* 101(1): 129–157.

Prelec, D. (1998). The Probability Weighting Function. *Econometrica* 66(3): 497–527.

Quiggin, J. (1982). A Theory of Anticipated Utility. *Journal of Economic Behavior and Organization* 3(4): 323–343.

Rabin, M. (2000). Risk Aversion and Expected-Utility Theory: A Calibration Theorem. *Econometrica* 68(5): 128–192.

Savage, L. J. (1954). *The Foundations of Statistics*. New York: Wiley and Sons.

Smith, J. M. and Parker, G. A. (1976). The Logic of Asymmetric Contests. *Animal Behaviour* 24(1): 159–175.

Starmer, C. (2000). Developments in Non-expected Utility Theory: The Hunt for a Descriptive Theory of Choice under Risk. Journal of Economic Literature 38: 332–382.

Tversky, A. and Kahneman, D. (1981). The Framing of Decisions and the Psychology of Choice. *Science* 211(4481): 453–458.

Tversky, A. and Kahneman, D. (1992). Advances in Prospect Theory: Cumulative Representation of Uncertainty. *Journal of Risk and Uncertainty* 5(4): 297–323.

Wakker, P. P. (2010). *Prospect Theory for Risk and Ambiguity*. Cambridge: Cambridge University Press.

Problems for Part I

1. Prove Proposition 1.1. [Hint: Prove this result diagrammatically for the case of a two-outcome lottery, and then prove it more generally by invoking Jensen's inequality].
2. Consider the lottery $L = (5, 0.8; 30, 0.2)$ and $u(x) = \log x$. Show that the certainty equivalent is 7.17. What can you conclude about the risk aversion characteristics of the individual? Draw a diagram to illustrate your answer. Also compute your answers for the utility functions $u(x) = x$ and $u(x) = x^2$.
3. Suppose that one is compelled to play the game of *Russian roulette* using a revolver that can potentially fire six rounds, but all rounds are not loaded. Essentially the person takes a bet, points the revolver to his/her head and fires. If the revolver does not fire and the person survives, then the person wins the bet, otherwise the person loses the bet. Most reasonable people would be willing to pay much more to reduce the number of bullets from one to zero (elimination of risk) than from four to three (reduction, but not elimination of risk). However, in each case, the reduction in the probability of a bullet firing is 1/6. Show that under EUT, the decision maker should be willing to pay the same amount in both cases. This suggests nonlinear weighting of probabilities.
4. Show that for $\alpha = 1$, the Prelec probability weighting function takes the form $w(p) = p^{\beta}$, is strictly concave if $\beta < 1$ but strictly convex if $\beta > 1$. In particular, for $\beta = 1$, $w(p) = p$ (as under EU).
5. Draw the following two Prelec functions $w(p) = e^{-0.5(-\ln p)^{0.6}}$ and $w(p) = e^{-2(-\ln p)^{2}}$ and label clearly the *point of inflection* and the *fixed points* (you do not have to plot to an exact scale; a freehand drawing will be sufficient).
6. Is the following a probability weighting function? Give reasons for your answer.

$$w(p) = \begin{cases} 0 & \text{if } p = 0 \\ 1 & \text{if } p > 0 \end{cases}.$$

7. Do the following functions satisfy the conditions for a probability weighting function?

$$w(p) = \frac{p^{\tau}}{p^{\tau} + (1-p)^{\tau}}, \quad 0 < \tau < 1, p \in [0, 1].$$

$$w(p) = \frac{\delta p^{\eta}}{\delta p^{\eta} + (1-p)^{\eta}}, p \in [0, 1], \delta \geq 0, \eta \geq 0.$$

8. Show that RDU can explain the Allais paradox in Section 1.3.3. Use the Prelec function, $w(p) = e^{-0.5(-\ln p)^{0.15}}$.
9. Consider the lottery $L = (15, 0.8; 0, 0.2)$ that captures the risky returns associated with a financial decision. The utility function of the decision maker satisfies $u(0) = 0$. The

individual uses rank dependent utility (RDUT) to evaluate lotteries and has the probability weighting function $w(p) = p^2$. Relative to a decision maker who follows expected utility (EUT), is this decision maker optimistic or pessimistic?

10. Consider the lottery $L = (16, 0.4; 9, 0.6)$ that captures the risky returns associated with a financial decision. The utility function of the decision maker satisfies $u(x) = \sqrt{x}$. The individual uses rank dependent utility (RDUT) to evaluate lotteries and has the probability weighting function $w(p) = p^2$. Evaluate the rank dependent utility of the lottery L and determine the risk attitudes of the decision maker. How do these risk attitudes compare with those of a decision maker under expected utility.
11. Consider the lottery $L = \left(9, \frac{1}{3}; 16, \frac{1}{3}; 25, \frac{1}{3}\right)$ that captures the discounted risky returns associated with the purchase of a financial security. The utility function of the decision maker is $u(x) = \sqrt{x}$. [Restrict calculations to four decimal places]
    (a) Suppose that the decision maker follows EUT. Compute the expected utility of the lottery. Is the decision maker risk averse, risk neutral, or risk loving?
    (b) Suppose that the decision maker uses RDUT to evaluate lotteries and has the probability weighting function $w(p) = \sqrt{p}$. Is this decision maker risk averse, risk neutral, or risk loving?
    (c) If there is a difference in the risk attitudes found in parts (a) and (b), what accounts for the difference?
12. Does the following function satisfy the conditions of a utility function under prospect theory?

$$v(x) = \begin{cases} x^{1.6} & \text{if} \quad x \geq 0 \text{ (domain of gains)} \\ -0.5(-x)^{0.88} & \text{if} \quad x < 0 \text{ (domain of losses).} \end{cases} \tag{2.45}$$

    Give reasons for your answer.
13. Prove the assertion that the decision weights do not add up to one in prospect theory unless all outcomes are either in the domain of gains or losses. If there are both gains and losses, how can you construct decision weights such that they add up to 1, but do not have an effect on the prospect theory calculations.
14. Show that Example 2.4 in Section 2.3.3 is consistent with prospect theory by using the status-quo interpretation of reference points for each pair of lotteries. Use the value function $v(x) = x^{0.6}$ and the Prelec probability weighting function $w(p) = e^{-(-\ln p)^{0.65}}$.
15. A decision maker follows prospect theory. He faces the lottery $L = (-10, 0.5; -5, 0.5)$, where outcomes are already expressed relative to the reference point, so both outcomes are in the domain of loss. His utility function is given by

$$v(x) = \begin{cases} x & \text{if} \quad x \geq 0 \text{ (domain of gains)} \\ -2.5(-x) & \text{if} \quad x < 0 \text{ (domain of losses),} \end{cases} \tag{2.46}$$

    and the probability weighting function is $w(p) = e^{-(-\ln p)^{0.6}}$. What is the lottery L worth to the decision maker? Is the decision maker risk averse, risk loving, or risk neutral?
16. Suppose that two decision makers, Jim and Tom, follow prospect theory. They face the identical lottery $L = \left(16, \frac{1}{3}; 24, \frac{1}{3}; 45, \frac{1}{3}\right)$ that captures the risky returns associated with a financial decision. The reference points of Jim and Tom are, respectively, $r_J = 24$ and $r_T =$

45. Both decide to invest in the lottery if the prospect theory value for the lottery is positive. Both individuals have identical preferences, so the utility functions of both individuals are given in (2.46) and the probability weighting function for both is $w(p) = e^{-(-\ln p)^{0.6}}$. Will either one or both invest in the lottery?

17. This exercise is from Nicholas Barberis and Ming Huang (2001). An investor is thinking about buying a portfolio of two stocks, say, one share of each. The shares of both stocks are currently trading at \$100 so if he buys both stocks he spends \$200. After careful thought, the investor decides that for both stocks, the share value of each stock one year from now will be distributed as (150,0.5; 70, 0.5), independently across the two stocks. Suppose that the investor's utility function is given in (2.46). Suppose that the reference point is the purchase price, so if both assets are purchased, the reference point is \$200. For simplicity, assume that this decision maker engages in linear probability weighting, that is, $w(p) = p$.
    (a) Will an expected utility maximizer buy the two assets?
    (b) Will a prospect theory utility maximizer buy the two assets?

18. Consider a problem in the spirit of the Benartzi and Thaler (1995) explanation of the equity premium puzzle. Suppose that initial wealth I is 10 and the decision maker uses prospect theory with linear probability weighting. The reference income, R, is the status quo, so it also equals 10. There are two assets, each with a maturity period of one year. A safe asset offers a return of 0%. The value function is piecewise linear and given in (2.46). Assume that the return on the risky asset, θ, can take either of two values, a low level of return, $\theta_L = -5\%$ (with probability 0.5), or a high level of return, $\theta_H > 0$ (with probability 0.5).
    (a) What level of return, θ_H, is required for the decision maker to be indifferent between the two assets? What is the difference between the average returns on the risky and the safe asset when the decision maker is indifferent between the two assets?
    (b) How would your answer for θ_H have changed if the low level of return θ_L had been even lower and if loss aversion λ were lower?

19. Consider the following lottery $L = (9, 0.3; 16, 0.4; 36, 0.3)$. The utility function of the individual is

$$v(x) = \begin{cases} \sqrt{x} & \text{if } x \geq 0 \\ -2.5(\sqrt{-x}) & \text{if } x < 0 \end{cases}, \tag{2.47}$$

    The probability weighting function is given by $w(p) = e^{-(-\ln p)^{0.5}}$. The reference point of the individual is 18. Find the attitudes to risk (i.e., whether the decision maker is risk averse, risk neutral, or risk loving) under each of the three decision theories: expected utility, rank dependent utility, and prospect theory.

20. A decision maker who uses prospect theory faces the lottery $L = (0, 1-p; y, p)$ in incremental form and $y > 0$ (single outcome in gains only). Let the utility function be given by $v(y) = \sqrt{y}$. Since there are no outcomes in losses we need not specify utility for losses. Let the probability weighting function be $w(p) = e^{-(-\ln p)^{0.5}}$. Show that there exists a cutoff probability $\widehat{p} = 0.0183$ such that for any probability $p < \widehat{p}$, the decision maker is risk loving (despite having a concave utility function) and for any probability $p > \widehat{p}$, the decision maker is risk averse. What is the intuition for your results?

21. As decision maker who uses prospect theory faces the lottery $L = (y, p; 0, 1-p)$ in incremental form and $y < 0$ (single outcome in losses only). Let the utility function be given by $v(y) = -\sqrt{-y}$. Since there are no outcomes in gains we need not specify utility for gains. Let the probability weighting function be $w(p) = e^{-(-\ln p)^{0.5}}$. Show that there exists a cutoff probability $\widehat{p} = 0.0183$ such that for any probability $p < \widehat{p}$, the decision maker is risk averse and for any probability $p > \widehat{p}$, the decision maker is risk loving. What is the intuition for your results?
22. Consider the effect of the tax rate on evaded income under EUT in the model of tax evasion in Section 2.5.3. Suppose that a decision maker has the choice of investing a given income between a risky asset and a riskless asset. The assumption of *decreasing risk aversion* (DARA) implies that the decision maker will allocate a higher absolute amount of income to the risky activity as income increases. Under the assumption of DARA what is the intuition behind the following result: An EUT taxpayer will evade less taxes as the tax rate increases.
23. Consider the following series of examples from Heath et al. (1999). Explain the findings in each example.
    1. Alice typically scores around 80 on weekly 100-point quizzes in one of her classes. One week she sets a goal of scoring 90. She scores 87. Betty typically scores around 80 on weekly 100-point quizzes in one of her classes. One week she decides to do her best. She scores 83. Overall, who will be more satisfied with her performance?
    2. Sally and Trish both follow workout plans that usually involve doing 25 sit-ups. One day, Sally sets a goal of performing 31 sit-ups. She finds herself very tired after performing 35 sit-ups and stops. Trish sets a goal of performing 39 sit-ups. She finds herself very tired after performing 35 sit-ups and stops. Who is experiencing more emotion?
    3. Charles and David both follow workout plans that usually involve doing 25 sit-ups. One day, Charles sets a goal of performing 30 sit-ups. He finds himself very tired after performing 34 sit-ups and, at most, has the energy to perform 1 more. David sets a goal of performing 35 sit-ups. He finds himself very tired after 34 sit-ups and, at most, has the energy to perform 1 more. Who will work harder to perform the 35th sit-up?

Part II

Other-Regarding Preferences

Introduction to Part II

Individuals have *self-regarding preferences* if they derive utility exclusively from their "own" consumption of goods, services, or other intangible benefits and costs. On the other hand, individuals have *other-regarding preferences* when they derive utility not only from their "own" but also from the consumption of goods, services, and intangible benefits and costs of others.

In its *original conception*, as distinct from its *actual practice*, neoclassical economics did not rule out departures from self-regarding preferences. Indeed, there is important early work on *snob consumption*, *bandwagon effects*, and *keeping up with the Joneses*, dating back to the early twentieth century, that relies on interdependent preferences of individuals. Nor does the assumption of rationality in neoclassical economics require that homo-economicus be endowed exclusively with self-regarding preferences. However, it is the case that other-regarding preferences have been almost nonexistent in neoclassical economics.

We reiterate the point made earlier in the introductory chapter of the book that our usage of the term "neoclassical economics" refers purely to its "actual practice" over the last several decades in research and in teaching. This also applies to our use of the term homo-economicus which is the model of humans used in the actual practice of neoclassical economics. This caveat applies here, and to the rest of the book too. In its actual practice, economics did not always take account of the insightful set of ideas discussed more informally in the early twentieth century by the founding fathers of neoclassical economics.

The preferences of homo-economicus are typically assumed to be self-regarding and *amoral*, whereby moral virtues and human ethics play no role. Thus, homo-economics exhibits an absence of reciprocity, empathy, altruism, and envy towards others. Many economists believe that giving up these features of preferences to explain economic phenomena would dissipate hard-won theoretical discipline and rigor in the subject, and lead down a slippery slope of ad-hoc explanations. This view is mistaken and has no basis in science. No serious researcher would advocate ad-hoc changes in preferences to accommodate the empirical evidence. Equally, it is impossible to ignore the massive amount of evidence on *other-regarding preferences* (sometimes also referred to as *social preferences*) and *human moral virtues*, which are central to behavioral economics. The empirical evidence indicates that among humans, there is a mix of individuals with self-regarding and other-regarding preferences. Furthermore, this mix depends on the context, frame, and the situation.

The term "other-regarding" incorporates a range of human motivations such as altruism, envy, fairness, empathy, envy, and conditional reciprocity. Human social motivations also include an innate desire to cooperate and follow social norms; a deep concern about the fairness of procedures; and differentiating between social ingroups and outgroups in the exercise of prosociality. Pure altruism, that is, unconditional kindness, is probably more the preserve of saints than ordinary mortals. Most humans exhibit instead, *conditional reciprocity*, that is, they respond to kindness with kindness and unkindness with unkindness, and they typically begin by cooperating in a new social situation. These insights collectively alter how we think about economics, say, in the design of incentive schemes in private and public organizations, and in the exercise of public policy.

Homo-economicus cooperates and coordinates in a purely *instrumental* manner by calculating the material costs and benefits from actions. In the harsh, amoral, world of homo-economicus, people happily lie, cheat, break promises, and behave unethically, provided that this leads to higher material gains. By contrast, the evidence indicates that humans have an *intrinsic* desire to cooperate and coordinate, even with strangers, and this is the product of an evolutionary history stretching back at least 200,000 years. Human morality, and the desire to do the right thing, often underpins our actions, even at the cost of material gains, and sometimes even our lives. Human history is replete with examples where people have preferred death in preference to compromising on moral principles. The purely self-regarding and amoral view, central to the construction of homo-economicus, is not only rejected by the evidence, its continued use in research is ad-hoc and, put bluntly, bad science. However, note well that advocating other-regarding preferences does not mean that material self interest is not important. There is also substantial heterogeneity among humans in the degree of their other-regarding preferences.

Our discussion of other-regarding preferences and issues of morality and ethics are spread over two chapters. Chapter 3 introduces the nature of other-regarding preferences through a series of experimental games and presents the associated evidence. We also evaluate the model of self-regarding preferences against this evidence. Chapter 4 considers models of behavioral economic theory that are able to account for this evidence.

3 The Evidence on Other-Regarding Preferences, Morality, and Ethics

3.1 Introduction

In the first of our two chapters on other-regarding preferences, we consider the evidence on human prosociality, morality, and ethics. "Human prosociality" is a broad term. The experimental evidence from several different games has vastly improved and illuminated our understanding of the various dimensions of human prosociality. These experiments carefully control for confounds arising from reputation formation, limited attention, imperfect memory recall, and are relatively simple to understand. Hence, they give us a relatively clean snapshot of human prosociality.

We begin, in Section 3.2, with a discussion of experimental evidence from two games that have established some of the core foundations of this subject area. In the *ultimatum game*, a proposer has a fixed endowment and has to decide on a proposed split, that is, how much money to offer to a responder. The responder either accepts, in which case the proposed split is implemented; or rejects, in which case the proposer and the responder get nothing. The neoclassical prediction is that the proposer should offer the minimum amount, say, one cent, because the responder will strictly prefer to accept anything above zero cents. In experiments, the mean offers by proposers range between 40%–50% of the endowment. Low offers are rejected by responders on the grounds that they are unfair, suggesting the presence of *conditional reciprocity* in their rejection decision.

When the ultimatum game is modified so that the responder has no meaningful actions, and cannot reject the offer, then the resulting game is known as a *dictator game*. In a dictator game, any positive offers by the proposer reflect *pure altruism* because the responder cannot reject the offer to punish the dictator for a low offer. The evidence shows that dictators offer roughly 15% of the endowment in a dictator game, indicating the presence of altruism. We explore the rich evidence on these games, and variants of these games.

Section 3.3 discusses the *gift exchange game* which models wage determination between a firm and its workers. In a static game, if firms offer a binding wage to the worker, and effort is costly, self-regarding workers should accept the binding wage and put in zero effort; this is sometimes known as the "take the money and run" strategy. Anticipating this behavior, firms should offer a binding wage rate of zero. However, the experimental evidence shows that firms offer a binding wage that is greater than the outside option of the workers; the difference constitutes the rent offered to the workers by the firm. The higher is the rent offered to the workers, the greater is the costly, and voluntary, effort that they put in. This once again illustrates the importance of conditional reciprocity in determining human behavior.

Section 3.4 considers the *trust game*. This is a two-player game. The first player, the *trustor* is given a fixed endowment and decides on what part of the endowment to send across as an investment to the second player, known as the *trustee*. The amount of the investment sent by the trustor captures the extent of *trust* shown by the trustor. For every dollar sent as an investment by the trustor, the experimenter passes on three dollars to the trustee (or any multiple greater than one). The trustee must then decide on how much money to return to the trustor. The amount of money returned by the trustee is a measure of *trustworthiness*. If players had purely self-regarding preferences, then the trustee should not return any money. Anticipating this, rational trustors will not make any investment. By contrast, the results from experiments show that trustees return the trustor's investment, plus an extra amount that may be viewed as a return on the investment. Trustors make strictly positive investments and they do get a positive return on their investment. These experiments, which have been conducted in different cultures, have established the presence of trust and trustworthiness among humans.

Section 3.5 describes human behavior in *social dilemmas*, with particular application to *public goods games*. A social dilemma arises when there is a gap between the privately optimal and the socially optimal solutions. For instance, if a group of people use a common property resource, for example, fishing on a common lake, then the privately optimal solution that ignores the negative externalities caused to other fishermen, involves catching more fish relative to the socially optimal solution. Public goods games are relevant to this class of problems. Under self-regarding preferences it might be optimal for people to free-ride on the efforts of others to produce a public good. However, we observe that (i) in actual practice, humans are successful in devising rules to cooperate and coordinate in social dilemma situations, and (ii) in experiments on public goods games that allow contributors to punish noncontributors, there is very little free-riding.

Section 3.6 distinguishes between pure altruism (unconditional kindness) from conditional reciprocity whereby people respond to kindness with kindness and unkindness with unkindness.

Section 3.7 considers evidence on the differences in human behavior in WEIRD (western, educated, industrial, rich, democratic) and non-WEIRD societies. Most of the evidence in behavioral economics has been collected in WEIRD societies. There is now a greater recognition of the need to collect evidence in non-WEIRD societies and contrast it with the evidence from WEIRD societies. The literature has identified several differences in a comparative analysis of this evidence which point towards the importance of cultural factors. For instance, while in WEIRD societies one largely observes prosocial punishments in public goods games, in non-WEIRD societies we may observe antisocial punishments (punishments of contributors by noncontributors). Antisocial punishments result in low overall contributions to public goods and reduce the welfare of groups.

Section 3.8 explores the evolutionary origins of differences in preferences across and within countries, as applied to risk preferences, social preferences, and time preferences. We try to provide a quantification of the "Out of Africa" theory.

Section 3.9 gives an introduction to the important topic of *social identity*. Humans often associate themselves with other members of their group (the ingroup) relative to nongroup members (the outgroup). Many people conform with the mental models and beliefs of their ingroups and discriminate against, and hold stereotypical views, about outgroup members. However, social identity may also have beneficial consequences such as greater cooperation and coordination among ingroup members. Social identity has evolutionary origins and humans appear hardwired to follow it. In experiments, subjects often discriminate against outgroup members on the basis of even a minimum group identity, such as a blue group and a red group.

In neoclassical economics, the economic actor, homo-economicus, is self-regarding, amoral, and lacks any notion of ethics. Much of microeconomics is about designing clever incentive schemes and contracts for people who will gladly break promises and even lie if the probability of being caught is low enough and fines are not prohibitive. Any observed moral or ethical behavior on the part of homo-economicus is then explained on account of instrumental reasons, that is, doing so increases material gains. In Section 3.10, we present evidence to show that, by and large, humans are intrinsically moral and like to keep promises and are often averse to lying. Our morality and sense of ethics arise from intrinsic reasons, that is, we just "like" being good and upright people, rather than for instrumental reasons. Section 3.10.3 shows when apologies might be effective in repairing and maintaining relations. It also demonstrates the harmful effects of apologies, relative to no apologies, if the associated commitments are reneged upon.

Section 3.11 considers the *external validity* of lab experiments in the literature on prosocial preferences. External validity requires showing that what occurs in the lab is descriptive of real life behavior in some concrete sense. For instance, that people who are more prosocial in the lab are likely to be more prosocial in their real life. Or that people who cooperate more in, say, the public goods game in the lab are also more likely to engage in more cooperative ventures in the real world. The evidence overwhelmingly supports the external validity of lab evidence.

3.2 Fixing Ideas about Conditional Reciprocity: Ultimatum Game

Let us start with some terminology about strategic situations, which are dealt with in more detail in Part IV of the book. A *strategic situation*, known as a *game*, arises when a set of individuals, known as *players*, take actions that mutually affect the material payoffs of each other. When taking actions, players typically have *beliefs* about what has happened so far in the game, what is likely to happen in the rest of the game, and what actions the other players are likely to take. The analysis of strategic situations falls under the rubric of *game theory* and different approaches in game theory try to predict the outcome of a well-defined game. A game has *complete information* when all players know everything about the game and about each other's utility functions.

The *ultimatum game*, introduced by Güth et al. (1982), is a *two-stage, complete information, game* between two players, a proposer, P, and a responder, R; see Figure 3.1. In the first stage, the proposer, who has an endowment of \$10, is asked to propose a share, $s \in \{0.01, 0.02, \ldots, 10.00\}$, of the endowment to a responder. The proposer gets to keep the rest, $10 - s$. The endowment of the proposer can be a gift from the experimenter, or the proposer might have earned it by completing an experimental task. In the second stage, the responder either accepts the offer, so the proposed split is implemented, or rejects the offer, in which case both receive 0 each. What split should the proposer offer?

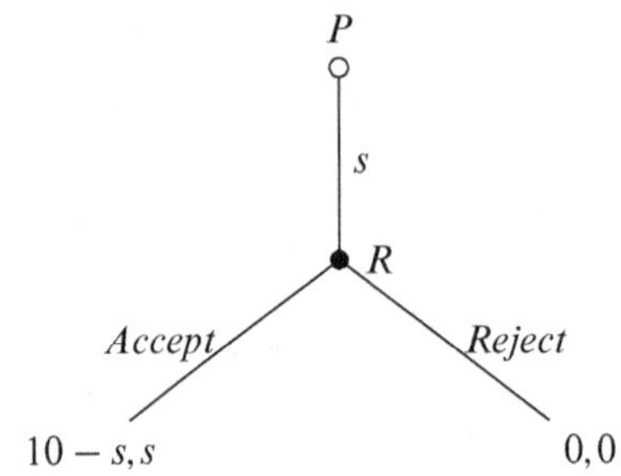

Figure 3.1 The ultimatum game

Two-stage games of complete information are solved in economics using *backward induction*. This implements an equilibrium concept in game theory, known as *subgame perfection*, which is explained in Chapter 5. Suppose that both players have self-regarding preferences and this is mutually known to the players. Then, backward induction is implemented as follows. In deciding on the optimal share, a rational proposer needs to calculate the responder's optimal response (accept or reject) "for all possible choices" of the share, s. If the responder is known to be self-regarding, the proposer knows that the responder will accept a minimum offer of $s = 1$ cent (because 1 cent is greater than 0 cents). Taking the responder's optimal response into account, a self-regarding proposer who wishes to maximize material gains will offer the share $s = \$0.01$, which will be immediately accepted by the responder. Hence, the proposer gets to keep \$9.99. This is the unique backward induction outcome under self-regarding preferences, and it can be empirically tested. One of the great strengths of neoclassical economics is that it offers precise predictions that can be tested against the evidence.

With student subjects, the evidence shows that the mean offer is 30%–40% of the proposer's endowment, and the median offer is 40%–50% of the endowment. There is, however, substantial cross-cultural variation in offers. Mean offers vary between 26%–58% of the proposer's endowment across 15 small scale societies in four different continents (Henrich et al., 2001). Small offers are rejected on the grounds of the "unfairness" of offers, an argument that lacks meaning in a world where everyone has self-regarding preferences. Thus, most responders appear to behave in a *conditionally reciprocal manner* – accept if the offer is high enough to be perceived as a fair offer, otherwise reject the offer and receive nothing but, in doing so, ensure that the proposer also gets nothing. This is typically anticipated by proposers who avoid making very low offers. These findings reject the predictions of a model based exclusively on self-regarding preferences.

An important finding in the cross-cultural study by Henrich et al. (2001) is that *greater prosociality* (i.e., higher proposer offers and expectations of the responders of a higher share) is associated with two factors.

1. Market integration in the community (incidence of buying/selling and working for a wage).
2. Cooperation in production, for example, team production rather than individual production.

Both factors are correlated with greater development of markets. Thus, *markets may promote prosociality*, which is the opposite of the basic lesson taught in many economics courses. However, we shall see later in this chapter that the evidence that *markets might reduce ethicality is mixed.*

As the *stake size*, that is, the size of the proposer's endowment, increases to a moderately high level, there is almost no change in the results. However, at very high stake sizes (say, several months, worth of work), the proposer's offers are still about 20% of the endowment and the rejection rate of responders also falls somewhat. However, remember that the prediction with self-regarding preferences is that the offer should be the smallest possible positive offer.

Although subjects in these experiments make their choices only once, could they be mistakenly, and automatically, applying some social norms of cooperation learnt from outside the lab? This does not appear to be the case because the evidence shows that subjects in lab experiments exhibit different behavior in games where they make choices once and where they make these choices repeatedly (Fehr and Fischbacher, 2002).

Does the proposer's offer reflect *altruism* towards the responder, or does it arise from a *strategic motive* that low offers will be rejected, resulting in a zero payoff? This question is addressed in a variant of the ultimatum game, called the *dictator game*. In this game, the proposer, known as the *dictator*, makes an offer but the responder, known as the *receiver*, is passive and must accept whatever is offered, including nothing. The evidence shows that dictators make offers that are, on average, between 15%–20% of their endowment. Although these offers are much lower than the corresponding figure of 40%–50% in ultimatum games, there is no strategic motive in the dictator game because the responder cannot reject offers. This enables us to identify altruism as the leading explanation for positive offers. The difference between the offers in the ultimatum and the dictator games reflects strategic considerations arising from the conditional reciprocity of the responders in the ultimatum game. In the ultimatum game and the dictator game, prosociality is reduced when the endowments of the proposer and the dictator are earned (say, by doing an onerous task in the experiment) rather than experimenter-provided (Cherry et al., 2002).

The degree of prosociality revealed in the dictator game may also predict behavior in other real world domains. In the US, the Democrats support greater redistributive taxation and a larger size of the social welfare state relative to the Republicans. Fisman et al. (2017) show that subjects who are revealed to have a higher degree of prosociality in dictator game experiments are also more likely to be Democrat voters than Republican voters. This evidence also speaks to the *external validity* of lab experiments, namely, that results in the lab predict well the behavior of subjects in real world domains.

The dictator game is a very stylized nonstrategic situation and the results from this game are not always robust to the introduction of strategic considerations as captured, say, in the ultimatum game. Hence, one should be careful in generalizing the results from dictator games. Consider two examples.

1. Putting pictures of human eyes in the room where the dictator game is played, induces higher dictator offers (Haley and Fessler, 2005), yet a similar effect is not found in the ultimatum game (Fehr and Schneider, 2010).
2. When dictators are given an opportunity to exit the experiment with a slight reduction in their endowment, in return for keeping their identity anonymous from the receiver, some dictators take up the offer; that is, they exercise *moral wiggle room* (Dana et al., 2007). This is akin to avoiding a beggar on the street by crossing over to the other side of the street. However, the moral wiggle room does not play a role when strategic interaction is introduced (van der Weele et al., 2014).

Yet, the ability of dictator games to predict other real world behaviors, as in the voting propensities of the subjects, or to classify subjects according to their prosociality, is useful in many areas of behavioral economics.

The degree of prosociality of humans can be correlated with other behavioral traits. For instance, preferences for *positive reciprocity* (reacting to kind behavior of others with kindness), trust, and altruism were found to be correlated in a study on global preferences of individuals in 76 countries, using the Global Preference Survey (Falk et al., 2018). The same study also reported several other interesting findings. First, prosociality is culturally determined, for instance, on average, prosociality is higher in Asia relative to sub-Saharan Africa. Second, lab evidence on social preferences has a high degree of external validity. The lab measures of prosociality were correlated with the real life charitable behavior of subjects, their gift of time to others, and their tendency to help friends/strangers. Third, preferences for positive reciprocity and *negative reciprocity* (reaction to unkind behavior with unkind behavior) were positively correlated with the cognitive ability of subjects. Fourth, the average level of negative reciprocity in a country is positively correlated with the frequency of armed conflict.

There is evidence that children might form social preferences at a relatively young age and that these preferences are influenced by the type of education that children receive. For instance, the prosociality of children, aged 3–4 years, is influenced by whether they go for preschool sessions or are exclusively home-schooled by parents (Cappelen et al., 2020). Data from Germany distinguishes between low socio-economic status (low SES) households who have low income, low education, and are headed by single parents, and families with the converse set of characteristics who have high socio-economic status (high SES). Children from low SES families exhibited relatively lower altruism, lower IQ, greater impatience, and more pronounced risk taking tendencies as compared to children from high SES families (Deckers et al., 2021). Children have a strong desire to conform to the social norms of the groups. Li et al. (2021) find that the desire for norm conformity overrides individual preferences of 3.5 year old children.

Remark 3.1 *It is possible to give an incomplete information version of all the main experimental games in this chapter where players do not fully know the utilities of other players, but have beliefs over these utilities. However, this does not add fundamentally new insights here, and requires additional game–theoretic machinery which we have not yet introduced. In the actual experiments, full information is implemented by announcing the material payoffs of the other players and hoping that for relatively small material payoffs, the utility functions are approximately linear. For this reason, we shall stick with the complete information variants of these games throughout.*

3.3 Wage Determination in Firms: The Gift Exchange Game

The idea that *gift exchange* underpins reciprocal exchange among humans is well established in sociology (Mauss, 1924; Gouldner, 1960). Important applications in behavioral economics commenced with the work of Akerlof (1982). The gift exchange game that we discuss below was developed in a series of papers (Fehr et al., 1993; Fehr et al., 1997).

Consider wage determination between a firm and a single worker in an employment relation. The worker can obtain an income $y \geq 0$ outside this employment relation; this is known as the *outside option* of the worker. The effort level, e, of the worker either cannot be observed, or even if observed, hard evidence of it cannot be produced before a third party, such as a court. Hence, because inadequate effort on the part of the worker cannot be legally established, it cannot be formally written down in a contract, giving rise to *incomplete contracts* in which effort is noncontractable. This is a situation of *moral hazard.*

In the first stage of this two-stage game, the firm offers a fixed, legally binding, wage, $w \in [0, w_{max}]$, where w_{max} is the maximum possible wage that the firm can offer. The firm also specifies some desired, but nonbinding, effort level, e_n. Given incomplete contracts, if the worker chooses actual effort level, e, below the desired effort ($e < e_n$), the firm has no recourse to legal action. The worker observes the labor contract (w, e_n) and then chooses actual effort, e, from a set of possible effort levels, say, $[0, e_{max}]$, where e_{max} is the maximum possible effort level.

This is a *two-stage game of complete information*, like the ultimatum game. The predictions for this game under neoclassical game theory, and self-regarding preferences, are obtained by solving it by backward induction. We now engage in this exercise.

The utilities of the players are likely to be linear over small material payoffs in experiments. Hence, a self-regarding worker's utility is given by

$$u = w - \frac{1}{2}e^2, \tag{3.1}$$

where effort $e \in [0, e_{max}]$ is chosen by the worker to lie between 0 (complete shirking) and e_{max}, the highest effort level. The worker derives utility from wage, w, but effort is costly and imposes an effort cost, $c(e) = \frac{1}{2}e^2$, on the worker. For instance, if the worker chooses $e = 4$, then the cost of effort is $\frac{1}{2}4^2 = 8$. Effort costs of the worker, $c(e)$, increase as effort increases, and they increase at an increasing rate. In other words, the marginal cost of effort for the worker is positive and increasing. [For readers familiar with calculus, it is straightforward to check that $c'(e) = e > 0$ and $c''(e) = 1 > 0$. Hence, the cost function is strictly convex.]

The firm's revenue, or production function, given by $f(e) = 10e$, increases as the worker puts in higher effort. Thus, the profit of the self-regarding firm, net of the fixed wage cost, w, is

$$\pi = 10e - w. \tag{3.2}$$

What wage $w \in [0, w_{max}]$ should the firm offer?

Using backward induction, the firm first calculates the optimal effort that will be chosen by the worker *for each possible choice of the wage* it offers. In other words, the firm wishes to compute the *reaction function* of the worker. From (3.1), for a given contractually binding wage, w, the utility of the worker is decreasing in the effort level. Hence, self-regarding and amoral workers will simply take the money (the contractually binding wage, w) and run, that is, choose actual effort $e_a = 0$. Thus, the reaction function of the worker,

$$e^*(w) = 0 \text{ for all } w,$$

shows that the worker chooses zero effort irrespective of the wage offered by the firm.

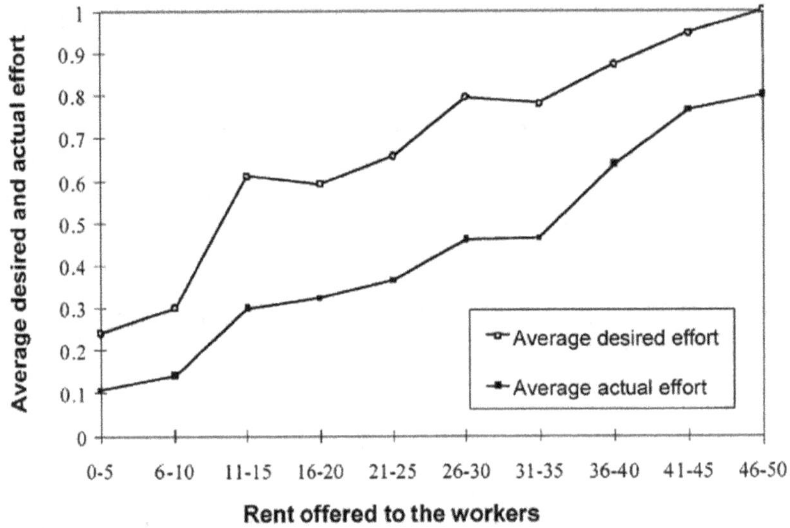

Figure 3.2 Average actual and desired effort levels of workers for different possible rents offered to them. Source: Fehr and Falk (2002)

The firm takes into account the reaction function of the worker, and substitutes it into the profit function in (3.2) to get

$$\pi = 10e^*(w) - w = -w.$$

The firm's optimal choice of a wage to offer is, thus, $w^* = 0$, because the worker will never respond with strictly positive effort. In sum, the backward induction solution under self-regarding preferences is $(w^*, e^*) = (0, 0)$.

In contrast to these predictions, the empirical findings are as follows. Figure 3.2 plots the actual effort, e, and the desired effort, e_n, levels of the workers, plotted against the rents received by the worker from the firm. The worker's *rent* in the employment relation is the wage offered, w, by the firm in excess of the worker's outside option, y (i.e., $w - y$). Figure 3.2 is based on data in the paper by Fehr et al. (1997) who allow effort, e, and desired effort, e_n, to vary in the normalized interval $[0, 1]$, so $e_{max} = 1$. The Figure shows clearly that the greater is the rent offered to the worker, the greater is the worker's actual effort e.

The best explanation of this finding is the *conditional reciprocity* of the workers who interpret a high wage as a kind action and respond with kindness by putting in a high effort level. This is the essence of gift exchange. On average, there is shirking by the workers, $e < e_n$, and they put in an effort level lower than the firm's desired, but contractually noninding, effort. Some workers choose the lowest possible effort $e = 0$. Thus, there is a mixture of other-regarding and self-regarding workers; Fehr and Falk (2002) provide a rough estimate of a 60–40 ratio between the two, which is likely to depend on the context, frame, and culture.

Many social norms are sustained by sanctions and punishment of norm violators. Firms too might have "internal work norms" that specify the effort expected in an employment relation and there is a shared understanding of the formal or informal sanctions that arise from violating the work norm, for example, disapproval by peers. Motivated by these observations, suppose that the experimenter allowed the firm to engage in voluntary, but costly, punishment of shirkers after observing the worker's effort level. This is implemented by adding a third stage in the gift exchange game after the firm has observed the second stage effort choice $e < e_n$ of the worker. The cost of the punishment to the firm is $\kappa > 0$ per unit. If the firm punishes the worker in proportion to the shortfall in effort, $e_n - e$, then the total cost of the punishment to the firm is $\kappa(e_n - e)$. Thus, the profits of the firm in the third stage, if it were to choose to punish the worker, are given by

$$\pi = 10e - w - \kappa(e_n - e); \kappa > 0. \tag{3.3}$$

Since the worker's effort choice, e, has already been determined in the second stage, the decision to inflict costly punishments on the worker only affects the third term on the RHS in (3.3). If the firm decides not to punish the worker, it can get even higher utility that equals $\pi = 10e - w$. But this is exactly what a self-regarding firm that wishes to maximize its profits in the third stage will choose to do. Hence, the firm treats bygones as bygones and chooses not to punish the worker.

In the second stage, rational self-regarding workers will look forward and predict that they will not be punished for shirking in the third stage, hence, they continue to shirk. In the first stage, a rational forward looking self-regarding firm can foresee the optimal choices in the second and third stages, so it offers a wage of zero. In effect, adding costly punishments in the neoclassical model with self-regarding preferences does not alter the outcome $(w^*, e^*) = (0, 0)$ because bygones are bygones and punishments are costly. This is a testable prediction.

Empirically, however, the introduction of the punishment option significantly reduces shirking. The firm actively punishes shirkers. Workers appear able to anticipate subsequent punishment, hence, the incidence of shirking falls from 83% in the absence of the punishment option to just 20%, and the average effort nearly doubles. The firm is rather more keen to punish workers from falling below its desired effort, e_n, than to reward workers who exceed e_n. Clearly, the model with self-regarding preferences cannot account for this data. But why won't firms let bygones be bygones? One possibility is other-regarding preferences such as inequity aversion which induce the firm to punish the worker and reduce the income inequity between the two parties (see Section 3.5). A second possibility is that firms find it hedonically attractive to punish workers for being opportunistic (see the neuroeconomic evidence in the online book chapter).

The average quantitative effects of gift exchange are often found to be weak and empirically not long-lived (Gneezy and List, 2006; Rajshri et al., 2016). However, field evidence shows that among workers with longer tenures at the firm, as compared to spot market workers, these effects are stronger and last longer (Bellemare and Shearer, 2007). Gift exchange has also been documented with field data, for example, strikes and industrial action when workers perceive they are unfairly treated. Gift exchange has a basis in an evolutionary account of human behavior and has led to important advances in contract theory, labor economics, and macroeconomic models among other areas (Dhami, 2019, Vol. 2).

Some further results in the literature merit mention.

1. Suppose that in competitive markets between buyers and sellers, buyers first offer a price and then sellers decide on the quality of the output to supply. Quality can be either high, which is costly to produce, or low, which is cheaper to produce. Assume that the quality cannot be verified to a third party, such as a court of law, hence, it cannot be written down in a contract,

so contracts are incomplete. The results from experiments in Fehr et al. (1998) showed that when buyers offered a high price, the conditional reciprocity of the sellers induced them to offer the costly high quality, even when they could have got away with offering the cheaper low quality. In these experiments, there are no future economic interactions between the two parties, and hence no reputational issues are at play.

2. Social comparisons between workers at the workplace were found to mediate gift exchange in the experiments of Cohn et al. (2014). With two workers, a wage cut applied to both workers by the firm reduces effort of both workers (negative reciprocity). However, an identical sized wage cut for the first worker alone, but not the second worker, reduces the effort of the first worker even more, relative to the first case (negative reciprocity and social comparisons).
3. Nonmonetary gifts might be more effective than monetary gifts in eliciting greater effort from workers (Falk, 2007). It is possible that non-monetary gifts have greater evolutionary salience– money is, after all, a relatively recent invention in human history. Malmendier and Schmidt (2017) show that small non-monetary gifts influence decisions by players in bilateral relations, even when these decisions harm a third party. For instance, doctors may be influenced by the small gifts that they receive from pharmaceutical companies to recommend their medicines to patients, even if a better medicine (or a similar, but cheaper medicine) manufactured by other companies is available. Another example is the small gifts by lobbyists to politicians that induce politicians to reciprocate with favors, potentially at the cost of more efficient public policies. Interestingly, the receivers of these small gifts often express unawareness of the bias in their decisions, which suggests that humans might be hardwired to respond to gifts in this manner without necessarily consciously realizing it.
4. Minimum wage laws, and the status-quo wage, might serve as reference points for the workers. Thus, the extent of gift exchange of effort by the workers might be determined by comparing the actual wage with the minimum wage (Akerlof, 1982). Even if minimum wage laws are repealed, there is a *ratchet effect* because workers consider the old minimum wage as a fair wage, below which they may not be willing to engage in gift exchange. A minimum wage is found to raise average wages, and a modest increase in effort levels of workers, leading overall to a Pareto improvement (Owens and Kagel, 2010).
5. The original formulation of gift exchange in Akerlof (1982) is more ambitious than the subsequent empirical attempts to test it. Akerlof highlighted the roles of *external wage norms*, which are wages offered in similar industries, and the role of *internal effort norms* that specify the acceptable levels of effort within the firm. Relatedly, workers might feel "guilty" from letting down the firm's effort expectations. Testing the effects of these factors on gift exchange requires a formal beliefs-based model and an unambiguous definition of guilt. Such models explicitly specify the beliefs that workers hold about others, and the expectations that workers have about the beliefs of others. Dhami et al. (2021) use a beliefs-based model to extend the gift exchange game to allow for the presence of external wage norms, internal effort norms, and the expectations of the firms about the worker's effort (roughly the analogue of e_n in the model above). These variables are found to significantly affect the optimal effort choice of workers. Furthermore, aversion to guilt plays an important part in explaining why workers respond to contractually non-binding effort injunctions by the firm. The formal account here relies on using psychological game theory that we discuss in Part IV of the book.

6. Relative to a baseline wage (Treatment 1), the experiments in Kube et al. (2013) induced an unexpected pay increase (Treatment 2), and an unexpected wage decrease (Treatment 3). The effort differences between Treatments 1 and 2 are not significant. However, effort in Treatment 3 is significantly lower than in Treatment 1. The elasticity of effort with respect to a wage reduction is 0.82 (Kube et al., 2013). However, the elasticity of effort with respect to an increase in wages is 0.15 in Gneezy and List (2006) and 0.30 in Kube et al. (2006). This appears reminiscent of the idea of loss aversion discussed in Part I of the book. This evidence is also related to the earlier empirical findings of Bewley (1999) who showed that in a recession, firms prefer to lay off workers but not cut the wages of the employed workers for fear of lowering worker morale. He demonstrated that maintaining worker morale and giving a fair wage provided a better explanation for the evidence on the downward stickiness of wages and the effect on unemployment relative to any of the leading theories of unemployment in modern macroeconomics.

A rejection of the predictions of the gift exchange model is a joint rejection of (i) self-regarding preferences and (ii) the backward induction outcome. So which one do we implicate? We shall see in our discussion of the empirical evidence in Chapter 5 that the backward induction outcome is generally not supported by the evidence when several iterative steps are required to solve the game, for example, centipede games that involve four or more moves. However, it is a dominant strategy for any self-regarding worker to choose $e = 0$, for any wage. Hence, even if firms do not use strict backward induction, but believe that the other player will not play their dominated strategy, we get exactly the same outcome, $(w^*, e^*) = (0, 0)$. For this reason, it is reasonable to implicate self-regarding preferences as the driving factor behind the prediction $(w^*, e^*) = (0, 0)$. A similar comment applies to the other two-stage games in this chapter.

3.4 Trust and Trustworthiness: The Trust Game

Most real life contracts are incomplete for a variety of reasons. For instance, it might not be possible to write down contractually binding terms in the presence of asymmetric information when information that is observable and verifiable to a third party might be hard to produce. Or, it might not be possible to specify all possible contingencies that might occur in the future. This potentially reduces the scale and scope of economic activity. However, informal, verbal, agreements based on *trust* have often been found to substitute for formal contracts and legal institutions (Greif, 1993). Measures of trust have been shown to be correlated with GDP, GDP growth, political stability, reduced transaction costs, and improved economic outcomes across countries (Putnam, 1993). Trust can also be influenced by experiences of war and conflict (Fehr, 2009; Bauer et al., 2016). The slave trade in Africa led to Africans being captured by fellow Africans to be sold off as slaves. Research has highlighted the long-term effects of the slave trade, giving rise to low levels of trust which have persisted for generations (Nunn, 2008; Nunn and Wantchekon, 2011).

The *trust game*, due to Berg et al. (1995), allows for a precise definition and measurement of terms such as *trust* and *trustworthiness*. In this game, the first player, the *trustor*, is given an initial endowment, $Y > 0$, by the experimenter and, in the first stage of the game, is asked to send an investment, i, to a second player, the *trustee*. The experimenter multiplies the investment, i, by a multiplier $m > 1$, and passes on the amount mi to the trustee. The trustee is also given an endowment of $Y > 0$ (this is not critical; trust game experiments can also be run by giving the trustee an endowment of 0). On receiving the amount mi, the trustee must decide on the amount, $r \in [0, mi]$, to return to the trustor in the second stage of the game. In many experiments, $Y = 10$ and $m = 3$, so let us use these figures. Since the utilities of the players are approximately linear for the small stakes used in experiments, we may take the incomes of the players to equal their levels of utilities. At the end of the trust game, the utility of a self-regarding trustor is

$$u_1 = 10 - i + r, \tag{3.4}$$

and the utility of a self-regarding trustee is

$$u_2 = 10 + 3i - r. \tag{3.5}$$

How much investment should the trustor send?

Definition 3.1 *The investment sent by the trustor, i, is a measure of trust, and the amount returned by the trustee, r, is a measure of trustworthiness.*

The trust game is a two-stage, two-player game of complete information, hence, we shall solve it by backward induction in the same manner as we solved the gift exchange game in Section 3.3.

In the first stage, the trustor first computes the optimal response of the trustee for each level of investment, i, that the trustor might send. From (3.5), for a given level of i that has already been committed to, the self-regarding trustee maximizes utility by choosing $r = 0$, hence the trustee should return nothing. Thus, the reaction function of the trustee is

$$r^*(i) = 0 \text{ for all possible levels of } i.$$

A forward looking trustor uses the trustee's reaction function to maximize her utility in (3.4),

$$u_1 = 10 - i + r^*(i),$$

or $u_1 = 10 - i$, which is maximized at $i^* = 0$. Thus, the unique outcome of the trust game under self-regarding preferences, and backward induction, is zero trust and zero trustworthiness, that is, $(i^*, r^*) = (0, 0)$. This is a testable prediction of the model, and one which has been repeatedly tested.

The self-regarding prediction, $(i^*, r^*) = (0, 0)$, has been shown to fail the empirical test. Define the variables

$$pSent = \frac{i}{10},$$

and

$$pReturn = \frac{r}{10 + 3i},$$

respectively, as the proportion of the respective incomes sent by the trustor, and returned by the trustee. The results of a meta study based on 161 replications of the trust game and 23,000 observations by Johnson and Mislin (2011) is shown in Figure 3.3. They found that across the 161 replications, mean *pSent* is 0.502 and mean *pReturn* is 0.372 (notice that the denominator in *pReturn* is larger). Thus, trustors send more than half their income as investment and trustees

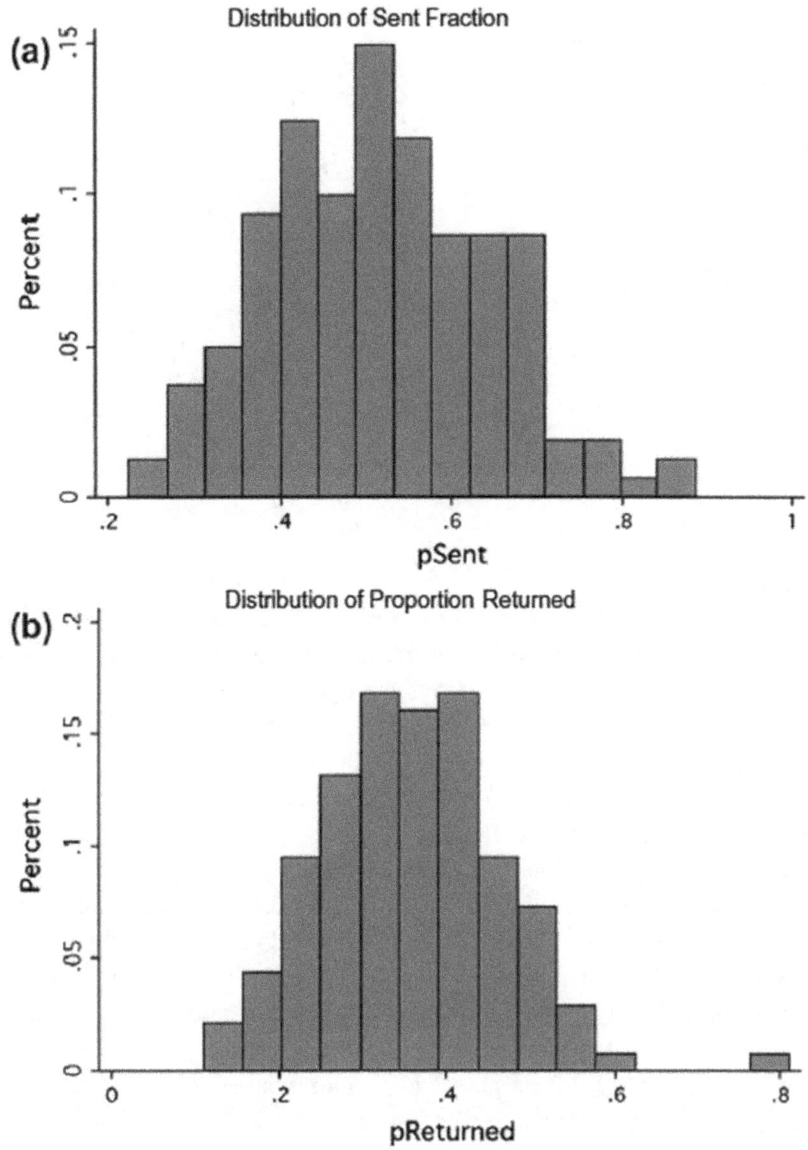

Figure 3.3 Measures of trust and trustworthiness in the trust game. Source: Johnson and Mislin (2011)

typically return an amount over and above the investment they receive ($r > i$), so both are better off. To see that $r > i$, based on the mean levels of *pSent* and *pReturn*, rewrite $\frac{r}{10+3i} = 0.372$ as $r = 0.372\,(10 + 3i)$. Divide both sides by 10 to get $\frac{r}{10} = 0.372\left(1 + 3\frac{i}{10}\right)$. Now subtract $\frac{i}{10}$ from both sides to get $\frac{r-i}{10} = 0.372\left(1 + 3\frac{i}{10}\right) - \frac{i}{10}$. Substituting the empirically observed value $\frac{i}{10} = 0.502$ we get

$$r - i = 4.302 > 0,$$

as claimed.

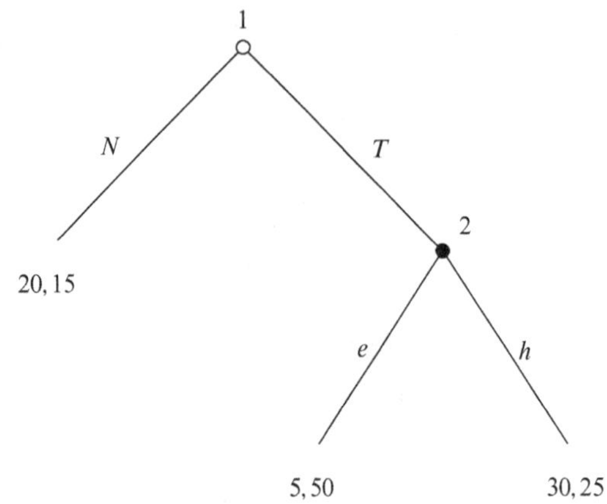

Figure 3.4 A depiction of the trust game in Huck et al. (2012).

In a significant finding, trust and trustworthiness were found to be related. In experiments by Charness et al. (2011), repeated over several rounds, players were paired anonymously to play the trust game. At the beginning of each round, players were given the option of knowing their partner's history of choices in previous trust games – 70% of the players took up this option. Suppose that in the current round of play, a player in the role of a trustor is matched with a trustee. Yet, in the past, this trustee might have only played the role of a trustor, so only the matched player's trust history is available. However, players were found to use past data on trust to infer their partner's trustworthiness.

Huck et al. (2012) consider the effects of market competition on trust, using the two-player game of complete information shown in Figure 3.4; this game was used earlier by Bohnet et al. (2005). The first number in any pair of payoffs in Figure 3.4 is player 1's payoff and the second number is player 2's payoff. Player 1, the trustor, can either choose N (no trust) to end the game for a payoff of 20 and a payoff of 15 to the other player; or choose T (trust), which allows player 2, the trustee, to exercise a choice. Player 2, if given an opportunity, can choose either to exploit trust (e) for a payoff of 50 and a payoff of 5 to player 1; or choose to honor trust (h) for a payoff of 25 and a payoff of 30 to player 1. Honoring trust is analogous to being trustworthy.

The prediction under neoclassical economics, if players are self-regarding, can be found readily by using backward induction. If player 2 is given a choice, then she always chooses e over h (because $50 > 25$). Looking forward, and taking account of the reaction function of player 2, a rational player 1 will know that the choice N gives a payoff of 20 and the choice T gives a payoff of 5, hence, she chooses N. Thus, the unique prediction of the game, if players use backward induction and are self-regarding, is the pair of choices (N, e). Notice that player 2 never gets to choose an action.[1] On the other hand, the trusting and trustworthy choices of

[1] Strategies are complete contingent plans of actions in game theory. Hence, even though player 2 never gets a chance to choose if player 1 plays N, we are required to compute the optimal choice of player 2, if player 2 were asked to make a choice.

Table 3.1 Each entry in a cell of the table shows three figures, expressed in percentages, in the following order: Efficiency rate, trust rate, and honor rate

	Random matching	Endogenous matching (competition)
Private information	50, 70, 36	86, 92, 79
Full information	51, 69, 36	90, 94, 85

the two players are shown along the lines T and h in Figure 3.4. They correspond to the pair of choices (T, h) and they lead to a joint payoff of 55, which is greater than the joint payoff of 35 from the pair of choices (N, e).

In order to analyze this game, the authors use the following definition.

Definition 3.2 *The "trust rate" is the percentage of times the trustor plays T. The "honor rate" is the percentage of times the trustee plays h. The "efficiency rate" is the percentage of times the outcome* (T, h) *occurs.*

Bohnet et al. (2005) find that the efficient outcome (T, h) is played only 5% of the time and the trust and honor rates are very low.

In order to examine the effect of market competition, Huck et al. (2012) play the trust game in Figure 3.4 over 30 rounds, and use the 2×2 design shown in Table 3.1. Each subject in the experiment is assigned either to the role of a trustor or a trustee over the duration of the experiment. In any market, in the experiment, there are four trustors and four trustees.
In the first dimension of the 2×2 design, information is varied in the following two ways.

(i) In the private information treatment (*pi*), each subject knows their own history of interaction with trustees over the previous rounds in the experiment, but others do not.
(ii) In the full information treatment (*fi*), all trustors in a market have full access to the histories of all the other participating trustees in the market.

In the second dimension of the 2×2 design, the nature of the matching between the players is varied in the following two ways.

(i) Under random matching (*r*), in each market, each of the four trustors is randomly assigned to one of the four trustees in the market, in each round of the experiment.
(ii) Under endogenous matching, or competitive matching (*c*), in each market, the trustors actively choose the trustees themselves.

The 2×2 design gives us the following four treatments, each of which takes one element from each of the two dimensions: *pi-r*, *pi-c*, *fi-r*, *fi-c*. For instance, in the treatment *fi-c*, the trustors have full access to the entire history of the trustworthiness of the trustees (*fi*) and compete for the trustees (*c*).

There is also a control treatment in which the trust game in Figure 3.4 is played over 30 rounds with randomly matched opponents in each round, chosen from the entire pool of subjects in the experiment. This gives similar results to those in Bohnet et al. (2005), so this is a successful replication of the earlier design. Consider first, random matching under private information and full information, that is, the two treatments *pi-r* and *fi-r*. The results are very similar in both cases, so varying information does not matter. However, relative to the control treatment, the efficiency rate improves from 5% to 50%, and the trust rate (70%) and the honor rate (36%) are very high. This changes even more dramatically when we introduce competition in the two treatments, *pi-c* and *fi-c,* in the third column of Table 3.1. Varying information does not produce vastly different results, but the best results are found in the treatment *fi-c*, which produces an efficiency rate of 90%, a trust rate of 94%, and an honor rate of 85%. In sum, market competition and access to the history of the participants are particularly important factors in fostering trust and trustworthiness.

Remark 3.2 *The results in Huck et al. (2012) are consistent with the narrative around the formation of merchant guilds in many societies, the role of social capital, and developing a reputation for honoring trust, which have historically led to relatively efficient outcomes, even in the absence of formal legal structures. In conjunction with the results from the ultimatum game in Section 3.2, which showed that markets enhance prosocial behavior, it is perhaps worth pointing out that first year textbooks in microeconomics sometimes paint a misleading picture of human motivation in markets. The following arguments are not uncommon. "If any market participants were other-regarding, or exhibited prosocial behavior, their profits would be lower than those who are self-regarding, hence, they would have to exit the market. Indeed, such behavior is irrational in markets." While this can be easily empirically rejected, there is a more general point here. Arguments in economic theory are sometimes stated in an axiomatic fashion and taken to be self-evidently true, without recourse to the gold standard in science, which is to let the empirical evidence play the decisive role in such choice.*

The gift exchange game and the trust game are related. In the gift exchange game, the economic surplus is created by the second player, the worker, through the choice of an effort level. Using (3.1) and (3.2), the sum of payoffs of both players in the gift exchange game is $u + \pi = 10e - \frac{1}{2}e^2$, which is independent of the wage choice, w, of firms. By contrast, in the trust game, the economic surplus is created by the choice of the first player, the trustor, through the choice of the investment level. The sum of utilities of the two players in (3.4) and (3.5) is $u_1 + u_2 = 20 + 2i$, which is independent of the return decision, r, of player 2, the trustee. The wage in the gift exchange game, w, and the amount returned in the trust game, r, do, however, influence the allocation of the total surplus between the two parties.

In their meta study of trust games, van den Akker et al. (2020) found that men trust more than women, but there are no gender differences in the extent of trustworthiness. They also found that in the gift exchange game, men did not announce significantly higher wage rates as compared to women. The authors conjecture that there is a *male multiplier effect* whereby men are more trusting in situations where there is an efficiency gain (money is multiplied before being passed on to the other party, as in the trust game). Gender differences are found in a range of other domains in behavioral economics such as in risk-taking behavior and in the extent of overconfidence; for surveys, see Croson and Gneezy (2009) and Niederle (2016).

3.5 Social Dilemmas and Managing the Commons: The Public Goods Games

Let us begin with some basics. *Negative externalities* arise when the actions taken by one party causes harm, or *negative spillovers*, to another party (or parties) and the harm-causing party pays no compensation for it. For instance, indoor smoking in the presence of nonsmokers; traffic congestion caused by using too little public transport; tax evasion that leaves less government revenues available for schools and hospitals; excessive exploitation of a *common property resource* such as fisheries, scarce underground water resources, and grasslands.

The word "commons" refers to a joint property resource owned by a group of people, who have common property rights over the resource, which itself is in limited supply. Given the joint ownership over the resource, there is a potential problem of excessive exploitation of the commons by individuals, which causes harm to other joint owners. In the absence of regulation or other voluntary arrangements, the harm-causing individuals may not fully take account of, or fail to *internalize*, the *negative externality* they cause for others, resulting in excessive harm to others relative to what is *socially optimal*. The socially optimal harm need not be zero – it depends on the trade-off between the marginal costs and marginal benefits of reducing harm.

Positive externalities are simply the flip side of negative externalities. They arise when the actions of one party benefit another by creating *positive spillovers*. Yet the party that causes positive externalities does not take account of the benefits to others, nor is it paid for these benefits by others. Hence, it takes a suboptimally low/inadequate action relative to the socially optimal action. The classic example is an individual who owns an aviary that helps to pollinate the neighbor's garden.

Public policy may find it socially optimal to (1) encourage actions involving positive externalities through subsidies and other forms of public policy such as regulation, and (2) discourage actions that create negative externalities by levying taxes on such actions, for example, taxing polluting firms, or use regulation to partially, or fully, ban these actions. Such subsidies and taxes that align the private net benefits of an individual's actions with the social net benefits are known as *corrective taxes* (subsidies are simply negative taxes). Sometimes corrective taxes are called *Pigouvian taxes*, after the Cambridge economist, A. C. Pigou, for his work in this area, first published in 1920. It might not be optimal for public policy to eliminate negative externalities completely, or to promote positive externalities to the maximum possible extent. It all depends on the trade-off between the marginal costs and the marginal benefits of public policy intervention.

Social dilemmas are situations where the *privately optimal action* of individuals that maximizes their self-regarding utility, is "suboptimal" relative to the *socially optimal action* that maximizes some composite (e.g., the sum) of the utilities of the group. The discrepancy between the privately and the socially optimal actions might arise, for instance, because private actions may cause harm to others by causing *negative externalities*. In this case, the privately optimal action is likely to be "suboptimally high" relative to the socially optimal action.

Within the class of social dilemmas, an important problem arises from *public goods* provision; the problem of the commons is an exemplar. A *pure public good*, in contrast to a *private good*, satisfies the following two conditions.

1. Non-rival in consumption, that is, one person's consumption does not reduce consumption of the good for another person.
2. Non-excludable, that is, it is not possible to exclude potential users from consuming the good.

Private goods, such as a hot meal in a university cafeteria, are rival (one person's consumption precludes another person from consuming it) and excludable (only those who pay for the good can receive it). Examples of public goods include national defense and radio airwaves. The classic example of a public good is a lighthouse that all ships in the harbor can use without affecting the ability of other ships to use it (nonrival), but none of the ships can be excluded from the use of the lighthouse (nonexcludable). Many goods satisfy these conditions only partially, and also have some features of private goods; these are known as *impure public goods.* Examples include parks and recreation facilities that are nonexcludable but may become congested and, hence, rival in consumption; or certain goods that may be nonrival, yet they are excludable, such as clubs of various sorts that require a membership. We simply use the generic label "public goods" below.

Freely functioning private markets may often fail to provide public goods, a situation known as *market failure*, which might call for public provision of the good. There are the following three main solutions to market failures caused by public goods.

1. Government provision, as in the case of national defense. Education and health, sometimes classed as impure public goods, are often both publicly and privately provided.
2. Private provision using community social norms and conventions, for example, managing common resources such as fisheries, grazing land, and forests through a variety of private arrangements (Ostrom, 1990).
3. Private provision, by assigning explicit legal property rights, and possible government regulation such as permits and leases.

Lab and field experiments provide a controlled environment to study human motivations in public goods games. Consider the following *public goods game*. There are $i = 1, \ldots, 6$ players (recall we refer to individuals as players in a game) and each is given an endowment of 20 tokens. Tokens is a unit of currency in experiments that is convertible into real money at the end of the experiment. All six players are risk neutral (see Part I for a definition) and they "simultaneously" choose their contributions to the public good, that is, without observing the contributions of each other. The contribution of any player i is denoted by $g_i \in [0, 20]$. The public good, G, is produced by using a linear production technology, so it equals the sum of all contributions

$$G = g_1 + g_2 + \ldots + g_6.$$

Since the public good is nonrival and nonexcludable, everybody benefits equally. Suppose that each player receives a benefit per unit of the public good equal to $b > 0$; in the typical experiment, $b = 0.3$, and we use this figure below. Thus, the utility of any player $i = 1, \ldots, 6$, net of the cost of contribution, g_i, and the benefit from the public good, $0.3G$, is given by

$$u_i = 20 - g_i + 0.3G;\ i = 1, \ldots, 6. \tag{3.6}$$

How much should each player contribute to the public good?

The once-played public goods game, described above, is a *static game of complete information*. The choice of an individual contribution $g_i \in [0, 20]$ is known as the strategy of player i, and the set of contribution choices of all players, $(g_1, g_2, \ldots, g_6)$, is known as the *strategy profile* of the game. Three examples of strategy profiles in this game are: $(0, 0, \ldots, 0)$, that is, everybody contributes 0; $(20, 20, \ldots, 20)$, that is, everybody contributes their entire endowment; and $(8, 0, 14, 16, 5, 18)$ where all players contribute different amounts. Let us use the concept of a *Nash equilibrium* to solve this game, which is described in more detail in Part IV of the book.[2]

A *strategy profile* $(g_1, g_2, \ldots, g_6)$ in the public goods game is a Nash equilibrium if, given the choices of all others, no player can improve their own utility by making a different choice. In other words, in a Nash equilibrium, each player is doing the best they can (in terms of maximizing their own utility), that is, playing a *best response*, given the choices of all others, even though all players make their choices simultaneously without observing what anyone else chooses. A Nash equilibrium may appear to some as intuitive and reasonable, and to others a circular concept. It continues to be the centerpiece of modern neoclassical game theory. However, there is a valid question of how players arrive at such a magical equilibrium outcome; whether experience or learning can aid in achieving this outcome; and, most importantly, whether it is supported by the empirical evidence. We examine the empirical evidence in Part IV of the book. The evidence is often unkind to the predictions of a Nash equilibrium, while the behavioral game theory models account for the evidence much better. There should be no presumption that human learning and experience will help achieve a Nash equilibrium.

One can show that the strategy profile $(0, 0, \ldots, 0)$ (hence, $G = 0$) is a Nash equilibrium. To see this, choose any player, say, for simplicity, player 1. Could player 1 improve utility, u_1, defined in (3.6), by changing her existing contribution, $g_1 = 0$, to any other contribution, *holding fixed the contributions of other players* at $g_2 = 0, g_3 = 0, \ldots, g_6 = 0$?

The answer is no. Suppose that player 1 contributes 1 extra token, so $g_1 = 1$ and $G = 1$. Using (3.6), this reduces the utility of player 1 because $-1 + 0.3 \times 1 = -0.7 < 0$; notice that this conclusion holds for any value $b < 1$ and not just $b = 0.3$. Hence, player 1 prefers $g_1 = 0$ to $g_1 = 1$. The same reasoning applies to any of the other players. For a Nash equilibrium, we needed to check that none of the six players has an incentive to deviate from zero contributions; and we have found this to be true. Thus, the choices $g_1 = 0, \ldots, g_6 = 0$ constitute a Nash equilibrium of this game. In effect, everybody prefers to be a *free-rider* and the utility of each player $i = 1, \ldots, 6$ equals their endowment, $u_i = 20$. In fact, this is the *unique* Nash equilibrium of this game; no other strategy profile satisfies the conditions for a Nash equilibrium.

The free-rider outcome is what Hardin (1968) referred to as the *tragedy of the commons*. The tragedy of the commons arises because each player creates a positive externality for all others by contributing. Yet, players do not take account of the beneficial effects of their contributions on others, that is, they "do not internalize the externality" caused to others. The consequence is they contribute "too little" relative to the socially optimal solution.

To find the *socially optimal solution*, consider a *benevolent social planner* whose objective is to maximize the sum of the utilities of all six players,

$$W = u_1 + u_2 + \ldots + u_6,$$

[2] This concept was proposed by the mathematician and Nobel Prize winner, John F. Nash; some readers might have seen the film *A Beautiful Mind* based on his life.

where the utility function of each player is given in (3.6). This objective function is also known as a *utilitarian social welfare function*. Substituting (3.6) in W, and using $G = g_1 + \ldots + g_6$, one can readily rewrite W as

$$W = 6 \times 20 - (g_1 + \ldots + g_6) + 6 \times 0.3 \times (g_1 + \ldots + g_6). \tag{3.7}$$

The social planner chooses the individual contributions $g_1, g_2, \ldots, g_6$, on behalf of the players, in order to maximize W. By adding utilities, the social planner *internalizes the positive externalities* caused by the actions of all players on others.

Free-riding is not socially optimal. To see this, suppose that the social planner starts from the Nash equilibrium strategy profile $(0, 0, \ldots, 0)$ and wishes to see if W can be improved by getting any player, say, player 1, to contribute one extra token. This increases G from 0 to 1. The total effect on social utility, W, in (3.7) is, $-1 + 6 \times 0.3 = 0.8 > 0$, which is positive. Proceeding in this iterative manner, the social planner will find that getting players to contribute additional tokens always improves the value of W. Hence, the socially optimal solution is for each player to contribute their entire endowment of 20 tokens, so that $G = 6 \times 20 = 120$. At the social optimum, the utility of any player $i = 1, \ldots 6$, u_i, can be found by substituting $g_i = 20$ and $G = 120$ in (3.6) to get $u_i = 36$, which is a large improvement over the utility, $u_i = 20$, in the privately optimal solution in a Nash equilibrium.

Given that the socially optimal solution is utility-improving, can we actually implement it in the absence of a social planner when players make voluntary choices? One possibility is that the government subsidizes the contribution of each player towards the public good at some subsidy rate $s > 0.7$ per unit of contribution. In the presence of subsidies, the utility function of player $i = 1, \ldots, 6$ in (3.6) becomes

$$u_i = 20 - g_i(1 - s) + 0.3 \times G. \tag{3.8}$$

The effective private cost of contributing one token towards the public good is now $(1 - s) < 1$, where $s > 0.7$. Let us now derive the Nash equilibrium strategy profile with subsidies. Let us begin from the Nash equilibrium strategy profile in the absence of subsidies, $(0, \ldots, 0)$. From (3.8), the change in the utility of player i from contributing one extra token is $-(1 - s) + 0.3 > 0$; this is positive because $s > 0.7$. The reader can check that this calculation holds for any strategy profile of contributions where all players have not yet contributed their entire endowments. Hence, in the presence of subsidies, each player finds it optimal to contribute their full endowment of 20 tokens towards the public good, as in the socially optimal solution. Essentially, the subsidy, s, allows players to internalize the positive externality that they cause for others. This is the essence of Pigouvian taxes, and in fact any $s > 0.7$ is an effective Pigouvian subsidy.

One drawback of corrective subsidies is that they rely on tax revenues raised elsewhere, which might create tax distortions elsewhere. For instance, if these tax revenues are raised by taxing labor incomes, then the suppliers of labor might partly switch from labor to leisure, reducing their labor supply – optimal policy would then need to calculate the cost of this distortion.

The Nobel prize winner Roland Coase showed that one can obtain the socially optimal solution simply by assigning property rights to one of the affected parties, provided that there are no transaction costs of bargaining between the parties. However, *bargaining impasse* is a common problem in real life bargaining problems (e.g., protracted strikes, costly divorces, difficulty of global agreements on climate change), so the "no transaction costs" assumption is unlikely to be met in practice.[3] Bowles (2004) terms solutions based on the Coasean method as *utopian capitalism*.

An alternative approach is to allow individuals to design their own rules in providing public goods, or equivalently, preventing exploitation of public goods, such as a common resource. This problem has been repeatedly solved in human history with much success. The Nobel Prize winner Eleanor Ostrom (1990, 1999) conducted pathbreaking work on the voluntary management of commons. This work shows that there is a wide range of private institutional arrangements, depending on cultures and communities, that have been used to restrict access to the commons and prevent its overuse.

An essential component of many voluntary institutional rules governing access to the commons is to form *social norms* around its usage. Social norms are often enforced through sanctions of norm violators. These sanctions may be carried out by those directly affected, or even by third parties that are not directly affected, a phenomenon known as *altruistic punishments*. Some of these insights have been used in experiments on public goods provision.

In a seminal contribution to this literature, Fehr and Gächter (2000) played the public goods game, outlined above, repeatedly over 20 different rounds. At the end of each round, players observe the contributions of others before choosing their own contributions in the next round. The first 10 rounds include a *punishment option*, that is, after observing the contributions of others at the end of each round, players can engage in costly punishment of others. For every token that a punisher gives up to punish a target player, the target player loses three tokens. For instance, contributors might wish to punish non-contributors, which is known as *prosocial punishment*. However, in the remaining rounds, 11–20, no punishment is allowed.

In the model with self-regarding preferences, the punishment option should have no bearing on contributions. The proof is along the same lines as sketched out for the gift exchange game in Section 3.3. The intuition is that at the time of punishment, all contributions and, hence, the level of public goods production, G, have already been determined. Bearing the extra costs of punishments would reduce a player's utility without any concurrent material benefits, hence, it is best to let *bygones be bygones*. When making the contributions decision, rational players should then be able to look forward and correctly guess that they will never be punished for making low contributions. This makes the punishment stage redundant, giving rise, once again, to zero contributions.

The findings of experiments in Fehr and Gächter (2000) are shown in Figure 3.5, which plots average contributions in each round, over 20 rounds. There are three treatments. In the "Partner treatment," the six players are matched at the beginning of round one and stay matched over the 20 rounds. In the "Stranger treatment," at the beginning of each round, players are randomly rematched from the pool of players attending the experiment. The "Perfect Stranger" treatment refines the "Stranger treatment" by preventing previously matched players to be matched again. Hence, we do not have complete data for this treatment as everybody got matched at least once

[3] For more discussion on bargaining problems, see Part IV of the book.

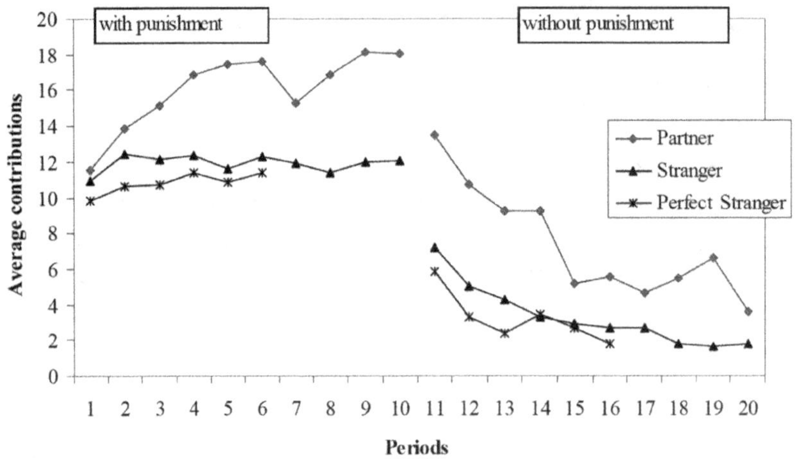

Figure 3.5 Pattern of public goods contributions over 20 rounds with and without punishments, in three different treatments. Source: Fehr and Gächter (1999)

in the first six rounds. Remember that the Nash equilibrium strategy profile is $(0,0,\ldots,0)$ and the socially optimal solution is $(20,20,\ldots,20)$.

When the punishment option is allowed (rounds 1–10) the "Partner treatment" achieves close to the socially optimal level of contributions by round 10. The other two treatments achieve about half of the socially optimal level of contributions. Thus, being paired together for a longer interval improves contributions relative to the other two cases, perhaps because it gives players a chance to develop a reputation and also a level of trust with players in the group inducing them to contribute more. However, as soon as the punishment option is removed (rounds 11–20), average contributions drop over successive rounds in all treatments to levels that are just above zero. This finding does not vindicate the neoclassical prediction of zero contributions. Rather, we need to explain the pattern of decay of contributions in rounds 11–20. The answer is provided by *conditional reciprocity*. Over rounds 11–20, contributors who observe others who do not contribute enough, perceive this as an unkind action, and react by reducing their own contributions in order to respond with unkindness. This elicits further rounds of negative reaction and counter-reaction from others, leading to a downward spiral in contributions. One of the exercises at the end of the chapter formalizes this intuition.

In rounds 1–10, we observe that high contributors punish low contributors at the end of each round. Low contributors typically respond by increasing their contributions in the next round. This virtuous cycle continues to build until contributions reach high levels. Thus, punishments are effective in inducing high contribution. But why do punishments occur in the first place? Should not *bygones be bygones*? This puzzle was resolved by findings from *neuroeconomics* – the application of neuroscience to economics. The idea here is to study brain activity when individuals make decisions, and then infer from existing neuroscience research the implications of such brain activity to explain as well as to predict. For instance, when punishing low contributors, an area of the brain, the dorsal striatum, associated with the brain's reward circuits, shows intense activity among high contributors. Put simply, the very act of punishing low contributors gives hedonic pleasure to those who punish. Revenge may be sweet after all. Since revenge is typically not incorporated in economic models, several models struggle to explain this empirical finding.

This particular example underlines the point made in the introduction that economics needs to be open to all sources of data – lab, field, and neuroeconomic data. There has been opposition to neuroeconomic data from some quarters in economics on the grounds that economic models make no assumptions on the workings of the brain. Ever since Colin Camerer wrote the provocatively titled article "Neuroeconomics: Do Economists Need Brains?" in 2004, opposition has waned, perhaps not causally. Neuroeconomics has confirmed several essential features of behavioral economics, including those in the area of decision theory in Chapter 2 (e.g., loss aversion, reference dependence, and nonlinear probability weighting). Importantly it can be used for prediction as well. The online chapter offers a detailed discussion of neuroeconomics.

There is a rich literature on the experimental evidence from public goods games; see Camerer (2003), and Dhami (2019, Vol. 2). Here is a subset of the key findings, developed through a series of examples.

Example 3.1 *Is the cost of punishment from punishing low contributors compensated by higher contributions from the low contributors? In other words, on net, are punishments beneficial in the sense that they improve the earnings of subjects? One would hypothesize that when the public goods game with the punishment option is played often, a norm of high contributions develops, so that very little actual punishment is required to ensure high contributions. Thus, the punishment option may be expected to be efficiency enhancing if the game is played for a sufficiently long period.*

This was demonstrated in the experiments by Gächter et al. (2008) who used a 2 × 2 design. Along one dimension, they varied the number of rounds over which the public goods game was played – either 10 rounds or 50 rounds. Along the second dimension, they varied the possibility of punishment – either no punishment (N) or punishment (P). The results are shown in Figure 3.6,

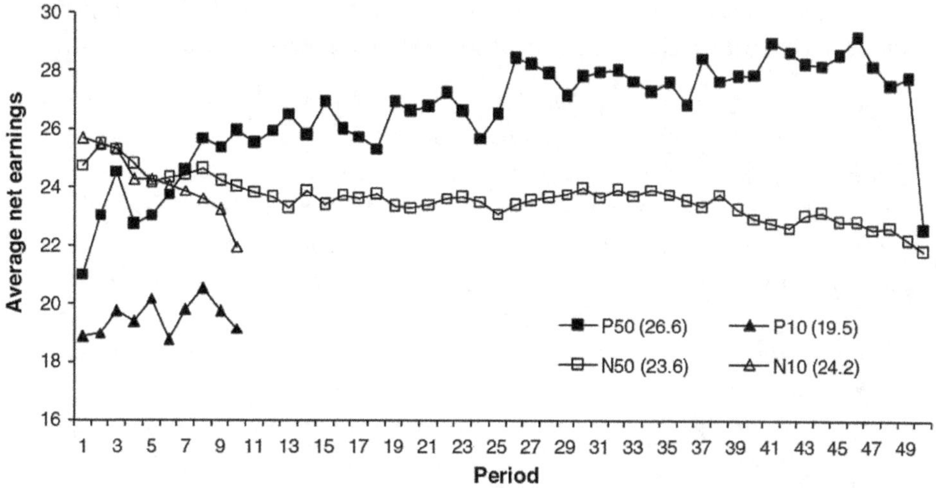

Figure 3.6 Average net earnings in four different treatments: 10N, 10P, 50N, 50P. Source: Gächter et al. (2008)

which plots average net earnings in the four different treatments: 10N, 10P, 50N, 50P. When the game is played over 10 rounds, average net earnings are higher in the absence of punishment, that is, in the treatment 10N rather than in the treatment 10P; punishments are effective for public goods provision but they are too costly, reducing average net earnings. However, when the game was played over 50 rounds, this conclusion flips. Now average earnings are relatively higher in the treatment 50P that allows for punishments, as compared to the treatment 50N, which does not. Contributions converged and stabilized at a high level, in response to the punishments in the previous rounds, and one observed very little punishment towards the final rounds.

Example 3.2 *Nonmonetary punishments are also very effective. Indeed, traditionally, one of the most effective and severe punishments was ostracization from the group. In small hunter-gatherer societies with a hostile external environment, it was often difficult to survive in isolation. Nonmonetary punishment in the form of social approval or disapproval by other group members is efficacious (Masclet et al., 2003; Dugar, 2013; Dhami et al., 2022), as is expulsion of low contributors from a group based on a majority vote (Cinyabuguma et al., 2005). From other social dilemma games, such as the prisoner's dilemma game, we know that when the methods of punishments are chosen democratically, they are more efficacious (Dal Bó et al., 2010).*

Example 3.3 *High-contributors often cooperate more with like-minded partners who have a higher propensity to contribute. Gächter and Thöni (2005) first conduct an initial round of a public goods game and then match players to play subsequent rounds of the public goods game, based on their initial level of contributions. The top three contributions in the initial round are grouped together, then the next three, and so on. For the top group with the highest initial contributions, the contributions in subsequent rounds of play are close to the socially optimal contributions, even in the absence of a punishment option. In the experiments, players know that they are grouped with like-minded players. This links nicely to the concept of "evidential reasoning" that we explore in Part IV. When players are matched with other like-minded players, they assign diagnostic significance to their own actions in forming beliefs about the actions of other players. Hence, high contributors, since they are predisposed to making high contributions, expect other like-minded players to contribute a high amount as well, which increases their own incentive to contribute.*

Example 3.4 *Bochet et al. (2006) allow players in public goods games to send messages through several methods. These messages include face-to-face communication; chat room communication where messages can be sent only over computer terminals in a lab; and messages that only convey the number of units of contributions that one intends to make. Of these three methods, face-to-face communication is the most effective and achieves nearly 96% of the contribution levels of the socially optimal solution. The effectiveness of face-to-face communication prior to the experiment suggests that players might feel "guilty" from breaking their promise. A proper analysis of guilt requires an explicit modeling of the beliefs of the players and an explication of the machinery of psychological game theory; for details, see Part IV of the book. Dhami et al. (2019) use this machinery to test for the presence of guilt-aversion in public goods games and find that when this channel is activated, it achieves close to the socially optimal solution. Players contribute more in this case because they feel guilty if their contributions fell below the expectations of others, when the expectations are conveyed to them.*

Example 3.5 *When there is a mixture of self-regarding and other-regarding subjects, then there are interesting dynamics (Fischbacher et al., 2001). It can be shown that even when there is a majority of other-regarding subjects, the presence of a small minority of self-regarding subjects (say, about 30%) can cause contributions to unravel to very low levels. The reason is that other-regarding subjects, who are conditionally reciprocal, react to the free-riding behavior of self-regarding subjects to hit back by free-riding themselves. This starts a downward spiral in contributions. We formalize this intuition in one of the exercises.*

Example 3.6 *Gürerk et al. (2006) give subjects a choice of two alternative institutions in a public goods game. Individuals can either choose to join a group where sanctions are allowed, sanctioning institution (SI), or a group where sanctions are not allowed, sanctioning-free institution (SFI). Subjects play this game over 30 rounds. At the end of each round, they can observe the payoffs of players under each institutional choice, and then they are allowed to self-select themselves into any of the two institutions, SI or SFI, in the next round. The results are shown in Figure 3.7. In the first round, the majority of the subjects, 63.1%, choose the SFI. However, over time, free-riding becomes prevalent in the SFI and payoffs are significantly lower relative to the SI where many subjects punish noncontributors, allowing for a norm of high contributions to gradually develop over time. As players observe higher payoffs in the SI, they gradually self-select themselves into it and the share of SI grows over time, at the expense of the SFI. Contributions converge to near zero in the SFI and close to the socially optimal levels in the SI. By round 19, contributions in the SI are 97% of the socially optimal level and after round 16, more than 90% of the subjects choose the SI. Subjects who switch institutions from SFI to SI, immediately increase contributions to relatively high levels, even if they were making low contributions in the SFI. This endogenous*

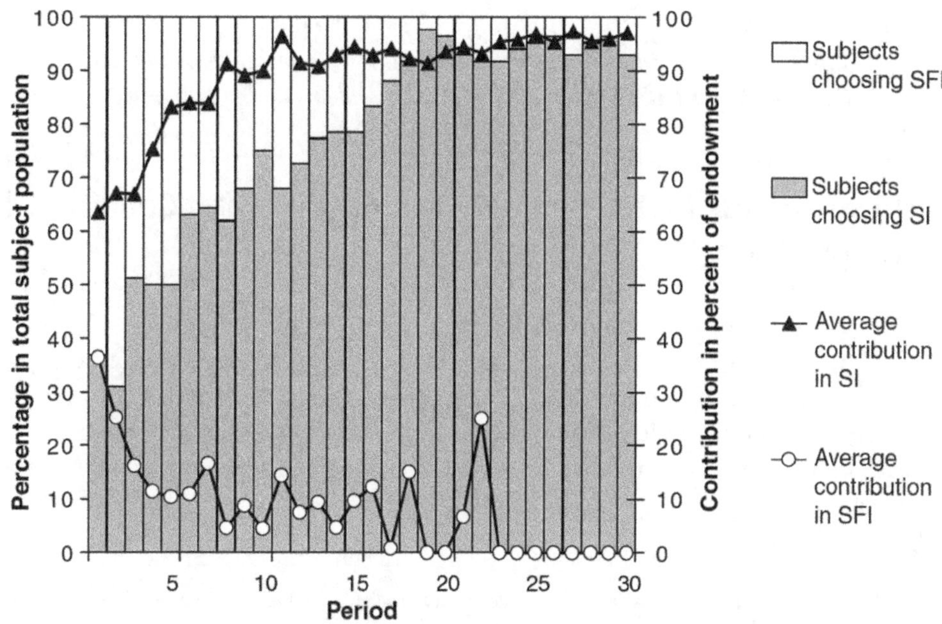

Figure 3.7 Voluntary choice of contributions and institutions. Source: Gürerk et al. (2006)

preference for SI over SFI mirrors how institutions and sanctions may have evolved naturally over human evolutionary history.

Example 3.7 *The typical lab experiment on public goods provides a simplified environment within which to analyze the salient features of human cooperation. Real world problems can often be more complicated. Consider, for instance, the problem of mitigating the effects of climate change. A clean environment is a public good and poses issues similar to the problem of the commons. Individual countries can choose free-riding and deplete the commons (the clean air) without internalizing the negative externalities caused for other countries. One multilateral response has been to try to reach global climate agreements. Examples include the Kyoto Protocol, 1997, and the Paris Agreement, 2005.*

These multilateral agreements have had limited success and it is difficult to assign specific targets for countries. A situation of strategic bargaining between countries develops and it is challenging to reach a successful agreement. Different countries might conflate between what is in their self-interest and what is a fair outcome, leading to a "self-serving bias in bargaining" that we discuss in Part IV of the book. Multilateral negotiations also have a high degree of complexity, and the politics behind the negotiations, as well as the probabilistic nature of the outcomes, impose further layers of complexity. In actual practice, the agreements typically break down, promises are not kept, often the treaty is not ratified, and countries resort to self-serving individual targets, say, to limit carbon emissions, rather than accept the targets set by an international agency.

Schmidt and Ockenfels (2021) conduct some of the first formal experiments in this direction. They introduce different treatments that look something like the Kyoto Protocol and the Paris Agreement, as well as a third treatment, uniform carbon pricing, that imposes an identical price-based rule on all the countries. They find that uniform carbon pricing provides a focal point in the form of an easy to understand number and enhances cooperation between experimental subjects who play the role of countries. It provides a superior outcome relative to Kyoto and Paris style negotiations. This is an intriguing result and calls for more theory and empirical analysis along these lines to address one of the most important problems facing humanity.

3.6 A Note on the Distinction between Altruism and Conditional Reciprocity

Altruism is defined as *unconditional kindness*.[4] Consider two players, $i = 1, 2$. Player 1 is altruistic to player 2 if player 1 derives utility from the well-being of player 2, irrespective of the actions chosen by player 2. In other words, if the monetary outcomes received by the two players are x_1 and x_2, then the utility of player 1, $u_1(x_1, x_2)$, is increasing not only in x_1, but also in x_2, irrespective of the actions taken by player 2. The requirements of unconditional kindness may be hard to satisfy for most people.

[4] This note developed out of my response to queries from Mehar Chauhan who in her first-year psychology and neuroscience course was grappling with the differences between these concepts. I am grateful to her for raising these queries with me.

The empirical evidence from the experimental games in Sections 3.2 to 3.5 suggests that people are conditional cooperators, which is more general than the concept of altruism. Conditional cooperators satisfy the first two of the following conditions.

1. They respond to the perceived kindness of others with kind behavior, and the perceived unkindness of others with unkind behavior.
2. Their initial instinct, say, in social dilemma situations, is to cooperate with the other players. If, in addition, we add the next condition, then conditional reciprocators are also known as *strong reciprocators*.
3. When they are a third party to a social or economic exchange, they are willing to punish those who engage in noncooperative behavior, or those who violate social or moral norms, even if this punishment does not give private material benefits to them, and is costly.

Note that there are alternative definitions of strong reciprocators in the literature, but we use it in the sense defined above.

These requirements are nicely captured in the definition of *strong reciprocators* in Gintis (2009, p. 48), which also explains several related terms:

> One salient behavior in social dilemmas revealed by behavioral game theory is strong reciprocity. Strong reciprocators come to a social dilemma with a propensity to cooperate (altruistic cooperation), respond to cooperative behavior by maintaining or increasing their level of cooperation, and respond to non-cooperative behavior by punishing the "offenders," even at a cost to themselves and even when they cannot reasonably expect future personal gains to flow therefrom (altruistic punishment). When other forms of punishment are not available, the strong reciprocator responds to defection with defection ... The strong reciprocator is thus neither the selfless altruist of utopian theory, nor the self-regarding individual of traditional economics.

We use the terms conditional reciprocators and strong reciprocators (also conditional reciprocity and strong reciprocity) interchangeably in this chapter. The predictions of models based on conditional reciprocity may differ from models based on inequity aversion (see Section 4.2.1 below), but in other contexts it is difficult to distinguish between the two. In particular, unlike inequity aversion, conditional reciprocity does not assign utility gains or losses to payoff differences with other players. However, payoff differences are often caused by the actions of others that may reveal a kind or an unkind intention. For instance noncontributors in public goods games may reveal through their contributions decisions that they are unkind. Conditionally reciprocal contributors may then punish noncontributors if they get a chance (e.g., in public goods games with punishments). However, inequity averse contributors might wish to do exactly the same because they find that their payoffs are lower than those of noncontributors.

Consider the following two examples.

Example 3.8 *John is terribly late for his flight and must rush to the departure gate, this very instant, if he is to catch the flight. Any delay, and he will miss the flight in this touch and go situation. However, he spots someone on a chair who is clutching his heart. John stops instead to alert the airport authorities, but misses his flight in the process. Can we conclude that John is altruistic and* *conditional reciprocity is a needless complication in understanding human behavior? Certainly not, as we argue below.*

Suppose that in a parallel universe, John is in a rush to catch his flight. But before entering the airport, he collides with another man (let us call him Mr. X) who is also in a rush. Mr X turns abusive, and when John protests, Mr. X uses foul language, threatens to punch John, and challenges him to a one-on-one fight. John quietly walks away, mindful of his flight departure time. Mr. X checks in before John and is already sitting on a chair, waiting for his flight. John checks in after, and while rushing to his flight, spots Mr. X clutching his heart. However, John does not stop this time and proceeds to his flight, boarding it just in time.

In this parallel universe, John is not altruistic. He views the behavior of Mr. X outside the airport as unkind, and feels no need to be kind to him when he appears in a spot of bother. The problem with concluding altruism from John's behavior in the first case, which causes him to miss the flight, is that there was no history between the two men that would allow John to infer any intentions on the part of Mr. X. John might simply have been following sound internal moral norms, or personally held standards of behavior, that specify the following injunction: "Help other 'good people' during health emergencies, even at a cost to yourself."

Example 3.9 *Jane rushes into a burning apartment building, risking her own life, in order to save her child. Can we not conclude, therefore, that Jane is altruistic? Not necessarily. Jane might not be kind to other people who are unkind to her, and her hardwired maternal instinct was probably responsible for her earlier behavior. In a distant future, where the child who was saved, turns into an adult, and commits an unspeakably violent act, Jane publicly disowns the child, never to speak to him again. Jane cannot bear to be unconditionally kind (altruistic) to her adult child.*

3.7 Social Sanctions in WEIRD and Non-WEIRD Societies

WEIRD is an acronym for *western, educated, industrialized, rich, democratic* societies, which includes mainly Western and American societies. Many social scientists, most prominently Joseph Henrich, have argued that the culture and social psychology of WEIRD and non-WEIRD societies is very different. Recently Henrich (2020) has traced the origins of this difference to the role of the Christian church since the middle ages, particularly its promulgations against cousin marriage. His thesis is that this destroyed the close kinship network in clan based societies, circa 1000AD to 1500AD. In looking for marriage partners beyond their immediate kinship network and clans, members of Western societies increasingly opened up to strangers. This required the development of trust and social dynamism that fueled invention, patience, meritocracy, and representative democracy. By contrast, non-WEIRD societies continued to rely on close kinship networks, a strong sense of local community, and stayed more closed to outsiders, missing out on the social dynamism occurring in the West.

The body of empirical evidence on which behavioral economics typically relies, comes mainly from WEIRD societies. Since the majority of the world's population lives in non-WEIRD societies, it becomes important to engage in a comparative analysis with the existing findings

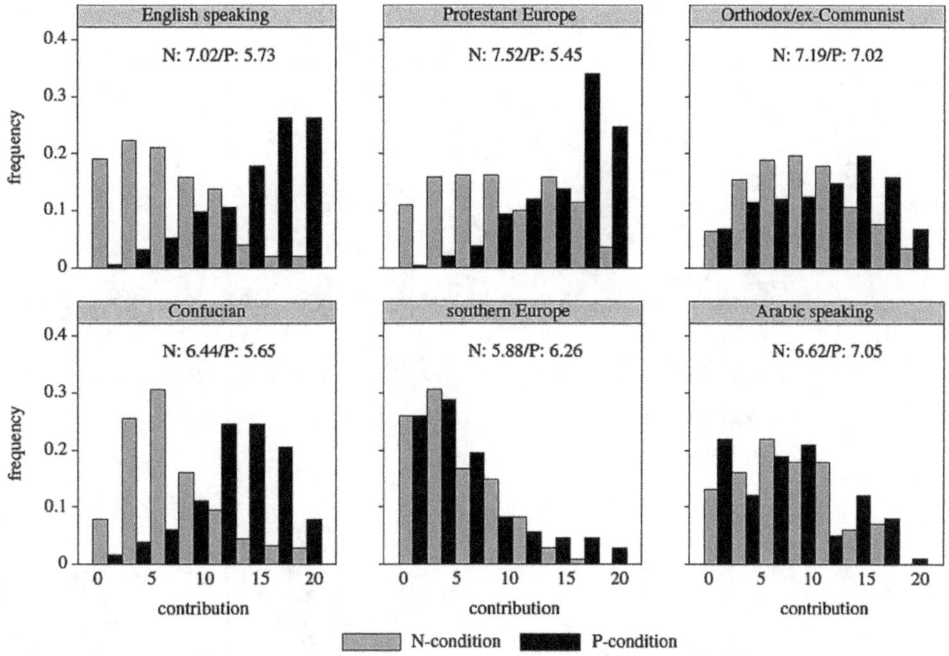

Figure 3.8 Histograms of culture-specific average contributions in the no punishment condition (N-condition) and the punishment condition (P-condition). Source: Gächter et al. (2010)

in non-WEIRD societies. We are currently only fitting the basic pieces of this jigsaw and much remains to be done. In Section 3.2, we have already noted the variation in results from ultimatum game experiments across cultures. Another important piece of evidence comes from behavior in public goods games that we consider below.

Recall that in the public goods game with the punishment option, the evidence reported in Section 3.5 (all from WEIRD societies) is that players mainly, although not exclusively, engage in *pro-social punishments* (i.e., high-contributors punish low-contributors). When conducted in non-WEIRD societies, the opposite pattern of *anti-social punishments* is often found, that is, low contributors may punish high contributors in revenge for being punished in the past. As one might expect, this has a detrimental effect on public goods contributions – the sanctioning role of punishments in sustaining high contributions is lost.

In Figure 3.8, we plot histograms of average contributions in public goods experiments conducted in six different cultures when the punishment option is present (P-condition) and when it is absent (N-condition). Average contributions in the P-condition are (1) high in the English speaking, Protestant-European, and Confucian cultures, but (2) much lower in the Orthodox Christian/Ex-communist societies, Southern European societies, and in Arabic-speaking countries. These results are highly correlated with prosocial punishments in societies with high contributions and antisocial punishment in societies with low contributions. This point is illustrated separately in Figure 3.9. Antisocial punishments, shown in the darker histograms, are lowest in the English speaking, Protestant-European and Confucian cultures.

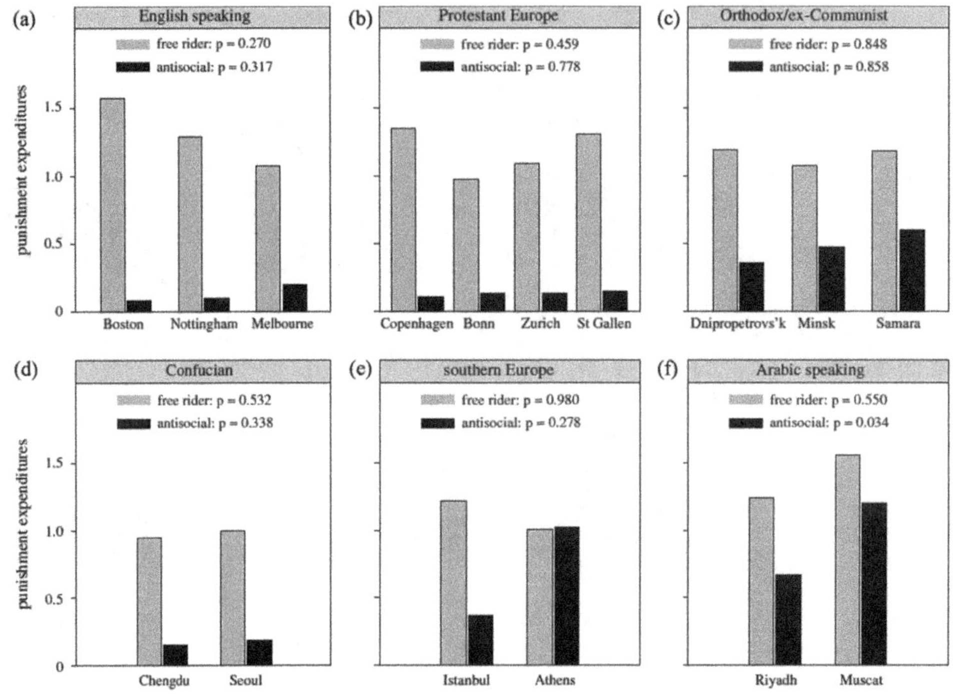

Figure 3.9 Histograms of the frequency of prosocial and antisocial culture-specific punishments. Source: Gächter et al. (2010)

3.8 "Out of Africa" and the Evolutionary Origins of Preferences

There is significant inter-country and intra-country variation in several types of preferences, such as risk preferences, social preferences, and time preferences; and these preferences explain a great deal of human behavior (Falk et al., 2018; Dohmen et al., 2022). Indeed, these preferences are the subject matter of the first three parts of this book. What accounts for this variation, or heterogeneity, in preferences?

A leading explanation is in terms of the "Out of Africa" theory. Namely, that homo-sapiens originated in Africa and then spread across the world through successive migration of breakaway subgroups. Typically, once a population had migrated to an area, and grown in size, a subgroup of that parent population would begin a new migration, restarting the process once again, and continuing over many successive subgroups. Two factors are likely to have played an important role in determining differences in preferences between successive subgroups that settled in different locations.

1. Location-specific evolutionary selection processes may create differences in preferences. For instance, locations where food was scarce might, over time, self-select those individuals who have a proclivity for sharing food (prosocial preferences) in order to survive, and possibly greater risk aversion too.

2. Historical experiences, such as wars and famines, might also influence risk and social preferences. Human preferences are malleable and transmitted across generations giving rise to long-lasting environmental influences on preferences (Fehr and Hoff, 2011; Dohmen et al., 2012)

In an interesting study, Becker et al. (2020) try to quantify some of these ideas. They use the public data set in Falk et al. (2018), which constructs individual-specific measures of risk aversion, patience, negative reciprocity, altruism, positive reciprocity, and trust, for 80,000 individuals in 76 countries.

Becker et al. (2020) then construct proxies for the "genetic distance" between subgroups of populations. For any two populations, the genetic distance is the length of time since the two populations shared a set of common ancestors who lived in one place. When a subgroup separates from the parent population, "genetic drift" leads to an increase in the genetic distance between the parent population and the subgroup. These genetic differences may manifest in, for instance, skin color, hair color, eye color, average height, average weight, and blood types. The authors also employ linguistic differences between subgroups, which also proxy for the elapsed time since subgroups separated from their parent groups. The genetic and linguistic measures are combined into a measure of the "ancestral distance" between populations.

With these two separate data sets, one on preferences, and the other on ancestral distance between populations, we can now answer some of the questions posed above. The authors first run regressions that compare each pair of countries, sometimes known as dyadic regressions, in their list of 76 countries. This gives them 2,850 pairs of countries. A typical dyadic regression that regresses differences in average preferences between country i and country j, on the ancestral difference between the countries, may be written as follows.

$$\left|p_i - p_j\right| = a_0 + a_1 d_{ij} + a_2 f_i + a_3 f_j + \varepsilon_{ij},$$

where p_i, p_j are, respectively, the average preferences in countries i and j, say, altruism, trust, or positive reciprocity. Thus, the independent variable, $\left|p_i - p_j\right|$, is the absolute value of the difference in the average preferences between the two countries. On the RHS, $a_0, \ldots, a_3$ are the regression coefficients; d_{ij} measures ancestral distance between the two countries; f_i, f_j are country-specific fixed effects; and ε_{ij} is a random term that is specific to this pair of countries. We are mainly interested in the regression coefficient a_1, which quantifies the extent to which ancestral distance determines average preference differences.

The estimates show that a one standard deviation increase in ancestral distance causes an increase of 22% of 1 standard deviation in differences in preferences. The coefficient a_1 is the highest when we consider risk preferences and prosociality; that is, ancestral distance most strongly determines the differences in these preferences. The coefficients for negative reciprocity and patience are positive, but their magnitudes are relatively small and their statistical significance is marginal.

Similar regressions can also be run to analyze preferences within countries. The authors study pairs of immigrant subjects in countries whose preference differences are now the dependent variable in a regression. They control for country fixed effects in the parent country from where the subjects migrated and the host country. Similar results to those for differences in preferences in pairs of countries are found. Ancestral distance is, thus, an important determinant of preference differences.

3.9 Social Identity

Humans typically feel a sense of belonging to some *social identity* or *social category*, for instance, Protestant or Catholic, Democrat or Republican, African-American or Asian-American, and black or white. Within each social category, there are shared norms of behavior and shared beliefs, possibly enforced by sanctions, or a desire to conform, which partition members of society into those inside that category (*ingroup members*) and those outside (*outgroup members*). It is possible for an individual to hold many overlapping identities. For instance, one may live in Edinburgh, but support the Manchester United football team, yet in the football World Cup, support Scotland if they play against England. Different contexts may trigger different identities, for instance, a family identity, a regional identity, or a national identity.

The study of differences in individual behavior towards ingroup and outgroup members is the subject matter of *social identity theory*. Most people favor ingroups over outgroups in matters of prosociality, trust, cooperation, and coordination. On the flip side, this can also lead to favoritism towards ingroups, and nepotism, prejudice, and long-lasting stereotypes towards outgroups. Thus, social identity has both beneficial and harmful effects. Henri Tajfel, a Polish Jew, one of the founders of this approach, lost family members in the Holocaust and switched from the study of chemistry to social psychology in order to contribute towards laying the foundations of the nature of human prejudice.

There are evolutionary reasons for favoring ingroups over outgroups. Over most of their evolutionary history, humans evolved in small hunter-gatherer societies where intergroup conflict was common. Successful groups required group members to be highly cooperative and prosocial towards each other and be willing to repel outsiders, including invaders, even at the cost of their lives. This possibly led to the evolutionary and cultural development of social identity. Another contributory factor, arising from low geographical mobility, is that in such societies, individuals interacted almost exclusively with other ingroup members, hence, they worried more about developing a good reputation with them than with outsiders.

Romano et al. (2021) conduct a variant of the *prisoner's dilemma game* (see Part IV of the book) in a set of 42 diverse countries with 18,411 observations. Two players are matched and each is given 10 tokens (a unit of experimental currency). Both must simultaneously choose to send any amount between 0–10 tokens to the other player, which is doubled by the experimenter. Each player makes the decision without knowing the other's choice. The highest material payoff for each player occurs if both simultaneously send 10 tokens, so that each receives 20 tokens. When matched with ingroup members from the same country, players sent relatively higher amounts as compared to outgroup members from other countries. The extent of discrimination towards outgroup members, which the authors term as *national parochialism*, is similar across all countries and, surprisingly, not influenced by culture, institutions, and income levels. However, the degree of cooperation towards ingroup members varies by country. Some of the factors conducive to greater cooperation were greater historical exposure to western churches; more egalitarian values; informal and tolerant social norms; and, individualistic and self-expression values.

There is a rich body of evidence on social identity in behavioral economics. Even a *minimum group identity*, for example, labeling subjects as belonging to "blue" and "green" groups, is sufficient for group members in experiments to discriminate against outgroup members and in favor of ingroup members. There is also robust evidence that priming individuals for their social identity enhances ingroup/outgroup discrimination. For a survey see Dhami (2019, Vol. II), but below we give several examples.

Example 3.10 *In an insightful design, Eckel and Petrie (2011) introduce the possibility that subjects playing a trust game (see Section 3.8 above) can view photographs of the partners they are matched with. Subjects can voluntarily buy a picture of their partner at a price set by the experimenter. As the price increases, the demand for photographs falls, so there is a well-defined demand curve for photographs. Many players do wish to know the identity of their partners before they make decisions. For instance, at the lowest price of $0.20, 50% of the players wish to buy the partner's photograph. Trustors are more keen to buy photographs of their partners as compared to trustees, because their choice determines the social surplus in a trust game.*

Conditional on having seen a photograph of their partner, white trustors discriminate favorably towards other white trustees, although black trustors do not discriminate between white and black trustees. The authors conjecture that this is perhaps because many of the role models for blacks growing up (e.g., teachers, doctors) are white. However, white trustors generally exhibit higher average trust levels than black trustors. In their role as trustees, both white and black trustees send higher amounts to trustors of the same ethnicity. Thus, the informational value of a face is non-zero.

Example 3.11 *Dhami et al. (2021) play the ultimatum game (see Section 3.2 above) with registered political party members of five main British political parties (Labor, Conservative, Liberal Democrat, Green, UKIP). They find significant ingroup-outgroup effects at the level of political parties, and generally left party proposers transferred less money to right party responders. Responders are also less likely to accept low offers from outgroup proposers as compared to ingroup proposers. When the income of the proposer is taxed and the proceeds redistributed to the poorer of the two, then the typical offer by the proposer falls and the typical minimum acceptable offer of the responder also falls by a roughly similar amount. This suggests that there is a "shared understanding" of the reduction in prosociality of the proposer in the presence of redistributive taxes.*

Example 3.12 *In a study of Ashkenazi and Eastern Jews in Israel, Fershtman and Gneezy (2001) find that both Ashkenazi and Eastern Jew trustors exhibited lower trust when the trustee was an Eastern Jew, that is, lower amounts were invested in Eastern Jew subjects. The observed behavior of Ashkenazi Jews could either be due to "taste-based discrimination" (say, inherent dislike for Eastern Jews) or "statistical discrimination" (Eastern Jews statistically return lower amounts in general, i.e., they are less trustworthy). In order to distinguish between these two kinds of discrimination, the authors play the same trust game, but with the second stage missing, so the trustor has no decision to make. Hence, this effectively becomes the dictator game. In this game, Ashkenazi and Eastern Jew dictators do not send significantly different amounts to Ashkenazi and Eastern Jew receivers, thus, ruling out taste-based discrimination. Hence, the authors conclude that* *the social identity effects in the trust game are picking out statistical discrimination only. Both Ashkenazi and Eastern Jew trustors predict, correctly, that Eastern Jew trustors will return a lower amount, so they trust less.*

Example 3.13 *Social identities can be consciously changed. Akerlof and Kranton (2005) describe how the military changes the identity of new recruits from a civilian identity to a military identity by minimizing the role of self-regarding preferences, and stressing injunctive norms to put "country before self" and the team before self; and stressing the need for a high degree of obedience to authority. On p. 9, they describe the following initiation at the US West Point military academy, which does not make any apparent sense when viewed from any known principles in economics.*

> *On plebes' first day ... they strip down to their underwear. Their hair is cut off. They are put in uniform. They then must address an older cadet, with the proper salute ... must stand and salute and repeat, and stand and salute and repeat, until they get it exactly right, all the while being reprimanded for every tiny mistake.*

Yet, this ritual, repeated every year, is used to make plebes feel a part of the ingroup, and different from the outgroup. Corporate cultures also often try to change the social identity of new employees in a variety of ways, for instance, by using a particular dress or a dress code, or by stressing corporate-specific goals, or by referring to members of the corporation as a "family."

Example 3.14 *We have noted above that a minimum group (MG) identity is sufficient to induce subjects in experiments to engage in ingroup/outgroup discrimination, say, based on blue and green groups. By contrast, in the real world, subjects belong to real social groups (SG), such as blacks or whites. What is the difference in ingroup-outgroup discrimination between groups who have a MG identity and those who have a SG identity? In order to explore this question, Goette et al. (2012) use Swiss Army recruits. Within the set of army recruits, the cadets are assigned to platoons of 21 members and membership of a platoon may be taken as one's SG identity; members of the same platoon is the ingroup while members of other platoons is the outgroup. Candidates for the MG identity are army cadets who are matched based on their social security numbers but do not know if their partner is of the same platoon or not.*

A modified version of the prisoner's dilemma game is played with the subjects. Each player has 10 tokens and players simultaneously choose to send any number of tokens between 0 and 10 to the matched partner. The experimenter doubles the amount sent, hence, the highest material payoffs for both players arise when they send all 10 tokens to the other player and each receives 20 tokens at the end of the game. The cooperation rate is taken to be the number of tokens sent by the players as a fraction of the total endowment of 20 tokens. The results are shown in Figure 3.10. In both MG and SG groups, there is significant ingroup-outgroup discrimination. However, SG groups discriminate even more. The cooperation rate is 65% when averaged across both groups. However, the difference in cooperation rates when the partner is an ingroup member as compared to an outgroup member is 10% for the MG group and 20% for the SG group. The actions of the players are consistent with their beliefs. Players expect that ingroup members will cooperate more with them relative to outgroup members.

The authors also look into altruistic third party punishment whereby a third party is given the opportunity to punish players based on their observed cooperation rates. In the SG group, low levels of cooperation with ingroup members are punished more by third parties, relative to low levels of

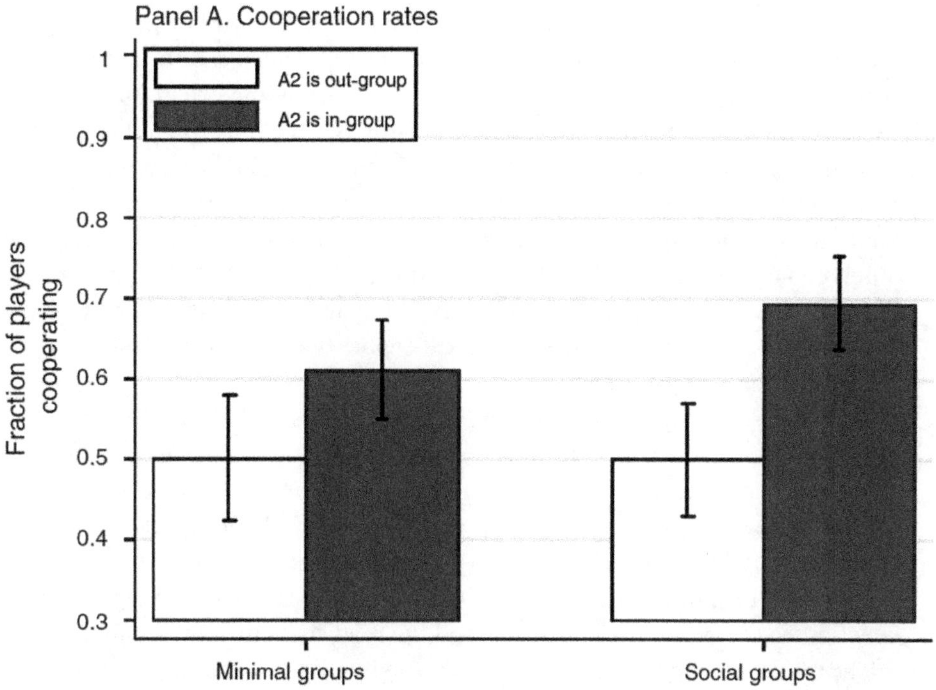

Figure 3.10 Cooperation rates for MG identity and SG identity for Swiss army cadets. Source: Goette et al. (2012)

cooperation with outgroup members. However, this effect is not found for MG groups where the third parties do not punish low cooperation rates towards ingroup members relative to outgroup members.

Example 3.15 *In a simple, but clever, field experiment, Bertrand and Mullainathan (2004) sent 5,000 fictitious applications for 1,300 job-wanted ads in Boston and Chicago newspapers. All applications were identical, but on half the applications they used white sounding names (e.g., Emily, Greg) and on the other half they used African-American-sounding names (e.g., Lakisha Washington, Jamal Jones). The applications with white-sounding names received* 50% *more call-backs for interviews. This suggests taste-based discrimination, unless it can be shown that statistically African-Americans are somehow less productive on the same jobs (see statistical discrimination, above), but there is no evidence for this.*

The interested reader can pursue a more wide-ranging survey of the evidence on social identity and economic behavior in Charness and Chen (2020).

3.10 Human Virtues, Morality, and Ethics

Homo-economicus is amoral, devoid of ethical considerations, and has no compunction in telling *selfish black lies* that materially benefit the teller even if others are harmed (see

Gneezy (2005) for this terminology). The main subject matter of *neoclassical incentive theory* is to design clever incentives to reduce or eliminate the incidence of selfish black lies. In recent years, many experiments have been conducted to study the extent and determinants of lying behavior and they form an important part of the evidence base on human virtues and morality.

In an ingenious design, Fischbacher and Föllmi-Heusi (2013) propose the *die-cup experiment*. Subjects privately toss a fair, six-sided die, with the numbers one to six on it, and privately observe the outcome. Suppose that they receive as many dollars as their *self-report* of the privately observed number (e.g., $3 if they self-report that they observed the number three), except that they receive $0 for reporting the number six. What number should they report? If they are willing to tell selfish black lies, then they must self-report the number five because it gives the highest possible material payoff of $5.

Since subjects privately observe and self-report the numbers, we cannot infer if a particular subject has lied. However, if we have a large number of subjects, we can infer the distribution of subjects who lie. The reason is that if we randomly throw a fair six-sided die, statistically, there is a $\frac{1}{6}$ probability that any particular side comes up. So, if all self-reports were completely truthful, then we should observe a sixth of the subjects reporting each of the six numbers, which gives rise to a uniform distribution at $\frac{1}{6} = 0.167$ or 16.7%. If there is lying, we expect a difference between the self-reported distribution and the predicted uniform distribution.

The results are shown in Figure 3.11. The numbers above the histograms show the percentage of self-reports corresponding to the numbers, 1–6, on the X-axis. The predicted uniform distribution under complete honesty is shown as the horizontal line at 16.7%. There is a statistically significant difference between the actual distribution of self-reports and the predicted uniform distribution. Less than 16.7%, but still a fairly high percentage, of subjects self-report the lower numbers one, two, and three and the number six for which they receive $0, when they could all have self-reported five. More than 16.7% of the subjects self-report each of the numbers four and five. We summarize the results as follows.

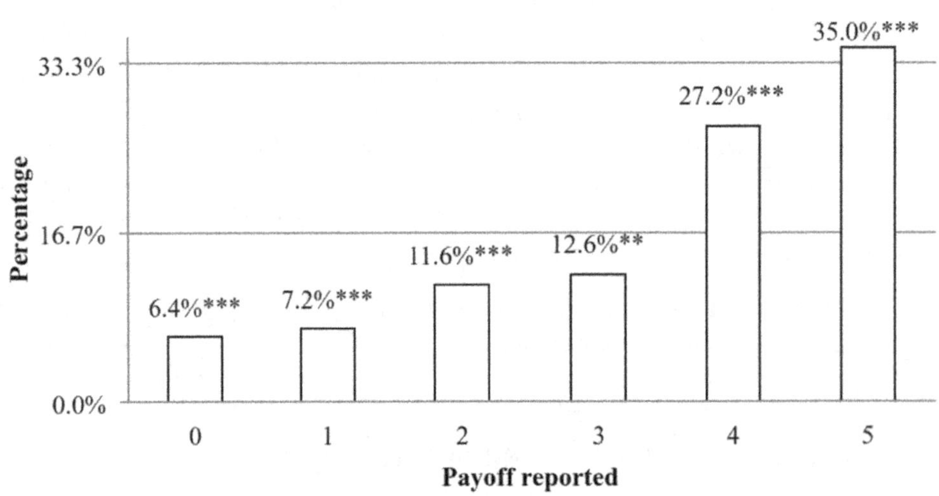

Figure 3.11 The predicted distribution under truth-telling and actual distribution of self-reports in the die-cup experiments. Source: Fischbacher and Föllmi-Heusi (2013)

1. There is a significant amount of *partial lying*. The distribution of self-reports suggests that subjects could have overstated their self-reports even more to increase their material payoffs. The fact that they do not overstate more, suggests that they may feel guilt, say, from a violation of internal moral norms, from even greater lying.
2. Suppose that honesty is not correlated with the number that comes up on the die. Then, we can determine the percentage of honest subjects in the following manner. 16.7% of the subjects should have observed the number six, yet only 6.4% self-report the number six, hence, the percentage of subjects who are fully honest is $\frac{6.4}{16.7} \times 100 = 38.32\%$.
3. Consider only unethical income maximizers who always wish to self-report the number five. 16.7% of the total number of subjects would have privately observed five, so they do not need to lie. But the rest would have privately observed the remaining numbers, one, two, three, four, six, yet report the number five. Overall 35% subjects report the number five, hence, the percentage of unethical income maximizers is $\frac{6}{5}(35 - 16.7) \times 100 = 21.96\%$.

These results have been successfully replicated in a large number of empirical studies in a very active field of research. There is already a huge literature in behavioral economics that examines individual lying. For a survey and the references, see Dhami (2017) and Dhami and al-Nowaihi (2019) which discuss some of the following key findings. Lab and field evidence shows that the extent of lying depends on the strength of one's other-regarding preferences; on whether one lies individually or as part of a team, which spreads responsibility for lying; on whether there are competitive incentives between players or team incentives; and on whether there are injunctive norms against lying such as highlighting the potential benefits of public services to potential tax evaders.

3.10.1 A Selection of Results From Empirical Studies on Lying

In this subsection, we examine some examples from the fascinating empirical evidence from studies on lying below.

Example 3.16 *The results on gender differences in lying are somewhat mixed, and depend on the type of the lie, and the stake sizes involved. Erat and Gneezy (2012) show that men are relatively more likely to tell a selfish black lie and a Pareto white lie (a lie that benefits all, but does not harm anyone), while women are more likely to tell altruistic white lies (lies that benefit others but not them).*

Example 3.17 *We observe two kinds of behaviors when an individual has lied before.*

(a) Previous lies may sometimes reduce the guilt from lying more; this is known as the "slippery slope of dishonesty" which has been confirmed by neuroeconomic evidence (Engelmann and Fehr, 2016).

(b) Previous lies may lead to a short-term increase in honesty on account of the "conscience accounting hypothesis" which proposes that guilt from lying is highest after lying and depreciates over time. Dai et al. (2018) consider the relation between fare evasion by passengers using public transport in Lyon and their lying behavior in the die-cup experiments. There is considerable dishonesty in the field. The experimenters offered a day pass in exchange for

the ticket, if the passenger could produce a ticket; clearly the day pass is a superior option. However, 41.8% *of the passengers could not produce a ticket and the self-reports of passengers suggested that* 54.92% *traveled without a ticket once every 10 trips. The authors classify individuals into the following* 2×2 *categories. Those who were traveling with a ticket and without; and those who confessed to cheat on the fare in the past, and those who did not. We can now compare the distribution of self-reports in the die throwing task for each group of individuals with the predicted statistical distribution. Those who had evaded the fare today were less likely to lie in the die throwing task. This is consistent with the conscience accounting hypothesis.*

Example 3.18 *It is commonly believed that some individuals would not lie if the stakes are low, but could be persuaded to lie when the stakes are higher. In other words, morality might not be an "absolute" for some people, and they might be willing to loosen their morality if the temptation were high enough. However, the meta study by Abeler et al. (2019) of 90 experimental studies containing a total of 429 treatment conditions does not support this view. It shows that the propensity to lie in the Fischbacher and Föllmi-Heusi type die-cup experiments does not increase appreciably even when there is a considerable increase in stake sizes.*

Example 3.19 *Subjects may care about the harm caused by a lie, and not just the monetary consequences of a lie. For identical monetary consequences, a lie that causes more harm is rated more unfair. Gneezy (2005) asked University of Chicago students to judge which of the following two scenarios is more unfair. A seller sells a car to a buyer but withholds information that:*

(a) the car has a faulty pump that will cost $250 *to fix, or*
(b) the car has faulty brakes that will cost $250 *to fix.*

Subjects rated the second scenario to be more unfair, hence, they are not merely consequentialists in material terms. If this sense of morality is widely shared, then used-car salesmen are more likely to inform us of faulty car brakes than faulty pumps.

Example 3.20 *Lying behavior also depends on the structure of incentives in organizations. In a field experiment, Balafoutas et al. (2020) gave professional German internal auditors a set of 30 calculations and told them that 10 were incorrect. The auditors were required to check the calculations in a real effort experiment but they had varying incentives to report the number of correct answers. For instance, under competitive incentives, auditors who get the highest number of correct answers win a prize, but their peers may check their work and report on the number of correct answers. Under team incentives, auditors are constituted into a team and report on the number of correct answers of their team members. In another treatment, the evaluation is done objectively, say, by the experimenter against the objectively true answers; this provides the benchmark evaluation. Under competitive incentives and peer evaluation, the number of correct answers of the partner are under-reported by their peers by about 22%. However, under team incentives, peers over-report the number of correct answers by 16%. Under team incentives, but objective evaluation (so the evaluation by peers is not taken into account but the experimenter's evaluation prevails), peers still under-report the number of correct answers of their partners. In this case, the under-reporting might be caused by self-image or status perceptions of the peers.*

Example 3.21 *How important is moral suasion for lying behavior? In their empirical study, Hallsworth et al. (2017) used five different messages and randomized them while sending them to 100,000 taxpayers who had declared their incomes, but had not yet paid their taxes. The control group received a standard reminder to pay their taxes but no moral suasion was used. In two messages, two kinds of factors were highlighted. (a) Descriptive norms provided information to subjects about the timeliness of the "actual" payments of other taxpayers and (b) injunctive norms informed taxpayers what they "ought" to do, for example, pay in a timely manner. Two further messages stressed the public service aspect of tax payments, for example, that taxes fund useful public services. The messages were able to induce more timely payment of taxes relative to the control treatment. Relative to the control treatment, the most successful of the messages produced a treatment effect of 5.1%. Descriptive norms are relatively more effective than injunctive norms. Other literature, not related to lying, shows that when descriptive and injunctive norms are in conflict, it is the descriptive norms that are relatively more effective in determining human behavior (Bicchieri and Xiao, 2009).*

Example 3.22 *In an interesting design, Houser et al. (2016) asked parents to "privately" toss two coins; each coin had a green and a blue side. If the parent reports that both sides came up green then they received a reward whose nature depended on the treatment (see below). Individual lying could not be discovered because the method relies on self-reports of parents about a privately observed event. However, one can compute the probability that both randomly tossed coins will show up as green,* $\frac{1}{2} \times \frac{1}{2} = \frac{1}{4}$ *or* 25%, *which can be compared with the percentage of parents who claimed the prize. The authors used a* 2×2 *design (a) the reward was either $10 to the parent, or a toy to the child and (b) the self-report is made either privately by the parent, or in front of their child. This design is shown in Table 3.2. The individual cells are deliberately left empty and will contain relevant information (e.g., the percentage of truthful reports) for the corresponding treatments.*

We can find the average percentage of self-reports of two green sides of a coin for each parent, in each of the four categories of the 2×2 *design shown in Table 3.2. We can then compare these average self-reports to see if the differences are statistically significant. This is a common technique used to make inferences from experimental data. When the self-report is made privately (sum of the two figures in the second column)* 46% *of the parents claimed a win (as against the predicted* 25% *under full honesty). But in the presence of the child (sum of the two figures in the third column), the claimed win rate at* 33% *was closer to the predicted win rate of* 25% *under full honesty. However, the difference of* 8% *is still statistically significant at the* 10% *level.*

Of the four treatments, the greatest win rate, 58%, *arises when the reward is a toy and the parent reports privately (second row, first column). When the self-report is made in front of a girl child (column three specialized for the case of daughters only) the claimed win rate is only* 28%, *which is quite close to the* 25% *win rate under full honesty. The corresponding figure for sons is* 42%, *which*

Table 3.2 The 2×2 design in Houser et al. (2016)

	Self-report privately	Self-report in front of child
$10 reward	–	–
Toy for child	–	–

is significantly higher. The authors conclude that their results show that the lower incidence of lying for women arises because they are socialized differently from men when they are young.

Example 3.23 *Kocher and Schudy (2018) use a variant of the die-cup experiments in which subjects give self-reports after observing the throw of a die on a computer screen. Unknown to them, the experimenter can also observe the outcome of the die toss. Hence, direct evidence on individual level lying can be discovered. In the "individual treatment" individuals choose their self-reports. However, in the two "group treatments" a group of individuals collectively choose their group report after being given the opportunity to chat about the number to self-report.*

(a) *In the treatment GroupPC, if all group members report an identical number, then each receives a payoff equal to the reported number (as in other die-cup experiments, the payoff is zero if the number six is reported). If members do not report a common number, then all get a payoff of zero.*
(b) *In the treatment GroupNoPC, the payoff of each group member depends only on their individual self-report, irrespective of what other group members report. Hence, there is an absence of social concerns about the other group members.*

The percentage of subjects who lie in the individual treatment, the GroupPC treatment, and the GroupNoPC treatment is, respectively, 61.5%, 89.7%, and 86.3%. Thus, while there is no significant difference in the extent of lying in the two group treatments, there is a significantly greater incidence of lying in groups as compared to the individual treatment. There is a high degree of coordination on the number to self-report for the group in the GroupPC treatment where the absence of a coordinated report leads to zero payoffs for all players. However, perhaps surprisingly, there is also a high degree of coordination among group members in the GroupNoPC treatment where such coordination is not required (33 of the 39 groups coordinate on a common number).

Why do groups lie more? There are two reasons. First, chatting with other group members increases the beliefs of the members about the dishonesty of other members. Second, in group chats, arguments for dishonesty are made in 51% of the groups, while arguments for honesty are made in only 24% of the groups. In groups where relatively more arguments for honesty are made, lying decreases. However, there is no appreciable difference in the proportion of arguments for honesty across the two group treatments.

Example 3.24 *Garbarino et al. (2019) explore another dimension of "lying under risk" that uses the concept of loss aversion, introduced in Part I of the book. Suppose that an individual faces two possible outcomes* x_1, x_2 *such that* $0 \leq x_1 < x_2$*; the two outcomes occur with respective probabilities* $p, 1-p$*. In effect, a priori, the individual faces the lottery* $L = (x_1, p; x_2, 1-p)$*. Suppose that the reference point of the individual is an outcome that lies between the two outcomes. In particular, suppose that the reference point is the average outcome,* $\overline{x} = px_1 + (1-p)x_2$*. Thus, if the outcome* x_1 *occurs, then the individual is in the domain of losses where loss aversion bites, and if the outcome* x_2 *occurs, then the individual is in the domain of gains where loss aversion is absent. Suppose that the outcomes are generated randomly, as given in the lottery L, and the individual is asked to report the privately observed outcome, either* x_1 *or* x_2*, with higher rewards given for reporting the higher outcome. As p falls, the reference point,* $\overline{x}$*, increases, so the individual feels an even greater utility loss from reporting the low outcome. In terms of the prospect theory utility* *function (see Part I of the book), the disutility from reporting* x_1 *is* $-\lambda(\overline{x} - x_1)$*. As p increases,* $\overline{x}$ *increases, so the disutility from reporting* x_1 *also increases, thereby increasing the incentive to lie and report the high outcome* x_2 *instead. The results from the experiments are consistent with this prediction.*

3.10.2 A Note on Markets and Ethicality

We have seen from the crosscultural studies on the ultimatum game in Section 3.2 that *markets may enhance prosociality*. However, evidence of the relation between markets and ethicality is more contentious. The experiments in Falk and Szech (2013) showed that *markets may diminish ethicality*. They conduct experiments in which successful bargaining between people would lead to the life of a mouse being lost. If bargaining is unsuccessful, the life of the mouse is saved. These are lab mice used for biological experiments who are put down after the experiments are completed. Saving a mouse's life involves buying these lab mice and letting them live for the rest of their lives, typically about two more years.

In particular, the authors show that people are less willing to bargain successfully when they make the decision individually, relative to making this decision in a bilateral market setting. Furthermore, people are less willing to bargain successfully in a bilateral market setting as compared to a multilateral market setting. Thus, the life of the mouse is more likely to be lost when institutions are chosen in the following order: multilateral decisions in a group, bilateral decisions, and individual decisions. This is partly because the responsibility for taking the mouse's life is more diffused in a group decision relative to a bilateral decision, which in turn is more diffused relative to individual decisions. The larger the number of partners in a decision, the lower the level of guilt from being instrumental in the decision to end the mouse's life. Furthermore, conversations between the group members might draw greater attention to a nonmoral frame, say, the material advantages from a successful bargaining outcome.

Related research shows that firms may sometimes be willing to engage in unethical practices in markets on account of the "replacement excuse," for example, "if they did not do it, some other firm may do it and increase profits" (Bartling and Özdemir, 2021). In their experiments, Bartling et al. (2015) introduce two possible products for firms.

1. A product that is costless to produce, but causes negative externalities for third parties, reducing the payoffs of third parties by 60 units.
2. An externality-free product that costs 10 units.

The value of both types of products is 50 units for consumers. Thus, if the externality-causing product is produced, then the net value to society is $50 - 60 = -10$. If the externality-free product is produced then it imposes an extra cost on firms without eliciting a higher price because both types of products are valued at 50 units by consumers. Thus, the choice of producing the externality-free product is a *socially responsible or ethical choice*.

When the experiment is conducted with Swiss subjects, the externality-free product accounts for 45% of the total product produced. The corresponding figure for Chinese subjects is 16%, suggesting cultural differences in ethicality in markets. However, when an identical game is played, with identical payoffs, which is set in a "nonmarket frame" and labeled the "non-market allocation game," there is little difference in the choices between Chinese and Swiss subjects. However, the degree of ethicality, as measured by the mitigation of harm on third parties, is higher in the nonmarket settings. Thus, markets again reduce ethicality in this sense.

Bartling et al. (2021) point to a potential confound in the experiments of Falk and Szech (2013). In their individual treatment, Falk–Szech play a one period game, however, when allowing for bilateral bargaining they play a 10 period game. Bartling et al. (2021) conduct a related experiment in which the life of a mouse is not lost, but the money goes to Leprosy patients in India if parties do not successfully bargain with each other. They also consider a single period and 10 period interaction for individual choices and multilateral bargaining. Within a single period setting for individual choices, they recover the results in the Falk–Szech experiments. However, when individual choices are also made over 10 rounds in all cases, the authors ascribe differences in ethicality to the distinction between static play and repeated play in games, and not necessarily to the nature of bargaining – individual or multilateral. This calls for further research into this area.

This is the state of play at the time of writing this book. It would appear that this is a highly fruitful area for future research that is likely to clarify the precise relation between ethicality and markets.

3.10.3 The Effectiveness of Apologies

Humans often apologize to restore relationships that are under strain or are broken. In neoclassical game theory, apologies are implicitly considered to be cheap talk that could also be used by those who are not sincere. Hence, they have not played an active part in the discourse within economics. However, humans do apologize to each other, and apologies often aid in repairing relationships and inducing forgiveness. Firms also sometimes apologize to customers, and in other contexts, politicians have sometimes been known to apologize to the electorate. Why does this occur?

If apologies are costly, and sincere, then they might be a signal of trustworthiness and contribute towards greater future interaction between the two parties (Ho, 2012). However, apologies may also worsen relationships if they are perceived to be insincere (Fischbacher and Utikal, 2013; Gilbert et al., 2017).

Halperin et al. (2021) conduct a large scale experiment with Uber customers to analyze the efficacy of different types of apologies in separate treatments. Their paper was motivated by an empirical problem arising from the Uber customer experience. When Uber drivers delivered their customers late to their destinations (e.g., the driver took a wrong turn or arrived slightly late), or when similar bad experiences occurred, customers spent 5%–10% less on Uber rides in the future, as compared to customers who did not have a bad experience. The authors wondered if an apology might help restore customers confidence, and if so, what form should that apology take.

In order to answer the question, they tracked 1.5 million Uber customers who had a bad experience in the past, and randomly assigned them to one of the following eight groups. Subjects in the control group received nothing. Subjects in the baseline treatment (labeled "just promo") received a $5 coupon. Finally, subjects in six other treatment groups received one of the following three types of apologies. In each of these treatments, half of the subjects received a "$5 coupon" and the remaining half received only an email; hence this gives $3 \times 2 = 6$ treatments.

1. A monetary cost (basic apology): Apologies in this treatment take the form of a box of chocolates, or a litigation settlement. For half the subjects who received the "$5 coupon" this treatment is known as "basic apology + promo"; for the other half who only received an email, but no coupon, this treatment is known as "basic apology." A similar naming terminology applies to the remaining two cases discussed below.
2. A commitment cost (commitment apology): A commitment is offered to the customer that they will not have similar bad experiences with the company in the future. This is costly because if the commitment is carried through, it is fine. However, if the commitment is reneged on, it might anger/frustrate the customer even more, leading them to reduce spending on Uber even more drastically than in the absence of an apology.
3. A status cost (status apology): This is a simple apology that appeals to Uber's reputation, such that breaking the promise may entail a loss of status for the company.

Figure 3.12 shows the change in spending by customers in each treatment group in the 84 days following the original bad experience, which is a late ride. In general, apologies are effective but only when they are costly. For instance, the "$5 promo coupon" was generally effective across treatment conditions; this includes the four treatments, promo, basic apology + promo, commitment apology + promo, and status apology + promo. Apologies are effective in the sense that they result in positive returns for Uber as compared to the control group, even when we

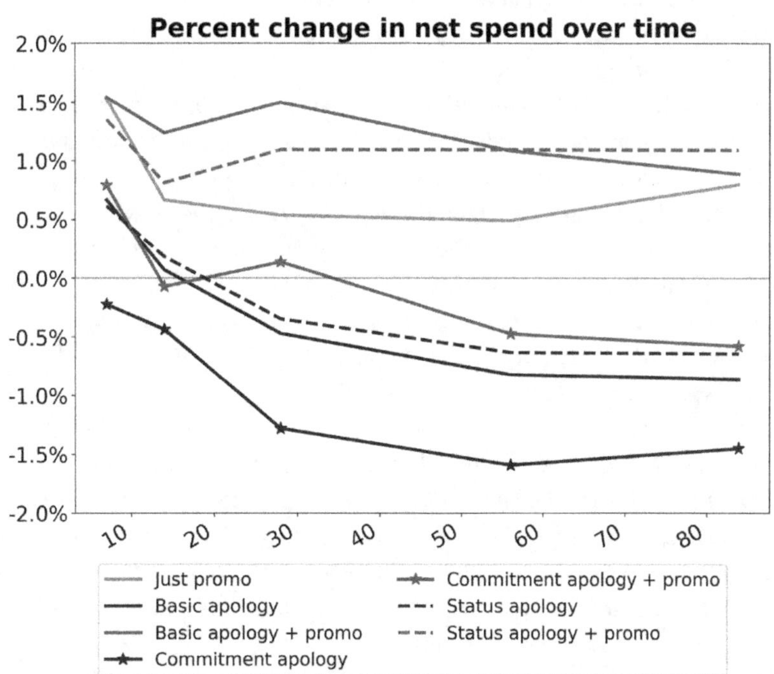

Figure 3.12 The effectiveness of different types of apologies with Uber consumers. I am grateful to Basil Halperin for providing me with this high resolution image

take account of the "$5 promo coupon" cost. Of these treatments, apologies + promo worked better than promo alone.

Apologies can backfire, when apologies are followed by further bad experiences. This is particularly the case when the promise of good future conduct was made explicit in the emails sent to customers but the promise was not kept. Such apologies did result in positive short term returns for Uber. However, Uber would have earned higher more from these customer if no apology had been made. This was also true for the customers who received a "$5 promo coupon." Finally, the effects of emails which stressed a reputation cost alone (status apology) had indistinguishable results from the baseline treatment.

3.11 External Validity of Lab Experiments

In the introductory chapter, we have briefly discussed the issue of external validity of lab experiments. This is the issue of the portability of findings from lab experiments to real world settings. Do people exhibit similar preferences in lab decisions and when they go about their business in real life? Doubts that this was the case were expressed in Levitt and List (2007). The accumulated weight of the evidence now suggests that lab experiments on other-regarding preferences have a high degree of *external validity*. We give some illustrative examples below.

Example 3.25 *In the early days of lab experiments, one concern was that the typical subject pool in lab experiments is university students. It was argued that this might somehow bias the results against the established neoclassical theories based on self-regarding preferences. The experiments in Falk et al. (2013) demonstrated two main results. First, it is not the case that more prosocial students self-select themselves into economics experiments. Second, if anything, students are less prosocial than the typical non-student subject pools. The second of these findings has been strengthened with several supporting experiments replicating the same result. Paradoxically, if we wish to find evidence for self-regarding preferences, the student subjects are the most suitable subject pool. However, on average, students too are sufficiently prosocial to reject the exclusive use of self-regarding preferences. Furthermore, the student subject pool is highly educated with relatively high cognitive abilities which, in the presence of incentivized experiments, must give standard neoclassical theory a better chance of success. Yet, the predictions of models with exclusively self-regarding preferences fail in a disconcertingly high number of cases.*

Do students with particularly behavioral preferences self-select themselves into lab experiments? Thiemann et al. (2022) show that there is no significant difference between students who select themselves for lab experiments, relative to others, in terms of time preferences, risk preferences, overconfidence, trust, and reciprocity. However, students with higher cognitive skills are more likely to participate in experiments. This makes it more likely that the students understand better the experimental instructions and this factor may improve the quality of data in lab experiments.

Example 3.26 *Another concern with experiments on other-regarding preferences has been that subjects might offer exactly the answers that the experimenter wants to hear; this is the issue of "experimenter demand effects." Experimenters often approach an experiment not knowing what* *they will find. The good experimenters keep an open mind with well-specified null and alternative hypotheses, and leave it to the data to pick one.*

Economic theories take several years for undergraduate students in economics to master, so non-economics subjects are unlikely to guess the underlying economic theories that are being tested in these experiments. It would be remarkable if the subjects could at all guess the null and alternative hypotheses that are being tested in experiments, except perhaps in the most trivial problems. There is, of course, the danger that unscrupulous experimenters might "lead" subjects to a particular response, but there are stringent checks and balances in modern experiments, and replications of experiments provide further checks. There is also no reason why unscrupulous applied scientists should be disproportionately represented in experimental economics relative to any other applied area in the social and behavioral sciences.

Barmettler et al. (2012) test one feature of experimenter demand effects, which is the degree to which the responses of subjects are anonymized from the experimenter. This can be a concern in some experiments, particularly where subject responses may reveal aspects of their moral virtues. For instance, experiments on lying behavior may give misleading results if subjects perceive that they are being watched by the experimenter. The authors consider three games – a dictator game, an ultimatum game, and a trust game. In the single anonymized treatment (S), at the end of the experiment the subjects reported their ID numbers to the experimenter who matched the ID numbers to sealed envelopes on the table that contained payment to the subjects. Payments took the form of a participation fee in the experiment plus incentive payments based on the answers given in the experiments. In the second treatment, the double anonymized treatment (D), the experimenter was not present when the payments were given. Rather the subjects had to match their own ID numbers with the envelopes which had been left on the table. In all games, the responses of players in each role were statistically indistinguishable between the two treatments, S and D.

Example 3.27 *In Toyama Bay, Japan, two kinds of fishermen operate. The "poolers" who cooperate to pool resources and share the catch, and the "non-poolers" who fish on an individual basis. Carpenter and Seki (2011) gave both kinds of fishermen an opportunity to play a modified public goods game in the lab in groups of four; within each group the members were either all poolers or all non-poolers. The public goods game was played over 10 rounds. In the first five rounds, there was no punishment option, but in the next five rounds there was a punishment option which took the form of costly social approval or disapproval on observing randomized data on the contributions of other players in the group. To indicate social approval or disapproval, players could buy, at a cost, either a "smiley face" to indicate approval or a "sad face" to indicate disapproval.*

A regression was run with individual contributions in any of the $t = 2, \ldots, 10$ rounds as the dependent variable, and contributions in the previous round, $t - 1$, as the independent variable. The intercept term in this regression indicates unconditional cooperation while the slope term (coefficient on the contributions in the previous round) indicates conditional cooperation. The lab measure of conditional cooperation is higher among poolers as compared to non-poolers, and it is the best predictor of productivity of the fishermen in their real life vocation. Unconditional cooperation is also found to be higher among poolers relative to non-poolers. The authors conclude that many years of real life cooperation and coordination among poolers has altered their preferences, and this is reflected in a lab experiment on public goods game. Or, perhaps those who had such an initial

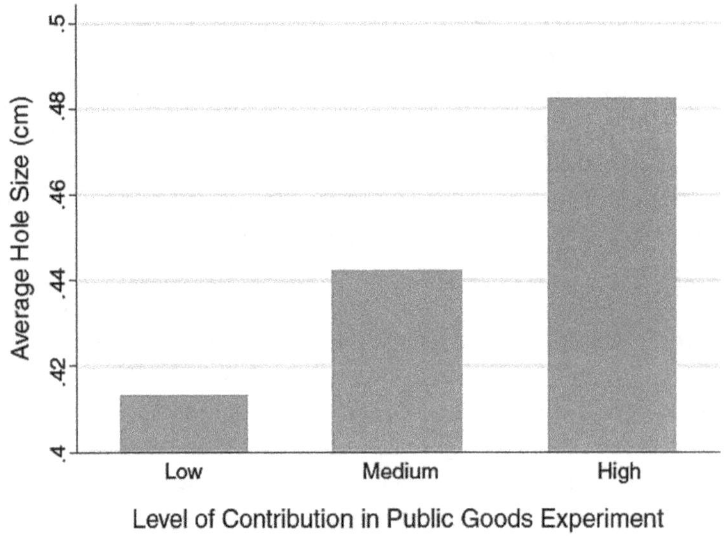

Figure 3.13 The relation between the hole sizes in fishing nets and the level of contributions in a public goods game. Source: Fehr and Leibbrandt (2011)

propensity to be more cooperative, self-selected themselves to be poolers rather than non-poolers. However, we cannot determine the answer to this question with the given data.

Example 3.28 *In rural fishing villages in northeastern Brazil, fishermen operate on a lake with common property rights, and there are no time limits or quotas on fishing. The fishermen have the option of using fishing nets with small holes (higher fish catch, but also trapping younger fish, not yet of mature size, hence, detrimental for the commons) or with larger holes (smaller fish catch, but younger adult fish not yet grown to maturity escape, hence, beneficial to the commons). Large holes correspond to greater real world cooperation in what is essentially a public goods problem of resource extraction on the commons.*

When the same fishermen play a lab public goods game, Fehr and Leibbrandt (2011) find that there is a strong correlation between those who cooperate more in the lab experiment and those who choose larger hole sizes in their nets. Figure 3.13 shows the striking results obtained by the authors, which make this point explicit. In a follow up study, Leibbrandt (2012) finds that shrimp fishermen who are found to be more prosocial in the lab public goods game are also less likely to lose important buyers in their real life vocation; more likely to get a better price for their shrimp; and more likely to have longer-term trading relations with buyers. In this case too, there is a strong link between what happens in the lab and what happens in the real world.

Example 3.29 *Recall our introduction to microfinance contracts in the introductory chapter that we continue in Part IV of the book. Karlan (2005) plays a lab trust game with microfinance borrowers in Ayacucho, Peru. A higher degree of trustworthiness (recall this corresponds to a higher returned amount in the trust game in Section 3.4) in the lab experiment is associated with a higher probability that the subject will repay their microfinance loan. A higher degree of trust (i.e., higher amounts* *sent by the trustor) in the lab experiment may reflect a gambling instinct; such subjects save less in real life.*

Example 3.30 *The Bale Oromo people in Ethiopia were given property rights over a forest and were required to manage the forest (a common resource) through a range of conservation efforts. Rustagi et al. (2010) played a two-player public goods game in the lab with these subjects. It was found that subjects who cooperated more in the lab public goods game also undertook a greater degree of conservation of the common resource, say, spending more time on costly personal monitoring of the forest to prevent its misuse by others.*

In sum, we now have a rich body of evidence that ought to lay to rest misgivings about the external validity of lab experiments on other-regarding preferences. Most of the original concerns about lab experiments have turned out to be unfounded. However, the potential criticisms have improved the practice of experimental economics by alerting experimental economics to potential pitfalls. Experiments these days are run with fairly stringent controls, and a careful consideration of the potential confounds that might arise. As such, experiments provide high quality data that can be safely used to make critical inferences about human nature.

4 Theoretical Models and Applications of Prosocial Behavior

4.1 Introduction

In Chapter 3, we considered the evidence from human behavior on prosociality in a variety of contexts. This evidence rejected the notion that humans exhibit exclusively self-regarding preferences. Human nature does have a strong self-regarding component, but also exhibits important and well-defined prosocial tendencies. A great deal of the evidence on human behavior is accounted for by the presence of conditional reciprocity which is fairly robust across contexts, frames, and domains.

The documentation of the empirical evidence, while enormously important, is not sufficient. In order to organize this evidence, to understand further the human motivations involved and, importantly, to make predictions, we need to construct rigorous theoretical models. Any prospective model must explain the evidence from the experimental games in Sections 3.2 to 3.5 in Chapter 3. This fundamentally differentiates behavioral economic theory from existing neoclassical models. The elegance, intuitiveness, usefulness, or beauty, of theoretical models are not primary criteria for the acceptance of models in behavioral economics. Conformity with the empirical evidence is the key element and the other elements are secondary.

In Section 4.2, we consider some of the main theoretical developments in the area of other-regarding preferences. Issues of *intentions-based reciprocity* that require the development of psychological game theory are postponed to Part IV of the book. We begin with the *Fehr–Schmidt model of inequity aversion* which is simple, tractable, and organizes well the evidence from many experimental games. It identifies three main human motivations, *selfishness* from caring about one's own material payoffs; *altruism* that arises from caring about the payoff differences between one's own payoff relative to those who are poorer; and *envy* that arises from caring about the payoff differences between one's own payoff relative to those who are richer. The *equity, reciprocity, and competition* (ERC) model takes account of selfishness from one's own payoff; and prosocial concerns that cause disutility if one's income is too high relative to the total income of a reference group. Models of *interdependent preferences* allow for individuals with different types of prosociality to exhibit preferential treatment to their own types. For instance, those who are more altruistic might be more prosocial towards others who are also more altruistic. Finally, the *Charness–Rabin model* incorporates both equity and efficiency concerns.

Another aim of this chapter is to demonstrate the usefulness of the alternative theoretical approaches in a wide range of domains. Section 4.3 applies social identity concerns to the ultimatum game by first deriving the predictions of a theoretical model of inequity aversion with Akerlof–Kranton type social identity concerns and then providing empirical tests that support the predictions.

Section 4.4 shows how prosocial preferences can be used in the domain of political economy. We consider the implications of having a mix of self-regarding and other-regarding preferences among voters in choosing the redistributive tax rate. We also show how lab determined prosociality plays a key role in determining voting in referenda on important issues, using Swiss data. Related empirical findings are also briefly surveyed.

Section 4.5 considers the problem of contractual choice in the employment relation by comparing several kinds of contracts such as incentive contracts, trust contracts, and bonus contracts. The trust and the bonus contracts are fairly incomplete contracts and would be taken advantage of by economic actors who have purely self-regarding preferences. As such, the prediction of neoclassical economic theory is that we should not observe these contracts in the presence of incentive contracts. However, once we allow for other-regarding preferences, this prediction changes. Conditional reciprocity, and human morality, ensure that when greater trust is reposed in workers, or a higher bonus is promised, then workers respond by putting in greater effort. The evidence is supportive of these predictions.

Neoclassical economics has paid almost exclusive attention to the power of economic incentives, typically understood to mean monetary incentives, in influencing economic actions. The evidence from behavioral economics has challenged this position. We review some of this evidence in Section 4.6. Economic incentives are not redundant, but their effect is fairly nuanced. Sometimes non-economic incentives that take account of human prosociality, when used in conjunction with economic incentives, are even more effective.

4.2 Models of Other-Regarding Preferences

In this section, we consider the main behavioral models that have been proposed to explain the empirical evidence in Sections 3.2 to 3.5 in Chapter 3. Some of these models have also proved popular in applied work in the area.

4.2.1 Inequity Aversion: The Fehr–Schmidt Model

Models of inequity aversion play an important role in capturing some of the central features of human motivations under other-regarding preferences. The *model of inequity aversion* due to Fehr and Schmidt (1999) (henceforth, the FS model) can explain a great deal of the evidence outlined in Sections 3.2 to 3.5 in Chapter 3.

Consider two players, 1 and 2, who have respective incomes $x_1 > 0$ and $x_2 > 0$. The FS utility of player 1, denoted by U_1, depends separately on the two cases where the income of player 1 is (i) relatively higher, $x_1 \geq x_2$ (*advantageous inequity*) or (ii) relatively lower, $x_1 < x_2$ (*disadvantageous inequity*):

$$U_1 = \begin{cases} x_1 - \beta_1 (x_1 - x_2) & if \quad x_1 \geq x_2 \\ x_1 - \alpha_1 (x_2 - x_1) & if \quad x_1 < x_2 \end{cases} ; \alpha_1 \geq 0, \beta_1 \geq 0. \tag{4.1}$$

In (4.1), for player 1, α_1 is the parameter of disadvantageous inequity, and β_1 is the parameter of advantageous inequity. Each of these parameters measure the additional effect of a unit increase in, respectively, disadvantageous inequity and advantageous inequity, on the utility of player 1. The utility function in (4.1) captures three motivations. Player 1 cares about her own income, x_1; this captures self-regarding preferences. From the first row of (4.1), player 1 derives disutility from having a relatively higher income, as shown by the term $\beta_1 (x_1 - x_2)$; this captures *altruism*. From the second row of (4.1), player 1 derives disutility from having a relatively lower income, reflected in the term $\alpha_1 (x_2 - x_1)$; this captures *envy*. In other contexts, say, in competitive contests, such as tournaments and races, players may derive utility from finishing ahead of others. In this case, it may be more appropriate to specify that $\beta_1 < 0$.

A similar FS utility function for player 2, U_2, can be readily written down, but needs no further explanation except that the two inequity aversion parameters, α_2, β_2, are allowed to be different from the corresponding parameters, α_1, β_1, for player 1.

$$U_2 = \begin{cases} x_2 - \beta_2 (x_2 - x_1) & if \quad x_2 \geq x_1 \\ x_2 - \alpha_2 (x_1 - x_2) & if \quad x_2 < x_1 \end{cases} ; \alpha_2 \geq 0, \beta_2 \geq 0. \tag{4.2}$$

Self regarding preferences are a special case of FS preferences, found by setting

$$\alpha_1 = \beta_1 = 0 \text{ and } \alpha_2 = \beta_2 = 0.$$

Throughout this chapter, we make the following empirically supported restriction about the parameters $\alpha_i, \beta_i, i = 1, 2,$

$$0 \leq \beta_i < 1; \ \beta_i < \alpha_i. \tag{4.3}$$

The upper bound of 1 on β_i ensures that people do not just throw away their incomes to reduce inequality with others, and we do not observe this occurring. The condition $\beta_i < \alpha_i$ requires that a unit increase in disadvantageous inequality gives rise to more disutility relative to a unit increase in advantageous inequality. So envy appears to be a more powerful emotion than altruism, at least on average, in the human population.

Consider, for instance, the public goods game with punishments, where high contributors punish low contributors in WEIRD societies. Since low contributors contribute less, yet derive the same benefits from the public good, hence, they have relatively higher income than high contributors. Thus, a potential explanation is that the disutility arising from disadvantageous inequality induces high contributors to punish low contributors. Punishment in public goods games is particularly hard to explain for many other theories of other-regarding preferences. Using inequity aversion, the Fehr–Schmidt utility function is able to explain the evidence from the experimental games in Sections 3.2–3.5. For instance, strictly positive amounts given in dictator games can be explained by altruism alone, or by aversion to advantageous inequity.

The FS utility function in (4.1) does not explicitly consider the beliefs of players. In some cases, one may wish to invoke conditional reciprocity to explain behavior. For instance, in the gift exchange game, a firm's high wage offer might be perceived to be a "kind" offer to which the worker wishes to respond in "kindness" by putting in high effort. But what does "kind" mean? Perhaps it means a wage offer greater than the worker's expectations, or greater than some wage norm. Expectations require explicit modeling of beliefs (*beliefs-based reciprocity*). Part IV of the book shows how we might take account of this by using *psychological game theory*.

In the FS model, one's own income serves as a reference point and departures from it reflect advantageous and disadvantageous inequity (*self-centered inequity aversion*). Other possible reference points could be a fair income, or a fair income based on some social norm. The FS model can be readily extended to any finite number of players. For instance, one may simultaneously feel disadvantageous inequity relative to a set of players whose income is higher and advantageous inequity relative to another set of players whose income is lower. For instance, if there are n players with respective incomes $x_1 < x_2 < \ldots < x_n$, then the FS utility of player i is given by

$$U_i = x_i - \frac{\beta_i}{n-1}\sum_{j=1}^{i-1}\left(x_i - x_j\right) - \frac{\alpha_i}{n-1}\sum_{j=i+1}^{n}\left(x_j - x_i\right). \tag{4.4}$$

In (4.4), player i feels advantageous inequity with respect to the incomes of players $j = 1, 2, \ldots, i-1$ and disadvantageous inequity with respect to the incomes of players $j = i + 1, i+2, \ldots, n$. The FS model does not specify the reference group of players for which one might suffer inequity aversion. The appropriate reference group is to be determined empirically, say, by individual case studies. The FS model in (4.4) is the *linear version* of the model, where the differences in incomes directly translate into changes in utility on account of inequity aversion. However, there is nothing which rules out a *nonlinear version* of the following form

$$U_i = x_i - \frac{\beta_i}{n-1}\sum_{j=1}^{i-1} v_i\left(x_i - x_j\right) - \frac{\alpha_i}{n-1}\sum_{j=i+1}^{n} v_i\left(x_j - x_i\right), \tag{4.5}$$

where v_i is a utility function defined over differences in one's incomes relative to the income of others (not to be confused with the prospect theory utility function in Part I of the book, although that might be one candidate example). In some cases, it might be more convenient to use the nonlinear form instead. In applications, the FS model has proved enormously useful in testing the predictions of other-regarding preferences and it is one of the most popular models in applied work.

We present a range of applications of the FS model in the rest of the chapter. These include finding a formal solution to the ultimatum game (Section 4.3), applications to political economy (Section 4.4), and deriving key results in the economics of incentives (Section 4.5).

4.2.2 The ERC Model

Bolton and Ockenfels (2000) propose the *equity*, *reciprocity*, and *competition* (ERC) model. Consider a set of n players with incomes $x_1 < x_2 < \ldots < x_n$ and the sum of incomes given by $S = \sum_{j=1}^{n} x_j > 0$. Define the relative income share of player $i = 1, 2, \ldots, n$ by

$$\sigma_i = \frac{x_i}{S}. \tag{4.6}$$

Then, the ERC utility of player *i* is given by a twice continuously differentiable function,[1]

$$u_i = u_i\left(x_i, \sigma_i\right). \tag{4.7}$$

The ERC model makes two assumptions about the utility function in (4.7); we state them first, followed by a description.

A1. For a given value of σ_i, the utility function, u_i, is increasing and concave in x_i.
A2. For a given value of x_i, the utility function, u_i, is maximized, with respect to σ_i at the value $\sigma_i = \frac{1}{n}$.

Assumption A1 shows that self-regarding preferences play a role in increasing utility, for a given level of relative income. In other words, fixing one's income relative to others (holding inequality fixed), one prefers to have a higher income. However, from assumption A2, for a given level of own-income x_i, the utility of player *i* is maximized if everyone shares the total income equally. Thus, $\sigma_i = \frac{1}{n}$ provides a *social reference point*. The conflict between the desire to maximize own-income (assumption A1) and a desire to achieve equitable social distribution of income (assumption A2) determines the preferred outcome of the decision maker.

Example 4.31 *This example requires familiarity with basic differentiation. For two players $i = 1, 2$, with incomes $x_1 < x_2$, an example of a utility function that satisfies the restrictions on the utility function in the ERC model is the following*

$$u_i = u_i\left(x_i, \sigma_i\right) = x_i - \frac{a_i}{2}\left(\sigma_i - \frac{1}{2}\right)^2; a_i > 0. \tag{4.8}$$

In (4.8), there is a single parameter a_i that gives the relative weight on the second term on the RHS. It can be checked that (4.8) satisfies both assumptions, A1 and A2. To check for A2, fix a value of x_i and differentiate both sides of (4.8) with respect to σ_i to get $\frac{\partial u_i}{\partial \sigma_i} = -a_i\left(\sigma_i - \frac{1}{2}\right)$. Differentiate this expression again to get $\frac{\partial^2 u_i}{\partial \sigma_i^2} = -a_i < 0$. Thus, u_i is a strictly concave function of σ_i. Both derivatives are continuous. Thus, there is a unique maximum value, which can be found from the first order condition $\frac{\partial u_i}{\partial \sigma_i} = 0$. This implies $-a_i\left(\sigma_i - \frac{1}{2}\right) = 0$, so the optimal value of σ_i found by solving the first order condition is $\sigma_i^* = \frac{1}{2}$, which verifies assumption A2. One can proceed analogously to verify assumption A1, but this time keeping σ_i fixed.

The FS model in Section 4.2.1, and the ERC models are non-nested models; neither is a special case of the other. They take a different approach to modeling inequity. In the FS model, inequity is self-centered, while in the ERC model inequity arises with respect to some notion of a socially fair income level, given by an "equal share" of the income for all players. The choice between

[1] A continuous function is roughly one that we can draw without lifting pen from paper (so it has no gaps). A twice differentiable function can be differentiated twice (so that we can derive first order and second order conditions in the usual manner to determine the optimal value). A twice continuously differentiable function is one where both derivatives of the function can be plotted on paper without lifting pen from paper. For instance, $y = f(x) = \sqrt{x}$, and $y = f(x) = x^2$.

the two models must, therefore, be an empirical one. The ERC model can also explain a range of empirical findings from Sections 3.2 to 3.5 in Chapter 3.

For instance, the ERC model can explain the behavior in ultimatum and dictator games. The self-regarding equilibrium in these two games is extremely inequitable (proposer offers only 1 cent in the ultimatum game, and the dictator offers nothing in the dictator game). In particular, these two outcomes are too far away from the notion of social justice in the ERC model. As players trade-off their own self-regarding material payoffs against the notion of social justice in the ERC model, they will typically find the self-regarding outcomes too removed from their most preferred outcome. Hence, proposers with ERC preferences in the ultimatum game, and dictators with ERC preferences, will wish to give away more of their endowments in a direction that is consistent with the empirical evidence. The next example shows how the ERC model explains giving in dictator games.

Example 4.32 *Consider a dictator game where the endowment of the dictator is $Y > 0$. Suppose that the utility function of the dictator is given in (4.8) and player $i = 1$ is the dictator while player $i = 2$ is the passive receiver. Thus, the utility function of the dictator is given by*

$$u_1 = x_1 - \frac{a_1}{2}\left(\frac{x_1}{x_1 + x_2} - \frac{1}{2}\right)^2 ; a_1 > 0, \tag{4.9}$$

where x_1 is the share of the dictator and x_2 is the amount offered by the dictator to the receiver, such that $x_1 + x_2 = Y$. Substituting $x_1 + x_2 = Y$ in (4.9), we get the unconstrained maximization problem of the dictator. The dictator chooses the optimal amount to keep, $x_1 \in [0, Y]$, in order to maximize

$$u_1 = x_1 - \frac{a_1}{2}\left(\frac{x_1}{Y} - \frac{1}{2}\right)^2 ; a_1 > 0 \tag{4.10}$$

Differentiating (4.10) with respect to x_1, we get the first order condition

$$\frac{du_1}{dx_1} = 1 - a_1\left(\frac{x_1}{Y} - \frac{1}{2}\right)\frac{1}{Y} = 0. \tag{4.11}$$

The second order condition, $\frac{d^2u_1}{dx_1^2} = \frac{-a_1}{Y^2} < 0$, is satisfied, hence, it is sufficient to solve out for x_1 from the first order condition, (4.11), to get the unique optimal value, x_1^*.

$$x_1^* = Y\left(\frac{Y}{a_1} + \frac{1}{2}\right). \tag{4.12}$$

Suppose that we use the following numerical values for the two parameters: $Y = 1$ and $a_1 = 4$, then we have

$$x_1^* = \frac{3}{4},$$

so the dictator keeps 3/4 of the endowment and leaves the rest, that is, 1/4, for the passive receiver. For other parameter values, we get different values of x_1^*. Recall that a_1 is the weight assigned by the dictator to the second term in (4.10), which captures a desire for social justice, relative to the first term, which is the self-regarding material payoff. As a_1 gets close to zero (or $a_1 \longrightarrow 0$) the optimal offer of the dictator approaches the case of purely self regarding preferences ($x_1^* = Y$)

and as a_1 becomes infinitely large (or $a_1 \longrightarrow \infty$) the dictator cares exclusively about social justice and chooses $x_1^* = 0$. Thus, the higher is the dictator's concern for social justice, the greater is the amount x_2 that the dictator passes on to the receiver.

The ERC model can explain why firms would like to give strictly positive rents to workers in the gift exchange game. The behavior in the ultimatum game and in the gift exchange game can also be accommodated within the ERC model. The ERC model can also accommodate the possibility that players might have asymmetric information about the type of the other players. Since interpersonal comparisons of inequity aversion are not allowed within the ERC model (only one's relative income, σ_i, matters) its predictions differ from the FS model. For instance, any changes in the existing income distribution that do not affect the income, x_i, of player i and the relative income, σ_i, of player i have no effect on the utility of player i. Yet, such changes are likely to affect advantageous and disadvantageous income inequity that player i faces, hence, if player i has FS preferences, the utility of the player will change. This is shown in the next example.

Example 4.33 *This example is based on the work of Charness and Rabin (2002) who show that following a mean preserving spread of incomes, the utility of a player might fall; this is consistent with the FS model but not the ERC model. This suggests that interpersonal inequity comparisons might be relatively salient. Consider three individuals, $i = 1, 2, 3$ who have respective incomes $6, 9, 12$ so that the sum of incomes is $S = 27$ and the mean income is $\overline{x} = \frac{27}{3} = 9$.*

We are only interested in the utility of player 2, whose relative income is given by $\sigma_2 = \frac{9}{27} = \frac{1}{3}$. Using (4.8), the ERC utility of player 2 is

$$u_2 = u_2\left(9, \frac{1}{3}\right) = 9 - \frac{a_2}{2}\left(\frac{1}{3} - \frac{1}{3}\right)^2 ; a_2 > 0. \tag{4.13}$$

Under FS preferences, from (4.5), and noting that $n = 3$, player 2 feels advantageous inequity with respect to player 1 whose income, 6, is lower and disadvantageous inequity with respect to player 3, whose income, 12, is higher. Hence, the FS utility of player 2 is

$$U_2 = 9 - \frac{\beta_2}{2}(9 - 6) - \frac{\alpha_2}{2}(12 - 9),$$

or,

$$U_2 = 9 - \frac{3}{2}\beta_2 - \frac{3}{2}\alpha_2. \tag{4.14}$$

Suppose now that there is a change in the income distribution. We increase the income of player 3 by 3 and decrease the income of player 1 by 3, but the income of player 2 is unchanged. The new income distribution is $3, 9, 15$ so that the sum of incomes, $S = 27$, and the mean income, $\overline{x} = \frac{27}{3} = 9$, are unchanged. However, the incomes are now more spread out than before. The ERC utility of player 2 under the new income distribution continues to be given by (4.13). However, the FS utility of player 2 has changed because player 2 now faces more advantageous inequity (with respect to player 1) and more disadvantageous inequity (with respect to player 3). The reader can readily check that the FS utility of player 2 under the new income distribution, given by

$$U_2 = 9 - \frac{6}{2}\beta_2 - \frac{6}{2}\alpha_2, \tag{4.15}$$

is now even lower. This accords with the empirical results in Charness and Rabin (2002). However, ERC cannot explain this evidence.

The ERC model also finds it difficult in some cases to explain indirect reciprocity or third party altruistic punishment. One of the exercises highlights this point. Finally, the ERC model cannot explain why contributors punish non-contributors in public goods games with punishments. Nevertheless, it remains a useful model and may provide a starting point to think about how social justice can be used as a reference point of comparison in evaluating utilities.

4.2.3 Models of Interdependent Preferences

In the model of *interdependent preferences*, or *type based reciprocity,* individuals who are altruistic might wish to be more prosocial to others who are also altruistic, but not necessarily to others who are not altruistic. This is entirely plausible, but it is already subsumed more generally within the concept of conditional reciprocity. Furthermore, inferring the types of other players, for example, altruistic or spiteful, requires the explicit formation of beliefs, and beliefs about beliefs, so the most appropriate machinery for this type of analysis is *psychological game theory* (see Part IV of the book). However, a reduced form approach was given in Levine (1998) and Rotemberg (2008) that illustrates the main idea; we consider the model due to Levine below.

Suppose that there are two players $i = 1, 2$, although the model can be readily extended to any finite number of players. Suppose that the incomes, or consumption bundles, of the two players are x_1 and x_2, respectively. The utility of player 1 (the utility of player 2 is analogously written) can be written as

$$v_1 = x_1 + b_1 x_2, \tag{4.16}$$

where the relative weight placed on the material outcome, x_2, of player 2 is

$$b_1 = \left(\frac{a_1 + \mu a_2}{1 + \mu}\right) \gtreqless 0; \mu \in [0, 1], \ a_1, a_2 \in (-1, +1). \tag{4.17}$$

Thus, player 1 derives utility directly from own material payoff, x_1, so in this sense player 1 is self-regarding. However, player 1 also derives utility, or disutility, from the the material outcome of player 2, x_2, depending on the sign of $b_1 \gtreqless 0$. In (4.17), the type of a player $a_i \in (-1, +1)$ reflects the altruism of a player. For $i = 1, 2$, if $a_i = 0$, the player is self-regarding; if $a_i > 0$, the player is altruistic; and if $a_i < 0$, the player is spiteful. Thus, for $i = 1, 2$, when $a_i > 0$, altruism is increasing in the size of the parameter a_i.

A special case of this model arises when $\mu = 0$. In this case, the utility of player 1 is given by

$$v_1 = x_1 + a_1 x_2. \tag{4.18}$$

We can use (4.18) to classify player 1 as (i) *altruistic* if $a_1 > 0$, so player 1 places a positive weight on player 2's material outcome, x_2, (ii) *spiteful* if $a_1 < 0$, so player 1 places a negative weight on player 2's material outcome, x_2, and (iii) *self-regarding* if $a_1 = 0$, so player 1 is unaffected by player 2's material outcome. The utility of player 2 is given analogously by $v_2 = x_2 + a_2 x_1$.

Consider now the case $\mu > 0$, and the utility function of player 1 in (4.16). We have two subcases.

1. $a_1 > 0$, so player 1 is altruistic. If player 2 is also altruistic, $a_2 > 0$, then from (4.17) $b_1 > 0$, so that player 1 derives higher utility when x_2 increases. If, however, player 2 is spiteful, $a_2 < 0$, then both cases are possible: (i) $b_1 > 0$ if $\frac{a_1+\mu a_2}{1+\mu} > 0$, or if $a_1 > \mu |a_2|$, where $|a_2|$ is the absolute value of a_2, and (ii) $b_1 < 0$ if $a_1 < \mu |a_2|$, which requires that the spitefulness of player 2 should be high enough, that is, a_2 should be closer to -1 and the altruism of player 1 should be low enough, that is, a_1 should be positive but closer to 0. This is the sense in which this is a model of type based reciprocity. In sum, if an altruistic player 1 figures out that
   (a) player 2 is altruistic, then player 1 derives greater utility from the well being, x_2, of the partner,
   (b) player 2 is spiteful and $a_1 < \mu |a_2|$, then the greater well being of player 2, x_2, causes disutility for player 1.
2. $a_1 < 0$, so player 1 is spiteful. We leave it to the reader to show that if player 2 is also spiteful, then $b_1 < 0$, but if player 2 is altruistic enough and the spitefulness of player 1 is low enough, then it is possible that $b_1 > 0$.

In this model, players privately know their type, and the type of player i is given by the sign of a_i, altruistic or spiteful. There is assumed to be a distribution of types in the population and players signal their types to other players through their actions. The underlying equilibrium concepts (see Part IV), a Bayesian Nash equilibrium in static games, and a Perfect Bayesian Nash equilibrium (PBNE) in dynamic games, impose an enormously high degree of cognitive burden on the players. There is also the possibility of multiple equilibria in these models, but there is very little empirical support for the refinements of a PBNE that are used to narrow down the set of multiple equilibria.

This model can explain why strictly positive, but low, offers in ultimatum games are rejected. The reason is that low offers might signal to the responder that the proposer is spiteful. If so, then even an otherwise altruistic responder might respond with spite towards the proposer by rejecting the low offer, for example, if $a_1 < \mu |a_2|$. The model can also explain why some players contribute in public goods games. If altruistic players have beliefs that other players in the game are also altruistic, then they positively internalize the payoffs of other players. Hence, they take account, at least partially, of the externality caused for other players from one's own contribution (recall this was also the mechanism in the socially optimal solution in Section 3.5 in Chapter 3). Thus, such players will find it optimal to contribute a strictly positive amount. However, the model is not able to explain positive giving in dictator games. Since the passive receiver takes no actions in the game, the dictator cannot form beliefs about the type of the receiver. Since the dictator cannot infer that the receiver is altruistic, there is no reason why, in a model of type based reciprocity, the dictator should offer any positive amount to the receiver.

4.2.4 The Charness–Rabin Model

Charness and Rabin (2002) argue for widening the scope of problems studied under other-regarding preferences by allowing decision makers to express a preference for more general social objectives. They propose two sets of other-regarding utility functions and also an equilibrium concept, *reciprocal fairness equilibrium*. The second of the two utility functions that they propose nests the FS model and the ERC model, but it contains four parameters that need to be estimated separately from the data, which is not a trivial task. Hence, we simply outline the first of their utility functions in this section.

Suppose that there are n individuals with material outcomes $x_1, x_2, \ldots, x_n$. Then, the utility function of any individual $i = 1, \ldots, n$, which is a weighted average of their own material outcome, x_i, and a social outcome, W, is given by

$$u_i = \gamma x_i + (1 - \gamma) W; \gamma \in (0, 1), \tag{4.19}$$

where

$$W = \theta min \{x_1, x_2, \ldots, x_n\} + (1 - \theta)(x_1 + x_2 + \ldots + x_n); \theta \in (0, 1). \tag{4.20}$$

In (4.20), the social outcome, W, is a weighted average of *equity considerations* (first term on the RHS) and *efficiency considerations* (second term on the RHS). Equity takes the form of a *Rawlsian social welfare evaluation* in which the welfare of society is given by the material outcome for the worse off member of society, $min\{x_1, x_2, \ldots, x_n\}$. Efficiency takes the form of a *utilitarian social welfare function* in which the sum of material outcomes for all members of society is maximized.

When there are only two individuals, $n = 2$, with material outcomes x_1, x_2, then using (4.19) and (4.20), we can write the utility function of player 1 as

$$u_1 = \begin{cases} [1 - \theta(1 - \gamma)] x_1 + (1 - \gamma) x_2 & \text{if} \quad x_1 \geq x_2 \\ x_1 + (1 - \gamma)(1 - \theta) x_2 & \text{if} \quad x_1 < x_2 \end{cases}. \tag{4.21}$$

Readers will recall from their basic microeconomics courses how to draw indifference curves corresponding to a particular utility function. Suppose that we drew the indifference curves of player 1, measuring x_1 along the horizontal axis and x_2 along the vertical axis. The indifference curve will have a kink at the point $x_1 = x_2$. In the region where $x_1 < x_2$, the absolute value of the slope of this indifference curve will be higher as compared to the region $x_1 \geq x_2$ (one of the exercises asks you to confirm this). This implies that player 1 will be more reluctant to give up an extra unit of x_1 in exchange for x_2 in the region $x_1 < x_2$.

This model can explain why dictators give a positive amount to passive receivers. The reason is that dictators care about equity. If (i) θ in (4.20) is high enough, and (ii) γ in (4.19) is low enough, then the concern for equity is high enough for the dictators to give a positive amount. The reason dictators will typically give less than half their endowments to receivers is that they are more reluctant to give up an extra unit of x_1 in exchange for x_2 in the region $x_1 < x_2$. The reader can use this intuition to demonstrate this point more formally. The model can also explain behavior in the trust game, but it is more difficult to explain punishments in public goods games with punishments. The second of their proposed other-regarding utility functions is able to explain punishments in public goods games because the FS model is a special case of those preferences.

4.3 Social Identity and Inequity Aversion in the Ultimatum Game

In this section, we outline a version of the model in Dhami et al. (2021), although we simplify their model by excluding redistributive taxation of incomes from the rich to the poor. Using this model, we demonstrate how (i) we can use FS preferences to explain prosocial behavior in the *ultimatum game described* in Section 3.2 in Chapter 3, and (ii) incorporate social identity issues (see Section 3.9 in Chapter 3) into the model.

The particular social identity that the authors were interested in, and tested using field data from the UK, was the political identity of the registered members of all the main UK political parties. However, for our exposition below, we will simply refer to a generic "social identity." The social identity is either an *insider social identity* ($S = I$) or an *outsider social identity* ($S = O$).

Suppose that the proposer and the responder in an ultimatum game have FS preferences. Thus, a player can either be a proposer ($i = 1$) or a responder ($i = 2$). The monetary endowment of the proposer is $y > 0$, and this is known to both players. The proposer first offers a share $s \in [0, y]$ to the responder, which is observed by the responder. If the responder accepts the offer, then the proposer gets to keep $x_1 = y - s$ and the responder receives $x_2 = s$. Thus,

$$x_1 = y - s; x_2 = s. \tag{4.22}$$

If the responder rejects the offer, both players get a zero payoff ($x_1 = x_2 = 0$). Assume that the endowment, y, of the proposer is infinitely divisible.

If both players have self-regarding preferences, then the responder will accept any positive outcome s. Since the monetary amount is infinitely divisible, the responder will accept $s = 0$. Looking forward, the proposer will offer $s = 0$, which will be accepted. Thus, the outcomes under self-regarding preferences are

$$x_1^* = y, x_2^* = 0. \tag{4.23}$$

Recall, from Section 3.2 in Chapter 3, that when the endowment is not infinitely divisible, and $y = \$10$, the equilibrium outcome under self-regarding preferences is $x_1^* = \$9.99, x_2^* = \$0.01$.

Using (4.1), the *FS utility* of the proposer, player $i = 1$, is given by

$$U_1 = \begin{cases} x_1 - \beta_S [x_1 - x_2] & if \quad x_1 \geq x_2 \\ x_1 - \alpha_S [x_2 - x_1] & if \quad x_1 < x_2 \end{cases}, \tag{4.24}$$

where $\alpha_S \geq 0$ and $\beta_S \geq 0$ are, respectively, the parameters of disadvantageous and advantageous inequity; the subscript S on these parameters indicates the social identity of the responder. For instance, when the proposer is paired with an ingroup responder, we have the case α_I and β_I; and when paired with an outgroup responder, we have the case α_O and β_O.

Social identity theory, discussed in Section 3.9 in Chapter 3, suggests that individuals are relatively more altruistic towards ingroup members, that is, $\beta_I > \beta_O$, so they derive greater disutility from coming out ahead of them. However, theory does not predict whether the envy parameter, α_S, is relatively higher or lower towards ingroup members, so any of the three possibilities, $\alpha_I \lesseqqgtr \alpha_O$, can arise. We summarize these observations as follows,

$$\beta_I > \beta_O \text{ but } \alpha_I \lesseqqgtr \alpha_O. \tag{4.25}$$

The determination of the relative sizes of α_I, α_O, is an empirical matter. One of the purposes of outlining this model is to show how empirical evidence can feed back into the relevant theory and determine which of the three possibilities, $\alpha_I \lesseqqgtr \alpha_O$, arises.

Similarly, the FS utility of the responder, player 2, is given by

$$U_2 = \begin{cases} x_2 - \beta_S [x_2 - x_1] & \text{if} \quad x_2 \geq x_1 \\ x_2 - \alpha_S [x_1 - x_2] & \text{if} \quad x_2 < x_1 \end{cases}. \tag{4.26}$$

We assume, for simplicity, that the parameters α_S, β_S are identical for both players, although this assumption can be easily relaxed. We also assume that both players know each other's preferences. In actual practice, players might have beliefs about the preferences of other players. This requires the use of expectations about others, which we shall not need in our model.

Using (4.22), we can now compare the monetary payoffs of the two players as follows

$$x_1 \gtreqqless x_2 \Leftrightarrow \frac{y}{2} \gtreqqless s, \tag{4.27}$$

where $s = \frac{1}{2}y$ is the offer of a share to the responder that equalizes the payoffs of both players. We simplify our exposition further by assuming that the proposer never offers the responder a share s more than one half the endowment, so $s \leq \frac{y}{2}$. This will be the case if the proposer is not too altruistic. We have

$$s \leq \frac{y}{2} \Leftrightarrow x_2 \leq x_1. \tag{4.28}$$

We now define the responder's *minimum acceptable offer* (MAO).

Definition 4.1 *Let s_M be the minimum share $s \in [0, y]$ offered by the proposer to the responder that satisfies $U_2 \geq 0$. Then s_M is the minimum acceptable offer (MAO) for the responder.*

The condition $U_2(s) \geq 0$ in Definition 4.1 is imposed because the responder can always guarantee a payoff of 0 by rejecting the offer. From (4.26) and (4.28) we have $U_2 = x_2 - \alpha_S [x_1 - x_2]$. Substituting the values of x_1 and x_2 from (4.22) we get

$$U_2 = s - \alpha_S [y - 2s]. \tag{4.29}$$

The requirement $U_2 \geq 0$ in Definition 4.1 and (4.29) imply that $s - \alpha_S [y - 2s] \geq 0$, or

$$U_2 \geq 0 \Leftrightarrow s \geq \left(\frac{\alpha_S}{1 + 2\alpha_S}\right) y.$$

Thus, the minimum share that the responder will accept in preference to rejecting the offer is

$$s = s_M = \left(\frac{\alpha_S}{1 + 2\alpha_S}\right) y. \tag{4.30}$$

Notice that s_M in (4.30) is independent of β_S. This is because the responder's income is never higher than the proposer's income. Under self regarding preferences, $\alpha_S = 0$, hence, from (4.30), $s_M = 0$, which gives rise to the result in (4.23). We can think of (4.30) as the *responder's reaction function*. It specifies that the responder will accept any offer by the proposer that is greater than or equal to s_M and reject any offer that is below s_M, that is,

$$\text{Accept proposer's offer if } s \geq s_M, \text{ otherwise reject.} \tag{4.31}$$

From (4.30), the MAO of the responder, s_M, is strictly increasing in (i) the endowment of the proposer, y and (ii) the disadvantageous inequity parameter of the responder, α_S, whenever the responder feels disadvantageous inequity, that is, $\alpha_S > 0$. This can be easily seen from a visual inspection of (4.30). More formally, these results follow from direct differentiation of (4.30).[2] When α_S is high, the responder experiences greater disutility from any disadvantageous income differences with the proposer. Hence, the responder wishes for the disadvantageous inequity to narrow down, which requires stating a higher MAO.

From (4.25), we know that theory does not predict which of the three cases, $\alpha_I \lesseqgtr \alpha_O$, is likely to occur. However, since we now know that s_M, is strictly increasing in α_S, when $\alpha_S > 0$, we can derive testable implications of all three cases and then let the data decide which of the three cases is supported by the data. These testable implications are:

1. If $\alpha_I > \alpha_O$, then the responder feels more disadvantageous inequity from ingroup proposers as compared to outgroup proposers. Since s_M is increasing in α_S, if $\alpha_I > \alpha_O$, then the responder's MAO when matched with an ingroup proposer must be higher than the MAO when matched with an outgroup proposer. If we can now get responders to state their MAO when matched with ingroup proposers and outgroup proposers, we can determine if this prediction is confirmed.
2. If $\alpha_I = \alpha_O$, then there is no difference between the responder's stated MAO when matched with ingroup proposers and outgroup proposers.
3. If $\alpha_I < \alpha_O$, then the responder's stated MAO when matched with ingroup proposers is predicted to be less than the MAO when matched with outgroup proposers.

The data in Dhami et al. (2021) shows that responders exhibit a strictly lower MAO when matched with ingroup proposers relative to outgroup proposers. From this, and our discussion above, we can conclude that the third case, $\alpha_I < \alpha_O$, must be true. Thus, there is relatively lower ingroup envy relative to outgroup envy. These results are consistent with the results of Chen and Li (2009) but, relative to their paper, they require weaker assumptions and rely on using a real world identity.

Let us now consider the proposer's choices.

We assume that the proposer chooses the optimal offer, $s = s^*$, in order to maximize her utility in (4.24), subject to the responder's reaction function in (4.31), where s_M is given in (4.30). This solution method is analogous to solving a Stackelberg game that many readers are likely to be familiar with. From (4.24) and (4.28) we have $U_1 = x_1 - \beta_S [x_1 - x_2]$. Substituting the values of x_1 and x_2 from (4.22) we get

$$U_1 = (1 - \beta_S)\, y - (1 - 2\beta_S)\, s. \tag{4.32}$$

From (4.32), we have three cases to consider, depending on the value of β_S. First note that

$$1 - 2\beta_S \gtreqless 0 \iff \frac{1}{2} \gtreqless \beta_S. \tag{4.33}$$

[2] Let $\alpha_S > 0$. Differentiating both sides of (4.30) with respect to y, we get $\frac{\partial s_M}{\partial y} = \frac{\alpha_S}{1+2\alpha_S} > 0$. Similarly, differentiating both sides of (4.30) with respect to α_S, we get $\frac{\partial s_M}{\partial \alpha_S} = \frac{y}{(1+2\alpha_S)^2} > 0$.

1. $\beta_S < \frac{1}{2}$: This implies that $1 - 2\beta_S > 0$, so from (4.32) the proposer's utility U_1 is strictly decreasing in the share offered to the responder, s. Thus, the proposer will wish to offer the smallest share possible. Given the reaction function of the responder in (4.31), the proposer must give a share $s \geq s_M$. Hence, the proposer chooses the smallest possible share $s^* = s_M$.
2. $\beta_S = \frac{1}{2}$: This implies that $1 - 2\beta_S = 0$, so the proposer's objective function in (4.32) is $U_1 = (1 - \beta_S)\,y$. Since U_1 is independent of s, so any share in the interval $\left[s_m, \frac{y}{2}\right]$ is optimal, that is, $s^* \in \left[s_m, \frac{y}{2}\right]$.
3. $\beta_S > \frac{1}{2}$: This implies that $1 - 2\beta_S < 0$, so the proposer's utility U_1 in (4.32) is strictly increasing in the share, s, offered to the responder. Thus, the proposer offers the maximum possible share which is $\frac{y}{2}$ (recall we have assumed that the proposer never offers more than $\frac{y}{2}$), that is, $s^* = \frac{y}{2}$.[3]

It follows from the three calculations above that the degree of altruism of the proposer, as captured by the size of β_S, is the key in determining the responder's share. An increase in β_S from below $\frac{1}{2}$ to above $\frac{1}{2}$, leads to a discontinuous increase in the optimal offer, s^*, from $s^* = s_M$ to $s^* = \frac{y}{2}$.

An important application arises when altruism towards ingroup members is high in the sense that $\beta_O < \frac{1}{2}$ and $\beta_I > \frac{1}{2}$, which satisfies the restriction $\beta_O < \beta_I$ in (4.25). In this case, the prediction of the model is that a proposer will offer more to an ingroup responder relative to an outgroup responder. It is probably fair to say that the modal empirical estimate is one of $\beta < \frac{1}{2}$, but these estimates come from studies where subjects are not primed for their social identity. We know very little about the size of β in the presence of social identity. The cut-off value of $\beta_S = \frac{1}{2}$ in the result above follows from the linear form of FS preferences. If we had used the nonlinear form of FS preferences in (4.5), then the proposer's share will depend in a continuous manner on β_S. The data in Dhami et al. (2021) show that proposers transfer 11.65% more of their endowment to an ingroup responder relative to an outgroup responder. This confirms the assumption made in (4.25) that $\beta_I > \beta_O$.

4.4 Political Economy and Other-Regarding Preferences

Public spending, which includes public expenditure on health, pensions, and unemployment insurance, is a major component of GDP in Western democracies. Among OECD countries, France accounts for the highest percentage of public spending relative to GDP, which is 30%. But in several other countries, this figure is between 25%–30% of GDP (e.g., in decreasing order for the 2020 data: Finland, Belgium, Denmark, Italy, Austria, Germany, Sweden, Norway, and Spain). What accounts for the desire of society to redistribute income towards the poorer and needy citizens? One also observes redistribution in the US to be smaller relative to the average in Western Europe. Why are attitudes to redistribution potentially different? A separate field of

[3] It is possible that there is an upper limit, $\overline{y} \leq \frac{y}{2}$ to the share that the proposer will offer to the responder, say, on account of social norms or customs. In this case, we have $s \in \left[0, \overline{y}\right]$ and $s^* = \overline{y}$.

economics, *political economy*, has developed to explain the interaction between economic and political institutions to determine voting and redistributive outcomes.

In the specific case of redistribution, is it the case that the human attributes of prosociality, that we evidenced in Sections 3.2–3.5 in Chapter 3, form the basis of observed redistribution levels? In this section we examine this question.

Let us first make some key points through Examples 4.34 and 4.35 which are drawn from the work of Dhami and al-Nowaihi (2010).

Example 4.34 *(Dhami and al-Nowaihi, 2010) Suppose that the three individuals in Example 4.33 are voters in a democratic system. Voters are given a choice between two income distributions (or options), A and B, where each distribution lists, successively, the income of the three voters.*

$$(A)\ 6, 9, 12 \text{ and } (B)\ 3, 9, 15.$$

Under option A, voters 1, 2, and 3 have the respective incomes 6, 9, and 12; and in option B, these incomes are 3, 9, and 15. One can think of voter 1 as poor, voter 2 as middle class, and voter 3 as rich; or one may think of these as representative voters from each of the three income classes. In a more complete model that allows for redistributive taxation, the first income distribution can be obtained from the second income distribution by taxing away three units of income from the richest voter and giving these three units to the poorest voter. We assume that the choice between the two distributions is made by majority voting, so the income distribution with the most votes in its favor is implemented.

Suppose, for the sake of illustration, that we assume that voters 1 and 3 are self-regarding, while voter 2 (who has income 9 under both distributions) is other-regarding and has FS preferences. A purely self-regarding voter 2 would have been indifferent between options A and B because income equals 9 in both cases. A voter 2 with ERC preferences would also have been indifferent between the two options because the income of the voter and the relative income are identical under both options (see Example 4.33). However, we know from Example 4.33 that a voter 2 with FS preferences prefers the first income distribution because her utility from the first distribution, given in (4.14), is larger than the utility from the second distribution, given in (4.15). We can now see why voter 2 will be decisive in any majority vote between options A and B.

Since voters 1 and 3 are both self-regarding and care only about their own incomes, voter 1 prefers option A (because $6 > 3$) while voter 3 prefers option B (because $12 < 15$). Thus, voters 1 and 2 prefer option A, while voter 3 prefers option B. Hence, a coalition of voters 1 and 2 will win the majority vote in favor of option A. It is as if the preference of voter 2 for option A was decisive. Thus, even a minority of voters with other-regarding preferences in the population can be decisive in determining the policy outcome.

Example 4.35 *(Dhami and al-Nowaihi, 2010) Rich voters typically prefer lower income redistribution because they are worse-off in material terms. However, some rich voters may also be egalitarian and compassionate about those who are not well off in society. This may push them towards supporting greater redistribution by aligning with poor voters or middle class voters who support greater redistribution. In Example 4.34, voters 1 and 3 were self-regarding. Suppose now that the rich voter 3, like, the middle class voter 2, has FS preferences but only the poor voter is self-*

regarding. Suppose that the two possible income distributions that are chosen through a majority vote are now given by

$$(A)\ 6,9,12 \textit{ and } (B)\ 1,9,15.$$

Distribution A is identical to the one that we considered above, but distribution B is different, and it results in a particularly bad outcome for the poorest voter. Denote the incomes of voters 1, 2, and 3, respectively, in any income distribution by x_1, x_2, x_3. *For option A,* $x_1 = 6, x_2 = 9, x_3 = 12$, *and for option B,* $x_1 = 1, x_2 = 9, x_3 = 15$. *The self-regarding voter 1 prefers option A to option B (because* $6 > 1$*). Using (4.4), and noting that* $n = 3$, *the FS utility of voter 2 from any of the two options is*

$$U_2 = x_2 - \frac{\beta_2}{2}(x_2 - x_1) - \frac{\alpha_2}{2}(x_3 - x_2). \tag{4.34}$$

Substituting $x_1 = 6, x_2 = 9, x_3 = 12$ *in (4.34), the FS utility of voter 2 from option A is*

$$U_2(A) = 9 - \frac{3}{2}\beta_2 - \frac{3}{2}\alpha_2.$$

Substituting $x_1 = 1, x_2 = 9, x_3 = 15$ *in (4.34), the FS utility of voter 2 from option B is*

$$U_2(B) = 9 - \frac{8}{2}\beta_2 - \frac{6}{2}\alpha_2.$$

It is clear that $U_2(A) > U_2(B)$, *so voter 2 prefers option A to option B. Using (4.4), and noting that* $n = 3$, *the FS utility of voter 3 is given by*

$$U_3 = x_3 - \frac{\beta_3}{2}\left[(x_3 - x_2) + (x_3 - x_1)\right].$$

We can write the FS utility for voter 3 from the two income distributions A and B, respectively, by

$$U_3(A) = 12 - \frac{\beta_3}{2}\left[(12 - 9) + (12 - 6)\right] = 12 - \frac{9}{2}\beta_3.$$

$$U_3(B) = 15 - \frac{\beta_3}{2}\left[(15 - 9) + (15 - 1)\right] = 15 - \frac{20}{2}\beta_3.$$

Thus voter 3 strictly prefers option A to option B if $U_3(A) > U_3(B)$, *or if* $12 - \frac{9}{2}\beta_3 > 15 - \frac{20}{2}\beta_3$, *which requires that voter 3 be altruistic enough in the sense that* $\beta_3 > \frac{6}{11}$.

Thus, if $\beta_3 > \frac{6}{11}$, *then all three voters prefer option A to option B. In this case, the rich voters vote with the poor and middle class voters for greater redistribution. Perhaps something like this occurs in countries that develop a consensus for more redistributive taxes.*

In an important contribution, Epper et al. (2020) use Swiss data to show that social preferences play a key role in accounting for observed societal redistribution. We outline this study in some detail, not only because of its innate importance, but also because it illustrates various aspects of the experimental method, and gives the reader an insight on how to conduct high-quality empirical research, should they be considering writing a research project themselves as part of their degree. The authors assemble a rich dataset that allows them to test competing models of redistribution. The social preferences of subjects are elicited by asking them to make choices

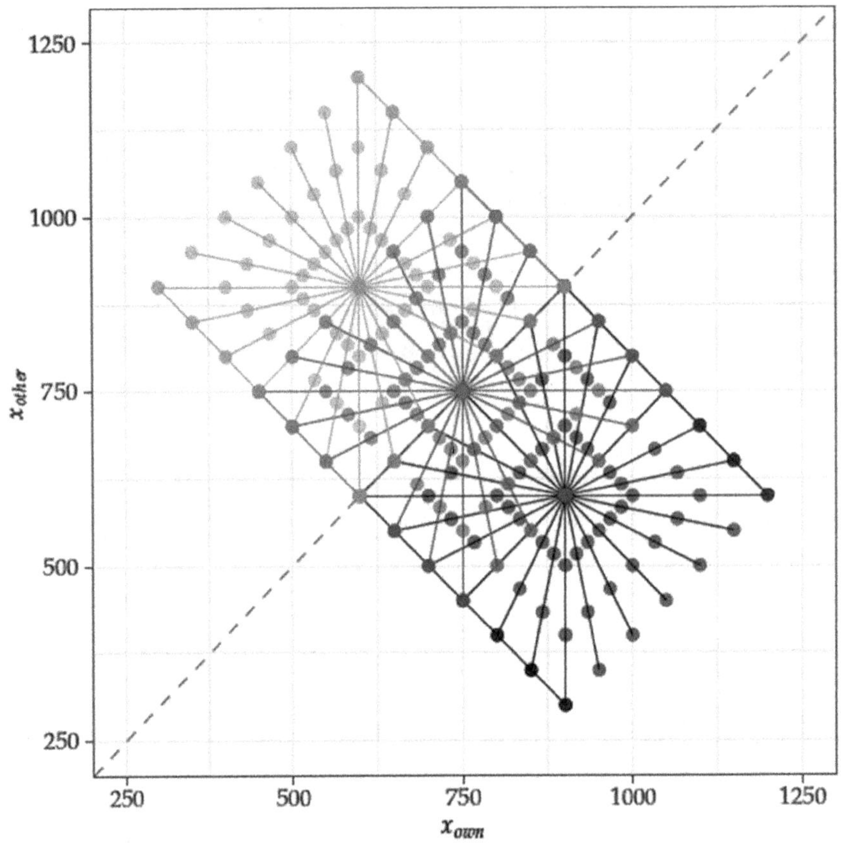

Figure 4.1 Budget lines across which players make choices of allocations between themselves and another player. Source: Epper et al. (2020)

between an allocation for themselves and another player, as in a dictator game. Figure 4.1 shows the sets of choices offered.

The income of the player whose social preferences we are interested in eliciting, is denoted by x_{own} and it is measured along the horizontal axis in Figure 4.1. The income of the other player is measured along the vertical axis, and denoted by x_{other}. Players are given a budget line along which they choose one allocation as their most preferred allocation. All the straight lines in Figure 4.1, with dots on them, represent different budget lines. Each dot on a budget line is an allocation and the subject picks one of these allocations. Along the diagonal line, where $x_{own} = x_{other}$, the incomes of both players are identical. All dots on the budget constraints that lie along the diagonal line represent allocations with identical incomes for both players.

The budget lines themselves are shown in three different regions. (1) In the north region, $x_{own} \leq x_{other}$, so all allocations, on each of the 14 lightest colored budget lines, lie on or above the diagonal line indicating higher income of the other player. This region is used to measure disadvantageous inequity. (2) In the south region, $x_{own} \geq x_{other}$, so all allocations, on each of the 14 darkest colored budget lines, lie on or below the diagonal line indicating that the income of the other player is lower. This region measures advantageous inequity. (3) The final region is the central region in which all budget lines, that are intermediate dark colored, go through the equal allocation (750, 750), and contain allocations for both advantageous and disadvantageous inequity.

For each of the three regions, we have budget lines that slope upwards and also slope downwards. A downward sloping line with slope, say, -3, indicates that if a subject gives up one unit of own income, x_{own}, the other player gets 3 extra units of income. Thus, a set of choices made along the negatively sloped budget lines in each region tells us how much of one's own income a subject is willing to sacrifice to enable the other player to receive extra income. Along the upward sloping budget lines, the incomes of both players increase. Hence, along these lines, choosing allocations lower down the line shows how much a subject is willing to sacrifice her own income, x_{own}, in order to reduce the income of the other player. Perhaps the other subject has a higher income and one might wish to pay a cost to reduce that income in order to achieve relatively greater income equality.

In any of the three regions, some of the 14 budget lines are used to estimate the social preferences of the individuals. Once the individuals are classified into different other-regarding types, predictions are made about which allocation they might choose in the remaining budget lines. These predictions are then used to validate the classification of subjects into different types.

The reader should pause for a moment to evaluate the usefulness of the experimental method relative to observational data for some purposes. In observational data, one is almost never able to obtain data in such detail, where such stringent controls are being used. Observational data is typically noisy, often collected for another purpose, and does not always allow for stringent testing of theories. The gold standard is randomized control trials (RCTs) but they too are often not able to provide the level of control of the underlying environment that one may find in experiments as, for instance, with the collection of data on social preferences that is based on Figure 4.1. Ultimately, however, all sources of data are important.

The elicited social preferences of the subjects are then matched to their support for various forms of redistributive policies. Political economists distinguish between two kinds of democratic institutions. In a *representative democracy*, voters vote for political parties, who then choose public policies, including redistributive policies. On the other hand, under *direct democracy*, voters vote directly for various policy choices, as in voting for or against Brexit, or exercising redistributive choices, through referenda or plebiscites. Several plebiscites for redistributive choices have taken place in Switzerland, where such policies are exercised at three levels, federal, canton, and municipal. In the experiments, subjects were asked to express a choice among the options in four such referenda; the experimental instructions were worded to reflect the spirit of these actual choices.

The referenda included the following. The *1 to 12 initiative* was offered to Swiss voters in 2013 and it proposed that the highest salary in any company should not exceed 12 times the lowest salary in the company. This referendum lost the popular vote, so it was reworded in the experiments as a less radical 1 to 20 initiative. The *initiative for a minimum wage* proposed a minimum wage of CHF 22 per hour (CHF 1 $\approx$ USD 1). The proposal for *unconditional basic income* proposed that all Swiss adult citizens should receive an unconditional basic income of CHF 2500 per month (and CHF 625 for a child). The *initiative for a fair tax code* proposed to end wasteful tax competition between cantons, say, to attract the rich by promising lower taxes.

For each of these referenda, subjects were asked to make one of five possible choices: Support, Rather Support, Don't Know, Rather Reject, Reject. An individual's support for a particular referendum item $i = 1,\ldots,4$ is represented as a binary variable, S_i: $S_i = 1$ if they choose Support or Rather Support, and $S_i = 0$ if they choose Rather Reject or Reject. If the choice for a particular referendum is Don't Know, then it is excluded. Across all the referenda items where subjects do express a definitive choice, an aggregate support variable AS is constructed for each subject as follows,

$$AS = \frac{1}{n}\sum_{i=1}^{n} S_i,$$

where n is the number of referenda items for which the subject does not give the answer, Don't Know.

The dependent variable in regressions is AS, one data point for each subject. The independent variables are (i) the various types of social preferences that have been identified from the allocation task shown in Figure 4.1 and (ii) a range of other important variables that test competing theories (e.g., age, education, gender, income, expected income, beliefs about the determinants of success in life such as luck or hard work). We describe these variables, as needed, below.

The results on the shares of individuals with various types of social preferences are as follows.

1. Individuals who have *inequity averse* preferences: The largest share of individuals, about 50%, makes choices that are consistent with the FS model of inequity aversion in Section 4.2.1. These subjects care for their own payoffs, but also, in addition, care about advantageous inequity (in the south region, they are willing to reduce their own payoffs to increase the payoffs of others in order to reduce inequity), and disadvantageous inequity (in the north region, they are willing to reduce the other person's payoffs at a cost to themselves in order to reduce inequality).
2. Individuals with *altruistic social welfare concerns*: About 35% of the subjects trade-off a concern for efficiency over equity. Their preferences are similar to those proposed in the Charness and Rabin (2002) model in Section 4.2.4; see equations (4.19), (4.20). Consider a budget line in Figure 4.1 that has a negative slope of -2. Giving up one unit of their own income, x_{own}, results in a two unit increase in the income, x_{other}, of the other player. The net gain, across both individuals, is one unit of income, which is efficiency enhancing. Such subjects are willing to make these efficiency enhancing choices (second term on the RHS of (4.20)). In the south region of Figure 4.1, where the other player has a lower payoff, such players are willing to choose an allocation that increases the payoff of the other player, even if it reduces the overall sum of payoffs of the two players. This behavior indicates a concern for the least well-off person (first term on the RHS of (4.20)).
3. Individuals who are *self-regarding*: The remaining 15% of individuals are self-regarding.

We can now run a regression of the following form:

$$AS_{jc} = \beta_0 + \beta_1 SW_j + \beta_2 IA_j + \alpha \mathbf{X} + \phi_c + \varepsilon_{ic}, \tag{4.35}$$

where the index j is for the jth subject in the experiment; the index c is for identifying the canton in which the individual resides; ϕ_c is a variable that captures canton fixed effects; and ε_{ic} is a random term. A dummy variable is constructed for the social type of the individual that takes a value (i) '0' if individual j is self-regarding, so this is the control group, (ii) "1" if individual j has inequity-averse preferences (IA_j), and (iii) "2" if individual j has altruistic social welfare concerns (SW_j). Notice that while we have three categories of preferences, we include only two categories in the regression to avoid the dummy variable trap. Hence, self-regarding individuals serve as the control category, which we have omitted from the regression. **X** is a vector (hence, in boldface) of all other variables such as age, gender, occupation, income, and beliefs. The regression coefficients are β_0 (which is the intercept term), β_1, β_2, and α (which are the coefficients on the independent variables).

The OLS regression estimates of this equation are shown in Table 4.1. This table is produced for the benefit of undergraduate readers who might wish to learn how to professionally report regression estimates. The first column contains all the independent variables; the names are self-explanatory. The next five columns report four regressions in which there are increasing numbers of independent variables (all contained within the vector X in (4.35)). The estimates reported in the table are the α and β coefficients in (4.35), including the intercept term, β_0. The stars on the estimates denote the corresponding p values of the estimates, where $p^* < 0.1$, $p^{**} < 0.05$, and $p^{***} < 0.01$. The main results are as follows.

1. Individuals with inequity averse preferences are 11% more likely to support redistribution as compared to the control group of self-regarding individuals ($p < 0.01$). Those with altruistic social welfare concerns are 9% more likely to support redistribution relative to the control group ($p < 0.05$). However, the corresponding regression coefficients β_1, β_2 are not significantly different. Adding controls in various regression coefficients does not influence the size of these regression coefficients, suggesting that these other variables do not interact with the deep underlying social preference variables. The self-reported political identity of the subjects on a left-right scale of the political spectrum is also a statistically significant determinant of desired redistribution.

   A *placebo initiative* or referendum, unrelated to redistribution, is also introduced. This is a vote on reducing the influence of political parties on the selection of federal judges by using an alternative method in which judges are selected using a random draw from a pool of skilled applicants. Social preferences are not found to be influential in determining how subjects vote for this initiative. Hence, social preferences influence societal redistribution, but not necessarily non-redistributive policies.

   Similar results on the relation between social preferences and desired redistribution also hold for the US Presidential elections. In the US, the Democratic party favors greater social redistribution relative to the Republican party. Fisman et al. (2017) find that subjects who are more prosocial in the role of dictators in lab experiments on dictator games, are also more likely to vote for Democratic party candidates. Kerschbamer and Müller (2020) use German data to show that inequity averse subjects comprise the main type of social preferences, and lab preferences predict political choices in elections quite well. Inequity averse subjects are more likely to vote for a left-wing party, more inclined to favor redistribution, and more likely to hold favorable views towards immigration. Subjects identified as having more self-

Table 4.1 Social preferences and aggregate political support for redistribution

	Aggregate support for redistribution			
	(1)	(2)	(3)	(4)
Social welfare concerns	0.094**	0.089**	0.090**	0.087**
	(0.039)	(0.038)	(0.039)	(0.039)
Inequality averse	0.114***	0.110***	0.110***	0.111***
	(0.036)	(0.036)	(0.036)	(0.036)
Income: above-median	-0.068**	-0.072***	-0.071**	-0.069**
	(0.028)	(0.028)	(0.028)	(0.028)
Male	-0.004	0.000	0.001	-0.012
	(0.026)	(0.027)	(0.027)	(0.027)
Age	0.008	0.007	0.008	0.003
	(0.006)	(0.006)	(0.006)	(0.006)
Have been unemployed in past	0.055**	0.055**	0.054**	0.038
	(0.025)	(0.025)	(0.026)	(0.026)
Beliefs about future mobility:			0.027	0.037
upwardly mobile (dummy)			(0.027)	(0.026)
Perceived past mobility:			0.000	0.009
upwardly mobile (dummy)			(0.024)	(0.023)
Perceived inequality (share				0.006
top/share bottom, z)				(0.013)
Mistrust in politicians (1-4)				0.032*
				(0.018)
Success under individuals' control				-0.077***
factors (risk, effort, education)				(0.022)
Success determined by external				0.049***
(luck, inheritance)				(0.016)
Above-median estimation of				0.016
absolute number of poor in CH				(0.023)
Constant	0.321**	0.325**	0.301**	0.409**
	(0.140)	(0.142)	(0.144)	(0.186)
Other socio-demographics	Yes	Yes	Yes	Yes
Education	Yes	Yes	Yes	Yes
Occupation	Yes	Yes	Yes	Yes
Other preference measures and general trust	No	Yes	Yes	Yes
Canton FE	Yes	Yes	Yes	Yes
R^2	0.085	0.096	0.097	0.132
Observations	812	810	810	810

Notes: OLS regression. The dependent variable is the aggregate support for redistribution (AS_i). Other socio-demographics include age squared, a dummy variable indicating whether the respondent's native language is french, a dummy indicating whether the respondent is married, and a dummy indicating whether the respondent did not disclose his/her income. Education includes dummies indicating a respondent's highest educational achievement (compulsory school, vocational training, high school, university or other), and occupation includes dummies indicating whether the individual currently has a full-time job, a part-time job, is unemployed or is not in the labor force. In addition, regressions 2-4 also control for subjects' risk aversion, patience, negative and positive reciprocity and general trust in people ("other preference measures and general trust"). Levels of significance: $^{*}p < 0.1, ^{**}p < 0.05, ^{***}p < 0.01$

regarding preferences in the dictator game behave in the opposite manner. This further supports external validity of lab experiments on other-regarding preferences.

2. Redistributive policies are likely to (i) materially benefit individuals with incomes below the median income as they are the main recipients of public income transfers and (ii) materially harm individuals with incomes above the median income, who are likely to pay higher taxes. Thus, one would imagine greater support for redistributive policies among those with below median income. Indeed, the data shows that those with incomes below the median are 7% more likely to support redistribution as compared to those whose incomes are above the median income. This is a standard prediction of many political economy models of redistribution with a linear progressive income tax. Politicians may use such taxes to signal their redistributive type to voters (Dhami, 2003).
3. Alesina and Angeletos (2005) invoke beliefs to explain why redistribution is lower in the US relative to Europe; this is sometimes known as the *American exceptionalism hypothesis*. They argue that in the US, people tend to believe that actual incomes are the result of hard work rather than luck, while the converse is true for Europeans who believe that luck plays the main role in being rich. For this reason, it is hypothesized, there is lower support for redistribution in the US (people get what they deserve and the ones who get less, deserve to get less). Alesina and La Ferrara (2005) and Alesina and Giuliano (2011) report empirical support for this hypothesis. Comparing American and Norwegian subjects, Almås et al. (2020) show that Americans are more tolerant of income inequality arising from differences in productivity and skills. In general, Norwegians choose a more equal distribution of income.

   Epper et al. (2020) asked their Swiss subjects to indicate the reason for why some people get ahead and succeed in life while others do not. The choices were:

   (a) the willingness to take risks,
   (b) inheritance,
   (c) hard work and initiative,
   (d) luck, and
   (e) having the right education are important reasons why some people get ahead and succeed in life while others do not.

   For each of these five factors, subjects had to report their beliefs on a five-point Likert scale where 1 meant "not at all important" and 5 meant "extremely important." The answers to (a), (c), (e) determined whether individuals believed that factors under the individual's control are important determinants of success and the answers to (b), (d) determined if they thought luck was important. The findings supported the earlier known results. A high degree of belief that luck was a significant determinant of success increased desired redistribution, and conversely a belief that factors under the individual's control were a significant determinant of success, reduced desired redistribution. The corresponding regression coefficients are statistically significant ($p < 0.01$).
4. Separate measures of trust elicited from the subjects found that greater trust increases support for redistribution ($p < 0.01$), but several other factors that play an important role elsewhere in behavioral economics do not matter for redistributive choices. These include: risk aversion, impatience, and positive and negative reciprocity. Separately the authors construct a proxy variable of people's mistrust in political institutions. Subjects are asked to state on a four-point scale how much they believe that Swiss politicians work to enrich themselves and

the lobbies they support instead of working for the benefit of the majority of the citizens. Greater mistrust in politicians increases desired redistribution, although the effects are only marginally statistically significant.

5. Bénabou and Ok (2001) propose that individuals care about their expected future incomes in determining their demand for redistribution. For instance, an individual with good future prospects might wish to vote for lower redistribution to avoid larger expected tax payments in the future. Similarly, individuals who have been upwardly mobile in the past may expect to continue to be upwardly mobile in the future, and also vote for lower redistribution. However, these factors are not found to matter in the Swiss data. Nor do subjective perceptions of poverty and income inequality influence the choice for redistribution.
6. All sociodemographic factors are found to be statistically insignificant determinants of redistribution. These variables include age, gender, occupation, race, religion, and marital status. The only exception is a history of unemployment, which positively influences demand for redistribution.
7. Poorer individuals who are more prosocial typically vote for greater redistribution on two counts. First, they are the beneficiaries of redistributive policies and, second, greater prosociality induces a demand for greater redistribution. The situation is different for affluent households who are more prosocial. Since they will be required to pay more taxes to fund greater redistribution, this reduces their support for redistribution. However, greater prosociality is associated with higher redistribution. The net effect of these two factors for affluent households is not clear. In the Swiss data, when the more affluent individuals are classed as inequity averse types, then relative to self-regarding individuals, they are 20% more likely to support redistribution; this is reminiscent of Example 4.35. The corresponding figure when they are classed as having a concern for social welfare is 12.6%.

4.5 Optimal Employment Contracts

In this section, we use an illustrative and simple exercise to determine the optimal employment contracts between a single firm and a single worker. A more general and realistic model could be presented, but we choose pedagogical simplicity over greater realism. The advantage is that we can completely characterize the solution using a range of alternative contracts.

The worker chooses costly effort, $e \in \{0, 1\}$, that can take two possible values, 0 and 1. The cost of effort function of the worker is given by $c(e)$. The worker either chooses to work hard ($e = 1$) at a cost $c(1) = c > 0$, or chooses to shirk ($e = 0$), which is costless, $c(0) = 0$. The worker's outside option, that is, the wage received in the next best job, is normalized to equal 0.

The firm's production function is $f(e) = \theta e$, where $\theta > 0$ is the per unit benefit to the firm when the worker puts in an extra unit of effort e. We assume that

$$0 < c < \theta, \tag{4.36}$$

so that the marginal benefit from effort to the firm is greater than the marginal cost of effort to the worker when the worker works hard. The firm cannot obtain verifiable information about the effort level of the worker unless the firm invests in a monitoring technology that costs the firm $\kappa > 0$. The worker knows if the firm has invested in the monitoring technology. The monitoring technology produces hard evidence of the worker's shirking with probability $p \geq 0$. However, with probability $1-p$, the monitoring technology fails to produce verifiable evidence that could be produced before a third party, such as a court or a labor tribunal, in order to prosecute the worker for inadequate effort.

4.5.1 Traditional Approach to Incentives in Economics

The traditional approach to incentives in economics is designed specifically for interacting parties that have self-regarding preferences, and this is the assumption we make in this subsection. Suppose that the firm offers a contract (w, e_n, f), which specifies a contractually binding wage, w, a desired but non-contractable effort, e_n, and a fine, $f > 0$, should verifiable evidence of the worker putting in an effort strictly below e_n be obtained.

If the firm does not invest in the monitoring technology, then it is unable to obtain verifiable evidence of low effort. The worker's utility, u, and the firm's profits, π, when no investment is made in the monitoring technology are

$$\begin{cases} u(e) = w - c(e) \\ \pi(e) = \theta e - w \end{cases}. \tag{4.37}$$

We assume that the firm sells its output θe at a price per unit of 1, so θe is also the total revenue of the firm when the worker puts in effort e. Given the contract, (w, e_n, f), and the fact that the firm has not invested in the monitoring technology, the worker knows that fines will never be levied. A self-regarding worker will, therefore, always shirk, irrespective of the contract offered because $w - c(0) > w - c(1)$. The firm will see through the self-regarding worker's incentives, hence, it will offer a wage $w = 0$. The respective payoffs of the two parties are $u = 0, \pi = 0$.

If the firm invested in the monitoring technology at a cost $\kappa > 0$, then the outcomes for both players are probabilistic. Outcomes depend on the effectiveness of the monitoring technology in producing verifiable evidence of low effort by the worker, which occurs with probability p. Since shirking ($e = 0$) produces zero output for the firm, we assume in the rest of the section that the firm always wishes to induce the worker to work hard ($e = 1$).

Assumption 4.A1: The firm always wishes to induce effort $e = 1$ and its desired effort is $e_n = 1$.

Using Assumption 4.A1, the incentive contract can be written as $(w, e_n, f) = (w, 1, f)$. The utility function of the worker is now dependent on the outcome of the monitoring technology.

If the worker works hard, then $e = e_n = 1$ and the cost of effort is $c(1) = c > 0$. Since $e = e_n$, the worker can never be fined, irrespective of the outcome of monitoring, so

$$u(1) = w - c. \tag{4.38}$$

If the worker shirks, $e = 0$, then monitoring produces verifiable evidence of shirking with probability p which results in a fine, f, for the worker. Otherwise, with probability $1 - p$, the monitoring technology is not successful in discovering evidence of shirking, so the worker cannot be fined. Hence, the utility function of the worker is given by

$$u(0) = \begin{cases} w - f & \text{with probability} \quad p \\ w & \text{with probability} \quad 1 - p \end{cases}. \tag{4.39}$$

Purely for pedagogical reasons, we assume that the firm and the worker use expected utility to evaluate risky situations. Hence, using (4.39), the expected utility of the worker from shirking is $Eu(0) = p(w - f) + (1 - p)w$, or

$$Eu(0) = w - pf. \quad (4.40)$$

From (4.38) and (4.40), the worker prefers to work rather than shirk if $u(1) \geq Eu(0)$ or if[4]

$$pf \geq c. \quad (4.41)$$

The condition (4.41) is known as the *no-shirking condition* of the worker. The term pf is the expected fine from being caught shirking (or the expected cost of shirking), while c is the saving in cost to the worker from shirking rather than working (or the expected benefit of shirking). Thus, workers are deterred from shirking if the expected cost of shirking exceeds the expected benefits of shirking.

It remains to check if the firm will wish to invest in the monitoring technology. If the firm does not invest in the monitoring technology, its profits have already been shown to equal zero. Hence, the firm will invest if the profits from investing in the technology are positive. There are two cases to consider.

If the firm invests, and the worker works hard ($e = 1$), then the profits of the firm equal

$$\pi(1) = \theta - w - \kappa. \quad (4.42)$$

Since the worker works hard, the output/revenue produced for the firm equals $\theta \times 1 = \theta$ and the firm incurs two costs: (1) Wage cost, w, and (2) the cost of the monitoring technology, κ.

If the firm invests and the worker shirks, $e = 0$, the revenue of the firm equals 0, and the profits of the firm are

$$\pi(0) = \begin{cases} -w - \kappa + f & \textit{with probability} \quad p \\ -w - \kappa & \textit{with probability} \quad 1 - p \end{cases}.$$

The expected profit of the firm equals $E\pi = p(-w - \kappa + f) + (1 - p)(-w - \kappa)$, or

$$E\pi(0) = -w - \kappa + pf. \quad (4.43)$$

Suppose that the monitoring technology is effective enough to induce the worker to work hard, $e = 1$, and the no-shirking condition $pf > c$ in (4.41) holds. From (4.42), the firm invests in the monitoring technology if $\pi(1) \geq 0$ (recall, not investing gives $\pi = 0$) if

$$\theta \geq w + \kappa. \quad (4.44)$$

We have used the tie-breaking rule that when indifferent between investing and not investing, $\pi(1) = 0$, the firm invests.

So how does the firm decide on the mix of wages and fines? Since the outside option of the worker is normalized to 0, the *participation constraint* (or the *individual rationality constraint*) of the worker is $u(1) = w - c \geq 0$. Paying higher wages directly reduces the firm's profit in (4.42), hence, the firm pays just enough to keep the worker in the job, so $w = c$.[5] Thus, we can rewrite the condition for investment in the monitoring technology in (4.44) as

[4] We have assumed that when indifferent between working and shirking, that is, $u(1) = Eu(0)$, the worker prefers to work. This is known as a *tie-breaking rule* and we shall use similar tie-breaking rules below.

[5] If the outside option of the worker were strictly positive, say, $\overline{u} > 0$, then the wage offered to the worker would have been $w = \overline{u} + c$.

$$\theta \geq c + \kappa. \tag{4.45}$$

The fine, f, is now chosen so that the *no-shirking condition* of the worker in (4.41) is satisfied. It is sufficient to choose a fine such that the condition is just satisfied, that is, $f = \frac{c}{p}$. Thus, the final contract offered by the firm, if (4.41) and (4.45) hold, is

$$(w, e_n, f) = \left(c, 1, \frac{c}{p}\right).$$

Substituting $w = c$ in (4.42), the profit of the firm is

$$\pi(1) = \theta - c - \kappa. \tag{4.46}$$

Summary 4.1 *If the no-shirking condition in (4.41) holds in the presence of fines, and the marginal productivity of the worker is high enough in the sense that (4.45) holds, then the worker exerts a high effort level. The problem of contractual incompleteness, that is, the non-verifiability of effort of the worker to a third party can be solved by using appropriate economic incentives. Of course, either of the two conditions (4.41) and (4.45) may fail. For instance, the monitoring technology might not be very effective, so p is low, which requires "too high" a value of the fine $f = \frac{c}{p}$. There might be an upper limit on the level of the fine that the firm can impose, say, due to legal and business reasons, which precludes imposing very high fines. Above all, this ignores the fact that workers might have other-regarding preferences, and might reciprocate high wages with high effort, as in the gift exchange game. If so, then the firm might not need to invest in the costly monitoring technology at all, obviating the need to incur the expense on the monitoring technology, κ, on the RHS of (4.46).*

4.5.2 Trust Contracts and Bonus Contracts under Self-Regarding Preferences

Suppose that the firm no longer invests in a monitoring technology but relies on the conditional reciprocity of workers to design contracts. We maintain the economic structure of the worker-firm problem, as above, but we explore alternatives to the incentive contract.

A *trust contract* offered by the firm to the worker specifies a binding wage, w, and a desired, but noncontractable, effort, e_n. The actual effort level of the worker continues to be nonverifiable to a third party. The firm offers the trust contract (w, e_n), which is observed by the worker, who then chooses actual effort $e \in \{0, 1\}$. We continue to use Assumption 4.A1, so the firm desires an effort level $e_n = 1$. The worker's utility and the firm's profits are given in (4.37). The trust contract is even more incomplete than an incentive contract because in an incentive contract, high effort, $e = 1$, can be ensured by setting the fine level high enough to satisfy the no-shirking constraint. By contrast, there are no formal economic incentives to guarantee that the worker will choose $e = 1$ in a trust contract.

A *bonus contract* (w, e_n, b) offered by a firm to a worker specifies a binding wage, w, a desired but noncontractable effort, e_n, and a nonbinding bonus payment, $b > 0$, from the firm to the worker. This is a three-stage game. In Stage 1, the firm offers the contract (w, e_n, b), which is observed by the worker who, in Stage 2, chooses actual effort $e \in \{0, 1\}$. In Stage 3, after having observed the effort chosen by the worker, the firm decides whether to pay a bonus, $b > 0$, or not.

Under both trust and bonus contracts, if the worker and the firm are self-regarding, then the worker will put in zero effort level, $e = 0$. In the trust contract, a self-regarding worker will accept the contractable wage payment, w, but since high effort is noncontractable and costly, the worker chooses to shirk and picks the costless effort level, $e = 0$ (this is known as a 'take-the-money and run' strategy). In a bonus contract, in Stage 2, a self-regarding worker will realize that a self-regarding firm will not pay any bonus in Stage 3. Hence, Stage 3 is redundant, and the first two stages are identical to a game with trust contracts. Hence, workers will optimally choose $e = 0$. Essentially, each player believes that a self-regarding partner will behave in an opportunistic manner in the future. We state this as a result.

Result 4.1 *When workers and firms are self-regarding, the worker chooses* $e = 0$ *in trust and bonus contracts. The firm chooses* $w = 0$ *in a trust contract, and* $w = b = 0$ *in a bonus contract.*

4.5.3 Trust and Bonus Contracts under Other-Regarding Preferences

We now depart from self-regarding preferences and make the following two assumptions.

Assumption 4.A2: The firm and the worker are other-regarding. Other-regarding players have Fehr–Schmidt (FS) preferences.

In Assumption 4.A2, we could also have considered alternative models of other-regarding preferences, but as noted earlier the FS utility function is very tractable. One of the exercises asks you to consider the possibility that a fraction $\lambda \in (0, 1)$ of the workers are self-regarding while the rest, $1 - \lambda$, are other-regarding.

The next assumption is in the spirit of *intentions-based reciprocity* (i.e., players reciprocate the kindness of actions of others, depending on the intentions behind the actions, as perceived by them).

Assumption 4.A3: If the firm chooses a trust or a bonus contract, when an incentive contract with monitoring technology is available, other-regarding workers interpret the intentions of the firm as "kind intentions" and reciprocate by demonstrating other-regarding preferences. Conversely, if the firm chooses the incentive contract, when the trust and the bonus contracts are available, other-regarding workers interpret this choice as revealing "unkind intentions" so they respond by demonstrating self-regarding preferences.

Assumption 4.A3 is empirically supported (Fehr and Gächter, 2001; Fehr and Rockenbach, 2003; Dickenson and Villeval, 2008). A related point arises from the literature that shows explicit incentives may crowd out the intrinsic motivation of employees.

Trust Contracts under Other-Regarding Preferences

As noted above, the material payoffs of workers and firms are given in (4.37). We solve this game by backward induction, solving first the Stage 2 problem of the effort choice of the worker after observing the trust contract, (w, e_n) offered in Stage 1. From (4.37), we have

$$\pi(e) - u(e) = \theta e - 2w + c(e). \tag{4.47}$$

From Assumption 4.A1, the firm desires to induce an effort level $e = 1$, and $e_n = 1$. Since $c(1) = c$, $c(0) = 0$, a simple calculation, using (4.37), shows that

$$u(1) = w - c;\ u(0) = w;\ \pi(1) = \theta - w; \pi(0) = -w. \tag{4.48}$$

Hence, using $c < \theta$ (from (4.36)), the payoff differences between the firm and the worker in (4.47) can be written as

$$\begin{cases} \pi(1) - u(1) = \theta - 2w + c \lesseqgtr 0 & if \quad e = 1 \\ \pi(0) - u(0) = -2w < 0 & if \quad e = 0 \end{cases}. \tag{4.49}$$

From the first row of (4.49), we have $\pi(1) - u(1) \lesseqgtr 0$, hence, we need to consider all three cases. We shall assume that when the worker works hard ($e = 1$), the firm's profits exceed the utility of the worker, that is,

$$\pi(1) - u(1) > 0,$$

leaving the interested reader to consider the remaining two cases, $\pi(1) - u(1) \leq 0$.

Thus, if $e = 1$ the firm experiences advantageous inequity and the worker experiences disadvantageous inequity. From the second row of (4.49), the opposite occurs when $e = 0$. Using (4.1), when the worker chooses $e = 1$, the FS utility of the worker, U_2, in the domain of disadvantageous inequity is given by

$$U_2(1) = u(1) - \alpha_2\,(\pi(1) - u(1)), \tag{4.50}$$

where α_2 is the worker's parameter of disadvantageous inequity. When $e = 0$, the corresponding utility of the worker in the domain of advantageous inequity is

$$U_2(0) = u(0) - \beta_2\,(u(0) - \pi(0)), \tag{4.51}$$

where β_2 is the worker's parameter of advantageous inequity. Using (4.48), we get

$$\begin{cases} U_2(1) = w - c - \alpha_2\,(\theta - 2w + c) & if \quad e = 1 \\ U_2(0) = w - \beta_2\,(2w) & if \quad e = 0 \end{cases}. \tag{4.52}$$

From (4.52), the worker prefers to work hard rather than shirk if $U_2(1) \geq U_2(0)$, or if

$$w \geq \frac{1}{2\,(\alpha_2 + \beta_2)}\,[c(1 + \alpha_2) + \alpha_2\theta] \equiv w_2^* > 0. \tag{4.53}$$

The condition (4.53) is known as the worker's no-shirking condition under trust contracts. It specifies that the wage, w, should be at least as high as w_2^* in order to induce the worker to choose $e = 1$ rather than $e = 0$. The reason that a high enough wage can prevent shirking is that this increases the advantageous inequity experienced by the worker when $e = 0$ (the firm gets $-w$ but the worker gets w). The greater is the aversion of the worker to advantageous inequity, or the higher is β_2, the easier it is for the firm to satisfy the no shirking condition by choosing a lower wage (notice that w_2^* is decreasing in β_2). On the other hand, the greater is the aversion of the worker to disadvantageous inequity, or the higher is α_2, the higher must be the wage, w_2^*, that satisfies the no-shirking constraint of the worker. The intuition for this result follows directly from the first line of (4.52); an increase in α_2 increases the disutility of the worker from working hard rather than shirking, hence, the firm must pay the worker a higher wage to compensate for the extra disutility of working hard. More formally, this follows from direct differentiation of the RHS of (4.53) with respect to α_2, which shows that the RHS is increasing in α_2.

In Stage 1, the firm chooses the optimal wage to pay to the worker, taking into account the no-shirking condition in (4.53). Let us use (4.1) to compute the FS utility of the firm. From (4.49), the firm is in the domain of advantageous inequality when $e = 1$ and its FS utility is $\pi_1(1) = \pi(1) - \beta_1 (\pi(1) - u(1))$; and in the domain of disadvantageous inequity if $e = 0$, where its FS utility is $\pi_1(0) = \pi(0) - \alpha_1 (u(0) - \pi(0))$. Using (4.48), we get

$$\begin{array}{ll} \pi_1(1) = \theta - w - \beta_1 (\theta - 2w + c) & \textit{if} \quad e = 1 \\ \pi_1(0) = -w - \alpha_1 (2w) & \textit{if} \quad e = 0 \end{array} . \tag{4.54}$$

The firm prefers to induce the worker to work hard rather than shirk if $\pi_1(1) \geq 0 > \pi_1(0)$. Using (4.54), this requires

$$w \geq \frac{1}{2\beta_1 - 1} [\beta_1 c - \theta(1 - \beta_1)] \equiv w_1^*. \tag{4.55}$$

A trust contract must simultaneously satisfy both conditions in (4.53) and (4.55). Two cases arise.

(a) From the first row of (4.54), if the firm is not overly altruistic in the sense that $\beta_1 < \frac{1}{2}$, then, an increase in the wage paid, w, reduces the FS utility of the firm.
(b) If however, the firm is too altruistic, $\beta_1 > \frac{1}{2}$, then an increase in the wage paid to the worker increases the FS utility of the firm.

Both cases are possible.

Suppose that for illustration purposes, we choose the case $\beta_1 < \frac{1}{2}$ (the reader can use the other case, $\beta_1 \geq \frac{1}{2}$, for practice). Since the FS utility of the firm is decreasing in the worker's wage, w, in this case, hence, the firm will pay the smallest possible wage such that

(1) the no-shirking condition of the worker in (4.53) is satisfied (i.e., $w \geq w_2^*$), and
(2) it is optimal for the firm to induce the worker to work hard rather than shirk, which requires, from (4.55), that $w \geq w_1^*$. But when $\beta_1 < \frac{1}{2}$, the condition $0 < c < \theta$ in (4.36) implies that $\beta_1 c - \theta(1 - \beta_1) < 0$, thus, (4.55) implies that $w_1^* < 0$. In effect, since negative wages cannot be paid, the condition in (4.55) only requires that a positive wage be paid, $w \geq 0$. Thus, the wage paid in a trust contract, w_T, is simply one that satisfies the worker's no-shirking condition at equality, because higher wage reduces the firm's profits. So,

$$w_T \equiv w_2^* = \frac{1}{2(\alpha_2 + \beta_2)} [c(1 + \alpha_2) + \alpha_2 \theta], \tag{4.56}$$

pins down the wage in a trust contract. We are not there quite yet. We need to check two more conditions; we leave the reader to check the details by simple substitution. First, we need to check that the FS utility of the firm is non-negative (otherwise the firm could just shut shop and receive zero utility). From the first row of (4.54), this requires checking that $\pi_1(1) = \theta - w_T - \beta_1 (\theta - 2w_T + c) \geq 0$. Second, we need to check that the worker gets a utility no lower than the outside option of zero. From the first row of (4.52) this requires checking that $U_2(1) = w_T - c - \alpha_2 (\theta - 2w_T + c) \geq 0$.

Summary 4.2 *In a trust contract with self-regarding workers, the worker shirks, choosing $e = 0$. Taking account of the worker's shirking, a self-regarding firm chooses a zero wage, $w = 0$. This result changes in the presence of other-regarding preferences. Despite relatively greater contractual incompleteness in the trust contract relative to the incentive contract, the worker can be induced to work hard, $e = 1$, and receive a positive wage, $w_T > 0$, given in (4.56). It is possible that the profits of the firm are greater in a trust contract with other-regarding workers, relative to incentive contracts, if the cost of the monitoring technology, κ, is high enough, and if the technology is not too effective, that is, low p. The reader may wish to show this more formally.*

Bonus Contracts under Other-Regarding Preferences

Consider a bonus contract (w, e_n, b), as described above. The three-stage game is solved by backward induction. Hence, we need to first calculate the optimal behavior in Stage 3, where the firm contemplates paying a bonus, $b > 0$, or not paying a bonus, $b = 0$, to the worker, having observed all that has occurred in the first two stages. Let the actual effort chosen by the worker in Stage 2 be $e \in \{0, 1\}$.

The worker's utility, u, and the firm's profits, π, in Stage 3 are given by

$$\begin{cases} u(e) = w - c(e) + b \\ \pi(e) = \theta e - w - b \end{cases} ; e \in \{0, 1\}; b > 0 \text{ or } b = 0. \tag{4.57}$$

In order to compute the FS utility of the firm in Stage 3, when it makes the decision to pay the bonus, we first need the following intermediate calculations.

$$u(1) = w - c + b;\ u(0) = w + b;\ \pi(1) = \theta - w - b;\ \pi(0) = -w - b. \tag{4.58}$$

The payoff differences between the firm and the worker are given by

$$\begin{cases} \pi(1) - u(1) = \theta + c - 2(w + b) \lesseqgtr 0 & \text{if} \quad e = 1 \\ \pi(0) - u(0) = -2(w + b) < 0 & \text{if} \quad e = 0 \end{cases}. \tag{4.59}$$

From the first row of (4.59), the sign of $\pi(1) - u(1) \lesseqgtr 0$ cannot be determined a priori. In what follows we assume that

$$\pi(1) - u(1) > 0, \tag{4.60}$$

that is, when the worker works hard, the profits of the firm are greater than the worker's utility. The reader can work through the other two cases for practice.

From (4.60), the firm faces advantageous inequity, hence, the FS utility of the firm when $e = 1$ is $U_1(1) = \pi(1) - \beta_1 (\pi(1) - u(1))$. When $e = 0$, the firm faces disadvantageous inequity, hence, the FS utility of the firm is $U_1(0) = \pi(0) - \alpha_1 (u(0) - \pi(0))$. Using (4.58), we have

$$\begin{cases} U_1(1) = \theta - (w + b) - \beta_1 (\theta + c - 2(w + b)) & \text{if} \quad e = 1 \\ U_1(0) = -(w + b) - \alpha_1 (2(w + b)) & \text{if} \quad e = 0 \end{cases}. \tag{4.61}$$

Notice from (4.61) that wage, w, and the bonus, b, are substitute instruments for the firm on account of the terms $w + b$. However, note that w is chosen in Stage 1 by the firm, and is predetermined in Stage 3, but b is determined in Stage 3. The only choice of the firm in Stage 3 is to choose b.

The Stage 2 effort choice of the worker has also already been determined. Suppose that the worker has chosen $e = 1$. Then the utility of the firm is given by the first row of (4.61), which can be rewritten as

$$U_1(1) = b\,(2\beta_1 - 1) + [\theta - w - \beta_1\,(\theta + c - 2w)]\,. \tag{4.62}$$

Only the first term on the RHS of (4.62) is under the control of the firm through its choice of b. If $2\beta_1 - 1 \geq 0$, or equivalently the altruism of the firm is high enough in the sense that

$$\beta_1 \geq \frac{1}{2}, \tag{4.63}$$

then the utility of the firm is increasing in the bonus that it pays out to the worker, so it will indeed pay out the noncontractable bonus to the worker. If, however, $\beta_1 < \frac{1}{2}$, then the firm's Stage 3 FS utility is strictly decreasing in b. No bonus is paid in this case. To make the problem interesting we assume that (4.63) holds, so that $\beta_1 \geq \frac{1}{2}$. This condition may not be as strong as it looks due to two possible reasons.

1. The cutoff value $\frac{1}{2}$ for β_1 arises due to the linear form of FS utility that we have assumed. Under the non-linear form of FS utility in (4.5), we get continuous dependence on the parameters.
2. We have used a bare-bones model that ignores several other important human motivations. Evidence shows that humans are reluctant to break promises and pledges. Indeed, they might experience either direct disutility from lying (Vanberg, 2008), or they may experience guilt from the act of breaking a promise (Charness and Dufwenberg, 2006). By excluding these factors to ensure greater tractability of our analysis, we have also placed the entire burden of adjustment on the parameter β_1. Hence, we have needed the more stringent condition, $\beta_1 \geq \frac{1}{2}$. If we had included these factors, then a lower value of β_1 would also have ensured that the firm keeps its promise of paying a bonus.

From the second row of (4.57), the profit of the firm, when the worker works hard, is $\pi(1) = \theta - w - b$. The firm will wish to ensure that it can meet its outside option of 0, so we require $\pi(1) \geq 0$. As noted, the condition $\beta_1 \geq \frac{1}{2}$ ensures that the Stage 3 FS utility of the firm is strictly increasing in b. Hence, the maximum possible bonus that the firm will pay out can be found by setting $\pi(1) = \theta - w - b = 0$, or

$$b = \theta - w, \tag{4.64}$$

where w has already been determined in Stage 1; note that w can never be strictly greater than θ otherwise, $\pi(1) < 0$.

If, however, in Stage 2, the worker chooses $e = 0$, then from the second row of (4.61), in Stage 3 the firm's utility

$$U_1(0) = -b(1 + 2\alpha_1) - w(1 + 2\alpha_1),$$

is strictly decreasing in b. So the firm will choose $b = 0$ in this case.

We can summarize these findings in the following result.

Result 4.2 *(a) Suppose that the worker chooses $e = 1$ in Stage 2. If $\beta_1 \geq \frac{1}{2}$ then the firm chooses a positive bonus given in (4.64). If $\beta_1 < \frac{1}{2}$, then the firm chooses a zero bonus, $b = 0$. (b) If the worker chooses $e = 0$ in Stage 2, then the firm always chooses a zero bonus, $b = 0$.*

Backward induction now requires us to fold back the game one stage. In Stage 2, the worker needs to choose the optimal effort, having observed the first stage contract of the firm (w, e_n, b) and being able to foresee correctly the firm's optimal choice of bonus in Stage 3, as summarized in Result 4.2.

In order to compute the FS utility of the worker in Stage 2, we first need the following intermediate calculations that are found by substituting $b = \theta - w$ in (4.58) when $e = 1$, and $b = 0$ when $e = 0$.

$$u(1) = \theta - c;\ u(0) = w;\ \pi(1) = 0;\ \pi(0) = -w. \tag{4.65}$$

Thus, we have

$$u(1) > \pi(1) \text{ and } u(0) > \pi(0),$$

so the worker faces advantageous inequity in both cases where $e = 1$ and $e = 0$. Thus, the FS utility of the worker, in Stage 2, for any effort level e is given by $U_2(e) = u(e) - \beta_2 (u(e) - \pi(e))$, which on using (4.65) results in

$$\begin{cases} U_2(1) = (\theta - c)(1 - \beta_2) & \text{if} \quad e = 1 \\ U_2(0) = w(1 - 2\beta_2) & \text{if} \quad e = 0 \end{cases}. \tag{4.66}$$

To keep the exposition and the number of cases manageable, and analogous to (4.63), we assume that

$$\frac{1}{2} \leq \beta_2 < 1. \tag{4.67}$$

It follows from (4.66) that $U_2(0) < 0$ and $U_2(1) > 0$. These conditions are sufficient to ensure that the worker will optimally choose to work hard, $e = 1$, rather than shirk. We summarize this finding.

Result 4.3 *If $\frac{1}{2} < \beta_2 < 1$, then the worker optimally chooses to work hard, $e = 1$.*

In Stage 1, given our assumptions in (4.63) and (4.67), namely, $\beta_1 \geq \frac{1}{2}$ and $\beta_2 \geq \frac{1}{2}$, the firm knows that the worker will exert effort level $e = 1$ in Stage 2, and it will pay a bonus $b = \theta - w$ to the worker in Stage 3. It must now choose its optimal wage, w. Given the anticipation of $e = 1$, in Stage 1, we need the following intermediate calculations $u(1) = w + b - c; \pi(1) = \theta - w - b$. Substituting $b = \theta - w$ we get

$$u(1) = \theta - c; \pi(1) = \theta - w - b = 0. \tag{4.68}$$

Since $u(1) > \pi(1)$, the firm is in the domain of disadvantageous inequity. Its FS utility is given by $U_1(1) = \pi(1) - \alpha_1 (u(1) - \pi(1))$. Using (4.68), we get

$$U_1(1) = 0 - \alpha_1 (\theta - c),$$

which is independent of w. The firm must make positive profits, $\pi(1) \geq 0$, which is satisfied in (4.68). Thus, any combination of wage, w, and bonus, b, that satisfies the condition $b = \theta - w$, is optimal for the firm. For instance, $w = 0$ and $b = \theta$ is as good as $b = 0$ and $w = \theta$.

Result 4.4 *If $\beta_1 \geq \frac{1}{2}$ and $\beta_2 \geq \frac{1}{2}$, then the worker optimally chooses to work hard, $e = 1$, and any pair (b, w) that satisfies $b + w = \theta$ is optimal for the firm.*

4.5.4 Incomplete Contracts and the Theory of the Firm

There is a rich and impressive literature on the theoretical analysis of incomplete contracts in neoclassical economics and these models form the basis of courses in contract theory and industrial organization. In the basic model, there are two contracting parties, say A and B, who choose each other from a competitive pool of potential partners. Entering into a joint contract effectively turns their relation into a bilateral monopoly. The interaction between the two parties has the following three Stages.

1. In Stage 1, the two parties decide on the contracts that will govern their interaction over the next two stages.
2. In Stage 2, both A and B choose *relation-specific and non-contractable investments*, respectively, i_A and i_B, either simultaneously or in sequence. The investments are chosen from some set $[0, I]$ of potential investments, at respective costs $c(i_A)$ and $c(i_B)$. Investments are relation-specific in the sense that they are useless outside the bilateral relation, hence, they are subject to ex-post expropriation by the other party.
3. In Stage 3, the investments from Stage 2 produce a joint surplus $v(i_A, i_B)$ between the two parties.[6] The contracts that were chosen in Stage 1 determine the allocation of the surplus $v(i_A, i_B)$ between A and B in Stage 3.

What type of contracts must both parties write down in Stage 1? This is the main question addressed in the *theory of incomplete contracts*, albeit in models with a richer structure. The basic elements of this approach were laid out in Hart (1995) and Grossman and Hart (1986). The main idea is that each player will be concerned about protecting the Stage 2 investment, fearful that the investments might be expropriated in Stage 3 by the other party; this is known as the ex-post *hold-up problem*.

Suppose, for instance, that in Stage 1, the two parties wrote down a *joint ownership contract*, which guaranteed each party an "equal share" of the surplus $v(i_A, i_B)$. Suppose also that A and B make their investment choices 'simultaneously' in Stage 2.

In Stage 2, A chooses i_A in order to maximize expected profits

$$\pi_A = \frac{1}{2}v(i_A, i_B) - c(i_A). \tag{4.69}$$

Simultaneously, B chooses investment i_B in order to maximize expected profits

$$\pi_B = \frac{1}{2}v(i_A, i_B) - c(i_B). \tag{4.70}$$

The problem each player faces is that when they increase their investment by one unit, they get only one half of the full marginal product of their effort, but must pay the full marginal cost of their investment. Joint ownership is not conducive for high investment in the relationship as each

[6] Technically, $v : [0, I] \times [0, I] \to \mathbb{R}$.

player realizes that one half of the benefits from their Stage 2 investment will be expropriated by the other player. Hence, each player makes low investments under joint ownership. The investment is "low" relative to what would be chosen by a benevolent social planner who chooses the investments i_A, i_B to maximize the sum of the expected profits of A and B, given in (4.69) and (4.70) to get

$$W = \pi_A + \pi_B = v(i_A, i_B) - c(i_A) - c(i_B). \tag{4.71}$$

When the social planner chooses either of i_A and i_B to maximize (4.71) the full marginal benefit (and not $\frac{1}{2}$ the marginal benefit) of investment is equated to the full marginal cost. This leads to a socially optimal investment that is higher than the privately optimal investments under joint ownership.

At the other extreme, suppose that only one of the players were to make the relation-specific investment, say, player A, but player B makes no relation-specific investment. For instance, player A sets up a firm and hires player B as an employee who is paid a wage w in return for supplying a contractable investment i_B in Stage 2. Player A, as the owner of the firm, now chooses investment, i_A, to maximize

$$\pi_A = v(i_A, i_B) - c(i_A) - w. \tag{4.72}$$

The privately optimal choice of i_A that arises from maximizing (4.72) is identical to that arising from the social planner's problem. If the underlying functions are continuously differentiable, then the first order condition to each of these problems is identical. It is given by the condition $\frac{dv(i_A, i_B)}{di_A} - \frac{dc(i_A)}{di_A} = 0$, which specifies that the full marginal benefit of investment equals the full marginal cost of investment, leading to socially optimal investment.[7] The lesson then is to vest *ownership rights* with the party that makes the critical relation-specific investment, and who might otherwise invest inadequately under joint ownership. If both parties were to make noncontractable relation-specific investment, then it might be optimal to vest the residual control rights with the party that makes the more important or critical investment. These, in a nutshell, are some of the key insights of the classical theory of ownership rights under incomplete contracts. We consider the empirical evidence for this theory in Subsection 4.5.6 below.

4.5.5 A Note on Observable but Non-Verifiable Information

In a variety of experimental games in this chapter, we have motivated the existence of incomplete contracts through assumptions on what actions of the two parties to a contract are observable and/or verifiable. For instance, in our discussion of the gift exchange game, we said that the worker's effort level is either

(1) not observable to the firm, or that
(2) it is observable, but not verifiable to a third party.

In either of these two cases, the firm cannot write down the worker's effort level in the contract, although it can specify a nonbinding effort level, e_n, that cannot be contractually enforced. The

[7] If the function v is strictly concave and the function c is strictly convex, then the second order condition holds. In this case, the first order conditions can be used to solve for the optimal value of investment, i_A.

reason is that if the firm cannot produce hard evidence of a worker's shirking behavior to a third party, then the firm cannot insinuate legal proceedings, or third party arbitration, against the worker for breach of contract. Since the worker's effort cannot be contractually enforced, the contract is necessarily incomplete.

However, there is a difference between the two cases (1) and (2) above. If the effort level is observable to the contracting parties, even though it might not be verifiable to a third party (case (2) above), then the two parties can achieve a better outcome. Maskin and Tirole (1999) showed that if case (2) occurs, then the contracting parties can write side contracts and reward/punish each other, based only on their commonly observed information, and essentially achieve the same outcome as under complete contracts. The side contracts cannot be legally enforced because they are based on information that cannot be verified to a third party, but they are so structured as to be in each party's individual interests to follow. As an example, consider the gift exchange game and suppose the firm can observe the worker's effort but cannot verify it to a third party. Then, the claim is that by writing side contracts, the firm and the worker can obtain essentially the same outcome as can be obtained if the worker's effort were observable and verifiable to a third party, and there was no contractual incompleteness.

So how should these side contracts be written? This falls under the remit of the *mechanism design* literature in economics. For each of the games in Sections 3.2 to 3.5 in Chapter 3, we specified the rules of the game that governed the interaction between the two parties: worker-firm in the gift exchange game; proposer-responder in the ultimatum game; trustor-trustee in the trust game. These rules specified, for instance, which player moves first, what the player chooses, what the other player observes, and then what the other player chooses. For instance, in the gift exchange game, these rules specified that the firm moves first, chooses an employment contract that is observed by the worker, who then chooses the effort level. Each of these sets of rules gave rise to an outcome in the game, which we computed using backward induction. In Chapter 5, you will see that this outcome is the subgame perfect outcome of the corresponding game.

Suppose now we turned this problem on its head and asked the following question: Given a particular subgame perfect outcome of the game, what "rules of the game" should be designed so that they lead to the desired subgame perfect outcome? Finding these "rules of the game" is the subject matter of mechanism design. So essentially, the work of Maskin and Tirole (1999) showed that one can find a mechanism that will implement the side contracts necessary to create an equivalence between the results when we have incomplete contracts (but actions are mutually observable to the two parties), and when we have complete contracts.

In general, the experimental evidence is not supportive of the efficacy of several different kinds of mechanisms that have been proposed in the literature; readers interested in a detailed discussion and the evidence may consult Dhami (2020). Fehr et al. (2021) put the predictions of Maskin and Tirole (1999) to the test. In their experiments, a seller sells a good to a buyer, and the seller may exert costly effort to improve the quality of the good that is sold to the buyer. However, the seller's effort is not verifiable to a third party, although it is observable to both parties. Hence, the two parties cannot write down the seller's effort level in a contract. The prediction of the model in Section 4.5.4 under self-regarding preferences is that the seller will fear that costly effort will be expropriated by the buyer who will take advantage of the higher quality but not pay a higher price. Hence, the seller is predicted to choose low effort.

Fehr et al. (2021) then propose a mechanism that allows for side contracts between the buyer and the seller that should, if the predictions of the Maskin–Tirole theory hold, result in high effort level of the seller (as under complete contracts). The mechanism requires the buyer to announce the quality received from the seller. If this announcement is untruthful (e.g., the buyer announces low quality to justify low payments but the quality is actually high), then the seller can punish the buyer. The mechanism is so constructed that a self-regarding buyer will prefer to make a truthful announcement and the self-regarding seller will only punish if the buyer is untruthful. In other words, the mechanism induces both self-regarding parties to stay honest. The mechanism specifies that both parties will also be fined if they depart from the rules of the mechanism.

In principle, this mechanism should implement the Maskin–Tirole theory. But the predictions are not supported by the evidence. Buyers often lie, understating the quality of the good, and sellers put in low effort. If a seller initiates punishment procedures against a buyer for lying about the quality, the buyer retaliates against the seller in future interaction. Since both parties to the side contract flout the rules of the mechanism, they are both fined.

As always, such empirical tests are a joint test of the theory and of the ability of the subjects to understand the relevant solution concepts on which they are based. However, tests of understanding carried out on the subjects showed that they understood the logic of backward induction and the rules of the game. Thus, the most reasonable conclusion is that the theory fails.

But why does the theory fail? The authors identify *conditional reciprocity* as the main reason. When a seller challenges the buyer's claim of a low quality, which results in a fine on the buyer, the buyer in turn retaliates against the seller, which, by the rules of the mechanism, initiates a counter-fine on the seller. In other words, theory fails because it does not take account of conditional reciprocity. The authors then incorporate conditional reciprocity into the theory, which leads to a different mechanism that is fairly successful in inducing high effort from the seller and truthful claims from the buyers in 90% of the cases. Yet, the take-up of the new mechanism, based on conditional reciprocity, is only 20%–60% which is relatively low and needs further exploration. In general, these results show that ignoring conditional reciprocity has serious implications for the mechanism design literature.

4.5.6 Evidence on the Choice of Incomplete Contracts

In this section, we consider the evidence from three different types of contractual arrangements.

Evidence on Incentive, Trust, and Bonus Contracts

Fehr et al. (2007) gave their subjects, in the roles of workers and firms, a choice between incentive contracts, trust contracts, and bonus contracts. The experiment lasted for 10 rounds, and different firms and workers were matched in each round. The effort choices of subjects are 11 possible discrete levels, $e \in \{0, 1, 2, \ldots, 10\}$. The results are shown in Figures 4.2 and 4.3. When the choice is between incentive contracts and trust contracts, firms increasingly chose the incentive contract over successive rounds; by rounds 7–10, 80% of the contracts offered

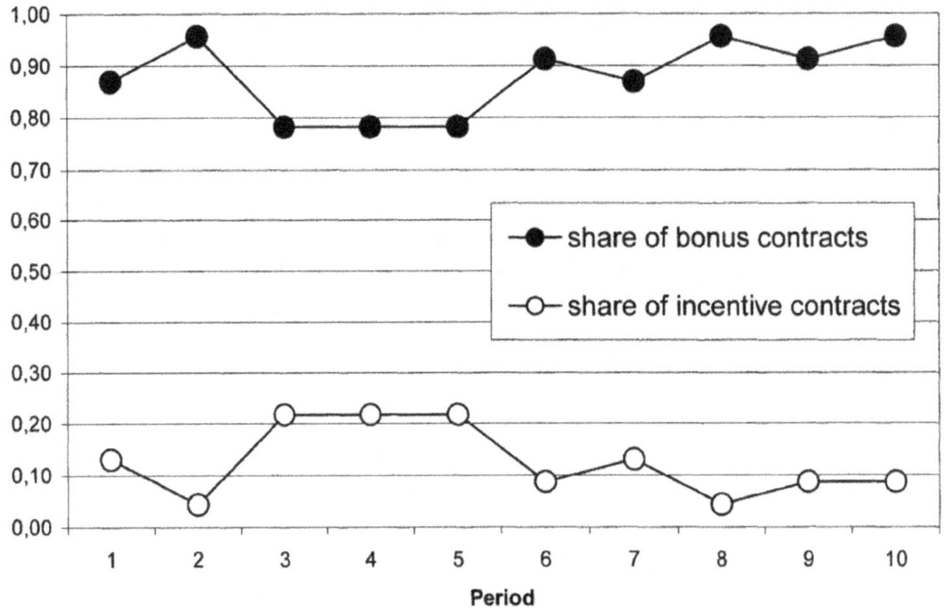

Figure 4.2 The share of bonus contracts and incentive contracts when there is a choice between them. Source: Fehr et al. (2007)

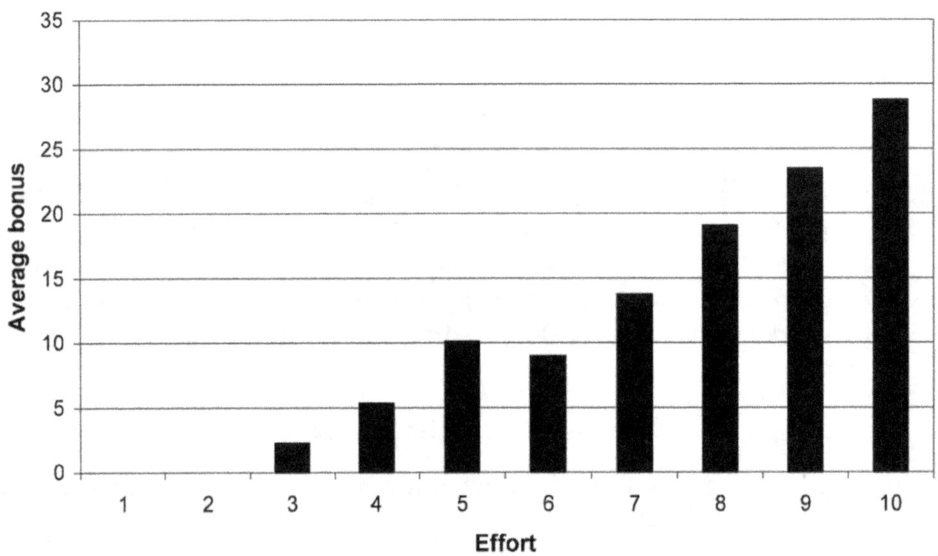

Figure 4.3 The average bonus paid for each level of effort when there is a choice between bonus and incentive contracts. Source: Fehr et al. (2007)

by firms were incentive contracts. However, 58.5% of the incentive contracts violated the no-shirking condition of the worker, leading, on average, to negative profits from the incentive contracts. Firms tried to choose the maximum possible fine in the incentive contract. When the no-shirking condition was satisfied, the incentive contracts were designed to lead to greater profits as compared to trust contracts.

The situation changes dramatically when subjects are given a choice between incentive contracts and bonus contracts. When averaged across all sessions, the overwhelming choice of firms is bonus contracts (about 90% of the firms) while a minority of the firms chose the incentive contract (about 10%). In the final period, 96% of the firms chose bonus contracts. Of all the contracts, the gap between the effort desired by the firm and the actual effort (the difference, $e_n - e$, in our theoretical model) is the smallest for bonus contracts. The profits of the firm are four times higher in the bonus contract relative to the incentive contract. On average, 40% of the payment to the worker is in the form of bonuses while the rest is paid as wages; this is consistent with Result 4.4. Higher bonuses are paid for higher effort levels. In sum, the bonus contract, the most incomplete of the three contracts, performs the best out of the three. These findings run counter to a basic prediction in neoclassical incentive theory, which essentially has at its heart a flawed view of human motivations as exclusively self-regarding.

Fehr and Schmidt (2007) allow, in addition to a simple bonus contract, a slightly more complex contract that allows simultaneously for bonuses for high effort and fines for low effort, a sort of carrot and stick policy. However, despite the presence of the more complex contract, $\frac{2}{3}$ of the firms still choose the simple bonus contract. It appears that workers interpret negatively, the choice of the more complex bonus contract in the presence of the simple bonus contract, perhaps interpreting this as a signal that the firm is self-regarding, who might pay a lower bonus in the end. This is consistent with Assumption 4.A3.

Evidence on Incomplete Contracts and the Theory of the Firm

The experiments of Fehr et al. (2008) test the model of incomplete contracts in Section 4.5.4 that is based on self-regarding preferences. The three stages in their experiments are as described above with the following amendment. In Stage 2, player B first chooses investment i_B, which is observed by player A, followed by the choice of investment, i_A, by player A. Thus, the investment decisions are sequential. The investments $i_A, i_B \in \{0, 1, 2, \ldots, 10\}$. In Stage 1, only player A makes the choice between the following two forms of contracts.

1. Under A-ownership, player A hires player B on a fixed wage contract that pays a wage, w, to player B. Thus, the respective profits of player A and player B, at the end of the game, are given by

$$\begin{cases} \pi_A = v(i_A, i_B) - c(i_A) - w \\ \pi_B = w - c(i_B) \end{cases}.$$

2. Under joint-ownership, both players receive half the benefits from the joint surplus and their expected profits, at the end of the game, are given in (4.69) and (4.70). The payoff structure of the game was chosen so that the solution to the socially optimal investment level (the solution to maximizing (4.71) with respect to i_A, i_B above) is $i_A = i_B = 10$.

In the model of incomplete contracts with self-regarding preferences, player B has zero incentive to invest. The reason is that B gets a fixed wage, w, independent of the level of investment i_B. So, the marginal benefit of investment to B is zero, but the marginal cost is positive, hence, it is optimal to choose $i_B = 0$. Under joint ownership, as already noted above, both players have insufficient incentive to invest because they receive only $\frac{1}{2}$ of the marginal benefits of their investment. The benefit and cost functions are so chosen in the experiments that under joint ownership, the optimal investment choice for A and B is $i_A = i_B = 1$.

The empirical results reject the model of incomplete contracts based on self-regarding preferences. In Stage 1, player A picks joint ownership over A-ownership in more than 80% of the cases and in Stage 2, the average investments under joint ownership are $i_A = 6.5$ and $i_B = 8.9$. In cases where A chooses joint-ownership, she makes higher profits as compared to cases where she chooses A-ownership. The main mechanism that gives rise to these results is that joint ownership allows players to tap into each other's reciprocity, while A-ownership does not. When player B knows that A chose joint-ownership rather than A-ownership, player B responds in a reciprocal manner by choosing a higher investment, i_B, that results in a higher surplus, $v(i_A, i_B)$. Once again, the predictions of the neoclassical model fail the empirical test because of an incorrect view of human motivation.

Evidence on Long-Term Contracts

Brown et al. (2004) consider long term relations between firms and workers. The intuition can be conveyed by the following simple stylistic example; readers interested in a richer game theoretic model and the underlying signaling equilibrium may consult the original paper. Suppose that a firm and its workers interact for two time periods. The worker's "type" can either be self-regarding or other-regarding, but the firm does not know the type of any worker. Workers get better at their jobs if they work for the firm for longer; perhaps their productivity improves over time on account of job-specific learning by doing. If on the other hand, the firm were to hire workers on the spot market in each of the two time periods, then it cannot take advantage of the job-specific learning-by-doing of the workers. In this case, in every period it will hire a new worker from the spot market who will need to be trained from scratch.

Firms would like to take advantage of the improved productivity of workers, from hiring them on a long-term basis. Since the wage level must reflect the productivity of the workers, as the long-term workers learn on the job and improve their productivity, their wages must increase. Thus, the contractable wages offered in the two periods for any worker who signs a long-term contract are: $0 \leq w_1 < w_2$. If a worker is hired on the spot market in any of the two periods, she is offered the base wage w_1 that is paid to someone who has not had a chance to learn on the job yet. At the end of each period, the firm can observe a verifiable signal of the actual effort put in by any long-term worker and if this is low, the worker is fired.

Suppose, as a benchmark case, that all workers were self-regarding and a long-contract were offered. We can solve the model by backward induction. In the second period, self-regarding workers will take the money and run, essentially they will take the contractable wage, w_2, but not exert any costly effort. In the first period, the firm correctly anticipates the opportunistic behavior of the worker in period 2, hence, it is not worth offering a long-term contract to such a worker. The firm will do equally well by hiring spot market workers in each period.

But in real life, we do observe long-term contracts between workers and firms. Suppose now that a fraction of the workers $\lambda > 0$ is other-regarding who engage in gift exchange, while the remaining fraction $1 - \lambda$ is self-regarding who take the money and run. In period 2, other-regarding workers will respond to the high wage w_2 by exerting high effort levels (gift exchange).

If the fraction λ is high enough, then it might be worthwhile for the firm to pay high second period wages. Looking forward in period 1, the firm will correctly anticipate this and wish to offer long term contracts. Interestingly, self-regarding workers will put in high effort in the first period, mimicking the high effort level of other-regarding workers, so that they are not fired. The firm benefits from the high effort levels from all workers in the first period and the other-regarding workers in the second period. This might result in higher profits for the firm than hiring workers from the spot market. Essentially, this argument explains the existence of long-term contracts.

The results of the experiments in Brown et al. (2004) showed that such endogenous long-term contracts do form between workers; they allowed a 15-period model in their experiments. The average effort level and the average wage was higher in such long-term contracts relative to short-term, or spot market, contracts. The difference was statistically significant. Not all interactions between firms and workers led to successful long-term relations. Of the ones that were successful, history played an important role. Long-term contracts that started with the firm paying a high wage and relationships that initially lasted at least two time periods, were more likely to be successfully maintained over time.

4.6 Are Humans Motivated Only by Economic Incentives?

The standard remedy to alter the behavior of homo-economicus in the presence of externalities is to design appropriate economic incentives that alter the material costs and benefits from an action. What if homo-behavioralis, as strongly suggested by the evidence, is a better description of human behavior? This alters the nature of economic incentives – one that needs to take account of the other-regarding preferences and the intrinsic motivation of humans.

Consider a firm designing an employment contract with a worker who puts in costly effort under *moral hazard* (i.e., worker's effort is not observable to the firm). The effort exerted by the worker translates into a noisy output level for the firm, perhaps because output is also influenced by other random factors. Thus, output is a noisy signal of the worker's effort, but it is the only signal of effort. If both parties have self-regarding preferences, then it may be possible to make workers work harder if they are paid a wage that is conditioned closely on the final output. This leads to the well-known prediction of *high-powered incentives*; by contrast we observe lower-powered incentives in actual practice. We have already seen in Section 4.5 that bonus contracts may outperform incentive contracts. These findings contradict much of what is taught in the traditional theory of incentives in the homo-economicus model.

In some cases, high powered incentives might even be counter-productive without invoking other-regarding preferences. This is the case in the theory of multi-task agency, in which a principal, say, a firm, hires an agent, say, a worker, who chooses several distinct kinds of effort levels (Holmstrom and Milgrom, 1991). But effort is either unobservable, or it is unverifiable, so that effort cannot be directly specified in a contract. Consider, for instance, a school teacher who must allocate scarce time between several competing tasks for children that include covering the basic curriculum, looking out for mental health issues in children, spurring their creativity, encouraging extra-curricular work, and so on. If explicit economic incentives are given to teachers, conditional on the grades received by the students, then teachers might switch their effort and time towards more easily measurable activities. But this comes at the cost of more difficult to measure activities that might be equally important, such as spurring creativity and encouraging extra-curricular work. The optimal contract for school teachers in the presence of these consideration might be to offer them a fixed wage with *low powered incentives*.

Bénabou and Tirole (2003, 2006) highlight the difference between *intrinsic motivation* and *extrinsic motivation*. Intrinsic motivations such as the desire to do one's job properly, work hard on the job, and take pride in the product of one's labor, are likely guided by one's internal moral norms. They do not depend on extrinsic incentives such as wage and piece rate payments. Individuals might wish to signal to themselves and to their relevant social group that they are "good people" or that they are altruistic and kind, but extrinsic incentives might prevent such signaling. For instance, Ariely et al. (2009a) find that introducing incentives reduces charitable donations when those donations are publicly revealed to others. This takes away the self-signaling value of donations and an outside observer may surmise that the donations were made not on account of one's underlying altruism but to gain praise from others. However, when the donations are not publicly revealed to others, incentives (e.g., tax-exempt charitable contributions) increased donations.

The classic example of the unintended consequences of incentives is work by Titmuss (1971) which showed that incentives for blood donation reduce the amount of blood donated. In the presence of such incentives, an external observer might confound the underlying motivations for blood donations – Is one donating blood because the person is kind and altruistic, or because they are motivated by economic incentives? The act of blood donation then becomes a noisy signal of motivations and outside observers face what is known as a "signal extraction problem" of the underlying motivations. This makes it difficult for individuals who donate blood to signal to themselves and to their social group, their real underlying motivations, resulting in reduced blood donations. Subsequent empirical research paints a mixed picture. Incentives can induce greater blood donation (Lacetera et al., 2012; Goette and Stutzer, 2020), have no effect on blood donations (Reich et al., 2006), or no effect for men but significant reduction in blood donation for women (Mellström and Johannesson, 2008). In any case, economic incentives for blood donation do not appear to have unambiguously large and positive effects that one might have expected in the neoclassical theory of incentives.

In a classic study, Gneezy and Rustichini (2000a) study late arrivals in 10 private day care centers in Haifa over a period of 20 weeks. In six out of the 10 care centers, a fine for late arrivals of parents to pick their children was introduced in weeks 5–17 (the remaining four centers were used as a control group). There was no fine for late arrivals in the first four weeks, and the fine was removed in weeks 18–20. The average number of parents who arrived late is shown in Figure 4.4. Surprisingly, when a fine was levied on latecomers, the incidence of late arrivals increased; and it increased almost immediately in week five. The reason is that in the absence of the fine, conditional reciprocity on the part of the parents prevented them from delaying the carers too much. However, the fine, by specifying a price for being late, induced those who could afford to pay, to come late. Once a price was paid, parents felt no qualms in arriving late to pick up their children, as they believed they owed nothing to the carers. The basic relation between parents

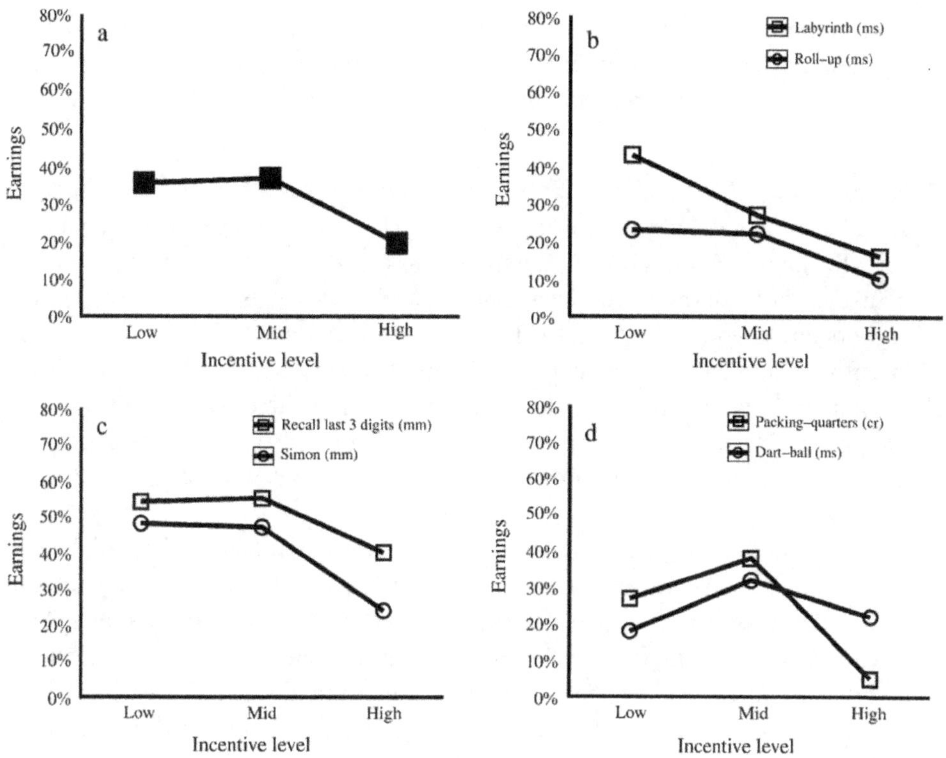

Figure 4.4 Average number of parents who arrive late during each of the 20 weeks. Source: Gneezy and Rustichini (2000a)

and carers was changed from a reciprocity-based relation to an exchange relation. This illustrates again the point that *extrinsic incentives* may crowd out *intrinsic incentives.* A similar effect was found in Norway when a fine was introduced in hospitals for patients who stay for too long, which ended up extending the hospital stay for those who could afford to pay (Holmås et al., 2010).

In the standard principal-agent model in economics, when the principal designs incentive schemes that *control* the agent, the agent does not experience any extra disutility beyond the pure monetary consequences of actions. However, psychologists have identified *control aversion* as a demotivating factor for human effort – people do not like to be controlled by others, and have a *preference for autonomy* (Deci and Ryan, 1985; Deci et al., 1999). Controlling incentives that push agents to take particular actions in preference to other actions (e.g., through the incentive compatibility constraints) may well be aversive and conflict with a desire for autonomy and independence.

In their experiments, Falk and Kosfeld (2006) have two treatments.

1. In the *trust treatment*, principals ask agents to freely choose an action, x, from the interval $[0, b]$, where b is the maximum possible action. A higher action chosen by the agent is costly to the agent, but is more profitable to the principal.

2. In a second treatment, the *incentive treatment*, the contract specifies that the agent must choose an effort from the interval $[a, b]$, where $0 < a$. Thus, the incentive treatment tries to control the agent by specifying a minimum action $a > 0$.

For low levels of the minimum action, a, the agent takes a higher action in the trust treatment and the principal's profits are higher in a trust contract relative to an incentive contract. Only for high enough levels of the minimum action, a, does the incentive contract do better than the trust contract. To check that control aversion is responsible for these results, the authors implement a third treatment, the control treatment. This treatment is identical to the incentive treatment, except that it is the experimenter (and not the principal) who chooses the minimum action, a. Thus, the principal does not directly control the agent, so the agent should not feel negative reciprocity for the principal in this case. As expected, the action of the agent and the principal's profits are higher in the control treatment relative to the incentive treatment.

High incentives may have another negative effect on agents. They might *over-arouse* them and create excessive anxiety and pressure (e.g., ex-ante feeling of regret should they fail in a high stakes task) to do well. The *Yerkes–Dodson law* in psychology shows that when rats are aroused with increasingly larger incentives, then their effort first increases, reaches a maximum, and then decreases. This suggests that there is an optimal level of incentives which arouses them just enough to maximize their efforts. We observe a similar phenomenon with humans too. For instance, people may choke under pressure – even elite athletes are not immune to such choking. Coaches typically understand this phenomenon and try to keep their wards reasonably relaxed before big events – the mental conditioning aspect of modern coaching addresses this potential problem.

Ariely et al. (2009b) give six tasks in a between-subjects design to subjects in an experiment in India. The tasks test memory (m), motor skills (ms), and creativity (cr). The tasks were administered through simple games. For instance, in Packing-quarters, which measures creativity, subjects are required to fit nine metal pieces into a wooden frame in a timed task. Two of the games test memory by requiring subjects to recall a series of numbers; these are "Simon" and "Recall last three digits." The games Labyrinth, Dart Ball, and Roll-Up test for motor skills.

There are three different levels of incentives, low, medium, and high. As a measure of the performance of subjects in any task, the authors use "share of earnings relative to maximum possible earnings." The results are shown in Figure 4.5. High monetary incentives can reduce performance, but there is no noticeable difference in performance between the low and the medium incentive conditions. One potential criticism is that the tasks might not be familiar to the subjects. Hence, they conducted a separate set of experiments on MIT student subjects who were given two tasks. (i) A cognitive task (adding a set of numbers in a time bound task), and (ii) a physical task (repeatedly pressing a set of keys in sequence). For the cognitive task, the results in Figure 4.5 are confirmed – high incentives are detrimental to performance. However, for the physical task, higher incentives enhance performance. This suggests that the effectiveness of incentives depends on the nature of the task.

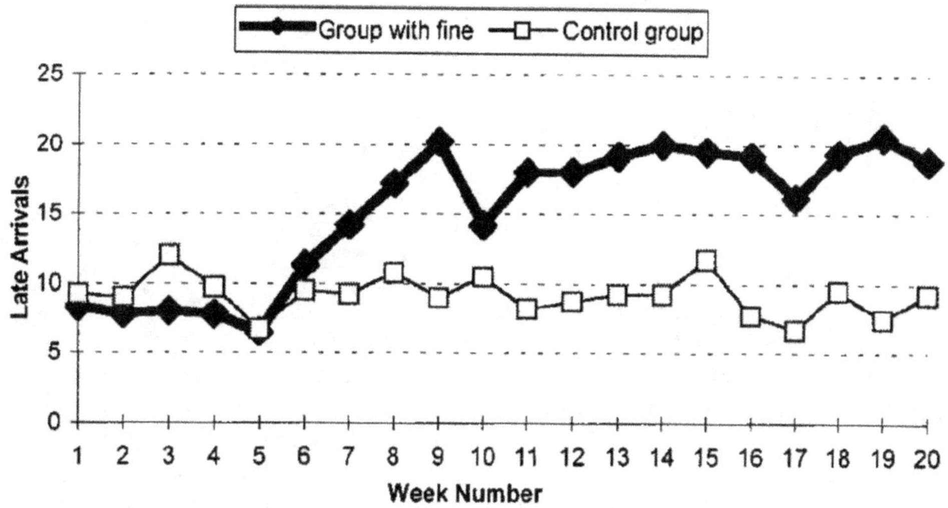

Figure 4.5 The mean of actual earnings to maximum possible earnings for each set of games, and for three different levels of incentives, low, medium, and high. The data is pooled together from all the games. Source: Ariely et al. (2009b)

The discussion in this section should not be taken to mean that incentives are not useful; that would be a misreading of the lessons learnt from the behavioral theory of incentives. Increasing incentives can often improve performance, but the outcomes under various non-economic incentives and moral suasion that rely on intrinsic incentives can sometimes do equally as well, if not better.

This point is nicely made in a study by Gneezy and Rustichini (2000b). They asked GMAT-style questions under four possible incentive treatments that offered, respectively, 0, 0.1, 1, and 3 New Israeli Shekels (NIS) for each correct answer. They found that the average number of correct answers in these four treatments was, respectively, 28.4, 23.075, 34.7, 34.1. There is obviously not a linear relation between the number of correct answers and the size of the incentives. However, if we pool together the number of correct answers for low incentives (0 and 0.1 NIS) and compare them with the number of correct answers for high incentives (1 and 3 NIS), the difference is statistically significant. Hence, high incentives do work.

In a second set of experiments, the donations experiment, groups of two students were asked to collect donations for a good cause. Three different treatments were used. In treatment 1a, the moral suasion treatment, subjects were told that the results of their efforts would be made public and that society wishes for them to collect as much money as possible. In treatment 1b, students received a monetary incentive equal to 1% of the donations collected, and in treatment 1c, a monetary incentive of 10% of the donations collected. The average collections in the three treatments, 1a, 1b, and 1c, respectively, were NIS 238.67, 153.67, 219.33. As one moves from the moral suasion treatment to the low incentives treatment (1a to 1b), there is a statistically significant fall in collections. However, as we improve the level of incentives (1b to 1c), there is a significant increase in collections. Thus, incentives are effective. Yet, the average collections under moral suasion are still greater than the collections under high incentives (treatments 1a versus 1c).

References

Abeler, J., Nosenzo, D., and Raymond, C. (2019). Preferences for Truth-Telling. *Econometrica* 87(4): 1115–1153.

Akerlof, George A. (1982). Labor Contracts as Partial Gift Exchange. *The Quarterly Journal of Economics* 97(4): 543–569.

Akerlof, G. A. and Kranton, R. E. (2005). Identity and the Economics of Organizations. *Journal of Economic Perspectives* 19(1): 9–32.

Alesina, A. and Angeletos, G.-M. (2005). Fairness and Redistribution: US vs. Europe. *American Economic Review* 95(4): 913–935.

Alesina, A. and La Ferrara, E. (2005). Preferences for Redistribution in the Land of Opportunities. *Journal of Public Economics* 89(5–6): 897–931.

Alesina, A. and Giuliano, P. (2011). Preferences for Redistribution. In J. Benhabib, A. Bisin, and M. O. Jackson (eds.), *Handbook of Social Economics*. Vol. 1. Elsevier: North Holland, pp. 93–131.

Almås, I., Cappelen, A. W., and Tungodden, B. (2020). Cutthroat Capitalism Versus Cuddly Socialism: Are Americans More Meritocratic and Efficiency-Seeking than Scandinavians? *Journal of Political Economy* 128(5): 1753–1788.

Ariely, D., Bracha, A., and Meier, S. (2009a). Doing Good or Going Well? Image Motivation and Monetary Incentives in Behaving Prosocially. *American Economic Review* 99(1): 54455.

Ariely, D., Gneezy, U., Loewenstein, G., and Mazar, N. (2009b). Large Stakes and Big Mistakes. *Review of Economic Studies* 76(2): 45169.

Balafoutas, L., Czermak, S., Eulerich, M., and Fornwagner, H. (2020). Incentives for Dishonesty: An Experimental Study with Internal Auditors. *Economic Inquiry* 58(2): 764–779.

Barmettler, F., Fehr, E., and Zehnder, C. (2012). Big Experimenter is Watching You! Anonymity and Prosocial Behavior in the Laboratory. *Games and Economic Behavior* 75(1): 17–34.

Bartling, B., Fehr, E., and Özdemir, Y. (2023). Does Market Interaction Erode Moral Values? *Review of Economics and Statistics* 105(1): 226–235.

Bartling, B., and Özdemir, Y. (2021). The Limits to Moral Erosion in Markets: Social Norms and the Replacement Excuse. Available at SSRN: https://ssrn.com/abstract=3043728 or http://dx.doi.org/10.2139/ssrn.3043728.

Bartling, B., Weber, R., and Yao, L. (2015). Do Markets Erode Social Responsibility? *Quarterly Journal of Economics* 130(1): 219–266.

Bauer, M., Blattman, C., Chytilova, J., Henrich, J., Miguel, E., and Mitts, T. (2016). Can War Foster Cooperation? *Journal of Economic Perspectives* 30(3): 249–274.

Becker, A., Enke, B., and Falk, A. (2020). Ancient Origins of the Global Variation in Economic Preferences. *American Economic Review Papers and Proceedings* 110: 319–323.

Bellemare, C. and Shearer, B. S. (2007). Gift Exchange within a Firm: Evidence from a Field Experiment. IZA, Discussion Paper 26–96.

Bénabou, R. and Ok, E. A. (2001). Social Mobility and the Demand for Redistribution: The POUM Hypothesis. *The Quarterly Journal of Economics* 116(2): 447–487.

Bénabou, R. and Tirole, J. (2003). Intrinsic and Extrinsic Motivation. *Review of Economic Studies* 70(3): 489–520.

Bénabou, R. and Tirole, J. (2006). Incentives and Prosocial Behaviour. *American Economic Review* 96(5): 1652–1678.

Berg, J., Dickhaut, J., and McCabe, K. (1995). Trust, Reciprocity, and Social History. *Games and Economic Behavior* 10(1): 122–142.

Bertrand, M. and Mullainathan, S. (2004). Are Emily and Greg More Employable Than Lakisha and Jamal? A Field Experiment on Labor Market Discrimination. *American Economic Review* 94(4): 991–1013.

Bewley, T. (1999). *Why Wages Don't Fall During a Recession.* Harvard University Press: Cambridge, MA.

Bicchieri, C. and Xiao, E. (2009). Do the Right Thing but Only If Others Do it. *Journal of Behavioral Decision Making* 22: 191–208.

Bochet, O., Page, T., and Putterman, L. (2006). Communication and Punishment in Voluntary Contribution Experiments. *Journal of Economic Behavior and Organization* 60(1): 11–26.

Bohnet, I., Harmgart, H., Huck, S., and Tyran, J.-R. (2005). Learning Trust. *Journal of the European Economic Association* 3(23): 322–329.

Bolton, G. E. and Ockenfels, A. (2000). ERC: A Theory of Equity, Reciprocity, and Competition. *American Economic Review* 90(1): 166–193.

Bowles, S. (2004). *Microeconomics: Behavior, Institutions, and Evolution.* Princeton University Press: Princeton and Oxford.

Brown, M., Falk, A., and Fehr, E. (2004). Relational Contracts and the Nature of Market Interactions. *Econometrica* 72(3): 747–780.

Camerer, C. F. (2003). *Behavioral Game Theory: Experiments in Strategic Interaction.* Princeton University Press: Princeton, NJ.

Cappelen, A., List, J., Samek, A., Tungodden, B. (2020). The Effect of Early Childhood Education on Social Preferences. *Journal of Political Economy* 128(7): 2739–2758.

Carpenter, J. P. and Seki, E. (2011). Do Social Preferences Increase Productivity? Field Experimental Evidence from Fishermen in Toyama Bay. *Economic Inquiry* 49(2): 612–630.

Charness, G. and Chen, Y. (2020) Social Identity, Group Behavior, and Teams. *Annual Review of Economics* 12: 691–713.

Charness, G., Du, N., and Yang, C. L. (2011). Trust and Trustworthiness Reputations in an Investment Game. *Games and Economic Behavior* 72(2): 361–375.

Charness, G. and Dufwenberg, M. (2006). Promises and Partnership. *Econometrica* 74(6): 1579–1601.

Charness, G. and Rabin, M. (2002). Understanding social preferences with simple tests. Quarterly Journal of Economics 117(3): 817–69.

Chen, Y. and Li, S. (2009). Social Identity and Group Preferences. American Economic Review 99(1): 431–457.

Cherry, T. L., Frykblom, P., and Shogren, J. F. (2002). Hardnose the Dictator. *American Economic Review* 92(4): 121–821.

Cinyabuguma, M., Page, T., and Putterman, L. (2005). Cooperation Under the Threat of Expulsion in a Public Goods Experiment. *Journal of Public Economics* 89(8): 1421–1435.

Cohn, A., Fehr, E., Herrmann, B., Schneider, F. (2014). Social Comparison in the Workplace: Evidence from a Field Experiment. *Journal of the European Economic Association* 12(4): 877–898.

Croson, R. and Gneezy, U. (2009). Gender Differences in Preferences. *Journal of Economic Literature* 47(2): 448–474.

Dai, Z., Galeotti, F., Villeval, M.C. (2018). Cheating in the Lab Predicts Fraud in the Field. An Experiment in Public Transportations. *Management Science* 64(3): 1081–1100.

Dal Bó, P., Foster, A., and Putterman, L. (2010). Institutions and Behavior: Experimental Evidence on the Effects of Democracy. *American Economic Review* 100(5): 2205–2229.

Dana, J., Weber, R. A., and Kuang, J. X. (2007). Exploiting Moral Wriggle Room: Experiments Demonstrating an Illusory Preference for Fairness. *Economic Theory* 33: 67–80.

Deci, E. L., Koestner, R., and Ryan, R. M. (1999). A Meta-Analytic Review of Experiments Examining the Effects of Extrinsic Rewards on Intrinsic Motivation. *Psychological Bulletin* 125(6): 627–668.

Deci, E. L. and Ryan R. M. (1985). *Intrinsic Motivation and Self-Determination in Human Behavior*. Springer: Berlin.

Deckers, T., Falk, A., Kosse, F., Pinger, P., and Schildberg-Hörisch, H. (2021). Socio-economic Status and Inequalities in Childrens IQ and Economic Preferences. *Journal of Political Economy* 129(9): 2504–2545.

Dhami, S. (2003). The Political Economy of Redistribution Under Asymmetric Information. *Journal of Public Economics* 87(9–10): 2069–2103.

Dhami, S. (2017). Human Ethics and Virtues: Rethinking the Homo-Economicus Model. CESifo Working Paper Series No. 6836.

Dhami, S. (2019). *The Foundations of Behavioral Economic Analysis: Behavioral Game Theory. Vol IV*. Oxford University Press: Oxford.

Dhami, S. (2020). *The Foundations of Behavioral Economic Analysis: Other-Regarding Preferences. Vol II*. Oxford University Press: Oxford.

Dhami, S. and al-Nowaihi, A. (2010). Redistributive Policy with Heterogeneous Social Preferences of Voters. *European Economic Review* 54(6): 743–759.

Dhami, S. and al-Nowaihi, A. (2019). Human Ethics and Virtues: Rethinking the Homo-Economicus Model. In M. D. White (ed.), *Oxford Handbook of Ethics and Economics*. Oxford University Press: Oxford.

Dhami, S., Arshad, J., and al-Nowaihi (2022). Psychological and Social Motivations in Microfinance Contracts: Theory and Evidence. *Journal of Development Economics* 158: 102921.

Dhami, S., Manifold, E., and al-Nowaihi, A. (2021). Identity and Redistribution: Theory and Evidence. *Economica* 88(350): 499–531.

Dhami, S., Wei, M., and al-Nowaihi, A. (2019). Public Goods Games and Psychological Utility: Theory and Evidence. Special issue on Psychological Game Theory in *Journal of Economic Behavior and Organization* 167(C): 361–390.

Dhami, S., Wei, M., and al-Nowaihi, A. (2021). Classical and Belief-Based Gift Exchange Models: Theory and Evidence. CESifo Working Paper No. 8992, available at SSRN: https://ssrn.com/abstract=3826068.

Dickenson, D. and M.-C. Villeval (2008). Does Monitoring Decrease Work Effort? The Complementarity between Agency and Crowding-Out Theories. *Games and Economic Behavior* 63(1): 56–76.

Dohmen, T., Enke, B., Falk, A., Huffman, D., and Sunde, U. (2022). Patience and Comparative Development. *Review of Economic Studies* 89(5): 2806–2840.

Dohmen, T., Falk, A., Huffman, D., and Sunde, U. (2012). The Intergenerational Transmission of Risk and Trust Attitudes. *Review of Economic Studies* 79(2): 645–677.

Dugar, S. (2013). Non-Monetary Incentives and Opportunistic Behavior: Evidence from a Laboratory Public Good Game. *Economic Inquiry* 51(2): 1374–1388.

Eckel, C. C. and Petrie, R. (2011). Face Value. *American Economic Review* 101(4): 1497–1513.

Engelmann, J.B. and Fehr, E. (2016). The Slippery Slope of Dishonesty. *Nature Neuroscience* 19: 1543–1544.

Epper T., Fehr, E., and Julien, S. (2020). Other-Regarding Preferences and Redistributive Politics. ECON – Working Papers 339, Department of Economics – University of Zurich.

Erat, S. and Gneezy, U. (2012). White Lies. *Management Science* 58(4): 723–733.

Falk, A. (2007). Gift Exchange in the Field. *Econometrica* 75(5): 1501–1511.

Falk, A. and Kosfeld, M. (2006). The Hidden Costs of Control. *American Economic Review* 96(5): 1611–1630.

Falk, A. and Szech, N. (2013). Morals and Markets. *Science* 340(6133): 707–711.

Falk, A., Becker, A., Dohmen, T. J., Enke, B., Huffman, D., and Sunde, U. (2018). Global Evidence on Economic Preferences. *Quarterly Journal of Economics* 133(4): 1645–1692.

Falk, A., Meier, S., and Zehnder, C. (2013). Do Lab Experiments Misrepresent Social Preferences? The Case of Self-Selected Student Samples. *Journal of the European Economic Association* 11(4): 839–852.

Fehr, E (2009). On the Economics and Biology of Trust. *Journal of the European Economic Association* 7(2–3): 235–266.

Fehr, E. and Falk, A. (2002). Joseph Schumpeter Lecture: Psychological Foundations of

Incentives. *European Economic Review* 46(45): 687–724.

Fehr, E. and Fischbacher, U. (2002). Why Social Preferences Matter: The Impact of Non-Self-Regarding Motives on Competition, Cooperation and Incentives. *Economic Journal* 112(478): C1–C33.

Fehr, E. and Fischbacher, U. (2003). The Nature of Human Altruism. *Nature* 425: 785–791.

Fehr, E. and Fischbacher, U. (2005). Human Altruism: Proximate Patterns and Evolutionary Origins. *Analyse & Kritik* 27(1): 6–47.

Fehr, E. and Gächter, S. (1999). Cooperation and Punishment in Public Goods Experiments. Institute for Empirical Research in Economics Working Paper No. 10; CESifo Working Paper Series No. 183.

Fehr, E. and Gächter, S. (2000). Cooperation and Punishment in Public Goods Experiments. *American Economic Review* 90(4): 980–994.

Fehr, E. and Gächter, S. (2001). Do Incentive Contracts Crowd Out Voluntary Cooperation? University of Zurich, Institute for Empirical Research in Economics, Working Paper 34.

Fehr, E., Gächter, S., and Kirchsteiger, G. (1997). Reciprocity as a Contract Enforcement Device: Experimental Evidence. *Econometrica* 65(4): 833–860.

Fehr, E. and Hoff, K. (2011). Tastes, Castes, and Cultures: The Influence of Society on Preferences. *The Economic Journal* 121(556): F396–F412.

Fehr, E., Kirchsteiger, G., and Riedl, A. (1993). Does Fairness Prevent Market Clearing? An Experimental Investigation. *Quarterly Journal of Economics* 108(2): 437–459.

Fehr, E., Kirchsteiger, G., and Riedl, A. (1998). Gift Exchange and Reciprocity in Competitive Experimental Markets. *European Economic Review* 42(1): 1–34.

Fehr, E., Klein, A., and Schmidt, K. M. (2007). Fairness and Contract Design. *Econometrica* 75(1): 121–154.

Fehr, E., Kremhelmer, S., and Schmidt, K. M. (2008). Fairness and the Optimal Allocation of Ownership Rights. *Economic Journal* 118(531): 1262–1284.

Fehr, E. and Leibbrandt, A. (2011). A Field Study on Cooperativeness and Impatience in the Tragedy of the Commons. *Journal of Public Economics* 95(910): 1144–1155.

Fehr, E., Powell, M., and Wilkening, T. (2021). Behavioral Constraints on the Design of Subgame-Perfect Implementation Mechanisms. *American Economic Review* 111(4): 1055–1091.

Fehr, E. and Rockenbach, B. (2003). Detrimental Effects of Sanctions on Human Altruism. *Nature* 422: 137–140.

Fehr, E. and Schmidt K. M. (1999). A Theory of Fairness, Competition and Cooperation. *Quarterly Journal of Economics* 114(3): 817–868.

Fehr, E. and Schmidt, K. M. (2007). Adding a Stick to the Carrot? The Interaction of Bonuses and Fines. *American Economic Review* 97(2): 177–181.

Fehr, E. and Schneider, F. (2010). Eyes Are on Us, but Nobody Cares: Are Eye Cues Relevant for Strong Reciprocity? *Proceedings of the Royal Society B: Biological Sciences* 277: 1315–1323.

Fershtman, C. and Gneezy, U. (2001). Discrimination in a Segmented Society: An Experimental Approach. *The Quarterly Journal of Economics* 116(1): 351–377.

Fischbacher, U. and Föllmi-Heusi, F. (2013). Lies in Disguise: An Experimental Study on Cheating. *Journal of the European Economic Association* 11(3): 525–547.

Fischbacher, U., Gächter, S., and Fehr, E. (2001). Are People Conditionally Cooperative? Evidence from a Public Goods Experiment. *Economics Letters* 71(3): 397–404.

Fischbacher, U. and Utikal, V. (2013). On the Acceptance of Apologies. *Games and Economic Behavior* 82: 592–608.

Fisman, R., Jakiela, P., and Kariv, S. (2017). Distributional Preferences and Political Behavior. *Journal of Public Economics* 155: 1–10.

Fréchette, G. R., Kagel, J. H., and Lehrer, S. F. (2003). Bargaining in Legislatures: An Experimental Investigation of Open versus Closed Amendment Rules. *American Political Science Review* 97(2): 221–232.

Gächter, S., Herrmann, B., and Thöni, C. (2010). Culture and Cooperation. *Philosophical Transactions of the Royal Society* B 365: 2651–2661.

Gächter, S., Renner, E., and Sefton, M. (2008). The Long Run Benefits of Punishment. *Science* 322(5907): 1510.

Gächter, S. and Thöni, C. (2005). Social Learning and Voluntary Cooperation among Like-minded People. *Journal of the European Economic Association* 3(23): 303–314.

Garbarino, E., Slonim, R., Villeval, M. C. (2019). Loss Aversion and Lying. *Journal of Economic Behavior & Organization* 158: 379–393.

Gilbert, B., James, A., and Shogren, J. F. (2018). Corporate Apology for Environmental Damage. *Journal of Risk and Uncertainty* 56(1): 51–81.

Gintis, H. (2009). *The Bounds of Reason: Game Theory and the Unification of the Behavioral Sciences*. Princeton University. Press: Princeton, NJ.

Gneezy, U. (2005). Deception: The Role of Consequences. *American Economic Review* 95(1): 384–394.

Gneezy, U. and List, J. A. (2006). Putting Behavioral Economics to Work: Testing for Gift Exchange in Labor Markets Using Field Experiments. *Econometrica* 74(5): 1365–1384.

Gneezy, U. and Rustichini, A. (2000a). A Fine Is a Price. *Journal of Legal Studies* 29(1): 1–17.

Gneezy, U. and Rustichini, A. (2000b). Pay Enough or Don't Pay at All. *Quarterly Journal of Economics* 115(3): 791–810.

Goette, L. F., Huffman, D., and Meier, S. (2012). The Impact of Social Ties on Group Interactions: Evidence from Minimal Groups and Randomly Assigned Real Groups. *American Economic Journal: Microeconomics* 4(1): 101–115.

Goette, L. F. and Stutzer, A. (2020). Blood Donations and Incentives: Evidence from a Field Experiment. *Journal of Economic Behavior & Organization* 170(C): 52–74.

Gouldner, A. W. (1960). The Norm of Reciprocity: A Preliminary Statement. *American Sociological Review* 25(2): 161–178.

Greif, A. (1993). Contract Enforceability and Economic Institutions in Early Trade: The Maghribi Traders' Coalition. *American Economic Review* 83(3): 525–548.

Grossman, S. J. and Hart, O. D. (1986). The Costs and Benefits of Ownership: A Theory of Vertical and Lateral Integration. *Journal of Political Economy* 94(4): 691–719.

Gürerk, Ö., Irlenbusch, B., and Rockenbach, B. (2006). The Competitive Advantage of Sanctioning Institutions. *Science* 312(5770): 10811.

Güth, W., Schmittberger, R., and Schwarze, B. (1982). An Experimental Analysis of Ultimatum Bargaining. *Journal of Economic Behavior and Organization* 3(4): 367–388.

Haley, K. J. and Fessler, D. M. T. (2005). Nobodys Watching? Subtle Cues Affect Generosity in an Anonymous Economic Game. *Evolution and Human Behavior* 26(3): 245–256.

Hallsworth, M., List, J. A., Metcalfe, R. D., Vlaev, I. (2017). The Behavioralist as Tax Collector: Using Natural Field Experiments to Enhance Tax Compliance. *Journal of Public Economics* 148: 14–31.

Halperin, B., Ho, B., List, J. A., and Muir, I. (2021). Toward an understanding of the Economics of Apologies: Evidence from a Large-Scale Natural Field Experiment. *The Economic Journal* 132(641): 273–298.

Hardin, G. (1968). The Tragedy of the Commons. *Science* 162: 1243–1248.

Hart, O. (1995). *Firms, Contracts, and Financial Structure*. Oxford University Press: Oxford.

Henrich, J. (2020). *The Weirdest People in the World: How the West Became Psychologically Peculiar and Particularly Prosperous*. Allen Lane: London.

Henrich, J., Boyd, R., Bowles, S., et al. (2001). Cooperation, Reciprocity and Punishment in Fifteen Small-Scale Societies. *American Economic Review* 91: 73–78.

Ho, B (2012), Apologies as Signals: With Evidence from a Trust Game. *Management Science* 58(1): 141–158.

Holmås, T. H., Kjerstad, E., Lurås, H., and Straume, O. R. (2010). Does Monetary Punishment Crowd Out Pro-Social Motivation?

A Natural Experiment on Hospital Length of Stay. *Journal of Economic Behavior and Organization* 75(2): 261–267.

Holmstrom, B. and Milgrom, P. (1991). Multitask Principal-Agent Analyses: Linear Contracts, Asset Ownership and Job Design. *Journal of Law, Economics and Organization* 7: 24–52.

Houser, D., List, J. A., Piovesan, M., Samek, A., and Winter, J. (2016). Dishonesty: From Parents to Children. *European Economic Review* 82: 242–254.

Huck, S., Lünser, G. K., and Tyran, J.-R. (2012). Competition Fosters Trust. *Games and Economic Behavior* 76(1): 195–209.

Johnson, N. D. and Mislin, A. A. (2011). Trust Games: A Meta-Analysis. *Journal of Economic Psychology* 32(5): 865–889.

Karlan, D. (2005). Using Experimental Economics to Measure Social Capital and Predict Financial Decisions. *American Economic Review* 95(5): 1688–1699.

Kajackaite, A. and Gneezy, U. (2017). Incentives and Cheating. *Games and Economic Behavior* 102: 433–444.

Kerschbamer, R. and Müller, D. (2020). Social Preferences and Political Attitudes: An Online Experiment on a Large Heterogeneous Sample. *Journal of Public Economics* 182: 104076. https://doi.org/10.1016/j.jpubeco.2019.104076.

Kocher, M. G. and Schudy, S. (2018) I Lie? We Lie! Why? Experimental Evidence on a Dishonesty Shift in Groups. *Management Science* 64(9): 3971–4470.

Kube, S., Maréchal, M. A., and Puppe, C. (2006). Putting Reciprocity to Work: Positive Versus Negative Responses in the Field. University of St. Gallen, Economics, Discussion Paper 2006–27.

Kube, S., Maréchal, M. A., and Puppe, C. (2013). Do Wage Cuts Damage Work Morale? Evidence from a Natural Field Experiment. *Journal of the European Economic Association* 11(4): 853–870.

Lacetera, N., Macis, M., and Slonim, R. (2012). Will There Be Blood? Incentives and Displacement Effects in Pro-Social Behaviour. *American Economic Journal: Economic Policy* 4(1): 186–223.

Leibbrandt, A. (2012). Are Social Preferences Related to Market Performance? *Experimental Economics* 15(4): 589–603.

Levine, D. K. (1998). Modeling Altruism and Spitefulness in Experiments. *Review of Economic Dynamics* 1(3): 593–622.

Levitt, S. D. and List, J. A. (2007). What Do Laboratory Experiments Measuring Social Preferences Reveal About the Real World? *Journal of Economic Perspectives* 21(2): 153–174.

Li, L., Britvan, B., Tomasello, M. (2021). Young Children Conform More to Norms than to Preferences. *PLoS ONE* 16(5): e0251228.

Malmendier, U. and Schmidt, K. (2017). You Owe Me. *American Economic Review* 107(2): 493–526.

Masclet, D., Noussair, C., Villeval, M.-C., and Tucker, S. (2003). Monetary and Non-Monetary Punishment in the Voluntary Contributions Mechanism. *American Economic Review* 93(1): 366–380.

Maskin, E. and Tirole, J. (1999). Unforeseen Contingencies and Incomplete Contracts. *Review of Economic Studies* 66(1): 83–114.

Mauss, M. (1924). The Gift: The Form and Reason for Exchange in Archaic Societies. Routledge & Kegan Paul: London. (Translated by W. D. Halls. London: Routledge, 1990).

Mellström, C. and Johannesson, M. (2008). Crowding Out in Blood Donation: Was Titmuss Right? *Journal of the European Economic Association* 6(4): 845–863.

Niederle, M. (2016). Gender. In John Kagel and Alvin E. Roth (eds.), *Handbook of Experimental Economics*. Second edition. Princeton University Press: Princeton, NJ, pp. 481–553.

Nunn, N. (2008). The Long-Term Effects of Africa's Slave Trades. *Quarterly Journal of Economics* 132(1): 139–176.

Nunn, N. and Wantchekon, L. (2011). The Slave Trade and the Origins of Mistrust in Africa. *American Economic Review* 101(7): 3221–3252.

Okada, A. and Riedl, A. (2005). Inefficiency and Social Exclusion in a Coalition Formation Game: Experimental Evidence. *Games and Economic Behavior* 50(2): 278–311.

Ostrom, E. (1990). *Governing the Commons: The Evolution of Institions for Collective Action*. Cambridge University Press: Cambridge.

Ostrom, E. (1999). Coping with Tragedies of the Commons. *Annual Review of Political Science* 2: 493–535.

Owens, M. F. and Kagel, J. H. (2010). Minimum Wage Restrictions and Employee Effort in Incomplete Labor Markets: An Experimental Investigation. *Journal of Economic Behavior and Organization* 73(3): 317–326.

Putnam, R. (1993). *Making Democracy Work: Civic Traditions in Modern Italy*. Princeton University Press: Princeton, NJ.

Rajshri, J., Ray, D., and de Véricourt, F. (2016). Anatomy of a Contract Change. *American Economic Review* 106(2): 316–358.

Reich, P., Roberts, P., Laabs, N., et al. (2006). A Randomized Trial of Blood Donor Recruitment Strategies. *Transfusion* 46(7): 1090–1096.

Riedl, A. and Vyrastekova, J. (2002). Social Preference in Three-Player Ultimatum Game Experiments. Tilburg University, Center for Economic Research, Discussion Paper 20025.

Romano, A., Sutter, M., Liu, J. H. et al. (2021). National Parochialism Is Ubiquitous across 42 Nations around the World. *Nature Communications* 12:44–56.

Rotemberg, J. J. (2008). Minimally Acceptable Altruism and the Ultimatum Game. *Journal of Economic Behavior and Organization* 66(34): 457–476.

Rustagi, D., Engel, S., and Kosfeld, M. (2010). Conditional Cooperation and Costly Monitoring Explain Success in Forest Commons Management. *Science* 330(6006): 961–965.

Schmidt, K. and Ockenfels, A. (2021). Focusing Climate Negotiations on a Uniform Common Commitment Can Promote Cooperation. *PNAS* 118(11): e2013070118; https://doi.org/10.1073/pnas.2013070118.

Schindler, S. and Pfattheicher, S. (2017). The Frame of the Game: Loss-Framing Increases Dishonest Behavior. *Journal of Experimental Social Psychology* 69: 172–177.

Thiemann, P., Schulz, J., Sunde, U., and Thöni, C. (2022). Selection into Experiments: New Evidence on the Role of Preferences, Cognition, and Recruitment Protocols. *Journal of Behavioral and Experimental Economics* 98: 101871.

Titmuss, R. M. (1971). *The Gift Relationship: From Human Blood to Social Policy*. Pantheon Books: New York.

Vanberg, C. (2008). Why Do People Keep Their Promises? An Experimental Test of Two Explanations. *Econometrica* 76(6): 1476–1480.

van den Akker, O. R., van Assen, A. L. M., van Vugt, M., and Wicherts, J. M. (2020). Sex Differences in Trust and Trustworthiness: A Meta-Analysis of the Trust Game and the Gift-Exchange Game. *Journal of Economic Psychology* 81: 102329.

van der Weele, J. J., Kulisa, J., Kosfeld, M., and Friebel, G. (2014). Resisting Moral Wiggle Room: How Robust Is Reciprocal Behavior? *American Economic Journal: Microeconomics* 6(3): 256–264.

Problems for Part II

1. This exercise is of the nature of a "project" for undergraduate students. Consider the ultimatum and gift exchange games in Section 3.2. Suppose you are given the task of determining the outcomes in these games with a sample size of 30 subjects (perhaps your friends, family, and others on social media). Write the experimental instructions for these two games that will enable your subjects to understand well the game, and give considered answers to the questions. You might not have any funding to provide economic incentives to your subjects for the answers, so you will need to rely on their intrinsic incentives. In designing your instructions pay particular attention to the clarity of the instructions that faithfully implement the underlying game. If you were given a small budget to run these experiments, how would you incentivize your subjects?
2. Consider the two-player utility function of player 1 given in (4.1). Draw the indifference curves for player 1, measuring x_1 on the horizontal axis and x_2 on the vertical axis. Interpret the indifference curves.
3. (Fehr and Fischbacher, 2003, 2005) Fischbacher et al. (2001) play a repeated public goods games. The evidence shows that 10% of the subjects always match the expected average contribution of others, 14% fully match the expected contributions of others until they spend half their endowments, 40% match the expected contributions of others to a lesser extent, 30% are free-riders, and the remaining 6% have no well-defined behavioral pattern.We are interested in finding the rational expectations equilibrium of the model. Denote the expected average contribution of others by y^e. Suppose that subjects have spent less than half their endowments. For each of the groups identified in the empirical evidence, but ignoring the 6% who have no well-defined preferences, write an equation describing their actual contributions indicating the dependence on expected contributions, y^e. Aggregate across all the groups of players and write the aggregate total contributions, y, as depending on y^e. Write this equation as

$$y = f(y^e).$$

A rational expectations equilibrium is a fixed point of this equation, that is, a value y^* such that $y^* = f(y^*)$. Find this fixed point. Suppose that the initial expected average contributions, y^e, of the players are 80% of the maximum contributions and subjects best respond to the observed contributions in the previous period. Show how you would explain the results shown in Figure 4.6
4. (Charness and Rabin, 2002) Consider the Charness–Rabin two-player utility function in (4.21). Compute the marginal rate of substitution of this utility function in (x_1, x_2) space. Show that the indifference curve will have a kink at the point $x_1 = x_2$ and that individuals

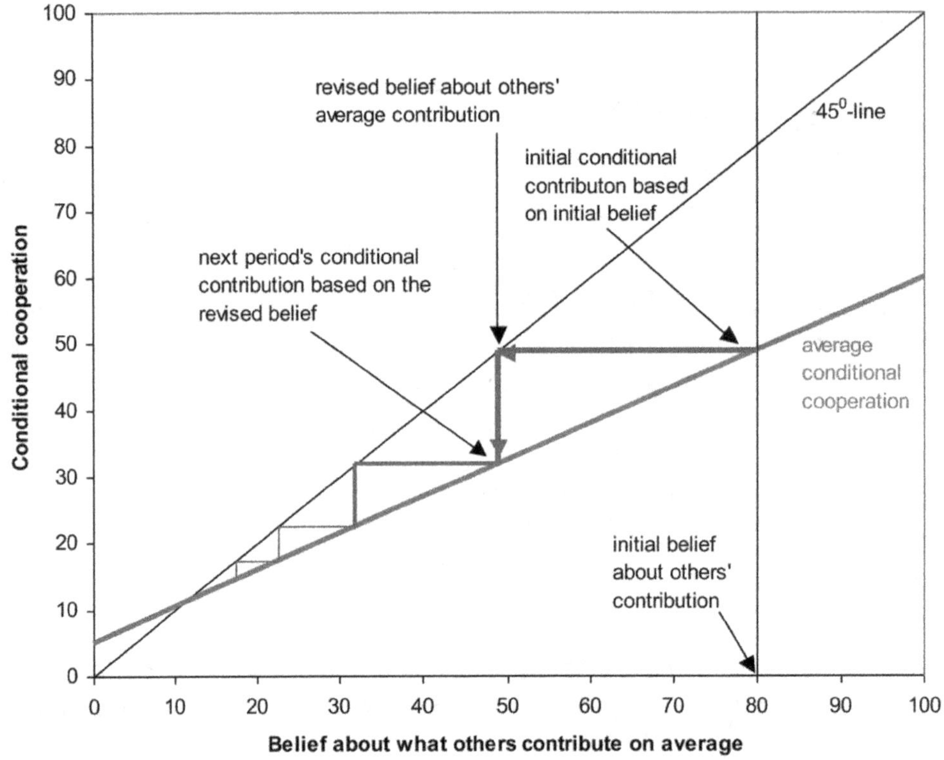

Figure 4.6 Temporal decay of cooperation when there are heterogeneous preferences. Source: Fehr and Fischbacher (2003)

are more reluctant to accept a reduction in their payoffs when their income is lower, than when their income is higher.

5. Suppose that all players have ERC preferences. Two players play the dictator game in Section 3.2. A third player, a passive observer, who also has the same endowment as the dictator, watches the share of the endowment shared by the dictator with the passive receiver. Show that the passive observer will never engage in third party punishment of the dictator even when the dictator makes a low offer. What are the implications for social norms?
6. Consider the maximin motive in the Charness–Rabin preferences in (4.20) and (4.21) in which individuals are hypothesized to care about the poorest member of society. Is the following evidence, summarized in Dhami (2019, Vol. 2, p.146), consistent with maximin preferences?
   (a) In the three-player ultimatum game, the experimental evidence is that the passive receiver typically gets nothing (Riedl and Vyrastekova, 2002).
   (b) In Fréchette et al. (2003), among a group of five players, one player is asked to make a proposal to allocate a fixed sum of money among the five players. The support of at least three players (majority rule) is needed to implement the proposal. In 65% of the cases, the winning proposal made no allocation to two of the five players.

(c) In Okada and Riedl (2005) there is one proposer and two responders. The proposer allocates a given amount to himself and the other two players; any particular allocation is denoted by (x_1, x_2, x_3). If the proposer decides to form a three-person coalition, the total amount to be allocated is 3000. If he decides to form a two-person coalition, the total amount available is an element of the set $\{1200, 2100, 2500, 2800\}$. A unanimity rule is imposed. Hence, for the proposer's offer to be successful, both responders must accept the offer in the three-person coalition and the single responder must accept the offer in the two-person coalition. When the amounts available for the two-player coalition are high enough (2500; 2800), then 90% of the proposers choose the two-player coalition. The three-player coalition is chosen by most proposers only when the amount available to the two-player coalition is very low, 1200.

7. Carry out the analysis of trust contracts in Section 4.5.3 with the following change. A fraction $\lambda \in (0, 1)$ of the workers are self-regarding while the rest are other-regarding. What effect does the fraction λ have on the wage offered in the trust contract?
8. Consider the case of bonus contracts in Section 4.5.3. Suppose that the principal's altruism parameter $\beta_1 < \frac{1}{2}$. Outline the optimal contractual solution when the worker's altruism parameter $\beta_2 < \frac{1}{2}$, and when it is $\beta_2 > \frac{1}{2}$.
9. Schindler and Pfattheicher (2017) used a variant of the die-cup experiments and asked subjects to privately roll a die 75 times and report the number of occurrences of 4. Can this experiment be used to determine the extent of lying behavior of each individual, unlike the Fischbacher–Föllmi–Heusi experiments that can determine lying behavior only at the aggregate level? Suppose that we put subjects into two different treatments. (i) In the gain frame, subjects are told that they will gain 10 cents for each reported 4. (ii) In the loss frame, subjects are initially endowed with 7.5 Euros and told that they will lose 10 cents for every report of a number that is not 4. Should we expect identical incentives to lie in the two treatments? If the data shows that lying behavior is different in the two domains, what can we conclude.
10. Kajackaite and Gneezy (2017) propose the mind game in which subjects first think of a number, then they roll a six-sided die. They then self-report to the experimenter if the number on the die is identical or different to the number they originally thought of. If they self-report an identical number, they receive a prize that was varied in different treatments. What advantages might this experiment offer relative to the Fischbacher–Föllmi–Heusi die-cup experiments? What if we find the results on lying in the two experiments to be different?

Part III

Behavioral Time Discounting

Introduction to Part III

Some of the most important individual decisions have a time dimension, for example, the choice of a university degree; marriage partner; pension plan; number of children; purchase of consumer durables; and a house purchase. Decisions by firms also often have a time dimension, such as: the introduction of a new product; mergers; acquisitions; and capital restructuring. Many government decisions that have important welfare consequences are also temporal in nature, such as: changing the mix between income and consumption taxes; timing of elections; giving choices in referenda such as the Brexit referendum; making commitments to contribute to a climate fund; and currency devaluations.

The third part of the book focuses on individual temporal decisions. However, the insights developed are also likely to apply in some form to firms and governments because ultimately these entities are also comprised of individuals themselves.

In making decisions over time, people may in "some domains" act in a far-sighted manner. For instance, we may postpone a pleasant experience to the future and derive *anticipal utility* in the interim periods. Or, we may sometimes get over an unpleasant experience as quickly as possibly and avoid negative emotional states, such as dread, that would accompany delay. In other domains, however, the evidence suggests that people make current choices in an impatient manner. Such behavior appears to reveal a taste for instant gratification, yet the same individual might be reasonably patient while making choices that apply to the more distant future. We shall refer to such preferences as *present-focused preferences*. We prefer the term "present-focused preferences" to the commonly used term "present-biased preferences" in the literature (Ericson and Laibson, 2019). The term "present-biased" behavior can only be used relative to some benchmark, which in this case is the neoclassical benchmark of exponential discounted utility (EDU). However, such an interpretation imparts normative significance to the EDU model and "bias" has the connotation of "undesirability" of behavior. The actual degree of impatience of humans, and its heterogeneity, is a matter of the *empirical evidence* and is not a bias in any normative sense. To avoid getting into these arguments, it may be desirable to use present-focused preferences.

The examples of present-focused behavior span a wide terrain in economics, as highlighted in the following quote from O'Donoghue and Rabin (2007):

> Topics now or soon to be studied with the perspective that present-focused preferences matter include: general savings rates, credit-card borrowing, cigarette consumption, welfare enrollment, procrastination in personal investment, unemployment and procrastination in employment search, purchase quantities under non-linear pricing for "virtue" vs. "vice" products, the effects of payday timing on monthly consumption patterns, food stamps, the effects of coupons and rebates on demand for products, organizational incentives, retirement timing, finishing school, returning to school for G.E.Ds, unsafe sex and AIDS and pregnancy, procrastination in seeking medical attention, compliance with medical prescriptions, alcohol

consumption, unhealthy eating, exercise, obesity, procrastination in research, and seeing too few Johnny Depp movies.

This should not be taken to mean that some of the behaviors ascribed to present-focus do not have other potential explanations. For instance, Loewenstein (2018) points out that in the US, the rise in obesity and the fall in savings are phenomena that arose after 1980. It is not as if Americans suddenly became so impatient as to become obese and undersavers, and there might be structural reasons for these phenomena that are not rooted in present-focused preferences. In the case of obesity, these factors include: the fast food culture; drop in the prices of processed foods; increase in the portion sizes, perhaps due to competitive pressures; changes in habits on snacking; and the changing and sedentary nature of work and leisure. A possible explanation for the decrease in savings is the growth in credit card debt. This alerts us to considering a range of alternative explanations before ascribing a given problem to present-focused preferences. Yet, in many domains, even after accounting for alternative explanations, present-focus is a real and important phenomena, and this is the subject matter in this part of the book.

Individuals may differ in their degree of awareness of future self control problems. The possibilities range from being completely aware (*sophisticates*) to complete unawareness of future self-control problems (*naifs*); there is also an intermediate category of *partial naifs* who have some, but not perfect, awareness of future self-control problems. If individuals have some degree of awareness of future self-control problems, they may wish to take actions to constrain their own future behavior; such actions take the form of *commitment strategies*. For instance, a drug addict who is desperate to quit may enroll in an expensive rehab clinic. The demand for commitment is driven by one's individual preferences. It is quite different from the commitment arising through strategic concerns between a set of players; for instance, an army General may order that his boats be burned on alighting on a foreign shore for the purposes of capturing territory. We shall not be interested in this form of strategic commitment in this part of the book.

While the theory is straightforward, identifying present-focus in actual practice and distinguishing it from other competing explanations such as limited attention, temptation preferences, or subadditive discounting, is often not straightforward. It may require careful causal identification.

There is a separate class of temporal models in economics that fall under the umbrella term of *habit formation models*. In these models, as individuals get habituated to a product, say, smoking or drugs, they need to consume ever-increasing quantities to get the same fix. In other words, their current marginal utility from consumption falls with a greater stock of consumption of the habit formation good in the past. It is often optimal in these models to choose an increasing profile of consumption (Ryder and Heal, 1973; Becker and Murphy, 1988). This results in behavior that is not present-focused, but the basic idea that individuals choose their consumption profiles of harmful projects in a fully rational manner, comparing the present discounted value of rewards and costs, does not appear consistent with the evidence from behavioral economics. We shall not discuss this class of models, but the interested reader can consult Dhami (2019, Vol. 3) for an exposition.

Our discussion is organized in two chapters. In Chapter 5 we describe the traditional model of time preferences in economics, the exponential discounting utility model, and its limitations. In Chapter 6, we consider the behavioral alternatives and their applications.

5 The Traditional Approach to Time Preferences

5.1 Introduction

In this chapter, we consider the *exponential discounted utility* (EDU) model, which is the main model in neoclassical economics that is used to study intertemporal choices. The EDU model adds up utilities received at different points in time, but discounts future utilities, and discounts them more, the further out in the future these utilities are received.

The EDU model was initially proposed by Paul Samuelson in 1937 who was looking for a method of measuring the marginal utility of money in the domain of intertemporal choices. Samuelson was interested in a purely technical result, did not claim any empirical evidence in support of the EDU, and cautioned against its use for welfare analysis. However, it was shown later, in the mid 1950s, that the EDU model is the unique model in an interesting class of models, known as *delay-discounting models*, that leads to a *time consistent* choice of outcomes (these terms are formally explained later in this chapter). This cemented the use of the EDU model in all areas of economics, including in welfare analysis.

We begin in Section 5.2 by introducing *time preferences*, and binary preferences over outcome-time pairs. We then use a simple example to fix basic ideas such as *preference reversals*, *time inconsistency*, and *limited awareness of future self-control problems*. We also introduce the concept of *utility representation of time preferences*.

In Section 5.3, we give an introduction to the ideas of simple and continuous time interest compounding. This is followed by a discussion of the preference foundations of the EDU model. This requires an examination of the restrictions on the underlying time preferences of individuals such that their time preferences can be represented by a utility function of the EDU form. We also introduce models of delay-discounting.

The EDU model describes complex human behavior over time, by encapsulating it in a single parameter, *the discount rate*; this turns out to be too parsimonious to account for the data. In the EDU model, the discount rate is constant between any two time periods, no matter when they occur, provided the gap is the same between them (e.g., today vs. tomorrow; or 100 days vs. 101 days from now). This is known as *stationarity of preferences*. Furthermore, the same discount rate applies to all outcomes, large or small, gains or losses, and to different types of goods.

It should not come as a surprise, given the restrictive nature of the EDU model, that the empirical evidence rejects it. In Section 5.4, we consider several rejections of the EDU model. These include the *common difference effect*, which is a violation of the stationarity of preferences;

the *magnitude effect* (larger outcomes are discounted less than smaller outcomes); gain-loss asymmetry (losses are discounted less than gains); and subadditive discounting (discounting over an interval depends on how that interval is subdivided). Finally, unlike the prediction under EDU, people attach significance to the shapes of consumption profiles. For instance, in many cases, people prefer an increasing stream of outcomes over time (e.g., we prefer dessert at the end of a meal).

5.2 Fixing Basic Ideas in Temporal Choice

5.2.1 Preferences over Outcome-Time Pairs

In this section, we briefly set out some of the preference foundations of intertemporal choices. These aid in testing the underlying theories. Starting from the next section, we shall mostly dispense with the preference foundations and talk only in terms of intertemporal utility functions.

Two important attributes of any temporal problem are the following.

1. The set of dates, $\Gamma = \{0, 1, 2, \ldots, T\}$, which capture the passage of time; we denote a typical element of this set by t. The current date is $t = 0$, and the terminal date beyond which there is no future is T. The choice of an appropriate time interval between two successive dates, for example, day, month, year, or some other unit, depends on the nature of the problem considered.
2. The set Z of possible outcomes, where a typical outcome is denoted by z. When outcomes are monetary outcomes, then we can write $Z \subset \mathbb{R}$. However, outcomes can be almost anything you might imagine, including nonmonetary outcomes, such as bundles of goods/services; or something abstract, such as a candlelit dinner, or playing frisbee in the park with your dog.

We will be interested in *outcome-time pairs*, denoted by (z, t), which signify an outcome $z \in Z$ to be received at time $t \in \Gamma$. The outcome is received with certainty. A different framework is needed if there were to be a risk of not receiving the outcome; see Section 6.9 for a brief discussion. All possible outcome-time pairs are drawn from the Cartesian product of the two sets $C = Z \times \Gamma$. The main question under time discounting is this: How do people choose between different outcome-time pairs drawn from the set of all possible outcome-time pairs, C?

Example 5.1 *Suppose that there are only two possible outcomes, so* $Z = \{5, 7\}$*; and there are two possible time periods* $\Gamma = \{1, 2\}$*. Then the Cartesian product* $C = Z \times \Gamma$ *is the set* $\{(5, 1), (7, 1), (5, 2), (7, 2)\}$*. Thus, for instance, the pair (5,1) is the outcome 5 received at time 1, and the pair (5,2) is the outcome 5 received at time 2. The problem of the individual is to choose between these 4 outcome-time pairs.*

We assume that individuals possess a *binary preference* relation between any two outcome-time pairs in the set of all possible outcome-time pairs, C. These binary preferences are represented by the symbol $\succeq$ which means "at least as good as." It is also useful to specify the related preferences $\sim$ (indifferent between) and $\succ$ (strictly preferred to). Consider, for instance, any two arbitrary outcome-time pairs in the set C, given by (z,t) and (z',t'). Here are some of the possible preferences that the individual might express.

1. If the individual considers the pair (z,t) "at least as good as" the pair (z',t'), then we write $(z,t) \succeq (z',t')$.
2. If the individual is "indifferent between" the pairs (z,t) and (z',t'), then we write $(z,t) \sim (z',t')$. This is a special case of the "at least as good as" preference relation where $(z,t) \succeq (z',t')$ and $(z',t') \succeq (z,t)$ are simultaneously true.
3. If the individual "strictly prefers" (z,t) to (z',t'), then we write $(z,t) \succ (z',t')$. Strict preference is a special case of the "at least as good as" preference when $(z,t) \succeq (z',t')$ is true but $(z',t') \succeq (z,t)$ is false.

In many problems of interest, individuals are confronted by a choice between a *smaller-sooner* (SS) option, denoted by (z_S, t_S), and a *larger-later* (LL) option, denoted by (z_L, t_L). Both options (z_S, t_S) and (z_L, t_L) are chosen from the set C and satisfy $z_S < z_L$ (z_S is the smaller of the two outcomes) and $t_S < t_L$ (t_S is the earlier of the two times). For instance, using the outcome-time pairs in Example 5.1, a choice between $(z_S, t_S) = (5,1)$ and $(z_L, t_L) = (7,2)$ would have been a choice of this nature. In such choices, the individual's degree of impatience is critical.

It is also important to state the time at which an individual makes a decision. The preferences that an individual has at one point in time might not be the preferences of the same individual at another point in time. For instance, as a child one might prefer chocolate ice cream to pistachio ice cream. However, the same person, as an adult, might prefer pistachio ice cream to chocolate ice cream. Hence, in stating an individual's preferences, $\succeq$, the time at which these preferences apply can be critical. Thus, the more complete notation $\succeq_t$ denotes the binary preference relation "at least as good as" but also records the time $t \in \Gamma$ when this preference is expressed. The corresponding "indifference" and "strictly preferred" preference relations that record the time t when the preferences are held are written as $\sim_t$ and $\succ_t$.

Let us consider the following example, due to Thaler (1981), popularly known as *Thaler's apples example.*

Example 5.2 *Suppose the outcomes in the set Z are apples. An individual, at time $t = 0$, strictly prefers 1 apple received today to 2 apples received tomorrow, that is,*

$$(1,0) \succ_0 (2,1), \tag{5.1}$$

where the subscript "0" on $\succ_0$ indicates that these preferences are time $t = 0$ preferences. The same individual, also at time $t = 0$, prefers 2 apples in 51 days to 1 apple in 50 days, that is,

$$(2,51) \succ_0 (1,50). \tag{5.2}$$

Do you find anything peculiar in this example? Example 5.2 can be used to illustrate three important issues in time discounting.

1. *Nonconstant time discounting and preference reversals*: Example 5.2 illustrates *preference reversals* from the perspective of the current time, $t = 0$. For choices over a short horizon (today versus tomorrow), the individual is impatient and prefers the SS reward, $(1,0)$, to the LL reward, $(2,1)$. However, over a longer horizon (51 and 50 days from now, but still from

the perspective of $t = 0$), the individual is patient, preferring the LL reward, $(2, 51)$, to the SS reward, $(1, 50)$. The time difference between both rewards is identical in both choices, that is, 1 day, and the outcome sizes are identical. Yet, impatience depends on whether the horizon is short or long; this, as we shall see later, is on account of *nonconstant discounting*.

2. *Time inconsistency of choices*: Given the preferences expressed in Example 5.2, let us consider the individual's choices at time $t = 50$. We ask the individual again, at time $t = 50$, using the time $t = 50$ preferences, $\succeq_{50}$, which outcome-time pair he would prefer, $(1, 50)$ or $(2, 51)$? Suppose that the individual prefers, at time $t = 50$, the option $(1, 50)$ to $(2, 51)$ (i.e., the SS option over the LL option) which is an impatient choice,

$$(1, 50) \succ_{50} (2, 51). \tag{5.3}$$

Comparing (5.2) and (5.3), the preference expressed at time $t = 0$ for the LL option over the SS option is overturned at time $t = 50$, when the outcomes and the time gap between the two dates are identical. In such cases, the individual's preferences are said to be *time inconsistent*, that is, the individual does not go through with the stated future plans when the future actually arrives. If, however, at time $t = 50$, the individual keeps unchanged his earlier preference for the LL option over the SS option, that is, $(2, 51) \succ_{50} (1, 50)$, then he is said to be *time consistent*.

3. *Lack of awareness of future self-control problems*: Suppose that the individual's choice is actually time inconsistent, that is, (5.2) and (5.3) both hold true. Suppose also that we asked the individual at time $t = 0$, to guess what he would choose at time $t = 50$, that is, the SS option or the LL option.
   (i) An individual who correctly guesses, at time $t = 0$, that preferences will be reversed towards the SS option in the future, is fully aware of self-control problems. Such an individual is known as a *sophisticate*.
   (ii) An individual who asserts, at time $t = 0$, that preferences will not be reversed at time $t = 50$ (when, in fact, they are), lacks awareness of future self-control problems. Such an individual is known as a *naive* individual. It is also possible to be *partially naive* by having some, but imperfect, awareness of future self-control problems.

5.2.2 The Utility Representation of Preferences

We can continue discussing the rest of this chapter in terms of time preferences over outcome-time pairs. We can, in addition, include the possibility of risky choices; for a recent treatment, see al-Nowaihi and Dhami (2021). However, it is simpler and analytically more convenient to express such preferences in terms of utility functions.

Suppose that we are interested in the preferences of an individual at time t, $\succeq_t$. The individual states that the outcome time pair (z, t) is at least as good as another outcome-time pair (z', t'). Then, a utility function U that represents these preferences, has the following two properties.

(i) For any outcome-time pair (z, t) in the set C, the corresponding utility $U(z, t)$ is a real number; this property is expressed as $U : C \to \mathbb{R}$.
(ii) The utility from (z, t) is no lower than the utility from (z', t').

In other words, we are looking for the following condition for a utility function,

$$(z,t) \succeq_t (z',t') \Longleftrightarrow U(z,t) \geq U(z',t');\ \forall (z,t),(z',t') \in C. \tag{5.4}$$

The condition in (5.4) can be used to derive the following two results that the reader should try to prove.

1. If $(z,t) \sim_t (z',t')$ then $U(z,t) = U(z',t')$, that is, utilities are identical for outcome-time pairs over which an individual is indifferent.
2. If $(z,t) \succ_t (z',t')$ then $U(z,t) > U(z',t')$, that is, utility is strictly higher from the strictly preferred outcome-time pair.

If the utility function U represent the preferences, $\succeq_t$, then we can analyze temporal choices either through the lens of the underlying preferences, or through the utility function. Both methods are equivalent. We choose to work with the utility function. This does not require that people go about their daily business carrying a utility function in their heads, but it does require people to have "well-defined" underlying preferences. The meaning of "well-defined" will be clarified later. In explaining evidence from temporal problems, there have been many different proposals for the utility function. We outline several such proposals in this chapter.

5.3 The Traditional Approach: Exponential Discounted Utility Model

In this section, we consider the main utility function that has been used to represent temporal preferences in economics. We shall also examine what sort of restrictions on temporal preferences give rise to such a utility function.

5.3.1 A Refresher on Simple and Compound Interest Rates

If one lends an amount $Y > 0$ at time $t = 0$ at an "annual interest rate" of $r > 0$, then one year from now this amount becomes $(1+r)Y$; two years from now it becomes $(1+r)^2 Y$; and t years from now it becomes

$$(1+r)^t Y; t = 1, 2, 3, \ldots \tag{5.5}$$

Conversely, suppose that at some time t in the future, one is to receive an amount W and we are interested in computing its *present discounted value* Y *at* $t = 0$. Suppose that $W = (1+r)^t Y$. Divide both sides by $(1+r)^t$ to get the present discounted value,

$$Y = \frac{1}{(1+r)^t} W; t = 1, 2, 3, \ldots \tag{5.6}$$

What if, instead, the interest were to be compounded several times during a year? Suppose that one invested a principal amount $Y > 0$ in a bank that compounded the interest rate every four months, or three times during the year. If the annual interest rate is $r > 0$, then at the end of four months, one receives $Y\left(1 + \frac{r}{3}\right)$. This principal is then invested again by the bank for another four months, so that at the end of eight months, one receives $\left[Y\left(1+\frac{r}{3}\right)\right]\left(1+\frac{r}{3}\right)=Y\left(1+\frac{r}{3}\right)^2$. At the end of the year, one receives $Y\left(1+\frac{r}{3}\right)^3$. If one left the money in the bank and the bank continued to pay compound interest, three times a year, then at the end of t years, the original principal amount of Y would have grown to

$$Y\left(1+\frac{r}{3}\right)^{3t};t=1,2,3,\ldots \tag{5.7}$$

If instead of compounding the interest rate three times a year, the bank had compounded the interest rate n times during each year, then after t years, the principal would have grown to

$$Y\left(1+\frac{r}{n}\right)^{nt};t=1,2,3,\ldots \tag{5.8}$$

Note that (5.7) is just a special case of (5.8) when $n=3$. Recall, from your first year courses, the definition of the number $e=2.718281693$, which is given by

$$e=lim_{m\to\infty}\left(1+\frac{1}{m}\right)^m. \tag{5.9}$$

The operator $lim_{m\to\infty}$ is read as "limit of the the expression as m becomes infinitely large." Define a new variable $m=n/r$. Then, we can rewrite (5.8) as

$$Y\left(1+\frac{1}{m}\right)^{mrt};t=1,2,3,\ldots$$

Let us now take the limit of this expression as $m\to\infty$. We get $lim_{m\to\infty}Y\left(1+\frac{1}{m}\right)^{mrt}$, which can be written as

$$Y\left[lim_{m\to\infty}\left(1+\frac{1}{m}\right)^m\right]^{rt}. \tag{5.10}$$

Using (5.9), the term in the square brackets in (5.10) equals e. Hence, we can rewrite (5.10) as

$$e^{rt}Y. \tag{5.11}$$

In words: Starting with an initial amount Y, and an interest rate, r that is continuously compounded, after t years, the initial amount grows to $e^{rt}Y$.

Let us continue to maintain the assumption of continuous compounding. If a decision maker receives an amount W at some time t in the future, what is the present discounted value, Y, of this amount at time $t=0$? Using (5.11), we guess that the relation between Y and W must be

$$W=e^{rt}Y. \tag{5.12}$$

Divide both sides of (5.12) by e^{rt} to get

$$Y=e^{-rt}W. \tag{5.13}$$

Thus, Y, given in (5.13), is the present discounted value of W received at some future date t, when interest is continuously compounded.

5.3.2 The Exponential Discounted Utility Model

Let $u(z)$ be the utility from an outcome, $z \in Z$. In models of time discounting, the function u is sometimes known as an *instantaneous utility function*, or *felicity*. It is typically assumed to be time-invariant, although this choice must be dictated by the empirical evidence. If time is discrete, $t \in \Gamma = \{0, 1, 2, \ldots, T\}$, then the *exponential discounted utility* (EDU) of the outcome-time pair (z, t) at time $t = 0$ is the present discounted value of the utility $u(z)$ from outcome z, that is,

$$EDU(z,t) = \frac{1}{(1+\theta)^t} u(z); \theta > 0. \tag{5.14}$$

In (5.14), $\theta > 0$ is the individual's *discount rate* between any two consecutive time periods. The parameter θ, which is the individual's preference parameter, reflects impatience by shrinking the value of future utility, and plays the same role as the interest rate, r, in (5.6), although the two are different entities. The interest rate is determined in markets, while the discount rate is a deep underlying preference parameter of an individual. More generally, we could impose the restriction $\theta \geq 0$ to include the case of no impatience, $\theta = 0$. The higher is θ, the lower is the weight $\frac{1}{(1+\theta)^t}$ put on the utilities from future outcomes. When this is the case, we say that future outcomes are *discounted more* or that they are *less salient*. For notational convenience, let us denote by δ, the *discount factor*, which is defined as

$$\delta = \frac{1}{(1+\theta)} < 1.$$

Raising both sides to the power t, it follows that

$$\delta^t = \frac{1}{(1+\theta)^t}. \tag{5.15}$$

Then, we can rewrite (5.14) as

$$EDU(z,t) = \delta^t u(z); 0 < \delta < 1, \tag{5.16}$$

where δ is known as the *discount factor*. From (5.15), δ^t decreases as t increases, hence, the further out in the future is the receipt of outcome z, the more highly it is discounted, or shrunk, reflecting greater impatience.

The empirical evidence indicates that there is substantial heterogeneity in the discount rate among people and it captures differences in many different dimensions (Dhami, 2019, Vol. III). For instance, the discount rate tends to be higher, reflecting greater impatience, for the young relative to the old, hence, younger drivers end up paying higher car insurance premiums; and for gamblers, smokers, drug users, and heavy alcohol drinkers who find it more difficult to quit harmful habits. Those with higher measured IQs tend to be more patient, that is, have low discount rates. We do not know for sure if this is due to their ability to better recognize their impatience and its potentially harmful effects, or whether higher IQ is innately correlated with greater patience. Individuals also exhibit different discount rates for different goods (Ubfal, 2016).

If time is measured continuously over the time interval, $\Gamma = [0, T]$, then we can rewrite the discrete version of EDU, given in (5.14), as

$$EDU(z,t) = e^{-\theta t} u(z). \tag{5.17}$$

This is just the analogue of (5.13) in which we replace the annual interest rate r by the annual discount rate θ, and take account of the utility u from outcomes. Continuous time is often a convenient technical assumption, but it may sometimes be approximately satisfied, for example, in continuous time trading in stock markets.

To ensure that we are comfortable with the formulae used so far, consider the following numerical examples.

Example 5.3 *Suppose that time is discrete. Tom is choosing between alternative pension plans. He also expects to receive an inheritance of* \$2,225,000, *10 years from now. His annual subjective discount rate is $\theta = 0.02$, or 2%, and his utility function is $u(z) = \sqrt{z}$. Using (5.14), the present discounted utility of the inheritance is*

$$\frac{1}{(1+0.02)^{10}}\sqrt{2,225,000} = 1223.70.$$

We can also see that the discount factor in this case is $\delta = \frac{1}{(1+\theta)} = \frac{1}{1.02} \approx 0.98$. If, however, the discount rate increases five times, $\theta = 0.10$, then the new discount factor is $\delta = \frac{1}{(1+0.1)} \approx 0.91$.

Example 5.4 *Suppose that Jane is a trader in the stock market who trades in continuous time. She expects to receive a return of* \$256 *at the end of six months. Her annual subjective discount rate is $\theta = 0.05$, or 5%, and her utility function is $u(z) = \sqrt{z}$. We use (5.17) to compute the present discounted utility of the return that accrues six months from now, to be*

$$e^{-0.05\left(\frac{1}{2}\right)}\sqrt{256} \approx 15.61.$$

In this calculation, we have used $t = \frac{1}{2}$. The reason is that θ is Jane's annual discount rate, we measure time in years and six months is half a year.

Moreover, EDU is easily extended to *streams of outcome-time pairs*. Suppose you are offered the outcome z_0 today, z_1 tomorrow, and so on until you receive z_T at date T. This could be a stream of temporal outcomes such as returns from an asset, monthly salary, or consumption levels. Denote the entire stream of outcomes by $\mathbf{z} = (z_0, z_1, \ldots, z_T)$ which is drawn from some underlying set Z of outcomes. Thus, $\mathbf{z}$ is a vector of $T+1$ outcomes. Then the EDU from this stream of temporal outcomes is a straightforward extension of (5.16).

$$EDU(\mathbf{z}) = \sum_{t=0}^{t=T} \delta^t u(z_t); 0 < \delta < 1, \mathbf{z} \in Z. \tag{5.18}$$

We remind readers that the summation notation in full is

$$\sum_{t=0}^{t=T} \delta^t u(z_t) = u(z_0) + \delta u(z_1) + \delta^2 u(z_2) \ldots + \delta^T u(z_T).$$

In (5.18), the outcome z_0 is received today at time $t = 0$, so the term $u(z_0)$ does not need to be discounted. The remaining outcomes are received in the future and the future utilities from these outcomes are discounted back to time $t = 0$.

Remark 5.1 *It is important to distinguish between (i) a discount rate, (ii) a discount factor, and (iii) a discount function. In the EDU model, the discount rate is θ, and the discount factor is $\delta = \frac{1}{1+\theta}$. The discount function, $D(t)$, specifies the discount factor at each of the dates $t = 0, 1, 2, \ldots$ Hence, for EDU, it is given by*

$$D(t) = \begin{cases} 1 & \text{if} \quad t = 0 \\ \delta^t & \text{if} \quad t > 0 \end{cases}.$$

A similar distinction between these three concepts also applies to other models of time discounting.

Let's familiarize ourselves with the formulation in (5.18) through the next example.

Example 5.5 *Suppose that Sahaj is interested in computing his EDU for a stream of outcomes over three consecutive time periods $\Gamma = \{0, 1, 2\}$. Sahaj's annual discount rate is $\theta = 0.05$, or 5%, his utility function is $u(z) = lnz$, and he receives the stream of outcomes, $z_0 = 14$ (today), $z_1 = 18$ (next year), and $z_2 = 27$ (the year after next). Using (5.18), the present discounted utility of this stream of outcomes is*

$$ln14 + \frac{1}{1 + 0.05} ln18 + \frac{1}{(1 + 0.05)^2} ln27 \approx 8.38.$$

Suppose now that time is measured continuously over the interval $[0, T]$ and the set of outcomes $Z \subset \mathbb{R}$. We can write the analogue of (5.18) in continuous time by replacing the summation sign with an integration sign

$$EDU(\mathbf{z}) = \int_0^T e^{-\theta t} u(z_t) dt; 0 < \theta < 1, \mathbf{z} \in Z. \tag{5.19}$$

From (5.19), we can see that the name "exponential discounting" is appropriate because the exponential discount function, $e^{-\theta t}$, is used to discount future utilities at time t. The second Nobel Prize winner in economics, Paul Samuelson, who proposed EDU in 1937, was looking for a convenient method of measuring marginal utility of money when people make choices over time. He expressed reservations about the use of this theory to represent actual human behavior. Referring to the integral in (5.19) Samuelson (1937, p. 159) wrote: "In the first place, it is completely arbitrary to assume that the individual behaves so as to maximize an integral of the form envisaged in (2)." He also cautioned against using it for welfare analysis by writing (p. 161): "In conclusion, any connection between utility as discussed here and any welfare concept is disavowed."

One reason for the subsequent popularity of EDU was due to the following result that was derived in Strotz (1955–56). It can be shown that EDU is the unique functional form in the class of *discounted utility models*, discussed below in Section 5.3.3, that always guarantees time consistency of choices (see Section 5.2 for this concept). This further established the almost exclusive use of EDU in economics, a practice that has continued until recently, despite the availability of empirically superior alternatives.

Despite the reservations expressed in Samuelson (1937), EDU quickly became the workhorse model while analyzing temporal choices in economics. This adoption occurred without proper and stringent empirical testing of the model itself. Unfortunately, the EDU model is not supported by a wide range of empirical evidence, which we discuss in Section 5.4. Although one is always wiser in hindsight, it would have been surprising if EDU had succeeded in accounting for the evidence on temporal choice. After all, the entire psychology of human choice in the EDU model is encapsulated in a single parameter, the discount rate, θ, which is an unreasonable burden on any model.

5.3.3 The Class of Discounted Utility Models

The EDU model is an example of a more general class of models, known as the class of *discounted utility models* (DU models). Consider discrete time, where time $t \in \Gamma = \{0, 1, 2, \ldots, T\}$. The general form of discrete time DU models is given by

$$DU(\mathbf{z}) = u(z_0) + D(1)u(z_1) + D(2)u(z_2) \ldots + D(T)u(z_T), \tag{5.20}$$

where $D(t)$, $t = 0, 1, \ldots, T$, known as the *discount function*, is the weight that is placed, at time 0, on the utility of the time t outcome, $u(z_t)$. The function $D(t)$ is a decreasing real-valued function, $D(1) > D(2) > \ldots > D(T)$, so that outcomes in the more distant future are assigned successively lower weights. Comparing (5.18) and (5.20) we can see that EDU is a special case of DU where

$$D(t) = \delta^t; t = 0, 1, 2, \ldots \tag{5.21}$$

The hyperbolic discounting utility model that we consider below in Section 6.2 is also a special case of the DU model.

If we know the discount function, D, then the discount rate, $\theta(t)$, at any time t, is defined as the rate of change of this function at time t. When time is discrete, we have

$$\theta(t) = -\frac{D(t) - D(t-1)}{D(t)}; t = 1, 2, \ldots \tag{5.22}$$

We prefix the minus sign on the RHS of (5.22) because $D(t) < D(t-1)$, hence multiplying by a negative sign makes the RHS positive, just as we do when we calculate the price elasticity of demand. Thus, a higher value of the RHS is interpreted as a higher discount rate. One of the exercises asks you to use (5.21) and (5.22) to find the discount rate under EDU.

For the case of continuous time, $t \in \Gamma = [0, T]$, if D is differentiable, then the discount rate at any instant in time t is simply the rate of change of the discount function, D, given by

$$\theta(t) = -\frac{D'(t)}{D(t)}; t \in [0, T], \tag{5.23}$$

where $D'(t)$ is the first derivative of the discount function.

The DU model has several potential limitations, which also apply to all other models that are special cases of the DU model. Some of these limitations are as follows.

1. The RHS of (5.20) is additively separable in outcomes over time. Thus, the marginal utility of an outcome that arises at time $t + 1$ is independent of an outcome that arises at time t. In some cases this is a reasonable assumption, but in other cases it might not be. Suppose that the outcomes themselves are meals at various times of the day, and that you have had an extremely heavy and unhealthy lunch. It is quite possible that this suppresses your appetite for dinner. The marginal utility of dinner is then not independent of what you had for lunch.

2. In (5.20) there is independence between the terms that contain time and the terms that contain outcomes. More generally, if there is dependence between the two, then we ought to write the term $D(t)u(z_t)$ as one composite term $u(z_t, t)$, $t = 1, 2, \ldots$ For instance, if Jim likes having a cup of tea with breakfast in the morning, but not with any other meal, then there is a dependence between the outcomes and the time when they are received.
3. Temporal decisions are often taken in emotional states. For example, one might be in a hot or a cold emotional state. Yet, emotions play no role in (5.20). For instance, consider Alexandra mulling over a divorce decision at time t which has implications for her outcomes at times $t+1, t+2, \ldots, T$. Her outcomes if she does not get a divorce are $\mathbf{z} = (z_{t+1}, z_{t+2}, \ldots, z_T)$, and if she does get a divorce the outcomes are $\mathbf{z}' = \left(z'_{t+1}, z'_{t+2}, \ldots, z'_T\right)$. If Alexandra were to make her decision in a cold state of mind by using the DU formulation given in (5.20), she finds that she should not divorce, that is, $DU(\mathbf{z}) > DU(\mathbf{z}')$. However, if she makes the divorce decision in a hot state of the mind, then she uses a simple decision rule. If her anger/frustration threshold exceeds a certain critical level, she chooses to divorce and then does not look back to regret her decision. Otherwise, she chooses not to divorce. Alexandra's decision in a hot state will appeal to many as a realistic possibility, yet the dependence of time preferences on emotions is not taken account of in the class of DU models. We indicate later how such dependence can be allowed.

5.3.4 Time Preferences and the EDU Model

Recall our discussion of the utility representation of preferences in Section 5.2.2. Can we find restrictions on the underlying time preferences of the individual, such that, if an individual satisfies those restrictions, then the individual follows the EDU model in Section 5.3.2? We now address this question.

As in Section 5.2, suppose that an individual's preferences over the set of all outcome-time pairs, $C = Z \times \Gamma$, at time $t = 0, 1, \ldots$ are given by the binary preference relations $\succeq_t$ (at least as good as), $\sim_t$ (indifferent to), and $\succ_t$ (strictly preferred to).

A decision maker who subscribes to the following set of axioms is said to be rational when making decisions over time. Hence, these are also sometimes known as the *axioms of rationality for time preferences*. It is sufficient to state these axioms in terms of the binary preference relation $\succeq_t$. It can be shown that similar conditions can be written in terms of the "indifference" and "strictly preferred to" binary preference relations, respectively, $\sim_t$ and $\succ_t$. We first state the axioms, followed by a discussion.

Definition 5.1 *(Axioms of rationality over time) Let z_j, z_k, and z_l be "any" three outcomes in the set Z and let t_j, t_k, and t_l be "any" three times in the set Γ. Let $\succeq_t$ be a binary preference relation on the set $C = Z \times \Gamma$ that represents the individual's time t preferences. A decision maker is said to be rational for decisions made over time, if $\succeq_t$ satisfies the following axioms for all times $t \in \Gamma$.*[1]

[1] We have omitted a technical axiom in this list, that of continuity of preferences.

(*a*) *Reflexivity: For any* $z \in Z$, *and any* $t \in \Gamma$, *we have* $(z,t) \succeq_t (z,t)$.

(*b*) *Completeness: For any two outcome-time pairs* (z_j, t_j) *and* (z_k, t_k), *either* $(z_j, t_j) \succeq_t (z_k, t_k)$, *or* $(z_k, t_k) \succeq_t (z_j, t_j)$, *or both are true.*

(*c*) *Transitivity: For any three outcome-time pairs* (z_j, t_j), (z_k, t_k), *and* (z_l, t_l), *if* $(z_j, t_j) \succeq_t (z_k, t_k)$ *and* $(z_k, t_k) \succeq_t (z_l, t_l)$, *then transitivity implies that* $(z_j, t_j) \succeq_t (z_l, t_l)$.

(*d*) *Monotonicity: Consider two outcome-time pairs,* (z_j, t_i), (z_k, t_i), *where the outcomes differ but they are received at the same time* t_i, *and* $z_j > z_k$. *Then monotonicity requires* $(z_j, t_i) \succ_t (z_k, t_i)$.

(*e*) *Impatience: Consider two outcome-time pairs,* (z, t_j), (z, t_k), *where the outcomes are identical, but they are received at different times* $t_k > t_j$. *Then, impatience requires* $(z, t_j) \succ_t (z, t_k)$.

(*f*) *Stationarity: For any two outcome-time pairs* (z_j, t_j) *and* (z_k, t_k), *we have*

$$(z_j, t_j) \succeq_t (z_k, t_k) \Rightarrow (z_j, t_j + t_i) \succeq_t (z_k, t_k + t_i) \; \forall t_i > 0.$$

Reflexivity is an obvious axiom; any outcome-time pair is at least as good as itself. The completeness axiom requires that any two outcome-time pairs can be compared, so, for instance, the decision maker is not allowed to say: "I am confused, but I cannot compare these options." Transitivity requires that if option 1 is at least as good as option 2, which in turn is at least as good as option 3, then it must be the case that option 1 is at least as good as option 3. Monotonicity requires that larger outcomes are strictly preferred to smaller outcomes when both are received at the same time. Impatience requires that for identical outcomes, the one that is received at the earlier time is preferred. In Definition 5.1, the most critical axiom is the stationarity axiom and it has been used extensively to test the EDU model. Stationarity requires that if option 1 is at least as good as option 2, then delaying both options by an identical number of time periods into the future, does not change the underlying preferences.

It can be shown that a decision maker who satisfies the axioms of rationality for time preferences (Definition 5.1) also follows the EDU model, and vice-versa. In this sense, and using the language introduced in Section 5.3.2, the *EDU model represents preferences that satisfy the axioms of rationality*. We record this result in the following Proposition.

Proposition 5.1 *(Fishburn and Rubinstein, 1982) Suppose that a decision maker's preferences,* $\succeq_t$, *when making choices over the set* $C = Z \times \Gamma$, *satisfy the axioms of rationality over time in Definition 5.1. Then, for some* $\delta \in (0,1)$ *and for any two outcome-time pairs* (z_j, t_j), (z_k, t_k) *in the set C, there is an increasing real-valued utility function u for outcomes such that the following holds.*

$$(z_j, t_j) \succeq_t (z_k, t_k) \Leftrightarrow \delta^{t_j} u(z_j) \geq \delta^{t_k} u(z_k). \tag{5.24}$$

From (5.16) and (5.24), the utility of an outcome z received at time t, $\delta^t u(z)$, corresponds to the EDU model. Comparing (5.4) with (5.24), and noting that $U(z,t) = \delta^t u(z)$, we can see that the EDU model represents preferences that satisfy the axioms of rationality over time. The equivalence relation in (5.24) gives rise to two alternative ways of testing the EDU model. One can test the EDU model directly using the predictions arising from the use of this model, but this may require estimating the unobserved utility function from outcomes, u. Alternatively, one can directly test the axioms of rationality over time in Definition 5.1, without requiring an estimation of the underlying utility function, u; hence, this is often the easier and more direct option. A rejection of any of the axioms in Definition 5.1 is a refutation of the EDU model.

The most tested of these axioms is the stationarity axiom and, as we show below, it is often rejected by the evidence.

5.4 Empirical Evidence on the Exponential Discounted Utility Model

In the EDU model, the discount rate, θ, is fixed across any time interval of a given length; it is identical for all goods and services; it is invariant to changes in emotions; and it is invariant to the magnitudes of different outcomes and for gains and losses. These features are rejected by the empirical evidence. However, we have learnt a great deal on the psychology of temporal choice from the empirical rejections of the EDU model. We describe some of this evidence below, based on Thaler (1981).

5.4.1 Magnitude Effect

The measured discount rate turns out to be relatively smaller for larger magnitudes; that is, larger magnitudes are discounted relatively less, so they are more salient. This is known as the *magnitude effect*. For instance, subjects in an experiment were indifferent between the following outcomes.

(i) \$15 received now and \$60 received in a year's time,
(ii) \$250 received now and \$350 received in a year's time, and
(iii) \$3000 received now and \$4000 received in a year's time.

The implied discount rate, θ, can be easily calculated from each of these indifferences. We shall use (5.17) and assume that utility from outcomes is linear, so $u(z) = z$. In (i), the amount \$15 received now is not discounted, so it is worth \$15 under EDU. The amount \$60 received in a year's time is worth $e^{-\theta}60$ now under EDU (we have set $t = 1$ in this calculation because the time delay is $t = 1$ year). Hence, the indifference between \$15 received now and \$60 received in a year's time implies

$$15 = e^{-\theta}60.$$

Taking log to the base e on both sides, it is straightforward to solve this equation in one unknown to get $\theta = \ln 4 = 1.386$. The remaining two calculations are analogous and the corresponding values of θ can be found from the calculations, $250 = e^{-\theta}350$, and $3000 = e^{-\theta}4000$. The discount rates, θ, in the three cases are respectively: (i) 1.386, (ii) 0.336, and (iii) 0.288. Thus, the larger the magnitude of the outcome, the smaller the discount rate, and the more weight assigned by the decision maker on the future outcomes.

5.4.2 Gain-Loss Asymmetry

Thaler (1981) calculated that the discount rate is much smaller for losses relative to gains. Thus, losses are discounted less; that is, they are more salient. This is known as gain-loss asymmetry. In other experiments, it has been shown that many subjects preferred to incur an immediate

Table 5.1 Implied annual discount rates in brackets, for gains and losses

Gain and Loss/Time	3 months	1 year	3 years
15	30 (3.923)	60 (1.386)	100 (0.632)
−15	−16 (0.258)	−20 (0.288)	−28 (0.208)

loss than delay the loss. The gain-loss asymmetry is reminiscent of losses being more salient than gains in static choices (loss aversion). The median responses reported in Thaler (1981), summarized in Table 5.1, show that individuals are indifferent between a current gain of \$15 and gains of \$30 in 3 months' time; \$60 in 1 year's time; and \$100 in 3 year's time. At the same time, individuals are indifferent between a current loss of \$15 and a loss of \$16 in three months' time; a loss of \$20 in one year's time; and a loss of \$28 in three years' time. Below each of the figures in Table 5.1, in brackets, is the implied annual discount rate calculated using the same method as in the magnitude effect; an exercise asks you to calculate these discount rates. The discount rates are higher, in each case, for gains relative to losses (compare the figures in brackets in each individual column). Thus, gains are discounted relatively more than losses and future losses are more salient than future gains.

5.4.3 Violation of Stationarity and Taste for Immediate Gratification

The most critical of the axioms of rationality of time preferences is the *stationarity* axiom (Definition 5.1f). A violation of the stationarity axiom is known as the *common difference effect*. From Example 5.2, stationarity is violated. From (5.1), in Thaler's apples example, we have $(1,0) \succ_0 (2,1)$. The stationarity axiom implies that if we move both rewards further out into the future by $t = 50$ time periods, then we should observe

$$(1, 0 + 50) \succ_0 (2, 1 + 50) \Rightarrow (1, 50) \succ_0 (2, 51).$$

However, from (5.2), we have $(2, 51) \succ_0 (1, 50)$, which violates stationarity and gives rise to the finding of the common difference effect.

In an experiment, when asked how much money in one month, one year, and ten years, repetition would make them indifferent to receiving \$15 now, the median response of subjects was \$20, \$50, and \$100, respectively. The implied annual discount rates can be readily calculated using the method already described to be, respectively, 3.452, 1.204, and 0.190 (for the one month calculation you will need to use $t = \frac{1}{12}$). Thus, over shorter horizons, the discount rate is higher and the individual is relatively more impatient, or less weight is assigned to future utilities.

5.4.4 Choices over Consumption Profiles

Loewenstein and Prelec (1993) gave subjects the option of having five weekend meals at either a French restaurant, a Lobster restaurant, or a meal at Home; see Table 5.2. Subjects had to

Table 5.2 Choice between the consumption profiles {$A1$,$A2$} and {$B1$,$B2$}. The percentage of subjects choosing each option is shown in brackets.

Options/Weekends	1	2	3	4	5
A1 (11%)	French	Home	Home	Home	Home
A2 (89%)	Home	Home	French	Home	Home
B1 (49%)	French	Home	Home	Home	Lobster
B2 (51%)	Home	Home	French	Home	Lobster

Source: Loewenstein and Prelec (1993)

pick one option from the set {A1, A2} and another option from the set {B1, B2}. For instance, in option A1, subjects get a coupon for a meal at a French restaurant for week 1, followed by Home meals for the remaining four weekends. From the set of choices {A1, A2}, 89% of the subjects chose option A2, and from the set of choices, {B1, B2}, subjects were split nearly equally between the two options.

These choices can be rationalized. A1 offers a front-loaded choice with the most exciting option upfront, while A2 offers a more balanced choice with the French meal in week 3. Subjects might, for instance, enjoy the anticipation of the French meal for the first three weeks and, hence, find A2 an attractive option. The choice between B1 and B2 is less obvious and depends on individual preferences and how much anticipated utility they are perceived to offer. But anticipated utility plays no role in the EDU model.

In contrast to the empirically observed choices, EDU predicts that people should either make odd numbered choices (A1 and B1) or even numbered choices (A2 and B2). In particular, they are not predicted to make an odd numbered choice from one set and an even numbered choice from the other set. To see this, let the utility from a French meal be $u(F)$, utility from a Home meal be $u(H)$, and utility from a Lobster meal be $u(L)$. Then the EDU evaluation of the choices A1 and A2, from the perspective of the current time period, say, at week $t = 0$, is:

$$EDU(A1) = \delta u(F) + \delta^2 u(H) + \delta^3 u(H) + \delta^4 u(H) + \delta^5 u(H). \tag{5.25}$$

$$EDU(A2) = \delta u(H) + \delta^2 u(H) + \delta^3 u(F) + \delta^4 u(H) + \delta^5 u(H). \tag{5.26}$$

When choosing between A1 and A2, EDU recommends choosing the option whose EDU valuation is the highest. However, when we subtract $EDU(A2)$ from $EDU(A1)$, the very last term, $\delta^5 u(H)$, cancels out. Hence, week 5's choice is inconsequential and the decision between A1 and A2 rests on evaluating the choices *for the first four weeks only*; indeed, since week 4 options are also identical, *the choice between A1 and A2 really depends on the options in the first three weeks only*.

Similarly, when we make an EDU evaluation of the choices B1 and B2 (which the reader should check), the very last term in both choices, $\delta^5 u(L)$, is common, hence it cancels out in a comparison of $EDU(B1)$ and $EDU(B2)$. Since the week 4 options are also identical, *only the first three weeks of choices matter for the comparison between B1 and B2*.

In sum, only the first three weeks of choices matter for choices from each of the two sets {A1,A2} and {B1,B2}. Thus, we can safely strike out the last two columns in Table 5.2 as being

Table 5.3 Choice between seven different shapes of income profiles. Figures in thousands of dollars. The last column reports the present discounted value of each income profile using an interest rate of 10%.

Shape/Year	1	2	3	4	5	6	Present-Value
Job 1 (decreasing)	27	26.2	25.4	24.6	23.8	23	120.8
Job 2 (flat)	25	25	25	25	25	25	119.8
Job 3	24	24.4	24.8	25.2	25.6	26	119.2
Job 4	23	23.8	24.6	25.4	26.2	27	118.7
Job 5	22	23.2	24.4	25.6	26.8	28	118.2
Job 6	21	22.6	24.2	25.8	27.4	29	117.6
Job 7	20	22	24	26	28	30	117.1

Source: Redrawn from Loewenstein and Sicherman (1991)

irrelevant to the choices. But then, focusing just on the first three weeks, A1 and B1 are identical, and A2 and B2 are identical too. So if a decision maker picks A1 over A2, they must pick B1 over B2; or if they pick A2 over A1, then they must pick B2 over B1. But this pattern is violated for a significant number of the subjects.

Experiments also find that people like increasing consumption profiles. For instance, in most cultures people prefer desserts at the end of a meal. Would you like to eat at a restaurant that offered the following three-course meal: Desserts, followed by the main course, which is followed by starters? This sequencing is potentially puzzling to explain using EDU, which recommends comparing only the numerical values of EDU for each option and picking the one that is the highest. This does not impose any conditions on the shapes of the consumption profile – whether they are increasing, decreasing, or constant.

Loewenstein and Sicherman (1991) conduct experiments to explore these ideas further. They offer subjects seven different profiles of outcomes spread over six years; see Table 5.3 for the exact numerical values in thousands of dollars. In Treatment 1, the profile of outcomes is framed as a yearly wage for the next six years from seven different kinds of jobs; in Treatment 2, the profile of outcomes is framed as the annual rental income from seven different properties for the next six years. The 80 adults who participated in the experiment were split equally into the two treatments. The final column in Table 5.3 uses an interest rate of 10% to compute the present discounted value (PDV) of the outcomes in each job/rental property over the six years.

Job 1 shows a decreasing outcomes profile, but it has the highest PDV of the seven options. Job 2 offers a flat outcomes profile. Jobs 3–7 offer an increasing profile of outcomes that become increasingly steeper but the PDV falls gradually. Subjects are also shown the same information in the form of seven different graphs, each graph corresponding to a different job. Subjects had to rank the jobs from 1–7 in terms of their preferences.

If a decision maker follows EDU and utility is approximately linear, then Job 1 ought to be the most attractive (highest PDV) and the Jobs 2–7, respectively, ought to be ranked in decreasing order of preference. However, the results are as follows.

1. Only 7.3% of the subjects in Treatment 1, and 23.1% of the subjects in Treatment 2 can be classified into those who followed the PDV calculations. The difference between the two is

statistically significant at the 5% significance level. In particular, only 12.1% of the subjects in Treatment 1, and 33.3% of the subjects in Treatment 2 choose Job 1 with a decreasing outcomes profile as their first preference, although it has the highest PDV.

2. Suppose we compared Job 1, the only decreasing wage profile, with its mirror image increasing wage profile, Job 4 (notice the numbers in Job 4 are the numbers in Job 1, written in reverse order). Then 83% of the subjects in Treatment 1, and 56% of the subjects in Treatment 2 preferred the increasing outcomes profile to the decreasing outcomes profile. Thus, the majority of subjects prefer increasing outcomes profiles to decreasing outcomes profiles. The preference for increasing outcomes can arise due to a variety of possible causes (Loewenstein and Prelec, 1993) that we list below.
    (a) Coping with self-control problems that lead to early splurges on consumption, hence, choosing an increasing outcomes profile is a form of self-control device. Self-control issues are considered later in this chapter.
    (b) Adaptive behavior where one adapts to the most recent income or interprets it as a reference point, so that an increasing income profile puts one perpetually in the domain of gains rather than slipping into the domain of losses where costly loss aversion bites (see Part I). This explanation is related to the "contrast effect" where lower initial outcomes create a favourable contrast with higher later outcome, leading to an increase in utility (Elster and Loewenstein, 1992).
    (c) Anticipal utility which creates utility purely from the anticipation of higher future incomes, and its flip side, disutility from dread which creates a tendency to get losses over with as quickly as possible (Loewenstein, 1987). This factor is likely to create a preference for decreasing sequences when the outcomes are losses.
3. Another way of looking at the differences in choices is to see how much money in PDV terms individuals are willing to sacrifice when they pick increasing outcomes profiles (Jobs 2–7) relative to the decreasing outcomes profile (Job 1). For instance, anyone who picks Job 1 over Job 7 is sacrificing \$120800 − \$117100 = \$3700. On average, those who chose one of the increasing outcomes profiles, sacrificed \$2851 in Treatment 1 and \$1764 in Treatment 2. The treatment difference is marginally significant at the 7% significance level.
4. From our discussion of points 1–3, there appears to be a greater tendency to choose increasing wage profiles in jobs as compared to increasing rental profiles in property incomes. Clearly, these are viewed as two distinct sources by many subjects. To delve more into the reasons for why this might be the case, subjects were asked to read one paragraph each on the arguments for decreasing and increasing outcomes profiles, prior to making their choices.

    The paragraph in favor of decreasing payments reads as follows: "Some researchers believe people should prefer option A [the declining sequence]. Their argument is that you can put part of the extra money you get at the beginning into the bank and withdraw it with interest later on. In fact, by choosing option A you could have more money every year."

    The paragraph in favor of increasing payments reads as follows: "Other researchers believe people should prefer option B [the increasing payment profile]. Their argument is that, first, it is satisfying to get a bigger payment each year. Second, even though you could save money in the first few years, it is often difficult to save money. Option B gives more spending later without worrying about putting money away in the first few years."

These two paragraphs speak to very different motivations. The argument in favor of decreasing payments is essentially one that would be advocated by someone who is likely to follow EDU. By contrast, the arguments in favor of increasing payments favors an explanation where subjects might have some form of self-control problems. If they receive high income early, they might splurge on consumption and not save adequately. This follows directly from models of hyperbolic discounting that we discuss in the next chapter, but not from the EDU model. Hence, it is interesting to see which of the two arguments the subjects were swayed by in making their choices in the two treatments.

In Treatment 1 (yearly wage profiles), 68% of the subjects were swayed by the arguments for increasing wage profiles and 30% by arguments for decreasing wage profiles. The opposite was true for Treatment 2 (rental income profiles), where these respective percentages were 40% and 57%. These proportions were significantly different ($p < 0.02$). Exposure to the arguments for decreasing outcomes profiles had a relatively larger impact for wage incomes than rental incomes. Yet, the majority of subjects still preferred increasing outcomes profiles.

Despite the relatively small sample size in the study reported above, the argument for increasing outcomes profiles is generally accepted, although replications with larger sample sizes are always important. One of the exercises asks you to think about a related problem. An important task for behavioral economists is to figure out the objective functions that decision makers might be trying to maximize if there is a preference for increasing outcomes profiles. Perhaps the EDU model needs to be amended along the following lines. Suppose, in a model with discrete time, that at any time $t = 1, 2, 3, \ldots$ the change in outcome over the previous period is $\Delta z_t = z_t - z_{t-1}$. Then, we may amend the EDU expression in (5.18) as

$$EDU(\mathbf{z}) = \sum_{t=0}^{t=T} \delta^t u(z_t, \Delta z_t); 0 < \delta < 1, \mathbf{z} \in Z,$$

where the utility function $u(z_t, \Delta z_t)$ is increasing in both arguments. This amendment may explain a preference for increasing outcomes profiles. It will not, however, save EDU from refutations on the grounds of violations of stationarity (or even of the magnitude effect and the gain/loss asymmetry), which require us to come up with more suitable discount functions. This is the subject matter of Section 6.2.

5.4.5 Subadditive Discounting

Suppose that, while situated at time $t = 0$, an individual is promised the following outcome-time pair (z, t_2), at time $t_2 > 0$. The present discounted value of this option under the EDU model, from the perspective of time $t = 0$, is

$$\delta^{t_2} u(z). \tag{5.27}$$

Suppose now that instead of discounting the reward z from time t_2 to time, $t = 0$, denoted by $0 \leftarrow t_2$, the individual discounts the reward in two successive steps. First, the reward is discounted back from time t_2 to an earlier time t_1 and then back from time t_1 to time $t = 0$ in two successive steps, which is denoted by $0 \leftarrow t_1 \leftarrow t_2$. In this case, under EDU, the present discounted value of the reward at time t_1 is $\delta^{t_2 - t_1} u(z)$ (this is the step $t_1 \leftarrow t_2$). Then, this present discounted value, $\delta^{t_2-t_1}u(z)$, is discounted from t_1 to $t = 0$ (this is the step $0 \leftarrow t_1$). Thus, the present discounted value at time $t = 0$ is

$$\delta^{t_1}\delta^{t_2-t_1}u(z) = \delta^{t_2}u(z). \tag{5.28}$$

Notice from (5.27) and (5.28) that the present discounted value is identical in each case. In general, under EDU it does not matter how we split the time interval into subintervals. Discounting over an entire interval leads to the same amount of discounting of future rewards as does discounting over successive subintervals. This is known as the *additivity property* of discount functions.

By contrast, the empirical evidence in Read (2001) violates the additivity property. They find that subjects in their experiments exhibited the following:

$$\delta^{t_1}\delta^{t_2-t_1}u(z) < \delta^{t_2}u(z).$$

Thus, discounting over an interval is smaller when we view the aggregate interval, but discounting increases as we subdivide the interval. This is known as *subadditive discounting*, which can also explain present-focused preferences.

5.5 Summary

It is fair to say that the refutations of the EDU model, like the refutations of expected utility theory that we looked at in Part I, are now so well established that it is pointless to test EDU any further. Indeed, the literature has moved on to developing alternatives to the EDU model and explaining the pattern of refutations of the EDU model. This is a task that we turn to next. At the same time, the descriptive and normative analysis in modern neoclassical economics continues to be based on the EDU.

6 Behavioral Approaches to Time Preferences

6.1 Introduction

This chapter describes the behavioral alternatives that have arisen from the need to explain the empirical evidence that rejects the EDU model. Of the many empirical rejections of the EDU model, the one that has garnered the most attention is the violation of stationarity. This violation is also known as the *common difference effect*. Empirical evidence indicates that the discount rate over a time interval of fixed size depends on the time at which that interval occurs. In other words, the discount rate is different when making a choice between today versus tomorrow; and a choice, today, between identical outcomes received over the same time interval, say, 50 days and 51 days from now. This forms the basis of *Thaler's apples example* that we discussed in the previous chapter. Most people prefer an apple today to two apples tomorrow but are willing to wait, today, to receive an extra apple in 51 days' time to receiving an apple in 50 days' time.

Section 6.2 describes the leading behavioral alternative that can account for the common difference effect, which also enables it to explain Thaler's apples example. This is the model of *hyperbolic discounting*. It takes account of the observed pattern of hyperbolically decreasing discount rates when discount rates are plotted against the time delay with which a future outcome is received. We focus on a particularly convenient form of hyperbolic discounting, *quasi-hyperbolic discounting*, also known as the (β, δ) model. This model allows for a sudden increase in impatience when making a choice between today and tomorrow, relative to making a choice, today, between any two dates in the future. This sudden increase in (current) impatience gives rise to *present-focused preferences* with a taste for *instant gratification*.

Section 6.4 introduces the idea of *multiple selves* of the same individual. This requires us to imagine that different selves of the same individual reside in different time periods. The current self of an individual cannot perfectly control a future self. For instance, alcoholics/smokers/drug users may not be able to commit that their future selves will not engage in such activity. Furthermore, the current self of an individual might not be fully aware of the self-control problems of their future selves. We can classify individuals into different types depending on their degree of awareness of future self-control problem. For instance, *sophisticates* are fully aware of their future self-control problems, while *naifs* are completely unaware; *partial naifs* lie somewhere in between in terms of their degree of awareness. We also present empirical evidence on the degree of awareness of future self-control problems.

Several sections that follow provide applications of present-focused preferences under limited awareness of future self-control problems.

Section 6.5 considers an application to the choice of optimal consumption profiles over an individual's lifetime. We show how the current self of an individual might seek to protect against splurges in consumption of future selves by investing in illiquid assets. The current self may also wish to seek protection from the early retirement decisions of future selves by altering the amount of current savings.

Section 6.6 shows how *procrastination* and its flip side, *preproperation*, might arise in the case of activities that need to be done only once, but could be done either today, or at some time in the future. Naifs, for instance, may procrastinate and believe that their future selves will do the activity, incorrectly believing that they will not have future self-control problems.

Under hyperbolic discounting, individuals may have time inconsistent preferences, as in Thaler's apples example. In Section 6.7, we consider an alternative framework that explains a desire for commitment when an individual's underlying preferences are time consistent.

Section 6.8 considers the empirical evidence on commitment devices that individuals might buy into in order to deal with future self-control problems.

Section 6.9 is a brief note on the relation between time preferences and risk preferences. The basic idea is that there might be a probability that a promised future reward does not materialize, giving rise to risky future outcomes. This requires us to introduce, within the model, a theory of decision making under risk.

Finally, Section 6.10 provides a much richer approach to behavior over time that draws on recent thinking in psychology. This approach is more holistic and arguably more persuasive than the standard time preferences approach in economics. However, it is not formalized in the same way as economic models are formalized. Economists can fruitfully incorporate this approach and enrich their models.

6.2 Hyperbolic Discounting

In testing the EDU model, stationarity, a key axiom in its derivation (Definition 5.1f), does not conform with the empirical evidence, although this is not the only axiom that fails. The evidence demonstrates a desire for instant gratification over shorter horizons and relatively more patient choices over a longer horizon, as in Thaler's apples example (Example 5.2). *Hyperbolic discounting* is able to account for this evidence.

The evidence for instant or short-run gratification comes from many sources, including animal studies on pigeons and rats. Animals have very high discount rates over short horizons and make highly impatient choices relative to humans. Some animals are hardwired to make apparently patient choices, such as squirrels storing nuts for the winter, adult honey bees storing honey, beavers patiently constructing beaver dams, weaver birds patiently constructing their nests. But, unlike in humans, these are not conscious choices, rather these choices are directly encoded into the brains of these animals – after all no gene in these animals has been directly implicated for these choices. Among humans, some individuals might exhibit an awareness of their preference for instant gratification, and choose to remove smaller-sooner (SS)

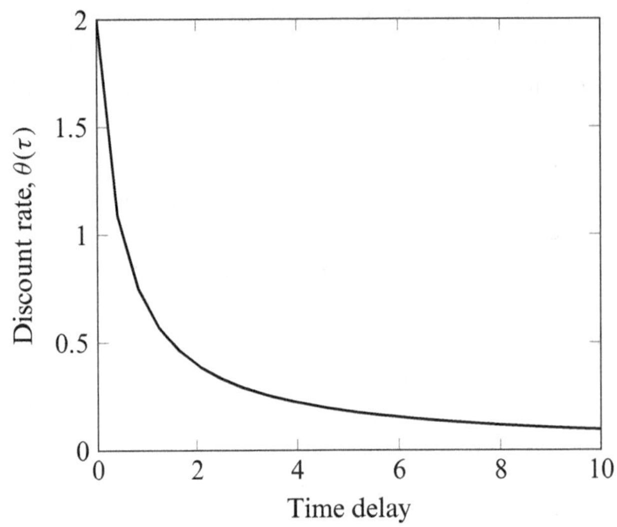

Figure 6.1 A plot of the time-varying discount rate

options from the menu of choices, leaving more patient larger-later (LL) options as the only alternative.

George Ainslie did important early work in the 1970s establishing the evidence for short-run impatience; see Ainslie (1992) for a summary. He found that the discount rate is not constant across intervals of fixed length but, in *earlier* versus *later* choices, it depends on how far out into the future the choices lie. In particular, discount rates are high for immediate choices, say today versus tomorrow, indicating higher impatience. However, the discount rates are lower when comparing more distant choices, indicating higher patience. Furthermore, one observes a pattern of *hyperbolically declining discount rates*, as shown in Figure 6.1.

The plot in Figure 6.1 was generated as follows. Suppose that τ is the time gap between the current period, $t = 0$, and some future time period $t = \tau > 0$. Ainslie showed that the discount rate over a fixed interval of time, say, the annual discount rate, for an outcome received at time τ is well approximated by the following function,

$$\theta(\tau) = \frac{k}{1 + k\tau}, \tau = 1, 2, \ldots, \tag{6.1}$$

where $k > 0$ is the single parameter. The plot in Figure 6.1 uses $k = 2$. Note that in (6.1), *the discount rate depends on time itself* (see the presence of the term τ on the RHS), in particular, how far out in the future the outcome is to be received. By contrast, under EDU, the discount rate θ over a fixed interval of time is independent of time (stationarity).

Impatience for choices over short horizons, but patience for choices over longer horizons, say, on account of the hyperbolic discount rate in (6.1), can explain violations of stationarity. But there is no presumption that this proposed solution can explain the other refutations of EDU that we highlighted in Section 5.4, such as the magnitude effect and gain-loss asymmetry. In a seminal paper, Loewenstein and Prelec (1992), with amendments in al-Nowaihi and Dhami (2006), explained the magnitude effect and gain-loss asymmetry by imposing restrictions on the utility function for outcomes, u, in (5.18); they also used hyperbolic discounting instead

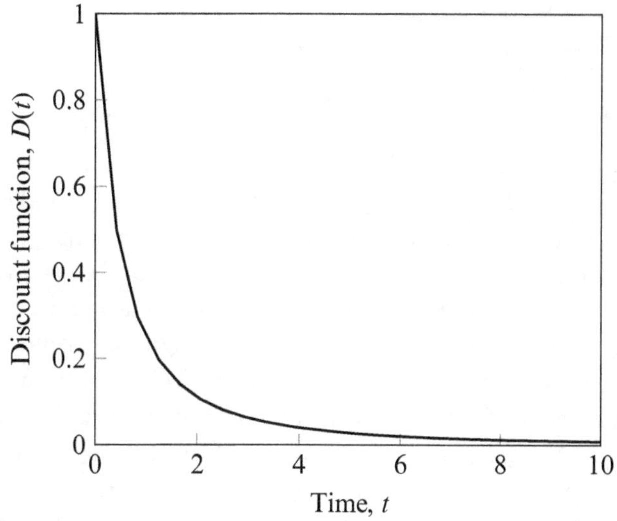

Figure 6.2 A plot of the discount function for the generalized hyperbolic discount function

of exponential discounting. We refer the reader for a detailed discussion of these issues in Dhami (2019, Vol. III). Below, we focus mainly on violations of stationarity because they provide some of the most interesting applications.

Two forms of *hyperbolic discounted utility* (HDU) models have been proposed. The most general form of hyperbolic discounting is due to Loewenstein and Prelec (1992). The discount function (see Section 5.3.3 for a definition), in this case is given by

$$D(t) = (1 + \alpha t)^{-\frac{\sigma}{\alpha}}\ ; \alpha > 0, \sigma > 0. \tag{6.2}$$

There are two strictly positive parameters, α and σ, in this function. If we specify values of α and σ we can plot this function. Suppose that we take $\alpha = 1$ and $\sigma = 2$, then we can rewrite (6.2) as

$$D(t) = (1 + t)^{-2}. \tag{6.3}$$

A plot of the discount function in (6.3) is shown in Figure 6.2. The reader can verify that the assumptions that we made on the discount function in Section 5.3.3 hold. At time $t = 0$, the discount function takes the value $D(0) = 1$, so that the utility from current outcomes is not discounted. However, D is a decreasing function that puts lower weight on more distant outcomes, and finally becomes extremely small in value, although never really becoming zero. Readers who are familiar with basic calculus can formalize the last bit of the previous sentence by noting that $lim_{t \to \infty} D(t) = 0$. We can find the discount rate corresponding to the discount function in (6.3) by using (5.22) or (5.23), depending on whether time is discrete or continuous. One of the exercises asks you to do this.

In empirical work, the *quasi-hyperbolic* or (β, δ) model which was originally proposed by Phelps and Pollack (1968) and later popularized by Laibson (1994, 1997) is more favored. Our discussion of hyperbolic discounting will rely on it. Recall our discussion of the EDU model for streams of outcome-time pairs in (5.18). The *quasi-hyperbolic discounted utility* (QHU) model, which is a member of the class of discounted utility models in Section 5.3.3, is only a slight modification of (5.18), and given by

$$QHU(\mathbf{z}) = u(z_0) + \beta\left[\delta u(z_1) + \delta^2 u(z_2) + \cdots + \delta^T u(z_T)\right]; 0 < \beta < 1, 0 < \delta < 1. \quad (6.4)$$

QHU has two parameters, β and δ, hence it is sometimes referred to as the (β,δ) model. In (6.4), if we set $\beta = 1$, then the QHU and EDU models are indistinguishable (the parameter δ is common to both). The parameter $0 < \beta < 1$ shrinks the present discounted utility from all future outcomes $z_1,\ldots,z_T$. This, in effect, increases the relative weight put on the current outcome, z_0, versus all future outcomes and leads to a taste for immediate gratification.

The EDU model also captures impatience, through the term $0 < \delta < 1$, but QHU captures an extra element of impatience in the current period through the term β. The lower is β, the more impatient is the decision maker. In their original formulation, Phelps and Pollack (1968) were interested in intergenerational optimal profiles of consumption, hence, $u(z_0)$ was the utility of the current generation, $u(z_1)$ the utility of the generation at time $t = 1$, and so on. It is also possible to write down a continuous time version of the discrete time formula in (6.4), but we shall conduct our analysis with the discrete time version only.

The term β plays no role if all the choices arise in the future, so that $u(z_0) = 0$. Continue to assume streams of outcome-time pairs. Suppose, for illustration, that there are only two outcome-time pairs in the stream, say z_1 tomorrow and z_2 the day after (there is no current outcome, z_0). Then, we can rewrite (6.4) as

$$QHU(\mathbf{z}) = \beta\left[\delta u(z_1) + \delta^2 u(z_2)\right]. \quad (6.5)$$

From (6.5), the ratio of the weights on the utilities arising from the two terms is $\frac{\beta\delta^2}{\beta\delta} = \delta$, which is independent of β. In effect, β plays no role when the decision maker makes a choice now between outcomes received at two dates in the future. The parameter β is only relevant if one of the outcomes is a current outcome.[1] For instance, if the decision maker receives two outcome-time pairs, say, (z_0,t_0) (which is a current outcome) and (z_1,t_1) (the outcome-time pair for the next time period), then we can rewrite (6.4) as

$$QHU(\mathbf{z}) = u(z_0) + \beta\delta u(z_1).$$

The ratio of weights on the two terms is $\frac{\beta\delta}{1} = \beta\delta$, which depends on β. Since $0 < \beta < 1$, the utility from the outcome z_1 shrinks further.

In Figure 6.3, we plot the discount function for the quasi-hyperbolic discounted utility model in (6.4). This is the sequence of terms $1, \beta\delta, \beta\delta^2, \beta\delta^3, \ldots$. We have used the numerical values $\beta = 0.5, \delta = 0.975$ suggested by Laibson (1994). As in Figure 6.2 for the general hyperbolic discount function, the quasi-hyperbolic discount function starts from $D(0) = 1$ and then slopes downwards. However, an important difference is that there is a sharp, discontinuous, downward jump in the quasi-hyperbolic discount function as we go from $t = 0$ to $t = 1$, followed by a more gradual decline from time $t = 1$ onwards. This captures a taste for immediate gratification in the current period, $t = 0$.

[1] Readers may recall that maximizing a function $f : X \to R$ is equivalent to maximizing the function βf, where $\beta > 0$. In other words scaling functions by a positive constant does not change the optimizing solution.

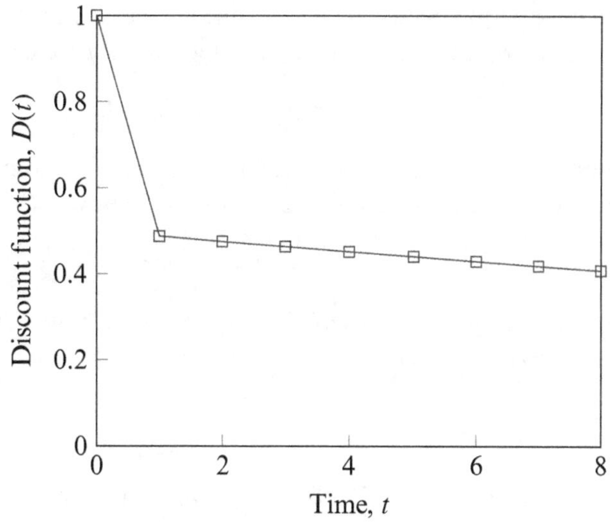

Figure 6.3 A plot of the discount function for the quasi-hyperbolic discount function

Quasi-hyperbolic discounting can explain behavior in Thaler's apples example in Example 5.2. Let us use (6.4), and assume that $u(x) = x$, so that the utility from consuming x units of a good equals x (in Example 5.2, x is the number of apples). Then the preference $(1,0) \succ_0 (2,1)$ in (5.1) implies that

$$1 > 2\beta\delta. \tag{6.6}$$

On the other hand, the preference $(2,51) \succ_0 (1,50)$ in (5.2) implies $\beta\delta^{50} < 2\beta\delta^{51}$. Dividing both sides by $\beta\delta^{50}$, we can rewrite this as

$$1 < 2\delta. \tag{6.7}$$

In order to be able to explain the behavior in Example 5.2, we need both inequalities in (6.6) and (6.7) to hold simultaneously. Using the empirically representative values $\beta = 0.5$ and $\delta = 0.975$, the first inequality is satisfied ($1 > 0.975$) and so is the second ($1 < 1.95$). Thus QHU can explain the violation of stationarity in Example 5.2.

6.3 Estimating Discount Rates

So far in this chapter, we have reported several calculations of the discount rates using models of EDU and the hyperbolic discounting utility model. However, in most calculations, particularly for those under EDU, we used monetary outcomes rather than utilities. The relevant objective functions in the EDU model (see (5.18)) and the QHU model (see (6.4)) are based on flows of utilities from outcomes, not on the monetary outcomes. However, we do not typically observe the underlying utility functions of the participants in the experiment, hence resort has often been made to using monetary rewards to measure discounting.

Suppose that a decision maker in an experiment expresses the following indifference between an amount z_0 received today at time 0 and an amount z_t received at a future date, time t, that is,

$$(z_0, 0) \sim_0 (z_t, t); t > 0. \tag{6.8}$$

We are interested in calculating the individual's underlying discount rate. Suppose that the individual follows EDU. Then, using (5.17), the indifference in (6.8) gives

$$u(z_0) = e^{-\theta t} u(z_t).$$

Dividing both sides by $u(z_t)$ and taking logarithms to the base e on both sides we get $ln\frac{u(z_0)}{u(z_t)} = -\theta t$, which on simplification gives the "true" underlying discount rate of the individual to be

$$\theta = \frac{-1}{t} ln \frac{u(z_0)}{u(z_t)}. \tag{6.9}$$

Yet, we do not observe an individual's utility function. Hence, we may attempt to proxy the calculation of θ by using direct monetary rewards as follows. Let us denote an estimate of the discount rate based on monetary rewards by $\widetilde{\theta}$, sometimes known as the *required rate of return* (RRR), that makes an individual indifferent between two outcome-time pairs. Then we have

$$\widetilde{\theta} = \frac{-1}{t} ln \frac{z_0}{z_t}. \tag{6.10}$$

When is $\widetilde{\theta}$ a good proxy for θ? Clearly this arises when the terms $ln\frac{u(z_0)}{u(z_t)}$ and $ln\frac{z_0}{z_t}$ are close to each other. This occurs when the utility function is relatively flat over the monetary rewards available to the individual. There are good grounds to suspect that the utility function is flat over the small rewards typically offered in experiments. An important justification is based on *Rabin's paradox* that we considered in Section 1.3, and it relies on the following intuition. If the individual is too risk averse over small rewards (i.e., exhibits too much concavity over small stakes relative to a flat utility function), then the individual can be shown to be infinitely risk averse over moderately sized rewards, which is absurd.

Measured RRRs in experiments are often high. For instance, Harrison et al. (2002) find an annual RRR for Danish subjects to be 28%, while Dohmen et al. (2010) find a similar median value, 30%, for the RRR of German subjects. When the delay to a future reward is only a few days, then experiments find a higher measured RRR; for a survey, see Frederick et al. (2002). These estimates of θ are quite high and certainly exceed the rates of returns on most assets. However, we are often interested in the relative magnitudes of the discount rate, and not on the absolute magnitudes.

When attempts have been made to account for the curvature of the utility function, the estimates of RRR, on an annual basis, turn out to be lower; for example, 10% for Danish subjects in Andersen et al. (2008). Some of the newer methods attempt to measure the discount rate by comparing choices over time-dated consumption profiles. A popular method is the *convex time budget constraint method*, but estimates of the discount rate for student subjects can still be high using this method; e.g., Andreoni and Sprenger (2012) estimate a number between 25% to 30%. All of these methods assume that the money is consumed on the day it is received. However, most empirical estimates suggest that the marginal propensity to consume out of money is not 1.

Another potential solution is to let subjects in experiments choose directly between *non-monetary rewards*. In early studies, Mischel and Ebbesen (1970) and Mischel et al. (1989) conducted the *marshmallow test* with children (the actual experiments are often conducted with cookies and chocolates). Children were given a choice of having a marshmallow now or waiting until the experimenter returns and having two marshmallows instead. The children do not know when the experimenter will return but in the typical experiments this takes about 15 minutes. The RRR for nonmonetary rewards often turns out to be even higher than for monetary rewards. Some early studies found a correlation between patience, as measured by the marshmallow test, and academic achievements in later life, for example SAT scores (Shoda et al., 1990), but subsequent studies with better econometric controls have found that the correlation is weaker (Watts et al., 2018).

There is a large literature on estimating the parameters β and δ in the lab and in the field; see Dhami (2019, Vol. III). There is a range of parameter estimates available, reflecting not only individual heterogeneity, but also context dependent preferences. Read and van Leeuwen (1998) offered temporal choices between healthy and unhealthy snacks to their subjects. When the choice was offered for immediate consumption, 83% chose the unhealthy snacks. However, when an identical choice was offered, now, for one week in the future, a smaller number of subjects, 51%, chose unhealthy snacks. Furthermore, the subjects were more likely to choose unhealthy snacks for current and future choices when they were in a nonsatiated state relative to a satiated state. This is reminiscent of *projection-bias*, where people project their current tastes and preferences disproportionately into the future. Note that we do not necessarily need to measure the curvature of the utility function in estimating the discount rates. If our only interest is in checking for the presence or absence of present-focus, then a large number of experimental findings are consistent with it. As always, we should strive to eliminate potential confounds, e.g., limited attention, subadditivity, or temptation preferences (see Section 6.7).

Imai et al. (2021) conduct a meta analysis of 31 studies of the estimates of the parameter β, where all the studies use a particular method of estimation known as *convex time budget constraints* which was originally suggested in Andreoni and Sprenger (2012). Figure 6.4 shows a funnel plot of the estimates of β. The null hypothesis is $\beta = 1$, which corresponds to EDU, in which case there is no present-focus; in Figure 6.4 this corresponds to the vertical grey line. Each of the dots in the Figure corresponds to an empirical estimate of β. On the vertical axis, we measure 1 divided by the standard error of the estimates, which is a measure of the precision of the estimates. Larger studies with higher sample size have lower standard errors (and higher precision), so the dots corresponding to them appear at the top of the graph. Smaller studies with lower precision appear at the bottom.

The dashed funnel-shaped lines are the boundaries for rejection of the null hypothesis, $\beta = 1$, at the 5% level. In other words, all dots below the dashed line, inside the funnel, indicate studies where the estimated β is not significantly different from 1. The funnel is not symmetric on both sides of $\beta = 1$, which suggests that there is a publication-bias in favor of studies that report $\beta < 1$. Studies lie on both sides of the dashed boundary of rejection. However, those studies that reject the null hypothesis typically find that $\beta < 1$ (present-focus) rather than $\beta > 1$ (future-focus). Overall, the average β is about 0.95 with there being greater evidence of present-focus for non-monetary rewards than monetary rewards.

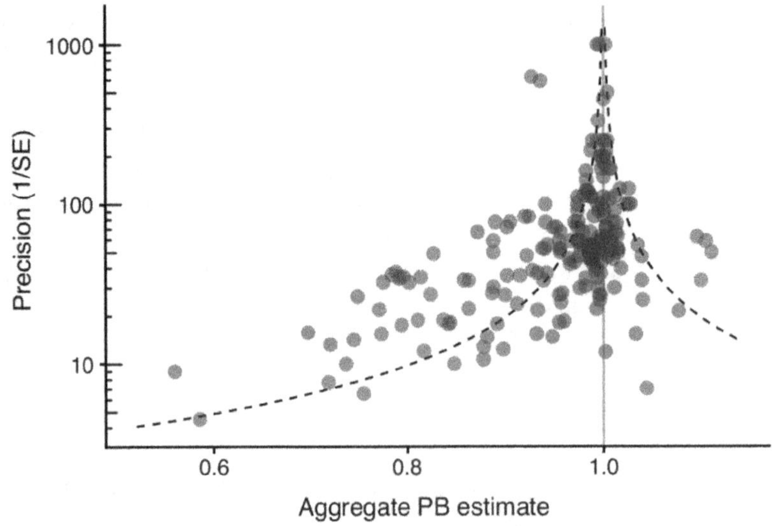

Figure 6.4 The y-axis (precision; inverse SE) is presented in the log scale. The dashed curves indicate the boundaries for rejection of the null hypothesis of no present focus (PB = 1; vertical grey line) for a two-sided test at the 5% significance level. Source: Imai et al. (2021)

The parameter β can also be estimated with methods other than convex time budget constraints, such as offering subjects *choice lists*. Furthermore, the quasi-hyperbolic model is one particular characterization of present-focused preferences, albeit an extremely tractable and useful one. Henderson and Bateman (1995) find that the hyperbolic discount function $D(t) = \frac{1}{1+0.21t}$ fits their data well. Viscusi et al. (2008) estimate β to be in the range $0.48 - 0.61$. Ikeda et al. (2010) find in a sample of 2,987 Japanese adults that subjects with a higher body mass index (BMI) make more impatient choices (lower values of β). Salaois and Moss (2011) find that β ranges between $0.304 - 0.637$ for US data.

Blow et al. (2021) propose a third approach to measuring choices that are consistent with quasi-hyperbolic discounting by using the *method of revealed preference* for survey data on consumption. This essentially involves checking a set of inequalities that are predicted to be satisfied by a proposed model. Only 2% of the choices of subjects are consistent with the EDU model, while 44% of the choices are consistent with quasi-hyperbolic discounting. Paserman (2008) finds that the degree of present-focus differs for workers of different wage levels. For workers earning a moderate wage, the degree of present-focus is high (β lies between 0.4 and 0.5), while for high wage workers, the present focus is lower ($\beta = 0.9$). Using a different econometric technique, the method of simulated moments, Laibson et al. (2020) estimate $\beta = 0.5$ and $\delta = 0.987$.

The meta analysis of Cheung et al. (2021) takes account of both convex budget methods as well as choice lists methods, and uses a larger dataset than the Imai et al. (2021) study reviewed above. Their main findings are as follows.

1. Studies that use convex budget constraints are more likely to estimate a value of β close to 1 (a lower present-focus) relative to the method of choice lists.

2. Comparing studies in which the choices of subjects are either consequential, or hypothetical, does not have a significant effect on estimates of β. In theory, the curvature of the utility function, u, in (6.4) might influence the estimate of β. However, empirically, an adjustment for the curvature of u does not have a systematic effect on estimates of β.
3. The degree of present-focus is stronger, that is estimates of β are lower, in the following three comparison groups: (a) General adult population compared to university students, (b) studies using bank transfers for payments to subjects in experiments as compared to using cash payments, and (c) when experiments are conducted with European subjects compared to North American subjects.
4. Funnel plots show evidence for selective reporting and publication bias. When the experiments are conducted for monetary rewards, the average value of β is 0.82, and the 95% confidence interval for β is $[0.74, 0.90]$. However, present-focus is higher, $\beta = 0.66$, for nonmonetary rewards, and the 95% confidence interval for β is $[0.51, 0.85]$.

6.4 Multiple Selves and Awareness of Future Self-Control

The term β in the (β, δ) model imparts extra short-run impatience relative to the EDU model, which might lead to issues of *self-control*, a form of succumbing to temptation for immediate choices. In order to make plans for the future, individuals need to guess the degree of their own future self-control problems. But how aware are individuals of their own self-control problems? In order to answer this question, we will assume that time is discrete, although there is no conceptual difficulty in extending the analysis to continuous time.

In order to model awareness of future self-control problems, we invoke the notion of *multiple selves* of the same individual. The idea is that different selves of the same individual live in different time periods, one for each of the dates $t = 0, 1, 2, \dots, T$. The present-self (say, the self at time $t = 0$) has beliefs about the self-control problems of future selves; such beliefs could be realistic (sophisticated individuals) or could be too optimistic (naive individuals). The present-self is patient over long horizons which, as we have seen above, does occur under hyperbolic discounting, but cannot directly control future selves who might succumb to short-term future temptations. How might the present self try to influence the actions of future selves?

Homer's epic poem, Odessey, describes the moment that Ulysses with his ship and crew is about to pass the island of the Sirens who sing melodiously to attract sailors to their doom. In this classic tale, the present-self of Ulysses is sophisticated and fully aware that neither he, nor his sailors, will be able to resist the sirens' songs. He designs a *commitment device*, ordering his ship's crew to tie him up before they approach the island of the sirens, while they are to block their own ears with beeswax, so that the sirens' songs cannot be heard. This successfully ensures safe passage for Ulysses and his crew.

Consider another example. Suppose the present-self of an individual, the night-self, sets an alarm to wake up at 6am. However, the morning-self of the individual might hit the snooze button more than once and overturn, at least partially, the decision of the night-self. If the night-self is sophisticated and fully aware of the self-control problems of the morning-self, then the night-self could place the alarm clock some distance away to make it more costly for the morning-self to press the snooze button; or even strategically set the alarm a bit earlier. If clock manufacturers did not have the snooze button, then the morning-self might have hit the "alarm off" button that completely overrides the decision of the night-self. This might prevent the individual from buying the alarm clock in the first place as it would then offer little in the way of a commitment device. So alarm clock manufacturers seem to provide about the right level of commitment to individuals through a prominent snooze button.

In the (β, δ) model, the utility function of the present-self at time $t = 0$ is given by (6.4). The present-self knows his own β value, that is, the weight that he puts on future utilities relative to the current utility. But the present-self might not know the β values of his own future selves. Let $\widehat{\beta}$ denote the expectation, or best guess, of the present-self about the β values of all future selves. We simplify the analysis by assuming that the present-self applies the same guess to the β values of all future selves.

The present-self, therefore, imagines that the self in the next period, at time $t = 1$, has the intertemporal utility function given by

$$QHU(\mathbf{z}) = u(z_1) + \widehat{\beta}\left[\delta u(z_2) + \delta^2 u(z_3) \cdots + \delta^{T-1} u(z_T)\right]; 0 < \widehat{\beta} < 1, 0 < \delta < 1. \tag{6.11}$$

Notice that (6.11) shifts time forward by one period relative to (6.4). In general, the present-self, say located at time $t = 0$, believes that the intertemporal utility function of the self at any future time $t = 1, 2, \ldots, T$ is given by

$$QHU(\mathbf{z}) = u(z_t) + \widehat{\beta}\left[\delta u(z_{t+1}) + \delta^2 u(z_{t+2}) \cdots + \delta^{T-t} u(z_T)\right]; 0 < \widehat{\beta} < 1, 0 < \delta < 1, \tag{6.12}$$

where $\widehat{\beta}$ is the value of β that the current self, self-0, estimates to apply to self-t.

6.4.1 Degrees of Awareness of Future Self-Control Problems

The relation between β and $\widehat{\beta}$ determines the degree of awareness of future self-control problems. We distinguish between three cases below. In each case, individuals know they have current self-control problems (because $0 < \beta < 1$) but they differ in their optimism about their future self-control problems (the relation between β and $\widehat{\beta}$). We shall use the terms "the self at time t" and "self t" interchangeably.

1. An individual is said to be *sophisticated* if
$$0 < \beta = \widehat{\beta} < 1. \tag{6.13}$$
Such an individual knows that identical self-control problems persist in the future (because $\beta = \widehat{\beta} < 1$).
2. An individual is said to be a *partial naif* if
$$0 < \beta < \widehat{\beta} < 1. \tag{6.14}$$
Such an individual believes that there will be future self-control problems but they will be less severe (because $\beta < \widehat{\beta} < 1$).
3. An individual is said to be a *naif* if
$$0 < \beta < \widehat{\beta} = 1. \tag{6.15}$$

Such an individual knows that there are current self-control problems (because $\beta < 1$) but also believes there are no future self-control problems at all (because $\widehat{\beta} = 1$), effectively believing that future selves will follow the EDU model in (5.18). Naifs have the most optimistic beliefs about their lack of future self-control problems.

Models of multiple selves are convenient to use, but there is a choice of other models which also allow one to incorporate the idea that the degree of patience varies between the present and the future self of an individual. The basic idea has been recognized since Plato and emphasized by Adam Smith who distinguished between short-sighted human passions that manifest in short-run impatient preferences, and a long-run patient spectator-self of the individual who is more concerned about the long-run consequences of their choice. Kahneman (2011) uses the distinction between Systems 1 and 2. These are hypothetical parts of the brain that dictate, respectively, impatient and patient choices, and there is conflict between them in determining temporal choices. Thaler and Shefrin (1981) distinguish between a planner-self of an individual, similar to a spectator in Smith's account, and a doer-self of an individual, similar to passions in Smith's account. These frameworks have also been formalized in the modern literature, although we omit them due to space limitations; for a survey see Dhami (2019, Vol. III) and for a dual selves framework, see Fudenberg and Levine (2006).

6.4.2 Empirical Evidence on the Degree of Self-Awareness

The empirical evidence is supportive of the view that many people are naifs or partial naifs.

Firms might take advantage of the lack of awareness of future self-control problems of individuals. For instance, gym attendance falls under the class of problems that have a current cost and future benefits. Individuals who are imperfectly aware of future self-control problems may overestimate their future gym attendance (DellaVigna and Malmendier, 2004). Firms can take advantage by offering long-term gym membership contracts that have a high sign-up fee and a low fee per visit. Since the gym does not get attended as often by individuals subject to self-control, the high initial sign-up fee maximizes the profits of the firm. However, present-focused consumers end up paying more per visit when they sign up for a long-term contract, relative to signing a "pay per visit" contract. For instance, those who sign a monthly contract pay an average price per gym visit of about \$17, over the first six months. They could have chosen instead to pay \$10 per visit by purchasing daily passes (DellaVigna and Malmendier, 2006). Firms build in automatic contract renewal for monthly contracts. Users procrastinate in cancelling their contracts, even when they are not using the gym. On average, there is a gap of 2.29 months between the last use of the gym, and cancellation of the gym membership. This is an instance where firms design contracts to take advantage of the present-focus in the time preferences of users (this is related to the idea of phishing that we consider in Section 11.3).

If consumers are naifs in credit markets, then firms might take advantage of their overly optimistic beliefs about their future self-control problems. Naifs are more likely to take up contracts that impose large penalties for non-repayment of loans in the mistaken belief that their future selves will be time consistent. However, this leads to a reduction in their welfare relative to individuals who are sophisticated (Heidhues and Kosegi, 2010).

In an interesting result, Fedyk (2021) shows that individuals have little awareness of their own future self-control problems, estimating the β parameters of their own future selves to be $\widehat{\beta} = 1.03$. Thus most people act as if they were naifs (see (6.15)). But individuals estimate the present-focus parameter of others to be $\widehat{\beta} = 0.82$, which is close to the actual value of $\beta = 0.87$ in the sample. Hence, most people are *asymmetrically naive*, that is, unaware of their future self-control problems, but sophisticated about their awareness of the self-control problems of others. Why do individuals fail to learn about their own degree of present-focus over time? The answer to this question has not been formally established. But one possibility is *motivated beliefs* whereby individuals wish to have a positive self-assessment of their own future selves, and a belief in the lack of self-control in the future may be viewed as a negative trait.

6.5 Life Cycle Models and Hyperbolic Discounting

There are interesting applications of QHU to the savings behavior of individuals, which fall within the domain of *behavioral macroeconomics*. On account of a taste for instant gratification ($0 < \beta < 1$), individuals might spend too much on current consumption, leaving them with inadequate savings for retirement. Data from the US shows that consumption follows income too closely, and there is a sharp fall in consumption on retirement. The multiple selves framework allows us to make these and other predictions on lifetime choices, as we show below.

Suppose that time is discrete and there are only three time periods, $t = 0, 1, 2$. There are three selves of the same individual over the individual's lifetime. At time $t = 0$, the individual is young (young-self); at time $t = 1$, the individual is middle-aged (middle-self); and at time $t = 3$, the individual is retired (old-self). The consumption of the individual at time t is denoted by c_t. The individual has exogenously given income y at time $t = 0$ only, and there is no other source of income. Thus, the only way to consume at times $t = 1, 2$ is to rely on savings that have been made in the immediately previous period. The savings vehicle is a one period bond that pays a zero interest rate. Hence, the only purpose of savings is to smooth consumption over time. Given this information, we can write the budget constraints of the three selves as follows,

$$\begin{cases} t_0: & c_0 + s_0 = y;\ s_0 \in [0, y] \\ t_1: & c_1 + s_1 = s_0;\ s_1 \in [0, s_0]\ . \\ t_2: & c_2 = s_1 \end{cases} \tag{6.16}$$

In (6.16), the first row shows the budget constraint of the young-self. The young-self has income y which is allocated between consumption, c_0, and savings, s_0, for the next period. In the second row, the only source of income for the middle-self is savings, s_0, made by the young-self which are allocated to consumption, c_1, and savings, s_1, for the old-self. In the third row, the only source of income for the old-self is savings, s_1, made by the middle-self. Since this is the last period, the old-self spends their entire income on consumption, c_2. Thus, the old-self is passive and has no decisions to make, while the young-self and the middle-self have to make a savings decision.

The utility function, u, from consumption at time t is given by

$$u(c_t) = \sqrt{c_t}; t = 0, 1, 2. \tag{6.17}$$

We assume that all three selves have (β, δ) preferences and each self believes that the preferences of the future selves are given in (6.12). Since our focus is mainly on the effects of present-focus, we can further simplify the exposition by assuming that $\delta = 1$; this version of the (β, δ) model is known as the $(\beta, 1)$ model. This is not unreasonable because empirically, the magnitude of δ is quite close to 1. Using (6.4), we can write the $(\beta, 1)$ model as follows,

$$QHU(\mathbf{z}) = u(z_0) + \beta\left[u(z_1) + u(z_2) \cdots + u(z_T)\right]; 0 < \beta < 1, \delta = 1. \tag{6.18}$$

Using (6.4), (6.12), and (6.17), we can write the intertemporal utility function, U_t, of self $t = 0, 1, 2$, as perceived by self 0, as follows,

$$\begin{cases} t_0: & U_0 = \sqrt{c_0} + \beta\left[\sqrt{c_1} + \sqrt{c_2}\right] \\ t_1: & U_1 = \sqrt{c_1} + \widehat{\beta}\sqrt{c_2} \\ t_2: & U_2 = \sqrt{c_2} \end{cases} ; \beta, \widehat{\beta} \in (0, 1). \tag{6.19}$$

In (6.19), the first row gives the intertemporal utility of the young-self, which depends on undiscounted current utility, $\sqrt{c_0}$, and the sum of utilities of the two future selves which are discounted by $\beta \in (0, 1)$. The middle row gives the intertemporal utility of the middle-self, as estimated by the young-self. It equals the current utility of the middle-self, $\sqrt{c_1}$, plus the discounted utility of the old-self. The young-self must form an estimate, $\widehat{\beta}$, of the present-focus parameter of the middle-self. The relation between β and $\widehat{\beta}$ can be used to classify the individual into one of three types, as shown in (6.13), (6.14), and (6.15). The last row corresponds to the utility of the old-self who has no future to worry about, hence, the intertemporal utility equals $u(c_2) = \sqrt{c_2}$.

The young-self knows that each of the selves would like to maximize their own utility in (6.19), subject to the corresponding budget constraint in (6.16). If we substitute out consumption using the budget constraints in (6.16) into (6.19), we can obtain the unconstrained objective function of each self, as perceived by the young-self.

$$\begin{cases} t_0: & U_0 = \sqrt{y - s_0} + \beta\left[\sqrt{s_0 - s_1} + \sqrt{s_1}\right] \\ t_1: & U_1 = \sqrt{s_0 - s_1} + \widehat{\beta}\sqrt{s_1} \\ t_2: & U_2 = \sqrt{s_1} \end{cases} ; \beta, \widehat{\beta} \in (0, 1). \tag{6.20}$$

The solution to this problem is by backward induction, which readers of this book should be familiar with by now. The old-self is passive and makes no economic decisions. In deciding on the level of optimal savings, s_0^*, the young-self needs to figure out how much the middle-self will save for old age, conditional on every possible level of savings $s_0 \in \left[0, y\right]$ made by the young-self. In other words, the young-self would like to figure out the reaction function of the middle-self. But this requires first determining the optimal choice of the middle-self, conditional on all possible levels of s_0.

From (6.20), the middle-self takes as given the savings by the young self, s_0, and chooses $s_1 \in [0, s_0]$ in order to maximize

$$U_1 = \sqrt{s_0 - s_1} + \widehat{\beta}\sqrt{s_1}.$$

Notice that we have used $\widehat{\beta}$ which is the guess of the young-self about the present-focus parameter of the middle-self. The first order condition, using the fact that the derivative of $\sqrt{x}$ equals $\frac{1}{2\sqrt{x}}$, is

$$\frac{\partial U_1}{\partial s_1} = \frac{-1}{2\sqrt{s_0 - s_1}} + \widehat{\beta}\frac{1}{2\sqrt{s_1}} = 0. \tag{6.21}$$

In order to reduce the number of cases, we shall consider only interior solutions, $s_1 \in (0, s_0)$ and $s_0 \in (0, y)$. The reader can check that the second order condition, $\frac{\partial U_1^2}{\partial s_1^2} < 0$, is satisfied at an interior solution. Solving out (6.21) for s_1 we get that the optimal savings of the middle-self, as perceived by the young-self, is a constant fraction of the savings inherited from the young-self,

$$s_1(s_0) = \mu s_0, \tag{6.22}$$

where the constant fraction μ equals

$$\mu = \left(\frac{\widehat{\beta^2}}{1 + \widehat{\beta^2}}\right). \tag{6.23}$$

The optimal choice of the middle-self will depend on the privately known value of β, which the young-self does not know. Hence, the best that the young-self can do is form an estimate, $\widehat{\beta}$, of this parameter, as in (6.23). The reaction function of the middle-self in (6.22) gives the optimal amount of savings of the middle-self, for all possible savings levels of the young-self, $s_0 \in (0, y)$. Given the savings of the middle-self in (6.22), the utility of the old-self is given from the last row in (6.20)

$$U_2 = \sqrt{\mu s_0}. \tag{6.24}$$

The reader can easily check from (6.23) that the fraction μ is increasing in $\widehat{\beta}$. Thus, the greater is the estimated present-focus of the middle-self, or the higher is $\widehat{\beta}$, the lower will be the anticipated savings of the middle-self for the old-self.

We can now solve for the optimal choice of savings of the young-self, given the young-self's best guess of what is to happen in the future, as captured by the reaction function in (6.22). Substituting (6.22) and (6.24) into U_0 given in the first row of (6.20), we get the intertemporal utility of the young-self

$$U_0 = \sqrt{y - s_0} + \beta\left[\sqrt{s_0 - s_1(s_0)} + \sqrt{s_1(s_0)}\right].$$

Substituting $s_1(s_0) = \mu s_0$ in this expression we get

$$U_0 = \sqrt{y - s_0} + \beta\gamma\sqrt{s_0}, \tag{6.25}$$

where

$$\gamma = \sqrt{1 - \mu} + \sqrt{\mu}. \tag{6.26}$$

The young-self chooses $s_0 \in (0, y)$ (recall our assumption of an interior solution) in order to maximize (6.25). The first order condition is

$$\frac{\partial U_0}{\partial s_0} = \frac{-1}{2\sqrt{y - s_0}} + \frac{\beta\gamma}{2\sqrt{s_0}} = 0. \tag{6.27}$$

Solving (6.27) for the optimal saving, s_0^*, we get (the reader should check that the second order condition holds)

$$s_0^* = \left(\frac{\beta^2\gamma^2}{1+\beta^2\gamma^2}\right)y. \tag{6.28}$$

Thus, the optimal savings is a fixed fraction of the income, y.

In the remaining cases in this section, except for time consistents who have $\beta = 1$, for pedagogical simplicity we shall only consider the case $\beta = 0.6$.

6.5.1 The Benchmark Case of Time Consistent Preferences

If we set $\beta = \widehat{\beta} = 1$, then we get the EDU model with $\delta = 1$. In this case, the decision maker has time consistent preferences, because EDU preferences are time consistent. Let us refer to individuals with such preferences as *time consistents*, that is,

$$\beta = \widehat{\beta} = 1.$$

Substituting $\widehat{\beta} = 1$ in (6.23), we get $\mu = \frac{1}{2}$. Substitute $\mu = \frac{1}{2}$ in (6.26) to get $\gamma = \sqrt{2}$. Substituting $\beta = 1$ and $\gamma = \sqrt{2}$ in (6.28), we get

$$s_0^* = \left(\frac{2}{3}\right)y. \tag{6.29}$$

Substituting $\mu = \frac{1}{2}$ and (6.29) in (6.22), we get

$$s_1^* = \frac{1}{3}y. \tag{6.30}$$

Substituting (6.29) and (6.30) in the budget constraints for the three selves in (6.16), we can find the optimal consumption levels for the case of time consistents to be

$$c_0^* = c_1^* = c_2^* = 0.33y. \tag{6.31}$$

Thus, time consistents engage in perfect consumption smoothing, sharing equally the income when young, across the three time periods.

6.5.2 Naif Individuals

From (6.15), a naif satisfies $0 < \beta < \widehat{\beta} = 1$. Since $\widehat{\beta} = 1$, as in the case of time consistents, we get $\mu = \frac{1}{2}$ and $\gamma = \sqrt{2}$. We have assumed $\beta = 0.6$, hence, we have $\left(\frac{\beta^2\gamma^2}{1+\beta^2\gamma^2}\right) = 0.42$. Thus, using (6.28), we get

$$s_0^* = 0.42y. \tag{6.32}$$

Substituting $\mu = \frac{1}{2}$ and (6.32) in (6.22), we get

$$s_1^* = 0.21y. \tag{6.33}$$

Substituting (6.32) and (6.33) in the budget constraints for the three selves in (6.16), the optimal consumption profile for naifs, as planned by the young-self, is

$$c_0^* = 0.58y; c_1^* = c_2^* = 0.21y. \tag{6.34}$$

However, the young-self has incorrect belief about the middle-self's self control problems. At time $t = 1$, the middle-self will not comply with the expectations of the young-self. The middle-self will save using their own "true" preference parameter $\beta = 0.6$. Thus, the actual value of μ is $0.36/1.36 = 0.26$, hence, the actual saving made by the middle-self is $s_1 = 0.26s_0 = 0.26 \times 0.42y = 0.11y$. Hence, the realized intertemporal consumption profile of a naif will be: $c_0 = 0.58y; c_1 = 0.31y; c_2 = 0.11y$.

Comparing (6.31) and (6.34), the naif overconsumes in the first period relative to time consistents by 1.76 times, and does not save enough for the two future selves.

6.5.3 Sophisticated Individuals

Consider now the case of sophisticates given in (6.13), $0 < \beta = \widehat{\beta} < 1$. We have assumed $\beta = 0.6$, hence, we get $\widehat{\beta} = 0.6$. Substitute $\widehat{\beta} = 0.6$ in (6.23) to get $\mu = 0.26$. Substitute $\mu = 0.26$ in (6.26) to get $\gamma = 1.37$. Substitute these calculations in (6.28) to get

$$s_0^* = 0.40y. \tag{6.35}$$

Substituting (6.35) in (6.22), we get

$$s_1^* = 0.10y. \tag{6.36}$$

Substituting (6.35), (6.36) in the budget constraints for the three selves in (6.16), the optimal consumption profile for sophisticates is quite similar to naifs, and it is given by

$$c_0^* = 0.60y; c_1^* = 0.3y; c_2^* = 0.10y. \tag{6.37}$$

Summary *Time consistents smooth income perfectly over the three time periods. However, naifs and sophisticates overconsume in the first period, hence saving inadequately for the future. One might have expected sophisticates to save more than naifs, given that they are more aware of their future self-control problems. However, in this class of problems, there is a delicate tradeoff between risk aversion, as captured by the shape of the utility function, and the degree of awareness about future self-control problems (O'Donoghue and Rabin, 2003). In other contexts, such as procrastination and preproperation, which we consider below, the contrast between the behaviors of naifs and sophisticates is quite stark.*

Since individuals with present-focus overconsume early on, they do not save enough for retirement. The empirical evidence supports this prediction and, for US data, there is a drop of 30% *to* 40% *in consumption at retirement (Kotlikoff et al., 1982; Bernheim et al., 2001). Some of the factors that are relevant but not considered in our model, above, are a reduction in work-related expenses when one retires; more time to shop around and seek lower-priced bargains; less interest in buying new and expensive gadgets; and reduced calorie intake.*

6.5.4 Illiquid Assets and Retirement Decisions

If the young-self could find a way of bypassing the middle-self and directly transfer resources to the old-self, then the welfare of the young-self can improve. Angeletos et al. (2001) suggest that the young buy illiquid assets that cannot be easily liquidated for cash by the middle-self. An example is buying a house that requires the payment of a mortgage over a sufficiently long period of time. This commits the middle-self to paying the mortgage and controlling, at least partially, the extent to which the middle-self can splurge on consumption. This also ensures greater savings for the old-self who can, at a minimum, participate in an equity release scheme, to gain liquidity when old.

The middle-self could, of course, try to sell the house, but selling houses incurs transactions costs and the middle-self must live somewhere, making this asset relatively illiquid in practice. This plan might not work if a credit card company comes along and offers cheap credit to the middle-self. Liquidity-constrained middle-selves might latch on to credit card debt all too eagerly, potentially reversing the young-self's long-term plan designed to discipline the middle-self. It has proven difficult for neoclassical theories to explain why individuals hold credit card debt and illiquid assets simultaneously. As we have seen above, the explanation under behavioral economics is straightforward. In the West, declining savings rates have been associated with the easy availability of credit, which is consistent with a behavioral explanation. One of the exercises asks you to formalize these insights.

Suppose that, within the same model as in this section, we consider a different decision, the retirement decision. The young-self might be worried that the middle-self will take early retirement, reducing the retirement income for the old-self. The young-self cannot directly control the retirement decision of the middle-self. But through the choice of savings, the young-self may have an indirect influence on the retirement decision of the middle-self. For instance, if the young-self strategically saves too little, then the middle-self might not have a choice but to continue working. If, however, the young-self guesses that the savings choices will not have any effect on the middle-self, then the young-self might have to be resigned to over-save for the old-self. These issues are formally considered in Diamond and Köszegi (2003).

6.6 Procrastination and Preproperation

Another important application of present-focus and the multiple selves framework is to issues of *procrastination* and its polar opposite, preproperation. Suppose that an individual has to undertake a single activity, only once, over T time periods, $t = 1, 2, \ldots, T$. The benefits of the activity to the individual, if undertaken at time t, equal v_t, and the costs are c_t. Thus, the pattern of benefits over the T time periods is $\mathbf{v} = (v_1, v_2, \ldots, v_T)$ and the pattern of costs is $\mathbf{c} = (c_1, c_2, \ldots, c_T)$.

The individual has $(\beta, 1)$ preferences given in (6.18). We consider a model of multiple selves, so each self guesses that the future selves have $(\widehat{\beta}, 1)$ preferences. The relation between β and $\widehat{\beta}$ gives us three kinds of present-focused individuals, described in (6.13), (6.14), and (6.15): Sophisticates, partial-naifs, and naifs. In the special case in which $\beta = \widehat{\beta} = 1$, we get the case of time-consistent individuals who follow the EDU model.

The main question posed in this section is: During which time period will the individual find it optimal to undertake the activity? We assume that decision makers will find it optimal to do the activity at least once in the T time period.

We distinguish between two polar cases: (i) Immediate costs and future benefits; (ii) Immediate benefits and future costs.

6.6.1 Immediate Costs and Future Benefits

Consider a single "project" that has current costs but future benefits. Examples include cleaning your room/car, mowing the lawn, quitting an addiction, and preparing for a trip. Current costs are not discounted, but future benefits are discounted and, hence, shrunk, due to the parameter β in $(\beta, 1)$ preferences. Thus, each self may disproportionately overweight the current costs over the future benefits and decide not to undertake the project. This tendency is likely to be heightened if each self has incomplete awareness of future self-control problems. For instance, a naif believes that future selves have no self-control problems at all, hence, that a future self will most likely do the project. For many people this may occur on a repeated basis, even if such expectations turn out to be repeatedly dashed, for example, chronic procrastination to clean one's room.

Let us give a slightly more formal treatment. Denote by $U_t(\tau)$ the $(\beta, 1)$ utility function of a decision maker at time t, if the activity is undertaken at time $\tau = t, t+1, t+2, \ldots$ Thus, the case $U_t(\tau = t)$ corresponds to the time t utility from doing the activity at time t, while $U_t(\tau = t+2)$ denotes the time t utility from doing the activity at time $t+2$, and so on. We define

$$U_t(\tau) = \begin{cases} \beta v_t - c_t & \text{if} \quad \tau = t \\ \beta(v_\tau - c_\tau) & \text{if} \quad \tau > t \end{cases}. \tag{6.38}$$

The first row of (6.38) corresponds to the case $U_t(\tau = t)$. If the activity is done now, the immediate costs are not discounted, but the future benefits are discounted. From the $(\beta, 1)$ preferences given in (6.18), notice that all future utilities are discounted by the term β; it does not matter in which future period the benefits arise. The second row of (6.38) gives the decision maker's utility at time t if the activity is undertaken at a future date τ; in this case, both benefits and costs arise in the future, so they are both discounted equally by β.

A "strategy" for the decision maker is a "complete contingent plan of action." This means that, for each of the T time periods, the decision maker chooses either to (i) do the activity (Y, short for "yes") or (ii) chooses not to do the activity (N, short for "no"). We denote the choice of action at time t of a decision maker of type j, by s_t^j, where $t = 1, 2, \ldots, T$ and $j = c, s, n$ ("c" for time consistents, "s" for sophisticates, and "n" for naifs; we omit the case of partial naifs). Since the action choice at time t can take only one of two possible values, Y and N, $s_t^j \in \{Y, N\}$. A strategy for the T time periods for a decision maker is given by

$$\left(s_1^j, s_2^j, \ldots s_T^j\right).$$

An example is the strategy $(N, Y, N, \ldots, N)$ where the decision maker chooses to perform the activity at time $t = 2$, but chooses not to do it in every other time period.

Since we have a finite period game of full information, we solve it by backward induction. We invoke an intuitive equilibrium concept known as a *perception perfect equilibrium*. We define it next, first for time consistents and naifs who both believe that they have no future self-control problems (the beliefs of naifs are, however, incorrect), and then for sophisticates. We state the definitions first, which are due to O'Donoghue and Rabin (1999a, 1999b), followed by an explanation of what they mean. Some of the early intuition about these ideas can be found in Akerlof (1991) who did not use a (β, δ) model, but relied instead on the salience of current versus future costs and benefits.

Definition 6.1 *Consider time consistents and naifs. A perception perfect strategy* $\left(s_1^j, s_2^j, \ldots s_T^j\right)$, $j = c, n$, *satisfies the following condition. For all* $t < T$, *the decision maker chooses to do the activity,* $s_t^j = Y$, *if the utility from doing it now exceeds the utility from doing it at any time in the future, i.e.,*

$$U_t(t) > U_t(\tau);\tau = t+1, t+2, \ldots, T. \tag{6.39}$$

Definition 6.2 *Suppose that the decision maker is a sophisticate. A perception perfect strategy* $\mathbf{s}^j = \left(s_1^j, s_2^j, \ldots s_T^j\right)$, $j = s$, *satisfies the following condition. For all* $t < T$, *the decision maker chooses to do the activity,* $s_t^j = Y$, *if the utility from doing it now exceeds the utility from doing it at the earliest time in the future that the decision maker expects a future self to do the activity, that is,*

$$U_t(t) > U_t(\tau), \tag{6.40}$$

where τ *is the first time period after time* t *when a future self is expected to do the activity.*

There is only a slight difference between Definitions 6.1 and 6.2. A sophisticate knows that all future selves will have the same self-control problems, hence, quite a few future selves may succumb to the temptation of not doing the activity due to self-control problems. Hence, a sophisticate wishes to find out that among those future selves who might succumb to temptation, who will be the first to do so. By contrast, the time consistents and naifs believe that all future selves are time consistent; hence, they believe that none will succumb to temptation. Thus, they do not need to figure out who among the future selves will be the first to succumb.

Let us take a concrete example. Suppose that $T = 4$ and the pattern of costs is an increasing one

$$\mathbf{c} = (4, 6, 10, 16) \tag{6.41}$$

and the future benefit from the activity is fixed at

$$\overline{v} = 34.$$

This ensures that the activity is always done at time $T = 4$ (because $34 > 16$), if it is not done earlier. At which time $t = 1, 2, 3, 4$ should a decision maker of type $j = c, s, n$ undertake the activity? This example fits, for instance, the case of cleaning one's room (as the clutter increases over time, it takes longer to sort it out, increasing the cost), or mowing the lawn (the grass gets increasingly bigger, so more difficult to mow, increasing costs), preparing for a trip (the longer one leaves it, the shorter the time in which to plan all the things, which raises stress costs), or quitting an addiction (as the addiction gets more entrenched, it is more costly to quit).

Let us now explore the optimal behavior for different types of decision makers. Our solution method is based on Definitions 6.1 and 6.2, hence it is a form of backward induction. In order to model the case of naifs and sophisticates, in addition to $\overline{v} = 34$, we shall assume in this example that if an individual is not time consistent, then

$$\beta = \frac{1}{2},$$

so that (6.38) can be written as

$$U_t(\tau) = \begin{cases} \frac{1}{2}34 - c_t & \text{if} \quad \tau = t \\ \frac{1}{2}(34 - c_\tau) & \text{if} \quad \tau > t \end{cases}. \tag{6.42}$$

Time Consistents

Time consistent individuals are characterized by $\beta = 1$. Using (6.38), we have $U_t(t) = \overline{v} - c_t = 34 - c_t$; and $U_t(\tau) = \overline{v} - c_\tau = 34 - c_\tau$ if $\tau > t$. Thus, (6.39) implies that the decision maker does it at time t, that is, $s_t^c = Y$, if $U_t(t) > U_t(\tau)$, or if $34 - c_t > 34 - c_\tau$, which can be rewritten as

$$c_\tau > c_t; \tau > t, \tag{6.43}$$

otherwise the decision maker chooses $s_t^c = N$. This is intuitive because if there is no discounting, then a decision maker will do it only if the current cost is lower than all the future costs of doing the activity. Since costs are increasing in (6.41), each self of the individual will find that current costs are low relative to future costs, so that (6.43) is always satisfied. Hence, each self chooses $s_t^c = Y$, $t = 1, 2, 3, 4$. Thus, the perception perfect strategy of time consistents is

$$\mathbf{s}^c = (Y, Y, Y, Y). \tag{6.44}$$

Since all selves will wish to do it, if given an opportunity, the activity gets done by the earliest self and there is no procrastination.

Naifs

Each of the current selves of a naif have the preference parameter $\beta = \frac{1}{2}$ but imagines that future selves have the preference parameter $\widehat{\beta} = 1$. Since all future selves are mistakenly believed to be time consistent, the naif mistakenly believes that they will all do the activity (this follows from (6.44)). We use this fact repeatedly in the calculations below. Let us first compute the utility to each of the four selves from doing it in the present period using (6.41) and the first row of (6.42).

$$U_1(1) = 13; U_2(2) = 11; U_3(3) = 7; U_4(4) = 1. \tag{6.45}$$

Since $U_4(4) = \frac{1}{2}34 - 16 = 1 > 0$, thus, at time $t = T = 4$, the naif will do it, so $s_4^n = Y$.

We now use (6.42) to show the following.

- Self 3 finds that it is better to wait for the self at $t = 4$ to do it because $U_3(3) = 7 < U_3(4) = \frac{1}{2}(34 - 16) = 9$. Hence, using Definition 6.1, we have $s_3^n = N$.

- The self at $t = 2$ believes that all future selves will do it, hence, expecting mistakenly that $s_3^n = Y$. Self 2 finds that it is better to wait for self 3 to do it because $U_2(2) = 11 < U_2(3) = \frac{1}{2}(34 - 10) = 12$. Hence, using Definition 6.1, we have $s_2^n = N$.
- The self at $t = 1$ expects mistakenly that $s_2^n = Y$. Hence, self 1 finds that it is better to wait for self 2 to do it because $U_1(1) = 13 < U_1(2) = \frac{1}{2}(34 - 6) = 14$. Hence, using Definition 6.1, we have $s_1^n = N$.

It follows that the perception perfect strategy of a naif is

$$\mathbf{s}^n = (N, N, N, Y).$$

Thus, naifs procrastinate to the maximum possible extent and do the activity in the very last time period at time $t = 4$.

Sophisticates

Each current self of a sophisticate has the preference parameter $\beta = \frac{1}{2}$, and correctly expects that future selves also have the same preference parameter, $\widehat{\beta} = \frac{1}{2}$. The utility to each of the four selves from doing it in the present period is already stated in (6.45), which we repeat below.

$$U_1(1) = 13;\ U_2(2) = 11;\ U_3(3) = 7;\ U_4(4) = 1. \tag{6.46}$$

The self at time $t = 4$ will do it because $U_4(4) = 1 > 0$. Thus, $s_4^s = Y$.

We now use (6.42) to show the following.

- Self 3 finds that it is better to wait for self 4 to do it because $U_3(3) = 7 < U_3(4) = \frac{1}{2}(34 - 16) = 9$. Hence, using Definition 6.2, we have $s_3^s = N$.
- Self 2 correctly forecasts that $s_3^s = N$ and $s_4^s = Y$ and this differentiates a sophisticate self 2 from a naif self 2. Thus, the choice is between doing it now or waiting for self 4 to do it. We have $U_2(2) = 11 > U_2(4) = \frac{1}{2}(34 - 16) = 9$, so self 2 prefers to do it, hence, $s_2^s = Y$.
- Self 1 correctly forecasts that $s_2^s = Y$, $s_3^s = N$ and $s_4^s = Y$ (unlike a naif self 1). Thus, the choice is between doing it now or waiting for self 2 to do it. We have $U_1(1) = 13 < U_1(2) = \frac{1}{2}(34 - 6) = 14$, so self 1 prefers not to do it, hence, $s_1^s = N$.

It follows that the perception perfect strategy of a sophisticate is

$$\mathbf{s}^S = (N, Y, N, Y).$$

Thus, a sophisticate procrastinates by one time period relative to a time consistent, but not as much as a naif. The sophisticate correctly predicts that some of the future selves will have a self-control problem, which ensures an early completion of the task relative to a naif.

6.6.2 Immediate Benefit and Future Costs

In some activities, the benefits from an action accrue to a decision maker immediately, but the costs of the action arise in the future. For instance, watching a late night movie might be currently pleasurable, but could reduce productivity the next day; buying a large house might give current benefits, but result in high mortgage payments in the future; succumbing to temptation during shopping and running a credit card debt might lead to immediate gratification but lead to painful high interest repayments later.

We use the same problem, a single activity to be undertaken only once in T time periods, and the same notation as in Section 6.6.1. In this case, the utility of self t, the analogue of (6.38), is given by

$$U_t(\tau) = \begin{cases} v_t - \beta c_t & \text{if} \quad \tau = t \\ \beta(v_\tau - c_\tau) & \text{if} \quad \tau > t \end{cases}. \tag{6.47}$$

The only difference between (6.38) and (6.47) is in their first rows. In (6.38) future benefits are discounted, while in (6.47) future costs are discounted. Definitions 6.1 and 6.2 on the perception perfect equilibrium for the different types of decision makers continue to apply unchanged in this case.

As a concrete example, let us consider a four period problem, $T = 4$, and $\beta = \frac{1}{2}$. Suppose that the net temporal benefits (benefits minus costs) of an activity over four time periods are

$$\mathbf{v} = (4, 6, 10, 16). \tag{6.48}$$

Since the costs are already incorporated into the net benefits, we assume that $\mathbf{c} = (0, 0, 0, 0)$. Below, we consider the optimal choices of different types of decision makers.

Time Consistents

For time consistent individuals, $\beta = 1$, hence using (6.47), we have $U_t(t) = v_t - 0$, and $U_t(\tau) = v_\tau - 0$ if $\tau > t$. Thus, (6.39) implies that $s_t^c = Y$ if $U_t(t) > U_t(\tau)$, or if $v_t > v_\tau$. However, from (6.48) we see that v_t increases over time and reaches a maximum value at $t = 4$, $v_4 = 16$. Hence, the condition $U_t(t) > U_t(\tau)$ does not hold for selves 1, 2, and 3, who therefore choose $s_t^c = N$ at $t = 1, 2, 3$. Finally, at $t = 4$, self 4 finds that none of the previous selves have done it, but $U_4(4) = 16 > 0$, so $s_4^c = Y$. Thus, the optimal strategy of time consistents is

$$\mathbf{s}^S = (N, N, N, Y). \tag{6.49}$$

Time consistents optimally procrastinate till the end, where the benefits are the highest.

Naifs

Any current self of a naif has the preference parameter $\beta = \frac{1}{2}$, but mistakenly believes that all future selves have the preference parameter $\widehat{\beta} = 1$. Hence, future selves are mistakenly believed to choose the strategies in (6.49). The utility of each of the four selves from doing it now is found from (6.47).

$$U_1(1) = 4 - 0; U_2(2) = 6 - 0; U_3(3) = 10 - 0; U_4(4) = 16 - 0. \tag{6.50}$$

Self 4 will do it because it cannot be done in the future and the utility from doing it now is $U_4(4) = 16 > 0$, so $s_4^n = Y$. We can now solve for the optimal actions of the naif in various time periods, using backward induction and applying Definition 6.1.

- Self 3 believes that self 4 will choose $s_4^n = Y$. We have $U_3(3) = 10 > U_3(4) = \frac{1}{2}(16) = 8$. Hence, using Definition 6.1, we have $s_3^n = Y$.
- Self 2 believes mistakenly that self 3 is time consistent and will choose $s_3^n = N$, but believes correctly that self 4 will choose $s_4^n = Y$. So the choice is between doing it now or letting self 4 do it. We have $U_2(2) = 6 < U_2(4) = \frac{1}{2}(16) = 8$. Hence, using Definition 6.1, we have $s_2^n = N$.
- Self 1 believes mistakenly that time consistent selves 2 and 3 will not do it, and that the only future self who will do it is self 4, $s_4^n = Y$. So the choice is between doing it now or letting self 4 do it. We have $U_1(1) = 4 < U_1(4) = \frac{1}{2}(16) = 8$. Hence, using Definition 6.1, we have $s_2^n = N$.

It follows that the perception perfect strategy of a naif is

$$\mathbf{s}^n = (N, N, Y, Y).$$

Thus, naifs do it before time consistents; they preproperate relative to the optimal solution for the time consistents. If they had waited one more time period till $t = 4$ they would have achieved a 60% higher payoff (from 10 to 16).

Sophisticates

The current self of a sophisticate in any time period has the preference parameter $\beta = \frac{1}{2}$ and correctly perceives that all future selves have the identical preference parameter $\widehat{\beta} = \frac{1}{2}$. The utility of each of the four selves from doing it now is found from (6.50).

Self 4 will do it because the utility from doing it now is $U_4(4) = 16 > 0$, so $s_4^s = Y$. We now solve for the optimal actions in each of the remaining time periods, using backward induction, and applying Definition 6.2.

- Self 3 anticipates correctly that self 4 will choose $s_4^n = Y$. We have $U_3(3) = 10 > U_3(4) = \frac{1}{2}(16) = 8$. Hence, using Definition 6.2, we have $s_3^s = Y$.
- Self 2 anticipates correctly that the earliest self who will choose to do it is self 3. Hence, the choice is between doing it at $t = 2$ or leaving it to self 3 to do it. We have $U_2(2) = 6 > U_2(3) = \frac{1}{2}(10) = 5$. Hence, using Definition 6.2, we have $s_2^s = Y$.
- Self 1 anticipates correctly that self 2 will do it. Definition 6.2 requires us to check if it should be done at $t = 1$ or left for self 2 to do it. We have $U_1(1) = 4 > U_1(2) = \frac{1}{2}(6) = 3$, thus we have $s_1^s = Y$.

It follows that the perception perfect strategy of a sophisticate is

$$\mathbf{s}^n = (Y, Y, Y, Y).$$

Thus, in the case of future rewards, the sophisticates do it even before the naifs; they preproperate the most. Paradoxically, the knowledge of their own self-control problems, and a awareness that their immediate future selves will succumb to the temptation of doing it, makes them do it even quicker. If they had waited till $t = 4$ to do it they would have achieved a 400% higher payoff (from 4 to 16).

6.6.3 Empirical Evidence on Procrastination

If one is aware of self-control problems in the future that might delay a task, then the imposition of "deadlines" may ensure that the task is completed on time. Ariely and Wertenbroch (2002) conduct an experiment on executive education students in a university who need to complete three assignments. One set of subjects was given experimenter-provided evenly spaced deadlines. The other set of students was offered the choice of self-imposed deadlines with financial penalties levied by the experimenter. Two-thirds of the subjects chose the self-imposed deadlines option, indicating an awareness of potential self-control problems in the future. However, self-imposed deadlines turned out to be less binding; did not lead to early completion of the assignments; and the performance on the assignments was lower relative to experimenter-provided deadlines.

The positive effects of deadlines has not been supported in some later studies. Burger et al. (2011) find that evenly spaced interim deadlines did not improve task completion rates in their experiment. When the "willpower" of subjects was depleted, it affected their performance for the first day of a two-day task, but the completion rates were higher. In their experiments, Bisin and Hyndman (2020) find that there is a demand for self-imposed deadlines, but these too do not lead to an increase in the task completion rates. Present-focus is widespread among the subjects, and although those who are more present-focused procrastinate more on single one-off tasks, they are able to demonstrate much higher self-control on repeated tasks. Thus, the relation between deadlines and procrastination may require further exploration.

Other evidence shows that procrastination on a task leads to poorer outcomes. Brown and Previtero (2020) define a procrastinator as someone who makes their health care open enrollment choice on the last day when such a choice can be made. Relative to non-procastinators, they find that procrastinators take longer to sign-up for 401(k) plans; contribute less to the plan; are more likely to stick with default portfolios; and retire earlier. These mechanisms are consistent with a model of present-focused preferences.

The observation of procrastination and insufficient awareness of future self-control problems is consistent with the standard model of present-focused preferences that we have outlined. However, the empirical evidence indicates that other factors could also be at play. For instance, Choi et al. (2002) find that 68% of their subjects felt that their savings rates were too low and their intention was to increase their savings rate in the future. However, we observe an *intentions-actions divide*. Only one eighth of these subjects went on to actually increase their savings rate. Present-focus is one possible explanation. But there are other possibilities also, for example, subjects may just forget; and they may have limited attention so that other events take priority. Lengthening deadlines does not lead to an improvement in task performance (Shu and Gneezy, 2010). Under present-focused preferences, lengthening deadlines should not reduce task completion rates, depending on one's degree of awareness of future self-control problems. However, the "lack of a positive effect" is also consistent with a model of limited memory. Ericson (2017) finds that in this case, reminders have a positive effect on task completion rates and overconfidence about memory and attention leads to a reduction in task completion rates. It is an open question if present-focused preferences lead to the willful suppression of memories that might induce either procrastination or preproperation.

Kosse and Pfeiffer (2013) separately measure the present-focus of mothers and their children, assuming that they follow the quasi-hyperbolic model. The (β, δ) parameters of mothers are first elicited by offering them choices between smaller-sooner and larger-later rewards. In order to elicit the (β, δ) parameters of the children, they were given a choice of receiving a pack of gummy bears at the start of the mother's interview or two packs at the end of the interview. A probit regression where the mother's elicited β was the independent variable and the child's elicited β was the dependent variable, showed that the marginal effects were statistically significant. More patient mothers, on average, had more patient children. Thus, patience may be transmitted intergenerationally, although the study does not identify if the channel is genetic or cultural. Since patience may be correlated with a range of later life outcomes, the early life experiences of children, or their genetic dispositions, may at least partially predetermine these outcomes.

Individuals might underestimate the costs of future actions and overestimate the future benefits. This is a form of planning fallacy and may also lead to an underestimation of the time taken to complete a task, hence leading to procrastination (Kahneman and Tversky, 1979). The planning fallacy is empirically supported (Augenblick and Rabin, 2019; Fedyk, 2021).

6.7 Dynamically Consistent Temptation Preferences

Preferences under the EDU model cannot explain time inconsistency, as that would violate the stationarity axiom (Definition 5.1f). Since we can explain time inconsistency under the QHU model, the stationarity axiom does not hold under QHU. In other words, the QHU allow for time inconsistent preferences.

An alternative approach is to continue to assume that *preferences are time consistent*, yet explain observed behavior that appears to be present-focused and time inconsistent. Some of the basic ideas were laid out in a series of papers that model *temptation preferences* (Dekel et al., 2001, 2009; Gul and Pesendorfer, 2001, 2004). The basic idea in this literature is that individuals make *choices over menus*. Each menu has several possible choices. The individual can then pick a menu at an earlier date that, from the perspective of the earlier date, leads to higher welfare, when the choices from the chosen menu are made at a later date.

As an illustrative example, suppose that there are only two choices in any possible menu.

(1) A healthy meal choice, H, and
(2) an unhealthy meal choice, U.

Then, all possible menus of choices are

$$\{H\}, \{U\}, \{H, U\}. \tag{6.51}$$

Suppose that the individual makes a choice at time $t = 0$ between the three menus in (6.51). Once the menu is chosen at date $t = 0$, the individual then makes the actual choice from the chosen menu at a future date, $t = \tau > 0$. We are now interested in the individual's date $t = 0$ preferences between menus. There are two possible cases.

1. *Commitment with strong temptation*: The date $t = 0$ preferences between the menus are given by

$$\{\mathbf{H}\} \succ \{H, \mathbf{U}\} \sim \{\mathbf{U}\}, \tag{6.52}$$

where the binary relation $\succ$ means strictly preferred to, and $\sim$ means indifferent to. In each menu, the individual knows which choice will be made at date $t = \tau$. The preferred choice in each menu is indicated in bold. Thus, in the menu $\{H, \mathbf{U}\}$, the individual will choose the unhealthy meal in preference to the healthy meal at date $t = \tau$. In the singleton menus, the choice is trivially the only one available.

From (6.52), at date $t = 0$ the individual knows that picking the menus $\{H, \mathbf{U}\}$ and $\{\mathbf{U}\}$ gives rise to an identical date $t = \tau$ choice, U, and so the individual expresses indifference between them. In other words, the individual foresees correctly that they will give in to temptation at date $t = \tau$; this is what we mean by "strong temptation." What if the individual, at date $t = 0$, prefers to eat a healthy meal at date $t = \tau$? One possibility, that is captured in (6.52), is for the individual to eliminate unhealthy meals from the menu altogether. Thus, at date $t = 0$, the individual expresses a strict preference for $\{\mathbf{H}\}$ over $\{H, \mathbf{U}\}$ and chooses the menu $\{\mathbf{H}\}$.

This model can also generate present-focus and preference reversals. In making long-term choices, the individual appears to act patiently, ruling out menus with unhealthy meals. However, in the short run, if the choice among options in the menu $\{H, \mathbf{U}\}$ at date $t = \tau$ were to be made, the individual makes the unhealthy choice. Thus, for empirical researchers, it can often become difficult to disentangle the effects of temptation preferences from present-focused preferences. The next case identifies a method to distinguish between the two cases.

2. *Commitment with weak temptation*: Suppose that the date $t = 0$ preferences between the menus are given by

$$\{\mathbf{H}\} \succ \{\mathbf{H}, U\} \succ \{\mathbf{U}\}. \tag{6.53}$$

At date $t = 0$, the individual knows that they will be successfully able to resist the temptation of unhealthy meals; this follows from the highlighted options in the preference $\{\mathbf{H}, U\} \succ \{\mathbf{U}\}$. However, the individual still wishes to eliminate the unhealthy choice from the menu; this follows from $\{\mathbf{H}\} \succ \{\mathbf{H}, U\}$. But if the individual is not going to be tempted at date $t = \tau$, why rule out the unhealthy option? The reason is that despite having strong enough willpower to not pick the unhealthy choice, the very act of exerting willpower is costly. Hence, the individual prefers not to pick a menu where such willpower costs are required, yet make no difference to the actual choice.

The last of these observations can give us a method of distinguishing between temptation preferences and present-focused preferences. Under present-focused preferences, the individual's utility is not affected by items that are not chosen. However, under temptation preferences, utility may be affected by items not chosen on account of the willpower costs to resist them. Thus, we can try to observe if preferences such as the one in (6.53) exist in the data.

6.8 Commitment Devices

Individuals who use QHU, but have some awareness of their future self-control problems (say, sophisticates or partial-naifs) might wish to pay for a *commitment device* to help control their future selves. For instance, an individual who desires to get fit might sign a costly contract with a personal trainer to get fit. Since the money must be contractually paid in the future, this is a form of commitment. Some of the experimental evidence on commitment devices, say on the effect of deadlines, has already been discussed earlier in this chapter.

Evidence on commitment devices using observational data has proven surprisingly difficult to obtain due to potential confounds with other explanations, and on account of the general difficulty of controlling for confounding factors in the field. However, the evidence from experiments, in the lab and the field, for commitment devices is clearer. For instance, in Section 6.5.4 we explained investment in illiquid assets using mortgages as a form of commitment to discipline one's own future selves from excessive consumption binges. But another potential explanation is that individuals engage in this behavior, at least in the US, because interest payments on mortgages are tax exempt.

Gruber and Mullainathan (2005) use data on excise taxes on cigarettes and the propensity of individuals to smoke in the US and Canada. They show that those with a propensity to smoke self-report higher happiness after the excise tax. This link is not found for other kinds of taxes. The tax reduces the consumption of future selves, even if the present-self cannot directly control the future selves; hence, it provides a potential commitment device. Wertenbroch (1998) reports that smokers might purchase a single pack of cigarettes rather than take advantage of quantity discounts on multiple packs. This increases the transaction costs of buying more cigarettes (more frequent trips to the shops), partially curbing their future self-control problems. An alternative explanation is that smokers might be too overconfident of their ability to make do with a smaller number of cigarettes. Alcohol drinkers aware of their future self-control problems might also sign into costly rehab with high initial costs to try to discipline their future selves.

Duflo et al. (2011) demonstrate an intentions-actions divide for farmers in Kenya who have an opportunity to raise productivity and farm incomes significantly by using fertilizers. In their sample, 97.7% of the farmers reported an intention to use fertilizers, but only 36.4% were able to implement their intentions. The scheme that worked best to encourage the take-up of fertilizers was the following. The experimenter offered a small subsidy to purchase fertilizers, just before the harvest of a crop (say, Crop 1), with a commitment to supply fertilizers when needed at the time of the next crop (say, Crop 2). This is consistent with a model of present-focused preferences; indeed 69% of the farmers in the sample were found to be present-focused. Present-focused farmers are likely to overestimate their ability to save enough money, post the harvest of Crop 1, to buy fertilizers for Crop 2. If these beliefs are too optimistic, then they are likely to find that they do not have enough money left to buy fertilizers for Crop 2, creating the intentions-action divide outlined above. The commitment technology embodied in the specific contract offered, plus the small subsidy that acts as an additional inducement, ensures much greater take-up of fertilizers. The increased take-up rates under the commitment contract are comparable with a noncommitment contract where farmers need to be offered a much larger price subsidy later in the season to induce fertilizer use.

While it is difficult to get subjects to make a payment for commitment devices in lab and field experiments, there are some exceptions. In a study on cycle-rickshaw drivers in Chennai, Schilbach (2019) offered them a choice between (1) unconditional payments, and (2) sobriety payments that are conditional on a daily check for alcohol consumption. A third of the rickshaw drivers were willing to forego 10% of their daily earnings for a week in order to choose the commitment device of sobriety payments. Casaburi and Macchiavello (2019) find that when given a choice between receiving daily payments or infrequent payments over a longer horizon, say, a month, a majority of milk producers chose the infrequent payments, even when the daily payments would have been larger. The authors interpret this as willingness to invest in a costly commitment device. Alternatively, this could have arisen from a desire to avoid the transactions costs of daily payments.

Ashraf et al. (2006) find that a commitment savings device, which restricted the withdrawal amounts, in the Philippines, increased savings by 81%. More patient individuals were more likely to choose this commitment device. In their study on data entry workers in the Philippines, Kaur et al. (2015) offered a commitment device that penalized low output. Among those who took up the commitment device, output increased by 6%. Commitment devices have also been shown to lead to improvements in several different domains; these include completion rates of degrees (Himmler et al., 2019), gym attendance (Milkman et al., 2013), and reduction in smoking (Giné et al., 2010).

The experiments in Sadoff et al. (2020) offer insights into the relation between time consistency, choice of commitment devices, and the degree of awareness of future self-control problems. In a study conducted over four weeks, subjects are initially given a budget. In week 1, they can order food items, using a food delivery service in Chicago and in Los Angeles, for delivery a week later. When the delivery was actually made, subjects were unexpectedly given a choice to exchange some already ordered food items for others that they had not ordered. The unordered items had appeared on the original list of choice items that the subjects used a week earlier. The 46% of subjects who exchanged at least one item, overriding their earlier decision, are classed as time inconsistent. Most of the exchanges were to gain unhealthy items at the expense of healthy items.

In weeks 3 and 4, a voluntary commitment option was introduced that forbade subjects to change their minds at delivery. This option was taken up by 53% of the subjects. However, of those who were previously identified as time inconsistent in weeks 1 and 2, only 40% chose the commitment option. It would appear that the remaining 60% of the time inconsistent subjects are unaware, or at best partially aware, of their self-control problems. Thus, the commitment device is largely chosen by those who already have no time-inconsistency problems. Thus, one potential reason why we observe low demand for commitment devices might be imperfect awareness of future self control problems. Using data from gym attendance, Royer et al. (2015) also find that those seeking commitment devices are mostly the time consistent individuals. This data is consistent with the model of temptation preferences, whereby decision makers try to remove a tempting option from the menu (Section 6.7).

Commitment technologies may also have some drawbacks. An important drawback arises from the conflict between commitment and flexibility (Amador et al., 2006). The typical feature of commitment is that it binds one's actions for the future, hence taking away the ability of individuals to respond flexibly to changing circumstances. Here is an example.

Example 6.6 *One may commit to retiring at 45, by working very hard early, and hoping to enjoy a good life later. However, after having carried out the plans and retiring early, the individual feels that retiring early has been a mistake. Not having an active routine in life is not as attractive after all, and the individual feels that life has lost a sense of direction which causes distress. But by then,* *the sacrifice in terms of not enjoying one's early life has been irreversibly made, and having been retired for a few years, work technology has moved on, making it difficult to reenter work.*

Another drawback of buying into a commitment product may be that one overestimates one's capability to stick to their stated commitments. This could be because one is too naive and overconfident in one's future self-control abilities. For instance, one may publicly announce one's intentions to carry out an action (a form of costly commitment), but find later that they do not have the resolve, or the ability, to go through with the action. Thus, they lose valuable social capital among their social group. In this case, the original commitment has proved to be welfare reducing for the individual. Giné et al. (2010) offered smokers in the Philippines a contract to quit smoking. Those who violated the contract faced a penalty in terms of losing a small amount of their savings. In the event, 66% of the smokers violated the contract and forfeited their savings of 277 pesos (a bit less than £5). It is possible that the penalty is weak, but the evidence is suggestive.

John (2020) considers the possibility of welfare losses from commitment devices by offering three different kinds of savings products in the Philippines. In a baseline product, there is no commitment other than to open a savings account with a fixed initial deposit of 10 pesos, about US $2.40, made for the subject by the experimenter. The other two savings products offer commitment devices. (i) In the *installment savings group*, subjects were offered an installment savings account which committed subjects to making fixed biweekly deposits. Failure to make the agreed-upon deposits incurred a monetary penalty. (ii) In the *withdrawal-restriction account*, the withdrawals of individuals from the account incurred a penalty. For all three savings products, a goal date (about 130 days on average) and a goal amount for savings was set. The results were as follows.

1. Despite the availability of the baseline savings account, 27% of the subjects chose the installment savings account and 42% chose the withdrawal-restriction account. Hence, there is a demand for commitment even among those who had not previously had a savings account.
2. In terms of the volume of savings in the account, the installment savings account was the most successful and savings increased by 429 pesos (US $10.20), followed by the withdrawal-restriction account, which led to an increase in savings of 148 pesos (US $3.50). The baseline savings account offered an increase of only 27 pesos in savings. Hence, there are relatively strong treatment effects arising from commitment devices.
3. There is substantial heterogeneity in the performance of individual savings accounts. Despite the overall success of the installment savings account, 55% of the individuals who took up this account incurred penalties for inadequate deposits. The penalties ranged from 150 to 300 pesos, roughly worth a day's wage. In the case of the withdrawal-restriction account, 79% of the individuals who chose this account made no further deposits in addition to the "free of cost" initial opening balance contributed by the experimenter. Thus, individuals overestimated their use of the commitment technology. It is conceivable that sophisticates who are aware of their future self-control problems may not sign up for the commitment technology and the largest welfare losses accrue to the naifs who chose weak commitments.

6.9 A Note on Risk and Time Preferences

So far, we have considered outcome-time pairs (z, t) taken from a set $C = Z \times \Gamma$. However, there might be *uncertainty* associated with future rewards that could arise from several sources. We identify two different sources.

(i) (Risk) There could be a probability $0 \leq p \leq 1$ that the promised future reward is delivered to an individual, but with the complementary probability $1-p$ the future reward is withheld from the individual. The smaller is p, the greater is the risk faced by an individual.
(ii) (Hazard) There is also a possibility that the individual might no longer be alive to collect the reward in the future, even if the reward is dutifully delivered. This captures the *hazard* $0 \leq \Pi \leq 1$ faced by the individual; it is the probability that the individual survives until the time the future reward is delivered. The case $\Pi = 1$ corresponds to no hazard, and $\Pi = 0$ corresponds to the case of full hazard.

The net result of this uncertainty is that individuals expect to receive a future reward with the probability $0 \leq p\Pi \leq 1$. In effect, the individual faces outcome-time-probability triplets $(z, t, p\Pi)$. Such a framework can also give rise to present-focused preferences. Because the individual is uncertain about whether future rewards will materialize, there is likely to be a preference for current rewards that are certain (instant gratification); this preference is likely to get stronger as the extent of uncertainty faced by the individual increases.

We already know from Part I that a range of nonexpected utility theory models describe well individual choices under risk and uncertainty. These include, for instance, rank dependent utility, and prospect theory. Epper et al. (2011) show that individuals whose probability weighting function (see Section 2.2) exhibits a more pronounced departure from linearity also discount more hyperbolically. Thus, risk preferences and time preferences might be related. It has also been shown that by making various assumptions on the shape of the hazard function faced by individuals one can get discount functions that are hyperbolic, as well as other kinds of discount functions used in the literature (Sozou, 1998; Halevy, 2008, 2015; al-Nowaihi and Dhami, 2021). A detailed consideration of these important issues requires a more advanced and technically demanding treatment.

6.10 A More General Psychological Approach

A common argument used in models of time preference, say, in models of dual selves, such as the planner-doer model, is that the patient long-run self of an individual might wish to control the impatient short-run future selves through the exercise of costly willpower. A rich psychological literature appears to have moved beyond a consideration of issues of willpower alone and has identified a range of factors that are important in temporal choices.

Psychologists often like to think about temporal problems as a conflict between *want* (go to a late night club; not exercise) and *should* (have an early night; live a healthy life) (Milkman et al., 2008). This idea is expressed more clearly in Loewenstein (2018, p. 95): "My own

Table 6.1 A 2 × 2 classification of different approaches to deal with self-control problems.

	Self-Deployed	Other-Deployed
Situational	Commitment Devices Temptation Bundling Situation Modification Behavior Therapy	Hard Paternalism Microenvironments Defaults Active Choice Choosing in Advance Planned Interruptions
Cognitive	Goal Setting Planning MCII Self-Monitoring Psychological Distancing Mindfulness Cognitive Therapy	Descriptive Social Norms Social Labeling Making the Future Self-Relatable Joint Evaluation Fresh-Start Framing Licensing Prevention

Source: Duckworth et al. (2018). Note that MCII stands for "mental contrasting/implementation intentions."

perspective ... views self-control as a conflict between affect (encompassing emotions, drives, and motivational feeling states such as pain) on the one hand and deliberation on the other."

Table 6.1 shows a useful 2 × 2 classification from Duckworth et al. (2018) of the alternative approaches to understanding and dealing with self-control problems. Our description below is based on their discussion. Along one dimension, they measure the following.

(i) Changes in either the environment or the situation faced by the individual (*situational*), and
(ii) beliefs about the environment (*cognitive*).

Along the second dimension they classify strategies used to counter present-focus in terms of whether they are

(i) deployed by the individual (*self-deployed*), or
(ii) deployed by a third party such as a firm or a government (*other-deployed*).

Self-deployed strategies require some degree of awareness of one's own self-control problems, while individuals might not even be aware of other-deployed strategies.

Table 6.2 gives an example of each of the entries in Table 6.1 applied to the problem of promoting healthy eating. The examples are self-explanatory. We describe many of these factors in this book, for example, goals, social norms, hard paternalism, defaults, and active choice. Thus, it suffices to briefly outline some of the newer terms. *Temptation bundling* refers to combining an unproductive activity, for example, watching TV out of boredom, with a productive activity such as using the exercise bike while watching TV. *Behavioral therapy* draws from the tradition of *behavioralism* in psychology that tried to explain human behavior, independent of human cognition and beliefs. In this view, behavior arises from unobserved mental states or impulses. The behavioral therapy approach to addictions, for instance, emphasizes avoiding cues and situations that might reinforce addiction, for example, hanging out with friends who smoke

Table 6.2 Examples of various strategies to promote healthy eating.

Strategy	Example
Self-deployed situational strategies	
Commitment devices	Decision maker commits to eat a serving of fruit and vegetables at dinner every night, asks spouse to serve as a referee, and puts money on the line that will be forfeited to spouse in case he or she fails to meet this commitment.
Temptation bundling	Decision maker listens to a favorite music album only when cooking dinner from scratch (rather than eating fast food).
Situation modification	Decision maker stocks up on bags of Halloween candy for trick-or-treaters—but only candy that she does not like.
Behavior therapy	Decision maker works with a therapist, learning to identify triggers that result in junk food binges (e.g., deadlines at work) and also alternatives (e.g., taking a walk) that can meet the same needs (e.g., stress relief).
Self-deployed cognitive strategies	
Goal setting	Decision maker decides: "I will eat a fruit or vegetable with every meal!"
Planning	Decision maker plans: "If it is 8 a.m., then I will look in the refrigerator for some fruit to have with my breakfast."
Mental contrasting with implementation intentions	Decision maker thinks: "The best outcome of eating healthy is that I will have more energy. The obstacle that stands in the way is that I don't have time to go shopping. My plan is: 'If it is Saturday morning, then I will take a nice walk to the grocery store to buy fresh fruit that I'll then eat.'"
Psychological distancing	Decision maker reframes situation using third-person perspective: "Angela is hungry and has a choice between a bag of potato chips and an apple. Which should she choose?"
Psychological distancing	Decision maker reframes situation using third-person perspective: "Angela is hungry and has a choice between a bag of potato chips and an apple. Which should she choose?"
Psychological distancing	Decision maker introspects: "I notice that I'm craving potato chips. I accept that I have this urge. I may or may not act on it."
Cognitive therapy	Decision maker works with a therapist, learning to ask, "What thoughts lead me to snack on potato chips in the afternoon? Do I think, 'I can't resist junk food. I have no self-control at all!' And is that a reasonable thought? Or am I exaggerating?"
Other-deployed situational strategies	
Hard paternalism	Lawmaker issues city-wide soda tax and prohibits sale of junk food within 1 mile of public schools.
Microenvironments	Grocery stores use "traffic light labeling" to indicate healthy (green) versus unhealthy (red) choices and strategically place healthy choices where they are more convenient.
Defaults	Employer makes the default lunch provided at all meetings a healthy salad, but allows employees to opt out of salad and into other menu options through an easy-to-use online portal.
Active choice	When ordering supplies for the following week, employers ask employees to actively choose between break room snacks that are healthy (e.g., fresh fruit) or unhealthy (e.g., donuts).
Choosing in advance	School cafeterias ask students to select their preferred lunch entrees one week in advance.
Planned interruptions	Snack manufacturers offer sets of five 20-calorie chocolates, each wrapped individually, instead of one, 100-calorie chocolate bar.
Other-deployed cognitive strategies	
Descriptive social norms	Employer shares statistics from recent company survey showing that 80% of employees say they eat fresh fruit daily.
Social labeling	Physician counsels a struggling dieter as a committed "health enthusiast" and praises their commitment to their new eating plan.
Making the future self relatable	During a checkup, physician shows young adults age-adjusted photos of themselves so they can imagine what middle age will be like and prompts them to make wise dietary choices from now on to benefit their future self.

Table 6.2 ***(Cont.)***

Strategy	Example
Joint evaluation	Cafeteria offers a daily special as well as a healthy option each day and features side-by-side nutrition information on both choices, leading diners to think through the pros and cons of the two choices.
Fresh-start framing	Employer sends email reminders about healthy options in the cafeteria on New Year's and after employees' birthdays noting that it is a great time to kick-start a healthy habit.
Self-licensing prevention	Employer uses data from the company cafeteria to remind employees of their junk food purchases in the previous month.

Source: Duckworth et al. (2018)

which creates a craving to smoke. *Planning* is an important prerequisite to goal setting, and may be enhanced by internal or external planning prompts. *Self-monitoring* has been shown to be important in achieving goals, particularly in weight loss. *Psychological distancing* can be spatial, temporal, and social. *Mindfulness* refers to the objective evaluation of one's current experiences.

Cognitive therapy tries to alter one's mental states, beliefs, and the mental representation of the world, as perceived by the individual. For instance, when craving the next cigarette, to think about the effect on one's health, and the implications it might have on one's children. *Cognitive behavioral therapy* (CBT) combines behavioral and cognitive therapies. It has been shown to be highly successful in countering anger and aggression and somewhat weaker, but positive, effects have been found for substance abuse and addictions. *Social norms*, particularly descriptive social norms that provide information to an individual about others (e.g., their energy use, or conformity with the law, or their take-up of pension/savings plans) have been found to significantly influence behavior.

Joint evaluation implies looking at the pros and cons of alternatives, side by side, in an evaluative manner, rather than looking at the two options separately. *Fresh start* refers to altering the recent status quo based on an external event such as a new year, or a new term/season. *Microenvironments* refer to the physical structure of an individual's environment, for example, whether healthy or unhealthy snacks are placed close to the check-out counter at a store. Many individuals appear to use the *default options* for various reasons that include the following. (i) Defaults could be a reference point from which departures create a tendency for loss aversion. (ii) One may be overconfident in revisiting the default options in the future with the aim of changing them, but one may procrastinate and never get down to changing the default. (iii) One may believe that defaults contain useful information and embody a desirable suggestion.
Choosing in advance refers to decisions that are made now about the future (these tend to be more patient choices) relative to making *on the spot decisions* (these tend to be more impatient choices). Building *planned interruptions* into one's activities can allow one to evaluate if a desirable course of action is being followed, for example, rest might be used to counter fatigue and low productivity.

References

Ainslie, G. W. (1992). *Picoeconomics*. Cambridge University Press: Cambridge.

Akerlof, G. (1991). Procrastination and Obedience. *American Economic Review* 81(2): 1–19.

al-Nowaihi, A. and Dhami, S. (2006). A Note on the Loewenstein–Prelec Theory of Intertemporal Choice. *Mathematical Social Sciences* 52(1): 99–108.

al-Nowaihi, A. and Dhami, S. (2021). Preferences over Time and under Uncertainty: Theoretical Foundations. CESifo Working Paper No. 9215.

Amador, M., Werning, I., and Angeletos, G-M. (2006). Commitment vs. Flexibility. *Econometrica* 74(2): 365–396.

Andersen, S., Harrison, G. W., Lau, M. I., and Rutström, E. E. (2008). Eliciting Risk and Time Preferences. *Econometrica* 76(3): 583–618.

Andreoni, J. and Sprenger, C. (2012). Estimating Time Preferences from Convex Budgets. *American Economic Review* 102(7): 333–356.

Angeletos, G.-M., Laibson, D., Repetto, A., Tobacman, J., and Weinberg, S. (2001). The Hyperbolic Consumption Model: Calibration, Simulation and Empirical Evaluation. *Journal of Economic Perspectives* 15(3): 47–68.

Ariely, D. and Wertenbroch, K. (2002). Procrastination, Deadlines, and Performance: Self-Control by Precommitment. *Psychological Science* 13(3): 219–224.

Ashraf, N., Karlan, D., and Yin, W. (2006). Tying Odysseus to the Mast: Evidence from a Commitment Savings Product in the Philippines. *Quarterly Journal of Economics* 121(2): 635–672.

Augenblick, N. and Rabin, M. (2019). An Experiment on Time Preference and Misprediction in Unpleasant Tasks. *The Review of Economic Studies* 86(3): 941–975.

Becker, G. S. and Murphy, K. M. (1988). A Theory of Rational Addiction. *Journal of Political Economy* 96(4): 675–700.

Bernheim, B. D., Skinner, J., and Weinberg, S. (2001). What Accounts for the Variation in Retirement Wealth among U.S. Households? *American Economic Review* 91(4): 832–857.

Bisin, A. and Hyndman, K. (2020). Present-Bias, Procrastination and Deadlines in a Field Experiment. *Games and Economic Behavior* 119: 339–357.

Blow, L., Browning, M., and Crawford, I. (2021). Nonparametric Analysis of Time-Inconsistent Preferences. *Review of Economic Studies* 88(6): 2687–2734.

Brown, J. R. and Previtero, A. (2020). Saving for Retirement, Annuities and Procrastination. Mimeo. Available online at www.aleprevitero.com/wp-content/uploads/2020/06/027PreviteroWPProcrastination.pdf

Burger, N., Charness, G., and Lynham, J. (2011). Field and Online Experiments on Self-Control. *Journal of Economic Behavior and Organization* 77(3): 393–404.

Casaburi, L. and Macchiavello, R. (2019). Demand and Supply of Infrequent Payments as a Commitment Device: Evidence from Kenya. *American Economic Review* 109(2): 523–555.

Cheung, S. L., Tymula, A., and Wang, X. (2021). Quasi-Hyperbolic Present Bias: A Meta-Analysis. IZA Discussion Paper No. 14625.

Choi, J. J., Laibson, D., Madrian, B. C., and Metrick, A. (2002). Defined Contribution Pensions: Plan Rules, Participant Choices, and the Path of Least Resistance. In J. M. Poterba (ed.), *Tax Policy and the Economy*, Vol. 16, National Bureau of Economic Research. MIT Press: Cambridge.

Dekel, E., Lipman, B. L., and Rustichini, A. (2001). Representing Preferences with a Unique Subjective State Space. *Econometrica* 69(4): 891–934.

Dekel, E., Lipman, B. L., and Rustichini, A. (2009). Temptation-Driven Preferences. *The Review of Economic Studies* 76(3): 937–971.

DellaVigna, S. and Malmendier, U. (2004). Contract Design and Self-Control: Theory and Evidence. *Quarterly Journal of Economics* 119(2): 353–402.

DellaVigna, S. and Malmendier, U. (2006). Paying Not to Go to the Gym. *American Economic Review* 96(3): 694–719.

Dhami, S. (2019). *The Foundations of Behavioral Economic Analysis. Vol. III. Behavioral Time Discounting*. Oxford University Press: Oxford.

Diamond, P. and Köszegi, B. (2003). Quasi-Hyperbolic Discounting and Retirement. *Journal of Public Economics* 87(910): 1839–1872.

Dohmen, T., Falk, A., Huffman, D., and Sunde, U. (2010). Are Risk Aversion and Impatience Related to Cognitive Ability? *American Economic Review* 100(3): 1238–1260.

Duckworth, A. L., Laibson, D., and Milkman, K. L. (2018). Beyond Willpower: Strategies for Reducing Failures of Self-Control. *Psychological Science in the Public Interest* 19: 102–129.

Duflo, E., Kremer, M., and Robinson, J. (2011). Nudging Farmers to Use Fertlizer: Theory and Experimental Evidence from Kenya. *American Economic Review* 101(6): 2350–2390.

Elster, J. and Loewenstein, G. (1992). Utility from Memory and Anticipation. In G. Loewenstein and J. Elster (eds.), Choice Over Time. Russell Sage: New York.

Epper, T., Fehr-Duda, H. and Bruhin, A. (2011). Viewing the Future through a Warped Lens: Why Uncertainty Generates Hyperbolic Discounting. *Journal of Risk and Uncertainty* 43(3): 169–203.

Ericson, K. M. (2017). On the Interaction of Memory and Procrastination: Implications for Reminders, Deadlines, and Empirical Estimation. *Journal of the European Economic Association* 15(3): 692–719.

Ericson, K. M. and Laibson, D. (2019). Intertemporal Choice. In D. Bernheim, D. Laibson, and S. DellaVigna, (eds.), *Handbook of Behavioral Economics: Foundations and Applications 2*. Elsevier.

Fedyk, A. (2021). Asymmetric Naivete: Beliefs About Self-Control. Available at SSRN: https://ssrn.com/abstract=2727499 or http://dx.doi.org/10.2139/ssrn.2727499.

Fishburn, P. C. and Rubinstein, A. (1982). Time Preference. *International Economic Review* 23(3): 677–694.

Frederick, S., Loewenstein, G., and O'Donoghue, T. (2002). Time Discounting and Time Preference: A Critical Review. *Journal of Economic Literature* 40(2): 351–401.

Fudenberg, D. and Levine, D. K. (2006). A Dual-Self Model of Impulse Control. *The American Economic Review* 96(5): 1449–1476.

Giné, X., Karlan, D., and Zinman, J. (2010). Put Your Money Where Your Butt Is: A Commitment Contract for Smoking Cessation. *American Economic Journal: Applied Economics* 2(4): 213–235.

Gruber, J. H. and Mullainathan, S. (2005). Do Cigarette Taxes Make Smokers Happier? *B. E. Journals: Advances in Economic Analysis and Policy* 5(1): 145.

Gul, F. and Pesendorfer, W. (2001). Temptation and Self-Control. *Econometrica* 69(6): 1403–1435.

Gul, F. and Pesendorfer, W. (2004). Self-Control and the Theory of Consumption. *Econometrica* 72(1): 119–158.

Halevy, Y. (2008). Strotz Meets Allais: Diminishing Impatience and the Certainty Effect. *American Economic Review* 98(3): 1145–1162.

Halevy, Y. (2015). Time Consistency: Stationarity and Time Invariance. *Econometrica* 83(1): 335–352.

Harrison, G. W., Lau, M. I., and Williams, M. B. (2002). Estimating Individual Discount Rates in Denmark: A Field Experiment. *American Economic Review* 92(5): 1606–1617.

Heidhues, P. and Kosegi, B. (2010). Exploiting Naïvete about Self-Control in the Credit Market. *American Economic Review* 100(5): 2279–2303.

Henderson, N. and Bateman, I. (1995). Empirical and Public Choice Evidence for Hyperbolic Social Discount Rates and the Implications for Inter-Generational Discounting. *Environmental and Resource Economics* 5(4): 413–423.

Himmler, O., Jäckle, R., and Weinschenk, P. (2019). Soft Commitments, Reminders, and Academic Performance. *American Economic Journal: Applied Economics* 11(2): 114–142.

Ikeda, S., Kang, M.-I., and Ohtake, F. (2010). Hyperbolic Discounting, the Sign Effect, and the Body Mass Index. *Journal of Health Economics* 29(2): 268–284.

Imai, T., Rutter, T. A., and Camerer, C. F. (2021). Meta-Analysis of Present-Bias Estimation using Convex Time Budgets. *The Economic Journal* 131(636): 1788–1814.

John, A. (2020). When Commitment Fails: Evidence from a Field Experiment. *Management Science* 66(2): 503–529.

Kahneman, D. (2011). *Thinking, Fast and Slow*. Farrar, Straus and Giroux: New York.

Kahneman, D. and Tversky, A. (1979). Prospect Theory: An Analysis of Decision Under Risk. *Econometrica* 47(2): 263–291.

Kaur, S., Kremer, M., and Mullainathan, S. (2015). Self-Control at Work. *Journal of Political Economy* 123(6): 1227–1277.

Kosse, F. and Pfeiffer, F. (2013). Quasi-Hyperbolic Time Preferences and their Inter-Generational Transmission. IZA. Discussion Paper 7221.

Kotlikoff, L. J., Spivak, A., and Summers, L. H. (1982). The Adequacy of Savings. *American Economic Review* 72(5): 1056–1069.

Laibson, D. (1994). Essays in Hyperbolic Discounting. MIT, Ph.D. Dissertation.

Laibson, D. (1997). Golden Eggs and Hyperbolic Discounting. *Quarterly Journal of Economics* 112(2): 443–478.

Laibson, D., Maxted, P., Repetto, A. and Tobacman, J. (2020). *Estimating Discount Functions with Consumption Choices over the Lifecycle*. Mimeo Harvard University.

Loewenstein, G. F. (1987). Anticipation and the Valuation of Delayed Consumption. *Economic Journal* 97(387): 666–684.

Loewenstein, G. F. (2018). Self-Control and Its Discontents: A Commentary on Duckworth, Milkman, and Laibson. *Psychological Science in the Public Interest* 19(3): 95– 101

Loewenstein, G. F. and Prelec, D. (1992). Anomalies in Intertemporal Choice: Evidence and an Interpretation. *Quarterly Journal of Economics* 107(2): 573–597.

Loewenstein, G. F. and Prelec, D. (1993). Preferences for Sequences of Outcomes. *Psychological Review* 100(1): 91–108.

Loewenstein, G. F. and Sicherman, N. (1991). Do Workers Prefer Increasing Wage Profiles? *Journal of Labor Economics* 9(1): 67–84.

Mayer, T. and Russell, T. (2005). Income Smoothing and Self-Control: The Case of Schoolteachers. *Economic Inquiry* 43(4): 823–830.

Milkman, K. L., Minson, J. A., and Volpp, K. G. M. (2013). Holding the Hunger Games Hostage at the Gym: An Evaluation of Temptation Bundling. *Management Science* 60(2): 283–299.

Milkman, K. L., Rogers, T., and Bazerman, M. H. (2008). Harnessing Our Inner Angels and Demons: What We Have Learned About Want/Should Conflicts and How that Knowledge Can Help us Reduce Short-Sighted Decision Making. *Perspectives on Psychological Science* 3: 324–338.

Mischel, W., Shoda, Y., and Rodriguez M. I. (1989). Delay of Gratification in Children. *Science* 244(4907): 933–938.

Mischel, W. and Ebbesen, E. B. (1970). Attention in Delay of Gratification. *Journal of Personality and Social Psychology* 16(2): 329–337.

O'Donoghue, T. and Rabin, M. (1999a). Incentives for Procrastinators. *Quarterly Journal of Economics* 114(3): 769–816.

O'Donoghue, T. and Rabin, M. (1999b). Doing It Now or Later. *American Economic Review* 89(1): 103–124.

O'Donoghue, T. and Rabin, M. (2003). Self-Awareness and Self-Control. In R. Baumeister, G. Loewenstein, and D. Read (eds.), *Time and Decision: Economic and Psychological Perspectives on Intertemporal Choice*. Russell Sage Foundation: New York, pp. 217–243.

O'Donoghue, T. and Rabin, M. (2007). Incentives and Self-Control. In R. Blundell, W. Newey, and T. Persson (eds.), *Advances in Economics and Econometrics: Volume 2, Theory and Applications* (Ninth World Congress). Cambridge University Press: Cambridge, pp. 215–245.

Paserman, M. D. (2008). Job Search and Hyperbolic Discounting: Structural Estimation and Policy Evaluation. *The Economic Journal* 118(531): 1418–1452.

Phelps, E. and Pollack, R. A. (1968). On Second Best National Savings and Game Equilibrium Growth. *Review of Economic Studies* 35(2): 185–199.

Read, D. (2001). Is Time-Discounting Hyperbolic or Subadditive? *Journal of Risk and Uncertainty* 23(1): 5–32.

Read, D. and van Leeuwen, B. (1998). Predicting Hunger: The Effects of Appetite and Delay on Choice. *Organizational Behavior and Human Decision Processes* 76(2): 189–205.

Royer, H., Stehr, M. and Sydnor, J. (2015). Incentives, Commitments, and Habit Formation in Exercise: Evidence from a Field Experiment with Workers at a Fortune-500 Company. *American Economic Journal: Applied Microeconomics* 7(3): 51–84.

Ryder, H. E. and Heal, G. (1973). Optimal Growth with Intertemporally Dependent Preferences. *Review of Economic Studies* 40(1): 1–31.

Sadoff, S., Samek, A., and Sprenger, C. (2020). Dynamic Inconsistency in Food Choice: Experimental Evidence from Two Food Deserts. *The Review of Economic Studies* 87(4): 1954–1988.

Salois, M. J. and Moss, C. B. (2011). A Direct Test of Hyperbolic Discounting Using Market Asset Data. *Economics Letters* 112(3): 290–292.

Samuelson, P. A. (1937). A Note on Measurement of Utility. *Review of Economic Studies* 4(2): 155–161.

Schilbach, F. (2019). Alcohol and Self-Control: A Field Experiment in India. *American Economic Review* 109(4): 1290–1322.

Shoda, Y., Mischel, W., and Peake, P. K. (1990). Predicting Adolescent Cognitive and Self-Regulatory Competencies Reschool Delay of Gratification: Identifying Diagnostic Conditions. *Developmental Psychology* 26(6): 978–986.

Shu, S. and Gneezy, A. (2010). Procrastination of Enjoyable Experiences. *Journal of Marketing Research* 47: 933–944.

Sozou, P. D. (1998). On Hyperbolic Discounting and Uncertain Hazard Rates. *Proceedings of the Royal Society B: Biological Sciences* 265(1409): 2015–2020.

Strotz, R. H. (1955–1956). Myopia and Inconsistency in Dynamic Utility Maximization. *Review of Economic Studies*. 23(3): 165–180.

Thaler, R. H. and Shefrin, H. M. (1981). An Economic Theory of Self-Control. *Journal of Political Economy* 89(2): 392–406.

Thaler, R. H. (1981). Some Empirical Evidence of Dynamic Inconsistency. *Economics Letters*. 8(3): 201–207.

Ubfal, D. (2016). How General Are Time Preferences? Eliciting Good-Specific Discount Rates. *Journal of Development Economics* 118: 150–170.

Viscusi, K. W., Huber, J., and Bell, J. (2008). Estimating Discount Rates for Environmental Quality from Utility-Based Choice Experiments. *Journal of Risk and Uncertainty* 37(23): 199–220.

Watts, T. W., Duncan, G. J., and Quan, H. (2018). Revisiting the Marshmallow Test: A Conceptual Replication Investigating Links between Early Delay of Gratification and Later Outcomes. *Psychological Science* 29(7): 1159–1177.

Wertenbroch, K. (1998). Consumption Self-Control by Rationing Purchase Quantities of Virtue and Vice. *Marketing Science* 17(4): 317–337.

Problems for Part III

1. O'Donoghue and Rabin (2007) write: "Most economists wouldn't bat an eye if someone suggested that people care 1% more about today than tomorrow—it's just discounting. But under the standard model of exponential discounting, such seemingly reasonable short-term impatience implies manifestly unrealistic long-term impatience." By how much more would such an individual care about present utility relative to utility in a year's time? Is your calculated amount of present-focus a reasonable description of human behavior?
2. (O'Donoghue and Rabin, 2007) Consider a realistic yearly discount factor of 0.7 (which implies that people care six times more about their well-being 10 years from now than 15 years from now). What does this imply about how much people care about today versus tomorrow under exponential discounting? Suppose that you prefer not to quit smoking today. What does this imply about your behavior about quitting smoking tomorrow?
3. O'Donoghue and Rabin (2007) describe the following statistics about credit card debt in the US:

   > There are a billion credit cards in use in the United States, with an average annual interest rate of 18.9%. About 60% of active credit-card accounts are not paid off monthly. The average credit-card debt among all American households is \$8,400, with an average card debt of \$9,205 among people who have at least one card. A typical American family today pays about \$1200 annually in credit-card interest.

   They go on to write:

   > And most dramatically in terms of recent growth, massive numbers of employed (and pensioned) people in U.S. have taken out one or more payday loans—borrowing against their next pay check. A typical transaction is that a person borrows \$300 using his or her paycheck or social-security check as collateral, and pays back \$354 when this check arrives. This is 18% interest for a month or (more commonly) two weeks.

   What can we conclude about the nature of human time preferences from these observations?
4. Use (5.21), (5.22), and the definition of the discount factor $\delta = \frac{1}{1+\theta}$ under EDU to show that θ is the discount rate under EDU.
5. Given the utility representation of preferences in (5.4) based on the *at least as good as* binary relation, $\succeq$, prove the following for the indifference relation ($\sim$) and the strictly preferred to ($\succ$) relation.
   (a) If $(z,t) \sim_t (z',t')$, then $U(z,t) = U(z',t')$ [Utilities are identical for outcome-time pairs over which an individual is indifferent].
   (b) If $U(z,t) \succ_t U(z',t')$, then $U(z,t) > U(z',t')$ [Utility is strictly higher from the strictly preferred outcome-time pair].
6. Calculate and verify the six discount rates shown in Table 5.1 in brackets.

Table 6.3 Choice between options A and B to be made at time $t = 1$ and $t = 2$. Numerical values in the table are utilities from the two options at various times

Utility/Time	1	2	3
A	0	4	0
B	0	0	6

7. Mayer and Russell (2005) used data from teachers in California. They showed that teachers preferred equally spread salaries over 12 months, rather than receiving the same salaries in 10 equal installments over 10 months (and not receive anything for the remaining two months). Is this consistent with EDU? What might account for the preferences of the teachers?
8. Write down the discount function in the QHU model, corresponding to (6.4).
9. Suppose that time is continuous. Calculate the discount rate corresponding to the general hyperbolic discount function in (6.3).
10. Consider the intuition provided in Section 6.5.4, following the work of Angeletos et al. (2001). Use the model of life-cycle consumption in Section 6.5 with the constant relative risk aversion utility function $u(c) = \frac{1}{1-\rho}c^{1-\rho}; \rho > 0$ and $\rho \neq 1$, to answer this question.
   (a) Suppose that a commitment technology allows the young-self who has $(\beta, 1)$ preferences to make savings choices for himself as well as for the middle-self. Find the optimal consumption profile under commitment.
   (b) Suppose now that the young-self at time $t = 0$ can invest in illiquid assets that mature only in period $t = 2$. The middle-self cannot encash these illiquid assets. No commitment technology is available and the young-self cannot control the savings choices of the middle-self. Show that illiquid assets allow the young-self to obtain the optimal solution under commitment.
11. Suppose that time $t = 1, 2, 3$, and a decision maker makes a choice between two possible options – A and B. The utilities corresponding to the two choices for each of the three time periods are shown in Table 6.3. For instance, option A gives a utility of 4 at $t = 2$ and option B gives a utility of 6 at $t = 3$. What is the optimal choice of the decision maker if the choice is made at (a) time $t = 1$, and (b) time $t = 2$. In answering your question, consider the two cases where the decision maker follows (i) EDU with the discount factor $\delta = 1$, and (ii) the (β, δ) model such that $\beta = \frac{1}{2}$ and $\delta = 1$.
12. Consider the case of immediate costs and future benefits described in Section 6.6.1. Suppose that $T = 4$ and the pattern of costs is an increasing one, $\mathbf{c} = (4, 8, 12, 20)$, and the future benefit from the activity is fixed at $\overline{v} = 44$. Find the perception perfect equilibrium for time consistents, naifs, and sophisticates when the present-focus parameter is (a) $\beta = \frac{3}{4}$, and (b) $\beta = \frac{1}{2}$.
13. Consider the case of immediate benefits and future costs described in Section 6.6.2. Suppose that $T = 4$ and the pattern of benefits net of costs is an increasing one, $\mathbf{v} = (4, 8, 12, 20)$, so the pattern of costs, already taken account of in the net benefits, is $\mathbf{c} = (0, 0, 0, 0)$. Find the perception perfect equilibrium for time consistents, naifs, and sophisticates when the present-focus parameter is (a) $\beta = \frac{3}{4}$, and (b) $\beta = \frac{1}{2}$.

Part IV

Behavioral Game Theory

Introduction to Part IV

In this part of the book, we present a more systematic analysis of *strategic situations* that we began in Part II of the book. Recall that in a strategic situation, the strategies of the participants (known as *players*) influence not just their own payoffs but also the *payoffs* of others. A detailed description of a strategic situation that specifies the participants, their payoffs, their actions, their beliefs, and who can do what and when, is known as a *game*. *Game theory* is the study of games. It has the potential to provide a common language and a unifying framework for the social and the behavioral sciences (Gintis, 2009).

The following two questions precede the construction of any game theoretic model.

1. What are the *motivations*, for example, self-regarding or other-regarding, and what assumptions do we impose on the *degree of rationality* of the players, for example, on the cognitive ability of the players?
2. What *principles* do we apply to determine the outcome, or prediction, of a given game? The predictions typically specify the chosen strategies and beliefs of the players in a game.

The answers to these questions are contentious, to say the least. Modern neoclassical economics is couched in the language of game theory, a transformation that gathered pace in the 1980s, although some of the foundational papers had been written by that time. Mainstream neoclassical economics has favored quite specific answers to the two questions posed above and adopted a version of game theory that we shall refer to as *neoclassical game theory*.

Neoclassical game theory typically assumes self-regarding motivations of the players who aim to maximize their own *material payoffs* or utilities from a game.[1] Players are also ultra-rational and are endowed with the ability to perform extremely complex strategic calculations in a sense that we make clearer below. To the second question, neoclassical game theory takes a *circular equilibrium approach* that has been criticized by some of the founders of modern game theory such as Reinhard Selten, and the principle of *methodological individualism*.

Roughly put, the equilibrium approach imposes two conditions. (i) Given the beliefs of the players and the actions of all players in a game, each player takes an action to maximize own material payoffs, that is, players play mutual *best replies* or *best responses*. (ii) Given the actions, the beliefs of the players are consistent with Bayes' Law, and conditional on the beliefs, the actions maximize material payoffs; this is the principle of *consistency of actions and beliefs*. Both conditions play a role in the two equilibrium methods, a *Nash equilibrium* and the *backward*

[1] Recall that our usage of the word "neoclassical" refers to the "actual" practice of the subject, and not what it could have been or could be. As such, readers should not take it as a loaded word, but one that is merely used to taxonomize the literature.

induction outcome, that were outlined and studied through a variety of games in Part II of the book.

The principle of methodological individualism implies that individual choices and actions determine social norms and institutions. Thus, primacy is given to individual choices and actions in determining all aggregate economic and social phenomena. However, the use of modern complexity theory in economics (see Part VI of the book) shows that *emergent phenomena* that characterize aggregate outcomes cannot be construed as having been "consciously" created by individual actions or choices. For instance, "starling murmurations" are emergent phenomena but not consciously created by the decisions of individual birds. For a discussion of methodological individualism, see Arrow (1994). For a discussion of the role of complexity in economics that goes beyond this book, and some of the references in this field, see Dhami (2020, Vol. VI, Sections 4.2, 4.3).

The formal study of game theory was developed initially to solve practical problems, say, in the determination of optimal strategies in World War II. However, the development of neoclassical game theory, particularly from the 1970s onward, was typically driven by a desire to build a logically consistent mathematical theory of strategic interaction. It was not always motivated by the desire to solve practical real-world strategic problems, but rather by the game theorist's subjective notion of what is plausible human strategic behavior. It was rarely felt necessary to pit the predictions of the models against the empirical evidence. The models were "believed" to be self-evidently true, and many in economics continue to subscribe to this view, including the surprising and retrogressive view that game theory is a branch of mathematics and needs no empirical testing. This approach is reflected in the widespread current practice of teaching neoclassical game theory in economics in an axiomatic, theoretical, manner without any mention of the relevant evidence. This practice extends to related courses in microeconomics where game theory plays an important role. This approach has been hugely damaging for economics. Bluntly put, it is bad science and it shortchanges the students in such courses.

The best practice would have been to subject the predictions of neoclassical game theory to stringent empirical testing right from the beginning and then try to improve the theory where it failed. Fortunately, such a parallel effort has already gained a head of steam in the last three decades or so. In a nutshell, the evidence has rejected many of the core features in neoclassical game theory. The evidence shows that players are not super-rational machines, and the equilibrium predictions in neoclassical game theory often do poorly. This has led to parallel developments in the study of strategic environments in behavioral economics, known as *behavioral game theory*. Behavioral game theory attempts to take account of the evidence from strategic environments and proposes models based on more persuasive psychological foundations, and varying degrees of less stringent nonequilibrium requirements. Importantly, the predictions of these models are in better conformity with the evidence.

A parallel development in evolutionary biology, *evolutionary game theory*, models the outcome of strategic interaction between different human genes. Neoclassical game theory typically focuses on an equilibrium, but not on how the equilibrium is arrived at. However, a central feature of evolutionary game theory is to study the *time path to an equilibrium*. The study of such time paths to an equilibrium is not behavioral game theory's forte either, but behavioral game theory allows for nonequilibrium outcomes to arise, while neoclassical game theory and evolutionary game theory allow for only equilibrium outcomes. The result is that there is a closer connection between equilibrium concepts in neoclassical game theory and evolutionary game theory.

The next two chapters are an account of these alternative theoretical approaches, neoclassical game theory, behavioral game theory, and evolutionary game theory. The central questions in the social and the behavioral sciences are ultimately about various aspects of *human cooperation and coordination* and the flip sides, conflict and miscoordination. We keep to this theme in these two chapters. Although some prior exposure to game theory is desirable, readers who have no prior knowledge of game theory should not find the material too difficult to follow. The appropriate machinery and concepts, including fairly basic ones, are introduced when they are needed, in the context of specific games.

7 Introduction to Behavioral Game Theory

7.1 Introduction

We begin in Sections 7.2 and 7.3 by outlining the basics of static and dynamic games of complete information. As templates for these two types of games, we use, respectively, the *prisoner's dilemma game* and the *centipede game*. We introduce the solution concepts for solving these games under neoclassical game theory, respectively, *pure and mixed strategy Nash equilibrium* and *subgame perfect equilibrium* (which is operationalized through *backward induction* for this class of games). We then examine the predictive success of these solution concepts.

In Section 7.4 we ask if cooperation can be sustained purely on account of *instrumental motivations* in *repeated games*. By instrumental motivations is meant that the reason people cooperate is based entirely on a calculation of the material costs and benefits from the act of cooperating. Or, is it the case that *intrinsic motivations*, that is, the innate desire to cooperate, independent of the costs and benefits, are important too.

Section 7.5 shows that history plays a powerful role in choosing between multiple Nash equilibria. By contrast, under neoclassical game theory, the choice between multiple Nash equilibria is often not clear. The empirical support for some of the selection mechanisms that have been proposed to select among multiple equilibria in neoclassical economics, such as payoff dominance and risk dominance, is not definite. The precise transmission channels through which history influences subsequent actions is not well established, but behavioral economics offers several promising candidates that we explore in this part of the book. These include *focal points* and *social norms*.

Section 7.6 is a note on the basics of *games of incomplete information* and an intuitive understanding of the requirements for an equilibrium in this class of games. Section 7.7 provides evidence on *coordination failures* in simple games. Coordination failures can arise in many ways. For instance, there could be multiple Nash equilibria in a game and one of the equilibria is Pareto optimal. Coordination failures would arise if we observed the outcome of the game to be the non-Pareto optimal Nash equilibrium.

Having shown that the empirical evidence is not supportive of the predictions of several aspects of neoclassical game theory, in the second half of the chapter we begin our study of behavioral models of game theory. In Section 7.8, we present four main models in behavioral game theory, and the associated empirical evidence. These models are the *level-k model*, and the closely related *cognitive hierarchy (CH) model*, which keep the feature of best replies under neoclassical game theory, but relax consistency of equilibrium actions and beliefs; *quantal response equilibrium* (QRE), which relaxes the feature of best replies under neoclassical game theory, but keeps the requirement of consistency of beliefs and actions; and a model of *cursed equilibrium* which applies to games of incomplete information whereby players assume that with some probability each type of a player plays the average action across all possible types.

Each of these models provides an improvement over neoclassical game theory, but the empirical success of none of these models is universal, across all categories of games. Yet, these models provide plausible directions in which we can amend neoclassical game theory, imparting it with a better capability to explain the empirical evidence. Of these models, the level-k model and the CH models impose the weakest and most plausible cognitive requirements on the part of the players. The other two models require fairly strong cognitive requirements. It is possible that the context determines which of these models is used by players in a game. There should be no presumption that a single behavioral model applies to all classes of games, and to all contexts. Hence, we should not be surprised if these models, and the estimated model parameters from one game, are not portable to another. We live in a complex world where many competing psychological and social motivations determine our behavior. There are no clean and easy answers.

We then go on to consider three more interesting classes of behavioral models that are given less attention in behavioral economics courses, but there is no reason why these models should occupy a hierarchically inferior position.

The first two models appear in Section 7.9. The first model, in Section 7.9.1, moves away from the concept of *private rationality* to *social rationality*. We discuss the ideas of team reasoning; joint intentionality; Kantian equilibrium; and universalist preferences whereby altruism exhibited by one person to another is not dependent on the social distance of the recipients of the altruism. The rules of behavior that humans use and the beliefs that they have could be determined by social norms of behavior. Social norms, in turn, might arise from long periods of learning and introspection, or might emerge accidentally without conscious individual effort. It is even possible that social norms might be "emergent phenomena" in a world that operates under complex adaptive dynamics (see Part VI of the book for these ideas). Either way, this relaxes the assumption of strict methodological individualism on which neoclassical game theory is based. We shall give several examples of this insight in this part of the book.

The second model, in Section 7.9.2, shows why we should be interested in a *correlated equilibrium*. We present insights from the work of Herbert Gintis who assigns to social norms, the role of a choreographer in a correlated equilibrium. The choreographer observes a randomizing device, and based on the realization of signals from such a device, gives recommendations to players in the game about which actions to follow. In a correlated equilibrium, players find it in their best interests to follow the recommendations, and improve their payoffs, often relative to a Nash equilibrium of the game. Think, for instance, of anarchy in traffic when there is no system of traffic lights. Now contrast it to the successful operation of traffic lights, where the choreographer observes a random signal and gives either a recommendation to go (green light) or stop (red light). This coordinates the beliefs and actions of the players, allowing for a better outcome for all players.

The third model, outlined in Section 7.10, imposes limited cognitive requirements on players, relative to the alternative behavioral proposals. In this case, players resort to using relatively *simple rules of thumb* to solve games. These rules of thumb could be derived from the evolutionary history of humans; from personal experiences; from internal moral values; or from social norms. In particular, we focus attention on one simple rule of thumb that has extensive empirical support in psychology, *evidential reasoning*, which also goes by the alternative names of *projection bias* and the *false consensus effect*. Under evidential reasoning, when players have to guess what other like-minded players will do in a game, they use their own predispositions as having diagnostic evidence about what others might do. This simplifies an essentially strategic situation to a decision theoretic situation, just as in Part I of the book; an identical simplification also occurs under a correlated equilibrium.

7.2 Static Games of Complete Information

7.2.1 The Prisoner's Dilemma Game and Basic Terminology

The archetypal strategic situation studied in the social and behavioral sciences to analyze human cooperation is the *prisoner's dilemma game* (henceforth, the PD game) which is described in Table 7.1. It was proposed by the Canadian mathematician Albert W. Tucker who studied mathematics at the University of Toronto. We shall use the PD game as a template to explore the nature of human cooperation in this chapter, using alternative frameworks.

We begin with some useful terminology from game theory. The PD game is a *static game* (i.e., each player takes an action only once and there is no time dimension) of *complete information* (i.e., both players have access to all relevant information in Table 7.1). Since this is a static game, both players make their choices simultaneously without observing what the other player chose (*simultaneous moves*). Table 7.1 presents the *normal form* of the PD game, which specifies three things: the set of players, their possible strategies, and their payoffs for each possible combination of strategies of the players.

Here's the story behind the PD game, which also illustrates how to set up a basic normal form game. Two petty criminals, who are the two players in this game, have committed a crime. They get locked up on suspicion of the crime, but the police lack evidence to convict them. They are interrogated in separate rooms and each has two possible actions, which are synonymous with "strategies" in this game. Players can choose either "defect" D (i.e., snitch and give evidence against the other player) or "cooperate" C (i.e., deny any involvement of both players in the crime). The two players make their choices simultaneously; each does not know what the other will choose.

Table 7.1 The prisoner's dilemma game

	C	D
C	2, 2	0, 4
D	4, 0	1, 1

The actions C, D are shown in Table 7.1 for each player. The choice of action for the *row player* is a choice of a row (either C or D) and a choice of action for the *column player* is a choice of a column (either C or D). For each pair of actions by the row and the column players, there is a pair of two numbers in each cell of Table 7.1; the first number is the row player's payoff, or utility, and the second number is the column player's payoff, or utility. All payoffs are expressed in some monetary units that we have suppressed.[1]

If both players choose C, they receive a payoff of 2 each. If both choose D, that is, both snitch, then each receives a low payoff of 1. If the row player chooses to cooperate, C, and the column player chooses to snitch, D, then the row player gets 0 (because evidence has been given against him) and the column player gets a payoff of 4 (no evidence against him, and perhaps an extra reward for helping the police). If the column player cooperates, C, and the row player snitches, D, then the payoffs are reversed to 0 and 4, respectively. When payoffs can be reversed in this manner, we say that the underlying game is *symmetric*, that is, we could have interchanged the identities of the row and the column players and nothing would change in Table 7.1. This is a game of complete information because both players can see the information provided in Table 7.1.

In a static game of complete information, such as the PD game, we can refer to *actions* and *strategies* interchangeably. However, strategies are more complicated constructs when we move to *dynamic games* where players can make sequential choices after observing what other players have chosen (more on this below). Any list of strategies of all players is known as a *strategy profile*. In the PD game, there are four possible strategy profiles: (C, C), (C, D), (D, C), and (D, D). A utility function, or payoff function, specifies what each player receives as a payoff from each of these four possible strategy profiles. All these concepts can be easily extended to games with many players and many strategies.

An *outcome* or *prediction* of this game is a single strategy profile (*unique equilibrium*) or possibly several strategy profiles (*multiple equilibria*), such that none of the players wish to depart from their part of the predicted strategy profile, given their beliefs about what others will do. What is the predicted outcome of the game in Table 7.1 in neoclassical game theory? Consider the row player first. If the column player chooses C, the row player prefers D to C (because $4 > 2$) and if the column player chooses D, the row player still prefers D to C (because $1 > 0$). Such strategies that give a higher payoff to a player over another strategy, irrespective of the strategy chosen by the other player, are known as *dominant strategies*. If the payoff from a strategy is "strictly" higher in every case, then we have a *strictly dominant strategy*. In the PD game, D is the strictly dominant strategy for the row player and C is the strictly dominated strategy. Since this is a symmetric game, exactly the same calculations apply for the column player who too finds D to be a strictly dominant strategy and C to be a strictly dominated strategy. In neoclassical game theory, it is taken as self-evidently true that rational players will never play strictly dominated strategies. Hence, the prediction under neoclassical game theory is that a "unique equilibrium" exists in the PD game in which each player chooses to defect, D. Thus (D, D) is the unique predicted *equilibrium strategy profile* for the game under neoclassical game theory.

[1] The payoffs in the payoff matrices, such as in Table 7.1, will be taken to reflect the underlying preferences of the players unless otherwise specified.

This completes the analysis of the PD game in neoclassical game theory and in similar games where each player has a unique strictly dominant strategy. However, this prediction is a hypothesis about how people behave. It stays as a hypothesis until tested stringently against the evidence. When tested, it is found that about 50–60 percent of the players choose to cooperate, C, depending on how the PD game is framed (for instance, as a cooperative game, a competitive game, or as a coordination game). Interestingly, this also holds true when the game is played with prison inmates who cooperate even more than university students. As such, theories that make the prediction (D, D) in a static PD game are not able to account for the evidence.

7.2.2 Pure Strategy Nash Equilibrium

Before we go further, recall our discussion of a *Nash equilibrium* in Part II while discussing the outcome of the public goods game. In a static game of complete information, a strategy profile is a Nash equilibrium if given the action of the other players, each player gets "at least as high" a payoff from choosing their part of the strategy profile, rather than choosing any other available strategy, that is, each player *plays a best reply to the equilibrium actions of all others.*

This definition implies that the outcome (D, D) that we obtained in the PD game by deleting strictly dominated strategies is a Nash equilibrium. Given that the column player plays D, if the row player keeps to his part of the strategy profile by playing D, then he gets a payoff of 1. But if he switches to the other strategy C, while the column player continues playing D, then the row player gets a lower payoff of 0. Hence, the row player prefers to play his part of the strategy profile (D, D). Since the PD game is symmetric, exactly the same calculations apply to the column player who cannot do any better by switching from D to C, given that the row player plays his part of the strategy profile, D. This result is not accidental. If a unique strategy profile results from deleting strictly dominated strategies, then it must be a Nash equilibrium (we omit the simple proof). This gives an obvious way of predicting an outcome in this class of games under neoclassical game theory and has often been employed in experimental tests of neoclassical game theory (see below). In many games, a unique strategy profile might not exist after we have deleted all dominated strategies of the players. However, in this case, a Nash equilibrium still gives us the obvious way of predicting the outcome of the game under neoclassical game theory.

Let us formalize a Nash equilibrium in the context of static two-player games of complete information, so as to make the concept absolutely clear. Let the two players choose their strategies from some set of n possible strategies $S = \{s_1, \dots, s_n\}$; for example, in the PD game, $S = \{C, D\}$. It is straightforward to extend the analysis to different strategy sets for the two players, say, S_1 and S_2, but we give the simpler case here. The *strategy profiles* for the game are pairs of strategies, one for each player, and we save on notation by denoting them by (s_1, s_2), where s_1 is the strategy chosen by the first player and s_2 by the second player. For instance, in the PD game, all possible strategy profiles are (C, C), (C, D), (D, C), and (D, D).

The respective utilities of the two players, $u_1(s_1, s_2)$ and $u_2(s_1, s_2)$, depend on the chosen strategy profile (as can be directly verified for the special case of the PD game in Table 7.1).[2] The *normal form of a game* is simply a description of the set of players, their strategies, and their

[2] Technically, we have $u_1 : S \to \mathbb{R}$ and $u_2 : S \to \mathbb{R}$.

utilities from all possible strategies. For the static two-player game of complete information, the normal form can be written as $\Gamma = \{2, S, u_1, u_2\}$. When players choose one of their strategies with probability 1, these are known are pure strategies.

Let us denote a Nash equilibrium strategy profile by (s_1^*, s_2^*) where each of s_1^*, s_2^* are chosen from the set S. A Nash equilibrium simply requires that each player plays a *best reply*, given the equilibrium strategy of the other player.

Definition 7.1 *(Pure strategy Nash equilibrium) Consider the two-player normal form game, $\Gamma = \{2, S, u_1, u_2\}$. In a Nash equilibrium strategy profile (s_1^*, s_2^*), each player must receive "at least as high" a utility from playing their part of the equilibrium strategy profile, as from playing any other available strategy in the set S, given that the other player sticks to their part of the equilibrium strategy profile. In other words,*

$$u_1(s_1^*, s_2^*) \geq u_1(s_1, s_2^*) \text{ for all } s_1 \text{ in } S,$$

and

$$u_2(s_1^*, s_2^*) \geq u_2(s_1^*, s_2) \text{ for all } s_2 \text{ in } S.$$

Readers should check that Definition 7.1 implies that (D, D) is a Nash equilibrium strategy profile in the PD game. It is possible that there is more than one Nash equilibrium in a game, in which case we may need other criteria to choose between them (we discuss this possibility later in the chapter; see e.g., coordination games below).

7.2.3 Iterated Deletion of Dominated Strategies When There Are More than Two Strategies

What if players have more than two strategies? Consider, for instance, the static two-player game of complete information shown in Table 7.2, which was studied in Schotter et al. (1994). Here the row and the column players have three strategies each, T, M, B and the payoffs corresponding to each pair of strategies can simply be read off from the corresponding cells in the table. In order to solve this game, we use *iterated deletion of dominated strategies*. We start by deleting the first dominated strategy for any player, delete it, and then try to spot another dominated strategy among the remaining strategies, delete it, then keep doing successive rounds of this exercise. If, at the end of this exercise, and this can be proved formally, we end up with a unique strategy profile, then it must be a Nash equilibrium.

Table 7.2 A 3 × 3 game solved by iterated deletion of dominated strategies

	T	M	B
T	4, 4	4, 4	4, 4
M	0, 1	6, 3	0, 0
B	0, 1	0, 0	3, 6

Let us apply this method to the game in Table 7.2. Notice first that B is a dominated strategy for the row player, so delete it (literally strike it out; it is no longer a part of the game). For the column player, strategy T is dominated by strategy M because $4 \leq 4$ and $1 < 3$. Let us pause for a remark.

Remark 7.1 *T is known as a weakly dominated strategy because $4 = 4$. By contrast, if all payoffs are strictly lower from a strategy then we have a strictly dominated strategy. For the game in Table 7.2, we are engaging in iterated deletion of "weakly dominated strategies." If this exercise leads to a unique surviving strategy profile, it is a Nash equilibrium of the game, as stated above. However, in this case, relative to the case of deletion of strictly dominated strategies, we might well have deleted another Nash equilibrium strategy profile during the exercise; we shall see this below. Hence, the resulting Nash equilibrium might not be "unique." By contrast, with iterated deletion of "strictly dominated strategies," if there is a unique surviving strategy, then it is the "unique" Nash equilibrium of the game.*

Let us now continue with the exercise and strike out the dominated strategy T for the column player. B for the row player and T for the column player have already been deleted. Of the remaining strategies for the column player, B is dominated by M, so delete it too. Only strategy M survives for the column player and strategies T, M survive for the row player. Of these, T is dominated by M (because $4 < 6$). This leaves a unique surviving profile (M, M), which is also a Nash equilibrium of the game. From Remark 7.1, we know that iterated deletion of "weakly dominated strategies" may delete one of the Nash equilibria for the game – in this case the Nash equilibrium (T, T) was deleted (check using Definition 7.1 that this is a Nash equilibrium).

When this game is played in an experiment, only 16% of the row players and 26% of the column players play M. What do we learn?

The games in Tables 7.1 and 7.2 differ not just in their specific context but also in the level of complexity; the first is a 2×2 game and the second is a 3×3 game. Hence, the game in Table 7.2 is cognitively more challenging, which should make no difference to the super-rational players assumed in neoclassical game theory. But, conformity with the Nash equilibrium often falls as the level of complexity of the game increases. In general, as players need to engage in larger and larger numbers of iterated deletion of dominated strategies, conformity with a Nash equilibrium falls. Two possible reasons could give rise to this observed outcome. First, players may have cognitive limitations that preclude more than a few steps of iterated deletion of dominated strategies. In this case, models that wish to aspire to explain the data must take this into account. Second, as the number of iterations increase, players need to be even more confident of the rationality of other players engaged in these successive steps.

7.2.4 Mixed Strategies

The strategies that we have considered so far (e.g., the play of C or D in the PD game) are also known as "pure strategies." It is possible that no Nash equilibrium exists when players choose a pure strategy. Consider, for instance, the matching pennies game in Table 7.3.

Each of two players has a coin and they privately, and simultaneously, turn their coins to either a heads, H, or a tails, T, without observing the choice of the other player. If the choices

Table 7.3 The matching pennies game

	H	T
H	$-1,1$	$1,-1$
T	$1,-1$	$-1,1$

match (both have heads or both have tails) then player 1 gives \$1 to player 2, and if the choices do not match (one heads, one tails), then player 2 gives player 1 an amount \$1. The four pure strategy profiles in this game are $(H,H),(H,T),(T,H),(T,T)$. The reader can readily check, by applying Definition 7.1, that none of these is a pure strategy Nash equilibrium.

Suppose that we allow both players to pick their pure strategies probabilistically. So the row player plays H with probability $0 \leq p \leq 1$ and T with probability $1-p$; while the column player plays H with probability $0 \leq q \leq 1$ and T with probability $1-q$. Such strategies that are played probabilistically are known as *mixed strategies* to differentiate them from pure strategies.

Since both players play their strategies probabilistically, players face a risky situation in which their payoffs depend on the probabilities p and q. We assume that players use expected utility theory (EUT) for decision making under risk (see Chapter 2 for EUT).[3] We denote the expected utility of the row player by $EU^r(p,q)$, where the superscript "r" stands for the row player. Suppose, for simplicity, that the payoffs in Table 7.3 capture the direct utilities to the players. We can use Table 7.3 to compute

$$EU^r(p,q) = p\left[-q + (1-q)\right] + (1-p)\left[q - (1-q)\right]. \tag{7.1}$$

In (7.1), the first term on the RHS is the expected utility to the row player from playing H (with probability p) and the second term is the expected utility to the row player from playing T (with probability $1-p$). We can also write the corresponding expected utility calculations for the column player (superscript "c" for the column player) from playing the two strategies probabilistically as

$$EU^c(p,q) = q\left[p - (1-p)\right] + (1-q)\left[-p + (1-p)\right]. \tag{7.2}$$

Let us now define a *mixed strategy Nash equilibrium* (MSNE) for a static two-player game of complete information where players have only two strategies and the strategy sets of the two players are identical, $S = \{s_1, s_2\}$; the matching pennies game is an example. This framework is easily extended to more than two players and more than two strategies, but we simply wish to provide a basic understanding of the concept in order to interpret the evidence below. The strategies of the players now are choices of the probabilities with which they play their available pure strategies; $0 \leq p \leq 1$ is a strategy for the row player and $0 \leq q \leq 1$ is a strategy for the column player.

Definition 7.2 *(Mixed strategy Nash equilibrium (MSNE)) Consider a two-player normal form game of complete information, $\Gamma = \{2, S, u_1, u_2\}$, where each player has two pure strategies and an*

[3] This is not an innocuous point. We know from Part I that expected utility theory is rejected by the evidence. Hence, it would be desirable to replace it by behaviorally realistic theories, such as prospect theory. However, this is typically not carried out in the actual practice of neoclassical game theory. There is, thus, no knowing which of the standard results in neoclassical game theory would survive the introduction of more realistic decision theories.

identical strategy set, denoted by $S = \{s_1, s_2\}$. *Player 1 plays* s_1 *with probability* $0 \leq p \leq 1$ *and* s_2 *with probability* $1 - p$*; while player 2 plays* s_1 *with probability* $0 \leq q \leq 1$ *and* s_2 *with probability* $1 - q$. *Then a MSNE is a set of probabilities,* (p^*, q^*)*, which satisfy two properties.*

(i) Conditional on player 2 playing his part of the strategy profile, q^**, player 1 cannot improve his expected utility by playing his pure strategies with any other probability, that is,*

$$EU(p^*, q^*) \geq EU(p, q^*) \text{ for all } 0 \leq p \leq 1.$$

(ii) Conditional on player 1 playing his part of the strategy profile, p^**, player 2 cannot improve his expected utility by playing his pure strategies with any other probability, that is,*

$$EU(p^*, q^*) \geq EU(p^*, q) \text{ for all } 0 \leq q \leq 1.$$

For the matching pennies games, the MSNE is $(p^*, q^*) = (\frac{1}{2}, \frac{1}{2})$, so each player chooses each of the pure strategies with equal probability. Thus, none of the players can do better, if the other player picks their strategies with equal probability. In order to find this, use (7.1) to compute the best reply of player 1 for any choice of player 2; this is known as player 1's reaction function, and we denote this by $p(q)$. Then carry out a similar exercise for player 2. Using (7.2), find the reaction function of player 2, $q(p)$, which gives the best reply of player 2 to any choice of p by player 1. The intersection point of these two reaction functions gives $(p^*, q^*) = (\frac{1}{2}, \frac{1}{2})$. However, there is an alternative method to find the MSNE, which we now outline.

Since both pure strategies are being played as part of the MSNE, they must give the player an identical payoff. If this were not the case, and one of the pure strategies gave a higher payoff, then the player could increase his payoff by playing that pure strategy with a higher probability. For the matching pennies game, given that the column player plays H and T with equal probabilities, the row player gets an identical expected payoff of 0 from both strategies H and T. The same is true for the column player in this symmetric game. Thus, in a MSNE, players play their pure strategies in the proportion that makes their opponents indifferent between their pure strategies.

This insight allows us to readily calculate a MSNE. Let us use the calculations already implicit in (7.1), (7.2). The expected utility of the row player from H and T, respectively, is $1 - 2q$ and $2q - 1$. For the row player to be indifferent between H and T, we require $1 - 2q = 2q - 1$; solving this equation for q, we get $q^* = \frac{1}{2}$. Similarly, the column player receives the expected utility $2p - 1$ and $1 - 2p$, respectively, from H and T. Indifference between these two payoffs requires $1 - 2p = 2p - 1$, or $p^* = \frac{1}{2}$. Thus, in a MSNE, $p^* = q^* = \frac{1}{2}$.

Suppose we restricted attention to only finite normal form games (finite numbers of players and strategies). Nash (1950a) showed that such games are guaranteed to have at least one MSNE even if there is no pure strategy Nash equilibrium in the game, as in the matching pennies game. The MSNE provides the underlying foundation for most University game theory courses, if not for most modern theoretical research in economics. It would be highly problematic, to say the least, if the MSNE were to be empirically rejected. For a start, the derivation of the result in Nash (1950a) requires that all players use EUT in computing their expected payoff (see, for instance, (7.1), (7.2) above). Yet, we know from Part I that EUT is rejected by the evidence. There is no guarantee that the result in Nash (1950a) holds if EUT does not hold. Furthermore, there is no intuitive reason why players should feel compelled to play their pure strategies with probabilities that makes the other player indifferent between their pure strategies, as is required in a MSNE.

In real life, one can imagine many contexts where it appears that players are playing mixed strategies by randomizing between their pure strategies. Some of the clearest examples come from sports contexts. For instance, a penalty kicker in football may kick to the left or to the right of the goalie with some probability; or a tennis player may serve to the left or to the right of the receiver with some probability. However, what is at stake here is the question: Do players play mixed strategies in the proportions required by a MSNE? A large literature exists on this question and it is surveyed in Camerer (2003) and Dhami (2020, Vol. IV). Here are some of the salient points.

1. Suppose that a game with a unique MSNE is played over many rounds and that game does not have a pure strategy Nash equilibrium. For instance, a penalty kicker in football who always uses the pure strategy of kicking to the right of a goalkeeper will be completely predictable and have low payoffs. Hence, the penalty kicker must follow a mixed strategy. If, say, we play the matching pennies game over many rounds, then in each round, the players must pick one of the two strategies, H or T, with equal probability, as required in a MSNE of the matching pennies game. If the game is played over sufficiently many rounds, we should observe H and T to be played about as many times and, in particular, the past play of strategies should have no influence on the current play of H or T which are chosen afresh with a 50-50 chance every round. This finding is rejected from sports and non-sports contexts. The current actions by the players are strongly influenced by their chosen actions in the past (serial correlation in actions) and the chosen actions by the opponent. There is little evidence of learning, for example, players are not able to pick out the serial correlation in the play of their opponent and use it to their advantage. Brown and Rosenthal (1990) is a classic study that establishes these points for a non-sports context.
2. The underlying mixed strategy resides, so to speak, inside the heads of the players who play it. We only observe the pure strategies chosen by the player. For instance, in the matching pennies game, the row player may toss a coin to choose between H and T (because $p^* = \frac{1}{2}$). However, we only observe a particular action chosen by the row player: H or T. If a large number of pairs of players were matched to play the matching pennies game, we will then observe a fraction who play H and the remaining fraction who play T. Some have interpreted the MSNE to apply to the fractions across all players (aggregate MSNE) and not just at the level of the individual players (individual MSNE). While Definition 7.2 is about individual MSNE, the aggregate MSNE interpretation, say, for the matching pennies game is that across large number of player, half will play H and the other half will play T.

   However, Mookherjee and Sopher (1994, 1997) reject both aggregate MSNE and individual MSNE. They use a two-player symmetric game where each player has four strategies, $1, 2, 3, 4$; see Table 7.4. Players either win an amount W which is either Rupees 5 or Rupees 10; or they can lose an amount W denoted by $-W$. The payoff labeled $\frac{1}{3}W$ in Table 7.4 denotes that a player has a $\frac{1}{3}$ chance of winning W and a $\frac{2}{3}$ chance of winning zero; the payoff labelled $-\frac{1}{3}W$ denotes a $\frac{1}{3}$ chance of losing W and a $\frac{2}{3}$ chance of losing zero. The explanations for $\frac{2}{3}W$, $-\frac{2}{3}W$ are analogous. This is known as a *constant sum game* because the payoffs of both players, when added together in any cell of Table 7.4, result in a zero payoff; the gains to any player are exactly offset by the losses to the other. The MSNE for

Table 7.4 Testing for a MSNE in Mookherjee and Sopher (1997)

	1	2	3	4
1	$W, -W$	$0, 0$	$0, 0$	$W, -W$
2	$0, 0$	$0, 0$	$W, -W$	$W, -W$
3	$0, 0$	$W, -W$	$\frac{1}{3}W, -\frac{1}{3}W$	$\frac{1}{3}W, -\frac{1}{3}W$
4	$0, 0$	$0, 0$	$\frac{2}{3}W, -\frac{2}{3}W$	$W, -W$

this game can now be calculated using any of the methods given above. For Games 1 and 3 in their paper, the MSNE is for players to play strategies 1, 2, 3, and 4 with respective probabilities: 37.25%, 25%, 37.25%, 0%. By contrast, row players in Game 1 play these four strategies with the respective probabilities: 28.75%, 20.50%, 44.0%, 6.75%. In Game 2, these respective probabilities were: 34.75%, 13.25%, 42.25%, 9.75%. A chi-squared statistical test rejects the hypothesis that the observed probabilities of play are equal to the probabilities predicted in a MSNE. Mookherjee and Sopher (1997) write (p.109) that these rejections of a MSNE "at the aggregate level, and not just at the level of individual decision making, implies that it cannot even be treated as an acceptable 'as if' theory."

In the *equilibrium in beliefs interpretation* (Binmore, 1991), players exclusively play pure strategies, but across all players, the proportions playing various strategies is consistent with a MSNE. But players do play mixed strategies; we do not observe some football players who always kick only to the left or only to the right of a goalie. When they play mixed strategies, the probabilities with which players choose their strategies is not consistent with a MSNE (Shachat, 2002).

3. The evidence from sports contexts is often cited as the best evidence for a MSNE (Palacios-Huerta, 2003; Walker and Wooders, 2001). We have noted the serial correlation in such data that is not predicted by a MSNE. There are additional issues related to

   (i) the temporal aspects of choice in, say, penalty kicks in football and the difference in conditions and levels of training/skills of the players over time, and

   (ii) the fact that there is not just a left and a right in tennis serves but many other multidimensional aspects such as the slice, speed, topspin, and depth of serve that are difficult to take account of in the data.

   In addition, one may query the external validity of this evidence. Sports contexts involve human motor skills that are instinctive and learned over a long evolutionary history; for example, body feints in football and tennis, that are used to implement a mixed strategy play, may be evolutionary in nature. It is not clear if this has external validity for other explicitly social or economic contexts, say, for savings behavior, or for the choice of a pension scheme, or for firms competing to introduce a new product. In an explicitly economic context, the individual and aggregate MSNE predictions were rejected by the evidence (Collins and Sherstyuk, 2000). Furthermore, even in a sports context, the presumed success (or lack of it) of MSNE, is not portable across different contexts. When successful penalty kickers or tennis servers play a lab game that has a MSNE, then they often fail to play it (Levitt et al., 2010; Wooders, 2010).

To summarize, the evidence in favor of MSNE is weak, while the evidence against it is reasonably strong. We should, of course, be interested in how players play mixed strategies, but we need to move beyond a MSNE.

7.3 Dynamic Games of Complete Information

So far we have looked at static games of complete information. However, in many situations, players may be asked to make choices sequentially, after observing the choices of others; this gives rise to the class of *dynamic games*. We have seen several examples of dynamic experimental games in Part II (e.g., ultimatum game, gift exchange game, public goods game with punishment, trust game). All these were games of complete information, that is, when making their choices, each player knew the past actions taken by the other players in the game, and their utility functions. Thus, we use the generic name, *dynamic games of complete information*. The main solution method that we use to solve such games is subgame perfect equilibrium that is implemented by *backward induction* in this class of games.

7.3.1 An Introduction to the Basic Concepts

Let us offer a brief introduction to the basic concepts first, which also have a bearing on understanding the *strategy method in experiments*.

The *centipede game*, drawn in Figure 7.1, is a dynamic game of complete information. It plays the same generic role in this class of games, as was played by the PD game in static games of complete information. It was introduced by Robert W. Rosenthal in 1981 in the context of the discussion of the chain store paradox. However, Binmore (1987) christened it as the *centipede game*; on account of the unmistakable resemblance between the game in Figure 7.1 and the metameric multilegged creature with two legs per each body segment.

In Figure 7.1, we show a four-move centipede game from McKelvey and Palfrey (1992). This is a game played between two players who choose one of their two actions, Across (A) or Down (D), *sequentially*, and player 1 gets to make the first choice. When it is the turn of any player to move, they can either choose (1) D and end the game so that each player receives the payoffs, measured in US dollars, shown in Figure 7.1, or (2) choose A and give the other player an opportunity to take an action, either A or D. The first payoff in any pair of payoffs is player 1's

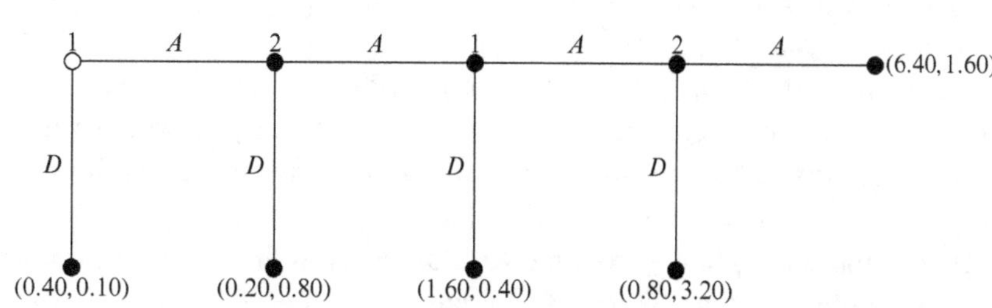

Figure 7.1 A four-move centipede game

payoff and the second payoff is player 2's payoff. For instance, when player 1 makes the initial move, a choice of D ends the game with respective payoffs of 0.40 and 0.10 to players 1 and 2. If player 1 chooses A, then player 2 is given the chance to make a choice between A and D. Player 2 can either choose D and end the game with respective payoffs of 0.20 to player 1 and 0.80 to player 2, or choose A and pass the move back to player 1. The remaining game can be read-off in this manner.

The representation of the dynamic game under complete information in Figure 7.1 is known as a *game tree* representation, or an *extensive form representation* of the game (compare this to the normal form representation of static games of complete information). The construction of the extensive form obeys certain rules and the basic unit of the game tree is a *node*. We use the centipede game to illustrate the concepts. There is an *initial node* at which the first mover makes a choice (in this case player 1). There are *decision nodes* at which players make their choices. In the game in Figure 7.1 there are four nodes, hence it is known as a four-move centipede game. There is a set of nodes where no decisions are made. These are the *terminal nodes* and they list the payoffs of the players (there are five terminal nodes in Figure 7.1). Starting from any node, we can always find a unique path back to the initial node (think of trees and how starting from any branch you can find a unique path back to the root of a tree). This is all we need at the moment, but we would need more machinery if we were describing a dynamic game of incomplete information.

Strategies in dynamic games are *complete contingent plans of action* for each player, specifying what each player will choose whenever the player has a chance to make a choice in the game. Some examples of a strategy for a player in the centipede game are: (1) Always play D whenever asked to move; (2) Always play A whenever asked to make a move; (3) Play A unless it is the last decision node, otherwise play D. Thus, the actions by the players at any decision node are still A and D, but strategies are more complicated in dynamic games.

Within the class of dynamic games of complete information, let us now introduce the distinction between the *backward induction outcome*, the *subgame perfect equilibrium*, and a *Nash equilibrium of an extensive form game*. This will show why we need to modify the solution concept of a Nash equilibrium for static games; the difference between an outcome and an equilibrium; and the rationale for the strategy method in experiments.

A *subgame* of an extensive form game of complete information begins at any of the decision nodes, say, it begins at node n. A subgame contains node n and includes all the decision nodes and the terminal nodes that can be arrived at following node n. For instance, in the four-move centipede game, we have a new subgame starting at nodes 1, 2, 3, and 4. The subgame starting with the node $n = 1$, or the initial node, is of course the entire game, which is trivially also a subgame of itself.

A subgame perfect equilibrium is any equilibrium of an extensive form game such that the strategies of the players constitute a Nash equilibrium in every possible subgame. We show that the subgame perfect equilibrium refines the set of Nash equilibria by ruling out noncredible threats by players to take a particular action.

Let us choose a concrete example to illustrate the difference between the three concepts. Consider the two-player extensive form game in Figure 7.2. Player 1 who gets the first move can choose either T or B. Having observed the choice of player 1, which constitutes the history

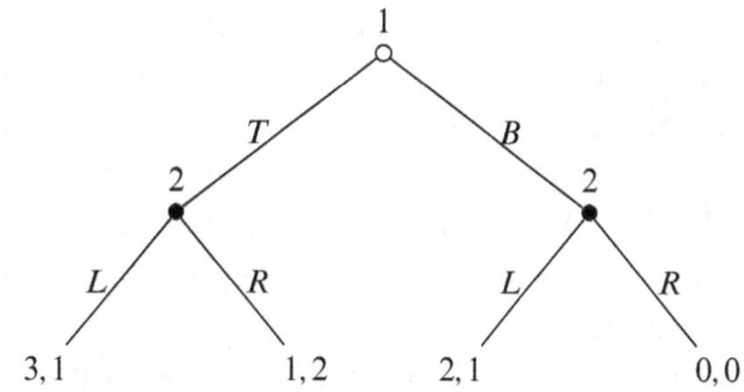

Figure 7.2 A two-player, two-stage extensive form game

of the game for player 2, player 2 can then choose either L or R. The payoffs for each possible strategy profile of the two players are shown at the four terminal nodes; the first payoff belongs to player 1 and the second payoff to player 2.

Backward induction outcome: If player 1 plays T, then player 2 optimally chooses R (because $2 > 1$) and if player 1 chooses B, then player 2 optimally chooses L (because $1 > 0$). Player 1 is assumed capable of computing the optimal choices of player 2 for each possible history of the game where player 2 might be called upon to make a choice; this is part of the rationality requirements for the game. If this assumption holds true, then player 1 knows that if he plays T, the outcome will be (T, R), giving player 1 a payoff of 1. If player 1 chooses B, he knows that player 2 will play L, so the outcome will be (B, L), giving player 1 a payoff of 2. Since $2 > 1$, player 1 chooses B. Thus, the unique backward induction outcome of the game is (B, L).

Subgame perfect equilibrium: The backward induction outcome is a specific outcome. By contrast, a subgame perfect equilibrium is a choice of strategies by each player for the entire game, such that when that choice is restricted to any subgame, it is a Nash equilibrium in that subgame. Recall that in extensive form games, a strategy is a complete contingent plan of action. Thus, player 2's strategy specifies a choice of L or R, corresponding to each possible choice made by player 1: T or B. Thus, the possible strategies of player 2 are, (L, L), (L, R), (R, L), (R, R); the first strategy in any pair of strategies denotes player 2's choice when player 1 plays T and the second strategy is the choice when player 1 plays B. For, instance, the strategy (L, R) of player 2 means that player 2 will play L if player 1 plays T and play R if player 1 plays B; while the strategy (R, R) means that player 2 will choose R, irrespective of the strategy chosen by player 1.

For the extensive form game in Figure 7.2, the subgame perfect equilibrium is $(B, (R, L))$. If we take the entire game starting from the initial node as a subgame, then in the strategy profile $(B, (R, L))$ each player plays a best response to the strategies of the other. Given the strategies of player 2, it is a best response for player 1 to play B rather than T because $2 > 1$. Given that player 1 has played B, the choice of L by player 2 is optimal (the choice of R in response to T is payoff irrelevant in this case). Now let us consider the two subgames where player 2 makes the initial move. Within each of these subgames, and conditional on having reached any of these subgames, player 2 must play a best response. For the subgame starting with the node where player 1 has already played T, the best response of player 2 is to play R; and in the other subgame, the best response is to play L. Hence, $(B, (R, L))$ is indeed a subgame perfect equilibrium.

To summarize, the backward induction outcome is (B, L) and the subgame perfect equilibrium is $(B, (R, L))$. The distinction highlights the difference between an "outcome" and an "equilibrium." Note that, in experiments, we only observe the actual choices of the players, and not the strategies that they might hold in their heads. So, if we played the game in Figure 7.2, say, in a lab experiment, then we would only observe the actual choices made by players 1 and 2. This can allow us to check if the backward induction prediction (B, L) is successful or not in explaining the data. However, for whatever reason, we might also wish to elicit the strategies of players in all possible situations, including the ones that differ from the actually observed equilibrium outcomes.

In order to check for the entire strategy profile in a subgame perfect equilibrium in experiments, we can employ the *strategy method*. In the strategy method, applied to the game in Figure 7.2, an experimental economist will typically proceed as follows.

1. Ask player 1 about the optimal choice. Say, player 1 reveals the optimal choice to be B.
2. Without revealing the optimal choice of player 1 to player 2, ask player 2 to state the optimal choice for every possible node in the game where player 2 has a chance to make a choice. Suppose player 2 says: "If player 1 plays T, I will play R; and if player 1 plays B, I will play L."
3. Once both players have made their strategy choices, the actual strategies of both players are implemented. In this case, the implemented choices are simply (B, L).

What have we learned? Given the hypothetically elicited choices above, we can not only confirm the backward induction outcome for this game, but we can also confirm the subgame perfect equilibrium. Of course, Figure 7.2 presents a very simple game where one of the two choices of player 2 is always dominated. But real life is almost always more complicated. We shall see a similar example of a two-stage extensive form game in Example 8.8, which presents a more nuanced situation where player 2 tries to infer the intentions of player 1 from the actions chosen by player 1.

Some experimental economists express skepticism about the strategy method on the grounds that:

(i) it may impose excessive cognitive load on experimental subjects, and
(ii) their choices at one node might be influenced by what they have chosen at another node.

It is true that the time horizon over which subjects have to make choices in experiments is a short one. However, in real life strategic environments, surely people do consider the implications of alternative actions, even those that they do not take, in a range of eventualities that they might be asked to act upon in. This basic idea is implemented in the strategy method. Another argument in favor of the method is that unless someone comes up with a clever alternative, this provides the only way of getting a self-report (typically incentivized in experiments) from players about their deep underlying contingent strategies.

Nash equilibrium: We now compute the Nash equilibria of this game. We write the normal form for this game in Table 7.5, which shows strategies as complete contingent plans of actions. There are two Nash equilibria, $(B, (R, L))$ and $(T, (R, R)$; the payoffs corresponding to these equilibria are shown in bold in Table 7.5. However, the Nash equilibrium $(T, (R, R)$ relies on a non-credible threat on the part of player 2 to play R whenever player 1 plays B (player 2 prefers L in this case). In other words, in the subgame starting with the play of B by player 1,

Table 7.5 The normal form corresponding to the extensive form game in Figure 7.2

	(L, L)	(L, R)	(R, L)	(R, R)
T	3, 1	3, 1	1, 2	**1, 2**
B	2, 1	0, 0	**2, 1**	0, 0

the choice of R by player 2 cannot be a part of the Nash equilibrium in that subgame. Hence, the requirement of subgame perfection allows us to rule out the Nash equilibrium $(T, (R, R))$. Subgame perfection, thus, rules out non-credible threats by players to choose certain actions.

7.3.2 An Analysis of the Centipede Game

In light of our discussion above, we now ask: What is the predicted outcome of the centipede game (see Figure 7.1), or what equilibrium strategy choices can we expect under neoclassical game theory?

The joint payoffs of the players are maximized if each player were to keep choosing A; this leads to the terminal payoffs 6.40 for player 1 and 1.60 for player 2, for a grand total payoff of 8.00, as shown in Figure 7.1. Will players be sufficiently patient and keep choosing A to end up with a pot of gold in the end? We use *backward induction* to solve this game. If we go to the very last decision node, player 2 prefers D to A because $3.20 > 1.60$. Let us now fold the game tree back one node and consider the decision at the penultimate node, where player 1 chooses between A and D, knowing fully well that a rational player 2 will pick D at the last node, giving player 1 a payoff of 0.80. This is part of the rationality requirements for players in neoclassical game theory. Player 1 now prefers D to A because $1.60 > 0.80$. Folding the game tree backwards, one decision node at a time, we find that each decision maker, when they get a chance to make a choice, and believing others are rational and believing they believe in the rationality of the player and so on, picks D (the reader should check this).

Thus, the unique prediction under neoclassical game theory is that player 1, at the very first node, will pick D, and end the game, ensuring respective payoffs of 0.40 for himself and 0.10 for player 2, for a total of only 0.50. By contrast, if players had continued to play A, the joint payoffs could have been 8.00 in the end. The equilibrium outcome is the most suboptimal outcome possible (just as the Nash equilibrium outcome (D, D) was in the PD game). When McKelvey and Palfrey (1992) put this prediction to the test, they found that there is a probability of only 7% that subjects play D at the very first node. When they added two more nodes to the game in Table 7.1, effectively turning it into a six-move centipede game, then they found that there is a probability of only 1% that players play D at the first node. By contrast, the probability of playing D at the third and fourth nodes in the four-move game is found to be much higher, respectively, 65% and 75%. Thus, while players might not always achieve the pot of gold at the end of the rainbow, in actual practice they go a fair distance towards it.

Someone who is steeped in neoclassical game theory may defend the rejection of the neoclassical prediction by arguing along the following lines. “Rational subjects” are not confident of the rationality of others, hence, they play A rather than D because they expect the other "irrational" player to play A. This is a common defense of neoclassical game theory in the face of experimental violations, but nevertheless it needs to be addressed. Empirical evidence rules out this possibility (Fey et al., 1996; McKelvey and Palfrey, 1998, García-Pola et al., 2020). Furthermore, we can also rule out the possibility that players play A simply because they are altruistic towards the other player (García-Pola et al., 2020).

Could rejections of the neoclassical game theory predictions based on backward induction arise because student subjects are not well-versed in backward induction, that is, perhaps these experiments lack external validity? In order to test this potential objection, an unusual subject pool, highly ranked chess players based on their Elo points rankings, has been used to play the centipede game as well as other related games that can be solved by backward induction. In carefully controlled experiments, Levitt et al. (2011) showed that conformity with the backward induction play is low, even when chess players played against each other. Thus, even if chess players routinely use backward induction in the game of chess, this skill is not easily portable to other games.

In the centipede game, the observed failure to play the outcome predicted by neoclassical game theory does not appear entirely to be a failure of backward induction. It could also arise from boundedly rational play such as that from level-k models or from a quantal response equilibrium. These possibilities are examined in Section 7.8 (Kawagoe and Takizawa, 2012; García-Pola et al., 2020). Or perhaps the explanation for behavior in the centipede game is even simpler – subjects may perceive this to be a cooperative game and being conditionally reciprocal and having an initial desire to cooperate (see Part II) play A at the first few nodes. We take up the centipede game again in Section 7.8 and consider alternative explanations for it.

Part II has already considered several rejections of the homo-economicus model. This includes evidence from the gift exchange game with and without punishment; the trust game; the public goods game with and without punishment. However, such tests are a joint test of self-regarding preferences and the ability to solve a game using backward induction. Both features, of course, are essential components in neoclassical economics and the rejection of the predictions from these games is also a rejection of the homo-economicus model. Since individual preferences are typically unobservable, as is the ability to perform backward induction, it is difficult to pinpoint the source of this rejection – failure of self regarding preferences alone; failure of backward induction alone; or a failure of both. This leads to a potential confound in the interpretation. However, the games in Part II (unless we add the punishment options) are simple two-stage games where failure of backward induction is unlikely to be a problem. For instance, it seems unlikely that when making an offer, the proposer in an ultimatum game does not try to calculate if the offer will be accepted or rejected by a responder. But this is the essence of what is required in backward induction in this case. Thus, the rejection of the homo-economicus predictions in Part II are most likely to have arisen from a failure of self-regarding preferences.

However, moving away from two-stage games, in slightly more complicated contexts, it is implausible that humans have the cognitive ability to engage in the backward induction outcome. Let us consider a fairly simple bread and butter example in economics. An individual lives for 30 time periods and in each period his income is uncertain. Income can take one of three possible values Y_1, Y_2, Y_3, with associated probabilities $p_1, p_2, 1 - p_1 - p_2$. In every period, the individual knows which of the three possible income levels has materialized, and makes a consumption-savings choice, that is, how much to consume and how much to save from the current income. This is a dynamic game of complete information and the solution method is backward induction. Economists use a technique called *dynamic programming* to solve such problems; see Section 9.3 for more details. It can be shown that an individual needs to make 68 trillion calculations in order to solve this problem. The interested reader can pursue more details in Dhami and Sunstein (2022). It is implausible that anyone could do these calculations. Yet, the maintained assumption in neoclassical economics is that the man in the street can effortlessly do these calculations or at least act "as if" they can. The calculations needed to solve such problems increase exponentially with the number of decisions and with the number of income levels; indeed the required calculations can easily exceed the number of particles in the universe making the entire exercise pointless.

We shall once again encounter dynamic games of complete information in Section 8.3 where we consider a three-stage bargaining game. We shall use it, in conjunction with another useful method of testing for backward induction, the mouselab software.

7.4 Human Cooperation in Repeated Games

Let us revisit the topic of human cooperation that we took up in Part II through various experimental games. The main motivation for human cooperation in neoclassical game theory is a desire to maximize one's own long-run material payoffs. So players cynically cooperate if the gains from cooperation outweigh the losses from noncooperation. In other words, the desire for cooperation is purely *instrumental*, and not *intrinsic*, which goes against the grain of much empirical evidence.

Consider again the PD game in Table 7.1 and suppose, for simplicity, that the utilities of players are identical to material payoffs. Assume that the two players repeatedly play the PD situation forever, an infinite number of times. Suppose that the strategy for each player is to start by choosing cooperation, C, but if the opponent ever chooses D, then punish the opponent by choosing defect, D, forever. Let us assume that players discount future payoffs by a factor $0 < \delta < 1$, as, say, in the EDU model in Part III.

Can the strategy profile in which both players choose to cooperate, C, be sustained in this repeated game? If any player chooses C forever, given that the other player continues to play their part of the strategy profile by choosing C, then each gets a payoff of 2 in every period of their lives (see Table 7.1). Thus, the lifetime payoff of player 1 from cooperating is $U(C) = 2 + 2\delta + 2\delta^2 + \ldots..$, where $0 < \delta < 1$. But this is just the sum of a infinite geometric series, so it can be written as

$$U(C) = \frac{2}{1-\delta}.$$

Now suppose that player 1 were tempted to defect just this once to get a higher payoff of 4 rather than 2 (see Table 7.1), given that player 2 chooses to cooperate as part of their strategy. Player 2 immediately finds out that player 1 defected, so as part of his strategy player 2 chooses D forever in the future. The best response of player 1, when player 2 chooses D, is also to choose D forever in the future. This gives player 1 a payoff of 1 in every subsequent time period. In other words, the lifetime payoff from this one-off temptation to defect is $U(D) = 4 + \delta + \delta^2 + \delta^3 + \ldots$. This too is the sum of a simple infinite geometric series, thus we can rewrite it as

$$U(D) = 4 + \frac{\delta}{1-\delta}.$$

Clearly, cooperation in the current time period is better than defection for any player, in any time period, if $U(C) \geq U(D)$ or $\frac{2}{1-\delta} > 4 + \frac{\delta}{1-\delta}$, which can be simplified and written as the restriction

$$\delta > \frac{2}{3}. \tag{7.3}$$

While many variations of this story and many extra complications can be added, the basic insight is captured in (7.3).[4] Players will cooperate, and not succumb to the temptation to defect, only if they are sufficiently patient; in the example above this requires that $\delta > \frac{2}{3}$. The evolutionary biologist and sociobiologist, Robert Trivers, proposed an explanation along these lines and called it *reciprocal altruism* (Trivers, 1971). However, he was thinking in terms of a trait of *reciprocal altruism* being hardwired into us as a product of human evolution and not of conscious deliberation.

If players instead interacted only a finite number of times, and not infinitely many numbers of times, as in the derivation of (7.3) above, the results are very different. A finite dynamic game of complete information can be solved by backward induction. Here self-regarding and amoral players (typical assumptions in neoclassical game theory) will both choose their strictly dominant strategy, D, in the last round of the game because there is no future to worry about. In the penultimate round, both players will know that rational players will defect in the last round, so there are no benefits to cooperating and sustaining a reputation for cooperation. Hence, they both choose the strictly dominant action D again. We can keep unraveling the choices of players backwards every period, and find that rational players always defect (as in the centipede game). Thus, cooperation cannot be sustained, under the conditions stated above, unless the interaction between players lasts forever.

We can achieve partial or full cooperation in the following two extensions of the theory.

1. If players are unsure of the rationality of each other, then they might cooperate for a few rounds, develop a reputation for being cooperative, cynically milking this reputation for a while, and towards the end of the finitely repeated game choosing to defect; this is sometimes known as the *gang of four model*, due to Kreps and Wilson (1982) and Kreps et al. (1982). It is unclear how relevant this purely theoretical argument is to explain either real world cooperation, or the results from experiments. It presents a cynical and opportunistic view of human behavior that we do not always observe in the data. In the context of centipede games, this explanation is rejected, as argued above in Section 7.3.
2. If there is probability, $0 < p < 1$, that the game ends at the end of each round and continues with a probability $1 - p$, then this effectively becomes an infinitely repeated game

[4] For instance, players might receive noisy signals of the cooperation levels of others. These signals could be privately observed or publicly observed by all players and players then have to base their decisions on how high or low these observed signals are.

because there is always a chance the game is played forever. This is the preferred method of implementing infinitely repeated games in lab experiments. For a comprehensive survey, organized around the repeated PD game, see Dal Bó and Fréchette (2018), which suggests that it is not easy to sustain cooperation in the lab. One confounding factor with such experiments is that the time horizon in lab experiments is very short and subjects might be making decisions over successive rounds very quickly. The impatience between today and tomorrow, if tomorrow is one minute away, is unlikely to be meaningful, which is problematic in testing theories that rely on a purely impatience-based instrumental explanation for cooperation. Furthermore, the estimation of the discount factor, δ, may be confounded by issues of hyperbolic discounting (see Part III).

The explanation for cooperation in repeated games, also known as the *folk theorem* in economics, relies on a dismal view of human nature that is contradicted by the evidence in Part II. In particular, neoclassical game theory does not entertain the idea that homo-economicus has an *intrinsic desire* to cooperate with others. The folk theorem runs into two kinds of problems. The first is that the theoretical framework is problematic; these arguments are fairly technical and rely, partly, on the suitability of mixed strategies and the purification agenda for repeated games and the interested reader is referred to Gintis (2009, Chapter 10). The second, which is perhaps more fundamental and important, is that the folk theorem ignores the evidence on how humans actually cooperate. There is widespread evidence of human cooperation in finitely repeated interactions where the two caveats to finite game cooperation mentioned above, do not apply readily. Cooperation in the static PD game is not predicted by the folk theorem, yet we observe that a majority of the subjects cooperate. The evidence from Part II indicates that humans are not solely cynically instrumental, amoral, cooperators driven by material gains alone, although this too happens in the rich tapestry of human behavior. But rather, that many individuals have an intrinsic desire to cooperate and that they are conditional cooperators.

7.5 Cooperation as a Historical Accident

Players often work in teams/groups and the outcome that they receive depends on the actions they take, as well as the actions taken by other team/group members. Players might take their actions simultaneously and not know what other team members have chosen, although they might have beliefs about what others are likely to choose. At least two kinds of games have been considered in the literature to study these issues. In *minimum action games*, the outcome for the members of the team depend on the slowest mover in the team, or one who takes the minimum action. Consider, for instance, Adam Smith's classic example of the division of labor in a pin factory. The output, a pin, is produced only when each of the team members have completed their individual task in producing the pin. A second class of games is *median action games*. In these games, the payoff or utility of a player in the team depends on the action chosen by the player and the median action chosen by the team members.

A *continental divide* is an imaginary line that can be drawn across a continent (except Antartica, which does not have a known continental divide) such that if a drop of water falls on either side of the line, it goes on to a different sea or ocean. Thus, purely historical accidents, say, the air speed on that day, lead to significantly different outcomes; two water droplets that accidentally collided and fell on either side of the continental divide, face a very different future. Let us consider a *continental divide game* below, due to Van Huyck et al. (1997), which is an example of a median action game.

Suppose that we have a set of n players. The strategy s_i of any player $i = 1, \dots, n$ is to simultaneously choose a number from the set of first 14 natural numbers $S = \{1, 2, \dots, 14\}$. Once the players have chosen their strategies, the median, M, which will also be a number between 1 and 14, can be determined. The utility, u_i, of player $i = 1, \dots, n$, depends on the chosen strategy, s_i, and the group median, M. One example of such a utility function for player $i = 1, \dots, n$ is the following

$$u_i(s_i, M) = aM - b\,[s_i - M]^2\,;\ a, b > 0. \tag{7.4}$$

In (7.4), a, b are the two parameters, both are strictly positive. The utility of the player is increasing in the group median M (first term) and decreasing in the distance between the strategy chosen by the player and the median value M. Thus, players would like the median value to be as high as possible, and their own choice of strategy to be as close as possible to the median. Using such a utility function for specific parameter values, Van Huyck et al. (1997) use the payoff matrix shown in Figure 7.3 and ask a set of n players to simultaneously choose their strategies from the set $S = \{1, 2, \dots, 14\}$.

In Figure 7.3, player i is the row player who can choose any number from the set $S = \{1, 2, \dots, 14\}$ and the group median value, M, plays the role of the column player. For any combination of a row and a column, we can read off the utility/payoff for player i. Let us first make a prediction for the outcome of this game.

		The median choice of the group, M													
		1	2	3	4	5	6	7	8	9	10	11	12	13	14
Your Choice, s_i	1	45	49	52	55	56	55	46	-59	-88	-105	-117	-127	-135	-142
	2	48	53	58	62	65	66	61	-27	-52	-67	-77	-86	-92	-98
	3	48	54	60	66	70	74	72	1	-20	-32	-41	-48	-53	-58
	4	43	51	58	65	71	77	80	26	8	-2	-9	-14	-19	-22
	5	35	44	52	60	69	77	83	46	32	25	19	15	12	10
	6	23	33	42	52	62	72	82	62	53	47	43	41	39	38
	7	7	18	28	40	51	64	78	75	69	66	64	63	62	62
	8	-13	-1	11	23	37	51	69	83	81	80	80	80	81	82
	9	-37	-24	-11	3	18	35	57	88	89	91	92	94	96	98
	10	-65	-51	-37	-21	-4	15	40	89	94	98	101	104	107	110
	11	-97	-82	-66	-49	-31	-9	20	85	94	100	105	110	114	119
	12	-133	-117	-100	-82	-61	-37	-5	78	91	99	106	112	118	123
	13	173	-156	-137	-118	-96	-69	-33	67	83	94	103	110	117	123
	14	217	-198	-179	-158	-134	-105	-65	52	72	85	95	104	112	120

Figure 7.3 Payoff matrix in the continental divide game. Redrawn from Van Huyck et al. (1997)

Suppose that all players $i = 1, \ldots, n$ are assumed to be identical, that is, they have an identical utility function $u_i = u$. Then, it is plausible that they will choose an identical strategy, say, s, from the set S. If all n players choose an identical strategy, s, then the median for the group also equals s, that is, $M = s$.

We now look for a *symmetric Nash equilibrium* in this game in which all players choose an identical strategy, s^* (so the median is $M = s^*$). A symmetric Nash equilibrium requires that none of the players can improve their utility by picking another strategy s_i from the set S, given that everyone else in the group sticks to their equilibrium strategy, s^*. In other words, we require that for each player $i = 1, \ldots, n$,

$$u(s^*, s^*) \geq u(s_i, s^*); s_i \in S. \tag{7.5}$$

Since the utility functions of all players are identical, we only need to check the condition in (7.5) once. In (7.5), we have assumed that the number of players is large, so each player ignores the effect of their own chosen strategy on the median. Otherwise, as player i changes the strategy from s^* to s_i, the median will not stay fixed at s^*. Alternatively, players simply ignore the effects of their own strategy choices on the median value.

From the payoff matrix in Figure 7.3, it is not hard to see when the inequality in (7.5) is satisfied. If the median, M, is between 1 to 7, then the payoffs of player i are high from a choice of a number between 1 to 7, and low from a choice of a number between 8 to 14 (shown by the shaded region). However, if the median, M, is between 8 to 14, then the payoffs of player i are high from a choice of a number between 8 to 14, but low from the choice of a number between 1 to 7 (also shown by the shaded region). Thus, players never make choices in the two shaded regions in Figure 7.3. There are two symmetric Nash equilibria in Figure 7.3 that satisfy the requirement in (7.5) and are shown in bold: $s^* = 3$ (with median $M = 3$) and $s^* = 12$ (with median $M = 12$). Notice that player i cannot improve own-payoff by choosing any other strategy in either of these two cases (compare the payoffs of 60 and 112, respectively, with other payoffs in the same columns to verify this).

Suppose that the continental divide game is played repeatedly with subjects, over 15 rounds. Figure 7.4 shows the results for 10 different groups who played the game (see the legend just above the X-axis of the Figure for the groups). The dotted horizontal line between the numbers 7 and 8 is known as a separatix, and is the analogue of the continental divide that we described above. When initial play in a group starts below the separatix (i.e., the median lies between 1 and 7), then play over successive rounds converges towards a choice of $s^* = 3$. However, when play starts above the separatix, so the median lies between 8 and 14, then play converges towards the second symmetric Nash equilibrium of $s^* = 12$.

Thus, pure historical accidents (in this case, the first round play) can determine the subsequent path of play. We reach this conclusion through many different routes in this chapter. It also arises in the case of conventions that can be purely accidental, such as driving on the left or the right of the road (Section 7.9). In evolutionary game theory (Section 8.4) the choice among different equilibria is also history-dependent. Thus, purely historical accidents also provide us with a selection criterion when we have multiple Nash equilibria.

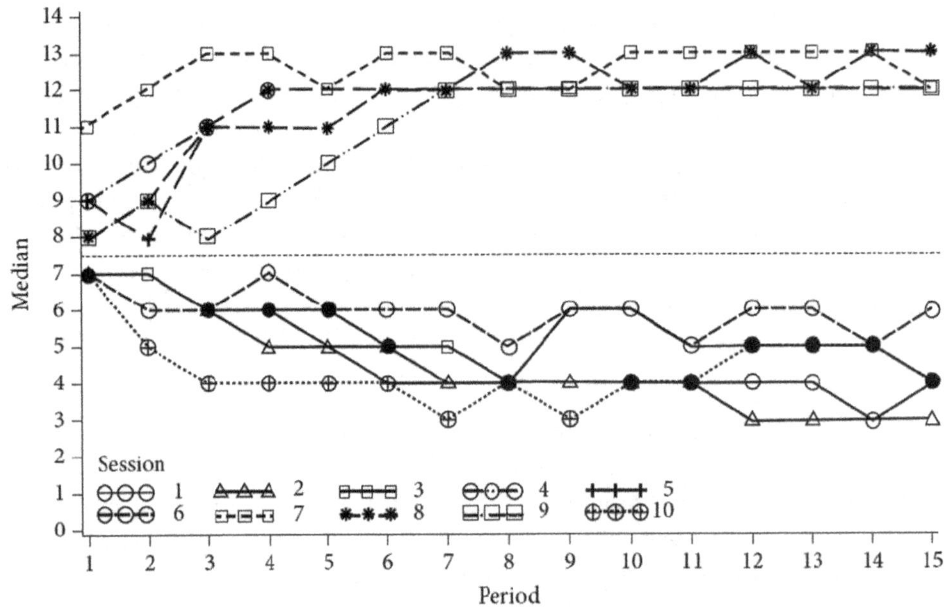

Figure 7.4 Time pattern of play over 15 rounds of the continental divide game. Source: Van Huyck et al. (1997)

7.6 A Brief Note on Incomplete Information

In our discussion of static and dynamic games above, we have assumed that all players have complete information, that is, they know everything there is to know about the game. However, in many cases, players may be unaware of relevant aspects of information about the other players, for example, about their utility or cost functions. This book does not require readers to have the pre-requisite knowledge to understand this class of games. Hence, our discussion in this section is fairly informal. We analyze this class of games in Section 7.8.4 in more detail through a concrete example.

Consider the following three examples.

1. A firm hiring a worker might not know the worker's ability, say, high or low, which is critical in the hiring and salary decisions. Workers are more likely to know their own abilities.
2. Buyers of used cars might not know if a car on the market is of low quality (a lemon) or of high quality (a peach), although the seller of the car is likely to know this information.
3. Firms competing in a market and simultaneously choosing their quantities know their own cost functions, but might not know each other's cost functions, an important factor in deciding how much they should produce themselves.

Examples 1, 2 illustrate *one-sided asymmetric information*, where one side to a transaction possesses the relevant information but the other side does not. Example 3 illustrates *two-sided asymmetric information*, where both sides do not know payoff relevant features of the other side. More generally, these are examples of *incomplete information*. The informed side of the market may often wish to lie about the relevant characteristics of their product, for example, low-ability workers claiming to be high-ability workers; sellers of lemons claiming their cars to be peaches; firms signaling that they have low costs to dissuade competitors from producing too much output.

We can extend the analysis in Sections 7.2, 7.3 to, respectively, static games of incomplete information, and dynamic games of incomplete information. Several observations are pertinent here.

1. Incomplete information is important. Economic actors in the real world do face these situations on a regular basis and try to solve them (the three examples above are realistic). However, several institutional features, mentioned below, may mitigate its impact.
2. There are often institutional solutions to the problem of incomplete information. For instance, used cars could be checked by an independent mechanic for quality before purchase; governments may mandate full disclosure of the contents of packaged retail food; and independent letters of reference and previous record may give a reasonable picture of a worker's ability.
3. There are also many private solutions to the asymmetric information problem. Either the informed side, or the uninformed side, may engage in actions that either *signals high quality* (*signaling games*) or *screens out low quality* (*screening games*). For instance, in *signaling games*, the informed party, say, sellers of high quality cars (peaches) may offer a long enough warranty that cannot reasonably be matched by sellers of low-quality cars (lemons), hence, successfully signaling their type. Such an equilibrium where the two types can be distinguished, or separated, through their actions is known as a *separating equilibrium*. On the other hand, if warranties are simply too costly to offer and car sellers of peaches and lemons cannot offer any warranties, then we have a *pooling equilibrium*, whereby one cannot distinguish between the two qualities of cars.

   In *screening games*, on the other hand, the uninformed party, say, an insurance firm offering life insurance to an applicant whose health status is uncertain, offers clever contracts that screen out applicants whose health status is bad. For instance, the insurance firm may offer a contract that gives low payouts for the first two years, hence, guarding against the possibility that the applicant has a hidden/terminal health condition that requires high immediate payouts.

The experimental study of static and dynamic games of incomplete information often focuses on signaling games. It uses the relevant theory to predict a separating or a pooling equilibrium, and then tests it with data. Signaling and screening games, as well as the solutions suggested above to the simple problems appear reasonable and persuasive. However, the neoclassical game theoretic analysis of these situations imposes even more stringent cognitive requirements on the players, as compared to games of complete information. This includes incredibly strong restrictions on the beliefs of the players that are nothing short of heroic. The relevant notion of equilibrium in this case is a *perfect Bayesian Nash equilibrium*, of which the separating and pooling equilibria considered above are two special cases. In particular, there can be a multiplicity of equilibria and in order to narrow the set of equilibria down, one needs further restrictions. These are refinements of a perfect Bayesian Nash equilibrium such as the intuitive criterion, but a discussion lies outside the scope of this book. Empirical support for the refinements is poor and the support for a perfect Bayesian Nash equilibrium in simple signaling games is mixed (Camerer, 2003; Dhami, 2020, Vol. IV).

Readers who wish to explore these issues further will need a good course in game theory as a prerequisite, which this book does not impose. However, the following observations are in order.

1. In strategic interactions between players, the typical assumption in neoclassical game theory is one of *common priors* – all players have identical beliefs about the unknown "types" of the other players. For instance, in the used car market, the two types are lemons and peaches. Buyers in markets for used cars are all assumed to have identical beliefs about what percentage of cars are lemons and what percentage are peaches. Neoclassical game theory fails to specify the source of the common priors. Common priors can be relaxed, and players can have their own individual prior beliefs, but the analysis can then become extremely complicated; one would need to specify beliefs of players about the individual priors of others, and beliefs about such beliefs. It is highly unlikely that players in most situations would have the cognitive capacity to reason in this manner. If individuals struggle to find the Nash equilibria in complete information games beyond very basic games, then conforming with the requirements for equilibria in signaling and screening games is fairly unlikely.
2. Players update their beliefs in static and dynamic games of incomplete information using *Bayes' Law* (see Part V). There is good evidence that compliance with Bayes' Law is low, certainly not high enough to justify its use in economic models (see Chapter 9).
3. The plausible predictions listed above (sellers of high-quality cars offering long warranties to separate themselves, insurance firms offering low payouts for the first two years to separate out high health risk applicants) can also arise from a variety of other frameworks. For instance, from trial and error in low rationality environments; from simple human deduction; or a Eureka moment that is followed by others, without ever requiring the cognitive complexity embedded within a perfect Bayesian Nash equilibrium.
4. In situations where there is one-sided asymmetric information, such as bargaining under one-sided asymmetric information, there is little empirical support for the predictions of neoclassical game theory (see Dhami, 2020, Vol. IV).
5. Under asymmetric information, players have "beliefs" about things that they do not know about the other players. In signaling and screening games, the appropriate equilibrium concept in neoclassical game theory, perfect Bayesian Nash equilibrium, requires consistency between beliefs and actions. For an example, see Section 7.8.3 below where we discuss a quantal response equilibrium. This is an extremely challenging cognitive requirement that is not supported by the empirical evidence in many different games. There is no guarantee that this condition will hold even when the game is repeated a large number of times.

7.7 Coordination Failures

The problems of human cooperation and coordination are closely related and difficult to separate. We begin with a definition.

Definition 7.3 *(Pareto improvement and Pareto optimality) Suppose that we have a set of $i = 1, \ldots, n$ players who face several potential alternatives from some set of alternatives, S. Each alternative is characterized by a distinct allocation that specifies the utility received by each of the n*

Table 7.6 A 2 × 2 coordination game

	O	*T*
O	200, 600	0, 0
T	0, 0	600, 200

players. Suppose that X and Y are two possible alternatives. Each of these alternatives is associated with the following respective allocations, or utilities to the n players.

$$(x_1, x_2, \ldots, x_n), (y_1, y_2, \ldots, y_n).$$

Then the alternative X offers a Pareto improvement relative to the alternative Y, if the utilities of all players are relatively higher in X as compared to Y, and the utility of at least one player is strictly higher under X. Thus $x_i \geq y_i$ *for all i, and there exists some j such that* $x_j > y_j$*. An alternative, say P, is a Pareto optimal alternative, if starting at P, no further Pareto improvements are possible.*

We can illustrate *coordination failures* by using the public goods game experiments in Part II. Recall that in the solution to the privately optimal problem, all players free-ride on others, and receive a payoff of zero.[5] However, if all of them had contributed their full endowments to the public good, then, as in the socially optimal solution, each would have received a payoff of 36. The receipt of 36 instead of 0 for each player is a *Pareto improvement*. In fact, the socially optimal solution, where each receives a payoff of 36, is the *Pareto optimal solution*, where no further Pareto improvements are possible. Coordination failures arise when players, through their actions, are unable to fully exploit all possible Pareto improvements that are possible, that is, when they fail to reach a Pareto optimal solution. Insofar as reaching the socially optimal solution in the public goods game might require players to cooperate, a high degree of cooperation is required to eliminate coordination failures.

Coordination failures have been extensively studied in game theory. One kind of coordination failure arises in games such as the PD game in Table 7.1. In this game, there is only one Nash equilibrium where both players defect, that is, (D, D), but the Pareto optimal equilibrium which arises when both players cooperate, (C, C), is not a Nash equilibrium at all.

A second type of coordination failure arises when there are multiple Nash equilibria within the same game and both are Pareto optimal. Table 7.6 gives an example of a static, simultaneous move, two-player *battle of sexes game*, taken from Cooper et al. (1990), where each player has two strategies, O and T. The basic story is as follows. The row player, say, the husband prefers the theater (strategy T) while the column player, the wife, prefers the opera (strategy O), but they would rather go with each. Going separately gives them a payoff of zero each. There are two pure strategy Nash equilibria in this game (O, O) and (T, T); the reader should check that starting from any of these two equilibria, and holding fixed the strategy of the other player, no player can increase their payoff by altering their equilibrium strategy. Both equilibria are Pareto optimal and the total payoffs across both players equal 800 in each. There is also a mixed strategy Nash equilibrium (see discussion in Section 7.2.4 above) in which the column player

[5] In our discussion of the public goods problem in Part II, players were self-regarding and, approximately risk neutral over the small monetary payoffs in the experiment. Hence, we may treat monetary payoffs and utilities synonymously in this case.

Table 7.7 A 3 × 3 coordination game

	A	B	C
A	350, 350	350, 250	700, 0
B	250, 350	550, 550	0, 0
C	0, 700	0, 0	600, 600

plays O with probability of 75% and T with a probability of 25%, and the row player plays O with probability 25% and T with a probability of 75%. Each player receives an expected payoff of 150 from each strategy, which is worse than the payoffs in both pure strategy Nash equilibria. However, the two pure strategy Nash equilibria were found to occur less than 42% of the time in the data, suggesting widespread coordination failures.

A third type of coordination failure arises when there are two Nash equilibria but only one of the equilibria is Pareto optimal while the other is not. Coordination failures now arise if players do not choose the Pareto optimal Nash equilibrium. Table 7.7 shows a two-player game from Cooper et al. (1990), where each player has three strategies, A, B, C, and players simultaneously choose their strategies without knowing the strategy of the partner. There are two Nash equilibria in this game, (A, A) and (B, B). The reader should check this by the standard method of no profitable deviations in strategy for any player starting from the equilibrium strategies, and holding fixed the equilibrium strategy of the other player. However, of the two Nash equilibria, (B, B) is Pareto optimal because each player receives a strictly higher payoff relative to (A, A). Across the entire game, the pair of strategies (C, C) is Pareto optimal, but this is not a Nash equilibrium, and it is risky to play C (if your opponent did not play C, then you would get 0). In another treatment, the payoff of 700 was changed to 1000, but this does not alter anything we have said above.

In most cases, players played one of the two Nash equilibria, (A, A) or (B, B). However, they mainly played A, so that widespread coordination failures were observed; each player could have received an extra payoff of 200 if they had managed to coordinate on (B, B). Another reason for playing A is that it appears to be the less risky of all the strategies – players do get a positive payoff irrespective of what the other player does. This is known as a *risk dominant strategy*, and it can be stated more formally, while the Nash equilibrium (B, B) is *payoff dominant* among the two Nash equilibria.[6]

Strategy C is dominated, but it has the obvious appeal that it is the Pareto optimal outcome for the entire game, much like the social planner's solution in the public goods game. However, in neoclassical game theory, only the Nash equilibrium is believed to be the obvious way of playing the game. For this reason, many discussions of coordination failures omit our first category of coordination failures based on our example of free-riding in public goods games. If we changed the payoff of 600, 600 from the strategy profile (C, C) in Table 7.7 to 500, 500, then the strategy profile (C, C) loses its special status and the Nash equilibrium (B, B) is now Pareto optimal across all possible strategy profiles. In this case, we observe more players coordinating on (B, B).

How might we solve coordination problems? In neoclassical economics, there are two main solutions that are taught to students in economics degrees.

[6] Readers interested in formal statements of risk dominance and payoff dominance can consult Dhami (2020, Vol. IV).

(i) Competitive markets are predicted to arrive at a Pareto optimal outcome for all participants under certain extremely stringent conditions such as no public goods, no externalities, and no asymmetric information; this is the *first welfare theorem in economics*. However, the associated conditions are unlikely to be ever met, so the first welfare theorem serves mainly as a benchmark result.
(ii) In the second solution, the Nobel Prize winner Roland Coase proposed a private market solution that takes the form of definite assignment of property rights to the players. In the presence of externalities, when parties can freely and costlessly bargain with each other, this proposal results in an efficient solution, albeit one with distributional consequences.

Bowles (2004) refers to the two solutions discussed above as *utopian capitalism* because while they are elegant and form a useful benchmark, their practical relevance in solving real life coordination problems is limited.

Thomas Schelling proposed that in some coordination problems, *focal points* might serve to coordinate expectations and solve coordination problems. He asked: If two individuals agree to meet in New York at a specified time, but have failed to specify the location, where should they both head off to? New York central train station (known as the Grand Central Terminal) or the Statue of Liberty could be good *focal points* to coordinate on. Hence, focal points may serve to ease the coordination problem by narrowing down the set of possible actions. Focal points need not be geographical or locational. Social norms and conventions may also serve as powerful focal points by coordinating expectations about the behavior of others.

Mehta et al. (1994) found that student subjects perform reasonably well in several familiar coordination problems. Students were given a reward for correctly answering two kinds of questions.

(i) In the "picking condition" subjects simply state their "personal favorite."
(ii) In the "coordinating condition" the reward depended on how closely aligned the answers of subjects were with the answers given by others.

We now state some of these questions, with the modal (most common) response in the brackets. In the brackets we give first the response to the picking condition and then the response to the coordinating condition.

Any year (1971, 1990);
Name any flower (Rose, Rose);
Name any car manufacturer (Ford, Ford);
Write any colour (Blue, Red);
Write any boys name (John, John).

For the first question, most students were born circa 1971 and the experiment was done circa 1990. For favorite color, most people preferred blue, but in the coordinating condition they chose red. This indicates a degree of sophistication in making choices in the coordination condition that are distinct from personal preferences as revealed in the picking condition.

Human language and communication may also serve as a coordination device. In the battle of the sexes game in Table 7.6, consider the possibility of either *one-way communication* (1W) in which one of the two players can send messages (e.g., that "I will play the strategy *T*")

Table 7.8 A simple coordination game

	A	B
A	$800, 800$	$800, 0$
B	$0, 800$	$1000, 1000$

to the other player prior to making choices; or *two-way communication* (2W) in which both players can send such messages. Recall that, in the absence of communication, the coordination rate on any one of the two Nash equilibria was 42% in this game. Under 1W communication, the coordination rate is 96% and under 2W communication it is 58%. Thus, communication enhances coordination, but the type of communication is critical. When the row player sends a message (say, an intention to play T) then in 95% of the cases the coordination is on the row player's preferred outcome (T, T). The reason 2W communication does not work is that both players end up stating their preferred outcome and the coordination conflict is not resolved.

In some cases, 2W communication works rather well. Consider the coordination game in Cooper et al. (1992) shown in Table 7.8. The two Nash equilibria are (A, A) and (B, B) and the Pareto optimal equilibrium is (B, B). The Nash equilibrium (A, A) is the *risk dominant equilibrium* because when each player plays the strategy A, they are guaranteed a safe payoff of 800 irrespective of what the other player chooses. Under 1W communication, the coordination rate on the Pareto optimal Nash equilibrium (B, B) is 53%. However, under 2W communication, the coordination rate on (B, B) increases to 97%. The reason 2W communication works well in this case is that both players send an identical message to play B; there is no conflict of interest here, unlike the battle of the sexes game.

Coordination problems can also be solved through historical accidents such as conventions (Sugden, 1989). Consider, for instance, the convention of driving on the left side of the road (say, the UK) or on the right side of the road (say, the US). Both are Nash equilibria but a choice of one over the other is a historical accident and possibly traceable to small, chance, events; similar examples abound. The literature on coordination games in behavioral economics is very rich and several other important facets of the problem have been explored. These include the roles of loss aversion, group size effects, role of financial incentives, role of intergenerational advice, and recommendations of an external arbitrator; the interested reader can pursue these in Dhami (2020, Vol. IV, Section 1.4).

7.8 Models in Behavioral Game Theory

In contrast to the stringent cognitive requirements in neoclassical game theory, behavioral game theory has developed a range of models to incorporate the boundedly rational behavior of humans who have limited cognitive abilities. In this section, we consider two main behavioral models that have been developed as a response to the violations of the predictions of neoclassical game theory. These are the (1) *level-k model*, and a variant of it, the *cognitive hierarchy* (CH) model, and (2) a *quantal response equilibrium* (QRE). These models apply to the case of games with complete and incomplete information, although our discussion mainly uses static and dynamic games of complete information. We also briefly discuss the concept of a *cursed equilibrium* which offers a way of thinking about introducing cognitive simplifications in the presence of asymmetric equilibrium.

These are not the only models that have been developed as a response to the refutations of neoclassical game theory. There are many other interesting classes of models in behavioral economics that we either omit or discuss very briefly. Some of these require a greater development of the material in Section 7.6 under asymmetric information, hence, a slightly more advanced treatment is called for. The interested reader can consult Camerer (2003) and Dhami (2020, Vol. IV).

Neoclassical game theory imposes very stringent requirements on human cognition and computation. These requirements are unlikely to be met, unless, say, the proposed neoclassical solution coincides with an outcome recommended by a successful social norm, which is then followed on account of the human propensity to follow social norms. But social norms are often different from the equilibria proposed in neoclassical game theory. The Nash equilibrium in the PD game and the backward induction outcome in the centipede game lead to dismal outcomes for the players. One can conjecture that social norms or conventions might help coordinate the player's expectations on more cooperative outcomes that ensure higher payoffs for the players. This forms the subject matter of Section 7.9.

7.8.1 The Level-k Model

We first consider the level-k model; some of the early ideas came from Nagel (1995), Stahl and Wilson (1995), and Ho et al. (1998). Let us motivate the level-k model through a simple game, the *p-beauty contest*. Suppose that a set of $n \geq 2$ players simultaneously choose a number from the interval $[0, 100]$. Denote the choice of player i by x_i, $i = 1, \dots, n$ and the average of these choices across all players by $\overline{x} = \frac{1}{n}(x_1 + \cdots + x_n)$. Let $p > 0$ be a positive number. The winner of the p-beauty contest is the player whose guess is closest to the target number $p\overline{x}$. If there is more than one winner, the prize, say, $z > 0$, is shared equally between the winners.

Suppose, for instance, we pick $p = \frac{2}{3}$, and suppose, hypothetically, that the average is $\overline{x} = 51$, then the target number is $p\overline{x} = \frac{2}{3} \times 51 = 34$, so the winner is the player whose choice x_i is closest to 34. Of course, when making their choices, players do not know what others have chosen, so they cannot know $\overline{x}$ either. Which number in the interval $[0, 100]$ should any player choose? Pause for a moment to make your own choice as if you were one of the players, before reading on.

Since this is a static game of complete information where players choose actions simultaneously, neoclassical game theory requires us to compute the Nash equilibrium. We claim that the Nash equilibrium of this game is for each player $i = 1, \dots, n$ to choose the number $x_i = 0$, so that the average $\overline{x} = 0$. The target number is $\frac{2}{3}\overline{x} = 0$ so that a guess of zero will win the prize. To verify that this is a Nash equilibrium, we use Definition 7.1 to check if any of the players can improve their payoff by choosing a different number in the interval $[0, 100]$. If any player, say, player $i = 1, \dots, n$ chooses a strictly positive number $x_i > 0$ (when all others choose 0), then $\overline{x} = \frac{x_i}{n}$ and the new target number is $\frac{2}{3}\overline{x} = \frac{2x_i}{3n}$. The absolute value of the gap between the new target number and the choice of player i is $x_i - \frac{2x_i}{3n} > 0$. But the absolute value of the gap between the new target number and the choice of any of the other players who chooses 0 is even smaller, $\frac{2x_i}{3n} - 0$, hence they win (the reader should check this using simple algebra). Thus, starting from a choice of zero, no player can improve their payoff by choosing any other number, confirming that the Nash equilibrium is for each player to choose 0. In fact, it can also be shown that this is the unique Nash equilibrium of the p-beauty contest for any $0 < p < 1$.[7] Did you choose the number 0, when you were invited to make your own choice above?

Here is what happens under a level-k model and this might help you to understand your own choice better. People have different cognitive abilities or levels; we denote the level of a player by Lk, where $k = 0, 1, 2, \ldots$ Each player of level Lk, other than level $L0$, believes that all others are one level below. Thus, level Lk players believe that all other players are level $Lk - 1$ players; perhaps players are overconfident of their own abilities, which is consistent with the evidence from many contexts. The levels are built up recursively starting from level $L0$, as we now show.

Level $L0$ players choose uniformly randomly over the interval $[0, 100]$ and pick, on average, the number 50. Level $L1$ players believe that all others are level $L0$ players who choose on average, 50, so they choose the number $\frac{2}{3}50 = 33.33$, which they hope will win. Level $L2$ players believe that all others are level $L1$ players, who they believe will choose 33.33, so they choose the number $\frac{2}{3}33.33 = 22.22$, or $\left(\frac{2}{3}\right)^2 50$. Level $L3$ players believe that all others are level $L2$ who are expected to choose 22.22, so they choose $\frac{2}{3}22.22 = 14.81$, or $\left(\frac{2}{3}\right)^3 50$. By now the pattern of recursion should be clear. For any value of k, type Lk believes that all other players are type $Lk-1$, so type LK chooses the number $\left(\frac{2}{3}\right)^k 50$. In other words, we should expect to see spikes in the data at the numbers 50, 33.33, 22.22, 14.81,.... By contrast, under neoclassical game theory, all players have the level Lk, $k \to \infty$, so they will all choose $\left(\frac{2}{3}\right)^\infty 50 = 0$, confirming what we have already directly checked above.

The predictions of the level-k model are consistent with the data although they do not fully explain all the choices. Figure 7.5 gives a summary of the results from several studies with different subject pools including students, university professors, readers in newspaper polls, and chess players; n is the number of subjects in the experiment. These results stay unchanged if we play the p-beauty contest game with subjects who have high cognitive abilities, such as PhD students, Caltech graduates, and CEOs of companies (Camerer, 2003). There is a heterogeneous pattern of contributions across the players and most players do not choose 0. Neoclassical game theorists may defend their theory on the grounds that players believe that others are irrational, so they do not choose 0; and if they believed that all others were perfectly rational, they would choose 0. However, we have no evidence that the choices are driven by these considerations, and these arguments also run the risk of making neoclassical game theory nonfalsifiable. Furthermore, we do see spikes in the data in Figure 7.5 at the numbers predicted in the level-k model, that is, at 50, 33.33, 22.22, 14.81,.... Thus, the Nash equilibrium prediction is contradicted by the data for a large majority of the subjects.

[7] Readers who would like to verify this claim can try picking any other putative Nash equilibrium in which each player chooses $\widetilde{x} : 0 < \widetilde{x} \leq 100$, and check that any player has a profitable deviation by choosing a smaller number, assuming that everyone else continues to choose $\widetilde{x}$, as required by Definition 7.1.

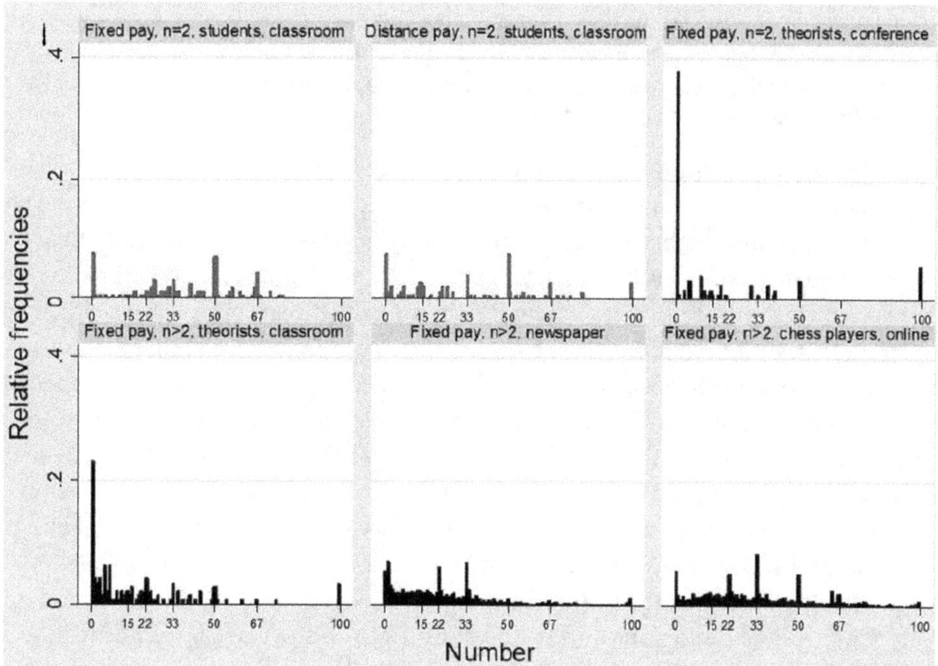

Figure 7.5 Results of the p-beauty contest game from a variety of subject pools. Relative frequencies of choices in the two-person games with fixed payoffs (upper left), distance payoffs (upper middle) and with economics professors in various conferences (upper right); lower left $n > 2$ games with economic professors and students in advanced economic classes; in lower middle newspaper contestants; lower right chess players online. Source: Nagel et al. (2017) with permission

The level-k model is a step in the right direction to relax the unreasonably demanding cognitive requirements in neoclassical game theory, and its predictions are reasonably successful in explaining the data for the p-beauty contest. However, we observe a distribution of choices, including choices of numbers that are not predicted by the level-k model. This suggests that other types of non-level-k players also exist (see below), but nevertheless the level-k model provides a promising base to build on.

While level-k models share with a Nash equilibrium, the feature that players play a *best response to beliefs*, it relaxes the assumption of *equilibrium beliefs*, namely that the beliefs and the actions of the players should be consistent with each other. This is the reason that after playing the p-beauty contest, players are often "surprised" by the outcome, as we often might be at the conclusion of strategic situations. In a widely cited quote, the eminent British macroeconomist, John Maynard Keynes likened stock market investment with newspaper beauty contests of his day, and his description appears consistent with a level-k model. In Keynes (1936, p. 156) he wrote:

professional investment may be likened to those newspaper competitions in which the competitors have to pick out the six prettiest faces from a hundred photographs, the prize being awarded to the competitor whose choice most nearly corresponds to the average preferences of the competitors as a whole; [. . .] It is not a case of choosing those [faces] which, to the best of one's judgement, are really the prettiest, nor even those which average opinion genuinely thinks the prettiest. We have reached the third degree where we devote our intelligences to anticipating what average opinion expects the average opinion to be. And there are some, I believe, who practise the fourth, fifth and higher degrees.

Keynes who was a twelfth wrangler in the mathematics Tripos at Cambridge in 1905 might well have been thinking of himself when he imagined that there are those who practise "the fourth, fifth and higher degrees." However, empirical evidence suggests that most people are distributed between levels $L0$, $L1$, $L2$, and $L3$. Costa-Gomes et al. (2001) use mouselab software experiments[8] in 18 normal form games between two players who have either two, three, or at most four strategies. Each of these games has a unique pure strategy Nash equilibrium. The estimates of the incidence of levels $L1$ and $L2$ are between 67%–89% of the players. Another common type whose incidence is 1%–20% in the games is a type $D1$, who uses a *simple heuristic* (more on this below) to solve the game. Type $D1$ deletes just one dominated strategy (but no more, even if there is the possibility of iterated deletion of further dominated strategies) and then plays a best response assuming that the opponent will choose the remaining strategies with equal probability. If the game cannot be solved by one or two rounds of iterated deletion of dominated strategies, then conformity with a Nash equilibrium is often found to be weak.

Costa-Gomes and Crawford (2006) consider 16 static two-player normal form games called guessing games that can be solved by iterated deletion of dominated strategies. The players choose their guesses over intervals of numbers and are required to hit a target guess that also depends on the opponent's guess. Out of 88 subjects, the guesses of 43 subjects were an exact match to the prediction of the level-k model in 10 out of 16 games. The econometric analysis revealed that 20 subjects were $L1$, 12 subjects were $L2$, three subjects were $L3$, and eight subjects were *equilibrium types* who conformed to the predictions of neoclassical game theory. No $D1$ types were found. When the search and decision data from mouselab software was used, the main types of players found were levels $L1$, $L2$, and equilibrium types. One advantage of the mouselab software was that the search and lookup patterns could be used to rule out social preferences as an explanation.[9]

Do we expect the levels in a level-k model to be stable across games, or in other words: Are levels portable across games? The evidence suggests that this is not necessarily the case (Georganas et al., 2015; Hargreaves et al., 2014). However, this is not fatal for the level-k model because a central insight of behavioral economics is that preferences are context and frame dependent. As Georganas et al. (2015) also note, certain contexts and frames may trigger the use of level-k models. In other contexts, players may use team reasoning (see Section 7.9). Indeed, this is also explicitly recognized in Crawford et al. (2008) who write: "Overall, our results suggest a synthesis of level-k thinking and team reasoning in which team reasoning supplements or supplants level-k thinking in some settings."

[8] An application of mouselab software is described in more detail in Section 8.3 below, which explains the basic use of this software.

[9] Players who have social preferences would be expected to alternate clicking between boxes (see description of the mouselab software in Section 8.3) that contained their payoffs and the payoffs of the opponents.

The level-k model has been applied to a wide range of problems such as auctions, bargaining, and salience of focal points. The base level $L0$ might not exist in reality, but could simply be an artificial construct in the minds of level $L1$ players about the world. Yet, there is some evidence that the level $L0$ is real (Dhami, 2020, Vol. IV; Section 2.4.6); see, for instance, the spike in the data at 50 in Figure 7.5, or perhaps some of you chose 50 when you were invited to make a guess above. The results in level-k models are sensitive to assumptions about the choices of level $L0$ players (or how the level $L1$ players perceives the level $L0$ players will play). These assumptions are important to determine the optimal choices of each of the higher levels, $L1$, $L2$, $L3$.... This is sometimes cited by critics as a major drawback of the model. But it is mainly an argument about gathering more empirical evidence to determine if level L0 players exist, and how level $L1$ players form mental models of the world in which players of level $L0$ are situated in different contexts.

García-Pola et al. (2020) provide a careful analysis of the centipede game that we considered in Section 7.3. Their study is also important because they run a horse race between several competing explanations of behavior in the centipede game, using *mixture models*. Mixture models is a statistical technique that allows us to simultaneously uncover several kinds of behavior, or preferences, when we examine the data from a game. They consider 16, six-move centipede games with varying payoffs that allow them to distinguish between alternative explanations. They group games by four types: constant-sum (the sum of payoffs at any terminal node is the same); increasing-sum (the sum of payoffs at the terminal nodes increases from left to right in the game); decreasing-sum (the sum of payoffs at the terminal nodes decreases from left to right in the game); and variable (no distinct pattern). The centipede game in Section 7.3 was an increasing-sum game.

Let us illustrate how level-k models may explain behavior in the centipede game. In Figure 7.6, we show an increasing-sum six-move centipede game; it is one of the 16 centipede games used in García-Pola et al. (2020). The backward induction outcome under neoclassical game theory is that player 1 should play D at the very first node and end the game, as in the centipede game in Figure 7.1.

We are now interested in the *reduced normal form representation* of the extensive form game in Figure 7.6. Recall from Section 7.2 that a normal form game simply contains information on the set of players, the strategies (which are just the actions in a static game), and the associated payoffs from the strategies. However, as noted in Section 7.3, strategies in extensive form games are more complicated – they provide a complete contingent plan of action, which can be difficult to capture in a normal form game. The reduced normal form representation of the

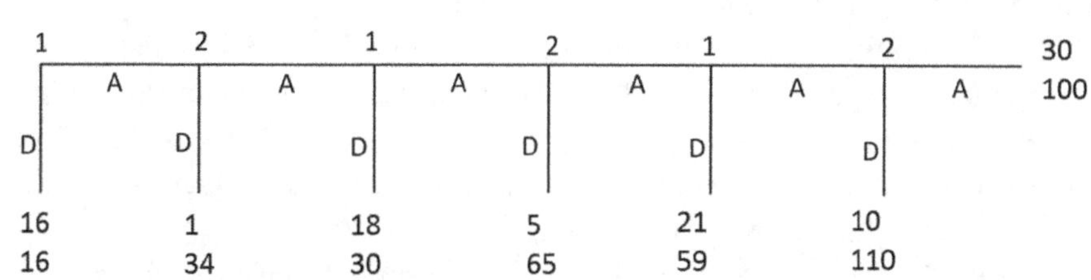

Figure 7.6 A six-move increasing-sum centipede game. Redrawn from García-Pola et al. (2020)

Table 7.9 The reduced normal form game corresponding to the extensive form game in Figure 7.6

	$D1$	$D2$	$D3$	AA
$D1$	16, 16	16, 16	16, 16	16, 16
$D2$	1, 34	18, 30	18, 30	18, 30
$D3$	1, 34	5, 65	21, 59	21, 59
AA	1, 34	5, 65	10, 110	30, 100

centipede game, therefore, gives only partial information about the underlying extensive form game. It essentially shows the payoffs and strategy profiles, starting from any of the nodes of the centipede game that lead to the closest terminal node. This should become clear in Table 7.9 where we show the reduced normal form representation of the centipede game in Figure 7.6.

In Figure 7.6, in order to reach any of the terminal nodes (which show the payoffs), one of the players chooses D except at the very last set of payoffs, $(30, 100)$, which requires both players to "always choose A," a strategy that we label as AA in Table 7.9. In Table 7.9, player 1 is the row player and player 2 is the column player. When both players choose AA, the corresponding payoff is $(30, 100)$; this is listed in the last row and last column of Table 7.9. We now describe the remaining strategies in Table 7.9. In the centipede game in Figure 7.6, each player gets to chose D a maximum of three possible times. Let $D1$ be the choice of D, the first time, a player gets this opportunity (first node for player 1 and second node for player 2). Similarly, let $D2$ be the choice of D, the second time a player gets this opportunity (third node for player 1 and fourth node for player 2); and let $D3$ be the choice of D, the third time a player gets this opportunity (fifth node for player 1 and sixth node for player 2). This completes the description of strategies used in Table 7.9.

We now describe the payoffs in Table 7.9 using the information given in Figure 7.6. If player 1 plays D at the very first node (strategy $D1$ of the row player), then the payoffs are $(16, 16)$ irrespective of the strategy choice of player 2; this gives the first row of payoffs in Table 7.9. If player 2 plays D at the very first time at node 2 (strategy $D1$ of the column player), then payoffs are $(1, 34)$ irrespective of what player 1 might do subsequently; this gives the first column of payoffs below the payoff $(16, 16)$ in Table 7.9. If player 1 plays D a second time, at the third node (strategy $D2$ for the row player) then the payoffs are $(18, 30)$ irrespective of what player 2 does subsequently; this gives the second row of payoffs to the right of the payoff of $(1, 34)$ in Table 7.9. The reader can construct the remaining payoffs in Table 7.9 analogously. Thus, the reduced normal form in Table 7.9, reduces the corresponding extensive form game to a two-player normal form in which each player has four pure strategies.

There is a unique Nash equilibrium in the game in Table 7.9 in which each player chooses the strategy $D1$ for a payoff of 16 each. In the extensive form game in Figure 7.6, this corresponds to player 1 playing D at the very first node and ending the game with payoffs of 16 each for both players. The authors use the reduced normal form to make predictions for the centipede game, for different theories, as we now explain.

In order to use the level-k model we need to first specify the choices of level $L0$ players. We make the simplifying assumption that a level $L0$ player, whether it is a row or column player, chooses randomly between the 4 pure strategies, so each strategy is chosen with a 25% probability. Let us now calculate the best reply for each of the row and column players for levels $L1, L2, L3$. In the literature, there is very little evidence of players being of higher levels, so we omit a consideration of the optimal strategy of these levels.

1. $L1$ row and column players: A row player who is level $L1$ believes that he is facing a column player who is level $L0$, and plays each strategy with a 25% chance. Among the four strategy choices of the row player of level $L1$, the strategy $D1$ gives the highest expected payoff of 16. The reader can check that any other strategy will give a lower payoff, for example, the strategy $D3$ gives the expected payoff of 12.[10] A column $L1$ player's best reply to the belief that the row player is level $L0$ is to choose strategy $D3$ to receive a payoff of $16 \times 0.25 + 30 \times 0.25 + 59 \times 0.25 + 110 \times 0.25 = 53.75$ which exceeds the payoff from any other strategy choice.
2. $L2$ row and column players: Row players who are level $L2$ believe that all column players are level $L1$. They also know (from the calculations done above) that column $L1$ players play $D3$. Therefore, from Table 7.9, the best response of a level $L2$ row player is to also play $D3$ for a payoff of 21. Level $L2$ column players believe that all row players are level $L1$ who play $D1$, so they get a payoff of 16 irrespective of which strategy they play. Hence, they are equally likely to play any of the four strategies, $D1, D2, D3, AA$.
3. $L3$ row and column players: Row players who are level $L3$ believe that all column players are level $L2$ who are equally likely to choose any of the four strategies, $D1, D2, D3, AA$. This situation is identical to a level $L1$ row player who faces a $L0$ column player (see calculations above). Hence, the optimal choice of the $L3$ row player is $D1$. An $L3$ column player believes that all row players are level $L2$ who play $D3$. The best response of $L3$ column players is, thus, to play $D2$ for a payoff of 65.

In order to rule out the role of other-regarding preferences, several plausible behavioral considerations are entertained. *Altruistic types*, denoted by A, simply maximize the sum of payoffs of both players. So, in increasing-sum games, they always play "across" to reach the highest possible joint payoffs; for the game in Figure 7.6 this is the payoff pair $(30, 100)$. For decreasing-sum games, they choose down, D (which is the strategy $D1$), at the first opportunity because this maximizes joint payoffs, and for constant sum games, they are indifferent between all their actions. One can also consider a *modified altruistic type*, A(γ), who maximizes the sum of their own payoff and γ times the payoff of the other player. The parameter γ can be varied to generate different predictions. Notice that both altruistic types are non-strategic – they follow a simple heuristic that is conditional on their degree of altruism. One can also introduce players who always pick the Pareto optimal outcome; call these players as *PE types*. In all the increasing-sum games, only the last two payoff pairs are Pareto optimal. In Figure 7.6 this is the payoff pair $(30, 100)$ (the reader should use Definition 7.3 to make sure to check this).

In order to take account of inequity aversion (see Part II for the Fehr–Schmidt model of inequity aversion), an inequity-averse type, or IA type, is introduced who minimizes the absolute value of the difference between any two pairs of payoffs. For the centipede game in Figure 7.6, such a player in the role of player 1 would play D at the very first node (strategy D1 for the

[10] This is calculated as follows: $1 \times 0.25 + 5 \times 0.25 + 21 \times 0.25 + 21 \times 0.25 = 12$.

row player in Table 7.9) so that the payoff difference between the players is zero. A column IA player in Table 7.9 would also play D at the first opportunity in Figure 7.6 (strategy $D1$ for the column player in Table 7.9). Another type IA(α, β) has the Fehr–Schmidt preferences where α is the parameter of disadvantageous inequity and β is the parameter of advantageous inequity. Varying these parameters produces different predictions.

To take account of optimism, an optimistic type, denoted by "O" plays a maximax strategy (choosing the highest of the maximum payoffs while varying the strategies of the other player). In Table 7.9, a type O row player first takes his maximum payoff in each column of the table to get the following sequence of payoffs: 16, 18, 21, 30. The maximum of these payoffs is 30, so he picks the maximax strategy AA (always pass). A final type of player, QRE(λ), plays the quantal response equilibrium (see Section 7.8.3) which has a single parameter, λ; the estimates below use $\lambda = 0.38$. We postpone a detailed discussion of this type of player to Section 7.8.3 below. In a QRE, players play each of the pure strategies with some probability, so the notation z_{QRE} means that in a QRE the player plays that strategy with a z% probability.

This completes our discussion of all the possible types of players and the predictions on their behavior in the centipede game in Figure 7.6 (the authors consider 15 other such games, each having its own distinct set of predictions).

For the centipede game in Figure 7.6, the predictions of each theory and the percentage of row and column players choosing each of the strategies, $D1, D2, D3, AA$, is shown in Table 7.10. By BI we denote the predictions under backward induction under neoclassical game theory. Consider, for instance the first column of results for the strategy labeled $D1$. In the first row, 51.32% of player 1s (row players in Table 7.9) choose $D1$; and in the second row, 10.67% of player 2s (column players in Table 7.9) choose $D1$. Back to the first row and first column of payoffs, the following theories did predict the play of $D1$ by player 1: $BI, L1, L3, IA, A(\gamma), IA(\alpha, \beta), 0.15_{QRE}$. Thus, several theories are able to account for the 51.32% of row players who picked $D1$. Neoclassical game theory can explain this outcome through backward induction (BI), as can models of inequity aversion ($IA, IA(\alpha, \beta)$), models of altruism (A), level-k models through the optimal play of levels $L1, L3$, and a model of quantal response equilibrium that predicts row players will choose strategy D1 with a 15% probability (denoted by 0.15_{QRE}). All these predictions have been explained above in the various models, except the QRE model that we take up in Section 7.8.3.

Table 7.10 The empirical results corresponding to the play of the four strategies, *D*1,*D*2,*D*3,*AA*, in Table 7.9. The results are given separately for the row player (player 1) and the column player (player 2). Within each cell, the percentage of the players who play that particular strategy is given first, followed by the list of theoretical models that predict the play of that strategy

	$D1$	$D2$	$D3$	AA
Player 1	51.32% $BI, L1, L3, IA$ $A(\gamma), IA(\alpha, \beta), 0.15_{QRE}$	15.79% 0.31_{QRE}	19.74% $L2$ 0.41_{QRE}	13.16% A, PE, O 0.13_{QRE}
Player 2	10.67% $BI, L2, IA$ $A(\gamma), IA(\alpha, \beta), 0.0_{QRE}$	34.67% $L2, L3, IA$ $IA(\alpha, \beta), 0.14_{QRE}$	40.00% $L1, L2, PE, O, IA$ $IA(\alpha, \beta), 0.53_{QRE}$	14.67% $A, L2, PE, IA$ $IA(\alpha, \beta), 0.32_{QRE}$

This empirical study is exemplary in two ways. First, the wide range of models that is considered in making predictions; running horse races between models is an important part of model evaluation. Second, the use of mixture models to simultaneously account for the predictions of all the models within the same dataset. The main empirical findings in García-Pola et al. (2020) are as follows. In constant-sum and decreasing-sum games, the incentive to choose strategy A (i.e., play "across") is reduced, hence, the backward induction outcome, choose D at the first node, is more likely to be observed. But in increasing-sum games, the backward induction outcome is often violated and players typically do not play D at the first move, which is contrary to the predictions of the BI outcome under neoclassical game theory. The authors show that this evidence can be explained by two different kinds of behavioral models – a level-k model, and the quantal response equilibrium model that we consider in Section 7.8.3 below. Rather than being competitors, the empirical results indicate that the level-k model and the QRE model apply to different games.

The final point is important enough to stress separately. Even when the backward induction (BI) outcome under neoclassical game theory appears to do well, there is a range of other competing models that explain the outcome equally well. For instance, in the 11th of the 16 games that García-Pola et al. (2020) consider, a decreasing-sum game, the outcome $D1$ is played by 64.47% of player 1s and 70.67% of player 2s; see the exercises at the end of this chapter for this game. On the face of it, this would appear to be strong support for the BI outcome. Yet the behavior of player 1s is equally well explained by the $A, L2, L3, PE, A(\gamma), IA(\alpha, \beta), 0.43_{QRE}$ models, and the behavior of player 2s is equally well explained by the $A, L1, L2, L3, PE, A(\gamma), IA(\alpha, \beta), 0.42_{QRE}$ models.

This appears generally true. The predictions of neoclassical game theory often fail the empirical test, and when they appear to succeed, there are typically are other behavioral models which can also account for the predictions. We shall see another example of this general point below, when we discuss the market entry game. The continued, and exclusive, use of neoclassical game theory in game theory courses in economics is a puzzle, as is the absence of any empirical evidence in these courses.

7.8.2 The Cognitive Hierarchy Model

The *cognitive hierarchy* (CH) model is related to the level-k model. It assumes that any player of level Lk believes that there is a distribution of players of all possible lower types, $Lk - 1$, $Lk - 2, \ldots, L0$ (Camerer et al., 2004). These are sometimes known as *step Lk players* rather than level-k players to differentiate them from players in the level-k model. The perceived distribution of players of lower levels is typically assumed to be a Poisson distribution, which has a single parameter that needs to be empirically determined. The predictions of the level-k model and the CH model are similar for most games, so we need more empirical evidence to distinguish between the two.

The Poisson distribution specifies the objectively correct proportion of players who are of type Lk as

$$f(k) = \frac{e^{-\tau}\tau^k}{k!}; k = 0, 1, 2, \ldots, \tag{7.6}$$

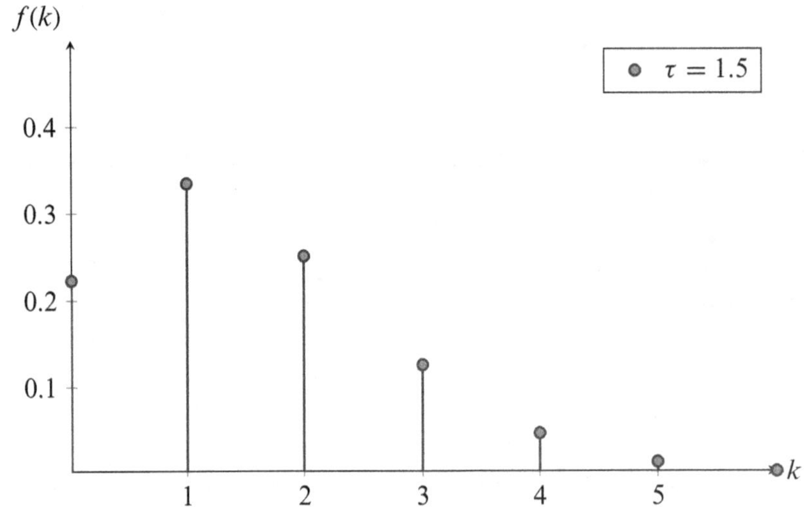

Figure 7.7: The Poisson distribution, as we vary the levels of the players: $k = 0, 1, 2, \ldots, 5$

where the single parameter, τ, is the mean and the variance of the distribution. The denominator $k!$ (read, k factorial) equals the product $k(k-1)(k-2)\ldots 1$. For a specific value of τ, we can determine the value of $f(k)$ for different values of $k = 0, 1, 2, \ldots$. In an important paper in this area, Camerer et al. (2004, p. 863) write: "In 24 beauty contest data sets, the median estimate is $\widehat{\tau} = 1.61\ldots$ Indeed, values of τ between 1 and 2 explain empirical results for nearly 100 games, suggesting that assuming a value of 1.5 could give reliable predictions for many other games as well." We assume below that $\tau = 1.5$.

Figure 7.7 shows the Poisson distribution as we vary $k = 0, 1, 2, \ldots, 5$; we stop at $k = 5$ because the evidence shows the preponderance of low values of k in the data. The six plotted values in Figure 7.7 are:

$$f(0) = 0.223;\ f(1) = 0.334;\ f(2) = 0.251;\ f(3) = 0.125;\ f(4) = 0.047;\ f(5) = 0.014. \qquad (7.7)$$

Thus, of the total number of players, type $L0$ are 22.31%; type $L1$ are 33.47%; type L3 are 12.55%; and so on. The proportion of the players drops off rapidly as we increase k and $L5$ types are just 1.41% of the total. From (7.6), we can write $f(k-1) = \frac{e^{-\tau}\tau^{k-1}}{(k-1)!}$. Dividing the two, we get

$$\frac{f(k)}{f(k-1)} = \frac{\tau}{k}.$$

Thus, the ratio of the successive proportions of the players drops off at a rate that depends on k itself, and as k increases, the decline becomes precipitous. This is one of the reasons why the Poisson distribution is used.

The density f in (7.6) is the objectively correct density of the players that describes the fraction of each Lk type. However, players have incorrect beliefs and a "step Lk player" believes that 100% of the other players in the population are distributed among the lower levels $Lk-1, Lk-2, \ldots, L0$. As in the level-k model, the reader may find it useful at the moment to think of players being overconfident of their own cognitive abilities. Hence, they need to normalize the objectively correct estimates in (7.6) to form their subjectively (incorrect) estimates. Consider, for instance, step $L2$ players who follow the CH model and, hence, view that everyone else is either level $L0$ or $L1$. From (7.7), $f(0) = 0.2231, f(1) = 0.3347$, which adds upto 55.78% of the population. Yet, step $L2$ players believe, incorrectly, that this accounts for 100% of the population. Hence, the *subjective belief distribution*, g_2, of step $L2$ players about the two lower types is

$$g_2(0) = \frac{f(0)}{f(0) + f(1)} = 0.40; g_2(1) = \frac{f(1)}{f(0) + f(1)} = 0.60. \tag{7.8}$$

From (7.8), step $L2$ players believe that 40% of the other players in the population are level $L0$ and 60% are level $L1$; from (7.7), the objectively correct respective percentages are 22.31% and 33.47%. In general, for any step Lk player the *subjective belief distribution* about all the lower types is given by

$$g_k(n) = \frac{f(n)}{f(k-1) + \cdots + f(0)}; n = 0, 1, 2, \ldots k-1. \tag{7.9}$$

In the CH model, players choose an action that maximizes their expected payoff (i.e., they *play a best response*, as in level-k models), given their subjective beliefs in (7.9). The parameter τ can be estimated from the choices of players, assuming that they follow the CH model. There is no presumption that the value of τ is portable across different games, and we have addressed this issue also for level-k models – the context and frame dependence of preference parameters is not uncommon in behavioral economics.

Consider an application to the *market entry game*, originally due to Selten and Güth (1982). There is a market with N potential entrants who simultaneously make the decision to Enter the market or stay Out of the market. Let us fix $N = 100$ for simplicity so that the fraction of firms and actual numbers of firms are identical. Each entrant can, for simplicity, supply only one unit of a good. The market size is $d < 100$ units of the good, that is, there are more potential entrants relative to the size of the market. Suppose that there are $e \leq 100$ actual entrants. If $e \leq d$ entrants enter, they all get a payoff of 1. If $e > d$ entrants enter (the "Enter" decision), then all entrants get a payoff of 0, say, due to wasteful competition, which swamps all profits. If a potential entrant does not enter (the "Out" decision), then the payoff is 0.5; sometimes known as the outside option.

How many of the potential entrants should enter? The reader will recognize the similarity of this game with the median action game in Section 7.5, where the payoff of a player depends on "own action" and a statistical measure of the actions of others, although these are different classes of games.

We show the normal form of this game in Table 7.11, which is similar to the normal form of a median action game (see Figure 7.3). The table shows only the payoffs of a potential entrant (the row player) who considers the entry decision, not knowing how many other potential entrants have chosen to enter. In lieu of the column player, we have the two mutually exclusive outcomes arising from the aggregate decision of all players; either $e < d$ or $e \geq d$ (notice that if $e = d$ then by entering, a potential entrant tips the scales to $e > d$ resulting in 0 profits).

Table 7.11 The market entry game

	$e < d$	$e \geq d$
Enter	1	0
Out	0.5	0.5

From (7.7), 22.313% are level $L0$; 33.47% are level $L1$; and 25.10% are level $L2$. Suppose that all $L0$ players randomize equally between Enter and Out. Thus, the objectively correct situation is that $\frac{1}{2}$ of the level $L0$ players, or $\frac{1}{2}22.313 = 11.16\%$ of 100 enter, which is the same as 11.16 players (we can round this up to 11 players but let us continue with decimals for simplicity).

All step $L1$ players think that everyone else is a $L0$ player, so, their subjective probability estimate is $g_1(0) = 1.00$ (and $g_1(n) = 0, n \geq 1$). Since they believe that half of these players, who comprise the entire population, will enter, so they believe, mistakenly, that 50 out of 100 players will enter. In reality, only 11.6 players enter, as we have seen above. Hence, using the payoffs in Table 7.11, step L1 players follow a simple decision rule:

$$\text{Enter if } 50 < d, \text{ otherwise choose Out.} \tag{7.10}$$

If $50 < d$ then step $L1$ players choose Enter. In this case, the "objectively correct" total number of potential entrants who have entered are $\frac{1}{2}22.313 + 33.470 = 44.63\%$ of 100, which is the same as 44.63 entrants. Otherwise, if step $L1$ players choose Out, then objectively only 11.16 $L0$ players enter.

Consider step $L2$ players and suppose that $50 < d$. Using their subjective probability distribution in (7.8), they believe that 40% of 100 potential entrants are $L0$ (half of which enter) and 60% of the 100 potential entrants are $L1$ (all of them enter using (7.10)). Thus, in their mistaken subjective beliefs, a total of 80% of the 100 potential entrants have entered. It follows that their optimal decision rule is

$$\text{Enter if } 80 < d, \text{ otherwise choose Out.} \tag{7.11}$$

If $80 \geq d$, then step $L2$ players will choose not to enter, although objectively only 44.63 potential entrants have chosen to enter. If $80 < d$ then step $L2$ players will enter, in which case the objectively correct number of players who enter is $\frac{1}{2}22.313 + 33.470 + 25.10 = 69.73\%$ players, which is the same as 69.73 players.

We can now proceed in this manner to step $L3, L4, L5, \ldots$ players. However, we have done enough to uncover the pattern of this recursion. Players use simple cutoff rules of the form given in (7.10) and (7.11) to make their decisions. These decisions are of the following form. If $c_k < d$ then choose Enter, otherwise choose Out, where c_k is a constant that is specific to a step Lk player; from (7.10) and (7.11) we have $c_1 = 50$ and $c_2 = 80$.

When the market entry game is played repeatedly one often obtains the efficient solution $e = d$ over a few rounds, that is, the number of entrants equals the market size. The Nash equilibrium of this static simultaneous move game is also that exactly $e = d$ entrants enter (the reader should check this as an exercise). This outcome was achieved over a few rounds of play in the pilot experiments conducted by Daniel Kahneman, which moved him to write in Kahneman (1988) "to a psychologist, it looks like magic." However, behavioral models, such as the CH model, can also explain the empirical data, as we show below. Our analysis above is not of a repeated market entry game that requires an explicit consideration of models of learning, but of a static game. Yet, we can use it to highlight some of the key behavioral regularities in this game.

Suppose that $d = 52$. From (7.10), step $L1$ players will enter but from (7.11), step $L2$ entrants will not enter, so 44.63 potential entrants will have simultaneously chosen to enter in a market size of 52. This is close to the efficient outcome. However, if d is very small, say, $d = 10$, then only $\frac{1}{2}$ of the $L0$ players will enter, which is 11.16 players. Hence, we have over-entry ($11.16 > 10$). If, however, d is large, say, $d = 75$, then (1) from (7.10), step $L1$ players will enter, and (2) from (7.11), step $L2$ players will not enter, so 44.63 potential entrants will have simultaneously chosen to enter in a market size of 75, which is a case of under-entry. The findings of over-entry for low values of d and under-entry for high values of d is also an empirical finding that the CH model successfully explains, but the Nash equilibrium cannot. As d goes up entry goes up, which is also an empirical finding that the CH model explains. Camerer et al. (2004, p. 873) remark: "The Poisson-CH can therefore explain the magic of approximate equilibration—monotonicity of entry with the demand d—as well as systematic departures from equilibrium observed in the data."

7.8.3 Quantal Response Equilibrium (QRE)

An alternative behavioral approach, the *quantal response equilibrium* (QRE), takes a different route and relaxes the Nash assumption of best replies, but maintains the challenging cognitive assumption of *consistency of actions and beliefs*. In the QRE model, players play all their strategies "noisily" with some probability, but they play their best replies with a higher probability – so they play a *better reply* rather than a *best reply*. The cognitive requirements in a QRE can be extremely challenging, at least relative to the level-k model, but it also has the ability to explain behavior in several kinds of games while in others its predictions are not consistent with the data. For surveys of QRE that are favorable to it, and advocate its use, see Goeree et al. (2016) and Goeree et al. (2020).

The basic idea that players might play their strategies with some noise has a long tradition in *stochastic choice models* (Thurstone, 1927; Luce, 1959). The source of the noise in QRE models is not too clear. The initial studies in psychology were conducted on subjects who observe two psychophysical stimuli, such as sources of sound or light, of slightly different intensities. It was found that the choices of subjects in identifying the stronger of the two stimuli were stochastic in the sense that the choices kept randomly flipping between two options. However, what might be the source of the noise if subjects chose among, say, the two strategies in the PD game in a stochastic manner? These questions are not properly addressed in the literature and require further exploration of the microfoundations of these theories. There is, however, supporting evidence from neuroeconomics that locates the reason for such stochastic choice in the human neural architecture and this literature may provide useful microfoundations in the future (Fehr and Rangel, 2011; Woodford, 2012, 2014; Konovalov and Krajbich, 2019). We deal with this interesting set of questions in the online chapter on neuroeconomics.

To fix ideas, let us consider the prisoner's dilemma (PD) game shown in Table 7.1 and let the payoffs be the utilities of the players. For simplicity, we assume that there are homogeneous beliefs in the sense that each player believes that the other plays the respective strategies C and D with probabilities p and $1-p$. We also consider heterogeneous beliefs in the next example. Then the expected utilities of any of the players from the two strategies C, D are, respectively,

$$\pi(C) = 2p \text{ and } \pi(D) = 4p + (1-p) = 1 + 3p. \tag{7.12}$$

In (7.12), we are using the simpler notation $\pi(C)$, $\pi(D)$ for the standard notation for expected utility, $EU(C)$, $EU(D)$, that we used in Part I. Since the PD game is symmetric and we assume that beliefs are also symmetric, we dispense with subscripts on the payoff functions. One method of introducing stochastic choice among strategies is to use the *Luce ratio probabilistic choice rule*. Denoting by $P(C)$ the probability with which the row player plays C in the PD game, this rule specifies

$$P(C) = \frac{\pi(C)}{\pi(C) + \pi(D)}. \tag{7.13}$$

In the place of a best response, which is the case under a Nash equilibrium, the choice rule in (7.13) is a *better response*. The higher is $\pi(C)/\pi(D)$, the higher is $P(C)$, thus, strategies with relatively higher expected utilities are played with higher probabilities. An equilibrium arises, when the probability, $P(C)$, with which the first player actually plays C equals the second player's belief, p, about the probability with which the first player plays C, that is,

$$p = P(C). \tag{7.14}$$

The requirement in (7.14) is also known as computing a *fixed point in beliefs*. This is an extremely stringent requirement and reflects the "equilibrium in beliefs" requirement that is also central to neoclassical game theory. The weight of the evidence would suggest that there is inadequate support for it from games that are played over a few time periods. It is possible, although by no means guaranteed, that players may learn to satisfy (7.14) after many rounds of learning, particularly when the underlying economic environment is stationary, that is, an environment in which the rules of the game, the strategies, and the payoffs are unchanging. Many real world economic environments of interest may not have this property.

Substituting (7.12), (7.13) in (7.14), we get $p = \frac{2p}{1+5p}$. Simplifying this expression we get the following quadratic equation

$$5p^2 - p = 0. \tag{7.15}$$

There are two solutions to (7.15) and each constitutes a quantal response equilibrium, QRE (strictly speaking, this term applies to the case of a logit quantal response function in (7.23) below, but the underlying principles are identical). The first is $p = 0$ and the second is $p = \frac{1}{5}$; substitute each solution value in (7.15) to check that the equality holds on both sides. In terms of the notation in Table 7.10, we would write these two equilibria as 0.0_{QRE} and 0.20_{QRE}. Thus, a QRE can potentially explain cooperation in the PD game by allowing players to cooperate with a 20% probability. However, we know from the evidence in Section 7.2 that the cooperation rate in the static PD game is higher, and ranges between 50–60% depending on how the game is framed.

Table 7.12 An asymmetric matching pennies game; $x = 10, 2$

	L (heads)	R (tails)
T (heads)	$x, 1$	$1, 2$
B (tails)	$1, 2$	$2, 1$

The cognitive requirements for two-player asymmetric games where each player has two actions are even higher and require the explicit modeling of heterogeneous beliefs. In this case, the row and the column players play with different probabilities and they must have, in equilibrium, the correct beliefs about each other. For instance, in a two-player asymmetric normal form game, player 1's beliefs about the probability with which player 2 plays his strategies must, in equilibrium, be the probability with which player 2 actually plays his strategy; and vice-versa. For games with a large number of players and a large number of strategies, the cognitive requirements needed for a fixed point in beliefs increases exponentially with the complexity of the game. Thus, the study of quantal response equilibria does not offer a cognitive simplification over neoclassical game theory in seeking solutions to strategic situations.

Consider the asymmetric matching pennies game in Goeree et al. (2020) shown in Table 7.12; the symmetric version of this game is shown in Table 7.3 above. The strategies of the row player are Top and Bottom with acronyms T, B; these correspond respectively to heads and tails. The strategies of the column player are Left and Right with acronyms, L, R; these also correspond respectively to heads and tails. The payoff x can either equal 10 or 2 in two different cases that we consider below.

In this game, there are no pure strategy Nash equilibria. However, the row player prefers to match on heads, (T, L), rather than matching on tails, (B, R). The column player prefers a mismatch to a match on any strategy. Consider the payoff $x = 10$. Then, the mixed strategy Nash equilibrium (MSNE) is for the row player to play T and B with equal probabilities of 0.5 each, and for the column player to play L with probability 0.1 and R with probability 0.9. How would the MSNE change if x changed to $x = 2$? It turns out that the row player will still play T and B with equal probabilities of 0.5 each. The reason, recall from Section 7.2.4, is that the row player chooses the mixing probabilities so that the column player is indifferent between the two pure strategies L, R, and the payoffs of the column player have not changed. We have questioned this feature of a MSNE in Section 7.2.4. Indeed, the empirical evidence is consistent with what one might expect a-priori, namely, that as x increases, the row player plays T with a higher probability.

Let us now compute the QRE corresponding to the game in Table 7.12. Suppose that player 2, the column player, holds the following private beliefs: Player 1, the row player, plays T with probability $0 \leq p \leq 1$ and B with probability $1-p$. Similarly, the row player holds the following private beliefs: The column player, player 2, plays L with probability $0 \leq q \leq 1$ and R with probability $1 - q$. Players do not communicate with each other and choose their strategies simultaneously. Their beliefs are also not revealed to the opponents.

Given the beliefs, the expected payoff (or expected utility if the payoffs are measured in utilities) of the row player from each of the two pure strategies T and B is

$$\pi_1(T) = xq + (1 - q) \text{ and } \pi_1(B) = q + 2(1 - q) = 2 - q. \tag{7.16}$$

The expected payoffs of the column player, given the column player's beliefs, from the two pure strategies L, R are

$$\pi_2(L) = p + 2(1 - p) = 2 - p \text{ and } \pi_2(R) = 2p + (1 - p) = 1 + p. \tag{7.17}$$

Suppose that both players use the Luce ratio probabilistic choice rule in determining the probabilities of play of their pure strategies. Thus, the row player plays the strategy T with the probability $P(T)$:

$$P(T) = \frac{\pi_1(T)}{\pi_1(T) + \pi_1(B)}, \tag{7.18}$$

and the strategy B with the probability $P(B) = 1 - P(T)$.

The column player plays the strategy L with the probability $Q(L)$:

$$Q(L) = \frac{\pi_2(L)}{\pi_2(L) + \pi_2(R)}, \tag{7.19}$$

and the strategy R with a probability $Q(R) = 1 - Q(L)$.

The most critical requirement for a QRE is the analogue of (7.14). The suitability of the method depends on the empirical success of this requirement, namely, that in a QRE, *players play a fixed point in beliefs.* This requires two conditions in our two-player asymmetric game with two strategies.

$$p = P(T); q = Q(L). \tag{7.20}$$

Substituting (7.16)–(7.19) in (7.20), we get

$$p = \frac{xq + (1 - q)}{xq + 3 - 2q}. \tag{7.21}$$

$$q = \frac{2 - p}{3}. \tag{7.22}$$

The first equation in (7.21) gives the *quantal response function* for p in terms of q; we denote it by $p(q)$. The second equation in (7.22) gives the *quantal response function* for q in terms of p, which we denote by $q(p)$. The equilibrium quantal probabilities arise when both these equations are simultaneously satisfied. Essentially, these are two equations in two unknowns which can be readily solved, if a solution exists. The solution is the QRE of the game.

In Figure 7.8, we show a plot of the two quantal response reaction functions; the function $q(p)$ is the straight downward sloping line and the two different $p(q)$ functions correspond to two different values of $x = 10$ (continuous upward sloping curve) and $x = 2$ (dotted upward sloping curve). The intersections of the reaction functions gives the QRE. For instance, for the case $x = 2$, we can solve the two equations $p = \frac{1+q}{3}$ and $q = \frac{2-p}{3}$ to get the QRE: $p_{QRE} = q_{QRE} = \frac{1}{2}$. We can see directly from Figure 7.8 that as we increase x to $x = 10$, the value of p in a QRE increases, which can be calculated readily to be $p_{QRE} = \frac{3}{4}$, yet the probability with which the row player must play his strategies in a mixed strategy Nash equilibrium is unchanged. This prediction of the QRE is in accord with the empirical evidence (McKelvey et al., 2000; Goeree et al., 2003).

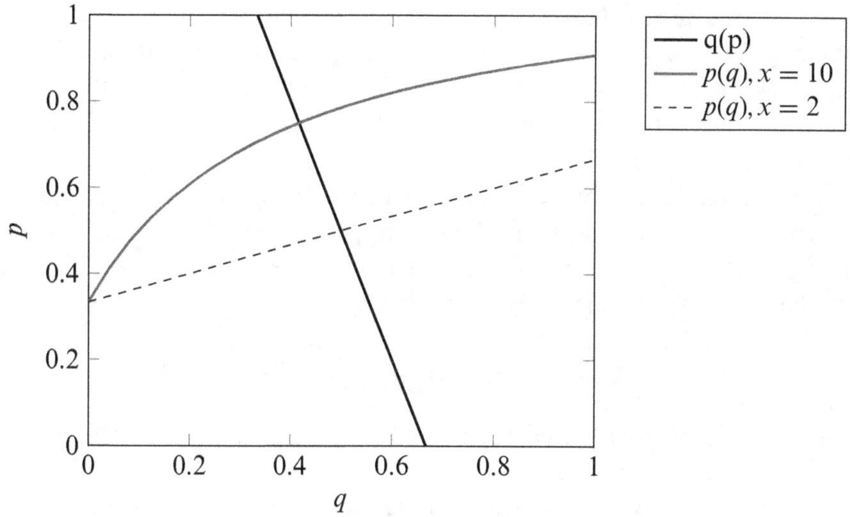

Figure 7.8 A plot of two quantal response functions

From (7.20), the probability with which the row player plays T, given by $P(T)$ (which is only privately known to the row player) is also the probability p with which the column player privately believes that the row player will play T. Similarly, the probability with which the column player plays L, given by $Q(L)$, is known privately only to the column player. Yet, it is also the probability, q, with which the row player privately believes the column player will play L. This is the essence of the fixed points in belief requirements with two players.

Remember that this is a static game in which players pick their strategies, and beliefs, simultaneously, without any communication with each other. Thus, the requirements for an equilibrium in (7.20) are extremely stringent. A similar condition on the consistency of actions and beliefs is a central requirement in equilibrium concepts in neoclassical game theory in games of incomplete information. Concerns about the nature of this requirement have been raised before. The Nobel Prize winner Rienhard Selten (1998, p. 421) wrote that "the natural way of looking at game situations … is not based on circular concepts, but rather on a step-by-step reasoning procedure." This would seem to favor the approach taken in the level-k model. Yet, the QRE model is able to account for several features of the experimental data, for instance, the variation in the probability of play as x varies, in a direction that is consistent with the evidence. Clearly, it captures some aspects of behavior and perhaps mirrors insights from another cognitively more realistic model. Yet, it is not able to explain many empirical phenomena, such as the label salience of actions in coordination games (see one of the exercises at the end of this part of the book).

The discussion above captures the key points in a QRE. However, one drawback of the Luce ratio probabilistic choice rule is that it is not designed for negative payoffs. For instance, if in (7.18), (7.21), the value of x were negative, then the associated probabilities will also be negative, but probabilities are always positive.

An alternative specification that can handle such cases, and is popular in applied work in economics, is a *logit quantal response function* which we now describe. While this can be stated generally for any finite number of strategies of players, let us first focus on the case of two players who have two strategies that they choose simultaneously (as in the 2×2 payoff matrix in Table 7.12).

Suppose that any player $i = 1, 2$ has two different pure strategies given by s_1, s_2 and the expected payoff from these strategies is, respectively, $\pi_i(s_1)$ and $\pi_i(s_2)$ (as before, this can be the expected material payoff, or the expected utility, of the players). Then, the probability with which player i plays the strategy s_1, is given by

$$P(s_1) = \frac{e^{\lambda \pi_i(s_1)}}{e^{\lambda \pi_i(s_1)} + e^{\lambda \pi_i(s_2)}}; \lambda > 0, \tag{7.23}$$

where λ is the *precision parameter* in the logit quantal response function that is estimated from the data on choices made by individuals.

Suppose that players have a utility function which takes the form of a payoff plus additive noise, and the additive noise follows an extreme value distribution (or a Weibull distribution). Then it can be shown using more advanced methods that it is optimal for the players to use the logit quantal response function in (7.23).[11]

Define the expected payoff differences from the two strategies for player $i = 1, 2$ by

$$\Delta_i = \pi_i(s_1) - \pi_i(s_2). \tag{7.24}$$

Divide the numerator and denominator of (7.23) by $e^{\lambda \pi_i(s_1)}$ to rewrite it in a slightly different but more convenient form as

$$P(s_1) = \frac{1}{1 + e^{-\lambda \Delta_i}}. \tag{7.25}$$

Remark 7.2 *We can use this method in more general games with m players. Suppose that any player $i = 1, .., m$ has n different pure strategies given by $s_1, s_2, \ldots, s_n$. Then the probability with which player i plays his strategy s_j, $j = 1, 2, \ldots, n$, is given by*

$$P(s_j) = \frac{e^{\lambda \pi_i(s_j)}}{e^{\lambda \pi_i(s_1)} + e^{\lambda \pi_i(s_2)} + \cdots + e^{\lambda \pi_i(s_n)}}; \lambda > 0.$$

We can now see the role played by the parameter λ. It is inversely related to the variance of the noise with which players play their strategies. When $\lambda = 0$, the players play their strategies completely randomly, i.e., with extreme noise. For instance, setting $\lambda = 0$ in (7.25), we get $P(s_1) = 0.5$ (and so $P(s_2) = 0.5$); the player randomizes equally between both pure strategies. At the other extreme when λ is as large as possible ($\lambda \to \infty$), then the variance of the noise term disappears and the behavior of players approaches a Nash equilibrium. Suppose that $\lambda \to \infty$, then from (7.25): If $\Delta_1 > 0$ then $P(s_1) = 1$; if $\Delta_1 < 0$ then $P(s_1) = 0$ (and $P(s_2) = 1$); and if $\Delta_1 = 0$ then $P(s_1) = P(s_2) = 0.5$. This is the case of *best replies* in a Nash equilibrium, where the strategy that offers a higher expected payoff is chosen with probability 1. In general, for a finite and strictly positive value of λ, strategies that give a higher payoff are played with a higher

[11] Readers interested in the detailed derivation of this result can consult Dhami (2020, Vol IV, Appendix B).

Table 7.13 An asymmetric matching pennies game $x > 0$

	H	T
H	$-1, 1$	$x, -1$
T	$1, -1$	$-1, 1$

probability. The reader can check that in (7.25), the RHS is strictly increasing in the size of the payoff difference term for player i, Δ_i.

Let us now apply the logit quantal response function to the asymmetric matching pennies game in Table 7.13.

In the special case where $x = 1$, Table 7.13 collapses to the symmetric matching pennies game shown in Table 7.3 which had a unique MSNE where both players play each of their two strategies with probabilities $\frac{1}{2}$ each. However, by varying the value of x we can study other aspects of the game.

Suppose that the row player (player 1) believes that the column player (player 2) will play his strategies H, T with respective probabilities $0 \leq q \leq 1$ and $1 - q$. Using identical notation as in our discussion of the asymmetric matching pennies game above, we have

$$\pi_1(H) = -q + x(1 - q) \text{ and } \pi_1(T) = q - (1 - q) = 2q - 1. \tag{7.26}$$

The logit quantal response function specifies that the row player will play the strategy H with a probability $P(H)$ given by

$$P(H) = \frac{e^{\lambda \pi_1(H)}}{e^{\lambda \pi_1(H)} + e^{\lambda \pi_1(T)}}; \lambda > 0. \tag{7.27}$$

We can rewrite this in the same form as (7.25):

$$P(H) = \frac{1}{1 + e^{-\lambda \Delta_i}}, \tag{7.28}$$

where we can use (7.24) and (7.26) to write

$$\Delta_1 = \pi_1(H) - \pi_1(T) = 1 - 3q + x(1 - q). \tag{7.29}$$

In Figure 7.9, we plot the logit quantal response function in (7.28) for three values of the precision parameter λ, as we vary the payoff differences, Δ_1, between -20 and 20. For low values of the precision parameter $\lambda = 0.1$ and $\lambda = 0.5$, the logit function is relatively flat and sloping upward gently. However, for a high value of $\lambda = 100$, the function transforms closer to its limiting shape of a step function that arises when $\lambda \to \infty$. The step function (when $\lambda \to \infty$) shows that when $\Delta_1 < 0$, $P(H) = 0$ and the logit function coincides with the X-axis; and when $\Delta_1 > 0$, $P(H) = 1$, so the logit function flatlines at 1.0; for $\Delta_1 = 0$ we have $P(H) = \frac{1}{2}$. The higher is the noise, that is, the lower is λ, the more the logit function departs from the step function.

It remains to find the QRE of the asymmetric matching pennies game in Table 7.13. In order to do this, we need to also construct the logit quantal response function for the column player (the analogue of the row player's logit function in (7.28)). The intersection of the two logit functions

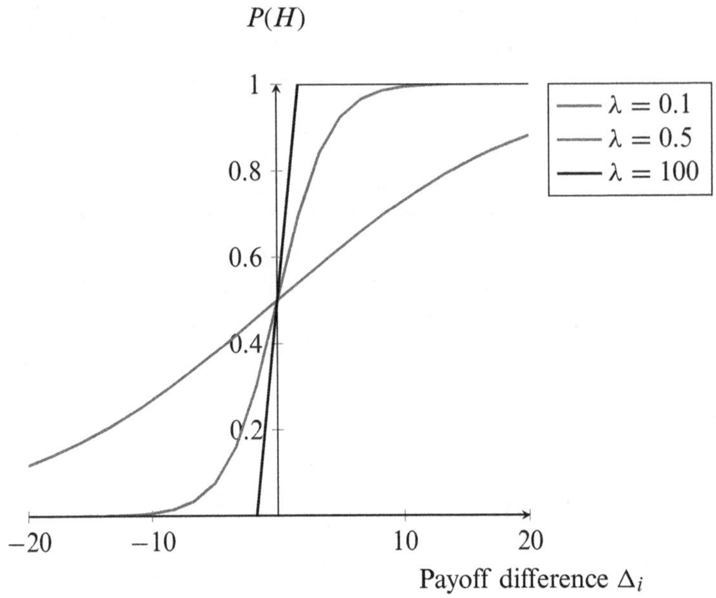

Figure 7.9 A plot of logit quantal response functions for different values of the precision parameter λ

will then give the QRE of the game. One of the exercises asks you to solve this – a graphical solution will do.

As the number of players and the strategies increases, calculation of the QRE is typically not possible with analytical methods and numerical solutions must be found using softwares such as Matlab and R. The QRE requires the players in these games to be able to either explicitly perform these calculations to arrive at the solution, or alternatively, act "as if" they can. In terms of the empirical estimation of λ, we face issues of a similar nature to those that arise in the estimation of the parameter τ for the Poisson distribution in the CH model. The parameters might not be portable across games and one would ideally like to measure individual-specific parameters based on a large number of individual choices, rather than group-level parameters. The maintained assumption in these cases, which is central to the estimation of the parameters, is that all individuals follow these theories. It is quite possible that many individuals use simple rules of thumb, or their own specific experiences, or the recommendations of their social groups, or social norms, when they make their strategic decisions. The relevant parameters are then likely to be measured with error. A desirable method is to use mixture models in which we can simultaneously allow different individuals to follow different models of play – a good example of this is the work of García-Pola et al. (2020) that we have examined in Section 7.8.1 above.

7.8.4 Cursed Equilibrium

A *cursed equilibrium* (Eyster and Rabin, 2005) incorporates the idea that when players form beliefs under asymmetric information about the unknown types of other players, they economize on scarce cognitive resources by grouping the types into categories. All types within a category, although distinct, are treated in an identical manner. The idea that when faced with "rich information" players may usefully categorize information into a relatively small number of categories to reduce their cognitive burden is found in many behavioral models, although the models differ in the details. These include models of *analogy based equilibrium* (Jehiel, 2005; Huck et al., 2011) and models of *coarse thinking and categorization* (Mullainathan, 2002; Mullainathan et al., 2008). More technically equipped readers interested in an exposition of these models can consult Dhami (2020, Volumes IV, V).

Consider a simple application of a cursed equilibrium using one of the examples introduced in Section 7.6, popularly known in economics as the *market for lemons* (Akerlof, 1970). A used car market has two types of cars: *Peaches*, or high quality cars, and *lemons*, or low quality cars. The quality of the car is privately known to the sellers only and it constitutes the seller's *type*; in this example there are two types of sellers. Suppose, for the moment, that we rule out considerations of warranties and third party checks (e.g., a mechanic chosen by the buyer to examine the car before buying). While this example is couched in terms of used car sales, it is widely applicable. This is a situation of *one-sided asymmetric information* because the sellers are informed about their type but the buyers are not. The uninformed party, the buyer, has prior beliefs that 50% of the cars sold are peaches and 50% are lemons.

Let us make the extreme assumption that lemons are worth zero to both sellers and buyers (perhaps the maintenance costs of these cars make them unprofitable in the long-run). A peach, on the other hand, is worth \$3000 to the seller and worth \$4000 to a buyer. Let us assume that the market price for a car is fixed at \$1500 (in a more complete model, the price itself would be endogenous). Sellers of peaches are not willing to accept this price because their cars are worth \$3000 to them. Sellers of lemons are obviously delighted with the price of \$1500 and would like to sell. In effect, all cars on the market are lemons and no peaches are on sale. The optimal strategy of the seller of a lemon is to sell with probability 1, and the optimal strategy of the seller of a peach is to sell with probability 0. There are now two possible ways of proceeding further, that we outline below.

In neoclassical game theory, we would close the model by imposing the condition of mutual consistency of beliefs and actions; the relevant equilibrium concept is known as a *Perfect Bayesian Nash equilibrium*. Given that the market contains only lemons, in equilibrium, the beliefs of the buyers must assign a probability zero to any peaches in the market. No cars are then sold. In other words, we have a situation of *market failure* that precludes the possibility of profitable trades. This is a market failure because a peach is worth \$3000 to the seller and worth \$4000 to a buyer so if the types could somehow be identified, mutually beneficial trade would occur.

A *cursed equilibrium* relaxes the rationality requirements under neoclassical game theory by giving up the requirement of mutual consistency of beliefs and actions. It assumes that players are not able to perfectly correlate the types with their optimal strategies. Suppose that buyers assume that:

(i) with probability $\chi \in [0, 1]$ each type of seller plays the average strategy of both types of sellers, and
(ii) with probability $1 - \chi$ each type of seller follows their optimal action.

The size of the parameter χ is referred to as the *degree of cursedness* of the buyers. A fully-cursed buyer is characterized by $\chi = 1$ and in neoclassical game theory, which assumes zero-cursedness, we have $\chi = 0$. Given the optimal strategies of both types of sellers (lemon sellers sell with probability 1 and peach sellers with probability 0), the average strategy of the two types is to sell the car with probability $\frac{1}{2}$. Given the description above of cursedness, the buyer's (incorrect) beliefs in a χ−cursed equilibrium are as follows.

1. With probability χ, the owner of a peach sells his car with probability $\frac{1}{2}$ (the average strategy) and with probability $1-\chi$ the peach owner does not sell (the optimal strategy of the peach owner).
2. With probability χ, the owner of a lemon sells his car with probability $\frac{1}{2}$ (the average strategy) and with probability $1-\chi$ the lemon owner sells his car with probability 1 (the optimal strategy of the lemon owner).

Conditional on a car being on sale in the market, what is the probability that it is a peach? To answer this question, we introduce *Bayes' Law*, which is the standard method used in neoclassical economics although not well supported by the evidence (see Section 9.4). Suppose that there is a sample space Ω that contains two mutually exclusive events X_1, X_2, such that their union is the sample space, that is, $X_1 \cup X_2 = \Omega$. For instance, if we throw a six-sided die then $\Omega = \{1, 2, \ldots, 6\}$. If X_1, X_2 are the events, even numbered and odd numbered outcomes on a random throw of the die, then $X_1 = \{2, 4, 6\}$ and $X_2 = \{1, 3, 5\}$. Suppose that some event in Ω is observed, say, $X = \{3\}$. What is the probability of X_1 conditional on having observed event X? We write this conditional probability as $P(X_1 \mid X)$. Or, we might wish to compute the conditional probability of the event X_2, $P(X_2 \mid X)$. Answers to these sort of questions require the use of Bayes' Law, which we formalize in the next definition.

Definition 7.4 *Let Ω be a sample space and let X_1, X_2 be two mutually exclusive events such that $X_1 \cup X_2 = \Omega$. Then, for any $X \in \Omega$, we have*

$$P(X_j \mid X) = \frac{P(X \mid X_j)P(X_j)}{P(X \mid X_1)P(X_1) + P(X \mid X_2)P(X_2)}; j = 1, 2, \tag{7.30}$$

where $P(X_j)$ is the "unconditional probability" of the event X_j.

Definition 7.4 can be easily extended to any number of events $X_1, X_2, \ldots, X_n$ that comprise the sample space.

Since the cars are differentiated by quality (high and low), let us denote the seller of a peach as a high type, H, and the seller of a lemon as a low type, L. Let us denote the event that a car is for sale in the market by M. Given the beliefs of the buyer, outlined above, we wish to find $P(H \mid M)$, that is, the probability that, conditional on a car being on the market for sale, it is of high quality (a peach). The sample space is $\Omega = \{H, L\}$, thus, we can directly use Bayes' Law from Definition 7.4 to compute

$$P(H \mid M) = \frac{P(M \mid H)P(H)}{P(M \mid H)P(H) + P(M \mid L)P(L)}. \tag{7.31}$$

The unconditional probability of a peach and a lemon (i.e., their respective proportions in the population) are, respectively, $P(H) = \frac{1}{2}$ and $P(L) = \frac{1}{2}$. Using the χ−cursed buyer's beliefs about the peach seller above,

$$P(M \mid H) = \frac{\chi}{2}.$$

Similarly, given the χ−cursed buyer's beliefs about the lemon seller, we have

$$P(M \mid L) = 1 - \chi + \frac{\chi}{2} = 1 - \frac{\chi}{2}.$$

Substituting this information in the Bayes' rule in (7.31) we get

$$P(H \mid M) = \frac{\frac{\chi}{2}\frac{1}{2}}{\frac{\chi}{2}\frac{1}{2} + \left(1 - \frac{\chi}{2}\right)\frac{1}{2}} = \frac{\chi}{2}. \tag{7.32}$$

It follows that $P(L \mid M) = 1 - P(H \mid M) = 1 - \frac{\chi}{2}$. Thus, the expected value of a car on the market to the buyer is

$$EV = P(L \mid M) \times 0 + P(H \mid M) \times 4000 = \frac{\chi}{2} \times 4000. \tag{7.33}$$

The buyer buys the car if the expected value of the car exceeds the fixed price of the car \$1500, that is, $EV \geq 1500$. Using (7.33), this requires

$$\frac{\chi}{2} \times 4000 \geq 1500 \Rightarrow \chi \geq \frac{3}{4}.$$

Thus, if the degree of cursedness is high enough, in the sense that $\chi \geq \frac{3}{4}$, then buyers should buy the car. However, an unpleasant surprise might await car buyers. Because their beliefs are mistaken, they will find that they have purchased a lemon, which does sometimes happen with used car buyers. However, in actual practice, car buyers are offered many different kinds of private and institutional protections that minimize the effects of such potentially problematic market outcomes arising from asymmetric information.

One of the exercises at the end of this part of the book asks you to explain the *winner's curse* described in Section 8.2 using a cursed equilibrium. Empirically, a cursed equilibrium does not explain all aspects of the winner's curse because subjects in experiments play with significant noise around the predictions of a cursed equilibrium. Yet, a cursed equilibrium explains the data better than the corresponding equilibrium concept under neoclassical game theory, a Bayesian Nash equilibrium, that we used above in explaining the outcome of the lemons market under neoclassical game theory.

7.9 Social Rationality, Norms, and Cooperation

Neoclassical game theory is based on the notion of *private rationality*, which is also known as *individual rationality*. This requires that players do the best that they can for themselves. However, in an alternative notion of rationality, *social rationality*, in addition, players take into account some notion of what is best for their group, and have beliefs that other group members might also behave in this manner. Consider, for instance, a member of a football team who exerts costly individual effort so that his team may win; or a member of an army unit on a joint mission with other soldiers willing to incur great personal costs to ensure the success of the mission; or a member of a voluntary fundraising unit striving to meet an aggregate contributions target.

In each of these examples there are elements of strategic interaction, and self-interest, yet there is also a concern for the collective interest. Several concepts of social rationality have been proposed in the literature.

7.9.1 Social Rationality

The concept of *joint intentionality* (Tomasello, 2014) assumes that players have a shared common goal and they trust each other to implement the shared goal. Humans appear hardwired to behave in this manner in many social contexts and the early insights arose from Tomasello's work on comparing infant humans and infant chimps with respect to cognition and sociality. Infant humans exhibit joint intentionality from an early age, but chimps do not.

Kantian rationality may also be used to explain human cooperation through a notion of social rationality based on the *Kantian protocol* (Roemer, 2015, 2019). In the Kantian protocol, a player wishes to take the action that he/she would like the other players to take. Social rationality then ensures that players believe that other players will also take the same action. Players do not take actions consistent with the Kantian protocol because they fear reprisals from other players (which is the main mechanism supporting cooperation in repeated games in neoclassical game theory) but because it feels the right or the moral thing to do so.

Suppose that the payoffs in Table 7.1 are the actual utilities of the players in a PD game. Recall our formalization of a Nash equilibrium in Section 7.2. We are interested in the special case where each player chooses the same strategy, say, s, which can be any member of the set of possible strategies $S = \{C, D\}$. Given such a pair of strategies, (s, s), (known as a *symmetric strategy profile*) chosen by the two players, the utility function of player $i = 1, 2$ is given by $u_i(s, s)$.

A *Kantian equilibrium* is a symmetric strategy profile that arises when the utilities of both players are the highest relative to any other symmetric strategy profile. For the PD game, this condition holds true for the case of the symmetric strategy profile (C, C) because, for each player, $u(C, C) = 2 > u(D, D) = 1$. Thus, there is no puzzle from the observation of the cooperative outcome in the PD game if players are using social rationality instead of private rationality.

Team reasoning predisposes players to strive towards a common team objective (Bacharach, 2006); think, for example, of the analogy of players in a football team. Suppose that the team objective is to maximize the sum of payoffs of all players in the team. In the PD this will predispose players to choose the cooperative outcome. This line of inquiry does appear promising, but its success relies on using empirical evidence to figure out the team objectives in different contexts and frames and then make predictions that can be tested. It is also important to hypothesize and test the underlying emotions that lead players to conform to team objectives. For instance, it could be the case that players in a team feel guilt and/or shame from letting down other team members. We deal with some of these issues while analyzing joint liability contracts in microfinance in Section 8.6, but the relevant mechanism there is peer pressure and social norms, not team reasoning.

We often observe individuals engaging in costly actions for the social good, even in cases where the withdrawal of their actions does not lead to perceptible changes in the social good. In such cases their actions are said to be *nonconsequentialist*. Gintis (2017) distinguishes between three kinds of preferences *self-regarding*, *other-regarding*, and *universalist*; we discussed the first two preferences in Part II, although we have not discussed the third type of preferences before. *Universalist preferences* induce us to engage in virtuous acts for their own sake, such as being honest, trustworthy, keeping promises, and exhibiting compassion. Furthermore, Gintis distinguishes between two kinds of *personas* of individuals – a *private persona* and a *public persona*. The private persona applies when engaging in consequentialist actions, for example, the choice of a strategy in the PD game to maximize material payoffs. The public persona applies when engaging in nonconsequentialist actions, such as voting in elections, participating in civil rights movements, and protesting against inadequate governmental response to climate change. Many individuals might be predisposed to turn-on their public personas and turn-off their private personas when they encounter nonconsequentialist social situations, while others with different preferences might not. One can then study the interaction between the three kinds of preferences with the two kinds of personas above to get six possible cases.

The interesting interaction, for our present discussion, arises when one has a public persona but we vary preferences. An individual with a public persona but other-regarding preferences may take actions to favor his ingroup members over outgroup members (a sort of *homo parochialis*). An individual with a public persona but universalist preferences (termed *homo universalist*) would typically be willing to take selfless actions over social issues that do not necessarily directly alter the individual's material payoffs. However, these actions would appear, to the individual, to be the moral, and socially virtuous, thing to do. The presence of homo universalist would also explain why many individuals choose to vote in national elections although their vote is of no practical consequence for the outcome of the elections. By contrast, in neoclassical game theory, an entire branch of the field, political economy, has struggled to explain voting in elections, and has often come up with increasingly contrived, but untested, explanations for voting. This illustrates yet another feature of behavioral economics. Because the underlying human motivations are not contrived, and are often based on reasonably good evidence, one does not need to invoke ad hoc auxiliary assumptions to explain observed phenomena.

Enke et al. (2023) conducted a survey with 11,000 subjects in Australia, France, Germany, Sweden, and the United States, to detect the presence of *universal altruism* and *universal trust*. Recall from Part II of the book that social identity concerns arise when people favor others whose social distance from them is shorter (ingroups such as family members, clan members, regional members, club members) as compared to outgroup members. By contrast, individuals are said to exhibit universal altruism (in the sense used by these authors) when their altruism is not dependent on the social distance of the recipients of the altruism. For instance, such individuals might not distinguish between nationals from their own country relative to foreigners; or not distinguish between local community members and other nationals of their country.

Suppose that we plotted measured altruism of an individual against the social distance of the recipient of their altruism. The smaller is the slope of the estimated degree of altruism (i.e., smaller are social identity concerns), the greater is the degree of their measured universal altruism. Universal trust can be measured in a similar way.

We can also distinguish between the degree of universal altruism of policies. Examples of highly universalist policies include foreign aid, affirmative action, environmental protection, and federal redistribution because the beneficiaries typically have high social distance. Examples of policies that have a low degree of universalism include military spending and stringent border controls because they are less favorable to those whose social distance is greater.

Individuals in the survey are asked to allocate a sum of $100 between two individuals with varying social distance (e.g., someone from their country and a foreigner; or someone from their family and a randomly chosen individual from their country). This allows the authors to determine the degree of universal altruism of their subjects. Universal trust can be similarly gauged by determining how much subjects trust others depending on their social distance. For instance, would they trust someone from their country the same as a foreigner?

The main findings are as follows. First, universal altruism and universal trust are highly correlated, although the former is quantitatively more important in explaining policy choice. The authors club these two phenomena under the more general heading of *moral universalism*. Second, there is a significant degree of heterogeneity in universal altruism and universal trust among the subjects. Measured universal altruism explains policy choices when subjects are asked to allocate a sum of money to alternative government policies. Subjects with relatively higher universal altruism report (1) relatively greater desired expenditure on welfare payments, environment, affirmative action, foreign aid, and universal health care, and (2) relatively lower desired expenditure on border control, military, and law enforcement and police.

The third of these findings suggests that universalism might play an important role in the actual determination of a diverse set of policy choices. Indeed, related research shows that the propensity to vote and the political ideology of voters reflects deep preferences related to universalism, rather than material concerns (Waytz et al., 2019; Enke, 2020). By contrast, the modern literature in neoclassical political economy has stressed the almost exclusive importance of material concerns. These findings may also help to enrich that literature.

Social norms play no essential role in neoclassical game theory, yet humans are social animals with an inherent evolutionary desire to conform to social norms (Gintis, 2017). Norms and conventions often, although not always, lead to cooperative outcomes. Following Bicchieri (2006), successful social norms have the following components that we have described in more detail elsewhere in the book. Society has "desired" or *normative expectations* of what its group members "ought" to do. Group members also observe the actual actions taken by others; this constitutes the *empirical expectations* of group members. Group members who fall short of the normative expectations of the group are typically *sanctioned or punished* in some manner. Finally, successful norms often have the feature that the empirical and the normative expectations are consistent with each other.

All four components, normative expectations, empirical expectations, consistency between the two kinds of expectations, and sanctions might be needed for the successful implementation of social norms. This leads to a *shared understanding* of actions and beliefs among adherents of the norm (Fehr and Schurtenberger, 2018). Emotions such as *guilt* and *shame* from violating social norms play an important role in norm conformity, a theme that we return to in more detail in Section 8.6 (Bicchieri, 2006; Elster, 2011). Social behaviors based on normative expectations alone are sometimes referred to as *injunctive norms*, and when based on empirical expectations alone they are sometimes known as *descriptive norms*. *Conventions* are social norms that are not backed by any sanctions or punishments.

Social norms, past and present, can also sometimes lead to outcomes that are pernicious for society. Examples include female genital mutilation in Africa, which still persists; and the ancient Hindu practice of sati, or wife burning on the husband's pyre, practiced in some parts of India, which was finally outlawed and eradicated in 1829. Social norms can be inertial and hard to change, which in the case of harmful norms can reduce societal welfare over an extended time period. In other cases, social norms and conventions can play a beneficial role by coordinating potentially heterogeneous expectations of group members on a suitable cooperative outcome.

The social norms of trust, reciprocity, and adherence to one's word/promise, popularized, for example, in the saying "a man is only as good as his word," facilitate exchange in market economies with incomplete contracts. The social norms of bravery in battle and "no greater honor than dying in a battle" allowed internal cooperation between group members in times of adversity (rather than choose the free-rider option and flee). However, viewed from the perspective of inter-group conflict, it might well have reduced overall welfare through excessive violence which has been a feature of the human historical record.

7.9.2 Correlated Equilibrium

Gintis (2009) has argued powerfully to limit the role of a Nash equilibrium because it is based on several implausible assumptions. These include the assumption of *common priors* (see, Section 7.6 when players have asymmetric information about other players) and *common knowledge*. Suppose that there are two players, player 1 and player 2, and an event, say, event A, that has occurred. Common knowledge requires the following conditions. Players 1 and 2 know about event A. Player 1 knows that player 2 knows A. Player 2 knows that player 1 knows A. Player 1 knows that player 2 knows that player 1 knows A. Player 2 knows that Player 1 knows that player 2 knows that player 1 knows A … and so on ad infinitum. Indeed, it becomes challenging to write these chains of reasoning beyond a few steps. Yet, the common knowledge assumption requires that each player be able to engage in these sorts of infinitely long chains of reasoning; This is sometimes known as the *infinite regress problem*. How do players in a game come to form *shared mental constructs* such as common knowledge or common priors?

Gintis (2009) suggests that social norms play this role and coordinate the expectations and beliefs of the players in a game, but this requires moving beyond a Nash equilibrium. The idea that Nash equilibria can be interpreted as social norms is an old one (Schelling, 1960; Lewis, 1969). However, this is not empirically supported and most social norms are not Nash equilibria. For instance, most people would not expect social norms to lead to the worst possible joint outcome in the PD game (Section 7.2), in the centipede game (Section 7.3), and in the public goods game (Section 3.5). One can also determine the conditions under which players will play a Nash equilibrium, and this is the subject matter of *epistemic game theory*. A discussion of these issues is beyond our scope, but the required conditions are unlikely to be satisfied in practice. Gintis instead proposes a *correlated equilibrium*. We explain this next.

Epistemic game theory is the study of how various assumptions about (i) the rationality of players, and (ii) their beliefs about what they know and believe about the beliefs of other players, lead to different behaviors in games. As such, the basic setup is quite different from the way we have set up normal form and extensive form games in non-cooperative game theory in Sections

Table 7.14 A two-player simultaneous move game with two strategies

	c_1	c_2
r_1	a_{11}, b_{11}	a_{12}, b_{12}
r_2	a_{21}, b_{21}	a_{22}, b_{22}

Table 7.15 A simple illustration of the game in Table 7.14

	c_1	c_2
r_1	5, 1	0, 0
r_2	4, 4	1, 5

7.2, 7.3. A *correlated equilibrium* is a Nash equilibrium of an epistemic game in which a social planner or a choreographer first observes a random variable and then, based on this observation, issues recommendations to the players in the game. Conditional on other players following the recommendation of the choreographer, in a correlated equilibrium, each player prefers to follow the recommendation given to them. One of the central insight of Gintis (2009) is to equate the choreographer with social norms and conventions.

Let us first define a *correlated strategy,* restricting attention to only two-player games where players have two strategies each; see Table 7.14. The extension to more players and more strategies is straightforward. The row player, player 1, has two strategies, r_1, r_2, and the column player, player 2, also has two strategies, c_1, c_2. The payoffs of player 1 are denoted by a_{ij} and the payoffs of player 2 by b_{ij}, where $i,j = 1,2$. The set of all possible strategy profiles for the game is given by $S = \{(r_1,c_1),(r_1,c_2),(r_2,c_1),(r_2,c_2)\}$ and we will denote a typical element of this set by s. For instance, if the strategy profile is $s = (r_2, c_1)$, then player 1 receives a payoff of a_{21} and player 2 receives a payoff of b_{21}.

Consider any probability distribution over the set S. For instance, the four possible strategy profiles in S could be played with the respective probabilities given in the vector $p = \left(\frac{1}{3}, 0, \frac{1}{4}, \frac{5}{12}\right)$, where (r_1, c_1) is played with probability $\frac{1}{3}$; (r_1, c_2) is never played; (r_2, c_1) is played with probability $\frac{1}{4}$; and (r_2, c_2) is played with a probability $\frac{5}{12}$. This is an example of a correlated strategy. In general, we can write down any probability distribution over the set S as $p = (p_{11}, p_{12}, p_{21}, p_{22})$, where all four probabilities are nonnegative and sum up to one.

Definition 7.5 *A correlated strategy p is any probability distribution over the set of possible pure strategy profiles, S.*

The expected payoffs of the two players, player 1 and player 2 (using the same notation as in Section 7.8.3) from the strategy profile p are

$$\pi_1 = p_{11}a_{11} + p_{12}a_{12} + p_{21}a_{21} + p_{22}a_{22}. \tag{7.34}$$

$$\pi_2 = p_{11}b_{11} + p_{12}b_{12} + p_{21}b_{21} + p_{22}b_{22}. \tag{7.35}$$

Let us now work our way through some examples that enable us to develop the notion of a correlated equilibrium. Consider the game shown in Table 7.15, which is a special case of Table 7.14. There are two pure strategy Nash equilibria in this game (r_1, c_1) and (r_2, c_2). There is also a MSNE in which each player plays both strategies with equal probability. Thus, the expected payoff of the row player in a MSNE is

$$\frac{1}{2}\left(\frac{1}{2}5 + \frac{1}{2}0\right) + \frac{1}{2}\left(\frac{1}{2}4 + \frac{1}{2}1\right) = 2.5.$$

The reader can check that the expected payoff of the column player is also 2.5.

Suppose that two players, who know each other well enough to be fully confident that any mutual agreement will be honored, shake hands on a gentleman's agreement on playing the game in Table 7.15 in the following manner. They will toss a fair coin. If the coin comes up heads, they will play the strategy profile (r_1, c_1) and if it comes up tails, they will play (r_2, c_2). The expected payoff for the row player is now

$$\frac{1}{2}5 + \frac{1}{2}1 = 3,$$

and it is the same for the column player. Thus, playing correlated strategies can help improve the payoffs over a MSNE.

Let us now explain the basic idea behind a correlated equilibrium. Suppose the two players do not know each other well enough and have no confidence that the other will respect the gentleman's agreement. Yet, they are attracted by the payoff improving possibilities offered by a correlated strategy. So they appoint a *mediator*. The mediator tells them that he will make a private recommendation to each player to play a particular strategy. The mediator gives a short speech in which he says that he will choose randomly among two possible strategy profiles (r_1, c_1) and (r_2, c_2), with a probability of $\frac{1}{2}$ each. The mediator has, thus, chosen a probability distribution over S given by

$$\alpha = \left(\frac{1}{2}, 0, 0, \frac{1}{2}\right) \tag{7.36}$$

that specifies the probability with which the four elements in S are respectively chosen by the mediator; we have used α instead of p to indicate the choice of the mediator. Let us denote by S_m the subset of the set of strategy profiles S that are played with strictly positive probability under a given vector of probabilities, α. This set is $S_m = \{(r_1, c_1), (r_2, c_2)\}$ and the elements of this set are sometimes also called as *states*. The mediator is completely trustworthy and honors his word under all circumstances.

Suppose that player 1 is given a private recommendation to play r_1 by the mediator. Since player 1 has heard the mediator's speech, he knows immediately that player 2 must have been given the recommendation to play c_1. Similarly when given a private recommendation to play r_2, player 1 knows that player 2 must have been given the recommendation to play c_2. The same applies to player 2. When given a private recommendation to play c_1 (respectively, c_2) player 2 knows player 1 must have been given a recommendation to play r_1 (respectively, r_2).

To indicate that this is an epistemic game, we specify a *knowledge partition* of the two players. This specifies which elements in the set S_m players are able to distinguish between, based on the recommendations that they get. From our discussion above, we know that both players accurately infer the two strategy profiles in S_m from the given recommendations. Hence, the respective knowledge partitions of players 1 and 2, denoted by P_1 and P_2, are:

$$P_1 = \{(r_1, c_1), (r_2, c_2)\}\,; P_2 = \{(r_1, c_1), (r_2, c_2)\}\,. \tag{7.37}$$

A necessary (but not sufficient) condition for a correlated equilibrium is that each player prefers to follow the recommendations, assuming that the other player follows the recommendations. Let $r_j, j = 1, 2$ be a recommendation to player 1 and let the player actually choose the strategy $r_i, i = 1, 2$ for an expected payoff of $\pi_1(r_i \mid r_j)$. Similarly, we define the expected payoff of player 2 as $\pi_2(c_i \mid c_j)$, where c_i, $i = 1, 2$, is the chosen strategy when the recommendation is $c_j, j = 1, 2$.

For player 1 we need to check the following two conditions, assuming that the other player follows the recommendations.

$$\pi_1(r_1 \mid r_1) \geq \pi_1(r_2 \mid r_1) \Rightarrow 5 \geq 4, \text{which is true.} \tag{7.38}$$

$$\pi_1(r_2 \mid r_2) \geq \pi_1(r_1 \mid r_2) \Rightarrow 1 \geq 0, \text{which is true.} \tag{7.39}$$

From (7.38), when the recommendation is r_1, player 1 prefers to play r_1 rather than r_2, and from (7.39), when the recommendation is r_2, player 1 prefers to play r_2 rather than r_1. Both conditions hold because the strategy profiles $(r_1, c_1), (r_2, c_2)$ are Nash equilibria. The analogous conditions for player 2, which we leave the reader to interpret, are

$$\pi_2(c_1 \mid c_1) \geq \pi_2(c_2 \mid c_1) \Rightarrow 1 \geq 0, \text{which is true.} \tag{7.40}$$

$$\pi_2(c_2 \mid c_2) \geq \pi_2(c_1 \mid c_2) \Rightarrow 5 \geq 4, \text{which is true.} \tag{7.41}$$

The four conditions (7.38) to (7.41) are known as the players' *strategic incentive constraints*. This is pretty much what is achieved by a system of traffic lights. In the absence of traffic lights, particularly in busy traffic, there would be utter chaos, as sometimes occurs when traffic lights fail. Traffic lights play the role of a mediator, who in this case is the designer of the traffic lights. The mediator observes some set of states, say, two placards with Go and Stop written on them. The mediator then chooses every minute, one of the two signs with a probability $\frac{1}{2}$. If the Go placard turns up, the mediator turns on the green light and if the Stop placard turns up, the mediator turns on the red light. This successfully regulates the traffic. Of course, more complicated schemes, depending on the traffic intensity, and whether this is a two-way or a four-way junction, can be constructed, but the basic idea remains the same.

An important feature of this mediator-driven solution is that the *strategic problem* faced by any player (e.g., how to negotiate the traffic in the absence of traffic lights) becomes a *decision theoretic problem*, which can be analyzed using the machinery of Part I of the book. Hence, the individual essentially faces a set of probabilities over the states of the world and picks an optimal action. Thus, this form of social rationality offers a convenient cognitive simplification of an underlying strategic problem, and can improve decision making.

We now describe a correlated equilibrium. Suppose that the objective of the mediator, W, is to choose a correlated strategy

$$\alpha = (p_{11}, p_{12}, p_{21}, p_{22})\,,$$

from the set of all possible correlated strategies, which we denote by A, in order to maximize the sum of the expected utilities of the two players. Thus, the mediator's optimization problem is as follows:

$$\alpha \in argmax_{\alpha \in A}\ W = \pi_1 + \pi_2. \tag{7.42}$$

The mediator must respect the following constraints.

First, each player must prefer to follow the recommendation of the mediator assuming that other players follow the recommendation. This requires us to check the four strategic incentive compatibility constraints under the correlated strategy α. We list these constraints below.

$$\text{Player 1: } \pi_1(r_1 \mid r_1) \geq \pi_1(r_2 \mid r_1) \text{ and } \pi_1(r_2 \mid r_2) \geq \pi_1(r_1 \mid r_2). \tag{7.43}$$

$$\text{Player 2: } \pi_2(c_1 \mid c_1) \geq \pi_2(c_2 \mid c_1) \text{ and } \pi_2(c_2 \mid c_2) \geq \pi_2(c_1 \mid c_2). \tag{7.44}$$

Second, the correlated strategy should be feasible, that is, all probabilities recommended by the mediator must be non-negative and sum up to 1 across all possible strategy profiles, S. Thus, we have[12]

$$\alpha(s) \geq 0 \text{ for all } s \in S \text{ and } \sum_{s \in S} \alpha(s) = 1. \tag{7.45}$$

A correlated equilibrium is the solution to the problem of maximizing W in (7.42), subject to the constraints in (7.43), (7.44), and (7.45). Since the objective function in (7.42) is linear in the payoffs, the basic method of solution may require linear programming. Some readers of this book may have had training in this technique. One of the exercises asks you to find the linear programming solution.

The probability distribution $\alpha = \left(\frac{1}{2}, 0, 0, \frac{1}{2}\right)$ given in (7.36) is not a correlated equilibrium in the sense that we have defined a correlated equilibrium because

1. the mediator can ensure even higher payoffs for both players by choosing the new probability distribution $\alpha = \left(\frac{1}{3}, 0, \frac{1}{3}, \frac{1}{3}\right)$ over the set $S = \{(r_1, c_1), (r_1, c_2), (r_2, c_1), (r_2, c_2)\}$, and,
2. players prefer to follow the mediator's new recommendations.

In the new recommendations, the subset of states played with strictly positive probability is

$$S_m = \{(r_1, c_1), (r_2, c_1), (r_2, c_2)\}.$$

This involves the state (r_2, c_1), which is not a Nash equilibrium, but the joint payoffs of $4+4 = 8$ from (r_2, c_1) constitute the Pareto optimal outcome for the game in Table 7.15. Players know the states and the probabilities with which the mediator chooses them.

The knowledge partitions of the players are now more complex. When given a recommendation to play r_1, player 1 knows for sure that player 2 is given a recommendation to play c_1. However, when given a recommendation to play r_2, player 1 does not know what recommendations have been given to player 2. If (r_2, c_1) is chosen by the mediator, then player 2 is recommended to play c_1 and if (r_2, c_2) is chosen by the mediator, then player 2 is recommended

12 Recall that we denote by $\alpha(s)$ the probability with which an element s in S is chosen by the mediator; for instance, for (7.36), we have $\alpha((r_1, c_1)) = \frac{1}{2}$.

to play c_2. Similarly, when given a recommendation to play c_2, player 2 knows that player 1 has been given a recommendation to play r_2. However, when given a recommendation to play c_1, player 2 does not know what recommendation has been given to player 1; it could either be r_1 if the mediator has chosen (r_1, c_1) or it could be r_2 if the mediator has chosen (r_2, c_1). Thus, the knowledge partitions for players 1 and 2 (the analogues of (7.35) above) are

$$P_1 = \{\{(r_1, c_1)\}, \{(r_2, c_1), (r_2, c_2)\}\}; P_2 = \{\{(r_1, c_1), (r_2, c_1)\}, \{(r_2, c_2)\}\}. \quad (7.46)$$

Using (7.46), when given a recommendation to play r_2, player 1 uses Bayes' rule to assign probabilities to the two states $(r_2, c_1), (r_2, c_2)$ as follows:

$$p_1(r_2, c_1) = \frac{\frac{1}{3}}{\frac{1}{3} + \frac{1}{3}} = \frac{1}{2}; \; p_1(r_2, c_2) = \frac{\frac{1}{3}}{\frac{1}{3} + \frac{1}{3}} = \frac{1}{2}. \quad (7.47)$$

In (7.47) we have used the subscript 1 on p to denote player 1's beliefs. Thus, when given a recommendation to play r_2, it is "as if" player 1 faces an opponent who plays c_1 and c_2 with equal probability. Likewise, and using (7.46), when player 2 is given a recommendation to play c_1, he also uses Bayes' rule to assign probabilities to the two strategy profiles $(r_1, c_1), (r_2, c_1)$ as follows:

$$p_2(r_1, c_1) = \frac{\frac{1}{3}}{\frac{1}{3} + \frac{1}{3}} = \frac{1}{2}; \; p_2(r_2, c_1) = \frac{\frac{1}{3}}{\frac{1}{3} + \frac{1}{3}} = \frac{1}{2}. \quad (7.48)$$

From (7.48), when given a recommendation to play c_1, player 2 assigns equal probabilities of $\frac{1}{2}$ to player 1 playing either r_1 or r_2.

Having specified the beliefs, we can now check to see if the strategic incentive compatibility constraints for the players are satisfied. Let us first check the relevant conditions for player 1. (1) Suppose player 1 is given the recommendation to play r_1 (so player 1 knows player 2 has been recommended to play c_1), then player 1 should not do better by playing r_2. In other words, we need to check

$$\pi_1(r_1 \mid r_1) \geq \pi_1(r_2 \mid r_1) \Rightarrow 5 \geq 4, \text{ which is true.}$$

Now suppose that player 1 is given a recommendation to play r_2 (so player 1 uses the probabilities in (7.47)), then player 1 should not get a higher expected payoff from playing r_1, that is,

$$\pi_1(r_2 \mid r_2) \geq \pi_1(r_1 \mid r_2) \Rightarrow \frac{1}{2}4 + \frac{1}{2}1 \geq \frac{1}{2}5 + \frac{1}{2}0, \text{ which is true.}$$

We now check the strategic incentive compatibility constraints for player 2. Given the knowledge partition for player 2 in (7.46), the relevant conditions for player 2 are as follows.

$$\pi_2(c_1 \mid c_1) \geq \pi_2(c_2 \mid c_1) \Rightarrow \frac{1}{2}4 + \frac{1}{2}1 \geq \frac{1}{2}5 + \frac{1}{2}0, \text{ which is true.}$$

$$\pi_2(c_2 \mid c_2) \geq \pi_2(c_1 \mid c_2) \Rightarrow 5 \geq 4, \text{ which is true.}$$

Thus, all four strategic incentive compatibility constraints are satisfied, so both players follow the recommendations of the mediator.

The expected payoff to either of the two players when $\alpha = \left(\frac{1}{3}, 0, \frac{1}{3}, \frac{1}{3}\right)$ over the set $S = \{(r_1, c_1), (r_1, c_2), (r_2, c_1), (r_2, c_2)\}$ is

$$\frac{1}{3}4 + \frac{1}{3}1 + \frac{1}{3}5 = \frac{10}{3} = 3.33 > 3.$$

The main difference between a correlated equilibrium and a MSNE is that in a correlated equilibrium, the mediator prescribes a probability distribution across the set of strategy profiles S of the two players. By contrast, in a MSNE, players form a probability distribution across the set of their own pure strategies, S_i. Hence, the two equilibrium concepts differ significantly and typically make different predictions.

We now consider some of the experimental evidence on correlated games. When non-binding preplay communication is allowed between players, then players typically follow the strategies recommended by a mediator (Moreno and Wooders, 1998). Cason and Sharma (2007) find that in the absence of preplay communication, recommendations are less likely to be followed and depend on other factors. For instance, when subjects play against robot opponents who are preprogrammed to follow recommendations (and this is known to the players), then players are more likely to follow recommendations, as compared to playing against human opponents. The main impediment to following the recommendations, as revealed from a belief elicitation exercise of the players, is a lack of belief that the anonymously matched opponent will follow the recommendations. When players did follow the recommendations, their payoffs were higher. It is not a surprise then, that the earlier results on the success of recommendations involved preplay communication which is likely to have strengthened the beliefs that the other players will follow the recommendations. Recall that our motivation for introducing a correlated equilibrium was to assign to social norms the role of a mediator in environments where players interact, possibly at arms length. The presence of preplay communication, rather than its absence, in such an environment, is the natural assumption to make.

Duffy and Feltovich (2010) run a more nuanced experiment in which they distinguish between several different kinds of recommendations in a two-player *game of chicken* (see Section 8.4 below for this game) in which each player has two pure strategies. This game has two pure strategy Nash equilibria and one MSNE. When no recommendations are given, the aggregate proportion of players who are split between the pure strategies are close to the MSNE. In Cason and Sharma (2007), the expected payoffs of the players from following the correlated equilibrium were always greater than the expected payoff in the MSNE in the game. Motivated by this observation, Duffy and Feltovich introduce several treatments. In the good recommendations treatment (Treatment G), the expected payoffs exceed the expected payoffs in the MSNE. In the bad recommendations treatment (Treatment B), the expected payoffs in a correlated equilibrium are below the expected payoffs in the MSNE. In the very good recommendations treatment (Treatment VG), the expected payoffs exceed the very highest expected payoffs that can be achieved in a correlated equilibrium.

The results are as follows. First, subjects do not follow the recommendations in Treatment B even though it is a correlated equilibrium. Second, subjects do not follow the recommendations in Treatment VG either, although it offers the very highest expected payoffs to the players. Thus, a correlated equilibrium is a necessary, albeit not a sufficient, condition for recommendations to be followed. This also suggests why social norms are followed – if they take the form of a correlated equilibrium, then the injunctions in a norm are self-enforcing and more likely to be accepted and adopted. Third, in Treatment G, the recommendations were followed 70%–75% of the time. Fourth, recommendations always move play in a direction away from the MSNE and towards the recommendations, but the extent to which the play moves, depends in a more nuanced way on the type of recommendations, as revealed in the different treatments.

In the discussion above, we have assumed that players have self-regarding preferences. However, if players have other-regarding preferences that reflect inequity aversion, such as the Fehr–Schmidt preferences described in Part II, then inequity aversion will have implications for whether the recommendations that underlie a correlated equilibrium will be followed or not. The experiments in Anbarci et al. (2018) show this to be the case. This result suggests checking the robustness of the results in the correlated equilibrium literature with respect to different types of preferences.

7.10 Using Simple Heuristics to Solve Games

Relative to the heroic rationality requirements under neoclassical game theory, players in experiments often appear to use simple rules of behavior. Lab experiments offer possibly the only way to stringently test the predictions of neoclassical game theory because we can directly manipulate the experiments to test if the relevant restrictions required by neoclassical game theory hold true or not. Stringent testing in this area using field data is difficult and tricky and there is hardly much evidence to report here. Neuroeconomic evidence offers another promising direction in which some of the basic assumptions of game theory could be tested.

In Section 7.8, we saw that placing limits or bounds on the cognitive abilities of players, for example, in the level-k and the CH models, is likely to explain several kinds of experimental evidence better. The evidence provided in García-Pola et al. (2020) also showed that the behavior of players who follow simple rules may have greater explanatory power; see, for example, the simple types listed in Table 7.10. But how limiting should be the cognitive limits? This is an interesting question whose answer is not fully clear at the moment despite several promising suggestions.

Humans might use simple heuristics based on moral or social norms to decide which actions to take in a game even at the cost of foregone material payoffs. For instance, a norm of cooperation under some notion of social rationality might drive the play of C in the PD game (see Section 7.9 above). In other cases, players could simplify a strategic situation and turn it into a simpler decision theoretic problem, as we saw with our discussion of correlated equilibrium in Section 7.9.2.

Another proposal in this direction is *evidential reasoning* that has been mainly applied to static games of complete information (al-Nowaihi and Dhami, 2015), although the tools are transferable to other classes of games also. Under evidential reasoning, which is also known as *projection-bias* and sometimes the *false consensus effect* in psychology, players use their own propensity to play a particular strategy as having diagnostic significance in guessing what other like-minded players will do.

In a classic experiment conducted in Stanford University, students were asked if they would walk around the campus wearing a sandwich board with the word REPENT written on it (Ross et al., 1977). Those who agreed to do so, estimated that 63.5% of their fellow students would also agree to wear the board. Similarly, those who disagreed estimated that 76.7% of their fellow students would also disagree. Each set of students appear to be using their own disposition to wear, or not to wear, the sandwich board as diagnostic evidence of whether others would choose to wear one. This is the false consensus effect.

Often, in static games, players need to form beliefs about what others will choose in the absence of information on what others actually choose. Indeed, this is true in any static simultaneous move game of complete or incomplete information, for example, in coordination games. Evidential reasoning provides a cognitive shortcut in forming the relevant beliefs, at least if other players are believed to be like-minded. The evidence on players using their own beliefs and actions as diagnostic evidence of what like-minded others are likely to choose comes from many sources. In US Presidential elections, Democrat voters overestimate the share of other Democrat voters in the population and Republican voters overestimate the share of Republican voters in the total population despite having access to identical public information. Similarly, one's affective or emotional states disproportionately influence one's estimate of future affective states. For instance, people tend to buy more groceries for the week ahead when they buy in a currently hungry affective state, relative to a more satiated state. For the details of this and the other empirical evidence on evidential reasoning, see al-Nowaihi and Dhami (2015).

Consider how evidential reasoning, in conjunction with conditional reciprocity, might lead players to cooperate in the PD game. From Part II, we know that conditional reciprocators respond to kindness with kindness and unkindness with unkindness, but in new social situations they have an initial disposition to cooperate. Evidential reasoners who are conditional cooperators, come to the PD game with an initial disposition to cooperate, and they use this as diagnostic evidence about what their partners are likely to do.

If the partners are, thus, expected to cooperate why does not a player defect and get a higher payoff of 4? The answer, using evidential reasoning, is that players think that if they were to wish to do this, then their partner is also likely to wish to do this (because they project their own dispositions) in which case both will defect and get the lowest payoff of one each. Hence, they do not wish to defect even though players fully realize that they have no control over the choices of others. The result is that a significant fraction of the population may be expected to cooperate. In this explanation for cooperation, which goes back to Lewis (1979), and is formalized using the language of game theory by al-Nowaihi and Dhami (2015), players use simple rules of thumb to decide on their actions.

The determination of which rules of thumb players use in which strategic situation will be an important question for future research. It will require creative interdisciplinary research that uses notions of social rationality, say, from sociology, and the suitability of alternative cognitive shortcuts from work done in cognitive and social psychology. The resulting framework might not appear as elegant to some who are trained in neoclassical game theory, but it is likely to explain the evidence better.

8 Topics in Behavioral Game Theory

8.1 Introduction

In this chapter we continue our study of *human cooperation and coordination* and the flip sides, *conflict and miscoordination*, in strategic environments.

We begin in Section 8.2 by studying the *winner's curse* in *common value auctions* and show that it is essentially a failure to compute the correct conditional probabilities. It leads winners in common value auctions to overbid relative to the true value of the auctioned object, which typically results in low profits and/or bankruptcy for the winner of such auctions. There is a sizable literature on auctions with private values that we do not review, but the reader can look up several excellent references, for example, Kagel and Levin (2010).

Section 8.3 considers the behavioral economics of bargaining. A great deal of important human behavior occurs within bargaining environments. We outline the *Nash cooperative bargaining solution*, and a simple *alternating offers bargaining game*. The neoclassical predictions from the alternating offers bargaining game do not provide a satisfactory account of the data. When the *pattern of searches and lookups* of the players is examined using *mouselab software*, they are not consistent with what we might expect under neoclassical game theory. Players trained in neoclassical game theory do better. The predictions from these bargaining models do not explain why there is so much *bargaining impasse* in the real world, for example, prolonged conflict, wars, strikes, and messy drawn-out divorces. We outline a simple model of bargaining impasse that can potentially account for such phenomena.

Section 8.4 gives an elementary exposition of *evolutionary game theory*. We outline the main solution concept, an *evolutionary stable strategy* (ESS) and the *replicator dynamics* which trace out the time path that leads to a steady state of such a system. One advantage of evolutionary game theory is that in the presence of multiple Nash equilibria, the concept of *asymptotic stability* in replicator dynamics provides an equilibrium selection device. The selected equilibrium is history-dependent, and initial conditions play a powerful role. We also introduce the reader to some of the other exciting topics within evolutionary game theory.

Our analysis of evolutionary game theory is restricted to deterministic systems, so once the dynamic system reaches the *basin of attraction* of an asymptotically stable steady state, the system rests there for all time, unless a *chance mutation* occurs. By contrast, most real world dynamic systems are in a constant state of flux. In Section 8.5 we introduce the reader to the study of *stochastic social dynamics*, where shocks constantly buffet the system, giving rise to *persistent randomness*. We outline the concept of *punctuated equilibria* and indicate how low-level rationality can be critical in the formation of institutions.

In the final section, Section 8.6, we consider the exciting field of *psychological game theory*, which is a branch of behavioral game theory. In psychological game theory, the beliefs of players about what others will do, and beliefs about such beliefs, directly enter into the utility functions of players. This allows us to directly incorporate many different kinds of emotions into our analysis, such as guilt, shame, anger, and frustration. These emotions underpin the formation of social norms (Bicchieri, 2006; Elster, 2011) and, as such, help us in explaining how social norms might be sustained. We provide an analysis of some of the important issues in this area.

8.2 Winner's Curse in Auctions

The optimal design of auctions is an important area of study within game theory. Economists are mainly interested in exploring alternative rules that govern auctions, for example, how are bids invited, who pays what, and which auction format maximizes revenues for the seller.

An interesting form of auctions arises in the case of *common value auctions*. Suppose that we have n bidders, $i = 1, 2, \ldots, n$, for a single indivisible object in an auction. It is possible that each of these bidders receives some private signals $X_1, X_2, \ldots, X_n$ that may be informative about the value of the object. All bidders might also observe a common public signal S that is also informative about the value of the object (e.g., an expert on the object writes an article in a newspaper opining on the value of the object).

In general, before the auction begins, the utility of any bidder is given by a utility function $v_i = v_i (X_i, S)$, $i = 1, \ldots, n$, that depends on the private signal and the public signal. Two polar cases may be considered. In the first, utility depends only on the private signal, so $v_i = v_i (X_i)$; this is known as the *independent private values auction*. In the second, utility depends only on the public signal, so $v_i = v_i (S)$; this is known as the *common values* auction or the CV auction. Behavioral game theory has focused on both cases, but here we shall look into the common values case only, which has uncovered a *winner's curse*.

The winner's curse was first identified in auctions for the drilling rights for oil on given tracts of land. A public signal S is available of the value of the oil in this tract of land; this signal is identical for all bidders, hence, this is a common value auction. However, at the bidding stage, companies cannot be sure of the drilling costs, although all of them can make their guesses, and even consult independent experts for their best estimate of the costs. Since these estimates are formed independently, companies are likely to differ in their estimates. Suppose that the estimate of the actual cost of drilling by company i is given by

$$C_i = c + \varepsilon_i,$$

where c is the true cost of drilling, and the term ε_i is an independently and identically distributed random term across companies that has zero mean. In effect, the term ε_i adds noise to the cost estimates of companies and its actual value is realized separately for each bidder before the auction.

On average, bidders will guess the costs correctly because ε_i has a mean value of zero, so $EC_i = c$. However, different companies are likely to observe a range of values, some low, some high, depending on the realization of their company-specific noise term ε_i. The lowest value of ε_i that is observed, perhaps a large negative value, results in a cost estimate that is unrealistically low. Such bidders are likely to be overoptimistic about the costs of drilling, and, hence, bid too high. Since all bidders are identical except for their cost estimates, the winner in the auction is the most optimistic bidder who has the lowest realization of ε_i.

An unpleasant surprise might await the winner once drilling begins – the actual costs are likely to turn out to be much higher than the estimated costs. This might result in the bidder going bankrupt (version 1 of the winner's curse), or the profits might turn out to be much lower than expected (version 2 of the winner's curse).

Some of the earliest evidence consistent with the winner's curse was produced by three engineers Capen, Clapp, and Campbell in the early 1970s using data from the outcomes of the US Federal government's outer continental shelf oil lease auctions. These auctions appear to be of the nature of common value auctions. There was significant heterogeneity in the bids and winners were consistently disappointed with the rates of return. Many of the empirical findings are summarized in Thaler (1988), which we now draw upon.

(i) The ratio of the highest to the lowest bids was between 5 to 10 and sometimes as high as 100.
(ii) The sum of the winning bids in the 1969 Alaska North Slope sale was \$900 million, and the sum of the second highest bids was \$370 million.
(iii) The winning bid was at least four times the second highest bid in 26% of the auctioned tracts and at least two times the second highest bid in 77% of the cases.
(iv) Based on the before-tax returns on 1223 leases over the period 1954–69 in the Gulf of Mexico, only 22% of the leases were profitable and the after-tax earnings were low.

Classroom experiments on the winner's curse were conducted by Bazerman and Samuelson (1983) with MBA students at Boston University. In each of their 48 auctions, which had $4-26$ bidders, subjects bid for a jar full of coins or nickels or small/large paper clips with a value of \$8. The winning bid that was closest to the actual value of the item, won a \$2 prize. Bidders observed the same object (common public signal), but they were not told the exact value of the items in the jar, so the bids had to be based on their own noisy guesses. Obviously, subjects who formed the most optimistic estimates would win the jar, which mimics outcomes in a common value auction. The mean bid across all auctions was \$5.13, however, the average winning bid was \$10.01, which is about \$2 above the actual value and led to losses in half of the auctions.

Neoclassical game theory struggles to explain the evidence on the winner's curse. It views players as sufficiently "rational" to see through the problem and realize that their cost estimate is unrealistically low, and so they should not bid too high. For instance, it predicts that as the number of bidders increases, the optimal bids of bidders should fall. The main intuition is that winning an auction in a larger group conveys even worse news, because the winner's signal of the measurement error term, ε_i, is even more extreme. By contrast, in experiments, bids do not reduce as the number of bidders increases (Kagel et al., 1995).

There is some evidence that high levels of experience with bidding may reduce the winner's curse, but this does not eliminate it. This only occurs when subjects play a very large number of rounds of an auction game in experiments, with feedback. However, in the real world one might not get a similar opportunity for experience and feedback. When there are claims of a mitigation of the winner's curse based on real-life subjects, such as sports card dealers, the claims have been challenged. For instance, Harrison and List (2008) gave sports card dealers a package of 10 sports cards with a publicly known retail value, hence, eliminating any scope for a winner's curse, and in other contexts simple heuristics can explain the claimed mitigation of a winner's curse (Kagel, 2015).

Example 8.1 *("Acquire a company" game) An interesting demonstration of the winner's curse was conduced in the experiments by Samuelson and Bazerman (1985) with their "Acquire a company" game. In this game, an acquiring firm (A) bids an amount $b \geq 0$ to acquire a target firm (T). Firm A announces a bid, which firm T can either accept or reject. The value of the target firm, $v \geq 0$, is private information to T and unknown to A. However, A knows that v is uniformly distributed over the interval* $[0, 100]$, *that is, each of the values in the interval are equally likely. Firm A also knows that if it acquires firm T, the value of firm T will increase to γv, $\gamma > 1$ (e.g., firm A, rightly or wrongly, believes that it can add value to its acquisitions). Firm T agrees to the bid by firm A if the bid is greater than the valuation of the firm by T, that is, $b \geq v$. How much should firm A bid?*

Before reading on, think how much you would bid if you were firm A.

When $\gamma = 1.5$ (i.e., A expects to increase the value of T by 1.5 times after the takeover), then about 90% of the subjects in their role as firm A, bid in the range 50–75. Subjects in their role as firm A appear to reason as follows. "Since the value of firm T is expected to be uniformly distributed over the interval $[0, 100]$, the average value of the company is 50. Since $\gamma = 1.5$, the post-acquisition expected value is $1.5 \times 50 = 75$." The key error in this reasoning is that subjects ignore what the value of the firm would be, conditional on their bids being accepted.

Here is the statistically correct reasoning behind the optimal bid that will avoid the problem of a winner's curse. Firm T accepts the bid only if $b \geq v$. Thus, if a bid b is accepted, then it must be the case that firm T is not worth more than b. Since A believes that the value of firm T is uniformly distributed over $[0, 100]$, each value of firm T below b (and greater than or equal to zero) must be equally likely. Thus, on average, firm T is worth no more than $b/2$. It follows that if firm T is taken over by firm A, then the firm is worth $\gamma \frac{b}{2}$ in expected value. Does it make sense to bid b for a firm that has an expected value for firm A equal to $\gamma \frac{b}{2}$? The answer depends on whether

$$\gamma \frac{b}{2} \geq b,$$

or $\frac{\gamma}{2} > 1$. Suppose, however, that $\frac{\gamma}{2} < 1$ (or equivalently $\gamma < 2$) as, say, when $\gamma = 1.5$. Then, for any bid b in the interval $[0, 100]$, the expected value of the firm, $\gamma \frac{b}{2}$, is lower than the bid, b. Hence, the firm will make negative expected profits from bidding any strictly positive amount. Thus, the optimal bid must be zero, yet the evidence shows that subjects typically bid $50 - 75$ when $\gamma = 1.5$. Hence, they are subject to the winner's curse.

Game theorists often cite the example of auction theorists using models of auctions from neoclassical game theory to design auctions that have raised an impressive amount of money for governments. However, the actual design of these auctions followed common sense heuristics in achieving efficiency and competition by employing existing real world auction formats. Two leading UK auction theorists who played an important role in the UK spectrum auctions describe this well in Binmore and Klemperer (2002) who write (p. C94): "The auction confirmed our view that industrial-organization issues are more important than the informational issues on which the auction literature has mostly focused ... The really bad mistake in running an auction is just to take an auction design off the shelf, as shown by a comparison of the British and subsequent European 3G auctions. Auction design is a matter of 'horses for courses', not one size fits all." Indeed, in formulating their advice, they often had to resort to lab experiments at short notice in order to test auction formats that are not directly taught in neoclassical game theory courses on auctions. Hence, the ability to raise high revenues is testament to the sound advice and common sense of the auction theorists, as well as their ability to adapt the auction format to features outside of auction theory in neoclassical game theory.

8.3 Bargaining and Conflict

Bargaining is a very common feature of human interaction and, hence, one whose fundamentals need to be well understood. Neoclassical game theory uses two alternative methods of finding bargaining solutions that rely on cooperative and noncooperative game theory; we consider these below. We also consider other models that do not fall within this tradition.

8.3.1 The Nash Bargaining Solution

The first method, due to the Nobel Prize winner John F. Nash, is the cornerstone of cooperative bargaining theory. It begins by specifying some desirable features of a bargaining process and then predicts the bargaining solution, conditional on these desirable features. For instance, suppose that two players/parties, 1 and 2, bargain over the division of an amount of money M. Their respective shares are x_1 and x_2, where

$$x_1 + x_2 \leq M,$$

and the respective utilities of the players from these shares are $u_1(x_1)$, and $u_2(x_2)$; we allow the utility functions of the two parties to be different. Suppose that we denote the *utility possibility set* by U. It is the set of all possible utilities of the two players from all possible shares x_1 and x_2, that satisfy $x_1 + x_2 \leq M$ (see example below).

The fallback positions of the two players, should bargaining fail, sometimes known as the *outside options*, are respectively, z_1 and z_2. We wish to find a *bargaining solution*, which specifies what utilities each player will get from their respective shares x_1 and x_2, under the following four desirable features (or axioms) of a bargaining outcome, which would appear to most readers to be reasonable.

1. Pareto optimality (P): The bargaining solution should be Pareto optimal (see Definition 7.3), that is, it should not be possible to improve one person's payoff without reducing another person's payoff.
2. Symmetry (S): The condition of symmetry requires that when the set of all possible utilities of the players, U, is symmetric, then the bargaining solution should give identical utilities to the two players. The concept of symmetry is described in Example 8.2, below.

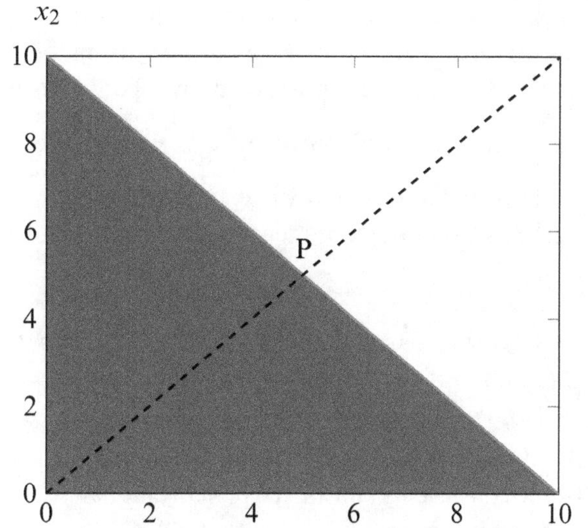

Figure 8.1 A symmetric bargaining set when dividing 10 between two players who have an identity utility function $u(x) = x$

Example 8.2 *To give a concrete example, suppose that $M = 10$; the individual utility functions are identity functions, that is, $u_1(x_1) = x_1$, and $u_2(x_2) = x_2$; and the outside options are zero, that is, $z_1 = 0$ and $z_2 = 0$.*

Then the set U is shown as the shaded region in Figure 8.1. It shows all possible utilities of the two players from all possible divisions of $M = 10$ between them; the X-axis measures x_1 and the Y-axis measures x_2. The point of origin $(0, 0)$ denotes the outside options of the two players (more generally, with $z_1 > 0$ and $z_2 > 0$, the origin of this figure is (z_1, z_2)). The dotted line is a 45° line that is at an equal distance from both axes. Symmetry requires that the bargaining solution lies at the intersection of this dotted line and the set U, which can occur at any point on the dotted line inside U. The assumption of Pareto optimality (P) requires that the solution must be on the boundary of the shaded region where $x_1 + x_2 = M$, that is, no resources should be wasted; this is shown as the point P in Figure 8.1. Otherwise, starting from any initial point in the interior of the shaded region, but on the dotted line, one can move in the direction of the boundary of the shaded region and improve the utility of both players. Hence, the initial interior point cannot have satisfied P. Thus, P implies that we can write the respective payoffs of the two players as x and $M - x$ (we use this in (8.1) below).

3. Independence of utility units (IUU): Suppose that we have a utility possibility set U and the bargaining solution gives the respective utilities u_1^* and u_2^* to the two players. Now multiply each possible utility of each player in the set U by a number $\alpha > 0$ so that we get a new utility possibility set denoted by U_1. Then IUU requires that in the new bargaining solution, the respective utilities of the two players are αu_1^* and αu_2^*, that is, they are scaled up by a factor α.
4. Independence of irrelevant outcomes (IRR): Suppose that the bargaining solution, when the utility possibility set is U, is given by u_1^* and u_2^*. Suppose that u_1^* and u_2^* belong to some subset $\widetilde{U}$ of U. Then, the bargaining solution, if we restricted attention only to the subset $\widetilde{U}$, is also given by u_1^* and u_2^*.

In a remarkable result, Nash (1950a) showed that any bargaining solution that satisfies these four desirable features (P, S, IUU, IRR) requires maximizing the product of utilities of the two players, net of the outside option. In other words, we should engage in the following exercise:

$$\text{Choose } x \text{ to maximize } W = (u_1(x) - z_1)\,(u_2(M - x) - z_2). \tag{8.1}$$

Consider the special case in Example 8.2 where $M = 10, z_1 = 0, z_2 = 0, u_1(x_1) = x_1\ u_2(x_2) = x_2$. In this case (8.1) asks us to choose x in order to maximize

$$W = x(10 - x). \tag{8.2}$$

The expression in (8.2) reaches a maximum value when $x = 5$, that is, a 50–50 split of the pie for each player. This solution is found from solving $\frac{dW}{dx} = 10 - 2x = 0$ to get the Nash bargaining solution $x^{NB} = 5$. This is a maximum value because $\frac{d^2W}{dx^2} = -2 < 0$.

Thus, when the outside options and utility functions are identical, the Nash bargaining solution formalizes what is widely considered in many human societies to be a fair split. A 50–50 split also appears to be incorporated into several kinds of social norms. The Nash bargaining solution does not specify an underlying bargaining method. It is viewed mainly as a *normative solution* to the bargaining problem, that is, "what ought to be" rather than "what is." However, the Nash bargaining solution does not allow us to compare the utilities of the two players. What if one player is more deserving on some ethical yardstick, for example, a severely handicapped person waiting at the end of a queue? Or what if the fallback positions of the players themselves are unfair, for example, one of the players is well provided for retirement while the other has prolonged spells of unemployment which have precluded any savings for retirement? In both cases, society is likely to come up with solutions that do not seem like the Nash bargaining solution. For instance, a separate queue for the physically handicapped, and a social security net for people retiring with low incomes.

These arguments suggest that we might need to drop the symmetry (S) requirement. This is accomplished in the *generalized Nash bargaining solution.* Suppose that $0 \le \mu \le 1$ is a number that denotes the relative *bargaining power* of player 1 and $1 - \mu$ is the relative bargaining power of player 2. Then, the generalized Nash bargaining solution, for the special case of Example 8.2 above, is given by

$$\text{Choose } x \text{ to maximize } W = x^{\mu}(10 - x)^{1-\mu}. \tag{8.3}$$

As an illustration, suppose that player 1 has all the bargaining power, so μ =1, then the solution is clearly $x = 10$ and player 2 gets nothing. At the other extreme, if player 2 has all the bargaining power, so $\mu = 0$, the solution is $x = 0$ and player 2 gets everything. For intermediate values of μ we get other solutions, tilted in favor of the party that has a higher bargaining power. To see this, differentiate (8.3) with respect to x to get

$$\frac{dW}{dx} = \mu x^{\mu-1}(10 - x)^{1-\mu} - x^{\mu}\,(1 - \mu)\,(10 - x)^{-\mu} = 0. \tag{8.4}$$

Dividing both sides of (8.4) by $x^{\mu}(10 - x)^{-\mu}$, we get the Nash bargaining solution $x^{NB} = 10\mu$, which shows that the share of player 1 is increasing in the player's bargaining power.

While the Nash bargaining solution is a milestone in game theory, it does not address issues about the *fairness of bargaining procedures*, nor does it tell us the source of the bargaining power of the players. It also does not tell us how parties should bargain with each other, say, how they should make offers and counteroffers to each other. Our next model explicitly addresses the second of these issues.

8.3.2 Alternating Offers Bargaining

The main bargaining procedure used in economics is the *alternating offers bargaining game* that explicitly incorporates a bargaining procedure and the assumption that time delays are costly because players are impatient. The main insight from this model is that relatively more patient players are more likely to achieve better bargaining outcomes.

While this method is quite general, we consider a specific example of two players who bargain over three time periods in an alternating offers bargaining game. We index the two players by 1 and 2 and denote time by $t = 1,2,3$. An offer by a player at the beginning of any time period specifies a split of a pie of given size. Players make offers and counteroffers sequentially, and only one player can make an offer in any period, starting with player 1 who makes the initial offer at time $t = 1$. This offer is either accepted by player 2, in which case the split offered by player 1 is implemented, or player 2 rejects the offer and makes a counteroffer at $t = 2$. This can either be accepted by player 1 at $t = 2$, or rejected, in which case player 1 makes a counteroffer at $t = 3$. No counteroffers can be made subsequent to the last time period $t = 3$.

The size of the original pie is \$5, but it shrinks to \$2.50 in the second round, and \$1.25 in the third round. This captures, in a reduced form manner, issues of time discounting and impatience of the players, although it cannot capture the relative impatience of the players. For simplicity, we assume that players do not discount future payoffs. The outside option of each player, should they exit bargaining without an agreement, is assumed to be zero.

Readers would have noticed that this is a dynamic game of complete information, so the solution under neoclassical game theory can be found by backward induction, starting from the last period $t = 3$, then unraveling or folding the game tree backwards, one time period at a time. Let us first state the bargaining solution that arises under backward induction.

Proposition 8.1 *Suppose that both players have common knowledge that they have self-regarding preferences, that they are rational, and there is an absence of conditional reciprocity. In the backward induction equilibrium, player 1 offers* \$1.26 *to player 2 at* $t = 1$*, keeping* \$3.74 *for himself, and this is immediately accepted by player 2, ending the bargaining game with an agreement.*

Proof of Proposition 8.1: Assume, as in neoclassical game theory, that both players have common knowledge that they have self-regarding preferences, that they are rational, and there is an absence of conditional reciprocity. Given the alternating offers structure, player 1 makes an offer at times $t = 1$ and $t = 3$, while player 2 makes an offer at time $t = 2$.

At the terminal time $t = 3$, when it is the turn of player 1 to make an offer, the size of the pie is \$1.25, so he offers \$0.01 to player 2 and proposes to keep \$1.24 for himself. It is individually rational for player 2 to accept this offer because the outside option is zero and $0.01 > 0$. Folding back the game tree one period, at time $t = 2$, when player 2 makes the offer, he knows that any offer that is less than or equal to \$1.24 will be rejected by player 1 who will be willing to wait for one time period, to get \$1.24 at $t = 3$. So, player 2 makes an offer of \$1.25 to player 1 (just 1 cent higher than \$1.24 to induce acceptance) and keeps \$2.50 – \$1.25 = \$1.25 for himself. At time $t = 1$, when player 1 makes the offer he knows that any offer to player 2, less than or equal to \$1.25 will be rejected by player 2 who would rather wait until $t = 2$ to get \$1.25. So, at $t = 1$, player 1 offers \$1.26 to player 2 and keeps \$5.00 – \$1.26 = \$3.74 for himself. Thus, in the backward induction outcome, player 1 offers \$1.26 to player 2 at time $t = 1$, keeping \$3.74 for himself and this is immediately accepted by player 2. This completes the proof.

Suppose that in Proposition 8.1, if we had assumed that when players are indifferent between an amount now or in the future, they accept the offer. Then, it is straightforward to show that an opening offer of \$1.25 instead of \$1.26 should also be immediately accepted by player 2.

The method of solution used in the proof of Proposition 8.1 underpins neoclassical game theory. Yet there are several problems. First, it relies on the backward induction solution method that is empirically rejected by a great deal of the evidence (see Section 7.3). Second, it is based on a misleading picture of human motivations that assumes self-regarding preferences and absence of conditional reciprocity. It also imposes unreasonable rationality requirements on the players when the same procedure is used for solving games with a large number of time periods and under more complicated assumptions such as incomplete information. Third, and most importantly, the prediction of the model that the very first offer is accepted, concluding a successful bargaining outcome, cannot explain persistent bargaining impasse in many areas, for instance, industrial disputes, strikes, lengthy divorce settlements, and wars between nations, despite recourse to third party arbitrators.

How might boundedly rational players with more realistic human motivations play the bargaining game outlined above? Johnson et al. (2002) offer the following conjecture that draws on insights from the level-k model (Section 7.8 above). Suppose that players are of two types, *naive* (similar to level $L0$) and *partially sophisticated* (similar to level $L1$).

A naive player, in his role as player 1, interprets any round of play as an ultimatum game (see Part II) and ignores the future rounds of play, capturing limited cognitive abilities. Suppose that such players make an offer of 40% of the pie, which is the average offer in ultimatum game experiments. With a pie size of \$5 at $t = 1$, this translates into an offer of \$2.00 to player 2.

A partially sophisticated player, in his role as player 1, believes (just like level L1 players) that all other players are naive. Such players look one step ahead, and ask what would be the counteroffer made by a naive player in the next round. Thus, at time $t = 1$, a partially sophisticated player 1 believes that at time $t = 2$, the offer made by a naive player 2 will be 40% of the pie of size \$2.50, which gives player 1 a payoff of \$1 and player 2 a payoff of \$1.50. Thus, looking ahead, at time $t = 1$, a partially sophisticated player 1 offers \$1.51 to player 2, which he believes will be immediately accepted.

We state these results in the Proposition.

Proposition 8.2 *When players are boundedly rational, the offers made by players at time $t = 1$ are as follows. Naive players offer \$2.0, and partially sophisticated players offer* \$1.51.

8.3.3 Testing the Predictions of Alternating Offers Bargaining with Mouselab Software

We can now play the bargaining game with real people, say, in a lab experiment, and test the predictions of Propositions 8.1 and 8.2. But we can also aspire to do a bit more. What if we made attempts to test the underlying human cognitive processes, proxied by the pattern of information acquisition of the players, which leads to a bargaining solution?

For instance, under neoclassical game theory, and using the logic of backward induction, this will require player 1 to first look to determine his own choices at time $t = 3$. It will also require player 2, at time $t = 2$, to first look ahead at the choices of player 1 at time $t = 3$ before deciding on her time $t = 2$ offer. Folding back the game tree, player 1 will now need to look ahead to infer the choices of player 2 at time $t = 2$. Thus, players should search for the relevant information "backwards" in the game as they figure out what they and the other players will choose in the future before making their current decisions.

But how can we peek inside the minds of players 1 and 2? A relatively direct method would be to use neuroeconomic methods, but they have their limitations when we wish to answer questions of the specificity that we seek here. The *mouselab software method* offers an ingenious way out. This method, in conjunction with other *psychophysical methods*, such as eye tracking information, pupil dilation, and skin conductance rates, along with inferring the cognitive processes of players through the time it takes them to deliberate in reaching a decision (deliberation times) now forms an important part of the arsenal of behavioral economists (Wang et al., 2010; Krajbich et al., 2015; Polonio and Coricelli, 2019; Alós-Ferrer and Buckenmaier, 2021).

The mouselab interface from Johnson et al. (2002), shown in Figure 8.2, was designed explicitly to test the three-stage bargaining game described above. The three time periods are identified as the three rounds on the left margin. The three boxes in the second column show the pie size corresponding to each of the three rounds and the three boxes in the third column show the player's role in that round (e.g., in rounds 1 and 3, player 1 makes the offer, while player 2 can only accept or reject). Each of the six boxes is blank. However, if the subject, who can see this interface, hovers the cursor on any box, the box opens to reveal its contents. In Figure 8.2, the subject has moved the cursor to the first box in column 1, which reveals the contents to be \$5.

If the subject were to move the cursor away from the box, the box closes, hiding its contents. Subjects who wish to make an offer when it is their turn to do so, move the cursor at the bottom of the box, which shows a dollar scale; clicking at a particular value on the scale enables them to make the offer. The software records the activity of the subjects every 16 milliseconds. This provides detailed information to the experimenter on the pattern of information acquisition in terms of the *look-ups and searches* of each player. An assumption of this method is that the pattern of information acquisition mirrors the structure of the cognitive process and information usage of the players.

Proponents of neoclassical game theory might object to the use of the mouselab software on the grounds that a Nash equilibrium does not make any assumptions about the underlying cognitive processes of the players. However, the Nash equilibrium also often fails direct tests (as outlined above in several sections), and the additional data on the observed cognitive processes of players may provide valuable information on refining existing theoretical models.

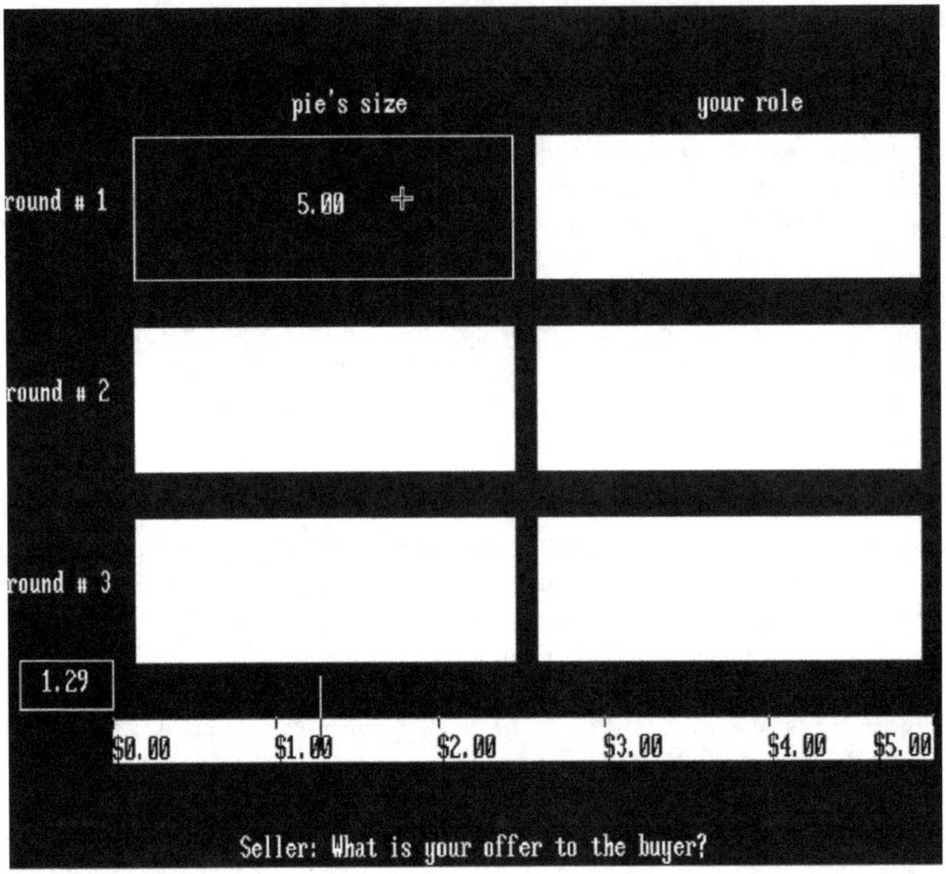

Figure 8.2 The mouselab interface for a three-round bargaining game between two players. Source: Johnson et al. (2002)

Furthermore, we can train subjects in the use of methods from neoclassical game theory, such as backward induction, in a "trained subjects treatment," and then compare the differences in their responses on the mouselab software to subjects untrained in neoclassical game theory in an "untrained subjects treatment."

Proponents of neoclassical game theory might also object to the mouselab method by arguing that the pattern of information acquisition of subjects could be searching forwards, memorizing that information, but really using it backwards, which is consistent with backward induction. However, why should players choose this more cognitively demanding method and not search backwards directly? Furthermore, players in the experiment were found to open the same box more than once, suggesting that it may have been difficult to memorize the contents.

The results were as follows. Consider first the baseline treatment in which subjects were not trained in neoclassical game theory. Subjects spent the majority of their time searching the boxes forward, and not backwards. Subjects who had to make offers, spent most of their time looking at the size of the pie in the first two rounds, and only 7% of their time looking at the size of the pie in the third round. The average first round offer by player 1 is $2.11, while offers below $1.80

are rejected half the time. This is inconsistent with the predictions of neoclassical game theory (see Proposition 8.1). The offers of players who searched the boxes backwards are closer to the predictions of the backward induction outcome, as compared to those who searched forwards. Thus, the mouselab method appears to have internal validity.

Could players be influenced by other-regarding preferences in making offers because they care for the other player's payoffs? In order to test for this, a "robot treatment" was used in which players played against a robot opponent; presumably humans do not exhibit the same degree of other-regarding preferences for robots. In this case, compared to the \$2.11 offer in the baseline treatment, the average offer falls to \$1.84. The robot is programmed to make an opening offer of \$1.25 at $t = 1$, yet unlike the predictions of neoclassical game theory (see Proposition 8.1), this is frequently rejected.[1] When subjects are trained in backward induction and asked to make an opening offer to the robot, they make an offer close to the expected offer under neoclassical game theory, \$1, 22. This suggests that people do not typically use backward induction unless they are trained in it. This is a more general point with respect to experiments in behavioral economics. When experiments are conducted using economics students, they are sometimes found to make more self-regarding choices relative to the general population.

Finally, in a mixture treatment, subjects trained in backward induction in the robot treatment were asked to play the bargaining game with untrained human subjects. Trained subjects initially make low offers that are rejected by untrained subjects. Untrained subjects initially make high offers but they find these are too easily accepted. When given an opportunity to learn, both groups of subjects adjust – trained subjects adjust towards higher offers and untrained subjects adjust towards lower offers. The effect of this tug of war is to give rise to an average first round offer, at time $t = 1$, of \$1.61. This is still quite some way from matching the predictions under neoclassical game theory.

8.3.4 Bargaining Impasse and Negotiation Models

While the evidence does not support the predictions of neoclassical game theory in the alternating offers bargaining model, we still have not answered why bargaining often stalls with disastrous consequences for both parties. For instance, messy divorces where the lawyers may end up being the happier of the three parties. The standard explanation in economics is *asymmetric information*. Suppose, for instance, that a couple who have just split up are arguing about the division of their assets, worth 100 (in some monetary units), but have had different incomes in the past. However, they have their own privately known sense of entitlement to the assets, which is unknown to the other party. Suppose that the husband believes that the wife's feeling of entitlement is equally likely to be either 60 or 30. So he offers a middle figure of 45. But unknown to him, the wife's entitlement is a 50–50 division of the assets, so she turns down his offer, which delays the bargaining outcome because she will now come up with a counter-proposal. She, in turn, might not know the husband's entitlement, and might make a low offer, which gets turned down, creating further delay.

[1] Recall our comment just after Proposition 8.1 that a different tie-breaking rule ensures that an opening offer of \$1.25 at $t = 1$ should be accepted.

Asymmetric information is undoubtedly important in the real world. Yet, economic theorists sometimes tend to invoke asymmetric information too easily and too quickly, without considering alternative explanations, and without subjecting the asymmetric information explanation to stringent empirical tests. The discussion below illustrates this point.

In the bargaining context, one of the most persuasive explanations for a bargaining impasse has come from behavioral economics without invoking asymmetric information (Babcock and Loewenstein, 1997). Bargaining parties may be subject to a *self-serving bias*, which arises from an attempt to rationalize actions by selective use of evidence to fit in with one's own self interest. Thus, the bargaining parties may confound between

(i) what really serves their own selfish interests, and
(ii) what is a fair bargaining outcome.

In other words, the outcome that they typically wish to implement gets identified, in their minds, as a fair outcome. This has two effects. First it narrows the set of possible outcomes to those that might be purely self-serving. Second, since the bargaining parties identify their self interests with (incorrectly) perceived fair outcomes, they interpret rejections of their offers by the other party as opportunistic and unfair. Since humans are also conditionally reciprocal, this incorrectly perceived intransigence of the other party elicits an unkind reaction by rejecting the other party's offers, even if that offer is reasonably fair by some objective criterion. Both effects serve to create a *bargaining impasse*.

But we can go further by creating a complete information environment inside the lab that lacks any elements of asymmetric information and test if there is a bargaining impasse. In the experiments conducted by Loewenstein et al. (1993), subjects are randomly allocated to the roles of a plaintiff and a defendant and given "identical" case material in which a plaintiff sues a defendant for damages worth \$$x$. The case material is fairly complete and independently checked. Subjects are asked to guess the damages awarded by a judge. The differences in the estimates of the subjects, in their roles as plaintiffs who assign high damages, and defendants who assign low damages, are statistically significant. Yet both parties have access to identical case information, so issues of asymmetric information are minimized.

A different approach to bargaining is taken in *negotiation research*, where the process of bargaining is not as structured as in models in economics. This has had little influence in economics, but Camerer et al. (2019) use the basic insights and machine-learning methods to try to identify which aspects of the bargaining process might play an important role in determining the bargaining outcomes under one-sided asymmetric information.[2] In unstructured bargaining, any party can make an offer at any time and can take as long as it wants to, subject to the overall time limit of the overall experiment.

The findings from this sort of work can potentially alert us to important shortcomings of the existing models of bargaining and also guide us in the development of future models. For instance, the authors found that as time increases within a round, the bids of the informed players increase, but the bids of the uninformed players decrease. They also observe a *deadline effect*

[2] The description of machine-learning methods is beyond the scope of this book (see Dhami, 2020, Vol. VI for an introduction).

because the majority of the deals were made within the last two seconds of any round, and deals were made more quickly when the pie size was larger. These predictions cannot be made by the other models of bargaining considered in this section, and point to newer factors that could enrich bargaining models. Empirically, the model based on "process data" was found to outperform competing models of bargaining.

8.4 Evolutionary Game Theory

Evolution is a slow and conservative process in which animals are "hardwired" to choose certain strategies. By contrast, in game theory, humans actively choose between alternative strategies. Yet, evolution provides the basis for the behavioral features that we see in behavioral models, such as loss aversion, reference dependence, altruism, reciprocity, and hyperbolic discounting.

One drawback of the Nash equilibrium solution is that there might be too many Nash equilibria in a game. For instance, the battle of the sexes game in Table 7.6 has two pure strategy Nash equilibria and one MSNE. *Evolutionary game theory* can potentially provide guidance on which of the multiple Nash equilibria is likely to get chosen, and also highlights the time path of choices of the players that lead to a particular equilibrium.

While behavioral traits are steeped in evolution and explained by evolutionary game theory, the same set of tools can be used to study the evolution of culture which can evolve much faster as compared to traits in biological evolution. As such, a basic knowledge of the tools of evolutionary game theory is indispensable for any social and behavioral scientist.

Here are the basic ideas in a nutshell. In evolutionary game theory, the basic unit of analysis is a gene. A gene can have several variants, or alleles. For instance, in humans, different alleles determine eye color, hair color, blood type, and height. Evolutionary game theory answers questions such as which allele, say, for eye color, will be the most successful in a given population. To simplify the analysis, we abstract from alleles, and assume simply that there are competing genes. Each gene is responsible for some behavior or trait, known as its *phenotype*. Different phenotypes have different levels of "fitness" that depends on (i) the environment that an animal lives in, and (ii) the competing phenotypes in the population.

Natural selection, in the sense of Darwin, ensures that phenotypes with greater fitness have higher reproductive success, that is, they make more copies of the animal, and hence of themselves. New phenotypes arise randomly by a process of *mutation*. We shall assume that there is only one mutation at a time. Phenotypes that can resist being invaded by mutants are said to be *evolutionary stable*. When we interpret phenotypes as strategies in a game, then we correspondingly search for *evolutionary stable strategies* (ESS). There could be no ESS, or one ESS (a *monomorphic population*), or more than one ESS (*polymorphic population*).

8.4.1 Evolutionary Stable Strategies (ESS)

We restrict our analysis to two-person simultaneous move games of complete information (see Section 7.2). We assume that players play pure strategies only. Suppose that the set of strategies for each player is identical, and denoted by S; it contains m pure strategies. The *strategy profiles* for the game are pairs of strategies, one for each player, denoted by (s_1, s_2), where $s_1 \in S$ is the strategy chosen by the first player and $s_2 \in S$ is chosen by the second player. The respective utility functions of players 1 and 2 are denoted by $u_1(s_1, s_2)$ and $u_2(s_1, s_2)$, that is, corresponding to any strategy profile (s_1, s_2), the utility function provides a numerical measure of the payoff or satisfaction of the player.[3]

We consider only *symmetric games*, which means that interchanging the row and column players in a normal form representation of the game does not make any difference. This is the case, for instance, in the PD game in Table 7.1, and the coordination games in Tables 7.6, 7.7. In a symmetric game, $u_1(s_1, s_2) = u_2(s_2, s_1)$, where the first strategy is always chosen by player 1 and the second strategy is always chosen by player 2. For instance, in the PD game in Table 7.1, $u_1(C, D) = u_2(D, C) = 0$ and $u_1(D, C) = u_2(C, D) = 4$. For this reason, we can dispense with the subscript on the utility function for players and simply refer to the utility of a player from the strategy profile (s_1, s_2) by $u(s_1, s_2)$. It is also for this reason that we have considered a common pure strategy set S for both players. In symmetric games, if we show that something is true for player 1, then it must also be true for player 2, and vice-versa. Thus, we need to show it is true for any player.

Next, we define an ESS, as first described by Maynard Smith and Price (1973), and then explain it in detail.

Definition 8.1 *Suppose that there is an existing strategy (or existing phenotype), s, that is played by both players, and there is any potential mutant strategy (or mutant phenotype),* $\widehat{s}$, *which is different from s. Then, the strategy s is an evolutionary stable strategy (ESS) if the following conditions hold:*

(i) Primary criterion: $u(s, s) > u(\widehat{s}, s)$.
(ii) Secondary criterion: If $u(s, s) = u(\widehat{s}, s)$, *then* $u(s, \widehat{s}) > u(\widehat{s}, \widehat{s})$.

The primary criterion requires that the utility, $u(s, s)$, of a player who plays strategy s against an opponent who also plays s is strictly higher relative to the utility, $u(\widehat{s}, s)$, where the player instead plays the mutant strategy $\widehat{s}$. If, however, the primary criterion is not able to differentiate between the two strategies, i.e., $u(s, s) = u(\widehat{s}, s)$, then we need to invoke a secondary criterion. Here the utility, $u(s, \widehat{s})$, from s against the mutant $\widehat{s}$, must be higher than the utility, $u(\widehat{s}, \widehat{s})$, from the mutant strategy $\widehat{s}$ against itself. If a strategy is an ESS, then it cannot be successfully invaded by a mutant strategy.

In Definition 8.1, we applied the concept of ESS to pure strategies only. One can equally apply the concept of ESS to mixed strategies. We do so in Section 8.4.5. However, until that section we will assume that players play only pure strategies.

Let us apply the requirement for an ESS to the symmetric hawk–dove game shown in Table 8.1 in which two players divide a prize $V > 0$ between them. Each of the two players has two identical strategies, Hawk (H), and Dove (D); Hawk has the connotation of being aggressive and Dove has the connotation of being a pacifist. If two Hawks meet, then they end up fighting for the prize, incurring an individual cost $c > 0$ each, so net of the cost, they share the remaining

[3] Technically, $u_i : S \times S \to \mathbb{R}$, $i = 1, 2$.

Table 8.1 The hawk–dove game

	Dove	Hawk
Dove	$\frac{V}{2}, \frac{V}{2}$	$0, V$
Hawk	$V, 0$	$\frac{V-c}{2}, \frac{V-c}{2}$

Table 8.2 The game of chicken

	C	M
C	2, 2	0, 4
M	4, 0	−3, −3

prize, that is, $\frac{V-c}{2}$ each. If two Doves meet, they agree costlessly to share the prize so that each receives $\frac{V}{2}$. If a Hawk meets a Dove, then the latter backs away from the contest, leaving the prize V to the former. We have two possible cases of interest.

1. If $V > C$, then we have the PD game. Here Hawk corresponds to defect and Dove corresponds to cooperate. Substituting $V = 4$ and $c = 2$ in Table 8.1, we immediately get the payoff matrix in our PD game in Table 7.1.
2. If $V < C$, then we have a *game of chicken* where there are two pure strategy Nash equilibria (H, D) and (D, H) (the reader should check this in the usual manner). Let us relabel the strategy Hawk as Macho (M) and Dove as Chicken (C) and use the values $V = 4$ and $c = 10$. We now get the game of chicken shown in Table 8.2. The metaphor is that of boy racers racing towards each other – the one who stops first is a Chicken and the one who stops last is Macho. Two Machos will damage each other for (negative) payoffs of −3 each, while two Chickens are grateful to escape unhurt with a payoff of 2 each. When a Macho meets a Chicken, the Macho wins and gets a payoff of 4, while the Chicken gets nothing. There are two pure strategy Nash equilibria of this game, (C, M) and (M, C). There is also a mixed strategy equilibrium, but we ignore it.

We are now interested in finding the ESS in these two games (PD game and the game of chicken) assuming that the numbers in each of the cells in Tables 7.1 and 8.2 are respective utilities of the two players from the corresponding strategy profiles.

Let us first consider the PD game. From Table 7.1, we can directly read off the utilities: $u(C, C) = 2$, $u(C, D) = 0$; $u(D, C) = 4$, and $u(D, D) = 1$. Recall that the only Nash equilibrium of the PD game is that both players play D. Is (D, D) also an ESS? To check this, we assume that initially all players play D, and then a small number of mutants who play the strategy C arise. We can now directly apply Definition 8.1 to check if (D, D) is an ESS. The primary criterion requires us to check it $u(D, D) > u(C, D)$, which is true because $1 > 0$. Thus, (D, D) is an ESS. The reader can check, using the same method, that if we started instead with all players playing C, then (C, C) cannot be supported as an ESS, that is, it can be successfully invaded by players playing D.

In fact (D, D) is the unique ESS of the game, as well as the unique Nash equilibrium of the game. This is not a surprise. It is true more generally that the set of ESS in the game is always a subset of the set of Nash equilibria of the game. Proving this is not hard. One simply needs to compare definitions 7.1 and 8.1. Notice that the primary criterion in the ESS is a strict inequality ($u(s,s) > u(\widehat{s},s)$ for all $\widehat{s} \in S$) relative to a weak inequality in a Nash equilibrium ($u(s,s) \geq u(\widehat{s},s)$ for all $\widehat{s} \in S$). Thus, every ESS must also be a Nash equilibrium. Because there is a secondary criterion in the ESS if the primary criterion fails, and this is not present in a Nash equilibrium, a Nash equilibrium need not be an ESS. Thus, the set of possible ESS lie within the set of Nash equilibria of the game.

Let us now consider the game of chicken in Table 8.2. Given the relation between ESS and a Nash equilibrium, the strategy profiles where all players play Chicken, (C, C), or where all players play Macho, (M, M), cannot be ESS, because each of the strategy profiles is not a Nash equilibrium. This is readily checked. Note that in the game of Chicken, we have

$$u(C,C) = 2, u(C,M) = 0; u(M,C) = 4; u(M,M) = -3.$$

(i) Suppose that we start with a monomorphic equilibrium in which all play C. Can a small fraction of mutants who play M invade this population successfully? Let us check the primary criterion, which requires $u(C,C) > u(M,C)$, but this is not true because $2 < 4$, hence, all play C is not an ESS. The intuition is that if everyone is a chicken, then a small fraction of macho mutants will find that they rarely encounter other machos and mostly encounter chickens, against whom they do rather well (payoff of 4).

(ii) By an analogous reasoning, if we start with a monomorphic population of all machos, then a small fraction of mutant chickens can successfully invade this population (the primary criterion $u(M,M) > u(C,M)$ is false because $-3 < 0$). In this case machos will mostly run into machos and incur large losses while the chicken will back out from contests and do better – the meek really do inherit the earth in this case.

It follows from the discussion above, that the only possible outcome of the game of Chicken is that we could have a *polymorphic equilibrium* in which a fraction $0 < x < 1$ of the players play chicken and the remaining fraction $1 - x$ play macho. Let us find a value of x that will ensure a polymorphic equilibrium.

Suppose that we have a large population of players and players meet each other randomly from the same population and play the game of Chicken with them. Then, with a probability x, a player who plays chicken meets another player who plays chicken, and with probability $1 - x$, meets another player who plays macho. Using Table 8.2, the expected utility of a player who plays chicken is

$$2x + 0(1 - x) = 2x. \tag{8.5}$$

Analogously, using Table 8.2, the expected utility of a player who plays macho is

$$4x - 3(1 - x) = -3 + 7x. \tag{8.6}$$

Using (8.5) and (8.6), if $2x > -3+7x$, then the fitness of chicken is greater and we should expect the fraction of players who play chicken to grow over time in the population, so this cannot be a stable equilibrium. If, however, $2x < -3 + 7x$ then the fitness of macho is greater and we should expect the fraction of players who play macho to grow over time, so this cannot be a stable equilibrium either. The only possibility left for a stable equilibrium is when

$$2x = -3 + 7x \Rightarrow x = \frac{3}{5} = 0.6. \tag{8.7}$$

Thus, in a stable polymorphic equilibrium, a fraction $x = 0.6$ of the players play chicken, and the remaining fraction $1 - x = 0.4$ play macho.

So far, we have considered equilibrium analysis (e.g., Nash equilibrium, ESS) and non-equilibrium analysis (e.g., level-k models, evidential reasoning), but we have been silent about the *time path to an equilibrium*. A great strength of evolutionary game theory is its ability to uncover the time path to an equilibrium. We now turn our attention to an explicit discussion of this issue.

The analysis of strategy choices over time in evolutionary game theory relies on the Darwinian idea of the *survival of the fittest*. Fitter strategies proliferate in the population and those that are less fit, decay over time. The process continues until we arrive at an equilibrium where the proportions of the strategies do not change over time. There could be multiple equilibria, some could be stable in the sense that small departures from those equilibria automatically bring the system back to the original equilibrium, while other equilibria might be unstable.

8.4.2 Replicator Dynamics

In order to formalize the idea of survival of the fittest, and the evolution over time of the various strategies, we use the method of *replicator dynamics* that was introduced by Taylor and Jonker (1978). Since we are also interested in polymorphic populations, we need to consider populations which contain mixtures of players playing different strategies. For ease of explanation, suppose first that time t is discrete, so $t = 0, 1, 2, \dots T$, where T is some terminal time; we allow for the possibility that $T \to \infty$.

Continuing with our example of the game of Chicken, at any time t, a fraction $0 \leq x_t \leq 1$ of the players play chicken and the remaining fraction $1 - x_t$ play macho. We are interested in how these fractions evolve over time, that is, starting from some initial value x_0, what are the values of $x_1, x_2, x_3, \dots$. Players in the population are randomly matched with each other to play the game of Chicken in Table 8.2.

Since opponents are randomly drawn from the population, at time t it is as if a player plays against an opponent who chooses chicken with probability x_t and macho with probability $1-x_t$. This is equivalent to saying that players face an opponent who plays the average strategy $\overline{s}$ which is an x_t probability of playing chicken and a $(1-x_t)$ probability of playing macho. Players, thus, face a risky situation and we assume that they use expected utility to evaluate these risky payoffs. The expected utility of each player will depend on the fractions x_t and $1 - x_t$; this will become clear below from the examples.

We only need to figure out how x_t changes over time because $1 - x_t$ can simply be calculated as a residual. We first state the formula for *replicator dynamics* that shows the evolution of x_t, and then we explain it in detail.

$$\frac{x_{t+1} - x_t}{x_t} = \pi(C, \overline{s}) - \pi(\overline{s}, \overline{s}); t = 1, 2, \dots T. \tag{8.8}$$

In (8.8), on the LHS, we have the rate of growth of the fraction of the population playing chicken at time t. On the RHS, the term $\pi(C,\bar{s})$ is the expected utility of a player who plays chicken against the average strategy $\bar{s}$ in the population; while the term $\pi(\bar{s},\bar{s})$ is the expected utility from playing the average strategy against an opponent who plays the average strategy. Note that we are using our convention of denoting expected utility by π in this chapter and the utility from an outcome by u.

If $\pi(C,\bar{s}) > \pi(\bar{s},\bar{s})$, then the fitness of chicken against the average strategy is greater relative to the average strategy against the average strategy, so the LHS is positive. Thus, between times t and $t+1$, the fraction of the population playing chicken will increase (and the fraction playing macho will decrease). The opposite takes place if $\pi(C,\bar{s}) < \pi(\bar{s},\bar{s})$. The relationship in (8.8) must hold in every time period.

What we have in (8.8) is a *difference equation* and it can be derived in many ways; see Bowles (2004), Bowles and Gintis (2011), and Dhami (2020, Vol. VI) for derivations.

It is analytically more convenient to analyze equation (8.8) when it is presented in continuous time, rather than discrete time. Assume, therefore, that time t belongs to some time interval $[0,T]$ and that equation (8.8) holds at each instant in time in this interval. Then we can rewrite equation (8.8) as

$$\frac{\dot{x}_t}{x_t} = \pi(C,\bar{s}) - \pi(\bar{s},\bar{s}); \text{ for all } t \text{ in } [0,T]. \tag{8.9}$$

The only difference between (8.8) and (8.9) is how we represent the LHS. In (8.9), $\dot{x}_t = \frac{dx_t}{dt}$ is the change in x_t at time t for a small instantaneous change in time, so the ratio $\frac{\dot{x}_t}{x_t}$ is the rate of change of x_t at time t. In particular, whenever $\pi(C,\bar{s}) > \pi(\bar{s},\bar{s})$ (fitness of chicken is relatively higher) we have $\dot{x}_t > 0$, the fraction playing C is increasing at time t. On the other hand, whenever $\pi(C,\bar{s}) < \pi(\bar{s},\bar{s})$, (fitness of chicken is relatively lower) we have $\dot{x}_t < 0$, the fraction playing C is decreasing at time t.

Letting

$$f(x_t) = x_t\,(\pi(C,\bar{s}) - \pi(\bar{s},\bar{s})),$$

we can rewrite (8.9) in its final form as

$$\dot{x}_t = f(x_t) = x_t\,(\pi(C,\bar{s}) - \pi(\bar{s},\bar{s})). \tag{8.10}$$

Thus, we wish to analyze the behavior of the differential equation $\dot{x}_t = f(x_t)$. Suppose we find a value of x_t such that when $x_t = x^*$ then $f(x^*) = 0$. Such a value of x^* is known as a *steady state* and there can be more than one steady state; see, for example, Figure 8.3. From (8.10), at a steady state

$$\dot{x}_t = f(x^*) = 0.$$

In other words, when the fraction of the population playing chicken is $x_t = x^*$, the rate of growth of the population playing chicken is

$$\frac{\dot{x}_t}{x_t} = 0,$$

because $\dot{x}_t = 0$. Thus, no further change over time in the fraction of the population that plays chicken will take place (and there is no change in the fraction that plays macho either). Notice that we have already derived the steady state $x^* = 0.6$ in (8.7) for the polymorphic population case. If we now plot $f(x_t)$, then we can find how the fraction playing chicken changes with time, and when and how the dynamic system in (8.10) arrives at a polymorphic equilibrium starting with an initial value x_0. Let us now undertake this task.

To determine the RHS of (8.10), we need to compute $\pi(C,\bar{s})$ and $\pi(\bar{s},\bar{s})$. To compute $\pi(\bar{s},\bar{s})$ notice that it is the expected utility from the average strategy $\bar{s}$ against itself, that is, as if an individual played C with probability x_t (to get $\pi(C,\bar{s})$) and M with probability $1 - x_t$ (to get $\pi(M,\bar{s})$) faces an opponent who played $\bar{s}$. Thus,

$$\pi(\bar{s},\bar{s}) = x_t\pi(C,\bar{s}) + (1 - x_t)\pi(M,\bar{s}). \tag{8.11}$$

We have already computed $\pi(C,\bar{s}) = 2x_t$ above in (8.5) and $\pi(M,\bar{s}) = -3 + 7x_t$ in (8.6). Substituting these values in (8.11) and simplifying we get

$$\pi(\bar{s},\bar{s}) = -5x_t^2 + 10x_t - 3.$$

Substituting $\pi(\bar{s},\bar{s})$ and $\pi(C,\bar{s})$ in (8.10), and simplifying, we get

$$\dot{x}_t = f(x_t) = x_t\left[5x_t^2 - 8x_t + 3\right]. \tag{8.12}$$

In Figure 8.3, we plot $f(x_t) = x_t\left[5x_t^2 - 8x_t + 3\right]$ as x_t varies between 0 and 1. We are interested in the *steady states* of this dynamic system, that is, the fraction, $x_t = x^*$, such that $\dot{x}_t = f(x^*) = 0$. From Figure 8.3, there are three steady states. Two of the steady states lie at the two extremities of this graph, $x^* = 0$ and $x^* = 1$. Both are monomorphic equilibria where all play M (at $x^* = 0$) or all play C (at $x^* = 1$). The third is an interior steady state at $x^* = 0.6$ (shown by the point E in Figure 8.3), which is a polymorphic steady state where both strategies, chicken and macho, coexist.

Is there any reason why the polymorphic steady state is particularly interesting? In order to answer this, we need some criterion which can separate the interesting from less-interesting

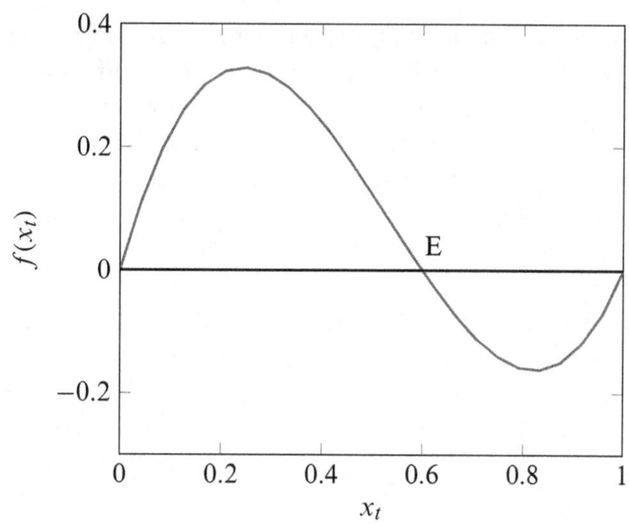

Figure 8.3 A plot of $f(x)$ for the game of Chicken

steady states. This criterion is *stability* of the steady state. A steady state is stable if starting from that steady state, any temporary departures, or perturbations, from it push the system back to the steady state, otherwise it is unstable.

Consider the steady state $x^* = 0$, where all play macho. Values of x smaller than 0 are meaningless. Immediately to the right of $x^* = 0$, where $x_t > 0$, in Figure 8.3, we have that $f(x_t) > 0$ (notice that $f(x_t)$ lies above the X-axis in region). It follows that $\dot{x}_t = f(x_t) > 0$ in that region, or the fraction of the population that plays chicken is increasing, so we continue to move further away from $x^* = 0$. Hence, this is an unstable steady state. By a similar reasoning, the steady state $x^* = 1$, where all play chicken, is unstable because just to the left we have $f(x_t) < 0$ ($f(x_t)$ lies below the X-axis). Any perturbation to the left, starting from $x^* = 1$, therefore, leads to $\dot{x}_t = f(x_t) < 0$, that is, a fall in the fraction, x_t, who play chicken, pushing the dynamic system further away from $x^* = 1$. Starting from $x^* = 1$, perturbations to the right are not possible because x_t cannot exceed 1.

However, the polymorphic steady state, $x^* = 0.6$, is stable. Using the same arguments as above, to the left of $x^* = 0.6$, we have $\dot{x}_t = f(x_t) > 0$ (the dynamic system is pushed back to $x^* = 0.6$) and to the right of $x^* = 0.6$, we have $\dot{x}_t = f(x_t) < 0$ (the dynamic system is again pushed back to $x^* = 0.6$). Such a state is said to be an *asymptotically stable steady state* because if the dynamic system starts from any initial state, x_0, except from the two extreme points ($x_0 \neq 0$ and $x_0 \neq 1$), then the dynamic system drifts over time to the polymorphic equilibrium steady state $x^* = 0.6$. If, however, the initial state is $x_0 = 0$ or $x_0 = 1$, then the dynamic system stays there for all time, unless a chance mutation takes place. If a dynamic system only reverts back to a steady state when perturbed in a small vicinity of the steady state, then the steady state is referred to as *locally stable*.

Note that from Figure 8.3, of the three steady states, the asymptotically stable steady state, $x^* = 0.6$, has the property that the function f cuts the X-axis from above, that is,

$$f'(x^*) < 0. \tag{8.13}$$

This condition for the stability of a steady state holds generally for any first order differential equation $\dot{x}_t = f(x_t)$ in one variable, provided that the first partial derivative of f is continuous.

Just like the set of ESS is a subset of the set of Nash equilibria of the game, the asymptotically stable steady states of the replicator dynamics is also a subset of the set of Nash equilibria of the game. We have proved the first of these two assertions above, but a proof of the second lies beyond the scope of this book. There is no presumption that a dynamic system will always have an asymptotically stable steady state. An example at the end of this section demonstrates this claim.

In other cases, one might have multiple Nash equilibria that are asymptotically stable. In this case, evolutionary game theory can predict which of the equilibria will arise, enabling us to make predictions that we cannot make under neoclassical game theory. An example is the *battle of sexes* game in Table 7.6. In Table 8.3, we use a slightly modified form of the game that expresses the payoffs in different units (relative to the payoffs in Table 7.6 these are divided by 100).

In Table 8.3, we have

$$u(A, A) = 2, u(A, B) = 0; u(B, A) = 0; u(B, B) = 6. \tag{8.14}$$

Table 8.3 A 2 × 2 coordination game

	A	B
A	$2,6$	$0,0$
B	$0,0$	$6,2$

Suppose that a fraction x_t of the population plays A and the remaining fraction, $1-x_t$, plays B. In a large population, players are randomly matched with each other to play the game in Table 8.3. Each player expects to meet an opponent who, on average, plays the strategy $\overline{s}$ which plays A with probability x_t and B with probability $1-x_t$. We would like to study the time evolution of the fraction x_t. As usual, we employ the replicator dynamics to answer this question, which is given by (note this is the analogue of (8.9)):

$$\frac{\dot{x}_t}{x_t} = \pi(A,\overline{s}) - \pi(\overline{s},\overline{s}); \text{ for all } t \text{ in } [0,T]. \tag{8.15}$$

Using (8.14), we can now readily calculate the following (as already explained for the game of Chicken).

$$\pi(A,\overline{s}) = 2x_t \text{ and } \pi(B,\overline{s}) = 6(1-x_t).$$

$$\pi(\overline{s},\overline{s}) = x_t(2x_t) + (1-x_t)6(1-x_t).$$

Substituting these calculations into (8.15), we get

$$\frac{\dot{x}_t}{x_t} = 2x_t - \left[2x_t^2 + 6(1-x_t)^2\right]. \tag{8.16}$$

Simplifying the RHS of (8.16), we can write it as $f(x_t) = x_t\left[-8x_t^2 + 14x_t - 6\right]$. Substituting back in (8.16), we can write the final form of replicator dynamics for the battle of the sexes game (the analogue of (8.12) for the game of chicken) as

$$\dot{x}_t = f(x_t) = x_t\left[-8x_t^2 + 14x_t - 6\right]. \tag{8.17}$$

In Figure 8.4, we plot the RHS in (8.17). This tells us how the fraction, x_t, of individuals playing the strategy A in the population varies. There are the following three steady states at which $\dot{x}_t = f(x^*) = 0$. There are two monomorphic equilibria $x^* = 0$ (all play B) and $x^* = 1$ (all play A); and there is one polymorphic equilibrium, $x^* = 0.75$, where 75% of the population plays A and 25% plays B (see point E in Figure 8.4).

Compare Figures 8.3 and 8.4. In Figure 8.4, when x_t lies in the interval $(0, 0.75)$ we have $\dot{x}_t = f(x_t) < 0$ ($f(x_t)$ lies below the X-axis), thus, the fraction playing A decreases until it reaches $x^* = 0$ (all play B). If, on the other hand, x_t lies in the interval $(0.75, 1)$ we have $\dot{x}_t = f(x_t) > 0$ ($f(x_t)$ lies above the X-axis), thus, the fraction playing A increases in this range until it reaches $x^* = 1$ (all play A). Thus, both monomorphic equilibria $x^* = 0$ (all play B) and $x^* = 1$ (all play A) are stable – any small perturbations from these equilibria bring the system back to these equilibria. Both are examples of asymptotically stable equilibria. However, the polymorphic equilibrium $x^* = 0.75$ is unstable in this case. If the system begins at time $t = 0$ at $x^* = 0.75$, then it stays there for all time, unless a mutation occurs. However, any perturbation to the right drives

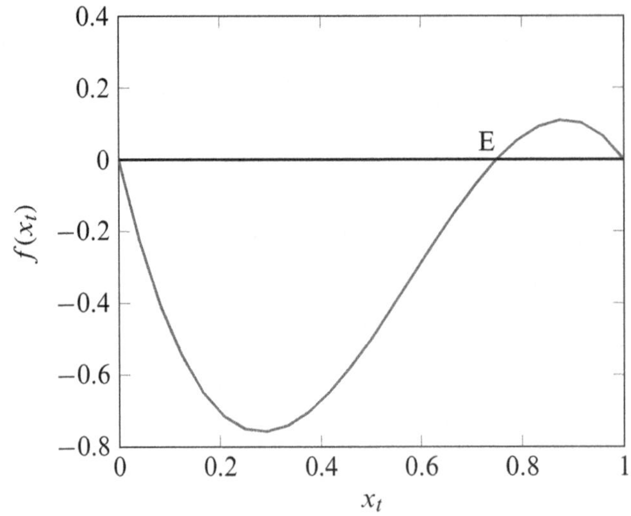

Figure 8.4 A plot of $f(x)$ for the battle of sexes game

the system to $x^* = 1$ and any perturbation to the left drives the system to $x^* = 0$. The reader can also check that each of the two monomorphic equilibria are also ESS by using Definition 8.1.

We already knew that (A, A) and (B, B) are Nash equilibria, but the predictions of neoclassical game theory could go no further. However, the extra insight that we draw from evolutionary game theory is when we might expect any of these equilibria to arise. We showed above that whenever the fraction x_t playing A lies in the interval $[0, 0.75)$, the system returns to $x^* = 0$ (all play B). This range, $[0, 0.75)$ is known as the *basin of attraction* of the monomorphic equilibrium $x^* = 0$. Similarly, the interval $(0.75, 1]$ is known as the basin of attraction of the monomorphic equilibrium $x^* = 1$ (all play A) because whenever the system is in this interval, it drifts to $x^* = 1$ over time. Thus, evolutionary game theory tells us that ultimately which of the two Nash equilibria arises, it is history dependent, that is, depends on the initial value x_0 where we start off the system at $t = 0$. If x_0 lies in $[0, 0.75)$, the system ends up at $x^* = 0$ and if x_0 lies in $(0.75, 1]$, the system ends up at $x^* = 1$.

8.4.3 Further Topics in Evolutionary Game Theory

The study of evolutionary game theory results in many other insights; for analysis and references the reader can follow up Bowles (2004), Bowles and Gintis (2011), and Dhami (2020, Vol. VI). Here is a brief taster of the many fascinating issues that can be addressed.

1. How might behavioral features such as loss aversion, reciprocity, or hyperbolic discounting have developed over human evolutionary history? In order to analyze them we need to specify appropriate models where these behavioral features play an important role as strategies in a well-defined game. We can then check if these features are ESS and also if they are asymptotically stable.
2. We can also study the evolution of culture. For instance, some cultures favor revenge, others forgiveness. In an appropriately defined game, one can then study which of these strategies

satisfies the conditions of ESS and asymptotic stability. It is important to appreciate that the relative fitness of these strategies depends on the relevant environment that they operate under, as well as the set of other competing strategies. Hence, the specification of these features assumes great importance.

3. In 1 and 2 above, we study the evolution of genes alone, or culture alone. There are interesting models of *gene-culture co-evolution* that combine the two. The idea is to create a feedback mechanism between genes and culture that mutually evolve to increase the reproductive success of an animal. A fascinating example comes from the fitness advantages of better oral communication (e.g., while our ancestors were cooperating and coordinating to hunt large animals) that were aided by genetic changes that facilitated richer communication. Gintis (2011, p. 3801) explains the genetic changes associated with the fitness-enhancing advantages of better communication (i.e., culture): "Expansion in the motor cortex region to facilitate speech production; development of brain regions such as Brocas and Wernickes areas, unique to humans, that facilitate grammatical speech; a gradual lowering of the larynx to increase the range and resonance of sounds; anatomical changes and developments in the tongue muscles that facilitate more precise speech; and changes in facial nerves and musculature that allowed a richer range of emotions to be displayed in a complementary manner with speech."
4. We can also use evolutionary game theory to study the evolution of human institutions. For an insightful book length account, the reader may wish to consult Bowles (2004).
5. In the analysis above, we have used gene as a unit of analysis and the sole purpose of a gene is to ensure that enough copies of it are passed on to the next generation; this formed the theme of Richard Dawkin's well-known book titled *The Selfish Gene*. However, human cooperation can often be hard to explain within the basic model. Several interesting directions have been proposed. These include *kin selection theories* which explain human cooperation among close family members. Shared genes within such close, genetically related, groups ensure that cooperation benefits individual genes. Selection may, however, operate on many levels. Within groups, altruism by individuals may be taken advantage of, lowering its fitness. However, across-groups, those groups who have a higher degree of cooperation, among themselves, possibly aided by individuals exhibiting altruism among themselves, are likely to do better in intergroup conflict. Cooperation can then arise as an evolutionary equilibrium depending on the degree of associative matching within-groups (e.g., how likely is it that two altruists within a group meet each other and not be mutually taken advantage of) and the degree of intergroup conflict. The interested reader can follow up these issues in Bowles and Gintis (2011) and Gintis (2017).

8.4.4 Advanced Topic 1: Non-Existence of an Asymptotically Stable Equilibrium

We now provide an example of the nonexistence of an asymptotically stable steady state. Some of this material might be easier to grasp for readers who have studied the basics of differential equations, but others might wish to try to persevere through the explanation.

Consider the two-player rock–scissors–paper game often played by children, where each player simultaneously chooses among three pure strategies, rock (R), paper (P), and scissors (S). The normal form game is shown in Table 8.4 with the corresponding strategies and payoffs;

Table 8.4 The rock–scissors–paper game

	R	S	P
R	0, 0	1, −1	−1, 1
S	−1, 1	0, 0	1, −1
P	1, −1	−1, 1	0, 0

note that the strategy scissors, S, is not to be confused with the set of strategies "S" that we have used earlier in this chapter. When the row and the column players pick identical strategies, their payoffs are 0. This is a zero-sum game (the sum of payoffs in each cell is 0). When two different strategies are played, one of the strategies wins to receive a payoff of 1 and the other loses for a payoff of -1. Rock beats scissors, scissors beat paper, and paper beats rock. The rock–scissors–paper game has no pure strategy Nash equilibrium (which the reader should check) and the only equilibrium is in mixed strategies, where each player picks all three pure strategies with an equal probability of $\frac{1}{3}$. Since this is the unique Nash equilibrium of the game, our discussion above shows that this is the only candidate for an ESS and an asymptotically stable steady state.

The presence of three strategies leads to a slightly more complex analysis because we need to solve a system of two differential equations. Suppose that the fractions of players who play the strategies R and S at any instant of time $t \in [0, T]$ are, respectively, x_t and y_t, while the fraction of players who play the remaining strategy P can be found as the residual $z_t = 1 - x_t - y_t$. Hence, we only need to study the behavior of the fractions x_t and y_t over time; the fraction z_t can always be found as a residual.

The average strategy $\overline{s}$ at time t is defined as playing R with probability x_t, S with probability y_t, and P with probability z_t. Players are randomly matched with each other in the population, thus it is as if each player is facing an opponent who plays the average strategy, $\overline{s}$. Since we are now interested in the time evolution of two different fractions, x_t and y_t, we need to write two differential equations, which are the analogues of (8.10). These are:

$$\dot{x}_t = f(x_t, y_t) = x_t\left(\pi(R, \overline{s}) - \pi(\overline{s}, \overline{s})\right); \tag{8.18}$$

$$\dot{y}_t = g(x_t, y_t) = y_t\left(\pi(S, \overline{s}) - \pi(\overline{s}, \overline{s})\right). \tag{8.19}$$

The differential equations in (8.18) and (8.19) show how the fraction of players playing R and S evolve, respectively. The expected utility from playing R against the average strategy is denoted by $\pi(R, \overline{s})$ and the expected utility from playing S against the average strategy is denoted by $\pi(S, \overline{s})$. Both expected utilities depend on x_t and y_t because of the presence of the average strategy $\overline{s}$ on the RHS. It is for this reason that the functions, f, g, depend on x_t, y_t. The reader can check in the usual manner that

$$\pi(R, \overline{s}) = 2y_t + x_t - 1;\ \pi(S, \overline{s}) = 1 - 2x_t - y_t;\ \pi(\overline{s}, \overline{s}) = 0. \tag{8.20}$$

Substituting (8.20) in (8.18) and (8.19), we get

$$\dot{x}_t = f(x_t, y_t) = x_t\left(2y_t + x_t - 1\right), \tag{8.21}$$

$$\dot{y}_t = g(x_t, y_t) = y_t\left(1 - 2x_t - y_t\right). \tag{8.22}$$

A steady state (x^*, y^*) of this system is a pair of fractions who play R and S such that we have

$$\dot{x}_t = f\left(x^*, y^*\right) = 0, \ \textit{and} \ \dot{y}_t = g\left(x^*, y^*\right) = 0.$$

The steady state value of the fraction P can be found as a residual, $z^* = 1 - x^* - y^*$. From (8.21), (8.22), we can readily solve out for the steady state (the reader should work this out)

$$\left(x^*, y^*\right) = \left(\frac{1}{3}, \frac{1}{3}\right); \text{and } z^* = 1 - x^* - y^* = \frac{1}{3}.$$

Suppose that we wish to check the *asymptotic stability* of the steady state $\left(\frac{1}{3}, \frac{1}{3}, \frac{1}{3}\right)$. Asymptotic stability requires that whenever the dynamic system is in the vicinity of the steady state, it arrives at the steady state over time. When we had a single differential equation in (8.12), the condition for asymptotical stability was given by (8.13). For a system of two differential equations, as in (8.21), (8.22), we need to check an analogous condition based on the following Jacobian matrix.

$$J\left(\frac{1}{3}, \frac{1}{3}\right) = \begin{bmatrix} \frac{\partial f\left(\frac{1}{3}, \frac{1}{3}\right)}{\partial x_t} & \frac{\partial f\left(\frac{1}{3}, \frac{1}{3}\right)}{\partial y_t} \\ \frac{\partial g\left(\frac{1}{3}, \frac{1}{3}\right)}{\partial x_t} & \frac{\partial g\left(\frac{1}{3}, \frac{1}{3}\right)}{\partial y_t} \end{bmatrix}.$$

Using (8.21), (8.22), direct differentiation of the functions f, g gives

$$J\left(\frac{1}{3}, \frac{1}{3}\right) = \begin{bmatrix} \frac{1}{3} & \frac{2}{3} \\ \frac{-2}{3} & \frac{-1}{3} \end{bmatrix}.$$

We now wish to find the eigenvalues of the matrix J. These are found as solutions to the determinant $\left|J\left(\frac{1}{3}, \frac{1}{3}\right) - \lambda I\right| = 0$ where I is a 2×2 identity matrix and λ is an eigenvalue. Solving this equation, we get the quadratic equation

$$9\lambda^2 + 3 = 0.$$

Using the standard formula for computing the roots of a quadratic equation, we find that both roots are imaginary numbers, given by $\lambda_1, \lambda_2 = 0 \pm i\sqrt{\frac{1}{3}}$, where $i = \sqrt{-1}$. From standard stability theory, when the real part of the imaginary roots is zero, the steady state is neutrally stable. By this is meant that it is not asymptotically stable (nor even locally stable), but if the dynamic system is started-off with an initial value (x_0, y_0, z_0) that is close enough to the steady state $\left(\frac{1}{3}, \frac{1}{3}, \frac{1}{3}\right)$, then the dynamic system stays close enough to $\left(\frac{1}{3}, \frac{1}{3}, \frac{1}{3}\right)$ as $t \to \infty$.

In Figure 8.5, we give a stylistic freehand representation of how the strategies evolve over time (a sort of artist's rendition of the underlying diagram) in a ternary diagram. Such diagrams are used to plot three variables x_t, y_t, z_t that always add up to a fixed number; here they add up to one. The vertices are marked with the respective fractions x_t, y_t, z_t. The steady state is marked with a dot and labeled with the letter s. The distance sa gives the value of x_t; the distance sb gives the value of y_t; and the distance sc gives the value of z_t.

In Figure 8.5 consider four possible initial states (x_0, y_0, z_0) that are marked in Figure 8.5 by $s, 1, 2, 3$. If the initial state is the steady state, s, the system stays there forever. However, the slightest perturbation will move the system away from s, never to return back to s. We show the

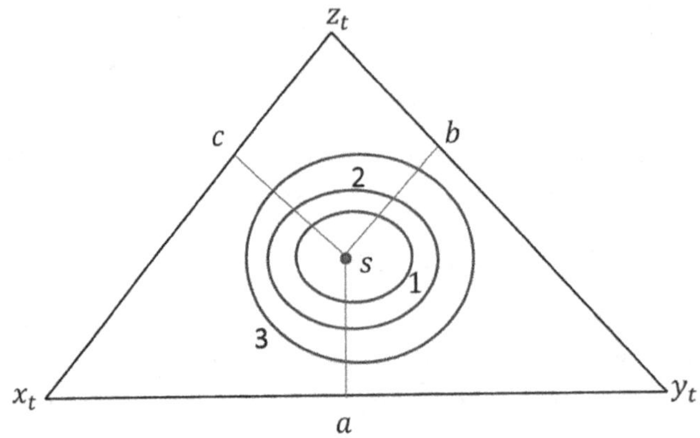

Figure 8.5 A stylistic representation of the time path of play in the rock–scissors–paper game

various time paths that this dynamic system traverses, starting from different initial states, 1, 2, 3, as the oval paths (this is not an exact plot) that stay close to the neutrally stable steady state, s, which is a requirement of neutral stability. Thus, to an outside observer, the dynamic path of the system keeps going in circles. The system appears in a constant state of flux without ever coming to a resting point, despite there being no random shocks to the system.

8.4.5 Advanced Topic 2: Evolutionary Stable Strategies in Mixed Strategies

A mixed strategy is a probability distribution over the set of pure strategies S. If, for instance, the set of pure strategies is $S = \{a_1, a_2, \ldots, a_n\}$, then a mixed strategy, p, specifies the probabilities $p_1, p_2, \ldots, p_n$ with which each of these n pure strategies is respectively played, thus, we can write $p = (p_1, p_2, \ldots, p_n)$. Denote the set of all possible mixed strategies by Δ. A mixed strategy $p \in \Delta$ is an ESS if it cannot be invaded by any mutant mixed strategy $q \in \Delta$. Under mixed strategies, players face a risky situation. We assume that they follow expected utility theory in evaluating their choices. Denote by $\pi\ (p, q)$ the expected utility of a player when he plays the mixed strategy p against an opponent who plays the mixed strategy q.

Suppose that all players initially play the mixed strategy $p \in \Delta$. Players in the population are randomly matched with each other. Hence, in any random meeting, the expected utility of a player is given by $\pi\ (p, p)$. Suppose now that there is small fraction $\varepsilon > 0$ of the players who turn mutant and play another mixed strategy q. Then, in any random meeting between players in the population, a player who plays p expects to meet an opponent who plays q with probability ε and p with probability $1 - \varepsilon$. In other words, this is an opponent who plays the average strategy

$$\overline{\sigma} = \varepsilon q + (1 - \varepsilon)p.$$

We can now state the analogue of Definition 8.1 in terms of mixed strategies.

Definition 8.2 *(ESS in mixed strategies) A mixed strategy $p \in \Delta$ is an ESS if for any mutant strategy $q \in \Delta$ played by some fraction ε of mutants, where $\varepsilon \in (0, \varepsilon_q)$, we have*

$$\pi\ (p, \overline{\sigma}) > \pi\ (q, \overline{\sigma}),$$

where $\overline{\sigma}$ is the average strategy given by $\overline{\sigma} = \varepsilon q + (1 - \varepsilon)p$, and ε_q is an upper bound on the fraction of mutants that can arise.

Definition 8.2 requires that the ESS, p, does strictly better against the average strategy as compared to the mutant strategy against the average strategy. We can also restate Definition 8.2 in a form that is analogous with Definition 8.1 by invoking a primary criterion and a secondary criterion.

Definition 8.3 *Consider a mixed strategy $p \in \Delta$ that is played by most players in the population and a mutant strategy $q \in \Delta$ played by some fraction ε of mutants, where $\varepsilon \in (0, \varepsilon_q)$. Denote the average strategy by $\overline{\sigma} = \varepsilon q + (1 - \varepsilon)p$. Then p is an ESS if:*

(a) Primary criterion: $\pi(p,p) > \pi(q,p)$.
(b) Secondary criterion: If $\pi(p,p) = \pi(q,p)$, then $\pi(p,q) > \pi(q,q)$.

In one of the exercises you are asked to apply this concept.

8.5 A Note on Stochastic Social Dynamics

In Section 8.4, we considered deterministic dynamics in which the only source of randomness was chance mutations. By and large, mutations are rare events, so in the long run the dynamic system spends most of its time in one of the asymptotically stable steady states. We demonstrated that the asymptotic steady state the system ends up in depends on the powerful role of history, as captured by the initial state of the system. Most people would agree that in contrast to this relatively serene state of affairs, the real world is buffeted by constant shocks, such as taste shocks, technology shocks, or even extreme unexpected weather events, that is, there is a state of *persistent randomness*. Deterministic dynamics would find it difficult to explain the stylized facts in such a world.

An alternative approach is provided in the study of *stochastic social dynamics* (Young, 1998; Dhami, 2020, Vol. VI). This framework recognizes that the world is in a constant state of flux and buffeted constantly by random shocks. Due to persistent randomness, any stochastic dynamic system is unlikely to stay forever in an asymptotic steady state. Even if the shocks are themselves of a small magnitude, persistent shocks can tip a system out of the basin of attraction of an asymptotically stable state.

Set your mind back to Figure 8.4, where the basin of attraction of the steady state $x^* = 0$ (all play B) is $[0, 0.75)$ and the basin of attraction of the steady state $x^* = 1$ (all play A) is $(0.75, 1]$. Suppose that the system is at one of these asymptotically stable steady states, say at $x^* = 1$. Then persistent shocks can slowly tip this system out of its basin of attraction in [0, 0.75). As soon as we have $x_t < 0.75$, the system automatically tips into the basin of attraction of the equilibrium $x^* = 0$, and over time, on account of persistent randomness, the dynamic system may reach $x^* = 0$, having started originally from $x^* = 1$. But the system does not get established at $x^* = 0$ forever; persistent randomness may again force a series of moves in the other direction that tip the system out of its basin of attraction of $(0, 0.75]$, back into the basin of attraction of the equilibrium $x^* = 1$.

So what are the predictions for these sorts of stochastic models? The first feature is *punctuated equilibria*, that is, the system keeps alternating between the various equilibria. Fashion watchers, for instance, are often amused by periodic changes in fashion; older fashions reappear, only to vanish again, to be replaced by newer fashions, but possibly reappear at some future time again. The second feature of these stochastic models arises from the analogue of asymptotic stability that characterized deterministic systems. This analogue, in this new framework, is called *stochastically stable equilibrium*. An equilibrium is stochastically stable if the system spends most of its time at that equilibrium, even if it keeps flitting about to other equilibria from time to time. If we study the long run frequency of play in such dynamic systems, we can identify where the system resides most of the time.

Let us now highlight the essential elements of this approach to give a flavor of how it works. While the approach under neoclassical game theory, and even in some behavioral models, such as quantal response equilibria, imposes fairly stringent rationality requirements on the players, stochastic social dynamics rely on *low level rationality*. Suppose that players were playing the hawk–dove game (of which the PD and the game of Chicken are special cases) repeatedly against randomly matched opponents from the population.

In this framework, players have *limited memory* of past play and remember only the play in the last few time periods, say, the last T_1 time periods (limited memory). They have access to the frequency of play during those remembered T_1 periods. Suppose they observe that in $\tau \leq T_1$ of these time periods, the other player played Hawk, and in the remaining $T_1 - \tau$ times periods they observe the opponent playing Dove. In the current period, they imagine that with probability $\frac{\tau}{T_1}$ they are facing an opponent who plays Hawk and with probability $1 - \frac{\tau}{T_1}$, an opponent who plays Dove. Then they play a *best reply* to these beliefs (known as a *myopic best reply*) with some probability $p > 0$, but with probability $1 - p$ they *experiment* by randomly choosing from one of the two strategies – Hawk or Dove (experimentation). So the essential features in this approach are: *limited memory*, *myopic best reply*, and *experimentation*. Thus, players are neither superrational, nor stupid, but they are boundedly rational and do the best they can for themselves.

While this approach paints a more realistic picture of human behavior and motivation under persistent randomness, the technical aspects of the analysis, at least in their full glory, are beyond the scope of this book. However, the intuition behind the main equilibrium concept, *stochastically stable equilibrium*, is not hard to grasp. A stochastically stable equilibrium is the one whose basin of attraction is the hardest to escape from.

The source of persistent randomness in the model is experimentation by the players. Let us start from any of the two monomorphic steady states in the battle of sexes game, ($x^* = 0$ and $x^* = 1$), say $x^* = 1$, where all play strategy A. We then ask: how many consecutive experiments by the players in favour of the other strategy, B, will result in the system tipping out of the basin of attraction of the $x^* = 1$ equilibrium, which is $(0.75, 1]$, and into the basin of attraction of the other equilibrium, $x^* = 0$, which is the interval $[0, 0.75)$. Clearly, the interval $(0.75, 1]$ is small as compared to the interval $[0, 0.75)$, thus, it will take fewer such experiments to escape it. In other words, it is easier to escape from the basin of attraction of the equilibrium $x^* = 1$ as compared to the basin of attraction of the other equilibrium $x^* = 0$. Thus, the stochastically stable equilibrium state is $x^* = 0$, and the system spends most of its time in that equilibrium state.

We can also interpret strategy profiles as leading to different institutions. For instance, in the PD game, the choice of a cooperative strategy might really reflect a choice of a cooperative institution and the choice of defect, a less cooperative institution. One of the interesting claims in this literature is that institutional choice is not the outcome of actions by major players (e.g., the importance of Napoleon to the legal code, Bismarck to social security, and Gandhi to nonviolence), but rather it is determined by the low level rationality of the players in a game (Young, 1998; Dhami, 2020, Vol. VI).

8.6 Psychological Game Theory

In neoclassical game theory, emotions are completely absent. By contrast, in our everyday decisions, emotions, such as guilt, shame, anger, and frustration, play a central role, and often provide the mechanism through which social norms and conventions are sustained. We develop this material gradually through the following six examples.

Example 8.3 *You are on a work trip to a city, where you are a stranger, and you are unlikely to visit again. In the evening, you decide to have dinner at a restaurant to sample the local cuisine. The food and the service are reasonably good. The waiter brings the bill at the end of your meal and you have a choice to tip the waiter or not to tip. If you did not tip, you do not lose any social capital (after all you are a stranger in the city), nor do you lose any reputation going forward in this particular restaurant as it is unlikely that you will visit the city again. Paying a tip reduces your material payoff. Why would you pay the tip?*

Neoclassical game theory predicts that homo-economicus would walk out without paying the tip, and the waiter will also assign a zero probability of receiving the tip. Will you pay or not pay the tip? In fact, many people are likely to pay the tip. As the waiter stands there in front of you, and you make eye contact while taking out your wallet, it might be hard for you to not feel "guilty" if you did not pay the tip, particularly "if you believed that the waiter expects the tip."

You might be in a similar position at the end of a taxi ride in the same city, where you have the option of paying a tip to the taxi driver. Or consider an even more extreme example, during the same trip. You hail a taxi from the street to go see a nearby picturesque beach on a moonlit night. You stop the taxi at a deserted spot along the beach with no one around, with the intention of taking a long walk. The driver is a handicapped old man, while you are a martial arts expert. If you do not pay and walk off, nobody will find out, and the taxi driver cannot harm you. Will you pay? Neoclassical game theory would suggest that you do not pay. However, most people are likely to feel immense "guilt" if they did not pay, and many others might feel the emotion of guilt from even imagining that they might do such a thing.

Example 8.4 *Recall our discussion of the public goods game in Section 3.5. Consider a static two-player public goods game. Before the players have had a chance to make their contribution decisions, the experimenter conveys to each of them the expectation held by the partner about their contribution level. Many players are likely to feel "guilty" from letting down the expectations of their partners, and this may induce them to contribute more, even if there are no punishments or sanctions. We will see concrete evidence later that this is the case.*

Example 8.5 *Consider the public goods game when punishments or sanctions are allowed once players have observed the contribution decisions of others (see Section 3.5 in Part II). As outlined in Part II, in neoclassical game theory bygones are bygones and players should not bother to engage in costly punishments of others because it would reduce their material payoffs. Yet, we often observe players punishing others for low contributions. One possible explanation for punishment is the inequity-aversion of players. However, another complementary possibility is that contributing players are frustrated and angry when they find that other players were free-riding. Hence, they wish to vent their anger at the free-riders through costly punishment. Having punished the noncontributors, the contributors feel better afterwards.*

Our next two examples come from *microfinance contracts* discussed in the introduction to this book. Recall that microfinance borrowers are small borrowers who engage in risky, but productive, projects, and lack any collateral to borrow money from the formal banking sector. A solution to this problem was discovered by Muhammad Yunus and the Grameen Bank through cleverly designed contracts (see the introduction) and these contracts resulted in a repayment rate in excess of 99%; this led them to winning the 2006 Nobel Peace Prize.

Example 8.6 *The Grameen Bank offered loans to groups of borrowers. Group members typically work on their individual projects (e.g., newspaper vendors, or vegetable vendors) that are risky. Despite working on independent projects, the group members are "jointly liable" for the repayment of the loan. Joint liability means that if one group member is unable to repay "her" loan (many borrowers are women), then all group members are refused future loans, even if they have repaid their individual loans. These loans are known as "joint liability loans" and they leverage the local information and the social capital of group members to ensure that group members locally monitor each others' effort levels on the independent projects. One can conjecture that "guilt" from nonrepayment of one's loan, which denies future loans to other group members, may spur individual effort that makes the individual projects more likely to succeed under joint liability, and ensure high overall loan repayments.*

Example 8.7 *Loan repayments to the Grameen Bank are often made in public in front of other members of one's social group. This is mainly because the loan officer is pressed for time and makes periodic visits to each region. During these visits, the microfinance borrowers in that region are gathered in a group and make their payment/default decisions publicly. Default in front of one's social group may invite the aversive emotion of "shame" from violating a social norm of repayment, and erode one's social capital. Could this too facilitate greater effort on the part of borrowers and, hence, higher loan repayment rates?*

The situation described above in Examples 8.6, 8.7 is generic to almost any problem where players work as part of a team with interdependent actions in the sense that one player's actions affects the payoffs of other team members. Guilt from letting down the perceived expectations of other team members is likely to be a key mechanism that spurs players to choose actions that are beneficial for the team. Shame from violating the team-specific social norms (say, *firm culture* when working within a firm) is likely to be another factor influencing the choice of individual decisions in a team. Thus, an important problem in incentive theory in economics is to design optimal team/group incentives that potentially take account of such social pressures.

Team incentives can play a complementary role to enhancing these emotions in a manner that is beneficial for team objectives. Such incentives have been shown to increase productivity in teams, relative to individual incentives. However, the literature on team incentives, some of it cited below, does not typically consider the role of beliefs that is central to our analysis in this section and to psychological game theory. By contrast, under neoclassical game theory, and under the conditions we shall specify, team incentives are typically predicted to be suboptimal because they induce a free-rider problem.

Hamilton et al. (2003) show that group piece-rate incentives increased productivity by nearly a sixth relative to individual piece rate incentives. Bandiera et al. (2005) show that productivity is higher when teams of players are given individual piece-rate incentives rather than relative incentives such as a bonus for producing higher output relative to other workers. Relative incentives may create guilt and envy among workers (although guilt is not the specific transmission channel studied by the authors) from unequal earnings relative to other workers who might be close friends and long-time coworkers. Babcock et al. (2015) explicitly identify guilt and shame as the relevant transmission channels through which team incentives are more productive than individual incentives. One can conjecture that being observed by peers may invoke the emotions of guilt and shame even more, contributing to an even greater increase in productivity in teams. Several empirical papers in the literature allude to the role of such social pressure in enhancing productivity (Charness et al., 2007; Andreoni and Bernheim, 2009; Bandiera et al., 2010).

Example 8.8 *Consider a simplified two-player ultimatum game in Figure 8.6 in which the proposer, P, has two choices only. This is a dynamic game of complete information, so we use backward induction to solve it. Player P moves first by choosing one of two actions, labeled "1" and "2." The responder, R, observes the action chosen by P, and then either accepts (action "a") or rejects (action "r"). The respective payoffs of the two players are shown as two numbers at the bottom of each terminal node in Figure 8.6; the first number is the payoff of player 1 and the second number is the payoff of player 2. For instance, if P chooses 1 and then R chooses reject, then both get zero, but if R had chosen accept, then their respective payoffs would be 8 and 2. If P chooses 2 and R chooses to accept then we can see two pairs of numbers that reflect the payoffs of P and R in two different treatments. In treatment T1, the payoffs are 5 each, and in treatment T2, the payoffs of player P and R (shown in brackets) are, respectively, 10 and 0.*

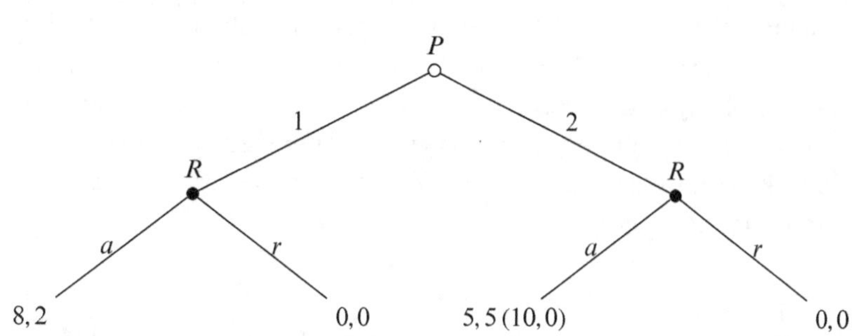

Figure 8.6 An ultimatum game to study the role of intentions. Source: Redrawn using numerical values from Falk et al. (2008)

In neoclassical game theory, in both treatments, a self-regarding R never receives a lower payoff from accept, relative to reject which gives a payoff of zero. Looking forward, and knowing this, P should choose the action "1" in treatment T1 (because $8 > 5$*) and the action "2" in treatment T2 (because* $8 < 10$*).*

A more nuanced answer follows if we relax the assumption of self-regarding preferences. Suppose that players are conditionally reciprocal (as in Part II) and care about the "intentions" of the other player in making their strategic choices. Players would like to reward other players for kind intentions and punish them for "unkind intentions." Think, for instance, of the difference in your reaction if someone accidentally steps on your foot and immediately apologies, and someone who deliberately stomps on your foot and sneers at you.

Consider treatment T1 first. If P plays "1" resulting in a payoff of 2 to R, then it reveals to player R that P is unkind. After all, P could have played '2' instead and ensured an equal payoff of 5 for both players. So, a strongly conditionally reciprocal player R might choose to reject, following a choice of "1" by P.

However, in Treatment T2, the choice of "1" by P provides a signal of kindness to player R. In this case, P could have played "2" instead, to achieve a payoff of 10 (and R gets 0) but chose instead to forego some of that payoff to play "1" instead and get a payoff of 8 and ensure that player 2 gets 2. Hence, player 2 is more likely to accept in treatment T2. This reasoning is consistent with the findings of Falk et al. (2008) who find that the rejection rate following the play of "1" by P in treatment T1 is 44.4% while it is only 8.9% in treatment T2; the 8.9% rejections possibly come from players who may believe that it is unfair that their payoffs are lower than player 1 in every case. The formation of the players' beliefs about the intentions of others is critical in explaining this data.

Examples 8.3–8.8 require the construction of a theoretical model in which the beliefs that players have about other players, and their beliefs about such beliefs, play a central role. Guilt, for instance, arises from falling short of the perceived expectations of others, or even falling short of the moral standards that one sets of oneself (Examples 8.3, 8.4, 8.6). Hence players need to form beliefs about the expectations of others, or sometimes even beliefs about their own expectations of themselves as in the case of moral norms of behavior. In Example 8.7, "shame" arises from falling short of the perceived expectations of one's social group, particularly if the social group expects one to repay third-party loans. So players may need to form beliefs about the expectations of one's social group.

It is eminently plausible that feelings of guilt and shame give us *direct disutility* and lower our well-being and happiness. But this requires introducing beliefs directly into the utility functions of players. However, neoclassical game theory does not allow beliefs to enter into the utility function; only outcomes, monetary or nonmonetary, are allowed to enter into the utility functions. Hence, we need a somewhat different framework, *psychological game theory* (PGT), to incorporate such factors.[4]

[4] For an authoritative review of all aspects of PGT see Battigalli and Dufwenberg (2022). This contains an extensive list of many seminal references in this literature that we have omitted. For a textbook treatment, see Dhami (2020, Vol. IV, Sections 2.5, 3.6).

Let us formalize guilt in Example 8.4 in a single-round public goods game considered in Part II with two players ($n = 2$), that we label as player 1 and player 2. Each player has an endowment of 20 tokens and both players simultaneously choose contributions to the public good. From Part II, the utility function of a self-regarding player $i = 1, 2$, reflecting the material payoffs alone, is

$$u_i = 20 - g_i + 0.3 \times G. \tag{8.23}$$

Player $i = 1, 2$ contributes an amount g_i to the public good and the partner contributes an amount g_{-i} (the subscript $-i$ denotes player i's partner) for total public goods contributions given by

$$G = g_i + g_{-i}. \tag{8.24}$$

We now wish to introduce beliefs into this utility function in order to introduce the possibility of guilt. Beliefs of different orders are built up in a hierarchical manner, as we now explain. Before player $i = 1, 2$ makes his contribution decision, he has beliefs about what the partner will contribute. These beliefs, known as the *first order beliefs of player i*, are denoted by b_i^1 and $0 \le b_i^1 \le 20$ (in b_i^1, the subscript denotes the player $i = 1, 2$, and the superscript "1" denotes the order of beliefs, here beliefs of the first order). If player 1 expects the partner to contribute 14 tokens then $b_1^1 = 14$, and if player 2 expects the partner to contribute 10 tokens, then $b_2^1 = 10$.

However, the expectations of the players (or their first order beliefs) are known privately to them, and not known to their partners, which is characteristic of many social situations. Yet, players might wish to figure out what their partner really expects from them to ensure, for instance, that they do not fall below these expectations. The beliefs of players about the first order beliefs of their partners are known as *second order beliefs*. The second order belief of player $i = 1, 2$ about the partner's first order belief is denoted by b_i^2 and $0 \le b_i^2 \le 20$ (the superscript 2 refers to the order and the subscript i indexes the player). For instance, player 1 might have the belief that player 2 expects a contribution of 12 from him (although the partner in fact expects only a contribution of 10; see above). In this case, we write $b_1^2 = 12$, although in fact $b_2^1 = 10$, so the second order beliefs are not entirely accurate. Misjudging the expectations of others is endemic in human interactions. By contrast, the mutual consistency of beliefs and actions precludes this possibility under neoclassical game theory.

Two further observations on beliefs are warranted, before we proceed to use them to model guilt.

1. One can proceed in this hierarchical manner and construct beliefs of order $3, 4, \ldots$.. For instance, b_i^3 denotes the third order beliefs of player $i = 1, 2$ about the second order beliefs of the partner. In neoclassical game theory, players are required to construct, and do effortlessly construct, beliefs up to an infinite order, that is, b_i^∞. However, it is difficult to write in plain English, a description of beliefs of order 3–4 and beyond. For our purposes, we will not need beliefs of order higher than 2.
2. What we have described above are "point beliefs." It is conceivable that players may also have belief distributions. For instance, consider the expectations of player 1 about the contributions of player 2, denoted by b_1^1. Player 1 might assign a 25% probability to player 2 contributing the amounts 12, 13, 14, and 15. Such belief distributions can be readily

accommodated within the theory; see Khalmetski et al. (2015) and Dhami et al. (2019) who use theory and experiments to demonstrate the usefulness of this framework.

3. How do we elicit the beliefs of players in order to test the predictions of PGT models? In a widely used method, *the direct elicitation method*, players are directly asked about their beliefs, and most of the early tests of PGT are based on this method. However, Ellingsen et al. (2010) pointed out a serious, and fatal, flaw with this method. Direct elicitation is subject to the *false consensus effect* (see the discussion on evidential reasoning in Section 7.10). Thus, when guessing the expectations of others, players assign to others, their own expectations of others.

   In response to this problem, Ellingsen et al. (2010) suggested the *induced beliefs design*, whereby players are asked to state their expectations of others, but not told why this is being asked, in order to prevent strategic mis-statement of beliefs. The experimenter then directly informs the other player about the expectations (b_j^1) of the partner. The result is that the second order beliefs of the player $i = 1, 2$, b_i^2, about the first order belief of the partner, b_j^1, are as accurate as possible. This method has been gradually improved in response to criticisms, such as subject deception. For instance, after the players are asked their beliefs about others, but before the experimenter conveys it to the partner, the consent of the players could be required before the beliefs are actually transmitted (Dhami et al., 2022). In properly incentivized and controlled experiments, the only valid concern with this method arises if subjects are to repeatedly participate in future experiments. This might then alter their behavior in future experiments. However, if subjects are participating in a one-off experiment, as in the lab-in-the field experiment in Dhami et al. (2022), then the induced-beliefs design remains the most satisfactory method of eliciting beliefs.

Let us now modify the utility function in (8.23) to incorporate guilt. Several different notions of guilt are possible. In its simplest formulation as *simple guilt*, Battigalli and Dufwenberg (2007) have suggested that guilt arises from falling behind the perceived expectations of the other players. Suppose that we have only two players ($n = 2$). We rewrite the utility function in (8.23) to include simple guilt as follows

$$u_i = (20 - g_i + 0.3G) - \alpha_i \gamma_i;\ 0 \leq \alpha_i. \tag{8.25}$$

In (8.25), the last term, $\alpha_i \gamma_i$, captures simple guilt. The magnitude of the parameter α_i captures the importance of guilt for the individual relative to material payoffs; for $\alpha_i = 0$ we get the special case under neoclassical game theory in (8.23). If $\alpha_i = 1$, guilt is as important as material payoffs and for $\alpha_i > 1$ guilt is relatively more important. The function γ_i is known as the *guilt function* for player $i = 1, 2$. We first state it and then explain it immediately below.

$$\gamma_i = \begin{cases} \left(b_i^2 - g_i\right)^2 & \text{if} \quad 0 \leq g_i < b_i^2 \\ 0 & \text{if} \quad g_i \geq b_i^2 \end{cases}. \tag{8.26}$$

The guilt function distinguishes between two possible cases.

(i) If $g_i < b_i^2$, then the actual contribution of player i falls short of what the player believes is expected by the partner. In this case, player i experiences guilt, which is increasing at an increasing rate in the gap between expectations and actual contributions, $b_i^2 - g_i$. In this case, the last term in (8.25) equals $-\alpha_i \left(b_i^2 - g_i\right)^2$, so player i faces direct disutility from falling behind the partner's perceived expectations.

(ii) If $g_i \geq b_i^2$ then player i contributes at least as much as he believes is expected by the partner, hence, player i feels no guilt. The last term in (8.25) is 0 in this case.

We can now substitute (8.24), (8.26) into (8.25) to get an unconstrained maximization problem for player i. Player i chooses his optimal contributions g_i in order to maximize his utility function, given (i) the contributions of the partner, g_{-i} (which player i does not know yet because the players choose contributions simultaneously), and (ii) the second order beliefs of player i as captured in the term b_i^2. Thus, we can write the optimization problem of player i by

$$Max_{(0 \leq g_i \leq 20)}\ u_i = \begin{cases} 20 - g_i + 0.3\left(g_i + g_{-i}\right) - \alpha_i \left(b_i^2 - g_i\right)^2 & \text{if} \quad 0 \leq g_i < b_i^2 \\ 20 - g_i + 0.3\left(g_i + g_{-i}\right) & \text{if} \quad g_i \geq b_i^2 \end{cases}. \tag{8.27}$$

Before, we can make further progress, an important question within PGT is about whether the beliefs of various orders should be equilibrium beliefs. This requires specifying an equilibrium in PGT. Suppose first that we stayed quite close to neoclassical game theory and forced consistency between the actions of players and the beliefs of various orders. In the two-player static public goods game outlined above (restricting attention to beliefs up to order two only), let us use stars as superscript for equilibrium values. We now define an equilibrium in pyschological game theory for the specific context of the public goods game described above, and restricting attention only to first and second order beliefs.

Definition 8.4 *An equilibrium of the public goods game in psychological game theory is*

(i) a pair of contributions by each player (g_1^*, g_2^*), $0 \leq g_i \leq 20$, $i = 1, 2$,
(ii) the first order beliefs of the two players (b_1^{1*}, b_2^{1*}), $0 \leq b_i^{1*} \leq 20$, $i = 1, 2$, *and*
(iii) the second order beliefs of the two players (b_1^{2*}, b_2^{2*}), $0 \leq b_i^{2*} \leq 20$, $i = 1, 2$

such that the following two conditions are satisfied.

1. *(Best response by players) For any player* $i = 1, 2$, *the chosen contribution* g_i^* *maximizes their utility in (8.27), given the contributions of the partner, their first order beliefs, and their second order beliefs.*
2. *(Belief consistency) The actions and beliefs of both players are consistent with each other. For player 1 this requires* $g_1^* = b_2^{1*} = b_1^{2*}$ *and for player 2, this requires that* $g_2^* = b_1^{1*} = b_2^{2*}$.

Most people would agree that the first of these requirements (best response) is less controversial, at least a priori. In problems that are not too complicated, we do expect people to do the best they can, given the beliefs that they hold about the world. However, the second requirement, that is also an essential part of the toolkit of neoclassical game theory, is controversial. For instance, the condition for player 1, $g_1^* = b_2^{1*} = b_1^{2*}$, requires the following. The chosen contribution of player 1, g_1^*, equals the expectation of player 2 about the contribution of player 1, as captured by the first order beliefs of player 2, b_2^{1*}; and both these objects must equal what player 1 believes that player 2 expects him to contribute, b_1^{2*}. A similar requirement holds for player 2 ($g_2^* = b_1^{1*} = b_2^{2*}$). In other words, beliefs of various orders of the players are themselves *endogenous*, or determined as part of the equilibrium. The requirement of belief consistency demonstrates the circularity of reasoning that is characteristic of equilibrium analysis in neoclassical game theory and in behavioral alternatives that adopt the equilibrium method.

Although we have stated the equilibrium for two players only, an equilibrium in PGT can be stated for games with any finite number of players, in static and dynamic games, and in games with complete and incomplete information; see Battigalli and Dufwenberg (2022) for a thorough survey.

The equilibrium in PGT described above is only a hypothesis about the outcomes in such games. It cannot prove how players actually behave, and it is the purpose of experiments to confirm or reject this hypothesis. In general, PGT specifies beliefs up to any order and then equilibrium requires belief consistency for these higher order beliefs as well; indeed neoclassical game theory requires such belief consistency for all beliefs up to an infinite order. This is not empirically supported. For instance, Bellemare et al. (2011) show that actions, first order beliefs, and second order beliefs are inconsistent with each other in experiments.

It is sometimes claimed in neoclassical game theory that a Nash equilibrium and belief consistency are the result of learning after playing many repeated rounds of a game. When put to the empirical test, the evidence is mixed; many learning experiments do not report convergence to a Nash equilibrium, although some do (Camerer, 2003; Dhami, 2020, Vol. VI). Typically when the economic environment is ever changing, and the game is not trivial, which describes most real world situations, then we should not expect learning to converge to a Nash equilibrium.

Social norms, conventions, and various notions of social rationality, can often coordinate the actions of group members (Section 7.9, above). In this case, all players know what actions are consistent with a social norm, know that other players are likely to take these actions, and know that these actions are expected of them by other group members. It is not implausible that actions and beliefs are, therefore, in sync, as required in the definition of equilibrium in PGT (see, e.g., Definition 8.4). But for the public goods game considered above, where no social norms exists, this is not the case.

A sensible, and empirically supported, response to these problems is to take the first part of the definition of an equilibrium under PGT, but to drop the second (consistency of beliefs of different order and actions). Some of the literature has already moved in this direction (Khalmetski et al., 2015; Dhami et al., 2019, 2022) and see, in particular, Battigalli and Dufwenberg (2022) for a discussion that is supportive of this idea. Let us refer to the resulting equilibrium notion that drops belief consistency with actions, as a *psychological equilibrium*; readers interested in alternative solution concepts can consult Battigalli et al. (2019).

Let us return to the public goods game to compute the psychological equilibrium of the game using the special case of point beliefs in Dhami et al. (2019) who consider general belief distributions. From (8.27), player i maximizes his utility u_i, taking as given the contribution of the other player, and his own privately held beliefs, b_i^1, b_i^2, with no presumption that beliefs will be consistent with equilibrium actions.

The objective function in (8.27) is not continuous in the contributions of the player, g_i. Hence, we need to find the maximum value of the utility function in each of the two domains, $g_i < b_i^2$ and $g_i \geq b_i^2$, and then pick the domain where the value of the utility function is the higher of the two. Within each domain, the utility function is continuous and has continuous partial derivatives, hence, within each domain, we can maximize the objective function in the usual manner. As a first step, differentiate the two rows in (8.27) with respect to g_i to get

$$\frac{du_i}{dg_i} = \begin{cases} -1 + 0.3 + 2\alpha_i \left(b_i^2 - g_i\right) & \text{if} \quad 0 \leq g_i < b_i^2 \\ -1 + 0.3 < 0 & \text{if} \quad g_i \geq b_i^2 \end{cases}. \tag{8.28}$$

Let us now consider the maximum value of the objective function separately in each domain.

(i) The domain $g_i \geq b_i^2$: From the second row of (8.28), we have $\frac{du_i}{dg_i} < 0$, so the objective function is strictly decreasing at all points in the domain $g_i \geq b_i^2$, hence, it is optimal to choose $g_i^* = b_i^2$ which is the minimum permissible value of g_i in this domain. The maximum value of the utility function in this domain is found by substituting $g_i = b_i^2$ in the second row of (8.27),

$$u_i = 20 - 0.7b_i^2 + 0.3g_{-i}. \tag{8.29}$$

(ii) The domain $g_i < b_i^2$: From the first row of (8.28), we have $\frac{d^2u_i}{dg_i^2} = -2\alpha_i$, hence, there is a unique solution to g_i in this domain. Solve for $\frac{du_i}{dg_i} = -0.7 + 2\alpha_i \left(b_i^2 - g_i\right) = 0$ to get solution

$$g_i = b_i^2 - \frac{0.7}{2\alpha_i}. \tag{8.30}$$

As $\alpha_i \to 0$ (absence of guilt), we get the free-rider solution $g_i = 0$. At the other extreme, as $\alpha_i \to \infty$ (only guilt aversion matters), then $g_i \to b_i^2$. For intermediate values of α we get all possible solution values of g_i in the interval $\left(0, b_i^2\right)$. Substituting (8.30) in the first row of (8.27), the maximum value of the utility of player i in the domain $g_i < b_i^2$ is given by

$$u_i = 20 - 0.7b_i^2 + 0.3g_{-i} + \frac{0.49}{4\alpha_i}. \tag{8.31}$$

Comparing (8.29) and (8.31), we can see that the utility of the player in the domain $g_i < b_i^2$, given in (8.31), is higher for any finite level of guilt-aversion. Thus, the globally optimal solution across both domains is given in (8.31).

From (8.30), public good contributions are higher if the second order beliefs of players are high. If players believe that their partners expect high contributions from them, then they feel guilty contributing a lower amount. This is a testable prediction of the model. In (8.30), the number 0.7 on the RHS is 1 minus the return, $r > 0$, on the public good, which is set at $r = 0.3$ in this example (so $1 - 0.3 = 0.7$). More generally, we can rewrite (8.30) as $g_i = b_i^2 - \frac{1-r}{2\alpha_i}$. Clearly, g_i is also increasing in the rate of return, r, which is another testable prediction.

These predictions can be tested in actual experiments, but preferably not by using direct belief elicitation, which is subject to the false consensus effect (see discussion above). Dhami et al. (2019) test these predictions in experiments using the induced beliefs design, described above. They show that the second order beliefs of the players are a significant determinant of public goods contribution, which is consistent with the guilt aversion hypothesis. They also find that first order beliefs are also a significant determinant of public good contributions. This demonstrates the reciprocity motive, which is formally modelled in their paper. Players who expect other players to contribute more, also contribute more, reciprocating the expected kind behavior of the partners with kind behavior.

One typically expects reciprocity in dynamic games, where players have had a chance to observe a kind action by another player before reciprocating with kindness; see Example 8.8 above. However, reciprocity can also arise in static games purely based on the expectations of actions one holds about other players. This was highlighted in the seminal paper by Rabin (1993) that seeded the modern literature in PGT. Notice that when beliefs are subject to the false consensus effect as, say, in direct belief elicitation, one cannot use both first and second order beliefs within the same explanation (certainly not within the same regression analysis) because they are highly correlated and one cannot disentangle their separate effects. But in an induced beliefs design, the first and second order beliefs need not be correlated and one can separate out their effects.

Let us now use the notion of a *psychological equilibrium* to look into Example 8.4. So far, the beliefs that we have considered are about the expected "actual" actions of others and beliefs about such beliefs. Such beliefs are sometimes known as *positive beliefs* and we have used them above to demonstrate how guilt influences actions. In order to formally distinguish between *guilt* and *shame*, Dhami et al. (2022) use the distinction between positive and *normative beliefs* (see Bicchieri, 2006).

Normative beliefs apply when players are playing a game with respect to their social group or their peer group. The *first order normative expectations* of player i, $B_i^1 \in [0,20]$, are his beliefs about what other group members "ought" to do in a specific social situation. The *second order normative expectations* of player i, denoted by $B_i^2 \in [0,20]$, are his beliefs about what his social group thinks he (player i) "ought" to do in a specific social situation. We have used "point normative beliefs" for simplicity, but it is possible to extend this analysis to belief distributions over the actions of players.

Shame arises from falling below the normative expectations of the social group, as perceived by a player in terms of his beliefs, B_i^2. This is analogous to, but distinct from, guilt that arises from falling below the perceived positive expectations of other players, which relies on positive second order beliefs, b_i^2.

Sticking with the context of the two-player public goods game, an individual who is motivated by both guilt and shame has the following utility function, which is a modification of (8.25):

$$u_i = 20 - g_i + 0.3 \times G - \alpha_i \gamma_i - \beta_i \varphi_i;\ 0 \leq \alpha_i, 0 \leq \beta_i. \tag{8.32}$$

The last term on the RHS of (8.32) captures disutility arising on account of shame. The size of the parameter $0 \leq \beta_i$ captures the importance of shame; a player feels no shame if $\beta_i = 0$. The function φ_i that denotes shame, is constructed in a manner similar to (8.26) but uses normative expectations instead of positive expectations.

$$\varphi_i = \begin{cases} \left(B_i^2 - g_i\right)^2 & \text{if} \quad 0 \leq g_i < B_i^2 \\ 0 & \text{if} \quad g_i \geq B_i^2 \end{cases}. \tag{8.33}$$

One interprets (8.33) in the same way as (8.26). If contributions fall below the second order normative expectations with respect to a relevant social or peer group ($0 \leq g_i < B_i^2$) then player i experiences shame that is increasing at an increasing rate in the shortfall of contributions relative to expectations. Otherwise, if contributions are higher ($g_i \geq B_i^2$), then the player feels no shame.

The mechanism through which shame operates is often strengthened through several factors that are the hallmarks of successful social norms. These include the following.

(i) Observations of what other group members do, and forming beliefs about their actions based on these observations. Such beliefs are known as *empirical expectations*.
(ii) Punishments and social sanctions from the social group based on the observation of one's actions. Punishments need not be monetary. They can be nonmonetary, for instance, the social group might deny access to the activities of the social group and express disapproval of the actions through various means, all of which are costly for the player.
(iii) Empirical expectations and normative expectations must be consistent with each other. This is to say that one's expectations of the actions of other group members are similar to the actions one believes that group members expect members ought to take.

The reader can try to work through a solution of the public goods contribution problem outlined above in the presence of both guilt and shame. One of the exercises asks you to give this a try, with a hint on how to solve it.

Dhami et al. (2022) use the framework outlined above that is able to distinguish between guilt and shame to construct a two-period theoretical model of microfinance contracts that can address Examples 8.6 and 8.7. Contracts can either be joint liability (JL) contracts, or individual liability (IL) contracts. Under any of these contracts, players take a loan for their independent and risky projects that are more likely to succeed if they put in higher effort.

Under *JL contracts*, as explained in Example 8.6, borrowers might feel guilty from putting in low effort, and reducing the chances of their partner in the *JL* contract to get a future loan. By contrast, under *IL* contracts, borrowers take loans individually, for their individual projects, and are only responsible for paying their own loans, hence, they feel no guilt with respect to any other player. Thus, borrowers are likely to exert relatively more effort under *JL* contracts. From Example 8.7, we know that when borrowers make a public repayment (*P*) in front of their social group, they are likely to feel shame from nonrepayment, hence, they are expected to exert higher effort to ensure that their project succeeds.[5] By contrast, if repayments are made privately, or individually (*I*), to the bank, then nobody finds out if a borrower has defaulted, leading to no shame.

The authors then use a 2×2 design with four treatments and test these predictions with 400 actual microfinance borrowers in Pakistan. Along one dimension, they varied the liability structure, either joint liability (*JL*) or individual liability (*IL*). Along the other dimension they varied the mode of repayments, either publicly (*P*) or privately (*I*). This gives rise to four kinds of contracts that we have outlined in the introduction. *ILI* (individual liability and individual repayments); *ILP* (individual liability and public repayment); *JLI* (joint liability and individual repayment); and *JLP* (joint liability and public repayment). We can now compare the effort levels of the borrowers in the different treatments and draw inferences about the roles of the emotions of guilt and shame.

[5] Readers should note that this statement only holds when the other prerequisites for successful social norms, mentioned above, hold. These prerequisites include consistency between empirical expectations and normative expectations; observability of actions by peer group; and punishments of norm violators.

(i) The only difference between the contracts *ILI* and *ILP* is that the repayment is private in ILI and publicly in front of one's social group in *ILP*. Thus, if one experiences shame from nonrepayment in front of one's social group, then we should expect relatively higher effort by borrowers in *ILP* contracts. The authors find that in the first period of this two-period model, the average effort is relatively higher under ILP contracts by 60% and the repayment rate is higher by 23%. This is consistent with the *shame-aversion motive*.

(ii) In the contracts *ILI* and *JLI*, the repayment method is held fixed at private repayment, but the type of liability is varied. If borrowers experience guilt from letting down the perceived expectations of their partners, then we should expect relatively higher effort in JLI contracts. The average effort under *JLI* turns out to be almost double relative to *ILI*, and the repayment rate increases by 33%. This is consistent with the *guilt-aversion motive*.

(iii) In the contracts *JLI* and *JLP*, the liability is fixed at joint liability but the repayment method is varied. In *JLP* contracts, one experiences both guilt (with respect to the partner) and shame (with respect to the social group from nonrepayment) while in the JLI contract one experiences only guilt with respect to the partner.

What if guilt and shame are in conflict? For instance, suppose in a *JLP* contract, your partner wants you to put in a low effort, but the social group believes that you ought to put in a slightly higher effort. Which of these two emotions will win out? The main finding in the data here is that *shame trumps guilt* in the sense that players are more keen to avoid letting down their social group rather than their partner in the joint liability contract. Indeed, the data showed that in *JLP* contracts, that allowed for the simultaneous presence of guilt and shame, the partner's expectations that would have induced guilt, play a negligible role in influencing effort levels of borrowers. By contrast, the effort levels are highly influenced by beliefs of borrowers about the normative expectations of their social group. On average, borrowers exert exactly the effort level that the social group deems that its group members ought to exert. In *JLI* contracts, where the shame-aversion motive is absent, and the only motivation for putting in high effort levels is guilt-aversion, the effort level is also fairly high and, as noted above, 60% higher than ILI contracts. Hence, from the point of view of the lenders, where public repayment of loans is not possible (so the contract JLP cannot be offered), the JLI contract also performs quite well. This allowed the authors to explain the changing liability structure in Grameen banks from joint liability contracts (Grameen-I) to individual liability contracts (Grameen-II), that preserved public repayment of loans.

Overall, this work shows that peer pressure and social capital can be meaningfully defined, and used to explain real world contractual choices. Emotions, which play no role in neoclassical game theory, must form an essential component in explaining human cooperation and contract design. Psychological game theory currently provides the most satisfactory method of implementing these ideas.

References

Akerlof, G. A. (1970). The Market for Lemons: Quality Uncertainty and the Market Mechanism. *Quarterly Journal of Economics* 84(3): 488–500.

al-Nowaihi, A. and Dhami, S. (2015). Evidential Equilibria: Heuristics and Biases in Static Games of Complete Information. *Games* 6(4): 637–677.

Alós-Ferrer, C. and Buckenmaier, J. (2021). Cognitive Sophistication and Deliberation Times. *Experimental Economics* 24: 558–592.

Anbarci, N., Feltovich, N., and Gürdal, M. Y. (2018). Payoff Inequity Reduces the Effectiveness of Correlated-Equilibrium Recommendations. *European Economic Review* 108: 172–190.

Andreoni, J. and Bernheim, B. D. (2009). Social Image and the 50–50 Norm: A Theoretical and Experimental Analysis of Audience Effects. *Econometrica* 77(5): 1607–1636.

Arrow, K. J. (1994). Methodological Individualism and Social Knowledge. *American Economic Review* 84(2): 1–9.

Babcock, L. and Loewenstein, G. (1997). Explaining Bargaining Impasse: The Role of Self-Serving Biases. *Journal of Economic Perspectives* 11(1): 109–126.

Babcock, P., Bedard, K., Charness, G., Hartman, J., and Royer, H. (2015). Letting Down the Teams? Social Effects of Team Incentives. *Journal of the European Economic Association* 13(5): 841–870.

Bacharach, M. (2006). *Beyond Individual Choice: Teams and Frames in Game Theory*. (N. Gold and R. Sugden, eds.). Princeton University Press: Princeton, NJ.

Bandiera, O., Barankay, I., and Rasul, I. (2005). Social Preferences and the Response to Incentives: Evidence From Personnel Data. *Quarterly Journal of Economics* 120: 917–962.

Bandiera, O., Barankay, I., and Rasul, I. (2010). Social Incentives in the Workplace. *Review of Economics Studies* 77: 417–458.

Battigalli, P., Corrao, R., and Dufwenberg, M. (2019). Incorporating Belief-Dependent Motivation in Games. *Journal of Economic Behavior & Organization* 167(C): 185–218.

Battigalli, P. and Dufwenberg, M. (2007). Guilt in Games. *American Economic Review* 97(2): 170–176.

Battigalli, P. and Dufwenberg, M. (2022). Belief-Dependent Motivations and Psychological Game Theory. *Journal of Economic Literature* 60(3): 833–882.

Bazerman, M. H. and Samuelson, W. F. (1983). I Won the Auction but Dont Want the Prize. *Journal of Conflict Resolution* 27(4): 618–634.

Bellemare, C., Sebald, A.C., and Strobel, M. (2011). Measuring the Willingness to Pay to Avoid Guilt: Estimation Using Equilibrium and Stated Belief Models. *Journal of Applied Econometrics* 26(3): 437–453.

Bicchieri, C. (2006). *The Grammar of Society: The Nature and Dynamics of Social Norms*. Cambridge University Press: New York.

Binmore, K. (1987). Modeling Rational Players: Part 1. *Economics and Philosophy* 3: 179–214.

Binmore, K. (1991). *Fun and Games: A Text on Game Theory*. D. C. Heath: Lexington, MA.

Binmore, K. and Klemperer, P. (2002). The Biggest Auction Ever: The Sale of the British 3G Telecom Licences. *The Economic Journal* 112(478): C74–C96.

Bowles S. (2004). *Microeconomics: Behavior, Institutions, and Evolution*. Princeton University Press: Princeton, NJ.

Bowles, S. and Gintis, H. (2011). *A Cooperative Species: Human Reciprocity and Evolution*. Princeton University Press: Princeton, NJ.

Brown, J. N. and Rosenthal, R. W. (1990). Testing the Minimax Hypothesis: A Re-examination of O'Neills Game Experiment. *Econometrica* 58(5): 1065–1081.

Camerer, C. F. (2003). *Behavioral Game Theory: Experiments in Strategic Interaction*. Princeton University Press: Princeton, NJ.

Camerer, C. F., Ho, T.-H., and Chong, J.-K. (2004). A Cognitive Hierarchy Model of Games. *Quarterly Journal of Economics* 119(3): 861–898.

Camerer, C. F., Nave, G., and Smith, A. (2019). Dynamic Unstructured Bargaining with Private Information: Theory, Experiment, and Outcome Prediction via Machine Learning. *Management Science* 65(4): 1867–1890.

Cason, T. N. and Sharma, T. (2007). Recommended Play and Correlated Equilibria: An Experimental Study. *Economic Theory* 33(1): 11–27.

Charness, G., Rigotti, L., and Rustichini, A. (2007). Individual Behavior and Group Membership. *American Economic Review* 97(4): 1340–1352.

Collins, R. and Sherstyuk, K. (2000). Spatial Competition with Three Firms: An Experimental Study. *Economic Inquiry* 38(1): 73–94.

Cooper, R. W., DeJong, D. V., Forsythe, R., and Ross, T. W. (1990). Selection Criteria in Coordination Games: Some Experimental Results. *American Economic Review* 80(1): 218–233.

Cooper, R. W., DeJong, D. V., Forsythe, R., and Ross, T. W. (1992). Communication in Coordination Games. *Quarterly Journal of Economics* 107(2): 739–771.

Costa-Gomes, M. A. and Crawford, V. P. (2006). Cognition and Behavior in Two-Person Guessing Games: An Experimental Study. *American Economic Review* 96(5): 1737–1768.

Costa-Gomes, M., Crawford, V. P., and Broseta, B. (2001). Cognition and Behavior in Normal-Form Games: An Experimental Study. *Econometrica* 69(5): 1193–1235.

Crawford, V. P. (2007). Let's Talk it Over: Coordination via Preplay Communication with Level-k Thinking. Mimeo, UCLA Department of Economics.

Crawford, V. P., Gneezy, U., and Rottenstreich, Y. (2008). The Power of Focal Points is Limited: Even Minute Payoff Asymmetry May Yield Large Coordination Failures. *American Economic Review* 98(4): 1443–1458.

Dal Bó, P. and Fréchette, G. (2018). On the Determinants of Cooperation in Infinitely Repeated Games: A Survey. *Journal of Economic Literature* 56(1): 60–114.

Dhami, S. (2020). *The Foundations of Behavioral Economic Analysis. Volume IV. Behavioral Game Theory*. Oxford: Oxford University Press: Oxford.

Dhami, S. (2020). *The Foundations of Behavioral Economic Analysis. Volume VI. Behavioral Models of Learning*. Oxford University Press: Oxford.

Dhami, S. and Sunstein, C. (2022). *Bounded Rationality: Heuristics, Judgment, and Public Policy*. MIT Press: Cambridge, MA.

Dhami, S., Arshad, J., and al-Nowaihi, A. (2022). Psychological and Social Motivations in Microfinance Contracts: Theory and Evidence. *Journal of Development Economics* 158:102912.

Dhami, S., Wei, M., and al-Nowaihi, A. (2019). Public Goods Games and Psychological Utility: Theory and Evidence. *Journal of Economic Behavior and Organization* 167(C): 361–390.

Duffy, J. and Feltovich, N. (2010). Correlated Equilibria, Good and Bad: An Experimental Study. *International Economic Review* 51(3): 701–721.

Ellingsen, T., Johannesson, M., Tjøtta, S., and Torsvik, G. (2010). Testing Guilt Aversion. *Games and Economic Behavior* 68: 95–107.

Elster, J. (2011). Norms. In P. Bearman and P. Hedström (eds.), *The Oxford Handbook of Analytical Sociology*. Oxford University Press: Oxford, pp. 19W–217.

Enke, B. (2020). Moral Values and Voting. *Journal of Political Economy* 128(10): 3679–3729.

Enke, B., Rodriguez-Padilla, R., and Zimmermann, F. (2023). Moral Universalism and the Structure of Ideology. *The Review of Economic Studies* 90(4): 1934–1962.

Eyster, E. and Rabin, M. (2005). Cursed Equilibrium. *Econometrica* 73(5): 1623–1672.

Falk, A., Fehr, E., and Fischbacher, U. (2008). Testing Theories of Fairness: Intentions Matter. *Games and Economic Behavior* 62(1): 287–303.

Fehr, E. and Rangel, A. (2011). Neuroeconomic Foundations of Economic Choice: Recent Advances. *Journal of Economic Perspectives* 25(4): 3–30.

Fehr, E. and Schurtenberger, I. (2018). Normative Foundations of Human Cooperation. *Nature Human Behaviour* 2: 458–486.

Fey, M., McKelvey, R. D., and Palfrey, T. R. (1996). An Experimental Study of Constant-Sum Centipede Games. *International Journal of Game Theory* 25(3): 269–287.

García-Pola, B., Iriberri, N., and Kovářík, J. (2020). Non-equilibrium Play in Centipede Games. *Games and Economic Behavior*, 120(C): 391–433.

Georganas, S., Healy, P. J., and Weber, R. A. (2015). On the Persistence of Strategic Sophistication. *Journal of Economic Theory* 159(Part A): 369–400.

Gintis, H. (2009). *The Bounds of Reason: Game Theory and the Unification of the Behavioral Sciences*. Princeton University Press: Princeton, NJ.

Gintis, H. (2011). Gene-Culture Coevolution and the Nature of Human Sociality. *Philosophical Transactions of the Royal Society* 366(1566): 878–888.

Gintis, H. (2017). *Individuality and Entanglement: The Moral and Material Bases of Social Life*. Princeton University Press: Princeton, NJ.

Goeree, J. K., Holt, C. A., and Palfrey, T. R. (2003). Risk Averse Behavior in Generalized Matching Pennies Games. *Games and Economic Behavior* 45(1): 97–113.

Goeree, J. K., Holt, C. A., and Palfrey, T. R. (2016). *Quantal Response Equilibrium: A Stochastic Theory of Games*. Princeton University Press: Princeton, NJ.

Goeree, J. K., Holt, C. A., and Palfrey, T. R. (2020). Stochastic Game Theory for Social Science: A Primer on Quantal Response Equilibrium. In Capra, C.M., Croson, R. T. A., Rigdon, M. L., and Rosenblat, T. S. (eds.), *Handbook of Experimental Game Theory*. Edward Elgar Publishing: Cheltenham.

Hamilton, B., Nickerson, J., and Owan, H. (2003). Team Incentives and Worker Heterogeneity: An Empricial Analysis of the Impact of Teams on Productivity and Participation. *Journal of Political Economy* 111(3): 465–497.

Hargreaves Heap, S., Rojo-Arjona, D., and Sugden, R. (2014). How Portable is Level-0 Behavior? A Test of Level-k Theory in Games with Non-neutral Frames. *Econometrica* 82(3): 1133–1151.

Harrison, G. W. and List, J. A. (2008). Naturally Occurring Markets and Exogenous Laboratory Experiments: A Case Study of the Winner's Curse. *Economic Journal* 118(528): 822–843.

Ho, T., Camerer, C. F., and Weigelt, K. (1998). Iterated Dominance and Iterated Best Response in Experimental P-Beauty Contests. *American Economic Review* 88(4): 947–969.

Huck, S., Jehiel, P., and Rutter, T. (2011). Feedback Spillover and Analogy-Based Expectations: A Multi-game Experiment. *Games and Economic Behavior* 71(2): 351–365.

Jehiel, P. (2005). Analogy-Based Expectation Equilibrium. *Journal of Economic Theory* 123(2): 81–104.

Johnson, E. J., Camerer, C. F., Sen, S., and Rymon, T. (2002). Detecting Failures of Backward Induction: Monitoring Information Search in Sequential Bargaining. *Journal of Economic Theory* 104(1): 16–47.

Kagel, J. H. (2015). Laboratory Experiments: The Lab in Relationship to Field Experiments, Field Data, and Economic Theory. In G. R. Fréchette and A. Schotter (eds.), *Handbook of Experimental Economic Methodology*. Oxford University Press: Oxford, pp. 339–359.

Kagel, J. H. and Levin, D. (2010). Auctions: A Survey of Experimental Research. In J. H. Kagel and A. E. Roth (eds.), *The Handbook of Experimental Economics*, Volume II. Princeton University Press: Princeton, NJ, pp. 501–586.

Kagel, J. H., Levin, D., and Harstad, R. M. (1995). Comparative Static Effects of Number of Bidders and Public Information in Second-Price

Common Value Auctions. *International Journal of Game Theory* 24(3): 293–319.

Kahneman, D. (1988). Experimental Economics: A Psychological Perspective. In R. Tietz, W. Albers, and R. Selten (eds.), *Bounded Rational Behavior in Experimental Games and Markets: Proceedings of the Fourth Conference on Experimental Economics, Bielefeld, West Germany, September 21–25, 1986*. Springer: New York, Berlin, London, and Tokyo, pp. 11–18.

Kawagoe, T. and Takizawa, H. (2012). Level-k Analysis of Experimental Centipede Games. *Journal of Economic Behavior and Organization* 82(2–3): 548–566.

Keynes, J. M. (1936). The General Theory of Employment, Interest, and Money. Harcourt Brace and Co.: New York.

Khalmetski, K., Ockenfels, A., and Werner, P. (2015). Surprising Gifts. *Journal of Economic Theory* 159: 163–208.

Konovalov, A. and Krajbich, I. (2019). Over a Decade of Neuroeconomics: What Have We Learned? Organizational Research Methods 22(1): 148–173.

Krajbich, I., Bartling, B., Hare, T., and Fehr, E. (2015). Rethinking Fast and Slow Based on a Critique of Reaction-Time Reverse Inference. *Nature Communications* 6(7455): 1–9.

Kreps, D. M., Milgrom, P., Roberts, J., Wilson, R. (1982). Rational Cooperation in the Finitely Repeated Prisoners' Dilemma. *Journal of Economic Theory* 27(2): 245–252.

Kreps, D. M. and Wilson, R. (1982). Reputation and Imperfect Information. *Journal of Economic Theory* 27(2): 253–279.

Levitt, S. D., List, J. A., and Reiley, D. H. (2010). What Happens in the Field Stays in the Field: Professionals Do Not Play Minimax in Laboratory Experiments. *Econometrica* 78(4): 1413–1434.

Levitt, S. D., List, J. A., and Sadoff, S. E. (2011). Checkmate: Exploring Backward Induction among Chess Players. *American Economic Review*. 101(2): 975–990.

Lewis, D. K. (1969). *Convention: A Philosophical Study*. Harvard University Press: Cambridge, MA.

Lewis, D. K. (1979). Prisoners Dilemma Is a Newcomb Problem. *Philosophy and Public Affairs* 8(3): 235–240.

Loewenstein, G. F., Issacharoff, S., Camerer, C. F., and Babcock, L. (1993). Self-serving Assessments of Fairness and Pretrial Bargaining. *Journal of Legal Studies* 22(1): 135–159.

Luce, R. D. (1959). *Individual Choice Behavior: A Theoretical Analysis*. Wiley: New York.

Maynard Smith, J. and Price, G. R. (1973). *The Logic of Animal Conflict*. Nature 246 (5427): 15–18.

McKelvey, R. D. and Palfrey, T. R. (1992). An Experimental Study of the Centipede Game. *Econometrica* 60(4): 803–836.

McKelvey, R. D. and Palfrey, T. R. (1998). Quantal Response Equilibrium in Extensive Form Games. *Experimental Economics* 1(1): 941.

McKelvey, R. D., Palfrey, T. R., and Weber, R. A. (2000). The Effects of Payoff Magnitude and Heterogeneity on Behavior in 2 × 2 games with Unique Mixed Strategy Equilibria. *Journal of Economic Behavior and Organization* 42(4): 523–548.

Mehta, J., Starmer, C., and Sugden, R. (1994). The Nature of Salience: An Experimental Investigation of Pure Coordination Games. *American Economic Review* 84(3): 658–673.

Mookherjee, D. and Sopher, B. (1994). Learning Behavior in an Experimental Matching Pennies Game. *Games and Economic Behavior* 7(1): 62–91.

Mookherjee, D. and Sopher, B. (1997). Learning and Decision Costs in Experimental Constant Sum Games. *Games and Economic Behavior* 19(1): 97–132.

Moreno, D. and Wooders, J. (1998). An Experimental Study of Communication and Coordination in Non-cooperative Games. *Games and Economic Behavior* 24(12): 47–76.

Mullainathan, S. (2002). A Memory-Based Model of Bounded Rationality. *Quarterly Journal of Economics* 117(3): 735–774.

Mullainathan, S., Schwartzstein, J., and Shleifer, A. (2008). Coarse Thinking and Persuasion. *Quarterly Journal of Economics* 123(2): 577–619.

Nagel, R. (1995). Unraveling in Guessing Games: An Experimental Study. *American Economic Review* 85(5): 1313–1326.

Nagel, R., Buehren, C., and Frank, B. (2017). Inspired and Inspiring: Hervé Moulin and the Discovery of the Beauty Contest Game. *Mathematical Social Science* 90: 191–207.

Nash, J. F. (1950a). Equilibrium Points in N-Person Games. *Proceedings of the National Academy of Sciences of the United States of America* 36(1): 48–49.

Nash, J. F. (1950b). The Bargaining Problem. *Econometrica* 18(2): 155–162.

Palacios-Huerta, I. (2003). Professionals Play Minimax. *Review of Economic Studies* 70(2): 395–415.

Polonio, L. and Coricelli, G. (2019). Testing the Level of Consistency between Choices and Beliefs in Games Using Eye-Tracking. *Games and Economic Behavior* 113: 566–586.

Rabin, M. (1993). Incorporating Fairness into Game Theory and Economics. *American Economic Review* 83(5): 1281–1302.

Roemer, J. (2015). Kantian Optimization: A Microfoundation for Cooperation. *Journal of Public Economics* 127: 45–57.

Roemer, J. (2019). A Theory of Cooperation in Games with an Application to Market Socialism. *Review of Social Economy* 77(1): 1–28.

Ross, L., Greene, D., and House, P. (1977). The "False Consensus Effect": An Egocentric Bias in Social Perception and Attribution Processes. *Journal of Experimental Social Psychology* 13(3): 279–301.

Samuelson, W. F. and Bazerman, M. H. (1985). The Winner's Curse in Bilateral Negotiations. In V. L. Smith (ed.), *Research in Experimental Economics*, Volume 3. JAI Press: Greenwich, CT.

Schelling, T. C. (1960). *The Strategy of Conflict*. Harvard University Press: Cambridge, MA.

Schotter, A., Weigelt, K., and Wilson, C. (1994). A Laboratory Investigation of Multi-person Rationality and Presentation Effects. *Games and Economic Behavior* 6(3): 445–468.

Selten R. (1998). Aspiration Adaptation Theory. *Journal of Mathematical Psychology* 42(2): 191–214.

Selten, R. and Güth, W. (1982). Equilibrium Point Selection in a Class of Market Entry Games. In M. Diestler, E. Furst, and G. Schwodiauer (eds.), *Games, Economic Dynamics, and Time Series Analysis*. Physica-Verlag: Vienna-Wurzburg.

Selten, R. (1998). Features of Experimentally Observed Bounded Rationality. *European Economic Review* 42: 413–436.

Shachat, J. M. (2002). Mixed Strategy Play and the Minimax Hypothesis. *Journal of Economic Theory* 104(1): 189–226.

Stahl, D. O. and Wilson, P. W. (1995). On Players' Models of Other Players: Theory and Experimental Evidence. *Games and Economic Behavior* 10(1): 218–254.

Sugden, R. (1989). Spontaneous Order. *Journal of Economic Perspectives* 3(4): 85–97.

Taylor, P. and Jonker, L. (1978). Evolutionary Stable Strategies and Game Dynamics. *Mathematical Biosciences* 40: 145–156.

Thaler, R. H. (1988). Anomalies: The Winner's Curse. *Journal of Economic Perspectives*. 2(1): 191–202.

Thurstone, L. (1927). A Law of Comparative Judgment. *Psychological Review* 34(4): 273–286.

Tomasello, M. (2014). A Natural History of Human Thinking. Harvard University Press: Harvard.

Trivers, R. L. (1971). The Evolution of Reciprocal Altruism. *Quarterly Review of Biology* 46(1): 35–57.

Van Huyck, J. B., Cook, J. P., and Battalio, R. C. (1997). Adaptive Behavior and Coordination Failure. *Journal of Economic Behavior and Organization* 32(4): 483–503.

Walker, M. and Wooders, J. (2001). Minimax Play at Wimbledon. *American Economic Review* 91(5): 1521–1538.

Wang, J. T., Spezio, M., and Camerer, C. F. (2010). Pinocchio's Pupil: Using Eyetracking and Pupil Dilation to Understand Truth Telling and

Deception in Sender-Receiver Games. *American Economic Review* 100(3): 984–1007.

Waytz, A., Iyer, R., Young, L., Haidt, J., and Graham, J. (2019). Ideological Differences in the Expanse of the Moral Circle. *Nature Communications* 10(1): 1–12.

Wooders, J. (2010). Does Experience Teach? Professionals and Minimax Play in the Lab. *Econometrica* 78(3): 1143–1154.

Woodford, M. (2012). Prospect Theory as Efficient Perceptual Distortion. *American Economic Review* 102(3): 1–8.

Woodford, M. (2014). Stochastic Choice: An Optimizing Neuroeconomic Model. *American Economic Review* 104(5): 495–500.

Young, H. P. (1998). *Individual Strategy and Social Structure: An Evolutionary Theory of Institutions*. Princeton University Press: Princeton, NJ.

Problems for Part IV

1. This problem, and the next, are projects for students that could take the form of a mid-term assessment for an applied course in behavioral and experimental economics. Consider the ultimatum game in Part II. What is the backward induction outcome, the subgame perfect equilibrium, and the Nash equilibrium of this game? Write down experimental instructions for testing the predictions of these three alternatives, taking care of the following. (1) Individual choices must be incentivized. (2) *Experimenter demand effects*, namely, the possibility that subjects might give answers that the experimenter wishes to listen to, are minimized. (3) Anonymity of the subjects is preserved.
2. Consider the gift exchange game in Part II. What is the backward induction outcome, the subgame perfect equilibrium, and the Nash equilibrium of this game? Write down experimental instructions for testing the predictions of these three alternatives, taking care of the following. (1) Individual choices must be incentivized. (2) *Experimenter demand effects*, namely, the possibility that subjects might give answers that the experimenter wishes to listen to, are minimized. (3) Anonymity of the subjects is preserved.
3. (Crawford, 2007) Consider the battle of the sexes games shown in Table 8.5. The payoff $a > 1$. The two pure strategy Nash equilibria are (H, D) and (D, H). Define coordination as the play of either of the two pure strategy Nash equilbria.
   (i) Find the unique mixed strategy Nash equilibrium. What is the coordination rate (percentage of times that either of (H, D) and (D, H) is played)? For what value of a is the coordination rate maximized?
   (ii) Consider a level-k model in which there are four types of players: levels $L1$, $L2$, $L3$, and $L4$. Each of the row and the column players can be any of these four types of players. In a random meeting of a row player and a column player to play the battle of sexes games in Table 8.5, what equilibrium actions do we expect. What is the expected coordination rate, and when is it maximized?
4. (Crawford et al., 2008) Consider two coordination games in which each of two players simultaneously choose the actions X and Y. The two pure strategy coordination equilibria are (X, X) and (Y, Y). Table 8.6 shows a symmetric coordination game; 76% of the column players play X and 24% of the column players play Y. Table 8.7 shows a moderately asymmetric game, which is to be interpreted in a similar manner (the percentage of row and column players who play each strategy is again shown in brackets). The authors argue that the label X is more salient (e.g., "X marks the spot") than the label Y. All players follow the level-k model. We make the following assumption on the behavior of level $L0$ players. (a) If the coordination game is symmetric, then type $L0$ players choose the label salient action with probability $p > 0.5$. (b) If the coordination game is asymmetric, then type L0 players choose

Table 8.5 A battle of the sexes game with $a > 1$

	H	D
H	0, 0	a, 1
D	1, a	0, 0

Table 8.6 A symmetric coordination game

	X(76%)	Y
X(76%)	5, 5	0, 0
Y	0, 0	5, 5

Table 8.7 A moderately asymmetric coordination game

	X(61%)	Y
X(33%)	5, 6	0, 0
Y	0, 0	6, 5

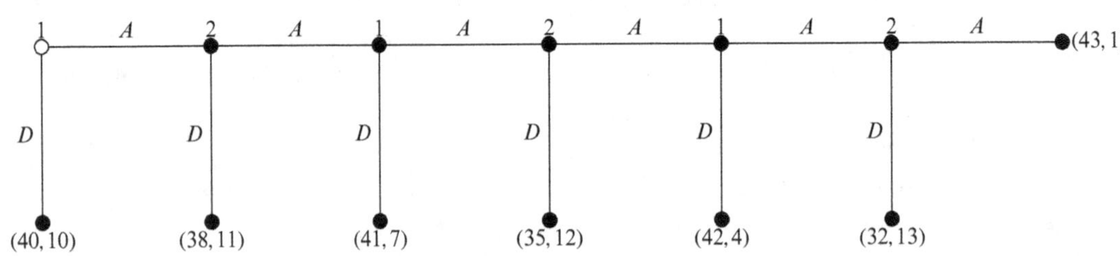

Figure 8.7 A six-move centipede game

the *payoff salient action* (the action that gives them a higher payoff) with probability $p > 0.5$ where $0.505 < p < 0.545$.

(i) Show that all row and column players choose X in the symmetric coordination game.

(ii) Consider the moderately asymmetric game. Show that players of type $L1$ play their own payoff salient action (row players play Y and column players play X). Also show that players of type L2 play the payoff salient action of their opponents (row players play X, column players play Y).

5. (García-Pola et al., 2020) Recall our discussion of the centipede game in Section 7.8.1 and the attempt to pit the predictions of a variety of models against the empirical evidence from this game. We shall use the same notation as in Figure 7.6 for the centipede game; in Table 7.9 for the description of the reduced normal form representation; and in Table 7.10 for the presentation of the results. First consider the six-move decreasing-sum centipede game shown in Figure 8.7.

(a) Write down the reduced normal form for this game (the analogue of Table 7.9).

Table 8.8 The empirical results corresponding to the play of the four strategies, $D1$, $D2$, $D3$, AA, (see Table 7.9 for these strategies). The results are given separately for the row player (player 1) and the column player (player 2). Within each cell, the percentage of the players who play that particular strategy is given first, followed by the theoretical models that predict the play of that strategy

	$D1$	$D2$	$D3$	AA
Player 1	64.47% $BI, A, L2, L3, PE$ $A(\gamma), IA(\alpha, \beta), 0.43_{QRE}$	10.53% $L1, PE$ 0.39_{QRE}	15.79% PE 0.05_{QRE}	9.21% IA, PE, O 0.12_{QRE}
Player 2	70.67% $BI, A, L1, L2, L3, PE$ $A(\gamma), IA(\alpha, \beta), 0.42_{QRE}$	16.00% $L3, PE$ 0.24_{QRE}	10.67% $L3, PE, O, IA$ 0.22_{QRE}	2.67% $L3, PE$ 0.13_{QRE}

Table 8.9 A two-player simultaneous move game from Costa-Gomes et al. (2001)

	L	R	*Data*	*Nash*
T	45, 66	82, 31	0.92	1
TM	22, 14	57, 55	0	0
BM	30, 42	28, 37	0	0
B	15, 60	61, 88	0.08	0
Data	0.64	0.36		
Nash	1	0		

(b) Interpret the empirical results shown for this game in Table 8.8 (the analogue of Table 7.10).

6. Consider the market entry game in Section 7.8.2. Suppose that the number of firms is $N = 200$. Players use the CH model with a Poisson distribution whose single parameter is $\tau = 1.6$. Type $L0$ randomizes between Enter and Out. Determine the optimal decisions and cutoff points for levels $L1, L2, L3$. How many entrants enter when the market size d equals (i) 30, (ii) 90, (iii) 140, (iv) 180?
7. (Camerer et al., 2004) Consider the two-player simultaneous move game in Table 8.9 from Costa-Gomes et al. (2001). The row player has four pure strategies T, TM, BM, B and the column player has two pure strategies L, R. The game has only one pure strategy Nash equilibrium (T, L); this is shown in Table 8.9 by an entry of 1 in the corresponding row and column labeled "Nash." 92% of the row players and 64% of the column players play their part of the Nash equilibrium; the percentage of players playing the remaining strategies is shown in the row and the column labeled "Data." Suppose that all players use the CH model and the single parameter of the Poisson distribution is $\tau = 1.7$. Derive the predictions of the CH model for the game in Table 8.9 and show that the proportion of column players who play the strategy L is 59% and the proportion of row players who play T is 85.5%, which is close to the observed data.

Table 8.10 A simple two-player static simultaneous move game, $x > 0$

	H	D
H	$x-1, x-1$	$x, 0.5$
D	$0.5, x$	$0.5, 0.5$

Table 8.11 A hawk–dove game

	H	D
H	$-3, -3$	$1, -2$
D	$-2, 1$	$0, 0$

Table 8.12 A hawk–dove game

	c_1	c_2
r_1	$6, 6$	$2, 8$
r_2	$8, 2$	$0, 0$

8. Consider the two-player symmetric simultaneous move game shown in Table 8.10 where each player has two pure strategies, H, D. Some of the payoffs are shown in terms of a variable payoff $x > 0$ that we can vary. We are interested in a symmetric equilibrium where all players play identical strategies.

   We are interested in computing a QRE to this game. Use the *Luce ratio probabilistic choice rule* in (7.13). Show that when $x = 1$, the QRE is $p = 0.5$ and when $x = \frac{5}{3}$ then $p = \frac{2}{3}$. [Hint: Proceed as in the solution to the PD game in Section 7.8.3 and find the fixed point in beliefs by forming the relevant quadratic equation which is $-p^2 + p\left(\frac{3}{2} - x\right) - x = 0$. Solve this out for the two values of a QRE.]
9. Consider the asymmetric matching pennies game in Table 7.13. Using the logit quantal response function, show that as x increases, in a QRE, the row player plays the pure strategy H with a higher probability.
10. Consider the Hawk–Dove two-player game in Table 8.11 where the strategy Hawk is represented by H and the strategy Dove by D. If it helps the reader, they can label the two strategies of the row player as r_1, r_2 and the two strategies of the column player as c_1, c_2.
    (i) What are the two pure strategy Nash equilibria in the game?
    (ii) Show that there is a MSNE in which each player randomizes equally between the two strategies for an expected payoff of -1 to each player.
    (iii) Consider the correlated strategy in which (H, H) is played with probability 0 and each of the remaining strategy profiles is played with a probability of $\frac{1}{3}$. Show that the expected payoff in this case is $-\frac{1}{3}$, which is greater than the expected payoff under a MSNE. Show that this correlated strategy satisfies the conditions for a correlated equilibrium.
11. Consider the two-player game in Table 8.12.

Table 8.13 A 2 × 2 normal form game

	A	B
A	1, 1	1, 1
B	1, 1	2, 2

Table 8.14 A 2 × 2 normal form game

	A	B
A	4, 4	1, 1
B	1, 1	2, 2

(i) What are the two pure strategy Nash equilibria in the game?

(ii) Show that there is a MSNE in which each player randomizes equally between the two strategies for an expected payoff of four to each player.

(iii) Consider a correlated equilibrium $\alpha = (a, b, c, d)$ in which the strategy profiles $(r_1, c_1), (r_1, c_2), (r_2, c_1), (r_2, c_2)$ are, respectively, played. First write down the four strategic incentive constraints for the game and use them to derive restrictions on the probabilities a, b, c, d. Use these probabilities to write down the expected payoff for each player, and add up the two expected payoffs. This is the objective function for the mediator to maximize by a suitable choice of the correlating probabilities a, b, c, d. Use the optimization problem of the mediator to derive the optimal values for a, b, c, d. Show that the expected payoff for each player is 5.333 which is greater than the expected payoff under a MSNE.

12. Consider the "Acquire a company game" in Example 8.1. Suppose that the acquiring firm, A, is fully cursed, that is, $\chi = 1$ in the terminology introduced in Section 7.8.4. Show that the optimal bid of the fully cursed firm A will be $b^c = 25\gamma$. [Hint: A fully cursed firm A always assumes that the target firm T will play the average strategy across all its types, where a type of the firm is its privately known valuation, v. Show that the average strategy of the target firm T is to accept any bid b by firm A, with probability $\frac{b}{100}$. Use this to write down the maximization problem of the fully cursed firm A. The solution to this problem will give $b^c = 25\gamma$.]
13. Can evolutionary game theory explain the empirical evidence in the PD game that a large number of players play the cooperative outcome (see Table 7.1)?
14. Find the steady states and the asymptotic stability under replicator dynamics of the games in Tables 8.13 and 8.14.
15. Consider the normal form game shown in Table 8.15. Show that only one of the two Nash equilibria satisfies the conditions for an evolutionary stable strategy (ESS). Can you conjecture what this means for the relation between ESS and those Nash equilibria which are achieved with the deletion of weakly dominated strategies?
16. Consider the normal form game in Table 8.16. Suppose that players only play mixed strategies. Find the unique MSNE of the game. Use the discussion in Section 8.4.5 to prove that the MSNE is also an ESS.

Table 8.15 A 2 × 2 normal form game

	A	B
A	1, 1	1, 1
B	1, 1	2, 2

Table 8.16 A 2 × 2 normal form game

	A	B
A	3, 3	2, 4
B	4, 2	0, 0

17. Consider the objective function of player $i = 1, 2$ in a two-player public goods game, given in (8.32). The player potentially experiences guilt from contributing an amount lower than the perceived positive expectations of the partner, b_i^2; and shame from contributing an amount lower than the perceived normative expectations of a social group, B_i^2. The guilt and shame functions are given, respectively, in (8.26) and (8.33). Derive the optimal contributions of player i under the following assumptions.
   (i) $b_i^2 < B_i^2$. [Hint: Consider the separate cases $b_i^2 < g_i \leq B_i^2$ and $g_i \leq b_i^2 < B_i^2$ and determine which domain the optimal decision lies in.]
   (ii) $B_i^2 < b_i^2$. [Hint: Consider the separate cases $B_i^2 < g_i \leq b_i^2$ and $g_i \leq B_i^2 < b_i^2$ and determine which domain the optimal decision lies in.]

Part V

Bounded Rationality

Introduction to Part V

How do individuals make optimal choices when they choose from a set of alternatives? The answer typically follows in two steps. In the first step, axiomatic foundations, under certainty, risk, subjective uncertainty, and in temporal problems are used to demonstrate that the underlying preferences of individuals can be represented by corresponding utility functions. We have given several examples in this book. For instance, in Part I, we showed how risk preferences can be represented by the expected utility function. In Part III, we showed how time preferences can be represented by the exponential discounted utility model. By establishing the equivalence between preferences and the corresponding utility function, choosing the most preferred alternative becomes equivalent to choosing the alternative that gives maximum utility. Thus, in the second step, individuals use mathematical optimization to maximize a well-defined utility function subject to the relevant constraints that depend on the problem being analyzed. Let us call this exercise *utility maximization*. Undergraduate students in economics are trained early in mathematical optimization. They are taught to set up the appropriate Lagrangians, first order conditions, and check appropriate conditions on bordered Hessians to determine if the second order conditions are satisfied. Often this becomes a default and mechanical exercise, which lacks a full appreciation of the underlying assumptions.

Utility maximization often requires the use of additional technical assumptions such as continuous differentiability of various orders whose preference foundations are not always plausible. More importantly, the underlying restrictions imposed on utility functions are often not empirically tested, so that utility maximization itself might not always rest on strong foundations. But this is not the only problem with strict utility maximization. The existence of a utility function requires the assumption of complete and transitive preferences (see Part I). Empirical evidence does not always support these assumptions. Many people may find it difficult to make a choice when the set of alternatives becomes too large; transitivity too is also violated in experiments (see Section 9.2 below). This evidence calls into question the very notion of a well-defined utility function that can be maximized.

Despite troubling evidence, many economists are likely to be reluctant to compromise on utility maximization. Gintis (2009), for instance, advocates keeping faith with this minimum degree of rationality in economics. The fear is that giving up utility maximization might result in giving up the highly desirable traits of rigor and precision in economic models, which also set it apart from some of the other social and behavioral sciences. There are also concerns that the empirical violations of the underlying axioms that give rise to a utility function might not take into account the context and frame dependence of preferences. Yet, the only tenable position in science is that we must always be guided by the evidence in making these decisions.

Individuals may also suffer from limited attention and pay inadequate attention to the set of alternatives over which they choose. Or, they may find the entire exercise of choosing a maximal element from the available alternatives to be excessively cognitively demanding. Hence, they may choose to *satisfice* by choosing an alternative that meets some minimum acceptable level of utility, rather than strictly *optimize* in a mathematical sense. We have good evidence that this might be the case.

Setting up and solving optimization problems in economics also often requires individuals to obey the known laws of classical statistics, not just mathematics. As we shall see in this chapter, the empirical evidence rejects this assumption. Many undergraduate students find probability theory challenging, and may, for instance, have difficulties in readily finding the solution to Bayes' Law. Yet, neoclassical economics assumes that people effortlessly obey the laws of classical statistics, or act "as if" they do so. Recall from our discussion in Part I that *true uncertainty* (the problem of unknown unknowns) is likely to be pervasive in real world problems. If this is the case, then strictly speaking, none of the existing optimization techniques apply.

Yet individuals who might have incomplete and intransitive preferences; violate the laws of classical statistics; possess limited attention, limited memory, and cognitive constraints; and possibly face true uncertainty, do make choices in the real world. How do they do it? This is an open problem in the social and behavioral sciences.

One possible answer is that individuals use *simple rules of thumb*, also known as *heuristics*, in making choices. Clearly, heuristics will lead to outcomes that never give higher utility than could be obtained with strict mathematical optimization, unless we are in a situation of true uncertainty where maximal utility is an undefined concept. In this sense, the solution with heuristics leads to *biases* relative to mathematical optimization.

Yet, the use of the term "bias" in this context is misleading on several counts. First, the optimization solution does not take account of cognitive costs and other costs of solving problems, for example, the *infinite regress problem in search costs*; see below. Second, if most humans use heuristics, then the use of the term "bias" to describe empirically observed behavior, relative to a hypothetical, and arguably unrealistic, benchmark is not a choice that everyone will agree with. Any use of the term "bias" in the literature, and in this book, must be subject to these caveats and as behavioral economics develops, we would do well to banish the usage of "bias" from the discourse.

In the 1970's, Daniel Kahneman and Amos Tversky published a set of seminal papers (Kahneman and Tversky, 1972a,b; Tversky and Kahneman, 1971, 1973, 1974) that provided a systematic treatment of the heuristics that people use. They showed that some of the central predictions in neoclassical economics are rejected by the evidence. Furthermore, people do not act "as if" they conformed to the assumption of neoclassical economics. The research program initiated by Kahneman and Tversky, one of the greatest achievements in the social and behavioral sciences, has come to be known as the *heuristics and biases research program*. Given our views on the term "bias," we prefer to call it the *heuristics research program*. We consider several heuristics in this research program. These include the *representativeness heuristic* and its variants, *the gambler's fallacy* and the *hot hand fallacy*; the *anchoring heuristic*; the *availability heuristic*; the fallacy that leads to the *hindsight bias*; *conjunction fallacy*; *neglect of base rates* and *underweighting the likelihood of a sample*; *regression to the mean*; and *attribute substitution*.

Any account of bounded rationality must highlight the work of Herbert Simon who won the Nobel Prize in the economic sciences, pioneered the use of bounded rationality, and is also one of the inventors of artificial intelligence. Simon was an early proponent of the view that there is too much rationality in economics relative to what we empirically observe. He emphasized the *procedural rationality* of methods that describe how people make their choices (Simon, 1957, 1978, 2000). For instance, if the procedure requires individuals to make trillions of calculations, as is often required in fairly modest problems in dynamic programming, then procedural rationality is likely to be violated. We shall describe Simon's proposal for *aspiration adaptation models* and the heuristic of *satisficing* that were designed to replace optimization.

A basic idea stressed in Herbert Simon's approach, and in other approaches that are motivated by it, such as the heuristics program of Kahneman–Tversky, and the work of Gerd Gigerenzer and his coauthors (Gigerenzer and Selten, 2001), is one of *fast* and *frugal* heuristics. The basic idea is that humans choose heuristics that are *fast* in terms of the computational time required to make decisions, and *frugal* in the use of information. While the heuristics program of Kahneman and Tversky dealt mainly with problems of risk and uncertainty, the work of Gigerenzer and his coauthors often speaks to human decision making under true uncertainty. Hence, the two frameworks are not necessarily competitors. We offer a critique of the Gigerenzer research program.

Let us consider two motivating examples of fast and frugal heuristics.

Example 1 *(Hospital checklists) Time is of the essence in making decisions in hospitals where the life of a patient could be in immediate danger. Rather than engage in potentially time consuming mathematical optimization to determine the optimal medical treatment to offer, hospitals employ simple heuristics in the form of checklists to classify patients into those who face high and low risks (Breiman et al., 1993). They employ decision trees that use only a limited number of variables. Here is an example: If the systolic blood pressure is below 91, the patient is immediately classified as high-risk and no further information is needed. If blood pressure is above 91, then patients older than 62.5 years and suffering from sinus tachycardia are classified as high risk. Otherwise they are classified as low risk.*

Example 2 *(The problem of catching a ball): Consider any ball and bat game (cricket and baseball are examples) in which the following situation arises. A batter, say, in baseball or in cricket, hits a ball from point A and the ball lands at point B after traveling through a parabolic trajectory. The objective of a fielder, stationed at point C, is to run and catch the ball before it lands at point B. What path should the fielder take from C to B? If the fielder uses mathematical optimization, then the fielder must have knowledge of parabolic curves, the weight of the ball, and how the trajectory of the ball might be influenced by wind speed and humidity at that time, to guess the location of point B. Since the shortest distance between two points is a straight line, the prediction under mathematical optimization is that the fielder must run in a "straight line" from point C to point B and catch the ball. Yet, when we observe successful fielders in baseball and in cricket, they do not run in a straight line from C to B. Rather they take a "curved path" from C to B to catch the ball. This is not consistent with mathematical optimization. Rather, they use a simple heuristic, the gaze heuristic, that evolved from millions of years of evolution during which we learned to (i) outwit predators running towards us, and (ii) run towards prey to catch them. The gaze heuristic requires* *fielders to run in a curved path from C to B. McLeod et al. (2006, p. 139) write: "the path of a fielder running to catch a ball is determined by the attempt to satisfy 2 independent constraints. The 1st is to keep the angle of elevation of gaze to the ball increasing at a decreasing rate. The 2nd is to control the rate of horizontal rotation necessary to maintain fixation on the ball." Thus, successful fielders use a heuristic that is fast in terms of computation time (fielders start running immediately towards the ball) and frugal in the use of information (only the angle of the gaze is required) relative to the complex solution under mathematical optimization.*

We take our working definition of *bounded rationality* to mean that (i) individuals use heuristics rather than strict mathematical optimization, and (ii) people use sensible goals such as "satisficing" (a neologism of "satisfy" and "suffice") to judge their actions. Thus, under bounded rationality, people engage in behaviors that are not predicted by the standard neoclassical economics models. In some cases neoclassical models may also predict the use of heuristics. Consider two well-known examples from macroeconomics (Blanchard and Fischer, 1989).

(i) Suppose that individuals are trying to predict the value of a random variable that occurs some time into the future. Under certain conditions on the random process that gives rise to the actual realization of the random variable, the requirements for rational expectations reduce to using adaptive expectations. Adaptive expectations require individuals to use a simple heuristic in making their current forecasts. They take their last period forecast and adjust it by a fraction of the last period's forecast error. Hence, in this special case, the prediction under rational expectation is observationally equivalent to using adaptive expectations.

(ii) Under certain conditions, such as restrictions on the utility functions, individuals engaging in intertemporal optimization may appear to an outsider to be using the following simple rule of thumb. They consume a fixed percentage of their income every period, and save the rest, which does appear to be a simple heuristic.

We do not treat these as examples of bounded rationality.

We consider a range of applications of bounded rationality in the second of the two chapters in this part, Chapter 10. These applications include *mental models*; *narrow bracketing* and *broad bracketing*; *mental accounting*; *projection-bias*; *aspiration adaptation*; and an introduction to *behavioral finance* and *behavioral corporate finance*.

9 Bounded Rationality I

Judgment Heuristics

9.1 Introduction

In the first of the two chapters on bounded rationality, we begin by exploring the basic rationale for why we might need to use simple heuristics. As part of this rationale, in Section 9.2 we explore the empirical evidence that violates some of the basic assumptions in neoclassical economics. These include the evidence contradicting completeness and transitivity of preferences; evidence on overconfidence, limited attention, inability to construct the full sampling distribution; and evidence on failures in the use of mathematical logic, such as the distinction between necessary and sufficient conditions.

We then outline the concept of *procedural rationality* in Section 9.3 and move on to explore the two main strands in the literature. In the first strand, which is the main focus of this chapter, we explore the *Kahneman–Tversky heuristics program* in Section 9.4. Within this program, we define, discuss, provide empirical evidence, and give applications of a large number of heuristics. These include, among others, the *representativeness heuristic* and its two exemplars, the *gambler's fallacy* and the *hot hand fallacy*; the *anchoring heuristic*; the *availability heuristic*; *hindsight-bias*; the *conjunction fallacy*; conformity with Bayes' law and reconciling the conflict between *base rate neglect* and *conservatism in the likelihood of a sample*; *regression to the mean*; and *attribute substitution*.

Section 9.5 shows that the departures of observed behavior from the neoclassical predictions, on account of judgment heuristics, are not reduced by offering high incentives. To be sure, very high incentives induce subjects in experiments to spend more deliberation time, hence, these incentives aid in motivation. However, since this does not influence the extent of the observed departures in behavior from the neoclassical predictions, the problem is a lack of cognitive ability and skill in solving the underlying problems.

We then discuss a second strand of the literature in Section 9.6, the *Gigerenzer fast and frugal heuristics program*, that places greater reliance on the procedural rationality of methods. Since this research program is often directed at problems under true uncertainty, there is no natural yardstick on which to compare the predictions. While promising, as it stands, this program does have several important limitations. We offer a critique.

9.2 Some Violations of the Neoclassical Rationality Assumptions

9.2.1 Completeness and Transitivity of Preferences

The axiom of *completeness* (see Part I) requires that in making choices between any two alternatives, say, A and B, from the set of choices, decision makers must be able to "rank" the alternatives. This requires them to say either that A is "at least as good as" B, or/and B is "at least as good as" A. They cannot say, for instance, that: "I am not sure which of the two options I prefer." The axiom of *transitivity* requires that, for any three alternatives, A, B, C, drawn from a choice set, if A is "at least as good as" B, and B is "at least as good as" C, then A is "at least as good as" C. Transitivity applies to any number of alternatives, not just three alternatives.

When decision makers are faced with riskless and static choices, then satisfaction of the axioms of completeness and transitivity is jointly sufficient for us to say that the decision maker has *rational preferences*. If preferences are rational, then these can be represented by a utility function (see Part I). However, even this most basic notion of rationality has been challenged by the empirical evidence.

When the choice set is "too large" and the alternatives too many, decision makers may find it cognitively challenging to rank the alternatives. In a well cited experiment, Iyengar and Lepper (2000) used two treatments. In a limited choice condition, they asked subjects to make a choice from a set of six varieties of jams. In an intensive choice condition, the choice had to be made from a set of 24 varieties of jams. Subjects were given a coupon of value $1 to buy a jar of jam. There was no difference in the percentage of jams sampled in both conditions, but the purchase decisions were quite different. Nearly 30% of the consumers in the limited choice condition purchased a jar of jam, but only 3% of the consumers in the intensive condition purchased the jar of jam.

A plausible inference is that decision makers find it cognitively difficult to make choices when there are too many options. This is sometimes known as the *choice overload hypothesis*. Another hypothesis is that the larger is the set of choices, the more could be the ex-post regret and disappointment from making an actual choice (Schwartz, 2000). Sethi-Iyengar et al. (2004) consider employee's contributions to 401(k) plans in the US. They find that as the number of funds offered in a plan increased, the likelihood of an employee participating in the 401(k) plan fell. For the addition of every ten funds, there was a 1.5%–2.0% drop in employee participation. In another study, reducing the number of loan options from four to one caused the same increase in borrowing as would be caused by a 2.3% reduction in the interest rate (Bertrand et al., 2010). The choice overload hypothesis has been replicated in other empirical studies with other objects such as pens, chocolates, coffee, and gift boxes.

Meta studies have sharpened our understanding of these results by showing that the extent of the choice overload effect depends on a range of other factors (Scheibehenne et al., 2010; Chernev et al., 2015). These include the similarity of the items; the familiarity of the subjects with similar choices in the past; the lack of an obviously dominant choice among the alternatives; and the difficulty/complexity of making the underlying choices. However, the meta-analyses often themselves require strong distributional assumptions across the comparison studies that are sometimes too heterogeneous and rely on very different qualitative data.

There is an argument that the assumption of transitivity might be more compelling under certainty. However, under risk and uncertainty, the presence of intransitivity was first demonstrated in the classic experiments by Lichtenstein and Slovic (1971). Recall, from Part 1, the concept of a lottery under risk, which specifies a set of outcomes and the associated objective probabilities of the outcomes. In their experiments, Lichtenstein and Slovic gave two different lotteries, a P-bet and a \$-bet, to the subjects.

$$P\text{-bet} = (0, 1-P; z, P), \ \$\text{-bet} = (0, 1-p; Z, p). \tag{9.1}$$

The relation between the two probabilities is $0 < p < P$, and the relation between the two outcomes is $0 < z < Z$. Thus, the P-bet offers a higher probability of winning a lower prize z (and a probability $1 - P$ of winning nothing). The \$-bet offers a lower probability p of winning a higher prize, Z (and a probability $1 - p$ of winning nothing).

Recall that the *certainty equivalent* of a lottery is an outcome which, when offered to the decision maker with certainty, makes the decision maker indifferent between the lottery and the outcome. Denote the *certainty equivalents* of the P-bet and the \$-bet by, respectively, C_P and $C_\$$. Recall from the notation introduced in Part I that $A \sim B$ means that a decision maker is indifferent between options A and B. By the definition of a certainty equivalent, we have

$$\$ - bet \sim C_\$ \text{ and } C_P \sim P - bet.$$

Subjects were asked to make two choices.

1. In the *lottery choice task*, subjects are asked to make a choice between the P-bet and the \$-bet.
2. In the *evaluation task*, subjects are asked to state the certainty equivalent for each of the two lotteries, the P-bet and the \$-bet.

Lichtenstein and Slovic (1971) showed that in the lottery choice task, subjects strictly preferred the P-bet over the \$-bet. Using the standard notation $A \succ B$ to mean that a decision maker strictly prefers A to B (see Part I), we can write this finding as

$$P - bet \succ \$ - bet.$$

However, in the evaluation task, they stated a higher certainty equivalent for the \$-bet, that is,

$$C_P < C_\$.$$

Transitivity fails because of the following chain:

$$\$ - bet \sim C_\$ \succ C_P \sim P - bet \succ \$ - bet. \tag{9.2}$$

From the first two comparisons in (9.2), transitivity requires that we must have $\$ - bet \succ C_P$. But from the last two comparisons in (9.2) we have $C_P \succ \$ - bet$. This violates transitivity. Lichtenstein and Slovic are psychologists, so these results were initially met with much skepticism in economics. Grether and Plott (1979), two experimental economists, expressed serious reservations about this evidence on the grounds that it was based on hypothetical situations/rewards and nonincentivized experiments. However, to their surprise, when they re-ran these experiments after addressing these potential confounds, they found the preference reversal effect was even stronger. This debate and some of the later studies are examined in

Lichtenstein and Slovic (2006). Several models in decision theory are able, in principle, to predict nontransitive choices, for example, regret theory (Loomes and Sugden, 1982; Loomes et al., 1991), but the pattern of intransitivities observed in the data is not always in conformity with this theory either. Recent research points to intriguing evidence that preference reversals might have genetic correlates and those who have a gene that results in more impulsive behavior are more likely to engage in preference reversals (Zeng et al., 2021).

9.2.2 Limited Attention

Neoclassical economics assumes that decision makers pay full, and unlimited, attention to all relevant alternatives. However, the empirical evidence from many domains reveals that decision makers pay *limited attention* to the available alternatives. We discuss some of this evidence below, postponing a discussion of the relevant theory to the last part of the book.

People tend to give more attention to the leftmost digits in a multi-digit number, and less attention to the digits on the right. Sellers often use this to their advantage by setting prices that end in the digit nine; for instance, a price of \$9.99 rather than \$10. There is also a well documented left digit bias in the used car market (Lacetera et al., 2012; Busse et al., 2013). The data on used cars reveals discontinuous drops in the prices of used cars at 10,000 mile thresholds. For instance, cars with 79,900–79,999 miles on the odometer sell for

(i) \$210 more than those with odometer readings in the range 80,000–80,100, but only
(ii) \$10 less than those with odometer readings 79,800–79,899.

Thus, prices exhibit a discontinuous jump at a mileage of 79,999 miles. Discontinuous jumps in prices are also found at thresholds of $X9,999$ miles where $X = 0, 1, 2, \ldots$. The data show that sellers display strategic behavior because there is a spike in the sales of cars just before they hit one of the relevant odometer thresholds.

The evidence also shows that many people pay differential attention to taxes and other charges that they face. In the US, the Federal taxes are added to the price displayed on the price stickers on store items, but the state taxes might only be added at the retail outlet. Using selected items in a grocery store, where the state sales tax was displayed for some consumer goods, but not for others, Chetty et al. (2009) showed that consumer purchases were influenced by whether state sales taxes were added or not, to price stickers. Consumers did display an awareness of the state sales taxes as this is public information, but the very fact that the taxes might not be added on the price stickers reduces their salience, inducing consumers to buy more of those goods. The poor who spend a greater proportion of their income on groceries pay greater attention to sales taxes that are not added to price stickers (Goldin and Homonoff, 2013). Customers who pay by manual tolls in car plazas, say, paying by cash relative to credit cards, demonstrate greater awareness of the amount paid (Finkelstein, 2009). The literature on the political economy of taxation has highlighted the use of less salient taxes, such as sales taxes, relative to more salient taxes, such as income taxes, in raising tax revenues, as the latter are less politically popular (Buchanan, 1967; Brennan and Buchanan, 1980).

Testing directly for limited attention faces the challenge of completely shutting down other competing channels of explanation. However, one can test for some of the possible indirect implications of limited attention. The 2015 World Bank Development Report gives supporting empirical evidence from developing countries. Consider the following examples.

1. Those with limited attention may pay more attention to information that is presented in a more readily understandable form. In an experiment with low-income individuals in Mexico City, Giné et al. (2014) asked subjects to spot the lowest-cost credit product in bank brochures. Only 39% of the subjects correctly spotted the lowest-cost product. However, when identical information was provided in the form of a user-friendly summary sheet, 68% of the subjects were able to spot the lowest-cost product.
2. Altering the information content of messages might also induce those with limited attention to pay greater attention. For instance, a chain smoker who smokes 20 cigarettes may not pay adequate attention if advised to resist the next cigarette. However, they might pay more attention if informed that over the course of a year they could be smoking 7,300 cigarettes at the current rate. Similarly, payday loans taken to tide over a few days often incur very high annual interest rates, but the amounts may not be very salient when considered for a week. When borrowers were informed about their effective loan repayments over a longer period, say, a month, then the amounts paid became more salient and this proved more effective in reducing their borrowing (Bertrand and Morse, 2011).
3. Attention among the poor in developing countries might be particularly compromised due to pressing everyday demands for basic necessities such as food, clean drinking water, shelter, and paying off loans borrowed at high interest rates. The constant anxiety about everyday survival, which might border on hopelessness, is a form of *cognitive tax* that might deplete willpower and the ability to pay adequate attention to other aspects of life (Banerjee and Mullainathan, 2008; Shah et al., 2012; Mullainathan and Shafir, 2013; Haushofer and Fehr, 2014). In other words, the poor may suffer from problems of *low bandwidth* and end up making suboptimal decisions, which in turn perpetuate their state of poverty. Supporting evidence comes from Mani et al. (2013) who show that farmers score up to 10 points lower on IQ tests before a harvest when they have high levels of financial stress.

   A corollary of these ideas is to ask the question if providing a cash transfer to people in financial stress improves their economic performance and attention, perhaps by reducing anxiety and stress. Banerjee et al. (2020) showed that asset transfers to the poor increase their labor supply. The subjects in Kaur et al. (2022) are 408 male agriculture workers in Odisha, India who, during the lean season, try to find temporary employment lasting over a few days to a few weeks. The two main worries reported by the subjects in this study are daily consumption and repayment of loans; 71% of these workers are under debt, and 86% report being worried about their finances. The workers are also highly liquidity constrained; 66% of the workers report that they did not have Rs 1000 (about US $15) to pay in case of an emergency.

   The authors implemented two treatments in which workers are paid piece rates (wages conditional on the amount of work done) for work done over 12 days. Workers in the "control treatment" receive a final payment on day 12. Workers in the "treatment group" received two payments. An interim payment on day 8 for the work done so far, and then a final payment on day 12 for the remaining four days of work. We can now compare the productivity of workers in the control and the treatment groups for days 9–12 in order to gauge treatment effects.

The results are as follows. Workers in the treatment group immediately use the cash received on day 8 on repayment of loans and on consumption. Insofar as this was the cause of their initial financial distress, and associated anxiety and stress, we may expect them to be more productive on the remaining days, days 9–12. On day 9, workers in the treatment group are 7% more productive than the control group, and this effect persists for the remaining days. The greatest productivity effects are concentrated among the poorest workers who would have been under the greatest financial stress. The 12-day task was to make leaf trays which required workers to plan and focus by stitching several leaves together. This enabled the authors to determine the extent of the worker's attention to work (e.g., the evenness of stitches and whether the workers could stitch them together in the first attempt). Measured in this way, attention was found to have increased in the treatment group on days 9–12, and the greatest effects were again found in the poorest workers.

Public policy on poverty that takes account of limited attention can have large welfare effects that are not very costly to implement and simply require altering the information content of messages; Datta and Mullainathan (2014) term this as *low hanging policy fruit*. This is not to suggest that these behavioral factors are the cause of poverty and that by addressing these factors, we might be able to eliminate poverty. Poverty has structural, political, social, historical, and institutional explanations whose exploration is beyond the scope of this book. The literature on behavioral economics, by highlighting the pernicious effect on the poor, adds to the weight of arguments for public policy to address poverty.

4. Individuals with limited attention might also benefit from reminders. Karlan et al. (2012) showed that goal-based text messages in Peru, Bolivia, and the Philippines, reminding individuals of their savings goals, improved savings by 16%.

9.2.3 Overconfidence

In neoclassical economics, there is no notion of *overconfidence* or *underconfidence*. When asked to make inferences, people use the laws of classical statistics to draw statistically accurate inferences. For instance, when they receive new information, people are assumed to use Bayes' Law in order to update their prior beliefs. Hence, confidence-neutral decision making is associated with using the correct statistical laws, and one important manifestation of overconfidence or underconfidence, depending on the situation, arises from an incorrect use of classical statistics.

Individuals need not always be overconfident, and may sometimes appear to be underconfident (see the discussion on the underweighting of the likelihood of a sample in Section 9.4.10). There is a large literature on overconfidence and we shall only provide readers with a brief introduction to the findings from this literature. However, we shall provide more references than usual in this section, so that the interested reader can follow up the relevant literature.

Following Moore and Healy (2008), we may classify overconfidence into one of the following three types.

1. *Overestimation* arises when individuals overestimate their performance in a task, for example, an IQ test.
2. *Overplacement*, or *better than average,* or the *better than median,* effect occurs when individuals rank themselves too favorably against some statistic of the rank order of some

characteristic of others, for example, the average or the median ability of others (Larrick et al., 2007).

3. *Overprecision* arises when subjects are asked to make predictions about a random variable, and they estimate overly narrow confidence intervals of their predictions, relative to the correct statistical benchmark.

These three categories may be related. In domains where overestimation is found to be high, underplacement (the opposite of overplacement) is also found to be high. One explanation is in terms of the *hard-easy effect* (Windschitl et al., 2003). People have imperfect information about their abilities and the abilities of others in the following manner.

(i) When the tasks are relatively easier, they underestimate their performance, but they underestimate the performance of others even more, leading to overplacement. Thus, for instance, many people rate their driving ability better than the average, or the median, driving ability of others.
(ii) For tasks that are hard, people overestimate their performance, but overestimate the performance of others even more, leading to underplacement.

A related explanation is in terms of the *Dunning–Krueger effect* (Krueger and Dunning, 1999). It arises when low-ability individuals overrate their skills/abilities and high-ability individuals underrate their skills/abilities, relative to their peers. In tests of grammar and logical reasoning, students in the bottom 25% of the subject pool rated their performance to be in the top 40 percentile and those who were in the top 25% underrated their performance (Dunning et al., 2003). Krueger and Dunning (1999) advance the argument that low ability subjects are doubly hampered. Their lower ability leads to low scores, and also hampers recognition of their relative rank among their peers. By contrast, high-ability individuals find the task easy, but mistakenly infer that others will find it even easier, so they underestimate their ranks. Competing explanations of the Dunning–Krueger effect include the *regression to the mean phenomena* (Krueger and Mueller, 2002) that we consider below, and the perceived difficulty of the task (Burson et al., 2006). However, a meta study by Ehrlinger et al. (2008) supports the original interpretation in Krueger and Dunning (1999) in preference of these alternative explanations.

Groups of individuals jointly making a decision, and firms estimating their future profitability, might also make overconfident decisions (Buehler et al., 2005; Staats et al., 2012). There are several possible reasons why consultations within teams might not necessarily weed out overconfident decisions (Meikle et al., 2016).

1. There might be only a few dominant team members who hold the ultimate power to make decisions, paying inadequate attention to any feedback that runs counter to their own subjective assessments.
2. Others in the team might anticipate that their feedback will not be taken seriously by the dominant team members, and be reluctant to offer contrary feedback.
3. The larger is the team size, the lower is the responsibility each individual team member may feel for a bad decision. Hence, they might be even more reluctant to offer contrary feedback.

The milestones achieved by firms, such as profit levels, are determined jointly by the actions taken by the managers of firms, and external factors over which firms have no control. Managers might have a tendency to ascribe bad outcomes to external factors, and good outcomes to their own actions. This phenomenon of *attribution bias* might be particularly preferred by the firm's managers as a way of maintaining a positive self image within the firm and raising the market prospects of firms. However, it might also give them a false sense of confidence (Chen et al., 2015).

Overconfidence among senior managers in firms is also likely to be correlated with other traits such as charm, passion, and decisiveness. This makes it even more difficult for outsiders, such as shareholders, to discover the underlying attribution bias of managers. The evidence suggests that those who rise to senior ranks in organizations are typically more risk-taking and more overconfident, and this may cost the firm in terms of lower profits (Mabe and West, 1982; Anderson et al., 2012; Bonner and Bolinger, 2013; Tenney et al., 2015). Overconfidence in terms of overprecision has been documented for experts who construct confidence intervals for their forecasts that are too narrow (Lin and Bier, 2008). Stock market traders, who are more overconfident, as measured by their self-assessed overplacement, also trade more (Glaser and Weber, 2007). Greater churning of asset portfolios in the stock market is often associated with lower returns.

There is a large literature that associates the overconfidence of CEOs with various outcomes for firms. More overconfident CEOs can help increase a company's patent count and increase innovation, but also lead to greater volatility in the company's stock market prices (Galasso and Simcoe, 2011; Hirshleifer et al., 2012). Overconfident leaders might also engage in more accounting fraud (Ahmed and Duellman, 2013; Hribar and Yang, 2015); are more likely to go to war (Johnson et al., 2006); but make less aggressive choices following government intervention (Banerjee et al., 2015); hold on to their own company stock for too long, hence, forgoing a profitable opportunity to sell company stock (Hall and Murphy, 2000, 2002; Meulbroek, 2001); more likely to engage in mergers that have a high failure rate (Malmendier and Tate, 2015); and more likely to believe that their stocks are undervalued by the market, avoiding profitable opportunities that rely on external borrowings (Malmendier et al., 2011). Markets exhibit a degree of rationality by reacting less to mergers undertaken by more overconfident CEOs (Malmendier and Tate, 2008). Aktas et al. (2016) measured narcissism in managers by the ratio of the number of times that CEOs used first person singular pronouns; more narcissist managers negotiate faster, and are more likely to have initiated and completed mergers that often fail.

It is not just CEOs of established firms who might be overconfident. Owners of startups overestimate the probability of success of their startups (Camerer and Lovallo, 1999). Moreover, 95% of such entrepreneurs believe that their odds are better than comparable enterprises, while a third believe that their success is assured (Cooper et al., 1988). French data shows that only 6% of startup entrepreneurs expect "difficulty" but three years on, 17% expect difficulty (Landier and Thesmar, 2009). In contrast to these subjective predictions, only half of all startups survive beyond three years (Scarpetta et al., 2002).

The literature on *motivated cognition* offers insights on why some people might be strategically overconfident. They might wish to maintain a positive self-image, or increase self-esteem, or improve their motivation, or signal desirable traits to themselves and to others (Akerlof and

Dickens, 1982; Bénabou and Tirole, 2002, 2016; Brunnermeier and Parker, 2005; Bénabou, 2015). There is some evidence that more optimistic people achieve better life outcomes in terms of savings, income, retirement, and marriage (Puri and Robinson, 2007; Huck et al., 2018). There does not seem to be any apparent link between IQ and motivated cognition (Kahan, 2013; Kahan et al., 2017).

Holding motivated beliefs may benefit an individual, but they might also impose a cost in terms of a reduction in the quality of decisions. *The literature on optimal belief management*, argues that individuals trade-off these benefits and costs to determine the optimal degree of motivated beliefs suitable for them. Strategic self-manipulation of beliefs to arrive at an optimal set of beliefs may involve several strategies, for example, information avoidance, that leads to confirmation-bias; or even by adhering to a particular religion or set of cultural values which might provide comfort/reassurance and self discipline (Bénabou and Tirole, 2016, p. 143).

9.2.4 Can Humans Successfully Construct the Full Sampling Distributions?

One of the basic foundational assumptions in the neoclassical approach is that people effortlessly use all the laws of classical statistics. This assumption is eminently testable, and tests of this assumption are an important part of the heuristics program of Kahneman and Tversky. We shall examine this program in more detail later. However, in this section we ask if individuals are able to produce the full probability distribution.

Consider a random sample of size N where each set of N observations, $x_1, \ldots, x_N$, is drawn from independent and identically distributed random variables, $X_1, \ldots, X_N$, each of which has finite mean μ and finite variance σ^2. Prior to the draw of the actual sample, the sample mean $\bar{x}(N) = \sum_{i=1}^{N} x_i/N$, depends on the unknown values of the N random variables, hence, the sample mean is also a random variable and has a sampling distribution.

The *law of large numbers* plays an essential role in statistics. It states that as the sample size, N, increases, the sample mean $\bar{x}(N)$ becomes closer to the population mean μ, and the sampling variance of $\bar{x}(N)$, given by σ^2/N, shrinks in size. The central limit theorem can be invoked to show that $\bar{x}(N)$ has a normal distribution with mean μ and variance σ^2/N. In the limit, as $N \longrightarrow \infty$, the distribution of $\bar{x}(N)$ becomes degenerate at μ.[1] We can now test to see if subjects in experiments satisfy these requirements.

So long as $N > 10$, the evidence indicates that subjects in experiments do not shrink the variance of the sample mean fast enough, as the sample size, N, increases. In fact, they tend to produce sampling distributions that show little variability with N. Kahneman and Tversky (1972b, p. 437) write: "Thus, the event of finding more than 600 boys in a sample of 1000 babies, for example, is as representative as the event of finding more than 60 boys in a sample of 100 babies. The two events, therefore, would be judged equally probable, although the latter, in fact, is vastly more likely."

[1] Here is a formal statement of the law of large numbers. Let $\{X_N\}$ be a sequence of independently and identically distributed random variables with a common mean μ and finite variance σ^2. Denote the sample mean based on N observations by $\bar{x}(N) = \sum_{i=1}^{n} x_i/N$, where x_i is the sample realization of the random variable X_i. Then $\bar{x}(N)$ "converges in probability" to the population mean, μ, i.e., $\lim_{N\to\infty} P[|\bar{x}(N) - \mu| \geq \varepsilon] = 0$, for all $\varepsilon > 0$.

In contrast to the statistically correct *law of large numbers*, most people seem to use the statistically incorrect *law of small numbers*, which we state informally, but not very precisely, below.

Definition 9.1 *(Law of small numbers) An individual subscribes to the law of small numbers, if the individual believes that for any finite sample size, N, the sample mean $\bar{x}(N)$ is either identical to the population mean, or "close" to it.*

Let us consider a problem similar to the one outlined in Kahneman and Tversky (1972b). A fair coin is tossed N times, and in each toss there is a binary outcome, Heads or Tails. We vary the sample size $N = 10, 100, 1000$, and ask subjects in an experiment to guess the percentage of heads in the sample for 11 bin sizes (0%–5%, 5%–10%,..., 95%–100%). For instance, for $N = 1000$, the subjects are asked the following question. How likely is that there are 0%–5% heads in 1000 tosses of the coin; 5%–10% heads in 1000 tosses; ...; 95%–100% heads in 1000 tosses? Subjects repeated this guessing exercise for different sample sizes.

Figure 9.1 shows the median beliefs for each of the bins for different sample sizes, $N = 10, 100, 1000$, shown as histograms that are in different colors. For each sample size, N, the statistically correct distribution is shown by the dotted curves. The variance of the statistically correct distributions shrinks as the sample size increases and the distributions become more and more concentrated around a mean of 50% heads. However, the variance of the empirically estimated distributions is unresponsive to the sample size N. For any bin size, the beliefs for any sample size are similar. Since the distributions do not shrink with an increase in sample size, the tails of the estimated distribution are "too fat" relative to the true distribution, even for a relatively large sample size of $N = 1000$. This fact has been leveraged by behavioral finance; fat tails lead subjects to give too much salience to extreme returns and this might be reflected in the pricing of assets (Barberis and Huang, 2008).

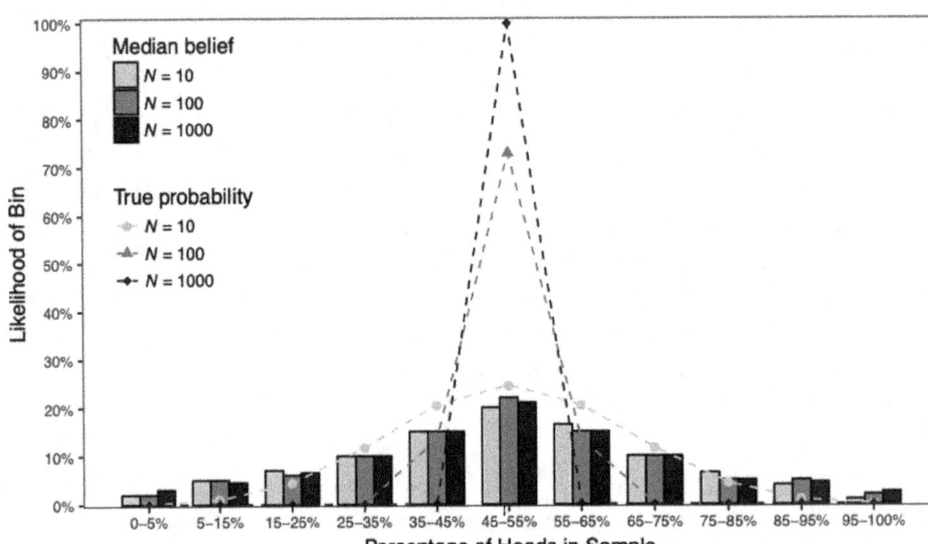

Figure 9.1 Sample size neglect for samples of 10, 100, 1000. Source: Benjamin (2018)

Is the choice of bin sizes important in eliciting the distribution of beliefs of the subjects? In neoclassical economics, the answer is in the negative. However, empirically, the bin sizes play a role in determining the elicited subjective beliefs distributions. This suggests a form of *subadditivity* of elicited belief distributions (see below) making it difficult to compare results across different studies. Subadditivity arises in many different domains in economics. We have already described subadditivity in time preferences in Part III.

Tversky and Koehler (1994) highlighted the role of subadditivity under risk. The probability assigned to an event is found to depend on how the event is unpacked into sub-events. Consider event A: "homicide in an area over the last year," and its two mutually exclusive subsets: (i) Event B: Homicide caused by strangers. (ii) Event C: Homicide caused by non-strangers such as family, spouse, and friends. Let $P(X)$ denote the probability of any event X. Since $A = B \cup C$, and B, C are mutually exclusive, the additive law of probabilities implies that

$$P(A) = P(B) + P(C).$$

The individual exhibits subadditivity under risk if

$$P(A) < P(B) + P(C). \tag{9.3}$$

From (9.3), people assign a lower aggregate probability of homicide relative to the sum of the individual probabilities of its two mutually exclusive parts. When people think of the constituent parts of an event, they can recall more cases from their memory, which leads them to assign a higher probability to the constituent parts.

Clemen and Ulu (2008) demonstrate subadditivity in the elicited belief distributions in their experiments. They asked subjects to assign probabilities to different ranges of temperatures in degrees Celsius, denoted by x. In the low partition condition, the set of possible temperatures was: $x \leq 18$, $18 < x \leq 20$, $20 < x \leq 22$, $x > 22$. In the high partition condition, it was: $x \leq 22$, $22 < x \leq 24$, $24 < x \leq 26$, $x > 26$. If subjects conform to the laws of classical statistics, then they will satisfy the following two conditions.

1. Since the probability of the entire sample space is one, hence, the sum of probabilities across all bins in each of the two partitions must also equal one. This condition was satisfied by 115/145 subjects.
2. In the low and the high partition conditions, it can be shown that six additivity conditions, such as the following condition, must hold

$$P(x \geq 20) = P(20 \leq x < 22) + P\left(x \geq 22\right).$$

All six conditions were satisfied by 54.5% of the subjects while 23.4% of the subjects satisfied $0 - 1$ conditions and 20% of the subjects satisfied 2–5 conditions. Thus, about 45% of the subjects failed on at least one of the additivity conditions. In the low partition condition, the median estimate of $P(x \leq 22)$ was 42% and in the high partition condition it was 10%. It follows that partitioning the domain of the random variable in different ways leads to different subjective estimates of probability distributions. This creates potentially serious problems in comparing the elicited belief distributions across studies that use different bin sizes.

9.2.5 Difficulty in Distinguishing between Necessary and Sufficient Conditions

Economic models often rely on the ability of individuals to distinguish between *necessary and sufficient conditions*. However, in experiments, many subjects fail to distinguish between these conditions. In mathematical logic, suppose that P and Q are statements. For instance, if Q is the statement that "the animal is a horse" and P is the statement that "the animal has a tail," then, we may write:

$$Q \Rightarrow P.$$

Q is said to be a *sufficient condition* and P is said to be a *necessary condition*. In particular, the statement $P \Rightarrow Q$ is false (e.g., an animal that has a tail could be a dog). Let the negation of these statements be $\sim Q$ (i.e., it is not a horse) and $\sim P$ (i.e., the animal does not have a tail). Then, the statement $\sim P \Rightarrow \sim Q$ is true, that is, if the animal does not have a tail it is not a horse. This is true, in general, for any such statements P and Q.

In the classic experiments in Wason (1968), four cards labeled E, K, 4, 7 were placed on a table. Subjects knew that each card has a number on one side and a letter on the other. Subjects were asked to pick all the cards that can test the following rule.

"*Every card with a vowel on one side has an even number on the other side.*"

We can rewrite this rule more formally as the following logical statement:

$$\text{Vowel on one side} \Rightarrow \text{even number on the other side.} \tag{9.4}$$

Thus, a vowel on one side (statement Q) is a sufficient condition for there to be an even number on the other side (statement P). But an even number on one side is only a necessary, but not a sufficient, condition for a vowel on the other side (i.e., $P \nRightarrow Q$). Since $\sim P \Rightarrow \sim Q$ is true, an implication of (9.4) is that

$$\text{not an even number on one side} \Rightarrow \text{ not a vowel on the other side.} \tag{9.5}$$

In order to check the given rule, (9.4) implies that we should choose card E, and (9.5) implies that we should choose card 7. Card 4 can neither confirm nor falsify the rule because an even number is not a sufficient condition for a vowel on the other side. However, about 65% of the subjects choose card 4.

9.3 Procedural Rationality and Dynamic Programming

Consider an informal description of the following dynamic problem in economics that is an essential part of its foundations when people make decisions over time. We do not need a full-blown formal description because it is not germane to the points that we make in this section. For a slightly more formal description of this problem, see Dhami and Sunstein (2022).

Consider a decision maker who lives for $T+1$ time periods and time t is discrete $t = 1, 2, \ldots, T+1$. In every period, $t = 1, \ldots, T$, the decision maker has the stochastic income Y which can take two possible values as shown in Figure 9.2, a high value, $H > 0$, with probability $0 < p < 1$ and a low value, L, with probability $1 - p$.

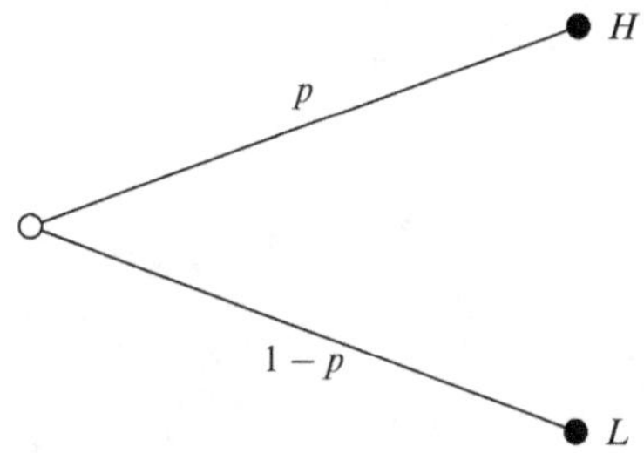

Figure 9.2 A simple decision tree when there are two outcomes, $n = 2$

The decision maker makes only one choice at any time $t = 1, \ldots, T$, namely, how much of the income to consume and how much to save for the next time period. Savings take the form of one-period bonds that pay an interest rate $r > 0$. There is zero income at time $T + 1$ and there are no consumption-savings decision to be made at time $T + 1$. Consumption at time $T + 1$ is financed solely by the savings made at time T. At any time $t = 1, \ldots, T$, the decision maker observes the realization of stochastic income Y and makes a consumption-savings decision. However, at time t, the decision maker does not know the future realizations of stochastic income, but does know its stochastic properties as shown in Figure 9.2.

A full description of the dynamic problem, which we do not need, will require us to specify at least two more things. (i) The objective function of the decision maker, which we assume is to maximize the present discounted utility of lifetime consumption. (ii) A transversality condition which ensures that the individual does not die in debt, that is, the present discounted value of lifetime income equals the present discounted value of lifetime consumption.

Let us now recursively outline the solution for different time periods, using dynamic programming. This requires us to solve the optimization problem backwards, starting with the last period and then unraveling back until we arrive at the initial time. We successively consider the cases $T = 1, 2, 3$ to uncover the underlying pattern of recursion.

1. $T = 1$: Suppose that the decision maker lives for two time periods, $t = 1, 2$, so $T + 1 = 2$. Thus, at time $t = 1$ the decision maker observes the realization of income, either H or L, and then decides how much to save for time $t = 2$. Time $t = 2$ is the last period in which there is no income and the decision maker only consumes from the savings made at time $t = 1$. The individual makes exactly two decisions in this problem, and both at time $t = 1$: (i) how much to consume/save if income is H, and (ii) how much to consume/save if income is L.
2. $T = 2$: Suppose that the decision maker lives for three time periods, $t = 1, 2, 3$, so $T + 1 = 3$. This case is shown in Figure 9.3. Recall that there is zero income at $T + 1$, which in this case corresponds to $t = 3$.

   - At time $t = 3$, the last period, the decision maker receives no exogenous income and makes no consumption/savings decisions. Thus, the decision maker is passive and makes no economically relevant decision. But in each possible state the decision maker inherits some savings from the past that finances consumption at time $t = 3$.
   - At time $t = 2$, the individual inherits the savings made from time $t = 1$, observes income to be either high, H, or low, L, and in each case makes an optimal consumption/savings decision.

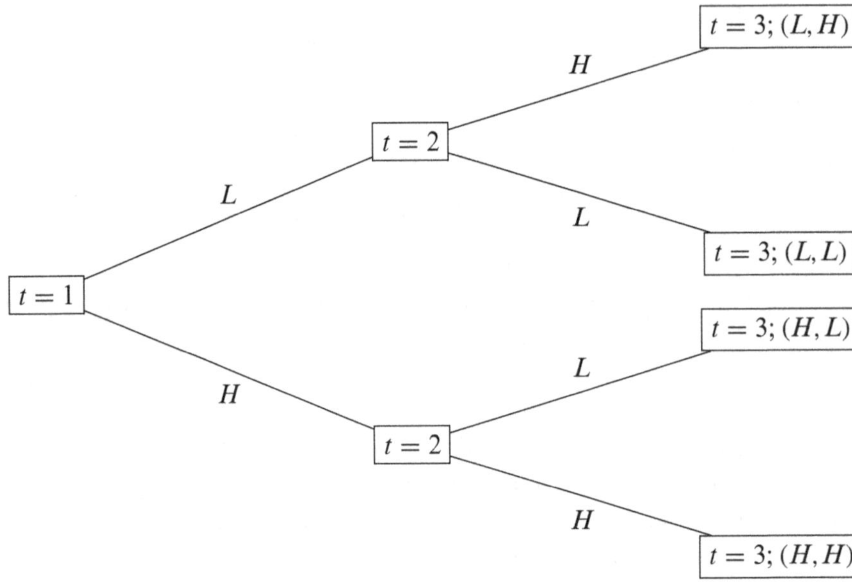

Figure 9.3 A decision tree with two time periods where income takes two possible values each period, high (H) and low (L)

- At time $t = 1$, the decision maker observes the current income (either H or L), but does not know the realization of income at time $t = 2$, which can be either H or L with probabilities p and $1 - p$. Each decision maker assumes that decision makers in all future time periods make their choices rationally. Hence, looking forward, at time $t = 1$, the decision maker must solve the optimal consumption/savings problem, also for $t = 2$, for each possible state of the world (H and L) that can arise at $t = 2$.

Let us now consider the two possible cases that arise at $t = 1$ when income is either L or H.

(2a) Suppose that the time $t = 1$ income is L. Then, the decision maker knows that there are two possible future worlds. One in which time $t = 2$ income is H, so the sequence of incomes over the first two time periods is (L, H) and another in which time $t = 2$ income is L, so the sequence of incomes over the first two periods is (L, L).[2] As noted, in dynamic programming, the time $t = 1$ decision maker assumes that at time $t = 2$, the choices will be optimal. Hence, such a decision maker needs to solve for the optimal consumption/savings choice at time $t = 2$ for each state (H and L) before solving for their own optimal time $t = 1$ consumption/savings choice. This involves making optimal choices for the two cases (L, H) and (L, L) for a total of "two" decisions.

(2b) Suppose that the time $t = 1$ income is H. Proceeding as above, the decision maker again makes "two" consumption/savings decisions for each of the two cases where the possible incomes over the first two time periods are (H, L) and (H, H).

From 2a and 2b, the time $t = 1$ decision maker makes $2 + 2 = 4$ decisions, or $2^T = 2^2 = 4$ decisions.

[2] Recall there is zero income at $t = 3$, so we need to only summarize the possible income realizations for the first two time periods. These income realizations are summarized in Figure 9.3 at the rightmost nodes at $t = 3$.

3. $T = 3$: Proceeding as above for the case $T = 2$, the time $t = 1$ decision maker makes $2^T = 2^3 = 8$ decisions.[3]

This sets the pattern of recursion when income takes only two possible stochastic values in any time period. For any T time periods, a decision maker, who lives for $T + 1$ time periods, makes 2^T decisions. In economics, it is routine to assume that the decision maker solves an infinite horizon problem, $T \to \infty$. The infinite horizon assumption is used purely on the technical grounds that it renders the long-run properties of the dynamic model, such as steady states, more "tractable." Students in courses where dynamic programming is taught are almost never invited to consider if this is a reasonable assumption. Indeed, it is a maintained assumption in economics that the man/woman on the street can solve such problems in their head in an instant, or act "as if" they can do so. But ultimately, the realism of this assumption is an empirical issue.

One explanation for this is that economics does not ask questions about the *procedural rationality* of the methods it uses. By contrast, the Nobel Prize winner Herbert Simon tried to bring procedural rationality to the forefront of economic analysis. Procedural rationality requires that the process by which decisions are made must be feasible and within the bounds of human abilities in relation to cognition, memory, attention, and perception. Does the dynamic programming method satisfy procedural rationality?

To answer this question, suppose that $T = 30$, which is an entirely benign assumption, given that courses in economics typically assume that $T \to \infty$. Then, the time $t = 1$ decision maker must make $2^{30} = 1,073,741,820$ calculations, that is, more than a billion calculations. If $T = 50$, so that the decision maker makes a consumption/savings decision 50 times in their life, then $2^{50} = 1125.89991 \times 10^{12}$, which requires more than a thousand trillion calculations. If on the other hand income Y takes on three possible probabilistic values, H, M, L, in every time period then the decision maker at time $t = 1$ will need to make 3^T calculations. For $T = 30$, this gives a total of $3^{30} = 717.897988 \times 10^{21}$ or more than 717 sextillion calculations.

Economic models routinely assume $T \to \infty$ and assume that stochastic income is distributed continuously. The number of calculations required to solve such problems exceed the number of particles in the universe! It is clearly absurd to assume that the man on the street makes such calculations when deciding on the consumption/savings choices; and the evidence shows that they do not act "as if" they do so. By contrast, economics assumes that for all manner of economic decisions, people effortlessly engage in such calculations or act "as if" they did so.

The main finding of the Kahneman–Tversky heuristics program is that, in many domains, people do not satisfy the predictions of the neoclassical model, even in an "as if" sense. Thaler (2015, p. 46) writes: "Even today, grunts of 'as if' crop up in economics workshops to dismiss results that do not support the standard theoretical prediction. Fortunately, Kahneman and Tversky have provided an answer to the 'as if' question. Both their work on heuristics and biases as well as that on prospect theory clearly showed that people do not act 'as if' they were choosing in accordance with the rational economic model."

For these reasons, studying bounded rationality is of critical importance to economics.

[3] Readers may wish to draw the corresponding decision tree along the lines of Figure 9.3. In this case, the time $t = 1$ decision maker will need to make a consumption/savings decision, factoring in the following eight possibilities for the incomes in the first three time periods: (L, L, L), (L, L, H), (L, H, L), (L, H, H), (H, L, L), (H, L, H), (H, H, L), (H, H, H).

9.4 The Kahneman–Tversky Heuristics Research Program

9.4.1 The Representativeness Heuristic

Suppose that the set of all possible outcomes arising from the realization of a random variable lie in the set S. Consider a partition $C_1, \ldots, C_n$ of the set S. By a partition, we mean that the sets $C_1, \ldots, C_n$ are mutually exclusive and the union of these sets is S. For example, if the set $S = \{1, 2, \ldots, 6\}$ arises from tossing a six-sided die once, then one possible partition is $C_1 = \{1, 3, 5\}$ and $C_2 = \{2, 4, 6\}$ and $n = 2$. However, the set S could be quite large, multidimensional, and the partition of the set could be fairly complex. The partitions could be provided to individuals by an external actor, such as their relevant social group or the experimenter; or perhaps individuals might use some heuristic to partition the set S.

Suppose that an individual is asked to guess the probability that an event, A, came from one of the sets C_i, $i = 1, \ldots, n$, in the partition. In other words, the individual is asked to compute the conditional probability $P(C_i \mid A)$. Under classical statistics, this is unproblematic. Individuals are assumed to use Bayes' Law (see Section 9.4.9) to compute the relevant conditional probability. However, people typically compute $P(C_i \mid A)$ not by using Bayes' Law, but by using the perceived "similarity" between the event A and the set C_i. This perceived similarity is often based on a small sample size and invokes the *law of small numbers* (see Definition 9.1). Thus, individuals might overinfer the similarity, or *representativeness*, of event A with the set C_i, giving rise to the *representativeness heuristic.*

Example 9.1 *Consider the following experimental instructions in Tversky and Kahneman (1974). "A town is served by two hospitals. In the larger hospital, about 45 babies are born each day, and in the smaller hospital, about 15 babies are born each day. As you know, about 50 percent of all babies are boys. However, the exact percentage varies from day to day. For a period of one year, each hospital recorded the days on which more than 60 percent of the babies born were boys. Which hospital do you think recorded more such days?"*

In terms of our notation above, event A is the number of days on which more than 60 percent of the babies born were boys. Let C_1 be the large hospital and C_2 be the small hospital. Then, subjects are being asked in effect to compare the two conditional probabilities $P(C_1 \mid A)$ and $P(C_2 \mid A)$. Subjects in experiments might not, of course, be thinking in terms of conditional probabilities.

In the sample, 53 students said that both hospitals are equally likely to have recorded such days; 21 students chose the larger hospital, and 21 students chose the smaller hospital. The statistically correct answer is the smaller hospital because the law of large numbers implies that as the sample size grows, the sample proportions become closer to the population proportions (and in the limit, as the sample size becomes very large, they equal the population proportions). Overall, the choices of 74% of the subjects violate the law of large numbers.

Let us consider another example of representativeness that requires calculating conditional probabilities. One of the problems asks you to calculate the exact conditional probabilities reported in this example.

Example 9.2 *Camerer (1987, 1990) reports the following example. Consider two urns, $i = A, B$. Urn A has one red ball and two black balls. Urn B has two red balls and one black ball. One of the* *urns is chosen randomly by nature and a sequence of three balls ($n = 3$) is drawn with replacement from one of the urns. Subjects know that nature chooses urn A with probability 0.6 and urn B with probability 0.4, so $P(A) = 0.6$ and $P(B) = 0.4$. But they do not know the exact urn from which the sample of three balls is drawn. Suppose that the observed sample is one red and two black balls, which we denote by RBB (the order is not important). Note that the sample RBB is "similar" to the composition of urn A. What is the posterior probability that the sample came from urn A? Using Bayes' law (see Section 9.4.9), the statistically correct answer is (an exercise asks you to compute this conditional probability)*

$$P(A \mid RBB) = 0.75.$$

By contrast, an individual who uses the representativeness heuristic assigns a subjective probability estimate between 0.75 and 1.00 to the sample RBB. Individuals exhibit "extreme representativeness" if they assign a subjective probability estimate equal to 1.00, based on the similarity, or representativeness, of the sample RBB to the composition of balls in Urn A.

There are now several formal models of the law of small numbers; for a survey, see Benjamin (2018) and Dhami (2020, Vol. V, Section 1.2.3). The representativeness heuristic takes two main forms, the gambler's fallacy and the hot hand fallacy. We consider these next.

9.4.2 Representativeness: The Gambler's Fallacy

The representativeness heuristic arises from using the law of small numbers. An important implication is that many people are (i) unable to generate a truly random sequence of numbers or events, and (ii) unable to identify if a given sequence of numbers is a random sequence.

When asked to write down a random sequence of coin tosses, subjects alternate too frequently between heads (H) and tails (T), giving rise to negative autocorrelation in what is essentially a random process. When asked to predict the outcome of a fifth coin toss when the first four tosses have given rise to the sequence H, H, H, H, the a priori, statistically correct, probability of a H or a T in the fifth toss is 0.5. Yet, many people assign a probability higher than 0.5 to the event T in the fifth toss (Bar-Hillel and Wagenaar, 1991; Rapoport and Budescu, 1992, 1997).

Definition 9.2 *(Gambler's fallacy) Suppose that a random sample of size n, $x_1, x_2, \ldots, x_n$, is to be drawn from a set of n identically and independently distributed random variables $X_1, X_2 \ldots, X_n$. Then, people are said to commit the gambler's fallacy, if their inference about the random sample $x_1, x_2, \ldots, x_n$ reveals negative autocorrelation. The greater is the extent of the inferred negative autocorrelation, the greater is the extent of the gambler's fallacy.*

In one illustration of the gamber's fallacy, subjects were informed of the outcome of three coin tosses. They had to assign a probability P that the fourth toss will result in the outcome H. For various sequences of the three coin tosses, the reported value of P is given below (Rapoport and Budescu, 1997; Rabin and Vayanos, 2010).

1. $P(H \mid HHH) = 0.30$.
2. $P(H \mid HTH) = 0.41$.
3. $P(H \mid THT) = 0.58$.
4. $P(H \mid TTT) = 0.70$.

In all of these cases, the ex-ante, statistically correct, probability of H in the fourth toss is 0.50, but the behavior of subjects is consistent with the gambler's fallacy in Definition 9.2. For a formal and more general model that can account for the gambler's fallacy when the outcomes are neither binary, nor independently and identically distributed, see Rabin and Vayanos (2010).

The term "gambler's fallacy" arose from observations on betting behavior. Clotfelter and Cook (1993) found that there is reduced betting on a winning number in subsequent lottery draws, which is consistent with the gambler's fallacy. Thus, many individuals appear to assign a low probability that the current winning numbers will be the winning numbers when the lottery is played the next time. This is reminiscent of the behavior of subjects captured in the estimate $P(H \mid HHH) = 0.30$ above. Other evidence for the gambler's fallacy has come from the study of betting behavior, for example, horse races (Metzger, 1984), dog races (Terrell and Farmer, 1996; Terrell, 1998), and gambling in casinos (Croson and Sundali, 2005). There are several applications of the gambler's fallacy in finance. People may sell winning stocks and hold on to loss-making stocks for too long (*disposition effect*) because they appear to believe that stocks that were winners in the past are due for a fall and vice-versa, which is consistent with the gambler's fallacy.

9.4.3 Representativeness: The Hot Hand Fallacy

Another manifestation of the representativeness heuristic is the *hot hand fallacy*. This is the statistical polar opposite of the gambler's fallacy in Definition 9.2.

Definition 9.3 *(Hot hand fallacy) Suppose that a random sample of size n, $x_1, x_2, \ldots, x_n$, is to be drawn from a set of n identically and independently distributed random variables $X_1, X_2 \ldots, X_n$. Then people are said to commit the hot hand fallacy, if their inference about the random sample $x_1, x_2, \ldots, x_n$ reveals positive autocorrelation. The greater is the extent of the inferred positive autocorrelation, the greater is the extent of the hot hand fallacy.*

The *hot hand fallacy* was first documented in betting behavior in sports such as basketball. The observed success of a player in a particular game in basketball arises from many different factors. There are two main types of factors.

1. Success might arise purely from being lucky on the day.
2. Success might arise from unobserved features of the player such as pre-match training, conditioning, and the mental health of the player on the day.

Observers who may be betting on the game are trying to infer which of these two factors (pure luck, or unobserved skill) is responsible for the player's performance; this is known as the *signal extraction problem*. If a player has been successful in making a sequence of good shots, then betting data indicates that bettors begin to assign a high probability that such a player will be successful for the rest of the game too (Camerer, 1989). The early studies did not find an actual hot hand effect. By this is meant that players perform at a mean level of skill that depends on their ability and there are random departures from the mean level, caused by variation in luck. Statistically, the observed sequence of successful basketball shots was found to be a random sequence (Gilovich et al., 1985; Tversky and Gilovich, 1989a,b).

By contrast, some of the recent research has raised the possibility of an actual hot hand phenomenon in basketball and baseball that differs from a purely random statistical process (Bocskocsky et al., 2014; Green and Zwiebel, 2017; Miller and Sanjurjo, 2018). However, advanced econometrics is needed to demonstrate the presence of an actual hot hand phenomenon and the quantitative effects found in the literature are not strong enough. Thus, there should be no presumption that bettors can see through the hot hand effect, or that they can successfully distinguish between the presence and the absence of a hot hand effect. This ability to differentiate between the two would be a critical advance in this literature, but it has not been done yet.

The most persuasive evidence for the hot hand phenomenon comes from a field experiment by Guryan and Kearney (2008). Lotto stores that, purely by luck, have sold a winning lotto ticket are no more likely to sell a winning lotto ticket in the future, as compared to any other lotto store. Hence, classical statistics dictates that people should not be more inclined to buy a ticket from a store that sold a winning ticket in the past, over another store that sells such tickets.

Yet, the empirical evidence shows that sales at lotto stores that have sold a winning ticket soar in the immediate weeks following the lotto win. Figure 9.4 shows a plot of the log sales at lotto stores that have sold a winning ticket at date t, for the previous 40 weeks and the subsequent 40 weeks, that is, for weeks in the range $\{t-40, t-39, \ldots, t, t+1, \ldots, t+40\}$. There is an immediate spike in sales from the winning lotto store, following the sale of the winning ticket in week $t+1$ and this positive effect on sales lasts for at least 40 weeks following the win. The result stays unchanged after controlling for several confounding factors such as a lottery win in a particular zip code may increase the salience of playing the lottery. One observes somewhat increased sales at other stores selling lotto tickets in the same zip code, but the increase in sales at the winning store is (i) significantly higher, and (ii) even higher for larger win sizes. This store-specific effect, found after controlling for confounding factors, is consistent with the hot hand fallacy.

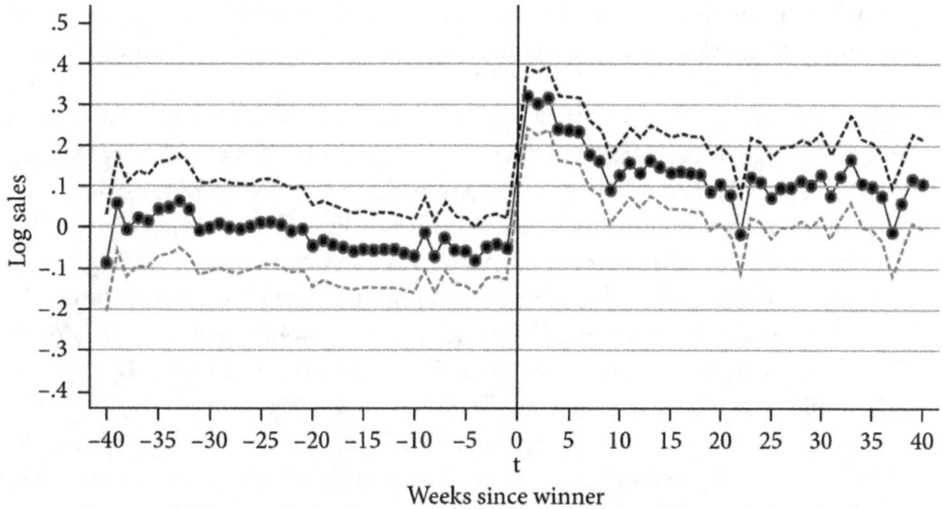

Figure 9.4 Retail level data for Lotto Texas wins. Source: Guryan and Kearney (2008)

9.4.4 How Can Representativeness Explain Event A and the Negation of Event A?

Recall that in an underlying random sequence, the gambler's fallacy is an inference of negative autocorrelation and the hot hand fallacy is an inference of positive autocorrelation. Yet both are explained in terms of the representativeness heuristic, which might sound paradoxical. For instance, Gigerenzer and Brighton (2011, p.18) criticize the representativeness heuristic thus: "No model of similarity can explain a phenomenon and its contrary; otherwise it would not exclude any behavior" They go on to write: "As it [representativeness heuristic] remains undefined, it can account even for A and non-A (Ayton and Fischer, 2004)"

We argue that there is no logical fallacy in using representativeness to explain the gambler's fallacy and the hot hand fallacy. The confusion, and the apparent paradox, arises from believing that they apply to the same domain. Ayton and Fischer (2004) argue persuasively that the domains in which these two fallacies apply are different. The hot hand fallacy typically arises in the domain of *animate processes*, for example, in basketball and tennis, and the gambler's fallacy typically arises in the domain of *inanimate processes*, such as throws of a die, or coin tosses.

Ayton and Fischer (2004) gave subjects different sequences of 21 binary outcomes. Each outcome in a sequence is classed as a success or a failure. For instance, in the toss of a coin, the outcome heads may be classed as success and tails as failure. Each of the given sequences of 21 outcomes had varying degrees of positive and negative autocorrelation. The *alternation rate* is the number of times a sequence changes direction, from success to failure, and vice-versa, divided by 10. Thus, sequences with high negative autocorrelation have high alternation rates and those with positive autocorrelation have low alternation rates. For each of the sequences, subjects were asked to guess if the sequences arose from (i) *human skilled performance*, such as basketball shots and tennis serves, or (ii) *inanimate process*, such as a coin toss and a binary outcome roulette wheel.

The results showed that sequences with low alternation rates were more likely to be judged to have arisen from animate processes such as basketball shots, and those with high rates of alternation from inanimate process, such as a coin tosses. Thus, the domains of the two fallacies are different, and the difference lies in the source of the underlying process, animate or inanimate. It is likely that subjects are solving different inference problems in each case, as we now describe.

1. For inanimate processes, such as a coin toss, subjects are fully aware of the underlying probabilities of heads and tails, 50% each. Thus, subjects switch "too often" in small samples to preserve the population proportions, because they follow the law of small numbers. This leads to negative autocorrelation. As Tversky and Kahneman (1974, p. 1125) put it quite beautifully: "Chance is commonly viewed as a self-correcting process in which a deviation in one direction induces a deviation in the opposite direction to restore the equilibrium. In fact, deviations are not corrected as a chance process unfolds, they are merely diluted."
2. For animate processes, the underlying distribution from which the binary outcomes, success or failure, are drawn, is unclear. Thus, the observer is trying to *infer the underlying model* that gives rise to the unobserved success/failure rates in a particular game. As noted above, streaks in basketball may arise either due to luck, or due to the unobserved player-specific characteristics such as pre-match practice and the state of mental health. Given an observed streak of success for a player, individuals use the law of small numbers to assign too high

a probability to factors conducive to the streak, for example, that the player has high confidence, low fatigue, high emotional stability, and good pre-match practice. Thus, they come to believe, in the small sample at their disposal, that the player will be more successful in the rest of the match, and are willing to bet money on this inference. Such an inference is not statistically correct. Analogously, for a streak of failures, perhaps arising purely from luck, they interpret the underlying distribution to imply the opposite.

9.4.5 Anchoring

How do people form expectations about events? Several heuristics have been proposed in the heuristics program to answer this question. *Anchoring* is a robust heuristic that highlights the influence of an initial suggestion on our subsequent subjective beliefs about events. Consider the following classic, and striking, example of anchoring.

Example 9.3 *Tversky and Kahneman (1974) rigged a wheel of fortune with the numbers 1–100 to come to a stop at either of the two numbers: 10 or 65. Subjects were first asked to write down the number that the wheel stopped at and then they were asked the following two questions in sequential order.*

(1) Comparative judgment question: Is the percentage of African nations among UN members larger or smaller than the number you just wrote?
(2) Absolute judgment question: What is your best guess of the percentage of African nations among UN members?

The answer to the comparative judgment question ought to be irrelevant for the correct answer to the absolute judgment question. Yet, the answers to the absolute judgment question were "anchored" too closely on the irrelevant outcome on the wheel of fortune. The median answer to the absolute judgment question of those who observed the number 10 was 25%, and the median answer of those who observed the number 65 was 45%. This is consistent with the idea that people anchor on irrelevant information in forming their beliefs about events.

Consider another example. Englich and Mussweiler (2001) conducted experiments on experienced trial judges with an average experience of 15 years. Subjects considered the case of a fictitious shoplifter who is accused of stealing from a supermarket for the twelfth time. The trial judges were given detailed case material including opinions from a psycho-legal expert, and testimonies by the defendant and a witness. In order to set a yardstick for the appropriate sentence to be given in this case, opinions were sought from other experienced and independent legal professionals who were not part of the experiment. The objective opinion indicated that (i) the case material was complete and realistic, and (ii) a mean sentence of 5.62 months was appropriate.

Trial judges in the experiment were asked to determine an appropriate sentence in two different treatments. In the high anchor treatment, the case material showed that the prosecutor had asked for a sentence of nine months. In the low anchor treatment, the corresponding sentence was shown as three months. The respective sentences chosen by the trial judges in the high and the low anchor treatments were eight months and five months. These findings are consistent with an anchoring effect and they show that even experienced professionals exhibit the anchoring effect.

Anchoring is one of the few heuristics that allows for a quantitative measurement of the extent of anchoring. Jacowitz and Kahneman (1995) proposed a method to calculate the extent of anchoring, through an *anchoring index*. Suppose that subjects in two different treatments are given a high anchor, a_H, and a low anchor, a_L. Suppose also that their respective answers in these treatments are x_H and x_L. Then, the anchoring index is defined by

$$\frac{x_H - x_L}{a_H - a_L} \times 100. \tag{9.6}$$

The higher is the value of this index, the greater is the extent of anchoring. In the wheel of fortune example above, we have $a_H = 65, a_L = 10$, $x_H = 45, x_L = 25$. Thus, the anchoring index gives a value of

$$\frac{45 - 25}{65 - 10} \times 100 = 36.36.$$

Northcraft and Neale (1987) provide additional field evidence of anchoring. In their experiment, estate agents were given a 10-page booklet with all relevant information about a property that was required for an evaluation of its price. The booklet also contained a suggested list price. In the high anchor condition, the list price was set at \$83,900 and in the low anchor condition, it was set at \$65,900. In the high anchor condition, the estate agents evaluated the property at a significantly higher price and, using (9.6), the *anchoring index* was 41%. When the experiment was repeated with business school students, they were only slightly more prone to anchoring and the value of their anchoring index was 48%. The estate agents refused to admit that the anchor provided to them had any effect on their calculations, but the calculated anchoring index suggests otherwise.

The anchoring phenomenon is remarkably robust across a wide range of domains, contexts, and frames; for a survey, see Dhami (2020, Vol. V, Section 1.6.3). These include the evaluation of lotteries and gambles; first offers in price negotiation; estimates of price; and the probability of a nuclear war. Anchoring can also explain other heuristics and phenomena that we consider in this book, including hindsight bias, preference reversals, and nonlinear probability weighting.

9.4.6 Availability

Individuals often need to make an inference about a random variable X, that either occurs concurrently, or in the future. Suppose that all the objectively available current information that is required to form an inference about X is contained in some information set I. In neoclassical economics, individuals make this prediction by computing the conditional mathematical expectation of the random variable, $E[X \mid I]$ (read as the expected value of X conditional on the information in the set I).

Neoclassical economics is less forthcoming about how individuals gain access to the information set I. This is a question about the procedural rationality of the method. But neoclassical economics typically does not provide guidance on procedural rationality.

It is possible that individuals might not have immediate access to all the information that goes into the set I. They might suffer from limited memory; limited attention; and limited, selective, strategic, and subjective, recall. The availability heuristic argues that some elements in the set I may be relatively more "salient" or "vivid" and such memories are likely to be more readily recalled. Hence, individuals might only be able to use a subset of the information $I_s \subseteq I$, and find that they are unable to use the rest. Thus, subjects might infer $E[X \mid I_s]$ and it is likely that

$$E[X \mid I_s] \neq E[X \mid I].$$

A central idea behind the availability heuristic is that predictions of future events, or estimates of concurrent events, are saliently determined by the "available information." By varying the information available to subjects, that is, the content of the set I_s by, for instance, diverting the subject's attention during recall, or making selective memories more salient, one can test for departures from the objective benchmark $E[X \mid I]$.

Lichtenstein et al. (1978) conducted important experiments on the availability heuristic that were successfully replicated in Pachur et al. (2012). For Swiss subjects, these experiments revealed a significant positive correlation between

(i) one's estimate of the annual mortality rate from various forms of cancer, and
(ii) the "availability" of information on cases of cancer from one's social network.

The more the instances of a particular type of cancer that can be recalled from one's social network, the higher was the estimate of the annual mortality rate from that type of cancer. Yet, the objective annual mortality rate from that type of cancer is a fixed number. Thus, a between-subjects design in which subjects differ in the availability of information on cases of cancer from their individual social network, reveals the use of the anchoring heuristic.

Events and stories that have been recently in the news in a prominent manner tend to be more vivid and easier to recall, so most people assign a greater probability to them (Lichtenstein et al., 1978; Eisenman, 1993). Kahneman (2011, p. 138) describes this with his usual brevity and depth: "The world in our heads is not a precise replica of reality."

Kuran and Sunstein (1999) propose the idea of *availability cascades* and apply it to two case studies – the *Love Canal affair* and the *Alar scare*. In each of these cases, there was some vivid/salient news, which facilitated recall of this information, leading to an emotional reaction, which led to increased news about these events, and further self-fulfilling bouts of emotional reaction. This heightened further the vividness/salience of these events, and facilitated easier availability of this information in subsequent recalls of information. Eventually, this created enough social and political pressure to give rise to the adoption of policies that may have been difficult to justify in cost-benefit terms.

In an interesting experiment, Tversky and Kahneman (1973) asked subjects to guess the probability that a randomly picked three-letter word from the dictionary begins with either the consonants r, k (event A), or ends with the consonants r, k (event B). Readers will find that words beginning with the letters r or k are much easier to remember, as compared to those that end with r or k. Hence, a high majority of subjects reported that event A was more probable, but the factually correct answer is event B.

9.4.7 Hindsight-Bias

Hindsight-bias arises when we feel wiser in hindsight. In judging how well we have made a prediction in the past, after having observed the actual outcome, hindsight-biased individuals judge their past predictions too favorably. They appear to believe that their past predictions are closer to the actually observed outcomes than they really are.

We can formalize the heuristic that lies behind this bias a bit more. Suppose that at some time t, an individual is asked to make a prediction of the expected value of a random variable X that will materialize at a future time period $t+j, j>0$. Denote by I_t, the time t information set which includes all possible information required by the relevant economic theory to predict the value of X. Denote by $E[X \mid I_t]$, the time t mathematical expectation of X, conditional on the information set I_t.

Under neoclassical economics, the relevant prediction is $E[X \mid I_t]$. It is also known as the *predictive judgment* at time t. Now suppose that at time $t+j$, having observed the actual outcome x of the random variable X, we ask the individual to remember the predictive judgment made at time t. However, the date $t+j$ information set, denoted by I_{t+j}, contains additional information which includes the observed value x, hence we have $I_t \subseteq I_{t+j}$. In remembering $E[X \mid I_t]$ at time $t+j$, the individual uses the new information set I_{t+j}, and forms the expected value of the remembered prediction, given by $E\left[E[X \mid I_t] \mid I_{t+j}\right]$. This is known as the *postdictive judgment* at time $t+j$.

In neoclassical economics, there is no notion of hindsight-bias, so individuals remember their predictions accurately, which leads to equality of the predictive judgment at time t and the postdictive judgment at time $t+j$, that is,

$$E[X \mid I_t] = E\left[E[X \mid I_t] \mid I_{t+j}\right]. \tag{9.7}$$

By contrast, for *hindsight-biased* individuals, the predictive and postdictive judgments differ. A simple way of describing hindsight-bias is to write the relation between the predictive and postdictive judgments as follows (Camerer et al., 1989),

$$E\left[E[X \mid I_t] \mid I_{t+j}\right] = \alpha x + (1-\alpha)E[X \mid I_t]; \alpha \in [0,1]. \tag{9.8}$$

In (9.8), the postdictive judgment is a linear combination of the actually observed value, x, of the random variable at time $t+j$ and the actual prediction made in the past at time t. If $\alpha = 0$, then the individual has no hindsight bias and this is the case presented in neoclassical economics. At the other extreme, if $\alpha = 1$, then the individual suffers from an extreme form of hindsight-bias in equating the postdictive judgment to the actually observed value x. Such an individual may assert or feel the following: "I fully knew it all along." However, intermediate values of α between 0 and 1 are probably more realistic as a description of human behavior. The equation in (9.8) can be thought of as the relevant heuristic that underpins hindsight-bias. In particular, hindsight-bias is itself not a heuristic.

Theories of learning analyze the dynamic process by which individuals learn to make decisions over time. However, hindsight bias is not related to learning models. It is about how accurately individuals remember their past predictions.

Early research on hindsight bias was done by Fischhoff (1975) who ran experiments in a between-subjects design. For each of the four events in the study, labeled A, B, C, D, there were two groups, a before and an after group. Each of the four events gives rise to four possible outcomes. The four events were chosen so that subjects were unlikely to know the actual outcome in each event.

1. The Before group was asked at date t to make a predictive judgment after reading a brief 150-word account of a historical or clinical event. They had to assign probabilities to "four possible mutually exclusive outcomes" that could arise at a future date $t+j$. Only one of the four outcomes actually occurred for each event.
2. For each of the events, an after group was then asked to read the same 150-word account at time $t+j$ in the experiment. These subjects were split up into four groups of 20 each. Although only one of the four outcomes, for each event, actually occurred, the subjects did not know which one. This was exploited in the following manner. The first group was told that the actual outcome that had occurred was the first outcome; the second group was told that the actual outcome that had occurred was the second outcome; the remaining two groups were told, respectively, that the actually occurring outcomes were the third and the fourth outcomes. Based on this information, the After group was required to make a postdictive judgment at time $t+j$ about what predictive judgment they might have made at time t, if they had been asked prior to reading the 150-word account.

We discuss the findings from the first event, event A. It used a historical account of the British–Gurkha struggle. Subjects were presented with the following 150-word account (Fischhoff, 1975, p. 305):

> For some years after the arrival of Hastings as governor-general of India, the consolidation of British power involved serious war. The first of these wars took place on the northern frontier of Bengal where the British were faced by the plundering raids of the Gurkhas of Nepal. Attempts had been made to stop the raids by an exchange of lands, but the Gurkhas would not give up their claims to country under British control, and Hastings decided to deal with them once and for all. The campaign began in November 1814. It was not glorious. The Gurkhas were only some 12000 strong; but they were brave fighters, fighting in territory well-suited to their raiding tactics. The older British commanders were used to war in the plains where the enemy ran away from a resolute attack. In the mountains of Nepal it was not easy even to find the enemy. The troops and transport animals suffered from the extremes of heat and cold, and the officers learned caution only after sharp reverses. Major-General Sir D Octerlony was the one commander to escape from these minor defeats.

The four possible outcomes offered to the Before and the After groups were:

(1) British victory,
(2) Gurkha victory,
(3) military stalemate with no peace settlement, and
(4) military stalemate with a peace settlement.

The actually observed historical outcome was (3) but different groups of the After subjects were informed of one of the factual outcomes (1)–(4) as the correct one to see how it would influence their postdictive judgment.

Table 9.1 shows the results for all four events in the study, A, B, C, D. Focus only on the results for event A. The probabilities assigned, in the form of percentages, by the Before group to the four outcomes, 1–4, in the absence of any information on which outcome occurred, are given in the first row (33.8 21.3 32.3 12.3). Consider the first After group which was told that the actual outcome was number 1. They assign a probability of 57.2% that they would have made the

Table 9.1 Mean probabilities assigned to each of four outcomes, 1–4, in the four events, A–D. The actual outcomes for events A, B, C, and D were, respectively, 1, 1, 4, and 2.

Experimental group	n	Outcome provided	Outcome evaluated			
			1	2	3	4
Event A: British–Gurka struggle (English-speaking subjects)						
Before	20	None	33.8	21.3	32.3	12.3
After	20	1	57.2	14.3	15.3	13.4
	20	2	30.3	38.4	20.4	10.5
	20	3	25.7	17.0	48.0	9.9
	20	4	33.0	15.8	24.3	27.0
Event B: Near-riot in Atlanta (subjects with knowledge of statistics)						
Before	20	None	11.2	30.8	43.8	14.2
After	20	1	30.6	25.8	23.3	20.3
	20	2	5.5	51.8	24.3	18.5
	20	3	2.9	23.9	50.8	21.4
	20	4	16.7	31.9	23.4	27.9
Event C: Mrs Dewar in therapy						
Before	19	None	26.6	15.8	23.4	34.4
After	13	1	43.1	13.9	17.3	25.8
	17	2	26.5	23.2	13.4	36.9
	16	3	30.6	14.1	34.1	21.3
	17	4	21.2	10.2	22.6	46.1
Event D: George in therapy						
Before	17	None	27.4	26.9	39.4	6.3
After	18	1	33.6	20.8	37.8	8.0
	18	2	22.4	41.8	28.9	7.1
	20	3	20.5	22.3	50.0	7.3
	17	4	30.6	19.5	37.7	12.3

Source: Fischhoff (1975)

predictive judgment that specified outcome number 1. This is their postdictive judgment (compare this to the predictive judgment of 33.8%); the probabilities assigned to the other outcomes, 2–4, by this group are much lower. Following on to the other diagonal elements, we can see that, in general, the postdictive judgments are the highest for the outcome that was revealed to the group as the actual outcome: 38.4% for After group 2 which was told that the actual outcome is number 2; 48.0% for After group 3 which was told that the actual outcome is number 3; 27.0% for After group 4 which was told that the actual outcome is number 4. In each case, these numbers are much higher than the corresponding predictive judgments of the Before group.

Thus, the evidence is consistent with there being a significant hindsight-bias. These results are not specific to event A. When the events are varied, events B, C, and D in Table 9.1, one obtains identical results. Event B is the near-riot in Atlanta, Georgia in July 1967, while events C and D are two clinical cases. In most of the cases (i) the numbers along the diagonal are the highest, indicating the highest postdictive judgment for events that the subjects were told had actually occurred, and (2) these numbers are higher than the predictive judgment made by the Before group.

There is extensive evidence of hindsight-bias in the literature; see Dhami (2020, Vol. V) and the meta study by Guilbault et al. (2004). Hindsight-bias has been found for all age groups and in many different contexts such as medical diagnosis, accounting decisions, sports contexts, legal liability, terrorist attacks, the verdict in the O. J. Simpson criminal trial, and labor disputes involving firefighters. Expertise does not automatically reduce the hindsight bias unless experts receive continual feedback.

9.4.8 Conjunction Fallacy

Consider two sets A and B. The intersection, $A \cap B$, of the two sets is always a subset of either of the two sets A and B, that is, $A \cap B \subseteq A$ and $A \cap B \subseteq B$. Figure 9.5 shows a graphical representation. A violation of this set inclusion principle is known as the *conjunction fallacy*. By assumption, the economic actors in neoclassical models can never engage in the conjunction fallacy. However, whether people do, in fact, make this error in real life, without perhaps realizing that they have made the error, is an empirical question.

In a classic experiment, known as the *Linda problem*, Tversky and Kahneman (1983) posed the following problem to their subjects.

"Linda is 31 years old, single, outspoken, and very bright. She majored in philosophy. As a student, she was deeply concerned with issues of discrimination and social justice, and also participated in anti-nuclear demonstrations." Which of the following statements is most likely?

1. Linda is a bank teller (B).
2. Linda is active in the feminist movement (F).
3. Linda is a bank teller and is active in the feminist movement (BF).

If subjects interpret these statements using the set inclusion principle, then the last of the three statements implies that the event BF is the intersection of B and F, that is, $B \cap F$. Hence, the event $BF \subseteq B$ and $BF \subseteq F$. From classical probability theory, we know that $P(BF) \leq P(B)$ and $P(BF) \leq P(F)$. A violation of any of these inequalities gives rise to a *conjunction fallacy*. Between 85% – 90% of the respondents rated either $P(BF) > P(B)$ or $P(BF) > P(F)$. Thus, the

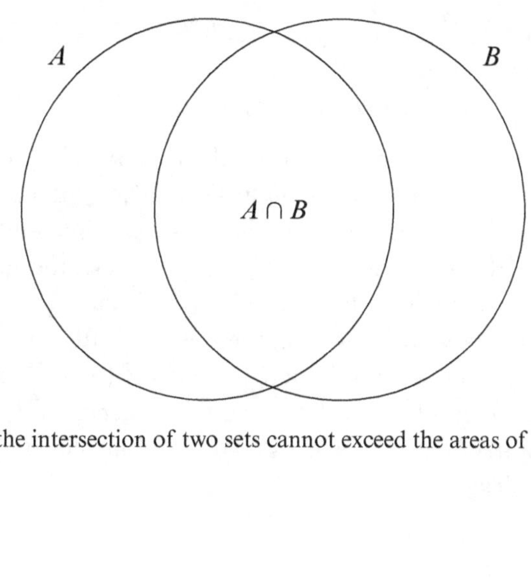

Figure 9.5 The area of the intersection of two sets cannot exceed the areas of any of the individual sets

conjunction fallacy is exhibited by the vast majority of the subjects. In another version of the Linda problem, 85% of the subjects who were Stanford doctoral students in the decision-science program and were well trained in the decision sciences, also exhibited the conjunction fallacy.

The explanation of the conjunction fallacy in the heuristics program is in terms of the representativeness heuristic. People judge the given description of Linda as a feminist and a bank teller as relatively more representative of the given description. Kahneman (2011, p. 158) writes: "we had pitted logic against representativeness, and representativeness had won!" If this is true then we should not observe the conjunction fallacy where the choices are not representative of the given description. For instance, Kahneman (2011) describes the following problem.

Which alternative is more probable?

(i) Mark has hair.
(ii) Mark has blond hair.

Representativeness plays no role here, and the conjunction fallacy was also absent – people rated the first alternative to be more probable than the second. There is a large literature on the conjunction fallacy that the interested reader can pursue; see the surveys in Moro (2009), Tentori et al. (2013), and Kahneman (2011, Chapter 15). For a review of the more recent literature, see Dhami (2020, Vol. V).

The *Linda problem* led to severe criticisms from those who were skeptical. Tversky and Kahneman (1983) and Kahneman and Tversky (1996) themselves addressed many potential criticisms. We summarize some of the critiques and responses below.

1. Natural frequency format: Hertwig and Gigerenzer (1999) make the claim that the conjunction fallacy disappears if the information in the Linda problem is posed in terms of natural frequencies. However, the experiments of Kahneman and Tversky (1996) show that the conjunction fallacy persists even when information is presented in terms of natural frequencies. They gave the following Linda problem to three groups of subjects (Groups 1, 2, 3) in a natural frequency format.

   Linda is in her early thirties. She is single, outspoken, and very bright. As a student she majored in philosophy and was deeply concerned with issues of discrimination and social justice. Suppose there are 1000 women who fit this description. How many of them are

   (a) High school teachers? [Groups 1, 2, 3]
   (b) Bank tellers? [Groups 1, 2]
   (c) Bank tellers and active feminists? [Groups 1, 3]

   Comparing the answers of group 1 for choices (b) and (c) (within-subjects design), 36% of Group 1 subjects exhibited the conjunction fallacy. Similarly, comparing the responses of group 3 for options (a) and (c) also uncovers a conjunction fallacy. Subsequent evidence in Tentori et al. (2004) replicates the result that presenting the information in the form of natural frequencies does not eliminate the conjunction fallacy.
2. Incentives and group decisions: Charness et al. (2010) find that the provision of incentives, and allowing for mutual consultation in groups of twos and threes, mitigates the conjunction fallacy in the Linda problem. However, the evidence on incentives is mixed. Bonini et al. (2004) and Stolarz-Fantino et al. (2003) find that monetary incentives do not reduce the conjunction fallacy.

3. Subject understanding: Another potential explanation of the conjunction fallacy concerns the role of "and" in the statement "Bank teller and active feminist" in the Linda problem (Camerer, 1995, p. 598). Does "and" here imply the intersection of the two sets? Hertwig et al. (2008) argue that the statement A and B, could be interpreted by experimental subjects as event A happening first, followed by event B. They claim that subjects who interpret "and" in the sense of set intersection are less susceptible to the conjunction fallacy. But these results are challenged in the experiments of Tentori et al. (2004). They show that although the conjunction fallacy may be lessened by taking account of literal differences and considering the set intersection implications of the term "and" but the conjunction fallacy survives. For a comprehensive and detailed discussion of these issues, see Tentori and Crupi (2012). They argue that the word "and" may have different meanings in different sentences, as pointed out by Hertwig et al. (2008), but within the same sentence its meaning is often unambiguous. They show that the multiple conjunctions considered in Hertwig et al. (2008) are assigned even lower probability than the single conjunctions in the Kahneman–Tversky results and these do not disprove the conjunction fallacy. One of the exercises considers a direct test of literal versus logical differences in the interpretation of choices in the Linda problem. Even in that case, the conjunction fallacy survives.

The following quote from Kahneman (2011, pp. 164–165) is instructive:

> The Linda problem attracted a great deal of attention, but it also became a magnet for critics of our approach ... These arguments were sometimes extended to suggest that our entire enterprise was misguided: if one salient cognitive illusion could be weakened or explained away, others could be as well ... The net effect of the Linda problem was an increase in the visibility of our work to the general public, and a small dent in the credibility of our approach among scholars in the field. This was not at all what we had expected.

9.4.9 Do People Conform to Bayes' Law?

In most economic models, people begin with a set of prior beliefs. They then observe some information which necessitates a revision of their prior beliefs into posterior beliefs that guide subsequent decision making. In transforming prior beliefs into posterior beliefs, economics has traditionally chosen to rely on Bayes' Law, due to The Reverend Thomas Bayes, whose work on Bayes' Law was published after his death in 1761.

Consider n mutually exclusive random variables $X_1, X_2, \ldots, X_n$ that comprise the sample space $X = X_1 \cup X_2 \cup \ldots \cup X_n$. Suppose that we pick any event $A \subseteq X$ such that $P(A) > 0$. What is the probability of event X_i, $i = 1, \ldots, n$, conditional on the event A having occurred, that is, $P(X_i \mid A)$? Bayes' rule uses the laws of conditional probabilities to provide the following answer,

$$P(X_i \mid A) = \frac{P(A \mid X_i)P(X_i)}{P(A)} = \frac{P(A \mid X_i)P(X_i)}{\sum_{j=1}^{n} P(A \mid X_j)P(X_j)}. \tag{9.9}$$

In (9.9), $P(X_i)$ and $P(A)$, the respective unconditional probabilities of the events X_i and A are referred to as the *base rates*. Empirical evidence shows that individuals neglect to take full account of base rates and, hence, they violate Bayes' law.

The classic illustration of base rate neglect was given by Kahneman and Tversky (1972b) through their *cab problem*.

Example 9.4 *(The cab problem) There are only two cab companies in the city, Green and Blue; 85% of the cabs are Green. There was an accident last night. A witness comes forward to testify that the cab involved in the accident was Blue. In similar conditions, the reliability of the witness is 80%, that is, the probability that the witness incorrectly identifies the cab is 20%. What is the probability that the actual cab involved in the accident was Blue? The median and modal response was a probability of* 80%, *which is also the probability with which the witness correctly identifies a Blue cab as the one involved in the accident.*

To find the statistically correct answer using Bayes' rule, define the events X_1 = Blue cab, X_2 = Green cab, and let the event, "identification by the witness that the cab is Blue" be A. Then, (9.9) implies that

$$P(X_1 \mid A) = \frac{P(A \mid X_1)P(X_1)}{P(A \mid X_1)P(X_1) + P(A \mid X_2)P(X_2)}. \tag{9.10}$$

Substituting $P(A \mid X_1) = 0.8$ (probability of a correct identification), $P(A \mid X_2) = 0.2$ (probability of an incorrect identification), $P(X_1) = 0.15$ (base rate), and $P(X_2) = 0.85$ (base rate) we get the statistically correct conditional probability, $P(X_1 \mid A) = 0.414$.

The median and the modal response in experiments is 80% and the statistically correct answer is 41.4%. The difference between these numbers arises because people underweight base rates and ignore the fact that only 15% of the taxis are actually Blue. When the attention of subjects is drawn to base rates, making them particularly salient, conformity with Bayes' law improves but base rate neglect does not disappear (Ajzen, 1977; Bar-Hillel, 1980). Ajzen (1977) makes a distinction between *causal base rates* and *incidental* base rates. A causal base rate conveys information on some causal factors relevant to the problem, while incidental base rates do not. Causal base rates create greater conformity with Bayes' law as shown in the following *modified cab problem*.

Example 9.5 *(Modified cab problem; Kahneman, 2011) There are only two cab companies in the city, Green and Blue, who own an equal number of cabs.* 85% *of the cabs involved in accidents are Green. The rest of this problem is identical to the earlier cab problem following the instruction: "There was an accident last night...." The median response that the cab involved in the accident was blue is* 0.60, *closer to the statistically correct answer of* 0.41.

The original and modified cab problems are mathematically equivalent and so must lead to identical conditional probabilities. Yet, empirically, subjects appear to give greater attention to base rates in the modified cab problem. The information provided under causal base rates suggests that drivers of Green cabs are particularly reckless, leading subjects to assign a lower probability to blue cabs being involved in the accident.

Subjects with higher cognitive ability do not conform better to Bayes' Law. One of the exercises addresses this issue.

Information to subjects in experiments can either be presented in a *natural frequency format* (e.g., 20 out of 100 students take action A) or in a *probability format* (20% of the students

Table 9.2 Percentage of responses consistent with Bayes' rule. Sample sizes in parenthesis. Source: Barbey and Sloman (2007)

Study	Format of Study	
	Probability Format	Frequency Format
Casscells et al. (1978)	18(60)	–
Cosmides and Tooby (1996, Exp. 2)	12(25)	72(25)
Eddy (1982)	5(100)	–
Evans et al. (2000, Exp. 1)	24(42)	35(43)
Gigerenzer (1996)	10(48)	46(48)
Gigerenzer and Hoffrage (1995)	16(30)	46(30)
Macchi (2000)	6(30)	40(30)
Sloman et al. (2003, Exp. 1)	20(25)	51(45)
Sloman et al. (2003, Exp. 1b)	–	31(48)

take action A). In neoclassical economics, so long as the information content of two messages is identical, it is irrelevant if information is presented in a frequency or a probability format. However, evolutionary accounts of human behavior have argued that a frequency format may induce greater understanding of a problem because, over their evolution, humans were more likely to have faced information in a natural frequency format (Gigerenzer and Hoffrage, 1995; Cosmides and Tooby, 1996; Pinker, 1997; Brase, 2002b). This is a testable hypothesis.

Table 9.2 presents a comparison of studies on base rate neglect that use both formats. The frequency format improves compliance with Bayes' law, but even when the evidence is most favorable to Bayes' Law, the majority of people do not conform to Bayes' Law. The Cosmides and Tooby (1996) result that is the most favorable for the frequency format could not be replicated by Sloman et al. (2003) and Evans et al. (2000). In experiments where the frequency format is used, the experimental instructions make the set inclusion relation too obvious relative to the probability format. When this confound is removed, the facilitation role of natural frequencies drops significantly (Girotto and Gonzalez, 2001). Brase (2002a) reports that both formats are perceived by their experimental subjects to be equally clear except when the probabilities are very low. The weight of the evidence, thus, suggests that the role of the frequency format in reversing or eliminating base rate neglect is much overstated.

9.4.10 Reconciling Conservatism and Base Rate Neglect

Conservatism refers to the phenomenon of underweighting the sample information. It is a form of underconfidence. This contrasts with base rate neglect that may lead to overconfidence in the sample. For instance, in the cab problem, subjects appear to overweight the conditional probability of the sample, $P(A \mid X_1)$, but underweight the base rate $P(A)$. So how do we reconcile overconfidence in one domain (base rate neglect) and underconfidence in another domain (underweighting the sample information).

To reconcile these conflicting ideas, Griffin and Tversky (1992) distinguish between the *strength* and the *weight* of evidence. We give two examples.

1. Consider an academic reference written for a student. The *weight* of the evidence is the academic standing of the referee, for example, the stature and reputation of the referee in the field. The *strength* of the evidence is how positive and warm the letter is, in its support for the student.
2. Suppose that we were to toss an unbiased coin, n times. The *strength* of the evidence is the number of times the coin comes up heads, and the *weight* is the sample size, n. Obviously if n is low then the number of times the coin comes up heads gives us very little statistical information (low weight), even if there is a large proportion of heads (high strength).

Griffin and Tversky (1992) argue that relative to the statistically correct answer, people give undue importance to strength as compared to the weight of the evidence. They write (p. 413): "Instead, we propose, people focus on the strength of the evidence – as they perceive it – and then make some adjustment in response to its weight." In our first example, the reader of an academic letter is likely to initially give too much importance to the strength of the letter (how supportive the letter is to the student), but then adjust it inadequately for the weight (how credible and well known the referee is). A moderately positive letter from a very credible referee leads to a feeling of underconfidence in the applicant because we overvalue the strength, yet we do not adequately take account of the credibility of the referee. In the opposite case where strength is high relative to weight, we feel overconfident in the applicant, akin to the case of base rate neglect.

One of the exercises for this chapter illustrates underweighting of the likelihood of the sample.

We now give a reduced form approach to thinking about both conservatism and base rate neglect. Consider two urns, $i = A, B$. Each of the urns contains a mixture of red balls and black balls, but in different proportions. A decision maker observes some signal S which is either (i) a single ball drawn from one of the urns, or (ii) n balls drawn with replacement from one of the urns. Let us for the moment consider only the first case of a draw of a single ball from one of the urns. The decision maker does not know which urn the ball was drawn from, but does know that nature chooses urns A and B with respective probabilities $p(A)$ and $p(B)$. We classify the event "success" as the draw of a red ball ($S = 1$) and the event "failure" as the draw of a black ball ($S = 0$) from an urn. The objective probability of success for urns A and B is, respectively, θ_A and θ_B; failure occurs with the complementary probabilities $1 - \theta_A$ and $1 - \theta_B$. For instance, if urn A has five red and 15 black balls, then $\theta_A = \frac{5}{20} = 0.25$.

Let us denote the objective and statistically correct probabilities by p and the subjective probabilities assigned by the decision maker by q. Using Bayes' Law, given in (9.9), the conditional probability of urn $i = A, B$, given the signal S, is

$$p(i \mid S) = \frac{p(S \mid i)p(i)}{p(S)}, \; i = A, B. \tag{9.11}$$

Using (9.11) to divide $p(A \mid S)$ by $p(B \mid S)$, we get that a decision maker who follows Bayes' law must satisfy

$$\frac{p(A \mid S)}{p(B \mid S)} = \left[\frac{p(S \mid A)}{p(S \mid B)}\right]\left[\frac{p(A)}{p(B)}\right]. \tag{9.12}$$

The empirical evidence shows that most people do not follow Bayes' law. In order to model departures from Bayes' law, let us follow Grether (1980) and modify (9.12). Suppose that the subjective beliefs of the decision maker are given by

$$\frac{q(A \mid S)}{q(B \mid S)} = \left[\frac{p(S \mid A)}{p(S \mid B)}\right]^a \left[\frac{p(A)}{p(B)}\right]^b, \tag{9.13}$$

where q denotes the decision maker's subjective beliefs, and p denotes the statistically correct beliefs. The size of the parameters, a, b, captures departures from Bayes' law. These parameters are likely to vary across individuals. The subjective beliefs of a decision maker who follows Bayes' law are identical to the objective beliefs in (9.12), that is,

$$\frac{q(A \mid S)}{q(B \mid S)} = \frac{p(A \mid S)}{p(B \mid S)},$$

so in this case, $a = b = 1$.

Denote the empirical estimates of a and b by, respectively, $\hat{a}$ and $\hat{b}$.

Definition 9.4

(i) *We define the case $\hat{a} < 1$ as underinference or underestimation of the likelihood of the sample. Conversely, $\hat{a} > 1$ is defined as overinference.*

(ii) *The case $\hat{b} < 1$ is defined as base rate neglect and $\hat{b} > 1$ is defined as base rate overuse.*

We now describe the results of the meta study of 16 studies by Benjamin (2018). Let us restrict attention to symmetric updating problems where the probability of a red ball from urn A is identical to the probability of a black ball from urn B; or

$$\theta_A = 1 - \theta_B = \theta.$$

The parameter θ is called the *diagnosticity parameter*.

Taking logs on both sides of (9.13):

$$\ln\left[\frac{q(A \mid S)}{q(B \mid S)}\right] = a \ln\left[\frac{p(S \mid A)}{p(S \mid B)}\right] + b \ln\left[\frac{p(A)}{p(B)}\right]. \tag{9.14}$$

The meta study contains both cases alluded to above, where the signal S can either be a random draw of a single ball from one of the urns, or a random draw of a sequence of balls with replacement from one of the urns.

Consider the case of *equal priors* where both urns are equally likely to be chosen by nature, $p(A) = p(B)$, so that (9.12) implies that

$$\frac{p(S \mid A)}{p(S \mid B)} = \frac{p(A \mid S)}{p(B \mid S)}.$$

Substituting this expression in (9.14), and noting that $\ln 1 = 0$, we get the following relation between subjective and objective beliefs of the decision maker

$$\ln\left[\frac{q(A \mid S)}{q(B \mid S)}\right] = a \ln\left[\frac{p(A \mid S)}{p(B \mid S)}\right].$$

The meta study estimates $\hat{a} = 0.20 < 1$, and restricting attention to incentivized studies it finds $\hat{a} = 0.38 < 1$. Hence, the data indicates underinference or underestimation of the likelihood of the sample. An increase in the sample size n (remember this is the case where n balls are randomly drawn in sequence, with replacement, from one of the urn), reduces $\hat{a}$. Thus, underinference is greater in larger samples. A value of $\theta > 0.5$ reduces $\hat{a}$, so underinference is found to be greater when the diagnosticity parameter is high. Underinference is also found when the signal S comprises a single random draw of a ball, that is, $n = 1$. If we relax the restriction $p(A) = p(B)$ and estimate (9.14), but restrict $a = 1$, then the meta study gives $\hat{b} < 1$ which is the finding of base rate neglect.

9.4.11 Other Heuristics in the Heuristics Program

In this subsection, we provide a brief discussion of some of the other heuristics in Kahneman–Tversky's heuristics program. Some of these heuristics such as the *false consensus effect* are discussed elsewhere in the book.

Confirmation-Bias

Individuals who suffer from *confirmation bias* interpret new information in a manner that supports their initial beliefs. This takes the form of biased assimilation of new information that ignores and underplays evidence that does not support the initial beliefs; and readily accepts confirming evidence. The interested reader can consult several surveys of this phenomenon; see Nickerson (1998), Lord and Taylor (2009), and Mercier and Sperber (2011).

Confirmation bias is succinctly described in the following quote from Lord et al. (1979, p. 2099):

> Thus, there is considerable evidence that people tend to interpret subsequent evidence so as to maintain their initial beliefs. The biased assimilation processes underlying this effect may include a propensity to remember the strengths of confirming evidence but the weaknesses of disconfirming evidence, to judge confirming evidence as relevant and reliable but disconfirming evidence as irrelevant and unreliable, and to accept confirming evidence at face value while scrutinizing disconfirming evidence hypercritically. With confirming evidence, we suspect that both lay and professional scientists rapidly reduce the complexity of the information and remember only a few well-chosen supportive impressions. With disconfirming evidence, they continue to reflect upon any information that suggests less damaging "alternative interpretations." Indeed, they may even come to regard the ambiguities and conceptual flaws in the data opposing their hypotheses as somehow suggestive of the fundamental correctness of those hypotheses. Thus, completely inconsistent or even random data—when "processed" in a suitably biased fashion—can maintain or even reinforce one's preconceptions.

Some situations and circumstance are more likely to lead to greater confirmation bias. Rabin and Schrag (1999) identify the following four factors:

(i) The evidence is ambiguous and bears alternative interpretations.
(ii) The collection and scrutinization of evidence is selective (*hypothesis-based filtering*).
(iii) People are asked to judge the correlation between temporally separated events.
(iv) Individuals need to aggregate information from various sources.

Greater cognitive abilities or open mindedness does not reduce confirmation bias (Stanovich and West, 2007, 2008). The biased information assimilation process, central to confirmation-bias, may make individuals too overconfident because they do not allow their initial beliefs to be sufficiently challenged. It might also contribute to prejudices and stereotypes.

In experiments on confirmation-bias, the prior beliefs of subjects for competing hypotheses are elicited. Examples from the literature include hypotheses about the football team that one supports; the party that one supports in US Presidential elections; whether one supports capital punishment or not; and whether one believes that nuclear technology is safe or not. The experimenter then provides subjects with information that is partial to one of the hypotheses and elicits the posterior beliefs of the subjects for the competing hypotheses. In each of these cases, one can compute the Bayesian benchmark for posterior beliefs using the formula in Section 9.4.10. If the elicited posterior beliefs adjust insufficiently relative to the Bayesian benchmark, then subjects may be subject to confirmation-bias. One of the exercises uses this method and asks you to think about the evidence from an experiment on confirmation-bias.

Regression to the Mean

In the Sydney Morning Herald, dated December 29, 2020, and just after India's historic second cricket Test match win over Australia, the sports correspondent Malcolm Knox wrote: "In their three Border-Gavaskar Trophy series since 2014–15, neither of these teams has managed to win two Test matches in a row. Indeed, two might be considered a streak. The same happened between Australia and England in the 2019 Ashes … The same alternation of win-loss-win characterizes State of Origin rugby league … By losing one match, each team becomes almost automatically the favorite to win the next."

In American professional sport, rookies who perform exceptionally well are typically unable to replicate their success in the following years. This is known as *sophomore slump*. In the Premier League in English football, a similar phrase, *second season syndrome*, highlights a slump in second season performance after a football team has done well in the previous season. Conversely, teams that might not have done too well in the previous season are often likely, on average, to do better, this season. What is going on here? These apparently disconnected observations are explained by a statistical phenomenon known as *regression to the mean*. This has a wide range of applications in many domains.

Francis Galton, a half-cousin of the biologist Charles Darwin, was interested in the heights of Victorian parents and their children. He first split parents in Victorian society into two groups: those whose heights were taller than the average (group 1), and those whose heights were shorter than the average (group 2). He found that the average height of adult children for group 1 was lower than the average height of their parents. However, the average height of adult children for group 2 was higher than the average heights of their parents. In other words, the average heights of the children in both groups tended to move towards the average heights in the respective populations that they came from, and away from the extremes of the heights of their parents. So, on average, taller than average parents will have slightly shorter children, and, shorter than average parents will have slightly taller children. In 1886, Galton termed this phenomenon as *regression to the mean*.

It turns out that this purely statistical result applies to many domains where there is an inherent randomness in the underlying process and the outcomes are partly governed by luck. In the

1960s, Daniel Kahneman faced an interesting problem, while he was advising the Israeli Air Force. He was told by flight instructors that pilots whose performance was praised did not perform as well in subsequent maneuvers. Conversely, pilots whose performance was criticized, performed better in subsequent maneuvers. The implication was that carrots, in the form of praise, diminish subsequent performance, while sticks, in the form of criticism, improve subsequent performance. Hence, the implication seemed obvious: avoid the carrot and use the stick.

Kahneman realized that this inference was mistaken because the flight instructors did not take account of regression to the mean. The pilots were required to perform extremely complicated maneuvers and the outcome was governed, in large part, by luck. Pilots who did well at any time, and performed above average, were just very lucky. On average, their performance, in their next attempt at the maneuvers, is statistically predicted to drop, just like parents with above average height produce, on average, shorter children. Similarly, pilots who performed worse than the average at any time, were unlucky. Regression to the mean dictates that their next attempt at the maneuvers would, on average, produce better performance. Carrots and sticks had nothing to do with actual performance and the flight instructors had mistakenly ascribed observed performance to such incentives.

To demonstrate this effect, Daniel Kahneman asked pilots to turn their backs towards a target line and aim to throw a coin that would hit the target line. Lucky pilots who were able to land a coin close to the target at any time found, that on average, in their next attempt at the target, the coin was further away from the target. Unlucky pilots experienced the reverse.

Let us revisit the cricket analogy at the start of this subsection. India's abysmal score of 36 all out that led to their defeat in Adelaide in the first "cricket Test match" of the 2020–21 series against Australia, despite being ahead for most of the match, was similarly a case of being very unlucky. This performance was below average against any historical yardstick. Regression to the mean would dictate that, on average, they would be expected to bounce back next time. They did so, quite spectacularly, winning the series for only the second time in their history, conditional on the series being played in Australia. Many commentators said after the first cricket test match that the only way for India was up. We do not know if they had an informal understanding of the phenomenon of regression to the mean – but they turned out to be right.

This phenomenon has an interesting application to finance. The outcomes of many stock market decisions are surprisingly decided by luck alone (Kahneman, 2011). Only very few financial investors have the skills to beat the market on a consistent basis. In a story narrated in Kahneman (2011), Daniel Kahneman was invited by a financial firm to suggest improvements. He found that the incentives within the firm were high-powered (i.e., the pay package was closely related to observed performance). Investors investing on behalf of the firm who did well in any particular year, earned high bonuses. Kahneman argued that those who did well were mostly lucky. The financial firm naturally resisted such an interpretation because it would make it difficult to justify the huge performance-related bonuses that were part of their culture. Kahneman asked for the earnings data for all investors in the firm for the past several years and computed the correlation between their performance in successive years. This correlation turned out to be nearly zero. In other words, above average performance in any year was matched, on average, by below average performance next year. Thus, those who did well at any point in time were mostly very lucky. Needless to say, this did not go down well with the financial firm.

Being aware of regression to the mean phenomenon can enable us to avoid errors of inference in many domains in life, and can enable firms to implement more efficient and fairer incentive schemes.

The Affect Heuristic

Recall that in our exposition of the availability heuristic above, we mentioned that salient and vivid memories of events are particularly amenable for recall. Salience and vividness are enhanced when there is an emotional, or *affective*, reaction to an event. The basic idea is that individuals tag the *affect* or the positive and negative quality/feeling *induced* by an event. The individual then draws on an *affect pool* of mental representations of the event in making judgments and decisions (Slovic et al., 2002).

Slovic et al. (2002, p. 398) write: "We sometimes delude ourselves that we proceed in a rational manner and weight all the pros and cons of the various alternatives. But this is probably seldom the actual case. Quite often 'I decided in favor of X' is no more than 'I liked X' … We buy the cars we 'like,' choose the jobs and houses we find 'attractive,' and then justify these choices by various reasons." This offers a completely different approach to consumer theory, relative to the one taught to students of economics. The work of Zajonc (1980) echoes these ideas when he notes that we do not just see a car, we see a *sleek car*, a *cool car*, an *ugly car*, depending on the *affect* of the car on us.

Why does "affect" play an important role in human judgment and decision making? Kahneman (2011) proposes that using "affective methods" offers a cognitive shortcut by substituting a hard question (What do I think about it?) by an easier question (How do I feel about it?). This provides a less cognitively challenging and less time-consuming method of making choices. This is especially the case when the underlying problems are complex and difficult, leading one to potentially freeze or procrastinate if one deliberated at length on the choices. It has become customary to refer to choices made through various affective shortcuts as using the *affect heuristic*.

The use of the affect heuristic creates potential difficulties for pubilc policy. On the one hand, Cass Sunstein has often recommended that public policy ought to be based on a cost–benefit basis taking account of the relevant risks, and this is often how public policy decisions are made. By contrast, Paul Slovic, a leading advocate of the affect heuristic, argues that there are no objective risks in an uncertain world where the public has a subjective notion of risk.

Empirical evidence on the affect heuristic tries to determine the effect of subjects' elicited emotional reaction to an event on their actual choices, often independent of the objective risks. For instance, Fischhoff et al. (1978) elicited the *subjective perception of risks* of various hazards depending on the *subjective dread* that these hazards induced. The hazards included antibiotics, X-rays, vaccines, smoking, and alcohol. Individuals are then asked to assign subjective risks of the various hazards and their subjective benefits. Individuals assign lower benefits to hazards that they dread more, even if there is no objective relation between the degree of risk and the benefits associated with an event. Similar results are given in Alhakami and Slovic (1994).

In an interesting extension to these results, the experimental results of Finucane et al. (2000) showed that varying risks give rise to varying perceived benefits. But the reverse is also true: By varying the benefits one can induce variations in perceived risk. For the specific case of nuclear power, they showed that subjects assigned low (high) risks when it was revealed to them that the benefits are high (low). These results are strengthened when decisions are made under greater time pressure.

The subjects in the experiments of Slovic et al. (1999) were experts who were members of the British Toxicology Association. The experts were first asked to rate 30 chemical items on an *affect scale* that ranged from bad to good. The chemicals included second-hand smoking, dioxins in food, benzene, and aspirin. Then, they were asked to make a risk assessment of exposure to each chemical, but the exposure level was 1/100 of the level rated to be dangerous. At these levels, the chemicals posed little or no risk. Yet, the affect ranking and the risk ranking of the chemicals was strongly negatively correlated for 95 out of the 97 experts. Chemicals that had a bad "affect" (as measured by the affect scale) on the experts were judged by them to be riskier, and this could not be justified in terms of objective risks.

Pachur et al. (2012) showed that a higher subjectively elicited dread score for different types of cancers, led to a higher estimate of the number of deaths from that cancer in the Swiss population. Thus, it would appear, that there are *better deaths* and *worse deaths*. Painful deaths, or deaths arising from a ghastly accident, elicit a more affective response, say, as compared to someone who died peacefully.

9.4.12 Attribute Substitution

Attribute substitution arises when one attribute of an object is substituted for another, perhaps because it comes more readily to mind (Kahneman and Frederick, 2002). An example is substituting "similarity" for "probability." Attribute substitution may be used to reduce the cognitive burden of solving a problem by substituting an easier, or easier to use, attribute for a more difficult to understand attribute. Strack et al. (1988) asked subjects the following two questions in this order and found low correlation between the answers.

(i) How happy are you with your life in general?
(ii) How many dates did you have last month?

When the order of the questions was reversed, the correlation in the answers increased to 0.66. Kahneman and Frederick (2002) propose the following explanation: "We suggest that thinking about the dating question automatically evokes an affectively charged evaluation of one's satisfaction in that domain of life, which lingers to become the heuristic attribute when the happiness question is subsequently encountered." These results were replicated by Schwarz et al. (1991).

9.5 Do Incentives Eliminate Biases?

We have already considered in this chapter, the relation between incentives and heuristics, particularly the resulting departures in observed behavior relative to the neoclassical prediction.

We may call these departures, for the purposes of this section, as cognitive biases. However, our discussion focused on studies that did not offer very large incentives.

Camerer and Hogarth (1999) showed that, in general, incentives do not necessarily eliminate cognitive biases, although they might reduce the variance of responses for certain kinds of experiments. However, they were comparing nonincentivized studies with incentivized studies that typically used small-sized incentives.

Enke et al. (2022) revisit this issue by using three different levels of incentives: No incentives; small incentives that are typical in lab experiments, or standard incentives; and large incentives that paid off the equivalent of a month's wages and are about 100 times the standard incentives. The experiments were conducted with 1236 University of Nairobi students in Kenya. The students were generally quite able and their performance on the *cognitive reflection test* (CRT) was comparable to US/European students.

The CRT was proposed by Frederick (2005) and it is a measure of people's reflective thinking. The correct answer requires some deliberation while the quick intuitive answer is typically incorrect. The authors included the following two questions (units in Kenyan currency).

1. A bat and a ball cost 110 KSh in total. The bat costs 100 KSh more than the ball. How much does the ball cost? (Intuitive answer is 10, correct answer is 5).
2. It takes 5 nurses 5 minutes to measure the blood pressure of 5 patients. How long would it take 10 nurses to measure the blood pressure of 10 patients? (Intuitive answer is 10, correct answer is 5).

The authors chose the following heuristics that we have considered in this chapter: base rate neglect; anchoring; failure of contingent thinking in the Wason selection task; and intuitive reasoning in the CRT. The last of these, the CRT, is not a heuristic. Furthermore, the experimental instructions for each of the heuristics employed two different types of framing. (1) Abstract framing presents only the essential elements necessary to solve a problem, but no context or simplification is given. (2) Intuitive framing include the context and is presented in a way that simplifies the problem.

So why should incentives reduce cognitive biases? There are two alternative hypotheses. First, subjects in experiments might have low motivation, so they might not spend enough time deliberating on the questions asked, hence, they might exhibit cognitive biases. To test this hypothesis, one can study the reaction times of subjects (time that it takes subjects to answer a question) with varying incentives. Second, the problem might not be motivational at all, but subjects lack the cognitive ability or skills required to solve the problems. In this case, varying the level of incentives will have little or no effect on cognitive biases.

The results are as follows. Cognitive biases do not respond to incentives, except for the CRT, which is not a heuristic. Rather, subjects appear to lack the cognitive ability or skills required to solve the problems given in experiments. Figure 9.6 demonstrates the results. Comparing standard incentives and large incentives, the performance of subjects in five out of six tasks is statistically indistinguishable (the only significant differences is for the CRT). Similarly, when we compare standard incentives and no-incentives, the performance is indistinguishable in five tasks. Using 95% confidence intervals, the results rule out performance increases of more than 318 percentage points in the presence of incentives. Cognitive biases do not disappear in the

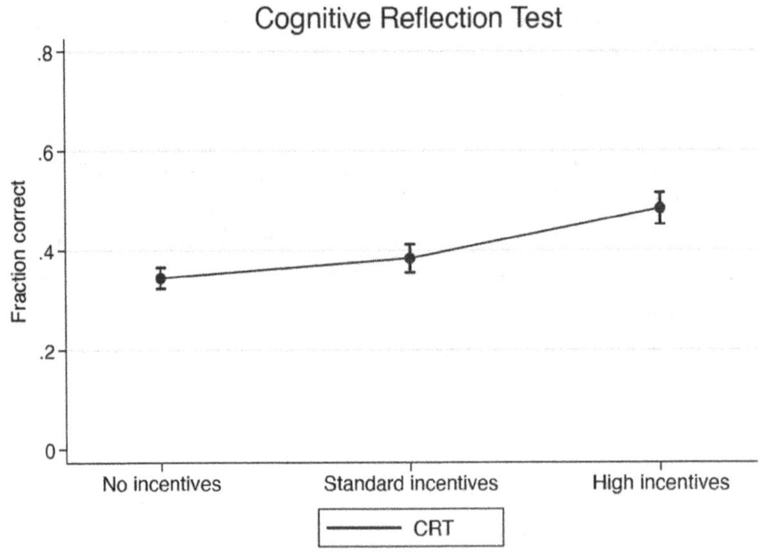

(a)

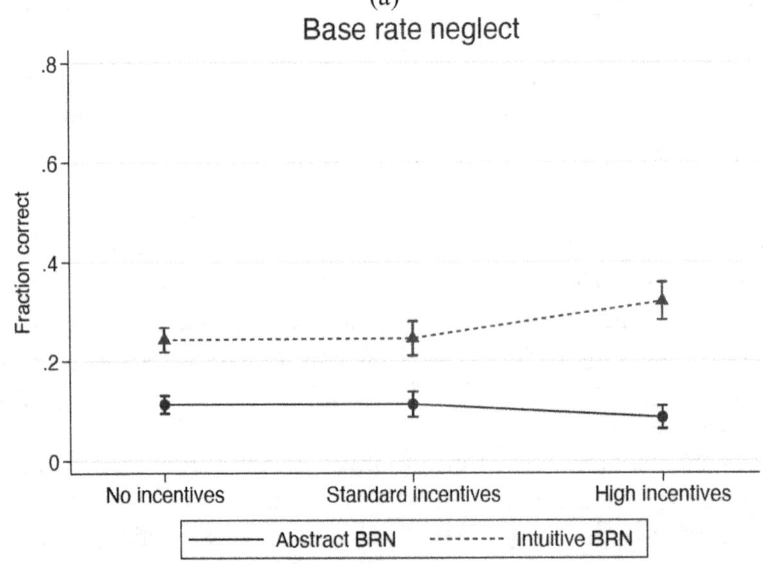

(b)

Figure 9.6 Average performance in different heuristics tasks for varying levels of incentives. I am grateful to Benjamin Enke for providing me with this high resolution image

presence of incentives, and even when incentives are the highest, the error rates (incorrect responses by subjects) range between 40% and 90%. When comparing the two frames (abstract and intuitive), performance improves with incentives the most in the intuitive frame for base rate neglect and the Wason task.

Response times increase by about 40% across all tasks when the incentives are highest, relative to no incentives. Hence, subjects deliberate significantly more in the presence of incentives.

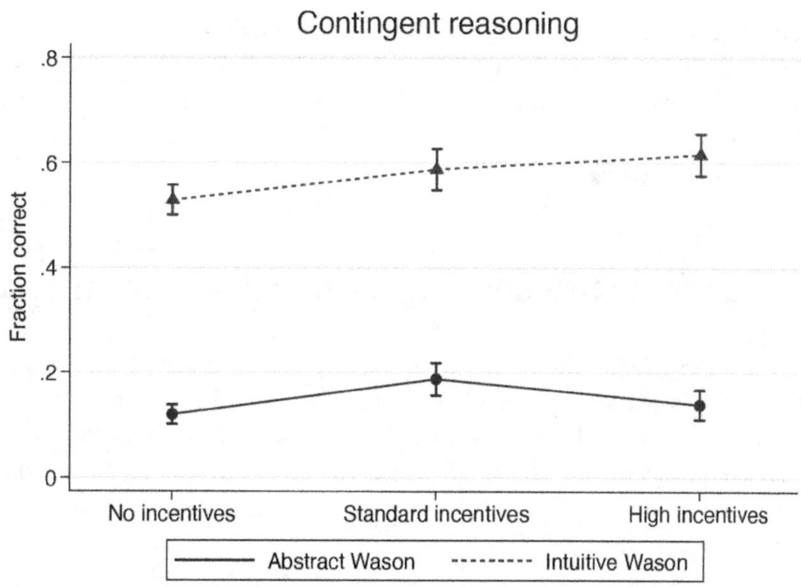

(c)

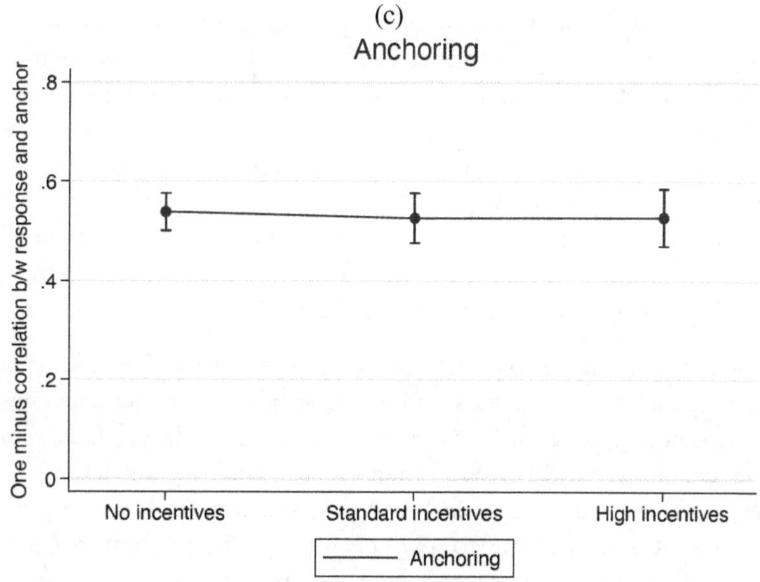

(d)

Figure 9.6 (*Continued*)

Yet, this increased deliberation makes no difference to the extent of cognitive biases. Hence, the hypothesis about the motivational effect of incentives is rejected. Rather, subjects lack the cognitive ability and the skills necessary to solve the given problems. But this is exactly what Kahneman and Tversky thought, and this has been one of their major findings. They argued that the predictions of neoclassical economics do not even hold in an "as if" sense.

Despite their findings, there has been push back from many economists who have dismissed the heuristics program on the grounds that they give no incentive or low incentives. The authors asked a sample of 68 Harvard researchers (experimental economists and students taking such courses) about their opinions on the efficacy of incentives. The experts predicted that moving from no incentives to low incentives will improve performance by 25%, and moving from low to high incentives will improve it by another 25%. Yet, the expert predictions did not turn out to be correct in this case.

9.6 The Gigerenzer Fast and Frugal Heuristics Program

We have noted above that in many contexts, people appear to use heuristics that are fast (in terms of the time taken to make a decision), and frugal (in terms of the information required to make a decision). These ideas have their intellectual origin in the work of the Nobel prize winner Herbert Simon (1957, 1978, 1982, 2000). The Kahneman–Tversky heuristics program is motivated, in principle, by similar concerns. Indeed, Herbert Simon himself approved of the direction taken in the heuristics program.

The focus of the Kahneman–Tversky heuristics program has been mainly on situations of certainty, risk, and subjective uncertainty. Gerd Gigerenzer and his coauthors, along with others, have tried to highlight procedural rationality in human behavior when choices lie in the domain of true uncertainty (unknown unknowns) that we discussed in Part I of the book. They explicitly distinguish between small worlds (risk and subjective uncertainty) and large worlds (true uncertainty). In order to distinguish it from the heuristics program, let us call this as the *Gigerenzer heuristics program* (GHP), but we note that there are many other important contributors in both programs; see Gigerenzer et al. (2011) for an edited collection of papers. The analysis of decision making under true uncertainty is extremely challenging, hence, it has been difficult to make as much headway. There are two main issues.

1. How does one create true uncertainty in experiments? It may not be clear if subjects are solving problems under risk/subjective uncertainty, or under true uncertainty.
2. There is no objective yardstick on which to evaluate the predictions of the program. In the Kahneman–Tversky heuristics program, the objective yardstick is extremely precise and it is to the great credit of neoclassical economics that its models make precise, testable predictions. However, it is unclear how to make decisions under true uncertainty, and economic theory is largely silent on the issue, so there is no objective yardstick. This raises great difficulty in evaluating any proposal, including the ones in the GHP. It is also unclear how to judge the efficiency of the heuristics proposed in the program. Should one judge them on an ex-ante basis before observing the unknown future, but based on some commonly agreed yardstick? Or judge them ex-post after observing the future? But these problems arise for any proposals that attempt to model human behavior under true uncertainty.

The GHP proposes that people have an *adaptive toolbox of heuristics* (Gigerenzer et al., 1999; Gigerenzer and Selten, 2001). People draw heuristics from this toolbox depending on the context/frame of the problem (*ecological rationality*). In principle, this is eminently plausible, and consistent with the stated objective of procedural rationality. The GHP begins with a *reference class of cues* and their *ecological validities*, which is their ability to differentiate, or discriminate, between the given options in the reference class. For instance, in the *take-the-best heuristic*, the cues are ordered by their ecological validities, which is their success rate in helping to choose between the given options (see below). Starting with the cue that has the highest ecological validity, we find the first cue than can *discriminate* between the given options.

When making a choice between options, an example of a simple cue is one that can *recognize* some of the objects in the given set of choices. For any two pairs of objects, the first two objects between which the cue can discriminate enables choice to be made, that is, choose the object that is recognized, in preference to the object that is not. In this case, the cue is able to discriminate between the options. This forms the basis for the *recognition heuristic*. The GHP also allows for more complex heuristics. For instance, decision makers may subjectively combine the cues in some manner (e.g., a linear combination of the cues) in order to make a decision. We might also require that cue discrimination must exceed a certain threshold value for it to be used to make a decisive choice.

The Kahneman–Tversky heuristics program has faced a great amount of scrutiny in the literature and we have examined many of the criticisms above. These include the use of a frequency format over a probability format; the use of incentives; and group decisions versus individual decisions. However, the GHP has not faced as much scrutiny, particularly from those who work outside this literature. There is almost complete neglect of GHP in economics. The GHP can benefit from a critical examination and from constructive criticism. A full treatment of this important topic is outside our scope here; for a detailed treatment, interested readers can consult Dhami (2020, Vol. V) and Dhami and Sunstein (2022).

Let us consider a simple example of how the GHP addresses the issue of procedural rationality, using a proposed explanation for hindsight-bias, drawn from Hoffrage et al. (2000). This example highlights many features of the GHP that we shall summarize in a critique below. We are not arguing that this is the leading and most successful example in the GHP, but our purpose is rather to illustrate the method that is used in the GHP.

Example 9.6 *Suppose that Patricia needs to decide, at Time 1, which of two foods, a cake and a pie, has more cholesterol. She lacks an objective answer to this question, so she decides to use "cues" to make an inference. The experimenter provides her with three cues: saturated fat, calories, and protein; this comprises the "reference class of cues." The experimenter also provides Patricia with the "ecological validities" of all three cues, stated as a percentage in the first column of Table 9.3. The ecological validity of a cue is the percentage of pairwise comparisons in the reference class of objects in which the cue can distinguish between the objects (in this case which of the two foods has*

Table 9.3 Determining which of two foods has more cholesterol

Cues/ecological validity	Time 1	Time 3
Saturated fat (80%)	cake ? pie	cake > pie
Calories (70%)	cake > pie	cake > pie
Protein (60%)	cake > pie	cake > pie
Choice	cake	cake
Confidence	70%	80%

greater cholesterol) in the sample. The "reference class of objects" selected by the experimenter, is a random sample of foods from a Chicago supermarket, cake and pie. If a cue favors object A over object B, we write A >B, and if the cue cannot discriminate between A and B, we write A ? B.

Consider Time 1. We now use the take-the-best heuristic, described above, to determine the optimal choice between the objects at Time 1. The cue with the highest ecological validity, saturated fat, cannot discriminate between the two objects (cake ? pie). Hence, Patricia is required to evaluate the two objects based on the cue with the next highest ecological validity, calories, which is able to successfully discriminate in favor of cake (cake > pie). Hence, at Time 1, Patricia is predicted to choose cake. The "confidence" that Patricia has in her judgment equals the ecological validity of the first cue that is able to discriminate, in this case calories, so the confidence is 70%.

Suppose that Patricia is now asked to make the same choice between cake and pie at a future time, Time 3. The authors assume that she has imperfect recall of her Time 1 choices, and they argue that "the cue values are not verdically remembered but show systematic shift towards feedback."[4] *The authors use this assumption to construct the information in column 3 of Table 9.3. The cue, saturated fat, which was not able to discriminate between cake and pie at Time 1, is able to discriminate at Time 3, in favor of cake over pie. Hence, the take-the-best procedure predicts that Patricia chooses cake at Time 3, and assigns 80% confidence to her judgment. This, the authors claim, explains hindsight-bias.*

We now offer a critique of this program.

1. By assuming that "cue values are not verdically remembered but show systematic shift towards feedback" assumes hindsight-bias, the very phenomenon that the authors wish to explain. Hence, this is not a persuasive explanation for hindsight-bias. The remaining part of the critique is not specific to the example above.
2. Since the stated aim of the GHP is to model procedural rationality, it is of critical importance for the theory to discover how individuals uncover the underlying reference class of cues and how they discover/compute their ecological validities. In particular, under true uncertainty, do they even know which information they should be searching for.

   Herbert Simon highlighted the "infinite regress in search costs problem" that motivated his satisficing approach (see Chapter 10). This problem arises because searching for any extra information (e.g., the reference class of cues and their ecological validities) requires computing the costs of searching for this information. However, this requires knowing the cost of the cost for searching for new information, and so on, giving rise to the infinite regress problem. The GHP invokes the work of Herbert Simon as its main motivation, but the experimenter-provided information on the reference class of cues, their ecological validities, and the reference class of objects, defeats the purpose of endogenizing procedural rationality.
3. Suppose that the cues and the reference class are "not" experimenter-provided. It is quite likely that different subjects in experiments will then choose a different reference class of cues, and there might be no obvious way of choosing a reference class. Subjects may also make mistakes in the computation of the ecological validities. Or perhaps, they might not even

[4] By "verdically" is meant the degree to which an experience, perception, or interpretation, accurately represents reality or is correctly remembered in this example.

know that ecological validities need to be computed as a part of whatever "true" underlying heuristics they are using. Providing identical information on the reference class of cues and their ecological validities in experiments ensures uniformity across subjects, but, at least partly, defeats the problem of finding out exactly how subjects make choices, particularly under true uncertainty.

Bröder and Schiffer (2003) partially address this problem in one of their treatments where subjects are narrated the relevant information, pictorially or verbally. Subjects then have to retrieve the relevant information from their memory. Although this method solves the criticism of cue-recall from identical information, it leaves unsolved the question of cue-search in the real world. It does not tell us how individuals would search for reference classes, cues values, and their ecological validities, if such information was not provided. Do subjects learn the ecological validity of cues, if given a chance? Newell and Shanks (2003) provided a set of cues to subjects and, unknown to the subjects, the ecological validity of these cues was, respectively, 0.80, 0.75, 0.70, 0.69. The authors set a learning trial period of 60 repetitions with feedback to enable the subjects to learn the ecological validity of the cues. Only three out of 16 subjects learned to order the cues in the correct order. Gigerenzer and Brighton (2011, p. 23) defend against this criticism by arguing that 60 rounds of learning is insufficient and at least 100 trials are needed. Yet, in the real world, in many decisions with significant consequences, opportunities to learn are limited. For instance, economic decisions such as the choice of savings/pension plans or purchase of consumer durables; decisions such as marriage, divorce, number of children; and altruistic decisions such as donating organs. Similarly, for firms, there are many infrequent decisions such as mergers, introduction of a new product, and capital restructuring.

4. The method proposed by GHP places it firmly in the class of "as if" theories, although curiously this is one of the grounds on which GHP criticizes theories in economics. In GHP, we only observe the final choices made. For instance, whether Patricia chose cake or pie in the example above. We really do not observe the mental process that Patricia engages in, or how, if at all, she uses the given cues and ecological validities. In principal, other competing theories may well have led to the same observed choices. We can match the observed choices of Patricia with the predictions of the theory. This is no different from other "as if" theories in behavioral economics, say, prospect theory, which also have a procedure for making choices that is based on reference points, a specific utility function, and a probability weighting function (see Part I). Let us consider two examples.

   Scheibehenne and Bröder (2007) used the recognition heuristic to show that mere name recognition of players for the 2005 Wimbledon tennis tournament correctly predicted 70% of the matches. Yet, there is a correlation between name recognition of the players and how highly seeded they are. Players who are more likely to be recognized, are more likely to be highly seeded, and more likely to win. So the claimed victory for the recognition heuristic in this case might well be a confound because these choices are likely to be indistinguishable from those that use a simple heuristic of predicting that "more highly seeded players will win."

   A similar problem exists in evaluating the use of the recognition heuristic in choosing among stocks based on whether people could recognize the name of the stock or not. Borges et al. (1999) claim that the use of such name recognition of stocks outperformed more traditional methods of stock market investment. However, more recognized stocks are also more likely to belong to larger, more established, and stable firms, as compared to newer, untried, and potentially more risky firms. Hence, the cautious choices made by a stock market participant for established firms in preference to risky newer entrants, are likely to be indistinguishable from someone who uses the recognition heuristic.

5. The GHP has pitted its proposed heuristics against other methods such as logistic regression and weighted tallying. Yet, none of these competitors is persuasive, certainty not under true uncertainty, while economics has little by way of objective benchmarks to offer in this case. As noted above, the lack of an objective benchmark under true uncertainty is a more general problem that goes well beyond the GHP.
6. Conformity of the evidence with some of the leading heuristics in the GHP is not satisfactory when pitted against other possible heuristics. In choosing between options A and B, *Dawes' rule* or *tallying*, picks the option that has the highest number of cues in its favor. *Franklin's rule* uses a weighted combination of the cues to choose between the options. Bröder (2011) showed that when compared with Dawes rule and Franklin's rule, only 28% of the subjects conformed to take-the-best, which is a prominent heuristic in the GHP. More people use Franklin's rule than take-the-best. One still does not know which heuristic in the GHP to use in which situation. In other words, we still appear a long way off from satisfying procedural rationality in opening the adaptive toolbox and picking a particular heuristic in a given situation.

In sum, while the GHP is to be commended for taking on the difficult problem of choices under true uncertainty, and despite a great deal of scholarship in the area, there are several areas of serious concern. How do people use these heuristics to make choices of pension plans, savings plans, job choices, marriage partners, choice of consumer durables, and University choices? More constructive criticism never hurt science, and this is often most fruitful when it is made by well meaning observers outside that literature.

10 Bounded Rationality II

Topics in Bounded Rationality

10.1 Introduction

In this chapter we continue our study of bounded rationality, but broaden it to consider several interesting applications. We begin by outlining in Section 10.2 how individuals use *mental models* to try to make sense of a complex world, possibly under true uncertainty, and under the constraints of limited cognition and limited attention. Mental models can be inertial, long-lived, and also contain inbuilt mechanisms that prevent falsification.

In Section 10.3, we distinguish between *narrow bracketing* and *broad bracketing*. In neoclassical economics, individuals use all available information (broad bracketing) but the evidence is consistent with people using a subset of the available information and ignoring the rest even when there are no issues of limited attention (narrow bracketing). Narrow bracketing can lead to suboptimal solutions. But it may also have certain benefits by making goals appear more manageable and less daunting; and enhancing self-image and confidence as in models of motivated reasoning.

In neoclassical economics, individuals diversify their portfolios using the expected values, variances, and covariances, of asset returns; as in the capital asset pricing model. In Section 10.4, we consider behavioral features of observed diversification strategies that often rely on simple rules of thumb. Although a range of such *diversification heuristics* have been proposed in the literature, we focus mainly on the implications of the $\frac{1}{n}$ *diversification heuristic*.

Section 10.5 makes the important distinction between *transaction utility* that is salient at the time of making purchases; and *acquisition utility* that relates to the actual consumption experience from a good. While acquisition utility is closely related to the concept of consumer surplus in neoclassical economics, transaction utility depends on the difference between a reference price (possibly determined by fairness, seller costs, and past prices) and the actual price. The higher the gap between the two, the more attractive it is to buy a good and more easily tempted one might be by "sales" and promises of "deals" and events such as "Black Friday." Yet, this concept is not directly related to consumer surplus, or to the subsequent consumption experience of the good, which are the only relevant factors to consider in traditional economic models.

Section 10.6 introduces *mental accounting*, an application of bounded rationality, that is rich and varied in applications. The essential idea is that people find it useful to code different sources of incomes and expenditures into different mental accounts. Mental accounts have two features.

First, money is not fungible across mental accounts. Second, it is aversive to leave mental accounts in the *red* (in debit) and people prefer to leave them in the *black* (in credit). We explore a range of evidence that supports these features and consider many diverse applications. Among the applications, we consider the implications for consumption choices; patterns of payments for goods (e.g., prepayment for vacations, and postpayments for consumer durables); the role of sunk costs in influencing behavior; and the behavioral economics of retirement savings.

In Section 10.7, we consider the possibility that current tastes might unduly influence our perception of future tastes. This is known as *projection bias* and it is likely to lead to departures of intertemporal consumption patterns from the optimal consumption profiles predicted under neoclassical economics. We also consider several applications of projection bias, for example, to medical decision making.

In Section 10.8, we consider choices made under *aspiration adaptation*, an idea proposed by Herbert Simon, which is an alternative to mathematical optimization in neoclassical economics. The basic idea is that people begin with initial *aspiration levels* and then search for alternatives that *satisfice* rather than *optimize*, in the sense that they satisfy existing aspirations. The aspirations themselves evolve over time; better outcomes relative to previous aspirations, increase current aspirations; while worse outcomes reduce current aspirations. We show how this method can be applied to explain the empirical evidence from simple games, including cooperation in the static prisoner's dilemma game.

In Section 10.9, we consider bounded rationality in financial markets. We examine and evaluate the assumptions that underlie the theory of efficient financial markets and general market efficiency in economics. We present insights from an alternative theoretical apparatus based on behavioral insights, and the empirical evidence on the suitability of these assumptions. This literature falls under the subject matter of *behavioral finance*, which is an entire field on its own. We end with a brief note on *behavioral corporate finance*.

10.2 Mental Models

In making decisions, people face an incredibly complex world where actions lead to uncertain outcomes, and they face cognitive and attentional constraints. For many important decisions there might not even be adequate opportunities for learning. In other cases, people might need to make decisions under "true uncertainty" (unknown unknowns) where economic models make no predictions. One potential solution is that people may employ a variety of *mental models* that simplify decisions under the given constraints.

An excellent discussion of mental models is provided in the World Bank Development report (WDR) that was published in 2015. WDR (2015, p. 11) gives a useful working definition of mental models drawing on Denzau and North (1994):

> When people think, they generally do not draw on concepts that they have invented themselves. Instead, they use concepts, categories, identities, prototypes, stereotypes, causal narratives, and worldviews drawn from their communities .... There are mental models for how much to talk to children, what risks to insure, what to save for, what the climate is like, and what causes disease. Many mental models are useful; others are not as useful and may even contribute to the intergenerational transmission of poverty.

Some mental models are formed due to the evolutionary history of humans, such as an inbuilt fear of snakes and spiders. Mental models can also arise due to historical accidents. Consider two examples.

Example 10.9 *In a series of studies, Nunn (2008) and Nunn and Wantchekon (2011) traced the current low levels of trust in parts of Africa to the slave trade that started in the sixteenth century. The slave traders roamed in Africa to capture slaves to sell. In response, Africans demanded guns to protect themselves against capture by the slave traders. Guns were expensive, and in order to afford them, some people resorted to kidnapping and selling other black Africans in the slave trade. This led to mistrust of strangers that still persists in some parts of Africa.*

Example 10.10 *The development of agriculture, which some estimates suggest began about 10,000 years ago, required the use of heavy equipment such as ploughs. The physical superiority of males gave them a comparative advantage in the use of this new technology. Empirically, a greater incidence of gender inequities is found in societies with an agricultural past (Alesina et al., 2013).*

There is a difference between mental models and *social norms* that we have examined elsewhere in the book (see Section 8.6 and the introduction to the book). Social norms typically require *normative expectations* (what a social group expects it's members "ought" to do) and are enforced by punishments of norm violators. By contrast, mental models do not require normative expectations, or sanctions. One may follow a particular mental model because one observes others following it, in much the same way as *descriptive norms* operate, based on *empirical expectations* (what one expects others actually do).

An exemplar of mental models is the literature on coarse thinking and persuasion. The early ideas were developed in Mullainathan (2002) and then formalized further in Mullainathan et al. (2008). One possible way of simplifying a large amount of information, for example, memories or experiences, is to categorize it into n mutually exclusive categories. Any separate items/objects in the same category are treated in an identical manner. For instance, if these items are similar problems, they might be solved by using the same heuristic. Neoclassical economics typically assumes that people are *sophisticated thinkers* rather than *coarse thinkers* because they have unbounded cognitive abilities. The solution arrived at by coarse thinking will typically not be an "optimal solution" in the sense this term is used in an economics problem. However, an optimal solution, so defined, may not be of much practical use if it is based on unrealistic cognitive assumptions.

Since objects in the same category are associated as similar, this may allow coarse thinkers to be exploited by others. For instance, advertisers might place a model or an actor/sports personality next to a car, although this adds no information about the car to a potential buyer. Yet coarse thinkers, using *associative thinking*, may transfer attributes they associate with the model/actor/sportsperson posing with the car, to the car itself. Hence, they might view the car as being more desirable, sporty, or sexy, than they would in the absence of such advertising. This is quite different from the standard view in economics that advertising only conveys essential information about a product.

Associative thinking explains the following examples of successful persuasion in Mullainathan et al. (2008).

1. American Express travelers cheques featured Karl Malden, an actor who played a detective in a well-known television show. The advertisements suggested that, for safety, people should carry American Express travelers cheques in preference to cash. Thus, the advertisement appears to be leveraging the reliability of Karl Malden and associating it with the reliability and safety of travelers cheques.
2. After the crash of the Internet bubble, the brokerage firm Charles Schwab launched an advertising campaign that featured judges, ship captains, crossing guards, doctors, grandmothers, and other steady and reliable individuals, each standing next to a Schwab investment specialist. The headline of one advertisement depicting a Schwab professional standing next to a pediatrician, said: "Both are seen as pillars of trust." Thus, desirable traits from an unrelated domain are being sought to be associated with a financial product (associative thinking).

Mental models have several important features.

1. They can be a good/accurate or bad/inaccurate description of the real world.
2. They can persist for long periods even when they cease to be useful. Individuals may get accustomed to using these mental models on autopilot in order to economize on cognitive costs.
3. Mental models can lead to outcomes that are harmful for others. Examples include stereotyping of others and racial discrimination based on one's social identity.

Mental models can sometimes be important in developing institutions and there could be a two-directional feedback between mental models and institutions. For instance, in Sierra Leone, Acemoglu et al. (2014) find that the degree of competition for the role of paramount chiefs, who are elected for a lifetime, is positively correlated with the quality of governance. However, in each area, paramount chiefs can only come from families that were originally recognized by the British colonial authorities, hence, in each area, the degree of competition is fixed. This has led to area-specific differences in respect towards authority. When the competition is lower, people are more respectful of authority, and less likely to question the actions of leaders, which perpetuates the existing lack of competition.

Consider the following two examples from Datta and Mullainathan (2014) of incorrect and harmful mental models.

Example 10.11 *The oral rehydration solution (ORS) is a relatively cheap and effective mix of essential salts to treat diarrhea. Yet, in many developing countries, the take-up rate is low; 35% of poor women surveyed in India believed that the best response to diarrhea is to reduce, not increase, fluid intake. They are possibly using a mental model of a leaky bucket, but this is an incorrect analogy. Since ORS eventually saves lives of those suffering from acute diarrhea, but does not reduce the symptoms of diarrhea, at least in the short run, many people continue to hold on to an incorrect and harmful mental model.*

Example 10.12 *Parents in Morocco and Madagascar pull their children out of school too early. In their incorrect mental models, they believe that primary education is not as beneficial as secondary education. There is an opportunity cost of sending children to school, because they could be earning* *wages outside school, making primary education nonviable for parents. However, the evidence shows that every extra year of schooling is equally valuable, including years spent in primary school. Thus, putting children through completion of primary school may, on net, be beneficial, but it is inconsistent with the mental models of the parents (Banerjee and Duflo, 2011).*

The examples considered above show that public policy has an important role to play in challenging harmful mental models through education and the provision of information. Policy also needs to create an environment that is conducive for the formation of appropriate mental models. The specifics of policy depend on the individual problems being addressed.

The literature on heuristics may also improve our understanding about the use and persistence of mental models. The *anchoring heuristic* and the *availability heuristic* make it more likely that "existing" mental models come to mind when taking decisions. *Confirmation bias* may prevent people from learning the defects of harmful mental models because people ignore/underplay strong evidence that is contrary to their mental models, but are too quick to accept weak confirming evidence. Mental models are often common within groups that share a social identity. Conformity with the group's shared mental models may serve as a signal of group membership, allowing mental models to persist even if they are harmful, such as stereotypes of outsiders.

Existing mental models may have inbuilt safeguards to prevent them from being falsified. Consider the following examples.

(i) Inadequate social exchange between communities that mistrust each other can allow mutual stereotypes to persist. Lack of trust prevents meeting people from the other group, perpetuating the possibly incorrect beliefs. Thus, individuals may be unwilling to experiment with alternative mental models (Mackie, 1996; Gollaher, 2000).
(ii) Female genital mutilation may persist because contact with the nonmutilated genitalia is perceived, among believers in this practice, to be harmful. Hence, individuals may never test the counterfactual.

Datta and Mullainathan (2014) argue that it might be more productive to provide evidence that falsifies the core beliefs in an incorrect mental model. Simply telling people that they hold incorrect mental models is likely to be ineffective. For instance, it has been found effective to provide people with a comparison of their activity relative to a set of peers, for example, their own neighborhood. Providing information on electricity consumption, relative to neighbors, reduced electricity use by an amount comparable to a 11%–20% increase in the price of electricity (Allcott and Mullainathan, 2010; Allcott and Rogers, 2014).

Ferraro and Price (2013) found that informing people of their water consumption in the form of a social comparison is more effective than simply providing people with technical information, or with prosocial messages that stress the positives for the environment. Here is a typical social comparison message that was found to be effective.

Your own total consumption June to October 2006: 52,000 gallons

Your neighbors' average (median) consumption June to October 2006: 35,000 gallons

You consumed more water than 73% of your Cobb County neighbors.

A combination of technical information, prosocial messages, and social comparisons is even more effective and achieves the same effect as an increase in the price of water by

12%–15%. Essentially, this package of information appears to change the mental model for water consumption in the minds of consumers.

There are many examples of behavioral changes that are consistent with changes in mental models. These changes have their basis in the provision of more information, and from appropriately framed messages. Information on the availability of jobs for girls with high school degrees made it more likely that villagers in poor countries provided education to girls (Jensen, 2012). Exposure to long-running soap operas in Brazil with appropriate social messaging, for example, small family sizes, led to a reduction in fertility (La Ferrara et al., 2012). A similar effect was found from exposure to cable TV in India that led to a reduction in fertility, increase in women's status, reduction in domestic violence, and an increase in children's school enrollment (Jensen and Oster, 2009). Legal or regulatory changes can also induce changes in mental models by altering attitudes towards slavery, wearing helmets, smoking, racism, and casteism (Sunstein, 1996).

10.3 Narrow Bracketing and Broad Bracketing

In neoclassical economics, individuals have unbounded cognitive abilities, hence, there is no need to ignore any information. Such individuals are said to engage in *broad choice bracketing*. By contrast, behavioral economics points to many reasons for ignoring some of the available information; we have explored some of the reasons elsewhere in this book. This could be to maintain a positive self-image; or in models of motivated beliefs to maintain a higher degree of optimism; or to strategically manipulate one's memory. *Narrow choice bracketing* typically occurs when individuals use only a subset of the available information or group/bracket information into categories and focus on selected categories in making decisions.

In neoclassical economics, individuals take account of the consequences of their current actions for all future periods and integrate incomes from all sources. This is an example of broad bracketing. However, people are often myopic and do not fully consider the consequences of their current actions for the future; and treat different sources of income differently, as in mental accounting (see Section 10.6); these are examples of narrow bracketing. In neoclassical economics, in deciding how much extra time they should work on a rainy day in New York, when the effective wage is high (broad bracketing), taxi drivers must consider opposing income/substitution effects, and all possible future effects of their decisions. However, the evidence in Part I suggests that taxi drivers set a daily earnings target, which is met earlier on a rainy day, so they quit early (narrow bracketing)

Read et al. (1999) provide another interesting example. In choosing to smoke each cigarette, a myopic smoker may take account of only the current costs and benefits but ignore the effect on long-term health outcomes. This is a form of narrow choice bracketing. If the individual were to engage in broad bracketing, and take into account the 7,300 cigarettes they will smoke in a year, at their current rate of smoking, they might make a different decision.

As one might expect, narrow bracketing can lead to suboptimal choices relative to the neoclassical benchmark. For instance, Rabin and Weizsäcker (2009) show that individuals who engage in narrow bracketing may choose stochastically dominated options. This is akin to leaving money on the table.

However, there are likely to be many benefits of narrow bracketing. Broad bracketing might be too cognitively challenging. For instance, in dynamic programming problems (see Section 9.3) broad bracketing requires individuals to make trillions of calculations before they can reach a decision. This is highly unlikely, and nor can these models be always justified using "as if" arguments. Hence, feasibility concerns may dictate simplification of the problem through narrow bracketing of some sort.

Narrow bracketing may also aid in achieving long-term goals through short-term interim goals/targets, because long-term targets/goals might be too daunting to pursue. For instance, successful sportspersons often break down a championship game into smaller segments that need to be won individually (e.g., win the next two games in a tennis match, or bat without losing a wicket for the next hour in cricket). Focusing on the more daunting task of winning the championship might not just be more daunting, one could also choke under the increased pressure and make unforced errors.

10.4 The Diversification Heuristic

In the presence of multiple risky assets, modern economics and finance is based on the ability of individuals to diversify their portfolios in order to optimally manage their risks. This typically requires taking account of the returns, variances, and covariances of individual assets in the portfolio, which is a cognitively challenging task. However, empirical evidence paints a different picture, one of *naive diversification* in which people seem to use simple rules of thumb, or heuristics, in deciding on their portfolio of assets. Read and Loewenstein (1995) and Benartzi and Thaler (2001) credit Simonson (1990) with the first demonstration of the *diversification heuristic*.

In a much studied form of the diversification heuristic, subjects split their budget equally between each of the available options. This rule is nicely illustrated in the following quote from Benartzi and Thaler (2001, p. 79): "Writing in about the fourth century, a Rabbi Issac bar Aha gave the following asset allocation advice: 'A man should always place his money, a third into land, a third into merchandise, and keep a third at hand.' There is anecdotal evidence that this rule is still in use."

Benartzi and Thaler (2001) show that when employees are asked to make a choice among alternative retirement funds, they use a simple heuristic. One of the retirement funds in their study contained one bond option and one stock option. Subjects allocated, on average, half the portfolio to each. When another stock was added to the possible portfolio, then the average allocation towards each stock was a third. It appears that the subjects are using a form of the diversification heuristic known as a $\frac{1}{n}$ *heuristic*: When allocating money between n funds, invest a fraction $\frac{1}{n}$ of the money in each of the n funds.

Experts may also exhibit the diversification heuristic. Thaler and Benartzi (2007) report the following quote from Harry Markowitz: "I should have computed the historic covariances of the asset classes and drawn an efficiency frontier. Instead, ... I split my contributions fifty-fifty between bonds and equities."

While some diversification is generally good, the extent of diversification is often naive, and suboptimal relative to the yardstick proposed in modern economic theory. However, if the calculations and information requirements in modern economic theory are beyond the ability of investors, then they must accept the associated "potential" suboptimality of the performance of heuristics, say, the $\frac{1}{n}$ heuristic.

One drawback of the $\frac{1}{n}$ heuristic is that the actual choice is skewed towards the more numerous option. For instance, when choosing from funds that mostly contain stocks, the $\frac{1}{n}$ heuristic will disproportionately skew the portfolio towards stocks. This is confirmed by a comparison of different pension plans in Benartzi and Thaler (2001). For instance, in the pension plan of Transworld Airlines, employees had the choice between five core stocks and one core bond which resulted in the average choice portfolio containing 75% stocks.

The experimental results in Baltussen and Post (2011) show that individuals do use the $\frac{1}{n}$ heuristic. But the heuristic is slightly modified to exclude those assets whose marginal returns are clearly unattractive. They also show that the use of this heuristic might involve the choice of first order stochastically dominated options.

Naive diversification takes many forms, of which the $\frac{1}{n}$ heuristic is an exemplar. In other forms of this heuristic, data from the US shows that individuals invest excessively in the stocks of their own companies (Mitchell and Utkus, 2002; Poterba, 2003). Individuals also invest too much in home stocks, perhaps on account of their greater familiarity, but in the process forgoing the diversification benefits from investing in foreign stock (French and Poterba, 1991; Solnik and Zuo, 2011).

Read and Loewenstein (1995) consider the behavior of trick-or-treaters on Halloween night. In their first treatment, the sequential choice condition, the children were offered a choice between two candies in two different houses. Three Musketeers in the first house and Milky Way, in the second house. The data show that 52% of the children picked up two pieces of their favorite candy at the two houses and 48% picked different candies. In the second treatment, at the first house the children visited they were told to "choose whichever two candy bars you like" from a large pile of both types of candies. In this case, they showed a strong desire to diversify and all children picked each candy of a different type.

10.5 Transaction Utility and Acquisition Utility

The concepts of transaction utility and acquisition utility that we introduce in this section can potentially explain a range of human behaviors (Thaler, 1985). Suppose that an individual places a subjective value, $v > 0$, on an object and pays a price p to acquire it. Then, the *acquisition utility*, u_A, of the individual is

$$u_A(v,p) = v - p. \tag{10.1}$$

The concept of acquisition utility corresponds to the traditional concept of *consumer surplus* in economics. It captures the extra utility received by an individual, over and above the price paid for it. This concept can be easily generalized to the purchase of multiple units of a good and a downward sloping demand curve for the good.

Transaction utility, u_T, is a different concept, which is not directly related to consumer surplus. For the purchase of an object at a price p, it is defined as

$$u_T(\overline{p},p) = \overline{p} - p, \tag{10.2}$$

where $\overline{p}$ is the *reference price* or the regular price that the consumer expects to pay for the object. There is no obvious link between v and $\overline{p}$. An important determinant of $\overline{p}$ is fairness, which depends on the seller's costs (Thaler, 1985).

Transaction utility is particularly salient at the time of making purchases, perhaps more salient than acquisition utility. Hence, it would dictate making a purchase when $\overline{p} - p$ is particularly high, even if acquisition utility is low. Humans appear to have a "taste for a good deal" or finding a "good bargain" on products. It would explain why retailers are keen to overemphasize the "great deals" that one gets in sales, and the popularity of events such as Black Friday in the USA and the UK (it is the Friday following Thanksgiving in the USA). In some cases, firms may artificially inflate initial prices at which very few people buy, and then subsequently drop them significantly to package it as an "amazing deal" in order to boost sales.

Example 10.13 *(Thaler, 1985, p. 189) You are lying on the beach on a hot day. All you have to drink is ice water. For the last hour you have been thinking about how much you would enjoy a nice cold bottle of your favorite brand of beer. A companion gets up to go make a phone call and offers to bring back a beer from the only nearby place where beer is sold at a fancy resort hotel [a small, run-down grocery store]. He says that the beer might be expensive and so asks how much you are willing to pay for the beer. He says that he will buy the beer if it costs as much or less than the price you state. But if it costs more than the price you state he will not buy it. You trust your friend, and there is no possibility of bargaining with the (bartender) [store owner]. What price do you tell him?*

The median willingness to pay for the beer from the resort in 1984 prices was \$1.50 from the grocery store and \$2.65 from the fancy resort hotel. Since the beer is identical from both sources, the acquisition utility is identical too, so this does not explain observed behavior. However, we can explain these findings if the decision criterion of the consumer is to use transaction utility to purchase the object, $u_T \geq 0$. If the reference price, $\overline{p}$, for the resort relative to the grocery shop is higher, then the consumer would also be willing to pay a higher actual price, p, for the resort beer.

10.6 Mental Accounting

Mental accounting has enormous significance for economics, but it is not a topic that most undergraduate students would have encountered. Thaler (1999, p. 186) defines mental accounting as follows: "I wish to use the term 'mental accounting' to describe the entire process of coding, categorizing, and evaluating events." This general definition subsumes several topics that we have considered under the broad heading of bounded rationality. These include coarse thinking and categorization, narrow and broad bracketing, and mental models, although these are often treated as separate topics.

We are also often interested in mental accounting in the domain of financial decisions. Thaler (1999, p. 183) provides a definition of financial mental accounting: "*mental accounting is the set of cognitive operations used by individuals and households to organize, evaluate, and keep track of financial activities.*" Consider the following interesting quote from Heath and Soll (1996, p.41) "in his study of unemployed workers in the 1930s, Bakke (1940, pp. 142–143) documented "all sorts" of budgeting arrangements from those that make use of small envelopes in which particular sums are put, or the series of china pitchers in the cupboard, to the ones who have checking accounts and carry on a fairly complicated bookkeeping." In their study of households in the 1950s, Rainwater, Coleman, and Handel (1959) described a process of "tin can accounting" in which households allocated funds into separate accounts symbolized by separate "envelopes, various drawers, or tin cans."

The following examples clarify some of the features of mental accounting.

Example 10.14 *(Thaler, 1999, p. 183) A former colleague of mine, a professor of finance, prides himself on being a thoroughly rational man. Long ago he adopted a clever strategy to deal with life's misfortunes. At the beginning of each year he establishes a target donation to the local United Way charity. Then, if anything untoward happens to him during the year, for example an undeserved speeding ticket, he simply deducts this loss from the United Way account. He thinks of it as an insurance policy against small annoyances.*

In Example 10.14, the Professor seems to have a mental account for "net miscellaneous outgoings" that include charitable giving, and misfortunes such as speeding ticket charges. By offsetting speeding ticket charges against a reduction in charitable giving, the Professor offsets two items within the same mental account against each other, so that the payment of a speeding ticket is not perceived as a loss; in other words the mental account does not go into the *red.*

Example 10.15 *(Thaler, 1999, p. 183) A few years ago I gave a talk to a group of executives in Switzerland. After the conference my wife and I spent a week visiting the area. At that time the Swiss franc was at an all-time high relative to the US dollar, so the usual high prices in Switzerland were astronomical. My wife and I comforted ourselves that I had received a fee for the talk that would easily cover the outrageous prices for hotels and meals. Had I received the same fee a week earlier for a talk in New York though, the vacation would have been much less enjoyable.*

Neoclassical economics assumes that the carriers of utility are the final wealth levels. In Example 10.15, the final wealth is identical in the two cases irrespective of whether the fee is received a week ago or after the talk; time discounting is hardly relevant over such a small time interval. Unless the Thalers were particularly liquidity constrained, neoclassical economic theory would find it difficult to explain their behavior.

Example 10.16 *(Thaler, 1999, p. 184) A friend of mine was once shopping for a quilted bedspread. She went to a department store and was pleased to find a model she liked on sale. The spreads came in three sizes: double, queen, and king. The usual prices for these quilts were $200, $250, and $300 respectively, but during the sale they were all priced at only $150. My friend bought the king-size quilt and was quite pleased with her purchase, though the quilt did hang a bit over the sides of her double bed.*

In Example 10.16, the friend (whose identity is revealed in Thaler, 2015) purchased an oversized quilt because it was a better deal relative to the normal price. Assuming that a better fitting quilt is more desirable, neoclassical economics would find it difficult to explain the oversized purchase. Also assuming that this behavior is not atypical, it is "as if" humans prefer a good deal. The distinction between transaction utility and acquisition utility (see Section 10.5) can address these sorts of puzzles.

In neoclassical economics, individuals have a global financial account that aggregates incomes and expenditures from all sources. In particular, this account is credited with an extra dollar whenever an extra dollar of income is earned, irrespective of the source of this income. The account is debited with an extra dollar whenever the individual spends an extra dollar on anything. Thus, *money is perfectly fungible* across all sources of income and all sources of expenditure. Even if the individual were to decide on classifying different sources of incomes or expenditures into different accounts, such a practice would be pointless in the sense that it would not alter observed behavior.

All this changes when we consider individuals who have bounded cognitive abilities and/or problems of self-control and limited attention. In this case, individuals may benefit from having a system of *mental accounts* that categorize incomes and expenditures into different accounts. These mental accounts have the following two important properties that are supported by the evidence, and can also be found in Examples 10.14, 10.15 (Thaler, 1999).

1. Money is not fungible across mental accounts. A credit or a debit into one account cannot be offset by a credit or debit into another account. For instance, mere labeling of the same amount of money in experiments under different headings (e.g., cash transfers, or in-kind transfers) influences how this money is spent, indicating nonfungibility across accounts (Abeler and Marklein, 2017). The behavior of people is consistent with the idea that different expenditure types, for example, food, energy, entertainment, are treated as different categories, or mental accounts, of expenditures. Similarly, different sources of earnings, such as money received as gifts, and money that is earned versus unearned, are also, in many cases, treated as being part of different mental accounts.

   Hastings and Shapiro (2013) provide evidence on nonfungibility of gas expenditures and other expenditure sources in the US. There is also a link between the source of income and how that income is spent. For instance, money that is received as gifts is more likely to be spent on frivolous expenditures (Levav and McGraw, 2009; Kardos and Castano, 2012). Kooreman (2000) shows that households are more likely to buy children's clothing out of exogenous child benefits as compared to other income sources. Epley et al. (2006) show that the marginal propensity of consumption is higher from income framed as a gain to current wealth relative to income that is framed as a return to past wealth. Many individuals are more likely to purchase a vacation when they receive a \$2000 gift as compared to a work bonus (Henderson and Peterson, 1992). Income received as windfall gains from dubious sources is more likely to be spent on utilitarian consumption such as school supplies rather than on hedonic consumption like ice cream (Levav and McGraw, 2009).
2. The objective of the individual is not necessarily to maximize overall financial wealth or minimize overall expenditure. Individuals desire to limit the size of the losses in the individual

accounts and they are particularly aversive to mental accounts going in the *red* (where the withdrawals exceed the deposits) and prefer them to stay in the *black* (deposits exceed withdrawals).

10.6.1 Mental Accounting and Consumption Choices

At the core of neoclassical economics is the temporal decisions made by individuals. The main method of solution is dynamic programming that we considered in Section 9.3. However, we showed that this imposes an unreasonable cognitive burden on individuals and invoking the "as if" argument to justify it is not empirically supported. An alternative method, that we discuss below, uses mental accounting and relies on the early work of Shefrin and Thaler (1988, 2004), Thaler and Shefrin (1981), and Thaler (1980, 1985).

Consider an individual who works for T periods and has a stream of income over the lifetime, given by $y_1, y_2, \ldots, y_T$. The individual retires in period T, so $y_T = 0$. Suppose that the individual uses a simple rule of thumb and saves a fraction, $\theta \in [0,1]$, of income each period for retirement and consumes the rest in that period. Shefrin and Thaler (2004) propose that in making consumption choices over the lifetime, individuals broadly have a system of three main mental accounts. The precise definitions of these accounts are not critical for us, but we are mainly interested in the implications that can follow from such a system of mental accounts.

1. A *current income account* (I) that is credited with income y_t at time t and an amount $(1-\theta)y_t$ is withdrawn from it for consumption at time t.
2. A *current asset account* (A) that at time t captures all the savings made to date. This is not simply the sum $\theta y_1 + \cdots + \theta y_{t-1}$ because the individual might also have received windfall gains/losses and other unexpected sources of incomes.
3. A *future wealth account* (F) that adds together all past savings and all anticipated future savings.

Shefrin and Thaler (2004, p. 401) write: "While the mental accounting system described here may seem bizarre to economists, it is remarkably similar to the accounting systems used by most private universities." Survey evidence in Graham and Isaac (2002) supports this mental accounting practice.

We highlight several features of interest arising from this framework.

1. Some mental accounts are more tempting to invade in the sense that it is easier to withdraw funds from them. Mental accounts that are labeled "wealth" rather than "income" are easier to invade. Other mental accounts that we have not considered in this framework might also be relatively more difficult to invade. For instance, people are reluctant to invade a "children's education mental account" that is designed to finance the future college/University education of a child. Some people find it useful to set up a book account that is credited with a sum of money every year to buy books, and they are reluctant to invade it for, say, entertainment expenses that are part of another mental account. For the three accounts that we have taken into consideration above, the evidence suggests that it is easiest to invade the current income

account, more difficult to invade the current asset account, and most difficult to invade the future wealth account.

2. The most obvious implication of the relative difficulty of invading different accounts is that people have an *account specific marginal propensity to consume* (this is the extra consumption for every $1 increase in credit into that account). Courant et al. (1986) report that the marginal propensity to consume out of the current asset account is about 0.25, but the marginal propensity to consume out of the future wealth account is significantly smaller. These results are also supported by the experiments with MBA students in Shefrin and Thaler (2004). Holbrook and Stafford (1971) find that the marginal propensities to consume out of labor and capital income are, respectively, 0.9 and 0.7. Shefrin and Thaler (2004) interpret the empirical evidence as suggesting that the marginal propensity to consume for (i) the current income account is approximately 1, (ii) the current asset account is between 0 and 1, and (iii) the future asset account is approximately 0. This is supported by the results in Levin (1998).

   Due to account-specific marginal propensities to consume, which account gets used to make higher contributions to pension plans is likely to impact on the savings rate. Choi et al. (2009) present evidence on this hypothesis from the 401(k) pension plans in the US, based on a change in rules in 2003. If an extra dollar in pension contributions comes out of the current income account, then it reduces savings one to one, because the marginal propensity to consume from this account is one. However, if this extra dollar comes out from the asset income account, then savings are not reduced one to one; in this case, part of the extra contribution to the pension plan comes about through a reduction in consumption. This has the overall effect of increasing savings (King and Dicks-Mireaux, 1982; Diamond and Hausmann, 1984). Similarly, if dividends and capital gains are allocated to different mental accounts by individuals, then the type of income from equity affects savings. Suppose, for instance, that dividends are classed as part of the current income account and capital gains as part of the future income account. Then, if firms decide to pay dividends to equity holders, the marginal propensity to consume of 1 from this account implies that the extra dividends will be entirely consumed. However, if the firm decides to pay no dividends and the income to equity holders takes the form of capital gains, then the marginal propensity to consume of zero from this account implies that no extra consumption will take place. The empirical results are supportive of this transmission channel (Baker et al., 2007).

   Small windfalls are coded by individuals as part of the current income account while larger windfalls are coded as part of the current asset account (Milkman and Beshears, 2009). Some individuals may place home equity in the current asset account, while others in the future wealth account. Dividend income might be placed in the current income account but asset income such as rents may be placed in the current asset account (Shefrin and Statman, 1984). Labor income is likely to be coded as current income and capital income as current asset income.

3. Mental accounting may arise from a desire to limit self-control problems. In other cases, self-control problems might influence how previously assigned mental accounts are misused. For instance, the assignment of income/expenditure into different mental accounts can be a grey area: Should an unexpected tax refund go into the current account or the asset account? Individuals might also engage in creative, or opportunistic, mental accounting to override

accounts set up to enhance self-control. Cheema and Soman (2006) cite the following example from Mark Twain. "Having limited himself to one cigar a day, he started shopping for bigger and bigger cigars until he had each made to such proportions that he 'could have used it as a crutch'." The loophole here arises because the original cigarette mental account of one cigar a day did not specify the size of the cigar. Soman and Cheema (2001) argue that windfalls, by their nature, are unexpected, hence, there is potential ambiguity about how they should be classified. Individuals may take advantage of this ambiguity to put windfall gains into those mental accounts that are in the red. For instance, such gains could be used to write off sunk costs.

4. At the time of forming mental accounts, individuals also need to estimate their future consumption levels. They might overestimate or underestimate future consumption, hence, they might set budgets for mental accounts that are too high or too low. Consider the following two examples from Heath and Soll (1996, p. 40) whose experimental results are consistent with the behavior exhibited in these examples.
   (a) "Mr. P recently went shopping for slacks. When he could not find any slacks he liked, he spent a similar amount of money on a sweater that he normally would not have purchased."
   (b) "Ms. C reluctantly declined a Sunday invitation to dinner because she had 'spent too much money' on tickets to the theater two days earlier. On questioning, she admitted that she would have enjoyed the dinner and was well able to afford it, but she felt compelled to decline because of the earlier theater expense."

It is quite likely that mental accounting is tied to the use of various judgment heuristics that we outlined in Chapter 9. For instance, an individual might wish to categorize items of income and expenditure based on how "similar" they are. Similarity may depend on the salience of different features of the outcomes, which in turn depend on the environmental cues available at the time of making decisions. One might then derive testable predictions for human behavior by varying the environmental cues and/or salience of different attributes of outcome. Evers et al. (2022) make progress in this direction. Our understanding of the foundations of mental accounting is likely to be much advanced in the coming years through a better understanding of the role of heuristics in this area.

10.6.2 Prospect Theory and Mental Accounting

Consider different sources of incomes that are either (i) gains relative to the reference point, or (ii) losses relative to the reference point, or (iii) mixed net gains relative to the reference point, or (iv) mixed net losses relative to the reference point. Would an individual prefer to integrate or segregate the different sources of income in each case (a form of mental accounting)? In each of these four cases, prospect theory (see Part I) predicts a pattern of aggregation and segregation that is consistent with the anecdotal evidence (Thaler, 1985).

One of the exercises, which is an essential accompaniment to this section, asks readers to check the following claims in a simple numerical example, although the results are general.

1. *Multiple gains are segregated*: If one receives a box of sweets one typically does not finish it in one go but tries to savor the enjoyment over time. Most people do not like to wrap all Christmas presents in one box. Both examples are a form of mental accounting and both are predicted to occur under prospect theory. Let $a > 0$ and $b > 0$ be two strictly positive outcomes relative to the reference point. Under prospect theory, the utility function for gains is strictly concave. Hence, the sum of the utilities of the individual gains is higher than the utility of the combined gains, so *gains should be segregated.*
2. *Multiple losses are integrated*: Sellers will often attempt to lump together items for sale; for instance, adding options to a car at the time of purchase. Consider two strictly negative outcomes, $a < 0$ and $b < 0$, expressed relative to a reference point. Most individuals prefer to incur the loss $a + b$ rather than incur two separate losses of a and b. Thus, it is optimal to integrate losses. Under prospect theory, the utility function for losses is strictly convex. Hence, the sum of the disutilities of the individual losses is higher than the disutility of the combined losses. Thus, prospect theory predicts that losses are integrated.
3. *Mixed net gains are integrated*: Consider two possible outcomes relative to a reference point, $a < 0$ and $b > 0$, such that we have mixed net gains, $a+b > 0$. The conjecture is that individuals will prefer to receive the combined amount $a + b$ rather than receive the separate amounts a and b. Under prospect theory, individuals suffer from loss aversion which magnifies perceived losses by a median value of about two times (see Part I). By combining the two outcomes for a net gain, they eliminate losses and prevent loss aversion from having a detrimental effect on utility. This is also sometimes known as the *principle of cancellation*; one can cancel the smaller loss against a larger gain.
4. *Mixed net losses and the silver lining principle*: In a bad year, CEOs of companies might particularly highlight a small positive news in the face of overwhelming negative news. Consider two possible outcomes relative to a reference point, $a < 0$ and $b > 0$, such that we have mixed net losses, $a + b < 0$. In general, we cannot say in this case if people will prefer to integrate or segregate the two amounts. However, there is one exception. Suppose that the absolute size of the gain is very small relative to a large loss. In other words, the very small gain appears as a silver lining against the large loss. In this case, individuals may prefer to receive the two amounts separately. This is known as the *silver lining principle*.

Evers et al. (2022) extend these ideas to choices over time. They first formalize the idea that objects belong to the same category (similar objects) or that they belong to different categories (dissimilar objects). Consider the following three events from their paper that are given to subjects. (1) You find out that the speed of your internet has decreased. (2) You find out that the cost of your internet has increased by 10. (3) You find out that the cost of your car insurance has since increased by 10. Clearly, events 1 and 2 appear similar to each other and are likely to be categorized together. However, event 3 is dissimilar to events 1 and 2 and likely to be classed in a different category.

The authors show experimentally that people prefer to receive similar losses close together in time, but they prefer to receive similar gains that are separated in time. However, this pattern reverses when the losses and gains are dissimilar. People prefer to receive dissimilar losses separated by time, but they wish to receive dissimilar gains close together in time.

By contrast, the findings from the previous literature were ambiguous. The authors assign the difference in findings to their experimental implementation of the idea of similarity and dissimilarity of items to categories.

10.6.3 Prepaying for Vacations and Postpaying for Consumer Durables

Many people like to prepay for vacations but prefer to buy consumer durables on credit and postpay for them. These different payment patterns are difficult to explain in neoclassical economics. The exponential discounted utility model in neoclassical economics (see Part III) would make two broad recommendations on payment methods.

1. Pay later rather than earlier because the future is discounted. Hence, the future costs are discounted and shrunk from the point of view of the present.
2. Compare the present discounted utility of the net benefits (benefits net of cost) arising from alternative payment streams and pick the one that offers the highest net present discounted utility of benefits. In particular, there is no preference for particular profiles of payments provided the net present discounted value of benefits is no higher.

Both features of EDU are violated in the following examples from Prelec and Loewenstein (1998) where individuals appear to give particular importance to the shapes of the payment profiles.

Example 10.17 *(Prepaying for vacations) Suppose that you are going to be away on vacation, six months from now. The cost of the vacation is* \$1200. *You can pay the total cost,* \$1200, *by one of two alternative methods. In method 1, you pay six monthly payments of* \$200 *prior to the vacation. In method 2, you pay six monthly payments of* \$200 *after returning from the vacation. In the experiments, 60% of the subjects preferred method 1 (preponement of payment) despite an implicit interest penalty of about* \$50 *arising from paying earlier.*

Two additional findings are as follows.

(i) Subjects also prefer to prepay for miscellaneous living expenses, and
(ii) a majority of subjects decline the offer of advance payment for work.

Example 10.18 *(Postpaying for consumer durables) Six months from now you will be purchasing a clothes washer-dryer that costs* \$1200. *There are two methods of paying. In method 1 you must pay in six equal monthly installments of* \$200 *starting now, while in method 2, you must pay in six equal monthly installments of* \$200 *with the first installment beginning in six months time. Now 84% of the subjects prefer method 2 (postponement of payment).*

In order to explain the preferences for alternative modes of payments, Prelec and Loewenstein propose a theory that is based on the following main ideas.

Hedonic Benefits or Net Experienced Utility

Suppose that the stream of utilities from a good, $u_t > 0, u_{t+1} > 0, \ldots, u_{t+j} > 0$, arise for j time periods, starting at time t. There is zero utility from the good beyond time $t + j$. The total price to pay for the good is P. For simplicity, we assume that the interest rate is zero.

Consider two polar opposite cases.

(a) The payments for the good have already been made prior to time t. Then, the good can be enjoyed at times $t, t+1, \ldots, t+j$ "as if" it were free in the current period. This is known as *prospective accounting*. Thus, the *hedonic benefits*, or *net experienced utility*, in each of the j future time periods is

$$u_t,\ u_{t+1}, \ldots,\ u_{t+j}. \tag{10.3}$$

(b) The payments for the good are made after time $t+j$ when the stream of utilities from the good have been exhausted. The payments last for l time periods (think of a mortgage), starting at a future time $k > t+j$, so payments occur at times $k, k+1, \ldots, k+l$. In this case, the stream of utilities at times $t, t+1, \ldots, t+j$ is mitigated by thoughts of future payments, and given by

$$u_t - \mu\hat{p}_t,\ u_{t+1} - \mu\hat{p}_{t+1}, \ldots,\ u_{t+j} - \mu\hat{p}_{t+j}, \tag{10.4}$$

where the constant term $\mu \geq 0$ is the the marginal utility of money. The terms $\hat{p}_t, \hat{p}_{t+1}, \ldots, \hat{p}_{t+j}$ capture, at each of the j time periods where the benefits are enjoyed, the *imputed future prices* to be paid. The imputed price at any time $\tau = t, t+1, \ldots, t+j$ is defined as

$$\hat{p}_\tau = \frac{\omega_\tau^c}{\sum_{s=\tau}^{t+j} u_s} P. \tag{10.5}$$

Thus, the imputed price at time τ depends positively on the total price, P, for the good to be paid in the future, and (ii) negatively on the remaining stream of utility or benefits from the good, $\sum_{s=\tau}^{t+j} u_s$. The term $\omega_\tau^c > 0$ is a time-dependent weight that shows what fraction of the future price contributes toward the imputed costs at time τ.

From (10.4) and (10.5) we can draw two conclusions. At the time of enjoying the benefits from a good, the thought of future payments is aversive in the sense that it reduces utility. Second, as the remaining benefits from the good diminish over the successive time periods $t, t+1, \ldots, t+j$, the imputed price increases. For instance, a ticking taxi meter in an unexpectedly expensive taxi trip in a foreign city might reduce one's enjoyment from the taxi ride. Furthermore, the closer one gets to one's destination, and the benefits from the ride diminish, the more miserable one might feel by the thought of impending payment for the expensive ride.

Hedonic Costs or Net Experienced Disutility

Let us now consider how the payment experience is influenced by thoughts of benefits received from the good. We introduce new time indices in this section, and these are not related to the previous case of hedonic benefits.

Suppose that the total price to pay for the good is P and it is paid over l time periods $t, t+1, \ldots, t+l$. There are two polar opposite cases depending on whether the stream of utilities (a) is to be received after the payments are made, or (b) whether it has already been received in the past.

(a) Suppose that the stream of utilities has already been received in the past, prior to time t. Then, the hedonic costs are identical to the actual stream of payments over the l time periods

$$p_t, p_{t+1}, \ldots, p_{t+l}.$$

(b) Suppose that the stream of utilities is to be received after all the payments have been made. In particular, suppose that the stream of utilities begins at time $k > t + l$ and lasts for j time periods, $u_k, u_{k+1}, \ldots, u_{k+j}$. The hedonic costs or *net experienced disutility* from making the payment in period $\tau = t, t+1, \ldots, t+l$ is

$$\hat{u}_\tau - \mu p_\tau, \tag{10.6}$$

where $\hat{u}_\tau$ is the imputed psychological benefit, at time τ, from the future consumption of the good. The imputed benefit offsets some of the payment p_τ at time τ, so that the net payment is experienced in the form given in (10.6). If $\hat{u}_\tau - \mu p_\tau > 0$, the imputed benefits more than fully offset the payment. We define

$$\hat{u}_\tau = \sum_{s=k}^{k+j} \omega_\tau^b u_s,$$

where the term $\omega_\tau^b > 0$ is a time dependent weight that shows what fraction of the future utility contributes towards the imputed costs at time τ. As an example, if the individual prepays in installments for a future vacation, then the thoughts of future enjoyment of the vacation mitigates the current costs of payment.

The feature of the model that (i) thoughts of future payments are aversive for current utility, and (ii) thoughts of future utilities reduce the perceived payments now, is known as *coupling*. Coupling is absent in the standard neoclassical model.

Another feature of the model that requires a more formal treatment than ours, is *prorating*. At any time, the remaining future benefits or costs are equally divided (prorated) over the remaining periods when the consumer constructs hedonic benefits and costs. This feature enters the model through the terms ω_τ^c and ω_τ^b that we have only discussed fleetingly; for a detailed treatment, see Prelec and Loewenstein (1998) and Dhami (2020, Volume V).

The purchase criterion of the individual is that the present discounted value of hedonic benefits is at least as high as the present discounted value of hedonic costs.

Figure 10.1 shows how the model explains prepayment for vacations (Example 10.17). The vertical axis measures hedonic costs of paying for the vacation (shown as vertical lines) and the stream of benefits (shown as the rectangular shape in panel A and the irregular polygon in panel B). The period of the vacation is marked along the horizontal axis, which measures time, with double-sided arrows. We consider two alternative payment options: prepayment before the vacations begins (panel A), and postpayment after the vacation ends (panel B).

Consider first prepayment, where the vacation is prepaid in equal monthly installments of \$$p$. Here, the benefit is received in the future, during the vacation period, when all costs have been prepaid. Since consumption that has been paid for can be enjoyed as if it were free (prospective accounting), the hedonic benefits, or net experienced utility, per period, equal the actual stream of utilities during each time period in the vacation, as in (10.3). For this reason, experienced

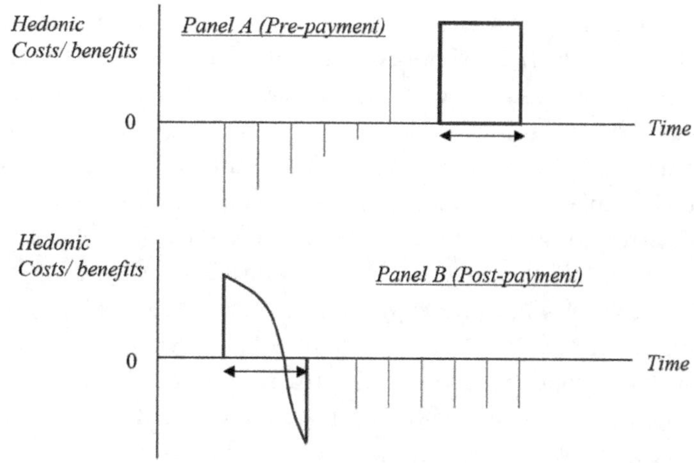

Figure 10.1 Hedonic costs (vertical lines) and hedonic benefits (shapes) for the two cases of prepayment (upper panel A) and postpayment (lower panel B) for vacations. The time period during which vacations are taken is shown by double-sided horizontal arrows

utility is shown by the area of the rectangle in panel A. By contrast, the hedonic costs (or net experienced disutility), shown by the vertical bars, fall over time because (i) the outstanding payments $\sum_{t\geq k} p_t$ get reduced, and (ii) thoughts of future benefits create anticipal utility and eventually outweight the cost of payment for the vacation towards the end of the payment period (the rightmost vertical line in panel A is above 0 to indicate this).

Now consider postpayment for the vacation in panel B, where all payments are made after the vacation. As the vacation progresses, some of the benefits have already been enjoyed, and the remaining benefits of the vacation fall. Hence, the hedonic benefits fall as the vacation progresses. Towards the end of the vacation, the remaining benefits are minimal while the complete set of payments looms large so the net hedonic benefits become negative (recall a ticking taxi meter towards the end of an expensive taxi ride). Thus, thoughts of future payment become increasingly aversive. Once the vacation ends, the vacation benefits have all been enjoyed in the past. Thus, the net hedonic costs are identical in every period, and equal to $\$p$ in every period, until all vacation costs are paid. Thus, all the lines in panel B are of identical length.

The optimal form of payment is made on the basis of present discounted value of hedonic benefits relative to the hedonic costs. Given the assumptions, prepaying for a vacation, and postpaying for consumer durables, is likely to turn out to be optimal.

10.6.4 Sunk Costs and Opportunity Costs

Neoclassical economics is based on *marginalist principles* that do not allow for sunk costs to influence decisions. For instance, firms produce at the point where marginal revenue equals marginal costs. The fixed costs of the firms, that are already sunk, do not influence how much the firm should produce. In choosing between alternative goods while facing a budget constraint, consumers choose in accordance with the following rule: equate the marginal rates of substitution to the ratio of prices. The sunk costs, which in this case might be the transport costs incurred by a consumer to reach a retailer, are not relevant. In contrast to these theoretical predictions, the experimental evidence shows that sunk costs influence human behavior.

Kahneman and Tversky (1984) highlight the role of sunk costs in an experiment where the first group of subjects were told that they had incurred sunk costs in purchasing a theater ticket for \$10. They were told that, however, they had lost the ticket before the event. The second group of subjects were told that they had lost an equivalent sum of money, \$10, but not in the form of the theater ticket. The subjects were then asked for their willingness to buy a theater ticket to attend a performance. Only 46% of the first group of subjects were willing to buy another ticket, but 88% of the second group was willing to buy a ticket. This is consistent with the theory that consumers create a mental account on "theater outings." Losing the ticket is seen as an outflow from this account, while losing an equivalent amount of money leaves this account unaffected.

In a variant of this experiment, the subjects in an experiment reported by Thaler (1980) were given the following information. Suppose that you purchased a ticket for \$100 to see a basketball game, but there is a blizzard on the day of the game. Will you go to see the game? The cost of the ticket is a sunk cost and, if the logic in neoclassical economics holds true, should not influence the decision to travel in a blizzard. Yet, those who already hold the ticket are more willing to travel in the blizzard. The mental accounting explanation is that there is a mental account for the basketball game which is debited for the \$100 when the ticket is purchased, hence, it goes in the red. If the game is missed, then the account must be closed in the red, which is aversive. However, for those who do not already hold a ticket, this is not true and they are more likely to be deterred from traveling in the blizzard.

Sunk costs do influence decisions, but they can depreciate over time, a phenomenon known as *payment depreciation*, as shown in the following example.

Example 10.19 *(Thaler, 1999) Suppose that you buy shoes that seem comfortable at the time of buying, but after wearing them for a day they feel uncomfortable. You try wearing them for the next few days but it gets worse. At this point, the shoes cannot be returned because of the wear and tear on them (hence, their purchase is a sunk cost). Thaler makes the following plausible conjectures:*

(1) If the shoes are more expensive, you will try to wear them more often, despite the discomfort.
(2) You will eventually stop wearing the shoes, but the more expensive are the shoes, the longer they will sit in the closet before being eventually thrown away.
(3) Irrespective of how expensive the shoes, they are eventually thrown away.

Conjectures 1 and 2 arise on account of the influence of *sunk costs*, while conjecture 3 illustrates *payment depreciation*, that is, sunk costs are eventually ignored. Sunk costs need not depreciate all the way down to zero for their effect to become unnoticeable. Using data on health club memberships, Gourville and Soman (1998) show that when sunk costs depreciate and fall below some lower, but still positive, threshold, the mental account is closed. The individual no longer worries at this stage if the account is in the red. We can use the concepts of *acquisition utility* and *transaction utility* (see Section 10.5) to understand how payment depreciation works in the next example.

Example 10.20 *In Section 10.5, we argued that people use transaction utility to make the purchase decision. However, it is also likely that they evaluate the subsequent experience in terms of acquisition utility. In Example 10.19, the shoe turns out to be smaller than expected, hence, ex post, the valuation of the shoe, v, is lower. Since the individual might find it impossible to wear an ill fitting shoe, perhaps because it hurts too much, let us assume that ex post the shoe is worthless, so* $v = 0$. *Thus, using (10.1), the acquisition utility is* $-p$ *per period. This turns the mental account for shoe purchase in the red by the dollar amount p. Suppose now that sunk costs depreciate continuously at the rate* δ *at each instant in time and the mental account is closed when the sunk costs depreciate and fall below a lower bound* $\underline{c}$. *This occurs at time t after the purchase of the shoe, where t can be found from the equality*

$$pe^{-\delta t} = \underline{c}. \tag{10.7}$$

The calculation on the LHS of (10.7) is the value of the depreciated sunk costs; see Part III for this calculation. The higher is the price p at which the shoes were purchased, the higher will be the time t at which the sunk costs will depreciate to a level beyond which they can be ignored. Hence, useless, but more expensive shoes are held on for longer before being thrown away.

Opportunity costs are the bedrock of modern neoclassical economics. In evaluating any action, individuals are assumed to take complete account of the opportunity cost of their action. For instance, when deciding on the purchase of a pint of beer in a student union bar in a UK university, a student must take complete account of the opportunity cost of a pint, which is its price, typically about £2.36. Sometimes, things do not have a market price. For instance, students volunteering their time for a good cause on campus must take account of the opportunity cost of their time, or the cost of the foregone activity that could have been undertaken in this time. Such costs are likely to vary between students.

Undergraduate students in economics are repeatedly tested on opportunity costs in lectures and classes. Shafir and Thaler (2006) put this concept to the test among subscribers of a wine newsletter. The wine newsletter in question, *Liquid Assets*, used to be published by the economist Orley Ashenfelter. The subscribers are extremely knowledgeable wine consumers who have substantial home cellars. In many cases, these are economists or business executives, so they should, in principle, be explicitly or implicitly aware of opportunity costs.

Example 10.21 *(Shafir and Thaler, 2006) "Suppose you bought a case of a good 1982 Bordeaux in the futures market for* \$20 *a bottle. The wine now sells at auction for about* \$75 *a bottle. You have decided to drink a bottle. Which of the following best captures your feelings of the cost to you of drinking this bottle?" The respondents chose from five different options:* \$0, \$20, \$20 *plus interest,* \$75, *and* $-$\$55. *The percentages of respondents choosing each answer was 30, 18, 7, 20 and 25.*

The opportunity cost of drinking a bottle of wine is \$75, because this is what must be paid now to buy a bottle of wine. The original cost of \$20 for the bottle is a sunk cost, which is irrelevant. Yet, 30% of the respondents report that drinking the bottle costs nothing. A total of 55% ($30 + 18 + 7$) of the respondents rate the current cost of drinking the wine to be less than the opportunity cost of \$75. There is substantial heterogeneity in answers, which suggests that the subjects are possibly using different heuristics in responding to the question.

People who choose the −$55 option, for instance, think that the value of the investment turned out to be $75, but they paid $20 in costs, so they saved $55. But this is not consistent with an opportunity cost calculation. When the experimental instructions were rephrased in terms of giving the bottle away rather than drinking it, then 30% of the subjects gave the correct answer, $75. Thus, "giving away the bottle" is more likely to induce the answer predicted by neoclassical economics. An even larger proportion of the subjects, 55%, exhibit behavior consistent with opportunity costs if the question is rephrased in terms of the wine bottle having been broken accidentally, which makes the replacement costs even more salient.

Consider a second experiment from the same paper.

Example 10.22 *(Shafir and Thaler, 2006) "Suppose you buy a case of Bordeaux futures at* $400 *a case. The wine will retail at about* $500 *a case when it is shipped. You do not intend to start drinking this wine for a decade. At the time that you acquire this wine, which statement more accurately captures your feelings?"*

(a) I feel like I just spent $400, *much as I would feel if I spent* $400 *on a weekend getaway.*
(b) I feel like I made a $400 *investment which I will gradually consume after a period of years.*
(c) I feel like I just saved $100, *the difference between the futures cost and what the wine will sell for when delivered.*

Participants were asked to give a score from 1 (strongly agree) to 5 (strongly disagree) to each of the three options. The mean scores for the three choices were, respectively, 3.31, 1.94, 2.88 (note that the lower the score the stronger the agreement). Hence, responders gave the highest approval to option (b), the investment option, rather than the saving option (c).

The two experiments lead the authors to conclude the following. The wine connoisseurs think of the initial purchase as an investment. At a later date, the wine is drunk as if it were free. This is identical to *prospective accounting* in the Prelec and Loewenstein (1998) model that we discussed in Section 10.6.3. Hence, the title of their paper: *Invest Now, Drink Later, Spend Never*.

The form of sunk costs, for instance, whether they are incurred in dollar value or in terms of "time" appears to matter. Soman (2001) shows that *sunk-time costs* have a smaller effect on actual actions relative to *sunk-dollar costs* and he offers conjectures for why this might be the case. First, time is a flow variable making it difficult for an individual to construct an inventory of the time expended on various activities. Second, in contrast to dollar costs, the disutility from expending time depends on how enjoyable/productive the activities undertaken during this time were. Third, people may have better training in accounting for money as compared to time. The evidence in Okada and Hoch (2004) shows that individuals' willingness to pay is higher for risky options that involve time rather than money. Rajagopal and Rha (2009) show that, like dollar amounts, time is not fungible across different mental accounts.

10.6.5 Mental Account and the Source of Earnings

Tasimi and Gelman (2017) propose that physical currency may inherit "moral valence" from its past use. Thus, whether the money was ethically or unethically obtained in the past may make a difference in terms of which mental account it ends up in the present, and hence how it is potentially spent. They write (pp. 524–525):

> In virtually all societies, money can be considered as either "clean" or "dirty" based on how it was acquired ... with implications for how it is spent, or even whether it can be spent. Moreover, anthropological fieldwork suggests that at least in some communities, moral history affects physical currency itself ... For example, among the Luo of Kenya, bad money – or bitter money – obtains its status through theft and harm; such money is considered dangerous and can only become good through an elaborate purification ritual. These provocative findings suggest that money, like other physical objects, may be viewed as retaining traces of its moral history.

Interestingly, the source of nonmonetary goods also alters their perceived value. For instance people may be reluctant to wear clothing worn previously by someone who is disliked or no longer alive. On the other hand, clothing previously worn by celebrities is highly valued in the market.

In their experiments, Tasimi and Gelman (2017) provided subjects with five different scenarios in which they could receive a dollar. Each scenario represents a different source of income. Subjects had to say for each dollar offered to them, from each source of income, how much they "wanted" the dollar on a Likert scale of 1–7, where 1 meant "not at all" and 7 meant "very much". The five different sources can be described as follows (Tasimi and Gelman, 2017, p. 526):

1. Neutral-giver/neutral-money (e.g., "Henry has a dollar in his desk. Henry says you can have the dollar, if you want.")
2. Bad-giver/neutral-money (e.g., "Paul stole a dollar from another person. The dollar that he stole is in his pocket. Paul has another dollar that he did not steal, in his desk. Paul says you can have the dollar in his desk, if you want.")
3. Neutral-giver/bad-money (e.g., "Frank found a stolen dollar in his desk. Frank says you can have the dollar, if you want.")
4. Bad-giver/bad-money (e.g., "Brian stole a dollar from another person. Brian says you can have the dollar, if you want.")
5. Dirty-money (e.g., "Marvin sneezed and used a dollar to wipe his nose. Marvin says you can have the dollar, if you want.").

The results are shown in Figure 10.2. The source of the money determines how much individuals want it. As one goes through sources 1 to 5, in that order, it is less desirable to have the dollar. In successive experiments, the authors control for potential confounds such as stake sizes, whether the stolen money can be traced by a third party, and whether anyone could find out that the subjects were in receipt of the stolen money. The qualitative results remained comparable despite taking account of these confounds.

Individuals are more likely to donate to charity a part of the money that they earned through unethical means, relative to ethical means (Gneezy et al., 2014). Imas et al. (2021) identify an intriguing *mental money laundering* phenomenon. If subjects are given an opportunity to launder unethical money and convert it into ethical money, then they spend this money as if it were earned ethically. In their experiments, the money laundering process took place as follows. Subjects were asked to deposit their earnings, potentially earned through unethical means, into

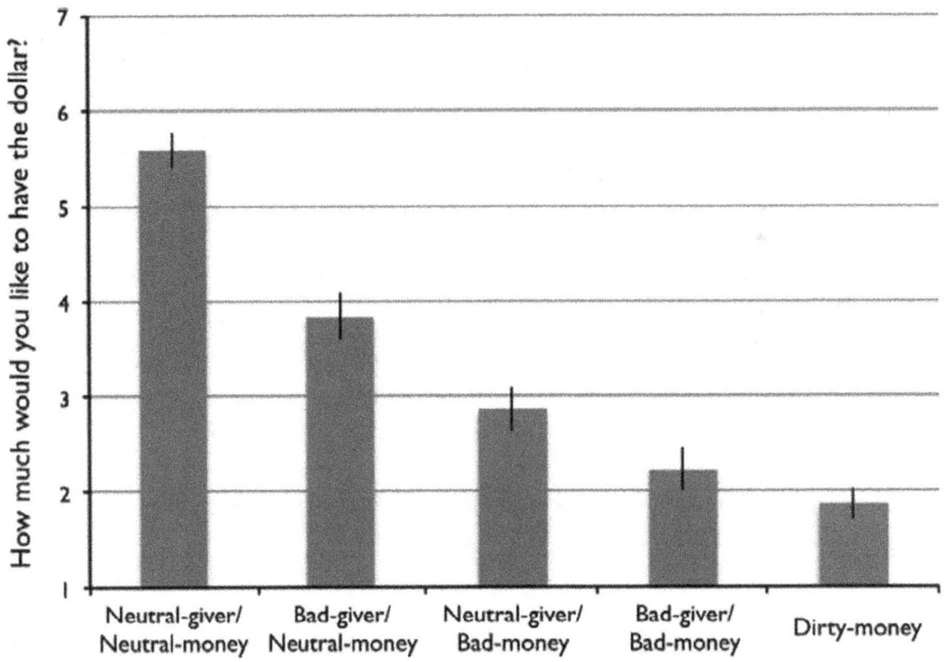

Figure 10.2 Mean ratings of how much subjects would want a dollar, on a scale of 1–7 (1 means "not at all" and 7 means "very much"), across five different scenarios. Error bars represent SE. Source: Tasimi and Gelman (2017)

a box and entered into a lottery. They won the lottery with a high probability, and the earnings from the lottery, which were identical to the original amount deposited in "dirty money," were given back to the subjects using a second box that contained physically different dollar bills. These new dollar bills were interpreted as "clean money" by the subjects. In another treatment, the subjects could pool together ethical and unethical money. In this case, they spent the pooled money as if it were all ethical money. Thus, pooling with ethical money appears to place the unethical money in a different mental account that has a different marginal propensity to consume. A final treatment allowed subjects to actively seek out such money laundering schemes but the findings suggested limited sophistication in realizing that such pooling could "clean" unethical money.

10.6.6 A Note on the Behavioral Economics of Retirement Savings

In this section, we briefly summarize some of the insights that have arisen from work on the behavioral economics approach to retirement savings; for informative surveys, see Thaler and Benartzi (2007), Benartzi and Thaler (2013), and Beshears et al. (2018).

The take-up of pension plans is often suboptimal. Many different reasons have been suggested, particularly present-biased preferences that give rise to procrastination and inertia in signing up for the plans. Governments across the world have tried to encourage pension contributions through favorable tax treatment of contributions, such as tax deductible contributions and tax deferred accumulations of pension savings. A particularly simple behavioral intervention, which is of the nature of a nudge, has been fairly effective in increasing enrollment in such plans. This intervention is an *opt-out default option* that automatically enrolls an individual in the plan, but individuals can choose to opt-out by filling in a form if they desire (Choi et al., 2002, 2004). In the converse case of the *opt-in default*, where individuals are automatically excluded from the plan but can choose to opt-in by filling in a form, participation is much lower.

Defaults can be effective in influencing choices for many reasons.

1. Initial preferences, particularly for new or unknown options, need to be constructed through a cognitively costly process. By contrast, accepting the default is cognitively simpler (Slovic, 1995).
2. Individuals might view defaults as being the option endorsed by a suitable choice architect.
3. Individuals might associate potential losses with moving away from a default option, a channel that might be strengthened in the presence of loss aversion.
4. Once a default option is established it becomes the status quo and individuals might have a status-quo bias in moving away from this option, inducing inertia to stick with the choice.

There is a negative correlation between the number of investment options offered in pension plans and the participation rates. A simplification of pension plans, for instance, in terms of a preselected contribution rate and asset allocation, improves the take-up of pension plans (Choi et al., 2009; Beshears et al., 2013). The initial contribution rates in many savings plans were, ex-post, found to be too low. The inbuilt default savings rate in many pension plans is $2\% - 3\%$ and the investment choices are conservative (e.g., money market account). Plan participants often appear to use heuristics to decide on contribution rates as multiples of five, or they simply save at the minimum rate required to get employers to match at the upper allowable limit.

If plan participants use the $\frac{1}{n}$ diversification heuristic, then adding options to the 401(k) plans might have little effect when the number of options is already large. Two additional features of portfolio allocation are of interest.

1. Thaler and Benartzi (2007) report that 33% of individuals who own company stock do not realize that it is more risky, relative to a diversified portfolio. Company stock is possibly a unique asset that is neither viewed as equity not as bonds (Benartzi and Thaler, 2001). Portfolios in retirement plans that lack company stock are normally split evenly between bonds and stocks. But in the presence of company stock, pension portfolios were found to invest 43% in company assets and the rest was split evenly between stocks and bonds. Hence, in the presence of company stock, pension portfolios end up investing a disproportionate amount of the pension savings, about 71%, in equities.
2. Individuals often overly extrapolate past performance of a stock for the foreseeable future, hence, portfolio allocation might not be optimal from a finance theory benchmark (Benartzi, 2001). The availability of faster information on the Internet and other newer communication media means that the variability of stock prices will be even more salient. The latter will possibly create even greater myopic loss aversion, distorting asset allocation.

Some elements of plan design can play a beneficial role in boosting savings. A leading example is the "Save more tomorrow" (SMarT program) plan (Benartzi and Thaler, 2004). It has three features that are likely to have contributed to its success.

(i) Suppose that workers were asked to commit to increasing their plan contributions now, conditional on the current wage. Since workers may be loss averse, current contributions may be viewed as a loss in current consumption, so this might not be successful in increasing savings. Hence, a more promising strategy, incorporated in the SMarT program, is to have workers agree, now, to deduct a fraction of a future wage increase as additional saving contributions, up to a certain limit; sometimes known as *automatic escalation*.
(ii) If the reference income level of workers is the current wage level, then additional contributions out of potential future income do not induce loss aversion.
(iii) Furthermore, if workers exhibit hyperbolic discounting and are present-biased, they are more likely to accept the SMarT plan because the costs and the benefits of this action arise in the future.

The evidence indicates that the SMarT plan has led to significant increases in savings (Benartzi and Thaler, 2013).

10.7 Projection-Bias

In making predictions about their own preferences or emotional states in the future, individuals are often unduly influenced by their current preferences and tastes. In this case, individuals are said to exhibit *projection-bias*.

Several experiments document the presence of projection-bias. For instance, when ordering a meal in a satiated state, people are likely to order healthier food and when ordering in a hungry state they are more likely to order unhealthy food. When ordering food for dinner, just after lunch, they order healthier food relative to ordering just before lunch (Read and van Leeuwen, 1998; Gilbert et al., 2002; VanEpps et al., 2016). The most likely explanation is that in a currently hungry state, subjects overestimate their future hunger, and in a currently satiated state, they underestimate future hunger. Thus, people project their current tastes onto future tastes.

Similarly, in smoking the next cigarette, an underappreciation of the effect on the future desire to smoke may lead smokers to greater current consumption. In their experiments, Smith et al. (2008) asked patients awaiting a kidney transplant to predict their quality of life in a year's time if they did, or did not, receive the transplant. Subjects predicted their quality of life to be much lower if they did not receive a transplant. A year later, subjects were invited to report on their actual quality of life. The subjective predictions made earlier, failed. The quality of life predicted by patients who received the transplant was lower relative to the actual quality of life. Those who did not receive the transplant rated their quality of life higher than their prediction a year ago.

Read and Loewenstein (1999) elicited subjects' willingness to accept money in return for accepting pain in the future. There were three groups of subjects. Group 1 had experienced pain (a dip of the hand in very cold water) just prior to the decision. Group 2 had experienced the same pain one week earlier and Group 3 had not experienced the pain. Group 1 asked for the highest money in return for experiencing future pain, Group 2 the next highest, and Group 3 the lowest. This is consistent with projection bias. Women who currently have no pain and have to predict whether they will need an epidural injection at childbirth, underpredict the chance that they will ask for the injection at childbirth.

In explaining projection bias, Loewenstein et al. (2003) highlight the following two salient features.

1. Individuals are able to predict the future *direction* of taste changes.
2. Individuals under-appreciate the true *magnitude* (or absolute value) of the future change in tastes.

Example 10.23 *Consider the following quote from Loewenstein (2005, pp. 96–97) that many academics will relate to. "Like many academics, I often face the decision of whether to accept an invitation to present at a conference or university … In such cases, I try to base my decision on benefits and costs … How I feel at the exact moment when I make the decision should not matter. But it does. If I'm already on a trip when the invitation arrives, my decision often depends on how tired I am. If I'm jetlagged in another country, I'm likely to reject an invitation for travel that involves crossing time zones or even for a conference near home if it seems likely to require effort. Yet, if fresh and rested, I probably would accept those same invitations. The same rule holds when I'm at home; in a good mood and feeling energetic, the prospect of travel seems pleasurable; in a funk or tired, the same trip looms onerously. I know that my immediate feelings should have no impact on the decision, and I try to correct for them, but not, I believe, with much success."*

Let us formalize projection bias in a simple manner. An individual lives for T time periods, $t = 1, 2, \ldots, T$. Suppose that the set $S = \{s_1, s_2, \ldots, s_k\}$ contains a list of k possible "states" of the individual; any of these states may occur at time t. We may take a "state" to mean the preferences/tastes, or even the emotional states of an individual, depending on what we are interested in modeling. The state of the individual at time t is denoted by $s_t \in S$. The instantaneous utility of the individual at time t is given by the utility function

$$u(c_t, s_t),$$

where c_t denotes the consumption at time t and s_t is the individual's state at time t.

For the rest of this section, we assume a simple case where there are only two possible states ($k = 2$) of the world: hungry "h" or satiated/full, "f" so that $S = \{h, f\}$. Let c_t denote the consumption of food. Then, at time t, $u(c_t, h)$ gives the utility of the individual when hungry; and $u(c_t, f)$ gives the utility of the individual when full. Consider the following two restrictions on the utility function.

$$(i)\ u(c_t, f) > u(c_t, h),$$

that is, for the same level of consumption, the utility of the individual is higher when satiated relative to when the individual is hungry.

$$(ii)\ \frac{du(c_t, f)}{dc_t} < \frac{du(c_t, h)}{dc_t},$$

that is, the marginal utility of consumption is higher when the individual is hungry relative to when the individual is full.

Suppose that, at time t, the current state of the individual is s_t, which is known to the individual. Since we want to hold fixed the level of consumption, we drop the prefix t and denote current consumption by c. The individual is now asked, at time t, to predict the utility from an identical level of consumption c at some future time $t+j, j > 0$, when the future state is $s_{t+j} \in S$ and the current state is $s_t \in S$. Denote this prediction by $\widetilde{u}(c, s_{t+j} \mid s_t)$.

Following Loewenstein et al. (2003), an individual exhibits projection bias if for all c, s_t and s_{t+j}, there exists a number $\alpha \in (0, 1]$ such that

$$\widetilde{u}(c, s_{t+j} \mid s_t) = \alpha u(c, s_t) + (1 - \alpha)u(c, s_{t+j}); \ \alpha \in (0, 1]. \tag{10.8}$$

Thus, the prediction made at time t about utility at time $t+j$ is a linear combination of the current instantaneous utility and the actual instantaneous utility in the relevant state. The current state, s_t, influences one's prediction of future utility. There are two polar opposite cases.

1. If $\alpha = 0$, then we have the neoclassical case of no projection bias, so $\widetilde{u}(c, s_{t+j} \mid s_t) = u(c, s_{t+j})$.
2. At the other extreme, when $\alpha = 1$, the individual is maximally projection-biased and $\widetilde{u}(c, s_{t+j} \mid s_t) = u(c, s_t)$. Thus, the individual predicts future utility to be identical to current utility, even if the future state is different from the current state.
3. If $0 < \alpha < 1$, then we have intermediate degrees of projection bias. In particular, the individual accurately predicts the direction of change in tastes, but underpredicts their magnitude.

Since, there are only two possible states in each of the time periods t and $t+j$, there is a total of $2 \times 2 = 4$ possibilities: $(h,h), (f,h), (f,f), (h,f)$, which are described below.

$$(i) \quad \widetilde{u}(c,h \mid h) = \alpha u(c,h) + (1 - \alpha)u(c,h) = u(c,h). \tag{10.9}$$

$$(ii) \quad \widetilde{u}(c,f \mid h) = \alpha u(c,h) + (1 - \alpha)u(c,f). \tag{10.10}$$

$$(iii) \quad \widetilde{u}(c,f \mid f) = \alpha u(c,f) + (1 - \alpha)u(c,f) = u(c,f). \tag{10.11}$$

$$(iv) \quad \widetilde{u}(c,h \mid f) = \alpha u(c,f) + (1 - \alpha)u(c,h). \tag{10.12}$$

From (10.9) and (10.11), if the current state is identical to the future state, then there is no projection bias. But when these states are different, as in (10.10) and (10.12), and $\alpha > 0$, then projection bias exists.

Consider the following numerical example.

$$u(c,h) = 8, \ u(c,f) = 16, \ \alpha = 0.5,$$

then for the two cases in (10.10) and (10.12), where the states are different in both time periods, we have

$$\widetilde{u}(c,f \mid h) = 12.$$

$$\widetilde{u}(c,h \mid f) = 12.$$

1. When the current state is h and the future state is f, predicted utility is $\widetilde{u}(c,f \mid h) = 12$, which is lower than the objectively correct estimate $u(c,f) = 16$. Hence, the direction of the change (from 8 to 12) is correctly predicted, but the magnitude of the change (4 instead of 8) is underappreciated.

2. When the current state is f and the future state is h, predicted utility is $\widetilde{u}(c,h \mid f) = 12$, which is higher than the objectively correct estimate $u(c,h) = 8$. Here too, the change (-4 instead of -8) is underappreciated but the direction of change, a fall in utility, is correctly anticipated.

Much empirical evidence is consistent with people behaving in the manner predicted by projection bias. Transitory emotional or environmental states may induce people to buy products that, under neoclassical economics, would require taking a longer term perspective. For instance, higher pollution on a given day might induce more people to buy health insurance plans (Chang et al., 2018). Using US data on 40 million new and used car transactions in car dealerships, Busse et al. (2015) show that temperature that is 10°F higher than normal, increases the sales of convertible cars by 2.7%. Furthermore, abnormally high snowstorms lead to an increase in the sales of four-wheel drive vehicles by 6% over the next few weeks when a snowstorm leads to snow accumulation of approximately 10 inches. Conlin et al. (2007) show that returns of cold weather items, ordered through catalogs, are influenced by projection bias arising from current weather conditions. They find that if the temperature on the date that an order is placed declines by 30°F, then the probability that the item is returned increases by 3.95%. The interpretation is that people overestimate their need for future cold weather items on a cold day, hence, they might need to make a correction to the order once the projection bias is discovered in the future.

Odermatt and Stutzer (2019) used data on 180,000 observations from the German Socio-Economic Panel. Participants were asked to predict their life satisfaction in five years' time. When compared to their actual life satisfaction five years later, significant prediction errors are found when the relevant states at the time of making the future predictions are unemployment, disability, and widowhood. In general, people make unduly pessimistic predictions of the future in these states. Loewenstein et al. (2003) consider the implications for intertemporal choice of consumption profiles in the presence of habit formation and projection bias.

Loewenstein (2005) explores the implications for medical decision making. Doctors sometimes struggle to get some people to complete their courses of antibiotics once their symptoms ease. This is because people project their current healthy state, as the symptoms ease, to the future, and believe that they need not take more antibiotics. Projection bias can be applied backwards in time. For instance, an individual who is depressed might report to a doctor that they have always been depressed in the past, projecting their current state backward in time. One's projection bias can also be used to judge others who might be in a different affective state. For instance, in a state where individuals are not craving for a drug, they judge the consumption of drugs by others more harshly, relative to the state where they themselves crave for the drug. Loewenstein (2005) gives several examples where projection bias might impact on the actual medical treatment received by a patient.

1. Doctors deciding on behalf of patients, or trying to maximize the welfare of patients, might not be in the same affective state (e.g., pain, discomfort) as the patient. Doctors might also vary in their feelings of empathy – how much they are able to place themselves in the patient's affective state. Hence, there are likely to be variations in the quality of treatment offered by doctors.

2. Suppose that patients are asked to make decisions on their future health/care plans at a time when they are in a state of shock having received a positive result, say, for cancer. Then their decisions might be quite different from those made a time when they have affectively calmed down.
3. Patients considering end of life decisions (e.g., on life support) in an affective state where they are in pain, extreme distress, and depression, may exaggerate their misery in the future. Hence, they might not be able to make decisions in their long-term interests.

10.8 Aspiration Adaptation

Recall issues of procedural rationality that were raised in the discussion on intertermporal mathematical optimization in Section 9.3. Even in relatively simple problems, trillions of calculations are required to determine the optimal solution. The work of Herbert Simon and Reinhard Selten provides us with a boundedly rational alternative to mathematical optimization (Simon, 1957; Selten, 1998). Simon proposed *satisficing*, a neologism that combines the words *satisfy* and *suffice.*

The idea behind satisficing is simple enough. Individuals and firms have an initial *aspiration level* which could be a level of utility, happiness, satisfaction level, goal, or a reference point, that they wish to achieve. In our discussion below, we take the aspiration level to be a level of utility. The aspiration level could be determined by the individual entity (individual or firms). Or it could be externally given, for instance, it might have legal, cultural, or social origins. Among the possible alternatives that an individual chooses from, an alternative is said to be *satisfactory* if it meets or exceeds the aspiration level.

Once an aspiration level is set, the individual needs to search for alternatives that will help achieve the aspiration level. This leads to the well-known *infinite regress problem in search.* In order to search for the alternatives, the individual needs to search for the unknown costs of searching for these alternatives. But searching for the unknown costs requires knowing the unknown costs for the search of the unknown costs, and so on, ad infinitum. In order to address this problem, Simon proposed the use of the following *simple stopping rule* which captures the limited sense in which individuals optimize in this model.

"Immediately stop searching for more alternatives when the utility from the current choice exceeds the aspiration level."

The aspiration levels are not fixed, and they are updated over time through a dynamic process that takes account of past payoffs and past aspirations. For instance, if payoffs from a choice are below (respectively, above) the aspiration level, then the aspiration levels may be adjusted downwards (respectively, upwards). Simon (1978, p. 503) writes: "In a benign environment that provides many good alternatives, aspirations rise; in a harsher environment, they fall."

We argued in Part IV that the prisoner's dilemma is a useful metaphor for human cooperation in the social and behavioral sciences. Yet, classical game theory cannot explain the choice of the cooperative outcome by 50% – 60% of the subjects in experiments on the static prisoner's dilemma game. Let us explore if aspiration adaptation can provide a potential explanation for

Table 10.1 The prisoner's dilemma game

	C	D
C	2,2	0,3
D	3,0	1,1

this evidence. The prisoner's dilemma game is shown in Table 10.1; readers may wish to refresh their understanding of this game by revisiting Part IV.

In order to explore the dynamic process through which aspirations arise, suppose that the prisoner's dilemma game is played repeatedly over time $t = 0, 1, 2, \ldots$ At time $t = 0$, no decisions are made; this time period is used only to define the initial "state" of the dynamic system, such as initial aspirations.

Strategies and Utilities

In the prisoner's dilemma game, there are two players, indexed by $i = 1, 2$; player 1 is the row player and player 2 is the column player. Each player chooses between one of two strategies, *cooperation* (C) and *defection* (D). At any time $t = 1, 2, \ldots$, both players simultaneously choose either C or D. The action/strategy of player i at time t is denoted by $s_{it} \in \{C, D\}$. The strategy profile of both players at time t is denoted by $s_t = (s_{1t}, s_{2t})$. For instance, if both players choose D at time t, the strategy profile is (D, D); and if player 1 chooses C and player 2 chooses D, the strategy profile is (C, D). The initial strategy profile is endogenously given by the history of the game, and denoted by $s_0 = (s_{10}, s_{20})$. The payoffs in the payoff matrix in Table 10.1 are assumed to represent utilities. For instance, if the strategy profile at time t is $s_t = (C, C)$, then the instantaneous utility of player $i = 1, 2$ at time t is given by $u_i(s_t) = u_i(C, C) = 2$.

In classical game theory, the choice of strategies in repeated games is a complete contingent plan of actions. However, under aspiration adaptation, strategies are chosen by simple rules of thumb that depend on the data on aspirations and the gap between aspirations and utility in the previous period, as we show below.

Aspirations

The aspiration level of player i at time t, measured in units of utility, is denoted by a_{it}, and the initial time $t = 0$ aspirations of the players, a_{10} and a_{20}, are exogenously given. The aspirations of the two players at any time t are given by the vector $a_t = (a_{1t}, a_{2t})$.

The process by which the aspiration levels of the two players evolve over time is determined as follows.

$$a_{it} = a_{it-1} + \gamma \left[u_i \left(s_{t-1} \right) - a_{it-1} \right]; 0 \leq \gamma \leq 1, t = 1, 2, \ldots \tag{10.13}$$

From (10.13), aspirations evolve according to a simple *adaptive expectations* rule. At the beginning of time t, the current aspiration of player i, denoted by a_{it}, equals the aspiration at time $t-1$, a_{it-1}, adjusted for the difference between the utility and the aspiration levels at time $t-1$, $u_i \left(s_{t-1} \right) - a_{it-1}$. The size of the parameter γ measures the weight of this past adjustment for current aspirations. In particular, if $u_i(s_{t-1}) - a_{it-1}$ is positive, then current aspirations are adjusted upwards; otherwise current aspirations are adjusted downwards.

Behavioral Rule for the Choice of Strategies

For any player $i = 1, 2$, we denote the strategy that is "chosen" by $s_{it}^c \in S_i = \{C, D\}$ and the "unchosen" strategy by $s_{it}^u \in S_i = \{C, D\}$. Suppose player i chooses strategy D at time t, then $s_{it}^c = D$ (chosen strategy) and $s_{it}^u = C$ (unchosen strategy). The individual uses the following simple behavioral rule to choose strategies at any time

$$s_{it+1} = \begin{cases} s_{it}^c & \text{if} \quad u_i(s_{it}^c) \geq a_{it} \\ ps_{it}^c + (1-p)s_{it}^u & \text{if} \quad u_i(s_{it}^c) < a_{it} \end{cases} ; 0 \leq p \leq 1. \tag{10.14}$$

In (10.14), there are the following two possible cases.

1. $u_i(s_{it}^c) \geq a_{it}$: In this case, at time t, the utility of player i from the strategy s_{it}^c is least as great as the current aspiration level. Hence, the individual feels satisfied and does not alter the strategy in the next time period, $t+1$, so $s_{it+1} = s_{it}^c$ (first row of (10.14)).
2. $u_i(s_{it}^c) < a_{it}$: In this case, the utility of the player at time t falls short of the aspiration level. The individual is not satisfied, and wishes to experiment with the alternatives. Hence, at time $t+1$, the individual chooses the same strategy s_{it}^c with probability p and the alternative strategy s_{it}^u with probability $1-p$ (second row of (10.14)). We may think of p as a measure of *inertia* arising from costs of switching strategies, although we do not formally model such costs. If $p = 0$, there is no inertia and the individual always switches to the alternative strategy; but if $p = 1$, then there is maximal inertia and the individual never switches. The case $0 < p < 1$ captures intermediate levels of inertia.

We consider the special case of no inertia, $p = 0$, but the results we give are more general and can be extended to the more general case $p > 0$.

We essentially have a *dynamic system*. A solution to a dynamic system takes as given the starting or initial values, which in this case are the initial aspiration levels, $a_0 = (a_{10}, a_{20})$, and the initial strategy profile, $s_0 = (s_{10}, s_{20})$, of the two players. It then solves for the time path of aspirations and the time path of the choice of strategies, $(a_1, s_1), (a_2, s_2), \ldots$, given (i) the rule for the evolution of aspirations in (10.13), and (ii) the behavioral rule for strategy choices in (10.14).

We shall assume, purely for illustrative purposes, that the initial aspiration levels for the prisoner's dilemma game are given by

$$a_{10} = a_{20} = 1.5. \tag{10.15}$$

We also assume, for simplicity, in (10.13), that

$$\gamma = 1.$$

The initial strategies, $s_0 = (s_{10}, s_{20})$, can be any of the four possible strategy profiles: (C, C), (D, C), (C, D), and (D, D). Of these, we take the case

$$s_0 = (D, D),$$

and leave the rest as exercises. In classical game theory, we should not observe the strategy profile (C, C) in a static prisoner's dilemma game because, as explained in Chapter 5, the strategy C is strictly dominated. However, in an infinitely repeated prisoner's dilemma game, the strategy profile (C, C) can arise due to reputational concerns that, in turn, rely on the material costs and benefits of actions. In other words, if the current benefits from defection, D, fall short of the discounted future costs of punishment by the other player, then players find it in their material self-interests to cooperate (instrumental rationality). However, we shall show that even when we begin with the strategy profile (D, D), in an aspirations adaptation model where players use simple behavioral rules and there are no punishments, the dynamic outcome can converge to (C, C).

To summarize, our assumptions in this special case are: The initial strategy profile is $s_0 = (D, D)$, the initial aspiration levels are given in (10.15), $\gamma = 1$, and there is no inertia, $p = 0$.

Using Table 10.1, the first period utilities of the two players from the strategy profile (D, D), are $(1, 1)$. Since $1 < a_{i0} = 1.5$, the aspiration levels of both players are not met. Given our assumption of no inertia, $p = 0$, in the next time period, $t = 1$, they both simultaneously switch strategies to the strategy profile (C, C). Using (10.13), at $t = 1$, their aspiration levels are given by $a_{i1} = 1 < u_{i1} = 2$. Hence, none of the players alters their strategy for $t = 2$ which remains unchanged at (C, C). Thus, $u_{i2} = 2$ for both players. Using (10.13), at $t = 2$, the aspiration levels of both players are given by $a_{i2} = 2$, and since $a_{i2} = u_{i2} = 2$, from the behavioral rule (10.14), both players leave unchanged their strategy for the next period at (C, C). This sequence is repeated for all time periods in the future. Hence, it gives a steady state of the system where the cooperative strategy profile (C, C) is played every period and the aspirations of both players and their respective utilities equal 2 in every time period.

The aspirations adaptation framework can be used to support the cooperative outcome in a variety of games (Colman et al., 2010).[1] One of the problems asks you to solve a two-player coordination game using the tools developed in this section.

The general framework of aspiration adaptation is supported by the evidence. Data on Ethiopian households shows that watching inspirational videos based on the actual life stories of successful people leads to increased savings and improved aspirations about the educational prospects of children (Bernard and Taffesse, 2014). Negative outcomes, such as poverty lower aspirations, and create greater hopelessness (Ray, 2006; Haushofer and Fehr, 2014). Poorer students, even in relatively richer countries, hold relatively lower aspirations towards education and employment (Guyon and Huillery, 2020). Lower aspirations may lower the motivation of the poor to put in higher effort giving rise to lowered economic outcomes that perpetuate poverty (Dalton et al., 2016).

10.9 Bounded Rationality in Financial Markets

10.9.1 The Basic Assumptions on Human Behavior

Financial markets are generally considered, mainly in economic theory, and sometimes in public discourse, as the epitome of efficiently functioning markets. The study of financial markets in

[1] Readers interested in other formalizations of these ideas can consult Börgers and Sarin (2000), Karandikar et al. (1998), Cho and Matsui (2005), Ray (2006), Genicot and Ray (2017).

neoclassical economics relies on several assumptions that are taken to be self-evidently true. Of these assumptions, we focus on three main ones.

1. *Investors are unboundedly rational*: It is assumed that investors are rational and in the long run only rational investors survive. In finance, rational investors are typically called *rational arbitrageurs* (sometimes the prefix "rational" is omitted). Rational arbitrageurs must satisfy the following two requirements.
   (a) Investors have complete and transitive preferences under certainty (so a utility function represents their preferences). Under risk, they use expected utility theory, and under subjective uncertainty they use subjective expected utility (see Part I). When making decisions over time, they use exponential discounted utility (see Part III). In general, they are unboundedly rational; have perfect memory and recall; have perfect attention; no problems with willpower; make cold, calculated emotionless decisions; and have complete familiarity with the tools of mathematics and statistics (or act "as if" they do so).
   (b) In response to new information, investors are assumed to update their priors in a Bayesian manner and use rational expectations to make predictions of random variables.
2. *There is no aggregate irrationality*: In the aggregate, investors are assumed to be rational. However, "some" irrational investors might exist. When they do exist, they make random individual errors, which when aggregated across all irrational investors, cancel out. Hence, the presence of irrational traders can be ignored.
3. *Irrational investors, if any, exit the market*: Suppose, for whatever reason, there exist irrational traders who bet on price departures from the fundamental values of assets. Then rational arbitrageurs are assumed to immediately spot an opportunity to make profits off them. Since nobody, including irrational traders, can continue to lose money, irrational investors must exit the market.

These three assumptions, or requirements, are nothing more than hypotheses. The first requirement is a set of behavioral assumptions about how people behave. The second and third requirements are hypotheses about what happens in actual markets. All three requirements are testable and have been rigorously tested. All three fail the empirical test.

Before we present the empirical evidence, it is curious to note that these requirements were accepted as self-evident truths for decades in the economics profession and continue to be taught noncritically in many programs. It also highlights the flaws in a methodological approach that establishes the truth value of hypotheses based on the plausibility of arguments rather than the only acceptable gold standard in the sciences – stringent empirical testing.

10.9.2 The Basics of Arbitrage and Risk in Financial Markets

In this section, we consider how arbitrage in financial markets results in market efficiency. We also demonstrate (i) how arbitrage can hedge against fundamental risk, but not against idiosyncratic risk, and (ii) the role of substitute securities in ensuring market efficiency. We also introduce readers to the concept of *shorting of an asset* that plays a key role in arbitrage.

Readers used to thinking about physical goods will know that sellers need physical possession of a good in order to sell it. However, in order to sell financial assets, one does not need physical possession. One can borrow a financial asset for a period, sell it, buy it back in the future, and return it to the lender.

Suppose that there are two time periods, $t = 1, 2$, during which the price of an asset is, respectively, P_1 and P_2. At time $t = 1$ investors do not know the actual price of the asset at time $t = 2$, so they form an expectation of this price, P_2^e. Suppose that an investor, who *does not own the asset*, believes that the future price will fall, that is, $P_2^e < P_1$. In this case, the investor, who we refer to as investor A, might wish to take a *short position* in the asset. Investor A approaches a broker who is able to borrow the asset from another investor, say, investor B, who owns the physical asset. The contract between the two investors states that investor A will borrow n units of the asset at time $t = 1$ from investor B and return the n units back at time $t = 2$. In return, investor A will pay the broker a small fee and also any earnings such as interest and dividends from the asset.

With the n units of the borrowed asset in hand, investor A sells the n units at time $t = 1$ at a price P_1 per unit, for a total revenue of nP_1. Investor A hopes to purchase back the n units of the asset in the market at time $t = 2$ incurring an expected cost of nP_2^e and then return them to investor B. The total expected profits of investor A are

$$n(P_1 - P_2^e).$$

Since the investor expects that $P_2^e < P_1$, hence, expected profits are positive, justifying, ex-ante, the decision to "short" the asset. However, expectations might not be fulfilled. Denoting the actual time 2 price by P_2, all three possibilities can occur:

$$P_1 \lesseqgtr P_2.$$

If, for instance, $P_1 < P_2$, then investor A will make a loss. These are the basics of shorting an asset. Legal restrictions constrain which types of securities can be shorted and, in part, the regulatory response to the 2007–8 financial crisis was a more detailed specification of these legal restrictions.

In order to illustrate how financial market arbitrage works through the process of shorting assets, consider the following example. There are two time periods $t = 1, 2$. An investor has the choice of investing in two close substitute securities, say, General Motors (GM) and Toyota securities. Both are car manufacturers and face the same *fundamental risk*, for example, energy shortages that threaten to disrupt demand for new cars. But they face different *idiosyncratic risks*, for instance, one of the car manufacturers might have tried a new technology that did not work very well and led to a significant number of car recalls. In the absence of any of these risks, suppose that the fundamental value of a security for each of the two car manufacturers is \$30.

Example 10.24 *(Arbitrage and efficiency in financial markets) Consider how arbitrage may bring about efficiency in financial markets, along the lines suggested by Friedman (1953) and Fama (1965). Suppose that, for whatever reasons, Toyota shares drop below their fundamental value to* \$20 *per share at $t = 1$. Arbitrageurs who spot an opportunity for profit take a "short position" in GM shares. Suppose that an arbitrageur borrows 10 GM shares at $t = 1$ and immediately sells them for* \$30 × 10 = \$300. *With this money, the investor buys $\frac{300}{20} = 15$ temporarily devalued Toyota shares. As more and more arbitrageurs spot this opportunity and create an excess demand for Toyota shares, these shares continue to increase in price and by time $t = 2$, the price of Toyota* *shares recovers back to its fundamental value of* \$30. *At* $t = 2$, *the arbitrageur sells the 15 Toyota shares for* $\$30 \times 15 = \$450$. *The investor then buys the 10 GM shares for* $30 \times 10 = \$300$ *to return back to the broker, making a profit of* $\$450 - \$300 = \$150$. *The efficient markets hypothesis now holds because each security equals its fundamental value.*

Several factors conspired to achieve the efficient outcome in Example 10.24. These include voluntary trade, rational arbitrageurs, presence of substitute assets, and unrestricted shorting of assets. If any of these factors is absent, then there is no guarantee that markets will arrive at an efficient outcome.

Example 10.25 *(Hedging against fundamental risk) Taking a short position in a substitute security, as in Example 10.24, protects the investor from fundamental risk. To illustrate this point, suppose that everything at time* $t = 1$ *is identical to Example 10.24. However, due to fundamental risk (e.g, an unexpected slump in the economy and poor forecasts for the future), the price of securities for each car manufacturer drops to* \$20 *per share at* $t = 2$; *this event could not have been predicted at* $t = 1$. *Thus, at time* $t = 2$, *the arbitrageur sells the 15 Toyota shares for* $\$20 \times 15 = \$300$. *Then, the investor buys the 10 GM shares for* $\$20 \times 10 = \$200$ *to return them back to the broker, making a total profit of* $\$300 - \$200 = \$100$. *The fundamental risk reduces the revenue at* $t = 2$ *from the sale of the Toyota shares from* \$450 *to* \$300, *but it also reduces the cost of purchasing the GM shares from* \$300 *to* \$200. *Thus, shorting reduces the exposure of the investor to fundamental risk.*

Legal constraints might prevent many investors from taking a short position, exposing them to fundamental risk. This might in turn induce a reduction in arbitrage activity.

Example 10.26 *(Exposure to idiosyncratic risk) This example makes the point that taking a short position does not protect the investor from idiosyncratic risk. Continuing with Example 10.24, suppose that there is no fundamental risk, unlike in Example 10.25. However, Toyota faces idiosyncratic risks, say, because a new technology that it used, forced a recall of some cars. The market views this information negatively and the price of a Toyota security drops to* \$20 *at* $t = 2$ *(the price of a GM share at* $t = 2$ *continues to be* \$30*). The arbitrageur now sells the 15 Toyota shares for* $\$20 \times 15 = \$300$ *at* $t = 2$. *The investor then buys 10 GM shares for* $\$30 \times 10 = \$300$ *to return to the broker, for a net profit of* $\$300 - \$300 = \$0$. *If, however, the idiosyncratic risk had forced the price of Toyota securities to fall below* \$20, *the investor would have made a loss.*

10.9.3 Efficient Markets Hypothesis

The *efficient markets hypothesis* (EMH) is the cornerstone of neoclassical finance and provides a natural yardstick for judging its predictions. Suppose that time $t = 0, 1, 2, \ldots, T$ and a decision maker can invest in a financial asset at time $t = 0$ that offers a stream of incomes over time $t = 1, 2, \ldots, T$. For instance, if the asset is an equity, then it offers a stream of dividends over time. Denote the stream of incomes by $D_1, D_2, \ldots, D_T$ and suppose that the decision maker uses an interest rate $r > 0$ to discount the future stream of incomes. The present discounted value of the asset, PDV, at time $t = 0$ is then written as

$$PDV = \frac{1}{1+r}D_1 + \frac{1}{(1+r)^2}D_2 + \cdots + \frac{1}{(1+r)^T}D_T. \tag{10.16}$$

The EMH postulates that the price of the asset *at any point in time* must equal its *fundamental value*, which is taken as the PDV of all the income streams for the asset. Thus, the price of the asset at time $t = 0$, denoted by P_0, equals the calculation for PDV in (10.16).

$$P_0 = PDV.$$

This formula can be extended to continuous time (continuous time trading is a commonly used assumption in finance) and it allows us to define the price of the asset *at any instant in time*. All publicly available information is immediately incorporated into security prices. Otherwise prices would not equal fundamental values at some instant in time. The idea that information is instantly incorporated into security prices requires the assumption that there is an instantaneous flow of information in financial markets. If, however, there is gradual flow of information (as suggested by the evidence below), then this assumption is violated.

The EMH gives rise to the following six testable implications, T1–T6.

T1: *Weak form of EMH*: Past information, sometimes known as stale information, *has no* affect on the current prices of securities. The activity of rational arbitrageurs in the past must have ensured that such information was already instantly incorporated into past security prices.

T2: *Semi-strong form of EMH*: Current prices of securities should be unaffected by any publicly available information. The reason is that such information is instantaneously incorporated into security prices. In Examples 10.24, 10.25, the information that led to the temporary mispricing of Toyota securities is corrected in the immediately next period in the sense that, under the assumptions of the model, prices equal fundamental values. In a continuous time trading model, this price correction will be instantaneous. Hence, prices of Toyota securities at time $t > 2$ should be unaffected by these past events.

T3: *Strong form of EMH*: Investors cannot earn excess market profits by using privileged information that is not available to others, that is, there is absence of *insider trading*. Insider information may be held fleetingly by some investors, however, their trading behavior would, so goes the argument under EMH, instantly reveal this information to others, wiping out any excess profits.

T4: Security prices react instantly to news, say, about the fundamental value of an asset; as in Examples 10.24, 10.25. In particular, we should not observe the following pattern in security prices. Security prices first gradually underreact to information, but then gradually overreact to it before finally reverting to the new fundamental value.

T5: Substitute securities cannot sell for different prices, except fleetingly. The assumption of continuous time trading ensures that any price differences between substitute securities are immediately exploited by investors in the form of a profitable trading opportunity, wiping out the price differences (see Examples 10.24, 10.25, above).

T6: Security prices should *not* react to *no news*. By no news is meant any news that is unrelated to fundamental values. In Examples 10.24, 10.25, investors will not need to engage in arbitrage if there is "no news" because the prices of both GM and Toyota shares are not predicted to depart from their fundamental values in this case.

10.9.4 Evaluating the Theoretical Case for Efficient Markets

Before we consider the empirical evidence on the EMH, we briefly consider some of the theoretical objections to the EMH.

Investor Sentiment and Judgment Heuristics

We briefly outlined the basic assumptions/requirements in neoclassical finance in Section 10.9.1. The evidence reviewed in this part demonstrated that several aspects of these requirements fail. People often fail to use Bayes' law correctly and underweight base rates, while at other times they underweight the likelihood of the sample. People are also often overconfident and use the law of small numbers, of which the *representativeness* heuristic is a leading exemplar. People do not have perfect memory, nor perfect recall, and often use the *availability heuristic* to search for salient information in their memory.

When investors exhibit any departure from the first rationality assumption in Section 10.9.1 (which required that investors are unboundedly rational), they are said to exhibit *investor sentiment*. Such investors are sometimes also known as *unsophisticated investors* (Kyle, 1985) and *noise traders* (Black, 1986).

Suppose that the decrease in the original price of Toyota securities in period 1 from \$30 to \$20 in Example 10.24 arises from the behavior of noise traders (investor sentiment). Rational arbitrageurs then face two kinds of risks when they take a short position in GM securities. (i) Potential fundamental or idiosyncratic risk in the future, (ii) risk from investor sentiment that could get worse at $t = 2$. One reason that the risk from investor sentiment could get worse in the future is the presence of *positive feedback traders*, who follow a simple rule of thumb: decide on buying the asset only if the asset performed well last period (De Long et al., 1990b). Such positive feedback traders will be even more reluctant to buy Toyota securities in period 2, possibly worsening the mispricing of Toyota securities, originally caused by investor sentiment. Suppose for the sake of argument, that this causes the prices of Toyota securities to drop to \$15 per share at $t = 2$. Then, at time $t = 2$, the investor will sell the the 15 Toyota shares for $\$15 \times 15 = \$225$, and purchase the 10 GM shares that cost $\$30 \times 10 = \$300$ in order to return them back to the broker. The total profit of the investor equals $\$225 - \$300 = -\$75 < 0$. This is the combined risk created due to noise traders and positive feedback traders. If investors know ex ante that such risk exists, then they may limit their arbitrage activity.

The problem is made worse for the predictions of neoclassical finance if rational arbitrageurs are able to foresee the behavior of noise traders and positive feedback traders. Rational arbitrageurs will then bet on the mispricing of Toyota shares at $t = 1$ getting worse at $t = 2$. In effect, if rational arbitrageurs read the market correctly, their actions will further worsen the mispricing of Toyota shares. Rational arbitrageurs might have to liquidate their positions before noise traders do, but this removes the market pressure to bring prices back to fundamental values (Figlewski, 1979).

We reiterate the dangers of arguing on the basis of ex-ante plausibility in economic theory rather than taking recourse to the relevant empirical evidence. Our discussion of judgment heuristics (Chapter 9) shows that laypersons and experts exhibit persistent and *systematic biases*. Hence, rather than investors making positive and negative errors that cancel out in the aggregate (see Section 10.9.1) it would appear likely that on many ocassions, errors accumulate in the same direction, leading to instability in financial markets.

We have also alluded to various other peices of evidence in this book on how judgment heuristics might violate the predictions of neoclassical finance. For instance, the underestimation of financial volatility on account of hindsight bias in Chapter 9 (Biais and Weber, 2009). We also observe far too much trading relative to the predictions of neoclassical finance, and this may be partly caused by the overconfidence of stock market participants (Barber and Odean, 2000). Empirically, it has been found that those who trade more earn the lowest average returns. Excessive trading by stock market participants contrasts with the puzzle of limited stock market participation. Barberis et al. (2006) explain this puzzle through narrow framing whereby individuals segregate stock market returns from other sources of income, hence, the perceived risk is higher. Combined with the tendency of individuals to reject small gambles, even those that are actuarially favorable, provides a potential explanation (Tversky and Kahneman, 1992).

In Part I we have also discussed several phenomena relevant to financial markets. These include the *equity premium puzzle* which results in returns on stocks relative to bonds that are too high to be justified by the increased risk of holding stocks (Benartzi and Thaler, 1995); the *disposition effect* which leads investors to hold losing stocks for far too long and sell winning stock too early (Odean, 1998); and overweighting of small probabilities that leads to a departure in asset prices from those predicted under neoclassical finance, and to pricing of the skewness in asset returns (Barberis and Huang, 2008). These phenomena are studied under the heading of the *psychology of tail events*.

Neoclassical finance is frame-invariant, but Benartzi and Thaler (1995) highlight *framing effects* on investor choice. They show that the decision of investors to buy stock depends on whether news about the performance is presented as *high, long-term, returns* or a *more finely presented series of fluctuating short-term stock returns*. Shleifer (2000, p. 10) summarizes some of the objections that we have raised in this section, which undermines the theoretical case for EMH

> it is difficult to sustain the case that people in general, and investors in particular, are fully rational. At the superficial level, many investors react to irrelevant information ... Investors follow the advice of financial gurus, fail to diversify, actively trade stocks and churn their portfolios, sell winning stocks and hold on to losing stocks thereby increasing their tax liabilities, buy and sell actively and expensively managed mutual funds, follow stock price patterns and other popular models. In short, investors hardly pursue the passive strategies expected of uninformed market participants by the efficient market theory.

Professional Arbitrageurs

Financial markets are characterized by a large number of small and dispersed investors who lack the skills and/or time to invest directly. They invest their money through professional arbitrageurs, such as mutual funds, who largely invest other people's money. This is often termed as the *separation of brains and capital* (Shleifer and Vishny, 1997). Since small investors may lack information on the ability of professional arbitrageurs, they rely on indirect signals of their ability, such as the following.

1. The end of year financial reports on the performance of professional arbitrageurs.
2. How well the professional arbitrageurs fare relative to each other, say, in terms of their end of year profitability; this is known as *relative performance evaluation.*
3. The performance of professional arbitrageurs relative to some publicly observed signal, such as the S&P 500 Index.

The first two features are likely to induce professional arbitrageurs to liquidate their loss making positions too soon, even when economic rationale requires them to hold on to such a position longer. This reduces the countervailing effect of the trades of professional arbitrageurs on the activities of noise traders. The second feature, relative performance evaluation, induces professional arbitrageurs to invest in similar assets so that each can avoid looking worse than each other (Scharfstein and Stein, 1990). The final feature induces professional arbitrageurs to choose portfolios whose returns are closely aligned to the S&P 500 Index. This may compromise the longer-term returns earned by professional arbitrageurs, even relative to passive investment strategies (Ippolito, 1989; Lakonishok et al., 1992).

Availability of Substitute Securities

In Examples 10.24, 10.25, a key institutional feature that allowed successful arbitrage, and for the prices of securities to equal their fundamental values, was the availability of substitute securities. However, substitute securities may not always be available (Shleifer, 2000; Barberis and Thaler, 2003). Not all assets can be shorted either; legal restrictions might prevent some assets to be shorted. Thus, investors might find it difficult to insure against fundamental risk, leading to a fall in arbitrage activity. Transaction costs of arbitrage include the cost of finding information about which shares are mispriced relative to their fundamental values, as well as the brokerage fees for taking a short position (D'Avolio, 2002). If these transaction costs are high, they might also prevent adequate arbitrage from taking place.

True Uncertainty or Knightian Uncertainty

Recall from Part I that true uncertainty, or Knightian uncertainty, arises when not all possible future outcomes/probabilities, arising from an action, can be known or even imagined (unknown unknowns). True uncertainty is likely to be pervasive in financial markets. Yet, the existing theories in finance are designed to deal only with risk and subjective uncertainty, with some progress under ambiguity (see Part I). Under true uncertainty, financial market participants might follow simple rules of thumb, or judgment heuristics. Insofar as many actual decisions in financial markets might be taken under true uncertainty, applying the predictions of models based on risk and subjective uncertainty is likely to be inappropriate. This is an unexplored dimension in finance.

Are Markets Efficient because It Is Hard to Beat Them?

The majority of investors find it hard to beat the stock market and make a profit. On average, even professional mutual and pension fund managers may not outperform passive investment strategies (Malkiel, 1990). This may be taken as evidence that the future performance of the stock market is not predictable using the current information set. Thus, one might invoke, say, the weak form of EMH, to argue that markets are efficient (Rubinstein, 2001).

Barberis and Thaler (2003) point out that this is a confusion between necessary and sufficient conditions (see Section 9.2.5 in Chapter 9). The EMH implies that

"Prices equal fundamental values $\Rightarrow$ no arbitrage opportunities."

However, the converse is not true, that is,

"No arbitrage opportunities $\nRightarrow$ prices equal fundamental values."

Thus, the difficulty of beating the stock market does not imply that prices equal fundamental values, or that the EMH holds.

10.9.5 Evaluating the Empirical Case for Efficient Markets

Many of the early tests of the EMH were conducted by the main proponents of EMH. They mainly tested the first two implications of EMH in Section 10.9.3, the weak form (T1) and the semi-strong form (T2) of the EMH, and found evidence supportive of EMH (Fama, 1965, 1970; Fama et al., 1969; Jensen, 1978). For instance, Jensen (1978, p. 95) opens with the following sentence: "I believe there is no other proposition in economics which has more solid empirical evidence supporting it than the Efficient Market Hypothesis. That hypothesis has been tested and, with very few exceptions, found consistent with the data in a wide variety of markets."

An early finding was that stock prices approximately follow a random walk (Fama, 1965). A popular method to test EMH was "event studies" whereby an event that might affect the fundamental value of the stock and the subsequent prices of the stock was studied. The event could be some important news about the company, such as the appointment of a new CEO, or an announcement by the CEO; or decisions taken by the company such as mergers, share repurchases, investment in new technology; or a change in management strategy. EMH predicts that these announcements should be immediately incorporated into stock prices and have no effect on future stock prices. The evidence reviewed in Fama (1970) was supportive of these predictions.

The empirical evidence since the late 1970s has focused on all six implications (T1–T6) and it has not been supportive of EMH. Our aim is not to provide a complete survey of the rich evidence. Readers can consult the surveys in Shleifer (2000), Barberis and Thaler (2003), Subrahmanyam (2008), and Barber and Odean (2013). For two book-length treatments from a behavioral economics perspective see Akerlof and Shiller (2008) and Shiller (2015). In this section, we mainly, and briefly, consider the evidence for the six main implications of EMH, T1–T6, outlined in Section 10.9.3.

Excess Volality of Stock Prices

Shiller (1981) presented an influential critique of the EMH. To understand his critique, we use a slightly more general form of (10.16), extended to the case of risk. Suppose that time is discrete $t, t+1, t+2, \dots, T$. Consider an investor who invests in a stock at time t. The price of the stock at time t is denoted by P_t. Ownership of the stock leads to a stream of uncertain future dividends. The investor tries to infer the expected value of each future value of the dividend, conditional on the information set at time t, denoted by I_t. Thus the present discounted value at time t of all future dividends from the stock, conditional on the information set at time t, denoted by $E[D \mid I_t]$, is

$$E[D \mid I_t] = \frac{1}{1+r}E\left[D_{t+1} \mid I_t\right] + \frac{1}{(1+r)^2}E\left[D_{t+2} \mid I_t\right] + \cdots + \frac{1}{(1+r)^{T-t}}E[D_T \mid I_t].$$

By definition, the EMH states that the price of the stock equals the fundamental value, which is $E[D \mid I_t]$, or

$$P_t = E[D \mid I_t]. \tag{10.17}$$

We can rewrite (10.17) as

$$P_t = D + u_t, \tag{10.18}$$

where u_t is a mean zero random variable, that is, $E[u_t \mid I_t] = 0$.[2] We can rewrite (10.18) as

$$D = P_t - u_t. \tag{10.19}$$

If EMH holds true, then all relevant information is instantly incorporated in prices, thus, u_t and P_t must be uncorrelated. Let the variance of the random variable X be denoted by $V(X)$. Then, taking conditional variances on both sides of (10.19), we get:[3]

$$V(D) = V(P_t) + V(u_t). \tag{10.20}$$

Variances are nonnegative, $V(u_t) \geq 0$, thus, (10.20) leads to the following immediate implication of EMH

$$V(P_t) \leq V(D). \tag{10.21}$$

Shiller's idea was to compute the variances of the price series and the dividend series for stocks and check if the implication in (10.21) held true.

Figure 10.3 plots P_t and D against time; these variables are labeled respectively as "Real Stock Price (S&P 500)" and "PDV, Constant Discount Rate." D was proxied by the present value of actual dividends paid in the future. In contrast to the prediction in (10.21), it is evident from Figure 10.3 that $V(P_t) > V(D)$, contradicting the prediction under EMH. There is too much stock price volatility relative to the prediction of EMH. Actual stock market decisions are often guided by investor sentiment and other behavioral features that create additional sources of price volatility, and systematic errors by investors that accumulate in one direction. However, these factors are ignored in neoclassical finance theory. Despite challenges to Shiller's findings on empirical grounds (e.g., the proxies used for D and P_t, and issues of time-invariant interest

[2] Taking conditional expectations on both sides of (10.18) gives us $E[P_t \mid I_t] = E[D \mid I_t] + E[u_t \mid I_t]$. P_t is known at time t, so $E[P_t \mid I_t] = P_t$. Since $E[u_t \mid I_t] = 0$, we are back to the equality, $P_t = E[D \mid I_t]$ that we started off with in (10.17).

[3] From (10.19), and using $E[u_t \mid I_t] = 0$, we have

$$V(D) = E[(P_t - u_t) - EP_t \mid I_t]^2 = E[(P_t - EP_t) - u_t \mid I_t]^2$$

$$= E[(P_t - EP_t) \mid I_t]^2 + E[u_t \mid I_t]^2 - 2E[(P_t - EP_t)u_t \mid I_t].$$

But $E[(P_t - EP_t) \mid I_t]^2 = V(P_t)$; $E[u_t \mid I_t]^2 = V(u_t)$ because u_t is a mean zero random variable; and $E[(P_t - EP_t)u_t \mid I_t] = 0$ because u_t and P_t are uncorrelated. Hence, $V(D) = V(P_t) + V(u_t)$.

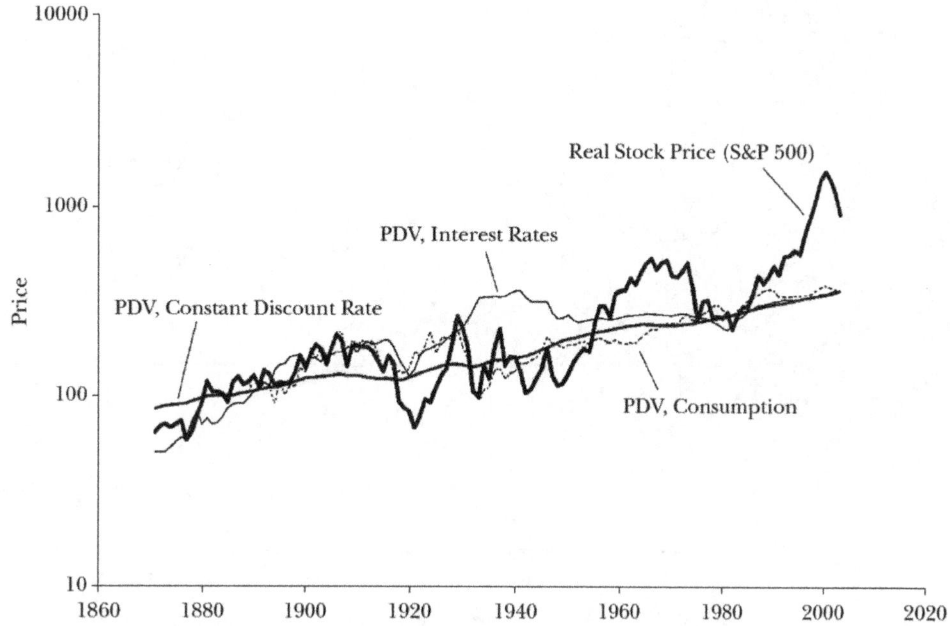

Figure 10.3 A plot of price and present discounted value of dividends against time. Source: Shiller (2003)

rates), the fundamental insights in his findings were borne out by subsequent research (Barberis and Thaler, 2003).

Violations of the Weak Form of EMH (T1 and T4)

Recall that the weak form of EMH states that stale information has no affect on the current prices of securities. But this is contradicted by the evidence from several studies. De Bondt and Thaler (1985) used data from stock prices at the New York Stock Exchange over the time period 1926–82. Among their sample of stocks, they first classified winners (W) or losers (L), based on their performance over the past three years, and then computed the returns on these stocks for the next five years, controlling for risks. Unlike the prediction of the weak form of EMH, they find that (i) W stocks give low returns over the next five years, while (ii) L stocks give high returns over the next five years. The L stocks were not found to be riskier than W stocks, hence, the higher subsequent returns on the L stocks could not be explained by their greater riskiness. Figure 10.4 plots the "cumulative average residuals" for Winner and Loser portfolios of 35 stocks over 60 months; the residual is an estimate of the difference between the return on the asset and the market portfolio.

The authors' preferred explanation is that stock prices have overreacted in the past and overshot the fundamental values, in either direction. The W stocks have overshot above their fundamental values and gradually fall back to their fundamental values, while the L stocks have overshot below their fundamental values and gradually increase to their fundamental values. In other words, we can, on average, predict the future performance of stocks based on their past

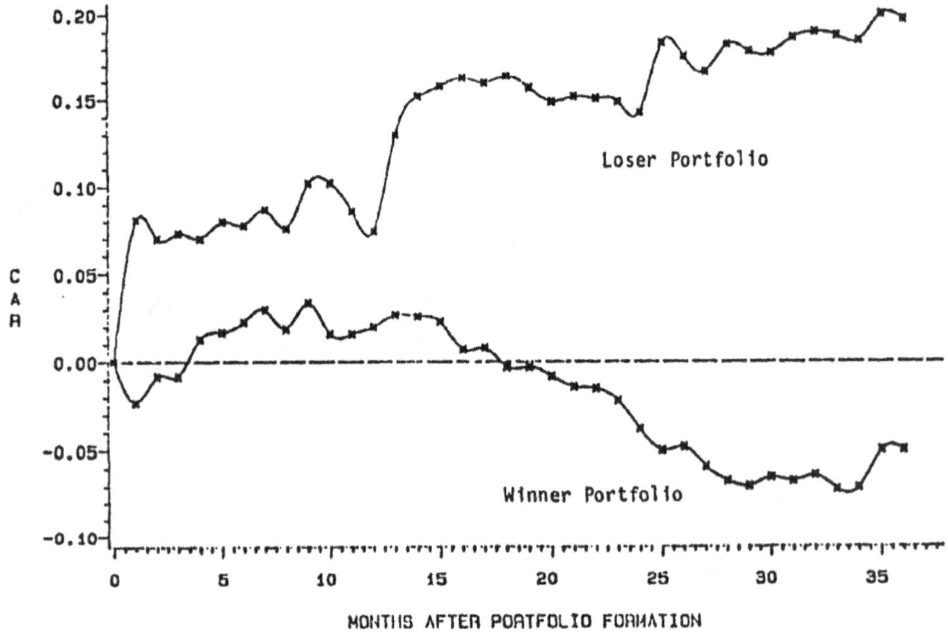

Figure 10.4 Cumulative average residuals (CARs) on the vertical axis for W and L portfolios of 35 stocks over five years. Source: De Bondt and Thaler (1985)

performance, which runs counter to the predictions of the EMH. These results were replicated in several studies that considered other countries, other time periods, and distinguished between small and large firms.

A similar explanation, in terms of overshooting, explains why stocks of companies with high *market to book value ratios* (MBVR) in the past (*glamour stocks*) do worse in the future (De Bondt and Thaler, 1985; Fama and French, 1992; Lakonishok et al., 1994). A high MBVR in the past may indicate overreaction that is gradually corrected through a fall in stock prices. Past MBVR constitutes stale information, yet it can be used to predict future returns, hence, this contradicts the weak-form EMH. Fama and French (1993, 1996a) have tried to rescue EMH on the grounds that a high MBVR is associated with higher risk and, hence, their lower subsequent returns are consistent with the theory. But serious doubts have been raised about the interpretation of MBVR as a measure of fundamental risk (Lakonishok et al., 1994; Daniel and Titman, 1997).

De Bondt and Thaler (1985) looked at returns over a long horizon. However, when returns are viewed over a shorter horizon, past high returns predict future high returns. This is known as the *momentum effect*. For instance, Jegadeesh and Titman (1993) classify portfolios into deciles based on their performance in the previous six months. They find that portfolios in the top deciles give about 10% higher returns relative to those in the bottom deciles for the next six months. Based on these findings, the authors show that a trading strategy that buys past winners and sells past losers earns a compounded excess annual return of 12.01% on average.

Fama (1970) and others have challenged the evidence against the EMH. Their main argument is that we need a model that incorporates both risk and return, embodied in, say, the capital asset pricing model (CAPM). As an illustrative example, suppose that there is some news about a security such that the expected level of return and the riskiness of the security increase simultaneously. If the prices of this security are below the fundamental value, yet we observe insufficient arbitrage, then the Fama (1970) critique argues this is not a refutation of the EMH. They would argue that rational arbitrageurs do not engage in sufficient arbitrage because the security is more risky now and the higher return justifies the greater risk.

Arguably a great deal of empirical evidence contrary to the EMH can be challenged on these grounds. However, this specific possibility was checked in the finding of stock market underreaction and overreaction by De Bondt and Thaler (1985), reported above. They measured risk using the CAPM. In this model, the only risk relevant for the pricing of an asset is the (i) variance of the market portfolio, and (ii) the covariance of the stock returns with the market portfolio. The "beta" of an asset (or portfolio) is covariance of this asset's (or portfolio's) returns with the returns of the market portfolio, divided by the variance of the market portfolio's returns. They found the beta value for winners (W) to be 1.37 and the beta value for losers (L) to be 1.03. Thus, losers were actually less risky than winners, which goes in the opposite direction to Fama's critique. One response in neoclassical finance has been to debunk the CAPM model (Fama and French, 1996a,b). Fama and French constructed three factor and five factor models with additional explanatory variables that were proposed to give a better measure of risk, but it is unclear if these models are supported by the empirical evidence (Fama and French, 2015).

The Semi-Strong Form of the EMH (T2)

The semi-strong form of the EMH requires that current prices of securities should be unaffected by any publicly available information. By contrast, empirical evidence reveals that prices move in the same direction as the initial public news ("up" if the news is good and "down" if it is bad) for a significant amount of time. This phenomenon, known as *post-earnings-news drift*, is documented for several kinds of public information, such as earnings news (Bernard and Thomas, 1989, 1990; La Porta et al., 1997), share repurchase news (Ikenberry et al., 1995), stock issue news (Loughran and Ritter, 1995; Spiess and Affleck-Graves, 1995), and new dividend issues (Michaely et al., 1995).

Rozeff and Kinney (1976) used data over the period 1904–74 to show that the average stock market returns during January were 3.48%, which is about eight times higher than the average monthly returns of 0.42% over remaining months. This is known as the *January effect* and it was replicated in other studies (De Bondt and Thaler, 1985). Several potential confounds such as firm size, risk, and tax liability, could not explain the effect either. Since the January effect should be public information, yet it continued to affect stock prices, it violates the semi-strong form of EMH.

Do Substitute Securities Sell for Identical Prices (T5)?

From Examples 10.24 to 10.26, unless constantly buffeted by idiosyncratic shocks, the prices of strictly substitute securities should be identical. Some of the most persuasive contrary evidence comes from large *Siamese twin* companies. Siamese twins are companies that have the following properties:

1. The companies have merged in the past, but operate in geographically separate areas.
2. The companies pool their cashflows, but each twin retains its own stock. For instance, suppose that companies A and B are Siamese twins who at the time of their merger have contributed the respective fractions x and y of the total equity of the firm ($x + y = 1$). Then all shareholders who buy shares in company A can claim $x\%$ of the total cashflows of the merged company. Thus, if prices of shares equal fundamental values, then the ratio of share prices of companies A and B should also be in the proportion $x : y$. Any departure of the ratio of the share prices from the proportion $x : y$ constitutes a violation of EMH. Rosenthal and Young (1990) demonstrated a significant departure of the relative share prices from the predicted $x : y$ ratio under EMH for two Siamese twin companies, (i) Royal Dutch-Shell and (ii) Unilever NV and Unilever PLC.

Froot and Dabora (1999) present data for three pairs of Siamese twin companies. Of these, we consider their treatment of Royal Dutch and Shell Transport. These companies merged in 1970 on a 60:40 or 1.5:1 basis. Thus, shares in Royal Dutch are a claim to 60% of the cash flow of the merged companies and EMH predicts that the ratio of share prices of the two companies should be in the proportion 1.5:1. Figure 10.5 plots the percent deviations of the ratio of prices from the predicted 1.5:1 ratio under EMH (so, the predicted curve under EMH should be a horizontal line at 0). These deviations are significant, violating EMH. They also find similar, and large, disparities from the predicted ratio of prices for the other two pairs of Siamese twin companies.

What explains the departures from the 1.5:1 ratio for Royal Dutch and Shell Transport? The authors find that the price of the stock of each twin is highly correlated with the market index shares where the twin predominantly trades. Royal Dutch is mainly traded on the US stock market while Shell is mainly traded on the UK stock market. When the US stock market performs well relative to the UK market, the share prices of Royal Dutch rise relative to Shell. The share prices of Royal Dutch also rise relative to Shell when the US dollar appreciates against the British pound.

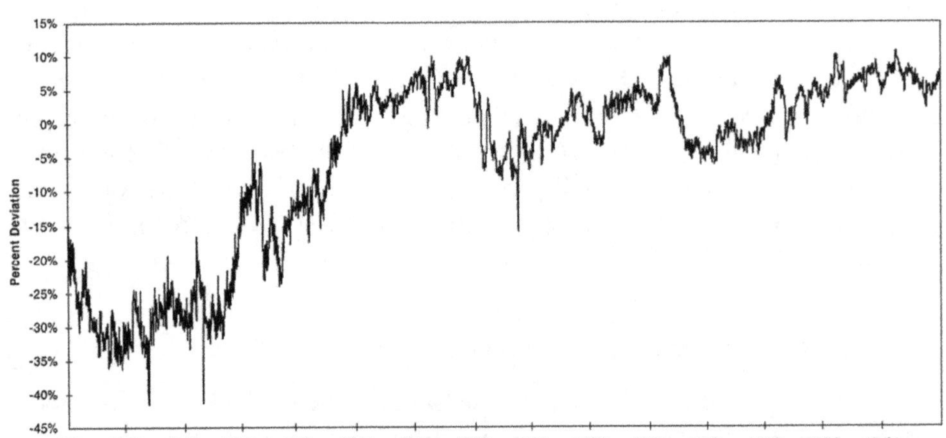

Figure 10.5 Log deviations from Royal Dutch/Shell parity of 1.5:1. Source: Froot and Dabora (1999)

Do Security Prices React to No News (T6)?

The last implication of EMH is that security prices should *not* react to no news. Several contrary examples exist. For instance, there was no news associated with the stock market crash of 1987, in which the Dow Jones fell by 22.6%. Cutler et al. (1991) find that no major news accompanied the 50 largest one-day stock price movements since World War II.

Over time, some of the existing stocks in the S&P 500 index are withdrawn because some companies might merge or are taken over. New stocks are then used to replace the withdrawn stocks with the objective of maintaining the representativeness of the index. The EMH predicts no change in the price of the newly inducted stock because induction into the index does not convey any new information about the company that was not available earlier. Yet, there is substantially increased trading in the freshly inducted stocks that contradicts T6 (Shleifer, 1986; Wurgler and Zhuravskaya, 2002).

Evidence violating T6 also comes from speculative bubbles in asset prices. Bubbles form when the price of an asset begins to increase well beyond fundamental values, possibly due to investor sentiment (Shiller, 2003). As the gap between the actual price and the fundamental price of the asset widens, it becomes unsustainable, and at some point the bubble bursts, with a huge fall in the price of the asset. There is often no apparent news that precedes a bursting bubble. Stock prices often react to a dividend announcement when such events convey no new news about fundamentals. The explanation in neoclassical finance is that firms may offer higher dividends to signal better market prospects to investors. However, Benartzi et al. (1997) do not find any evidence that dividends signal an increase in the future changes in earnings.

How Skilled Are Investors in Beating the Stock Market?

In a nutshell, the evidence shows that, on average, individual investors earn below market rates of pretax return on investments. For very short run investments, say, a week, the performance of individual investors may sometimes be better, at least based on US data. For a comprehensive review of the evidence, see Barber and Odean (2013) that we draw on below.

Odean (1999) provides evidence from the trading records of 10,000 investors in the US that reveals below-average returns to individual investors in the absence of transaction costs of trade. The trading records of another 78,000 investors show that these results extend to the inclusion of transaction costs in Barber and Odean (2000) who report the following two findings.

(i) Transaction costs are the prime reason for the underperformance of the portfolios of individual investors.
(ii) Investors who traded more are, on average, more likely to realize lower returns. The 20% of investors who trade the most, earn seven percentage points lower in annual rates of return, relative to the 20% who trade the least.

On average, data from Taiwan, Finland, and the US shows the following.

(i) Individual investors purchase stocks that subsequently perform poorly and sell stocks that subsequently perform strongly.
(ii) Institutional investors are more successful, selling stock that subsequently does poorly and buying stock that subsequently does well.

Thus, the *stock picking skills* of individual investors appear to be relatively unsuccessful, on average, while institutional investors have superior stock picking skills (Grinblatt and Keloharju, 2000; Hvidkjaer, 2008; Barber et al., 2009). There is variation across countries about how well individual investments perform over a short horizon, say, one week. The evidence from the US shows that individual investors perform quite well over these short horizons (Barber et al., 2009; Kaniel et al., 2012; Kelly and Tetlock, 2013). However, these results are not supported by Taiwanese data (Andrade et al., 2008; Barber et al., 2009). For Finland, the results are mixed: Investors make losses on limit orders[4] but profits on market orders (Linnainmaa, 2010). Yet, the opposite result is found for Taiwan (Barber et al., 2009). Thus, no general cross-country conclusions can be drawn.

A positive correlation between cognitive skills and investor performance has been found (Grinblatt et al., 2012; Korniotis and Kumar, 2013) but there is a negative correlation between age and investor performance (Korniotis and Kumar, 2009). Barber and Odean (2001) report two main gender effects from US data. (i) Men trade more than women, and (ii) those who trade more earn lower profits. Similar gender effects are also found for Germany, but these are weakened once we take account of risk aversion (Dorn and Huberman, 2005). One reason why men trade more and experience lower realized returns is that they might be more overconfident than women (Glaser and Weber, 2007; Grinblatt and Keloharju, 2009). The US data indicates a strong correlation between self-reported measures of competence and the extent of trading (Graham et al., 2009).

We have noted above that there is excessive trading relative to the predictions of neoclassical finance. One explanation is that this might arise from *sensation seeking* whereby individuals view trading activity as a form of entertainment, or sensation seeking. If there is a degree of substitutability between various sensation-seeking activities, then access to alternative sensation-seeking activities (for instance, a new legal lottery, higher stakes state lotteries) may reduce stock market trading (Dorn and Sengmueller, 2009; Gao and Lin, 2015).

There is also intriguing evidence to indicate that a very small percentage of the investors may be particularly skilled in doing quite well in the stock market. Such skillful individual investors earn abnormal persistent profits, which exceed the profits arising from other potential strategies (Coval et al., 2005). These results have been replicated for Taiwanese data (Barber et al., 2014). The special skills required to earn above-average returns in the stock market are more likely to reside with institutional investors (Grinblatt and Titman, 1989; Daniel et al., 1997).

10.9.6 A Brief Note on Behavioral Corporate Finance

Corporate finance studies the interaction between managers of firms and investors in the firm. Some of the issues explored in this literature are: decisions taken by the firm, such as the source of finance, for example, equity versus bonds; merger and acquisition decisions; capital restructuring; and the level of output. In neoclassical finance, the managers and investors are fully rational in the sense described in, say, Section 10.9.1. *Behavioral corporate finance* relaxes

[4] A limit order is an order placed with a brokerage firm to buy or sell a fixed number of shares at a specified price or better.

this rationality assumption. We outline, very briefly, some of the basic ideas focusing only on some of the implications of relaxing the rationality assumption for managers. For surveys of behavioral corporate finance, see Baker and Nofsinger (2010), Baker and Wurgler (2012), and Dhami (2020, Vol. V).

Unlike behavioral finance, which has an agreed-upon and falsifiable theory in the form of the efficient markets hypothesis, corporate finance does not have such a benchmark. Nor is data as readily available in corporate finance. For these two reasons, developments in corporate finance have been relatively slower, yet there is now a significant body of literature on the subject.

There is no reason to suppose that the top levels of management in firms (henceforth, CEOs) are not subject to the same behavioral biases as other individuals. However, it is a plausible hypothesis that markets might somehow develop mechanisms to get rid of CEOs who do not advance a firm's goals, say, profit maximization. However, there are several reasons why it might be difficult to get rid of CEOs who are either inefficient, or exhibit any of the behavioral biases that compromise on the firm's profits (Lazear, 2004). We explore some of these reasons below.

1. Some of the most important and critical decisions made by managers are of an infrequent nature. Thus, these decisions do not afford many opportunities for learning and improvement. Examples include making specialized investments, merger decisions, acquisition decisions, and capital restructuring. There is no agreed-upon yardstick to evaluate many of these decisions. For instance, consider the problem of evaluating a CEO's merger decision. Should the outcomes be evaluated in five months' time, two years' time, or 10 years' time? Should the outcomes be profits, increased synergies between divisions, greater external brand name reputation, or opportunities for long term growth? There is no clear answer.

   Unlike the standard theory of corporate finance, which is designed for risk and subjective uncertainty, managers often operate in a world of true uncertainty (unknown unknowns). This makes it even harder to evaluate the performance of CEOs. Risk, subjective uncertainty, and true uncertainty, also give the CEOs more wiggle room to defend their decisions through *attribution-bias*. The final outcomes experienced by a firm depend on the CEO's skills and random luck/external factors. The boards of directors and shareholders might find it difficult to disentangle these two factors and the problem is worsened by the CEO's *self-serving bias*. When the outcomes are poor, the annual company reports are likely to blame external factors beyond the CEO's control. However, good outcomes are attributed to internal factors such as CEO skills (Bettman and Weitz, 1983). Bertrand and Mullainathan (2001) report that the compensation of executives in oil companies increases as oil prices increase. Oil prices are typically determined by events outside the control of oil executives, such as the world demand and the strategic policies of the OPEC countries. Thus, in a good year for oil prices, executives might stake a claim for higher compensation based on the annual profits of their company and attempt to take credit for it.
2. In standard corporate finance, it is assumed that the board of directors maximizes the shareholder value. But the accuracy of this assumption is an empirical question. CEOs might have undue influence on the board of directors of the firm and take actions to protect themselves against market competition. They might influence the board, determine their own pay, and be able to extract rents (Bebchuk et al., 2002).

3. Why don't the firm's internal selection processes weed out "unsuitable" CEOs? Since performance can be difficult to judge under true uncertainty and a suitable theoretical benchmark is not available, overconfident middle managers might take more risks and leapfrog others purely due to luck (Goel and Thakor, 2008). Greater confidence might also be associated with other traits that are correlated with the "perception" of being a good manager, for example, having a positive and optimistic outlook, and being inspiring and charming.

We have already considered evidence on several managerial biases such as the effects of managerial overconfidence on their decisions in Section 9.2.3, so we omit it. An early contribution to this literature was by Roll (1986) who argued that overconfident CEOs assign too high a value on firms that they are keen to acquire, subjecting themselves to a "winner's curse". Overconfident CEOs might also hold on to company stock for too long, believing incorrectly that it is undervalued by the market, and forgoing profitable opportunities to sell it (Hall and Murphy, 2000, 2002; Meulbroek, 2001). If the firm does not have adequate levels of internal finance and lacks the capacity to absorb greater debt, then managerial overconfidence will result in lower levels of investment (Malmendier and Tate, 2005). On the other hand, if sufficient internal finance is available, then overconfident CEOs might invest too much (Heaton, 2002; Gervais et al., 2011). If this is coupled with high-powered managerial incentives, then it might lead to an even worse outcome for the firm by inducing CEOs to take on even greater risk.

Managerial overconfidence may also have some positive effects. For instance, in team production, overconfident CEOs overestimate their own marginal product, work harder, and induce others to work harder, increasing profits (Gervais and Goldstein, 2007). Managerial overconfidence is also associated with higher levels of risky R&D activity and higher patent counts (Hirshleifer et al., 2012).

References

Abeler, J. and Marklein, F. (2017). Fungibility, Labels, and Consumption. *Journal of the European Economic Association* 15(1): 99–127.

Acemoglu, D., Tristan R., and Robinson, J. A. (2014). Chiefs: Economic Development and Elite Control of Civil Society in Sierra Leone. *Journal of Political Economy* 122(2): 319–368.

Ahmed, A. S. and Duellman, S. (2013). Managerial Overconfidence and Accounting Conservatism. *Journal of Accounting Research* 51(1): 1–30.

Ajzen, I. (1977). Intuitive Theories of Events and the Effects of Base-Rate Information on Prediction. *Journal of Personality and Social Psychology* 35(5): 303–314.

Akerlof, G. A. and Shiller, R. J. (2008). *Animal Spirits: How Human Psychology Drives the Economy and Why It Matters for Global Capitalism.* Princeton University Press: Princeton.

Akerlof, G. and Dickens, W. (1982). The Economic Consequences of Cognitive Dissonance. *American Economic Review* 72(3): 307–319.

Aktas, N., de Bodt, E., Bollaert, H., and Roll, R. (2016). CEO Narcissism and the Takeover Process: From Private Initiation to Deal Completion. *Journal of Financial and Quantitative Analysis* 51(1): 113–137.

Alesina, A., Giuliano, P., and Nunn, N. (2013). On the Origins of Gender Roles: Women and the Plough. *Quarterly Journal of Economics* 128(2): 469–530.

Alhakami, A. S. and Slovic, P. (1994). A Psychological Study of the Inverse Relationship between Perceived Risk and Perceived Benefit. *Risk Analysis* 14(6): 1085–1096.

Allcott, H. and Mullainathan, S. (2010). Behavior and Energy Policy. *Science* 327(5970): 1204–1205.

Allcott, H. and Rogers, T. (2014). The Short-Run and Long-Run Effects of Behavioral Interventions: Experimental Evidence from Energy Conservation. *American Economic Review* 104(10): 3003–3037.

Anderson, C., Brion, S., Moore, D. A., and Kennedy, J. A. (2012). A Status Enhancement Account of Overconfidence. *Journal of Personality and Social Psychology* 103(4): 718–735.

Andrade, S. C., Chang, C., and Seasholes, M. S. (2008). Trading Imbalances, Predictable Reversals, and Crossstock Price Pressure. *Journal of Financial Economics* 88(2): 406–423.

Ayton, P. and Fischer, I. (2004). The Hot Hand Fallacy and the Gambler's Fallacy: Two Faces of Subjective Randomness? *Memory and Cognition* 32(8): 1369–1378.

Baker, H. K. and Nofsinger, J. R. (2010). *Behavioral Finance: Investors, Corporations, and Markets.* John Wiley & Sons, Inc.: Hoboken, NJ.

Baker, M., Nagel, S., and Wurgler, J. (2007). Effect of Dividends on Consumption. *Brookings Papers on Economics Activity* 1: 277–291.

Baker, M. and Wurgler, J. (2012). Behavioral Corporate Finance: A Current Survey. In G. M. Constantinides, M. Harris, and R. M. Stulz (eds.), *Handbooks in the Economics of Finance*, Volume 2. Elsevier: New York.

Bakke, E. W. (1940). *The Unemployed Worker.* Yale University Press: New Haven, CT.

Baltussen, G. and Post, T. (2011). Irrational Diversification: An Examination of the Portfolio Construction Decision. *Journal of Financial and Quantitative Analysis* 46(5): 1463–1491.

Banerjee, A. and Duflo, E. (2011). *Poor Economics: A Radical Rethinking of the Way to Fight Global Poverty*. Public Affairs: New York.

Banerjee, A. and Mullainathan, S. (2008). Limited Attention and Income Distribution. *American Economic Review* 98(2): 489–493.

Banerjee, A. V., Karlan, D., Trachtman, H., and Udry, C. (2020). Does Poverty Change Labor Supply? Evidence from Multiple Income Effects and 115,579 Bags. Global Poverty Research Lab Working Paper No. 20-104.

Banerjee, S., Humphery-Jenner, M., and Nanda, V. (2015). Restraining Overconfident CEOs through Improved Governance: Evidence from the Sarbanes–Oxley Act. *Review of Financial Studies* 28(10): 2812–2858.

Bar-Hillel, M. (1980). The Base Rate Fallacy in Probability Judgements. *Acta Psychologica* 44(3): 211–233.

Bar-Hillel, M. and Wagenaar, W. A. (1991). The Perception of Randomness. *Advances in Applied Mathematics* 12(4): 428–454.

Barber, B. M. and Odean, T. (2000). Trading is Hazardous to Your Wealth: The Common Stock Investment Performance of Individual Investors. *Journal of Finance* 55(2): 773–806.

Barber, B. M. and Odean, T. (2001). Boys Will Be Boys: Gender, Overconfidence, and Common Stock Investment. *Quarterly Journal of Economics* 141: 261–292.

Barber, B. M. and Odean, T. (2013). The Behavior of Individual Investors. In G. Constantinides, M. Harris, and R. Stulz (eds.), *Handbook of the Economics of Finance*. Elsevier: Amsterdam, pp. 1533–1569.

Barber, B. M., Lee, Y., Liu, Y., and Odean, T. (2009). Just How Much Do Individual Investors Lose by Trading? *Review of Financial Studies* 22(2): 609–632.

Barber, B. M., Lee, Y., Liu, Y., and Odean, T. (2014). The Cross-Section of Speculator Skill: Evidence from Taiwan. *Journal of Financial Markets* 18(c): 1–24.

Barber, B. M., Odean, T., and Zhu, N. (2009). Do Retail Trades Move Markets? *Review of Financial Studies* 22(1): 151–186.

Barberis, N. and Huang, M. (2008). Stocks as Lotteries: The Implications of Probability Weighting for Security Prices. *American Economic Review* 98(5): 2066–2100.

Barberis, N., Huang, M., and Thaler, R. H. (2006). Individual Preferences, Monetary Gambles, and Stock Market Participation: A Case for Narrow Framing. *American Economic Review* 96(4): 1069–1090.

Barberis, N. and Thaler, R. H. (2003). A Survey of Behavioral Finance. In G. Constantinides, M. Harris, and R. Stultz (eds.), *Handbook of the Economics of Finance*. North-Holland: Amsterdam, pp. 1051–1119.

Barbey, A. K. and Sloman, S. A. (2007). Base-Rate Respect: From Ecological Rationality to Dual Processes. *Behavioral and Brain Sciences* 30(3): 241–254.

Bebchuk, L. A., Fried, J. M., and Walker, D. I. (2002). Managerial Power and Rent Extraction in the Design of Executive Compensation. *University of Chicago Law Review* 69(3): 751–846.

Bénabou, R. (2015). The Economics of Motivated Beliefs. Jean-Jacques Laffont Lecture. *Revue d'economie politique* 125(5): 665–685.

Bénabou, R., and Tirole, J. (2002). Self-Confidence and Personal Motivation. *The Quarterly Journal of Economics* 117(3): 871–915.

Bénabou, R. and Tirole, J. (2016). Mindful Economics: The Production, Consumption, and Value of Beliefs. *Journal of Economic Perspectives* 30(3): 141–164.

Benartzi, S. (2001). Excessive Extrapolation and the Allocation of 401(k) Accounts to Company Stock? *Journal of Finance* 56(5): 1747–1764.

Benartzi, S., Michaely, R., and Thaler, R. H. (1997). Do Changes in Dividends Signal the Future or the Past? *Journal of Finance* 52: 1007–1034.

Benartzi, S. and Thaler, R. H. (1995). Myopic Loss Aversion and the Equity Premium Puzzle. *The Quarterly Journal of Economics* 10(1): 73–92.

Benartzi, S. and Thaler, R. H. (2001). Naive Diversification Strategies in Retirement Saving Plans. *American Economic Review* 91(1): 79–98.

Benartzi, S. and Thaler, R. H. (2004). Save More Tomorrow: Using Behavioral Economics to Increase Employee Savings. *Journal of Political Economy* 112(1): Part 2, S164–S187.

Benartzi, S. and Thaler, R. H. (2013). Behavioral Economics and the Retirement Savings Crisis. *Science* 339: 115253.

Benjamin, D. J. (2018). Errors in Probabilistic Reasoning and Judgment Biases. USC Dornsife Institute for New Economic Thinking Working Paper No. 18-21.

Bernard, T. and Taffesse, A. S. (2014). Aspirations: An Approach to Measurement with Validation Using Ethiopian Data. *Journal of African Economies* 23(2): 189–224.

Bernard, V. L. and Thomas, J. K. (1989). Post-earnings Announcement Drift: Delayed Price Response or Risk Premium? *Journal of Accounting Research* (Supplement): 1–36.

Bernard, V. L. and Thomas, J. K. (1990). Evidence that Stock Prices Do Not Fully Reflect the Implications of Current Earnings for Future Earnings. *Journal of Accounting and Economics* 13: 305–340.

Bertrand, M. and Morse, A. (2011). Information Disclosure, Cognitive Biases, and Payday Borrowing. *Journal of Finance* 66(6): 1865–1893.

Bertrand, M. and Mullainathan, S. (2001). Are CEOs Rewarded for Luck? The Ones Without Principals Are. *Quarterly Journal of Economics* 116(3): 901–932.

Bertrand, M., Karlan, D., Mullainathan, S., Shafir, E., and Zinman, J. (2010). What's Advertising Content Worth? Evidence from a Consumer Credit Marketing Field Experiment. *Quarterly Journal of Economics* 125(1): 263–305.

Beshears, J., Choi J. J., Fuster, A., Laibson D., and Madrian B. C. (2013). What Goes Up Must Come Down? Experimental Evidence on Intuitive Forecasting. *American Economic Review* 103(3): 570–574.

Beshears, J., Choi, J. J., Laibson, D., and Madrian, B. C. (2018). Behavioral Household Finance. In B. Douglas Bernheim, Stefano DellaVigna, and David Laibson (eds.), *Handbook of Behavioral Economics: Foundations and Applications*, Vol. 1. Elsevier: Amsterdam, pp. 177–276.

Bettman, J. R. and Weitz, B. A. (1983). Attributions in the Board Room: Causal Reasoning in Corporate Annual Reports. *Administrative Science Quarterly* 28(2): 165–183.

Biais, B. and Weber, M. (2009). Hindsight Bias, Risk Perception and Investment Performance. *Management Science* 55(6): 1018–1029.

Black, F. (1986) Noise. *Journal of Finance* 41(3): 529–543.

Blanchard, O. and Fischer, S. (1989). *Lectures in macroeconomics*. MIT Press: Cambridge, MA.

Bocskocsky, A., Ezekowitz, J., and Stein, C. (2014). The Hot Hand: A New Approach to an Old Fallacy, Paper presented at the MIT Sloan Sports Analytics Conference.

Bonini, N., Tentori, K., and Osherson, D. (2004). A Different Conjunction Fallacy. *Mind & Language* 19(2): 199–210.

Bonner, B. L. and Bolinger, A. R. (2013). Separating the Confident from the Correct: Leveraging Member Knowledge in Groups to Improve Decision Making and Performance. *Organizational Behavior and Human Decision Processes* 122(2): 214–221.

Börgers, T. and Sarin, R. (2000). Naïve Reinforcement Learning with Endogenous Aspirations. *International Economic Review* 41(4): 921–950.

Borges, B., Goldstein, D. G., Ortmann, A., and Gigerenzer, G. (1999). Can Ignorance Beat the Stock Market? In G. Gigerenzer, P. M. Todd, and the ABC Research Group (eds.), *Simple Heuristics that Make Us Smart*. Oxford University Press: New York, pp. 59–72.

Brase, G. L. (2002a). Which Statistical Formats Facilitate What Decisions? The Perception and Influence of Different Statistical Information Formats. *Journal of Behavioral Decision Making* 15(5): 381–401.

Brase, G. L. (2002b). Ecological and Evolutionary Validity: Comments on Johnson-Laird, Legrenzi, Girotto, Legrenzi, and Cavernis (1999) Mental-Model Theory of Extensional Reasoning. *Psychological Review* 109(4): 72–128.

Breiman, L., Friedman, J. H., Olshen, R. A., and Stone, C. J. (1993). *Classification and Regression Trees*. Chapman and Hall: New York.

Brennan, G. and Buchanan, J. (1980). *The Power to Tax: Analytical Foundations of a Fiscal*

Constitution. Cambridge University Press: Cambridge.

Bröder, A. (2011). The Quest for Take-the-Best: Insights and Outlooks for Experimental Research. In G. Gigerenzer, R. Hertwig, and T. Pachur (eds.), *Heuristics: The Foundations of Adaptive Behavior*. Oxford University Press: Oxford, pp. 363–380.

Bröder A. and Schiffer S. (2003). Take the Best Versus Simultaneous Feature Matching: Probabilistic Inferences from Memory and Effects of Representation Format. *Journal of Experimental Psychology: General* 132(2): 277–293.

Brunnermeier, M. and Parker, J. (2005). Optimal Expectations. *American Economic Review* 95(4): 1092–1118.

Buchanan, J. (1967). *Public Finance in Democratic Process: Fiscal Institutions and the Individual Choice*. University of North Carolina Press: Chapel Hill.

Buehler, R., Messervey, D., and Griffin, D. W. (2005). Collaborative Planning and Prediction: Does Group Discussion Affect Optimistic Biases in Time Estimation? *Organizational Behavior and Human Decision Processes* 97(1): 47–63.

Burson, K. A., Larrick, R. P., and Klayman, J. (2006). Skilled or Unskilled, but Still Unaware of It: How Perceptions of Difficulty Drive Miscalibration in Relative Comparisons. *Journal of Personality and Social Psychology* 90(1): 60–77.

Busse, M. R., Lacetera, N., Pope, D. G., Silva-Risso, J., and Sydnor, J. R. (2013). Estimating the Effect of Salience in Wholesale and Retail Car Markets. *American Economic Review* 103(3): 575–579.

Busse, M. R., Pope, D. G., Pope, J. C., and Silva-Risso, J. (2015). The Psychological Effect of Weather on Car Purchases. *The Quarterly Journal of Economics* 130(1): 371–414.

Camerer, C. F. (1987). Do Biases in Probability Judgment Matter in Markets? Experimental Evidence. *American Economic Review* 77: 981–997.

Camerer, C. F. (1989). Does the Basketball Market Believe in the "Hot Hand"? *American Economic Review* 79(5): 1257–1261.

Camerer, C. F. (1990). Do Markets Correct Biases in Probability Judgment? Evidence from Market Experiments. In J. Kagel and L. Green (eds.), *Advances in Behavioral Economics, Volume 2*. Ablex Publishers: Northwood, NJ, pp. 125–172.

Camerer, C. F. (1995). Individual Decision Making. In J. Kagel and A. E. Roth (eds.), *Handbook of Experimental Economics*. Princeton University Press: Princeton, NJ, pp. 587–703.

Camerer, C. F. and Hogarth, R. M. (1999). The Effects of Financial Incentives in Experiments: A Review and Capital-Labor-Production Framework. *Journal of Risk and Uncertainty* 19: 7–41.

Camerer, C. F. and Lovallo, D. (1999). Overconfidence and Excess Entry: An Experimental Approach. *American Economic Review* 89(1): 306–318.

Camerer, C. F., Loewenstein, G., and Weber, M. (1989). The Curse of Knowledge in Economic Settings: An Experimental Analysis. *Journal of Political Economy* 97: 1232–1254.

Casscells, W., Schoenberger, A., and Graboys, T. B. (1978). Interpretation by Physicians of Clinical Laboratory Results. *New England Journal of Medicine* 299(18): 999–1000.

Chang, T. Y., Huang, W., and Wang, Y. (2018). Something in the Air: Pollution and the Demand for Health Insurance. *The Review of Economic Studies* 85(3): 1609–1634.

Charness, G., Karni, E., and Levin, D., (2010). On the Conjunction Fallacy in Probability Judgment: New Experimental Evidence Regarding Linda. *Games and Economic Behavior* 68: 551–556.

Cheema, A. and Soman, D. (2006). Malleable Mental Accounting: The Effect of Flexibility on the Justification of Attractive Spending and Consumption Decisions. *Journal of Consumer Psychology* 16: 33–44.

Chen, G., Crossland, C., and Luo, S. (2015). Making the Same Mistake All Over Again: CEO Overconfidence and Corporate Resistance to Corrective Feedback. *Strategic Management Journal* 36(10): 1513–1535.

Chernev, A., Böckenholt, U., and Goodman, J. (2015). Choice Overload: A Conceptual Review and Meta-Analysis. *Journal of Consumer Psychology* 25(2): 333–358.

Cherry, T. (2001). Mental Accounting and Other-Regarding Behavior: Evidence from the Lab. *Journal of Economic Psychology* 22: 605–615.

Chetty, R., Looney, A., and Kroft, K. (2009). Salience and Taxation: Theory and Evidence. *American Economic Review* 99(4): 1145–1177.

Cho, I. K. and Matsui, A. (2005). Learning Aspiration in Repeated Games. *Journal of Economic Theory* 124(2): 171–201.

Choi, J. J., Laibson, D., Madrian, B. C., and Metrick, A. (2002). Defined Contribution Pensions: Plan Rules, Participant Decisions, and the Path of Least Resistance. In J. Poterba (ed.), *Tax Policy and the Economy* 16. MIT Press: Cambridge, MA, pp. 67–114.

Choi, J. J., Laibson, D., and Madrian B. C. (2009). Mental Accounting in Portfolio Choice: Evidence from a Flypaper Effect. *American Economic Review* 99(5): 2085–2095.

Choi, J. J., Laibson, D., Madrian, B. C., and Metrick, A. (2004). For Better or for Worse: Default Effects and 401(k) Savings Behavior. In D. Wise (ed.), *Perspectives in the Economics of Aging*. University of Chicago Press: Chicago, pp. 81–121.

Clemen, R. T. and Ulu, C. (2008). Interior Additivity and Subjective Probability Assessment of Continuous Variables. *Management Science* 54(4): 835–851.

Clotfelter, C. T. and P. J. Cook. (1993). The Gambler's Fallacy in Lottery Play. *Management Science* 39(12): 1521–1525.

Colman, A. M., Pulford, B. D., Omtzigt, D., and al-Nowaihi, A. (2010). Learning to Cooperate Without Awareness in Multiplayer Minimal Social Situations. *Cognitive Psychology* 61(3): 201–227.

Conlin, M., O'Donoghue, T., and Vogelsang, T. J. (2007). Projection Bias in Catalog Orders. *American Economic Review* 97(4): 1217–1249.

Cooper, A. C., Woo, C. Y., and Dunkelberg, W. C. (1988). Entrepreneurs' Perceived Chances for Success. *Journal of Business Venturing* 3(2): 97–108.

Cosmides, L. and Tooby, J. (1996). Are Humans Good Intuitive Statisticians After All? Rethinking Some Conclusions from the Literature on Judgment under Uncertainty. *Cognition* 58(1): 1–73.

Courant, P., Gramlich, E., and Laitner, J. (1986). A Dynamic Micro Estimate of the Life Cycle Model. In H. G. Aaron and G. Burtless (eds.), *Retirement and Economic Behavior*. Brookings Institution: Washington, DC.

Coval, J. D., Hirshleifer, D. A., and Shumway, T. (2005). Can Individual Investors Beat the Market? Working paper, Harvard University.

Croson, R. and Sundali, J. (2005). The Gambler's Fallacy and the Hot Hand: Empirical Data from Casinos. *Journal of Risk and Uncertainty* 30(3): 195–209.

Cutler, D., Poterba, J., and Summers, L. (1991). Speculative Dynamics. *Review of Economic Studies* 58: 529–546.

Dalton, P., Ghosal, S., and Mani, A. (2016). Poverty and Aspirations Failure. *Economic Journal* 126(590): 165–188.

Daniel, K., Grinblatt, M., Titman, S., and Wermers, R. (1997). Measuring Mutual Fund Performance with Characteristic-Based Benchmarks. *Journal of Finance* 52(3): 1035–1058.

Daniel, K. and Titman, S. (1997). Evidence on the Characteristics of Cross-Sectional Variation in Stock Returns. *Journal of Finance* 52: 1–33.

Darley, J. and Gross, P. (1983). A Hypothesis-Confirming Bias in Labeling Effects. *Journal of Personality and Social Psychology* 44(1): 20–33.

Datta, S. and Mullainathan, S. (2014). Behavioral Design: A New Approach to Development Policy. *Review of Income and Wealth* 60(1): 7–35.

D'Avolio, G. (2002). The Market for Borrowing Stock. *Journal of Financial Economics* 66: 271–306.

De Bondt, W. and Thaler, R. (1985). Does the Stock Market Overreact? *Journal of Finance* 40(3): 793–808.

De Bondt, W. and Thaler, R. (1987). Further Evidence on Investor Overreaction and Stock Market Seasonality. *Journal of Finance* 42: 557–581.

De Long, J. B., Shleifer, A., Summers, L., and Waldmann, R. (1990b). Positive Feedback Investment Strategies and Destabilizing Rational Speculation. *Journal of Finance* 45: 375–395.

Denzau, A. T. and North, D. C. (1994). Shared Mental Models: Ideologies and Institutions. *Kyklos* 47(1): 3–31.

Dhami, S. (2020). *The Foundations of Behavioral Economic Analysis: Bounded Rationality. Volume V*. Oxford University Press: Oxford.

Dhami, S. and Sunstein, C. R. (2022). *Bounded Rationality Heuristics, Judgment, and Public Policy*. MIT Press: Cambridge, MA.

Diamond, P. and Hausmann, J. (1984). Individual Retirement and Saving Behavior. *Journal of Public Economics* 23: 81–114.

Dorn, D. and Huberman, G. (2005). Talk and Action: What Individual Investors Say and What They Do. *Review of Finance* 9(4): 437–481.

Dorn, D. and Sengmueller, P. (2009). Trading as Entertainment. *Management Science* 55(4): 591–603.

Dunning, D., Johnson, K., Ehrlinger, J., and Krueger, J. (2003). Why People Fail to Recognize their Own Competence. *Current Directions in Psychological Science* 12(3): 83–87.

Dupas, P. and Robinson, J. (2013). Why Don't the Poor Save More? Evidence from Health Savings Experiments. *American Economic Review* 103(4): 1138–1171.

Eddy, D. M. (1982). Probabilistic Reasoning in Clinical Medicine: Problems and Opportunities. In D. Kahneman, P. Slovic, and A. Tversky (eds.), *Judgment under Uncertainty: Heuristics and Biases* Cambridge University Press: New York, pp. 249–267.

Edwards, W. (1968). Conservatism in Human Information Processing. In B. Kleinmutz (ed.), *Formal Representation of Human Judgment*. Wiley: New York, pp. 17–52.

Ehrlinger, J., Johnson, K., Banner, M., Dunning, D., and Krueger, J. (2008). Why the Unskilled Are Unaware: Further Explorations of (Absent) Self-Insight Among the Incompetent. *Organizational Behavior and Human Decision Processes* 105(1): 98–121.

Eisenman, R. (1993). Belief that Drug Usage in the United States is Increasing When It Is Really Decreasing: An example of the Availability Heuristic. *Bulletin of the Psychonomic Society* 31(4): 249–252.

Englich, B. and Mussweiler, T. (2001). Sentencing under Uncertainty: Anchoring Effects in the Courtroom. *Journal of Applied Social Psychology* 31(7): 1535–1551.

Enke, B., Gneezy, U., Hall, B., Martin, D., Nelidov, V., Offerman, T., and van de Ven, J. (2023). Cognitive Biases: Mistakes or Missing Stakes? *Review of Economics and Statistics* 105(4): 818–832.

Epley, N., Mak, D., and Idson, L. C. (2006). Bonus of Rebate?: The Impact of Income Framing on Spending and Saving. *Journal of Behavioral Decision Making* 19(3): 213–227.

Evans, J., Handley, S. J., Perham, N., Over, D. E., and Thompson, V. A. (2000). Frequency Versus Probability Formats in Statistical Word Problems. *Cognition* 77(3): 197–213.

Evers, E. R. K., Imas, A., and Kang, C. (2022). On the Role of Similarity in Mental Accounting and Hedonic Editing. *Psychological Review* 129(4): 777–789.

Fama, E. (1965). The Behavior of Stock Market Prices. *Journal of Business* 38(1): 34–105.

Fama, E. (1970). Efficient Capital Markets: A Review of Theory and Empirical Work. *Journal of Finance* 25(2): 383–417.

Fama, E., Fisher, L., Jensen, M., and Roll, R. (1969). The Adjustment of Stock Prices to New Information. *International Economic Review* 10: 1–21.

Fama, E. and French, K. (1992). The Cross-Section of Expected Stock Returns. *Journal of Finance* 47: 427–465.

Fama, E. and French, K. (1993). Common Risk Factors in the Returns of Bonds and Stocks, *Journal of Financial Economics* 33: 3–56.

Fama, E. and French, K. (1996a). Multifactor Explanations of Asset Pricing Anomalies. *Journal of Finance* 51: 55–84.

Fama, E. and French, K. (1996b). The CAPM Is Wanted, Dead or Alive. *Journal of Finance* 51(5): 1947–1958.

Fama, E. and French, K. (2015). A Five-Factor Asset Pricing Model. *Journal of Financial Economics* 116: 1–22.

Ferraro P. J. and Price, M. K. (2013). Using Nonpecuniary Strategies to Influence Behavior: Evidence from a Large-Scale Field Experiment. *Review of Economics and Statistics* 95(1): 64–73.

Figlewski, S. (1979). Subjective Information and Market Efficiency in a Betting Model. *Journal of Political Economy* 87(1): 75–88.

Finkelstein, A. (2009). E-Z Tax: Tax Salience and Tax Rates. *Quarterly Journal of Economics* 124(3): 969–1010.

Finucane, M. L., Alhakami, A., Slovic, P., and Johnson, S. M. (2000). The Affect Heuristic in Judgments of Risks and Benefits. *Journal of Behavioral Decision Making* 13(1): 1–17.

Fischhoff, B. (1975). Hindsight Biased Foresight: The Effect of Outcome Knowledge on Judgment under Uncertainty. *Journal of Experimental Psychology: Human Perception and Performance* 1(3): 288–299.

Fischhoff B., Slovic, P., Lichtenstein S., Read S., and Combs B. (1978). How Safe Is Safe Enough? A Psychometric Study of Attitudes Toward Technological Risks and Benefits. *Policy Sciences* 9: 127–152.

Frederick, S. (2005). Cognitive Reflection and Decision Making. *Journal of Economic Perspectives* 19(4): 25–42.

French, K. R. and Poterba, J. M. (1991). International Diversification and International Equity Markets. *American Economic Review* 81(2): 22–26.

Friedman, M. (1953). The Methodology of Positive Economics. In *Essays in Positive Economics*. University of Chicago Press: Chicago, pp. 3–43.

Froot, K. and Dabora, E. (1999). How Are Stock Prices Affected by the Location of Trade? *Journal of Financial Economics* 53(2): 189–216.

Galasso, A. and Simcoe, T. S. (2011). CEO Overconfidence and Innovation. *Management Science* 57(8): 1469–1484.

Gao, X. and Lin, T.-C. (2015). Do Individual Investors Treat Trading as a Fun and Exciting Gambling Activity? Evidence from Repeated Natural Experiments. *The Review of Financial Studies* 28(7): 2128–2166.

Genicot, G. and Ray, D. (2017). Asiprations and Inequity. *Econometrica* 85(2): 489–519.

Gervais, S. and Goldstein, I. (2007). The Positive Effects of Biased Self-Perceptions in Firms. Available at SSRN: http://ssrn.com/abstract= 963249.

Gervais, S., Heaton, J. B., and Odean, T. (2011). Overconfidence, Compensation Contracts, and Capital Budgeting. *Journal of Finance* 66(5): 1735–1777.

Gigerenzer, G. (1996). The Psychology of Good Judgment: Frequency Formats and Simple Algorithms. *Medical Decision Making* 16: 273–280.

Gigerenzer, G. and Brighton, H. (2011). Homo Heuristicus: Why Biased Minds Make Better Inferences. Appetizer in G. Gigerenzer, R. Hertwig, and T. Pachur, (eds.), *Heuristics: The Foundations of Adaptive Behavior*. Oxford University Press: Oxford, pp. 2–30.

Gigerenzer, G., Hertwig, R., and Pachur, T. (2011). *Heuristics: The Foundations of Adaptive Behavior*. Oxford University Press: Oxford.

Gigerenzer, G. and Hoffrage, U. (1995). How to Improve Bayesian Reasoning Without Instruction: Frequency Formats. *Psychological Review* 102(4): 684–704.

Gigerenzer, G. and Selten, R. (eds.). (2001). *Bounded Rationality: The Adaptive Toolbox*. MIT Press: Cambridge, MA.

Gigerenzer, G., Todd, P. M., and the ABC Research Group. (1999). Simple Heuristics That Make Us Smart. Oxford University Press: New York.

Gilbert, D. T., Gill, M. J., and Wilson, T. D. (2002). The Future Is Now: Temporal Correction in

Affective Forecasting. *Organizational Behavior and Human Decision Processes* 88(1): 430–444.

Gilovich, T., Vallone, R., and Tversky, A. (1985). The Hot Hand in Basketball: On the Misperception of Random Sequences. *Cognitive Psychology* 17(3): 295–314.

Giné, X., Cuellar, C. M., and Mazer, R. K. (2014). Financial Dis-information: Evidence from an Audit Study in Mexico. Policy Research Working Paper 6902, World Bank, Washington, DC.

Gintis, H. (2009). *The Bounds of Reason: Game Theory and the Unification of the Behavioral Sciences.* Princeton University Press: Princeton, NJ.

Girotto, V. and Gonzalez, M. (2001). Solving Probabilistic and Statistical Problems: A Matter of Information Structure and Question Form. *Cognition* 78: 247–276.

Glaser, M. and Weber, M. (2007). Overconfidence and Trading Volume. *Geneva Risk and Insurance Review* 32(1): 1–36.

Gneezy, U., Imas, A., and Madarász, K. (2014). Conscience Accounting: Emotion Dynamics and Social Behavior. *Management Science* 60(11): 2645–2658.

Goel, A. M. and Thakor, A. V. (2008). Overconfidence Leadership Selection and Corporate Governance. *Journal of Finance* 63(6): 2737–2784.

Goldin, J. and Homonoff, T. (2013). Smoke Gets in Your Eyes: Cigarette Tax Salience and Regressivity. *American Economic Journal: Economic Policy* 5(1): 302–336.

Gollaher, D. L. (2000). *Circumcision: A History of the World's Most Controversial Surgery.* Basic Books: New York.

Gourville, J. T. and Soman, D. (1998). Payment Depreciation: The Effects of Temporally Separating Payments from Consumption. *Journal of Consumer Research* 25(2): 160–174.

Graham, F. and Isaac, A. G. (2002). The Behavioral Life-Cycle Theory of Consumer Behavior: Survey Evidence. *Journal of Economic Behavior and Organization* 48(4): 391–401.

Graham, J. R., Harvey, C. R., and Huang, H. (2009). Investor Competence, Trading Frequency, and Home Bias. *Management Science* 55(7): 1094–1106.

Green, B. S. and Zwiebel, J. (2017). The Hot Hand Fallacy: Cognitive Mistakes or Equilibrium Adjustments? Evidence from Baseball. *Management Science* 64(11): 5315–5348.

Grether, D. M. (1980). Bayes' Rule as a Descriptive Model: The Representativeness Heuristic. *The Quarterly Journal of Economics* 95(3): 537–557.

Grether, D. M. and Plott, C. R. (1979). Economic Theory of Choice and the Preference Reversal Phenomenon. *The American Economic Review* 69(4): 623–638.

Griffin, D. and Tversky, A. (1992). The Weighing of Evidence and the Determinants of Confidence. *Cognitive Psychology* 24(3): 411–435.

Grinblatt, M. and Keloharju, M. (2000). The Investment Behavior and Performance of Various Investor Types: A Study of Finland's Unique Data Set. *Journal of Financial Economics* 55(1): 43–67.

Grinblatt, M. and Keloharju, M. (2009). Sensation Seeking, Overconfidence, and Trading Activity. *Journal of Finance* 64: 549–578.

Grinblatt, M. and Titman, S. (1989). Mutual Fund Performance: An Analysis of Quarterly Portfolio Holdings. *Journal of Business* 62(3): 393–416.

Grinblatt, M., Keloharju, M., and Linnainmaa, J. (2012). IQ, Trading Behavior, and Performance. *Journal of Financial Economics* 104(2): 43–67.

Guilbault, R. L., Bryant, F. B., Brockway, J. H., and Posavac, E. J. (2004). A Meta-Analysis of Research on Hindsight Bias. *Basic and Applied Social Psychology*, 26(2–3): 103–117.

Guryan, J. and Kearney, M. S. (2008). Gambling at Lucky Stores: Empirical Evidence from State Lottery Sales. *American Economic Review* 98(1): 458–473.

Guyon, N. and Huillery, E. (2020). Biased Aspirations and Social Inequality at School: Evidence from French Teenagers. *The Economic Journal* 131(634): 745–796.

Hall, B. J. and Murphy, K. J. (2000). Optimal Exercise Prices for Executive Stock Options. *American Economic Review* 90(2): 209–214.

Hall, B. J. and Murphy, K. J. (2002). Stock Options for Undiversified Executives. *Journal of Accounting and Economics* 33(1): 3–42.

Hastings, J. S. and Shapiro, J. M. (2013). Fungibility and Consumer Choice: Evidence from Commodity Price Shocks. *The Quarterly Journal of Economics* 128(4): 1449–1498.

Haushofer, J. and Fehr, E. (2014). On the Psychology of Poverty. *Science* 344(6186): 862–867.

Heath, C. and Soll, J. B. (1996). Mental Budgeting and Consumer Decisions. *Journal of Consumer Research* 23(1): 40–52.

Heaton, J. B. (2002). Managerial Optimism and Corporate Finance. *Financial Management* 31(2): 33–45.

Henderson, P. W. and Peterson, R. A. (1992). Mental Accounting and Categorization. *Organizational Behavior and Human Decision Processes* 51(1): 92–117.

Hertwig, R., Benz, B., and Krauss, S. (2008). The Conjunction Fallacy and the Many Meanings of *and*. *Cognition* 108: 740–753.

Hertwig, R. and Gigerenzer, G. (1999). The Conjunction Fallacy Revisited: How Intelligent Inferences Look Like Reasoning Errors. *Journal of Behavioral Decision Making* 12(4): 275–305.

Hirshleifer, D., Low, A., and Teoh, S. H. (2012). Are Overconfident CEOs Better Innovators? *Journal of Finance* 67(4): 1457–1498.

Hoffrage, U., Hertwig, R., and Gigerenzer, G. (2000). Hindsight-Bias: A Byproduct of Knowledge Updating? *Journal of Experimental Psychology: Learning Memory and Cognition* 26(3): 566–581.

Holbrook, R. and Stafford, F. (1971). The Propensity to Consume Separate Types of Income: A Generalized Permanent Income Hypothesis. *Econometrica* 39: 1–21.

Hong, H. and Stein, J. (2007). Disagreement and the Stock Market. *Journal of Economic Perspectives* 21(2): 109–128.

Hribar, P. and Yang, H. (2015). CEO Overconfidence and Management Forecasting. *Contemporary Accounting Research* 33(1): 204–227.

Huberman, G. and Regev, T. (2001). Contagious Speculation and a Cure for Cancer: A Non-event that Made Stock Prices Soar. *Journal of Finance* 56(1): 387–396.

Huck, S., Szech, N., and Wenner, L. M. (2018). *More Effort with Less Pay: On Information Avoidance, Belief Design and Performance.* Mimeo University College London.

Hvidkjaer, S. (2008). Small Trades and the Cross-Section of Stock Returns. *Review of Financial Studies* 21(3): 1123–1151.

Ikenberry, D., Lakonishok, J., and Vermaelen, T. (1995). Market Underreaction to Open Market Share Repurchases. *Journal of Financial Economics* 39: 181–208.

Imas, A., Loewenstein, G. F., and Morewedge, C. (2021). Mental Money Laundering: A Motivated Violation of Fungibility. *Journal of the European Economic Association* 19(4): 2209–2233.

Ippolito, R. A. (1989). Efficiency with Costly Information: A Study of Mutual Fund Performance, 1965–1984. Quarterly *Journal of Economics* 104(1): 1–23.

Iyengar, S. S. and Lepper, M. R. (2000). When Choice Is Demotivating: Can One Desire Too Much of a Good Thing? *Journal of Personality and Social Psychology* 79(6): 995–1006.

Jacowitz, K. E. and Kahneman, D. (1995). Measures of Anchoring in Estimation Tasks. *Personality and Social Psychological Bulletin* 21(11): 1161–1166.

Jegadeesh, N. and Titman, S. (1993). Returns to Buying Winners and Selling Losers: Implications for Stock Market Efficiency. *Journal of Finance* 48: 65–91.

Jensen, M. C. (1978). Some Anomalous Evidence Regarding Market Efficiency. *Journal of Financial Economics* 6(2/3): 95–101.

Jensen, R. (2012). Do Labor Market Opportunities Affect Young Women's Work and Family Decisions? Experimental Evidence from India. *Quarterly Journal of Economics* 127(2): 753–792.

Jensen, R. and Oster, E. (2009). The Power of TV: Cable Television and Women's Status in India. *Quarterly Journal of Economics* 124(3): 1057–1094.

Johnson, D. D. P., McDermott, R., Barrett, E. S., Cowden, J., et al. (2006). Overconfidence in

War Games: Experimental Evidence on Expectations, Aggression, Gender and Testosterone. *Proceedings of the Royal Society* B 273: 2513–2520.

Kahan, D. M. (2013). Ideology, Motivated Reasoning, and Cognitive Reflection. *Judgment and Decision Making* 8(4): 407–424.

Kahan, D. M., Peters, E., Dawson, E. C., and Slovic, P. (2017). Motivated Numeracy and Enlightened Self-Government. *Behavioral Public Policy* 1(1): 54–86.

Kahneman, D. (2011). *Thinking Fast and Slow.* Farrar, Strauss, Giroux: New York.

Kahneman, D. and Frederick, S. (2002). Representativeness Revisited: Attribute Substitution in Intuitive Judgment. In T. Gilovich, D. Griffin, and D. Kahneman (eds.), *Heuristics and Biases: The Psychology of Intuitive Judgment*. Cambridge University Press: Cambridge, pp. 103–119.

Kahneman, D. and Tversky, A. (1972a). On Prediction and Judgment. *Oregon Research Institute Bulletin* 12(4).

Kahneman, D. and Tversky, A. (1972b). Subjective Probability: A Judgment of Representativeness. *Cognitive Psychology* 3(3): 430–454.

Kahneman, D. and Tversky, A. (1984). Choices, Values, and Frames. *The American Psychologist* 39(4): 341–350.

Kahneman, D. and Tversky, A. (1996). On the Reality of Cognitive Illusions: A reply to Gigerenzer's Critique. *Psychological Review* 103(3): 582–591.

Kamin, K. A. and Rachlinski, J. J. (1995). Ex Post-Ex ante: Determining Liability in Hindsight. *Law and Human Behavior* 19: 89–104.

Kaniel, R., Liu, S., Saar, G., and Titman, S. (2012). Individual Investor Trading and Return Patterns around Earnings Announcements. *Journal of Finance* 67: 639–680.

Karandikar, R., Mookherjee, D., Debraj, R., and Vega-Redondo, F. (1998). Evolving Aspirations and Cooperation. *Journal of Economic Theory* 80(2): 292–331.

Kardos, P. and Castano, E. (2012). Money Doesn't Stink, or Does it? The Effect of Immorally Acquiring Money on Its Spending. *Current Psychology* 31(4): 381–385.

Karlan, D., Morten, M., and Zinman, J. (2012). A Personal Touch: Text Messaging for Loan Repayment. Working Paper 17952, National Bureau of Economic Research, Cambridge, MA.

Kaur, S., Mullainathan, S., Oh, S., and Schilbach, F. (2022). Do Financial Concerns Make Workers Less Productive? *Quarterly Journal of Economics* https://economics.mit.edu/sites/default/files/2022-09/financial-strain.pdf.

Kelly, E. K. and Tetlock, P. C. (2013). How Wise Are Crowds? Insights from Retail Orders and Stock Returns. *Journal of Finance* 68(3): 1229–1265.

King, M. A. and Dicks-Mireaux L. D. L. (1982). Asset Holdings and the Life Cycle Model. *Economic Journal* 92: 247–267.

Kooreman, P. (2000). The Labeling Effect of a Child Benefit System. *American Economic Review* 90(3): 571–583.

Korniotis, G. M. and Kumar, A. (2009). Do Older Investors Make Better Investment Decisions? *Review of Economics and Statistics* 93(1): 244–265.

Korniotis, G. M. and Kumar, A. (2013). Do Portfolio Distortions Reflect Superior Information or Psychological Biases? *Journal of Financial and Quantitative Analysis* 48(1): 1–45.

Krueger, J. and Dunning, D. (1999). Unskilled and Unaware of it: How Difficulties in Recognizing One's Own Incompetence Lead to Inflated Self-Assessments. *Journal of Personality and Social Psychology* 77(6): 1121–1134.

Krueger, J. and Mueller, R. A. (2002). Unskilled, Unaware, or Both? The Contribution of Social-Perceptual Skills and Statistical Regression to Self-Enhancement Biases. *Journal of Personality and Social Psychology* 82(2): 180–188.

Kuran, T. and Sunstein, C. (1999). Availability Cascades and Risk Regulation. *Stanford Law Review* 51(4): 683–768.

Kyle, A. S. (1985). Continuous Auctions and Insider Trading. *Econometrica* 53: 1315–1336.

La Ferrara, E., Chong, A., and Duryea, S. (2012). Soap Operas and Fertility: Evidence from

Brazil. *American Economic Journal: Applied Economics* 4(4): 1–31.

La Porta, R., Lakonishok, J., Shleifer, A., and Vishny, R. (1997). Good News for Value Stocks: Further Evidence on Market Efficiency. *Journal of Finance* 49: 1541–1578.

Lacetera, N., Pope, D. G., and Sydnor, H. (2012). Heuristic Thinking and Limited Attention in the Car Market. *American Economic Review* 102(5): 2206–2236.

Lakonishok, J., Shleifer, A., and Vishny, R. W. (1992). The Impact of Institutional Trading on Stock Prices. *Journal of Financial Economics* 32(1): 23–44.

Lakonishok, J., Shleifer, A., and Vishny, R. (1994). Contrarian Investment, Extrapolation and Risk. *Journal of Finance* 49: 1541–1578.

Landier, A. and Thesmar, D. (2009). Financial Contracting with Optimistic Entrepreneurs. *Review of Financial Studies* 22(1): 117–150.

Larrick, R. P., Burson, K. A., and Soll, J. B. (2007). Social Comparison and Confidence: When Thinking You're Better Than Average Predicts Overconfidence (and When It Does Not). *Organizational Behavior and Human Decision Processes* 102(1): 76–94.

Lazear, E. P. (2004). Balanced Skills and Entrepreneurship. *American Economic Review* 94(2): 208–211.

Levav, J. and McGraw, A. P. (2009). Emotional Accounting: How Feelings about Money Influence Consumer Choice. *Journal of Marketing Research* 46(1): 66–80.

Levin, L. (1998). Are Assets Fungible? Testing the Behavioral Theory of Life-Cycle Savings. *Journal of Economic Behavior and Organization* 36: 59–83.

Lichtenstein, S. and Slovic, P. (1971). Reversals of Preferences between Bids and Choices in Gambling Decisions. *Journal of Experimental Psychology* 89(1): 46–55.

Lichtenstein, S. and Slovic, P. (eds.) (2006). The Construction of Preference. Cambridge University Press: New York.

Lichtenstein, S., Slovic, P., Fischhoff, B., Layman, M., and Combs, B. (1978). Judged Frequency of Lethal Events. *Journal of Experimental Psychology: Human Learning and Memory* 4(6): 551–578.

Lin, S. W. and Bier, V. M. (2008). A Study of Expert Overconfidence. *Reliability Engineering and System Safety* 93(5): 711–721.

Linnainmaa, J. T. (2010). Do Limit Orders Alter Inferences about Investor Performance and Behavior? *Journal of Finance* 65(4): 1473–1506.

Loewenstein, G. (2005). Projection Bias in Medical Decision Making. *Medical Decision Making* 25(1): 96–105.

Loewenstein, G., O'Donoghue, T., and Rabin, M. (2003). Projection Bias in Predicting Future Utility. *Quarterly Journal of Economics* 118(4): 1209–1248.

Loomes, G., Starmer, C., and Sugden, R. (1991). Observing Violations of Transitivity by Experimental Methods. *Econometrica* 59(2): 425–439.

Loomes, G. and Sugden, R. (1982). Regret Theory: An Alternative Theory of Rational Choice under Uncertainty. *The Economic Journal* 92(368): 805–824.

Lord, C. G., Ross, L., and Lepper, M. R. (1979). Biased Assimilation and Attitude Polarization: The Effects of Prior Theories on Subsequently Considered Evidence. *Journal of Personality and Social Psychology* 37(11): 2098–2109.

Lord, C. G. and Taylor, C. A. (2009). Biased Assimilation: Effects of Assumptions and Expectations on the Interpretation of New Evidence. *Social and Personality Psychology Compass* 3(5): 827–841.

Loughran, T. and Ritter, J. R. (1995). The New Issues Puzzle. *Journal of Finance* 50: 23–52.

Mabe, P. A. and West, S. G. (1982). Validity of Self-Evaluation of Ability: A Review and Meta-Analysis. *Journal of Applied Psychology* 67(3): 280–296.

Macchi, L. (2000). Partitive Formulation of Information in Probabilistic Problems: Beyond Heuristics and Frequency Format Explanations. *Organizational Behavior & Human Decision Processes* 82(2): 217–236.

Mackie, G. (1996). Ending Footbinding and Inbulation: A Convention Account. *American Sociological Review* 61(6): 999–1017.

Malkiel, B. (1990). *A Random Walk Down Wall Street*. W. W. Norton: New York.

Malmendier, U. and Tate, G. (2005). CEO Overconfidence and Corporate Investment. *Journal of Finance* 60: 2661–2700.

Malmendier, U. and Tate, G. (2008). Who Makes Acquisitions? CEO Overconfidence and the Market's Reaction. *Journal of Financial Economics* 89(1): 20–43.

Malmendier, U. and Tate, G. (2015). Behavioral CEOs: On the Role of Managerial Overconfidence. *Journal of Economic Perspectives* 29(4): 37–60.

Malmendier, U., Tate, G., and Yan, J. (2011). Overconfidence and Early-Life Experiences: The Effect of Managerial Traits on Corporate Financial Policies. *Journal of Finance* 66(5): 1687–1733.

Mani, A., Mullainathan, S., Shafir, E., and Zhao, J. (2013). Poverty Impedes Cognitive Function. *Science* 341(6149): 976–980.

McLeod, P. and Dienes, Z. (1996). Do Fielders Know where to Go to Catch the Ball, or Only How to Get there? *Journal of Experimental Psychology: Human Perception and Performance* 22: 531–543.

Meikle, N. L., Tenney, E. R., and Moore, D. A. (2016). Overconfidence at Work: Does Overconfidence Survive the Checks and Balances of Organizational Life? *Research in Organizational Behavior* 36: 121–134.

Mercier, H. and Sperber, D. (2011). Why Do Humans Reason? *Behavioral and Brain Sciences* 34: 57–111.

Metzger, M. (1984). Biases in Betting: An Application of Laboratory Findings. *Psychological Reports* 56(3): 883–888.

Meulbroek, L. K. (2001). The Efficiency of Equity-Linked Compensation: Understanding the Full Cost of Awarding Executive Stock Options. *Financial Management* 30(2): 5–30.

Michaely, R., Thaler, R., and Womack, K. (1995). Price Reactions to Dividend Initiations and Omissions. *Journal of Finance* 50: 573–608.

Milkman, K. L. and Beshears, J. (2009). Mental Accounting and Small Windfalls: Evidence from an Online Grocer. *Journal of Economic Behavior and Organization* 71: 384–394.

Miller, J. B. and Sanjurjo, A. (2018). Surprised by the Gambler's and Hot Hand Fallacies? A Truth in the Law of Small Numbers. *Econometrica* 86(6): 2019–2047.

Mitchell, O. S. and Utkus, S. P. (2002). The Role of Company Stock in Defined Contribution Plans. Wharton Pension Research Council Working Papers No. 444.

Moore, D. A. and Healy, P. J. (2008). The Trouble with Overconfidence. *Psychological Review* 115(2): 502–517.

Moro, R. (2009). On the Nature of the Conjunction Fallacy. *Synthese* 171: 1–24.

Mullainathan, S. (2002). A Memory-Based Model of Bounded Rationality. *Quarterly Journal of Economics* 117(3): 735–774.

Mullainathan, S. and Shafir, E. (2013). *Scarcity: Why Having Too Little Means So Much*. Times Books: New York.

Mullainathan, S., Schwartzstein, J., and Shleifer, A. (2008). Coarse Thinking and Persuasion. *Quarterly Journal of Economics* 123(2): 577–619.

Newell B. R. and Shanks, D. R. (2003). Take the Best or Look at the Rest? Factors Influencing "One-Reason" Decision Making. *Journal of Experimental Psychology: Learning Memory and Cognition* 29(1): 53–65.

Nickerson, R. S. (1998). Confirmation Bias: A Ubiquitous Phenomenon in Many Guises. *Review of General Psychology* 2(2): 175–220.

Northcraft, G. B. and Neale, M. A. (1987). Experts, Amateurs, and Real Estate: An Anchoring-and-Adjustment Perspective on Property Pricing Decisions. *Organizational Behaviour and Human Decision Processes* 39(1): 84–97.

Nunn, N. (2008). The Long-Term Effects of Africa's Slave Trades. *Quarterly Journal of Economics* 123(1): 139–176.

Nunn, N. and Wantchekon, L. (2011). The Slave Trade and the Origins of Mistrust in Africa. *American Economic Review* 101(7): 3221–3252.

Odean, T. (1998). Are Investors Reluctant to Realize Their Losses? *Journal of Finance* 53: 1775–1798.

Odean, T. (1999). Do Investors Trade Too Much? *American Economic Review* 89: 1279–1298.

Odermatt, R. and Stutzer, A. (2019). (Mis-)Predicted Subjective Well-being Following Life Events. *Journal of the European Economic Association* 17(1): 245–283.

Okada, E. M. and Hoch, S. J. (2004). Spending Time Versus Spending Money. *Journal of Consumer Research* 31(2): 313–323.

Pachur, T., Hertwig, R., and Steinmann, F. (2012). How Do People Judge Risks: Availability Heuristic, Affect Heuristic, or Both? *Journal of Experimental Psychology: Applied* 18(3): 314–330.

Pinker, S. (1997). *How The Mind Works*. Norton: New York.

Poterba, J. M. (2003). Employer Stock and 401(k) Plans. *American Economic Review* 93(2): 398–404.

Prelec, D. and Loewenstein, G. (1998). The Red and the Black: Mental Accounting of Savings and Debt. *Marketing Science* 17(1): 428.

Puri, M. and Robinson, D. (2007). Optimism and Economic Choice. *Journal of Financial Economics* 86(1): 71–99.

Rabin, M. and Schrag, J. (1999). First Impressions Matter: A Model of Confirmatory Bias. *Quarterly Journal of Economics* 114(1): 37–82.

Rabin, M. and Vayanos, D. (2010). The Gambler's and Hot-Hand Fallacies: Theory and Applications. *Review of Economic Studies* 77(2): 730–778.

Rabin, M. and Weizsäcker, G. (2009). Narrow Bracketing and Dominated Choices. *American Economic Review* 99(4): 1508–1543.

Rainwater, L., Coleman, R. P., and Handel, G. (1959). *Workingman's Wife. Her Personality, World, and Life Style*. Oceana: New York.

Rajagopal, P. and Rha, J -Y. (2009). The Mental Accounting of Time. *Journal of Economic Psychology* 30(5): 772–781.

Rapoport, A. and Budescu, D. V. (1992). Generation of Random Binary Series in Strictly Competitive Games. *Journal of Experimental Psychology* 121(3): 352–364.

Rapoport, A. and Budescu, D. V. (1997). Randomization in Individual Choice Behavior. *Psychological Review* 104(3): 603–617.

Ray, D. (2006). Aspirations, Poverty and Economic Change. In R. Bénabou, A. Banerjee, and D. Mookherjee (eds.), *What Have We Learnt About Poverty*. Oxford University Press: Oxford, pp. 409–443.

Read, D. and Loewenstein, G. (1995). Diversification Bias: Explaining the Discrepancy in Variety Seeking between Combined and Separated Choice. *Journal of Experimental Psychology: Applied* 1(1): 34–49.

Read D. and Loewenstein G. (1999). Enduring Pain for Money: Decisions Based on the Perception of Memory of Pain. *Journal of Behavioral Decision Making* 12(1): 1–17.

Read, D., Loewenstein, G., and Rabin, M. (1999). Choice Bracketing. *Journal of Risk and Uncertainty* 19(13): 171–197.

Read, D. and van Leeuwen, B. (1998). Predicting Hunger: The Effects of Appetite and Delay on Choice. *Organization Behavior and Human Decision Processes* 76(2): 189–205.

Roll, R. (1986). The Hubris Hypothesis of Corporate Takeovers. *Journal of Business* 59(2): 197–216.

Rosenthal, L. and Young, C. (1990). The Seemingly Anomalias Price Behavior of Royal Dutch/Shell and Unilever N.V./PLC. *Journal of Financial Economics* 26: 123–141.

Roze., M. S. and Kinney, W. R., Jr. (1976). Capital Market Seasonality: The Case of Stock Returns. *Journal of Financial Economics* 3: 379–402.

Rubinstein, M. (2001). Rational Markets: Yes or No? The Affirmative Case. *Financial Analysts Journal* 57(3): 15–29.

Scarpetta, S., Hemmings, P., Tressel, T., and Jaejoon, W. (2002). The Role of Policy and Institutions for Productivity and Firm Dynamics: Evidence from Micro and Industry Data. OECD working paper No. 329.

Scharfstein, D. S. and Stein, J. C. (1990). Herd Behavior and Investment. *American Economic Review* 80(3): 465–479.

Scheibehenne, B. and Bröder, A. (2007). Predicting Wimbledon 2005 Tennis Results by Mere Player Name Recognition. *International Journal of Forecasting* 23(3): 415–426.

Scheibehenne, B., Greifeneder, R., and Todd, P. M. (2010). Can There Ever Be Too Many Options?

A Meta-Analytic Review of Choice Overload. *Journal of Consumer Research* 37(3): 409–425.

Schwartz, B. (2000). Self-Determination: The Tyranny of Freedom. *American Psychologist* 55(1): 79–88.

Schwarz, N., Strack, F., and Mai, H. P. (1991). Assimilation and Contrast Effects in Partwhole Question Sequences: A Conversational Logic Analysis. *Public Opinion Quarterly* 55(1): 3–23.

Selten R. (1998). Aspiration Adaptation Theory. *Journal of Mathematical Psychology* 42(2): 191–214.

Sethi-Iyengar, S., Huberman, G., and Jiang, G. (2004). How Much Choice is Too Much? Contributions to 401(k) Retirement Plans. In Olivia S. Mitchell and Stephen P. Utkus (eds.), *Pension Design and Structure: New Lessons from Behavioral Finance*. Oxford University Press: Oxford, pp. 83–97.

Shafir, E. and Thaler, R. H. (2006). Invest Now, Drink Later, Spend Never: The Mental Accounting of Delayed Consumption. *Journal of Economic Psychology* 27(5): 694–712.

Shah, A. K., Mullainathan, S., and Shafir, E. (2012). Some Consequences of Having Too Little. *Science* 338: 682–685.

Shefrin, H. and Statman, M. (1984). Explaining Investor Preference for Cash Dividends. *Journal of Financial Economics* 13: 253–282.

Shefrin, H. and Thaler, R. H. (1988). The Behavioral Life-Cycle Hypothesis. *Economic Inquiry* 26: 609–643.

Shefrin, H. M. and Thaler, R. (2004). *Mental Accounting, Saving and Self Control. Chapter 14 in Camerer C. (ed.) Advances in Behavioral Economics*. Princeton University Press: Princeton, NJ.

Shiller, R. (1981). Do Stock Prices Move Too Much to Be Justified by Subsequent Changes in Dividends? *American Economic Review* 71(3): 421–436.

Shiller, R. (2003). From Efficient Markets Theory to Behavioral Finance. *Journal of Economic Perspectives* 17(1): 83–104.

Shiller, R. (2015). *Irrational Exuberance.* 3rd edn. Princeton University Press: Princeton, NJ.

Shleifer, A. (1986). Do Demand Curves for Stocks Slope Down? *Journal of Finance* 41: 579–590.

Shleifer, A. (2000). *Inefficient Markets: An Introduction to Behavioral Finance.* Oxford University Press: Oxford.

Shleifer, A. and Vishny, R. (1997). The Limits of Arbitrage. *Journal of Finance* 52: 35–55.

Simon, H. A. (1957). *Models of Man.* Wiley: New York.

Simon, H. A. (1978). Rational Decision-Making in Business Organizations. Nobel Memorial Lecture, December 8, 1978.

Simon, H. A. (1982). *Models of Bounded Rationality. Volume 1: Economic Analysis and Public Policy. Volume 2: Behavioural Economics and Business Organization: 1982* (reprinted 1983). MIT Press: Cambridge, MA.

Simon, H. A. (2000). Bounded Rationality in Social Science: Today and Tomorrow. *Mind and Society* 1(1): 25–39.

Simonson, I. (1990). The Effect of Purchase Quantity and Timing on Variety-Seeking Behavior. *Journal of Marketing Research* 27(2): 150–162.

Sloman, S. A., Over, D., Slovak, L., and Stibel, J. M. (2003). Frequency Illusions and Other Fallacies. *Organizational Behavior and Human Decision Processes* 91(2): 296–309.

Slovic, P. (1995). The Construction of Preferences. *American Psychologist* 50(5): 364–371.

Slovic, P., Finucane, M., Peters, E., and MacGregor, D. G. (2002). The Affect Heuristic. In T. Gilovich, D. Griffin, and D. Kahneman (eds.), *Heuristics and Biases: The Psychology of Intuitive Judgment*. Cambridge University Press: New York, pp. 397–420.

Slovic, P., MacGregor, D. G., Malmfors, T., and Purchase, I. F. H. (1999). Influence of Affective Processes on Toxicologists Judgments of Risk (Report No. 992). Decision Research: Eugene, OR.

Smith, D., Loewenstein, G., Jepson, C., Jankovich, A., Feldman, H., and Ubel, P. (2008). Mispredicting and Misremembering: Patients with Renal Failure Overestimate Improvements in Quality of Life After a Kidney Transplant. *Health Psychology* 27(5): 653–658.

Solnik, B. and Zuo, L. (2011). A global equilibrium asset pricing model with home preference. *Management Science* 58(2): 273–92.

Soman, D. (2001). The Mental Accounting of Sunk Time Costs: Why Time is Not Like Money. *Journal of Behavioral Decision Making* 14(3): 169–185.

Soman, D. and Cheema, A. (2001). The Effect of Windfall Gains on the Sunk Cost Effect. *Marketing Letters* 12(1): 49–60.

Spiess, D. K. and Affleck-Graves, J. (1995). Underperformance in Long-Run Stock Returns Following Seasoned Equity Offerings. *Journal of Financial Economics* 38: 243–268.

Staats, B. R., Milkman, K. L., and Fox, C. R. (2012). The Team Scaling Fallacy: Underestimating the Declining Efficiency of Larger Teams. *Organizational Behavior and Human Decision Processes* 118(2): 132–142.

Stanovich, K. E. and West, R. F. (2007). Natural Myside Bias is Independent of Cognitive Ability. *Thinking and Reasoning* 13(3): 225–247.

Stanovich, K. E. and West, R. F. (2008). On the Relative Independence of Thinking Biases and Cognitive Ability. *Journal of Personality and Social Psychology* 94(4): 672–695.

Stolarz-Fantino, S., Fantino, E., Zizzo, D. J., and Wen, J. (2003). The Conjunction Fallacy: New Evidence for Robustness. *American Journal of Psychology* 116(1): 15–34.

Strack, F., Martin, L. L., and Schwarz, N. (1988). Priming and Communication: The Social Determinants of Information Use in Judgments of Life-Satisfaction. *European Journal of Social Psychology* 18(5): 429–442.

Subrahmanyam, A. (2008). Behavioral Finance: A Review and Synthesis. *European Financial Management* 14(1): 12–29.

Sunstein, C. R. (1996). Social Norms and Social Roles. *Columbia Law Review* 96(4): 903–968.

Tasimi, A. R and Gelman, S. A. (2017). Dirty Money: The Role of Moral History in Economic Judgments. *Cognitive Science* 41(S3): 523–544.

Tenney, E. R., Logg, J. M., and Moore, D. A. (2015). (Too) Optimistic About Optimism: The Belief That Optimism Improves Performance. *Journal of Personality and Social Psychology* 108(3): 377–399.

Tentori, K., Bonini, N., and Osherson, D. (2004). The Conjunction Fallacy: A Misunderstanding About Conjunction? *Cognitive Science* 28(3): 467–477.

Tentori, K. and Crupi, V. (2012). On the Conjunction Fallacy and the Meaning of *and*, Yet Again: A Reply to Hertwig, Benz, and Krauss (2008). *Cognition* 122: 123–134.

Tentori, K., Crupi, V., and Russo, S. (2013). On the Determinants of the Conjunction Fallacy: Probability vs. Inductive Confirmation. *Journal of Experimental Psychology: General* 142: 235–255.

Terrell, D. (1998). Biases in Assessments of Probabilities: New Evidence from Greyhound Races. *Journal of Risk and Uncertainty* 17(2): 151–166.

Terrell, D. and Farmer, A. (1996). Optimal Betting and Efficiency in Parimutuel Betting Markets with Information Costs. *The Economic Journal* 106(437): 846–868.

Thaler, R. H. (1980). Toward a Positive Theory of Consumer Choice. *Journal of Economic Behavior and Organization* 1(1): 39–60.

Thaler, R. H. (1985). Mental Accounting and Consumer Choice. *Marketing Science* 4(3): 199–214. Republished (2008) in *Marketing Science*.

Thaler, R. H. (1999). Mental Accounting Matters. *Journal of Behavioral Decision Making* 12: 183–206.

Thaler, R. H. (2015). *Misbehaving: The Making of Behavioral Economics.* W. W. Norton: New York.

Thaler, R. H. and Benartzi, S. (2007). The Behavioral Economics of Retirement Savings Behavior. AARP Public Policy Institute Working Paper 2007–02.

Thaler, R. and Johnson, E. (1990). Gambling with the House Money and Trying to Break Even: The Effects of Prior Outcomes on Risky Choice. *Management Science* 36: 643–660.

Thaler, R. H. and Shefrin, H. M. (1981). An Economic-Theory of Self-Control. *Journal of Political Economy* 89(2): 392–406.

Tversky, A. and Gilovich T. (1989a). The Cold Facts about the "Hot Hand" in Basketball. *Chance* 2(1): 16–21.

Tversky, A. and Gilovich T. (1989b). The Hot Hand: Statistical Reality or Cognitive Illusion? *Chance* 2(4): 31–34.

Tversky, A. and Kahneman, D. (1971). Belief in the Law of Small Numbers. *Psychological Bulletin* 76: 105–110.

Tversky, A. and Kahneman, D. (1973). Availability: A heuristic for Judging Frequency and Probability. *Cognitive Psychology* 5(2): 207–232.

Tversky, A. and Kahneman, D. (1974). Judgment under Uncertainty: Heuristics and Biases. *Science* 185: 1124–1131.

Tversky, A. and Kahneman, D. (1983). Extensional vs. Intuitive Reasoning: The Conjunction Fallacy in Probability Judgment. *Psychological Review* 90(4): 293–315.

Tversky, A. and Kahneman, D. (1992). Advances in Prospect Theory: Cumulative Representation of Uncertainty. *Journal of Risk and Uncertainty* 5(4): 297–323.

Tversky, A. and Koehler, D. J. (1994). Support Theory: A Nonextensional Representation of Subjective Probability. *Psychological Review* 101(4): 547–567.

VanEpps, E. M., Downs, J. S., and Loewenstein, G. (2016). Calorie Label Formats: Using Numbers or Traffic Lights to Reduce Lunch Calories. *Journal of Public Policy and Marketing* 35(1): 26–36.

Wason, P. C. (1968). Reasoning About a Rule. *Quarterly Journal of Experimental Psychology* 20: 273–281.

Windschitl, P. D., Krueger, J., and Simms, E. (2003). The Influence of Egocentrism and Focalism on People's Optimism in Competitions: When What Affects Us Equally Affects Me More. *Journal of Personality and Social Psychology* 85(3): 389–408.

World Development Report (2015). *Mind, Society, and Behaviour*. The World Bank: Washington, DC.

Wurgler, J. and Zhuravskaya, K. (2002). Does Arbitrage Flatten Demand Curves for Stocks? *Journal of Business* 75: 583–608.

Zajonc, R. B. (1980). Feeling and Thinking: Preferences Need No Inferences. *American Psychologist* 35(2): 151–175.

Zeng, J., Chen, H., Xiong, X., Su, L., Hou, X. (2021). A Genetic Determinant of the Preference Reversal Phenomenon. *The American Journal of Psychology* 134(2): 167–174.

Problems for Part V

1. Consider Example 9.2. Compute the statistically correct answer, $P(A \mid RBB) = 0.75$, using a binomial distribution and Bayes' Law.
2. Tversky and Kahneman (1974) asked two groups of subjects to take five seconds to make the following two calculations: (i) $1 \times 2 \times \cdots \times 8$, and (ii) $8 \times 7 \times \cdots \times 1$. The correct answer to the identical calculations is 40,320. However, the median answers to the ascending and descending sequences are, respectively, 512 and 2250. What accounts for the different answers of the subjects?
3. (Kahneman, 2011) Subjects were asked the following two questions in a San Francisco Exploratorium.
   (a) (Comparative judgment question) Is the height of the tallest redwood more or less than "a" feet?
   (b) (Absolute judgment question) What is your best guess about the height of the tallest redwood?

   In the comparative judgment question, the anchor value is "a" feet and it varies in different treatments. Two different values of the anchor, measured in feet, were given to two different groups of subjects; a high anchor value, $a = 1200$, and a low anchor value, $a = 180$. The answers to the absolute judgment question in the high and the low anchor treatments, respectively, were 844 and 282. Using the method introduced of Jacowitz and Kahneman (1995), calculate the *anchoring index*. Is the extent of anchoring in this problem greater or smaller than the extent of anchoring in Example 9.3?
4. (Casscells et al., 1978) Consider the following problem, a variant of which was given to students at Harvard Medical School. Suppose that a police breathalyzer test discovers false drunkenness in 5% of the cases when the driver is sober. However, the breathalyzers are always able to detect a truly drunk person with complete certainty. In the general population, 1/1000 of drivers engage in driving while drunk. Suppose that a driver is checked at random, and takes a breathalyzer test, which shows that the driver is drunk. How high is the probability that the driver is actually drunk?
   (a) Find the statistically correct answer.
   (b) The modal response of subjects in an experiment was 95%, the mean response was 56%, and a sixth of the students gave the statistically correct answer. What inferences can you draw from these results?
5. Explain the answers to these questions based on the heuristics that people might employ.
   (a) Why do some people become scared of flying after they observe a plane crash, even if statistically the probability of another crash is still the same? Which heuristic explains the behavior of people?

(b) A used car salesman has the following typical strategy for selling cars. His car is really worth £5000. But he starts his negotiations with a buyer by asking for a starting price of £6000. He then negotiates the price down to £5750 at which point the buyer is happy to buy the car. What heuristic is the salesman exploiting?

(c) Why are many stock market traders, who earned exceptionally high returns last year, likely to earn lower returns this year? Furthermore, those who earned very poor returns last year are likely to earn better returns this year. What statistical phenomena can explain this finding?

6. Consider the problem of *conservatism*, or the *underweighting of the likelihood of a sample*. Consider the following problem in Camerer (1995), originally proposed by Edwards (1968). Suppose that there are two urns A and B, each of which contains only red and blue balls. Urn A has seven red and three blue balls and urn B has three red and seven blue balls. A sample of 12 balls is drawn *with replacement* from one of the urns. Subjects do not know which urn was chosen to draw the balls from. But they do know that each urn was equally likely to be chosen, that is, $P(A) = 0.5$ and $P(B) = 0.5$.

   Denote the number of red balls in a sample of size 12 by $x \in \{0, 1, \ldots, 12\}$. Consider the sample of eight red and four blue balls, which does not equal the exact proportions in any of the two urns. Let p_A and p_B be the respective probabilities of drawing a red ball from urns A and B.

   (a) Find the statistically correct conditional probability of getting a sample of eight red and four blue balls from urn A, that is, $P(A \mid x = 8)$.

   (b) The typical response in experiments is that $P(A \mid x = 8) \approx 0.7$ to 0.8. What can we conclude.

7. (Biais and Weber, 2009) Suppose that risk averse investors are interested in investing in an asset, say, a stock. The underlying return on the asset has an unknown variance that is either high, σ_H^2, or low, σ_L^2. Obviously, the higher is the variance, or the risk, the lower is the amount that investors will wish to invest in the asset. They try to infer the unknown variance by using their observations of actual returns.

   Suppose that an investor invests in the asset at time t, and predicts that the asset will give a return y when it matures at time $t+j$. The actual random variable that denotes the random return on the asset is X. At time $t+j$, the actual return is x, which is the realization of the random variable X. Provide an argument in plain English why, in this postdictive judgment, investors subject to hindsight-bias will underestimate financial market volatility.

8. (Kamin and Rachlinski, 1995) Consider the following experimental instructions given to subjects. A municipality may undertake flood precautions that cost $\$10^5$ but if the floods do occur they cause damages worth $\$10^7$. The efficacy of flood precautions is ex-ante uncertain but subjects were provided with meteorological and anecdotal data. One group of subjects, group A, was asked to predict the probability of a flood (this is the group that makes the predictive judgment). Subjects in this group were told that if they find the probability of floods to be greater than 10%, based on the meteorological and anecdotal data, then they should decide to take the precaution.

   Another group of subjects, group B, was also provided with the same meteorological and anecdotal data and asked to make a postdictive judgment. Group B was informed that the precautions had not been taken by the municipality and a flood had occurred. They were instructed that if their postdictive judgment is that the probability of a flood was greater than 10%, based on the same data provided to group A, then they should find the municipality guilty. In Group A, 24% of the subjects thought that the precautions were merited, while 57% in group B found the municipality guilty. How can you explain this data?

9. In the context of the 9/11 tragedy in the US, Kahneman (2011) cites public reaction when it was revealed that in July 2001 the CIA had come across information to suggest that al-Qaeda might be planning an attack on the US. In this case, the CIA did not pass on the information to the President but did pass it on to the National Security Advisor. A former executive editor of the *Washington Post* wrote (p. 294): "It seems elementary to me that if you've got the story that is going to dominate history you might as well go right up to the President." How would you evaluate this statement?
10. In the experiments in Bonini et al. (2004), subjects allocated 7 euros among the following three possible options. To facilitate comparison with the Linda problem, we use the same acronyms, B and F, for the two events.

    1 Option B.
    2 Option $B \wedge F$ (where $\wedge$ is the logical operator "and").
    3 Option $B \wedge (\sim F)$, where $\sim F$ is the option "not F."

    The third option controls for the objection that subjects may actually be interpreting (1) as (3), that is, the option B as $B \wedge (\sim F)$. Across all blocks of experiments, the average amount allocated to the three options was, respectively, 1.99 euros, 3.15 euros, and 1.86 euros. The difference between the allocations to options 1 and 2 is statistically significant. Why do these results show that the subjects engaged in the conjunction fallacy (in fact, 85.32% of the subjects engaged in the conjunction fallacy, which is close to the figure of 85% reported in Tversky and Kahneman, 1983)?
11. In their experiments, in two different treatments, Darley and Gross (1983) create two different profiles of a girl in a between-subjects design. In Treatment 1, she is the daughter of college graduates who hold white-collar jobs and a video clip of the girl playing in a prosperous, middle-class, neighborhood is shown to subjects. In Treatment 2, she is the daughter of high school graduates who hold blue-collar jobs and a video clip of the girl playing in a poor, inner-city, neighborhood is shown to the subjects. The subjects in each treatment are divided into two groups. Group A is used to elicit prior beliefs of the girl's scholastic abilities, and group B is asked to form posterior beliefs of the girl's scholastic abilities. The idea is to see the differences between the prior and posterior beliefs of groups A and B, respectively, in the two treatments. Given the information provided, the average prior beliefs of group A about the reading abilities of the girl in the first treatment is slightly higher (4.29) as compared to the second treatment (3.90).

    Subjects in group B, in both treatments, are provided identical evidence on the girl's scholastic abilities in the form of a video clip in which the girl answers a series of questions with varying degrees of success. They are then asked to state their posterior beliefs. The average posterior beliefs in group B about the girl's reading abilities, in both treatments, were significantly different from the prior beliefs of the corresponding subjects in group A.

Table 10.2 A two-player coordination game

	C	D
C	$1, 1$	$-1, -1$
D	$-1, -1$	$0, 0$

Group B subjects in the Treatment 2 (inner-city) rated the girl's average ability to be 3.71, as compared to the prior belief, 3.90, of group A for that treatment. Group B subjects in the Treatment 1 (middle class) rated this ability to be 4.67, which is statistically higher than the prior estimate of group A individuals for this treatment, 4.29. Remember that subjects viewed identical evidence.

What can we conclude from this evidence?

12. How can we explain the endowment effect using projection bias?
13. (Mullainathan et al., 2008) Consider Arnold Schwarzenegger's memorable speech at the 2004 Republican National Convention. In the best remembered part of his speech, Schwarzenegger defended free trade: "To those critics who are so pessimistic about our economy, I say: Don't be economic girlie men!... Now they say India and China are overtaking us. Don't you believe it. We may hit a few bumps—but America always moves ahead. That's what Americans do." How might a neoclassical economist and a behavioral economist, respectively, try to understand this speech?
14. Consider the following observation from Datta and Mullainathan (2014). "Farmers might overuse nitrogenous fertilizers because they believe that such fertilizers promote greener plants. This model works well for plants like spinach but not as well for grains, because it over-encourages green healthy leafs at the cost of lower crop yields." How might a neoclassical and behavioral economist view this information?
15. Consider the prisoner's dilemma game in Table 10.1 and the aspiration adaptation framework in Section 10.8. The initial aspirations are given in (10.15), $\gamma = 1$ in (10.13), and there is no inertia, $p = 0$. In Section 10.8 we considered the case $s_0 = (D, D)$. Find the solution to the dynamic problem when $s_0 = (C, C)$ and show that in every subsequent time period, the strategy profile (C, C) is played. However, if $s_0 = (D, C)$, then trace the path of play for the first few time periods, say, till five, and show that play does not settle down to any particular pattern.
16. Consider the two-player coordination game in Table 10.2.

    In this game, coordination refers to choosing the strategy profile (C, C), which is also the Pareto optimal outcome. If both players coordinate on (C, C) they get the highest payoff of 1 each. If players do not coordinate their actions (any of the two profiles (D, C) or (C, D)) then each receives the lowest possible payoff of -1. However, if they coordinate on (D, D), then both get a zero payoff. In classical game theory, there are two Nash equilibria in this game (C, C) and (D, D). However, it is not clear without further refinements of equilibrium (e.g., imposing payoff dominance that would give rise to (C, C) in equilibrium), which of these two equilibria will be played.

Suppose instead that the players follow aspiration adaptation as outlined in Section 10.8. Assume that the initial aspiration levels are given by $a_{10} = a_{20} = -0.1$. Suppose that $\gamma = 1$ in (10.13), and there is no inertia, $p = 0$.

(a) Show that if the initial strategy profile is $s_0 = (C, C)$, then the prediction of the model is that players will continue coordinating at (C, C) for all time periods.

(b) Show that if the initial strategy profile is $s_0 = (C, D)$, the strategy profile settles at (D, C) for all time periods, starting at $t = 1$.

(c) Show that if the initial strategy profile is $s_0 = (D, D)$, then it is played in every future time period.

17. (Dupas and Robinson, 2013) In Kenya, many households do not invest sufficiently in health care activities such as buying insecticide-treated mosquito nets that are not prohibitively expensive. In the baseline intervention, individuals are provided with a lockable box with padlock, keys, and a passbook that they can use to keep track of the cash deposited in the lockable box. In three other treatments, they vary other aspects of the baseline such as not providing the keys, or exerting a degree of social pressure. After 12 months, the take-up rates were between 66% and 97% in the four treatments. How can you explain these findings?

18. Cherry (2001) finds that when dictators propose a split of an "earned" endowment, they exhibit self-regarding behavior 76% of the time. However, if they are using experimenter-provided, or "unearned" endowment, they exhibit self-regarding behavior only 26% of the time. How can you explain this finding?

19. Answer this question in terms of the standard neoclassical lifecycle model and the lifecycle model of Shefrin and Thaler (2004) in Section 10.6.1.

(a) What are the implications of rapidly rising house prices on the consumption and savings behavior of households?

(b) What are the implications for savings and consumption when income is received in the form of (i) bonuses versus small windfalls; (ii) bonuses versus large windfalls.

20. Denote wealth by y, and the reference point by r. Define $x = y - r$ as the increment in wealth relative to the reference point. Then, the power form of the utility function, u, in prospect theory (see Part I) is given by

$$u(x) = \begin{cases} x^{\beta} & \text{if } x \geq 0 \\ -\lambda(-x)^{\beta} & \text{if } x < 0 \end{cases}. \tag{10.22}$$

Let us use the experimentally observed typical values of the parameters of the utility function: $\beta = 0.88$ and $\lambda = 2.25$ (Tversky and Kahneman, 1992). All amounts in this question are expressed to a reference point.

(a) Show that an individual prefers to split the composite amount 100 into two equal gains of 50 each.

(b) Show that an individual prefers to incur the composite loss 100, rather than incur two separate losses of 50 each.

(c) Suppose that an individual has the choice of receiving two outcomes $a = -5$ and $b = 12.565$ either separately or by integrating the two (i.e., $a + b$). Show that the individual prefers to receive the integrated amount.

(d) Suppose that an individual has the choice of receiving two outcomes $a = -6000$ and $b = 10$ either separately or by integrating the two (i.e., $a + b$). Show that the individual prefers to receive the two amounts separately. How is this related to the silver lining principle and what possible applications can you think of?

21. Consider the Prelec and Loewenstein (1998) model described in Section 10.6.3. Using this model explain the following, but do not use arguments based on self-control issues:
    (a) Why do many people prefer to buy tokens at casinos upfront and then use them later in the casino?
    (b) Why do individuals who go on holiday to a foreign country report that things are much cheaper abroad even when they are not?
    (c) Prelec and Loewenstein (1998) report that in one study, about 65% of consumers selected a flat-rate telephone payment scheme when an alternative variable rate scheme would have saved them money. In contrast, only 10% of those who chose the variable rate payment option could have saved money by switching to the flat-rate scheme. How might you explain these empirical results?
    (d) Why do Club Med vacations cover several activities (travel, meals, lodging, and recreation) under a single fee (e.g., why not just add them to the ticket price of the vacation)?
22. (House money effect) Consider the following experiments and results in Thaler and Johnson (1990). Subjects in their experiments were given the following three problems. The percentage of subjects making each choice is given in square brackets.

    Problem 1. You have just won $30. Now choose between:
    (a) A 50% chance to gain $9 and a 50% chance to lose $9. [70]
    (b) No further gain or loss. [30]

    Problem 2. You have just lost $30. Now choose between:
    (a) A 50% chance to gain $9 and a 50% chance to lose $9. [40]
    (b) No further gain or loss. [60]

    Problem 3. You have just lost $30. Now choose between:
    (a) A 33% chance to gain $30 and a 67% chance to gain nothing. [60]
    (b) A sure $10. [40]

    How would you interpret the experimental findings?
23. (Huberman and Regev, 2001; Hong and Stein, 2007). News that a biotechnology firm, EntreMed had undertaken pathbreaking research into cancer treatment appeared in the journal *Nature* in November 1997. The news also appeared in the newspaper *The Times* on page A28 (not a particularly salient page), as well as in other media. This resulted in an increase in the price of EntreMed stocks. However, five months later, on May 3, 1998, *The Times* carried out a front page story (a very salient page) on topical cancer research innovations in which EntreMed's contributions were noted prominently. The stock price of EntreMed rose from $12/share to $52/share within a day. Is the observed behavior of stock prices consistent with the efficient markets hypothesis? What might account for the observed pattern of stock market price of EntreMed?

Part VI

Further Topics in Behavioral Economics

Introduction to Part VI

The final part of the book contains two chapters.

Chapter 11 provides an introduction to a range of important topics in behavioral economics. The organization of the chapter allows the topics to be read independently of each other.

We begin the chapter with the topic of *happiness economics*, which asks questions about the ultimate aim of economic policy. In neoclassical economics, individuals are the best judges of their own actions and they make considered choices that reflect their underlying preferences. Hence, the ultimate aim of policy, if individual welfare alone is of interest, is the maximization of individual utility. If, however, societal welfare is of interest, the aim is to maximize some aggregation of the utilities of all members of society. However, in practice, behavioral factors may uncouple preferences from choices; the utilities of members of society might not be fully known to policymakers; or alternative policies might require us to make interpersonal comparisons of utility that are potentially problematic. Happiness economics advances an alternative view, namely, that the purpose of any public policy is to maximize the happiness of society. Happiness itself is measured using the self reports of members of society. This gives rise to cardinal data on well-being. We examine the problems of basing a measure of well-being on cardinal data and the correlates of happiness that include the following: income, unemployment, inequality, age, gender, and the presence or absence of democratic institutions.

We then consider some of the main findings from the emerging literature on *behavioral industrial organization* that is organized around two themes. The first theme is an evaluation of the work of Akerlof and Shiller on *phishing for phools*. The basic idea here is that firms might take advantage of consumer psychology to increase profits, at the cost of consumer surplus. We examine the relevant notion of a market equilibrium in this case and the contrast between formal and informal approaches to theory building. The second theme is the examination of strategies followed by firms in the presence of limited attention by consumers towards some component of price, such as add-ons to prices. Both themes add valuable insights to classical industrial organization.

Two related topics, that we nevertheless treat in separate sections, are *salience* and *limited attention*. In a world where goods have many different attributes, and consumers compare those goods, we ask which attributes might be particularly salient, and how they impinge on optimal choices. We then propose a framework for modeling limited attention and discuss economic applications.

Complexity economics offers a promising alternative framework, or a very useful complement at the least, to the current mainstream school of macroeconomics. It envisages a world in which all economic agents use *low-level rationality* in the form of simple rules of thumb in the presence of true uncertainty (unknown unknowns). Economic agents use adaptive learning, using past data, to refine their choice of the rules of thumb, as they obtain more information about the feedback between aggregate outcomes and their own choices. Within this entirely plausible framework, we obtain striking results that are not possible within mainstream macroeconomics. These include *endogenous fluctuations* without any apparent external shocks, *emergent phenomena* that cannot be predicted from individual actions (the outcomes are greater than the sum total of the parts), and *chaotic dynamics* such that the system dynamics are overly sensitive to very small changes in the initial conditions. The emergent phenomena are complex and appear to an outsider to be choreographed by an intelligent social planner, although there is no such planner. We also describe several applications including the *choice of technology* among competing technologies in the presence of increasing returns, and *agent-based modelling*.

We offer a brief discussion on *learning models* while focussing on just two classical learning models, *reinforcement learning* and *belief-based learning*. These models differ in the extent of rationality that they assume. Reinforcement learning does not require players to know anything more than the past data on the actions they took and the payoffs that resulted. The conversion of their actions into payoffs can be a complex function of the strategies followed by their opponents and the economic environment, but they are not aware of this. Yet, players learn, even if they do so slowly. In belief-based models, players do understand the mapping between their actions, the actions of the opponent, and the payoffs. However, their beliefs are not as sophisticated as under neoclassical game theory. For instance, in a model of Cournot competition, firms might hold the belief that the opponent will simply pick the strategy they did in the last period. The model then determines the probabilities with which players play their current actions.

The last section examines the evidence on *double auction experiments*, a particular institution that is able to mimic the outcome of a perfectly competitive economy. However, the result is of more academic interest than practical use because the conditions required for a perfectly competitive equilibrium are rarely met. We also know from the "theory of the second best" that if all the required conditions do not hold, then there is no justification for satisfying the remaining conditions. The results in double auction experiments also rely on a "market improvement rule" that predisposes even zero intelligence robots in some cases to play a perfectly competitive equilibrium. However, in more complex environments, these results do not survive, nor do we see the institution of double auctions widely used. These experiments use an induced-value design (essentially tell people what their value for an object is). However, when such a design is not used and people can use their actual subjective values, then we know, from Part I, that an endowment effect arises, that does not give rise to market efficiency.

In the second chapter, Chapter 12, we outline and discuss some of the main issues in *behavioral welfare economics*. Welfare economics within the neoclassical tradition is relatively unproblematic. Individuals are the best judges of their actions, and they make considered, rational, deliberate, choices that reflect their underlying preferences. This gives rise to a well-defined correspondence between the true underlying preferences and the observed choices of individuals. Hence, we may place normative significance on the observed choices, recover the underlying preferences using revealed preference arguments, and then design policy to maximize the utility of the individual.

In this framework, paternalism is generally frowned upon, and liberalism in the form of respect for individual choices is the main guiding principle. When policy affects more than one individual, then other criteria, such as Pareto optimality, are invoked to decide among competing policies. When there is a conflict between equity and efficiency considerations (e.g., the poor might need subsidies, but taxes that are too high might disincentivize the rich), and when there are externalities, one observes a form of *hard paternalism*. This involves the imposition of distortionary taxes, such as redistributive taxes on income, or externality-correcting Pigouvian taxes. In other cases it involves regulation, mandates, and bans. Examples of regulation include speed limits on cars; pollution permits given to firms; the requirement on producers to label the food contents on jars; and the requirement on financial institutions to state the APR on their loans. Mandates and bans include prohibition on the sale of class A drugs; bans on cigarette advertisement; and various mandates enforced through the laws of the land.

The behavioral evidence shows that people might not always make decisions that are in their long-term interest. This could arise due to a variety of reasons, such as making decisions in a hot state of the mind; present-focused preferences; limited attention; subjective salience functions; or other forms of bounded rationality. This breaks the neoclassical correspondence between preferences and choices. Hence, observed choices do not provide a reliable guide to the true underlying preferences of individuals. An individual who is in poor health and checks into an alcohol rehab clinic does not necessarily have preferences that dictate excessive alcohol consumption; an individual who forgets a doctor's appointment does not necessarily have a preference to forget the appointment; a chain smoker who develops a serious lung condition does not necessarily have a preference for lung disease. In many cases, people get into a habit due to peer pressure, or without properly calculating the benefits and costs of an activity. If this is accepted then there might be a case for *nudging* people in a direction that might be in their long-term interests, as judged by themselves; this is known as the *informed desire criterion*.

In contrast to hard paternalism, the behavioral alternatives are sometimes referred to as *soft paternalism*. A leading alternative is known as *libertarian paternalism*, exemplified in public policy and popular debates through a variety of *policy nudges*. The basic idea is to minimally distort the behavior of the fully rational types, but potentially improve the welfare of the behavioral types whose behavior departs from the fully rational types (paternalism). However, all individuals voluntarily decide on the action to be taken, for example, they can ignore the nudge at a minimal cost (liberalism). This approach argues for the inevitability of some degree of paternalism as already embedded within any choice problem. It also argues for the inevitability of the existence of *choice architects* in any choice problem; after all, any choice is framed in a particular manner and embodies some choice architecture. However, there has been a debate about the reasonableness of the informed desire criterion that we discuss.

We also consider several other alternatives within this broad tradition, such as *asymmetric paternalism* and critiques based on the *contractarian approach*. Consider the class of activities/-goods that have a current benefit and a future cost; an example is *sin goods* such as harmful addictions. We provide a framework for analyzing the welfare implications arising for choices made for this class of goods and provide a concrete application to *optimal sin taxes*. In the last section in this chapter we give an introduction to the fast growing field of *behavioral public economics*. In particular, we consider the welfare implications of consumption taxes when there is limited attention in terms of the efficiency costs and tax incidence. We also outline the issues involved in the determination of an *optimal sugar tax*.

The final chapter, Chapter 13, gives an introduction to *neuroeconomics*. Neuroeconomics tries to bring together insights from neuroscience to establish correlation and causation with economic behavior. Its role is, therefore, not just to inform which brain regions might be activated when humans make particular decisions. The aim is also to go beyond the preference foundations of human behavior and locate the primitives for human behavior in neural activity in the brain. This typically takes the form of establishing the direction of causality from neuroeconomic data to human behavior and also predicting human behavior. Neuroeconomics can potentially unlock puzzles in observed behavior, such as punishments in public goods games, that neoclassical economic theory finds difficult to explain. No prior training in neuroscience is required to read this chapter.

We begin by introducing basic brain anatomy, the structure of the neuron, and the main brain regions of interest for neuroeconomic research. We also describe the main techniques for the *measurement* of brain activity, such as *positron emission tomography* (PET) and *functional magnetic resonance imaging* (fMRI); and for *manipulating* brain activity in the sense of upregulating or downregulating it, such as *transcranial magnetic stimulation* (TMS) and *transcranial direct current stimulation* (tDCS).

The remaining chapter has three main themes that are woven around several applications. These are as follows.[1]

1. Studies that document a causal impact of brain stimulation on decision making in economically important contexts.
2. Studies that take core insights from neuroeconomics and apply them to explain actually observed behaviors better or that solve important problems in economics.
3. An exposition of the attention-based *drift diffusion model* developed by Rangel and Krajbich, and its applications.

In addition to these themes, we discuss the neural correlates of human behavior outlined in the first four parts of the book. In particular, we consider the neural correlates of prospect theory; private versus social rewards; immediate versus future rewards; low-level and high-level strategic thinking; and ingroup favoritism in models of social identity. The richness in the scope of our discussion of the topics in neuroeconomics at the undergraduate level is unprecedented.

[1] I am very grateful to Ernst Fehr for suggesting this structure.

11 A Smorgasbord of Topics in Behavioral Economics

11.1 Introduction

In this chapter, we consider several topics that are of independent interest for teaching and research. The structure and organization of the chapter allows the topics to be read independently of each other.

In Section 11.2, we survey the literature on *happiness economics*. In neoclassical economics, the objective of public policy is to maximize the utility of a representative consumer, as is the case in macroeconomics, or to combine the utilities of a heterogeneous group of individuals through a social welfare function, as in welfare economics, and much of public economics. Utility itself is an ordinal concept (for instance, we can only say that utility from an outcome x is higher than utility from an outcome y, but not by how much), which is typically unobserved by third parties. However, given the empirical evidence on behavioral factors, the tight link between preferences and observed choices required in welfare economics cannot be justified. The literature on happiness economics advances the view that the ultimate aim of economic policy must be to maximize the happiness of people in society, as *self-reported* by people themselves. Hence, the resulting data is sometimes known as self-reported well-being (SWB) data. Happiness, in contrast to utility, is a cardinal concept (so its magnitude is measurable) and gives rise to qualitative data. The typical surveys ask people to self-report their own overall well-being, or aspects of well-being.

In Section 11.2.1, we first discuss the issue of appropriate theoretical and empirical foundations of happiness economics with a focus on recent criticisms of the use of cardinal data. The main spur for research in happiness economics was the *Easterlin parodox*. This paradox showed that while income may increase happiness in the short-run, it does not have a perceptible effect on happiness in the long-run because, say, the aspirations of people adjust to increased incomes. We outline the empirical evidence on the debate about the short-run and long-run effects in Section 11.2.2. Section 11.2.3 outlines the empirical evidence on several other correlates of self-reported well-being. These include unemployment, age, gender, education, health, income inequality, and how democratic the underlying institutions are.

Section 11.3 presents some of the key findings from the "modern" *behavioral industrial organization* literature. It is perhaps unfortunate that this literature has largely ignored the insights of the "traditional" behavioral literature developed in the 1950s and 1960s on the managerial theories of the firm and modeling firms as a formal and informal network of dynamic contracts. The nature of the questions asked in the traditional and the modern literature are somewhat different. The modern literature takes the more recent evidence on bounded rationality, such as limited attention, and examines the implications for consumer welfare, firm profits, and the nature of market competition.

Our discussion is organized around two main subsections. Subsection 11.3.1 considers the work of Akerlof and Shiller on *Phishing for Phools*. This is the strategic behavior by firms that is designed to increase profits by taking explicit account of the underlying psychology of consumer choice. We also describe what an equilibrium might look like in such a market. Finally, we consider the contrast between the informal discursive modeling of Akerlof and Shiller; and, following Ran Spiegler, a more formal style of modeling. Subsection 11.3.2 considers the effect of *limited attention* on the firm's optimal choice between an observed price component and a less visible price component (an add-on) that consumers with limited attention might not pay any attention to. We consider the implications for consumer welfare and firm's profits.

In neoclassical economics, when each of several possible objects have several attributes, then decision makers pay attention to all the attributes in making their "optimal" choice of an object. However, the empirical evidence suggests that people do not pay attention to all the attributes. We consider two departures from this assumption in Sections 11.4, 11.5. In Section 11.4, we show how to define the *salience* of different attributes in a set of choices and how salience can determine which object is optimally chosen. In Section 11.5, we model *limited attention* and show how it can be used to explain a range of economic phenomena.

Section 11.6 provides an introduction to *complexity economics* and its main features. In this framework, entities/agents (e.g., humans, neurons, individual cells, animals) use low level rationality in an environment characterized by true uncertainty (unknown unknowns). Agents use simple adaptive learning models based on the feedback between their actions and the aggregate outcomes in order to decide on their actions. The aggregate system-wide outcomes tend to be *complex* and characterized by *chaotic dynamics*. The complexity of the outcomes may lead one to believe that there is an intelligent choreographer or a central planner who is using sophisticated methods. Yet, there is no central planner or choreographer. The aggregate outcomes appear to be greater than the sum of the individual parts and they are *emergent phenomena*, in the sense that they cannot be predicted from individual actions. The observed fluctuations in the system arise *endogenously* through the actions of the individuals, rather than from stochastic exogenous shocks. This offers a different and alternative view to economic fluctuations as compared to standard models in macroeconomics that rely on exogenous shocks. We also briefly touch on *agent-based models*.

Section 11.7 introduces *learning models*. There is a large literature on the topic, and we do no more than present some of the classical ideas in the literature. We present two main models, *reinforcement learning* and *belief-based learning*. Under reinforcement learning, players know very little about the actual game they are playing, the strategies followed by the opponents, and the environment that gives rise to the payoffs. Hence, this is a relatively *low rationality environment*. Players do have data on the payoffs that arise following their strategy choices in the past. They use this data to play those strategies that have given rise to a higher payoff in the past. In belief-based models, players are more rational. They know the strategies of their opponents and payoffs that arise from various combinations of their strategies and the strategies of the opponents. They place a greater weight on the strategies followed by their opponents in the past, and convert these weights into the probabilities with which they play their own strategies. We also briefly describe some of the more recent developments.

A competitive general equilibrium in economics is an idealized environment in which there are no trading frictions, all markets are perfectly competitive, and there are no imperfections such as externalities or public goods. In such an environment, firms maximize profits, consumers maximize utility, and all markets clear. While the theory characterizes an equilibrium, it is less clear on the time path to an equilibrium, that is, the dynamics of the system. It requires a fictitious actor, the Walrasian auctioneer, to gradually nudge non-equilibrium trading towards an equilibrium. In the theory, there can be no trading outside of equilibrium and all trading happens instantly, in equilibrium.

In Section 11.8, we consider *double auction experiments* that create a competitive equilibrium environment in the lab and study whether it results in market clearing prices and quantities. In place of the Walrasian auctioneer, the double auction experiments introduce the *market improvement rule*. This rule only allows prices to go up when they are below the equilibrium and to go down when they are above the equilibrium. We argue that it plays a critical role in the success of the double auctions. The assumptions behind a competitive equilibrium are incredibly restrictive. Even if one were to demonstrate that any lab institution, such as a double auction experiment, can achieve convergence to an equilibrium, we need to check if it is of practical interest. In any case, the full set of double auction experiment rules are not widely observed in the real world.

11.2 Happiness Economics

What should be the ultimate aim of economic policy? The approach in neoclassical economics is to take account of an individual's lifetime utility, invoking the principle of liberalism to argue that the choices made by the individual are in the considered best interest of the individual. The objective of economic policy is take as inputs, the lifetime utilities of all individuals in society, and aggregate them through a social welfare function. For instance, when the lifetime utilities of all members of society are added together, one gets a *Utilitarian social welfare function*. When social welfare is equated with the utility of the worse off member of society, then one gets a *Rawlsian social welfare function*. Any number of intermediate social welfare functions arise from assigning different weights to the utilities of different individuals, perhaps to take account of equity and efficiency considerations.

As we have seen on several occasions in this book (e.g., Parts I and III), for the utility functions to exist, individuals must have suitably well-defined preferences over a set of objects. Revealed preference arguments can then be used to back out the true underlying preferences of individuals from the observed choices. This is the sense in which economists have typically argued that maximization of social welfare corresponds to maximizing some underlying notion of individual well-being, as determined by the individuals themselves.

In the revealed preference approach, utility is a purely *ordinal concept*. For instance, a higher indifference curve, say, in the space of two goods x and y, gives a "higher" utility as compared to a lower indifference curve, but we are not required to specify "how much more utility it gives."

This means that if a utility function $u(x, y)$ represents an individual's underlying preferences over bundles of goods, x, y, then a monotonic transformation of utility, say $v = f(u)$ where $f' > 0$, also represents identical preferences. For instance if $u = x^{0.3}y^{0.7}$ is a Cobb–Douglas utility function, then the utility function $v = 9x^{0.3}y^{0.7}$ represents identical preferences. Thus, we cannot make interpersonal comparisons of utility.

Example 11.1 *Is Mehar happier than her friend Sarah? We cannot answer this question simply by comparing Mehar's utility with Sarah's, since levels of utilities in an ordinal framework do not matter. If Mehar's utility function is* $u_M = 3x^{0.3}y^{0.7}$ *and Sarah's is* $u_S = x^{0.3}y^{0.7}$ *and they consume identical amounts of x and y, then it would appear that Mehar's utility is higher than Sarah's. Since monotonic transformations are allowed, we could equally write Sarah's utility as* $u_S = 6x^{0.3}y^{0.7}$, *which results in higher utility as compared to Mehar's. Yet, we do hear people making statements of the form: "Mehar is happier than Sarah," which suggests that people might have in their minds, a cardinal approach. But this is ruled out in an ordinal approach.*

What if individuals do not always make informed choices that are in their best long-term interests? We discuss these sorts of issues in the next chapter. What if we cannot use revealed preference arguments to back out the underlying preferences of individuals? Or even if we could, by imposing restrictions on the choice data that will allow us to back out the preferences, the restrictions themselves typically require us to invoke other objective functions based on non-choice data, which many might find unpersuasive (Bernheim and Taubinsky, 2018).

The literature on happiness economics advances the alternative view that public policy could be guided by the *subjective* well-being (SWB) of individuals, as self-reported by them. In other words this is self-reported preference data, not choice data as observed by an external observer. SWB is typically measured in ordinal terms as exemplified in the following questions asked directly to the respondents.

(i) Are you happier this year than you were last year?
(ii) All things considered would you say that you are unsatisfied/satisfied/very satisfied with your life?

However, in order to conduct statistical analysis, such ordinal data needs to be converted into cardinal units. In other cases, SWB may be directly measured in cardinal units, as exemplified in the following question. On a scale of 1–10, where "0" signifies not at all happy and "10" signifies "as happy as one could possibly be" how happy are you now? The answer to this question, say, 6.8, is in cardinal units.

Why should we be particularly interested in SWB? Here is how Richard Layard, who is one of the leading advocates of this approach, responded in written evidence given to a Select Committee of the House of Lords in England on September 7, 2021 (report number LBC0306).

> Governments have multiple objectives. But in the end, they have to decide whether one policy is better than another. Policy A may have a bigger impact on one objective and Policy B may on another objective. How to choose between the policies? The government must implicitly weight the importance of one objective compared with another. It would be much better to make this explicit, by having and applying a single overarching criterion, against which to judge the merit of different outcomes.

> That criterion should be the wellbeing of the people. There are of course many other good things – health, wealth, freedom and so on. But for each of these goods we can ask "Why are they good?" and expect an answer. For example, health matters because without it people feel lousy. Similarly with wealth, freedom etc. But if we ask "Why does it matter how people feel?", we can give no answer. It self-evidently matters, which is why the subjective wellbeing of the people is the most obvious candidate for the overarching good.

A great deal of the research in happiness economics is an attempt to measure the effects of socioeconomic variables on the underlying happiness levels of individuals, as proxied by self-reported well-being. Critics have highlighted the following two main drawbacks of happiness economics.

1. The preference foundations of the objective of happiness economics are suspect.
2. The measurement of happiness using qualitative data in the form of self-reports about "well-being" poses insurmountable problems and rules out policy analysis.

We shall consider these criticisms below in Section 11.2.1. In a nutshell, there are two considerations.

(1) Should public policy only be based on theories that have a rigorous preference foundation when preferences themselves are so malleable and often so difficult to infer from observed choice?
(2) Several new proposals on the measurement of cardinal variables make valuable suggestions for putting happiness economics on a firmer footing. How persuasive are these?

Happiness data has several features that make it attractive to use.

1. Plausible association: The SWB data has the expected sign when correlated with unemployment status, inflation, income inequality, social capital, health, and democratic institutions. We explore some of these associations below.
2. Predictive ability: The evidence links self-reported measures of well-being with important economic variables, for example, the SWP data predicts worker productivity (Oswald et al., 2015); job quits (Clark, 2001); probabilities of suicides (Helliwell, 2007); and the possibility of a future divorce among couples (Guven et al., 2012).
3. Inevitability of using happiness data: In some contexts, revealed choice data cannot be used. In these cases, we cannot change the exogenous variables such as prices and ask subjects to make choices such that their choices reveal their underlying preferences. The reason is that in these cases, each individual has little, if any, influence on the final outcome. Examples include environmental degradation, income inequality, fairness of the tax system, social capital, quality of governance, inflation, and unemployment. Yet, we may be interested, as a policy matter, to evaluate the effects of these hugely important variables on individual well-being. Hence, self-reported measures of *life satisfaction*, *well-being*, or *happiness*, which are sometimes used interchangeably in the literature, may provide valuable insights to policymakers in evaluating economic policy.
4. Nonpecuniary well-being: Economists are typically interested in pecuniary measures of well-being, for example, GDP per capita. However, well-being can also arise from nonpecuniary factors. For instance, unemployment has a scarring effect on people and has adverse effects on

well-being and mental health (see evidence below). Yet, by taking market clearing as a neutral construct[1] the existing measures of per capita GDP ignore the non-pecuniary effects on the unemployed. For instance, a highly trained engineer who has been laid off, might continue to look for another engineering job even if there is the possibility of working at the minimum wage elsewhere. If policy can tap into the SWP data of the engineer as an input, and others like him, then it may provide a better assessment of the overall well-being of society.

11.2.1 The Issue of Appropriate Foundations

The issue of appropriate foundations is at the very heart of the research agenda in happiness economics and raises some vexed and difficult questions. Readers who are not interested in the foundations can skim this subsection on a first read and then revisit it once they have read the entire section to get a better perspective on the literature.

Theoretical Foundations

The first question to ask is: What does SWB data measure? In this regard, Kahneman and Thaler (2006, p. 222) write: "In the older interpretation of utility, the question of whether choices maximize utility has a simple meaning: do people choose the options that they will most enjoy? In modern decision theory, which ignores the distinction, the question is quite different: are preferences consistent and do they satisfy the axioms of rational choice?"

Thus, the objective under happiness economics is to figure out which choices people most enjoy. When asked to report their current SWB, one suggestion is that people somehow aggregate the stream of past utilities that they have derived. Suppose that time is discrete, $t = 1, 2, \ldots, T$, and at any time t an individual derives *instantaneous utility* from n possible dimensions of life, such as health, absolute income, relative income with respect to one's peers, the extent of civil liberties, freedom, marital relations, public infrastructure, etc. Let us denote these dimensions at time t by

$$x_{1t}, x_{2t}, \ldots, x_{nt}. \tag{11.1}$$

Then, the utility function of the individual at time t is

$$u(x_{1t}, x_{2t}, \ldots, x_{nt}), \tag{11.2}$$

where the variables are so defined that u is increasing in each of its arguments. So an increase in the individual variables that, for instance, captures an improvement in health, an increase in income, an increase in civil liberties, and an increase in freedom, increase utility. Suppose that an individual were asked at time τ: All things considered, how satisfied are you with your life? Rate your answer on a 10-point scale where "0" denotes "not satisfied at all" and "10" denotes "completely satisfied." One possibility, in the spirit of experienced utility, is that at time τ, individuals sum up their utilities up to, and including, time τ, to compute their total utility so far,

[1] Market clearing implies that all those who are able to work at the existing wage can find work. All those whose reservation wage is higher than the market clearing wage are unemployed.

$$W_\tau = \sum_{t=1}^{\tau} \delta^{\tau-t} u(x_{1t}, x_{2t}, \ldots, x_{nt}); 0 < \delta < 1. \tag{11.3}$$

In (11.3), δ is the discount factor under exponential discounted utility, but applied backwards in time. Hence, individuals weight the more recent utilities the most and utilities in the more distant past, the least. The stream of instantaneous utilities in the past constitute *remembered utility*. What sort of challenges might the individual face in computing W and then converting W into a 1–10 scale? In neoclassical economics this is unproblematic because, by assumption, individuals have *perfect recall* of all past events, hence, computing W is straightforward. However, ruling things out by assumption may impose untenable restrictions on behavior, and may run contrary to the evidence.

Kahneman et al. (1997) outline the evidence on remembered utility, drawing on several empirical studies.[2] In these studies, subjects who are undergoing colonoscopy are asked to report their discomfort every 60 seconds, that is, their instantaneous utility, and then asked to state their remembered utility at the end of the procedure. The experimenters can then check to see if remembered utility is consistent with the stream of instantaneous utilities. It turns out that remembered utility is the relevant metric by which individuals evaluate their colonoscopy experience, once the procedure is completed. However, remembered utility is not formed in the manner suggested in (11.3). It is based on *peak-end evaluation*, which is based on two separate calculations.

1. The average of the remembered peaks of past instantaneous utilities.
2. The instantaneous utility towards the end of the experience.

Such a calculation has the following two implications.

1. *Duration neglect*: The overall duration of the experience, say, of the colonoscopy procedure, is not of first order importance, holding fixed the average of the remembered peaks.
2. *Violations of temporal monotonicity*: The second component of peak end utility is the most recent instantaneous utility, which may interfere with the average of the past peaks of instantaneous utilities. In the colonoscopy example, if the last few minutes of the procedure were relatively painless, then they reduce the effect of the peaks of the past pain levels during the entire colonoscopy experience, reducing remembered disutility. On the other hand if the average of the past peaks was relatively low, but the procedure was relatively painful towards the very end, the overall remembered disutility of the procedure is high.

Using the material from Parts IV and V, there are other problems that people face in recalling past events.

1. Subjects may be subject to projection bias; liable to framing effects implicit in the wording of the SWB questions; and answer questions when they are in an emotionally hot state.
2. Different subjects may interpret the same question in a different manner, or they might even use nonlinear scales while the experimenter interprets the 0–10 scale as a linear scale. A linear scale means that the change in SWB between, say, the numbers 3 and 4 is the same as that between the numbers 7 and 8.

[2] See the papers by Varey and Kahneman (1992), Fredrickson and Kahneman (1993), Kahneman et al. (1993), and Redelmeier and Kahneman (1996).

The first problem can be somewhat mitigated by increasing the sample size; asking questions when subjects are in an emotionally cold state; and running extensive pilots and post-pilot interviews with subjects to ensure that the inherent framing and contextual effects implicit in the SWB questions are well understood by the experimenter. The second problem is more serious, and we deal with it below. The seriousness of these objections also depends on the purpose for which the SWB data will be used. In many cases it does not invalidate the use of SWB data. Consider, for instance, the following quote from Alan Blinder (1990, p. 297) who is fully aware of the drawbacks of such qualitative data:

> In the other social sciences, the notion that you can learn things by asking people would hardly be revolutionary message. Indeed, it would hardly be a message at all, for asking people is a fundamental tool of inquiry in anthropology, sociology, psychology, and even, to some extent, political science. Yet it is something that economists not only rarely do, but often actually sneer at. After all, we don't want to act like sociologists and political scientists. Physicists and chemists do not ask their subjects why they behave as they do, so we shouldn't either – or so we think. But is that a scientific attitude? If molecules could talk, would chemists refuse to listen?

Currently, it is not possible to provide rigorous preference foundations of SWB data despite there being a compelling case to use it for policy purposes. Benjamin et al. (2021) build a simple framework to describe some of the problems that arise in interpreting the SWB data. In (11.1), we considered the well-being of an individual as being influenced by n different dimensions/attributes. Suppose that an individual is looking after old parents who are unwell, perhaps terminally ill. If such an individual is asked to complete an SWB questionnaire, the reported well-being may be influenced by the health status of the parents. Or consider an individual who feels undervalued at work because he receives too low a salary relative to peers in a comparable position. His self-reported SWB may be influenced by the relative income comparisons at his workplace (see evidence below).

For these reasons, we need to consider several other dimensions that might be relevant to an individual's well-being. Suppose that there are a total of $m+n$ attributes that are relevant for well-being. The first n are personal attributes and each of the remaining m attributes, $n+1,\ldots,n+m$, refer to attributes related to other members of the social group, for example, family and friends. Let x_t be a vector of these attributes

$$x_t = (x_{1t}, \ldots, x_{nt}, \ldots, x_{m+n,t}). \tag{11.4}$$

Denote the instantaneous utility of an individual at time t by $u(x_t)$. If one assumes that the utility function, u, is additively separable in its arguments, then we can write

$$u(x_t) = \sum_{i=1}^{n} \alpha_i u_i(x_{it}) + \sum_{i=n+1}^{n+m} \beta_i u_i(x_{it}), \tag{11.5}$$

where α_i, $i = 1,\ldots,n$ and β_i, $i = n+1,\ldots,n+m$ are the weights that the individual assigns to the various attributes and u_i is the utility function from a particular attribute.

Define the intertemporal utility of the individual at any time τ by

$$W_\tau = \sum_{t=1}^{\tau-1} \delta^{\tau-t} u(x_t) + u(x_\tau) + \sum_{t=\tau+1}^{T} \delta^{t-\tau} u(x_t); 0 < \delta < 1. \tag{11.6}$$

In (11.6), the first term on the RHS is discounted remembered utility, the second is current utility, and the third is discounted future utility. There are three main cases.

1. If $\delta^{\tau-t} = 0$ for $t < \tau$, then the first term on the RHS of (11.6) equals zero. In this case, W_τ is known as *forward looking utility*.
2. If $\delta^{\tau-t} > 0$ for some or all $t < \tau$, then W_τ is known as *lifetime utility*, a concept that welfare economics has favored.
3. The concept of *flow utility* corresponds to the case $\delta^{\tau-t} = 0$ for $t < \tau$ and $\delta^{t-\tau} = 0$ for $t > \tau$, so that $W_\tau = u(x_\tau)$.

When presented with a SWB questionnaire, a researcher might assume that individuals are filling in the questionnaire by using equations (11.5) and (11.6). By contrast, individuals filling in the questionnaire might interpret the SWB questions in their own subjective manner, and use instead their deep personal preferences parameters $\widetilde{\delta}, \widetilde{\alpha_i}, \widetilde{\beta_i}$ instead of the actual parameters $\delta, \alpha_i, \beta_i$ in (11.5). Discovering the relation between $\delta, \alpha_i, \beta_i$ (true model imagined by the researcher) and $\widetilde{\delta}, \widetilde{\alpha_i}, \widetilde{\beta_i}$ (actual model used by the individual conditional on the SWB questionnaire) is the key factor in making good inferences from SWB data. Here is a simple classification but not the only one by any means.

The individual is said to have *self-regarding utility* if in (11.5), $\widetilde{\beta_i} = 0$ for all i. The individual is said to have *family centered utility* if in (11.5), $\widetilde{\beta_i} = 0$ for all non-family members and $\widetilde{\beta_i} = \beta_i$ for all family members. *Other regarding utility* corresponds to the case $\widetilde{\beta_i} = \beta_i$ for all i.

The evidence indicates that there is a difference between the true model typically imagined by the researcher, say, in (11.6) and the actual model used by respondents with the parameters $\widetilde{\delta}, \widetilde{\alpha_i}, \widetilde{\beta_i}$ (Benjamin et al., 2012, 2014). Benjamin et al. (2021) make the recommendation that in using SWP data, the researcher must maintain clarity about which utility is being used, that is the relevant restrictions on $\delta, \alpha_i, \beta_i$. Thus, researchers must specify whether they are eliciting a response in terms of lifetime utility, flow utility, backward looking utility, self-regarding utility, family-centered utility, or other regarding utility. They are also critical of much of the existing literature for failing to specify these things. However, there are exceptions. Alesina et al. (2004) interpret the responses of their subjects as corresponding to experienced utility; Gruber and Mullainathan (2005) with a notion of forward looking utility; and Blanchflower and Oswald (2004) with flow utility. In the absence of such inferences, it might be difficult to draw policy implications from the data. They also show how one might be able to map the wording in the SWP questions into the utility notion that subjects could be using. If such a mapping can be refined and generally agreed upon, it will be a major step forward for the literature. Researchers in this area will be well advised to take this suggestion seriously.

Benjamin et al. (2021) also elicit the weights that subjects put on various attributes in the vector of attributes in (11.4); these are the weights α_i and β_i in (11.5). In their experiments, they find that their subjects assign the highest weight to themselves, followed by strictly positive weights to their immediate family and their social circle in that hierarchical order. Since weights are assigned to all three components, subjects have other-regarding preferences (see Part II of the book). Thus, a researcher who did not specify that the data captures other-regarding preferences and assumed that $\beta_i = 0$ for all $i = n+1, \ldots, m+n$, when in fact $\widetilde{\beta_i} > 0$, would draw mistaken policy inferences. Small changes in the wording of the SWP questions, for example, from those that stress "family well-being" rather than"personal well-being" lead to a predictable increase in the weights, β_i, assigned to others. The authors find that if the researcher wishes to specifically elicit self-centered flow utility, then the following question is the most appropriate: "On a scale from 0 to 10, how would you rate your overall personal well-being?" If such contextual changes lead to predictable changes in the responses, then the insights can be used to conduct SWB research on more sound foundations. Furthermore, Benjamin et al. (2021) show that the standard SWP questions appear to be answered in terms of flow utility by women and the unemployed. By contrast, men and the employed appear to consider a broader time horizon, more akin to lifetime utility, and put greater weights on their social circles rather than just their immediate families.

Benjamin et al. (2012) gave subjects 13 different scenarios. In some of the scenarios, subjects had to engage in two tasks. In the first task, they had to state which of the choices made them happier (SWB question) and in the second task they had to state which they would choose (utility maximizing choice). Consistency between the two sets of answers can potentially reveal if SWB is a good proxy for utility maximization. In one of these scenarios, subjects were asked to pick a trade-off between sleep and income.

"Say you have to decide between two new jobs. The jobs are exactly the same in almost every way but have different work hours and pay different amounts.

Option 1: A job paying $80,000 per year. The hours for this job are reasonable, and you would be able to get about 7.5 hours of sleep on the average work night.

Option 2: A job paying $140,000 per year. However, this job requires you to go to work at unusual hours, and you would only be able to sleep around 6 hours on the average work night.

Between these two options, taking all things together, which do you think would give you a happier life as a whole?"

Subjects indicated the intensity of their SWB for both options, based on a three-point scale.

Next, subjects were asked the following choice question.

"If you were limited to these two options, which do you think you would choose?"

Subjects again indicate the intensity of the preference for one of the jobs on a three-point scale.

In other scenarios, SWB was not a consideration. For instance, in Scenario 4, subjects make a choice between two career paths, one career path involves an easier life with fewer sacrifices, while another promises posthumous impact and fame. Scenario 2 subjects were given an ethical choice: A more convenient option versus one that is the "right thing to do."

Overall, the *SWB ranking* of the two options and the *actual choices* are consistent with each other for 83% of all respondents. For different samples the consistency levels are different; in the Denver sample, 87% of the SWB rankings and choices are consistent with each other while in the Cornell sample, only 76% are consistent. Yet, a test of proportions rejects the null hypothesis that the proportion of subjects picking Option 1 is the same in the subjective well-being question and the choice question. Subjects are more likely to choose the option that gives them more money, even if it is indicated to give lower SWB.

The authors then add additional explanatory variables to see if these would better predict the choices made. These variables, each measured on a seven-point scale include: your family's happiness; social life; control over life; level of spirituality; social status; and sense of purpose. The actual choices are then regressed on SWB and these additional 11 variables. However, SWB predicts choices better than all the other variables combined, and in most scenarios the new explanatory variables do not add sufficiently to explanatory power.

Benjamin et al. (2014) attempt to unpack the constituent parts of SWB. Their list includes happiness; goals; achievements; freedom; morality; and relationships. Happiness, health, and life satisfaction play a major role in explaining SWB, as do the quality of relationships, financial and physical security, morality, and freedom of choice. Several of these variables correspond to the use in Sen (1985, 1992) of *functionings* and *capabilities*; functionings refers to material standards of living and capabilities to opportunities to achieve the relevant functionings, and to individual freedoms.[3]

Empirical Foundations

Ordinal data has several well known limitations that we have outlined above. Bond and Lang (2019) show that by transforming the happiness scale on which subjects rate their SWB, they can reverse the estimated effects of many different variables on mean levels of happiness. Similarly, Schröder and Yitzhaki (2017) showed that the signs of coefficients on the variables in OLS regressions that regress SWB on independent variables such as income and health, can be reversed. These papers have implications for any research that is carried out with ordinal variables. As a matter of fact much research that informs government policy and the marketing/advertising strategies of firms relies on collecting data on ordinal variables.

In an important response to these papers, Kaiser and Vendrik (2021) acknowledge that such sign reversals of coefficients can take place. However, they show that the criticisms in these papers do not apply for empirically observed parameter values to the happiness literature. Chen et al. (2019) also show that replacing comparisons of mean levels of happiness by median levels of happiness avoids the criticisms of ordinal data in the Bond–Lang and Schröder–Yitzhaki papers. Another median-based approach that avoids these criticisms is proposed by Bloem and Oswald (2021).

We follow here the demonstration of the relevant issues in Kaiser and Vendrik (2021) using as an example the *Easterlin paradox* which examines the relation between mean self-reported measures of happiness and incomes. This paradox, that we explain in detail in Section 11.2.1, arises when, in the short-run, incomes can increase mean happiness but this effect disappears in the long-run.

Suppose that respondents are asked the question "Taken all together, how would you say things are these days – would you say that you are very happy, pretty happy, or not too happy?" Suppose that subjects "self-report" a happiness level H_r which can be in one of the following three categories $c = 1, 2, 3$.

- $c = 1$ for "not too happy."
- $c = 2$ for "pretty happy."
- $c = 3$ for "very happy."

[3] For the implications of these factors for social welfare see also Fleurbaey (2009) and Fleurbaey and Blanchet (2013).

Let us assume that subjects have a true, but unobserved, underlying happiness scale H_t. The subject then translates the true unobserved scale H_t into the "self-reported" three-point discrete happiness scale $H_r \in \{1, 2, 3\}$.

Example 11.2 *Consider the following purely illustrative example (we do not carry forward the structure of this example for the rest of this section). Suppose that H_t is continuous over some interval $[a_1, a_4]$ and $a_1 < a_2 < a_3 < a_4$. Suppose that the subject employs the following rule. If the subject's true happiness is in the interval $I_1 = [a_1, a_2)$ then the subject self reports $r = 1$; if it is in the interval $I_2 = [a_2, a_3)$ the subject reports $r = 2$; and if it is in the interval $I_3 = [a_3, a_4]$ the subject reports $r = 3$.*

We assume that the self-reports provide, on average, a correct reflection of the underlying true level of happiness measured on the scale $c = 1, 2, 3$, that is, $E[H_t \mid c] = c$. Using the expectation operator E to denote both population mean and sample mean, this requires imposing the following restrictions on the conditional sample mean

$$E[H_t \mid 1] = 1; \; E[H_t \mid 2] = 2; \; E[H_t \mid 3] = 3. \tag{11.7}$$

Thus, the sample mean, conditional on the self reports, provides a good approximation to the true underlying happiness scale, H_t. We relax this assumption below.

Denote by s_1, s_2, s_3 the respective proportions of the sample that report $r = 1, r = 2$, and $r = 3$. Then, using the standard formula for a weighted average, the mean unconditional happiness in the sample equals

$$E[H_t] = s_1 E[H_t \mid 1] + s_2 E[H_t \mid 2] + s_3 E[H_t \mid 3]. \tag{11.8}$$

Substituting (11.7) into (11.8) we get

$$E[H_t] = s_1 + 2s_2 + 3s_3. \tag{11.9}$$

By definition, $s_1 + s_2 + s_3 = 1$, so $s_2 = 1 - s_1 - s_3$. Hence, we can rewrite (11.9) as

$$E[H_t] = 2 - s_1 + s_3. \tag{11.10}$$

Suppose that we now wish to consider the effect of a change in some independent variable, say, the log of GDP per capita, denoted by X. We can then take partial derivatives on both sides of (11.10) with respect to X to get

$$\frac{\partial E[H_t]}{\partial X} = \frac{\partial s_3}{\partial X} - \frac{\partial s_1}{\partial X}. \tag{11.11}$$

Using data from Stevenson and Wolfers (2008) who used happiness data from the US-American General Social Survey, the relevant regression coefficients give us (** signifies $p < 0.05$, and *** signifies $p < 0.01$)

$$\frac{\partial s_1}{\partial X} = -0.0254; \; \frac{\partial s_2}{\partial X} = 0.079^{***}; \; \frac{\partial s_3}{\partial X} = -0.0535^{**}. \tag{11.12}$$

Thus, an increase in log of GDP per capita reduced the shares s_1 and s_3, respectively, of individuals who chose $c = 1$ (not too happy) and $c = 3$ (very happy). There is a corresponding increase in the share s_2 of individuals who chose $c = 2$ (pretty happy). Thus, while, in general, the sign of the RHS of (11.11) is indeterminate, $\frac{\partial E[H_t]}{\partial X} \lesseqgtr 0$, but for the specific estimates in (11.12), s_3 fell more than s_1 (the share of the very happy fell relatively more), hence we have

$$\frac{\partial E[H_t]}{\partial X} < 0. \tag{11.13}$$

This is consistent with the Easterlin paradox that in the long-run, an increase in income does not lead to a statistically significant increase in mean levels of happiness.

Suppose we had used the more general notation $E[H_t \mid 1] \equiv h_1$; $E[H_t \mid 2] \equiv h_2$; $E[H_t \mid 3] \equiv h_3$. Then, we can rewrite the more special case of the restriction in (11.7) as

$$h_1 = 1;\ h_2 = 2;\ h_3 = 3.$$

This special case of the restriction implies that the gaps in the reported happiness categories are identical, on average, to the gaps in the true underlying happiness, that is,

$$h_2 - h_1 = 1;\ h_3 - h_2 = 1.$$

Suppose that we now relax this restriction, so that we now have $E[H_t \mid c] \neq c$. Denote this new, unevenly spaced, happiness scale by

$$E[\widetilde{H}_t \mid 1] \equiv \widetilde{h}_1;\ E[\widetilde{H}_t \mid 2] \equiv \widetilde{h}_2;\ E[\widetilde{H}_t \mid 3] \equiv \widetilde{h}_3.$$

For instance, the case

$$\widetilde{h}_2 - \widetilde{h}_1 > \widetilde{h}_3 - \widetilde{h}_2, \tag{11.14}$$

implies that when individuals switch between $c = 1$ and $c = 2$ the true underlying difference in happiness between "pretty happy" and "not too happy" is greater than the case where individuals switch between $c = 2$ and $c = 3$, which is the difference between "very happy" and "pretty happy."

The analogue of (11.8) for the new unevenly spaced scale is

$$E[\widetilde{H}_t] = s_1\widetilde{h}_1 + s_2\widetilde{h}_2 + s_3\widetilde{h}_3.$$

Using, as before, the relation $s_2 = 1 - s_1 - s_3$, the mean unconditional sample happiness, the analogue of (11.10), is

$$E[\widetilde{H}_t] = s_3\left(\widetilde{h}_3 - \widetilde{h}_2\right) - s_1\left(\widetilde{h}_2 - \widetilde{h}_1\right) + \widetilde{h}_2.$$

Differentiating with respect to X we get

$$\frac{\partial E[\widetilde{H}_t]}{\partial X} = \frac{\partial s_3}{\partial X}\left(\widetilde{h}_3 - \widetilde{h}_2\right) - \frac{\partial s_1}{\partial X}\left(\widetilde{h}_2 - \widetilde{h}_1\right). \tag{11.15}$$

Using the empirical estimates in (11.12) and the restriction in (11.14) we get

$$\frac{\partial E[\widetilde{H}_t]}{\partial X} = -0.0535\left(\widetilde{h}_3 - \widetilde{h}_2\right) + 0.0254\left(\widetilde{h}_2 - \widetilde{h}_1\right) \lesseqgtr 0. \tag{11.16}$$

Unlike (11.13), the sign in (11.16) is indeterminate. When might the sign flip to $\frac{\partial E[H_t]}{\partial X} > 0$ and violate Easterlin's paradox? From (11.15) and (11.16) we have that this violation would require

$$\frac{\partial E[\widetilde{H}_t]}{\partial X} > 0 \Leftrightarrow \frac{\widetilde{h}_2 - \widetilde{h}_1}{\widetilde{h}_3 - \widetilde{h}_2} > \frac{\frac{\partial s_3}{\partial X}}{\frac{\partial s_1}{\partial X}} = \frac{0.0535}{0.0254} = 2.11. \tag{11.17}$$

Thus, if underlying true happiness scale is, on average, concave enough in the sense specified in (11.17), $\widetilde{h}_2 - \widetilde{h}_1 > 2.11(\widetilde{h}_3 - \widetilde{h}_2)$, while individuals continue to have only three categories to report, $c = 1, 2, 3$, then Easterlin's paradox is reversed. This is the essential point made in Bond and Lang (2019).

Kaiser and Vendrik (2021) show, however, that there is no happiness scale that is simultaneously (i) concave enough to violate Easterlin's paradox, and (ii) results in statistically significant positive coefficients of the effects of X on self-reported happiness. Indeed, even when the underlying happiness scale is infinitely concave

$$\frac{\widetilde{h}_2 - \widetilde{h}_1}{\widetilde{h}_3 - \widetilde{h}_2} \to \infty,$$

the highest statistical significance they can get on X is $p = 0.13$. Hence, while the Bond–Lang argument is theoretically correct, it has less empirical bite than was originally claimed by the authors; the title of Bond–Lang paper is "The Sad Truth about Happiness Scales." The actual demonstration of this result in the Bond–Lang paper is in terms of restrictions on the error term in the ordered probit regressions. Kaiser and Vendrik (2021) also address their criticism specifically in terms of ordered probit regressions and reach similar conclusions (theoretically possible, empirically implausible); interested readers can directly read their paper for such a demonstration. We make two additional points in this respect.

1. There is heterogeneity in responses across various categories, so $\frac{\partial s_3}{\partial X} \neq \frac{\partial s_1}{\partial X}$, which leads to potential reversals of results in happiness economics. One solution is to take account of omitted variables that might reduce the heterogeneity in responses, or control variables that are correlated with X.
2. A more direct test is to see if subjects in experiments view a given happiness scale as linear or nonlinear. Indeed, this would appear to have been an important building block for the happiness literature. There are surprisingly few papers in this area, but the existing evidence suggests that subjects view a given happiness scale in a linear manner. In an early experiment, subjects in Van Praag (1991) were asked to translate verbal labels, such as very bad, bad, not bad, not good, good, very good into a cardinal scale between 1 and 1000.

   As a first piece of experimental evidence, Van Praag (1991) tested how people translate ordered verbal labels (very bad; bad; not bad; not good; good; very good) into cardinal quantities in a context-free setting. In the first experiment he asked subjects to assign numbers between 1 and 1000 to each verbal label. Here, 1 stood for the "very worst" and 1000 for the "very best." In the second experiment, respondents were asked to produce lines of a certain length corresponding to each verbal label. Here a length of 1 unit stood for the "worst,"and a length of 40 units for "very good." In both tasks, subjects produced cardinal scales that are reasonably linear with the various categories roughly, although not exactly, equally spaced.

   The Dutch subjects in Studer (2012) engaged in two tasks.

   (a) Report their happiness on a slider task which allows them to move a slider on a continuous interval.
   (b) Report their happiness on a 10-point Likert scale $(0, 1, \ldots, 9)$.

   We may take the first task as a better proxy to quantify the underlying true happiness, H_t, of the subject and the second task as the usual self-reported happiness, H_r. The answers on the two scales can then be compared by setting cutoff points on the continuous slider scale that would correspond to the discrete Likert scale, as in Example 11.2. This will require the construction of 9 cutoff points to determine 9 intervals $I_1, I_2, \ldots, I_9$ so that an answer of 1 on the Likert scale corresponds to true happiness in the interval I_1; 2 on the Likert scale corresponds to the interval I_2;...; 9 on the Likert scale corresponds to the interval I_9. The main finding is that the intervals are not equally spaced as would be required for a perfectly linear scale. There is no predictable pattern in the intervals. However, the intervals do not systematically shrink in a manner that would be required to produce enough concavity for the theoretical possibility in the Bond–Lang and Schröder–Yitzhaki papers to reverse known results in the happiness literature.

11.2.2 Relation between Income and Well-Being: The Easterlin Paradox

One of the most celebrated results in the literature on happiness economics is the *Easterlin paradox*. This paradox is due to Easterlin (1974) who applied the nascent techniques of subjective well-being that had been developed in early work by Van Praag (1968, 1971). The Easterlin paradox refers to the following two sets of findings.

1. At any point in time, happiness increases in income, whether measured in cross country data or data within the same country.
2. Over a sufficiently long period of time, as income grows, there is zero correlation between happiness and income.

Figure 11.1, based on an illustration in Easterlin and O'Connor (2019), explains the Easterlin paradox through simple, hypothetical, plots. The a and b curve plots the movement of per capita GDP over time; we shall only be interested in real per capita GDP throughout, but omit the prefix "real." The cyclical movements reflect business cycles as the economy goes through booms and recessions; the peaks for income are shown as $a_1, \ldots, a_4$ and the troughs by $b_1, \ldots, b_4$. A linear trend line fitted through cyclical income is shown by the dashed curve, labeled T_I. The lower jagged curve shows SWB and it also exhibits cyclical movements with peaks $c_1, \ldots, c_4$ and troughs $d_1, \ldots, d_4$. A linear trend line fitted through the SWB curve is shown by the dashed line, labeled T_H. In the short-run, over any business cycle, as income increases, SWB also increases, and as income decreases, SWB also decreases. For simplicity, we have matched the peaks and troughs of both sets of curves although in actual practice one might expect a slight time delay. Such a pattern occurred, for instance in the Great Recession of 2007–2009 when the American economy slowed down, and self-reported happiness fell to its lowest level and then increased once the economy began to recover (Graham et al., 2010; Deaton, 2011).

This pattern changes over the longer run as can be seen by comparing the dashed trend lines. There is an upward trend in real incomes. However, the trend line for SWB is flat. Why does this occur? Drawing on the work of Veblen ([1899] 1973), Duesenberry (1949), and the work of Kahneman–Tversky on reference points (see Part I of the book), Easterlin (1974, 1995, 2001, 2021) gives an explanation in terms of *relative income concerns* and *shifting aspiration levels*. As income grows, people find that not only their own income has grown, the incomes of others have also increased, hence, their *relative incomes* do not change (Clark et al., 2008). Their

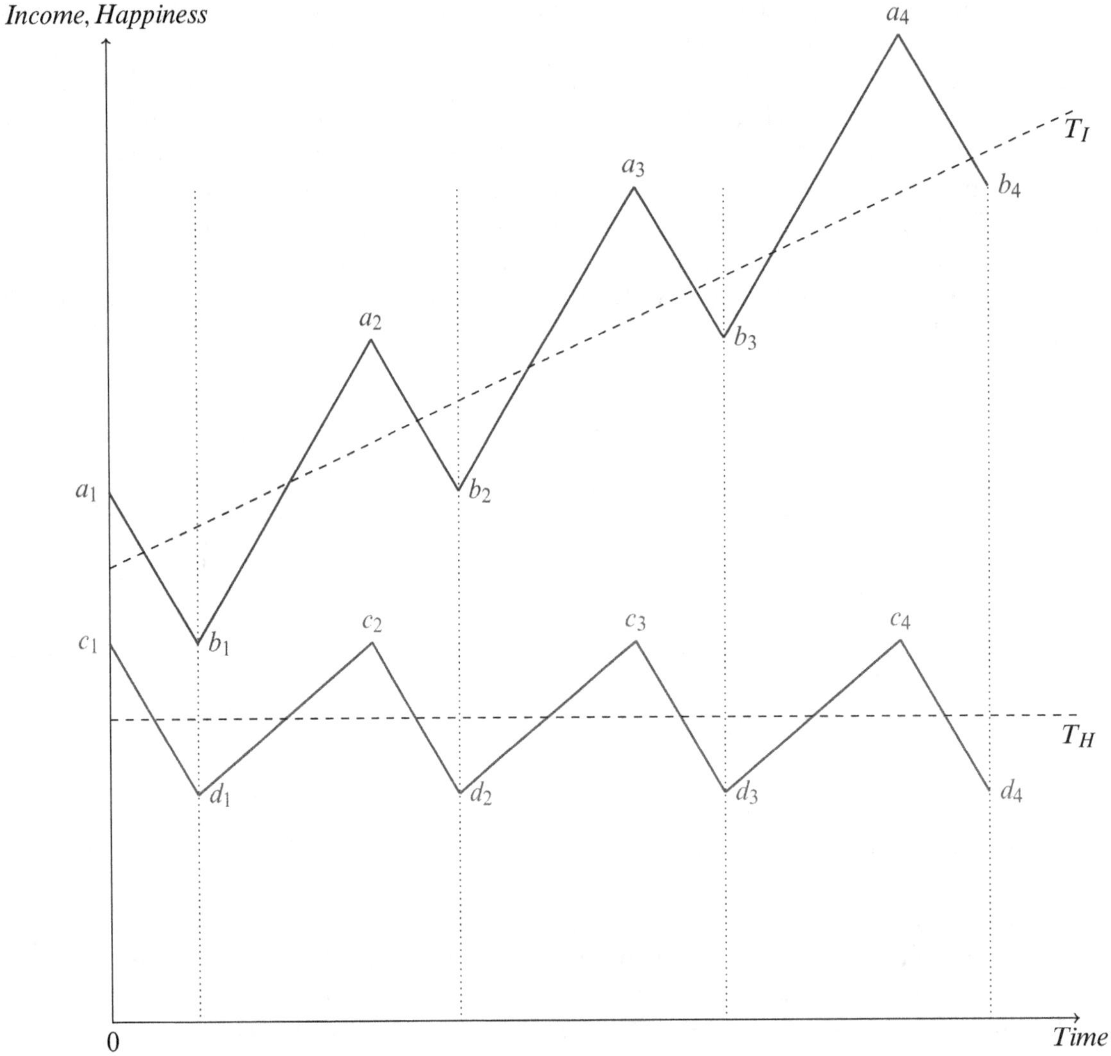

Figure 11.1 An illustration of the Easterlin paradox. The income series is shown by the a and b lines and the happiness series by the c and d lines. The dotted lines show the trend in income, T_I, and the trend in happiness, T_H

own aspirations also increase with an increase in their incomes through a dynamic process of aspiration adjustment.

As this hedonic process of adjustment takes place, people feel that they are no better off, relatively speaking, hence, their SWB does not change. This process is sometimes known as the *hedonic treadmill* (Brickman and Campbell, 1971; Diener et al., 2006). Empirically, well-being has been shown to depend on the difference between actual income and income aspirations (Stutzer, 2004; Knight and Gunatilaka, 2012). Regressions where life satisfaction is the dependent variable and the independent variables are lagged incomes, with various lags, show that individuals adapt to changes in income over a relatively short span of a few years.

German micro-level data revealed complete adaptation within four years of the unification of Germany (Di Tella et al., 2010).

Yet another explanation for the absence of a long-term relation between happiness and income is based on the *set point theory of happiness*. The theory postulates that individuals have an inherent, or latent, level of happiness. Temporary shocks, such as income changes may lead to short-term departures in happiness from the latent levels, but over time happiness reverts back to the latent level (Easterlin, 1995). The evidence suggests that about 33% of the variation in life satisfaction is on account of genetic factors, which is consistent with there being a latent level of happiness (De Neve et al., 2012).

Let us now illustrate the Easterlin pardox using data taken from the United States General Social Survey (Di Tella and MacCulloch, 2006). The self-reported measure of happiness is based on the following question: "Taken all together, how would you say things are these days – would you say that you are (3) very happy, (2) pretty happy, or (1) not too happy?"

Figure 11.2 shows the cross-sectional evidence on the relation between happiness (measured on a 3-point Likert scale) and per capita GDP for 1994. A continuous curve is fitted through the data points. The fitted line is increasing, so higher income is associated with higher happiness. It is also concave, so successive increases in income bring about smaller marginal increases in happiness. If happiness is a proxy for utility, then the concavity of the curve suggests diminishing marginal utility of income. Figure 11.3 moves beyond the short term to examine the long-term relation between happiness and income over 22 years. The income graph which joins the filled-in dots is clearly upward sloping over time, but the happiness graph is flat over time. This is consistent with Easterlin's paradox.

Variants of the Easterlin paradox arise when the "long-term" relation between happiness and income is upward sloping up to a certain income threshold, but the relationship is flat thereafter. For instance, for the *World Values Survey*, the relationship between life satisfaction and GDP is relatively flat for incomes above \$10,000 (Frey and Stutzer, 2002). Similar findings are reported by Diener and Seligman (2004), Di Tella et al. (2003), and Frey and Stutzer (2002). A potential

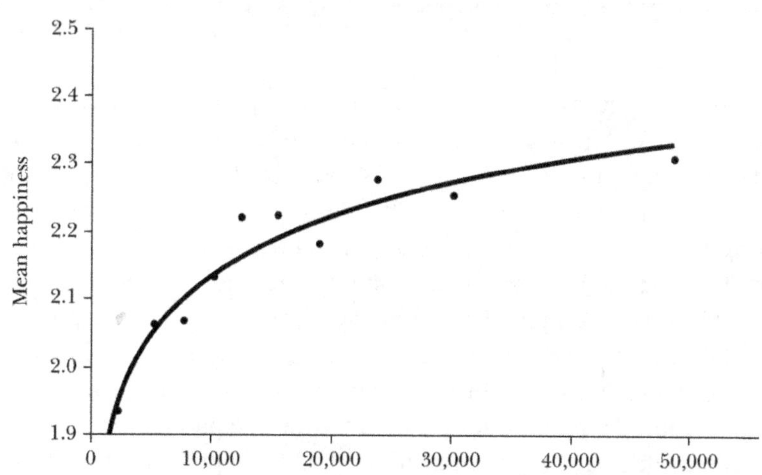

Figure 11.2 A snapshot of the relation between happiness and income for a cross section of Americans in 1994. Source: Di Tella and MacCulloch (2006)

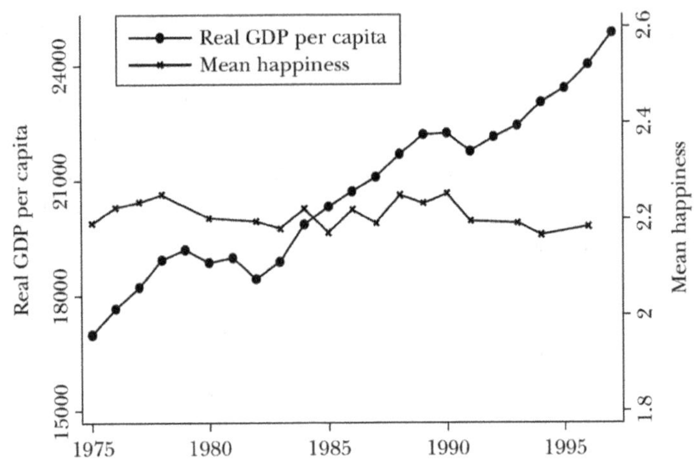

Figure 11.3 The relation between happiness and income for US data over the time period 1975–1997. Source: Di Tella and MacCulloch (2006)

explanation is that once basic needs are met at some income threshold, then extra increases in income do not lead to increased happiness. The threshold effect is not found for the Gallup World Poll data that we examine below (Deaton, 2008). There have been several replications of the Easterlin paradox for many countries, for example, Japan, France, Germany, United Kingdom, Switzerland (Easterlin, 1995; Frey and Stutzer, 2000; Myers, 2000; Di Tella et al., 2001; and Blanchflower and Oswald, 2004).

Figure 11.4 shows long-term, country-specific data for three countries, China, India, and Japan, together accounting for about 37% of the world population. There is no long-term trend in happiness in the three countries; the trend is virtually flat, despite impressive increases in real per capita GDP over a period of rapid economic progress in these countries; the shortest time period is that for India at 12 years.

This provides the main elements of Easterlin's hypothesis. We now consider some related issues.

1. Why does happiness decline in a recession? After all, the incomes of others fall too, as would aspirations, so why does one's SWB fall? The reason is that there is a different channel that operates during times of recession (De Neve et al., 2018). In a recession, people set as their reference point, the income levels that they were used to before the recession. The fall in the living standards is then perceived as a fall in well-being.
2. Suppose that the Easterlin paradox holds true, and societal happiness is the main objective of public policy. Is it the case that public policy is ineffective in poor countries if an increase in GDP will not increase long-term happiness? The answer is in the negative. The Easterlin paradox tells us that an exclusive reliance on GDP growth will not make the citizens of a poor country more happy in the long run. But social and public policy offer other channels through which people's well-being can be improved. An improvement in the social safety net and an increase in employment are likely to improve SWB (Easterlin, 2013). Supporting evidence comes from Chinese data (Easterlin et al., 2017) and Japanese data (Sarracino et al., 2019).

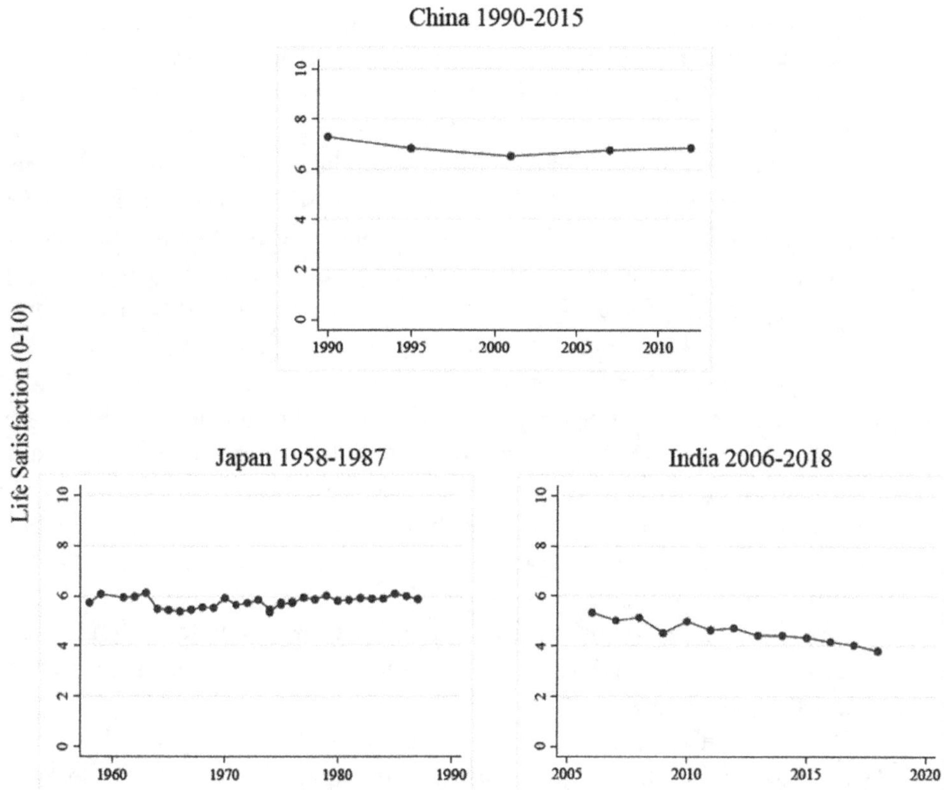

Figure 11.4 The long-term relation between happiness and income for three countries.
Source: Easterlin and O'Connor (2019)
Note: The horizontal axis reflects the time scale over which the data was gathered. On the vertical axis, we measure life satisfaction on a 1–10 scale. The response scale for Japan is 1–4 but was converted to 0–10 for comparable presentation. Sources: China – World Values Survey; Japan – (Veenhoven, 2000); India – Gallup World Poll

3. The Easterlin paradox cannot be disproved by using short-run data. For instance, suppose that a researcher observes data over short horizons, say, over one trough to the next peak, or from one peak to the next trough. In particular, in terms of Figure 11.1, suppose that the researcher observes data on GDP per capita from b_3 to a_4 and the corresponding SWB data from d_3 to c_4. Then, the researcher may mistakenly claim to have disproved Easterlin's paradox but what is being measured is really the first part of the paradox (short-run positive association between income and happiness). However, how long is a "short horizon" and a "long horizon"? The relevant time period has been a major bone of contention between Easterlin and his critics. Easterlin and O'Connor (2019) suggest a minimum time period of at least 12 years. They write (p. 7): "we exclude countries with time series less than 12 years in length in order to reduce the likelihood of including time series so short that our estimate is basically the short-run rather than long-run relation of happiness to income." Bartolini and Sarracino (2014) show that the relationship between happiness and income continues to weaken as the time horizon increases, which is consistent with Easterlin's paradox.

4. The positive association between happiness and incomes in cross sectional data establishes correlation, but not causation. Could it be that higher incomes make people happier, or happier people have higher incomes because they are more productive and have lower stress (Kenny, 1999; Graham et al., 2004)? One natural experiment to establish the direction of causality is to examine the "before" and "after" happiness of people who unexpectedly win the lottery. Gardner and Oswald (2007) use the British Household Panel Survey (BHPS) to examine this question. The survey contains a mental well-being measure based on 12 questions. For each question, the lowest well-being score is three and the highest is zero. Thus, the aggregate minimum well-being score is 36 and the maximum score is zero. A simple sum of these scores across the 12 questions for each subject gives the General Health Questionnaire score (GHQ) for the subject; higher scores denoted lower well-being. Using data over the period 1998–2001, the authors cull out individuals who have won differing amounts of money in the lottery. There are 4,822 observations for individuals who have won a small amount (less than £999) and 137 observations on medium-sized wins (greater than £1000). The control group of subjects is those who do not win anything. The data allows the authors to compare the GHQ score for subjects in each of the three categories (no wins, small-sized wins, and medium-sized wins) "before" and "after" the lottery win. The lottery win is the exogenous variation in income that can potentially uncover the direction of causality if, say, the GHQ score of the subjects improves (i.e., falls) after the lottery win. The main findings are as follows.

   There is an increase in mental stress in the year of the win, particularly for medium-sized wins. However, in the year immediately after the lottery win, there is no difference in the GHQ scores for subjects in the control group and those who win small amounts. The GHQ score improves for subjects who have medium-sized wins. In a nutshell, small wins do not matter but larger, medium-sized, wins raise happiness. So we can infer that the causality runs from income to happiness. Furthermore, the channel through which happiness arises in this data is through changes in the mental stress levels and not changes in aspirations.

   Kuhn et al. (2011) use the Dutch postcode lottery data to show that winning the lottery does not have any effect on a household's reported happiness six months after the win. One possibility is that there is aspiration adaptation after the win. It is plausible that the winners start to compare themselves to richer people, perhaps having purchased a house in a richer neighborhood, where they are not necessarily relatively richer. Alternatively, there could be cultural differences between the British and the Dutch. Lottery wins do not appear to result in better self-assessed physical or mental health outcomes (Apouey and Clark, 2015; Cesarini et al., 2016; Raschke, 2019). In particular, using German data, Raschke (2019) finds that the self reported mental health outcomes for lottery winners with low education significantly deteriorate following the lottery win, but there is no change in health outcomes for winners who are more educated. Using Swedish data, Cesarini et al. (2016) find that following large lottery wins, there is (i) no change in the children's health indicators (e.g., infant health data, body mass data, drug consumption data, and hospitalization data), (ii) nor any significant changes in health care utilization of adults, except for a fall in the consumption of mental health-related drugs. This suggests that when there is an extensive social security net, as in Sweden, childrens' developmental outcomes and adult health outcomes are not income dependent. Frijters et al. (2004) employ novel field evidence from Germany to study the causal effect from income to happiness. After the fall of the Berlin wall and the unification of Germany, the increase in income of East Germans appears to have had a causal effect on their self-reported happiness.

5. Kahneman and Deaton (2010) distinguish between two aspects of subjective well-being. The first "life evaluation," is about "the thoughts that people have about their life when they think about it." This is the sense in which happiness is mostly used in the literature. The second component, which they call "emotional well-being," refers to the quality of the emotional everyday experience. This includes "the frequency and intensity of experiences of joy, stress, sadness, anger, and affection, that make one's life pleasant or unpleasant." The authors analyze 450,000 responses to the Gallup-Healthways Well-Being Index, a daily survey of 1,000 US residents. Subjects who have higher incomes and better education are more likely to report better "life evaluation." However, the second component, emotional well-being is more directly related to the subjects' health, care giving, loneliness, and smoking. Emotional well-being is increasing in log income, upto an annual income of approximately $75,000, but further increases in income cease to improve emotional well-being. The authors conclude that "high income buys life satisfaction but not happiness, and that low income is associated both with low life evaluation and low emotional well-being."
6. Self-reported well-being in the Easterlin paradox is based on comparing one's own incomes relative to those of others. But this begs the question of who the relevant others are. The relevant reference group could be one's neighbours (Luttmer 2005; Kuhn et al., 2011); other workers who have shared labor market characteristics (Clark and Oswald, 1996); and other households in the same village (Knight et al., 2009). Clark and Senik (2010) use data from 18 European countries in Wave 3 of the European Social Survey in which income comparison questions were asked for the year 2006–7. The sample consists of the working age population, 16–65. The two income comparison questions asked in the Survey were the following:

   (i) "How important is it for you to compare your income with other people's income?" Subjects made a choice of answers on a 0–6 scale: 0 (not at all important) to 6 (very important). A total of 19,053 respondents answered this question about the intensity of income comparisons with others. Of these, 25% choose 0 (comparisons not important); each of the numbers 1–4 are chosen by about 15% of the subjects; the number 5 is chosen by 10% of the subjects; and the number 6 is chosen by approximately 5% of the subjects.
   (ii) "Whose income would you be most likely to compare with your own? Please choose one of the groups on this card: Work colleagues/ Family members/ Friends/ Others/ Don't compare/ Not applicable/ Don't know." The responses to this question are shown in Table 11.1. 35.9% of the 18,936 subjects report that they do not compare their incomes to others; by contrast, for Q1, this figure was 25% of the subjects, which suggests a slight inconsistency in responses. Yet, of those who stated that they did not compare incomes with others in Q1, 73% chose "Don't compare" in Q2, so there is also an element of consistency. From Table 11.1, when subjects compare their incomes to others, they overwhelmingly choose to compare with work colleagues, followed by their friends. For the first question, the evidence suggests that a greater intensity of income comparisons with others is associated with lower real per capita GDP across countries as well as within

Table 11.1 Responses to the the second question (relevant reference group for income comparisons). Source: Clark and Senik (2010)

	Observations	%
Work colleagues	6874	36.3
Family members	1103	5.8
Friends	2825	14.9
Others	1344	7.1
Don't compare	6789	35.9
Total	18936	100.0

countries. The categories of people who compare more include poorer households, the self-employed, and those who are single; no noticeable gender effects are found. There is also a cultural component to the intensity of income comparisons, for example, people in Eastern European countries compare more relative to Western European countries. For the second question, the self-employed are more likely to compare their income with family members and friends, while the employed are more likely to compare with colleagues. Women who compare their incomes are more likely to compare with other family members. Culturally, Eastern Europeans are less likely to compare to other family members while Continental Europeans are more likely to compare with colleagues. Overall, the correlation coefficient between the intensity of income comparison with others and self-reported happiness is negative and significant. This correlation is smaller for richer as compared to the poorer individuals. Those who compare with colleagues are significantly happier than others who compare with friends. Individuals who compare more are also more likely to favor greater income redistribution.

7. We have mostly considered evidence using the World Values Survey (WVS) above. A second source of data set is the Gallup World Poll (GWP) collected every year from 2005 to 2019. The country coverage has varied over different years and has expanded over time, which is also the case with WVS data. The GWP data set covers about 160 countries that comprise about 99% of the world population, so it is more complete in its coverage, especially of poorer countries, as compared to the WVS. The GWP asks questions about *life satisfaction* on an 11-point scale, while the WVS asks questions about *happiness* on a three-point scale. Much of the literature treats life satisfaction and happiness as synonymous; see Van Praag et al. (2011) for supporting arguments, but see Deaton (2008) who distinguishes between the two. Deaton identifies life satisfaction with making an overall evaluation of one's life, while happiness can be gauged from *experiential questions* such as asking the individual if they have been smiling a lot, or if they have been depressed. Figure 11.5 shows the relation between mean life satisfaction (vertical axis) and the log of per capita GDP (horizontal axis) for the Gallup World Poll data for 2003. Three curves are shown in the figure. The uppermost dotted curve is for subjects in the age group 15–25; the lowest dotted curve is for subjects who are 60 years and above; and the middle dashed curve is the average across all age groups. The size of the circles reflects the associated country sizes. The relationship is approximately linear. If, however, we had used the

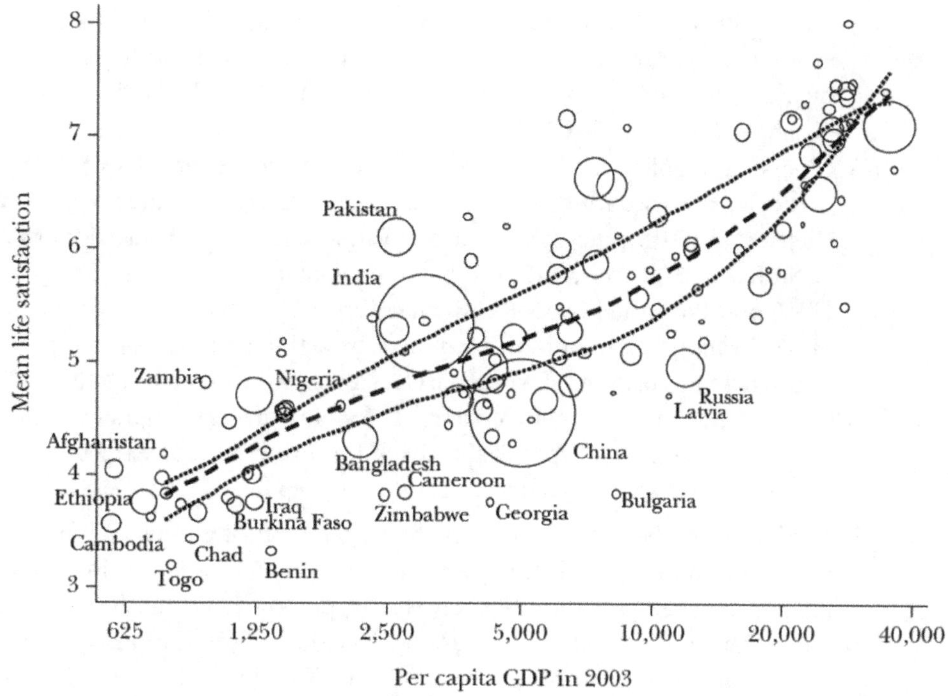

Figure 11.5 The relation between mean life satisfaction and log of per capita GDP for Gallup World Poll data in a cross section of countries for 2003. Source: Deaton (2008)

absolute level of per capita GDP (and not the log), the relationship between mean life satisfaction and income is increasing and concave. Figure 11.5 allows us to draw several conclusions.

(a) Happiness increases with income. People in richer countries (North America, Western Europe, Japan, Australasia) have relatively greater mean level of satisfaction, measured at 7.5–8.5 on an 11-point scale, as compared to some of the poorer countries where the mean level is below 4.

(b) The results from the WVS indicate a cutoff point of about $10,000 (Layard et al., 2003) or $20,000 (Layard, 2005) beyond which income is unrelated to happiness. However, no such cutoff point can be seen in Figure 11.5. If anything, the relation is more steep for richer countries. Deaton gives several reasons for the difference in results between the WVS and the GWP.

   (bi) The GWP includes a larger share of poorer countries. The share of Eastern European countries, who have relatively lower incomes and lower life satisfaction is larger in the WVS. Both these factors create greater variation in mean life satisfaction.

   (bii) The WVS in relatively poor countries such as Ghana, Nigeria, India, and China, sampled the relatively better-off individuals who were likely to report higher life satisfaction. This flattened the relation between income and happiness.

Some of the salient results from the GWP data are as follows.

(c) Mean Life satisfaction for those in the age group 15–25 is highest, while that of individuals aged 60 or above is the lowest. The exception is the highest income countries such as the US, Canada, the UK, Australia, and New Zealand, where this relation is U-shaped (Deaton, 2008).

(d) Others have replicated the main results reported above for the GWP. This includes, in particular, Stevenson and Wolfers (2008, 2013), Sacks et al. (2013), Inglehart et al. (2008), Diener et al. (2013), and Veenhoven and Vergunst (2013). Consider, for instance, the work of Stevenson and Wolfers (2013), based on data for a sample of 155 countries from the GWP over the period 2008–12, which covers 95% of the world's population. They find that the simple correlation between life satisfaction and log of per capita GDP is 0.79. The regression coefficient in a simple OLS regression of life satisfaction on log per capita GDP is 0.335 with a standard error of 0.018. No statistically significant threshold effects are found; the authors specifically check for a threshold of \$15,000. The relationship between life satisfaction and income is fairly steep for the 25 largest countries.

8. The findings from the GWP have been challenged by Easterlin in several publications. For instance, Easterlin et al. (2010) write in their abstract: "Recent critiques of the paradox, claiming the time series relationship between happiness and income is positive, are the result either of a statistical artifact or a confusion of the short-term relationship with the long-term one." A similar criticism is made in Easterlin and O'Connor (2019). Beja (2014) uses relatively long time series data (1973–2012) for a cross section of European countries. While the relation between happiness and income is positive, its magnitude is relatively weak and economically not significant enough. Easterlin and O'Connor (2019, p. 9–10) also highlight the lack of economic significance in the positive estimates: "if the GDP of a country were increased by one percentage point, it would take 1000 years to raise happiness by one point according to the WVS/EVS coefficient … and 500 years, by the GWP coefficient" (EVS refers to the European Values Survey). The results are sensitive to the inclusion of transition economies that belonged to the former Soviet Union. The reason is that for these countries, the relevant data are mostly available during their economic expansion phase. It would appear that the best test of the long-term relation is to use country-specific time series, as in the case of Figure 11.4.

9. Consider the second part of the Easterlin paradox which compares the trend levels of happiness and incomes. Ideally we would like to correlate an autonomous time trend with the trend in SWB (see Figure 11.1). This will require us to remove other factors that influence these time trends, such as the effect of an improvements in the quality of government. Kaiser and Vendrik (2019) aim to make a correction for such time trend factors. They find that the Easterlin paradox holds for North-Western European countries (i.e., Austria, Belgium, Denmark, Finland, France, Great Britain, Netherlands, Sweden, West Germany), but not for Southern European countries (Spain, Greece, Italy, Portugal) and Eastern European countries (Bulgaria, Czech Republic, Croatia, Estonia, Hungary, Latvia, Lithuania, Poland, Romania, Slovakia, Slovenia, Turkey). Southern and Eastern European countries, on average, have lower levels of GDP per capita, hence it is a plausible hypothesis that the Easterlin paradox may only hold after countries surpass some underlying threshold of economic development.

11.2.3 Other Correlates of Subjective Well-Being

The relation between income and well-being has been one of the most examined relationships in the happiness literature. In this section, we examine the relation between well-being and other aggregate variables such as unemployment, inflation, income inequality, social capital, health, and democratic institutions. We also consider *domain satisfaction* which refers to SWB in, say, the health domain.

Age and Well-Being

A fairly well-documented finding in the literature is of a U-shaped relationship between subjective well-being and age (Blanchower and Oswald, 2008; Cheng et al., 2017). Figure 11.6 shows the U-shaped relation between age and well-being from Eurobarometer data over the time period 2009–2019 for 1.25 million people. Average life satisfaction in the Eurobarometer data is based on the following question answered on a 1–4 scale: "On the whole, are you very satisfied, fairly satisfied, not very satisfied, or not at all satisfied with the life you lead?" Answers range on a four-point scale from "not at all" (1) to "very satisfied" (4). The "limited controls" curve in Figure 11.6 was estimated using single-year age dummy variables and controls for year and country. The curve labeled "With controls," in Figure 11.6, controls for gender, education, labor force status, and marital status.

The U-shaped relation in Figure 11.6 has been replicated several times and for different countries; e.g., Blanchflower and Graham (2021) show that it also holds for the US and for the UK. Happiness reaches a minimum around the age of 50 and then begins to recover. However, there is less agreement on why the relation is U-shaped. Graham and Pozuelo (2017) argue that the U-shaped curve in Figure 11.6 mirrors the inverse U-shaped curve in stress levels, which suggests that happiness and stress are inversely related over

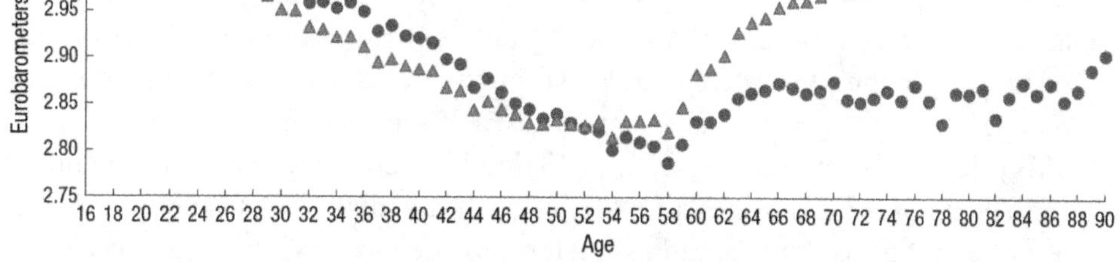

Figure 11.6 A plot of average life satisfaction in Europe, 2009–2019, against age using data from Eurobarometers. Source: Blanchflower and Graham (2021)

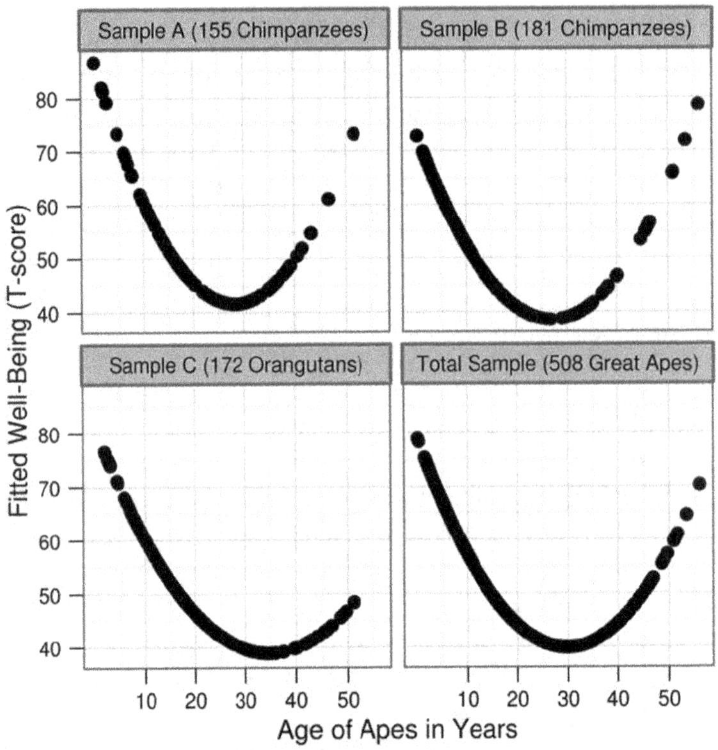

Figure 11.7 The U-shaped relation between age and well-being for the great primates. Source: Weiss et al. (2012)

the lifetime. Another social explanation is that there are high initial aspirations, which are gradually discovered as being too ambitious and unattainable in middle age, leading to a revision towards more modest aspirations that, in turn, lead to greater happiness beyond the age of about 50. However, curiously, the same U-shape also arises for the Great Apes (Weiss et al., 2012), which puts into doubt socially determined explanations for the relationship among humans.

Weiss et al. (2012) assigned "raters" to primates; raters are typically zoo keepers, volunteers, researchers, and caretakers who knew the primates well, usually for at least two years. The raters were asked to assess the degree to which a subject was in a positive versus negative mood; how much pleasure the subject derives from social situations; how successful the subject is in achieving their goals; how happy they would be if they were the subject for a week. For each of these questions, the raters used a 1–7 ranking scale. The well-being scores calculated in this manner are converted into a T-score. This is a well-established method for assessing positive affects in captive nonhuman primates. Figure 11.7 shows the results. The minimum point of the U-shaped curve for the great primates occurs around an age of 30, which is comparable to an age of about 50 for humans, adjusting for the different lifespans of the two.

Gender, Education, Race, and Well-Being

There are well-documented gender differences in self-reported SWB. In a typical study, Kahneman and Deaton (2010) use the *Cantril ladder*[4] to show that women report higher scores, which indicate higher SWB, yet their stress scores are higher. Using labor market data, Clark (1997) tested for several possible explanations such as differences in age, education, and self selection of more satisfied women in the labor force. Yet none of these could provide a decisive explanation. His preferred explanation, which was not tested, was that women have lower expectations in the labor market, as compared to men, hence, other things being equal, they are more satisfied with the outcomes. However, subsequent research has reported a fall in the happiness gender gap (Sousa-Poza and Sousa-Poza, 2003; Stevenson and Wolfers, 2009) or complete elimination of the gap (Green et al., 2018). The Cantril ladder scores also show that blacks report lower scores than whites for US data (Deaton and Stone, 2016), but other research shows that this gap might be shrinking (Stevenson and Wolfers, 2008).

The effect of education on SWB is complex. Higher education may be associated with higher incomes, in which case we might expect an increase in SWB. However, there are two countervailing factors. First, the more educated might have higher aspirations that reduce the perceived satisfaction from actual outcomes. Second, the more educated may, on average, engage in more sedentary and stressful jobs. The net effect is unclear. Since education, at least college and university education, is a choice that individuals make, one would also need to check if more (or less) happy people decide to be educated.

Unemployment and Inflation

Just lagging behind the important role of income, possibly the most important correlate of SWB is unemployment. The dominant approaches in macroeconomics over the last five decades have envisaged individuals making labor–leisure choices. Individuals, in this world, choose to be rationally and voluntarily unemployed if the actual wage falls below their current reservation wage. Encapsulated most strikingly within the real business cycle model, the conclusion is that *the unemployed have rationally chosen to enjoy leisure*.

The evidence from happiness economics paints a very different picture. The unemployed are significantly unhappy as compared to the employed whether we consider (i) a comparison between the employed and the unemployed in cross section data, or (ii) a "before" and "after" comparison for an individual who has become unemployed, by using panel data. Furthermore, macroeconomic policy often relies on minimizing a loss function that depends on deviations of unemployment and inflation from certain targets, such as their natural rates. This clearly appears to assume that unemployment is aversive in terms of social welfare.

[4] In the Cantril ladder, respondents answer the following question: "Please imagine a ladder with steps numbered from zero at the bottom to 10 at the top. The top of the ladder represents the best possible life for you and the bottom of the ladder represents the worst possible life for you. On which step of the ladder would you say you personally feel you stand at this time?"

Di Tella et al. (2001) find that unemployment and inflation reduce happiness, and that unemployment is more aversive to SWB relative to inflation. An increase in unemployment by one percentage point from 9% to 10% (9% was the mean unemployment rate in their data) reduces life satisfaction by 0.028 when happiness is measured on a 1–4 scale. However, an increase in inflation from 8% to 9% (8% was the mean inflation rate in their data) reduces happiness by 0.01 on the same 1–4 scale. On average, individuals are willing to trade a 1 percentage point increase in unemployment against a 1.7 percentage point increase in the inflation rate.

These findings have been replicated several times, for example, Blanchflower et al. (2014) confirm these results using Eurobarometer data. Wolfers (2003) uses data from 16 European countries to show that a one percentage point increase in unemployment results in 4.7 times as much unhappiness as a one percentage point increase in the inflation rate. The relative effects are mediated by the presence of other variables. Unemployment is less aversive in terms of its reduction in SWB if there is a higher unemployment rate; or if a partner is unemployed (Clark, 2003). Both effects can plausibly by explained in terms of reference point effects, and the effects of stigma from being unemployed that might depend on social comparisons.

Clark and Oswald (1994) and Clark (2018) argue that unemployment is more aversive for SWB as compared to any other individual characteristic or experience, say, divorce/separation, and it is relatively more aversive for the more educated. Winkelmann and Winkelmann (1998) show that unemployment causally leads to lower SWB. The drop in SWB among the unemployed is too large to be accounted simply by a drop in incomes. This suggests that there are important psychological costs of unemployment such as anxiety, depression, loss of self-esteem. There are also social costs such as alcoholism, stigma, scarring costs of unemployment, and strained social and personal relationships. Luechinger et al. (2010) report that relative to public sector workers in Germany who have much greater job security, private sector workers exhibit greater anticipatory anxiety towards potential economic shocks. This suggests that the anticipation of potential unemployment is aversive. Data from Italy shows that the suicide rates are highest in regions with the highest unemployment rates (Platt et al., 1992).

Using German panel data, Clark and Georgellis (2013) show that there is relatively complete adaptation of SWB of subjects to marriage, children, divorce and widowhood. However, unemployment stands out as an outlier where people do not adapt as well. SWB is lower not only for the currently unemployed but also for those who have had more spells of unemployment in the past three years. Thus, there is a *scarring effect* of unemployment. Being unemployed in the current period results in a lower drop in SWB if one has been unemployed in the past. This might reduce the incentive to find a job, and is consistent with the *hysterises hypothesis* for unemployment in macroeconomics. Those who self-report a higher fall in well-being on being unemployed are also more likely to have found a job a year later.

Health Satisfaction and Happiness

One may conjecture that healthier individuals are happier. However, this does not establish causality. Happier people may also be healthier (Diener and Chan, 2011). Both health status and happiness may be correlated with a third variable, such as genetic factors and hence they might move synchronously (De Neve et al., 2012). Individuals are fairly resilient in adapting to health

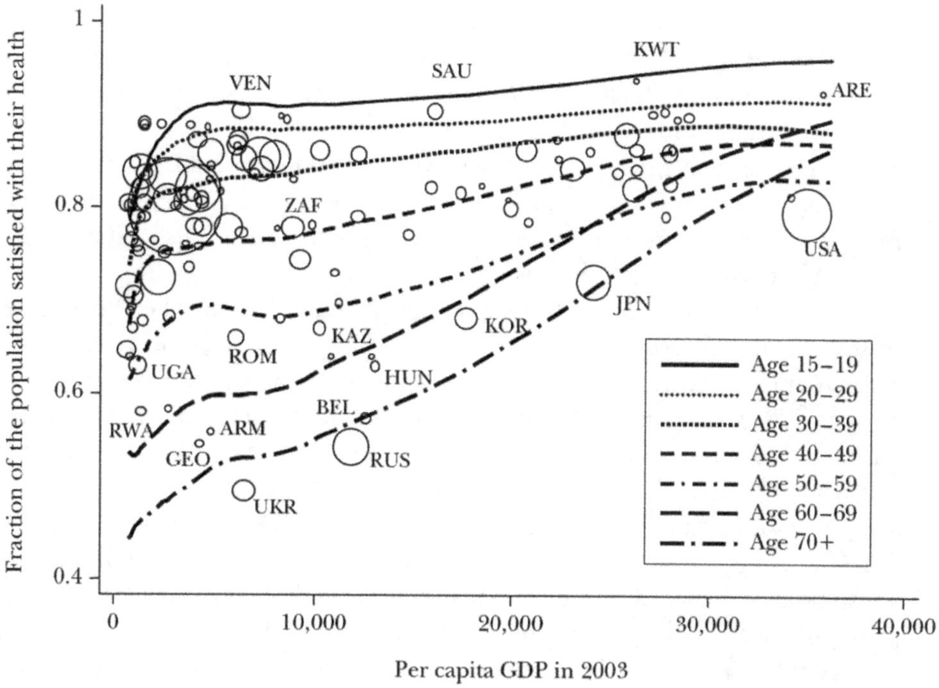

Figure 11.8 A plot of average health satisfaction against real GDP per capita in 2003 (measured at 2000 prices) for seven different age groups. Countries are plotted as circles with diameters proportional to population. The relevant data for each country is the fraction of people satisfied with their health in the population as a whole. Nonparametric regression curves are fitted for each of the age groups.
Source: Deaton (2008)

disabilities. The subjects in Smith et al. (2008) are patients waiting for a kidney transplant. They are asked to predict what their quality of life would be one year later if they did or did not receive a transplant. A year later, those who received (did not receive) the transplant rated their quality of life lower (higher) than their earlier prediction. Thus, individuals appear to have insufficient appreciation of their ability to adjust to changes in health. Oswald and Powdthavee (2008) report that within three years, individuals adjust to 30% of the effect of severe disability and 50% of the effect of moderate disability.

Deaton (2008, p. 56) writes: “Neither life satisfaction nor health satisfaction responds strongly to objective measures of health, such as life expectancy or the prevalence of HIV infection, so that neither provides a reliable indicator of population well-being over all domains, or even over health.” However, the main effect on health appears to arise through the mediating effect of age. Figure 11.8 shows Gallup World Poll data on health satisfaction (“are you satisfied or dissatisfied with your personal health?”) plotted against real GDP for different age groups. The vertical axis is the proportion of subjects in a country who report that they are satisfied with their personal health. The nonparametric regression curves plotted to the data are upward sloping, hence, higher income is associated with greater health satisfaction, although comparing the different curves, health satisfaction falls with age.

For the richest countries, the 50–59 age group has a lower health satisfaction relative to the 60–69 and the 70+ age groups. The gaps between the curves (higher gaps on the left and smaller gaps on the right) show that health satisfaction deteriorates with age at a greater rate in low and middle income countries as compared to in high income countries. It is plausible that the higher incomes in high income countries mitigate the reduced well-being expectations from poorer health in old age. Almost everyone in the age group 15–19 reports being satisfied with their health. In Eastern Europe, and in countries in the former Soviet Union, health satisfaction falls with age, but in the US it increase with age for those who are 50 and over.

Countries that were part of the former Soviet Union have low health satisfaction and 11 of these countries are in the bottom 20 in terms of health satisfaction. These countries with their ordered ranks in brackets are: Ukraine (1), Russia (3), Georgia (4), Armenia (5), Belarus (6), Moldova (8), Latvia (12), Estonia (13), and Kazakhstan (17). There is a similar story to tell for poor, and high mortality, countries such as Haiti, Rwanda, Burundi, Uganda, Cambodia, and Benin. There is also low health satisfaction in sub-Saharan Africa, but it cannot be fully accounted for by a fall in life expectancy due to HIV/AIDS (Deaton, 2008).

This does not mean that the health care systems in the countries in the former Soviet Union are so broken, or that they are poorer than those in Sub-Saharan Africa. The self-reports are perhaps indicative of the differences in the higher quality health care systems in the past in these countries relative to the current health care systems. These differences may bring into play reference dependence and loss aversion, in explaining the self-assessments. A similar explanation may hold for why African countries with high rates of HIV prevalence do not report even poorer health satisfaction. The existing morbidity in these countries has historically been high and people have become accustomed to low standards of health, so there are overall low health aspirations.

The influence of reference points on health-related well-being has been reported in other research too. In Eurobarometer data, self-reported perceptions of being overweight increase in one's own body mass index (BMI) but decrease when the BMI of the reference group is high (Blanchflower et al., 2009). A similar effect is found when the reference group is the BMI of one's partner (Clark and Etilé, 2011). Reference dependent reports of well-being are also found for Italian data (Carrieri and De Paola, 2012): Conditional on the height of a subject, subjects are more likely to report higher well-being when their height is greater than the average of their peer group.

For all these reasons, self-reported health satisfaction may not always be an objectively good indicator of the actual state of health in a country. Yet, these self-assessments and their covariates provide potentially important information for public policy. For instance, the British Household Panel Study (BHPS) data shows that the local quarterly crime rate reduces self-reported individual mental health (Dustmann and Fasani, 2016). The effect might arise not just from being a victim of crime, but rather from a change in expectations that one could become a potential victim.

One alternative approach is to use more objective measures of health, for example, the number of health problems, broken down by categories, such as disability, hearing problems, sight problems, heart problems, and kidney problems. This could be combined with data on the number of times that the respondents have visited the doctor, or the number of days spent in hospital over a time interval in the past. An example is the BHPS which asks subjects the question: "Please think back over the last 12 months about how your health has been. Compared to people of your own age, would you say that your health has on the whole been Excellent, Good, Fair, Poor and Very Poor." However, when these more objective measures are used, one continues to find a positive correlation between health and subjective well-being.

Health satisfaction appears to be a major component of life satisfaction. Easterlin (2006) decomposes overall life satisfaction into satisfactions in different domains, for example, health. In a regression analysis with a measure of SWB as the dependent variable, the coefficient on health satisfaction is statistically significant and large in magnitude. When the health variable is added, the coefficients on several other domains such as life expectancy, the change in life expectancy, and the rate of economic growth, are no longer statistically significant.

The correlation also seems to run from higher self-reported happiness to better health outcomes. Danner et al. (2001), in their often cited *Nun study*, found that nuns who wrote more positive short descriptions of their life in their late teens and early twenties were more likely to live longer. Subjects with higher SWB scores are also more likely to have stronger immune systems; experience less inflammation and cardiovascular disease and suffer from fewer infections (Diener and Chan, 2011); and suffer from less telomere shortening (Epel, 2009).

Income Inequality, Social Capital, and Happiness

Alesina et al. (2004) find that inequality reduces happiness. The relation between inequality and happiness is strong and statistically significant for Europe, but it is relatively weaker in magnitude for the US. The authors' preferred explanation is that in the US, upward income mobility is greater relative to Europe. Hence poorer individuals in the US do not view the presence of the rich as necessarily limiting their own aspirations or future prospects.

However, the relation between inequality and happiness is more complicated. Following a change in the income distribution, happiness appears to depend on how one's own position and the position of one's reference group of individuals changes. In their survey, Clark and D'Ambrosio (2014) write: "The broad conclusion from this work, which is by now far too voluminous to be listed in detail, is that others' incomes often do play a role in determining my well-being. As the income of others to whom I compare rises, my well-being falls; but this status effect may be diminished or even entirely neutralised by a signal effect if what happens to others today informs me about what may happen to me in the future."

Social capital is a broad phenomenon and it involves examining the effects of social networks and trust on production efficiency and well-being (Coleman, 1993; OECD, 2001). Helliwell and Putnam (2004, p. 1436) write: "Social capital can be embodied in bonds among family, friends and neighbors, in the workplace, at church, in civic associations, perhaps even in Internet based 'virtual communities'." They use cross-sectional data from the WVS, the European Values Study (EVS), and the Canadian Benchmark Survey. This allows them to examine the effects on SWB arising from variations in average trust, trust in neighbors and police, membership in associations, governance, the importance of God/religion, and marital status. The overall findings are supportive of the importance of social capital for well-being. The married report higher SWB relative to the divorced or separated; this perhaps reflects the effect of *family level social capital. Community level social capital* may be reflected in church attendance; those who attend church regularly, trust others more. Interactions with friends and neighbors are associated with higher SWB. Living in a high-trust neighborhood is associated with higher SWB and better health.

Anthropological studies have shown that the institution of marriage is present in all cultures and periods, ranging from hunter-gatherers to the current time. Gallup data show that over the period 2020–2023 there is a 20 percentage points gap between the SWB of those who are married and those who are not, even after adjusting for race, ethnicity, age, educational attainment, and gender. This gap transcends ethnic differences and, for US data, persists for American Indian, Asian, Black, Hispanic, Multiracial, or White. The Gallup data over the period 2020–2023, for the US, also shows that marital status is a better predictor of SWB as compared to education, race, age, and gender.

A positive relation between being married and having higher SWB leaves open the direction of causality (does marriage improve happiness, or are happier people more likely to get married). The work by Stutzer and Frey (2006) using the German Socio-Economic Panel (SOEP) data, which repeatedly surveys the same individuals over time, shows that individuals who are happier before marriage are more likely to marry. This does not rule out the possibility that, on average, marriage also improves SWB. Cetre et al. (2016) show that a similar relation also arises for the decision to have children. Individuals who have higher levels of life satisfaction are more likely to have children in the future, as compared to the group of individuals who never have children in the future. Lower levels of life satisfaction are also associated with a greater likelihood of future divorce and separation (Clark et al., 2008).

Those who report higher SWB scores are also likely to engage in behaviors that are more socially acceptable and, hence, more conducive to the building of social capital. Higher SWB scores are associated with greater generosity, cooperativeness and prosociality towards others (Clark, 2018); more volunteering (Thoits and Hewitt, 2001); and greater political participation (Flavin and Keane, 2012). The opposite direction of causality might also hold. Using British Cohort Study data, Layard et al. (2014) show that childhood emotional health over the ages 5–16 is negatively associated with the number of adult crimes between the ages of 16–34.

Democracy, Freedom, and Life Satisfaction

The literature has also examined the link between political institutions, economic freedom, and well-being. Economic freedom typically refers to the freedom to make personal choices, engage in voluntary exchange; the presence of competition; and the protection of private property rights. The Better Life Index, which is constructed using OECD data shows a positive relationship between economic freedom and most aspects of well-being (Nikolaev, 2014).[5] Economic freedom and health/education/environmental quality have been found to be positively related (Stroup, 2007). These relationships probably arise because economic freedom is higher in richer countries, who also have better health, education, and quality of environment.

[5] This index combines income and life satisfaction with nine other dimensions of well-being, including housing, jobs and earnings, community, education, environment, civic engagement, health, safety, and work-life balance.

Rode et al. (2013) use the life satisfaction data from the WVS which measures satisfaction on a 1–10 scale. They measure economic freedom using data in the *Economic Freedom of the World: 2012 Annual Report*. Countries are classed into autocracies and democracies using the framework of Cheibub et al. (2010). The authors report the following findings. The average life satisfaction in autocracies is 5.56 while that in democracies is 6.79. A regression analysis shows that the effects of economic freedom and democracy on life satisfaction are positive and statistically significant at 1%. The authors conjecture, following Frey and Stutzer (2002), that in a democracy, respect for the choices of people give them a feeling of well-being.

Data for 38 developed countries shows that indices of political freedom, economic freedom, and personal freedom have a statistically significant and positive correlation with happiness (Veenhoven, 2000). However, economic freedom enhances happiness relatively more in poorer countries, while political freedom enhances it relatively more in richer countries. It is likely that there is a greater expectation of political freedom in the richer countries, while in poorer countries basic needs must be met first before people aspire to the same level of political freedom. The average self-reported happiness in Swiss cantons with higher indices of direct democracy (e.g., direct voting in referenda) is also higher (Frey and Stutzer, 2000).

11.3 Behavioral Industrial Organization

Industrial organization is broadly the study of decisions taken by incumbent firms and potential entrants in a market; and the effect of these decisions on market outcomes. It also considers the determination of boundaries between firms and markets, that is, which transactions take place within firms and why, relative to taking place in markets. Behavioral industrial organization lies at the intersection of behavioral economics and industrial organization. The neoclassical view has traditionally been that firms maximize profits and the rationality requirements that hold for individuals also typically hold for firms. For instance, firms too are assumed to employ expected utility under risk/uncertainty; exponential discounting when making temporal decisions; and the same strategic reasoning as individuals do.

The early, and influential, empirical evidence in the Hall and Hitch (1939) report, showed that large corporations do not appear to behave as simple profit maximizing entities. They showed that firms do not produce at the point where marginal revenue equals marginal costs (which continues to be the equilibrium condition in microeconomic models of firms). Rather firms appeared to use a simple heuristic that covered their average costs plus a price markup, typically 10%. The reasons they gave for their findings would find sympathy among modern behavioral economics. First, firms operate under conditions of true uncertainty so that they do not know what their marginal cost and marginal revenue curves really are. Second, the average cost plus a transparent and reasonable markup was viewed to be "fair." Firms knew that customers disliked frequent price changes, so they kept prices constant for long periods of time. These findings cannot be explained by a simple profit maximizing view of the firm. Furthermore, when asked, managers of firms reported that short-run profit maximization was not their goal. Rather their goals were multidimensional, such as fair level of profit, building up their goodwill, and being fair to their competitors.

The insights on the boundedly rational behavior of firms by Herbert Simon in the 1950's highlighted the use of the *satisficing* heuristic to make decisions rather than *optimizing* (Simon, 1957); see Section 10.8. It also spoke about *procedural rationality*; the procedure used to arrive at a final decision must itself be plausible and believable. Firms face massive computational problems and there have been attempts to open the black box of decision making within firms. For instance, a range of theories have tried to peer inside the black box by considering firms as a formal and informal network of dynamic contracts (Simon, 1955; Cyert and March, 1963; Nelson and Winter, 1982; Radner, 1992, 1996). Some of this earlier work is nicely documented elsewhere, see for instance Koutsoyiannis (1979) for a textbook treatment. We do not wish to detract from the importance of this work, but space limitations dictate that our focus in this section will be on the more modern behavioral literature.

The modern behavioral industrial organization literature has not incorporated the early insights from the literature cited above; this is a potential drawback. It has preferred mainly to focus on profit maximizing firms that face consumers who depart in various ways from the neoclassical benchmark. It does allow the managers of such firms to be either rational, in a neoclassical sense, or not to be rational. For instance, the work by Malmendier and Tate (2005, 2008), that we have considered earlier, showed that overconfident CEOs may take decisions, such as mergers, that do not necessarily optimize in the sense of maximizing value for shareholders. For most of this section, we will consider rational managers who face consumers that depart from neoclassical rationality.

11.3.1 Phishing for Phools

The Oxford English Dictionary defines the word phish as: "To perpetrate a fraud on the Internet in order to glean personal information from individuals, especially by impersonating a reputable company; to engage in online fraud by deceptively 'angling' for personal information." In their book *Phishing for Phools* Akerlof and Shiller (2015) define "phishing" (page xi) as follows.

> We are creating a new, broader meaning for the word phish here. We take the computer definition as a metaphor. Rather than viewing phishing as illegal, we present a definition for something that is much more general and goes much further back in history. It is about getting people to do things that are in the interest of the phisherman, but not in the interest of the target. It is about angling, about dropping artificial lure into the water and sitting and waiting as wary fish swim by, make an error, and get caught. Thus, phishing is the strategic and well thought out behavior of large organizations designed to exploit either psychological or informational weaknesses of consumers.

This is not a very precise definition, but one that is in keeping with the informal nature of the discourse in their book. Several examples can be used to illustrate the phenomenon of phishing. Clever advertising may get us to buy the kinds of things that we might not have wanted; the convenience of credit cards may get us to spend more than we would like to; pharmaceutical companies might give small gifts to doctors to prescribe their own medicines; credit rating companies might use their reputation to give undeservedly high ratings to financial firms, for example, Goldman Sachs mined its reputation to sell highly rated, but worthless, securities to clients in the run-up to the financial crisis; a soap advertisement might convince us that it makes us not just clean, but beautiful; we might be sold diesel cars with "defeat software" that overstates the fuel efficiency; and the US pharmaceutical giant Merck tried to hide the serious side-effects of its miracle drug "Vioxx" and only admitted breach once third-party research discovered the problems.

Akerlof and Shiller write (p.171): "Phishing for phools is not some occasional nuisance. It is all over the place. Not only does it affect many decisions; in some cases it has sizable effects on welfare." In many of these cases, we buy into narratives and stories that dupe us and significantly influence economic decision making. The author write that this is "perhaps our book's most important takeaway."

In the spirit of behavioral welfare economics, Akerlof and Shiller distinguish between two kinds of preferences. Our "stated preferences" could be to eat better, save more, and stop smoking (we refer to these as normative preferences in our discussion of welfare economics). However, the choices arising from these preferences could also be guided by psychological impulses, which as they put it (p. 5), are the "monkeys on our shoulders" that entice us into poor decisions. Their thesis is that (p. 20) "Free markets do not just produce what we really want; they also produce what we want according to our monkey-on-the-shoulder tastes."

How do we protect ourselves from phishing? The authors' proposed solution is "sound government regulation" to protect us from fraud. But is there a tradeoff between such regulation and individual liberty? What precise form should such regulation take? These are not questions that the authors go into at great lengths, but our discussion on behavioral welfare economics in the next chapter should provide a complementary approach. For instance, the Dodd–Frank Act of 2010 increased the liability of credit ratings agencies for faulty ratings. Food and drug regulation, regulation of corporate accounting, securities regulation, campaign finance regulation, and insurance regulation are some other examples that are designed to reduce the impact of phishing. The actions of firms are endogenous, so they might try to get around loopholes in the existing regulations by designing newer forms of phishing. Hence, the design of regulation must be a dynamic process with constant feedback between market outcomes and economic policy.

Economics is based on the notion of a market equilibrium. What does a market equilibrium look like when phishing is a possibility? The authors are a bit sketchy on the details, but they motivate their reasoning using the example of the checkout lane at the supermarket. Everybody wishes to join the shortest lane. In equilibrium, the marginal benefit of any individual joining any of the lanes is identical. All the checkout lanes, in equilibrium, are almost the same length. In a similar manner, firms looking for phishing opportunities exhaust them in equilibrium. Any potential profits are competed away by the phishing activities of the firms. The authors write (p. 2) that a "phishing equilibrium" arises when "every chance for profit more than the ordinary will be taken up."

Spiegler (2019) argues that there are pros and cons of the purely informal style of reasoning as in Akerlof and Shiller (2015). On the one hand an "informal style" provides the flexibility to think of a wider range of operative factors and frameworks as compared to the "pure theory style" preferred in economics. This allows for a richer consideration of the issues. However, on the other hand, a theoretical framework might also provide insights that the purely informal style might not.

However, one has to be careful in making these arguments. Suppose the pure theory style provides us with "new insights" that the informal style of reasoning does not. Yet, it relies on invoking empirically rejected components such as expected utility, exponential discounting, use of mixed strategy Nash equilibrium, or backward induction. How confident can we be of the new insights, particularly their empirical relevance? Spiegler does not address this question. However, his criticisms merit attention, as illustrated in the following example.

Consider a single seller who has one object to sell to a single buyer. The seller is privately informed of the objectively correct value of the object, $v > 0$. The buyer's valuation of the object is $v + b$, where $b > 0$ represents the gains from trade, but the buyer does not know the exact objective value, v. Hence, we have a problem of adverse selection. The buyer believes that v is uniformly distributed over the interval $[0, 1]$. What price p should the buyer offer to the seller in a one-off interaction between the two parties? This problem is related to the phishing problem because it falls within the ambit of problems where the buyer might misperceive the seller's incentives under adverse selection (e.g., misperceiving the real value of mortgage backed securities).

We first remind readers of a basic result from statistics.

Remark 11.1 *Suppose that a random variable X is distributed uniformly over the interval $[a, b]$; we denote a particular realization of the random variable by x. Then, the probability density of the random variable is*

$$f(x) = \frac{1}{b-a}; x \in [a, b], \tag{11.18}$$

and $f(x) = 0$ for $x \notin [a, b]$. The cumulative distribution function F is given by

$$F(x) = \begin{cases} 0 & \text{if} \quad x < a \\ \frac{x-a}{b-a} & \text{if} \quad x \in [a, b] \\ 1 & \text{if} \quad x > b \end{cases}. \tag{11.19}$$

Suppose that a "rational buyer" chooses a price to offer to the seller, in order to maximize the expected value from trade. The buyer knows that the seller will only trade the object if $p \geq v$. Since v is unknown, let $Pr(v \leq p)$ be the objectively correct probability computed by the buyer that trade will take place. If trade does not take place, then both parties get a payoff of zero. Hence, the expected value of trade to the buyer, for any price p, is

$$\pi_B = Pr(v \leq p)\left[E\left[v \mid v \leq p\right] + b - p\right]. \tag{11.20}$$

In (11.20), the term $E\left[v \mid v \leq p\right]$ is the expected value of the object, conditional on the seller having accepted the offer. For instance, suppose the buyer offers a price $p = 0.6$, and the seller accepts it. Then the buyer must believe that the objectively correct value of the object is distributed uniformly over the interval $[0, 0.6]$. Thus, a rational buyer satisfies two conditions. (i) Computes the statistically correct probability $Pr(v \leq p)$, and (ii) uses the correct conditional expected value $E\left[v \mid v \leq p\right]$.

Using Remark 11.1, and noting that in our case $a = 0$ and $b = 1$, we can compute the following

$$Pr(v \leq p) = F(p) = p.$$

$$E\left[v \mid v \le p\right] = \int_0^p vf(v \mid v \le p)dv, \tag{11.21}$$

where $f(v \mid v \le p)$ is the probability density of v if v were distributed uniformly over the interval $[0, p]$ rather than over the interval $[0, 1]$. Thus, we now have the case $a = 0, b = p$, hence, using (11.18), we have $f(v \mid v \le p) = \frac{1}{p-0} = \frac{1}{p}$. Hence, we can write (11.21) as

$$E\left[v \mid v \le p\right] = \int_0^p \frac{v}{p}dv.$$

A straightforward calculation shows that

$$\int_0^p \frac{v}{p}dv = \frac{1}{p}\left|\frac{v^2}{2}\right|_0^p = \frac{p^2}{2p} = \frac{p}{2}.$$

Substituting these calculations back in (11.20), we get

$$\pi_B = p\left[\frac{p}{2} + b - p\right]. \tag{11.22}$$

The buyer chooses the price, p, to maximize π_B in (11.22). We have

$$\frac{d\pi_B}{dp} = -p + b; \quad \frac{d^2\pi_B}{dp^2} = -1 < 0. \tag{11.23}$$

From (11.23), π_B is a strictly concave function of p so we have a unique maximizer that can be found by setting $\frac{d\pi_B}{dp} = 0$. Hence, the optimal choice of price of a rational buyer to offer to the seller, denoted by p^*, is

$$p^* = b. \tag{11.24}$$

Since the valuation of the buyer is $v + b$, which is greater than the valuation of the seller, *it is efficient for the seller and the buyer to trade, irrespective of what the objectively correct value of v is*. However, since the objectively correct v is uniformly distributed over $[0, 1]$ and a price $p^* = b$ is offered, the *probability that trade takes place* is

$$F(b) = b. \tag{11.25}$$

It follows that with probability $1 - b$, trade does not take place. This is an illustration of the market failure that arises from the problem of adverse selection.

Consider now the optimal price chosen by a buyer who is "cursed" in the sense of Eyster and Rabin (2005). We have outlined a *cursed equilibrium* in Section 7.8.4 of the book. Essentially, such a buyer (i) knows that sellers do not accept an offer unless $p \ge v$, but (ii) does not take account of the correlation between v and p. Thus, the expected utility perceived by a cursed buyer is

$$\pi_B = Pr(v \le p)\left[E[v] + b - p\right]. \tag{11.26}$$

Comparing (11.20) and (11.26), a cursed buyer imagines the average value of the object to be $E[v]$ which is independent of the price, p. We have $E[v] = \int_0^1 vf(v)dv$. Using (11.18), and $a = 0, b = 1$, a simple calculation shows that $E[v] = \frac{1}{2}$. Hence, we can write (11.26) as

$$\pi_B = p\left[\frac{1}{2} + b - p\right].$$

Proceeding as above, we can find the optimal choice of price, p^c, for a cursed buyer to be

$$p^c = \frac{1}{4} + \frac{b}{2}. \tag{11.27}$$

The probability that trade takes place in this case is $F(p^c)$, which is given by

$$F(p^c) = \frac{1}{4} + \frac{b}{2}.$$

Adverse selection harms the buyer because trade might not sometimes take place even when it is efficient for all values of v. But is trade more unlikely to take place due to the phoolishness of the buyer (on account of cursed beliefs)? Not necessarily. The answer depends on the relative sizes of $F(p^*)$ and $F(p^c)$. Comparing (11.25), (11.27), trade is even more likely to take place under phoolishness when

$$F(p^c) > F(p^*) \Leftrightarrow b < \frac{1}{2}.$$

Thus, if $b < \frac{1}{2}$ then phoolishness actually benefits both parties involved in the trade by making trade more likely to occur. While this is an illustrative example, its characterization of phoolishness is much more limited than the one proposed in Akerlof and Shiller (2015) and does not diminish the insights of their work.

11.3.2 The Effects of Limited Attention

An important focus of the literature on behavioral industrial organization has been on exploring the effects of limited attention on the optimal prices chosen by firms.

The basic idea can be illustrated by thinking of the price charged by a firm, p, as having two components. A *directly observed price component*, q, and the *price of add-ons or surcharges*, a, that might be not as transparent and visible to all consumers. For instance, when booking a hotel, a consumer might be quoted the price of the room, q, but there could be add on components such as room service charges, laundry charges, room telephone charges, wifi-charges, and car parking charges. Hence, we can write

$$p = q + a; a \in [0, \overline{a}], \tag{11.28}$$

where $\overline{a}$ is some maximum possible add-on price. We assume that there are two types of consumers; sophisticated consumers who observe both q and a, and *naive consumers* who observe q but do not either observe, or do not pay attention, to the add-on component a.

The behavioral industrial economics literature has identified several channels that cause naive consumers to overlook the add on component, a. In their survey, Heidhues and Köszegi (2018) identify the following channels.

1. Limited attention: Naive consumers may be inattentive to the component a. For instance, empirical evidence suggests that consumers ignore state sales taxes that are only added at the cash register to the ticket price of an item, even when they are aware of the existence of such taxes (Chetty et al., 2009). By contrast, the federal taxes are added directly to the ticket price so consumers pay attention to them. Consumers have also been shown to be inattentive to bank overdraft charges when opening a bank account (Armstrong and Vickers, 2012).

2. Temporal preferences: In Part III of the book we considered present-focused preferences as, for instance, manifested in the hyperbolic discounting model. If "naive" consumers (see Part III for a definition) have present-focused preferences, they assign a lower weight on the future costs of actions. For instance, they might overestimate their future use of a gym. Hence, they are likely to be willing to sign a "fixed term contract" that has a relatively low pay-per-visit charge, but a high upfront fee. However, once the future arrives, their present-focus makes the current cost of gym attendance more salient, reducing the number of actual gym visits. Thus, they may end up paying more and are likely to have benefited from a pay-per-visit contract with low upfront fees instead (DellaVigna and Malmendier, 2004, 2006). It is "as if" the consumers are not paying enough attention to the high upfront charge in a fixed term contract and are overestimating their future gym usage. A second possibility is that naive consumers might be subject to *projection-bias.* Thus, their current usage of the product may heavily influence the prediction that they make about the future usage of the product (Loewenstein et al., 2003). For instance, consumers might enter into too much credit card debt, on the mistaken projection that they are unlikely to need to borrow much in the future (Ausubel, 1991).
3. Statistical misperceptions: Naive consumers might not obey the laws of classical statistics. Mobile phone consumers might underestimate the variance of their phone usage. Companies might take account of this misperception by offering convex pricing schemes that levy increasingly higher call charges as phone usage increases (Grubb, 2009). It would appear to an outsider that the consumer ignores these higher charges, but the consumer does not anticipate ever paying for them due to an underestimation of the variance. Believers in the *law of small numbers* assign to relatively small samples the properties of large samples (see Section 9.4). Naive consumers who use the law of small numbers might also be more willing to pay for the services of "quacks" because the quack has to be proved right only a small number of times for them to believe in the effectiveness of the quack (Spiegler, 2006). In reality, however, the predictions of the quack might be no better than chance.

Suppose that, for whatever reason, naive consumers (or naifs) do not pay attention to the add-on "a" in (11.28) while sophisticated consumers (or sophisticates) do pay attention to it. In order to study the implications of inattention, let us first outline the basic *Hotelling model of price competition.*

Suppose that consumers are uniformly located over the interval $[0, 1]$. One can think of this interval as a linear city of 1 mile. There are two competing firms, A and B, that sell a homogeneous good; both firms have an identical marginal cost of supplying one unit of the good, equal to $c > 0$. The two firms are located at the two ends of the city; firm A is located at 0 and firm B at 1. Denote a generic location in this city by $x \in [0, 1]$. The respective prices charged by firms A and B are p_A and p_B. The prices include a visible component q, but the add-on component, a, might not be visible to all consumers. Thus, the price charged by a firm is

$$p_i = q_i + a_i; i = A, B. \tag{11.29}$$

The firms compete in prices, p_i, by choosing the two components q_i and a_i, $i = A, B$.

Each consumer demands either zero unit of the good, which gives a utility of 0, or 1 unit of the good, which gives utility v. Since both firms sell a homogeneous good, it does not matter to the consumer whether the good is purchased from firm A or B. However, the consumer must incur a transportation cost $t > 0$ per unit of distance traveled to buy the good. A consumer who lives at the location $x \in [0, 1]$ incurs a transport cost of tx^2 when buying from firm A and a transport cost $t(1 - x)^2$ to buy from firm B.

Benchmark Case: All Consumers Are Fully Attentive

Suppose that all consumers are sophisticates, that is, are fully attentive to the two price components q_i and a_i. Since consumers ultimately only care about the composite price p_i, each firm optimally sets zero add-ons, that is,

$$a_i = 0; i = A, B.$$

Thus, we can directly consider competition between the two firms in the overall prices, $p_A = q_A$ and $p_B = q_B$. The utility of a consumer who is located at $x \in [0, 1]$ is given by,

$$U = \begin{cases} v - p_A - tx^2 & \textit{if} \;\; \text{buying from A} \\ v - p_B - t(1 - x)^2 & \textit{if} \;\; \text{buying from B} \end{cases}. \tag{11.30}$$

In (11.30), the consumer's utility from buying one unit of a good equals the value of the good, v, minus the two costs – the price paid, and the transportation cost incurred. Let us find a location $x_c \in [0, 1]$ such that a consumer who is located at x_c is indifferent to buying from firms A or B. Using (11.30), we have

$$v - p_A - tx_c^2 = v - p_B - t(1 - x_c)^2. \tag{11.31}$$

Solving out for x_c we have

$$x_c = \frac{p_B - p_A + t}{2t}. \tag{11.32}$$

The location x_c is depicted in Figure 11.9. As the traveling distance increases on either side of x_c, the rise in traveling costs reduces the consumer's utility; for simplicity we have shown the curves in Figure 11.9 to be linear. The utility of the consumer, at x_c, from traveling a distance $x_c - x$ towards firm A is shown on the left. When this consumer buys from firm A, the utility of the consumer is shown by the height of the dashed vertical line at $x = 0$ (this is the LHS of equation (11.31)). Similarly the utility of the consumer, at x_c, from traveling a distance $x - x_c$ towards firm B is shown on the right. When this consumer buys from firm B, the consumer's utility is shown by the height of the dashed vertical line at the location $x = 1$ (shown as the RHS of equation (11.31)). To the left of the location x_c, all consumers prefer to buy from firm A because their traveling cost to firm A is even lower (and the traveling cost to firm B is higher). By a similar argument, all consumers located to the right of location x_c prefer to buy from firm B.

Suppose that the consumer located at x_c always prefers to buy the good, that is,

$$v - p_A - tx_c^2 \geq 0. \tag{11.33}$$

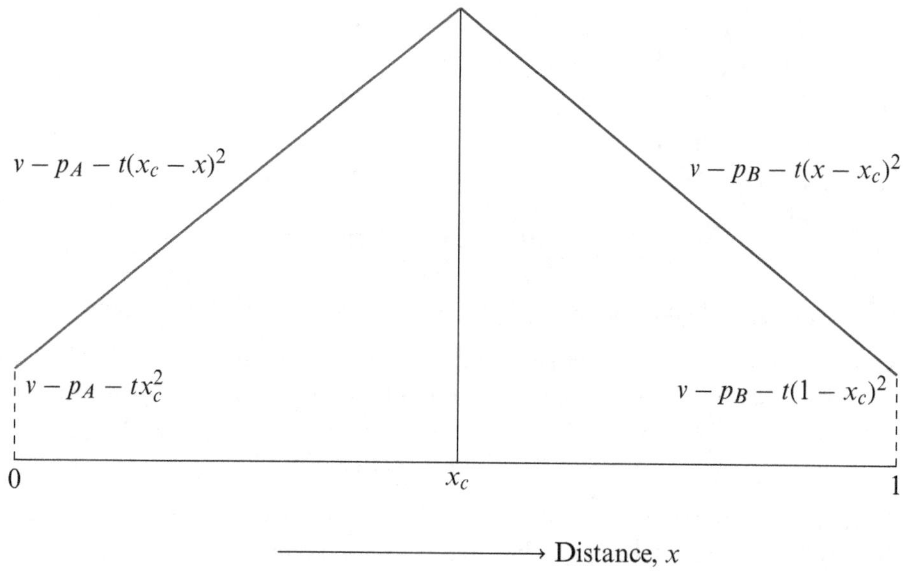

Figure 11.9 The Hotelling model. The consumer located at x_c is indifferent to buying from any of the two firms

It follows that all consumers in the city located anywhere in the interval $[0, 1]$ also prefer to buy the good. This holds true because on either side of x_c, everyone incurs a lower transport cost by buying either from firm A (all those to the left of x_c) or from firm B (all those to the right of x_c). Hence, they derive an even higher, and a strictly positive, level of utility relative to the consumer at location x_c.

Since everyone to the left of x_c buys from firm A, so the demand facing firm A is

$$D_A = \int_0^{x_c} f(z)dz,$$

where $f(z)$ is the density function of a uniform distribution (recall that consumers are uniformly distributed over the interval $[0, 1]$). Using Remark 11.1 and using $a = 0$ and $b = 1$ we get $f(z) = 1$. Hence, we get[6]

$$D_A = \int_0^{x_c} dz = x_c = \frac{p_B - p_A + t}{2t}. \tag{11.34}$$

Everyone to the right of x_c buys from firm B, so the demand facing firm B is

$$D_B = \int_{x_c}^{1} dz = 1 - x_c = 1 - \frac{p_B - p_A + t}{2t}. \tag{11.35}$$

Each firm maximizes its profits, given by

$$\pi_i = D_i (p_i - c) ; i = A, B, \tag{11.36}$$

[6] For the computation in (11.34), we have used $\int_0^{x_c} dz = |z|_0^{x_c} = x_c - 0 = x_c$. For the computation in (11.35) we have used $\int_{x_c}^1 dz = |z|_{x_c}^1 = 1 - x_c$.

where $D_i p_i$ is the total revenue and $D_i c$ is the total cost of firm $i = A, B$. Substituting (11.34) in (11.36), the profits of firm A are

$$\pi_A = \frac{p_B - p_A + t}{2t}(p_A - c). \tag{11.37}$$

Differentiating (11.37),

$$\frac{d\pi_A}{dp_A} = \frac{p_B - p_A + t}{2t} - \frac{1}{2t}(p_A - c). \tag{11.38}$$

Differentiating again, we get $\frac{d^2\pi_A}{dp_A^2} = \frac{-1}{t} < 0$. Hence, the profit function of firm A is strictly concave in its price, so a unique solution exists. For an interior solution, we solve $\frac{d\pi_A}{dp_A} = 0$ for p_A to get the *reaction function of firm A* as a function of the price of firm B

$$p_A = \frac{1}{2}(p_B + t + c). \tag{11.39}$$

The reaction function of firm A gives the best response of A, in terms of the choice of price p_A, to any price p_B set by B. Proceeding analogously, the reaction function of firm B is given by

$$p_B = \frac{1}{2}(p_A + t + c). \tag{11.40}$$

Solving the two reaction functions in (11.39), (11.40) simultaneously, we get the Nash equilibrium in prices $p_A^* = p_B^* = p^*$, where[7]

$$p_A^* = p_B^* = p^* = t + c. \tag{11.41}$$

Thus, in a Nash equilibrium, each firm sets its price above marginal cost, where the markup is given by the unit transportation cost, t. Since both firms set zero add-ons ($a_A = a_B = 0$), hence, using (11.29), we can also rewrite (11.41) as

$$q_A^* = q_B^* = q^* = t + c. \tag{11.42}$$

Substituting (11.41) in (11.34), (11.35), we can see that each firm gets half the market share ($D_A = D_B = \frac{1}{2}$). Substituting $D_i = \frac{1}{2}$ and $p_i = t + c$ in (11.36) the profit of each firm in equilibrium is

$$\pi_A = \pi_B = \frac{t}{2}. \tag{11.43}$$

In the perfectly competitive benchmark, each firm sets price equal to marginal cost. Hence, the perfectly competitive analogue of (11.41) would have been

$$p^* = c,$$

which corresponds to the case of zero transport cost, $t = 0$; it is "as if" each consumer could buy from a firm at its doorstep. The outcome $p^* = c$ is also identical to the outcome under Bertrand competition. As transport cost per unit, t, increases, the gap between the competitive and the imperfectly competitive outcome grows, as does the gap between the price and the marginal costs of firms.

[7] From (11.40) we get $p_A = 2p_B - t - c$. Substitute this in (11.39) to get $2p_B - t - c = \frac{1}{2}(p_B + t + c)$. Solving out for p_B we get $p_B^* = t + c$. Substituting p_B^* back in (11.39) we get $p_A^* = t + c = p_B^*$.

All Consumers Are Inattentive

Suppose now that all consumers are inattentive. They do not pay any attention to the add-ons, a_A and a_B, but they do pay attention to the visible component of prices, q_A and q_B. For each firm, the market demand is decreasing in the price that they set, in this case the visible component of price; see (11.34), (11.35). Hence, both firms set the invisible component, the add-on, at the maximum possible level,

$$a_i = \overline{a}; i = A, B. \tag{11.44}$$

But, the all-inclusive optimal price charged by each firm, $i = A, B$, stays as $p^* = t + c$; this can be checked by going through the same steps as in the case of fully attentive consumers. Denote the visible component of price for firms A and B by, respectively, $\widetilde{q}_A$ and $\widetilde{q}_B$. Hence, using (11.29), (11.41), (11.44), we get

$$p^* = \widetilde{q}_i + \overline{a} = t + c; i = A, B. \tag{11.45}$$

Solving out for $\widetilde{q}_i$ we get

$$\widetilde{q}_i = t + c - \overline{a}. \tag{11.46}$$

Comparing (11.42) and (11.46), we get that

$$\widetilde{q}_i < q_i^*. \tag{11.47}$$

The all-inclusive price paid in both cases (fully attentive and fully inattentive consumers) is $p^* = t + c$. Hence, inattention does not hurt the inattentive consumers. They actually pay $p^* = t + c$, although they believe that they are paying a lower price $\widetilde{q}_i$. This leads to the remarkable result that, in effect, market competition may protect boundedly rational consumers (Grubb, 2015).

From (11.46), if $\overline{a}$ is too high, then $\widetilde{q}_i$ will be too low. Yet, there could be *price floors* below which the visible price cannot drop. For instance there could be a price floor, $\underline{q}$ such that

$$\underline{q} < \widetilde{q}_i = t + c - \overline{a}. \tag{11.48}$$

In this case, the visible price might not be able to fall low enough. If both firms still wish to keep the add-ons to the maximum levels, $a = \overline{a}$, then this will raise the all-inclusive price that firms charge. In this case, fully inattentive consumers will not be protected by market competition. Several examples of price floors can be given. In the market for printers, inattentive consumers may ignore the prices of printer cartridges when buying a printer (Miao, 2010). To maximize profits, firms work on the add-ons margin, and make their printers incompatible with printer cartridges of other firms and set high prices for their cartridges. Raising the prices of add-ons too high and reducing the price of printers, $\widetilde{q}_i$, too low could induce consumers to buy a new printer rather than a new cartridge. This sets a lower bound $\underline{q}$ on printer prices. Another example of an add-on is the price of the warranty as part of the all-inclusive price of consumer durables (Michel, 2017). In this case, the firm could increase the price of a warranty and sell the consumer durable at too low a price. However, in some countries legal requirements prevent the retail price of a good to fall below the wholesale price, effectively setting a price floor.

Consider the case of perfect competition, $t \to 0$, so that from (11.46), $\widetilde{q}_i = c - \overline{a}$. If

$$c - \overline{a} < v < c,$$

then fully inattentive consumers will buy the good because the valuation of the good exceeds the price they believe they pay ($v > \widetilde{q}_i$). However, it is socially undesirable to produce the good because $v < c$. Thus, inattention may create economic inefficiencies and distortions in production.

From (11.34), (11.35), the demand facing each firm is decreasing in its price. Insofar as inattentive consumers cannot spot the add-ons and will focus on the visible component of price, q_i, firms have the incentive to innovate to produce new technologies of obfuscation that enable the maximum possible add-ons, $\overline{a}$ (Heidhues et al., 2016). Thus, an implication of inattention is that it might lead firms to pursue more devious strategies for obfuscation (Piccione and Spiegler, 2012; Murooka and Schwarz, 2018).

This might particularly be the case when there is a price floor given by $\underline{q}$ and (11.48) holds. In this case (price floors), an increase in competition, corresponding to a drop in the unit transportation cost t, will not reduce the price, $\widetilde{q}_i$ in (11.46). However, competition might also produce efforts to improve the technology of obfuscation that increases $\overline{a}$ (Spiegler, 2006; Carlin, 2009; Heidhues et al., 2016; Gamp and Krähmer, 2019). This runs counter to the argument in neoclassical regulation and antitrust economics that competition is almost always good, reducing the prices that consumers pay and leading to greater efficiency.

The lab experiments of Fehr and Wu (2021) give opportunities to sellers to obfuscate their products by employing add-ons to their products, on top of the headline prices, while buyers can spend time searching for the best products. In the benchmark case where no obfuscation is allowed, price equals marginal cost, so that the predictions of competitive markets hold. However, in the presence of obfuscation, sellers do use add-ons and buyers do not search enough. Competition between sellers reduces the headline price, but on account of the add-ons, price is greater than marginal cost, hence, giving rise to a reduction in consumer surplus and an increase in producer profits.

A Mixture of Attentive and Inattentive Consumers

Suppose that a fraction μ of the consumers is fully inattentive and the remaining fraction $1-\mu$ is fully attentive; and that firms know these fractions. If the objective of firms is to maximize expected profits, then the optimal price chosen by them, the analogue of (11.45), is

$$p^* = \widehat{q}_i + \mu\overline{a} = t + c. \tag{11.49}$$

Thus, the analogue of (11.46) is

$$\widehat{q}_i = t + c - \mu\overline{a}. \tag{11.50}$$

Notice that the fully attentive case, $\mu = 0$, corresponds to $\widehat{q}_i = t + c = q_i^*$ (as in (11.42)) and the case of fully inattentive consumers, $\mu = 1$, corresponds to $\widehat{q}_i = t + c - \overline{a} = \widetilde{q}_i$ (as in (11.46)).

Fully attentive consumers can directly observe the add-ons and react to them by protecting themselves from being exploited by the high prices of these add-ons. For instance, if hotels levy high charges for room telephone calls or room service charges, attentive consumers might bring along a mobile phone, use a public telephone booth, or limit their use of room service (Gabaix and Laibson, 2006). In other contexts, they might avoid bank accounts that have high overdraft charges, and avoid buying printers that are incompatible with cheaper printer cartridge brands. However, inattentive consumers cannot protect themselves from the high costs of add-ons.

Suppose that fully attentive consumers buy no add-ons and pay the price given in (11.50), but fully inattentive consumes use the add-ons and pay a higher price. The difference in the price paid by the two types of consumers equals $\mu\bar{a}$ which depends on the proportion μ of inattentive consumers. The higher is the proportion of inattentive consumers, the higher is the *cross subsidy from inattentive to attentive consumers* (Gabaix and Laibson, 2006). For instance, opening and maintaining a bank account may be free of cost to all consumers, including attentive consumers, but the bank recoups the costs through high overdraft charges on inattentive consumers. This practice may be regressive with respect to income because poorer consumers are more likely to pay overdraft charges (Armstrong and Vickers, 2012).

Would inattentive consumers benefit if they hired an expert, or used a third party, to give them advice on their purchase decisions? An example is the use of price comparison websites. However, the decisions of firms are endogenous. They are likely to respond by quoting low headline prices on the price comparison website, but use high surcharges (Ellison and Ellison, 2009; Armstrong and Zhou, 2011). On the other hand, if firms collude with intermediaries, say, by offering higher commissions, in return for overstating the quality of their products, they may increase prices, reducing consumer surplus (Murooka, 2015).

Heidhues and Köszegi (2018) offer a critical assessment of some unexpected effects of *soft paternalism* that we consider in Chapter 12. Suppose that society values the utilities of the inattentive and the fully attentive consumers. Consider any libertarian paternalistic policy, such as a nudge to inattentive consumers, for example, financial literacy or clearer labeling/description of products, that reduces the fraction, μ, of inattentive consumers. From (11.50), this reduces the cross subsidy received by fully attentive consumers who are worse off, while some of the inattentive consumers are better off. Thus, on net, we cannot say if policies that help inattentive consumers are overall welfare-improving. Or, consider a policy intervention that reduces the likelihood that inattentive consumers will pay late fees associated with credit card payments. Credit card companies might respond to lowered profits by imposing or increasing annual fees on all consumers. On balance, it is difficult to say if there has been a welfare gain.

Dhami and Sunstein (2022) offer several countervailing arguments. First, if interpersonal comparisons of utility are allowed, then the gainers might gain more in terms of welfare than the losers lose, allowing for compensatory changes in utility. Second, some evidence suggests that nudges can help inattentive consumers without harming the fully attentive consumers (see Agarwal et al., 2015; Sarin, 2019). However, we need more evidence on these countervailing factors before we can be sure.

Does regulatory intervention necessarily lead firms to choose new and more devious methods to increase profits? Dhami and Sunstein (2002) highlight the following possibilities from US regulatory policy:

(1) The Department of Transportation requires airlines to include taxes and other fees in posted prices.
(2) The Federal Trade Commission forbids hotels and resorts from adding "hotel fees" at checkout time.

(3) The Consumer Financial Products Bureau forbids online companies from automatically enrolling people into certain programs (such as costly insurance packages).
(4) The Department of Labor mandates fee and performance disclosures for investment options in certain plans.
(5) The Department of Energy requires various appliances, such as refrigerators and microwave ovens, to be sold with energy efficiency disclosures.

Whether firms choose to obfuscate more in the cases (1) through (5), and whether the net welfare gains are positive, is an empirical question irrespective of whether we consider soft paternalism or hard paternalism. As Dhami and Sunstein (2022) write: "There is evidence, for example, that something like (4) has helped investors (Kronlund et al., 2020), that something like (3) has helped consumers (Sarin, 2019), and also that something like (1) has helped travelers (Bradley and Feldman, 2020). One analysis suggests that something like (2) would help consumers (Sullivan, 2017). None of this demonstrates that the concern is baseless. But how companies will respond to soft paternalism, and whether the response will eliminate a potential welfare gain, is an empirical question, and cannot be answered in the abstract."

On balance, behavioral industrial organization has identified several new and interesting channels through which the pricing strategies of firms can be analyzed. However, empirical evidence has lagged behind the theory. The models are typically very simplified versions of reality and it is not always clear how closely they are able to explain actual empirical phenomena. Some of the game theoretic machinery typically used in these models has not found adequate empirical support (see Part IV). However, economic theory must continue to bear on the important issues in industrial organzation, as must the greater awareness of behavioral factors.

11.4 Salience

Suppose that a decision maker chooses among n objects in a choice set $C = \{x_1, x_2, \ldots, x_n\}$. An object may be a good, or a service, or some intangible thing such as an experience (e.g., a special tour-guided holiday). Each of the objects in C may have several attributes. Suppose that any object x_i, $i = 1, \ldots, n$, has $k = 1, \ldots, K$ attributes. The attributes of object x_i, which we take to be real valued numbers in our discussion, may be listed in the vector a_i as

$$a_i = (a_{i1}, a_{i2}, \ldots, a_{iK}), \tag{11.51}$$

where a_{ik} is the kth attribute of object x_i.

In neoclassical economics, multi-attribute problems are typically dealt with as follows. The decision maker has a well-defined utility function over objects that takes account of the utility from the individual attributes. The decision maker then carefully deliberates, taking account of all the attributes in all the objects, and chooses the option that maximizes the utility function.

In actual practice, decision makers are likely to have limited attention, and pay selective and uneven attention to the potentially large number of attributes on offer. In making their optimal choices, they might be attracted to a particular object because it rates very high on the "salience" of its attributes.

Consider the System 1/System 2 distinction, highlighted in Kahneman (2011). System 1 is the automatic, involuntary, brain mechanism that is guided by short-term goals, while System 2 is the deliberate, voluntary, brain mechanism that is guided by long-term goals. For instance, System 1 may be instinctively attracted by a tempting choice, while System 2 is likely to induce us to consider the longer-term consequences of our actions.

Bordalo et al. (2021) associate System 1 with a *bottom up* selection mechanism and System 2 with a *top down* selection mechanism. They argue that salience is conditioned by a bottom up selection mechanism and they highlight the following three main determinants of salience. In psychology, research on these determinants has largely been conduced for visual and auditory stimuli.

1. *High contrast with surroundings*: An object is more salient if a particular attribute stands out with respect to the environment. For instance, a black swan is salient in a group of white swans; an albino lion stands out from a pride of lions; and white handwriting stands out against a black background (as in the "dark mode" on the Mac).
2. *Unusual or surprising nature*: Attributes whose values are significantly different from the values experienced in the past, or are counter to social and cultural norms, may surprise us and attract bottom up, involuntary, attention (Kahneman and Miller, 1986).
3. *Prominence*: In psychology, attributes that immediately attract visual attention are more prominent. For instance, in supermarkets, the objects placed at eye level are often particularly prominent. Unlike surprise, that arises from a comparison of stimuli with experienced values, prominence does not directly depend on the stimuli.

One reason to be interested in the phenomenon of "salience" is that bottom up attention to attributes may shift our attention from other goals that require top down attention. For instance, the presence of a tempting sweet counter could induce us to compromise on the goal of losing weight. Thus, consumers might not always choose objects that are in their best longer term interests, or the objects they might have chosen had they been given a chance to reflect longer on their choices. This is one of the central themes in behavioral welfare economics (see Chapter 12). Our bottom up attention might also be exploited, or strategically manipulated, by third parties such as advertising agencies and politicians, as in our discussion on phishing in Section 11.3.1. Bordalo et al. (2021, pp. 2–3) provide the following example:

> One example is the use of Twitter by former U.S. President Donald Trump. As Lewandowsky et al. (2020) show, in response to bad news in the Mueller investigation of Russia's interference in the Presidential election, Trump would immediately send provocative tweets on an unrelated topic, such as China, jobs, or immigration. These "red herring" tweets would successfully capture the attention of even centrist and left-leaning news outlets, such as ABC News and the New York Times, distracting them from Muller's findings.

The origins of bottom up attention are probably evolutionary. It is likely to have evolved as a survival response, for example, the "fight or flee" response. However, as noted in Section 8.4, evolution is a slow and conservative process, and traits that have been acquired through evolution are unlikely to be shed easily even when the environment has changed to make those traits redundant. Human free will, in the form of strategies to strengthen System 2, or the top down mechanisms, provide one possible method of protection from the potentially harmful effects of certain traits. Kahneman (2011) makes practical suggestions along these lines, as well as pointing out the difficulty in doing so.

The solution to a problem might depend not just on the given data (e.g., prices, income, taxes), but also on its presentation and framing that might change the salience of attributes. For instance, alternative methods of framing the same problem may lead to different choices, and this is what we observe. The explanation under prospect theory (see Part I) lies in the association between the reference point and alternative methods of framing. However, the explanation in salience models is slightly different, as we see below.

In order to formally model problems of this sort, one needs to define salience, and the conditions under which an attribute might be more salient as compared to another attribute. In a series of papers, Bordalo, Gennaioli, and Shleifer (2012, 2013, 2020) provide one possible formalization. In this section we consider their work.

Example 11.3 *Bordalo et al. (2013) Suppose that a consumer must decide between n possible wines. Each type of wine has two possible attributes, quality, q, and price, p, so $K = 2$. The choice set in terms of the attributes of the n wines can now be written as*

$$C = \{(q_1, p_1), (q_2, p_2), \ldots, (q_n, p_n)\},$$

where (q_i, p_i) give the quality and price attributes of the ith wine. We can also define the average quality, $\overline{q}$, and the average price, $\overline{p}$, respectively, across all the objects in C as follows.

$$\overline{q} = \frac{1}{n}\sum_{i=1}^{n} q_i;\ \overline{p} = \frac{1}{n}\sum_{i=1}^{n} p_i.$$

One potential method of judging the salience of the "quality" of the ith wine is to compare its actual quality q_i with the average quality, $\overline{q}$. Similarly, one could try to judge the salience of the "price" of the ith wine by comparing its actual price p_i with the average price, $\overline{p}$. We pursue this insight below.

We can summarize the attributes of all n objects in the following attribute matrix.

$$A = \begin{bmatrix} a_{11} & a_{12} & . & . & . & a_{1K} \\ a_{21} & a_{22} & . & . & . & a_{2K} \\ . & & . & . & & . \\ . & & . & & . & . \\ . & & . & & . & . \\ a_{n1} & a_{n2} & . & . & . & a_{nK} \end{bmatrix}. \tag{11.52}$$

Each row of the matrix corresponds to the attributes of a particular object in the choice set C while each column fixes an attribute whose value can be read off for each of the n objects.

Suppose that the utility of a *rational thinker* (rational in a neoclassical sense) for object i is given by

$$V_i = \sum_{k=1}^{K} w_{ik} a_{ik};\ i = 1, \ldots, n, \tag{11.53}$$

where w_{ik} is the weight assigned to attribute k of object x_i.

By contrast, a *salient thinker* distorts the weights, w_{ik}, depending on the salience of the attributes of the objects. The utility of a salient thinker is given by

$$V_i = \sum_{k=1}^{K} \widetilde{w}_{ik} a_{ik};\ i = 1, \ldots, n, \tag{11.54}$$

where $\widetilde{w}_{ik}$ is the "salience distorted weight" assigned to attribute k of object x_i. The weights w_{ik} and $\widetilde{w}_{ik}$ are influenced by top down and bottom up factors.

Example 11.4 *Consider the problem of choosing between n wines in Example 11.3 when there are only two attributes. The first attribute, k* $= 1$*, is quality and we assume that the weight on it is* $w_{i1} = 1$ *for every wine. The second attribute, k* $= 2$*, is price and we assume that the weight on it is* $w_{i2} = 1$ *for every wine. Thus, the rational consumer derives the following utility from any wine i:*

$$V_i = q_i - p_i;\ i = 1, \ldots, n. \tag{11.55}$$

In contrast to a rational thinker, a salient thinker assigns salience to the two attributes, quality and price. Suppose, for the moment that, for whatever reason, in comparing two different wines from the list, wine i and wine j, a salient thinker has determined that the quality of wine i is relatively more salient and its price is relatively less salient. Then the salient thinker might assign the following utility to wine i:

$$V_i = 0.7q_i - 0.3p_i.$$

In other words, the salience adjusted weight on quality is 0.7 *while the salience adjusted weight on price is* 0.3*. By contrast, in (11.55), the rational thinker assigns an equal,* $50-50$*, weight to both attributes. We consider below how precisely such salience adjusted weights might be constructed.*

We now formalize the insight in Example 11.3 on comparing attributes to their average values in determining salience. For each of the K attributes shown in the matrix A, in (11.52), we can compute the average value of the attribute by finding the sum in each column and dividing by n. For instance, the average for attribute k is defined as

$$\overline{a}_k = \frac{1}{n} \sum_{i=1}^{n} a_{ik};\ k = 1, \ldots, K. \tag{11.56}$$

For each of the n objects, we now define a salience function for each attribute of the object, $\sigma(a_{ik}, \overline{a}_k)$, that depends on the value of the attribute for that object, and its average value across the choice set C.

Definition 11.1 *The salience function for attribute k of object i is given by a real valued function* $\sigma(a_{ik}, \overline{a}_k)$ *that is non-negative,* $\sigma \geq 0$*, and satisfies the following conditions.*

(i) Ordering: Suppose that for object i, there are two different values of the kth *attribute,* a_{ik} *and* a'_{ik}*. Also consider two different corresponding average values of the attributes* $\overline{a}_k$ *and* $\overline{a}'_k$*. Then, ordering implies that*

$$\sigma(a_{ik}, \overline{a}_k) < \sigma(a'_{ik}, \overline{a}'_k) \text{ if } [min\{a_{ik}, \overline{a}_k\}, max\{a_{ik}, \overline{a}_k\}] \subset [min\{a'_{ik}, \overline{a}'_k\}, max\{a'_{ik}, \overline{a}'_k\}].$$

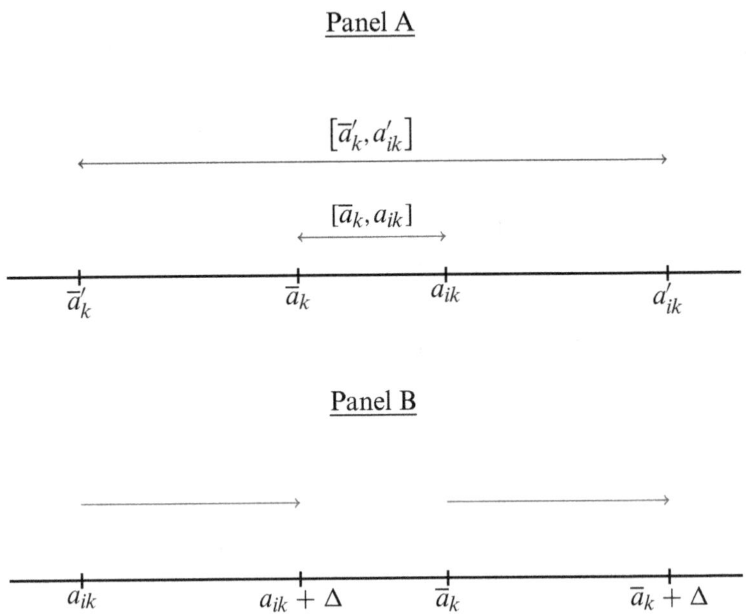

Figure 11.10 Properties of the salience function: Ordering (Panel A) and diminishing sensitivity (Panel B)

(ii) Diminishing sensitivity:

$$\sigma(a_{ik} + \Delta, \overline{a}_k + \Delta) < \sigma(a_{ik}, \overline{a}_k);\ \Delta > 0.$$

In Definition 11.1 we have used the notation σ for the salience function instead of lowercase alphabets, such as f or g to reflect the standard use of this notation in the salience literature. Ordering (Definition 11.1(i)) implies that an attribute that is at a greater distance from the average value is relatively more salient; recall that the notation $\subset$ means a "subset of." This is illustrated in the upper panel in Figure 11.10 for the case

$$\overline{a}'_k < \overline{a}_k < a_{ik} < a'_{ik}.$$

Thus, we effectively have the subset relation

$$[\overline{a}_k, a_{ik}] \subset [\overline{a}'_k, a'_{ik}],$$

as required in the definition of ordering and this is what we have used in Figure 11.10. Definition 11.1 allows us to compare two different values of the same attribute in terms of salience. By contrast, diminishing sensitivity fixes the object and the attribute and considers changes in the attribute value.

Example 11.5 *Suppose that we have only two objects, x_1 and x_2, in the choice set and there is a single attribute ($k = 1$) which is price. Suppose that last year the respective prices of x_1 and x_2 were 800 and 400 but this year they are both priced at 800. The price of x_1 has not changed, but salience theory predicts that the price of x_1 was more "salient" last year as compared to this year. This arises because the average price, across both objects, last year was 600, but it is 800 this year.*

Hence, $\sigma(800,800) < \sigma(800,600)$ *because, using Definition 11.1(i),* $[800,800] \subset [600,800]$*. It follows that the price of* x_1 *was more salient last year.*

Diminishing sensitivity (Definition 11.1(ii)) is the analogue of the assumption of diminishing marginal utility in economics. A given change in stimulus has a greater marginal effect when the stimulus is at a low level as compared to a higher level; see the lower panel in Figure 11.10. In psychology, this idea has been used in the context of sensory perception and is known as the *Weber–Fechner law of sensory perception*. For instance, in pitch darkness, a candle illuminates, but when it is bright sunlight, a candle makes an imperceptible effect.

An example of a salience function that satisfies Definition 11.1 is the following.

$$\sigma(a_{ik}, \overline{a}_k) = \frac{|a_{ik} - \overline{a}_k|}{|a_{ik} + \overline{a}_k|}. \tag{11.57}$$

The numerator of (11.57) captures the ordering property in Definition 11.1. If the attribute is at a greater distance from the average attribute value, then it is more salient. The denominator captures the diminishing salience property in Definition 11.1.

Once the salience function is defined, various possible formalizations of (11.54) are possible. The simplest case used in Bordalo et al. (2020) arises by setting $\widetilde{w}_{ik} = \sigma(a_{ik}, \overline{a}_k)$ to get

$$V_i = \sum_{k=1}^{K} \sigma(a_{ik}, \overline{a}_k) a_{ik};\ i = 1, \ldots, n. \tag{11.58}$$

In (11.58), the salience distorted weight $\widetilde{w}_{ik}$ of attribute k is increasing in the salience of the attribute k. An alternative formulation used in Bordalo et al. (2012, 2013) is to rank the K attributes for good i in order of salience, $r = 1, 2, \ldots, K$. Let the ranking of attribute k be denoted by r_k. We can now define the term $\widetilde{w}_{ik}$ in (11.54) as

$$\widetilde{w}_{ik} = \frac{\delta^{r_k - 1}}{\sum_{k=1}^{K} \delta^{r_k - 1} w_{ik}};\ \delta \in (0, 1],$$

where w_{ik} is the weight in (11.53). In this case, the salience distorted weight $\widetilde{w}_{ik}$ is increasing in the salience rank of attribute k.

We now describe how Bordalo et al. (2020) propose to introduce the element of "surprise" and "prominence." The usefulness of this exercise is to show how behavioral economics is trying to formalize models of salience while endogenizing the memory recall and attention allocation processes.

1. Modeling surprise: The attributes for good i, $a_i = (a_{i1}, a_{i2}, \ldots, a_{iK})$, serve as "cues" that lead to a recollection of past "normal values" of these attributes for good i, given by $a_i^n = (a_{i1}^n, a_{i2}^n, \ldots, a_{iK}^n)$. One can similarly form recollections of past normal values of attributes for all goods $i = 1, 2, \ldots, n$. We can now form a new matrix A_n of past remembered normal values of all the attributes for all goods,

$$A_n = \begin{bmatrix} a_{11}^n & a_{12}^n & . & . & . & a_{1K}^n \\ a_{21}^n & a_{22}^n & . & . & . & a_{2K}^n \\ . & . & . & & & . \\ . & . & . & & & . \\ . & . & . & & & . \\ a_{n1}^n & a_{n2}^n & . & . & . & a_{nK}^n \end{bmatrix}.$$

Averaging across the columns of the matrix A_n, gives us the respective average values

$$(\overline{a}_1^n, \overline{a}_2^n, \ldots, \overline{a}_K^n).$$

In determining how the past normal values are retrieved, the authors formalize the memory recall process of individuals using three features from psychological research – *frequency*, *similarity*, and *interference*. When faced with an attribute a_{ik}, individuals tend to recall experiences that are "frequent" and "similar" to it. As they do so, it "interferes" with the recall of less frequent and less similar experiences. Once the vector $(\overline{a}_1^n, \overline{a}_2^n, \ldots, \overline{a}_K^n)$ is constructed, salience can now be defined as $\sigma(a_{ik}, \overline{a}_k^n)$ and it satisfies the conditions in Definition 11.1 after we replace $\overline{a}_k$ by $\overline{a}_k^n$.

2. Modeling prominence: Suppose that, for good i, a decision maker is "visibly" (or saliently) presented with a subset of $m < k$ attributes from the set of possible attributes a_i in (11.51). We order the attributes so that the first m are the visible attributes $a_i^V = (a_{i1}, a_{i2}, \ldots, a_{im})$. The remaining attributes are the "invisible" attributes $a_i^I = (a_{im+1}, a_{im+2}, \ldots, a_{iK})$. Attributes may be visible because, say, they have been highlighted in an advertising campaign by a firm. For cars, these attributes could be fuel efficiency, compliance with the most stringent safety standards, and extended warranty. The visible attributes lead the individual to recall past normal values, as in the matrix A_n. However, there is some probability $p > 0$ that the decision maker might also recall past normal values of the invisible attributes. The utility of the individual is given by a variant of (11.58):

$$V_i = \sum_{k=1}^{m} \sigma(a_{ik}, \overline{a}_k^n) a_{ik} + p \sum_{k=m+1}^{K} \sigma(a_{ik}, \overline{a}_k^n) a_{ik};\ i = 1, \ldots, n.$$

We now consider an application of this framework. In Part I of the book we discussed the Allais paradox as a common ratio violation to show that the linear probabilities used in expected utility theory are not tenable. A second form of the Allais paradox is known as the *common consequence violation* (Allais, 1953). A leading application of salience theory is that it is able to capture this violation. It is worth outlining the common consequence violation first because it is used as an application in several literatures. We use the notation for lotteries introduced in Part I.

Definition 11.2 *(Common consequence violation) Suppose that A, B, C, D are lotteries and $\lambda \in (0, 1)$. These lotteries are used to form the following four compound lotteries, L_1, L_2 and L_3, L_4.*

$$L_1 = (A, \lambda; D, 1 - \lambda)\,;\ L_2 = (B, \lambda; D, 1 - \lambda)\,. \tag{11.59}$$

$$L_3 = (A, \lambda; C, 1 - \lambda)\,;\ L_4 = (B, \lambda; C, 1 - \lambda)\,. \tag{11.60}$$

These are compound lotteries because they are lotteries of lotteries. For instance, the lottery L_1 is read as: Lottery A is played with probability λ and lottery D is played with probability $1-\lambda$. Suppose that the decision maker is asked to choose lotteries in the following pairwise comparisons:

(i) Choose between L_1 and L_2 (where the common consequence is lottery D with probability $1-\lambda$).
(ii) Choose between L_3 and L_4 (where the common consequence is lottery C with probability $1-\lambda$).

The "common consequence violation" occurs if a decision maker prefers L_1 over L_2 and L_4 over L_3 (or L_2 over L_1 and L_3 over L_4).

Under expected utility theory, the common consequence violation should never occur. The reason is that the independence axiom allows us to cancel the common consequence in each pair of choices (D in the first and C in the second; each with a probability $1-\lambda$). Thus, if A is preferred to B, then L_1 must be preferred over L_2 and L_3 over L_4. If, B is preferred to A, then L_2 must be preferred over L_1 and L_4 over L_3.

Example 11.6 *(Allais paradox as a common consequence violation) Consider the following demonstration of the common consequence effect in Kahneman and Tversky (1979). All outcomes are expressed in units of Israeli pounds.*

Problem 1: (72 subjects) Choose between

$$L_1 = (0,0;2400,1) \text{ and } L_2 = (0,0.01;2400,0.66;2500,0.33). \tag{11.61}$$

Problem 2: (72 subjects) Choose between

$$L_3 = (0,0.66;2400,0.34) \text{ and } L_4 = (0,0.67;2500,0.33). \tag{11.62}$$

We can recast these choices as a common consequence violation using the same notation as in Definition 11.2. Let $\lambda = 0.34$ and define the following lotteries:

$$A = (2400,1); B = \left(0,\frac{1}{34};2500,\frac{33}{34}\right);$$
$$C = (0,1); D = (2400,1).$$

Then we can write the lotteries L_1, L_2, L_3, L_4 as follows.

$$L_1 = (A,0.34;D,0.66) = (0,0;2400,1;2500,0). \tag{11.63}$$

$$L_2 = (B,0.34;D,0.66) = (0,0.01;2400,0.66;2500,0.33). \tag{11.64}$$

$$L_3 = (A,0.34;C,0.66) = (0,0.66;2400,0.34;2500,0). \tag{11.65}$$

$$L_4 = (B,0.34;C,0.66) = (0,0.67;2400,0;2500,0.33). \tag{11.66}$$

The structure of lotteries in (11.63)–(11.66) is now exactly as in (11.59), (11.60) in Definition 11.2. The empirical evidence showed that 82% of the subjects chose L_1 in Problem 1 and 83% of *the subjects chose L_4 in Problem 11.2. This is a common consequence violation, which also rejects expected utility theory.*

The explanation for the choices described in Example 11.6 in terms of our discussion of prospect theory in Part I of the book is as follows. In the choice between lotteries L_1 and L_2, given in (11.61), most decision makers prefer L_1 due to the "certainty" of receiving 2400. The reason is that the "probability weighting function" is very steep near the end points of the probability interval (see Part I). In the choice between lotteries L_3 and L_4, given in (11.62), most decision makers prefer L_4 because the "probability weighting function" is relatively flat in the middle ranges, so that a probability of 0.33 and 0.34 are coded as relatively similar, thus, the decision maker chooses the relatively higher prize 2500 in lottery L_4.

In attribute based models, when considering situations of risk, it is typical to distinguish between the outcome attribute and the probability attribute. However, in applying salience theory to the lottery choices in (11.63)–(11.66), Bordalo et al. (2012) take a different approach. They distinguish between three states of the world that arise with different probabilities. For instance, suppose that we split the outcome 2400 with probability 1 in lottery L_1 into three outcomes: 2400 with probabilities 0.33, 0.66, and 0.01. Then, the comparison between lotteries L_1 and L_2 can be written as.

$$L_1 = (2400, 0.01; 2400, 0.66; 2400, 0.33). \tag{11.67}$$

$$L_2 = (0, 0.01; 2400, 0.66; 2500, 0.33). \tag{11.68}$$

We can now imagine the three states as follows.

1. State 1 arises with probability 0.01 and the respective outcomes in lotteries L_1 and L_2 are 2400 and 0.
2. State 2 arises with probability 0.66 and the respective outcomes in lotteries L_1 and L_2 are 2400 and 2400.
3. State 3 arises with probability 0.33 and the respective outcomes in lotteries L_1 and L_2 are 2400 and 2500.

In any state $s = 1, 2, 3$, let the minimum outcome be x_s^{min} and the maximum outcome be x_s^{max}. Then, the decision maker evaluates the salience of pairs of outcomes

$$x_s = (x_s^{min}, x_s^{max})$$

in each state. For the three states $s = 1, 2, 3$, when we are interested in comparing the salience of the states in lottery L_2, these pairs are:

$$(0, 2400), (2400, 2400), (2400, 2500). \tag{11.69}$$

Definition 11.1 was couched in terms of restrictions on pairs of the form $(a_{ik}, \overline{a}_k)$. For decisions under risk, Bordalo et al. (2012) provide an analogue of Definition 11.1 that is couched in terms of pairs (x_s^{min}, x_s^{max}).

We would now like to determine the salience of each state for each lottery. Suppose that the two lotteries are L_i and L_j. Then, in any state s, we are interested in pairs of outcomes (x_s^i, x_s^{-i})

where x_s^i is the outcome in state s in lottery L_i and x_s^{-i} is the outcome in state s in the other lottery, in this case lottery L_j.

Example 11.7 *Consider the lotteries L_1 and L_2 in (11.67), (11.68). Suppose that we are interested in the salience of state $s = 1,2,3$ for lottery L_1. For any state, s, denote the outcome that belongs to lottery L_1 by x_s^1 and the outcome that belongs to lottery L_2 by x_s^2 so that in any state, s, we have a pair of outcomes (x_s^1, x_s^2). For instance, in state $s = 1$, we have $x_1^1 = 2400$, $x_1^2 = 0$, $x_1^{min} = 0$, $x_1^{max} = 2400$. In state $s = 2$, we have $x_2^1 = 2400$, $x_2^2 = 2400$, $x_2^{min} = 2400$, $x_2^{max} = 2400$. In state $s = 3$, we have $x_3^1 = 2400$, $x_3^2 = 2500$, $x_3^{min} = 2400$, $x_3^{max} = 2500$. These pairs of outcomes will be reversed if we are interested in the salience of states $s = 1,2,3$ in lottery L_2. Then we would consider pairs of outcomes (x_s^2, x_s^1).*

Definition 11.3 *(Bordalo et al. 2012) The salience of state $s = 1,2,3$ for lottery L_i, $i = 1,2$ is a continuous and bounded function $\sigma(x_s^i, x_s^{-i})$ that satisfies the following two conditions.*[8]

(i) Ordering: Consider two different states s and s′. Then, ordering implies that

$$\sigma(x_s^i, x_s^{-i}) < \sigma(x_{s'}^i, x_{s'}^{-i}) \text{ if } [x_s^{min}, x_s^{max}] \subset [x_{s'}^{min}, x_{s'}^{max}].$$

(ii) Diminishing sensitivity: Suppose that all outcomes are positive. Then diminishing sensitivity implies

$$\sigma(x_s^i + \Delta, x_s^{-i} + \Delta) < \sigma(x_s^i, x_s^{-i});\ \Delta > 0.$$

A comparison of Definitions 11.1 and 11.3 shows that they are identical except that the latter uses pairs of the form (x_s^i, x_s^{-i}) while the former uses pairs of the form $(a_{ik}, \overline{a}_k)$. Notice that if the ordering property implies that state s' is more salient than state s for lottery L_i, it also implies that this states is more salient for lottery L_j. Hence, in this case, we may speak of the salience of a state without reference to the lottery.

Bordalo et al. (2012) propose the following salience function for this case which satisfies the conditions in Definition 11.3.

$$\sigma(x_s^i, x_s^{-i}) = \frac{\left|x_s^i - x_s^{-i}\right|}{\left|x_s^i\right| + \left|x_s^{-i}\right| + \theta};\theta > 0. \tag{11.70}$$

Let us now examine the salience of the three pairs of states in (11.69). Using Definition 11.3(i), since $[2400, 2400] \subset [2400, 2500]$, ordering implies that

$$\sigma(2400, 2400) < \sigma(2500, 2400). \tag{11.71}$$

We now wish to compare $\sigma(2500, 2400)$ with $\sigma(0, 2400)$. Directly using the salience function in (11.70) we get

$$\sigma(0, 2400) = \frac{2400}{2400 + \theta};\ \sigma(2500, 2400) = \frac{100}{2400 + 2500 + \theta}.$$

[8] The authors also give a third property, which they call "reflection." For any two states s and s', and all outcomes that are strictly positive, reflection implies that $\sigma(x_s^i, x_s^{-i}) < \sigma(x_{s'}^i, x_{s'}^{-i}) \Leftrightarrow \sigma(-x_s^i, -x_s^{-i}) < \sigma(-x_{s'}^i, -x_{s'}^{-i})$.

Since $\sigma(2500, 2400)$ has a smaller numerator and a larger denominator, it follows that

$$\sigma(2500, 2400) < \sigma(0, 2400). \tag{11.72}$$

From (11.71), (11.72), we can rank the salience of all three states as follows:

$$\sigma(2400, 2400) < \sigma(2500, 2400) < \sigma(0, 2400). \tag{11.73}$$

It follows that in a comparison of the lotteries L_1 and L_2, the most salient state for the risky lottery L_2 is state $s = 1$ in which the outcome 0 is received with probability 0.01. Hence, decision makers are more likely to choose lottery L_1 over L_2; they make a relatively risk averse choice in this case.

In comparing lotteries L_3 and L_4 in (11.62), we can rewrite them as follows.

$$L_3 = (2400, 0.32; 0, 0.01; 2400, 0.02; 0, 0.65) \tag{11.74}$$

$$L_4 = (2500, 0.32; 2500, 0.01; 0, 0.02; 0, 0.65)\,. \tag{11.75}$$

As before, we identify the four states which arise with respective probabilities 0.32, 0.01, 0.02, 0.65. The four pairs of outcomes in these states are

$$(2500, 2400), (2500, 0)(0, 2400), (0, 0).$$

In this case, the most salient state is (2500,0). This is easily checked by using the salience function in (11.70):

$$\sigma(2500, 0) = \frac{2500}{2500 + \theta}; \sigma(0, 2400) = \frac{2400}{2400 + \theta}; \ \sigma(2500, 2400) = \frac{100}{2500 + 2400 + \theta}.$$

We have, since $\theta > 0$,

$$\sigma(2500, 0) > \sigma(0, 2400) > \sigma(2500, 2400),$$

But in the most salient state $(2500, 0)$, lottery L_4 is at an advantage because the decision maker receives an outcome 2500 from choosing L_4 and an outcome of 0 from choosing L_3. Hence, the decision maker is likely to pick L_4 over L_3. Thus, the choice of lottery L_1 over L_2 and L_4 over L_3 is consistent with salience theory, so the Allais paradox with common consequences does not arise.

How should we evaluate the claims of salience theory relative to those of prospect theory? Salience is clearly of prime importance in any area of human choice and this line of reasoning needs to be encouraged. Yet, we should await more evidence before we accept the existing claims of salience theory. For instance, do decision makers really partition the lotteries into states in the manner that is assumed by salience theory? Why do they not think of the lottery L_4 in (11.75) as the perfectly reasonable form $(0, 0.67; 2500, 0.33)$? But when partitioned in this manner salience is not able to explain the Allais paradox. There is a large attribute-based literature in psychology and behavioral economics that argues that people think of attributes in lotteries as outcomes and probabilities, rather than the state space introduced in the above explanation of the Allais paradox. Why is that attribute-based framework less compelling? The domain over which the salience function is defined changes with different versions of the theory. Comparing Definitions 11.1 and 11.3, one version uses pairs of the form (x_s^i, x_s^{-i}) while the other uses pairs of the form

$(a_{ik}, \overline{a}_k)$. Which version should we use in a particular case? Unless the theory can specify this rigorously, the theory would appear to need further critical developments.

By contrast, the prospect theory explanations are based on specific components such as non-linear probability weighting, loss aversion, concavity of utility function in gains and convexity in losses (see Part I of the book). The explanations based on these components have been rigorously tested for a long time and the predictions are, by and large, consistent with them.

In sum salience theory, in its current form, while a promising development, cannot, as it stands, replace prospect theory as the dominant theory under risk, uncertainty, and ambiguity. For instance, we know very little about how salience might explain the Ellsberg paradox, or the many applications based on loss aversion and changes in reference points (see Part I of the book), while prospect theory is able to explain these phenomena successfully.

11.5 Modelling Limited Attention

We have already considered the evidence for limited attention in Part V. In this section, we outline simple theoretical models that can be used to formally model limited attention.

Consider a simple optimization problem in which a decision maker maximizes a utility function u that depends on a vector of K attributes of a good,

$$a = (a_1, \ldots, a_K),$$

and the action taken by the individual is denoted by x. For instance, consider an individual who is thinking of buying a car. The decision is either to buy the car, $x = 1$, or not buy the car, $x = 0$, so $x \in \{0, 1\}$. The attributes of the car might include the following: fuel economy (a_1); insurance cost (a_2); price (a_3); seating capacity (a_4), and so on. We could have introduced an index $i = 1, 2, \ldots, n$ for the n possible cars that the decision maker is considering, so that the attribute vector could have been defined as in (11.51), but we suppress that notation.

Assume that the decision maker's choice is a continuous one (e.g., choosing the quantity of a good or service to buy) and X represents the set of choices. For instance X could be an interval of the form $[0, \overline{X}]$ and $x \in X$. A decision maker in neoclassical economics will then take account of all the attributes on offer and choose $x \in X$ in order to maximize the utility function (we assume that the budget constraint is substituted and subsumed within the utility function)

$$u^n(x, a). \tag{11.76}$$

If the utility function is twice continuously differentiable, and strictly concave in x, then we can find the unique optimal action of the decision maker by solving the first order condition

$$\frac{\partial u^n(x, a)}{\partial x} = 0. \tag{11.77}$$

Denote by x^n the optimal, or rational, action of a neoclassical decision maker, obtained by solving (11.77),

$$x^n = x^n(a).$$

The optimal action depends on the entire vector of attributes a. Consider our car purchase example. In principle, a car will have hundreds of possible attributes that a potential buyer can obtain access to from the manufacturer. Yet, in buying a car, most people consider only a handful of attributes that they deem most important. The most likely explanation is that it is cognitively too costly to consider all possible attributes and the purchase of the car probably competes with other decisions that the decision maker might simultaneously be making. If attention is a scarce resource, then the rational solution $x^n(a)$ may provide misleading answers. For instance, suppose that a_j is an attribute that most buyers ignore. Then, public policy, or sellers' strategies, that attempt to influence the private decision x via changes in the attribute a_j are not likely to be very effective. These sorts of considerations make a case to formally model limited attention.

In contrast to a neoclassical decision maker, suppose that a "behavioral decision maker," who exhibits limited attention, pays attention to only a subset of the attributes in the attribute vector a. We assume that a behavioral decision maker chooses $x \in X$ in order to maximize the following attention-augmented utility function

$$u^b(x, a, \theta), \tag{11.78}$$

where the "attention vector" $\theta = (\theta_1, \theta_2, \ldots, \theta_K)$ captures limited attention. The kth element of the attention vector, $\theta_k \in [0, 1]$, captures the attention paid to the kth attribute. For any attribute $a_k \in a$ we assume that the subjectively perceived value of the attribute to the decision maker is denoted by a_k^s, such that

$$a_k^s = \theta_k a_k + (1 - \theta_k)\overline{a}_k; \theta_k \in [0, 1], k = 1, \ldots, K, \tag{11.79}$$

where $\overline{a}_k$ is the "default value" of the attribute. The theory does not specify what the default value is, but offers suggestions, such as previously experienced mean values of the attribute, or some cognitively simple interpretation of the attribute. For instance, if the attribute is price, then a price of \$9.99 may be coded as \$9.00; see, for instance, our discussion of "left digit bias" in used car prices in Part V. Thus, in (11.79), the subjectively perceived value of the attribute is a linear combination of the correct value of the attribute, a_k, and the default value of the attribute, $\overline{a}_k$. If $\theta_k = 0$ for some k, then the decision maker pays no attention to that attribute. At the other extreme, if $\theta_k = 1$, then the decision maker pays full attention to the attribute, ignoring the default value. For intermediate values $0 < \theta_k < 1$, the decision maker uses a combination of the attribute value and its default value.

Using (11.79), we can write a special case of (11.78)

$$u^b(x, a_1^s, a_2^s, \ldots, a_K^s), \tag{11.80}$$

where a_k^s, $k = 1, \ldots, K$ is defined in (11.79).[9]

Let us denote the value of x that maximizes the utility function (11.80) by

$$x^b = x^b(a, \theta),$$

which depends not only on the vector of attributes, a, but also the attention vector θ.

[9] Several papers in the inattention literature use the formalization in (11.80), such as Gabaix and Laibson (2006), Chetty et al. (2009), Gabaix (2014).

Let us compute the optimal choices, x^n and x^b, by using utility functions that are quadratic in the difference between actions and attributes. Consider first a neoclassical decision maker. A particularly simple utility function is

$$u^n(x,a) = \frac{-1}{2}\left(x - \sum_{k=1}^{K} w_k a_k\right)^2 ; w_k \geq 0, \tag{11.81}$$

where w_k is the weight assigned to attribute a_k in the utility function. The individual derives disutility from departures of the action x from a weighted average of the attributes. We would like to find the maximum value of the function. Since the utility function is negative throughout, it is maximized when the size of the loss is minimized.

Differentiating (11.81) with respect to x and using the simple chain rule of differentiation, we get

$$\frac{\partial u^n(x,a)}{\partial x} = \sum_{k=1}^{K} w_k a_k - x. \tag{11.82}$$

The second order condition, $\frac{\partial^2 u^n(x,a)}{\partial x^2} = -1 < 0$, is satisfied. Hence, we can solve out for the unique solution by setting the RHS of (11.82) equal to zero, which gives

$$x^n(a) = \sum_{k=1}^{K} w_k a_k.$$

Thus, the optimal neoclassical choice is a weighted average of the attributes. If there are several goods to choose from, this would imply choosing the good that has the highest weighted average of the attributes.

Similarly, using (11.79), (11.80), the utility function for a behavioral decision maker is given by

$$u^b(x,a,\theta) = \frac{-1}{2}\left(x - \sum_{k=1}^{K} w_k \left[\theta_k a_k + (1-\theta_k)\bar{a}_k\right]\right)^2 ; w_k \geq 0, \theta_k \in [0,1]. \tag{11.83}$$

The only difference between (11.81) and (11.83) is that in the behavioral decision maker's utility function we have replaced a_k by its subjectively perceived value a_k^s given in (11.79). We now minimize the utility function in (11.83) by choosing an optimal value x^b. Proceeding as in the case of the neoclassical decision maker, we get the unique optimal value

$$x^b(a,\theta) = \sum_{k=1}^{K} w_k \left[\theta_k a_k + (1-\theta_k)\bar{a}_k\right]. \tag{11.84}$$

Gabaix (2019) shows that several distinct behavioral phenomena can be interpreted in terms of a model of limited attention. These are hypotheses that need to be empirically tested against the alternative explanations for the same phenomena. We give a few examples below.

Example 11.8 *Consider the model of industrial organization in Section 11.3 where consumers may be inattentive to charges that are added-on to the price. For instance, a bank account that is free to open but has high overdraft charges that consumers ignore at the time of opening the account.*

Suppose that we imagine price to be an attribute associated with a bank account. Then, using (11.79), the subjectively perceived price, p^s, of the bank account is a combination of the actual price of the account, p, and a default price, $\overline{p}$,

$$p^s = \theta p + (1-\theta)\overline{p};\ \theta \in [0,1]. \tag{11.85}$$

An alternative formulation for add-ons is $p^s = p + \theta p^A$, where p is the visible price and p^A is the price of the add-on that is potentially diminished by a factor θ because not enough attention is paid to it.

Suppose, in a properly specified model, we could compute the demand of the neoclassical consumer $x^n(p)$. The corresponding demand for a behavioral consumer is $x^b(p^s)$, or

$$x^b(\theta p + (1-\theta)\overline{p}).$$

We might be interested in computing the elasticity of demand with respect to the price for the behavioral consumer, which requires us to compute the derivative[10]

$$\frac{dx^b}{dp} = \frac{dx^b}{dp^s}\frac{dp^s}{dp} = \theta \frac{dx^b}{dp^s}. \tag{11.86}$$

Thus, limited attention dampens the responsiveness of demand to prices. The greater is inattention, that is, the smaller is θ, the greater is this dampening effect.

Example 11.9 *Consider a model of limited attention in which a taxpayer perceives the after-tax price, q, of a good to be*

$$q = p + \theta\tau; \theta \in [0,1], \tag{11.87}$$

where p is the before-tax price and τ is a specific sales tax. A neoclassical taxpayer who does not suffer from limited attention has $\theta = 1$, that is, correctly perceives the after-tax price to be the sum of a pretax price and the tax rate, that is, $q = p+\tau$. On the other hand, an inattentive consumer who does not fully pay attention to the sales tax acts "as if" $0 < \theta < 1$. We develop the consequences of such limited attention in Section 12.10 in the next chapter. For a comprehensive application of these ideas see Farhi and Gabaix (2020).

Example 11.10 *Consider the model of projection bias due to Loewenstein et al. (2003) that we have considered in Section 10.7. At time t, the individual is asked to forecast the value of an attribute at time t+j, a_{t+j}, when the current value of the attribute is a_t. The statistically correct expectation formed at time t is $E\left[a_{t+j} \mid I_t\right]$. A behavioral decision maker subject to projection bias uses the subjective estimate*

$$a^s_{t+j} = \theta E\left[a_{t+j} \mid I_t\right] + (1-\theta)a_t.$$

More inattentive decision makers have lower θ, hence, the current value of the attribute a_t plays a disproportionately larger role in forming subjective expectations of the future.

[10] In computing this derivative we have used the chain rule and, using (11.85), the fact that $\frac{dp^s}{dp} = \theta$.

Measuring inattention is difficult. Using (11.86), we can write

$$\theta = \frac{\frac{dx^b}{dp}}{\frac{dx^b}{dp^s}}. \tag{11.88}$$

If we could measure the RHS of (11.88), then we can measure the attention parameter θ. The numerator can be observed from the data; it is the observed change in x when price changes. However, the denominator, change in x when price changes for a fully attentive consumer, is never observed. At the moment there is no completely satisfactory way of measuring it, although several proxies have been used. See Gabaix (2019) for a discussion which reports a mean value of $\theta = 0.44$ based on the existing studies. This value is likely to be highly dependent on the context/framing/type of the problem and it also likely to be heterogeneous across decision makers.

11.6 Complexity Economics

11.6.1 An Introduction to Complexity Economics

In nature, examples abound where the individual entities, for example, animals, cells, and neurons, engage in simple "rule of thumb behavior" in a *low rationality framework*. Yet, the *outcomes are complex* and appear as if they are guided by a *highly intelligent controller*. While none of the individual entities is consciously working towards producing the observed complex aggregate outcomes, the *aggregate outcomes exceed the sum of the individual parts*.

Examples include behavior in ant colonies where millions of ants using simple rules of thumb produce complex behaviors such as an ant bridge over a swollen creek; billions of individual neurons fire in the brain to produce complex thoughts, such as the theory of relativity; billions of individual white blood cells in an immune system follow simple rules of thumb to produce remarkable aggregate behaviors in controlling dangerous infections; billions of individual cells form an eye and although they may be performing simple and distinct functions, together they are instrumental in producing human vision; and billions of individual brain cells give rise to something as complex as human consciousness.

Millions of individual birds in a flock of starlings follow simple rules of thumb, for example, maintain a fixed flying distance from the immediate neighbors and follow the flight movements of a few immediate neighbors. Neverthess, the aggregate visual patterns observed by an outsider are complex and fascinating. These "starling murmurations" (readers who have not seen these before should see a video) appear to an observer as if they are controlled by an intelligent piece of software, or a central planner.

Yet, in all these cases, the individual entities possess relatively low intelligence, and there is actually no central planner/controller who controls and coordinates their behavior. Such complex aggregate patterns of behavior are known as *emergent behaviors* or *emergent properties of the system*. Such systems, because they appear so precisely organized to an observer, are also sometimes termed as *self-organizing systems*.[11]

[11] The interested reader can consult several surveys of complexity and agent-based models. Some of those surveys are suitable for economists, see Epstein and Axtell (1996), Tesfatsion (2002), Beinhocker (2006), Kirman (2010),

It is difficult to give a definition of complex systems that would be widely accepted. Hence, it is more natural to simply list some of the central features of complex systems. Mitchell (2009, p. 13) proposes the following definition of complex systems: "a system in which large networks with no central control and simple rules of operation give rise to complex collective behavior, sophisticated information processing, and adaptation by learning or evolution." She also gives an alternative definition on the same page: "a system that exhibits nontrivial emergent and self-organizing behaviors."

Complexity economics is the application of ideas from the literature on complexity to economics. It appears that the term complexity economics was first coined by Arthur (1999). Complexity economics deals with an economic environment and framework that is very different from that in neoclassical economics.

In neoclassical economics, *rational decision makers* interact in situations of *risk and uncertainty* to produce outcomes. Outcomes in neoclassical economics are almost always analyzed in an *equilibrium framework*. If the outcomes are "market outcomes" then economists are often interested in a *general competitive equilibrium*. In a competitive general equilibrium, all markets are competitive and all individuals are price takers. The objective is to find a set of equilibrium prices such that:

(i) all individuals maximize their utility,
(ii) all firms maximize their profits, and
(iii) demand equals supply in all markets.

Once an equilibrium is attained, no further arbitrage of goods and services is required because it raises neither the utility of the individuals, nor the profits of the firms.

In particular, in such models, the agents in the economy are *passive unless exogenous stochastic shocks occur*. If we relax the assumption of perfect equilibrium and consider oligopolistic models of firms that are not price takers (as in Section 11.3 above), the analysis remains an equilibrium analysis, although the equilibrium is defined in a game theoretic sense (for instance, a Nash equilibrium). Neoclassical game theoretic models too are essentially equilibrium models. Agents in such models use *deductive reasoning*, that is, they use facts, axioms, and premises to make judgments. For instance, under risk and uncertainty if decision makers conform to the axioms of rationality, then they follow expected utility theory in making decisions (see Part I).

The aim of complexity economics is to relax some of the central features of neoclassical economics discussed above. In relaxing the assumption of rational decision makers, it endeavors to follow insights from behavioral economics. But in modeling the system-wide dynamics of an economy, it develops its own unique framework. It is mainly interested in situations of *true uncertainty,* that is, where decision makers cannot imagine all the possible consequences of their actions (unknown unknowns). For instance, individual starlings cannot imagine all the possible outcomes that arise from their flying behavior. Starling murmurations are *spontaneous*, and they are emergent phenomena that are greater than the sum of their individual parts.

Hommes (2013), Haldane (2016). For a simple and engaging introduction to complexity, see Mitchell (2009). A technically more demanding treatment can be found in Hommes and LeBaron (2018).

Complexity economics assumes that economic agents have *limited rationality* and use simple strategies, for example, simple rules of thumb, in making decisions. As unpredictable complex patterns arise in the economy, there is a *constant feedback* between these patterns and the simple rules of thumb used by individuals. For instance, an individual might use a simple rule of thumb for a few periods, leading to *hysterisis in choices*, and then discard it in favor of a new rule of thumb if it does not work well enough. Limited rationality implies that instead of deductive reasoning, individuals use *inductive reasoning*, that is, they look at the past data and decide on their current actions. In making this decision, they are guided by simple learning rules and simple feedback rules between aggregate outcomes and their own choices in the past.

The entire system never settles down to a state of equilibrium. Rather, the norm for such economic systems is that they are in a constant state of flux with *persistent randomness*. Persistent randomness does not arise from exogenous shocks (which is the case in neoclassical economics) but from *endogenous shocks*. The source of these endogenous shocks may be *true uncertainty*, or *technological uncertainty*. For instance, changes in technology create ripple effects and subsequent endogenous technological developments. These ripple effects may never die down, for example, those arising from the invention of the steam train, air travel, computer chips, telephones, and gene splicing. One could have a *statistical equilibrium*, such as in physics, when particles move in a Brownian motion. But at other times, even such a statistical equilibrium might not exist. There is no notion of a competitive general equilibrium in such a framework. The outcomes of the system are *emergent phenomena* that cannot be predicted by examining individual actions, just as we cannot predict the exact pattern of starling murmurations by looking at the behavior of individual birds.

Neoclassical economics often, although not always, uses the normal distribution in theoretical models. However, the normal distribution is not the default in complexity economics. It has been shown that *cascades* of events that lead to further events (or *propagation effects*) may reveal *power laws* in the data, hysterisis over time, and *heavy tailed probability distributions* (Farmer and Geanakoplos, 2004; Arthur, 2006). From Part V, we know the elicited subjective probability distributions of people tend to be too fat-tailed to accord well with the typical assumptions in theoretical models in economics.

Example 11.11 *Consider the accordion or concertina effect in traffic flows that illustrates several ideas in complexity economics. In the normal flow of traffic, some cars might unexpectedly slow down due to drivers losing concentration or getting distracted with a phone call. This is an "endogenous shock" to the system. This causes the cars that are to the rear of such cars to slow down, potentially creating a cascade or propagation effect that slows down traffic and potentially creates a traffic jam. None of the cars that slowed down, did so with the intention of creating a traffic jam. However, the traffic jam is an emergent property of the system. It occurs from endogenous, not exogenous, shocks. While an outsider observer may feel that the jam is created by a central planner, but there is no planner. The traffic jam cannot be predicted with any certainty. The system is in a perpetual state of randomness with traffic jams occurring spontaneously and unpredictably from time to time.*

Complexity economics is young. Open problems remain about how to determine various pieces of the jigsaw such as the simple rules of thumb for individuals; and the feedback rules between aggregate outcomes and rules of thumb. Behavioral economics can provide a powerful framework for guiding these choices. Unlike many models in neoclassical economics, the models in complexity economics typically lack an analytical solution. Complexity models can have a very large number of economic agents and behavioral equations, hence, recourse has to be made to computational methods of solution. Progress in computational models has given a significant boost to this literature. On the issue of analytical versus the computational/algorithmic method, Bookstaber and Kirman (2018, p. 770) write: "And this in turn means that rather than seeking a theoretical result, we are in the world of pragmatism, of engineering, of case studies. And, it means we must delve into the real world."

Economists who are used to theoretical models in economics that draw on analytical techniques in mathematics may find the literature on complexity economics to be lacking rigor. In this context Arthur (2015, p. 21) explains the position of complexity economists very well:

> Consider a parallel with biology. Even now, 150 years after Darwin's *Origin*, no one has succeeded in reducing to an equation-based system the process by which novel species are created, form ecologies, and bring into being whole eras dominated by characteristic species... Equations do well with changes in number or quantities within *given* categories, but poorly with the appearance of new categories themselves... Biology then is theoretical but not mathematical; it is process-based, not quantity-based. In a word, it is *procedural*. By this token, a detailed economic theory of formation and change would also be procedural.

This quote is reminiscent of the notion of *procedural rationality* in the work of Herbert Simon that we have considered in Part V.

The individual entities in complexity models need not be economic agents. In Axelrod (1980a,b) the individual entities are "strategies" to play the prisoner's dilemma game (see Figure 11.2) that we have studied in several chapters in this book. Axelrod invited people to submit suggestions for strategies in a repeated prisoner's dilemma game. In Axelrod (1980b), a horse race was run between 63 strategies. Among the strategies were the following: "always cooperate," "always defect," and "cooperate with a 50% probability every round." One of the strategies that did well was the *tit-for-tat strategy*. This strategy required a player to initially cooperate and then mimic the previous period strategy of the opponent, ignoring all previous history. It was the overall winner, and adopted by the largest proportion of the subjects. Other variants of this strategy included the *tit-for-two-tats* in which a player initially cooperates but then defects only when the opponent has defected twice in succession. The two-tits-for-tat, strategy initially cooperates but defects two times in succession if the opponent has defected once.

Why was the tit-for-tat strategy so successful? Axelrod (1980b, p. 54) explains as follows:

> What accounts for TIT FOR TAT's robust success is its combination of being nice, retaliatory, forgiving, and clear. Its niceness prevents it from getting into unnecessary trouble. Its retaliation discourages the

Table 11.2 The prisoner's dilemma game

	C	D
C	2, 2	0, 4
D	4, 0	1, 1

other side from persisting whenever defection is tried. Its forgiveness helps restore mutual cooperation. And its clarity makes it intelligible to the other player, thereby eliciting long-term cooperation.

For a critique of the tit-for-tat strategy, see Rapoport et al. (2015) who argue that the results are sensitive to the design of the tournament, success criteria for alternative strategies, and the payoffs chosen in the prisoner's dilemma game.

In another contribution, Lindgren (1991) considers a variant of an iterated prisoner's dilemma game in which players choose their strategies with noise. By this is meant that they are hardwired to play particular strategies (e.g., the tit-for-tat), but with some probability players mutate and choose other strategies. All players play against all other players. The most successful strategies have a greater chance of being passed on to the subsequent rounds of play. The reader will notice that this structure is similar to our study of evolutionary dynamics in Section 8.4 of the book. A simulated tournament is played in which the strategies are pitted against each other and new mutations are allowed to arise freely. Initially, tit-for-tat is quite successful. But it is taken over by more complicated strategies that take advantage of the simple structure of tit-for-tat. As in our discussion of evolutionary dynamics, one observes strategies that are evolutionary stable, and as in our discussion on stochastic social dynamics, we observe punctuated equilibria (see Section 8.5). Over time, more complicated strategies with longer memories of the choices made in the previous periods arise. This is shown in Figure 11.11.

If one restarts the simulation in Figure 11.11 for another 30,000 periods, then in every restart we get different patterns. In some cases, the strategies with long memories appear early while in other cases they appear late in the simulations; in some simulations an evolutionary stable strategy makes an appearance while in other cases no such strategy appears and the available strategies keep mutating and evolving indefinitely. Arthur (2021, p. 138) writes:

> But, in spite of these variations, the experiment shows consistent phenomena: the exploitation of strategies by other strategies, emergence of mutual support among strategies, sudden collapses of strategies and takeover by novel ones, periods of stasis followed by ones of turbulent change. The overall scene looks like species competition in palaeozoological times.

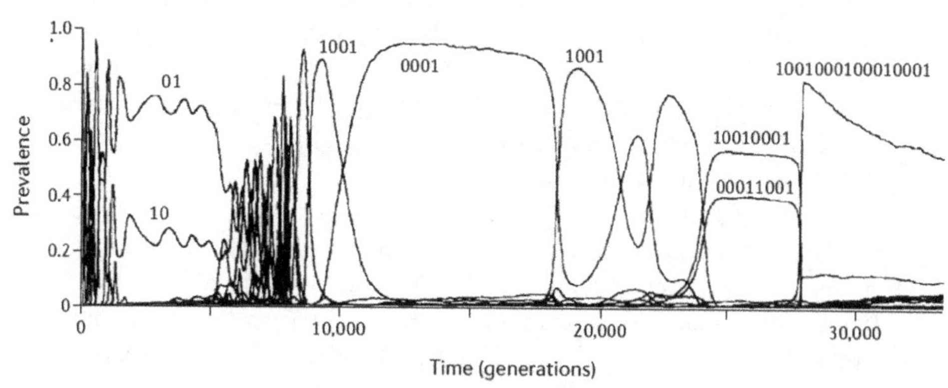

Figure 11.11 The time evolution of strategies over 30,000 generations. New strategies evolve to take advantage of existing strategies if they are able to improve the payoffs of players. The number of digits on the labels for the strategies indicate the number of previous moves in the game that each of the strategies takes into account. Source: Arthur (2021)

Figure 11.11 also illustrates what a solution looks like in complexity economics. Due to the feedback between individual actions and aggregate outcomes, the solution itself is ever-changing unless one reaches an evolutionary stable strategy. The solution at any point in time comprises several alternative competing strategies (or an *ecology of strategies*), some of which might suddenly go extinct only for their place to be taken up by new mutant strategies.

11.6.2 The El Farol Problem

El Farol is the name of a bar in Sante Fe.[12] Brian Arthur conceived of the relation between complexity economics and his observation of the behavior of customers in this bar; this has come to be known as the *El Farol problem* (Arthur, 1994).

The bar has a maximum capacity for 60 people. Suppose that the potential customer base is 100 people who must simultaneously decide in the evening whether to visit the bar or not. A trip to the bar is costly in terms of time and travel expenses, so each of the potential customers must make a guess about how many other people are likely to "simultaneously" make the decision to visit the bar. If the guess is 60 people or more, then it is not worth visiting the bar. However, none of the potential customers can predict with certainty the decision of others, nor is there any potential basis to make this prediction.

This problem is solved in neoclassical game theory in the following general way. Each player is typically required to have identical prior beliefs about the types of others. This is the assumption of common priors, but as noted in Part IV of the book it often lacks any empirical justification. In the Bayesian Nash equilibrium of a static game, players will use deductive reasoning and exactly 60 players will make the decision to visit; perhaps these players could be the ones that have the lowest costs of travel. But, empirically, one does observe disequilibrium outcomes. On any given day, one might see customers turning back from the El Farol bar because the bar already holds 60 people.

An alternative approach is to use inductive reasoning and simple rules of thumb to make the decision to visit the bar. This requires the use of past data on attendance rates to form inferences about how many others are likely to visit the bar on any given day. In making these decisions, individuals might often face disappointment and be turned back at the bar. If they are disappointed a large number of times, they might wish to change the rule of thumb that they are using. In due course, as people learn from the feedback of a trip to the bar (success or failure to enter), they might stumble upon other rules of thumb such that they are less disappointed. If we give people a long enough time to learn, the hope, in a model of complexity economics, would be that the distribution of rules of thumb across people (the "ecology of rules of thumb" as in Figure 11.11) is such that about 60 people turn up at the bar.

In the simulations that are reported in Arthur (1994), a set of predictors $P = \{p_1, p_2, \ldots p_m\}$ is used such that any predictor, p_i, takes the past attendance rates and converts it into a decision

[12] The Santa Fe Institute is at the cutting edge of research on complexity economics. Brian Arthur was asked to head a research program there in the late 1980's which led to several important developments in complexity economics, some of which we describe in this book.

to visit or not visit the bar. At time t, the past attendance rates for n time periods are given by the set $A = \{a_{t-1}, a_{t-2}, \ldots a_{t-n}\}$, where a_{t-j} is the number of people who visited the bar j time periods ago. Thus, any predictor is a mapping

$$p_i : A \to [0, 100],$$

that predicts the number of people who are likely to attend the bar at time t, conditional on the available data. If $p_i \geq 60$, a decision maker who is using predictor p_i decides not to go to the bar, and if $p_i < 60$, the decision maker goes to the bar. Some of the predictors used in the study were

$$p_1 = a_{t-1};\ p_2 = 100 - a_{t-1};\ p_3 = \frac{1}{4}\sum_{i=1}^{i=4} a_{t-i};\ p_4 = a_{t-2};\ p_5 = a_{t-5}.$$

For instance, the predictor p_1 just takes account of the attendance in the last period, while the predictor p_3 is the average attendance rate over the last four time periods. To complete the model, assumptions need to be made on the speed of learning, ex-post evaluation thresholds, and the specific learning/adaptation mechanisms. For instance, how quickly are predictors discarded if one is disappointed with the feedback from the current predictor, and how are new predictors chosen. Complexity theory does not yet provide us with concrete guidance on such choices and these features remain model-specific. However, the evidence from behavioral economics can be a useful resource for specifying these choices.

Figure 11.12 provides one such simulation with 100 artificial agents and 100 repetitions of the bar problem. It is also based on underlying model-specific assumptions of the type required in our discussion above. The purely inductive dynamic process results in mean attendance converging towards 60, which is an emergent property of the system. Each agent uses low-level rationality in the form of simple rules of thumb designed only to maximize the chances of gaining entry into the bar. Yet the actions of disorganized agents using low-level rationality guide the system towards an equilibrium outcome. By the end of the simulations, 60% of the predictors predict an attendance below 60 (these agents decide to visit the bar) and 40% of the predictors predict an attendance above 60 (these agents decide not to visit the bar).

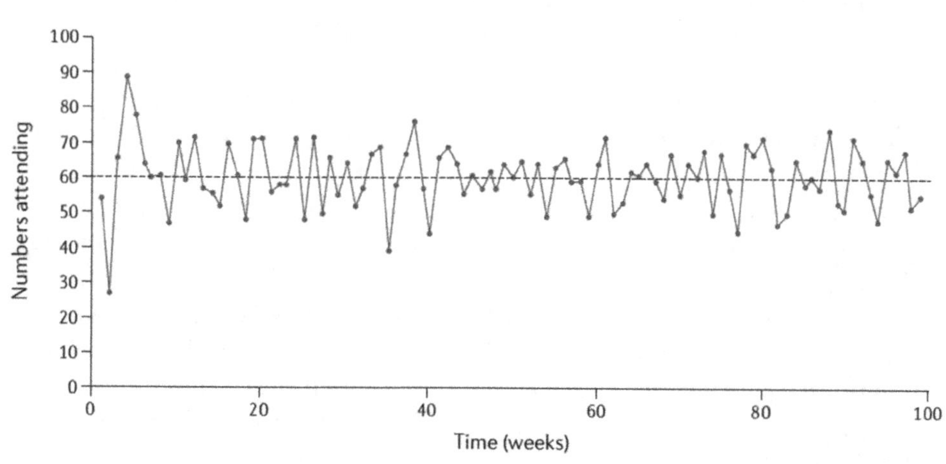

Figure 11.12 A particular simulation demonstrating the number of patrons attending the bar over 100 periods. Source: Arthur (2021)

To see how such an ecology of predictors arises, suppose that a time t, 10% of the predictors predict an attendance over 60 and 90% of the predictors predict an attendance below 60. Then 90 agents decide to go to the bar, but only 60 gain entry, so that 30 will be disappointed. These 30 disappointed agents may wish to switch to a new predictor. Suppose we assume a high enough speed of learning so that this switch to a new predictor is immediate. Then, those who successfully gained entry at time t will wish to continue using their existing predictors. Some of the new predictors used by the 30 disappointed agents will, at time $t+1$, predict that more than 60 agents will visit the bar. So, at time $t+1$, these agents will not visit the bar and they will not be disappointed. The remaining agents in the group of the set of 30 disappointed agents will have switched to a predictor that predicts less than 60 agents visiting the bar at time $t+1$. They will decide to go to the bar and continue to be disappointed and so switch predictors at time $t+2$. Such switching behavior continues until we get the required 60–40 ratio.

In this game, neoclassical game theoretic models can also make a similar 60–40 prediction when agents play a mixed strategy Nash equilibrium (Shubik, 2011). However, the empirical evidence raises serious concerns about the use of mixed strategies despite their popularity and continued use in economics; we discuss this at length in section 7.2. However, if the underlying problem is one of true uncertainty, then neoclassical game theoretic models cannot be used, but the inductive method described above remains highly suitable and effective.

11.6.3 Increasing Returns and Technological Choice

In this section, we examine a stylized problem of technology adoption under increasing returns following the model of Arthur (1989). Suppose that a large number of potential technology adopters (henceforth, agents) make the decision to adopt one of two new technologies, A or B. The choices are made sequentially across time, so only one agent makes a technology choice in each time period, followed by another in the next time period, and so on. Suppose that n agents have made the technology adoption decision (so the time itself also equals n). Denote by n_A the number of agents who have chosen A and n_B the number who have chosen B, so that

$$n_A + n_b = n.$$

We assume there are two types of agents, type 1 and type 2, that differ in their fixed and variable returns from the two technologies. Only the variable returns depend on the number of other previous adopters of the technologies; the fixed returns are independent of the number of previous adopters. The utilities of each type of agent from adopting each technology are shown in Table 11.3; for example, the utility of a type 1 agent from adopting technology A is $a_1 + rn_A$. Type 1 agents get a fixed return a_1 and b_1, respectively, from technologies A and B, while the variable return r per unit, for type 1 agents, is identical for both technologies. By contrast, type 2 agents get a fixed return a_2 and b_2, respectively, from technologies A and B, while the variable return, s per unit, for type 2 agents, is identical for both technologies.

The fixed return of technology A to type 1 agents is relatively higher, and the fixed return of technology B to Type 2 agents is relatively higher, that is,

$$0 < b_1 < a_1 \text{ and } 0 < a_2 < b_2. \tag{11.89}$$

Table 11.3 Types of agents and the fixed and variable returns from technology adoption, conditional on the number of other agents who have already adopted one of the two technologies, A and B.

Type/Technology	A	B
Type 1	$a_1 + rn_A$	$b_1 + rn_B$
Type 2	$a_2 + sn_A$	$b_2 + sn_B$

Thus, for instance, if 100 individuals adopt A and 100 adopt B ($n_A = n_B = 100$), then type 1 agents will prefer technology A ($a_1 + 100r > b_1 + 100r$, or $b_1 < a_1$ which is true from (11.89)). It can similarly be shown that type 2 adopters will prefer technology B.

The variable returns are positive

$$r > 0 \text{ and } s > 0.$$

Variable returns depend on the number of other agents who have already adopted a particular technology. For instance, if $r = 0.5$ and $n_A = 100$, then the variable return to a type 1 agent from adopting technology A is $0.5 \times 100 = 50$. If, however, $n_A = 500$, then the variable return goes up five times to 250. This is the sense in which there are "increasing returns" to technology adoption for both technologies.

Increasing returns typically arise when the adoption of a technology lowers its costs, or increases its benefits for subsequent adopters. For instance, prices of computers have dropped massively over time as the number of adopters has exponentially increased. The restriction $r > 0$ and $s > 0$ captures the case of increasing returns. In other cases, some industries that use difficult to obtain inputs may experience an increase in factor prices as demand increases. Such technologies exhibit decreasing returns, which are associated with the case $r < 0$ and $s < 0$. We do not consider this case but the interested reader can use the method described below to analyze this case.

At time $t = n$, n_A agents have adopted A and n_B have adopted B and $n = n_A + n_B$. Let us now consider the technology adoption decision of an agent whose turn it is to make a technology choice in the next time period, at time $n+1$. Let us consider the optimal decision for each of the two types:

1. A type 1 agent will choose B over A if the utility from B exceeds the utility from A, that is,

   $$a_1 + rn_A < b_1 + rn_B.$$

   Simplifying this inequality, we get

   $$n_A - n_B < \Delta_1 = \frac{b_1 - a_1}{r} < 0. \tag{11.90}$$

   If, however, $n_A - n_B > \Delta_1$, then the type 1 agent will choose technology A. If $n_A - n_B = \Delta_1$, then the type 1 agent is indifferent between A and B. In this case, we need a tie-breaking rule; we assume that B is chosen in this case. From (11.90), B is chosen if the fixed return from B,

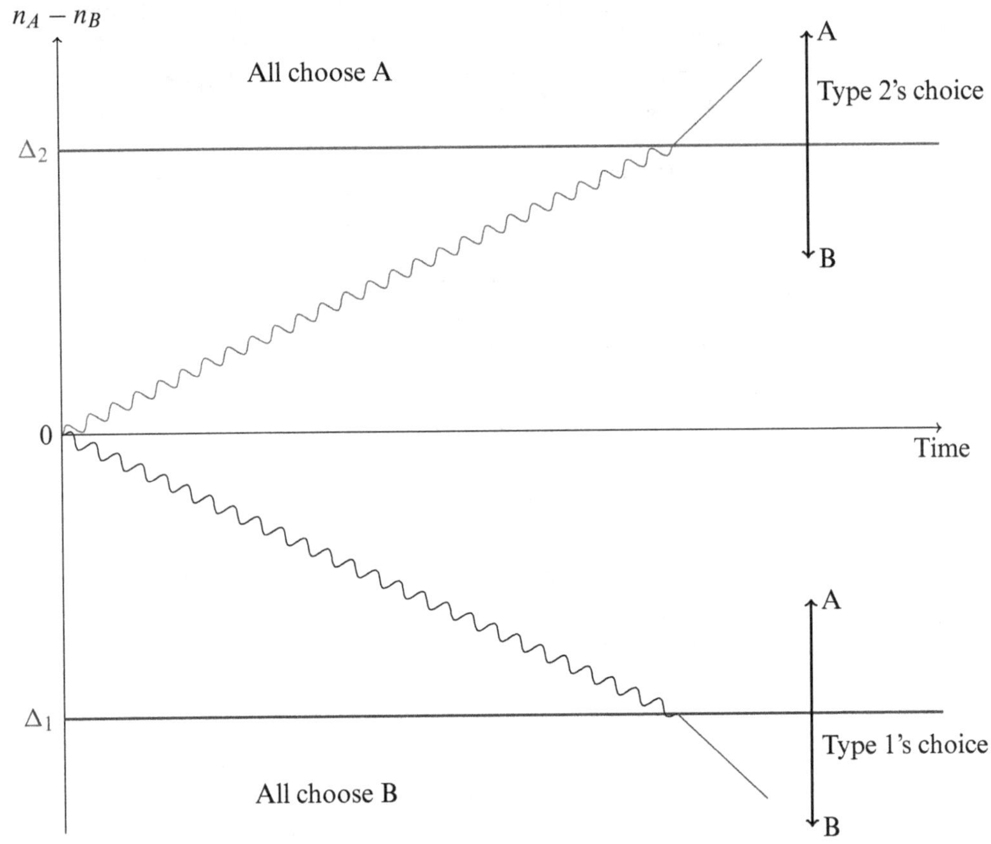

Figure 11.13 Increasing returns and technology adoption

b_1, is not too low; the variable return r is high; and the number of adopters of B in the past are high enough (so that $n_A - n_B$ is low enough).

2. A type 2 agent will choose A over B if

$$a_2 + sn_A > b_2 + sn_B.$$

Simplifying this inequality we get

$$n_A - n_B > \Delta_2 = \frac{b_2 - a_2}{s} > 0. \tag{11.91}$$

Otherwise, if $n_A - n_B < \Delta_2$, then the agent chooses technology B. If $n_A - n_B = \Delta_2$, then the agent is indifferent between A and B; we use the tie-breaking rule that A is chosen in this case. From (11.91), a type 2 agent is more likely to choose A if the number of previous adopters of A is high; and if the fixed return from A is not too low as compared to the fixed return of B.

Figure 11.13 plots the difference, $n_A - n_B$, between the number of agents adopting technology A and B against time, as successive agents make their technology choice. Ex-ante, the type of any agent is only privately known, hence, prior to the technology adoption decision by any agent, the subsequent choice is a random variable to an outside observer. The two "barriers" $\Delta_1 < 0$ given in (11.90) and $\Delta_2 > 0$ given in (11.91) are shown in Figure 11.13. The term $n_A - n_B$ is a random variable that goes up by one unit if an agent adopts A and down by one unit if an agent adopts B.

Consider first the lower barrier, $\Delta_1 < 0$. From (11.90), type 1 agents will choose A when they are above the barrier Δ_1 and B below the barrier. From (11.91), type 2 agents will choose A when they are above the barrier Δ_2 and choose B when they are below it. Both choices are shown by the up-down arrows in Figure 11.13 on the extreme right of the figure.

Given our tie-breaking rule, explained above, it follows that both types of agents choose technology A on or above the barrier Δ_2; and technology B on or below the barrier Δ_1. Hence, both barriers are known as *absorbing barriers* in the following sense. Once technology adoption hits one of the barriers, then all subsequent agents, irrespective of their type, will choose an identical technology (A at the barrier Δ_2 and B at the barrier Δ_1). Thus, in this case one of the two technologies completely dominates in all subsequent adoption.

Between the barriers Δ_2 and Δ_1, type 2 agents choose B and type 1 agents will choose A. The shape of the dynamic path depends entirely on chance, and it hinges on which type of agents get to move at what time. If fortuitously, many agents initially adopt one of the two technologies, then increasing returns will ensure that its adoption is subsequently favored. We show two hypothetical and purely illustrative time paths in Figure 11.13. The jagged upward sloping path hits the upper barrier Δ_2, leading everyone to adopt technology A. The dynamic system is now *locked-into* technology A. The jagged downward sloping path hits the lower barrier Δ_1, which leads everyone to be *locked-into* technology B.

Nobody can predict ex-ante which of the two technologies will eventually get adopted but there is an advantage of an early start. The less-favored technology is locked-out forever; and the outcome is purely accidental. Several examples illustrate this lock-in effect.

1. The choice between the QWERTY and the Dvorak keyboards (David, 1985).
2. Alternating current and direct current (David and Bunn, 1988).
3. Light-water nuclear reactors and gas-cooled nuclear reactors (Agnew, 1981).
4. Petrol-powered and steam-powered cars (Arthur, 2009).

Once the system is locked-into a technology for a long enough time, then public policy is unlikely to reverse the technology adoption decision. The reason is that increasing returns ensure that the large number of previous adoptions of a technology significantly reduce the cost of the technology, so in effect the variable returns are too high to make any other technology viable. Suppose, for instance, the government now wished everyone to adopt steam-powered cars by offering subsidies. This is unlikely to have a significant policy impact.

Ergodicity is an important property of dynamic systems. It implies that the eventual state of a dynamic system is history independent. However, this is not the case under increasing returns. It is not clear, ex-ante, in terms of Figure 11.13, which of the two paths, the downward sloping or the upward sloping, or any of the other infinitely possible shapes of these paths, will the dynamic system follow. The exact path followed depends on the particular history of adoptions. One of the technologies could, by chance, be adopted initially by a large number of agents, perhaps because they happened to be of the same type. Or it might initially seem that one of the technologies might win out, but then successive adoptions by one type of agent might tip the balance towards the other technology. Nothing can be predicted, so the outcome is history dependent and ergodicity fails. In particular, the unpredictability in the outcome is not caused by exogenous shocks, but by endogenous shocks relating to technology adoption. By contrast, in the macroeconomic literature, fluctuations are typically caused by exogenous shocks only.

11.6.4 Chaos and Sensitivity to Initial Conditions

An important feature of dynamic systems in complexity economics is that they can be very sensitive to initial conditions. For certain values of the parameters in the model, a minuscule change in the initial condition can lead to enormous changes in the time path of the dynamic system, leading to *chaos*. In the popular literature, one often encounters striking examples, such as the flapping of butterfly wings in one part of the world resulting in a tornado in another part of the world; or a single flap of a seagull's wings changing the global weather forever.

While these examples often draw gasps of amazement, they are probably empirically overstated although they cannot be ruled out on theoretical grounds. However, one can imagine other examples that leave one wondering if a small change in the initial conditions might have resulted in a completely different history of the world. What if the Academy of Fine Arts in Vienna had not rejected Adolf Hitler's application, twice? What if the assassination of Archduke Franz Ferdinand had not occurred? What if Alexander Fleming had not left an uncovered Petri dish near an open window which became contaminated with mold? What if a meteor had not struck the earth 65 million years ago? The list is endless. Another easy to remember example is reducing the temperature of water by a small amount at 0° Celsius, or raising it by a small amount above 100° Celsius. These small changes completely alter the liquid state to, respectively, a solid and a gaseous state.

We use a simple nonlinear first order difference equation to show how dynamic systems can have extreme dependence on initial conditions. In particular, we are interested in a deterministic first order difference equation known as the *logistic map* which was first used by Pierre Verhulst in 1845 as a model of population growth.

Suppose that time t is discrete, $t = 0, 1, 2, \ldots$, and we are interested in the population growth rate of some species of animal. At any time t the population is y_t and the initial population is y_0. Denote the birth rate in the population by $b \geq 0$, the death rate by $d \geq 0$, and their difference by

$$\lambda = b - d.$$

The maximum population that can be supported by the environment is given by $\overline{y}$. Then, the logistic map is given by

$$y_{t+1} = \lambda \frac{y_t}{\overline{y}} \left(\overline{y} - y_t \right); t = 0, 1, 2, \ldots . \tag{11.92}$$

In (11.92) we have a first order difference equation because the maximum time difference in the equation is one time period (due to the terms y_{t+1} and y_t). Suppose that we know the population at time y_t, then the difference equation gives us y_{t+1}, the population at time $t + 1$. Clearly, the higher is the positive difference between the birth and death rates (higher $\lambda > 0$), and the higher is the positive difference between the maximum carrying capacity of the environment and the

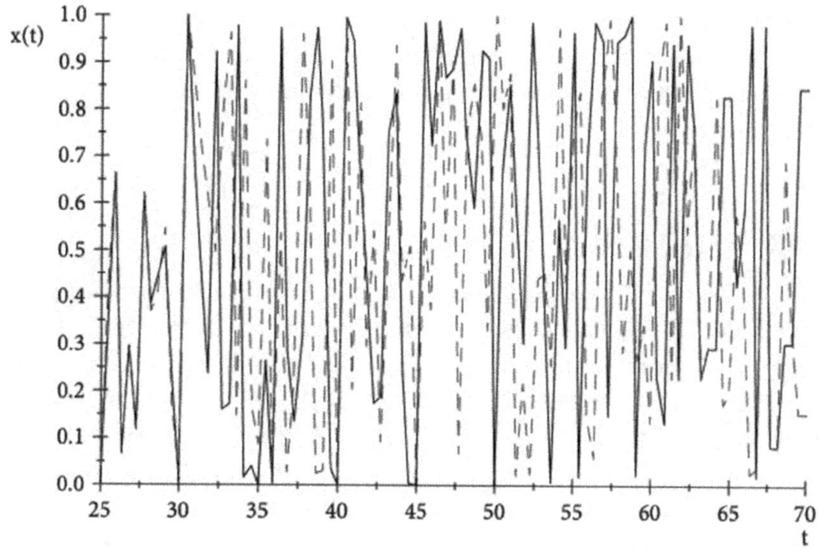

Figure 11.14 The logistic map and chaos for $\lambda = 4$. The time paths correspond to the initial values $x_0 = 0.5$ (solid curve) and $x_0 = 0.50000000001$ (dashed curve)

actual population (higher $\overline{y} - y_t > 0$), the higher will be y_{t+1}. A solution to the difference equation tells us the entire time path of the population, starting from a particular value of the initial population, y_0.

If we transform variables slightly so that $x_t = \frac{y_t}{\overline{y}} \in [0, 1]$ is the current population relative to the maximum carrying capacity of the environment, then (11.92) can be written as

$$x_{t+1} = f(x_t) = \lambda x_t (1 - x_t), \tag{11.93}$$

which is known as the *logistic map* and has the initial condition $x_0 = \frac{y_0}{\overline{y}}$.

As we vary the parameter λ, the logistic map exhibits interesting behavior. We are not interested in the solution to the logistic map, but in the extreme sensitivity of the logistic map to initial conditions (chaotic dynamics) that occurs when $\lambda \geq 3.56995$. In particular, consider the value $\lambda = 4$. In this case, we have an explicit solution given by

$$x_t = 0.5 \left(1 - cos\left(2^t cos^{-1}(1 - 2x_0)\right)\right),$$

which is plotted in Figure 11.14 for two different values of the initial condition, $x_0 = 0.05$ (solid curve) and $x_0 = 0.50000000001$ (dashed curve). The initial conditions are nearly identical and differ by 1 at the 11th decimal place. For the first 30 time periods, the two time paths are indistinguishable. However, thereafter the two paths trace out very different dynamics and it would be difficult to guess that they are both generated from the same underlying logistic map. This illustrates the extreme dependence on initial conditions that is a hallmark of complexity economics.

The logistic map is a low-dimensional, deterministic, difference equation. If it is able to produce such complicated dynamics, one wonders how much more complicated would be the dynamics arising in higher order difference equations embedded in a general model of the economy. The difference equation is nonlinear. Hence, introducing artificial linearities, as in the current practice of linearizing Euler equations in macroeconomics, rules out legitimately interesting dynamics.

11.6.5 Agent-Based models

The insights from complexity theory have been operationalized in economics through the use of agent-based models. In these models, it is typical to consider a very large number of heterogeneous agents ranging from a few hundreds to millions. Agents could be consumers, firms, banks, and other financial institutions. Each agent follows relatively simple rules of thumb, hence, this is low-rationality world. Within firms, for instance, the individual agents might be endowed with different rules. One can then simulate the effects of many diverse kinds of economic factors on the time path of eventual outcomes. For instance, we could ask what happens to the time paths of inflation, unemployment, financial solvency, profits of firms, and exports, when the government engages in macroprudential policy designed to regulate the financial sector. As one might imagine, typically no analytical solutions can be found.

Traditionally macroeconomic theory has been based on a representative agent model whereby a single entity represents all consumers and all firms; coupled with a very simple model of an economy. In recent years there has been some increase in the degree of heterogeneity introduced in macroeconomic models. However, the degree of heterogeneity allowed in agent-based models is unprecedented in economics. Several features of complexity economics arise naturally in agent-based models. These include fluctuations in the absence of exogenous shocks, and extreme dependence on initial conditions. Agent-based models also allow one to consider the effects of economic policy when such effects may be hard to examine with real life macroeconomic data. For instance: If required bank reserve ratios are mandated by policy to increase by 60%, then what is the effect on the stability of financial markets?

As a method, agent-based models are already well established in the physical sciences where they go by the name of Monte-Carlo simulations; in computer science they fall under the rubric of multi-agent systems. However, they also have their limitations when applied to economics. For more details on the drawbacks, as well as an explication of an agent-based model of the housing sector, see Dhami (2020, Vol. VI). Here we note only a few potential criticisms although some of these criticisms also apply to economic models in other frameworks too.

1. In agent-based models, the rules of thumb assigned to agents can sometimes appear to be no better than guesses and this literature is not yet as well informed by the modern developments in behavioral economics. Taking better account of behavioral insights can make these models more realistic.
2. There are too many degrees of freedom in specifying any agent-based model. This has to do with the specification of the types of economic agents, institutions, the behavioral rules of thumb followed by economic agents, and the outside data that is taken as given in the agent-based model. It is not too clear what the underlying model selection criterion is, although most agent-based models aim to reproduce economic time series in their simulations.

3. Agent-based models typically take as given the set of rules followed by economic agents. This practice is subject to the Lucas critique, namely, the behavioral rules of thumb that are used by the economic agents may not be invariant to changes in economic policy. In the real world, the behavioral rules of thumb are themselves endogenous and depend on the economic policy in operation.

The drawbacks of agent-based models should not distract us from their usefulness. Existing macroeconomic models cannot deal with the case of true uncertainty (unknown unknowns) which is arguably vital in explaining real world data. Agent-based models can accommodate true uncertainty and provide novel explanations for economic fluctuations. These models are still relatively young and only a relatively small proportion of the academic profession works on these models, as compared to the concentration of scholarship on neoclassical macroeconomic models. Hence, it is quite likely that with further developments, some of the existing drawbacks may be gradually addressed.

11.7 Learning Models

11.7.1 Reinforcement Learning

Reinforcement learning or *stimulus response learning* or *rote learning* is one of the oldest learning models in psychology (Bush and Mosteller, 1955; Luce, 1959; Suppes and Atkinson, 1960). This model has enjoyed a resurgence of interest in the modern artificial intelligence literature. It applies to a situation where "players" are not fully aware of the economic environment, the opponents, or indeed of the exact "game" that they are playing.[13] Players make a choice from their set of actions and then observe the payoffs arising from their action. The exact process through which their actions translate into payoffs is not known to them. Based on the empirically observed past relation between their own actions and payoffs, they make a choice of their current action. Hence, the informational and cognitive requirements in this model are minimal.

Reinforcement learning relies on the following three features.

1. *Law of effect*: If an action gives rise to a higher payoff (*stimulus*), then the *response* of the decision maker is to use that action with a higher probability in the future (Thorndike, 1911). For this reason, reinforcement learning is sometimes known as *stimulus–response learning*.
2. *Choice of actions is probabilistic*: Decision makers choose among their actions in a probabilistic manner. Actions that have led to higher payoffs in the past are more likely to be played in the present.
3. *Power law of practice*: The learning curves of decision makers are more steep initially, but then gradually flatten out. However, the evidence on this, unlike the first two features is not conclusive.

Reinforcement learning is potentially a useful tool in economic environments that are very complex and difficult to understand; for instance, in the case of true uncertainty. In simpler

[13] We use the terms "players" and "game" in the sense used in game theory (see Part IV).

games, reinforcement learning is less satisfactory and the predicted speed of learning is sluggish relative to the actual speed of learning observed in experiments.

The simplest model of reinforcement learning is the one-parameter model (Bush and Mosteller, 1955; Arthur, 1991, 1993). The model applies for any number of decision makers. However, for simplicity, let there be only two decision makers; 1 and 2. Suppose that player 1 can choose from the set A of m possible actions/strategies

$$A = \{a_1, a_2, \ldots, a_m\}, \tag{11.94}$$

and player 2 can choose from the set B of n possible actions/strategies

$$B = \{b_1, b_2, \ldots, b_n\}. \tag{11.95}$$

Let us consider things from the perspective of player 1 only; the situation for player 2 is analogous. The true underlying payoff of player 1, is generated by a function $\Pi_1(a, b; \theta)$, where a and b are the actions of the two players ($a \in A, b \in B$) and θ is a vector of some relevant aspects of the environment. However, player 1 does not observe the process by which the true underlying payoffs are generated, or the action chosen by player 2, or how environmental factors influence payoffs. All that player 1 observes is a payoff

$$\pi(a); a \in A,$$

that materializes when player 1 chooses $a \in A$.

Example 11.12 *Consider, for instance, the prisoner's dilemma game shown in Table 11.4. Suppose that the row player is player 1 and the column player is player 2. Neither of the players can observe the game shown in Table 11.4. Here $A = \{C, D\}$ and $B = \{C, D\}$. The true underlying payoffs of player 1 are determined by*

$$\Pi_1(C, C) = 2; \Pi_1(C, D) = 0; \Pi_1(D, C) = 4; \Pi_1(D, D) = 1. \tag{11.96}$$

Player 1 does not observe the true payoffs in (11.96). On playing C, player 1 sometimes observes $\pi_1(C) = 2$ (corresponding to the true underlying payoff $\Pi_1(C, C) = 2$) and at other times observes $\pi_1(C) = 0$ (corresponding to the true underlying payoff $\Pi_1(C, D) = 0$), depending on what player 2 has chosen.

Suppose that time $t = 0, 1, 2, \ldots$ is discrete. Players begin with initial *propensities* or *attractions* to play their pure strategies. For player 1, these are given by

$$q_0(a_1), q_0(a_2), \ldots, q_0(a_m).$$

One possibility is that the initial propensity to play any pure strategy is identical, that is, for any $a_i, a_j \in A$, $i \neq j$, we have $q_0(a_i) = q_0(a_j)$. But other possibilities can be easily incorporated. The

Table 11.4 The prisoner's dilemma game

	C	D
C	2, 2	0, 4
D	4, 0	1, 1

propensities at any time $t = 1, 2, \ldots$ are given by $q_t(a_1), q_t(a_2), \ldots, q_t(a_m)$ and we describe below how these are formed.

Let $\overline{\pi}_1$ be the minimum payoff of player 1. Then, the *reinforcement function*, R_1, for player 1 is defined as

$$R_1(\pi_1(a_i)) = \pi_1(a_i) - \overline{\pi}_1 \geq 0,\ a_i \in A. \tag{11.97}$$

Propensities are updated over time as the players gradually observe the empirical relation between their actions and payoffs. For player 1, the updating process for propensities is described as follows:

$$q_{t+1}(a_i) = \begin{cases} q_t(a_i) + R_1(\pi_i(a_i)) & \text{if } a_i \text{ is played at time } t \\ q_t(a_i) & \text{otherwise} \end{cases};\ a_i \in A,\ t = 1, 2, \ldots. \tag{11.98}$$

Since $R_1 \geq 0$ (from (11.97)), propensities are always positive. From the first row of (11.98), the propensity to play the strategy a_i is updated by the empirically observed payoff from playing a_i relative to the minimum payoff (see (11.97)). Otherwise, if a strategy is not played, then propensities are not updated (second row of (11.98)).

Finally, we convert propensities into probabilities of playing all pure strategies. Let $p_t(a_i)$ be the probability that player 1 chooses the pure strategy a_i at time t. Then

$$p_t(a_i) = \frac{q_t(a_i)}{Q_t},\ \text{where } Q_t = \sum\nolimits_{i=1}^{m} q_t(a_i),\ a_i \in A. \tag{11.99}$$

Q_t, known as the aggregate propensity, is the sum of propensities across all the strategies at time t. The probability with which strategy $a_i \in A$ is played at time t equals its propensity, $q_t(a_i)$, relative to the aggregate propensity Q_t.

The simple form for probabilities in (11.99) is sometimes not adequate to fit the data. Hence, in empirical work, the following one-parameter form is sometimes used, as in logit models.

$$p_t(a_i) = \frac{e^{\lambda q_t(a_i)}}{\sum_{i=1}^{m} e^{\lambda q_t(a_i)}};\ \lambda \geq 0. \tag{11.100}$$

The parameter λ captures the sensitivity of probabilities to reinforcements. To see this, we can write (11.100) for two different strategies $a_i, a_j \in A$ and then divide the two expressions to get

$$\frac{p_t(a_i)}{p_t(a_j)} = e^{\lambda[q_t(a_i) - q_t(a_j)]},\ a_i \neq a_j. \tag{11.101}$$

Thus, λ determines how strongly the difference in propensities $q_t(a_i) - q_t(a_j)$ translates into changes in the probabilities with which the two strategies a_i, a_j are played. At one extreme, as $\lambda \to 0$, all choices are made with equal probabilities. At the other extreme, as $\lambda \to \infty$, the strategy with the higher propensity is played with probability 1. For intermediate values of λ, the strategy with a higher propensity is chosen with a higher probability.

The reinforcement model has been extended in several directions that allow it to fit the empirical evidence better. These extensions enrich the feedback between players and their environment, and it also increases the speed of learning, which is an issue with the one-parameter reinforcement learning model. For a survey, the interested reader can refer to Dhami (2020, Vol. VI). Some of these directions are as follows.

Roth and Erev (1995) and Erev and Roth (1998) propose a *three-parameter reinforcement learning model*. They consider two psychological features.

1. *Experimentation*: Players identify strategies that are similar to each other. At any point in time they might experiment with choices that are similar to those that led to higher past rewards.
2. *Recency*: More recent experiences have a larger effect on the probabilities with which the current actions are played, relative to experiences in the more distant past.

Duffy and Feltovich (1999) allow players not only to learn from their own experiences, but also from the experiences of others. Hence, the updating of propensities also depends on the experiences of others. Bereby-Meyer and Erev (1998) and Huck et al. (2007) show that evidence is consistent with reinforcement models in which players update propensities relative to their aspiration levels rather than the minimum possible payoffs that can be achieved. The aspirations themselves can be updated in a manner that is suggested by models of aspiration adaptation (see Section 10.8).

11.7.2 Belief-Based Models of Learning

Under reinforcement learning, players are not required to know the true underlying economic environment. They play a *better response*, that is, they play a strategy whose propensity is higher with a higher probability, but they do not play a *best response* with probability 1, which is typically the case in neoclassical game theory.

Belief-based models of learning, by contrast to models of reinforcement learning, incorporate a greater degree of rationality, and players are aware of the game that they are playing. Such models formally describe how players form beliefs about others and their economic environment, and specify how these beliefs evolve over time. In belief-based models, players are not concerned with their own historically successful strategies. However, they are interested in the history of play of their opponents, which they use to predict their opponent's current choices; then they play a best response to these predictions with probability 1. However, the beliefs of players about others are not "rational" in the sense of neoclassical game theory and no mutual consistency of beliefs and actions is required.

Example 11.13 *As an example of a beliefs-based model, consider two Cournot oligopolistic firms, 1 and 2, who simultaneously choose their respective quantities, $a_t \in A$ and $b_t \in B$, at time t, in every time period $t = 1, 2, \ldots$ A and B are the respective strategy sets of the two players, in this case a set of possible quantities that can be produced. Each firm holds the beliefs that its opponent will choose the quantity that they chose in the previous time period. Given these simple beliefs, ex-post, in each period firms will find that their opponent did not choose the quantity that they expected, unless firms are already at the Cournot equilibrium. This leads us to ask some of the following questions. Will firms learn from their mistakes? More general belief-based models incorporate weighting of past actions of the opponent in order to form the relevant beliefs. In most models of learning, players are hardwired to play given behavioral rules. Different assumptions on the speed of revision of these rules in the light of new observations determine how fast, if at all, play converges in the model. Developing models that incorporate such "revision" in a more realistic manner will require us first* *to gather more empirical evidence on actual learning processes employed by real world economic actors.*

We illustrate belief-based models for the case of a two-player simultaneous move game. Time is discrete, $t = 0, 1, 2, \ldots$. The strategy sets of players 1 and 2, respectively, A and B, are given in (11.94) and (11.95). The payoffs (or utility functions) of the players are given, respectively, by π_1, π_2, and both players use expected utility to evaluate risky situations. The payoffs of both players depend on their own choice of a strategy and the strategy chosen by the opponent. Thus, the payoffs of both players (formally, $\pi_i : A \times B \to \mathbb{R}$, $i = 1, 2$) can be written as

$$\pi_1(a, b),\ \pi_2(a, b);\ a \in A,\ b \in B.$$

Below, we consider the analysis from the point of view of player 1. The analysis for player 2 is analogous.

At time t, player 1 assigns a weight $w_t^1(b_j) \geq 0, j = 1, \ldots, n$ to the pure strategy b_j of player 2. Hence, the vector of these weights on the n possible strategies of player 2 is given by

$$w_t^1 = \left(w_t^1(b_1), \ldots, w_t^1(b_n)\right).$$

The initial weights assigned by player 1 at time $t = 0$ are given by

$$w_0^1 = \left(w_0^1(b_1), \ldots, w_0^1(b_n)\right).$$

Starting from the initial weights, between any two successive time periods, t and $t+1$, the weights on each of the strategies of player 2 evolve in the following manner:

$$w_{t+1}^1(b_j) = \begin{cases} w_t^1(b_j) + 1 & \text{if } b_j \text{ is played at time } t \\ w_t^1(b_j) & \text{otherwise} \end{cases};\ b_j \in B. \tag{11.102}$$

From the first row of (11.102), if a strategy b_j is played by player 2 at time t, then its weight is increased by 1 unit at time $t + 1$, but the weight on all other pure strategies of player 2 is unchanged. The sum of weights at time t, across all strategies of player 2, is given by

$$\overline{w}_t^1 = \sum\nolimits_{j=1}^{n} w_t^1(b_j),\ t = 1, 2, \ldots \tag{11.103}$$

At any time t, the weights are converted into probabilities with which player 1 believes that player 2 will play each of the pure strategies in the set B, as follows. Denote by $p_t^1(b_j)$, the probability with which player 1 expects player 2 to play the pure strategy $b_j \in B$. Then,

$$p_t^1(b_j) = \frac{w_t^1(b_j)}{\overline{w}_t^1} \geq 0,\ t = 1, 2, \ldots. \tag{11.104}$$

To summarize, the vector listing the probabilities of play of player 2, as believed by player 1, is given by

$$p_t^1 = \left(p_t^1(b_1), \ldots, p_t^1(b_n)\right). \tag{11.105}$$

From (11.104), the reader can check that the probabilities are non-negative and that they sum up to 1. For any strategy $a_i \in A$, the expected utility of player 1 is (see Section 1.3)

$$EU_1(a_i, p_t^1) = \sum\nolimits_{j=1}^{n} p_t^1(b_j)\pi_1(a_i, b_j);\ a_i \in A. \tag{11.106}$$

Player 1 now chooses the strategy $a^* \in A$ that maximizes the expected utility of player 1, conditional on the beliefs of player 1 about the probabilistic play of player 2, as given in (11.105). Thus, the optimal strategy $a^* \in A$ chosen by player 1 at time t, satisfies the condition

$$EU_1(a^*, p_t^1) \geq EU_1(a_i, p_t^1);\ \text{for all } a_i \in A.$$

Thus, unlike neoclassical game theory, the choice of the optimal strategy in belief-based models does not take account of the strategic behavior of the opponent.

It can be shown that in special circumstances, reinforcement learning and belief-based models are consistent with fully rational behavior (Fudenberg and Levine, 1998). However, these special circumstances need not be empirically persuasive.

There is no clear winner when reinforcement learning is pitted against belief-based models in experiments. In games with mixed strategy equilibrium that have relatively low dimensional strategy spaces, reinforcement learning seems to do better (Mookerjee and Sopher, 1994; Erev and Roth, 1998). By contrast, in coordination games, belief-based models make relatively better predictions (Ho and Weigelt, 1996; Battalio et al., 2001). For more details on the empirical evidence, the reader can consult Camerer (2003) and Dhami (2020, Vol. VI).

Reinforcement learning and belief-based models appear to be two distinct models. However, Camerer and Ho (1999) showed that both these models are special cases of a more general model which they call *experience weighted attraction model of learning* (EWA). The EWA has a greater number of parameters than either of the special cases it gives rise to it. Its predictive ability is also superior to either reinforcement or belief-based models. Does this arise simply because it has more parameters? Camerer et al. (2001) used the Akaike and the Bayesian information criteria that allow for a tradeoff between greater explanatory power and a higher number of model parameters. In their data, EWA outperforms belief-based learning in all in-sample comparisons and better than reinforcement learning in 16 out of 20 comparisons. When the out-of-sample comparisons are made, EWA does better, often modestly as compared to the reinforcement learning model, in 11 comparisons and better than belief-based models in 9 out of 11 comparisons. A large number of other learning models have also been considered in the literature; for a survey see Dhami (2020, Vol. VI).

11.8 Competitive Equilibrium Experiments

The theory of competitive market equilibrium is an elegant construct in microeconomics. It applies to a world where all markets are assumed to be perfectly competitive, so no individual economic actor has any market power and everyone is a price taker; no trading and informational frictions exist; and no externalities or public goods exist. The aim is to find the equilibrium prices of all goods, services, and factors of production, so that (i) all consumers maximize utility; (ii) all firms maximize profits; and (iii) all markets for goods, services, and for factors of production, clear in the sense that demand equals supply in those markets. How do markets arrive at a competitive equilibrium, if they are initially not at equilibrium, is a bit of a mystery.

Economists rely on the fictitious construct of a "Walrasian auctioneer" who intervenes to bring markets to an equilibrium, for example, by raising prices when they are below the equilibrium price, and reducing prices when they are above the equilibrium price. But no such Walrasian auctioneer exists in actual practice, so will markets arrive at an equilibrium? We cannot answer this question by looking at real world data because it is unlikely that any market will satisfy the stringent assumptions that underlie a competitive equilibrium. We could, however, use experiments to create perfectly competitive markets inside the economics lab to see if the predictions of the theory are confirmed by the evidence. We consider below some of the classic experiments in this area.

Most experiments in this area use the *induced value mechanism*. In the typical experiment, subjects are divided into buyers (B) and sellers (S). Sellers have a single unit of a good to sell and buyers have unit demands. Buyer, $i = 1, 2, \ldots$ is given a card with a number B_i and is "informed" that the number on the card is their valuation for a single unit. Seller, $j = 1, 2, \ldots$ is given a card marked with a number S_j and is "informed" that the number on the card is their cost of supplying the good. All buyers and sellers have private information about their valuation or cost, that is, they are privately informed about the numbers on their respective cards. Buyer $i = 1, 2, \ldots$ is instructed not to pay a price higher than B_i and seller $j = 1, 2, \ldots$ is instructed not to accept any price lower than S_i.

Figure 11.15 considers a simple example with nine buyers who have respective valuations

$$B_1 > B_2 > \ldots > B_9,$$

and nine sellers with respective costs given by

$$S_1 < S_2 < \ldots < S_9.$$

The highest valuation is $B_1 = 10$, so the buyer is willing to pay up to 10 to acquire 1 unit of the object; and the lowest valuation is $B_9 = 1$, so this buyer is willing to pay a maximum of 1 to acquire 1 unit of the object. The lowest cost seller has cost $S_1 = 1$ and is willing to accept a price no lower than 1 to sell 1 unit of the object. The highest cost seller has cost $S_9 = 10$; such a seller is willing to accept a price of no lower than 10 to sell the object. In Figure 11.15, the demand curve is labeled by the letter D and the supply curve by the letter S.

The curves are step functions because we have only a small number of buyers and sellers. For large numbers of buyers and sellers, the curves smoothen out, at least to the naked eye. If we could draw these curves in a continuous manner, the (inverse) demand curve corresponds to the equation $p = 10 - q$ and the (inverse) supply curve to the equation $p = 1 + q$. The market clearing solution is $p^* = 5.5$ and $q^* = 4.5$. However, we have unit demands, so only integer quantities are feasible. From Figure 11.15, we can see that at a price of $p^* = 5.5$, the buyer with the valuation B_5 finds it worthwhile to buy and the seller with the cost S_5 finds it worthwhile to sell. Thus, $q^* = 5$ units of the good are exchanged in a competitive equilibrium at a price $p^* = 5.5$. The outcome is achieved for any price in the interval $[5, 6]$ over which the two curves D and S overlap.

The competitive equilibrium has desirable efficiency properties. It maximizes the sum of consumer surplus and producer profits. The markets are efficient in the sense that all buyers whose valuations exceed the equilibrium price, and all sellers whose marginal costs are below the equilibrium price are able to trade. No voluntary trades are left unexploited in equilibrium.

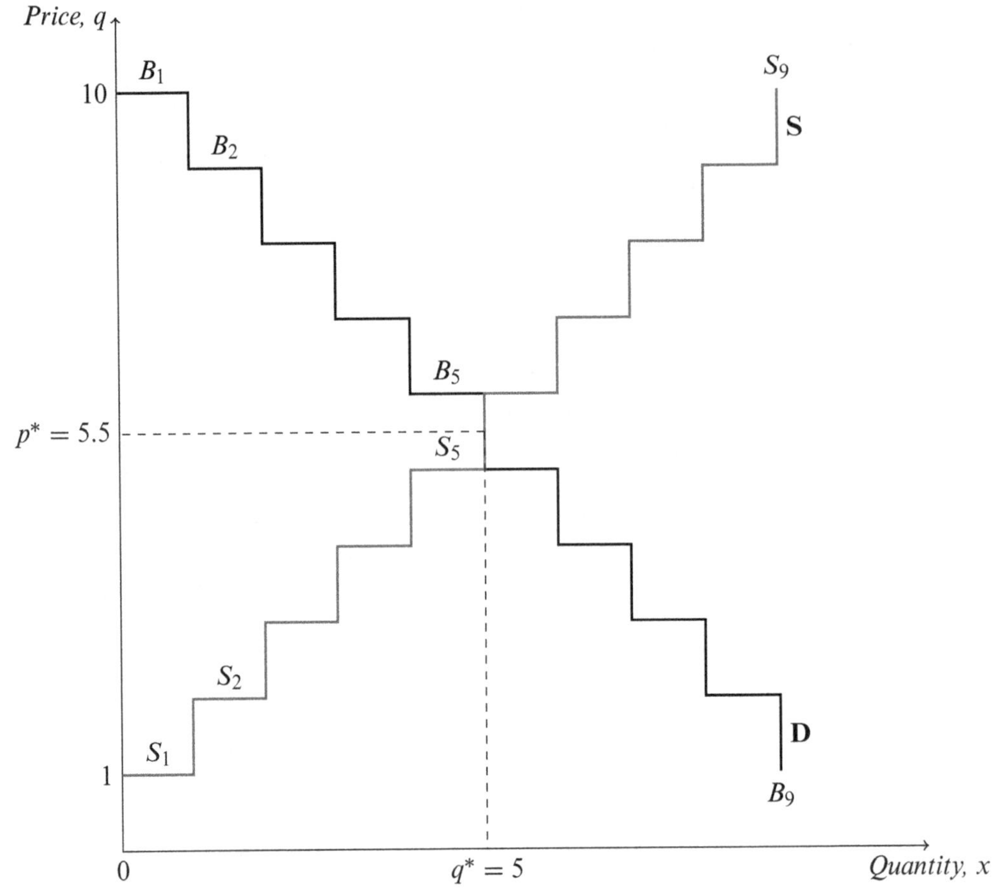

Figure 11.15 A plot of supply and demand curves in the induced value methodology

There is no inherent notion of "fairness" in the concept of an equilibrium price. For instance, if the good in question is private medical services, then efficiency requires that all those who are able to pay for the medical services gain access to the services. However, this sidesteps the question of whether the poorest can afford to pay for expensive medical services. Typically the answer is, they cannot. Most people would not wish to live in a society where the poorest had no access to medical facilities. Hence, governments typically intervene to provide medical services free, or heavily subsidized, at the point of delivery; as, for instance, in the case of the National Health Service in the UK and medicaid and medicare in the US. Thus, efficiency alone cannot be used as a guide to the desirability of particular market institutions. However, efficiency may still offer a benchmark while considering tradeoffs that involve fairness.

11.8.1 The Market Experiments by Chamberlin (1948)

Chamberlin (1948) who did pioneering work on monopolistic competition conducted some of the first experiments to test for a competitive equilibrium, using as subjects, students in his

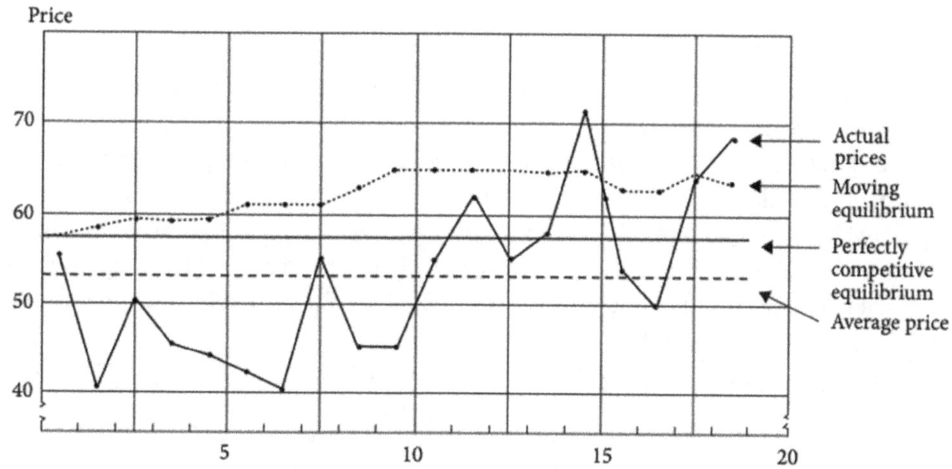

Figure 11.16 The time path of prices over successive rounds of the experiments in Chamberlin (1948). Source: Chamberlin (1948)

Harvard class. He used the induced value mechanism. In a design that is reminiscent of the actual functioning of many markets, he allowed subjects to mingle with each other and to freely strike bargains with each other. In any of these random encounters between buyers and sellers, say, a buyer with valuation B_i and a seller with cost S_j, the two parties could arrive at a mutually agreeable outcome if $S_j < B_i$. They can bargain and haggle to settle at any price p such that $S_j \leq p \leq B_i$ to share the gains from trade; the buyer's payoff is $B_i - p \geq 0$ and the seller's payoff is $p - S_j \geq 0$. After a fixed amount of time, the market closes, but within that time, the market experiment can be repeated several times.

Chamberlin repeated the experiment 46 times. The actual quantity traded was above the equilibrium quantity in 91.3% of the cases. The average price was higher than the equilibrium price 7 times, and lower 39 times. Figure 11.16 shows the typical experimental results over 20 rounds in which the competitive equilibrium price prediction is 57; this prediction follows from the underlying demand and supply curves used in the experiment.

The actual prices in each round of the experiment are shown by the curve labeled "Actual Prices" and a moving average of the actual prices is also shown. The dynamic path of prices did not show any tendency to move towards the competitive outcome, even during the later rounds of the experiment.

The experiments in Chamberlin (1948) allow for "out of equilibrium trading." By contrast, in the theory of competitive equilibrium, all trades take place at the equilibrium price. Economics has typically been interested in the characterization of an equilibrium rather than the related question of exploring the path to an equilibrium. Thus, one observes several trades taking place among the subjects in experiments that are not predicted to take place in the relevant theory that considers only equilibrium trades. Letting p^* be the price predicted by a competitive equilibrium, and p the price at which any bilateral trade takes place among sellers and buyers. These trades are typically of two kinds

$$p^* < S_j < p < B_i, \tag{11.107}$$

$$S_j < p < B_i < p^*. \tag{11.108}$$

Trades such as the one shown in (11.107) occur when a seller with cost S_j meets a buyer whose valuation B_i is higher. Clearly they can strike a mutually beneficial bargain if they agree on some price p such that $S_j < p < B_i$. In (11.108) the seller and buyer have an opportunity for mutually beneficial trade at a price below the equilibrium price. Both examples can be observed in Figure 11.16. Since buyers and sellers do not know the costs and valuations of others in the induced value mechanism (numbers on cards are private information), hence, they do not often want to forego the opportunity for a profitable trade (if $S_j < B_i$) in preference for obtaining a potentially better deal later.

In summing up the results of his experiments, Chamberlin (1948, p. 102) writes:

> My own skepticism as to why actual prices should in any literal sense tend toward equilibrium during the course of a market has been increased not so much by the actual data of the experiment before us which are certainly open to limitations as by failure, upon reflection stimulated by the problem, to find any reason why it should be so. It would appear that, in asserting such a tendency, economists may have been led unconsciously to share their unique knowledge of the equilibrium point with their theoretical creatures, the buyers and sellers, who, of course, in real life have no knowledge of it whatsoever.

Chamberlin's experimental design seems eminently plausible and natural, but it was abandoned by subsequent research. A great deal of the subsequent research was driven by Vernon Smith who had participated in some of these early experiments as a student.

11.8.2 Double Auction Experiments

Smith (1962) used an alternative method of implementing a competitive equilibrium, using a *double auction mechanism*. Unlike Chamberlin's model where subjects meet privately, and freely strike deals, in Smith's proposal subjects only make "public" announcements. Sellers announce offers/asks while buyers announce public bids. The underlying method of assigning values to buyers and costs to sellers uses the induced value mechanism that we have already explained; sellers sell one unit of an object and buyers demand one unit. The valuations and costs are expressed in dollars, and are private knowledge to, respectively, buyers and sellers.

Any seller or buyer can make a public announcement at any time. Buyers and sellers can move in any order to make their public announcements. Table 11.5 shows nine such moves that eventually result in a successful trade. There are nine sellers $S1, S2, \ldots, S9$ with respective costs $1, 2, \ldots, 9$ and nine buyers $B1, B2, \ldots, B9$ with valuations $1, 2, \ldots, 9$. Seller S8 who has the cost 8, moves first and asks for 10. This is immediately followed by an ask of 8.50 from seller S6 who has a cost of 6. Buyer B6 with valuation 6 then bids 2.50 for the object, followed by buyer B5 with a bid of 3.20. This continues, until in the ninth move, buyer B8 who has a valuation 8, accepts an offer of 6 from seller S4 who has cost 4. This results in a mutually beneficial trade between the two parties. Seller S4 makes a profit of $6 - 4 = 2$ and buyer B8 gains $8 - 6 = 2$, so the gains from trade are split equally. The market is then closed and immediately reopened for another round of trade in which the demand and supply curves may be altered by the experimenter.

A critically important role in the success of the double auction experiments is played by *the market improvement rule* (Davis and Holt, 1993, p. 128; Kagel and Roth, 1995, p. 369). Notice

Table 11.5 A hypothetical example of the sequence of moves in a double auction experiment

Moves	Bid	Offer
1		S8 asks \$10.00
2		S6 asks \$8.50
3	B6 bids \$2.50	
4	B5 bids \$3.20	
5		S5 asks \$7.50
6	B7 bids \$4.10	
7		S3 asks \$6.20
8		S4 offers \$6.00
9	B8 accepts	

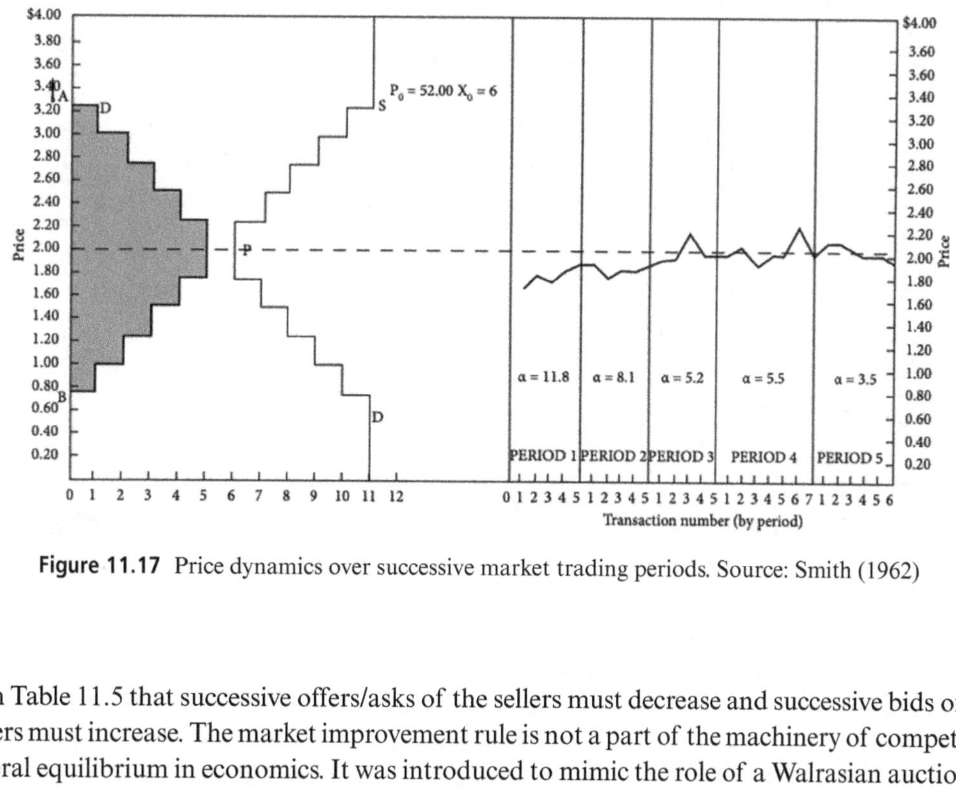

Figure 11.17 Price dynamics over successive market trading periods. Source: Smith (1962)

from Table 11.5 that successive offers/asks of the sellers must decrease and successive bids of the buyers must increase. The market improvement rule is not a part of the machinery of competitive general equilibrium in economics. It was introduced to mimic the role of a Walrasian auctioneer who plays the critical role in economic theory to bring about a competitive general equilibrium.

The left panel of Figure 11.17 shows the demand and supply curves used in one of the experiments in Smith (1962). The right panel shows the price dynamics over different market trading periods. In order to test the closeness of the actual results with the competitive equilibrium prediction, Smith used the *parameter of convergence*, α, defined as $\alpha = \frac{\sigma}{p^*} \times 100$, where σ is the standard deviation of the actual experimental price and p^* is the predicted equilibrium price. The variation in prices, as measured by α, tends to fall in successive trading periods. There is a tendency for the observed prices to converge towards the predictions of the competitive equilibrium price over time. These results also hold for other demand and supply curves. A large number of replications have since confirmed these results.

Another method of evaluating the success of the double auction experiments is to compute a measure of allocative efficiency, E. Define social surplus as the sum of consumer surplus and producer surplus. Let θ_P denote the "predicted social surplus" under the competitive outcome and θ_A the "actual social surplus" in experimental conditions. The allocative efficiency of the observed outcome in experiments is defined as

$$E = (\theta_A/\theta_P) \times 100. \tag{11.109}$$

The allocative efficiency in double auction experiments is impressive; it ranges between 97.3% and 99.4%; see Davis and Holt (1993, Table 3.4, p. 136).

11.8.3 Other Approaches

List (2004) uses field data from experienced traders from the sports cards and collector pin markets. In the sports cards market, for instance, the item exchanged is multiple copies of a sports card. As in Chamberlin (1948), buyers and sellers met each other freely to strike privately optimal deals by meeting, bargaining, and haggling. As in Smith (1962), the induced value mechanism is used. Two features separate these experiments from those in Chamberlin and Smith.

(i) As soon as a buyer and a seller exchanged an object, the price and the contract was publicly announced to all other participants in the session. The most recent publicly announced price is likely to serve as an anchor around which market participants post asks and bids in subsequent rounds.
(ii) Discussions among groups of sellers and groups of buyers that could lead to a collusive outcome were not allowed.

The experimental outcomes were found to converge to the predictions of the competitive market outcomes. These experiments show that the double auction method is one of potentially several methods that can achieve a competitive equilibrium.

We have discussed agent-based models in Section 11.6. Gode and Sunder (1993) provide an application of agent-based models to double auctions experiments. These are experiments in which the subjects in Smith (1962) are replaced by nonhuman robots who are endowed with fixed and mechanistic trading rules to draw bids and asks/offers randomly from a fixed set of numbers. The *jth* zero intelligence (ZI) robot in the role of a buyer is endowed with a valuation B_j, and is allowed to bid randomly, any number in the interval $[0, B_j]$. The *ith* robot seller is endowed with a cost S_i, and chooses an offer/ask randomly by announcing any price in the interval $[S_i, S_{max}]$, where S_{max} is the maximum over all buyer valuations. A critical assumption in this model is that the ZI robots follow the market improvement rule, as in Smith's original experiment. These agents are sometimes known as constrained robots or ZI-C traders because they respect the budget constraint and do not trade at a loss. Unconstrained zero intelligence traders, ZI-U traders, by contrast, are not required to respect a budget constraint, so they can incur a loss.

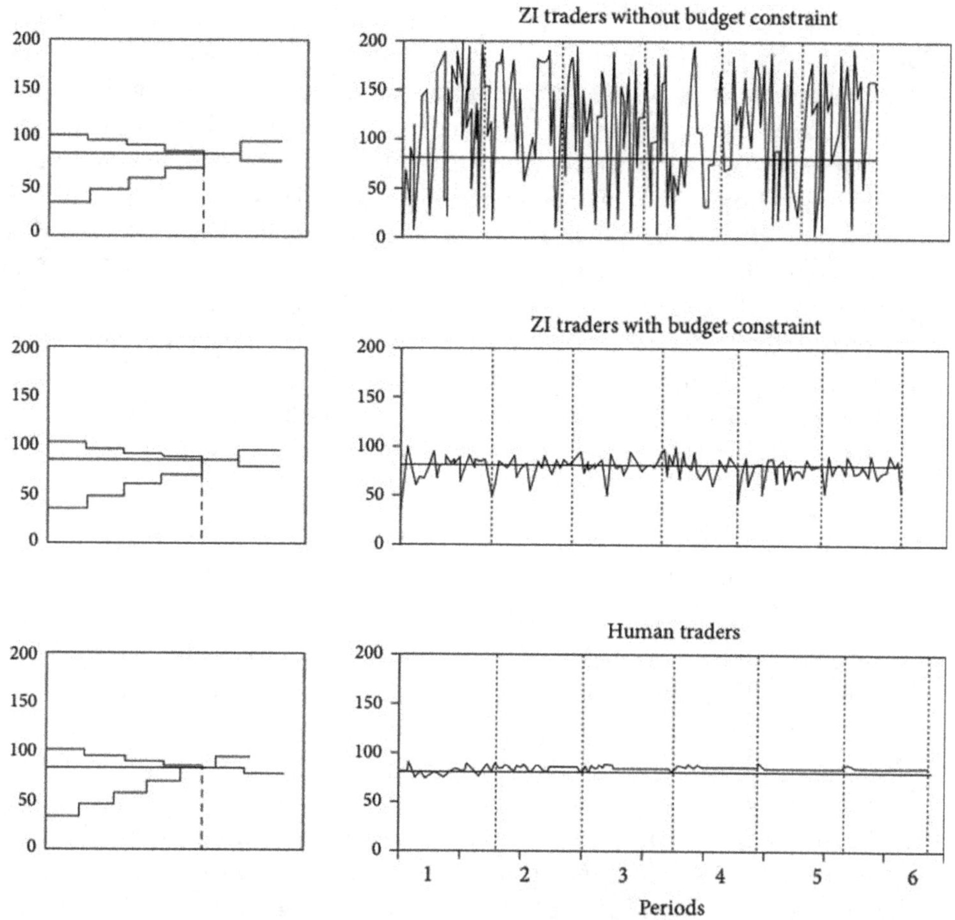

Figure 11.18 Price dynamics in competitive markets for zero intelligence robots in the right panel and the demand/supply curves in the left panel. Source: Gode and Sunder (1993)

Figure 11.18 shows the price dynamics for ZI-C traders, ZI-U traders, and human subjects, corresponding to the demand and supply curves shown in the left panel. The competitive equilibrium prediction is $p^* = 80$ and $q^* = 24$. Human subjects very quickly approach the competitive equilibrium prediction. The price dynamics for the ZI-C traders show relatively greater variance as compared to human subjects, but the variation declines over time. The allocative efficiency, E (see (11.109)), for ZI-C robots is 98.7%, while human subjects lag only a little behind at 97.6%. ZI-U robot traders show no tendency to converge to the competitive equilibrium predictions.

11.8.4 What Do We Learn from this Evidence?

The double auction experiments have no doubt been extremely successful in replicating the predictions of a competitive equilibrium, even when individual traders have private information on their valuations and costs. Convergence occurs reliably and relatively quickly. However, as noted above, the competitive equilibrium in economics is an idealized benchmark. The underlying assumptions are unlikely to be satisfied in any real world market setting. The confirmation of its predictions by the empirical evidence using lab data does not, therefore, inform us much about the real world. Hence, the results are probably of greater academic than practical value.

The results from the evidence on zero intelligence subjects show that the rationality of human subjects is not the key element in explaining the success of double auction experiments. It would seem that the market improvement rule plays the pivotal role in the success of double auction experiments. Whenever price is below (above) equilibrium, the market improvement rule forces the price upwards (downwards). Hence, there is a built-in mechanism within these experiments to achieve the very result that they seek to prove exists. For this reason, perhaps the observed success is less magical than is sometimes claimed in the literature.

Thaler (2015) expresses valid concerns about the induced value mechanism that are often missed in the discussion in this literature. He writes (p. 40, 41):

> But I had some worries about this methodology. When you go to a store and decide to buy a jacket for \$49, no one is telling you how much you are willing to pay for it. You have to decide that for yourself, and that value might depend on all sorts of issues.

A more natural way of assigning values to objects is to endow economic actors with the relevant objects and invite them to trade those objects for money. When they make their decisions they assign their "own" personal willingness to pay for those objects (by contrast, in the induced value methodology, the experimenter assigns values of objects to subjects, which are written on cards). Indeed, this is what was done in the case of experiments on the *endowment effect* that we reviewed in Section 2.5 of the book. The results are dramatically different. The widespread evidence on the endowment effect shows that there is a lot less trading relative to the competitive equilibrium benchmark. Yet, this sort of exercise might not be useful for, say, trading on the stock market, that the double auction mechanism seeks to mimic. Equally, the results from double auction mechanisms do not apply everywhere.

The double auction institution achieves nearly 100% allocative efficiency. However, if this market institution is so successful, why do we not observe it more often in practice? A potential explanation is that this institution ignores real world transaction costs and other important frictions that are not modeled in experiments. These institutions appear more applicable to the auction or stock market trading environment, which is unlikely to be the typical case. However, the growth of online trading platforms could increase the practical relevance of these results.

The equivalence of the results generated with ZI-C robots and human subjects breaks down in a more complex double auction setting. For instance, when there are fixed costs of trading for sellers that are actually incurred only if an exchange takes place, then the outcome might no longer be efficient (Van Boening and Wilcox, 1996). When the trading decisions are more complicated, for example, goods that need to be carried over from one season to the next, then ZI robots do considerably worse than human subjects (Miller, 2008). The economic environment in lab experiments is fairly stationary. When more temporal variability in demand and supply curves is introduced to mimic real life markets then ZI robots do not converge to a competitive equilibrium, and human subjects might not either (Brewer et al., 2002).

References

Agarwal, S., Chomsisengphet, S., Mahoney, N., and Stroebel, J. (2015). Regulating Consumer Financial Products: Evidence from Credit Cards. *The Quarterly Journal of Economics* 130(1): 111–164.

Agnew, H. (1981). Gas-Cooled Nuclear Power Reactors. *Scientic American* 244(6): 55–63.

Akerlof, G. A. and Shiller, R. J. (2015). *Phishing for Phools: The Economics of Manipulation and Deception*. Princeton University Press: Princeton, NJ.

Alesina, A., Di Tella, R., and MacCulloch, R. (2004). Inequality and Happiness: Are Europeans and Americans Different? *Journal of Public Economics* 88(9–10): 2009–2042.

Allais, M. (1953). Le comportement de l'homme rationnel devant le risque: critique des postulats et axiomes de l'école Américaine. *Econometrica* 21(4): 503–546.

Apouey, B. and Clark, A. E. (2015). Winning Big but Feeling No Better? The Effect of Lottery Prizes on Physical and Mental Health. *Health Economics* 24(5), 516–538.

Armstrong, M. and Vickers, J. (2012). Consumer Protection and Contingent Charges. *Journal of Economic Literature* 50 (2): 477–493.

Armstrong, M. and Zhou, J. (2011). Paying for Prominence. *Economic Journal* 121(556): F368–F395.

Arthur, W. B. (1989). Competing Technologies, Increasing Returns, and Lock-In by Historical Events. *Economic Journal* 99: 116–131.

Arthur, W. B. (1991). Designing Economic Agents that Act Like Human Agents: A behavioral approach to Bounded Rationality. *American Economic Review Papers and Proceedings* 81: 353–359.

Arthur, W. B. (1993). On Designing Economic Agents that Behave Like Human Agents. *Journal of Evolutionary Economics* 3: 1–22.

Arthur, W. B. (1994). Inductive Reasoning and Bounded Rationality. *American Economic Association Papers and Proceedings* 84: 406–411.

Arthur, W. B. (1999). *Complexity and the Economy. Science* 284(5411): 107–109.

Arthur, W. B. (2006). Agent-Based Modeling and Out-of-Equilibrium Economics. In K. Judd and L. Tesfatsion (eds.), *Handbook of Computational Economics, Volume 2, Agent-Based Computational Economics*. Elsevier B.V.: Amsterdam pp. 1551–1564.

Arthur, W. B. (2009). *The Nature of Technology: What It Is and How It Evolves*. Free Press: New York.

Arthur, W. B. (2015). *Complexity and the Economy*. Oxford University Press: Oxford.

Arthur, W. B. (2021). Perspectives: Foundations of Complexity Economics. *Nature Reviews: Physics* 3: 136–145.

Ausubel, L. M. (1991). The Failure of Competition in the Credit Card Market. *The American Economic Review* 81(1): 50–81.

Axelrod, R. (1980a). Effective Choice in the Prisoner's Dilemma. *Journal of Conflict Resolution* 24(1): 3–25.

Axelrod, R. (1980b). More Effective Choice in the Prisoner's Dilemma. *Journal of Conflict Resolution* 24(3): 379–403.

Bartolini, S. and Sarracino, F. (2014). Happy for How Long? How Social Capital and Economic Growth Relate to Happiness over Time. *Ecological Economics* 108: 242–256.

Battalio, R., Samuelson, L., and Van Huyck, J. (2001). Optimization Incentives and

Coordination Failure in Laboratory Stag Hunt Games. *Econometrica* 69: 749–764.

Beinhocker, E. D. (2006). *The Origin of Wealth Evolution, Complexity, and the Radical Remaking of Economics.* Harvard Business School Press: Harvard.

Beja E. Jr. (2014). Income Growth and Happiness: Reassessment of the Easterlin Paradox. Munich Personal RePEc Archive Paper No. 53360.

Benjamin, D. J., Guzman, J. K., Fleurbaey, M., Heffetz, O., and Kimball, M. S. (2021). What Do Happiness Data Mean? Theory and Survey Evidence. Working Paper 28438. www.nber.org/papers/w28438

Benjamin, D. J., Heffetz, O., Kimball, M. S., and Rees-Jones, A. (2012). What Do You Think Would Make You Happier? What Do You Think You Would Choose? *American Economic Review* 102(5): 2083–2110.

Benjamin, D. J., Heffetz, O., Kimball, M. S., and Szembrot, N. (2014). Beyond Happiness and Satisfaction: Toward Well-Being Indices Based on Stated Preference. *American Economic Review* 104(9): 2698–2735.

Bereby-Meyer, Y. and Erev, I. (1998). On Learning to Become a Successful Loser: A Comparison of Alternative Abstractions of Learning in the Loss Domain. *Journal of Mathematical Psychology* 42: 266–286.

Bernheim, B. D. and Taubinsky, D. (2018). Behavioral Public Economics. In B. Douglas Bernheim, S. DellaVigna, and D. Laibson (eds.), *The Handbook of Behavioral Economics*, Vol. 1. Elsevier: New York, pp. 381–516.

Blanchflower, D., Bell, D., Montagnoli, A., and Moro, M. (2014). The Happiness Trade-Off between Unemployment and Inflation. *Journal of Money, Credit and Banking* 46(S2): 117–141.

Blanchflower, D. G., and Graham, C. L. (2021). The U Shape of Happiness: A Response. *Perspectives on Psychological Science* 16(6): 1435–1446.

Blanchflower, D. G. and Oswald, A. J. (2004). Well-Being over Time in Britain and the USA. *Journal of Public Economics* 88(7–8): 1359–1386.

Blanchower, D. G. and Oswald, A. J. (2008). Is Wellbeing U-shaped over the Life Cycle? *Social Science and Medicine* 66(8): 1733–1749.

Blanchflower, D. G., Oswald, A. J., and Landeghem, B. V. (2009). Imitative Obesity and Relative Utility. *Journal of the European Economic Association* 7(2–3): 528–538.

Blinder, A. S. (1990). Learning by Asking Those Who Are Doing. *Eastern Economic Journal* 16(4): 297–306.

Bloem, J. R. and Oswald, A. J. (2021). The Analysis of Human Feelings: A Practical Suggestion for a Robustness Test. IZA DP No. 14632.

Bond, T. N. and Lang, K. (2019). The Sad Truth about Happiness Scales. *Journal of Political Economy* 127 (4): 1629–1640.

Bookstaber R. and Kirman, A. (2018). Modelling a Heterogeneous World. In C. Hommes and B. LeBaron, (eds.), *Handbook of Computational Economics, Volume 4*. Elsevier: Amsterdam, pp. 769–795.

Bordalo, P., Gennaioli, N., and Shleifer, A. (2012). Salience Theory of Choice under Risk. *Quarterly Journal of Economics* 127(3): 1243–1285.

Bordalo, P., Gennaioli, N., and Shleifer, A. (2013). Salience and Consumer Choice. *Journal of Political Economy* 121(5): 803–843.

Bordalo, P., Gennaioli, N., and Shleifer, A. (2020). Memory, Attention and Choice. *Quarterly Journal of Economics*, 135(3): 1399–1442.

Bordalo, P., Gennaioli, N., and Shleifer, A. (2021). Salience. NBER Working Paper 29274.

Bradley, S. and Feldman, N. (2020). Hidden Baggage: Behavioral Responses to Changes in Airline Ticket Tax Disclosure. *American Economic Journal: Economic Policy* 12(4): 58–87.

Brewer, P. J., Huang, M., Nelson, B., and Plott, C. R. (2002). On the Behavioral Foundations of the Law of Supply and Demand: Human Convergence and Robot Randomness. *Experimental Economics* 5(3): 179–208.

Brickman, P. and Campbell, D. T. (1971). Hedonic Relativism and Planning the Good Society. In M. H. Appley (ed.), *Adaptation Level Theory*. Academic Press: New York, pp. 287–302.

Bush, R. R. and Mosteller, F. (1955). *Stochastic Models for Learning*. John Wiley & Sons: New York.

Camerer, C. F. (2003). *Behavioral Game Theory: Experiments in Strategic Interaction*. Princeton University Press: Princeton, NJ.

Camerer, C. F. and Ho, T.-H. (1999). Experience-Weighted Attraction Learning in Normal Form Games. *Econometrica* 67: 827–874.

Camerer, C. F., Ho, T.-H., and Chong, J. K. (2001). Behavioral Game Theory: Thinking, Learning and Teaching. Paper presented at the Nobel Prize symposium.

Campbell, J. Y. (2016). Restoring Rational Choice: The Challenge of Consumer Financial Regulation. *The American Economic Review* 106(5): 1–30.

Carlin, Bruce I. (2009). Strategic Price Complexity in Retail Financial Markets. *Journal of Financial Economics* 91(3): 278–287.

Carrieri, V. and De Paola, M. (2012). Height and Subjective Well-Being in Italy. *Economics & Human Biology* 10(3): 289–298.

Cesarini, D., Lindqvist, E., Ostling, R., and Wallace, B. (2016). Wealth, Health, and Child Development: Evidence from Administrative Data on Swedish Lottery Players. *Quarterly Journal of Economics* 131(2): 687–738.

Cetre, S., Clark, A. E., and Senik, C. (2016). Happy People Have Children: Choice and Self-Selection into Parenthood. *European Journal of Population* 32(2): 445–473.

Chamberlin, E. H. (1948). An Experimental Imperfect Market. *Journal of Political Economy* 56(2): 95–108.

Cheibub, J. A., Gandhi, J., and Vreeland, J. R. (2010). Democracy and Dictatorship Revisited. *Public Choice* 143(1): 67–101.

Chen, L. Y., Oparina, E., Powdthavee, N., and Srisuma, S. (2019). Have Econometric Analyses of Happiness Data Been Futile? A Simple Truth about Happiness Scales. IZA DP No. 12152.

Cheng, T., Oswald, A. J., and Powdthavee, N. (2017). Longitudinal Evidence for a Midlife Nadir in Human Well-Being: Results from Four Data Sets. *Economic Journal* 127(599): 126–142.

Chetty, R., Looney, A., and Kroft, K. (2009). Salience and Taxation: Theory and Evidence. *American Economic Review* 99(4): 1145–1177.

Clark, A. E. (1997). Job Satisfaction and Gender: Why Are Women So Happy at Work? *Labour Economics* 4(4): 341–372.

Clark, A. E. (2001). What Really Matters in a Job? Hedonic Measurement Using Quit Data. *Labour Economics* 8: 223–242.

Clark, A. E. (2003). Unemployment as a Social Norm: Psychological Evidence from Panel Data. *Journal of Labor Economics* 21: 323–351.

Clark, A. E. (2018). Four Decades of the Economics of Happines: Where Next? *Review of Income and Wealth Series* 64(2): 245–269.

Clark, A. E. and D'Ambrosio, C. (2014). Attitudes to Income Inequality: Experimental and Survey Evidence IZA DP No. 8136. In A. Atkinson and F. Bourguignon (eds.), *Handbook of Income Distribution, Volume 2A*. Elsevier: Amsterdam, pp. 1147–1208.

Clark, A. E., Diener, E., Georgellis, Y., and Lucas, R. (2008). Lags and Leads in Life Satisfaction: A Test of the Baseline Hypothesis. *Economic Journal* 118(529): F222–F243.

Clark, A. E. and Etilé, F. (2011). Happy House: Spousal Weight and Individual Well-Being. *Journal of Health Economics* 30(5): 1124–1136.

Clark, A., Frijters, P., and Shields, M. (2008). Relative Income, Happiness, and Utility: An Explanation for the Easterlin Paradox and Other Puzzles. *Journal of Economic Literature* 46(1): 95–144.

Clark, A. E. and Georgellis, Y. (2013). Back to Baseline in Britain: Adaptation in the BHPS. *Economica* 80(319): 496–512.

Clark, A. E. and Oswald, A. J. (1994). Unhappiness and Unemployment. *Economic Journal* 104: 648–659.

Clark A. E. and Oswald A. J. (1996). Satisfaction and Comparison Income. *Journal of Public Economics* 61: 359–381.

Clark, A. E. and Senik, C. (2010). Who Compares to Whom? The Anatomy of Income Comparisons in Europe. *The Economic Journal* 120: 573–594.

Coleman, J. S. (1993). Social Capital in the Creation of Human Capital. *American Journal of Sociology* 94: 95–120.

Cyert, R. M. and March, J. G. (1963). *A Behavioral Theory of the Firm*. Prentice-Hall: Englewood Cliffs, NJ.

Danner, D., Snowdon, D., and Friesen, W. (2001). Positive Emotions

David, P. A. (1985). Clio and the Economics of QWERTY. *American Economic Review* 75(2): 332–337.

David, P. A. and Bunn, J. A. (1988). The Economics of Gateway Technologies and Network Evolution: Lessons from Electricity Supply History. *Information Economics and Policy* 3(2): 165–202.

Davis, D. D. and Holt, C. A. (1993). *Experimental Economics*. Princeton University Press: Princeton, NJ.

De Neve J. E., Christakis, N. A., Fowler, J. H., and Frey, B. S. (2012). Genes, Economics, and Happiness. *Journal of Neuroscience Psychology and Economics* 5(4): 193–211.

De Neve, J.-E., Ward, G., De Keulenaer, F., Landeghem, B. V., Kavetsos, G., and Norton, M. I. (2018). The Asymmetric Experience of Positive and Negative Economic Growth: Global Evidence Using Subjective Well-Being Data. *Review of Economics and Statistics* 100(2): 362–375.

Deaton, A. (2008). Income, Health, and Well-Being around the World: Evidence from the Gallup World Poll. *Journal of Economic Perspectives* 22: 53–72.

Deaton, A. (2011). The Financial Crisis and the Well-Being of Americans. *Oxford Economic Papers* 64(1): 1–26.

Deaton, A. and Stone, A. (2016). Understanding Context Effects for a Measure of Life Evaluation: How Responses Matter. *Oxford Economic Papers* 68(4): 861–870.

DellaVigna, S. and Malmendier, U. (2004). Contract Design and Self-Control: Theory and Evidence. *Quarterly Journal of Economics* 119(2): 353–402.

DellaVigna, S. and Malmendier, U. (2006). Paying Not to Go to the Gym. *American Economic Review* 96(3): 694–719.

Dhami, S. (2020). *The Foundations of Behavioral Economic Analysis: Learning Models (Volume VI)*. Oxford University Press: Oxford.

Dhami, S. and Sunstein, C. R. (2022). *Bounded Rationality Heuristics, Judgment, and Public Policy.* MIT Press: Cambridge, MA.

Di Tella, R. and MacCulloch, R. J. (2006). Some Uses of Happiness Data in Economics. *Journal of Economic Perspectives* 20(1): 25–46.

Di Tella, R., Haisken-De New, J., and MacCulloch, R. J. (2010). Happiness Adaptation to Income and to Status in an Individual Panel. *Journal of Economic Behavior and Organization* 76(3): 834–852.

Di Tella, R., MacCulloch, R. J., and Oswald, A. J. (2001). Preferences Over Inflation and Unemployment: Evidence from Surveys of Happiness. *The American Economic Review* 91: 335–341.

Di Tella, R., MacCulloch, R. J., and Oswald, A. J. (2003). The Macroeconomics of Happiness. *Review of Economics and Statistics* 85: 809–827.

Diener, E. and Chan, M. (2011). Happy People Live Longer: Subjective Well-Being Contributes to Health and Longevity. *Applied Psychology: Health And Well-Being* 3(1): 1–43.

Diener, E. and Seligman, M. E. P. (2004). Beyond Money: Toward an Economy of Well-Being. *Psychological Science in the Public Interest* 5(1): 1–31.

Diener, E., Lucas, R. E., and Scollon, C. N. (2006). Beyond the Hedonic Treadmill: Revising the Adaptation Theory of Well-Being. *American Psychologist* 61(4): 305–314.

Diener, E., Tay, L., and Oishi, S. (2013). Rising Income and the Subjective Well-Being of Nations. *Journal of Personality and Social Psychology* 104(2): 267–276.

Duesenberry, J. (1949). *Income, Saving, and the Theory of Consumer Behavior*. Harvard University Press: Cambridge, MA.

Duffy, J. and Feltovich, N. (1999). Does Observation of Others Affect Learning in Strategic Environments? An Experimental Study. *International Journal of Game Theory* 28(1): 131–152.

Dustmann, C. and Fasani, F. (2016). The Effect of Local Area Crime on Mental Health. *Economic Journal* 126(593): 978–1017.

Easterlin, R. A. (1974). Does Economic Growth Improve the Human Lot? Some Empirical Evidence. In P. A. David and M. W. Reder (eds.), *Nations and Households in Economic Growth: Essays in Honor of Moses Abramovitz*. Academic Press: New York, pp. 89–125.

Easterlin, R. A. (1995). Will Raising the Incomes of All Increase the Happiness of All? *Journal of Economic Behavior and Organization* 27(1): 35–47.

Easterlin, R. A. (2001). Income and Happiness: Towards a Unified Theory. *Economic Journal* 111(473): 465–484.

Easterlin, R. A. (2006). Life Cycle Happiness and Its Sources: Intersections of Psychology, Economics, and Demography. *Journal of Economic Psychology* 27(4): 463–482.

Easterlin, R. A. (2013). Happiness, Growth, and Public Policy. *Economic Inquiry* 51(1): 1–15.

Easterlin, R. A. (2021). *An Economist's Lessons on Happiness: Farewell Dismal Science*! Springer: New York.

Easterlin, R. A., and O'Connor, K. J. (2019). The Easterlin Paradox. IZA Discussion Paper No. 13923.

Easterlin, R. A., McVey, L., Switek, M., Sawangta, O., and Zweig, J. (2010). The Happiness Paradox Revisited. *Proceedings of the National Academy of Sciences* 107(52): 22463–22468.

Easterlin, R. A., Wang, F., and Wang, S. (2017). Growth and Happiness in China, 1990–2015. In J. F. Helliwell, R. Layard, and J. D. Sachs (eds.), *World Happiness Report* 2018. Sustainable Development Solutions Network: New York, pp. 48–83.

Ellison, G. and Ellison, S. F. (2009). Search, Obfuscation, and Price Elasticities on the Internet. *Econometrica* 77 (2): 427–452.

Epel, E. (2009). Telomeres in a Life-Span Perspective: A New "Psychobiomarker?" *Current Directions in Psychological Science* 18(1): 6–10.

Epstein, J. M. and Axtell, R. (1996). *Growing Articial Societies: Social Science from the Bottom up*. Brookings Institution Press and MIT Press: Cambridge, MA.

Erev, I. and Roth, A. E. (1998). Predicting How People Play Games: Reinforcement Learning in Experimental Games with Unique, Mixed Strategy Equilibria. *American Economic Review* 88: 848–881.

Eyster, E. and Rabin, M. (2005). Cursed Equilibrium. *Econometrica* 73(5): 1623–1672.

Farhi, E. and Gabaix, X. (2020). Optimal Taxation with Behavioral Agents. *American Economic Review* 110(1): 298–336.

Farmer, J. D. and Geanakoplos, J. (2004). *Power Laws in Finance and Their Implications for Economic Theory.* Mimeo Sante Fe Institute.

Fehr, E. and Wu, K. (2021). Obfuscation in Competitive Markets. University of Zurich, Department of Economics, Working Paper No. 391. Available at SSRN: https://ssrn.com/abstract=3864205.

Flavin, P. and Keane, M. (2012). Life Satisfaction and Political Participation: Evidence from the United States. *Journal of Happiness Studies* 13(1): 63–78.

Fleurbaey, M. (2009). Beyond GDP: The Quest for a Measure of Social Welfare. *Journal of Economic Literature* 47 (4): 1029–1075.

Fleurbaey, M. and Blanchet, D. (2013). *Beyond GDP: Measuring Welfare and Assessing Sustainability*. Oxford University Press: Oxford.

Fredrickson, B. L. and Kahneman, D. (1993). Duration Neglect in Retrospective Evaluations of Affective Episodes. *Journal of Personality and Social Psychology* 65: 45–55.

Frey, B. S. and Stutzer, A. (2000). Happiness, Economy and Institutions. *Economic Journal* 110(446): 918–938.

Frey, B. S. and Stutzer, A. (2002). What Can Economists Learn from Happiness Research? *Journal of Economic Literature* 40(2): 402–435.

Frijters, P., Haisken-Denew, J. P., and Shields, M. A. (2004). Money Does Matter! Evidence from Increasing Real Income and Life Satisfaction in East Germany Following Reunication. *American Economic Review* 94(3): 730–740.

Fudenberg D. and Levine, D. K. (1998). *The Theory of Learning in Games*. MIT Press: Cambridge, MA.

Gabaix, X. (2014). A Sparsity-Based Model of Bounded Rationality. *Quarterly Journal of Economics* 129(4): 1661–1710.

Gabaix X. (2019). Behavioral Inattention. In D. Bernheim, S. DellaVigna, and D. Laibson (eds.), *Handbook of Behavioral Economics*. Vol. 2. Elsevier: North Holland, pp. 261–343.

Gabaix, X. and Laibson, D. (2006). Shrouded Attributes, Consumer Myopia, and Information Suppression in Competitive Markets. *Quarterly Journal of Economics* 121(2): 505–540.

Gamp, T. and Krähmer, D. (2019). *Deception and Competition in Search Markets*. Mimeo Humboldt-Universität of Berlin.

Gardner, J. and Oswald, A. J. (2007). Money and Mental Well-Being: A Longitudinal Study of Medium-Sized Lottery Wins. *Journal of Health Economics* 26(1): 49–60.

Gode, D. K. and Sunder, S. (1993). Allocative Efficiency of Markets with Zero Intelligence Traders: Market as a Partial Substitute for Individual Rationality. *Journal of Political Economy*. 101(1): 119–137.

Graham, C., Chattopadhyay, S., and Picon, M. (2010). Adapting to Adversity: Happiness and the 2009 Economic Crisis in the United States. *Social Research* 77(2): 715–748.

Graham, C., Eggers, A., and Sukhtankar, S. (2004). Does Happiness Pay? An Initial Exploration Based on Panel Data from Russia. *Journal of Economic Behavior and Organization* 55(3): 319–342.

Graham, C. and Pozuelo, J. R. (2017). Happiness, Stress, and Age: How the U Curve Varies across People and Places. *Journal of Population Economics* 30(1): 225–264.

Green, C., Heywood, J., Kler, P., and Leeves, G. (2018). Paradox Lost: Disappearing Female Job Satisfaction. *British Journal of Industrial Relations* 56(3) 484–502.

Grubb, M. D. (2009). Selling to Overconfident Consumers. *American Economic Review* 99(5): 1770–1805.

Grubb, M. D. (2015). Consumer Inattention and Bill-Shock Regulation. *Review of Economic Studies* 82(1): 219–257.

Gruber, J. and Mullainathan, S. (2005). Do Cigarette Taxes Make Smokers Happier? B. E. *Journal of Economic Analysis and Policy* 5(1).

Guven, C., Senik, C., and Stichnoth, H. (2012). You Can't Be Happier Than Your Wife. Happiness Gaps and Divorce. *Journal of Economic Behavior and Organization* 82(1): 110–130.

Haldane, A. G. (2016). The Dappled World. Mimeo Bank of England (available at www.bankofengland.co.uk/publications/Documents/speeches/2016/speech937.pdf).

Hall, R. and Hitch, C. (1939). Price Theory and Business Behaviour. *Oxford Economic Papers* 2(1): 12–45.

Heidhues, P. and Köszegi, B. (2017). Naivete-Based Discrimination. *Quarterly Journal of Economics* 132(2): 1019–1054.

Heidhues, P. and Köszegi, B. (2018). Behavioral Industrial Organization. In D. Bernheim, S. DellaVigna, and D. Laibson (eds.), *Handbook of Behavioral Economics*, Vol. 1. Elsevier: North Holland, pp. 518–612.

Heidhues, P., Köszegi, B., and Murooka, T. (2016). Exploitative Innovation. *American Economic Journal: Microeconomics* 8(1): 1–23.

Helliwell, J. F. (2007). Well-Being and Social Capital: Does Suicide Pose a Puzzle? *Social Indicators Research* 81(3): 455–496.

Helliwell J. and Putnam R. D. (2004). The Social Context of Well-Being. *Philosophical Transactions of the Royal Society (London), Series B* [Internet] 359(1449): 1435–1446.

Ho, T. and Weigelt, K. W. (1996). Task Complexity, Equilibrium Selection, and Learning. *Management Science* 42(5): 659–679.

Hommes, C. H. (2013). *Behavioral Rationality and Heterogeneous Expectations in Complex Economic Systems*. Cambridge University Press: Cambridge.

Hommes, C. and LeBaron, B. (2018). *Handbook of Computational Economics, Volume 4: Heterogeneous Agent Modelling*. Handbooks in Economics Series. North-Holland: Amsterdam.

Huck, S., Konrad, K. A., Müller, W., and Normann, H.-T. (2007). The Merger Paradox and Why Aspiration Levels Let It Fail in the Laboratory. *Economic Journal* 117: 1073–1095.

Inglehart, R., Foa, R., Peterson, C., and Welzel, C. (2008). Development, Freedom, and Rising Happiness. *Perspectives on Psychological Science* 3(4): 264–285.

Kagel, J. H. and Roth, A. E. (1995). *The Handbook of Experimental Economics*. Princeton University Press: Princeton, NJ.

Kahneman, D. (2011). *Thinking, Fast and Slow*. Farrar, Straus and Giroux: Princeton, NJ.

Kahneman, D. and Deaton, A. (2010). High Income Improves Evaluation of Life but Not Emotional Well-Being. *PNAS (Proceedings of the National Academy of Sciences)* 107(38): 16489–16493.

Kahneman, D. and Miller, D. T. (1986). Norm Theory: Comparing Reality to Its Alternatives. *Psychological Review*, 93(2): 136–153.

Kahneman, D. and Thaler, R. H. (2006). Anomalies: Utility Maximization and Experienced Utility. *Journal of Economic Perspectives* 20(1): 221–234.

Kahneman, D. and Tversky, A. (1979). Prospect Theory: An Analysis of Decision under Risk. *Econometrica* 47(2): 263–292.

Kahneman, D., Fredrickson, B. L., Schreiber, C. A., and Redelmeier, D. A. (1993). When More Pain Is Preferred to Less: Adding a Better End. *Psychological Science* 4: 401–405.

Kahneman, D., Wakker, P. P., and Sarin, R. (1997). Back to Bentham? Explorations of Experienced Utility. *Quarterly Journal of Economics* 112: 375–405.

Kaiser, C. and Vendrik, M. C. M. (2019). Different Versions of the Easterlin Paradox: New Evidence for European Countries. In M. Rojas (ed.), *The Economics of Happiness: How the Easterlin Paradox Transformed Our Understanding of Well-Being and Progress*. Springer: Cham, pp. 27–55.

Kaiser, C. F. and Vendrik, M. C. M. (2021). *How Threatening Are Transformations of Happiness Scales to Subjective Wellbeing Research?* Mimeo Oxford University.

Kenny, C. (1999). Does Growth Cause Happiness, or Does Happiness Cause Growth? *Kyklos* 52(1): 3–26.

Kirman, A. (2010). *Complex Economics: Individual and Collective Rationality*. Routledge: New York.

Knight, J. and Gunatilaka, R. (2012). Income, Aspiration and the Hedonic Treadmill in a Poor Society. *Journal of Economic Behavior and Organization* 82(1): 67–81.

Knight, J., Song, L., and Gunatilaka, R. (2009). SWB and Its Determinants in Rural China. *China Economic Review* 20: 635–649.

Koutsoyiannis, A. (1979). *Modern Microeconomics*. Macmillan Education: New York.

Kronlund, M., Pool, V., Sialm, C., and Stefanesco, I. (2020). Out of Sight No More? The Effect of Fee Disclosures on 401K Investment Allocations. NBER Working Paper No. 27573. Available at www.nber.org/papers/w27573.

Kuhn, P., Kooreman, P., Soetevent, A., Kapteyn, A. (2011). The Effects of Lottery Prizes on Winners and Their Neighbors: Evidence from the Dutch Postcode Lottery. *American Economic Review* 101(5): 2226–2247.

Layard, R. (2003). Happiness: Has Social Science a Clue? Lionel Robbins Memorial Lectures 2002/3. Lecture given at the London School of Economics, London, March 3–5.

Layard, R. (2005). *Happiness: Lessons from a New Science*. Penguin Press: New York.

Layard, R., Clark, A. E., Cornaglia, F., Powdthavee, N., and Vernoit, J. (2014). What Predicts a Successful Life? A Life-Course Model of Wellbeing. *Economic Journal* 124(580): F720–F738.

Lewandowsky, S., Jetter, M., and Ecker, U. K. H. (2020). Using the President's Tweets to Understand Political Diversion in the Age of Social Media. *Nature Communications* 11(5764).

Lindgren, K. (1991). Evolutionary Phenomena in Simple Dynamics. In C. G. Langton, C. Taylor, J. D. Farmer, and S. Rasmussen (eds.), *Artificial Life II*. Addison-Wesley: Reading, CA, pp. 295–312.

List, J. A. (2004). Testing Neoclassical Competitive Theory in Multilateral Decentralized Markets. *Journal of Political Economy* 112(5): 1131–1156.

Loewenstein, G., O'Donoghue, T., and Rabin, M. (2003). Projection Bias in Predicting Future Utility. *Quarterly Journal of Economics* 118(4): 1209–1248.

Luce, R. D. (1959). *Individual Choice Behaviour*. Wiley: New York.

Luechinger, S., Meier, S., and Stutzer, A. (2010). Why Does Unemployment Hurt the Employed? Evidence from the Life Satisfaction Gap between the Public and the Private Sector. *Journal of Human Resources* 45(4): 998–1045.

Luttmer, E. (2005). Neighbors as Negatives: Relative Earnings and Wellbeing. *Quarterly Journal of Economics* 120(3): 963–1002.

Malmendier, U. and Tate, G. (2005). CEO Overconfidence and Corporate Investment. *Journal of Finance* 60(6): 2661–2700.

Malmendier, U. and Tate, G. (2008). Who Makes Acquisitions? CEO Overconfidence and the Market's Reaction. *Journal of Financial Economics* 89(1): 20–43.

Miao, C.-H. (2010). Consumer Myopia, Standardization and Aftermarket Monopolization. *European Economic Review* 54(7): 931–946.

Michel, C. (2017). Market Regulation of Voluntary Add-on Contracts. *International Journal of Industrial Organization* 54(C): 239–268.

Miller, R. M. (2008). Don't Let Your Robots Grow up to Be Traders: Artificial Intelligence, Human Intelligence, and Asset-Market Bubbles. *Journal of Economic Behavior & Organization* 68(1): 153–166.

Mitchell, M. (2009). *Complexity: A Guided Tour.* Oxford University Press: Oxford.

Mookherjee, D. and Sopher, B. (1994). Learning Behavior in an Experimental Matching Pennies Game. *Games and Economic Behavior* 7: 62–91.

Murooka, T. (2015). Deception under Competitive Intermediation. Working Paper.

Murooka, T. and Schwarz, M. A. (2018). The Timing of Choice Enhancing Policies. *Journal of Public Economics* 157(C): 27–40.

Myers, D. G. (2000). The Funds, Friends, and Faiths of Happy People. *American Psychologist* 55(1): 56–67.

Nelson, R. R. and Winter, S. G. (1982). *An Evolutionary Theory of Economic Change.* Harvard University Press: Cambridge, MA.

Nikolaev, B. (2014). Economic Freedom and Quality of Life: Evidence from the OECD's Your Better Life Index. *Journal of Private Enterprise* 29(3): 61–96.

OECD (2001). *The Well-Being of Nations: The Role of Human and Social Capital.* OECD Centre for Educational Research and Innovation: Paris.

Oswald, A. and Powdthavee, N. (2008). Does Happiness Adapt? A Longitudinal Study of Disability with Implications for Economists and Judges. *Journal of Public Economics* 92(56): 1061–1077.

Oswald, A., Proto, E., and Sgroi, D. (2015). Happiness and Productivity. *Journal of Labor Economics* 33(4): 789–822.

Piccione, M. and Spiegler, R. (2012). Price Competition under Limited Comparability. *Quarterly Journal of Economics* 127(1): 135–197.

Pigou, A. C. and Robertson, D. H. (1924). Those Empty Boxes. *Economic Journal* 34(133): 16–31.

Platt, S. R., Micciolo, R., and Tansella, M. (1992). Suicide and Unemployment in Italy: Description, Analysis and Interpretation of Recent Trends. *Social Science & Medicine* 34(11): 1191–1201.

Radner, R. (1992). Hierarchy: The Economics of Managing. *Journal of Economic Literature* 30: 1381–1415.

Radner, R. (1996). Bounded Rationality, Indeterminacy, and the Theory of the Firm. *The Economic Journal* 106(438): 1360–1373.

Rapoport, A., Seale, D. A., and Colman. A. M. (2015). Is Tit-for-Tat the Answer? On the Conclusions Drawn from Axelrod's Tournaments. *PLoS ONE* 10(7): 1–11.

Raschke, C. (2019). Unexpected Windfalls, Education, and Mental Health: Evidence from Lottery Winners in Germany. *Applied Economics* 51(2): 207–218.

Redelmeier, D. A. and Kahneman, D. (1996). Patients' Memories of Painful Medical Treatments: Real-time and Retrospective

Evaluations of Two Minimally Invasive Procedures. *Pain* 66(1): 3–8.

Rode, M., Knoll, B., and Pitlik, H. (2013). Economic Freedom, Democracy, and Life Satisfaction. In J. Gwartney, R. Lawson, and J. Hall (eds.), *Economic Freedom of the World: 2013 Annual Report*. Fraser Institute: Vancouver, pp. 215–233.

Roth, A. and Erev, I. (1995). Learning in Extensive-Form Games: Experimental Data and Simple Dynamic Models in the Intermediate Term. *Games and Economic Behavior* 8: 164–212.

Sacks, D. W., Stevenson, B., and Wolfers, J. (2013). Growth in Subjective Wellbeing and Income Over Time. Unpublished.

Sarin, N. (2019). Making Consumer Finance Work. *Columbia Law Review* 119(6): 1519–1596.

Sarracino, F., O'Connor, K. J., and Ono, H. (2019). Making Economic Growth and Well-Being Compatible: Evidence from Japan. Munich Personal RePEc Archive Working Paper No. 93010. https://mpra.ub.uni-muenchen.de/93010/.

Schröder, C. and Yitzhaki, S. (2017). Revisiting the Evidence for Cardinal Treatment of Ordinal Variables. *European Economic Review* 92: 337–358.

Sen, A. (1985). *Commodities and Capabilities.* North-Holland: Amsterdam.

Sen, A. (1992). *Inequality Reexamined.* Clarendon Press: Oxford.

Shubik, M. (2011). El Farol Revisited: A Note on Emergence, Game Theory, and Society. *Complexity* 16(6): 62–65.

Simon, H. A. (1955). A Behavioral Model of Rational Choice. *The Quarterly Journal of Economics* 69(1): 99–118.

Simon, H. A. (1957). *Models of Man*. Wiley: New York.

Smith, D., Loewenstein, G., Jepson, C., Jankovich, A., Feldman, H., and Ubel, P. (2008). Mispredicting and Misremembering: Patients with Renal Failure Overestimate Improvements in Quality of Life After a Kidney Transplant. *Health Psychology* 27(5): 653–658.

Smith, V. L. (1962). An Experimental Study of Competitive Market Behavior. *Journal of Political Economy* 70(2): 111–137.

Sousa-Poza, A. and Sousa-Poza, A. (2003). Gender Differences in Job Satisfaction in Great Britain, 1991–2000: Permanent or Transitory? *Applied Economics Letters* 10(11): 691–694.

Spiegler, R. (2006). The Market for Quacks. *Review of Economic Studies* 73(4): 1113–1131.

Spiegler, R. (2019). Behavioral Economics and the Atheoretical Style. *American Economic Journal: Microeconomics* 11(2): 173–194.

Stevenson, B. and Wolfers, J. (2013). Subjective Well-Being and Income: Is There Any Evidence of Satiation? *American Economic Review: Papers & Proceedings* 103(3): 598–604.

Stevenson, B. and Wolfers, L. (2008). Happiness Inequality in the United States. *Journal of Legal Studies* 37(S2): S33–S79.

Stevenson, B. and Wolfers, L. (2009). The Paradox of Declining Female Happiness. *American Economic Journal: Economic Policy* 1(2): 190–225.

Stroup, M. D. (2007). Economic Freedom, Democracy, and the Quality of Life. *World Development* 35(1): 52–66.

Studer, R. (2012). Does It Matter How Happiness Is Measured? Evidence from a Randomized Controlled Experiment. *Journal of Economic and Social Measurement* 37(4): 317–336.

Stutzer A. (2004). The Role of Income Aspirations in Individual Happiness. *Journal of Economic Behaviour and Organization* 54(1): 89–109.

Stutzer, A. and Frey, B. S. (2006). Does Marriage Make People Happy, or Do Happy People Get Married? *Journal of Socio-Economics* 35(2): 326–347.

Sullivan, M. W. (2017). Economic Analysis of Hotel Resort Fees. Economic Issues, Bureau of Economics Federal Trade Commission.

Suppes, P. and Atkinson, R. (1960). *Markov Learning Models for Multiperson Interactions*. Stanford University Press: Stanford, CA.

Tesfatsion, L. (2002). Agent-Based Computational Economics: Growing Economies from the Bottom up. *Articial Life* 8(1): 55–82.

Thaler, R. H. (2015). *Misbehaving: The Making of Behavioral Economics*. Norton: New York.

Thoits, P. and Hewitt, L. (2001). Volunteer Work and Well-Being. *Journal of Health and Social Behavior* 42(2): 115–131.

Thorndike, E. L. (1911). *Animal Intelligence*. Macmillan: New York.

Van Boening, M. V. and Wilcox, N. T. (1996). Avoidable Cost: Ride a Double Auction Roller Coaster. *American Economic Review*. 86(3): 461–477.

Van Praag, B. M. S. (1968). *Individual Welfare Functions and Consumer Behavior: A Theory of Rational Irrationality*. North-Holland: Amsterdam.

Van Praag, B. M. S. (1971). Individual Welfare Functions and Consumer Behavior: A Theory of Rational Irrationality. Dissertation, Contributions to Economic Analysis, No. 57. North-Holland Publishing Company: Amsterdam.

Van Praag, B. M. S. (1991). Ordinal and Cardinal Utility: An Integration of the Two Dimensions of the Welfare Concept. *Journal of Econometrics* 50(1–2): 69–89.

Van Praag, B. M. S. and Ferrer-i-Carbonell, A. (2011). Happiness Economics: A New Road to Measuring and Comparing Happiness. *Foundations and Trends in Microeconomics* 6(1): 1–97.

Varey, C. A. and Kahneman, D. (1992). Experiences Extended Across Time: Evaluation of Moments and Episodes. *Journal of Behavioral Decision Making* 5(3): 169–185.

Veblen, T. ([1899] 1973). *The Theory of the Leisure Class: An Economic Study of Institutions. Introduction John Kenneth Galbraith*. Houghton Mifflin: Boston, MA.

Veenhoven, R. (2000). Freedom and Happiness: A Comparative Study in 44 Nations in the Early 1990s. In E. Diener and E. M. Suh (eds.), *Culture and Subjective Wellbeing*. MIT Press: Cambridge, MA, pp. 257–288.

Veenhoven, R. (2020). *Distributional Findings on Happiness in Japan. World Database of Happiness.* Rotterdam: Erasmus University Rotterdam. https://worlddatabaseofhappiness.eur.nl.

Veenhoven, R. and Vergunst, F. (2013). The Easterlin Illusion: Economic Growth Does Go with Greater Happiness. EHERO working papers: Erasmus Happiness Economics Research Organization No. 2013/1.

Weiss, A., King, J., Inoue-Murayama, M., Matsuzawa, T., and Oswald, A. (2012). Evidence for a Midlife Crisis in Great Apes Consistent with the U-shape in Human Well-Being. *Proceedings of the National Academy of Sciences of the USA* 109(4): 19949–19952.

Winkelmann, L. and Winkelmann, R. (1998). Why Are the Unemployed So Unhappy? Evidence from Panel Data. *Economica* 65(257): 1–15.

Wolfers, J. (2003). Is Business Cycle Volatility Costly? Evidence from Surveys of Subjective Well-Being. *International Finance* 6(1): 1–26.

12 Behavioral Welfare Economics

12.1 Introduction

This chapter is an introduction to behavioral welfare economics. We begin in Section 12.2 by outlining the basics of neoclassical welfare economics. The essential idea is that individuals make considered, deliberate, choices that are in their own long-term interests. Optimal public policy is then based on the idea of liberalism and respect for individual choice. However, issues of conflict between equity and efficiency, and the presence of externalities, allow for various forms of *hard paternalism* in neoclassical public policy. Examples include taxes, subsidies, regulation, mandates, and bans that are justified on grounds of equity and efficiency conflicts; the presence of externalities; fairness; and merit goods.

Section 12.3 considers the behavioral evidence on the neoclassical assumptions made in Section 12.2 and makes a case for a degree of paternalism in policies. Section 12.4 considers alternative forms of paternalism in neoclassical and behavioral economics. In particular, we consider an intertemporal problem with current benefits and future costs and demonstrate the application of each of the paternalistic policies for this problem.

An important framework for thinking about behavioral policy is *libertarian paternalism*, which manifests in the practical form of *nudges* in popular discourse. This is a form of paternalism that falls under the umbrella term of *soft paternalism*. The basic idea is to minimally constrain the choices of the rational types that populate neoclassical welfare economics, but impart significant welfare improvements for the behavioral types that populate behavioral economics models. We introduce this framework in Section 12.4 and undertake a more detailed study of it in Section 12.5 that considers the inevitability of some degree of paternalism and the inevitability of *choice architects* in any decision. We also consider the difficulty of formalizing the *informed desire criteria*, but argue that this is not fatal for demonstrating the positive effects on welfare that arise from actually observed policy nudges. Section 12.6 considers another form of soft paternalism known as *asymmetric paternalism* that is based on a cost-benefit analysis of the effects of public policy.

Section 12.7 considers another variant of soft paternalism known as light paternalism that is based on the dominance and self-officiating criteria. Section 12.8 evaluates criticisms of soft paternalism. We show that many of these criticisms are generic and apply with equal force to neoclassical welfare economics, and to any form of public policy. We also evaluate the criticisms that are based on the *contractarian approach*.

Sections 12.9 and 12.10 consider two applications of the concepts. In Section 12.9, we consider the problem of designing optimal taxes on *sin goods*. These are goods that result in current benefits but future costs, such as excessive smoking or alcohol consumption, and consuming drugs. Section 12.10 contains a discussion of the emerging field of behavioral public economics. No prior knowledge of public economics is required, as our discussion is self contained. In particular, we focus on the effects of limited attention and bounded rationality on *tax efficiency* and *tax incidence*. We also discuss the problem of *optimal sugar taxes*.

12.2 The Basics of Neoclassical Welfare Economics

In neoclassical welfare economics, the underlying preferences of an individual are the primitives on which the individual choices are based. External observers do not observe the underlying preferences, but they can infer preferences from the observed choices. For instance, an individual might choose an electric car over a diesel car that costs a similar amount of money and has similar features. An external observer might infer that the individual prefers relatively environmentally friendly cars.

In this book, we have described how individual preferences lead to observed choices in several domains. For instance, in Part I, we showed how an individual's preferences over lotteries leads to an expected utility representation. The choice of the individual can then be found by maximizing the expected utility functional. In Part III of the book, we showed how an individual's time preferences lead to an exponential discounted utility representation of preferences. The individual's choice can then be found by maximizing the exponential discounted utility function.

In the cases considered above, the data on choice also reveals the underlying preferences. Thus, the nonobservability of underlying preferences poses no hindrance for welfare analysis. The *theory of revealed preference* ensures that preferences can be recovered from underlying choices (Samuelson, 1948; Houthakker, 1950; Afriat, 1967). Suppose that we do not know an individual's underlying preferences, or utility function. So, we also do not know if the individual maximizes a utility function. An individual who maximizes a utility function can be thought of as maximizing their well-being in the sense that they are the best judge of their own welfare. We do not, however, typically observe a utility function. What we observe is data on the prices, and the quantities that consumers buy at those prices, that is, the choice data of the individual. So how can we be sure, based on the choice data, that the consumer maximizes some well-defined utility function? The answer comes from *revealed preference analysis*.

Suppose that an individual has income I and consumes two goods, x and y, that sell for the respective prices p_x and p_y per unit. The budget constraint of the individual is

$$xp_x + yp_y \leq I. \tag{12.1}$$

Suppose that the following two bundles of goods are available, (x_1, y_1), (x_2, y_2). The individual chooses the bundle (x_1, y_1) at the prices p_x, p_y and income I. In this case, we say that the bundle (x_1, y_1) is "directly revealed preferred" to the bundle (x_2, y_2), and we write this as

$$(x_1, y_1)R^d(x_2, y_2).$$

In other words, the bundle (x_2, y_2) was affordable, yet the decision maker revealed through their choice that they prefer the bundle (x_1, y_1). Suppose that we knew for a fact that the individual makes choices in order to maximize a utility function u. Then, we can also write

$$u(x_1, y_1) \geq u(x_2, y_2).$$

But, of course, we might not know that the choices maximize utility, and we wish to infer if they do so. Suppose that we have a sequence of bundles (x_1, y_1), (x_2, y_2),...,(x_n, y_n) and by varying prices and incomes, we establish the following chain of preferences

$$(x_1, y_1)R^d(x_2, y_2); (x_2, y_2)R^d(x_3, y_3); \ldots; (x_{n-1}, y_{n-1})R^d(x_n, y_n).$$

Then, we say that the bundle (x_1, y_1) is revealed preferred to the bundle (x_n, y_n) and we write this as

$$(x_1, y_1)R(x_n, y_n). \tag{12.2}$$

Suppose we assume that the underlying utility function of the individual satisfies local non-satiation. This property implies that if we give the individual a greater quantity of any good, the individual's utility increases. In this case, if

$$x_1 p_x + y_1 p_y > x_n p_x + y_n p_y, \tag{12.3}$$

then we can show that (12.2) and (12.3) together imply that

$$u(x_1, y_1) > u(x_n, y_n). \tag{12.4}$$

In this case, we say that the bundle (x_1, y_1) is "strictly directly revealed preferred" to the bundle (x_n, y_n) and we write this as

$$(x_1, y_1)R^{sd}(x_n, y_n).$$

To prove the assertion above, suppose that (12.3) holds and in contravention of (12.4) $u(x_1, y_1) = u(x_n, y_n)$, where (x_1, y_1) is the utility maximizing bundle. We now derive a contradiction. We can find feasible bundle, say, (x_0, y_0), such that $x_0 = x_n + \varepsilon$ and $y_0 = y_n + \varepsilon$, where $\varepsilon > 0$ is a very small number. Local nonsatiation then implies that $u(x_0, y_0) > u(x_n, y_n)$. But this contradicts the initial choice of (x_1, y_1) as the utility maximizing bundle. Hence, the only possibility is that $u(x_1, y_1) > u(x_n, y_n)$, which is given in (12.4).

The main result in revealed preference theory is the *generalized axiom of revealed preference* (GARP) that we state next.

Definition 12.1 *Suppose that the bundle (x_1, y_1) is revealed preferred to the bundle (x_n, y_n), that is, $(x_1, y_1)R(x_n, y_n)$. Then, it can never be the case that (x_n, y_n) is strictly directly revealed preferred to (x_1, y_1), that is, it cannot be the case that $(x_n, y_n)R^{sd}(x_1, y_1)$.*

It can be shown that GARP is a sufficient condition for utility maximization. In other words, if an individual's choices satisfy GARP then the individual must maximize some underlying utility function. In this sense, the actual choices of individuals reflect a *considered judgment* that maximizes the *individual's welfare*. This is the key assumption in neoclassical welfare economics that is relevant for us and such preferences are also known as *normative preferences*. We now describe some basic elements of analysis in neoclassical welfare economics.

A social planner can be completely liberal, taking as given an individual's choice and respecting it in designing policy. When policy needs to be designed for many individuals, who are heterogeneous with respect to their preferences and choices, then the social planner needs to take into account *equity* and *efficiency* considerations. For instance, in a society with rich and poor individuals, the social planner might design redistributive taxes that transfer some of the wealth from the rich to the poor (equity); but ensure that the redistributive taxes do not overly reduce the motivation of the rich to work more and generate more wealth (efficiency). Several social objective functions that take account of such equity and efficiency considerations have been proposed in the literature.

In neoclassical economics, policy interventions to alter individual behavior are sometimes justified on account of externalities (Atkinson and Stiglitz, 1980; Stiglitz, 2000). Individuals or firms might cause *negative externalities* for others, for instance, individuals exposed to passive smoking; or a firm discharging harmful pollutants into the atmosphere. In these cases, the actions that cause the externality may need to be "reduced" through economic incentives, such as Pigouvian taxes (see Part II of the book), or through regulation. Optimal public policy needs to take account of the marginal costs and marginal benefits of externality reduction. Hence, it is often not optimal to completely eliminate negative externalities. Thus, Pigouvian taxes on pollutants discharged into the atmosphere might be used to incentivize firms to reduce pollution, but at their optimal levels, often do not eliminate pollution altogether.

Car drivers might be required to purchase mandatory car insurance. They might also be required to get a mandatory car check to certify that the car is roadworthy, before being legally allowed to drive. These are examples of regulation on consumers. Under complete certainty, regulation and Pigouvian taxes produce identical outcomes. However, under uncertainty, the source of uncertainty might determine which of the two policy options is preferred (Weitzman, 1974, 2011). Regulation and Pigouvian taxes are mandatory restrictions on the actions taken by individual entities, hence, this form of paternalism is sometimes referred to as *heavy-handed paternalism* (Loewenstein and Haisley, 2008).

12.3 Behavioral Evidence and the Implications for Welfare Economics

Neoclassical welfare economics justifies several regulatory responses on grounds of *merit goods*. These are regulations that, in the social planner's view, merit active consideration by individuals. Examples include mandatory seat belts; mandatory helmets for two-wheeler drivers; certificates of roadworthiness of vehicles; warnings on cigarette packs; public advice on the number of daily portions of fruits and vegetables; government recommendations on the number of drinks one could have before driving; mandatory cooling-off periods for consumer purchases and for divorce applications; and in some countries, mandatory primary education for children.

How does one justify these policy interventions in a neoclassical framework? After all, people are the best judges of their actions (liberalism) and they make *considered judgments*, having considered all the benefits and costs. The typical response in neoclassical welfare economics would be that people are not sufficiently aware of the costs and benefits of their actions, and/or of the risks that they face. But, if this is the case, then the solution is not necessarily regulation.

Since people are assumed to be unboundedly rational and fully attentive in neoclassical economics, they could be provided with the relevant information, which will serve to align their actions with those that are achieved through regulation.

An alternative rationale for such regulation, which is a form of paternalism, arises for factors highlighted in behavioral economics, but not entertained within neoclassical welfare economics. Perhaps the assumption that individuals are able to make considered judgments of their own welfare is too strong. Traditionally, neoclassical economists have shied away from paternalism – a term that is sometimes used in a pejorative sense in economics. However, as Jolls et al. (1998, p. 1545) note in their *anti-antipaternalistic approach*: "No axiom demonstrates that people make choices that serve their best interests; this is a question to be answered based on evidence."

The evidence from behavioral economics suggests that individuals may not always make decisions that are in their considered best interests. Part V of the book on bounded rationality, in particular, and other parts of the book, have summarized evidence which showed that people use simple rules of thumb in making decisions; they suffer from limited attention, limited memory, and limited cognition; they often conform to simple mental models, from cognitive limitations or from the desire to conform to the mental models of their group; they often make decisions based on social norms and social identity concerns that might not always be optimal or rational in a neoclassical sense; they might be myopic, taking account of only a short horizon in making decisions; people might make important decisions in a "hot" state of the mind that they regret later; people might be excessively present-focused and save inadequately for retirement, or procrastinate in making important decisions.

The cumulative evidence on these, and other factors, is now so large that the idea that people always make considered judgments of their own welfare does, and should, appear to be a very strong assumption. In some cases, people seek professional help to shed undesirable habits; invest in reading self-help and cognitive behavioral therapy (CBT) books; prefer the median portfolio to the one that they have chosen (e.g., because it is based on the use of a suboptimal $\frac{1}{n}$ heuristic); self-report that they would like to save more or give more to charity (Camerer et al., 2003; Beshears et al., 2008); or make New Year resolutions that are often broken, sometimes systematically.

Thus, it would appear that there is a deep wedge between one's underlying normative preferences, and the choices that one exhibits. Suppose that we grant that an individual has underlying normative preferences that can somehow be discovered if we switched off all possible behavioral channels relative to the neoclassical benchmark. But it is unclear how we can determine the relative contributions of normative and behavioral preferences to actual choices. Hence, there is no presumption that observed choices solely reflect underlying normative preferences. There is one of two possible routes that one could then follow.

1. Use choice data: Try to reconstruct underlying normative preferences from given choice data by purging the effects of behavioral factors. There is already a great deal of literature in this area, but its practical usefulness, as distinct from its theoretical contribution, has not yet been established. The basic idea is to trim down choices by eliminating the "problematic choices" to somehow reconstruct normative preferences. Trimming down problematic choices requires other welfare criteria that justify such trimming down, precisely the problem that we were trying to avoid in the first place.

2. Use preference-based welfare criteria: The basic idea is to use stated preferences in an "ideal state" to design policies even if the choices of the individual are not consistent with the stated preferences. This may seem quite hard to satisfy in the abstract but may make surprising sense when individual case studies are considered. Consider, for instance, the following quote from Loewenstein and Haisley (2008, p. 223) which makes a strong case for this approach:

> Our own opinion is that the welfare criterion for evaluating paternalistic policies should be based on preference. Much as a psychotherapist would likely take at face value a client's professed desire to become happier, more sociable, or less anxious, even if she engaged in patterns of thinking and behavior that led to the opposite result, we would argue that the economist-as-therapist should treat verbal statements of preference as useful information, even if choice is not in line with professed preference. If people express a desire to lose weight but make choices that cause them to gain weight; if they express a desire to be financially solvent, but make choices that lead to burdensome debt; if they want to stop smoking but continue to smoke; if they want to take prescription medications but fail to do so, these are all situations in which paternalistic interventions could be helpful.

The discussion above indicates that welfare economics in the presence of behavioral insights and evidence, a field known as *behavioral welfare economics*, is incredibly difficult. This is a world away from the sanitized framework of neoclassical welfare economics. Most practical applications of these ideas have come through the framework of *libertarian paternalism* to alter behavior. This has also captured the public's imagination, through various well-designed nudges, although it has also invited criticism from several quarters within and outside economics. We shall consider this idea in some depth below.

12.4 Alternative Forms of Paternalism

Suppose that the government, or a social planner, is concerned about the rising incidence of cigarette smoking in society and its burden on publicly provided healthcare (e.g., the NHS in Britain). The government wishes to reduce the incidence of smoking through public policy. We can distinguish between three alternative forms of paternalism to deal with this specific problem.

1. *Direct paternalism*: Direct paternalism arises when a third party directly determines individual actions through regulation. For instance, the government may ban the sale of cigarettes, particularly to vulnerable groups, say, those below the age of 16. Other examples of direct paternalism include mandatory seat belts in cars; ban on using mobile phones while driving; setting a minimum age for driving cars; requiring a successful driving test before one is allowed to legally drive; and mandatory car insurance.
2. *Indirect paternalism*: Under indirect paternalism, the government alters the economic incentives to taking actions, typically by levying taxes and subsidies, that alter relative prices. For instance, the government may increase the tax on cigarettes in order to reduce consumption. Other examples of indirect paternalism include levying road taxes on cars in proportion to their CO_2 emissions; subsidies on charitable giving; subsidies to buy electric vehicles; and taxes on sugary drinks.
3. *Libertarian paternalism or soft paternalism*: This form of paternalism recognizes that there are potentially two kinds of decision makers. Those who, like the economic actors in neoclassical

economics, always chose rationally – the *rational types*.[1] Such individuals are predicted, in neoclassical economics, to make a rational decision to smoke after carefully calculating the present discounted value of all the future marginal benefits and costs (Becker and Murphy, 1988). The evidence shows that most people do not in fact choose to smoke in this manner. They might initially get into a smoking habit due to peer group effects; or due to an inadequate appreciation of all the future health costs; or they might start smoking in a state of depression; or simply because someone in the family or close network smoked on a regular basis. Libertarian paternalism is directed mainly at this second group of people, who we might refer to as the *behavioral types*.

The aim of libertarian paternalistic policy is to minimally distort the behavior of the rational types or, even better, leave their behavior unchanged. However, such a policy aims to

(i) alter the behavior of the behavioral types in a manner that is consistent with their long-term best interests, as determined by their own underlying normative preferences, and
(ii) allow for voluntary choice by all individuals.

The content of (i) lies at the heart of the debate between the proponents and the critics of libertarian paternalism. We come back to the issues raised by the critics a bit later. One possible libertarian paternalistic policy is a graphic warning on cigarette packs about its health consequences. This policy is libertarian paternalistic because it should not, in principal, have an effect on the rational types who have already taken account of all benefits and costs, but it might "nudge" the behavioral types into reconsidering their decision to smoke. Yet, the behavioral types are, in principle, free to choose to smoke if they wish to; there is no mandate or ban on their behavior. This is the sense in which the policy respects individual liberty. But at the same time, it also provides information on the harmful consequences of smoking; in this sense it is paternalistic. Hence, *libertarian paternalism* is not an oxymoron, which is the title of the paper by Sunstein and Thaler (2003); see also Thaler and Sunstein (2003, 2009).

In order to contrast this sort of intervention with hard paternalism under neoclassical welfare economics, we may refer to it as *soft paternalism* which is an umbrella term for several non-coercive forms of paternalism including libertarian paternalism (Loewenstein and Haisley, 2008). *Default options* are a leading example of soft paternalism in which changing a default is nearly costless, at least in principle, because it requires one to tick the relevant box. For instance, in the context of a default option for pension plans, this specifies whether one is automatically enrolled, or not, in a pension plan.

In order to fix ideas, consider the following example. One of the problems asks you to solve a numerical problem based on this example.

Suppose that a decision maker can do an activity that has *current benefits and future costs*; we have considered such problems in Part III. Examples include smoking, drinking, having a late night out, and excessive consumer spending financed with debt or with mortgage payments. Suppose that the current benefit of an action is $v > 0$, but the future cost of the action is $c > v$.

[1] We use the term "rational" in the sense that we have defined rationality in this book. This requires consistency with various axioms of rationality, described in several parts of the book.

The reader may wish to think of the benefit v as the "consumer surplus" from the consumption of the good and c as any of the future costs such as health costs, or the opportunity cost of foregone earnings/reputation.

The individual has quasi-hyperbolic preferences and uses the $(\beta, 1)$ model, where $0 < \beta < 1$ (see Part III for details). In the absence of any intervention by a third party, the individual engages in the activity if

$$v - \beta c \geq 0 \Leftrightarrow \beta \leq \beta^* \equiv \frac{v}{c} < 1, \tag{12.5}$$

otherwise the individual does not do the activity. Thus, if the individual's present-focus is high enough in the sense that $\beta \leq \beta^*$ then the individual engages in the action.

By contrast, an individual who follows the exponential discounted utility model in neoclassical economics has $\beta = 1$ (see Part III). Hence, such an individual will only do the activity if

$$v - c \geq 0 \Leftrightarrow v \geq c, \tag{12.6}$$

which is false because $c > v$. Thus, the individual will never engage in this activity.

Let us now consider the outcome under various forms of paternalism described above.

1. Direct paternalism: The only two actions available to the decision maker are to either do the activity or not to do it. Under direct paternalism, a policymaker can ban the activity altogether if it is not deemed in the social interest. For instance, the government bans several kinds of drugs or allows their consumption only for medicinal purposes, for example, the use of cannabis in the UK for certain health conditions. If (12.5) holds, then the decision maker finds it privately optimal to engage in the activity but the policymaker may find it in the social interest to ban it.
2. Indirect paternalism: This takes the form of altering the economic incentives to undertake the activity. If the policymaker wishes to reduce the incidence of the activity, then such a policy may take the form of taxing the current benefits from the good (as, say, in the form of a cigarette tax). Suppose that the government imposes a tax $0 < t < 1$ on the activity, so that the after-tax benefits from the good are now $(1 - t)v$. In the presence of taxes, the individual engages in the activity if

$$(1 - t)v - \beta c \geq 0 \Leftrightarrow \beta \leq \beta^{**} \equiv \frac{(1 - t)v}{c} < 1, \tag{12.7}$$

otherwise the decision maker does not do the activity. Since $\frac{(1-t)v}{c} < \frac{v}{c}$, so from (12.5), (12.7), $\beta^{**} < \beta^*$. Thus, a tax on the activity reduces the likelihood that the activity is undertaken.
3. Libertarian paternalism: The graphic displays on cigarette packaging are typically justified on the grounds that they raise awareness among people on the future costs of smoking. Several other public campaigns to raise awareness about the costs of a potentially harmful activity have resulted in a reduction in the relevant activity, for example, campaigns by the UK and the US governments to raise awareness about teenage pregnancy rates. In other cases, the government requires producers to provide detailed nutritional and calorie information on food labels. In the spirit of soft paternalism, such policies ought to have no influence on the actions of the rational types (those with $\beta = 1$) who do not engage in the activity; see (12.6). However, it may "nudge" the behavioral types to take better account of the costs of their actions, perhaps by focusing their limited attention on these costs.

Suppose that the effect of such policies is to reduce the extent of present-focus of the behavioral types, that is, these policies lead to an increase in β to a new, and higher, value $\widetilde{\beta}$. For pedagogical simplicity, we assume that this increases the value of β by a factor of $\gamma > 1$, that is,

$$\beta < \widetilde{\beta} = \gamma\beta < 1; \gamma > 1.$$

The new value, $\widetilde{\beta}$, is less than 1 as required in quasi-hyperbolic discounting. Once the libertarian paternalistic policy is implemented, the decision maker engages in the activity if

$$v - \gamma\beta c \geq 0 \Leftrightarrow \beta \leq \widetilde{\beta}^* \equiv \frac{v}{\gamma c} < 1, \tag{12.8}$$

otherwise they do not. In effect, the graphic warnings on cigarette packaging serve to induce individuals to take better account of the future costs of smoking. Since $\frac{v}{\gamma c} < \frac{v}{c}$, hence, from (12.5), (12.8), we have $\widetilde{\beta}^* < \beta^*$. Thus, behavioral types who are faced with a libertarian paternalistic policy are less likely to engage in the action. For instance, if

$$\frac{v}{\gamma c} < \beta < \frac{v}{c}, \tag{12.9}$$

then the decision maker engages in the activity in the absence of the libertarian paternalistic policy (this follows from (12.5)) but does not engage in the activity in the presence of the policy (this follows from (12.8)).

4. Comparison of the policies: From a comparison of (12.7) and (12.8) it may appear that indirect paternalism and libertarian paternalism lead to identical welfare effects if $1 - t = \frac{1}{\gamma}$, or if the tax rate is chosen so that

$$t = \frac{\gamma - 1}{\gamma} > 0.$$

However, taxes may lead to *deadweight or efficiency losses* when there is the possibility of substituting between activities. Levying and collecting taxes also requires substantial administrative costs. By contrast, the efficiency and administrative costs are minimal for libertarian paternalistic policies, which is likely to tip the balance in their favor. Suppose that the condition in (12.9) holds. Then, is a policy of banning the activity (direct paternalism) not equivalent to a libertarian paternalistic policy? After all they both succeed in preventing the activity. This is not necessarily true. The reason is that banning activities often drives them underground leading to the emergence of black markets. The extra expenditure on policing black markets and enforcing the ban, and the costs of secrecy incurred by individuals, need to be factored into the success of a policy that imposes bans. By contrast, libertarian paternalism is not subject to these costs and may, hence, dominate the other policies.

12.5 Libertarian Paternalism

We have already outlined the proposal for libertarian paternalism, above. Thaler and Sunstein (2009) invite us to imagine a *planner* or a *choice architect* whose brief is to decide on a menu of options that are to be presented to an individual. In choosing the options, the choice architect makes a judgment about what options are in the best interests of the individual, as judged by the individual, if one could somehow tap into the individual's underlying normative preferences.

12.5.1 The Informed Desire Criterion

The need for the choice architect arises because there is considerable behavioral noise in the mapping from normative preferences into choices, for the reasons that we have considered above. Hence, in making choices, individuals might not be acting in their best long-term interests. Individuals do not act in their best interests if (Sunstein and Thaler, 2003, p. 1162): "they make decisions that they would change if they had complete information, unlimited cognitive abilities, and no lack of self-control."

Figuring out "best interest" is not an easy task and critics such as Sugden (2008, 2013) who term this as the *informed desire criterion*, have taken issue with it. Thaler and Sunstein would operationalize the informed desire criterion by having the choice architect use a cost–benefit analysis, or employ insights from psychology to filter out the noise from actual choices to arrive at normative preferences. Insofar as policy options such as defaults are, at least in principle, easy to override, the choice architect may experiment with such policy options in figuring out the underlying normative preferences. Advances in neuroeconomics might provide another avenue for the choice architect to uncover normative preferences.

It is not possible, at the moment, to offer a theoretical or empirical defense of the informed desire criterion that is watertight. However, in many cases of profound practical interest, the informed desire criterion has the potential to improve human lives. Consider the following examples.

Example 12.14 *The English footballer, Paul Gascoigne, rated by many to be the most creative footballer of his generation, has suffered from a well-publicized and long-running battle with alcohol addiction. This has led to embarrassing public displays of unexpected behavior, repeated check-ins into expensive rehab centers, deleterious effects on his personal relations with friends and family, emotional and mental issues, and even jail and suicide attempts. Indeed, several of Gascoigne's close mentors have played the roles of the choice architect at various points in his life. In 1998, his football manager Bryan Robson signed him into a well-known addiction clinic, the Priory Hospital, after Gascoigne became unconscious from a bout of drinking (reportedly, 32 shots of whisky). A similar intervention was made by the Everton FC chairman Bill Kenwright in 2001. Several such subsequent interventions were made on his behalf. In an interview on BBC Radio 5 Live in 2013, his agent, Terry Baker said: "He won't thank me for saying it but he immediately needs to get help … His life is always in danger because he is an alcoholic. Maybe no one can save him – I don't know. I really don't know."*

It would be absurd if from the observed choices we were to conclude that Gascoigne's normative preferences were to continue to suffer the repeated life-destroying bouts with alcohol addiction. Indeed, if Gascoigne were to be asked to state his considered judgment, in an emotionally cold state, when sober, on whether he would prefer to continue to suffer, he is most likely to say no. It would also be absurd if one had used the critic's argument to approach Bryan Robson and Bill Kenwright, who played the role of choice architects at critical moments, and advised them against offering options to Gascoigne on the grounds that economists cannot fully formalize the informed desire criterion.

Example 12.15 *Jim and his wife Alice fell on hard times after Jim, the only bread winner in the family, lost his job. They had meagre savings which soon ran out, and young children to feed. In desperation, and hopeful that Jim would get another job, they seek out a payday loan. In their poverty, and in their anxiety, they suffer from the problem of low bandwidth (see Part V of the book) and do not fully appreciate the astronomical interest rate charged on the loans, perhaps because the payments expressed in dollars per day. In the event, the Covid slowdown hits hard and Jim is unable to find a job. The loan is unpaid, and Jim needs to borrow even more money to (i) refinance the loan, and to (ii) tide them over for the next few weeks. This gets Jim into a downward spiral of debt from which he finds it hard to extricate himself, and he feels suicidal. It will be absurd to argue that Jim has normative preferences for making expensive payday borrowings and get into a downward spiral of debt. It would also be absurd to invoke the lack of formalism around the informed consent criterion to argue that choice architects (i) should not push for more clarity into the terms on which payday loans are offered, and (ii) should not push for more welfare support for people in Jim and Alice's position.*

Clearly, one can come up with an infinite number of such examples where the role of the choice architect is critical in potentially improving human welfare. One could also come up with examples where the informed consent criterion places us in a grey area. Consider, for instance, the following example.

Example 12.16 *(Sugden, 2017) Bill eats unhealthily and is obese, but he suffers no symptoms of ill health. However, he could suffer a potentially deadly heart attack at a future date. He must have been exposed to public information, warning of the potential consequences of unhealthy eating. Yet he continues to eat unhealthily. Should we interpret his behavior as an error or mistake that needs to be nudged? Would Bill wish to be nudged and would it be the best course of action as judged by Bill, to be in his best interest?*

Sugden is not against nudging per se, but he would take issue with the inference that we can conclude anything about informed desire from this example. The arguments and fears expressed against libertarian paternalism often come from abstract reasoning. The actual track record of applications of libertarian paternalism would appear to be welfare improving to many. However, the debate between Sugden (2017) and Sunstein (2018) suggests that there is a need to differentiate between two cases where the individual has well-defined normative preferences; and when the individual does not have well-defined normative preferences.

Consider first the following examples from Sunstein (2018, pp. 3–4), where the individual appears to have well-defined normative preferences. In these cases the policy interventions would appear to be consistent with the informed desire criterion.

1. Luke has heart disease, and he needs to take various medications. He wants to do so, but he is sometimes forgetful which could create potential health complications. His doctor sends him periodic text messages. As a result, he takes the medications. He is very glad to receive those messages.

2. Meredith has a mild weight problem. She is aware of that fact, and while she does not suffer from serious issues of self-control, and does not want to stop eating the foods that she enjoys, she does seek to lose weight. Because of a new law, many restaurants in her city have clear calorie labels, informing her of the caloric content of various options. As a result, she sometimes chooses low-calorie offerings – which she would not do if she were not informed. She is losing weight. She is very glad to see those calorie labels.
3. Edna is a professor at a large university, which has long offered its employees the option to sign up for a retirement plan. Edna believes that signing up would be a terrific idea, but she has not gotten around to it. She is somewhat embarrassed about that. Last year, the university switched to an automatic enrollment plan, by which employees are defaulted into the university's plan. They are allowed to opt out, but Edna does not. She is very glad that she has been automatically enrolled in the plan.

However, the informed desire criterion is less persuasive, by definition, when the individual might not have either well-defined normative preferences, or the normative preferences themselves are guided by the information provided in a nudge. Consider the following two examples from Sunstein (2018).

Example 12.17 *Thomas has a serious illness. The question is whether he should have an operation, which is accompanied by potential benefits and potential risks. Reading about the operation online, Thomas is not sure whether he should go ahead with it. Thomas' doctor advises him to have the operation, emphasizing how much he has to lose if he does not. He decides to follow the advice. In a parallel world (a lot like ours, but not quite identical), Thomas' doctor advises him not to have the operation, emphasizing how much he has to lose if he does. He decides to follow the advice.*

Example 12.18 *George cares about the environment, but he also cares about money. He currently receives his electricity from coal; he knows that coal is not exactly good for the environment, but it is cheap, and he does not bother to switch to wind, which would be slightly more expensive. He is quite content with the current situation. Last month, his government imposed an automatic enrollment rule on electricity providers: People will receive energy from wind, and pay a slight premium, unless they choose to switch. George does not bother to switch. He says that he likes the current situation of automatic enrollment. He approves of the policy and he approves of his own enrollment.*

Thomas appears to have no true underlying normative preferences about whether to have an operation or not. In two separate worlds, he follows two opposite bits of advice. Ex-post, it is likely that he might be equally happy in both scenarios. Suppose that in the first scenario Thomas is on the way to the operating theater, having accepted the earlier advice. However, the doctor stops him on the way and says that after consulting another specialist, and having reconsidered, it would be best after all for Thomas not to have the operation. It is quite conceivable that Thomas might have been equally happy ex-post in this case too, having never had a chance to experience the counterfactual. The nudge in this case, a nonbinding piece of advice from a doctor, cannot be said to be catering to Thomas' underlying informed consent criterion.

From the information given in the second example, it is not clear if George has underlying normative preferences for a cleaner environment or not.

12.5.2 Choice Architects

As hinted in Example 12.14, many types of individuals fit the description of choice architects. We give further examples. An accountant might advise a client on several alternative legal methods to reduce tax payments. A personal gym instructor hired by an individual might design alternative exercise plans for the individual to choose from. A dietitian might design alternative diet plans for a patient with low weight. Doctors advise patients on treatment alternatives with different pros and cons. An architect provides a client with alternative house designs.

In each case, the advice is likely to be based on what the advisor feels is in the best normative interests of the advisee, leaving the advisee to choose an alternative. The strict definition of a choice architect requires that (Thaler and Sunstein, 2009, ch. 5):

1. The interventions are designed to make individuals better off, *as judged by themselves*, and
2. the freedom of choice of individuals is not unduly compromised.

We may take the choices offered by the choice architect as the definition of a *nudge.*

Example 12.19 *We observe choice architecture around us all the time. For instance, the design of different nozzles for dispensing diesel and petrol fuel; cash machines that require cash to be collected before the card can be collected; beeping sound in cars if the driver is not wearing a seat belt; automatic electric switches that switch lights off if they do not detect any movement in the room for a length of time; various default options for savings plans, pension plans, and organ donation; color coded labels on supermarket food; bans on cigarette advertisements and warning labels on cigarette packs; regulations on the display of pricing information in supermarkets that requires quoting the price per standard unit, for example, per 100 grams or per liter; and bank and financial markets regulations on the provision of APR rates to borrowers.*

12.5.3 Two Misconceptions in Neoclassical Welfare Economics

Sunstein and Thaler (2003, p. 1163) highlight two widespread misconceptions in neoclassical welfare economics, the recognition of which is essential to appreciating the power of their own proposed framework.

1. Is there a viable alternative to paternalism?
   In neoclassical economics, which is built on the principles of liberalism, the answer is unambiguously: Yes. However, paternalism in the sense of advice given by a choice architect is ubiquitous in human life. Almost every choice that is offered to us is framed be someone else. Our normative preferences on beauty are often shaped by the models, actors, and brand ambassadors for some of the leading brands. These in turn are often determined by large advertisement firms. Our normative preferences for mobile phones are determined by the menu of options created by phone developers and software designers. Our normative preferences for filling in tax returns (or our dislike for them) is determined by the existing design of the tax forms. Our appreciation for building architecture is often determined by the existing menu of architectural designs available. The notion that we have normative

preferences independent of the actions of choice architects can be difficult to justify. Thus, some paternalism is always implicit in most human choice.

2. Does paternalism necessarily involve coercion?
   The view in neoclassical economics is that paternalism is coercive. However, paternalism need not be coercive; for instance, it is not coercive under libertarian paternalism. Under libertarian paternalism, the choice architect makes a suggestion, a frame, or a design, to individuals, but respects individual freedom in making the final choice. A literature in Law and Economics, and in the economics of contracts, views paternalism with suspicion on account of "regulatory capture" of institutions by firms and their lobbies; and the bounded rationality of bureaucrats (Posner, 1986; Laffont and Tirole, 1993). The force of these arguments applies equally to neoclassical welfare economics and behavioral welfare economics and is not central to the debate between the two.

If the two misconceptions are accepted, then Thaler and Sunstein (2003, p. 175) conclude that: "we can abandon the less interesting question of whether to be paternalistic or not and turn to the more constructive question of how to choose among paternalistic options." Consider the following cafeteria example.

Example 12.20 *(The cafeteria example; Sunstein and Thaler, 2003) The "cafeteria example" is useful to illustrate some of the central ideas in libertarian paternalism. Supermarkets spend a lot of time planning about the arrangement of food items (a form of framing) and alternative arrangements appear to have a significant effect on consumer choices. People appear more likely to choose items that are placed at "eye level" or pick tempting snacks placed near the checkout counters. Suppose that a cafeteria manager has the following options in deciding on the arrangement of food items in the store:*

1. *She could make choices that she thinks would make the customers best off, all things considered.*
2. *She could make choices at random.*
3. *She could choose those items that she thinks would make the customers as obese as possible.*
4. *She could give customers what she thinks they would choose on their own.*

Someone who is a thorough "anti-paternalist" must choose option 4. But this requires information on what would consumers choose on their own, which is not available. As noted above, normative preferences may themselves be constructed based on the existing choice architecture. Sunstein and Thaler (2003, p. 1164) are well aware of it: "If the arrangement of the alternatives has a significant effect on the selections the customers make, then their true 'preferences' do not formally exist."

Suppose for this reason we rule out option 4. Most people would object to the choice of options 2 and 3, although in some fast food restaurants, option 3 and profit maximization of the outlet may be aligned to an extent. This leaves option 1 as the only reasonable option although the precise meaning of "best off" might be debatable. But option 1 does involve a degree of paternalism and that is why it is likely to be ignored by the anti-paternalist. As noted above, paternalism has negative connotations in economics due to its perceived association with coercion. We have already noted the limitations of this view. The cafeteria manager, in the role of a choice architect, is simply making a decision on how to arrange the items in the cafeteria. The final choice rests with the consumers (liberalism).

If economic actors were indeed like the ones in neoclassical economics, then the assumption of framing invariance makes alternative arrangements irrelevant. However, if framing invariance is violated, as suggested by the evidence, then choice architecture is potentially welfare improving for the behavioral types. For instance, if an individual is subject to present-focused preferences, and tempting snacks are prevented from being placed at eye level, then the individual is likely to make healthier choices in their long term interests. Imagine Paul Gascoigne, in Example 12.14, trying to quit an alcohol addiction, entering into a grocery shop that has tempting bottles of alcohol arranged at eye level. This could just be the cue that leads to a downward spiral, which Paul in a sober state might dread happening. But if the bottles are placed elsewhere in a discrete place, the cue that leads to a downward spiral can be removed, at least for that moment. What if the cafeteria manager were purely a profit maximizer (Sugden, 2008, p. 236)? The answer is less clear cut in this case because we do observe grocery stores placing tempting snacks and alcoholic products near the check out counter. However, public policy, which is the main topic of interest to us, is enacted by governments and governments do not necessarily subscribe to the profit motive, but may often subscribe to the public interest motive. They might not do so as a matter of personal preference, but as a matter of electoral compulsions, particularly in the spheres of education, health, and public infrastructure that are easily observable and likely to determine electoral outcomes.

12.5.4 Some Empirical Evidence for the Effectiveness of Nudges

There is now much empirical evidence for the effectiveness of libertarian paternalistic policies that take the form of nudges. Some recent literature also highlights the importance of taking general equilibrium effects into account, but this is the case with any government policy, including neoclassical welfare policies.

We have considered several examples of libertarian paternalistic policies in the book. In many cases, the quantitative effects of nudges are equivalent to those that would arise from a policy that changed relative prices through high levels of taxes and subsidies, with associated distortionary costs (Benartzi et al., 2017; Sunstein, 2016, 2017). In this section, we consider some more examples. One potential candidate for intervention is the present-focused behavior of behavioral types that leads to interventions considered at various points in this book, such as graphic warnings on cigarette packs; color-coded labels on food; labeling the food contents on food containers; default options on savings and pension plans; and government advice on healthy eating habits such as the "five a day food portions" in the UK.

In other cases, the behavioral types may suffer from limited attention (see Part V of the book). In this case, reminders, say, in the form of text messages or letters may enable better decisions for the behavioral types without reducing the quality of decisions of the rational types. For instance, a text reminder about a doctor's appointment. Extensive empirical evidence supports the positive effects of reminders. Reminders have a positive effect on charitable giving (Huck and Rasul, 2010; Sonntag and Zizzo, 2015); individual savings (Karlan et al., 2016); take-up of social benefits (Bhargava and Manoli, 2015); medical treatment (Altmann and Traxler, 2014);

gym attendance (Calzolari and Nardotto, 2017); and the take-up of contraceptives in Kenya (McConnell et al., 2018). Reminders of the average energy consumption of a relevant reference group reduces energy consumption (Schultz et al., 2007; Goldstein et al., 2008; Nolan et al., 2008; Allcott, 2011; Hedlin and Sunstein, 2016).

In Czap et al. (2018), *empathetic nudges* take the following form in an interaction between two parties. Prior to the decisions taken by one party, the other party issues the following appeal: "Before making your decision, please understand my situation better by imagining how your decision looks from my perspective." In this study, financial nudges took the form of altering the incentives through subsidies, but by themselves these are only moderately effective. Empathetic nudges are more effective for females as compared to males. However, a combination of financial nudges and empathetic nudges is more effective than either considered separately.

Jung and Mellers (2016) find that individual-specific characteristics determine which kinds of nudges people will support, and whether they will support nudges or not. They distinguish between several kinds of individuals and their behavior towards nudges.

1. Measuring empathy by using the Interpersonal Reactivity Scale (Davis, 1983), more *empathetic individuals* are more likely to follow nudges, particularly when nudges highlighted social benefits and costs.
2. *Reactant individuals* are defined as those who resist imposition of goals on them by third parties. Measuring reactance, using a scale suggested by Hong and Page (1989), they find that more reactant individuals are more likely to oppose nudges, particularly nudges that are likely to engage System 1 (such as default options, changes in the placement of items in a grocery store, or smaller servings of meals).
3. *Individualist individuals* (measured using the Cultural Cognition Scale, due to Kahan et al. (2009), Kahan et al. (2011)) place greater trust in humans to pursue their own welfare while *communitarian individuals* believe that governments can be trusted to secure collective welfare. Individualists are more likely to oppose nudges relative to communitarians; and *conservatives* are more likely to oppose nudges relative to *liberals*.

The manner in which nudges are framed is also an important factor in their success. When nudges are framed in a manner that is consistent with people's political affiliation (say, either Democrats or Republicans in the US), then they are more likely to accept the nudge (Tannenbaum et al., 2017). Nudges framed as applicable to the general population rather than to the individual are more likely to be accepted (Cornwell and Krantz, 2014).

There are also cross-country differences in the propensity to follow nudges, for example, Swedes are more likely to follow nudges as compared to Americans (Hagman et al., 2015). Within Israeli society, there are differences in support for different types of nudges (e.g., prosocial nudges and proself nudges) depending on whether one belongs to the minority groups or to the majority Jews (Hagman et al., 2015). Minority groups, who might have a lower national attachment, are found to be relatively more receptive to proself nudges relative to prosocial nudges.

Pe'er et al. (2019) consider attitudes towards nudges of the majority Jews and the two minority groups in Israel, Israeli Arabs and Ultra-Orthodox Jews. Attitudes were elicited towards 17 different hypothetical nudges such as organ donation registration defaults; graphic warnings on cigarette packs; no exam-cheating pledge; automatic enrollment for donations in wills; health signals on food items capturing healthiness of food; credit limit alerts warning account holders who are about to go into the red; reminders for medical appointments; and distancing candy nudges that require placing tempting candies away from checkouts. Support for default nudges on organ donation was highest among majority Jews (59.13%) but much lower for Israeli Arabs (35.29%) and Ultra-Orthodox Jews (12%). For all other nudges, Israeli Arabs offered the lowest support among the three groups, suggesting cultural differences in the propensity to follow nudges. Ultra orthodox Jews gave the highest support among the three groups for automatic muting of messages while driving (they don't drive as much as the others), health signals, credit limit alert, self-breathalyzer tests before driving, and distancing from candy. The majority Jews gave the highest support for reminders for medical appointments, two-sided printing defaults, and privacy settings in posting social media content.

12.6 Asymmetric Paternalism

Camerer et al. (2003) propose another variant of soft paternalism which they refer to as *asymmetric paternalism,* or *paternalism for conservatives*. They write (p. 1212): "A regulation is asymmetrically paternalistic if it creates large benefits for those who make errors, while imposing little or no harm on those who are fully rational. Such regulations are relatively harmless to those who reliably make decisions in their best interest, while at the same time advantageous to those making suboptimal choices."

In this framework, alternative paternalistic policies are evaluated by using a simple cost–benefit framework that can be described as follows. Suppose that a fraction p of the consumers are behavioral, and the remaining fraction $1-p$ are fully rational consumers as in the neoclassical benchmark. Consider a paternalistic policy that requires implementation costs, I, imparts benefits $B>0$ to the behavioral consumers, imposes costs $C>0$ on the fully rational consumers; and changes the profits of the firms by $\Delta\pi$. The proposed policy benefits society if the following cost–benefit calculation holds.

$$pB-(1-p)\,C-I+\Delta\pi>0. \tag{12.10}$$

Factors conducive to a successful paternalistic policy on these grounds are: A high value of B and p; low values of C, I; and $\Delta\pi$ that is not too negative. In actual practice, the estimates of $p, B, C, I, \Delta\pi$ may be difficult to obtain. For instance, the perceived benefits, B, may depend on the psychological state of the consumers, the framing of actual policy, the context, and the status-quo bias from altering an existing policy. Measuring the net effect of these changes is likely to be a nontrivial exercise. An ideal asymmetrically paternalistic policy is one where $C=0$. Such a policy imparts benefits to behavioral consumers but imposes no costs on rational consumers; hence, the name – asymmetric paternalism.

12.7 A Pragmatic Approach

Loewenstein and Haisley (2008) propose a pragmatic approach, *light paternalism*. This is a form of soft paternalism that is based on two main criteria.

1. *Dominance*: In comparing two proposed policies, choose the one that clearly dominates another in terms of outcomes, or in terms of risk. For instance, if two policies have similar risk, then choose the one that gives a higher outcome. Or, among two policies that result in identical outcomes, choose the one that is less risky. An example of such a policy choice arises in 401(k) matching programs. Clearly, full-utilization of the plan (where employers make matching contributions) "dominates" under-utilization because it results in a higher outcome but identical risk. Hence, the dominance criterion will recommend choosing full utilization.
2. *Self-officiating*: This requires individuals to choose their own goals, which preserves liberalism. However, when individuals choose their own goals, the following conditions must be met. (i) They should have been provided with the necessary information and given the necessary incentives to allow for self-control. (ii) The goals should be chosen in a "cold state" rather than in a "hot state" of the mind.

Example 12.21 *Suppose that there is a soda machine on the premises of an office and it dispenses unhealthy drinks. The choice is either to keep the machine or remove it from the premises. There is a third choice, dispense healthy drinks. However, the vendor cites logistics costs to rule out supplying healthy drinks. We can now use the two criterion under light paternalism to determine the next step. The employees are given the necessary information on the consequences of consuming unhealthy drinks. They are then given a month to decide if they wish to keep the machine or not. After a month, the employees overwhelmingly vote to remove the machine. This satisfies the self-officiating criterion because employees have been given the necessary information and a sufficiently long period to deliberate to ensure that they make their choice in a cold state. The employees determine through their decisions, and after being given the relevant information, that the absence of the machine dominates it's presence, perhaps by offering them a higher utility/outcome (dominance criterion).*

In some domains, these criteria might be more difficult to apply. For instance, the dominance relation might not always be applicable to policy choices and one could have a tradeoff between outcomes and risk that requires yet another welfare criterion for its resolution. In Example 12.21, there is a hidden role for the choice architect, which does not play an explicit role in this approach. Who determines how much time employees will be given to deliberate, and who determines that the outcome will be decided by, say, a majority or super-majority vote? As noted earlier, choice architecture is ubiquitous.

12.8 Evaluating the Criticisms of Soft Paternalism

We have already considered some of the criticisms of soft paternalism above including the criticism of the *informed desire* criterion (see particularly the discussion around Examples 12.14 and 12.15). We also showed that (1) choice architecture is ubiquitous and paternalism need not be coercive (Section 12.5), (2) the argument of regulatory capture, lobbies, and nonbenevolent politicians apply equally to neoclassical and behavioral welfare economics, and (3) fears of a draconian government that will leverage nudges to achieve its own nefarious agenda are not borne by the immense practical good that nudges have achieved in actual practice.

In this section, we consider additional criticisms of soft paternalism.

Klick and Mitchell (2006) criticize soft paternalism on the grounds that it ignores long-run costs. These are costs that (p. 1625): "offset short-run gains because of the negative learning and motivational effects of paternalistic regulations." They argue that paternalistic policies prevent the learning-by-doing process via a moral hazard argument: Individuals protected by paternalistic policies face a reduced incentive to protect themselves against bad outcomes. However, there are several problems in this argument as a specific criticism of soft paternalism.

1. The argument applies with equal force to any social welfare program, and indeed to the social welfare state. This includes individuals who are enrolled in government health plans that are delivered free at the point of service, such as the NHS in England; employees who will have access to publicly provided health insurance if they face grievous injury at work; and employees who might potentially be laid-off from work and are protected by government regulation on unemployment support. But these cannot be used as arguments to get rid of social welfare programs; only a very heartless society would do so. Moral hazard concerns might well be important, although this is an empirical question, and they could be addressed through other means, such as public education programs, monitoring, and moral suasion.
2. Individuals often make many decisions in situations where there are not enough opportunities to learn. For instance, most people buy very few houses in their lives. Consider Peter and Alicia, a couple who are buying their first house and seeking a mortgage. They benefit enormously from a soft paternalistic policy which requires all lenders to state their APRs. Should Peter and Alicia have been left to fend for themselves in a confusing borrower's world that lacks an APR regulation on the grounds that this prevents their learning opportunities? Or consider a soft paternalistic policy of color-coded food labels. Should consumers be left to learn the composition of different food items, including those that harm their long-term health, on the grounds that color-coded labels will prevent learning opportunities?

Sugden (2013) describes and develops the *contractarian approach* to normative economics based on the work of Buchanan (1968, 1975, 1986). In neoclassical welfare economics, the relevant theory is a guidebook for a "social planner" while under libertarian paternalism, it is a guidebook for a "choice architect." Sugden's first point is that in both cases there is an absence of the relevant addressee, for example, there is no actual social planner to whom one might send the guidebook. However, we have argued above that choice architects are ubiquitous in real life, so the problem of a valid addressee does not always apply in the libertarian paternalistic case. For instance, it should not be too difficult to figure out who the choice architect is in the cases in Example 12.19.

In the contractarian approach, one appeals or makes a recommendation directly to the individual who exhibits behavioral biases, and provides the relevant information. The appeal stresses the personal advantage to each individual, but is not made to the common interest. If this appeal is harmful to some parties, then the proposal may include compensating mechanisms. However, and similar to Pareto optimality, a contractarian recommendation cannot impose net losses on any individual on the grounds that the recommendation gives high benefits to other individuals. Hence, there is no role for interpersonal comparisons of welfare.

A contractarian is a mediator, an actual policy maker, or a politician, who recommends a mutually beneficial outcome to all parties in strategic or nonstrategic situations. Some parties may gain more than others, but they are not advised to strategically out-think the others. For instance, in a market exchange between several buyers and a seller of an object, a contractarian might recommend a second price auction as a trading mechanism to realize gains from trade. The contractarian approach also considers the incentives of those entrusted with the role of a mediator to make recommendations. If the mediator is a politician, then the relevant incentives could be electoral gains.

A contractarian's approach to tackling problems, such as smoking and excessive alcohol consumption, would be to engage in direct information dissemination of the relevant scientific findings to the public. The typical method is to first discover a particular bias in individuals and then find a mediator who has the incentives to disseminate public information to them in order that they themselves make better choices. In particular, the contractarian cannot choose to nudge an individual who chooses not to be nudged, even if the contractarian is convinced that the nudge is in the individual's interest. This is a significant difference from the libertarian-paternalism approach. Sugden (2013, p. 537) writes: "Unless individuals themselves wish to license others to act as their guardians, there is no common interest in paternalism."

Practical implementation of this proposal runs into many problems. How does one find a mediator who has the "correct" incentives to disseminate public information? The answer to this question quickly runs into an infinite regress search problem. How does the contractarian know if individuals wish to be nudged, which will trigger the provision of the relevant information? If the contractarian does not have this information, then presumably one method would be to ask individuals. For instance, within this debate, Bleichrodt et al. (2001) and Li et al. (2014) suggest recovering the underlying normative preferences by conducting face-to-face interviews with individuals and confronting them with choices that are inconsistent with their normative preferences.

But is not asking individuals about their biases already a form of nudge? Suppose the mediator approaches an individual who frequently misses doctor's appointments to ask if they would like to be nudged with a reminder. By the very fact of being asked, the individual is nudged. In several parts of the book, we have demonstrated the importance of the framing of information. How does the contractarian decide how the relevant information is to be framed? Is not framing itself the relevant choice architecture? How does the contractarian determine if the same information will not be interpreted by different people in a different manner? Will such framing not, therefore, require the contractarian to use something like the informed desire criterion? These concerns will apply to different degrees depending on the problem. However, getting into the specifics of what this proposal actually requires, appears to push us in the direction of libertarian paternalism, precisely the framework to which this proposal is suggested as an alternative.

Neoclassical welfare economics relies on a relatively weak normative benchmark to determine the scope for policy improvements, Pareto optimality. However, some of the most important practical policy choices are between alternatives where Pareto optimality fails, that is, where there are clear winners and losers and no fair/affordable compensation of losers is possible.

Soft paternalism has also been criticized on the grounds that it does not go far enough. Loewenstein and Chater (2017) make a case for considering relatively more stronger policy interventions. For instance, in Example 12.18, should we perhaps be willing to override George's underlying normative preferences in favor of social human obligations to save the planet and take a more proactive stance on climate change? The standard approach in libertarian paternalism to induce people to reduce their energy consumption is to use a variety of nudges such as smart electricity meters that "nudge" people to reduce their consumption relative to their neighbors. Clearly such interventions will be inadequate to deal with the scale of the climate change problem that is faced by humanity. A well-thought-out policy response will need, in addition, the instruments already suggested by neoclassical welfare economics such as regulation and Pigouvian taxes on firms and individuals.

Another example is the growing problem of obesity in the US, which is sometimes ascribed to the present-focused preferences of individuals. As already explained in Part III, there are important structural factors at play in explaining the post-1980's increase in obesity in the US. The explanation in terms of a sudden increase in present-focused preferences appears less plausible.

Loewenstein and Chater are persuasive in their observations. However, soft paternalism does not rule out a more overarching policy, of which it is one component. Neither does it rule out using other policy instruments such as strong regulatory responses and Pigouvian taxes to deal with more serious structural societal problems. A combination of soft and hard paternalism is likely to be even more effective than their individual use in problems such as climate change.

Most analyses of nudges apply to a particular situation and context, often considered in isolation. Thus, there has been a greater focus on the local or *partial equilibrium effects* of soft paternalism. The nonlocal or *general equilibrium effects*, by contrast, will take account of the spillover effects on everything else in the economy; see examples below. One of the basic lessons in economics is that the general equilibrium and partial equilibrium effects can be quite different. This argument applies with equal force to any policy intervention, whether that is hard paternalism or soft paternalism.

In recent years, a literature has gathered pace in identifying the "unexpected effects of nudges" which take account of more nonlocal, general equilibrium, effects. As such, this is welcome because any policy intervention should be well piloted to consider all manner of effects before it is actually implemented. However, this insight is neither new as it applies to any conceivable public policy in economics, not just soft paternalism; nor does it negate the rationale or the principles of soft paternalism. Yet, claims contrary to these are sometimes mistakenly invoked in the literature. Similar comments apply to the literature that shows weaker longer term effects of nudges as compared to the short term effects. Yet, nudges can also have strong long-run effects as, say, in the choice of the Premium Pension Plan in Sweden (Cronqvist et al., 2018).

Let us consider some examples. It has been argued that calorie labeling of food may invoke negative emotions such as guilt that reduce welfare (Thunström et al., 2016; Thunström, 2019). Glaeser (2006) argues that graphic warnings on cigarette packs is a form of emotional tax on the smokers that can reduce welfare. If we take these findings as an empirical fact, then one option is to evaluate the appropriateness of the relevant soft paternalistic policy using the framework of asymmetric paternalism in (12.10). Suppose that calorie food labeling and graphic warnings on cigarette packs do not reduce the consumption of rational types. Then, there is an emotional cost $C > 0$ on the fully rational consumers and the behavioral consumers from observing food labels and graphic warnings (although they can choose to ignore them if they so wish). Suppose that there are no other costs to any consumers. It might be that these graphic warnings dissuade a fraction $0 < \lambda < 1$ of the behavioral types from consuming but the rest continue to consume, so the benefits B really accrue only to the fraction λ. Then we may modify (12.10) so that the relevant nudge is beneficial if

$$\lambda pB - C - I + \Delta\pi > 0.$$

This does not change the fundamental insights of the theory although there is a quantitative difference in the policy prescription that needs to be taken account of.

In an interesting and unexpected effect of a nudge, Tiefenbeck et al. (2013) showed that nudges used to decrease water consumption also increased the consumption of electricity. A possible explanation is that once having engaged in a moral action (reduced water consumption), the perceived immorality of the subsequent action (electricity usage) reduces. This is a valuable insight and should serve to inform policymaking in other domains too. In a field study on charitable donations, Damgaard and Gravert (2018) show that a "request for charitable contributions to a specific cause" (a nudge) increases aggregate charitable donations by two thirds, a highly significant amount. However, it also leads more people to unsubscribe from the mailing list, which is an unintended consequence of the nudge.

The spillover of a nudge are important. Hagmann et al. (2019) consider a plan that defaults consumers to a renewable energy plan (a green nudge) as compared to a more traditional neoclassical policy instrument, a \$40/ton carbon tax. When subjects could choose the tax alone, 70% supported the tax. But when given a choice between implementing (i) the tax only, or (ii) tax and nudge, then support for both (i) and (ii) falls, suggesting a crowding-out effect of nudges.

Della Vigna and Linos (2022) compare the quantitative sizes of the effects of nudges in (i) published journal articles, and (ii) in unpublished studies carried out by two nudge units in the United States. They find that for published studies, the effect of a nudge in the treatment group is a 33.4% increase in terms of the "take-up effect" over the control group. The corresponding effect for the unpublished studies in the nudge units is an 8% increase in take-up. Since nudges are not costly, the 8% increase in take-up is still a reasonably sized effect if one compares its effectiveness to other interventions such as taxes, subsidies, and other economic incentives.

What accounts for the differences in the quantitative effects in the two cases? There are three main contributory factors.

1. First, the statistical power of the tests is lower in the academic studies because they have limited budgets and, hence, can typically achieve a smaller sample size.[2] The median sample size in the treatment group in the academic studies is 484 participants while the corresponding figure for the nudge units is 10,006 participants.
2. The second contributory factor arises due to a selection-bias and publication-bias. The data from the nudge units is obtained for all possible nudges undertaken in their studies. This includes nudges that proved effective and may form the basis of actual policy, as well as nudges that proved ineffective and were never translated into actual policy. Hence, the sample from the nudge units includes data on good nudges and bad nudges. The bad nudges

[2] The statistical power of a test is the probability of rejecting the null hypothesis when the alternative hypothesis is true.

reduce the effect size observed. By contrast, in academic studies, if a researcher observes that a suggested intervention is a bad nudge, the researcher might just give up and try another intervention. Studies on bad nudges are also less likely to get published in academia (publication-bias).

3. Third, while the nudge units are more likely to explore interventions where the effects may be weaker, academic researchers are more likely to explore interventions where the effects are larger, as these are more likely to get published.

Hence, there is no direct correspondence between the type of nudges and interventions used in the academic studies and the nudge units. Thus, the significantly lower observed effect size for the nudge units is very likely to be a lower limit on the effectiveness of nudges, yet the size of the effects is economically significant.

For several examples of actually employed nudges in the field that have a large quantitative effect, see Benartzi et al. (2017). They also make the important point that in order to judge the effectiveness of nudges, one needs to compare nudges with the net benefit of employing alternative interventions such as taxes and subsidies with their potentially large administrative and distortionary costs.

In their review of 100 studies, Hummel and Maedche (2019) find that 62% of the nudging treatments are statistically significant, but the rest are not; and the median effect size is 21%. The most effective nudges are those that rely on default effects as compared to those that work through the precommitment channel.

As a general point, not all nudges need to have quantitatively large effects. This is as true for nudges as it is true for other economic policies. For instance, small marginal changes in the tax rate on cigarettes may have weak quantitative effects on cigarette consumption. This does not, in general, invalidate the point that Pigouvian taxes levied on individuals may be effective in internalizing externalities caused to others, or even internalities caused to one's own future selves in other contexts (see Section 12.10 below). Hence, this is not a fatal criticism of nudges but it alerts us to the need to conduct extensive pilot studies before implementing nudges in the form of actual policy.

12.9 Optimal Sin Taxes

Sin taxes are commonly used to refer to any tax on habit formation goods that cause harm to one's health, such as smoking, alcohol consumption, and the consumption of drugs. Such goods are characterized by current benefits, $v > 0$, and future costs, $c > 0$, as in the case outlined in Section 12.4, which we use as an exemplar in this section. Individuals who have present-focused preferences might particularly underweight the future costs and overweight the current benefits. Hence, they are likely to engage in greater consumption of the sin good relative to those who do not have present-focused preferences.

In a model of *multiple selves* of the same individual (see Part III), the current self of an individual might be unable to directly control the consumption of the sin good of the future selves. Furthermore, the consumption of the current self of the sin good may lead to two kinds of harms to the future selves.

1. "Direct increase in health costs" to the future selves from past consumption of the sin good.
2. "Habit formation costs" so that an increase in past consumption requires even greater consumption in the present in order to give rise to an identical level of marginal utility. For instance, long-term drug users might have to consume ever-increasing quantities of the drug to get the same fix, so to speak.

Thus, an increase in the consumption of the sin good creates negative externalities to one's own future selves. Such externalities, caused to one's own future selves, are known as *internalities*. In this case, a consumption tax on the sin good may curtail consumption of the sin good, providing a commitment device to the current self and helping to internalize the internalities from consumption of the sin good (Gruber and Köszegi, 2001, 2004).

The task of a benevolent social planner is to determine the optimal sin tax to levy, while taking into account that (i) possibly a fraction of the individuals are present-focused, while the rest might not be present-focused, and (ii) there is likely to be heterogeneity across present-focused consumers in the degree of their present-focus. A complete analysis requires a model of habit formation; see, for instance, O'Donoghue and Rabin (2006). One of the exercises asks you to work through a problem with these features. For the analysis below, we use the simple model in Section 12.4 without invoking multiple selves or habit formation to highlight some of the key issues.

We use quasi-hyperbolic $(\beta, 1)$ preferences as our example of present-focused preferences and we assume, as in Section 12.4, that an individual must choose whether to undertake an activity or not. We interpret the activity as consumption of a sin good with current benefit v and future cost $c > v$. An individual who is not present-focused has $\beta = 1$, hence, will not undertake the activity because $c > v$. An individual who is present-focused, $0 < \beta < 1$, has the utility

$$v - \beta c$$

from consumption of the sin good. From (12.5), such an individual undertakes the activity if the extent of present-focus is high enough in the sense that

$$\beta \leq \beta^* \equiv \frac{v}{c} < 1. \tag{12.11}$$

Suppose that there are N citizens, of which N_R are the rational types and N_B are the behavioral types such that

$$N_R + N_B = N.$$

There is a distribution of behavioral types in the population. The present-focus parameter β is distributed across the behavioral types over the interval $[0, 1]$. The probability density is given by f and the associated cumulative density function is given by F. Thus, $F(x)$ is the proportion of the behavioral types whose β value is less than or equal to $x \in [0, 1]$.

Now suppose that the government imposes a sin tax t on the consumption of the sin good, so that consumers of the sin good receive the post-tax benefit $(1 - t)v$. From (12.7), we know that a present-focused individual will undertake the activity if

$$\beta \leq \beta^{**} \equiv \frac{(1-t)v}{c} < 1. \tag{12.12}$$

From (12.11), in the absence of sin taxes, a fraction $F\left(\frac{v}{c}\right)$ of the present-focused population engages in the activity. After the imposition of the sin tax, from (12.12), a fraction $F\left(\frac{(1-t)v}{c}\right)$ of the present-focused population engages in the activity, which is lower.

Are sin taxes at the rate t, worth it for the social planner or the government to levy from a welfare point of view? We assume that the government evaluates welfare, taking as its objective, the maximization of the sum of utilities of all N citizens, correcting for their present-focused preferences (i.e., by setting $\beta = 1$ for all citizens). Thus, the government determines that in evaluating social welfare it will correct for the present-focus of the consumers.

What is the optimal sin tax for the government to levy? The answer to this question depends on the costs and benefits of levying sin taxes. Taxes are not costless to levy and may impose administrative and deadweight costs. The lack of a substitution effect in our model precludes deadweight costs, but in a more general model, taxes will have deadweight costs that increase with the square of the tax rate. Suppose that levying a tax imposes a welfare cost $\frac{\kappa}{2}t^2$, $\kappa > 0$, on society.[3]

The benefit of the tax is an elimination in the consumption of the sin good for those present-focused individuals whose preference parameter, β, lies in the interval $\frac{(1-t)v}{c} < \beta \leq \frac{v}{c}$. Since $v < c$, this increases the welfare of each of these consumers (as perceived by the social planner) by an amount $c - v > 0$. Suppose that starting from an initial tax rate of zero, $t = 0$, one changes the sin tax to a strictly positive level, $t > 0$.

The total change in the welfare of society, denoted by ΔW, from levying sin taxes is therefore

$$\Delta W = \lambda \left[F\left(\frac{v}{c}\right) - F\left(\frac{(1-t)v}{c}\right) \right](c - v) - \frac{\kappa}{2}t^2. \tag{12.13}$$

In (12.13), the first term on the RHS gives the total benefits from levying a sin tax at the rate t and the second term gives the total deadweight costs. The rational types, who comprise a fraction $1 - \lambda$ of the population do not consume the good anyway, so the sin tax does not alter their actions, hence, they do not figure into the calculations. The remaining fraction λ is present-focused. The change in the fraction of this population that derives the benefits of sin taxes is given in the square brackets, multiplied by the benefit per person, $c - v$.

A particularly simple case arises when the distribution of β is uniform over $[0, 1]$. In this case we have

$$F\left(\frac{v}{c}\right) - F\left(\frac{(1-t)v}{c}\right) = \frac{tv}{c}.$$

Thus, we can rewrite (12.13) as

$$\Delta W = \lambda \frac{tv}{c}(c - v) - \frac{\kappa}{2}t^2. \tag{12.14}$$

Suppose that the government's objective is to determine the sin tax $t \in [0, 1]$ that provides the largest increase in welfare starting from a position of zero sin tax, $t = 0$. Differentiating (12.14) with respect to t and setting it equal to zero, we get

[3] This essentially corresponds to taking account of the area of Harberger's triangle; see our discussion of deadweight costs in Section 12.10.

$$\frac{d\Delta W}{dt} = \lambda \frac{v}{c}(c - v) - \kappa t = 0. \tag{12.15}$$

The second order condition is satisfied because $\frac{d^2 \Delta W}{dt^2} = -\kappa < 0$. Solving (12.15) for the optimal tax rate, t^*, we get the unique optimizing value of the sin tax

$$t^* = \frac{\lambda}{\kappa} \frac{v}{c}(c - v). \tag{12.16}$$

From (12.16), the optimal sin tax is higher, the higher is the fraction of present-focused individuals, λ; the higher is the fraction of present-focused individuals who are affected by the change in tax, $\frac{v}{c}$; the higher is the benefit, $c - v$, to each present-focused individual who is dissuaded from the activity; and the lower is the unit cost, κ, of imposing taxes.

12.10 Behavioral Public Economics

Behavioral public economics lies at the interface of behavioral economics and public economics. This section outlines some of the basic concepts from this literature.[4]

12.10.1 Limited Attention and Deadweight Losses from Taxation

Governments have the power to raise revenues through taxation. Taxes also impose several costs on society. Two main costs that economists are interested in are *efficiency costs* and *equity costs*.[5] There is an increasing interest in revisiting the classical results in the theory of taxation by using the insights derived from behavioral economics. This has led to an active and fast-growing literature in behavioral public finance. In this section, we will be mainly interested in how the efficiency costs of taxation are influenced by limited attention on the part of taxpayers.

We have considered the evidence on limited attention in Part V of the book. Consider an individual with income $I > 0$ who consumes two goods, x and y. Both goods are produced under competitive market conditions and constant marginal costs of production. The price of good y, the numeraire good, is normalized to 1; so the marginal cost of production of good y may be taken to be 1. The marginal cost of production of good x is $c > 0$. Under competitive markets, the price of good x, denoted by p, equals the marginal cost, that is, $p = c$. In the absence of any taxes on goods, the budget constraint of the individual is given by

$$px + y = I. \tag{12.17}$$

We distinguish between three kinds of taxes.

1. *Lump sum tax, T*: A lump sum tax deducts a fixed amount, T, of the individual's income. In particular, the tax is not conditioned on individual-specific characteristics, such as income,

[4] For a detailed survey of some of the foundational issues, the reader can consult Bernheim and Taubinsky (2018). Some of the other papers that develop key ideas in this framework are Chetty et al. (2009); Mullainathan et al. (2012); and Farhi and Gabaix (2020).

[5] There are also other costs that we omit, such as the administrative costs of taxation, and in a political economy context, the wastage in resources arising from the lobbying activities of interested parties.

age, or other demographic information; or on the prices of the goods. The budget constraint of the consumer in the presence of the lump sum tax is

$$px + y = I - T. \tag{12.18}$$

Such a tax is also known as a nondistortionary tax because it leaves unchanged the relative prices of the two goods.

2. *Specific consumption tax, t*: A specific tax, $t > 0$, levied, say, on good x, is a tax on each unit of consumption of good x. The budget constraint of the consumer, in the presence of the specific tax, is given by

$$(p + t)\, x + y = I. \tag{12.19}$$

A key feature of the distortionary tax is that it alters the relative prices of the two goods. Denote the after tax price of good x by

$$q = p + t, \tag{12.20}$$

so that the budget constraint in (12.19) can be rewritten as

$$qx + y = I. \tag{12.21}$$

3. *Ad-valorem tax, τ*: An ad-valorem tax, $\tau > 0$, on good x is levied as a fixed percentage of the price. Hence, it alters the relative prices of the two goods, so it is distortionary. In this case, the consumer's budget constraint is given by

$$p\,(1 + \tau)\, x + y = I. \tag{12.22}$$

The efficiency costs of taxation in welfare economics hinge on a comparison of the behavioral responses to lumpsum and distortionary taxes. In our discussion below, of the two forms of distortionary taxes, we focus only on specific consumption taxes.

The objective of the individual is to maximize a utility function

$$u(x, y), \tag{12.23}$$

which is strictly increasing and strictly concave in x and y, subject to the budget constraint, which takes the form (12.18) for lump sum taxes and (12.21) for specific taxes.

The concavity of the utility function u plays a key role in determining the efficiency costs of taxation. Undergraduate students will know from basic microeconomic theory that a consumer who has a strictly concave utility function has strictly convex indifference curves.[6] Convex indifference curves imply a love for variety in the sense that the individual will prefer the average bundle of the goods to extreme bundles. For instance, the individual will prefer the bundle of goods $(x, y) = (5, 5)$ to any of the two extreme bundles $(x, y) = (0, 10)$ and $(x, y) = (10, 0)$.

We now motivate two intuitive explanations for the concept of efficiency costs of taxation.

1. *Comparing differences in utility for fixed tax revenues*: Lump sum taxes reduce the consumer's overall income, but they do not alter relative prices of the two goods. Hence, such taxes do not interfere with the "preference for variety" aspect of preferences. However, distortionary

[6] This argument can be weakened to quasi-concavity of the utility function.

taxes create a disincentive to consume the good that is taxed relative to the untaxed good. Hence, such taxes restrict the ability of the consumer to exercise a "preference for variety" thereby leading to lower utility. Thus, if distortionary taxes were restricted to raise the same revenue as lump sum taxes, the consumer's utility would still be lower under distortionary taxes relative to lump sum taxes. The extent to which utility is lower, keeping fixed the tax revenues, gives us a measure of the *efficiency cost of distortionary taxes.*

2. *Comparing differences in tax revenues for a fixed level of utility*: Suppose that we fixed a level of utility, $\overline{u}$, for the consumer. We now ask: Given the prices of the two goods (p and 1 for, respectively, goods x and y) what are the tax revenues raised under both types of taxes, provided that the consumer achieves a certain fixed level of utility, $\overline{u}$? This difference in tax revenues between lump sum and distortionary taxes, keeping utility fixed at $\overline{u}$, turns out to be positive, and provides a second measure of the efficiency cost of distortionary taxes.

We now show how limited attention plays a role in this analysis. Suppose that the individual maximizes the utility function in (12.23) subject to the budget constraint (12.21) in the presence of a specific tax on good x alone; good y, the numeraire good, is not taxed. The solution to this problem gives the optimal consumption levels of the two goods as,

$$x(q,I), y(q,I),$$

known as the *uncompensated* or Marshallian demand curves. These demand curves show how the demands for the two goods depend on the after-tax price, q, and income, I. Substituting these demands in the utility function, we get the indirect utility function of the consumer

$$v = v(q,I) = u(x(q,I), y(q,I)), \tag{12.24}$$

which shows how the consumer's utility changes when q and I change.

One commonly used measure of the degree of responsiveness of the optimal quantity demanded of good x to its after-tax price, q, is the price elasticity of demand of good x, defined as

$$\eta_q = -\frac{dx(q,I)}{dq}\frac{q}{x}. \tag{12.25}$$

From (12.20), $q = p + t$, so a given change in the after tax price, q, can come about either through a change in the pretax price of the good, p, or through a change in the specific tax, t. Let us now rewrite the elasticity in (12.25), taking account of the channel through which q changes, either through p ($p \to q$), or through t ($t \to q$).

$$\eta_{p\to q} = -\frac{dx(q,I)}{dp}\frac{q}{x}; \ \eta_{t\to q} = -\frac{dx(q,I)}{dt}\frac{q}{x}.$$

Under neoclassical economics, consumers have unbounded attention, so they pay full attention to the channel through which the change in the after-tax price, q, occurs. Ultimately, consumers are only interested in changes in the after-tax price. Hence, for such consumers

$$\eta_{p\to q} = \eta_{t\to q}.$$

However, the evidence shows that consumers are boundedly rational and do not pay full attention to nonsalient taxes. In particular, the data in Chetty et al. (2009) show that consumers do not pay attention to state taxes, t, in the US, which are added at the cash register, even though they are aware of these taxes. By contrast, they pay more attention to the price, p, on the sales stickers that already includes federal taxes. For the sake of argument, if there is a component of q that consumers do not pay any attention to at all, then changes in that component will not affect the after-tax price, leaving the demand for the good unaffected. In order to model the relatively greater attention to the price on the price stickers, relative to nonsalient taxes, we assume that

$$\eta_{t\to q} = \theta\eta_{p\to q};\ \theta \in (0,1). \tag{12.26}$$

From (12.26), since $\theta \in (0,1)$, the quantity demanded of x is more responsive to changes in the after-tax price arising from changes in the pretax price, as compared to changes in the specific tax. Gabaix and Laibson (2006) develop a related idea based on *shrouded attributes*. For instance, before choosing a hotel, potential guests might not pay attention to all possible hidden add-on costs such as telephone charges, differences in room service charges, or even in the quality of such service, and restrictions on car parking.

Let us now outline the implications of limited attention on the deadweight costs from taxation; we shall use our second measure of deadweight costs (comparing differences in tax revenues for a fixed level of utility). Suppose that we optimally choose the consumption of goods x and y in order to minimize consumer expenditures, and achieve a target level of utility, $\overline{u}$. In other words, using (12.21), the consumer chooses x and y to minimize expenditure

$$qx + y,$$

subject to the constraint

$$u(x,y) \geq \overline{u}. \tag{12.27}$$

The solution to this problem is given by a set of optimal demands for the two goods,

$$x^c(q,\overline{u}),\ \ y^c(q,\overline{u}).$$

The superscript "c" on the demands refers to "compensated demands" because they compensate the consumer for changes in prices, through corresponding changes in income (not shown as an argument in the demand functions), so that the consumer can continue to achieve the target utility level, $\overline{u}$. These demand curves are also sometimes known as Hicksian demand curves. The constraint in (12.27) binds at the optimal solution,

$$u(x^c(q,\overline{u}), y^c(q,\overline{u})) = \overline{u}, \tag{12.28}$$

because an increase in utility requires greater expenditures on the goods, and the objective is to minimize expenditures. The total tax revenue raised by the government equals (remember only good x is taxed)

$$tx^c(q,\overline{u}).$$

Suppose that we now conducted an identical exercise under lump sum taxes. From (12.18), the consumer chooses the consumption of the two goods so as to minimize

$$px + y - T,$$

subject to the constraint in (12.27). However, in this case, the lump sum tax T is simply subtracted from the objective function and does not distort the relative prices of the two goods. Denote the optimal choices as

$$x^c(p,T,\overline{u}),\ y^c(p,T,\overline{u}).$$

As before, the constraint in (12.27) will bind, so that the analogue of(12.28) holds. But in order for the constraint to bind, that is, to achieve the target utility level $\overline{u}$, we will need to adjust the value of T to, say, T^*, so that (recall we are in the world of compensated demands here)

$$u(x^c(p,T^*,\overline{u}),y^c(p,T^*,\overline{u}))=\overline{u}.$$

To recap, we have achieved the same level of utility, $\overline{u}$, under both taxes, a distortionary tax, t, and a lump sum tax, T^*. The deadweight loss from the distortionary tax, DWL, is now defined as the extra tax revenue raised under lump sum taxes relative to a distortionary specific tax.

$$DWL=T^*-tx^c(q,\overline{u})\geq 0. \tag{12.29}$$

The intuition for why the sign of the RHS in (12.29) is positive has already been explained above. The lump sum tax enables the consumer to exercise fully the preference for variety between the two goods by keeping unchanged the relative prices, while the distortionary tax does not allow for this. In the extreme case where the underlying preferences of the consumer do not allow for any substitutability between the two goods, for example, in the case of perfect complements such as left and right shoes, the RHS of (12.29) will be strictly zero. More generally, when such substitution is allowed for, the DWL is strictly positive.

Denote the compensated demand curve for x when the pretax price changes, but the specific tax is held fixed, by $x^c_{p\to q}(q,\overline{u})$; the corresponding demand elasticity is denoted by $\eta^c_{p\to q}$. Similarly, denote the compensated demand curve for x by $x^c_{t\to q}(q,\overline{u})$ when the pretax price is held fixed, but q changes due to a change in the specific tax; the corresponding demand elasticity is denoted by $\eta^c_{t\to q}$. We assume that under limited attention, the demand elasticities obey a similar relation as in (12.26), that is,

$$\eta^c_{t\to q}=\theta\eta^c_{p\to q};\ \theta\in(0,1)\,. \tag{12.30}$$

Thus, the compensated demand curve $x^c_{t\to q}(q,\overline{u})$ gives a relatively muted response to changes in the tax rate, as compared to the compensated demand curve $x^c_{p\to q}(q,\overline{u})$, which captures the response to a change in p. We now plot two inverse demand curves for good x. They describe the relationship between quantity demanded of x and the after-tax price q, when the change in q is induced, respectively, by a change in p and a change in t.

$$q^c_{t\to q}(x,\overline{u}),\ q^c_{p\to q}(x,\overline{u})$$

in the usual (*quantity,price*) space.[7]

[7] If we followed standard practice in mathematics, we would draw demand curves in (*price, quantity*) space with the dependent variable, quantity, in the vertical axis and the independent variable, price, on the horizontal axis. However, due to an accident of history in which the English economist Alfred Marshall drew these axis the other way around, in (*quantity,price*) space, we need to use the inverse demand curves.

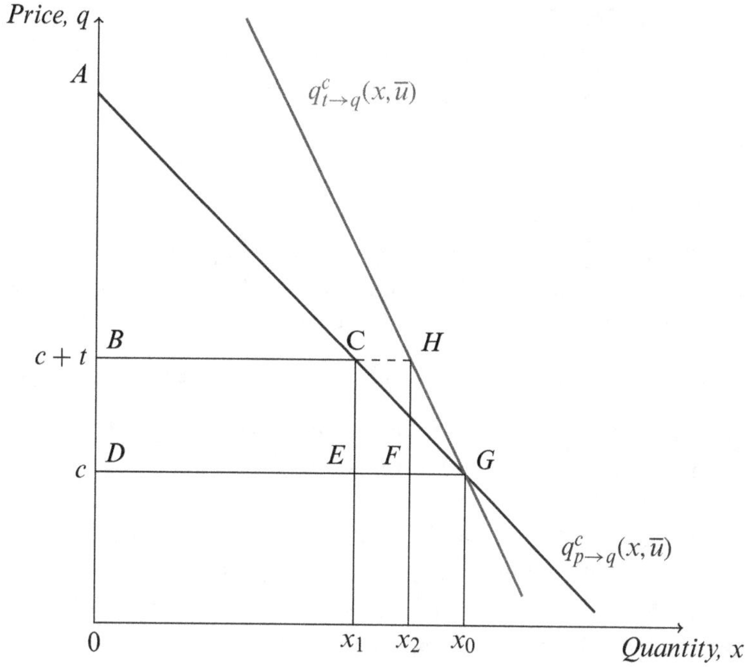

Figure 12.1 Limited attention and the deadweight costs from distortionary taxes

Example 12.22 *Suppose that the compensated demand curve is given by* $x^c(q,\overline{u}) = a - bq + c\overline{u}$. *Then the inverse demand curve is obtained by solving this equation for q in terms of x, which gives* $q(x,\overline{u}) = \frac{a}{b} + \frac{c}{b}\overline{u} - \frac{1}{b}x^c$.

From (12.30), the inverse demand curve $q^c_{t\to q}(x,\overline{u})$ is relatively steeper (more muted changes in demand in response to a unit change in price) relative to the inverse demand curve $q^c_{p\to q}(x,\overline{u})$. We drop the prefix "inverse" from "inverse demand curve" for the rest of the section.

Figure 12.1 shows the after-tax price, q, on the vertical axis, and the quantity of good x on the horizontal axis. The compensated demand curves $q^c_{t\to q}(x,\overline{u})$ and $q^c_{p\to q}(x,\overline{u})$ are labeled, and shown in Figure 12.1 as the two downward sloping lines. Under perfectly competitive market conditions, the initial price, in the absence of any taxes, is $p = c$, and the consumer demands a quantity x_0 at this price. The total revenue and total cost of profit maximizing competitive firms equals cx_0 and they make zero profits.

The Case under Full Attention

First consider a change in the after-tax price arising from a change in the pretax price, p, so that the relevant demand curve is the relatively flatter demand curve $q^c_{p\to q}(x,\overline{u})$. The area under the demand curve captures the *consumer's total willingness to pay for the good.* Thus, for x_0 units, the total willingness to pay is the area AGx_00. The consumer pays a total sum of money cx_0 for x_0 units of the good, so the *consumer surplus* is the area $AGx_00 - cx_0 = ADG$.

Now suppose that the government levies a specific tax, $t > 0$, so the marginal cost of the firm increases to $c + t > c$. Under competitive markets, the new market price is $p = c + t$ and the consumer now demands a quantity x_1 of good x. Since this is the case of full attention, the relevant demand curve is $q^c_{p \to q}(x, \overline{u})$. Proceeding as above, we can make the following inferences.

- The total revenue received by the firm is cx_1.
- The total tax revenue collected by the government is $BCED$, which equals tx_1.
- The consumer surplus is ABC; this is the consumer's total willingness to pay, ACx_10, minus the amount that the consumer actually pays, BCx_10.

Let us now compare the before-tax and the after-tax positions.

- The change in the consumer surplus is $ABC - ADG = -BCGD < 0$. Competitive firms make zero profits in both cases, so they are neither better off nor worse off.
- Can we account for the loss in consumer surplus $BCGD$? Of this area, the government receives a tax revenue of $BCED$, which it can spend in the form of government expenditure on the consumer to offset the fall in consumer surplus. However, we are unable to account for the remaining loss in consumer surplus, the area $BCGD - BCED = CEG > 0$. For this reason, the area $CEG > 0$ gives the *efficiency cost of taxation*.

Let us see how this area is related to our definition of deadweight loss. The compensated demand curve is drawn under the restriction (12.27), hence, it ensures that the consumer obtains the utility level $\overline{u}$.

Suppose that instead of imposing the specific tax $t > 0$, the government imposes instead, a lump sum tax $T > 0$. In particular, suppose that the government had imposed a lump sum tax equal to the area $BCGD$, when the consumer's demand curve is $q^c_{p \to q}(x, \overline{u})$ and there is no specific tax. Then, the consumer would have been as well off under a lump sum tax as under the specific tax (because utility is held fixed at $\overline{u}$ in both cases), yet the government would have collected an extra tax revenue equal to CEG, relative to the case of a specific tax. The government could have contributed the tax revenue CEG towards the welfare of the consumer through various government programs. Hence, this extra amount, which is lost while using a specific tax, is known as the deadweight loss from imposing a distortionary tax.

Alternatively, we can use the insight in (12.29). Before the imposition of the specific tax, the government could have imposed a lump sum tax $T^* = BCGD$ and the consumer would have achieved the utility $\overline{u}$. After the imposition of the specific tax, t, the total tax revenue of the government equals tx_1 which equals the area $BCED$; the consumer again achieves the utility $\overline{u}$. Thus, applying (12.29), we get

$$DWL = T^* - tx_1 = BCGD - BCED = CEG > 0.$$

The triangle CEG is sometimes referred to as *Harberger's triangle*.

The Case under Limited Attention

In this case, the relevant demand curve is the relatively steeper compensated demand curve $q^c_{t \to q}(x, \overline{u})$. The original pretax situation is as it was in the case under full attention. Suppose we impose a specific tax $t > 0$. The market price is now $c + t$ and it intersects the demand curve $q^c_{t \to q}(x, \overline{u})$ at point H. The new equilibrium quantity consumed is x_2 and the total tax revenues of the government now are tx_2. Proceeding as in the case of full attention, the reader can readily calculate the new deadweight loss by the area of the Harberger triangle HFG.

Comparing the size of the deadweight loss under the two cases, we find that the area of the triangle HFG is smaller than the area of the triangle CEG.[8] Thus, the efficiency losses due to distortionary taxes are lower under limited attention. The reason is that since the consumer pays lower attention to changes in distortionary taxes, relative to changes in pretax prices, the substitution away from the taxed good into the untaxed good is smaller, lowering the size of the deadweight loss. Political economy reasons often induce governments to levy taxes that are less salient. One potential reason is that changes in salient income taxes are politically unpopular, as compared to changes in consumption taxes. Yet consumption taxes are regressive with respect to incomes (the poor pay a disproportionately larger share of such taxes). Thus, one unexpected benefit of increasing less salient taxes, and restricting the increase in taxes to small magnitudes (so that salience is further reduced), is that the efficiency costs of such taxes may be lower.

The evidence in Taubinsky and Rees-Jones (2018) shows that taxes are relatively less visible at low levels as compared to high levels. Thus, the efficiency costs of marginal changes to taxes at low levels are also likely to be smaller. User charges and other add-on charges by firms that increase the relative price of their products in a hidden manner, particularly when one pays by direct debit, play a similar role in that they are less salient. Hence, they create a lower distortionary impact. However, if consumers pay greater attention to taxes when taxes are higher, then the efficiency costs of these taxes are even higher. For instance, suppose that at a low level of tax, $t_L > 0$, consumers pay no attention to it. However, when the government increases the tax to a high level, $t_H > t_L$, then consumers suddenly pay attention to the taxes. It is as if the tax has increased by a higher amount $t_H - 0$ rather than the lower amount $t_H - t_L$. The efficiency costs of taxation are higher, the higher is the tax; it increases the size of the Harberger triangle. The authors also identify allocational costs that arise from heterogeneity among consumers in the extent to which they pay attention. In their empirical study based on online shoppers in the US, the authors find that consumers pay attention to existing sales taxes "as if" they were only 25% of their actual size. When the taxes are tripled, consumers pay attention to them "as if" they were 50% of their actual size.

12.10.2 Tax Incidence and Limited Attention

Suppose that the government levies a specific tax, t, per unit, on the consumption of good x. For x units sold, the producer collects the tax revenue tx from the consumers, and hands the tax revenue to the government.

Tax incidence is the problem of determining what fraction of the tax t, per unit, is passed on by the producers to the consumers as an increase in the price of the good. Suppose that the producer passes on a fraction $\lambda \in [0, 1]$ of the tax as a price increase to the consumer and bears

[8] Triangle HFG has a smaller base but the same height as the triangle CEG. Hence, its area is smaller.

the rest, that is, $1 - \lambda$. Then consumers and producers share the tax burden in the proportions λ and $1 - \lambda$.

In this section, we are interested in how the fraction λ is determined when consumers are boundedly rational. In particular, we assume that they face limited attention in the sense that is specified in (12.26).

We consider the same basic two-goods setup as in Section 12.10.1, with competitive markets, but with two differences.

1. In Section 12.10.1, we were interested in the optimization problem of a single individual whose Marshallian demand curve for good x was given by $x(q, I)$. Now suppose that we have n consumers who are indexed by $i = 1, 2, \ldots, n$. Let us write the Marshallian demand curve of consumer i for good x by $x_i(q, I)$.
2. In Section 12.10.1, firms had a constant marginal cost of production of $c > 0$ per unit of good x produced. We now assume that the firms have an increasing marginal cost of production so that the supply curve of each competitive firm is upward sloping.

The problem of tax incidence requires us to first construct the market demand and market supply curves. By horizontally adding together the demand curves of all n consumers for good x, we can get the market demand curve

$$x = x_D(q, I) = \sum_{i=1}^{i=n} x_i(q, I), \tag{12.31}$$

where

$$q = p + t, \tag{12.32}$$

is the after-tax price of the good, and p is the price received by the sellers.

Similarly, by horizontally adding up the upward sloping supply curves of all competitive firms in the industry for good x, we get the industry supply curve

$$x = x_S(p), \tag{12.33}$$

which gives the aggregate market quantity sold by the competitive firms. The supply curve specifies for each price p, the amount supplied to the market by all the firms.

The market clearing condition requires that total market demand equals total market supply, or by using (12.31), (12.33)

$$x_D(q, I) = x_S(p). \tag{12.34}$$

In Section 12.10.1, we considered the effect of limited attention on the demand curves for individuals, which required us to compute the elasticities for these demand curves (see (12.25)). We now wish to study the effect of limited attention, on the part of individuals, on the aggregate demand and supply curves in the market.

From (12.32), changes in the after-tax price q can occur through two possible channels, p and t. Hence, we define two separate aggregate demand elasticities,

$$\epsilon_{p \to q} = -\frac{dx_D(q, I)}{dp} \frac{q}{x_D}, \quad \epsilon_{t \to q} = -\frac{dx_D(q, I)}{dt} \frac{q}{x_D}, \tag{12.35}$$

which capture the effect on the aggregate demand x_D for good x when changes in q arise, respectively, through p and t. Since aggregate demand is additive in the demands of individual consumers, we postulate an analogous form of limited attention at the aggregate level as at the individual level in (12.26):

$$\epsilon_{t\to q} = \theta\epsilon_{p\to q};\ \theta \in (0,1)\,. \tag{12.36}$$

Thus, changes in demand arising from changes in the tax rate are relatively more muted because consumers pay only partial attention to taxes but pay full attention to the price on the price stickers. When changes in q arise through changes in t, we may write the aggregate demand curve in (12.31) as $x_{Dt\to q}$; and when such changes arise through changes in p, we may write the aggregate demand curve in (12.31) as $x_{Dp\to q}$.

Before proceeding with a more formal derivation, let us give a diagrammatic exposition. As in Section 12.10.1, drawing the demand and supply curves in (quantity, price) space requires us to specify the inverse demand curve and the inverse supply curve. Since we wish to specify the channels through which the after-tax price changes, we define the inverse demand curves that arise from changes in p and t by, respectively

$$q = D_{p\to q}(x, I) \text{ and } q = D_{t\to q}(x, I).$$

Note that $D_{p\to q}$ is the inverse of $x_{Dp\to q}$; while $D_{t\to q}$ is the inverse of $x_{Dt\to q}$. As in Section 12.10.1, limited attention implies that the inverse demand $D_{t\to q}(x, I)$ is relatively steeper because consumers give less attention to changes in less salient taxes. Similarly define the "inverse supply curve" by $p = S(x)$, where S is the inverse of x_S, defined in (12.33).

Figure 12.2 shows the inverse demand and inverse supply curves in the same diagram; in what follows, we omit the prefix "inverse." The initial market equilibrium where demand equals supply is shown at point A and the market clearing quantity and price are, respectively, x_0 and p_0. Now suppose that a specific tax t is imposed per unit of consumption/sale of x. Since the tax can either be levied on consumption or on the sale of the same unit, we can study the effects of the tax by shifting either the demand curve or the supply curve. In Figure 12.2, we shift the supply curve upwards by the amount of the tax $t > 0$ for each value of x. Thus, the two supply curves $S(x)$ and $t + S(x)$ are parallel to each other and the vertical distance between the two, for any value of x, is identically equal to t.

Under unlimited attention, a change in q that arises through either a change in t or a change in p gives identical results. Consider first the case of unlimited attention so that the relevant demand curve is $D_{p\to q}(x, I)$. In this case, the new market equilibrium is at point B and the equilibrium quantity and price are, respectively, x_1 and p_c. The "consumer" pays the price p_c, the seller receives the price, p_s, and the difference between the two, $p_c - p_s = t$, is the tax per unit of the sale of the good that accrues to the government. The increase in the price paid by consumers from p_0 to p_c, which equals the distance BC, is less than the amount of the tax, t. Some of the tax per unit is absorbed by the sellers in the form of a fall in price. This equals the distance $p_0 - p_s$, which is equal to the distance CD. Thus, under unlimited attention, the answer

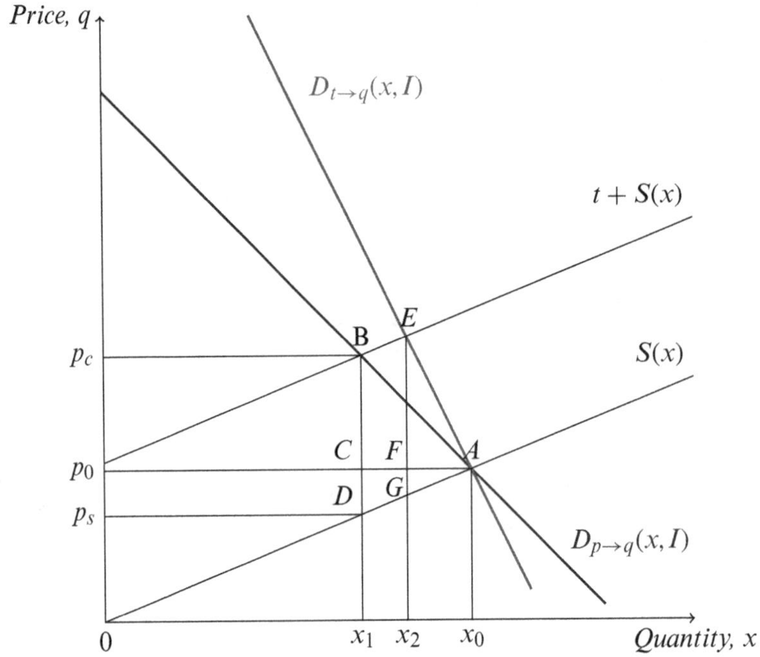

Figure 12.2 Limited attention and tax incidence

to our original question (the determination of λ) is that the ratio in which the burden of the tax is borne by the consumer and the producer is

$$\frac{BC}{CD}.$$

Clearly, this ratio depends on the relative elasticities of the underlying demand and supply curves.

Now consider the case of limited attention and a change in q arising from a change in the tax rate, t. The relevant demand curve is the relatively steeper demand curve, $D_{t\to q}(x, I)$. Proceeding as in the case of unlimited attention, we get the following result. The new market equilibrium point is E, and the ratio in which the tax burden is shared between consumers and sellers is

$$\frac{EF}{FG}.$$

We can see that

$$\frac{EF}{FG} > \frac{BC}{CD}.$$

Thus, under limited attention, the consumers bear a higher share of the tax burden as compared to sellers. This is intuitive. Since consumers pay insufficient attention to the increase in the post-tax price arising from an increase in taxes, sellers can pass on a relatively greater burden of the tax increase onto them. In the limit, if consumers failed to notice an increase in tax at all, their demand curve would be vertical and sellers would be able to pass on the entire burden of taxes to consumers.

On the other hand, if the supply curve gets steeper, then producers share a larger burden of the tax. Thus, the elasticities of demand and supply play a key role in determining what share of the increase in taxes is passed on to consumers in the form of a price increase, and what share is absorbed by the sellers. We examine this intuition more formally below in an algebraic analysis. Since we no longer need a graphical analysis, we will revert back to the demand and supply curves, rather than their inverses.

Keeping income I fixed, totally differentiate (12.34) to get

$$\left(\frac{\partial x_D}{\partial p} - \frac{\partial x_S}{\partial p}\right) dp + \frac{\partial x_D}{\partial t} dt = 0. \tag{12.37}$$

Since $q = p + t$, we have

$$\frac{dq}{dt} = 1 + \frac{dp}{dt}. \tag{12.38}$$

The price elasticity of supply, $\epsilon_s = \frac{dx_S(p)}{dp}\frac{p}{x_S}$, is defined as the percentage change in quantity supplied arising from a given percentage change in price. Using (12.34)–(12.38), simple calculations give rise to the following formula:

$$\frac{dq}{dt} = \frac{\frac{q}{p}\epsilon_s + (1-\theta)\,\epsilon_{p\to q}}{\frac{q}{p}\epsilon_s + \epsilon_{p\to q}}. \tag{12.39}$$

In (12.39), the LHS is the increase in the after-tax price paid by the consumer when the specific tax t increases by one unit. The RHS of (12.39) is decreasing in θ. Thus, greater inattention on the part of the consumers, that is, a lower θ, leads to a higher post-tax price paid by the consumer. In other words, firms are able to pass on a higher burden of the taxes to less attentive consumers.

This opens up a potential role for public policy. Suppose that for good x, consumption taxation is regressive with respect to income. For instance, because the good is consumed predominantly by the poor who also end up paying more taxes. Since producers can pass on a greater share of taxes to inattentive consumers, this further increases the regressivity of the tax system. One policy response is to avoid levying such taxes, or keeping them at low levels. Another policy response is to increase public awareness of such taxes, say, through a program of greater financial and tax literacy.

12.10.3 Optimal Sugar Taxes

The high levels of consumption of sugary drinks with excessive sugar content has been a cause for concern. The problem is particularly severe in the US, where consumption of sugary drinks is more than three to four times higher than the world average (Allcott et al., 2019a). Furthermore, the damage from such drinks is regressive with respect to income, as shown in Figure 12.3 which is based on "Nielsen Homescan," a 60,000-household, nationally representative panel data set of grocery purchases in the US. For instance, poorer individuals with an annual income below

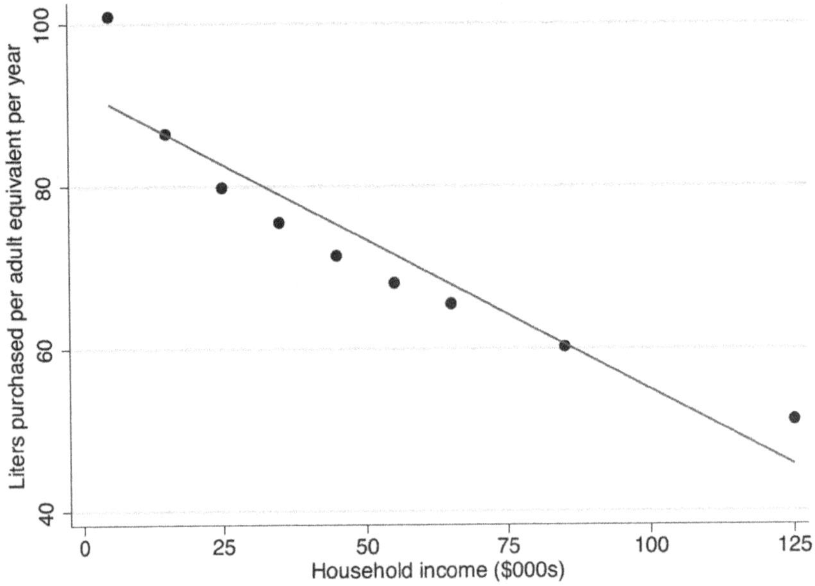

Figure 12.3 Regressivity of the damage from sugary drinks with respect to incomes. Source: Allcott et al. (2019a)

$25K consume 200 calories/day from sugary drinks while richer individuals with annual incomes above $75K consume 117 calories/day.

Should economists be concerned about the excessive consumption of sugary drinks? The answer in neoclassical welfare economics is, no. The reason is that people are assumed to make informed judgments of their welfare and they would have taken account of the present discounted value of all future costs and benefits (readily publicly available) and then rationally decided to consume in an "optimal" manner. Thus, in neoclassical welfare economics, health-related problems, such as obesity and diabetes, arising from excessive consumption of sugary drinks, are part of the rational, deliberate, considered, choices that people make. The opposition to paternalism in this literature then calls into question any interventions designed to reduce the consumption of sugary drinks.

By contrast, the view in behavioral economics is that people do not always make informed and considered judgments of their welfare. A range of factors may contribute to the choices made. For instance, individuals could be present-focused and a desire for instant gratification may prevent them from resisting the temptation afforded by tempting, but unhealthy, drinks. The instant food culture and changes in the technology of food production are some of the other factors that are likely to have led to an increased demand for such beverages (Loewenstein and Chater, 2017). Or it could be that individuals pay insufficient attention to the health advice that is offered to them by health professionals, including government advisories on public health.

Individuals may themselves be frustrated by their own weight and obesity problems, and may wish that they reduced their consumption of sugary beverages; this is evidenced by the multi-billion dollar dieting industry. Yet, their self-control problems may hinder such attempts. In such

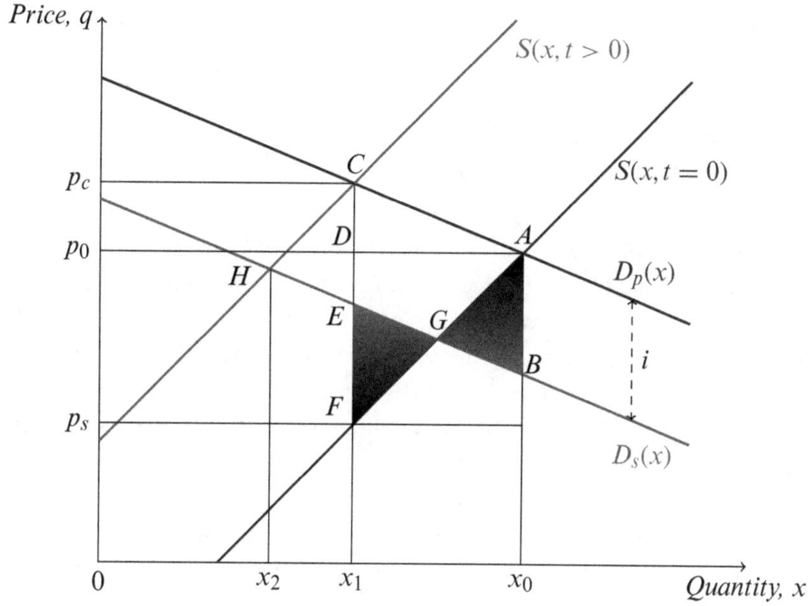

Figure 12.4 The optimality of sugar taxes

cases, there is a potential role for public policy, either in the form of soft paternalism that takes the form of nudges, or hard paternalism that takes the form of a tax on the consumption of such beverages.

Allcott et al. (2019b) list 39 countries that use or have tried to use such a tax on sugary drinks. Two kinds of taxes can be imagined. A general tax on sugary drinks by volume, is perhaps rather a blunt tax instrument. A more targeted approach is to tax the sugar content of drinks, yet this may be administratively more complicated to levy.

In Figure 12.4, we show why a tax on sugary drinks in competitive markets may be optimal. Let x be the quantity consumed of a sugary drink. The original inverse demand and inverse supply curves, in the absence of a specific tax on sugar consumption ($t = 0$), are shown as $D_p(x)$ and $S(x, t = 0)$. As in our previous analysis on tax incidence, we can consider a tax that applies either to the supply curve or to the demand curve. The rationale for the subscript p on the demand curve will be made clear below. The initial market equilibrium is shown at point A and the equilibrium quantity and equilibrium price are given, respectively, by x_0 and p_0.

Suppose now that the government levies a specific tax $t > 0$ per unit on the sale of good x. As in our analysis of tax incidence in Figure 12.2, the tax acts to increase the marginal cost of firms. Hence, the supply curve shifts upwards by the amount of the tax, t; the new supply curve is labeled $S(x, t > 0)$. The new equilibrium is shown by the point C and the equilibrium quantity and equilibrium price are, respectively, x_1 and p_c. The increase in price $p_c - p_0$ is lower than the per unit tax, $t > 0$. This follows from the arguments for tax incidence that we have already considered in Section 12.10.2.

The price received by the firm equals p_s while the price paid by the consumer is p_c; the difference $p_c - p_s$ equals the amount of the tax per unit, t. Hence, taking the initial price p_0 as the reference, the reader can readily check that the burden of taxes is shared between the consumers and the firms in the proportions

$$\frac{CD}{DF},$$

and the government collects total tax revenues equal to the area of the rectangle $p_c CFp_s$.

Consider a model of multiple selves of the same individual (see Part III). The inverse demand curve $D_p(x)$ gives the "private" marginal benefits to the current self of an individual from consuming good x. It does not take account of the harm from excess sugar that is caused to the future selves of the same individual, through the imposition of negative externalities that they cause on themselves. Recall that we have referred to externalities of this type as *internalities.* Suppose that each unit of consumption of x leads to an internality of a monetary amount $i > 0$, that is ignored by the current self of the individual.

Taking account of these internalities results in a lower *marginal social benefit* from the consumption of x, as compared to the *marginal private benefit* captured in $D_p(x)$; the subscript "p" captures private benefit.[9] The marginal social benefit is lower everywhere by an amount i that takes account of the per unit internalities caused, hence, it is shown by the "social" inverse demand curve $D_s(x)$. Suppose that the current self of the individual were somehow able to take account of the internalities caused, and treat $D_s(x)$ as the relevant demand curve. Then the post-tax equilibrium would occur at point H and the new equilibrium would be at a lower level of consumption $x_2 < x_1$.

For pedagogical simplicity, assume that there are no income effects on good x so that the compensated and uncompensated demand curves for good x are identical; for the distinction between the two kinds of demands, see Section 12.10.1. Thus, we can speak about the deadweight losses from taxes by using the (uncompensated) demand curves shown in Figure 12.4. Using our analysis in Section 12.10.1, the reader can readily calculate the deadweight loss *on consumers*, arising from the distortionary consumption tax on x, as the area of the Harberger triangle CDA.

However, in Section 12.10.1, we assumed that the marginal cost for the firm was constant and equal to $c > 0$, so that the supply curve was horizontal at the level of the marginal cost (see Figure 12.1). By contrast, we now have the case of increasing marginal costs and an upward sloping supply curve. Thus, the reduction in the quantity traded, $x_0 - x_1$, on account of the specific tax, reduces the producer surplus of firms by the area DAF. To see this, the reduction in the equilibrium quantity, $x_0 - x_1$, has two opposing effects.

1. There is a drop in total revenues of firms equal to $p_0 \times (x_0 - x_1)$ which equals the area of the rectangle DAx_0x_1.
2. There is a reduction in the costs of the firm, given by the area under the marginal cost curve. This equals FAx_0x_1.

[9] When health is publicly provided, free of costs, as under the NHS in the UK, excessive consumption of sugary drinks may result in public health costs to society. Hence, we use the term *marginal social benefit* rather than the more cumbersome expression *marginal internalized private benefit*.

Thus, the net effect, the area DAx_0x_1 minus the area FAx_0x_1, equals the area of the triangle DAF; this is the *deadweight loss on the sellers*. The total deadweight loss, DWL, is found by adding the deadweight loss to consumers (area CDA) and the fall in the net producer surplus of firms (area DAF). To summarize:

$$DWL = CDA + DAF = Area\ CAF. \tag{12.40}$$

In order to make a welfare evaluation, we also need to take account of internalities from the actions of the current self for all the future selves. The reduction in consumption, $x_0 - x_1$, benefits all future selves and the benefit per unit of x equals i. Hence, the total benefit to all future selves equals $i \times (x_0 - x_1)$, which equals the area of the parallelogram $ABEC$. Thus,

$$\text{Total benefits} = Area\ ABEC. \tag{12.41}$$

From (12.40), (12.41), the net welfare benefit is

$$\text{Net Benefit} = ABEC - CAF,$$

which can be rewritten in the following slightly different form that is obvious from Figure 12.4:

$$\text{Net Benefit} = ABG - EGF \lesseqgtr 0.$$

The net benefit can be positive or negative, as the reader can see from the shaded triangles in Figure 12.4. The calculation hinges on the relative elasticities of the demand and supply curves, the size of the specific tax, as well as on the extent of the per unit internalities, $i > 0$, caused to the future selves. If the net benefits are positive, then there is a good case for imposing a strictly positive level of such taxes.

Taxes on sugary drinks are a form of hard paternalism, but hard paternalism can also be used in conjunction with soft paternalism. For instance, a public awareness campaign of the dangers of sugary drinks (soft paternalism) can be combined with taxes on sugary drinks (hard paternalism). The analysis above applies for any other kind of sin good. For public policy directed at tobacco consumption see DeCicca et al. (2020), and for public policy towards sugary drinks see Allcott et al. (2019a,b).

As mentioned before, taxes on sugary drinks are likely to be regressive insofar as the poor spend a larger proportion of their budget on such drinks. Do distributional concerns preclude taxes on sugary drinks? The poor could also be disproportionately benefited by the tax because their internalities are taken care of, and their welfare might, on net, increase (Allcott et al., 2019a,b). It is conceivable that these benefits outweigh the costs to such an extent that the overall welfare effects are positive, despite taking tax regressivity issues into account.

Allcott et al. (2019a) consider issues of optimal taxes on sugary drinks. Two factors are critical to ensure that the optimal tax is strictly positive.

1. The higher is the price elasticity of demand of the poor, the more they will be deterred from consumption of the sugary drinks for a given increase in taxes.
2. The stronger is the degree of present-focus (e.g., a lower size of the parameter β in a (β, δ) model of hyperbolic discounting), the better is the case for a sugar tax.

If these two factors are critical enough, then redistributional concerns on the part of a social planner will work to increase sugar taxes, not decrease them. Pitted against these beneficial effects is the countervailing possibility that the tax is too distortionary, that is, the area of the relevant Harberger triangle that measures the efficiency loss from the tax, is too large. However, the empirical estimates reported in Allcott et al. (2019a) indicate that these deadweight losses are not large. They estimate the volume of sugary drinks that would be consumed by people if they had the same nutrition knowledge as dietitians and nutritionists, and no problems of self-control. The estimates suggest that those with incomes below \$10,000 would consume 37% to 48% less. For those with incomes above \$100,000 the corresponding figures are 27% to 32% less. This suggests that the poor are relatively more biased towards consumption of sugary drinks. The authors estimate the optimal tax on sugary drinks to be between 1 and 2.1 cents per ounce, and such a tax is likely to deliver welfare benefits between \$2.4 billion and \$6.8 billion a year.

References

Afriat, S. (1967). The Construction of a Utility Function from Expenditure Data. *International Economic Review* 8: 67–71.

Allcott, H. (2011). Social Norms and Energy Conservation. *Journal of Public Economics* 95(9–10): 1082–1095.

Allcott, H., Lockwood, B. B., and Taubinsky, D. (2019a). Regressive Sin Taxes, with an Application to the Optimal Soda Tax. *Quarterly Journal of Economics* 134(3): 1557–1626.

Allcott, H. Lockwood, B. B., and Taubinsky, D. (2019b). Should We Tax Soda? An Overview of Theory and Evidence. *Journal of Economic Perspectives* 33(3): 202–227.

Altmann, S. and Traxler, C. (2014). Nudges at the Dentist. *European Economic Review* 72(C): 19–38.

Atkinson, A. and Stiglitz, J. (1980). *Lectures on Public Economics*. McGraw-Hill: Maidenhead, Berkshire.

Becker, G. S. and Murphy, K. M. (1988). A Theory of Rational Addiction. *Journal of Political Economy* 96(4): 675–700.

Benartzi, S., Beshears, J., Milkman, K. L., Sunstein, C. R., Thaler, R. H., Shankar, M., Tucker-Ray, W., Congdon, W. J., and Galing, S. (2017). Should Governments Invest More in Nudging? *Psychological Science*. 28(8): 1041–1055.

Bernheim, B. D. and Taubinsky, D. (2018). Behavioral Public Economics. In B. D. Bernheim, S. DellaVigna, and D. Laibson (eds.), *The Handbook of Behavioral Economics*, Vol. 1. Elsevier: New York, pp. 381–516.

Beshears, J., Choi, J. J., Laibson, D., and Madrian, B. C. (2008). How Are Preferences Revealed? *Journal of Public Economics* 92(89): 1787–1794.

Bhargava, S. and Manoli, D. (2015). Psychological Frictions and the Incomplete Take-Up of Social Benefits: Evidence from an IRS Field Experiment. *American Economic Review* 105(11): 3489–3529.

Bleichrodt, H., Pinto, J.-L., and Wakker, P. (2001). Making Descriptive Use of Prospect Theory to Improve the Prescriptive Use of Expected Utility. *Management Science* 47(11): 1498–1514.

Buchanan, J. M. (1968). *The Demand and Supply of Public Goods*. Rand McNally: Chicago.

Buchanan, J. M. (1975). *The Limits of Liberty*. Chicago University of Chicago Press: Chicago.

Buchanan, J. M. (1986). *Liberty, Market and State*. Wheatsheaf: Brighton.

Calzolari, G. and Nardotto, M. (2017). Effective Reminders. *Management Science* 63(9): 2915–2932.

Camerer, C. F., Issacharoff, S., Loewenstein, G., O'Donoghue, T., and Rabin, M. (2003). Regulation for Conservatives: Behavioral Economics and the Case for Asymmetric Paternalism. *University of Pennsylvania Law Review* 151: 121–154.

Chetty, R., Looney, A., and Kroft, K. (2009). Salience and Taxation: Theory and Evidence. *American Economic Review* 99(4): 1145–1177.

Cornwell, J. F. and Krantz, D. H. (2014). Public Policy for Thee, but Not for Me: Varying the Grammatical Person of Public Policy Justifications Influences Their Support. *Judgment and Decision Making* 9(5): 433–444.

Cronqvist, H., Thaler, R. H., and Yu, F. (2018). When Nudges Are Forever: Inertia in the Swedish Premium Pension Plan. *American Economic Association Papers and Proceedings* 108: 153–158.

Czap, N. V., Czap, H. J., Khachaturyan, M., and Burbach, M. E. (2018). Conforming to or Defying Gender Stereotypes? Empathy Nudging vs. Financial Incentives in

Environmental Context. Papers in Natural Resources. 981. University of Nebraska-Lincoln.

Damgaard, M. T. and Gravert, C. (2018). The Hidden Costs of Nudging: Experimental Evidence from Reminders in Fundraising. *Journal of Public Economics* 157: 15–26.

Davis, M. H. (1983). A Multidimensional Approach to Individual Differences in Empathy. *Journal of Personality and Social Psychology* 44(1): 113–126.

DeCicca, P., Kenkel, D. S., and Mathios, A. (2020). Putting Out the Fires: Will Higher Taxes Reduce the Onset of Youth Smoking? *Journal of Political Economy* 110(1): 144–169.

DellaVigna, S. and Linos, E. (2022). RCTs to Scale: Comprehensive Evidence from Two Nudge Units. Forthcoming in *Econometrica* 90(1): 81–116.

Farhi, E. and Gabaix, X., (2020). Optimal Taxation with Behavioral Agents. *American Economic Review* 110(1): 298–336.

Gabaix, X. and Laibson, D. (2006). Shrouded Attributes, Consumer Myopia, and Information Suppression in Competitive Markets. *Quarterly Journal of Economics* 121: 505–540.

Glaeser, E. L. (2006). Paternalism and Psychology. *University of Chicago Law Review* 73(1): 133–156.

Goldstein, N. J., Cialdini, R. B., and Griskevicius, V. (2008). A Room with a Viewpoint: Using Social Norms to Motivate Environmental Conservation in Hotels. *Journal of Consumer Research* 35(3): 472–482.

Gruber, J. H. and Köszegi, B. (2001). Is Addiction Rational? Theory and Evidence. *Quarterly Journal of Economics* 116(4): 1261–1303.

Gruber, J. H. and Köszegi, B. (2004). Tax Incidence When Individuals Are Time-Inconsistent: The Case of Cigarette Excise Taxes. *Journal of Public Economics* 88(9–10): 1959–1987.

Hagman, W., Andersson, D., Västfjäll, D., and Tinghög, G. (2015). Public Views on Policies Involving Nudges. *Review of Philosophy and Psychology* 6(3): 439–453.

Hagmann, D., Ho, E. H., and Loewenstein, G. (2019). Nudging Out Support for a Carbon Tax. *Nature Climate Change* 9: 484–489.

Hedlin, S. and Sunstein, C. (2016). Does Active Choosing Promote Green Energy Use? Experimental Evidence. *Ecology Law Quarterly* 43(1): 107–141.

Hong, S.-M. and Page, S. (1989). A Psychological Reactance Scale: Development, Factor Structure and Reliability. *Psychological Reports* 64(3, Pt 2): 1323–1326.

Houthakker, H. S. (1950). Revealed Preference and the Utility Function. *Economica* 17(66): 159–174.

Huck, S. and Rasul, I. (2010). Transaction Costs in Charitable Giving. *B. E. Journal of Economic Analysis and Policy* 10(1): 31.

Hummel, D. and Maedche, A. (2019). How Effective Is Nudging? A Quantitative Review on the Effect Sizes and Limits of Empirical Nudging Studies. *Journal of Behavioral and Experimental Economics* 80: 47–58.

Jolls, C., Sunstein, C. R., and Thaler, R. H. (1998). A Behavioral Approach to Law and Economics. *Stanford Law Review* 50: 1471–1550.

Jung, J. Y. and Mellers, B. A. (2016). American Attitudes Toward Nudges. *Judgment and Decision Making* 11(1): 62–74.

Kahan, D. M., Braman, D., Slovic, P., Gastil, J., and Cohen, G. (2009). Cultural Cognition of the Risks and Benefits of Nanotechnology. *Nature Nanotechnology* 4(2): 87–91.

Kahan, D., Jenkins-Smith, H., and Braman, D. (2011). Cultural Cognition of Scientific Consensus. *Journal of Risk Research* 14(2): 147–174.

Karlan, D., McConnell, M., Mullainathan, S., and Zinman, J. (2016). Getting to the Top of Mind: How Reminders Increase Saving. *Management Science* 62(12): 3393–3411.

Klick, J. and Mitchell, G. (2006). Government Regulation of Irrationality: Moral and Cognitive Hazards. *Minnesota Law Review* 90: 1620–1663.

Laffont, J.-J. and Tirole, J. (1993). *A Theory of Incentives in Procurement and Regulation.* MIT Press: Cambridge, MA.

Li, C., Li, Z., and Wakker, P. (2014). If Nudge Cannot Be Applied: A Litmus Test of the Readers' Stance on Paternalism. *Theory and Decision* 76(3): 297–315.

Loewenstein, G. and Chater, N. (2017). Putting Nudges in Perspective. *Behavioral Public Policy* 1(1): 26–53.

Loewenstein, G. and Haisley, E. (2008). The Economist As Therapist: Methodological Ramifications of Light Paternalism. In A. Caplin and A. Schotter (eds.), *The Foundations of Positive and Normative Economics*. Oxford University Press: Oxford, pp. 210–245.

McConnell, M., Rothschild, C. W., Ettenger, A., Muigai, F., and Cohen, J. (2018). Free Contraception and Behavioural Nudges in the Postpartum Period: Evidence from a Randomised Control Trial in Nairobi, Kenya. *British Medical Journal: Global Health* 3: e000888.

Mullainathan, S., Schwartzstein, J., and Congdon, W. J. (2012). A Reduced-Form Approach to Behavioral Public Finance. *Annual Review of Economics* 4: 1–30.

Nolan, J. M., Schultz, P. W., Cialdini, R. B., Goldstein, N. J., and Griskevicius, V. (2008). Normative Social Influence Is Underdetected. *Personality and Social Psychology Bulletin* 34(7): 913–923.

O'Donoghue, T. and Rabin, M. (2006). Optimal Sin Taxes. *Journal of Public Economics* 90(1011): 1825–1849.

Pe'er, E., Feldman, Y., Gamliel, E., Sahar, L., Tikotsky, A., Hod, N., and Schupak, H. (2019). Do Minorities Like Nudges? The Role of Group Norms in Attitudes Towards Behavioral Policy. *Judgment and Decision Making* 14(1): 40–50.

Posner, R. A. (1986). *Economic Analysis of Law*. 3rd edn. Little, Brown: Boston.

Samuelson, P. A. (1948). Consumption Theory in Terms of Revealed Preference. *Economica* 15(60): 243–253.

Schultz, W., Nolan, J., Cialdini, R. B., Goldstein, N., and Griskevicius, V. (2007). The Constructive, Destructive, and Reconstructive Power of Social Norms. *Psychological Science* 18(5): 429–434.

Sonntag, A. and Zizzo, D. J. (2015). On Reminder Effects, Drop-Outs and Dominance: Evidence from an Online Experiment on Charitable Giving. *PLoS ONE* 10(8): e0134705 08.

Stiglitz, J. E. (2000). *Economics of the Public Sector.* 3rd edn. W. W. Norton & Company: New York.

Sugden, R. (2008). Why Incoherent Preferences Do Not Justify Paternalism. *Constitutional Political Economy* 19: 226–248.

Sugden, R. (2013). The Behavioural Economist and the Social Planner: To Whom Should Behavioural Welfare Economics Be Addressed? *Inquiry: An Interdisciplinary Journal of Philosophy* 56(5): 519–538.

Sugden, R. (2017). Do People Really Want to Be Nudged towards Healthy Lifestyles? *International Review of Economics* 64(2): 113–123.

Sunstein, C. R. (2017). The Council of Psychological Advisors. *Annual Review of Psychology* 67(1): 713–737.

Sunstein, C. R. (2017). Default Rules Are Better than Active Choosing (Often). *Trends in Cognitive Sciences* 21(8): 600–606.

Sunstein, C. R. (2018). "Better Off, as Judged by Themselves": A Comment on Evaluating Nudges. *International Review of Economics* 65(1): 1–8.

Sunstein, C. R. and Thaler, R. H. (2003). Libertarian Paternalism Is Not an Oxymoron. *University of Chicago Law Review* 70: 1159–1202.

Tannenbaum, D., Fox, C. R., and Rogers, T. (2017). On the Misplaced Politics of Behavioural Policy Interventions. *Nature Human Behaviour* 1: Article number 0130.

Taubinsky, D. and Rees-Jones, A. (2018). Attention Variation and Welfare: Theory and Evidence from a Tax Salience Experiment. *Review of Economic Studies* 85(4): 2462–2496.

Thaler, R. H. and Sunstein, C. R. (2003). Libertarian Paternalism. *American Economic Review: Papers and Proceedings* 93: 175–179.

Thaler, R. H. and Sunstein, C. R. (2009). *Nudge: Improving Decisions about Health, Wealth, and Happiness.* Penguin Books: New Haven, CT.

Thunström, L. (2019). Welfare Effects of Nudges: The Emotional Tax of Calorie Menu Labeling. *Judgment and Decision Making* 14(1): 11–25.

Thunström, L., Nordström, J., Shogren, J. F., Ehmke, M., and van't Veld, K. (2016). Strategic Self-Ignorance. *Journal of Risk and Uncertainty* 52(2): 117–136.

Tiefenbeck V., Staake T., Roth K., and Sachs O. (2013). For Better or for Worse? Empirical Evidence of Moral Licensing in a Behavioral Energy Conservation Campaign. *Energy Policy* 57: 160–171.

Weitzman, M. L. (1974). Prices vs. Quantities. *Review of Economic Studies* 41(4): 477–491.

Weitzman, M. L. (2011). Fat-Tailed Uncertainty in the Economics of Catastrophic Climate Change. *Review of Environmental Economics and Policy* 5(2): 275–292.

Problems for Part VI

1. Kuhn et al. (2011) exploit the exogenous variation in income caused by the Dutch postcode lottery in which the set of winners is all the buyers of the lottery tickets in a particular postcode. Each winner wins 12,500 euros per ticket and one of the postcode winners is chosen to additionally receive a brand new BMW. The data allow for tracking the consumption patterns of the winners and their neighbors. The neighbors of winners who receive a BMW, are also more likely to buy a BMW. How is this finding relevant to the Easterlin paradox?
2. (Spiegler 2019) In his Ely Lecture, Campbell (2016), considered the implication of imposing a tax on complex and potentially exploitative products when consumers are boundedly rational decision makers. Suppose that there are two products: (i) A *simple* product that has a fixed value, normalized to 0, which is correctly perceived by all consumers; (ii) A *complex* product whose value is heterogenous across consumers and denoted by u; thus, there is a distribution of u values across the population.

   A proportion $0 \leq \alpha \leq 1$ of consumers are sophisticated and the remaining fraction $1 - \alpha$ are naive. The valuation of the complex product by sophisticated consumers is unbiased. However, when a naive consumer values the complex product at u, its true value is actually $u - 1$; such consumers overvalue the complex product by 1 for all values of u. Suppose that we impose a fixed tax $\tau \in (0, 1)$ on the complex product and suppose that the tax revenues are not rebated back to the consumers.

   (a) Show that the only consumers whose behavior is affected by the intervention are those with $u \in (0, \tau)$.
   (b) Show that all consumers with $u > \tau$ are harmed by the tax, whereas all consumers with $u < 0$ are unaffected by it.
   (c) Consider consumers with $u \in (0, \tau)$. Show that sophisticated consumers are made unambiguously worse off but naive consumers are made better off.
   (d) What are the welfare implications?

3. Show that the salience function in (11.57) is homogeneous of degree 0, that is, $f(\alpha a_{ik}, \alpha \overline{a}_k) = f(a_{ik}, \overline{a}_k)$ for $\alpha > 0$.
4. (Bordalo et al. 2013) Consider Examples 11.3 and 11.4 where we considered the problem of choosing between $i = 1, 2, \ldots, n$ wines that have a quality and price attribute. Suppose that the higher quality or lower price of of a good i relative to the average attributes $(\overline{q}, \overline{p})$ is salient if and only if

$$\frac{q_i}{p_i} > \frac{\overline{q}}{\overline{p}}.$$

The utility function depends on whether quality is more salient than price ($\sigma(q_i,\overline{q}) > \sigma(p_i,\overline{p})$) or price is more salient than quality ($\sigma(q_i,\overline{q}) < \sigma(p_i,\overline{p})$) and is given by

$$U_i = \begin{cases} \frac{2}{1+\delta} q_i - \frac{2\delta}{1+\delta} p_i & if \quad \sigma(q_i,\overline{q}) > \sigma(p_i,\overline{p}) \\ \frac{2\delta}{1+\delta} q_i - \frac{2}{1+\delta} p_i & if \quad \sigma(q_i,\overline{q}) < \sigma(p_i,\overline{p}) \\ q_i - p_i & if \quad \sigma(q_i,\overline{q}) = \sigma(p_i,\overline{p}) \end{cases} ; \delta \in (0,1].$$

$\delta \in (0,1]$ captures the extent of salient thinking. The case $\delta = 1$ corresponds to the neoclassical case. However, as δ continues to fall, salient thinking increases in severity in the sense that the decision maker puts increasingly greater weight on the more salient attribute. Assume that the salience function is given in (11.57). Suppose that there are wines of two qualities. A high-end wine (q_h,p_h) and a low-end wine (q_l,p_l) such that $q_h > q_l$ and $p_h > p_l$.The average quality and average price are $\overline{q} = \sum_{i=1}^{n} q_i$, $\overline{p} = \sum_{i=1}^{n} p_i$.

(i) Show that when $\frac{q_h}{p_h} > \frac{\overline{q}}{\overline{p}} > \frac{q_l}{p_l}$ quality is salient for both wines.

(ii) Show that when $\frac{q_l}{p_l} > \frac{\overline{q}}{\overline{p}} > \frac{q_h}{p_h}$, then price is salient for both wines.

(iii) When prices are salient show that the low-end wine is more likely to be chosen by a salient thinker ($\delta < 1$) as compared to a fully rational thinker ($\delta = 1$).

(iv) When quality is salient show that the low-end wine is less likely to be chosen by a salient thinker ($\delta < 1$) as compared to a fully rational thinker ($\delta = 1$).

(v) Can you conclude that salience tilts preferences toward the wine offering the highest quality/price ratio.

5. (Gabaix, 2019) Consider the model of limited attention in Section 11.5. Show how this model might be used to provide an alternative interpretation of the model of quasi-hyperbolic discounting that we discussed in Part III of the book. What are the implications for behavioral welfare economics?

6. Consider the model of quasi-hyperbolic preferences in Section 12.4. Suppose that there are 5 individuals in a society with β values given, respectively, by $\frac{1}{8}, \frac{1}{4}, \frac{1}{3}, \frac{1}{2}, \frac{3}{4}$. Each individual is considering to undertake an activity that has a current benefit $v = 3$ and a future cost $c = 4$.

   (a) How many individuals find it optimal to undertake the activity in the absence of any government policy?

   (b) Consider a policy of indirect paternalism in which the policymaker levies a tax at the rate $t = \frac{1}{2}$ on the benefits from the activity. How many individuals find it optimal to undertake the activity?

   (c) Consider a libertarian paternalistic policy, such as provision of information about future costs, that results in an increase in the β value by a factor $\gamma = 3$ for all individuals. How many individuals find it optimal to undertake the activity?

   (d) What value of the tax rate in part (b) will ensure that the outcome is identical to that acheived under libertarian paternalism. Should we be indifferent between indirect paternalism and libertarian paternalism in this case?

7. Consider the detailed text that accompanies mortgage and lease contracts in the US. The detail in the text is a response to the Federal Truth in Lending Act. The text typically gives details of all costs and terms of the contract; multiple, mandatory, signatures certify that the reader has read the separate sections of the contract. Borrowers have to read the following

statement and sign that they understand it: "If you obtain this loan, the lender will have a mortgage on your home. You could lose your home, and any money you have put into it, if you do not meet your obligations under the loan."

(i) Show that this text exemplifies asymmetric paternalism.
(ii) What could be a potentially unexpected outcome of such a policy intervention?

8. Consider policy mandated *cooling-off periods*. Individuals are free to make their choices but they are allowed to reverse their decision within some legal time horizon, T. This typically occurs with the purchase of consumer durables and many services such as insurance products.
   (i) Are cooling-off periods needed under neoclassical welfare economics?
   (ii) How can cooling-off periods be justified in behavioral welfare economics?
9. Altmann and Traxler (2014) explore the effects of reminders to patients in a field study at a German dentist. Three different kinds of reminders were given. (i) Simple reminders without any further information. (ii) Reminders with information on the benefits of a preventive health checkup. (iii) Reminders that were framing positively and negatively. Relative to a control condition with no reminders, reminders doubled the fraction of individuals who contacted the dentist for a checkup from 8.9% to 19.3%. The fraction of individuals with reminders who visited the dentist increased by 10 percentage points higher relative to the control group. The form of the reminder had little effect on preventive checkups. Would such reminders have been effective in the neoclassical framework? How can we interpret the findings from the study?
10. Loewenstein and Chater (2017) compare the pension plans in the US and for Australia. The US pension plan is based along the lines of soft paternalism. A choice architect draws up a default option and plan participants can withdraw from pension funds before retirement, at no penalty. The Australian system, by contrast, is closer to the framework of hard paternalism. Employers are required to contribute 9% of their salary to the pension pot and employees make a mandatory contribution of 3% of their salary. Such mandatory requirements are not nudges. It is legally forbidden to withdraw money from the pension pot and withdrawals can be made only after retirement. The US population is 14 times larger, but the pension pot is not even double that of Australia. What can be concluded about the relative merits of soft and hard paternalism from this example?
11. Consider an individual whose multiple selves live over successive time periods $t = 1, 2, 3, \ldots, T$. The individual consumes two kinds of goods every period. A sin good x_t and a composite good, z_t which is an aggregate of all other goods consumed. The objective of individuals is to maximize present discounted utility. At any time t, the instantaneous, or time t utility, of an individual is given by

$$u_t = (lnx_t - ax_{t-1}) + z_t;\ a \in (0, 1). \tag{12.42}$$

The individual has income $I > 0$ in every time period. The unit price of the composite good at any time is normalized to 1. Assume that the marginal cost of production of sin goods is identical to the marginal cost of production of the composite good. Thus, under competitive market conditions, the unit price of the sin good is also 1. Self-t does not have any means of binding the choices of future selves. In other words, private individuals lack a commitment device to influence the choices of future selves. Thus, self-t is only able to choose the time t

consumption of the sin good, x_t, conditional on the history of choices, encapsulated in the time $t-1$ choice of the sin good, x_{t-1}.

The government levies a *specific consumption tax*[1] at the rate $\tau \in [0,1]$ on the sin good only, and the resulting tax revenues are returned as lumpsum transfers to individuals. Each individual receives a lumpsum transfer α from the government.

There is a total population of N individuals of which N_1 individuals, or a fraction $\lambda = \frac{N_1}{N} \in [0,1]$, are *present focused* and have identical quasi-hyperbolic $(\beta, 1)$ preferences such that $\beta \in (0,1)$. The remaining $N_2 = N - N_1$ individuals, or a fraction $1-\lambda$, are the rational types who do not discount the future at all and satisfy $\beta = 1$. The self-t of a present focused individual, $t = 0, 1, 2, \ldots, T$, has the following intertemporal preferences

$$U_t(\beta, 1) = u_t + \beta \sum_{j=1}^{T-t} u_{t+j};\ \beta \in (0,1). \tag{12.43}$$

The preferences of the rational types are a special case of (12.43) when $\beta = 1$, that is, they are given by $U_t(1,1)$.

(i) Show that the utility function in (12.42) captures a habit formation model in which negative internalities are created by the current self of the individual for the future selves of the same individual.

(ii) Write down the budget constraint of an individual at time t.

(iii) Use the index $j = b, r$ respectively for behavioral and rational types. Show that the unique solution to consumption of the sin good for a behavioral type at time t is

$$x_t^b = \frac{1}{(a\beta + 1 + \tau)}, \tag{12.44}$$

and the optimal consumption of the sin good for a rational type is

$$x_t^r = \frac{1}{(a + 1 + \tau)}. \tag{12.45}$$

Show that $x_t^r < x_t^b$.

(iv) Consider the *first best allocation* where there are no distortionary taxes, $\tau = 0$, although lumpsum taxes are available, and all individuals are rational types. Denote the optimal consumption of the sin good by any individual by x^* and show that

$$x^* = \frac{1}{(a+1)}. \tag{12.46}$$

(v) Is there a level of the distortionary tax, τ^*, such that present focused individuals, operating under this tax, will choose a level of sin good consumption that is identical to the first best allocation in (12.46)? Interpret your answer.

(vi) Show that the indirect utility of the self at time t is

$$v_t^j(\alpha, \tau) = \left(\ln x^j - a x_{t-1}\right) + \left(I + \alpha - (1+\tau) x^j\right);\ j = b, r, \tag{12.47}$$

[1] Economists distinguish between two kinds of consumption taxes. Ad-valorem taxes are imposed as a percentage of the price of a good. Specific taxes are imposed per unit of consumption of a good.

where x^j, $j = b, r$, is given in (12.44), (12.45).

12. Consider the problem described in Section 12.9 on sin taxes. Suppose that the objective function of the government (or the fiscal authority) is a utilitarian social welfare function. In each time period, $t = 1, 2, \ldots, T$, it wishes to choose its public policy optimally in order to maximize the sum of utilities of all individuals in society at time t. The sequence of moves is as follows. At the beginning of every time period, t, the government announces the consumption tax rate, τ, and the lumpsum transfer, α, which is observed by individuals who then choose their optimal consumption of the sin good and the composite good. Looking forward, the rational government knows that the consumption choices of individuals are given by (12.44), (12.45), thus the government behaves like a *Stackelberg leader*.

    Following O'Donoghue and Rabin (2006), assume that for any individual, the government at time t cares about the following measure of social utility for an individual of type $j = b, r$.

$$W_t^j(\alpha, \tau) = \left(lnx^j - ax^j\right) + \left(I + \alpha - (1 + \tau) x^j\right), j = b, r. \tag{12.48}$$

    In other words, the social planner sets $\beta = 1$ in evaluating the social utility of the present focused individuals. By contrast, the rational types already have $\beta = 1$ as part of their preferences. Hence, the government has the following weighted utilitarian social welfare function in which the sum of social utilities of the two types of individuals, weighted by the proportions of the two types, is maximized.[2]

$$W(\alpha, \tau) = \lambda W_t^b(\alpha, \tau) + (1 - \lambda) W_t^r(\alpha, \tau), \tag{12.49}$$

    where $W_t^j, j = b, r$, is given in (12.48) and λ, $1 - \lambda$ are the relative fractions of the behavioral and rational types. The government is assumed to follow a balanced budget. Thus, total tax revenues from the collection of consumption taxes equal total tax expenditures on making lumpsum payments to the taxpayers, that is, $N\alpha = N_1 \tau x^b + N_2 \tau x^r$ where N_1 and N_2 are the absolute numbers of the behavioral and rational types.

    (i) Write down the first order condition of the government's optimization problem and interpret it.
    (ii) Show that when there are no present focused individuals ($\lambda \to 0$), then the government optimally sets a zero optimal consumption tax, $\tau^* = 0$.
    (iii) How is the optimal tax related to the degree of present focused preferences as captured in the term $1 - \beta$ if all individuals are present-focussed?

13. Evaluate the following two quotes from Allcott et al. (2019b).
    (i) "A tax on soda and juice drinks would disproportionately increase taxes on low-income families in Philadelphia." – US Senator Bernie Sanders (2016)
    (ii) "They've [big soda] made their money off the backs of poor people, but this money [soda tax revenue] will stay in poor neighborhoods." – Philadelphia Mayor Jim Kenney (quoted in Blumgart, 2016)

[2] Technically, we have $W(\alpha, \tau) = N_1 W_t^b(\alpha, \tau) + N_2 W_t^c(\alpha, \tau)$. Maximizing W is equivalent to maximizing the function W/N. Using the definition of $\lambda = N_1/N$ gives rise to (12.49).

Index